THE OXFORD HANDBOOK OF

BRITISH POLITICS

D0862673

THE OXFORD HANDBOOK OF

BRITISH POLITICS

Edited by

MATTHEW FLINDERS
ANDREW GAMBLE
COLIN HAY
and
MICHAEL KENNY

OXFORD

UNIVERSITY PRESS

This book has been printed digitally and produced in a standard specification
in order to ensure its continuing availability

OXFORD
UNIVERSITY PRESS

Great Clarendon Street, Oxford OX2 6DP
United Kingdom

Oxford University Press is a department of the University of Oxford.
It furthers the University's objective of excellence in research, scholarship,
and education by publishing worldwide.

Oxford is a registered trade mark of Oxford University Press in the UK
and in certain other countries

British Library Cataloguing in Publication Data
Data available

Library of Congress Cataloging in Publication Data
Data available

ISBN 978-0-19-960444-9

PREFACE

The study of British politics has been reinvigorated in recent years as a generation of new scholars seeks to build upon a distinct disciplinary heritage while also exploring new empirical territory. It is very much in this context that the *Oxford Handbook of British Politics* has been designed and published. However the central ambition of this collection is not just to illustrate both the breadth and depth of scholarship that is to be found within the field. It is also concerned with promoting the study of British politics. It seeks to do so by demonstrating the vibrancy and critical self-reflection that has cultivated a much sharper and engaging—notably less insular—approach to the terrain it seeks to explore and understand. In this emphasis on critical engagement, disciplinary evolution, and a commitment to *shaping* rather than *restating* the discipline, the *Oxford Handbook of British Politics* is consciously distinctive. It is not intended as a standard text on British politics, nor a set of review articles, and it certainly does not replicate the various encyclopaedic survey-like collections on British politics that are now available. In showcasing the diversity now to be found in the analysis of British politics, the *Oxford Handbook of British Politics* is built upon three foundations.

The first principle that underpins this collection is a broad understanding of 'the political'. It is exactly this inclusive approach that has allowed us to embrace a much broader range of topics, themes, and issues than would commonly be found within a text on British politics. As a result, topics that would generally be viewed as core elements of British politics—for example Parliament, the core executive, political parties, and economic management—are set alongside those which might at first glance appear outliers when viewed through a traditional lens, like generational change, risk analysis, political marketing. But what is immediately obvious on reading such chapters is how readily they complement and build upon more established themes within the discipline, and how they aid our understanding in teasing apart the challenges and complexity of modern governance.

This emphasis on an inclusive approach also characterizes the second principle that has shaped this collection—namely, diversity in relation to commissioned authors. As a glance at the contents page reveals, the *Oxford Handbook of British Politics* includes chapters from both established and emerging names. It also includes contributions from scholars and practitioners alike. And, reflecting the genuinely international scope of the contemporary analysis of British politics, the collection includes chapters written by scholars based in North America, Australia, and mainland Europe.

The final principle underpinning this collection is a focus on the very nature of the distinctiveness to which we have already pointed. Every chapter in its own way and through a number of approaches seeks to reflect on what is distinctive about British politics—in terms of both the empirical nature of the issue of concern, and the theories and methods that have been deployed to unravel the nature and causes of the debate. The issue of distinctiveness is of critical significance in relation to a long-standing epistemological and methodological tension between what can (and has) been termed 'British political studies' and those approaches that commonly fall within the rubric of 'political science'. The first section of this collection— 'Approaches'—seeks to engage with this debate and challenge, or at least soften, the sub-disciplinary barriers that have so often tended to demarcate the study of British politics. In many ways this aspiration dovetails with the inclusive nature of this collection, while also fitting with the generally more pluralistic approach to theories and methods that has formed a defining feature of British political studies since its emergence as a distinct profession during the middle of the twentieth century.

Taken together these three principles have provided the reference points within which each author has been asked to prepare their chapter. The result is a unique collection of commentaries that: draw upon the intellectual strengths of the study of British politics; reflect the innate diversity and inclusiveness of the discipline; isolate certain distinctive issues and then reflect on their broader international relevance; and finally seek to point towards emerging or overlooked areas of research in order to maintain a certain momentum or dynamism in relation to each particular sphere. In some chapters the nature of the topic or the approach of the author has encouraged an emphasis on some of these issues more than others. As with all projects of this nature, the editors have sought gently to steer whilst resisting the temptation to row, setting down the key principles and ambitions but leaving it up to each author to interpret and emphasize these markers as they see fit. However, a degree of independent assessment and refinement was achieved through an editorial process in which each chapter was independently refereed by at least three established scholars. We are immensely grateful to all those scholars who were willing to contribute some of their time to this project by acting as reviewers.

The *output* of this process is a collection of chapters that, we feel, reflects the resurgence of British politics as a discipline while also seeking to probe and extend its boundaries in order to draw upon new approaches and perspectives. We hope the *outcome* of this project is a more refined and sophisticated appreciation not only of the British political tradition but also of the varied insights that the analysis of British politics can contribute more broadly.

The editors were saddened to hear of the death of Sir Bernard Crick, one of our contributors, shortly before this volume went to press. Bernard's essay in this collection is one of the last essays he wrote, and provides an excellent illustration of his significance and originality as a commentator on our political culture and life.

Matthew Flinders
Andrew Gamble
Colin Hay
Michael Kenny

CONTENTS

PART I APPROACHES

PART II   INSTITUTIONS

PART V   PROCESSES

LIST OF FIGURES

LIST OF TABLES

LIST OF CONTRIBUTORS

Richard J. Aldrich is Professor of International Security at the University of Warwick.

Mark Bevir is Professor of Political Science at the University of California, Berkeley.

Jim Buller is Senior Lecturer in Politics at the University of York.

Peter Burnham is Professor of Politics and International Studies at the University of Warwick.

Ben Clift is Senior Lecturer in Political Economy at the University of Warwick.

Bernard Crick was an Honorary Fellow in Politics and International Relations at the University of Edinburgh.

Colin Crouch is Professor of Governance and Public Management at the University of Warwick Business School.

Jonathan Davies is Reader in Public Policy at the University of Warwick.

Fiona Devine is Professor and Head of the School of Social Sciences at the University of Manchester.

Brian Doherty is Senior Lecturer in Politics at Keele University.

Keith Dowding is Professor of and Head of Political Science at the Research School of Social Sciences at the Australian National University.

Richard English is Professor of Politics at Queen's University, Belfast.

Keith Ewing is Professor of Public Law at King's College London.

Kevin Featherstone is Professor of Contemporary Greek Studies at the London School of Economics.

Matthew Flinders is Professor of Parliamentary Government and Governance at the University of Sheffield.

Andrew Gamble is Professor of Politics and a Fellow of Queens' College at the University of Cambridge.

Howard Glennerster is Professor Emeritus at the London School of Economics.

Robert E. Goodin, FBA, is Distinguished Professor of Social and Political Theory and of Philosophy at the Research School of Social Sciences at the Australian National University.

Randall Hansen is an Associate Professor and holds a Canada Research Chair in Political Science at the University of Toronto.

James Hampshire is a Lecturer in Politics at the University of Sussex.

Christopher Harvie is a Member of the Scottish Parliament and formerly Professor of British and Irish Studies at the University of Tübingen, Germany.

Colin Hay is Professor of Political Analysis and Co-Director of the Political Economy Research Centre at the University of Sheffield.

Richard Heffernan is Reader in Government at the Open University and a Visiting Professor at the University of Notre Dame.

Oliver James is Professor of Political Science at the University of Exeter.

Charlie Jeffery is Professor of Politics and Co-Director of the Institute of Governance at the University of Edinburgh.

Robert Johns is Lecturer in Politics in the Department of Government at the University of Strathclyde.

Ron Johnston is a Professor in the School of Geographical Sciences at the University of Bristol.

Grant Jordan is Professor of Politics at the University of Aberdeen.

Dennis Kavanagh is Professor of Politics at the University of Liverpool.

Michael Keating is Professor of Political Science at the European University Institute, Florence; and at the University of Aberdeen.

Paul Kelly is Professor of Political Theory at the London School of Economics.

Alexandra Kelso is Lecturer in British Politics at the University of Southampton.

Michael Kenny is Professor of Politics at Sheffield University and a Visiting Research Fellow at the Institute for Public Policy Research.

Steven Kettell is Associate Professor of Politics and International Studies at the University of Warwick.

Joel Krieger is the Norma Wilentz Hess Professor of Political Science at Wellesley College.

Fiona Mackay is Senior Lecturer in Politics at the University of Edinburgh.

Peter Mair is Professor of Comparative Politics at the European University Institute, Florence.

David Marquand is former Principal of Mansfield College, Oxford and currently a Visiting Fellow in the Department of Politics, University of Oxford and Honorary Professor of Politics at the University of Sheffield.

Tariq Modood is Professor of Sociology, Politics and Public Policy and the founding Director of the Centre for the Study of Ethnicity and Citizenship at the University of Bristol.

Michael Moran is Professor of Government at the University of Manchester.

Oliver Morrissey is Professor in Development Economics and Director of the Centre for Research in Economic Development and International Trade (CREDIT) in the School of Economics, University of Nottingham.

Charles Pattie is a Professor in the Department of Geography at the University of Sheffield.

B. Guy Peters is Maurice Falk Professor of American Government at the University of Pittsburgh.

Vicky Randall is Professor in the Department of Government, University of Essex.

Peter Riddell is Assistant Editor at *The Times*.

Henry Rothstein is a Senior Lecturer in the Department of Geography and Deputy Director of the King's Centre for Risk Management at King's College London.

Heather Savigny is Lecturer in Politics at the University of East Anglia.

Julia Stapleton is Reader in Politics at Durham University.

Helen Thompson is Senior Lecturer in Politics at the University of Cambridge.

Adam Tomkins is John Millar Professor of Public Law at the University of Glasgow.

Alan Walker is Professor of Social Policy and Social Gerontology at the University of Sheffield.

Paul Whiteley is Professor of Government at the University of Essex.

Abbreviations

AFDC	Aid for Families with Dependent Children
AHA	American Historical Association
AHRC	Arts and Humanities Research Council
AM	Assembly Member
APG	All Party Group
APPC	Association of Professional Political Consultants
APSA	American Political Studies Association
AWM	adult worker model
B&R	Bevir and Rhodes
BCS	British Cohort Study
BES	British Election Study
BGOP	Better Government for Older People
BHPS	British Household Panel Survey
BIS	Bank for International Settlements
BISA	British International Studies Association
BME	Black and Minority Ethnic
BNP	British National party
BP	basic pension
BSE	bovine spongiform encephalopathy
BT	British Telecom
CA	Countryside Alliance
CAP	Common Agricultural Policy
CBI	Confederation of British Industry
CD	Collier and Dollar
CEDAW	Committee on the Elimination of Discrimination Against Women
CFSP	Common Foreign and Security Policy
CIPR	Chartered Institute for Public Relations
CMEB	Commission on the Future of Multi-Ethnic Britain

CND	Campaign for Nuclear Disarmament
CRE	Commission for Racial Equality
DCLG	Department of Communities and Local Government
DFID	Department for International Development
DM	Deutschmark
DSEi	Defence Systems and Equipment International
DTI	Department of Trade and Industry
DUP	Democratic Unionist Party
DVLA	Driver and Vehicle Licensing Agency
ECB	European Central Bank
ECHR	European Convention on Human Rights
ECJ	European Court of Justice
EEA	European Economic Area
EHRC	Equalities and Human Rights Commission
EMA	Education Maintenance Allowance
EMU	Economic and Monetary Union
EO	equal opportunities
EOC	Equal Opportunities Commission
ERM	Exchange Rate Mechanism
ESRC	Economic and Social Research Council
ESS	European Security Strategy
EU	European Union
FCO	Foreign and Commonwealth Office
FDI	foreign direct investment
FE	further education
FSA	Financial Services Authority
FSA	Food Standards Agency
FSM	free school meal
GBS	General Budget Support
GCHQ	Government Communications Headquarters
GCSE	General Certificate of Secondary Education
GDP	gross domestic product
GE	gender equality
GHS	General Household Survey

GM	Gender Mainstreaming
GNP	gross national product
HC	House of Commons
HE	higher education
HEFCE	Higher Education Funding Council for England
HMT	Her Majesty's Treasury
HRA	Human Rights Act
HSE	Health and Safety Executive
HSMP	Highly Skilled Migrant Programme
IGO	intergovernmental organization
ILP	International Labour party
IMF	International Monetary Fund
IRA	Irish Republican Army
ISC	Intelligence and Security Committee
IT	information technology
ITO	International Trade Organization
JAC	Judicial Appointments Commission
JIC	Joint Intelligence Committee
JTAC	Joint Terrorism Analysis Centre
LME	liberal market economy
MAFF	Ministry for Agriculture, Fisheries and Food
MCB	Muslim Council of Britain
MCS	Millennium Cohort Study
MDG	Millennium Development Goal
MEP	Member of the European Parliament
MMR	measles, mumps, rubella
MoD	Ministry of Defence
MP	Member of Parliament
MSP	Member of the Scottish Parliament
MVT	median voter theorem
NAFTA	North American Free Trade Agreement
NAIRU	non-accelerating inflation rate of unemployment
NATO	North Atlantic Treaty Organization
NCDS	National Child Development Study

NDPB	Non-departmental public body
NGO	non-governmental organization
NHS	National Health Service
NIMBY	not in my back yard
NMW	National Minimum Wage
NPC	National Pensioners Convention
NPM	New Public Management
NSM	new social movement
ODA	Overseas Development Administration
ODM	Ministry for Overseas Development
OECD	Organization for Economic Cooperation and Development
OMC	open method of coordination
OMS	Oxford Mobility Study
ORR	Office of Rail Regulation
PASC	Public Administration Select Committee
PFI	private finance initiative
PM	Prime Minister
PPP	public–private partnership
PR	public relations
PRSP	Poverty Reduction Strategy Paper
PSA	Political Studies Association
PSA	Public Service Agreement
QMV	qualified majority voting
RDM	Russian Doll Model
RDR	Rural Development Regulation
RIPA	Regulation of Investigatory Powers Act
RRB	Race Relations Board
SGP	stability and growth pact
SDLP	Social Democratic and Labour party
SDP	Social Democratic party
SEA	Single European Act
SES	socio-economic status
SF	Sinn Fein
SEPA	Scottish Environment Protection Authority

SMPS	single-member plurality system
SNP	Scottish National party
SRO	self-regulatory organization
SSA	sub-Saharan Africa
SSRC	Social Science Research Council
SV	*Satanic Verses*
TCG	Tasking and Coordinating Group
TUC	Trades Union Congress
UKACIA	UK Action Committee on Islamic Affairs
UKIP	United Kingdom Independence party
UUP	Ulster Unionist party
WDF	waste-derived fuel
WEU	Western European Union
WM	Westminster Model
WMD	Weapons of Mass Destruction
WPR	Western Peripheral Route
WTO	World Trade Organization
WUNC	worthiness, unity, numbers, commitment

PART I

APPROACHES

SECTION ONE: THE BRITISH TRADITION

CHAPTER 1

....

POLITICS AS AN ACADEMIC VOCATION

....

MICHAEL KENNY

1.1 INTRODUCTION

....

Has there been a distinctively British approach to teaching and studying politics in its universities? If so, how best should we characterize the amalgam of indigenous traditions, prejudices, and interests that comprise such a tradition? Is it the case, as some now argue, that a distinctly British variant of political science has given way before the pressures to conform to the standards and approaches associated with the global hegemon in this subject area—American political science? Does British political studies fit more naturally with continental European practice? Or does the very notion of a singular national tradition of political scholarship belie the multiplicity of perspectives and theories that have been in contention throughout the lifetime of this subject?

Answers to these questions continue to divide the majority of those whose professional careers involve the scholarly analysis and teaching of the subject known variously as political studies, political science, Government, or Politics in British universities. The unresolved disagreement on these issues, manifest in the multiplicity of names which departments in this subject still carry, is far from novel. It is, according to some commentators, one of the hallmarks of the eclectic, tolerant, and diverse community of scholarship that has grown up in British universities throughout the twentieth century (Kavanagh 2003; 2007). Others, however, see dysfunction and weakness in this eclecticism (Dunleavy, Kelly, and Moran 2000; Aspinall 2006). Many practitioners believe that a fully independent and mature political science has only just begun to emerge in the UK, because the subject was for years held back by the influence of powerful rival disciplines—History, Philosophy, and Law—and was too enthralled to the gentlemanly amateurism that infused the study and teaching of politics in the early twentieth century, at Oxford University above all (Hayward 1999; Barry 1999).

In this chapter I aim to shed some light on these different perspectives, and probe some of the assumptions about the development of Politics as an academic discipline that shape contemporary thinking. I argue in particular that some deeply entrenched assumptions underpin commonly held ideas about the purpose and character of political studies as a modern, professionalized academic discipline. These largely unspoken presuppositions represent encumbrances that deserve critical reflection at a time when the subject needs fresh, imaginative, and historically minded thinking about its current status and future development. Academic practitioners have tended to avoid rather than address these questions about the identity and purpose of the subject during the intensive years of self-conscious professionalization. Recently there has been something of a move back to such questions, typically in the context of critical arguments about what political scientists and thinkers have assumed about the character and limits of politics (Dunn 2000; Freeden 2005; Gamble 2000; Hay 2007; Philp 2006; Stoker 2006). But it remains the case that for most practitioners, the ethos of political science professionalism is combined with a grudging pluralism about questions of method and theory (Beer 1977: 5), and a growing acceptance of the idea that the different subfields of study, such as comparative politics, area studies, and political theory, need to be granted greater autonomy. The centrifugal dynamic associated with this last idea is combined with and offset by the presumption that one of the most important bonds uniting the disciplinary field is the ethos and status of professionalism (Bevir 2001).

The identity supplied by such thinking is an uneasy one in key respects for the subject and is limited as a guide in the face of the challenging and increasingly competitive environment associated with Higher Education in the UK. Among the myriad challenges facing the subject are such questions as: how to promote the academic study of Politics, when politics itself is viewed with increasing indifference and cynicism; how to defend the funding quota it receives from the major funding body in the social sciences—the Economic and Social Research Council; how to compete in a more competitive struggle for research funding from other sources; how to convince university managers ever more inclined to invest in sure returns that some of the subjects, courses, and centres in areas that have drifted out of intellectual fashion are still worthy of support; and how to compete with other national and international rivals for students and prestige. Other ongoing intellectual challenges include questions about whether the boundaries between the subject and its nearest neighbours—Sociology, Economics, History, and Law—are aids or hindrances, and how to present as coherent a subject which increasingly looks like a set of quasi-independent sub-disciplinary fiefdoms (Almond 1988). Whether professionalism itself offers sufficiently robust and persuasive answers to these issues is an increasingly vexed issue for the subject as a whole.

The question of what if anything binds political studies practitioners in the UK needs to be more openly aired. We operate currently with only the dimmest sense of how the current outlook of practitioners in this field compares with our predecessors. Indeed a strengthening commitment to the ethos of professionalism is itself likely to hamper, not help, our thinking in this regard. For it tends to encourage a rather condescending and occasionally disdainful perspective towards the merits and worth of earlier contributions (see Robert Goodin's contribution to this volume, Chapter 3). A widely held view is that political studies has achieved an overdue rigour and seriousness on the back of the disciplinary independence that was won, rather late in the day for many contemporary tastes, from the late 1960s onwards. Until that point Politics figured on the curriculum of a handful of universities in the form of papers taught by scholars associated with the older established disciplines of History, Philosophy, Economics, and Law (Kavanagh 2007). The development of modern political analysis, it is therefore assumed, required the formation of a separate disciplinary field, with clearly defined intellectual boundaries, new departments, and the paraphernalia of professional self-organization. While this narrative captures something of the importance and benefits that the practice of a strengthened sense of 'disciplinarity' (Collini 1988) (including new departments, courses, and a recent upsurge in UK and overseas students) have undoubtedly brought into being, it is unduly one-eyed and historically stunting as a guide to the subject's complex intellectual past. In the remainder of this chapter I discuss the three major intellectual props that have nourished a good deal of the hubris that contemporary practitioners feel towards the subject's earlier history—the ethos of professionalism, a critical stance towards the intellectual insularity and parochialism of the indigenous intellectual culture which is assumed to have held political science back, and the presumption that mature political analysis requires an epistemologically grounded distance from politics itself.

1.2 ON PROFESSIONALISM

The values and ethos associated with professionalism have over the last twenty years become one important source of the shared identity of researchers and teachers in what has become a more diversified academic subject.[1] Since its inception in British universities, Politics has permitted important differences of focus, method,

---

[1] As far back as 1977, Dennis Kavanagh and Richard Rose reported that 'in style the study of politics has become self-consciously professional and specialized' (1977: 21).

and theory. This pluralistic approach was, however, nested within a widely shared set of intellectual and normative values for much of the last century. These had to a considerable extent been set down in the early decades of the twentieth century (Kavanagh 2003), and comprised a rich interweaving of Whiggish liberalism, a laudatory account of domestic political institutions, and a normative commitment to the values of liberty and representative democracy (Kenny 2004; 2007).

These coordinates all began to lose their hold on British-based scholars in the two decades after the Second World War. In the political and intellectual ferment of the mid- to late 1970s, they were all subjected to extensive criticism (Gamble 1990). The diversity of focus which once prevailed has become more entrenched and extensive, and 'the discipline' has come to assume the form of a large, loosely demarcated arena in which there coexist a number of fairly separate enclaves, under such headings as comparative politics, public policy, political behaviour, political economy, and political theory. International relations, which has developed in a semi-independent relation to Politics, typically occupies the most separate of spaces within this broad field, despite its many intellectual overlaps with and borrowings from the Politics lexicon (Schmidt 1998).

Associated with the construction and separation of these enclaves have been such developments as: the establishment of more journals covering smaller patches of intellectual territory; the emergence of leading figures and gatekeepers with reputations as leaders in particular subfields; and an increasingly disparate set of reference literatures. Where once there were relatively few border posts and low or absent fences between Politics and neighbouring subjects, there are now higher walls and a stronger sense of commitment to the identity conferred by association with a specialist field. The broad interwoven pattern of 'ideas and institutions' thinking which had shaped a good deal of political study in Britain undertaken until the 1960s began to wane in the 1970s (Adcock and Bevir 2005). While some important differences and debates subsisted within this broad paradigm, it also exerted a unifying effect on this fragmented intellectual community. In the context of these changes, as well as some significant shifts in the cultures and organizational structures of British universities, the subject has been encouraged to take up the mantle of social science professionalism as the medium through which it presents itself to external funders, university administrators, and its potential student 'customers'. The widespread diffusion of the notion that, despite differences of specialist focus and interest, those employed to undertake the study and teaching of Politics are united in respect of the professionally sanctioned competence and skills which they demonstrate, can be seen as one small instance of the much larger story of the emergence and power of professionals in the public sector (Perkin 1990).

David Marquand develops this interpretation, pointing to the steady displacement of 'the nineteenth-century citizenship ideal' in twentieth-century Britain by a:

> discourse of professionalism and the self-image of the professional class. The nineteenth-century themes of service, equity and trust remained central to both, but they came to be articulated in a language of positivist rationality rather than one of civic

engagement. More and more, professionals saw themselves, and (more importantly) presented themselves to the wider society, as technocratic specialists rather than members of, and contributors to a broader civic community.   (2004: 75)

The greater 'hermeticism and self-confidence' (76) which he detects among public-sector professional groups in the second half of the last century found direct echoes in the academy:

> The growing prestige of the natural sciences, and the associated, almost exponential growth in scientific knowledge and the effectiveness of applied science, led academics in the humanities and, still more, in the social sciences to imitate their scientific colleagues in certain key respects. Formerly, they had seen themselves as part of a broader public culture, to whose development they were duty-bound to contribute, and which they enriched by doing so. Now they tended increasingly to turn their backs on the public culture, and on the concerns of those who inhabited it.   (76)

Considering such changes in the context of the social sciences, he sees a common shift within Economics, Sociology, and Politics towards an emphasis on high theory and the growth of technical expertise in relation to research methodology, and a concomitant waning of the aspiration for each to play a broader public role. A major consequence of these changes has been the transformation of the academic profession into 'a secular priesthood, preoccupied by its own, increasingly arcane internal arguments, all too often expressed in a rebarberative and inaccessible jargon, and developed in obscure journals whose editorial practices aped those of the natural sciences' (76).

The kind of critical response to disciplinary developments that Marquand enunciates presents the subject's past as something very different to an 'amateurish prequel' (Hayward 1986) to today's professionalism. His reading is echoed in arguments that are still advanced at the margins of today's disciplinary thinking, some of which emanate from the hinterlands of the history of political thought and Oakeshottian thinking in particular (Johnson 1989). This kind of analysis sheds important light on the poverty of historical awareness displayed by today's professional political scientists (Nash 1995). Many of the latter caricature those who preceded them as gentlemanly-amateurs lacking the requisite training, expertise, theoretical tools, or properly collected data to deliver rigorous political understanding (Barry 1999). Little of value, it seems, lies in the scholarly output associated with the subject prior to its professionalized recent past. Only with the adoption of the theories and methodological approaches favoured by political scientists elsewhere, or by other, non-British, theoretical paradigms, did the cloying hold of a weak, underdeveloped, and inferior indigenous tradition begin to fade.

This forceful critique offers an inverted mirror image of the conventional account of how the subject has developed. Where most contemporaries assume a broadly linear pattern of progression away from our amateurish forebears, Marquand speaks for those who decry the intellectual effects of the rise of professionalism and its associated modes of technical reason. This perspective offers a powerful counter-image of the state of political studies. Its greatest merit for those seeking a more sinuous and independent perspective on the intellectual history of this academic subject is to remind us of the existence and interplay of rival conceptions of its ulterior purpose and character. That these have all but disappeared from view ought to give us pause for thought. Reconnecting with this lineage of critical and imaginative thinking is itself an important step towards greater historical awareness within political studies.

1.3 THE USES OF HISTORY

The weakening sense of anchorage within the resources associated with an array of familiar traditions of political thinking is closely bound up with some of the trends and developments that Marquand and other disciplinary critics discuss. It is, therefore, worth pausing to consider how key figures from the past deployed and connected with the traditions available to them as they developed arguments for a more independent and developed political analysis. This assessment has a direct bearing on the adequacy of the presumption that the subject was for a long time inhibited from becoming independent by a combination of the imperialism of subjects like History and Philosophy, and other supposedly ingrained indigenous intellectual weaknesses.

In his influential overview of the disciplinary field, *The Study of Political Science Today*, published in Britain in 1971, W. J. M. Mackenzie, Professor of Government at the University of Manchester, presented political studies as 'awkwardly posed between two strategies of teaching and research in political science'. The first of these was a distinctively English liberal humanism in which the idea of political education as an apprenticeship in coming to understand and deploy the insights of a (national) political culture was fostered. This was a lineage he had imbibed, and come to reflect critically upon, during his own years at Oxford. Also influential, Mackenzie observed, was a rival perspective, the heir to an indigenous pattern of radicalism that viewed politics as amenable to scientific analysis (understood predominantly as the gathering and objective interpretation of facts about social issues), which would be deployed on behalf of schemes of social and political reform. In his inaugural lecture as Professor of Political Science at LSE, Harold Laski nodded towards the merits and impact of the thinking of the School's inaugural Chair in the subject, Graeme Wallas (Laski 1940). Widely viewed as one of the founding fathers of the lineage later labelled behaviouralism, Wallas was convinced of the merits of the scientific study of mass political psychology (Adcock 2007; Wallas 2006). But this tradition was, Laski observed, always tempered by the political morality and sensibilities associated with the philosophical liberalism associated with Oxford University. Like Wallas, Laski conceived of the creation of citizens as an integral aspect of the work he undertook as scholar and teacher. As Mackenzie also observed, the ambition to foster and deepen a culture of citizenship, and a related focus upon a growing number of threats to the civic culture associated with mass democracy, were some of the key motifs around which the subject developed in the first half of the last century.

These themes were central to the writing and thought of the inaugural Cambridge Chair of Political Science, Sir Ernest Barker. For him, the study of social and political thought was the centre-ground of what amounted to 'a speculation about a group of facts in the field of social conduct, a speculation intended to result in a general schema which connects the facts systematically with one another and thus gives an explanation of their significance' (1928: 4). Such reflections took their bearings, Barker believed, from the welter of insights and thinking associated with the grand tradition of Western political philosophy.

These and other leading figures were thoroughly versed in the thinking and methods of a range of conventionally separated intellectual fields—history, political thought, constitutional government, and philosophy above all. All combined their historical awareness and familiarity with a range of intellectual traditions with a commitment to the development of the promotion of greater independence for, and seriousness about, the undertaking of the study and teaching of politics. The ideas of Wallas, Laski, Barker, and McKenzie were thus important resources for the formation of a stand-alone discipline, rather than obstacles to, or encumbrances upon, later developments. A detailed survey of what was being taught in this field which G. D. H. Cole completed for UNESCO in 1950 offered an especially important (and latterly forgotten) statement of the case for more extensive and coordinated teaching of Politics, and pointed towards the necessity for disciplinary independence.[2]

Similar arguments apply to earlier periods as well. As the historian Dorothy Ross has demonstrated, the winning of professional independence for political science in the United States at the very start of the twentieth century was mirrored and influenced by currents of thinking from England (2007: 26). The decades from the 1880s to 1920s represent an important transitional period in which scholars began to formulate an understanding of the historical past as a terrain that ought to be understood in more analytical ways, and when important debates about the character of the methods appropriate to the collection of data took hold. At Cambridge, the historian J. R. Seeley called for the adoption of a greater sense of analytical detachment in both the public discussion and the academic analysis of political phenomena. At least a century before the same kinds of arguments had become de rigueur, he suggested that politics itself should be looked at 'as a field of study, if not of science', and called for it to be offered as a separate subject in British schools and universities (1923: 7). Different kinds of 'scientific' approach to the study of politics, reflecting some of the major competing characterizations of science itself, were propounded at all of the universities where the subject was taught in the first half of the twentieth century.

These examples illustrate how wide of the mark are most conventional ideas about the subject's past. But, it might be countered, does a discipline need to be accurate

---

[2] See also William Robson's historically informed account of the subject, 'Political Science in Great Britain' (1950).

or indeed curious about its own past to be successful? Historical awareness is not an instrumental force dictating the health of a subject. Nevertheless there are good prudential and intellectual reasons for taking seriously this deficiency. First, given that judgements about originality and quality of interpretation are intrinsic to scholarly practice, with what confidence can we gauge whether current analysis is truly original or distinctive without a proper sense of what has come before (Dryzek and Leonard 1988)? Second, as with any other collective human entity, the adoption of future trajectories is best undertaken with reference to, and in dialogue with, the shared past. As a body of social-psychological and philosophical thought attests, it is only through the establishment of a healthy relationship with the past that a collective entity makes grounded and confident decisions about its future direction (Taylor 1992). And, third, a more developed sense of discipline-history is bound to return to the horizons of contemporaries' insights from earlier periods as well as forgotten but fertile paths of intellectual enquiry. These may be of worth in their own right, providing sources for new kinds of enquiry, or serving as benchmarks for the evaluation of current ways of thinking.

A more reflective, proportionate, and open-minded consideration of the discipline's development, current dilemmas, and different possible futures is long overdue. And there is no better terrain from which to undertake such an evaluation than the canvass of history. In the United States, a small but influential band of disciplinary historians have kept alive memories of the noble and significantly political purposes that infused the subject throughout its history (Dryzek and Leonard 1988; Farr 1988; Gunnell 1993). They show too that the nature and impact of professionalism have long figured within the subject's historiography (Ricci 1984), and have become prominent again in the wake of the recent perestroika movement that has campaigned against the drive towards quantitative research and rational choice models (Miller 2001). In the UK, by contrast, historical analysis of the subject is, with only a few exceptions, regarded as the property of the great and the good—appropriate subjects for inaugural lectures and Festschrifts, rather than being of more general worth or interest (Adcock and Bevir 2005).

Inadequate though conventional understandings may be, it does not follow that the tale of unadulterated decline that Marquand and others offer provides an especially robust alternative. For this perspective is in serious danger of giving undue causal prominence to professionalism and of misrepresenting its novelty. Anxieties about the implications of a creeping professionalization have been a recurrent presence in thinking about the social sciences in universities for well over a century (Collini, Winch, and Burrow 1983). Declinist arguments tend to posit a pre-professional golden age, when scholars were driven by civic concern and organically linked to wider political debates, that is belied by the complexities of any given period that results from closer historical examination. More specialist and technically focused scholarship existed side-by-side with the kind of politically engaged generalism that Marquand and others applaud, right throughout the last century. The changes he and others lament are in fact better understood as shifts in the balance between the competing and interlocked discourses of generalism and intra-disciplinary specialism that have, as Stefan Collini (2006) argues, been constitutive of intellectual practice throughout this period.

We should also bear in mind the distinctive ways in which different subject fields have embraced, interpreted, and internalized the values associated with the concept of the professional. A spectrum runs from subjects such as Law, Medicine, and Management across to some of the most established Arts and Humanities fields. Among the former a major rationale for the curriculum is the preparation of students for professional qualifications. Departments in these areas are usually closely attuned to the ethos of particular professions. Among the latter, older liberal-humanist ideas about the intrinsic value of educational attainment and the independence of forms of knowledge and thought associated with subjects such as Philosophy or Theology remain stronger, though are not entirely untouched by the winds of professional modernity.

Politics as a subject has tended to occupy points between these two poles, though it has shifted its centre of gravity somewhat over the last two decades from the latter towards the former. And yet despite this movement, it is not accurate to suggest that it has been drawn decisively towards the model of the professional scientist that has been one of the leading self-images of its American counterpart. In the UK, professionalism has been cross-fertilized with a sense of *modus vivendi* about the legitimacy of a range of methodological and theoretical approaches that research in the subject may deploy (Finer 1980; Crick 1980; Kavanagh and Rose 1977). No single theory or research paradigm has emerged into the leading position occupied by quantitative political science methodology and formal modelling in the USA. Some scholars fear or hope that this may change, not least because of the influence which the main funding council for social science research has exerted over the last decade over the methods of training younger cohorts of students.

An additional reason for avoiding the perils of golden-ageism in our evaluation of the development of the subject concerns the ambivalent character of the practices and values associated with professionalism. A 'for' or 'against' stance gives us little analytic purchase on the complexities of these phenomena. Instead we might separate more clearly in our thinking an appreciation of the ideas and power of the ethos associated with 'professionalism' from the institutional practices and legally shaped processes that might be described under the heading of 'professionalization'. The first of these concepts helps us understand the different, not always mutually consistent, values that have been advanced through this notion. Under this heading we should assess the cogency and rigour of the claims that are developed through the normative ideal of the professional, including adjacent concept-ideas such as impartiality, detachment, rigour, expertise, and objectivity.

In relation to 'professionalization', we should consider the legal, political, and institutional processes that have resulted, for instance, in greater equity and transparency in terms of hiring, training, and the wider regulation of workplace behaviour. Through such a conceptual separation, we might become more adept at distinguishing between the epistemological and ethical claims advanced when scholars claim the mantle of professionals, and more nuanced in our judgements of the character and implications of these processes. In the case of political studies, therefore, an appreciation of the undoubted egalitarian and democratic benefits of some of the changes associated with professionalization does not require that we also celebrate uncritically the hegemony of professionalism as an account of the identity of the subject.

1.4 THE PECULIARITIES OF ENGLISH THOUGHT?

One of the most recurrent motifs to surface in discussions of the history and character of the subject in the UK is the suggestion that political science in the UK developed slowly and painfully because the intellectual culture in which it sought to develop was exceptionally inhospitable (Smith 1986; Hayward 1991). A clutch of recent retrospective essays on the history of the main subfields within the wider subject couch their accounts in terms of the quintessentially 'English' values which their development reflects (Hayward, Barry, and Brown 1999). These are taken to include a scepticism towards rationalistic theories and formal modelling, a preference for historical and empirical modes of thinking, and a disinterest in the kinds of systematic or comparative analytical models that political science requires. The frequency with which characterizations of a purportedly dominant strain of the national intellectual culture are invoked as sources of explanation for developments in this and related subjects is striking (Easthope 1998). Also significant in these arguments is the related accusation that political studies has spawned analyses of the indigenous polity that are irreducibly tainted by a parochial solipsism.

But how accurate are these twin charges about Politics as an academic subject? Has it been unduly held back by intellectual insularity and unreflective exceptionalism? As is the case with the historical caricatures posited by linear narratives of the subject's development, these generalized assertions carry enough plausibility and resonance to ensure their ready reproduction and largely unquestioned status. And yet, neither is as easily demonstrable as is often assumed.

Characterizing the development of the subject in four different national contexts—Scotland, Wales, Northern Ireland, and England—through reference to the posited characteristics of a supposedly hegemonic English intellectual character is highly problematic. Quite clearly, the subject has developed in these contexts in close relation to, but also somewhat differently from, its counterpart in England. Presenting a singular British tradition as the aggregate or core to these national-intellectual differences is itself a problematic move. Equally, if we consider the two decades following the end of the Second World War, a period characterized by one commentator as a kind of amateurish prologue to the professionalized present (Hayward 1986), it is hard to reconcile the multiplicity of theoretical positions, ideological perspectives, and interpretative methods that circulated among those teaching and studying the subject in England with the image suggested by these characterizations of English intellectual culture. Major comparative studies—across time as well as space—were produced in this period (Rose 1995; Finer 1956). And these came well before American political science made serious inroads. A more important and complex set of intellectual changes slowly unfolded prior to the sudden expansion of the university sector in the late 1960s. A younger cohort of scholars (including Samuel Finer, Mackenzie, and Bernard Crick) sought in different ways to generate a more theoretically aware approach to political studies that combined historicism, philosophy, political science theory, and a comparative focus (Kenny 2007). The influence of members of this grouping on subsequent generations of practitioner has been considerably underplayed in standard historiographies of the discipline.

And yet the notion that political science has now emerged from the cloying embrace of a parochial national-intellectual tradition has been reiterated to the point where it has assumed the status of a bedrock myth. It is surely time to acknowledge the blind-spots of such a blanket generalization. Characterizations of 'the national' culture that emphasize English insularity, antipathy to theory, and narcissistic investment in its own singularity are drawn from a lineage of thought that itself has a lengthy history. Such laments have been aired since at least the late nineteenth century and gained a particular hearing in political circles because of a gathering anxiety about Britain's economic performance and diminishing role as a world power in the years after 1955. The attack upon the cloistered, insular, and blinkered character of domestic intellectual life that was variously advanced by Edward Shils, Perry Anderson, and Tom Nairn in the middle of the last century was taken up by political thinkers of left and right in later decades (Anderson 1992; Anderson and Nairn 1992; Shils 1972). It has also however become a major target for historians of the intellectual and cultural life (Collini 2006). Its weaknesses include: the mistaken tendency to project onto the whole of Britain what is essentially an account of English intellectual life; a downgrading of the continuing impact of non-liberal traditions of thought; and an overstatement of the hermetic and insular nature of indigenous thinking across a range of fields. These objections should give practitioners of political studies pause for thought. For each of them applies just as well to the ways in which the 'Englishness' of British political studies is routinely caricatured, and sometimes granted independent causal status in explaining disciplinary developments (or non-developments). While it is not hard to find evidence of an abiding empirical idiom and some strongly anti-theoretical and indeed anti-intellectual prejudices among figures in this field in England especially, the question of whether this offers a sufficient explanation of the subject's development needs to be posed much more sharply.

One consequence of the overuse of this standard account of the failings of England's intellectual culture is an understatement of the patterns of cross-national ideational exchange and mutual influence that shaped the subject in its different locations. In the early twentieth century, political scholarship and teaching at England's elite universities were deeply marked by the influence of European philosophy,

German constitutional thought, and professional developments in the United States. The last two decades of the nineteenth century and first couple of the twentieth witnessed a fairly continual pattern of dialogue and mutual influence between groups of scholars in the USA and Britain:

> Considerable Anglo-American contact, and even more frequent reference, occurred among these scholars, and for good reasons. In both countries, liberal academic elites wanted to carve out an authoritative place in the university and to salvage their political heritage in the face of new challenges posed by industrialization and mass democracy.
>
> (Ross 2007: 18)

On both sides of the Atlantic, political science emerged during these decades as a 'specialized field of study at the intersection of philosophy, history, and law' (2007: 18). Ross highlights the development at this time of an important Anglo-American 'left-liberal network anchored on Toynbee Hall, the Fabian Society, and the LSE on one side, and Jane Addams's Hill House, Progressive reform circles, and the social science departments of the new American universities on the other' (20). Elsewhere, the English liberal scholar and MP James Bryce exercised a very direct impact upon the way in which early twentieth-century American scholars approached the interpretation of their own institutions and political history, through the publication of his two-volume study, *The American Commonwealth* (1910). His importance was reflected in his award of the Presidency of the American Political Science Association in 1907.

A parallel process occurred in reverse and had a lasting impact upon the British subject. This has occurred through both the employment of American-trained figures in British departments, and the establishment of some important trans-Atlantic networks and research collaborations. Thus, the highly unlikely partnership that developed between the quantitative specialist Donald Stokes and the doyen of informed commentary upon the workings of the Westminster elite, David Butler, utterly transformed the content of the influential Nuffield Electoral Studies series (Butler and Stokes 1969; Kenny 2007). This has had a long-lasting impact upon the intellectual character and methodological tools of the subfield of electoral studies in the UK in subsequent years (Dunleavy 1990).

Certainly the volume of traffic between these different national-intellectual spaces has fluctuated in different periods. In the years after the Second World War, the USA became a more regular exporter than importer of ideas in this field. As with its overseas trade, Britain meanwhile was never disposed to deal with one partner at a time. New waves of Continental European thinking, in the fields of philosophy, political and social theory, and sociology, gained an influence over many younger British scholars from the 1950s onwards. Indeed, in conceptual and historical terms, British traditions evolved within a wider European framework of thinking in a way that belies simplistic conceptions of exclusively national traditions of scholarship and thought. Consideration of the impact of the migration of individual scholars and of thinking provides an important counterpoint to reified ideas about the national disciplinary past (Farr 2006). Key figures and traditions of thought, including those that have presented themselves as guardians of indigenous virtues or approaches, have developed their ideas against the backdrop of a deep familiarity with European *and* American intellectual traditions. Only in more recent years have political scientists, whose training and educational backgrounds mean that they are less likely to enjoy such a hinterland, come to the fore.

In fact a proper consideration of the nature and impact of these intellectual transactions would lead us to adopt a more widely angled perspective as an interpretative default in this area. This might enable practitioners to begin to appreciate[3] the degree to which Empire and Commonwealth have been overlooked as sources of influence upon academic thinking about politics in the last fifty years. Political studies reflected and helped engender some of the thinking that flowed into the practice and justification of formal imperial rule, and was then greatly affected by thinking associated with the politics of anti-colonial struggle. Yet despite the many ways in which the period of Empire shaped the priorities and infrastructure of British governance, provided the coordinates for a good deal of its political culture, and impacted upon Britain's foreign and economic policies, these themes are absent from both the historiography and self-assessment of the discipline as a whole.

The broader point arising from these reflections is that the endless reiteration of the myth of English insularity and its supposedly deleterious impact on the subject's development may perversely have the effect of obscuring the many non-English influences on the thinking that has fed into political studies. The migration of individuals and ideas across national borders has been a constitutive feature of the growth of universities. Amidst the many disagreements about the strengths and weaknesses of the subject in the UK, there has lurked a largely unquestioned consensus, that political science is alien to indigenous modes of thought, which needs serious reconsideration. Rather strikingly, scholarly investigation into other national-cultural thinking in Europe about the same issues has unearthed a very similar sense of anxiety about the degree to which indigenous idioms are hostile to a serious intellectual culture and theoretical worth, and the latter are routinely seen as typical of various 'elsewheres' (Collini 2006). England's intellectual culture may well be far less exceptional in kind than is widely assumed. And the widely held notion that political science, or indeed the social sciences as a whole, developed outside its parameters, and needed to be imported to its inhospitable terrain, simply does not stand up to any serious account of the intellectual history of subjects like political science and sociology.

1.5 ACADEMICS AND THE POLITICAL

The steadily increasing influence of the ideal of professionalism over British-based practitioners has elicited a growing sense of unease. One sign of the latter is the

[3] There are important exceptions to this generalization, not least the development of a field of study associated with 'Development', specialist studies of African and Asian politics, and the newer subfield known as international political economy.

intensification of a long-standing debate about whether political studies has been weakened by its distance from, and supposed irrelevance to, politics itself. This theme has been aired by a number of senior figures within this field, and posed by external bodies and groups that should be among the most important consumers of its outputs (Crick 1998; Marquand 2004; Pearce 2005).

A particular tributary of discussion branching off this larger debate has focused on whether the principal mechanism introduced by government's reforms since the 1980s—the Research Assessment Exercise (RAE)—to guide the allocation of research funds, has combined with a rising professionalism to generate cohorts of political scientists who excel at producing technically adept but intellectually narrow research that is designed above all to impress seniors in their specialist enclave. Many stake-holders involved in Higher Education have begun to wonder if scholars lack both the incentives and the cultural environment conducive to translate their work into more widely accessible kinds of intervention.

The system of peer review bound up in the RAE has actually operated as a brake on the drive towards specialism and 'technical reason' within British political science research. The outcomes of its deliberations have, probably relatedly, achieved a wide amount of legitimacy within this subject. Nevertheless, a growing perception in the Higher Education policy-making community is that it has buttressed a growing disinclination towards public dissemination and engagement. In the case of political studies, some important stakeholders see professionalism as a partial obstacle to the reanimation of a broader sense of civic purpose and democratic commitment, values that are central to the stated mission and evaluative criteria of the Economic and Social Research Council, the major funding body for many British political analysts. There exists too a tradition of thinking within the British politics community that is markedly sceptical of what one scholar has termed 'the illusions of utility' bound up in the occupation of the role of 'social engineer' (Johnson 1989).

Yet despite these opposed kinds of worry, it is striking to observe that many individual practitioners have communicated their research to stakeholders and users, and occasionally enjoyed influence with political actors and policy-makers. The dissemination of ideas about 'social capital', that originated in the reappropriation of this term in the work of American political scientist Robert Putnam, provides one of the most spectacular instances of such impact (Field 2008; Putnam 2001). Indeed, the growth of more technically adept and rigorous models of analysis in some areas of the study of politics has actually opened up avenues for public commentary and impact— most obviously in relation to extensive media treatment of elections and the increased quantity of coverage of 'high' party politics associated with the development of rolling news coverage and the proliferation of media outlets. Nevertheless, the emergence of the political-scientist-as-pundit is not quite what some of the high-minded civic and democratic visionaries of the subject had in mind when they urged it to remain engaged with the public culture. Is media presence quite the same thing as public influence?

More generally, simplistic assertions about whether the subject as a whole has become more or less engaged with politics and public life are bound to miss their target, not least because of the volume and range of activities now associated with departments and individual academics. Equally, judgements about whether research has succeeded in having influence and impact is a very different matter to the evaluation of whether the subject is more or less publicly engaged and outward facing than previously. Here too there is much to be gained by turning to the past when considering an apparently novel dilemma. Such a move leads us to appreciate that worries about a perceived growing 'irrelevance' on the part of political analysis and theorizing, as well as the invocation of a putative golden age when a more organic interrelationship purportedly existed between scholarship and political action, enjoy long precedents. Similar anxieties were aired when the subject became more prominent in the late nineteenth-century university, surfaced again in the face of the rise of Marxist thought in the 1930s, and were expressed by the clutch of mid-century figures discussed above (including Mackenzie, Crick, the Finers, and Samuel Beer) of their more cloistered and complacent elders. Related anxieties about a drift to greater specialization and the proliferation of technical language, as opposed to the vernaculars deployed in relation to more 'general' publics, are in fact as old as the academic study of politics itself.

But discursive continuity is not the whole story to be told on this issue. This emphasis needs to be leavened with a sense of the very significant changes that have occurred to the foundational ideas about its purpose and character which the subject has held about itself. The historical amnesia encouraged by the ethos of professionalism has tended to obscure the protean character of debate about these issues that prevailed in political studies until the greater consensus of recent times. The subject was variously endowed with such missions as: providing an important part of the education required for the next generation of public administrators; promoting and disseminating the ideals of the civic culture; providing data about and dispassionate expert analysis of policy issues to improve policy-making; and furnishing avowedly ideological perspectives upon British politics. The first of these notions was undoubtedly dominant at the turn of the nineteenth and twentieth centuries but was soon in contention with rival versions of these different ambitions. A broadly civic conception of the discipline was apparent in the thinking and public involvements of figures as disparate as Wallas, Barker, and McKenzie—though some important differences marked their views of who were the intended recipients of this education and what kinds of democratic effect it ought to have. Bernard Crick in the early 1960s called on political studies teachers to adhere to the civic-republican ambitions which he believed animated the foundation of the subject in the United States (Crick 1959; Kenny 2006). This translated into a long-standing conviction that university-based academics should do much more to develop and promote the subject in schools.

Alongside, and occasionally intertwined with, civic idealism, there persisted through much of the century the social-reforming impulse that stemmed from the Fabian milieu, and was embodied by Wallas at LSE. This tradition has favoured rigorous empirical study and the achievement of direct access to and influence upon members of the political elite. Politics at university level was on this view a policy science that ought to be directed towards the betterment of the community as a whole. Some other potent ideological conceptions of the purpose and rationale of the subject have also been in play across this period. Thus, Anglo-Marxists like Ralph Miliband saw political analysis as committed to the revelation of the veiled power relations that lay behind the frontage of the British state (Adcock and Bevir 2005; Kenny 2007). Conservative scholars of various hues have regarded the study of politics and political ideas as replete with lessons about the perils of rational design, social engineering, or Enlightenment thinking (Minogue 1985; Gray 1995).

The demise of some of the democratic and civic aspirations that flowed through the teaching and scholarship undertaken in this field provides an important backdrop to current anxieties about an apparent decrease in the amount of public engagement undertaken by political science professionals, even if the relationship between these two developments is not one of direct causation. It is notable that the figures mentioned above—Wallas, Barker, McKenzie, and Crick—all had the experience of teaching and performing public service roles outside the Oxbridge tutorial. Wallas was a University Extension Lecturer before he took up a Lectureship at LSE. He served on the London School Board (and was later Chair of its School Management Committee), as well as being a member of the Technical Education Board for London and of the Education Committee of London County Council. Such experiences undoubtedly helped engender and sustain the ambition of extending educational opportunity as widely as possible, and education figured prominently in his distinctive account of the importance and dangers of mass democracy. Mackenzie's experience of teaching local government officials in Manchester likewise bolstered a sense of commitment to a civic dimension for the subject. Barker meanwhile combined high scholarship and classical learning with a commitment to journalistic writing that ensured he had a mixture of audiences for his political thinking at the forefront of his mind.

And yet, judging the degree to which an academic subject has influence over, or relevance to, domains and practices outside it, is harder than we tend to think. The evaluative criteria associated with the terms 'impact', 'influence', and 'relevance' are multiple in kind and depend crucially upon the wider conceptual fields in which they are deployed. Put simply, one person's indirect impact may well be another's indication of irrelevance. Further epistemological complications arise because the act of interpretation which is central to political analysis invariably requires some process of abstraction—either through the explicit deployment of theoretical categories, methods, and hypotheses, or through the processes of simplification central to the assessment of relations of causality. Nor is the language in which a piece of research is expressed a necessary guarantee of, or inhibitor to, influence or relevance. Some of the most highbrow and 'technical' kinds of theory have been used by authors who also convey a tremendous sensitivity to political phenomena (Michael Oakeshott and Isaiah Berlin could be placed in this camp). And many writings in the straightforward empirical or journalistic veins have very little 'carry' into wider public argument and debate. A range of external contextual factors as well as qualities internal to a piece of research determine whether influence is achieved. And much depends on which are taken to be the audiences over whom influence is exerted.

Authoritative judgements about whether a subject has assumed greater or less political relevance and public engagement over time imply an empirical support that does not currently exist. What we can determine however is the content of the mental frameworks that prevail in a subject at a given time and their impact on thinking about what constitutes relevance, and at what proximity to politics political analysts choose to operate (Freeden 2005). Here, some discernible trends across the various subfields of Politics towards a greater emphasis on methodological expertise, the greater take-up of deductive theories, and important changes to the incentive structures facing individual academics and whole departments, can be judged to have tilted the equilibrium of the subject away from a greater sense of political connectedness and proximity typical of earlier decades. For many political science professionals this is undoubtedly a move in the right direction, concomitant with adjacent ideas about detachment and objectivity. But, considered against the backdrop of once powerful democratic and civic ideas of the subject's role, there are some losses to be calibrated, and perhaps compensated for, in this regard.

A less obvious, but nevertheless important, intellectual shift has played a role here as well. There has been a very broad movement across the last two decades in political studies towards theoretical approaches to political life that posit 'the political' as an essentially debased simulacrum of the idealized constructs developed in the world of theory (Newey 2001), or as an irredeemably irrational and corrupt domain (Hay 2007). Is there a danger that the political gets endowed with a series of implicitly pejorative connotations, or denied any sense of its autonomy or singularity as an aspect of social behaviour by the models scholars use to interpret and teach political phenomena? And, has the steady march of deductively derived theoretical models into the scholarship, textbooks, and curricula of the contemporary subject had the effect of relegating some of the most banal but distinctive features of 'the political'— emotions, passions, rhetoric, messy compromises, coalition building—to the status of irrational or anti-rational tools of manipulation? Are not these and other recurrent facets of the political equally deserving of analysis (Dunn 2000)?

It is certainly striking that across this field a discernible counter-trend has gathered force over the last decade, committed to the reclamation and exploration of what one scholar calls 'a political theory of politics' (Freeden 2005)—the conceptual discussion of the properties, attributes, virtues, and norms that are distinctive to the practices and logics of the political domain which appear to have been relegated in importance in the scholarly mind. A broad range of theoretically inclined authors, including John Dunn, Quentin Skinner, Mark Philp, Andrew Gamble, and Gerry Stoker, have in their very different ways and voices lately sought to remind us of the importance of the specific character of political reasoning. The foundational question, 'what is politics?', and its more rarely articulated subsidiary, 'what is the study of politics for?', would seem to be moving back to the top of the agenda for some of today's political scholars. Whether their centrality stems from the entrenchment of a confident sense of professional authority or from anxiety about a growing distance and detachment from the political and civic cultures we inhabit, is a matter worthy of wider discussion.

1.6 CONCLUSIONS

This chapter has sought to identify and question the validity of three of the main props that together have bolstered the sense of collective identity that prevails in the academic community involved in political studies in British universities. All characterizations of collective identities run the risk of distorting their inchoate, fluid, and complex contents. And certainly it would be wrong to assume that a sense of professionalism is the only frame through which members of this community understand its ulterior purpose. For many, a sense of commitment to the unique properties of politics, or an addiction to the peculiarities and processes of politics, are far more significant as sources of motivation. Yet these values are not reflected in the public representations that the subject makes of itself.

Highlighting the impact of a commitment to professionalization is not to argue *in toto* against its values and practices. Many of the latter should be welcomed for egalitarian and democratic reasons. However, adopting professionalism as an encompassing, overarching identity has, I suggest, banished from our minds an awareness of the implications and potential losses it brings in its wake. One such consequence has been the entrenchment of a weak historical understanding of the subject's development and the bolstering of an unduly hubristic approach to the contributions made at earlier stages of its development. This sensibility has been entrenched too, I suggest, by the recessive quality of a favourite theme among some of those who have offered explanations about the relative underdevelopment of British political science—the exceptional insularity and anti-theoretical bent of English intellectual culture.

Having identified these interpretative failings and criticized some of their distorting simplifications, I close with some indications of the kinds of approaches and mechanisms through which this narrowed collective identity might be broadened and imaginatively renewed. The most urgently needed development is the hardest to will into existence—the development of a specialist field of enquiry into the subject's history that may feed into the wider consciousness of this intellectual community. One way in which such a focus could be stimulated is through a reform to the many courses devoted to the teaching of 'methods' at undergraduate and postgraduate levels, so that these include and promote historical comprehension of the history of Politics as a subject, and of the variety of themes, traditions, and ideas that gave shape to the understandings of politics which have been in contention throughout its lifetime.

A related second development is equally overdue. This involves a more sustained and exploratory examination of the relations between how politics, in its institutional, cultural, and ideological guises, has shaped Politics as a subject. This most obvious and interesting of relationships is, curiously, one of the most elusive within the scholarly output of this community. Some insightful suggestions about political factors that may have shaped political studies have occasionally been forthcoming—for instance Michael Moran's (2006) discussion of the importance of the context and influence of the state in shaping social sciences in the UK. Yet, no systematic, conceptually informed analysis of the role and impact of environmental factors has been offered. And, most glaringly of all, political factors have rarely been granted serious attention as variables shaping the subject's development in the UK. It may be that an overly strong sense of professional pride and identity inhibit the recognition of the degree to which political scientists, like the subjects they consider, are also to some degree shaped by the political circumstances and influences of their age. Yet the opening up of a serious examination of the complex relations and interchanges between these domains would not only benefit contemporary scholars but would most likely bring to life for students an interest in the historical development of the subject in which they are enrolled.

The third concrete implication of the argument pursued here concerns the need for a more confident challenge to the dominant myths of British national-intellectual character to be mounted from within and beyond this community. Lazy references to 'English empiricism' and assumed contrasts with a singular 'American political science' lock us into a cramped and self-limiting way of thinking about the subject. A richer and more challenging sense of the resources and themes associated with its intellectual history involves a greater commitment to unearthing trans-national conversations, influences, and arguments. Approached thus, the history of political studies may become a more interesting and less familiar terrain, one that is both alien and surprisingly relevant in different respects. It is above all time for a reconsideration of whether it makes sense to talk so confidently of 'the British tradition' of political study. I have not addressed this question head-on in this chapter, though some of the critical reflections that I have offered about some conventional forms of thinking about the identity and history of the subject do have a bearing upon it. I close with two more concrete proposals in relation to this question. A first, minimalist one, is that we encourage our students, our colleagues, and ourselves to elucidate what they/we mean when we invoke such a tradition. We ought to expect more than some of the stultifying and self-serving arguments about the study of politics too often entrenched by its usage. And a second, more ambitious (and no doubt contentious) experimental suggestion is that we consider giving up the habit of talking about the subject, its standing, purpose, and historical development, through reference to such a construct. In so doing, we may quickly become more attuned to wider—European, American, post-imperial—circles of influence and intellectual fellowship, and more sensitive to the many important differences—of approach, methodology, and ideology—that have contributed to the development of political studies in the UK context.

References

ADCOCK, R. 2007. 'Interpreting Behavioralism'. In R. Adcock, M. Bevir, and S. C. Stimson (eds.), *Modern Political Science: Anglo-American Exchanges since 1880*. Princeton, NJ: Princeton University Press.

—— and BEVIR, M. 2005. The History of Political Science. *Political Studies Review*, 1/3: 1–16.

ALMOND, G. A. 1988. Separate Tables: Schools and Sects in Political Science. *PS: Political Science and Politics*, 21/4: 828–42.

ANDERSON, P. 1992. Components of the National Culture. Pp. 48–104 in P. Anderson (ed.), *English Questions*. London: Verso.

—— and NAIRN, T. 1992. 'Origins of the Present Crisis'. In P. Anderson (ed.), *English Questions*. London: Verso.

ASPINALL, M. 2006. 'Studying the British'. *Politics*, 26/1: 3–10.

BARKER, E. 1928. *The Study of Political Science and its Relation to Cognate Studies*. Cambridge: Cambridge University Press.

BARRY, B. 1999. 'The Study of Politics as a Vocation'. In J. Hayward, B. Barry, and A. Brown (eds.), *The British Study of Politics in the Twentieth Century*. Oxford: Oxford University Press.

BEER, S. H. 1977. 'Politics and Political Science'. In D. Kavanagh and R. Rose (eds.), *New Trends in British Politics*. Beverly Hills, Calif.: Sage.

BEVIR, M. 2001. 'Prisoners of Professionalism: On the Construction and Responsibility of Political Studies; A Review Article'. *Public Administration*, 79/2: 469–509.

BRYCE, J. 1910. *American Commonwealth: volume 1*. New York: Macmillan.

BUTLER, D., and STOKES, D. 1969. *Political Change in Britain: Forces Shaping Electoral Choice*. New York: St Martin's Press.

COLE, G. D. H. 1950. 'The Study of Politics in British Universities'. In W. A. Robson (ed.), *The University Teaching of Social Sciences: Political Science*. Paris: UNESCO.

COLLINI, S. 1988. ' "Disciplinary History" and "Intellectual History": Reflections on the Historiography of the Social Sciences in Britain and France'. *Revue de Synthèse*, 3/4: 387–97.

—— 2006 *Absent Minds: Intellectuals in Britain*. Oxford: Oxford University Press.

—— WINCH, D., and BURROW, J. 1983. *That Noble Science of Politics: A Study in Nineteenth-Century Intellectual History*. Cambridge: Cambridge University Press.

CRICK, B. 1959. *The American Science of Politics: Its Origins and Conditions*. Berkeley: University of California Press.

—— 1980. 'The British Way'. *Government and Opposition*, 15/3–4: 297–307.

—— 1998. 'The Decline of Political Thinking in British Public Life'. *Critical Review of International Social and Political Philosophy*, 1/1: 102–20.

DRYZEK, J., and LEONARD, S. 1988. 'History and Discipline in Political Science'. *American Political Science Review*, 82: 1245–60.

DUNLEAVY, P. 1990. 'Mass Political Behaviour: Is There More to Learn?' *Political Studies*, 38/3: 453–69.

—— KELLY, P., and MORAN, M. 2000. 'Characterizing the Development of British Political Science'. In P. Dunleavy, P. Kelly, and M. Moran (eds.), *British Political Science: Fifty Years of Political Studies*. Oxford: Blackwell.

DUNN, J. 2000. *The Cunning of Unreason: Making Sense of Politics*. London: HarperCollins.

EASTHOPE, A. 1998. *Englishness and National Culture*. London: Routledge.

FARR, J. 1988. 'The History of Political Science'. *American Journal of Political Science*, 32/4: 1175–95.

—— 2006 'Transactions of European-American Political Science'. *European Political Science*, 5: 171–82.

FIELD, J. 2008. *Social Capital*. London: Routledge.

FINER, H. 1956. *The Governments of Greater Foreign Powers: A Comparative Study of the Governments and Political Culture of Great Britain, France, Germany and the Soviet Union*. London: Methuen.

FINER, S. E. 1980. 'Political Science: An Idiosyncratic Retrospect'. *Government and Opposition*, 15/3–4: 346–63.

FREEDEN, M. 2005. 'What should the "Political" in Political Theory Explore?' *Journal of Political Philosophy*, 13: 113–34.

GAMBLE, A. 1990. 'Theories of British Politics'. *Political Studies*, 38/3: 404–20.

——2000 *Politics and Fate*. Cambridge: Polity.

GRAY, J. 1995. *Enlightenment's Wake: Politics and Culture at the Close of the Modern Age*. London: Routledge.

GUNNELL, 1993. *The Descent of Political Theory: Genealogy of an American Vocation*. Chicago: University of Chicago Press.

HAY, C. 2007. *Why We Hate Politics*. Cambridge: Polity.

HAYWARD, J. 1986. 'The Political Science of Muddling Through: The *De Facto* Paradigm?' In J. Hayward and P. Norton (eds.), *The Political Science of British Politics*. Brighton: Harvester Wheatsheaf.

——1991. 'Political Science in Britain'. *European Journal of Political Research*, 20/2: 301–20.

——1999. 'British Approaches to Politics: The Dawn of a Self-Deprecating Discipline'. In J. Hayward, B. Barry, and A. Brown (eds.), *The British Study of Politics in the Twentieth Century*. Oxford: Oxford University Press.

——BARRY, B., and BROWN, A. 1999. *The British Study of Politics in the Twentieth Century*. Oxford: Oxford University Press.

JOHNSON, N. 1989. *The Limits of Political Science*. New York: Oxford University Press.

KAVANAGH, D. 2003. 'British Political Science in the Inter-war Years: The Emergence of the Founding Fathers'. *British Journal of Politics and International Relations*, 5/4: 594–613.

——2007. 'The Emergence of an Embryonic Discipline: British Politics without Political Scientists'. Pp. 97–117 in R. Adcock, M. Bevir, and S. C. Stimson (eds.), *Modern Political Science: Anglo-American Exchanges since 1880*. Princeton, NJ: Princeton University Press.

——and ROSE, R. 1977. *New Trends in British Politics*. London: Sage.

KENNY, M. 2004. 'The Case for Disciplinary History: British Political Studies in the 1950s and 1960s'. *British Journal of Politics and International Relations*, 6/4: 565–83.

——2006. 'History and Dissent: Bernard Crick's "The American Science of Politics"'. *American Political Science Review*, 100/4: 548–53.

——2007. 'Birth of a Discipline: Interpreting British Political Studies in the 1950s and 1960s'. Pp. 158–79 in R. Adcock, M. Bevir, and S. C. Stimson (eds.), *Modern Political Science: Anglo-American Exchanges since 1880*. Princeton, NJ: Princeton University Press.

LASKI, H. 1940. 'On the Study of Politics'. Pp 32–56 in *The Danger of Being a Gentleman and Other Essays*. London: Basic Books/George Allen and Unwin.

MACKENZIE, W. J. M. 1971. *The Study of Political Science Today*. Basingstoke: Macmillan.

MARQUAND, D. 2004 *The Decline of the Public: The Hollowing Out of Citizenship*. Cambridge: Polity.

MILLER, D. W. 2001. 'Storming the Palace in Political Science'. *Chronicle of Higher Education*, 48/4 (21 September).

MINOGUE, K. 1985. *Alien Powers: The Pure Theory of Ideology*. London: Weidenfeld and Nicolson.

MORAN, M. 2006. 'Interdisciplinarity and Political Science'. *Politics*, 26/2: 75–83.

NASH, F. 1995. 'Political Science, History, and Contemporary History'. Paper delivered at the Annual Conference of the Political Studies Association at the University of York; available at http://psa.ac.uk/publications/psd/1995/nash2.htm.

NEWEY, G. 2001. *After Politics: The Rejection of Politics in Contemporary Library Philosophy*. Basingstoke: Palgrave.

PEARCE, N. 2005. 'Mix in with Mandarins'. *Times Higher Education Supplement*, 15 April.

PERKIN, H. 1990. *The Rise of Professional Society: England Since 1880*. London: Routledge.

PHILP, M. 2006. *Political Conduct*. Cambridge, Mass.: Harvard University Press.

PUTNAM, R. 2001. *Bowling Alone: The Collapse and Revival of American Community*. New York: Simon and Schuster.

RICCI, D. M. 1984. *The Tragedy of Political Science: Politics, Scholarship, and Democracy*. New Haven, Conn.: Yale University Press.

ROBSON, W. 1950. 'Political Science in Great Britain'. Pp. 294–312 in *Contemporary Political Science: A Survey of Methods, Research and Teaching*. Paris: UNESCO.

ROSE, R. 1995 *The Art of Writing about Politics*. Glasgow: Centre for the Study of Public Policy, University of Strathclyde.

ROSS, D. 2007. 'Anglo-American Political Science'. Pp. 18–36 in R. Adcock, M. Bevir, and S. C. Stimson (eds.), *Modern Political Science: Anglo-American Exchanges since 1880*. Princeton, NJ: Princeton University Press.

SCHMIDT, B. C. 1998. *The Political Discourse of Anarchy: A Disciplinary History of International Relations*. Albany: State University of New York Press.

SEELEY, J. R. 1923. *Introduction to Political Science: Two Series of Lectures*. London: Macmillan.

SHILS, E. 1972. 'British Intellectuals in the Mid-Twentieth Century'. In *The Intellectuals and the Powers: and Other Essays*. Chicago: University of Chicago Press; originally published 1955.

SMITH, T. 1986. 'Political Science and Modern British Society'. *Government and Opposition*, 21/4: 420–36.

STOKER, G. 2006. *Why Politics Matters: Making Democracy Work*. Palgrave: Basingstoke.

TAYLOR, C. 1992. *Sources of the Self: The Making of Modern Identity*. Cambridge: Cambridge University Press.

WALLAS, G. 2006. *Human Nature in Politics*. BiblioBazaar: London; originally published 1908.

CHAPTER 2

ANTECEDENTS

DENNIS KAVANAGH

2.1 INTRODUCTION

THE study of politics in Britain, specifically the study of British politics, long precedes the emergence of a discipline of political science. The origins of something akin to a disciplinary approach to the study of politics, based perhaps inevitably in universities, are visible in the late nineteenth century. A mix of politicians, constitutional lawyers, academic historians, political commentators, and journalists wrote about politics, principles of government, and relations between the state and the citizen, and courses were taught at universities.

The antecedents nourished: (a) a distinctively British approach to the subject, with strong roots in history and philosophy, both the product of a particular context and culture; (b) an enduring framework which may be termed the Westminster model; and (c) a legacy that has resulted in a proliferation of overly empiricist studies and a neglect of theoretical perspectives. All three of these features have been in decline over the past three decades because of the march towards professionalization.

Professionalizing trends—the growth of disciplinary self-awareness and autonomy, international conferences, scholarly networks and journals, and an emphasis on training—have combined to undermine distinctive national traditions of political science—and other sciences. But there has been a distinctive British approach over the twentieth century, one that is now under pressure. The emphasis has largely been on empirical works and there have been relatively few contributions in terms of theories, concepts, or methods. It has always lacked the hard positivism or interest in general theory found in the United States and never been subject to the influence jurists have exercised in France and Germany, where the subject was often taught in

I am grateful for the comments on an earlier draft from Michael Kenny and George Jones.

Law faculties. Because the British acceptance of the behavioural revolution across the Atlantic was muted (see below) the negative reaction to it was less marked than in the United Sates or the Continent. In the United States there were calls for a post-behavioural revolution in which relevance and reform would be key elements. In West Germany and Italy, where Marxism was stronger in the social sciences, the left mounted a vigorous attack on the new science. One is almost tempted to compare the gradual changes in the British approach to the study of politics with, to use a traditional language, the Whig narrative of the development of the mixed British constitution.

Over the past century the growing professionalization cum specialization of political science (see below) limited the scope for scholars to double as scholar-activists. In the 1920s and 1930s, for example, Laski, Muir, and Cole were heavily involved in political party activity, often at a high level. For Graham Wallas, 'The political scientist was to be not a philosopher but a social engineer' (Weiner 1971: 67).

Another change has been in the nature of the audience. For the first half of the twentieth century the major British figures in political studies wrote for an audience outside academe too, simply because the latter was too small. Laski, Cole, Barker, and Jennings also saw themselves as 'citizen-scholars', expressing views on the issues of the day in newspapers, magazines, on radio, and serving on public committees. Shaping public opinion and helping to make better citizens was a justification for studying and teaching politics (Kavanagh 2003). By the end of the century, however, scholars primarily address fellow scholars who, thanks to technology, journals, and conferences, form an audience across national borders.

As Kerr and Kettell (2006) report, there has been some decline in interest in the study of British politics. Reasons for the decline are various but one is the British tradition of studying politics, 'Whiggish developmentalism ... replete with its anti-intellectual aversion to theoretically informed debate' (6).

The chapter analyses British approaches over three periods—pre-1914, inter-war years, and post-1945—and discusses their merits. Some might want to make a division around the late 1960s in the last period. The first period is dominated by historians and a consensus around the Whig interpretation; the second sees the emergence of a number of academic political scientists based in universities; and the final period witnesses the stresses and pressures from the expansion and specialization of the discipline.

2.2 PRE-1914

A recognizable British approach to political science had already emerged in the late nineteenth and early twentieth centuries (Hayward 1999). The subject, as reflected in the teaching and writing on the subject at Oxford and Cambridge, was part of a humane tradition, deeply rooted in the classics, literature, and history, providing a liberal elite education. Its supporters argued that studying the relationship between political ideas and past events and the actions of politicians provided practical knowledge and wisdom for future political leaders. Because of this practical orientation, the approach 'tended to be prescriptive and make judgements, proclaiming its values and priorities openly' (Gamble 1990: 408). It was a means of inducting would-be rulers into a political tradition and an appreciation of the wisdom embedded in British political institutions and culture. The London School of Economics and Political Science, founded by the Webbs in 1895, provided a different approach, one wedded to empirical research and the development of a practical social science which would be useful for rulers.

Historians wrote legal-institutional studies such as *The Government of England* (1908) by A. L. Lowell and *English Political Institutions* (1910) by Sir John Marriot. In a different vein there was the journalist Sydney Low's *Governance of England* (1904). The lawyers dominated the study of constitutional history and above all fashioned the doctrine of parliamentary sovereignty. The key pre-1914 figures of Maine, Bryce, Pollock, and Dicey all held chairs in law. In an autobiographical essay W. J. M. Mackenzie (1975) recalls that these 'Knights of the textbooks' (his phrase) dominated student reading at inter-war Oxford. Yet in the post-1945 period this strand, apart from the work of W. I. Jennings and, to an extent K. C. Wheare and William Robson, virtually disappeared from British political science and revived only recently.

History, for this generation, including ancient history, was a source of methods, knowledge, and values. In late nineteenth-century Cambridge, Benthamite proponents of a deductive approach, which would lead to a science of legislation, lost out to advocates of an inductive approach, based on history (Collini et al. 1983). Maitland, Sidgwick, and Seeley provided a historical analysis of politics. Rather than working from hypotheses to universal generalizations, they claimed that their inductive approach furnished the knowledge for a so-called 'noble science' of politics, a victory that left 'an enduring anti-scientistic mark upon the study of politics in Britain' (Hayward 1999: 3).

The path adumbrated in Graham Wallas's *Human Nature and Politics* (1908) found no followers in Britain, but did so eventually in the USA. He urged that psychology should figure more prominently in political analysis, not least to achieve a more realistic perspective. His warning against the 'rationalist fallacy', or exaggeration of the intellectuality of public opinion, discussion of voters' use of the party image, and advocacy of more quantitative techniques sketch out an early behavioural approach to politics, but one that was in Britain largely stillborn. Although Wallas did not develop his suggestions into anything resembling a programme, his was one of the two seminal 'unmasking' books before 1914. Walter Bagehot's *The English Constitution* attempted to describe 'the living reality' behind the pieties of the constitution. Where Bagehot made the best of human irrationality (for example, popular deference to 'the outward show' of monarchy and the 'dignified' aspects of the constitution), Wallas feared it. Over forty years ago Richard Rose, one of the first students of behaviouralism in Britain, invoked the social and psychological insights of Wallas and Bagehot in his *Politics in England*. He regarded them, as well as Low, Lowell, and Ostrogorski, as pioneering students of the relationship between English politics and society.

Crucial to an understanding of the British approach at the time is the higher education context in which it emerged. Few British writers on politics before 1914—and the point holds as late as the 1950s—regarded themselves as political scientists. Most drew on other disciplines for their methods and would have shuddered at the idea that the subject should seek to emulate the natural sciences. Politics in the universities was a small subject operating in the small world of British higher education. The subject lacked a distinct identity; it was studied alongside economics, philosophy, law, and history, all of which were more securely established as separate subjects and even departments in universities. Politics operated under the shadow of more dominant subjects and departments and few held the view that politics was a self-contained subject. In the United States, however, political scientists had already begun to assert their identity as a distinct discipline by forming a separate Political Science Association in 1903, breaking away from the American Historical Association.

The small scale may have helped coherence but it also meant there was no specialized audience of a reasonable size, the academics were generalists, and there was a 'pervasive amateurishness' (Barry 1999: 431). The writers lacked a distinctive methodology, or at least one separate from philosophy or history. They were less concerned to define politics as a discipline separate from history or philosophy or law, than to stress its interconnections with them; most had graduated in history or classics and even as late as 1966 nearly 40 per cent of university teachers of politics in Britain had taken history as a first degree (Crick 1966). Ernest Barker was unhappy at his title as Cambridge's (first) Professor of Political Science and stated his preference for the study of 'moral phenomena of human behaviour in political studies' to be called 'Political Theory'.

Important for an understanding of the British approach was the dominance of the Whig view of the British political system. In the late nineteenth century such constitutional historians as J. R. Green, Stubbs, and Freeman developed the Whig interpretation of Britain's political development. They told a narrative of the rise of representative institutions, the gradual broadening of liberty and cumulative change in which institutions and elites adapted to new challenges. The genius of the British constitution was its adaptability, in implicit contrast to France. According to the historians, Britain was fortunate in its island position, which provided relatively 'free' security, and its moderate centralization of political authority. The attempts by the Stuarts to subvert the balanced constitution had been defeated and from the 1688 Glorious Revolution emerges the idea of English 'exceptionalism'. Britain had successfully resisted absolute monarchy, a royal standing army, and destruction of embryonic representative institutions. In contrast to France or Prussia, it developed as a 'low profile' state.

Many Americans (and Europeans) shared the Whig view of the merits of the mixed or balanced British constitution. Starting with Professor Woodrow Wilson, would-be reformers of the US parties and the civil service, as well as critics of the Madisonian model of the US system, looked to Britain for lessons (Kavanagh 1974). Hayward notes that a similar admiration for the British system was widespread at the time among Continental political scientists (1999: 28).

By the end of the nineteenth century the Whig view was being transmuted into the Westminster model—a set of institutions and conventions. Its main features were: Cabinet government, parliamentary sovereignty, the rule of the law, ministerial and collective responsibility to parliament, institutionalized and legitimate political opposition to the government in parliament, and accountability of parliament through regular competitive elections.

Features of this Whig tradition were coming under challenge. Den Otter (2007: 48 ff.) notes that the modernist empiricism of Maitland, Pollock, and Dicey developed an 'inductive study of law and politics that shaped a new discipline of political studies'. Maitland's explorations of medieval law undermined the Whig constitutional narrative of the continued expansion of English liberty. Such key stages in the making of the 'free-born Englishman' as trial by jury or habeas corpus or the origins of parliament were shown to have begun under royal auspices (Blaas 1978: 264). More critical historians claimed that the Whig view was teleological, a narrative in which the past moved smoothly and continuously to the present, eliminating the role of chance and conflict.

A more 'realist' school of writers undermined the Whig narrative, particularly on the role of parliament. The work of Mosei Ostrogorski on the emergence of the extra-parliamentary caucus, of Henry Maine and W. H. Lecky on the rise of 'popular government' (Maine), and A. Lowell on the development of disciplined mass political parties and the growing pressure of legislation in the Commons suggested that relations between the executive and legislature were being reshaped.

Yet the Whig interpretation still influenced much thinking on the constitution. As Blaas (1978: 34) admits:

> The Whig myth concerning the constitution was so irresistible that the constitution had come to be regarded as the sole explanation for the development of English history as such. It became the ideal angle from which to illustrate the growth of the British nation, and its development was the axis of the history of England *tout court*, the factor explaining especially the uniqueness of British political development it came to be almost regarded as an autonomous political force: the object to be interpreted had developed into a means for interpretation.

2.3 INTER-WAR YEARS

It is during the inter-war years that the founding fathers of British political science—Ernest Barker, W. I. Jennings, Ramsay Muir, H. J. Laski, and G. D. H. Cole—emerge.

In this period the Whig view of Britain's political system endures, perhaps because most of the writers had been educated in such values in the late nineteenth century. The first three clearly write within the Whig/Westminster model, Barker about the values of the institutions and political practice, Jennings and Muir more narrowly as institutionalists. But Laski and Cole are also aware of the shortcomings of a model developed when the electorate was small and the role of government limited. Pluralists, including the early Laski, attacked the idea of the omnicompetent parliament and the sovereign state and the collectivists (reflecting the rise of the Labour party after 1918) welcomed a more active state even if this made inroads on individual liberty.

Julia Stapleton (1994: 4) notes that in his blend of pluralism, Whiggism, and Idealism Barker mounts essentially a rearguard defence of the political order that prevailed before the First World War. He was committed to what he called the 'parliamentary system of government' and its importance in upholding English liberties. These values emerge strongly in two of the chapters in *Essays in Government* (1945), on 'The Parliamentary System of Government' and on 'British Statesmen'. For Barker, the essence of civilized (and British) politics is the place of discussion, rather than the will of a majority, as a means of reconciling differences. In his *Reflections on Government* (1942) he argues that the British political system facilitated discussion in four stages— the discussions within and between political parties, the choices voters make between political parties at general elections, the debates in parliament, and, finally, in the deliberations of Cabinet. It is a deliberative democracy in which the checks on the influence of public opinion allow it to be winnowed and settled before it is brought to bear on the rulers.

The public lawyer, W. I. Jennings, was comfortable with the British system and its political checks and balances. (But he was also a collectivist; see below.) British government was 'government by opinion', since parliament and the institutionalized opposition in the House of Commons provided the opportunity for the views of the public to be expressed. In his years at the LSE (1929–40) he produced eleven substantial books on British and other political institutions. His *Law and the Constitution* (1933), *Cabinet Government* (1936), and *Parliament* (1939) were heavily descriptive, drawing on statutes, legal cases, and available nineteenth-century political memoirs and biographies.

Ramsay Muir's *How Britain is Governed* (1930) was the first recognizable textbook on the British system. It had chapters on the Prime Minister and Cabinet, the Commons, the Lords, the civil service, the parties, and elections. As befits a prominent Liberal activist, he anticipated many of the criticisms and recommendations made by reformers some fifty years later. The book's subtitle was *A Critical Analysis of Developments in the British System of Government*, and the author expressed concern over what he regarded as threats to the Westminster constitution. He complained about the Cabinet's 'dictatorship' over parliament, the stifling effects of party discipline, the rise of interest groups, and the power of 'the Permanent Civil Service' (on which, he noted, historians and textbooks had been 'strangely silent'), all of which had caused the bypassing of parliament. Muir proposed what has become a litany of familiar reforms—specialized departmental committees in the Commons, elections by proportional representation to the two Houses of Parliament, and devolution to Scotland, Wales, and the English regions. In contrast to other critics, his purpose was to reinvigorate rather than replace the Westminster model.

Pluralism was another important theme in the inter-war period. In the early twentieth century there was, variously, a reaction against earlier individualist notions; the Whig emphasis on the superiority of territorial representation in an elected parliament; and the legal doctrine of state sovereignty. Pluralists favoured the dispersal of power between many groups and sought to limit the increasing powers of the state, even though the British state at the time was relatively weak. The young Laski and Cole, as well as Ernest Barker, no doubt influenced by their student reading of Gierke, Maitland, and Figgis, were all sympathetic to pluralism. They valued liberty and thought it was best gained and preserved by the spread of power among different institutions and groups. Dismissing the idea that society was either a collection of individuals or an organic whole, they asserted that it consisted of self-governing units and voluntary groups which had rights before and independent of the state. They rejected the claims that the sovereign state could be realized in practice or, even if it could, was desirable. Laski argued the case in his *Problems of Sovereignty* (1917), *The Foundations of Sovereignty* (1921), and *Authority in the Modern State* (1919). In his early work he advanced a liberal case for pluralism, praising a 'federal' society of different groups and the checks and balances which follow from the interplay of separate political institutions wielding separate powers. By the time of his *A Grammar of Politics* (1925), however, his support for pluralism had waned and the active collectivist state was held up for admiration (see below).

Cole argued for a more thoroughgoing pluralism and advocated self-government by workers in their industries. In his *Social Theory* (1920) he argued that representation should be based on a person's function in society. Because work was directly experienced and better understood, it was more meaningful than residence. His advocacy of creating a series of functional representative bodies challenged prevailing ideas about representation and the role of the state.

Another counter to the Westminster approach came from supporters of collectivism. Writers of a centre-left persuasion, including the Webbs, believed the actions or intervention of the state were more beneficial than those of the market and were confident that the tide was gradually but inevitably turning in their direction. An elected socialist government could use parliamentary sovereignty and the unitary state to implement its programme. Within striking distance of achieving power after 1918, Labour supporters had little interest in promoting more checks and balances for the benefit of their opponents. Laski, in his *Grammar*, had dismissed such devices as the referendum, devolution, proportional representation, and MPs electing their own select committees in the House of Commons because they could be restraints on the majority party and therefore on the electorate. He restated this view in his posthumous *Reflections on the Constitution* (1951).

In moving to his neo-Marxist phase, Laski was profoundly affected by the 1926 General Strike and the political and economic crisis that caused the collapse of the minority Labour government in 1931. In *Democracy in Crisis* (1933) he expressed fears that the coming economic crisis and sharper social class divisions, reflected in the Labour and Conservative parties, would tempt the ruling class to abandon the traditional rules of the game. He doubted there could be a peaceful path to the social and economic transformation promised by a radical Labour government. Parliamentary democracy might not survive the strains of sharp social and economic inequalities. He warned that to overcome 'unconstitutional' resistance from the holders of capital, normal parliamentary procedures might have to be suspended and emergency rule introduced. Here is a rejection of the Whig beliefs in the state's neutrality and optimism about progress—restated in *Parliamentary Government in England* (1938). Anticipating the later idea of Lord Hailsham's elective dictatorship he does not defend checks and balances or independence of the courts and local government.

This generation, like that of the late nineteenth-century comparative historians, was also aware of other countries. Herman Finer's *Theory and Practice of Modern Government* (1932) was a comparative study of the political similarities and differences across Britain, Germany, France, and the United States. But where James Bryce's *Modern Democracies* (1921) was a country-by-country study, Finer broke new ground in comparing topic by topic and institution by institution across his chosen states. Jennings was an authority on the constitutions of Commonwealth states, Laski wrote well-received books on the American presidency and the rise of European Liberalism, and Barker was steeped in classical Greek politics and wrote perceptively on the emerging totalitarian states of Russia and Germany.

Although the works are legal-institutional, they are not *only* legal-institutional. The literature covers the activities of pressure groups, the influence of the permanent civil service, the effects of party discipline on MPs, and the influence of the House of Commons and the rise of the Cabinet and how such features were challenging the Westminster model. However, with the exception of Laski, there is a failure to relate the politics to social and economic forces; much of the work is narrowly political in its focus on institutions. Some express doubts that the system might survive. The early behaviouralist ideas of Wallas and the criticisms of the neo-Marxist Laski resonate with themes in British political science from the late 1960s onward. The ideas of corporatism, so important to political scientists, economists, and sociologists in the 1960s and 1970s, were anticipated in the work of Laski and Cole.

2.4 POST-1945

The efforts of the inter-war figures did much to define the character and development of political science in Britain for at least the first two decades of the post-1945 period.

Many of the immediate post-war generation still regarded politics as a subject that properly borrowed from history and philosophy. A practical consideration in 1950 for naming the national professional association the Political Studies Association was that the new body had to accommodate the historians, constitutional lawyers, and philosophers who formed a majority of those teaching politics. Most members explicitly rejected the ideas of a science of politics and of competing with or emulating developments in the USA. In the 1950s the subject was still often taught in departments of law, history, or philosophy and no department offered a single degree in politics.

The experience of other European states during the first half-century, and success in the 1939–45 War, strengthened a sense of British exceptionalism and vindicated the political system. Its political stability, peaceful change, and legitimacy still stood out in comparison with European states. Over the course of the previous fifty years many European states had experienced military dictatorship, occupation or military defeat, fascist dictatorship, and large regime-challenging communist parties. Britain remained an outlier as a stable democracy, and a generation later the absence of proportional representation, coalition governments, a written constitution, or federalism still made it distinctive. Richard Rose began his *Politics in England* with a claim that few contested, that England 'is important as deviant case, deviant because of its success in coping with the many problems of the modern world' (1964: 1).

In the immediate post-war years students had no general textbook on British politics and the works of the past masters still clung heavily. A typical reading list still included Bagehot's *English Constitution*, Jennings's *Cabinet Government*, and Mill's *Representative Government*. In the late 1960s the first generation of textbooks on British politics was published to meet the demands of the growing number of students. The literature still operated within the old paradigm, reflecting a confident view of the British system and culture (often encouraged by empirical US studies). The themes of stability, strong government, consensus, social homogeneity, and pride in the political system were still prominent.

Adherence to traditional approaches stemmed from what Vout (1990: 24) calls an Oxford style, which involved the study of politics not as a science but a subject more appropriately approached in historical and philosophical modes. He quotes the founding editor of *Political Studies*, Wilfred Harrison, who in 1958 in the course of a review article of an American book, 'Some Aspects of American Political Science', expressed his distaste for American political scientists who 'dabble in social science; and some of what they have to say has been repugnant, depressingly narrow, frighteningly naïve, frighteningly arrogant or just irritatingly verbose' (Vout 1990: 24, 26). His was not a lone voice. Michael Oakeshott, Laski's successor at the LSE, was dismissive of any scientific analogy and held that politics had to be studied historically because of the need to understand political activity as a tradition.

Oakeshott, writing in the idealist tradition, offered a variant of the Whig approach. He argued that because a political system operates in its own distinctive tradition political analysis calls for a particular mode of understanding, involving the study of a tradition of behaviour. His work accords a central place to history and philosophy in political analysis and spurns so-called scientific methods. He and other historicists complained that behaviouralism was ahistorical and sacrificed a crucial understanding of context and change. Oakeshott influenced several writers on political thought and political philosophy, a number of Conservative political commentators, and some students of political institutions. For example, a passionate dismissal of the idea that politics was a science, coupled with the assertion that it can be studied only through history and philosophy, is found in Nevil Johnson's *The Limits of Political Science* (1989). A student of institutions and constitutions, he is Oakeshottian in his insistence on the historical-philosophical path as the only valid one. Bernard Crick, in his *American Science of Politics* (1959), complained that behaviouralism/political science was culture bound and, rather than being value free, was shot through with liberal American values. His later *In Defence of Politics* (1963) restated the idea of politics as a civic humanist activity, dating back to Aristotle.

Kenny (2007) has argued that by the late 1960s the older traditions were being challenged by—and soon coexisted with—the modern empiricism of younger academics, the latter the product of university expansion and the influence of the United States. Politics was looking at least as much to the social sciences as to history and philosophy. 'Whiggish ideas about the history, values and character of the British polity were intermingled with newer emphasis upon empirical verification and a degree of methodological rigour'. This 'methodological pluralism' established 'a distinctively British variant of the international political science community' (Kenny 2007: 179). From this fusion emerged a British approach that continues to the present.

Jean Blondel's *Voters, Parties and Leaders* (1963), an examination of the social fabric of British politics, had chapters on voters, party members, interest groups, bureaucracy, and the establishment. Richard Rose's *Politics in England* used the structural-functional categories of Talcott Parsons and Gabriel Almond. The book does not have chapters on Parliament, Cabinet or the civil service, or monarchy, but on political socialization, political culture, and communications. In the mid-1960s David Butler and the American Donald Stokes conducted their first wave of interviews for a landmark study of British voting behaviour and Richard Rose embarked on his surveys in Northern Ireland.

In the United States political behaviouralism developed rapidly in the 1950s and was dominant by the 1960s. It was applied mostly to phenomena that were observable and about which quantitative data could be collected. It involved a turning away from the traditional legal-institutional approaches (except insofar as they were amenable to the new techniques) and political philosophy. The emphasis was on surveys of mass political behaviour (particularly voting), hypothesis testing, and statistical techniques for establishing relationships. It was a challenge to the emerging mixture of historicism, philosophy, and empiricism in Britain. The new political science departments at Essex and Strathclyde acted as midwives of the new approach, explicitly following the American model and emulating the postgraduate training in research methods found across the Atlantic (Blondel 1997).

2.5 LINKAGES

During the 1960s the subject significantly expanded; new departments of politics were created, the number of academics and students of the subject grew, and more journals were established. But, according to one critical narrative of 'discipline history', the subject still reflected too much of the influence of the inter-war years, particularly the same tendencies to amateurishness and insularity, the continuing influence of history and philosophy, focus on institutions, and Whiggish assumptions. Such a view is heavily influenced by the claims that the discipline today is more professional, autonomous, and methodically self-aware. Kenny (2004: 587) complained that the 1950s and 1960s are viewed 'as a kind of amateurish prequel to the establishment of a modern autonomous discipline'.

Yet during the 1950s and 1960s a number of scholars were challenging some assumptions of the Westminster model, particularly the important place it accorded parliament. S. E. Finer's 'The Individual Responsibility of Ministers' (1956) drew on case studies to dismiss the claim that parliament's control of the executive extended to the dismissal of ministers where the minister had clearly blundered. Geoffrey Marshall and Graham Moodie (1959) further argued that the doctrine of ministerial responsibility was undermined by the strength of party government; the troubled minister could usually rely on the support of the majority party in the Commons to see him through. They added that the doctrine was damaging because of the courts' reluctance to intervene in cases where public authorities were abusing their power. The courts often claimed it was for parliament to provide remedies in the case of proven abuses. Finer and W. J. M. Mackenzie in their work on pressure groups challenged the assumed primacy of political parties in policy-making. Robert McKenzie (1955) challenged the portraits and 'myths' the Conservative and Labour parties presented of themselves and of each other. He claimed that the distribution of power within the parties was broadly similar; borrowing from Michels, he argued that in both parties the parliamentary leadership was dominant over the membership outside parliament. Another example of 'realism' was Mackenzie's translation of the 1961 Plowden Committee report on public spending. Drawing on his experience of Whitehall and his classical philological training, he claimed it was a classic Whitehall ruse of speaking in public but in code so that the public could not understand the subject matter. In other words, there was a good deal of 'unmasking' of myths of the British constitution.

During this period two figures, both educated in the 1930s, stand between American and British methods. Neither was entirely comfortable with the new science but they adapted to it and in their hands forged a British approach (Vout 1990; Kenny 2004; 2007). W. J. M. Mackenzie at Manchester acted as a filter for American political science and tried to reconcile what he described as the separate 'idioms' of the two political science communities, one based on history and philosophy, the other on behavioural science. This fusion was most evident in his work on pressure groups, community power, and public administration. A classics don who grew bored with teaching the subject, he switched to Philosophy, Politics, and Economics in 1936, teaching himself the subject by reading widely and drawing on his knowledge of ancient history, philosophy, and constitutional law. In his 'The Conceptual Framework and the Cash Nexus' (1962) he noted the older generation of political scientists wrote as pupils of linguistic classical scholars, historians, lawyers, and philosophers. He added that the study of politics could never be a hard science (although that was a useful aspiration), but it could be organized knowledge and communicable as a set of propositions. 'The job (of political science) is to talk in an orderly manner, paying regard to consistency and verifiability, about a unique situation which is extremely complex and changes rapidly', he wrote in his *Politics and Social Science* (1967). Despite the move to professionalism (e.g. graduate research training) he acknowledged that: 'our standards have been acquired by disciplines in the humanities and not in mathematics or natural science [and] ... we regard ourselves as scholars, rather than scientists, as learned men and careful writers, not as discoverers of new truths' (1975: 311). Vout asserts that Mackenzie wanted to strike a middle ground between historical and philosophical analysis and modern empiricism. While preserving the former dimensions, he encouraged the use of quantitative and sociological methods.

The other key figure is S. E. Finer. He kept up with American political science, although maintaining his distance. He dismissed the idea of a pure science of politics—'an empty set of mechanical calculations', he once called it. But he employed the techniques of classification, typologies, and models, and used the language of variables and relationships to make generalizations about political phenomena. In an autobiographical essay, he described his work as variously '*interpreting* a body of factual knowledge, making a *pattern* out of it ... making *sense* out of it', rather than seeking universal laws (1980: 363). Like his older brother Herman, he regarded comparison as the nearest approximation to the scientific method, classifying cases and looking for patterns of regularities and causal interrelationships.

Finer had little time for general theoretical frameworks and wrote critically of structural functionalism and systems analysis. His aversion to grand theory is, as Vernon Bogdanor notes (1999: 148–9), a British characteristic; there are no British counterparts to Easton, Almond, or Deutsch. Instead, Finer advocated a problem-centred approach; why, for example, did military dictatorship occur in so many newly independent states, or why had the military been so important in the formation of the great European states, or what were the circumstances in which British pressure groups succeeded?

A reason why Finer was suspicious of mainstream American political science/behaviouralism was because of its tendency to reduce the political factors to a dependent variable. Too often the political was analysed as being determined by economic, psychological, or social factors. The systems approach relegated to a political 'black box' government which converted inputs from the environment into outputs. But, in contrast to Oakeshott, he held that governmental and political data were not unique to time and place but could be classified, analysed, and compared. He became more convinced of the case for taking the historical route as the best means to explaining causation. Ultimately he took the historical path with a vengeance, going back over 5,000 years for *The History of Government from the Earliest Times* (1997).[1]

Another challenge to the Westminster model emerged from what Bevir and Rhodes (2007: 248 ff.) call a quasi-Marxist or socialist approach. Miliband (1961; 1969), a former student of Laski at the London School of Economics, claimed that British politics should be studied in the framework of an advanced capitalist society, and the latter's consequences for the opportunities and constraints on political actors. A particular target for Miliband was the Labour Party, which he thought had been crippled by its acceptance of Whig values and the Westminster model. Its commitment to achieving socialism by the parliamentary route and acceptance of the culture of parliamentarism caused the containment of pressure from below for transformation. Miliband claimed that the Labour party has, in history, been only reformist, making marginal and ameliorative changes, while capitalism remains intact.

What Miliband—and the neo-Marxist insights of Jessop, Marsh, Leys, Kingdom, Dearlove, and Saunders—bring to British politics is a discussion of political economy, of elites (and their socio-economic backgrounds), of structured inequalities, and of interests. They show how such agents of legitimization as the media and education system buttress inequality. Although a challenge to the consensus, their analysis may be viewed as a backhanded tribute to the strength of the Westminster model. They may refute some of the claims to be scientific made by behaviouralists, notably those of value neutrality—accusing behaviouralism of peddling pluralist views and masquerading as science—but they still employ their methods of data collection and analysis.

2.6 THE END OF A BRITISH APPROACH?

Challenges have emerged from outside the discipline, particularly from: (a) significant recent changes in British political institutions and behaviour, (b) dissatisfaction with the performance of British political institutions and by extension with the mindset associated with the Westminster model, and (c) the growing tendency to study British politics as part of a European system or polity.

---

[1] During a faculty meeting at Oxford in the 1970s Finer, then the Gladstone Professor of Government and Public Administration, shocked many of his colleagues by claiming that history and politics were different subjects and he had taught both. His immediate predecessor as the holder of the Gladstone chair, Max Beloff, and his immediate successor, Peter Pulzer, regarded politics as a branch of history, the first openly so. The first two holders of the chair, W. G. S. Adams and Sir Arthur Salter, regarded the subject as the insights of practical men, in their cases drawn from their considerable experience of government.

Since 1997 the introduction of devolution for Scotland, Wales, and Northern Ireland—a form of quasi-federalism—and continued membership of the European Union have imposed limits on the sovereignty of the parliament. The steady decline in popular support for the two main parties has led to coalition and minority rule, aided by proportional representation, in executives outside of the House of Commons. There has been greater use of referendums and a more important role accorded the judiciary. For some the Westminster model has been overtaken by a Differentiated Polity Model (Rhodes 1997) in which governance has replaced government, and is marked by segmented pluralism, policy networks, and a hollowing out of the state.

Dissatisfaction with the performance of the British political system has come from various quarters. On the free market right wing there developed in the 1970s a critique of government, particularly in the wake of the claims in the 1970s that government was 'overloaded'. Government, it was claimed, was too big and too interventionist, and, according to the new public management school, it was allegedly too often captured by special interests and government actors, whether elected or not, who had interests of their own to protect and promote. Their answer involved breaking up state monopolies and providing greater consumer choice through privatization, markets, and contracting out. New Labour's acceptance of neo-liberal views of economic management went some way to accepting the above analysis as well as abandoning a key feature of socialism—public ownership; the party promoted constitutional reform involving freedom of information, devolution, and a Human Rights Act. The Liberals and their successor party, the Liberal Democrats, claimed the Westminster political system had come to be a frail defence against the elective dictatorship of the executive. They have long advocated (cf. Ramsay Muir) a stronger House of Commons, more decentralization, stronger local government, and electoral reform.

British membership of the European Union and collaborative trans-European political studies encouraged and facilitated by the European Consortium of Political Research may have caused a relative reduction in scholarly interest in British politics per se. The constitutional changes of the past decade have made the British political system today less different from that in mainland Europe. The 'Europeanization' of British politics (however incomplete) is being reflected in a Europeanization of British political science.

These developments raise the question of whether it is still possible to have a distinctive national approach to the study of politics, while adhering to cross-national criteria and norms of professionalism. The latter are not about subject matter or approach but ideals of objectivity, theorizing, and rigour.

There have been three main drivers towards this professionalization/institutionalization. The first comes from the United States. On some calculations over 80 per cent of political scientists work in the United States (in 1960 there were 160 members of the PSA and already some 7,000 in the American Political Science Association); the USA is the home of large graduate and research schools of great prestige which train students in the latest techniques and house big social science projects. American universities place a greater emphasis than British on research, which in turn is encouraged by the greater availability of funds. The outcome of these forces is that professionalization is easily seen as approximating to American norms. Britain is particularly exposed to its influence because of a shared language as well as the number of Americans writing on British politics and of academic exchanges between the two countries. In virtually any branch of the subject, particularly rational choice, voting, the new institutionalism, and new public management, America is the market leader and Britain has drawn on 'homeopathic doses of American political science' (Hayward 1991: 104).

A qualification to the US hegemony is the influence of 'the English school' in the quasi-discipline of international relations. As Dunne (1998: 18) notes, the 'school' preferred a more interpretive approach over a positivist one, a more historical than a social science one. Its concern for rigour and precision pays less obeisance to models, measurements, and testing propositions

The financial support and remits of state-funding agencies (starting with the creation of the Social Science Research Council in 1965) and charities, as well as the type of publications favoured in the periodic research assessment exercises in higher education, are a second influence. Certain topics and research methods are favoured, notably policy-relevant or 'useful' projects, and proposals employing 'harder' social science techniques, again a force for Americanization.

A final force is the fragmentation of the discipline, both of topics and of methods. As late as the 1960s it was widely expected that most British political scientists would teach political institutions and political ideas and be familiar with most of the topics covered in the few academic journals (Barry 1999: 447 ff.). The Founding Fathers in the inter-war period sat at the same table, to borrow Terence Rattigan's metaphor, a consequence partly of the small London and Oxbridge axis but also of a shared educational background and interest in both political institutions and political theory. The pre-1914 interest in history and philosophy was still strong, as was the caution about positivism and scientism. The subject lost the old coherence, based on historical analysis of political ideas and institutions, in the wake of the expansion and greater specialization in which sub-disciplines have their separate journals, conferences, and working parties.

For some critics the pace of professionalization has been too slow. Kerr and Kettell complain that the study of British politics in particular has not kept pace with other areas of the discipline. This allegation is probably true, but may be part of a general decline in single-country studies. Despite the long history of attacks on their shortcomings, both the Westminster model and Whiggish assumptions—Britain as a model stable democracy and therefore a key topic for study—survived until the last twenty-five years. A consequence of the field's historical inheritance for Kerr and Kettell is 'its overly circumscribed conception of, and its theoretically underdeveloped approach towards, its own subject matter' (2006: 7). Only in recent years have scholars used theoretical perspectives, often imported from the United States, in analyses of British political institutions and processes—yet more examples of Bernard Crick's 'tolerant eclecticism'.

2.7 CONCLUSION

This chapter has argued that there have been trends to professionalization and positivism in British political science. But, as Bevir and Rhodes note (2007: 257), these forces have not driven out other traditions from the discipline. A legacy of the British inclination of some fifty years ago for an inductive, reflective, and largely atheoretical approach rather than a quest for general theories and deductive models remains the chief characteristic today. If the sense of professionalism and scientism in Britain still lags behind the United States, the same judgement applies to other countries. This characteristic has allowed a variety of approaches to flourish, including history, social humanism, idealism, and a post-Marxian socialism. As a result of the improved scholarship, in quantity and quality, political scientists are much better informed across virtually all areas of political science than our predecessors were.

REFERENCES

ADCOCK R. et al. (eds.) 2007. *Modern Political Science*. Princeton, NJ: Princeton University Press.

BARKER, E. 1942. *Reflections on Government*. Oxford: Oxford University Press.

—— 1945. *Essays on Government*. Oxford: Oxford University Press.

—— 1953. *Age and Youth*. Oxford: Oxford University Press.

BARRY, B. 1999. 'Politics as a Vocation'. In Hayward et al. 1999.

BEVIR, M., and RHODES, R. 2007. 'The Remaking of Political Theory'. Pp. 209–33 in R. Adcock et al. (eds.), *Modern Political Science*. Princeton, NJ: Princeton University Press.

BLAAS, P. B. M. 1978. *Continuity and Anachronism: Parliamentary and Constitutional Development in Whig Historiography and the Anti-Whig Reaction between 1890 and 1930*. The Hague: Martinus Nijhoff.

BLONDEL, J. 1963. *Voters, Parties and Leaders*. Harmondsworth: Penguin.

—— 1997. 'Amateurs into Professionals'. Pp. 115–26 in H. Daalder (ed.), *Comparative European Politics*. London: Cassell.

BOGDANOR, V. 1999. Comparative Politics. Pp. 147–80 in Hayward et al. 1999.

COLE, G. D. H. 1920. *Social Theory*. London: Methuen.

COLLINI, S., et al. 1983. *That Noble Science of Politics*. Cambridge: Cambridge University Press.

CRICK, B. 1959. *The American Science of Politics*. London: Routledge.

—— 1966. 'The Tendencies in Political Studies'. *New Society* (3 November).

DEN OTTER, S. 2007. 'The Origins of a Historical Political Science in Late Victorian and Edwardian Britain'. Pp. 37–65 in Adcock et al. 2007.

DUNNE, T. 1998. *Inventing International Society: A History of the English School*. London: Macmillan.

FINER, H. 1932. *Theory and Practice of Modern Government*. London: Methuen.

FINER, S. E. 1980. 'Political Science: An Idiosyncratic Retrospective of a Putative Discipline'. *Government and Opposition*, 15: 346–65.

—— 1997. *The History of Government from the Earliest Times*. Oxford: Oxford University Press.

GAMBLE, A. 1990. 'Theories of British Politics'. *Political Studies*, 38/3: 404–20.

HAYWARD, J. 1991. 'Cultural and Contemporary Constraints upon the Development of Political Science in Great Britain'. In D. Easton (ed.), *The Development of Political Science*. London: Routledge.

—— 1999. 'British Approaches to Politics'. In Hayward et al. 1999.

—— et al. (eds.) 1999. *The British Study of Politics in the 20th Century*. Oxford: Oxford University Press.

JENNINGS, I. 1933. *Law and the Constitution*. London: University of London Press.

—— 1936. *Cabinet Government*. Cambridge: Cambridge University Press.

—— 1939. *Parliament*. Cambridge: Cambridge University Press.

JOHNSON, N. 1989. *The Limits of Political Science*. Oxford: Clarendon Press.

KAVANAGH, D. 1974. 'The American Science of British Politics'. *Political Studies*, 22: 251–70.

—— 2003. 'British Political Science in the Inter-war Years: The Emergence of the Founding Fathers'. *British Journal of Political Science and International Relations*, 5: 594–613.

KENNY, M., 2004. 'The Case for Disciplinary History'. *British Journal of Politics and International Relations*, 6: 565–83.

—— 2007. 'Birth of a Discipline: Interpreting British Political Studies in the 1950s and 1960s'. Pp. 158–79 in Adcock et al. 2007.

KERR, P., and KETTELL, P. 2006. 'In Defence of British Politics: The Past, Present and Future of the Discipline'. *British Politics*, 1: 3–25.

LASKI, H. J. 1925. *A Grammar of Politics*. London: Allen and Unwin.

—— 1933. *Democracy in Crisis*. London: Allen and Unwin.

—— 1938. *Parliamentary Government in England*. London: Allen and Unwin.

LOW, S. 1904. *The Governance of England*. London: Fisher Unwin.

McKENZIE, R. 1955. *British Political Parties*. London: Heinemann.

MACKENZIE, W. J. M. 1975. *Explorations in Government: Collected Papers 1951–68*. London: Macmillan.

—— 1967. *Politics and Social Science*. London: Penguin.

MARSHALL, G., and MOODIE, G. 1959. *Some Problems of the Constitution*. London: Hutchinson.

MILIBAND, R. 1961. *Parliamentary Socialism*. London: Allen and Unwin.

—— 1969. *The State in Capitalist Society*. London: Weidenfeld and Nicolson.

MUIR, R. 1930. *How Britain is Governed*. London: Constable.

RHODES, R. A. W. 1997. *Understanding Governance*. Buckingham: Open University Press.

ROSE, R. 1964. *Politics in England*. Boston: Little, Brown.

STAPLETON, J. 1994. *Englishness and the Study of Politics*. Cambridge: Cambridge University Press.

VOUT, M. 1990. *Oxford and the Emergence of Political Science in England 1945–1960*. Strathclyde: Centre for the Study of Public Policy.

WALLAS, G. 1908. *Human Nature and Politics*. London: Constable.

WEINER, M. J. 1971. *Between Two Worlds*. Oxford: Oxford University Press.

CHAPTER 3

....

THE BRITISH STUDY OF POLITICS

....

ROBERT E. GOODIN

MY assessment of the British study of politics—forgive me, I shall call it 'political science', everyone else in the world does[1]—inevitably takes the form of a set of traveller's tales. Like all good travellers, I lingered for a time in new-found lands before moving on again. Like all good travellers, I revisit from time to time. But the eye I bring to this task is as much an outsider's as others in this section of the *Oxford Handbook of British Politics* are insiders'.

3.1 THE REVOLUTION OF 1975

....

I first encountered British political science en masse in 1975, at the Political Studies Association annual conference at St Catherine's College, Oxford. It was an auspicious

I am grateful for comments on earlier drafts from Brian Barry, Albert Weale, and the editors of this volume. Conversations with participants in the 2007 ESRC International Benchmarking exercise have also fed powerfully into this chapter. None of course is to be blamed for the use I have made of that advice.

[1] What else to call it? 'British Politics', as in the title of this volume, conflates the practice of politics in Britain with the academic study thereof. That there is no convenient phrase for referring to British students of politics is itself telling evidence of weak professional self-identity in the UK.

year for making a first acquaintance. That was the year the Old Guard was decisively routed by a slate of Young Turks, organized by Brian Barry and consisting more or less wholly of the professionalized subprofessoriate who formed the Editorial Board of the *British Journal of Political Science* at the time.[2] The revolution succeeded. (The Warden of Nuffield, Norman Chester, muttered darkly that it would not have done, had he been present—and the darkness of his utterance convinced me he was probably correct.) After the vote was announced at the AGM, the head of the Electoral Reform Society, Enid Lakeman, rose to express the hope that there would be no more talk of 'slates' and 'contested elections' in the PSA ever again. From the back of the hall Ian Budge offered the observation, 'Some of us spend a lot of our time on elections, and think they are pretty good things on the whole'.

The event marked a sea change in British political science.[3] *Political Studies* jolted decades forward: Jim Sharpe replaced Fred Ridley as editor with his post-doc, Patrick Dunleavy, as editorial assistant; and peer reviewing was systematically introduced. And polytechnic lecturers were welcomed into PSA membership on the same basis as university lecturers. Of course it would be wrong to exaggerate the depth of this revolution, as any other. The great bulk of people always invariably carry on doing things much as before. But even if not everyone cared to practice the profession in the new way themselves, the back of the rearguard resistance to contemporary political science was broken, and the institutional barriers to those who those who were tempted by that mode of political analysis were beginning to crumble.

Nowadays, in certain quarters on both sides of the Atlantic, there is nostalgia for the 'amateurish prologue to the professionalized present' (Kenny, this volume; cf. Gunnell 2005; Kavanagh, this volume; Kenny 2004). Certainly something was lost—and now is happily being reclaimed (more of which below)—when technical professional language cut the discipline off from its civic roots and undercut its capacity to make relevant contributions to politics and policy, popular discourse, and civic education (Crick 1975; Farr 2004). Still, I defy anyone hankering for a return to the pre-professional past to say in all honesty that they wish they had written any of the chapters in, for example, the (pre-Royal) Institute of Public Administration's survey of *British Government Since 1918* (Campion et al. 1950).

Emblematic of the Ancien Régime was the dispute raging within the Oxford Sub-faculty when I had first arrived to do a D.Phil. there. The debate was over when 'history' ended and 'politics' began. Like all demarcation disputes, that one was heated. But much more revealing was what was not at dispute. It was agreed on all sides that there is no real difference in the methodology used in studying history and politics.[4] Both were purely a matter of storytelling, well-crafted narratives laced with

---

[2] Prescient, the Old Guard of the Political Studies Association had tried (as one former editor puts it) to 'strangle *BJPolS* at birth', protesting to its publisher that they could not produce a journal under that title, since PSA was the official organization representing British political studies and already published the official British journal.

[3] The difference can be calibrated by reference to a pair of memoirs of the profession, written by the leaders of the opposing forces a quarter century apart: Chester (1975) and Barry (1999).

[4] Of course the US profession grew out of History, too: the American Political Science Association was founded at the 1903 meeting of the American Historical Association, and twelve of its first sixteen

telling anecdotes collected by mining the archives or, better yet, by plying the key players with sherry in some SCR or St James club.[5]

Oakeshott's (1962) talk of 'traditions' provided the fig leaf for British insouciance towards the new science of politics. But only the Cambridge 'ideas in context' school of political theorists and the English School of constructivists in international relations really engaged in the depth required to make good that claim. Most of the best work in this pre-professional past was hard to distinguish from quality journalism.[6] For all the time spent picking politicians' and civil servants' brains, it ironically took two American blow-ins—Heclo and Wildavsky (1974)—to provide the first richly ethnographic account of the 'Whitehall village' on a par with Evans-Pritchard's (1937) account of the Azande.[7]

It is wrong to suppose that those stories always lacked any theoretical edge. Many writers about politics (as about history) did so from a very particular point of view: Whiggish or Marxist or Fabian or whatever (Rhodes 2006). It would be fair to say, however, that those stories were written in almost complete innocence of any theories emerging out of twentieth-century social science. Opening the British profession to those vistas was the aim, and the accomplishment, of the Young Turks of 1975.

There are exceptions in every generation, and Bill Mackenzie certainly was one in his.[8] His *Politics and Social Science* (1967)—written during a sabbatical alongside Stein Rokkan in Bergen—gives a glimmer of what it must have been like to have studied with him at Manchester. It is unsurprising that so many of the Young Turks of 1975 hailed from there one way and another.[9]

Essex and Strathclyde came to symbolize the new ways of studying of politics, although from the inside (and I did time inside both) neither was as monolithic as outsiders imagined. The Essex-based European Consortium for Political Research

meetings were held jointly with AHA (Farr 2004: 38; 2007: 90–1). Whereas that practice ceased in 1927 in the USA, such affinities persisted in the UK for the next half-century.

[5] As Crick (1980: 302) describes the period, 'There were always the good old fellows who had no fancy thoughts about . . . problems of theory and practice, but who simply assumed that if you lived in London or Oxford . . ., you simply talked to civil servants and Cabinet Ministers, as in the good old days of the war'. Hayward (1999: 2) says, 'Not until the subject was recognized as an autonomous discipline, with its own professionally qualified practitioners, did political zoologists become separated from the denizens of the political zoo'.

[6] Compare e.g. Williams (1972), Sampson (1962). Far from being just some snide outsider's swipe, this is their self-description of their preferred research technique: the way Philip Williams announced he had terminated the academic study of French Politics was by announcing in the Common Room one day, 'I've made a big decision: I've stopped reading *Le Monde* every day'.

[7] Although for delightful anecdotes, journalists-cum-contemporary-historians such as Hennessy (1989) cannot be beat.

[8] As were Sammy Finer and Hugh Berrington, albeit in this period placed in outposts with less pervasive professional impact. Kavanagh (this volume: n. 1) reports that 'during a faculty meeting in Oxford in the 1970s Finer, then Gladstone Professor of Government and Public Administration, shocked many of his colleagues by claiming that history and politics were different subjects and he had taught both. His immediate predecessor as holder of the Gladstone chair, Max Beloff, and his immediate successor, Peter Pulzer, regarded politics as a branch of history, the first openly so'.

[9] For a delightful memoir of the department see Birch and Spann (1974).

powerfully furthered the cause. Initially built by Blondel and Rokkan around an axis of the four pre-eminent new-look political science groupings in Europe (Essex–Mannheim–Leiden–Bergen), its summer school modelled on Michigan's proselytized the new political science to junior staff and students Europe-wide; and its Joint Sessions of workshops, initially drawing participants disproportionately from the UK, Scandinavia, and the Netherlands, further solidified links among new-style political scientists across Europe, just as the 'Madison exchange' solidified Essex's link to a pre-eminent centre of US behaviouralism.

But as I have said, even Essex and Strathclyde were never as monolithically new-look political science as all that. And even in the early years after the 1975 revolution, there were new-look political scientists dotted all around: at ancient universities, redbricks, new universities, and polytechnics alike. Nowhere were they quite so predominant as at Essex or Strathclyde, but in many surprising places they were at least a minor presence.[10] That was UK political science as I found it upon returning in 1979.

3.2 STILL 'A SELF-DEPRECATING PROFESSION'

All ancient history, you might say. But skipping three decades ahead, I find things interestingly the same (as well as, of course, interestingly different). The remarks that follow are another set of traveller's tales, these from my sojourn chairing an International Benchmarking Panel on Politics and International Studies, convened by the Economic and Social Research Council jointly with the Political Studies Association and the British International Studies Association. The official report of the Panel is available for all to read (ESRC 2007). What follows are my own impressions, based on observations, evidence, and interviews as part of that exercise. In what follows, I shall obviously be speaking for myself; not for the ESRC, PSA, BISA, other members of that Panel, or anyone else.

To an outsider, much the most striking feature of British political science is its overwhelming modesty. Asked what 'big ideas' it had contributed to the discipline, people insistently refused to answer.[11] It is, as Jack Hayward (1999) wrote, a deeply

---

[10] As Crick (1980: 300) puts it, 'Behaviourism only really dominated Essex and then Strathclyde, most of the other new departments hedged their bets and lazily or wisely added a behaviourist or so to political ideas and institutions men'.

[11] Nor is this merely a recent development, apparently. Ridley (1980: 471) begins his contribution to the twenty-fifth anniversary issue of *Government and Opposition* devoted to 'a generation of political thought' by saying, 'It was only when I came to reflect on what I might write that I realized the folly of my acceptance. That shock of the exercise, indeed, was that I could make no list of developments in political science to trigger off this article; clearly, no thoughts on the important books of the past generation were stored at the back of my mind, awaiting this invitation for their release'. See similarly Dunleavy, Kelly, and Moran (2001: 7), reflecting back on the first fifty years of *Political Studies*.

'self-deprecating profession'. The general sentiment, as the Panel met with departmental representatives up and down the country, was that 'flashy Americans up themselves parade "big ideas"; we don't do that sort of thing, around here...'[12]

That modesty is unwarranted. Within my home sub-discipline of political theory I can think of several 'big ideas' that have emanated from Britain: conceptual analysis (Barry 1965), participatory democracy (Pateman 1970), analytical Marxism (Cohen 1978), the politics of presence (Phillips 1995). Within electoral studies, dealignment (Särlvik and Crewe 1983) was a pretty 'big thing', at least until it was overtaken by disaffection. Buzan, Weaver, and de Wilde (1997) coined the term 'securitization' before it became a worldwide phenomenon. Goodhart and Bhansali (1970) introduced the 'political business cycle' five years before Nordhaus (1975) gave it its name; and Sanders, Ward, and Marsh's (1987) study of 'Government Popularity and the Falklands War' remains one of the most dramatic demonstrations of it. The Cambridge School of ideas in context is one of the dominant influences on political theory worldwide, as is the English School on international relations. As we point out in the ESRC (2007: 12) report, 'some of the earliest work on what has come to be known as "international political economy" was British' and 'some of the earliest work on "networked governance" and "new public management" came from the UK'. It is simply not true that 'big ideas' do not come out of Britain. It is merely the case that there is a reluctance there to brag about them.

The other constant refrain, linked with the first, is the self-conception of the British profession as an insistently 'pluralist' one.[13] There is no big idea, still less any methodological orthodoxy, that anyone is trying to sell everyone else. It is a matter of live and let live. '[F]rom the 1950s and through the 1960s', Crick (1980: 303) reports, 'there was no possible general characterization of British political studies, except to say "tolerant eclecticism"'.[14] That mood very much remains to this day.

One way in which this can be seen most clearly is in the way in which sub-disciplines are fiercely fenced off in the UK. This is most evident with international studies, which in some places in the UK is a separate department and which throughout the UK is represented by a separate professional association, BISA, which has virtually no overlap with the PSA (ESRC 2007: 11). But as Kenny (this volume) points out, various other sub-disciplinary groups—in comparative politics, area studies, and political theory—stake greater claims to autonomy within British political science than they do even within the US discipline, where numbers are larger and critical mass within sub-disciplines is easier to obtain (more of which below). Whether this is a manifestation of genuine sub-disciplinary exceptionalism or mere sub-disciplinary protectionism is a matter of judgement.

[12] For elaboration of the (largely US) phenomenon of 'big things', see Barry (1974) and Goodin (2009).

[13] 'There are many styles in political science', writes Ridley (1980: 480), and, 'The freedom of the scholar to choose his own is essential to our academic tradition: pluralism is a "good thing" in this respect as in others'.

[14] This chimes, of course, with Crick's (1962: 21, 32, 141, 160) distinctively British conception of politics itself: as the 'conciliation of differing interests', as 'a way of ruling in divided societies without undue violence'; for 'conciliation is better than violence' and 'diversity is better than unity'.

In his valedictory lecture, Adam Roberts (2008: 335–6) celebrates what he sees as the characteristically British 'pluralist approach both to the actual conduct of international relations and to the academic subject'. He elaborates:

> It is a pluralism that accepts the relevance of many different approaches to international relations: not just the proper emphasis on power and interest that is found in realist theories, but also approaches that stress the significance of ideas and norms, the impact of domestic political and economic structures on international politics, the roles of transnational movements and international organizations, and the existence of new challenges. It is a pluralism of theories, a pluralism of political systems, a pluralism of different cultures and mindsets, a pluralism of methods of analysis and a pluralism of academic disciplines.

Roberts concludes by quoting approvingly from Mill's *Autobiography*: 'Goethe's device, "many-sidedness", was one which I would most willingly...have taken for mine'.

One can easily imagine some bedraggled American departmental chair saying those sorts of things, after the wars of methodology have been fought to a standstill. Such things are said in Britain, however, less out of war weariness than out of something more akin to a failure to engage. These are simply not things to be fought over in the first place. To each his or her own, methodologically. Funnily enough, that is precisely what the revolution of 1975 itself was fought in the name of: the right to practice modern political science if you wanted to, not any serious attempt to impose that practice on everyone else around you.[15]

In one way, that might sound like bad news. It might sound as if people do not care enough about their profession to insist that others practise it right. Or it might sound like post-modernism before its time: there is no truth, only perspectives. Or it might sound like best scientific practice: triangulate on the truth from as many angles as you can. There is evidence of all three, in Britain as elsewhere. But much the most interesting is the third. Colin Hay dedicates his marvellous primer on *Political Analysis* to the thought that 'there may be more than one way to explore the political world' (2002: 1), and to showing the ways in which they can be fruitfully combined.

Of course there are similarly synthetic projects afoot in many corners of the world, with many (different and hotly contested) suggestions for uniting qualitative and quantitative methods, for example (King, Keohane, and Verba 1994; Oakley 2000; Box-Steffensmeier, Brady, and Collier 2008). A pluralist synthesis is not a peculiarly British project. But in the UK it seems now to be a major part of the self-conception of the discipline as a whole, in a way it is not elsewhere.

These first two phenomena are, perhaps, connected. The puzzle of why big ideas do come out of Britain, but there is a reluctance to brag about them, might be explained by the simple fact that there is a live-and-let-live reluctance to try to shove one's own ideas, however big, down the throat of the profession as a whole. It is a reluctance to proselytize, not a reluctance to think big, that characterizes the UK profession.

---

[15] That right had to be fought for, in the face of stiff resistance: pluralism of this sort was far from the hallmark of the pre-1975 profession; anyone who doubts that needs only consult Johnson (1989).

The size of the UK discipline, compared to the US, might go some way towards explaining that, in turn. There are around 1,500 academics in UK departments of Politics and International Studies; in the USA more than ten times that number are members of APSA. Combine that fact with the observation that the 'big things' dominating the discipline—' "behaviouralism" in the previous generation or "rational choice" in the present one'—'are practiced to any high degree by only perhaps five percent of the...discipline' (ESRC 2007: 9). In the USA, 5 per cent amounts to 750 people, critical mass for a specialist conference every year. In the UK, 5 per cent would amount to only 75. That is not really critical mass, assuming you could only ever get half of them in the same room at once.[16] Any temptation to form a clique locally is further tempered by the ease, nowadays, of making common cause with the much greater numbers of like-minded colleagues globally. Such is the fate of locals and cosmopolitans in all professions (Gouldner 1957).

Of course, 5 per cent of the UK profession is a much larger number of people than it would have been a couple generations ago (Barry 1999: 431). Still, I think some truth remains in Ridley's (1975: 2) observation in introducing the issue of *Political Studies* commemorating the twenty-fifth anniversary of the PSA: 'The size of our own [UK] profession makes generalizations even harder to sustain. We know too many of our colleagues individually, too much of their individual work, to accept trends...: most will seem to us typical only of themselves'.

There is a cost as well as a benefit to all this think-small self-deprecation and modesty. It shows up clearly in the bibliometric analyses conducted for the ESRC Panel. Overall, UK journal articles get cited in roughly the proportion that should be expected: 'the UK accounts for around 15 per cent of journal articles indexed in [ISI/Thompson] databases, and around 14 per cent of citations there are to articles from the UK' (ESRC 2007: 10). That is 92 per cent of what you would expect—just a shade off the pace.

But when we look at *important* articles—at those most often cited—the UK political science profession is increasingly underrepresented the further you go up the academic food chain. Some 9.5 per cent of UK journal articles in political science are among the 10 per cent most cited—merely half a per cent less than expected. But only 4.1 per cent of UK articles are among the 5 per cent most cited. And only 0.7 per cent are among the 1 per cent most cited (ESRC 2007: 15). Among those 'very most important articles', UK political science scores only 70 per cent of what should be expected—way off the pace.

That suggests that UK political science probably is not pulling its weight at the very highest levels of political science worldwide. There is plenty of solid good work, and nearly as much very good work as there should be. But there is less than there should

---

[16] And it depends on how the sub-discipline conceptualizes itself. The UK is strong in the history of political thought, for example: but if people identify themselves with particular periods or particular authors rather than as 'historians of political thought' as such, the critical mass evaporates. Ditto for area studies: if people see themselves primarily as country specialists rather than as 'area studies' or 'comparativists', what could have been a critical mass ceases to be so.

be of the very highly innovative work that attracts really widespread professional notice worldwide.[17]

At the institutional level, too, UK political science is rather off the pace, internationally. One way to see this is to look at the comparative impact of the main UK-based journals. Since impact factors (ISI 2008) fluctuate substantially from year to year, Table 3.1 reports three-year averages.

Looking first at generalist political science journals, two US journals—the *American Political Science Review* and the *American Journal of Political Science*—have far greater impact than any others, due partly (but only partly) to their status as journals of the largest professional associations in US political science.[18] One UK-based journal, the *British Journal of Political Science*, joins the next tier of important journals worldwide. But the main journal of the UK Political Studies Association—*Political Studies*—has only half as much impact as *BJPolS*, and a quarter that of *AJPolS* and less than a fifth that of *APSR*.[19] Its performance is broadly on a par with that of lesser regionally based journals, such as the *Australian Journal of Political Science* and *Scandinavian Political Studies*.

The second set of columns in Table 3.1 reports similar statistics for journals of international relations. One US-based journal, *International Organization*, clearly dominates the field, with another (*Foreign Affairs*) following at some distance. Another pair of US-based journals, *International Studies Quarterly* and *World Politics*, are a little way behind that. The highest-impact UK-based journal, *International Affairs*, is that distance again further back, followed by the *Review of International Studies* and *Millennium*. One way of looking at these statistics, again, is to say that the official organ of the British International Studies Association, *Review of International Studies*, has only two-thirds the impact of *World Politics* or *International Studies Quarterly* and one-third the impact of *International Organization*.

A second set of institutional markers relate to world rankings of political science departments, based on impact-weighted journal publications of their members. Scorecards of this sort are regularly produced for US departments; and a more deeply informed ranking of UK departments is produced by periodic Research Assessment Exercises. But so far as I know the only systematic attempt at ranking departments worldwide is that of Hix (2004). These data too display considerable variability year to year, so I shall focus on Hix's report of departmental rankings based on sets of rolling five-year averages.

As seen in Table 3.2, there are fourteen UK departments that, at one time or another over the decade 1993–2002, figured among the world's top fifty departments

---

[17] One explanation might be that, once they begin writing high-impact articles, UK scholars are poached abroad. Certainly it is true, looking at the list of most-cited political scientists in the *Oxford Handbooks of Political Science*, that twice as many moved from the UK overseas as moved from overseas to the UK at the height of their careers (Goodin 2009: appendix 3).

[18] Subscription to which is included as part of membership in the American Political Science Association and the Midwestern Political Science Association, respectively.

[19] Other journals of the PSA—the *British Journal of Politics and International Relations*; *Politics*; and *Political Studies Review*—are not included in the ISI database at the time of writing, likewise other journals of the APSA.

Table 3.1. Journal impact factors, 2005–7

Political science	Impact factor			Average
	2005	2006	2007	
American Political Science Review	3.233	3.023	2.317	2.858
American Journal of Political Science	1.845	2.167	2.032	2.015
Annual Review of Political Science	0.860	1.368	1.359	1.196
British Journal of Political Science	0.785	1.205	1.311	1.100
Political Studies	0.575	0.500	0.488	0.521
Australian Journal of Political Science	0.538	0.397	0.582	0.506
Scandinavian Political Studies	0.457	0.342	0.553	0.451

International relations	Impact factor			Average
	2005	2006	2007	
International Organization	2.060	2.200	3.000	2.871
Foreign Affairs	2.058	1.482	1.854	1.795
International Studies Quarterly	1.415	1.369	1.386	1.390
World Politics	1.308	1.132	1.568	1.336
International Affairs	0.992	0.674	1.131	0.932
Review of International Studies	1.015	0.451	0.855	0.774
Millennium	0.400	0.500	0.673	0.524

Source: ISI 2008.

Table 3.2. Department rankings in global top fifty, 1993–2002

	1993–7	1994–8	1995–9	1996–2000	1997–2001	1998–2002
Essex	7	8	4	7.5	16	16.5
Warwick	14	14	27	31	–	–
Oxford	17.5	21	13	20	22	19
Birmingham	25	16	24	13	17	22
Strathclyde	37	45	–	–	–	–
Cambridge	38	33	32	22	20	23
Glasgow	40.5	35	50	–	–	–
LSE	40.5	39	37	37	24.5	15
Sheffield	–	49.5	38	26	35	25
Hull	–	49.5	48	–	–	–
Bristol	–	–	31	25	36	34
Aberystwyth	–	–	–	–	40	38.5
Cardiff	–	–	–	–	44	37
UCL	–	–	–	–	–	46

Source: Hix 2004: 311.

of political science assessed in this fashion. But of those fourteen, only five departments have continuously ranked in the top fifty, and only Essex consistently in the top twenty.

Put that way, it does not look as if UK political science overall has exactly been a world leader. But looking at those statistics another way, a more encouraging picture emerges. In the beginning of that period, there were eight UK departments in the global top fifty, four of them in the global top twenty-five. By the end of that period, there were ten in the global top fifty, six in the global top twenty-five. Clearly, there was movement in the right direction over that decade. And although I know of no data to confirm it, my sense is that that movement has continued and perhaps accelerated since.

These three ways of assessing the British profession converge on the same conclusion: good, but not great; doing well, but at the very top end could be doing better. Of course all these three ways of looking at the profession view it through the bibliometric lens of the ISI database; and there are well-known problems with bibliometrics in general and that database in particular.[20] For all their shortcomings, however, bibliometrics are surely the clearest indication that others take notice and make use of what you write. Of course, most social scientists doing the citing are American, so citation counts inevitably reflect American academic preferences. But those wishing to claim that they do something important but different need to explain why others so systematically fail to notice their contributions.

Many institutional factors impact upon UK political science. In many ways, constant reviews and compliance costs associated with an increasingly demanding

[20] Two of the most glaring are its underrepresentation of non-English-language journals and its indexing only references in journals and not in books.

regulatory culture and accountability regime doubtless impede academic performance. In other ways, they help to enhance it. No doubt the recurring Research Assessment Exercises have been a mixed blessing. However mixed, I am nonetheless inclined to think them definitely a blessing, on balance. Without the incentives that they provided, the improvements just remarked upon would almost certainly never have occurred.

The UK discipline is in very good health on a vast array of indicators, ranging from student numbers to the demographic profile of the profession (ESRC 2007). Most strikingly, there has been an internationalization (largely but not exclusively a 'Europeanization') of the junior ranks of the UK profession, making it more outward looking and comparative in nature (ESRC 2007: 34–5). That development, in particular, is much to be celebrated.

3.3 CONTRIBUTIONS TO PUBLIC LIFE

While this chapter has primarily focused on providing an academic assessment of British political science, as seen from afar and on intermittent revisitings, I close with some comments on the contribution of the profession to British public life more broadly.

There is anxiety, both within some sectors of the scholarly community and particularly among funders, that by becoming hyper-professionalized British political scientists have lost both the capacity and the willingness to contribute to the civic life of the community. The fear is that they have become 'eunuchs or voyeurs', in Crick's (1980: 307) acidic phrase. But that is simply not what our ESRC Panel found. British political science makes a massive contribution indeed to public life.

Much of that contribution comes through deep-background influence on public values and public culture, through media appearances and helping to shape public debates. Research Councils UK (2006)—an umbrella organization which includes both the ESRC and AHRC—rightly emphasizes that those are as important as direct economic impacts. Our ESRC Panel found much evidence of British political scientists doing just that.

Even just in terms of direct engagement with non-academic users 'in industry, Government, the professions and the voluntary sector' (which is ESRC's narrower specification), members of the British profession make a very considerable contribution:

They have served as advisors to Parliamentary committees at home and abroad; to the UK Cabinet Office, the Scottish Executive, the Wales Office and the Northern Ireland Office of First Minister and Deputy First Minister; and to various departments of state at home and abroad. At home, the discipline has provided members of the House of

Commons, the House of Lords, and the Scottish Constitutional Convention; it has provided directors of the Home Office Research Programme and the Scottish Public Sector Ombudsman, as well as members of the Competition Commission and the Defence Advisory Board. Overseas, UK Politics and IS scholars have testified to the Lebanese National Assembly, to the International Energy Agency, to the US Defense Intelligence Agency and NATO Defence College. UK Politics and IS scholars assist a wide range of international organizations, including the European Central Bank, European Commission and the Council of Europe, the International Monetary Fund, NATO, the UN Development Programme, the UN Human Rights Commission and the UN World Food Programme. They advise foreign governments on electoral reform in Australia, Bermuda, Canada, China, Lebanon and the Netherlands. They advise NGOs like Oxfam and businesses like Siemens and Shell.

I reiterate our conclusion: 'We would be hard-pressed to name any other country in which a larger proportion of the Politics and IS profession was directly engaged with high-level policy-makers in this way' (ESRC 2007: 26; see similarly British Academy 2004; 2008: 16–20). Furthermore, in 'the special survey of end-users we commissioned . . . well over half of potential end-users report that they do use UK Politics and International Studies Research, and use it heavily and appreciatively' (ESRC 2007: 26).

No profession with three so distinguished of its practitioners as Philip Norton, Bhikhu Parekh, and Raymond Plant sitting in the House of Lords, commenting on matters of great public concern on the basis of their considerable professional expertise, can be said to be failing its larger public mission.

References

Barry, B. 1965. *Political Argument*. London: Routledge and Kegan Paul.
——1974. 'Review Article: Exit, Voice and Loyalty'. *British Journal of Political Science*, 4: 79–107.
——1999. 'The Study of Politics as a Vocation'. Pp. 425–67 in J. Hayward, B. Barry, and A. Brown (eds.), *The British Study of Politics in the Twentieth Century*. Oxford: Oxford University Press, for the British Academy.
Birch, A. H., and Spann, R. N. 1974. 'Mackenzie at Manchester'. Pp. 1–23 in B. Chapman and A. Potter (eds.), *W.J.M.M. Political Questions*. Manchester: Manchester University Press.
Box-Steffensmeier, J., Brady, H., and Collier, D. (eds.) 2008. *Oxford Handbook of Political Methodology*. Oxford: Oxford University Press.
British Academy 2004. *'That Full Complement of Riches': The Contributions of the Arts, Humanities and Social Sciences to the Nation's Wealth: A British Academy Report*. London: British Academy. Available at: www.britac.ac.uk/reports.
——2008. *Punching Our Weight: The Humanities and Social Sciences in Public Policy Making: A British Academy Report*. London: British Academy. Available at: www.britac.ac.uk/reports.
Buzan, B., Weaver, O., and de Wilde, J. 1997. *Security: A New Framework for Analysis*. Boulder, Colo.: Lynne Rienner.
Campion, Lord, Chester, D. N., Mackenzie, W. J. M., Robson, W. A., Street, Sir A., and Warren, J. H. 1950. *British Government Since 1918*. London: Allen and Unwin, for the Institute of Public Administration.

CHESTER, N. 1975. 'Political Studies in Britain: Recollections and Comments'. *Political Studies*, 23: 151–64.

COHEN, G. A. 1978. *Karl Marx's Theory of History*. Oxford: Clarendon Press.

CRICK, B. 1962. *In Defence of Politics*. Harmondsworth: Penguin.

——1975. 'Chalk-Dust, Punch-Card and the Polity'. *Political Studies*, 23: 165–82.

——1980. 'The British Way'. *Government and Opposition*, 15: 297–307.

DUNLEAVY, P., KELLY, P. J., and MORAN, M. 2001. 'Characterizing the Development of British Political Science'. In *British Political Science: Fifty Years of* Political Studies. Oxford: Blackwell.

ECONOMIC AND SOCIAL RESEARCH COUNCIL (ESRC) 2007. International Benchmarking Review of UK Politics and International Studies. Swindon: ESRC, in partnership with the British International Studies Association and the Political Studies Association. Available at: http://www.esrc.ac.uk/ESRCInfoCentre/Images/P_IBR-Final_Report_tcm6-23426.pdf.

EVANS-PRITCHARD, E. E. 1937. *Witchcraft, Oracles, and Magic among the Azande*. Oxford: Clarendon Press.

FARR, J. 2004. 'The Science of Politics—as Civic Education—Then and Now'. *PS*, 37: 37–40.

——2007. 'The Historical Science(s) of Politics: Principles, Association and the Fate of an American Discipline'. Pp. 66–96 in R. Adcock, M. Bevir, and S. C. Stimson (eds.), *Modern Political Science: Anglo-American Exchanges since 1880*. Princeton, NJ: Princeton University Press.

GOODHART, C. A. E., and BHANSALI, R. J. 1970. 'Political Economy'. *Political Studies*, 18: 43–106.

GOODIN, R. E. 2009. 'The State of the Discipline, the Discipline of the State'. In R. E. Goodin (ed.), *Oxford Handbook of Political Science*. Oxford: Oxford University Press.

GOULDNER, A. W. 1957. 'Cosmopolitans and Locals: Toward an Analysis of Latent Social Roles'. *Administrative Science Quarterly*, 2: 281–306, 444–80.

GUNNELL, J. G. 2005. 'Political Science on the Cusp: Recovering a Discipline's Past'. *American Political Science Review*, 99: 597–609.

HAY, C. 2002. *Political Analysis: A Critical Introduction*. Houndmills: Palgrave.

HAYWARD, J. 1999. 'British Approaches to Politics: The Dawn of a Self-Deprecating Discipline'. Pp. 1–36 in J. Hayward, B. Barry, and A. Brown (eds.), *The British Study of Politics in the Twentieth Century*. Oxford: Oxford University Press, for the British Academy.

HECLO, H., and WILDAVSKY, A. 1974. *The Private Government of Public Money*. London: Macmillan.

HENNESSY, P. 1989. *Whitehall*. London: Secker and Warburg.

HIX, S. 2004. 'A Global Ranking of Political Science Departments'. *Political Studies Review*, 2: 293–313.

ISI WEB OF KNOWLEDGE 2008. Journal citation reports. <http://admin-apps. isiknowledge. com/JCR/JCR?SID=2CHfffDLOL7PJg996D7>

JOHNSON, N. 1989. *The Limits of Politics*. Oxford: Clarendon Press.

KENNY, M. 2004. 'The Case for Disciplinary History'. *British Journal of Politics and International Relations*, 6: 565–83.

KING, G., KEOHANE, R. O., and VERBA, S. 1994. *Designing Social Inquiry: Scientific Inference in Qualitative Research*. Princeton, NJ: Princeton University Press.

MACKENZIE, W. J. M. 1967. *Politics and Social Science*. Harmondsworth: Penguin.

NORDHAUS, W. D. 1975. 'The Political Business Cycle'. *Review of Economic Studies*, 42: 169–90.

OAKESHOTT, M. 1962. *Rationalism in Politics and Other Essays*. London: Methuen. 2nd expanded edn. Indianapolis, Ind.: Liberty Press, 1991.

OAKLEY, A. 2000. *Experiments in Knowing: Gender and Method in the Social Sciences*. New York: New Press.

PATEMAN, C. 1970. *Participation and Political Theory*. Cambridge: Cambridge University Press.

PHILLIPS, A. 1995. *The Politics of Presence*. Oxford: Oxford University Press.

RESEARCH COUNCILS UK 2006. Research Councils' Evidence for the Economic Impact Group—24 April 2006. <http://www.rcuk.ac.uk/cmsweb/downloads/rcuk/documents/rcsubtoeig.pdf>

RHODES, R. A. W. 2006. 'Old Institutionalisms'. In R. A. W. Rhodes, S. A. Binder, and B. Rockman (eds.), *Oxford Handbook of Political Institutions*. Oxford: Oxford University Press.

RIDLEY, F. F. 1975. 'Editor's Preface'. *Political Studies*, 23: 123–5.

——1980. 'If the Devil Rules, What Can Political Science Achieve?' *Government and Opposition*, 15: 47–185.

ROBERTS, A. 2008. 'International Relations after the Cold War'. *International Affairs*, 84: 335–50.

SAMPSON, A. 1962. *Anatomy of Britain*. London: Hodder and Stoughton.

SANDERS, D., WARD, H., and MARSH, D. 1987. 'Government Popularity and the Falklands War'. *British Journal of Political Science*, 17: 281–313.

SÄRLVIK, B., and CREWE, I. 1983. *Decade of Dealignment: The Conservative Victory of 1979 and Electoral Trends in the 1970s*. Cambridge: Cambridge University Press.

WILLIAMS, P. M. 1972. *Crisis and Compromise: Politics in the Fourth Republic*. London: Longman.

SECTION TWO: POLITICAL SCIENCE

CHAPTER 4

....

INSTITUTIONALISM

....

B. GUY PETERS

4.1 INTRODUCTION: INSTITUTIONAL THEORY IN POLITICAL SCIENCE

....

INSTITUTIONS are central to our understanding of politics and government. Their importance can be seen easily in day-to-day discourse about government, as citizens and scholars alike discuss the importance of parliament, the courts, or political parties in making policy and exercising the authority of the public sector. In addition to this quotidian sense of institutionalism in understanding government, the roots of political science are in the study of formal institutions (see Eckstein 1963). Even as early as Aristotle's discussions of comparative politics, institutions and the constitutions that created them constituted the core of political analysis. Central to this form of analysis was the idea that formal structures would shape behaviours and shape the outcomes of political processes.

Much of the 'old institutionalism' in political science (see Peters 1996; Greenwood and Greenwood 1996) did not involve explicit theorizing about institutions but remained largely descriptive and normative. The description of institutions in this extensive body of research was often very detailed and intensive, but generally did not attempt to use that evidence to construct explicit theories about the performance of institutions. That having been said, however, there were often implicit theories about the structure of government, and about the manner in which institutions themselves functioned. For example, the study of electoral laws has long assumed that those laws (an institution) influenced, and in some ways determined, the outcomes of elections (Duverger 1951). Indeed, to the extent that there was theory in the old institutionalism it was legal and constitutional, and tended to lack the more behavioural assumptions that would inform later theoretical developments.

The 'new institutionalism' in political science (March and Olsen 1986; Steinmo, Thelen, and Longstreth 1992) was built on the background of the old institutionalism, but also reflected the more theoretical turn in the discipline. The new institutionalism remains concerned with using institutional variables to explain important dependent variables in the discipline. For example, the fundamental differences between presidential and parliamentary institutions appear to have a major impact on policy choices (Weaver and Rockman 1994), and federal systems have been assumed to produce very different outcomes in public finance than unitary systems (Breton 1996). As new institutional theory developed, it imported ideas from rational choice theories (Shepsle 1989), sociological organization theory (March and Olsen 1986), and a variety of other sources such as institutional economics (Pierson 2000).

All of these theoretical approaches to institutions have at their core some assumptions about political behaviour and also have some interest, if limited in some important cases, in testing their assumptions empirically using quantitative as well as qualitative methodologies. Institutionalism therefore has now returned as one contender for a paradigm in political science. Unlike the other contenders that rely on individual-level variables, institutionalism bases its explanations on the structure of formal (and sometimes informal) organizations, or on the values, symbols, and routines that those institutions inculcate into their members. Those institutionalist explanations, however, further have been informed by an increased understanding of political behaviour coming from the 'behavioural revolution' in the discipline. Further, unlike most other explanations in most versions of institutionalism, the preferences of individuals are assumed to be derived from their membership in institutions, rather than exogenous to those memberships. Those preferences may be commitments to particular policy solutions or to particular institutional structures.

In this chapter I will examine the role of institutional theory, and institutional analysis more broadly, in British political science. Institutional analysis has been central to the British science of politics, but often has focused more on the nature of individual institutions than on developing more general theories of institutional formation and/or behaviour. That having been said, however, there have been some notable contributions to theory, and I will discuss and evaluate these theoretical statements. Finally, institutional analysis poses some interesting paradoxes about analysing and understanding British politics, and I will develop several of these and explore their implications.

4.2 INSTITUTIONALISM AS THE ROOT OF BRITISH POLITICAL ANALYSIS

The development of British political science has not been significantly different from that of the discipline outlined briefly above. There was an extremely strong tradition of the 'old institutionalism' in British political analysis, some of it from well before political science developed as a separate academic discipline. To some extent that tradition persists more clearly than in most other national political science professions. There are a continuing number of interesting and important studies of Parliament and other institutions, many without explicit attempts to develop political theories about those institutions. At the same time, however, the new institutionalism has become a significant part of the language of political science, and may serve as an explicit theoretical foundation for expanding understanding of those structures.

Some of the leading figures in the development of British political science, or perhaps more aptly 'political studies', can be easily identified with the old institutionalism. For example, one could easily begin with Walter Bagehot's (1873) study of the English (*sic?*) constitution as a central institutionalist document for British government. This study of the constitution was followed by other notable studies such as Dicey (1908) and Jennings (1941) that focused on the importance of the written and unwritten elements of that constitution, and especially the legal foundations of public action. At the same time, very much as would a contemporary normative institutionalist, they emphasized the myths, symbols, and routines that shaped the performance of politics in Britain.

While the above scholars were concerned primarily with British government, others among the old institutionalists were more concerned with comparative politics and the impact of institutions in shaping other political systems. For example, while Britain has been and remains a very centralized political system, K. C. Wheare (1947) produced one of the most important studies of federal systems, as well as important comparative studies of legislatures (1955) and the nature of the British Commonwealth (1960). Likewise, Samuel Finer (1962; 1999) has made a number of significant contributions to understanding governance and political institutions in a broad comparative manner. Again, the list of significant contributors to 'old' institutional understandings of politics coming from British political scientists could be extended to a substantial length, but it is clear from the sampling presented here that there has been a notable, and continuing, contribution.

4.2.1 Analysis of Particular Institutions

The persistence of the 'old institutionalism' in British political science can be seen in the large number of studies that continue to be published with an explicit focus on particular institutions and that seek to describe the internal dynamics of those institutions. Again, these studies constitute major contributions to the understanding of politics and governing and should not be demeaned. Further, they have often been addressed to significant analytic questions of British government, e.g. the increasing power of the Prime Minister relative to Cabinet and Parliament, or the increasing judicialization of governing in Britain and other EU countries. At the same time, however, many of these studies have not contributed to the broader development of the discipline, and are often unseen outside the specialist community. This is perhaps especially true because of the tendency not to consider the British parliament in comparative context, even of its close relatives in the other Westminster systems.

The study of Parliament is one of the clearest examples of the persistence of the 'old institutionalism' as a mode of research in British political science (Giddings 2005). Despite some notable exceptions (Judge 2003; Patterson 1989) the study of Parliament has produced primarily the type of descriptive studies of institutional dynamics described above. These studies describe one or more aspects of parliaments extremely well, and fit them into broader patterns of governance in the United Kingdom, but they do not move the theoretical literature forward, nor locate the British parliament in a comparative context—indeed, to the extent that the European Parliament appears to have been more of a focus for theory development, e.g. in agenda setting, than has the national parliament.

The same story told about the legislative branch might be extended to cover the executive, both the political executive and the permanent executive in the public bureaucracy. To some extent the relative absence of theory about the political executive may be a function of the United Kingdom being a 'majoritarian' political system and therefore being denied the issues of coalition formation and maintenance that have been at the centre of a good deal of theorizing about cabinets (Müller and Strøm 2000; Laver 1998). Crafting theories about prime ministers is often extremely tricky, given that they occur one at a time and their behaviour is often seen to be determined by individual factors. Likewise, much of what happens in Cabinet happens in private, especially given the tradition of secrecy in the United Kingdom, making studying the institution that much more difficult.

On the other hand, however, one area in which British political science appears to have made major theoretical contributions is in the area of studying the public bureaucracy (see below). Not all of that theorizing might fit into the usual institutionalist model, but it has certainly illuminated the bureaucracy as a public institution and served as a foundation for further theorizing about this institution. This work is especially significant given the tendency of political science in some other countries (notably my own) to denigrate public administration, and to exclude it from the usual canon in the discipline. Further, British political science has provided a number of interesting theoretical analyses of the relationship between political executives and their civil servants (Hood and Lodge 2006).

Finally, the study of local government in the United Kingdom has a long and honourable tradition, again much of it highly descriptive. There have been seemingly endless studies of local government and the various formats through which both management at the local level and the relationships between central and local government have progressed. That having been said, however, here too there has been greater effort at building theory for local government than for some other institutions in British government. For example, the 'resource dependency' approach (Rhodes 1988) has been central to the analysis of central–local relations in the United Kingdom, and has been extended to other elements of government as well. Urban regime theory (Mossberger and Stoker 2001; Pierre 2005) has been a more recent contribution to that important strand of research.

I should be careful to reiterate that these descriptions of the old institutionalism as a style of research are meant to be far from entirely negative. These studies illuminated the central institutions in British government and their role in governing. Further, they formed the foundation for the subsequent development of more theoretical approaches to institutions and governance. Indeed, contemporary political science has had some tendency to forge ahead with theories and analysis while lacking the type of information and understanding these studies would provide and the conclusions reached are worse for that lack of background.

4.2.2 New Institutionalism and Conscious Theorizing

The 'old institutionalism' in British political science was an extremely rich tradition of analysis of the institutions of British government, and to a lesser extent comparative analyses of other political systems. There was, however, little if any self-conscious theorizing about the way in which institutions worked or their complex interrelationships, or their relationships with the broader social system. There often was a theory that was informing the institutional research, but that theory was well hidden through the close attention to detail and it was mostly expressed in the form of specific understandings of particular institutions, or perhaps of the British constitution taken as an entity (Johnson 2004).

Partially in response to the development of the 'new institutionalism' as a major approach to political analysis, and its more explicit theorizing about the nature and role of institutions, British political science has undertaken more extensive and explicit analyses of institutions. These analyses have built on the tradition of detailed analysis of British institutions but have added more explicit concerns with theory and comparison. This shift in the style of analysis occurred at approximately the same time that British institutions were undergoing significant and perhaps unprecedented change. Thus, the 'real world' of government provided academics with an interesting laboratory for analysis, and helped to elucidate the nature of institutions in British government.

4.2.2.1 *Whitehall Series*

One of the most important applications of institutional analysis in the British public sector has been the Whitehall Series, a major study of the centre of government funded by the Economic and Social Research Council. This project produced an extremely large number of scholarly publications (see, for example, the review by Wilson 2001) about the changing nature of structure and behaviour within the central institutions of the state. This research project followed closely after large-scale changes in Whitehall, and therefore had significant practical as well as academic value. The project also reinforced the resource dependency approach of Rod Rhodes that had been applied to other aspects of British government, notably local government, and therefore helped to move the British study of central institutions in the public sector away from the descriptive emphasis of old institutionalism.

Although the Whitehall Series itself was concerned primarily with the British public sector, it appeared to have encouraged a number of other more comparative studies examining the role of central government institutions. The work of Vincent Wright, Jack Hayward, and Edward Page, among others, who have examined the core executive in a number of countries, was also influenced by the Whitehall Project. And the group of younger scholars trained by Rhodes, Smith, Wright, and the other scholars has helped to develop further this strand of institutionalist research in British political science. This continuing interest in institutions is in marked contrast to developments in American political science that too often ignores the complexity of institutions in the search for more easily quantifiable variables.

4.2.2.2 *Christopher Hood and the Public Sector*

British political science has also had one of the major international students of the public bureaucracy and the public sector taken more broadly. Although not explicitly working in an institutionalist paradigm, Hood has applied a range of theories to public administration and other political institutions. For example, his book on 'Bureaumetrics' (Hood, Huby, and Dunsire 1981) was an attempt to measure the nature of public organizations and to represent their differences in a more understandable manner. More importantly, Hood applied cultural theory to the study of the public sector (1998) and generated a number of insights into how organizations link to society, using that approach which is not entirely dissimilar to normative institutionalism.

The research by Hood and his colleagues has not only kept public administration in the centre of political science in Britain but has also advanced institutionalist thinking. This research has helped to understand the interactions of institutions in areas such as accountability and the relationships of ministers and their mandarins, and has also provided ways of linking various strands of social and political theory to the analysis of political institutions.

4.2.2.3 *Rational Choice Institutionalism*

British political science has also made a number of important contributions to rational choice studies of institutions, again especially the public bureaucracy. For example, Patrick Dunleavy (1985) developed a useful critique and alternative to more simplistic assumptions about the budget-maximizing behaviour of bureaucrats. The 'bureau-shaping' model has been applied primarily in the United Kingdom but should be applicable in a wider range of settings. Dunleavy and Keith Dowding have also developed more general rational choice approaches to the role of the civil service in governing.

British political science has been less taken with the rational choice approach than has American political science, but has been perhaps more conscious of the existence of policy networks and policy communities that generally function in an institutional manner. Indeed, there has been substantial intellectual conflict over the relative utility of these approaches and their relative contributions to the scientific aspects of political science (Dowding 2001). The two approaches to political science represent ways of thinking about politics that involve structure but which also elaborate the workings of institutions, or sets of institutions. Thus, their interactions add some aspects of agency to the study of structure.

4.2.2.4 *The Welfare State and Path Dependence*

Much of the discussion of institutions focuses on formal institutions in government, but long-standing policies and programmes can also acquire the status of an institution. Indeed, much of the 'historical institutionalism' in political science is more concerned with policies than with structures, and the welfare state in the United Kingdom and the rest of the Western Europe has become institutionalized, by any interpretation of that term. With that level of institutionalization it is important to understand the political logic of these institutions as well as their persistence and the possibilities for transformation. In the United Kingdom the level of attention given to the politics of the welfare state, and perhaps especially the National Health Service (Castles 2002), helps to understand institutionalism as well as this complex set of public policies (Jessop 1999).

The decisions concerning the welfare state made over half a century ago continue to have importance for contemporary policy decisions, but contemporary political values and social change challenge the existing institutional understandings. The demographic, fiscal, and ideological pressures on the welfare state constitute one of the important sources of institutional change in European politics (Leibfried and Zürn 2006), and the United Kingdom is certainly no exception. The logic of historical institutionalism and path dependence (Torfing 2001) has been central to understanding the retrenchment and the persistence of the welfare state, including the comparatively gradual reforms in the United Kingdom.

4.2.2.5 *Devolution and Federalism*

The devolution of powers to Scotland and Wales has created greater interest in the nature of federalism and other devolved forms of governing in British political science. As noted, the old institutionalism in British political science produced several interesting studies of federalism, but these were not directly relevant to British politics. However, with the changing status of Scotland and Wales (Bogdanor 2001; Laffin and Thomas 1999) understanding intergovernmental dynamics becomes increasingly important. Likewise, British membership in the European Union (see below) adds another dimension to the analysis of intergovernmental relations.

The Constitution Unit has played a major role in the study of devolution in the United Kingdom, and in studying the relationships among the various components of the country. For example, the Unit has published a series of studies monitoring devolution and regionalization within the United Kingdom (Trench 2001; Hazell and Rawlings 2005). These studies correspond very much to the description above of the old institutionalism. They have concentrated on the formal aspects of constitutional and institutional change in the United Kingdom, and especially on the devolution of powers to Scotland and Wales.

4.2.2.6 *Institutional Analyses of the EU*

British political science has made major contributions to the institutional analysis of the European Union. A great deal of the academic discussion of the EU continues to be mired in the debate between 'neo-functionalist' and 'liberal intergovernmentalist' theories. While this debate was important as this proto-political system was being developed, it appears to have little continuing relevance for understanding the system as it now exists. Many of the institutions now in place in the EU are not at all dissimilar to those of the constituent national governments, and can be understood through the same modes of analysis, including institutional analysis.

Although certainly not alone (Tsebelis and Garrett 1996) a number of British scholars have been central in understanding individual institutions within the European Union, and as understanding the entire structure in institutional terms. For example, Anand Menon (2003) and John Peterson (1999) have both made important statements about the use of an institutionalist perspective to understand the EU. Likewise, Keith Dowding (2000) has applied rational choice versions of institutionalism to critique some of the existing research in the area. Other British scholars (Radaelli 2004; Featherstone and Radaelli 2003) have been concerned with institutional isomorphism and the process of 'Europeanization' of national policy and administrative systems. This process has perhaps been especially interesting in the United Kingdom, given the perceived differences between its institutions, and governance traditions, and those of the EU.

The list of British scholars concerned with the institutions of the European Union could be extended greatly. Indeed, like political science in many other European countries, the study of the EU approaches being an obsession. Even with that the complexity of the EU structures and procedures provides an interesting locus for applying institutional analysis. Further, to some extent the development of ideas such as multi-level governance (Flinders 2008) has added to the armamentarium of institutionalist scholars.

4.3 Questions Arising from the Institutional Approach

To this point I have been describing the changing nature of institutional analysis in British political science. The picture that has emerged from this very personal account of the contributions that this approach has made to the discipline in Britain raises some more general questions. Phrased rather broadly, we need to ask what institutionalism has contributed to British political analysis, and in turn what the British version of institutionalism has contributed to the discipline more broadly.

The first question is what institutional analysis, especially the more theoretical versions, has contributed to British political science. In particular, what has it demonstrated that other approaches to politics could not have? The most obvious answer to that question is that the other dominant approaches in contemporary political science rely primarily on the individual level for explanation; institutional answers tend to focus more on the collective properties of organizations and institutions. Perhaps especially in a political system with such well-developed institutions this approach to politics can explain some patterns of behaviour that others could not. In particular, as discussed below, institutionalism helps explain how even individuals with strong political views appear to adapt those views to conform to institutional contexts.

Of course, this strength for institutional approaches to politics is also their weakness. While the institutional approaches emphasize the role of institutions they tend to ignore, or at least to de-emphasize, the role of the individual and of social context. Further, institutionalism may ignore agency, and needs to provide some place for individual actions if the explanations involving these structures are to be active, and the decisions required of the institutions are to be understandable. This role for agency is especially important for explaining changes in institutions and their policy choices. Likewise, institutions are anchored in a cultural and social environment and must be understood as reflections of that environment.

Given the complementary strengths and weaknesses of institutional approaches and the alternative paradigms for contemporary political science, the obvious question is can these approaches be blended to provide a more complete picture, and if so how? One such composite approach has been suggested by Fritz Scharpf (1997) in his 'actor-centered institutionalism'. The notion here is that institutions may comprise a great part of the landscape for any political system, but those institutions act only if the individuals within them make decisions and activate the capacity of the institutions. Likewise, institutions are not atomistic but they also must be understood as a part of that institutional context.

We also need to ask what is distinctive about British institutional analysis. I have also demonstrated the deep roots of institutional analysis in British political science, and the persistence of that mode of analysis. Indeed, the persistence of older styles of institutional analysis is one aspect of the distinctiveness of the British style of analysis. Much of American political science has lost that detailed institutional knowledge in its pursuit of methodological rigour. There is certainly nothing wrong with rigour, and generally it is to be applauded, but the implicit assumption that methodology should drive research, rather than vice versa, will ultimately undermine research.

Finally, we need to think about the reasons for the persistence of such a strong institutionalist strand in British political science. Perhaps the simple answer is the historical institutionalist response to questions such as this—path dependence. This style of research has been successful in the past, and has tended to be reinforced by education and graduate training, so that the rather distinctive style has persisted. Further, British political science has tended to maintain a stronger sense of the political than most other versions of political science. That is, there is less sense that politics is merely a poor relation of economics in British political science than in many, if not most, other national approaches to the discipline. The maintenance of this keener sense of the political requires a continuing concern with the formal institutions through which that politics is manifested.

4.3.1 Intellectual Puzzles and Paradoxes in Institutionalism

While in many ways the story that emerges about British institutions is familiar and predictable, still a more careful examination of these institutions produces some interesting paradoxes. These puzzles become more apparent when the analytic tools provided by the new institutionalism are applied to the existing, but still changing, institutions of the public sector. Indeed each of the major approaches to institutional theory (Peters 2002) appears to provide at least one interesting puzzle about the formal institutions in British political life. These paradoxes are not dissimilar to those identified by scholars dealing with institutional theory in a more abstract manner (Fernandez-Alles and Valle-Cabrera 2006). Further, in several of the paradoxes I have identified, one of the other approaches to institutionalism offers a means of resolving the apparent paradox in institutional life.

4.3.1.1 *Few Formal Veto Points but Deliberative Processes*

The structure of institutions can be described in a number of ways. The old institutionalism tended to describe institutions and the constitutions in exacting detail, and to focus on the legal underpinnings of institutional performance. Rational choice institutionalism, on the other hand, considers those formal structures as a collection of 'veto-points' (Tsebelis 2002). The fundamental idea behind this analysis is that the more points at which decisions can be blocked—the greater the number of veto points—the more difficult making decisions will be. So, for example, presidential political systems with their multiple independent actors will, everything else being equal, find making decisions more difficult than parliamentary systems without separation of powers (Weaver and Rockman 1994; Ackerman 2000). And even individual institutions may vary significantly in the number of veto points with, for example, the US House of Representatives being much simpler for decision-making than with the more complex rules of the Senate.

Beginning with the veto-point model of institutions and their decision-making, the British appears to place fewer restrictions on the political executive than most other democratic governments. Not only is the system parliamentary, but it has had single-party governments and thus has not faced the complexities and constraints of coalition government that tend to impose restraints on most continental parliamentary governments (Müller and Strøm 2000). This majoritarian (Lijphart 1984) style of governing should enable quick and decisive action, a property that may have been accentuated by the increasing power of the cabinet, and especially by the prime minister (Heffernan 2003). Thus, as has been noted any number of times, the British constitution provides relatively few veto points and hence has the capacity to run roughshod over its opposition, and over the wishes of much of the public.

The puzzle then is that government, and especially the Prime Minister, in the United Kingdom does run roughshod rather infrequently, although critics will certainly point to examples, perhaps notably involvement in the war in Iraq. Why is that the case? One answer is that it is easy to underestimate the number of veto points, especially as long as the electoral mechanism functions. The familiar example of Mrs Thatcher and the poll tax is still apt (Butler, Adonis, and Travers 1994), and backbench rebellions also constrain just how far a Prime Minister and the Cabinet can go in pushing their own policy priorities. Likewise, the House of Lords, despite major constraints on its powers, continued to function as a veto point for important legislation during the Blair government (Flinders 2005). The view of scholars such as Martin Smith (1999) also is that there are a number of levels of mutual dependence among actors in the core executive so that alliance building rather than imposition is the fundamental dynamic.

Perhaps the other answer to the absence of as strong a government as we might expect from the veto-point argument comes from normative institutionalism, and the 'logic of appropriateness'. That is, governments do not act in that way because it is not appropriate to do so. The normative structure of the public sector therefore produces a more deliberative and cooperative style of governing than might be necessary, albeit always conducted within the 'shadow of hierarchy'. The intellectual 'compost' (Hennessy 2000) in which British political institutions grow stresses custom and collegiality, so that an emphasis on hierarchy may not be as acceptable as it might in other settings.

4.3.2 Large-scale Change but Path Dependency

A standard critique of institutional theory in political science is that while it is very good at explaining stability, it is much less successful in explaining change (see Peters, Pierre, and King 2005). In particular, the development of historical institutionalism as an approach to political phenomena has made the persistence of programmes and organizations once adopted a central analytic concern (Steinmo, Thelen, and Longstreth 1992; Pierson 2000). The historical institutionalism has had at its core a concept of 'path dependency', originally developed to analyse the persistence of sub-optimal economic structures, but then adapted to describe the persistence of public programmes. In addition to the importance of sheer inertia (see Rose and Davies 1993) in explaining persistence, scholars have argued that even programmes that are sub-optimal provide positive feedbacks to political elites and to clients, and therefore produce political pressures for maintaining them (Pierson 2000).

British government is usually taken as a clear case of the persistence of policy and formal institutions in the face of massive social change outside the public sector. Many of the formal institutions of government have elements and procedures that are centuries old. All governments have procedures that are employed not only simply to process their business but also to constrain conflict as well as to legitimate laws and other public decisions. The British political system has maintained more of these vestigial elements than have most others, and reform of some of these elements, e.g. the House of Lords, has been accomplished only through overcoming substantial difficulty.

The experiences during the Thatcher government might be taken as a clear refutation of the perspective of historical institutionalism (Marsh and Rhodes 1992). Both the institutional structure of the public sector, e.g. the nature of the civil service, and the general style of governing were altered dramatically during the eleven years that she was Prime Minister. In particular the organizational structure of the public sector and the manner in which services were delivered were transformed significantly. Likewise, the Blair government was able to make even more transformations of the public sector, some following in the Thatcherite direction, others embarking in new directions.

The post-Thatcher period provides an interesting test for the historical institutionalist arguments. One part of that strand of theory would argue that the Thatcher reforms that went so far from the underlying institutional pattern would be reversed, and the dominant features of the *status quo ante* would be restored. Although that return has not been as pronounced as for some other major reformers, e.g. New Zealand (Scott 2000), there was some return to the former style of governing. On the other hand, however, the often-made, if exaggerated, argument that the Blair government is really a continuation of the Thatcher years appears to argue that the tradition could be changed, and that a new pattern of governing could be established without the extreme levels of disruption implied by some notions of 'punctuated equilibrium'. Gordon Brown's becoming Prime Minister now presents another interesting challenge to these arguments concerning persistence and the power of underlying traditions in government.

4.3.3 Myth and Symbol, but Substantial Efficiency

A third paradox in an institutional analysis of British government might be seen as the flip side of the first discussed above. We have argued that conventions and customs in the public sector have been used as a constraint on the capacity of a prime minister to exercise what might be virtually autocratic power. Here, however, we return to Bagehot's familiar distinction between the dignified and efficient components of government. Commentators on British government, especially coming from abroad, may be quick to note the numerous ceremonial and seemingly antiquated elements of political practice. The symbolic elements of governing are important in the United Kingdom, and cannot really be avoided.

On the other hand British government can be extremely efficient, and reforms over the past several decades have been attempting to modernize government and make it even more efficient (Burch and Holliday 2004). The massive changes in the civil service and the delivery of public services makes some parts of government appear fully modernized and efficient, especially when compared to other presumably more efficient governments, e.g. the United States or France (see Smith 1998). The British delegation also has the reputation of being by far the most efficient in dealing with the Brussels bureaucracy, so that the United Kingdom has been able to influence policy more than might have been expected, even being one of the larger members of the European Union (Kassim 2001).

Again, the paradox may be more apparent than real. As Richard Rose (1963) argued some time ago, there may be some 'modernity in tradition' in British government, and the persistence of common political symbols serves important functions for the political system. As the normative institutionalists (March and Olsen 1986; Olsen 2008) have argued, myths, symbols, routines, and so on are crucial for legitimating institutions, so that indeed without the persistence of many seemingly vestigial functions of the political system the desired level of economic efficiency in the public sector might not be attainable. In those terms the understanding of the numerous symbolic elements of British institutions may be important for making them work effectively and efficiently.

4.3.4 Institutional Power but Personal Leadership

The final puzzle that arises in an institutional analysis of government in the United Kingdom is to some extent endemic in any institutional analysis. Although institutional analysis tends to focus on formal institutions in the public sector, those institutions are to a great extent shaped by the individuals who occupy them. The office of prime minister, for example, was to some extent transformed by the Thatcher years, and perhaps again during the Blair years. In turn, however, individuals and their personal values are shaped by their involvement in institutions or, phrased differently, individual preferences can be conceptualized as being endogenous to institutions. Politicians often disappoint their supporters by becoming a part of an institution once elected and seeming to abandon the preferences that those supporters had found attractive. Individuals must learn how to survive and be successful in their institutions, and often also adopt the prevailing institutional ideologies as their own.

Both of these points of mutual influence are apparent at all levels of the political system, but are perhaps most apparent for the political leaders at the top of the government pyramid. Each prime minister, for example, to some extent redefines the office, and the massive literature on the changes—real and imagined—brought about by the Blair government is the most recent example of that simple fact (Seldon and Kavanagh 2005). If institutions, especially those in the centre of government, are as powerful as they are often argued to be, then how can any individual reshape them so readily (see Grafstein 1992)? Likewise, why do individual political leaders who clearly have their own political personalities and goals permit themselves to be shaped by the often amorphous character of the institutions within which they happen to find themselves? This is by no means just an issue in British government, but the centrality of the prime minister in the system makes it more evident.

4.4 WHERE NEXT?

The rich tradition of institutional scholarship in the United Kingdom is unlikely to melt away, nor should any serious scholar of politics hope that it would. That having been said, however, the limits of uni-dimensional accounts are also apparent, and some of the scholarship already discussed has demonstrated those limits. One of the major limitations demonstrated above is that to apply just one form of institutional analysis risks obtaining an imbalanced and limited perspective. Just as triangulation (Flick 2006) using more varied techniques may help understanding social phenomena, so too can the use of alternative forms of institutionalism.

In addition to understanding the complexity of institutional explanations for politics, we need to identify the limitations of the approach both in general and especially as it is applied within the United Kingdom. Most fundamentally, by its very nature institutional theory emphasizes the impact of the structures of the public sector, and therefore has the tendency to become static. To be effective in explaining how British government, even as one of the more stable governing systems in the world, actually functions, those formal institutional structures must be instead placed in motion and their interactions better understood. Thus, institutional analyses must be supplemented by a more encompassing concern with public governance.

Therefore, like the rest of the discipline, British political science may need to integrate more dynamic elements into the study of institutions. The strong institutionalist strand in British political science may actually facilitate that integration. Having the rich body of information about their own institutions, as well as those of the European Union and many European countries, providing a more complete understanding of the evolution of these institutions is more than feasible. To some extent it has already been achieved in a number of studies of specific institutions (Flinders 2007; Gamble 2003), but not at a broader level of analysis.

4.5 Conclusions

Institutional analysis has been, and in many ways continues to be, at the centre of British political science. Unlike many national versions of the discipline, the 'old institutionalism' involving detailed analysis of particular institutions, or of the entire political system, continues to be practised and to produce useful analyses of politics. That version of institutionalism now, however, is complemented and to a great extent displaced by a more theoretically motivated version of institutionalism. The coexistence of these two styles of political analysis does appear to provide a more complete understanding of institutions and governance than is true in many other national 'brands'.

The use of institutional analysis also reveals some interesting paradoxes about the practice of governing in the United Kingdom, and also illuminates the theories that bring forth the paradoxes. The formalism and presumed static nature of institutions in much institutional theory can provide part of an explanation for governance, in the United Kingdom or elsewhere, but can go only so far in providing that explanation. The other dimension of institutions, their symbolic and social elements, provide a complement to the formal discussion of institutions but also raise several paradoxes of their own.

A final point to be made is that institutional analysis, as practised, is both a strength and a weakness of British political science. On the one hand the tradition has produced a number of rich and important studies of institutions, largely in the British central government. At the same time that strong tradition of institutional analysis has tended to isolate many aspects of British scholarship from comparative analysis. This separation of scholarly traditions is unfortunate for the individuals, but even more unfortunate because of the relative failure to place British institutions in a broader comparative context. Again, that problem is also very evident for political science in the United States, but it certainly has limited a more nuanced understanding of British institutions as well.

References

ACKERMAN, B. 2000. 'The New Separation of Powers'. *Harvard Law Review*, 113: 633–729.

BAGEHOT, W. 1873. *The English Constitution*. Boston: Little, Brown.

BOGDANOR, V. 2001. *Devolution in the United Kingdom*. Oxford: Oxford University Press.

BRETON, A. 1996. *Competitive Governments: An Economic Theory of Politics and Public Finance*. Cambridge: Cambridge University Press.

BURCH, M., and HOLLIDAY, I. 2004. 'The Blair Government and the Core Executive'. *Government and Opposition*, 39: 1–21.

BUTLER, D., ADONIS, A., and TRAVERS, T. 1994. *Failure in British Government: The Politics of the Poll Tax*. Oxford: Oxford University Press.

CASTLES, F. G. 2002. 'The Future of the Welfare State: Crisis Myths and Crisis Realities'. *International Journal of Health Services*, 32: 255–77.

DICEY, A. V. 1908. *Introduction to the Study of the Law of the Constitution.* London: Macmillan.

DOWDING, K. 2000. 'Institutionalist Research on the European Union: A Critique'. *European Union Politics*, 1: 125–44.

——2001. 'There Must be an End to Confusion: Policy Networks, Intellectual Fatigue, and the Need for Political Science Methods Courses in British Universities'. *Political Studies*, 49: 89–105.

DUNLEAVY, P. 1985. 'Bureaucrats, Budgets and the Growth of the State: Reconstructing an Instrumental Model'. *British Journal of Political Science*, 15: 299–328.

DUVERGER, M. 1951. *Les Partis politiques.* Paris: Colin.

ECKSTEIN, H. 1963. 'A Perspective on Comparative Politics, Past and Present'. In H. Eckstein and D. Apter (eds.), *Comparative Politics.* New York: Macmillan.

FEATHERSTONE, K., and RADAELLI, C. M. (eds.) 2003. *The Politics of Europeanization.* Oxford: Oxford University Press.

FERNANDEZ-ALLES, M., and VALLE-CABRERA, R. 2006. 'Reconciling Institutional Theory with Organizational Theories: How Neoinstitutionalism Resolves Five Paradoxes'. *Journal of Organizational Change Management*, 19: 503–17.

FINER, S. E. 1962. *A Man on Horseback: The Role of the Military in Politics.* New York: Praeger.

——1999. *A History of Government from the Earliest Times.* Oxford: Oxford University Press.

FLICK, U. 2006. *An Introduction to Qualitative Research.* London: Sage.

FLINDERS, M. 2005. 'Majoritarian Democracy in Britain'. *West European Politics*, 28/1: 61–93.

——2007. 'Analyzing Reform: The House of Commons, 2001–5'. *Political Studies*, 55: 174–200.

GAMBLE, A. 2003. 'Remaking the Constitution'. In P. Dunleavy and G. Peele (eds.), *Developments in British Politics 7.* Basingstoke: Palgrave.

GIDDINGS, P. 2005. *The Future of Parliament.* Basingstoke: Palgrave.

GRAFSTEIN, R. 1992. *Institutional Realism: Social and Political Constraints on Rational Actors.* New Haven, Conn.: Yale University Press.

GREENWOOD, C. R., and GREENWOOD, R. 1996. 'Understanding Radical Organizational Change: Bringing Together the Old and New Institutionalism'. *Academy of Management Review*, 21: 1022–54.

HAZELL, R., and RAWLINGS, R. 2005. *Devolution, Law Making and the Constitution.* London: Constitution Unit.

HEFFERNAN, R. 2003. 'Prime Ministerial Predominance? Core Executive Politics in the United Kingdom'. *British Journal of Politics and International Relations*, 5/3: 347–72.

HENNESSY, P. 2000. *The Prime Ministers.* London: Allen Lane.

HOOD, C. 1998. *The Art of the State.* Oxford: Oxford University Press.

——HUBY, M., and DUNSIRE, M. 1981. *Bureaumetrics: A Quantitative Comparison on British Central Government Agencies.* Farnborough: Gower.

——and LODGE, M. 2006. *The Politics of Public Service Bargains: Reward, Competency, Loyalty, and Blame.* Oxford: Oxford University Press.

JENNINGS, I. 1941. *The British Constitution.* Cambridge: Cambridge University Press.

JESSOP, B. 1999. 'The Changing Governance of Welfare: Recent Trends in Its Primary Functions, Scale and Performance'. *Social Policy and Administration*, 33/4: 348–59.

JOHNSON, N. 2004. *Reshaping the British Constitution: Essays in Political Interpretation.* Basingstoke: Palgrave.

JUDGE, D. 2003. 'Legislative Institutionalization: A Bent Analytic Arrow?' *Government and Opposition*, 38: 497–516.

KASSIM, H. 2001. 'Representing the United Kingdom in Brussels: The Fine Art of Positive Policy Coordination'. In H. Kassim, A. Menon, B. G. Peters, and V. Wright (eds.), *The National Coordination of EU Policy: The Brussels Dimension*. Oxford: Oxford University Press.

LAFFIN, M., and THOMAS, A. 1999. 'The United Kingdom: Federalism in Denial?' *Publius*, 29: 89–108.

LAVER, M. 1998. 'Models of Government Formation'. *Annual Review of Political Science*, 1: 1–25.

LEIBFRIED, S., and ZÜRN, M. 2006. *Transformation of the State*. Cambridge: Cambridge University Press.

LIJPHART, A. 1984. *Democracies: Patterns of Majoritarian and Consensus Government in Twenty-One Countries*. New Haven, Conn.: Yale University Press.

MARCH, J. G., and OLSEN, J. P. 1986. *Rediscovering Institutions: The Organizational Basis of Political Life*. New York: Free Press.

MARSH, D., and RHODES, R. A. W. 1992. *Implementing Thatcherite Policies: Audit of an Era*. Buckingham: Open University Press.

MENON, A. 2003. 'Member States and International Institutions: Institutionalizing Intergovernmentalism in the European Union'. *Comparative European Politics*, 1/2: 171–201.

MOSSBERGER, K., and STOKER, G. 2001. 'The Evolution of Urban Regime Theory'. *Urban Affairs Review*, 36: 810–35.

MÜLLER, W., and STRØM, K. 2000. *Coalition Governments in Western Europe*. Oxford: Oxford University Press.

OLSEN, J. P. 2009. 'Change and Continuity: An Institutional Approach to the Institutions of Government'. *European Political Science Review*, 1/1.

PATTERSON, S. C. 1989. 'Understanding the British Parliament'. *Political Studies*, 37/3: 449–62.

PETERS, B. G. 1996. 'Political Institutions, Old and New'. In R. E. Goodin and H.-D. Klingemann (eds.), *New Handbook of Political Science*. Oxford: Oxford University Press.

—— 2002. *Institutional Theory in Political Science: The New Institutionalism*, 2nd edn. London: Continuum.

—— PIERRE, J., and KING, D. S. 2005. 'Beyond Path Dependency: Political Conflict in Historical Institutionalism'. *Journal of Politics*, 67: 1275–1300.

PETERSON, J. 1999. 'The Santer Era: The European Commission in Normative, Historical and Theoretical Perspective'. *Journal of European Public Policy*, 6: 46–65.

PIERRE, J. 2005. 'Comparative Urban Governance: Uncovering Complex Causalities'. *Urban Affairs Review*, 40: 446–62.

PIERSON, P. 2000. 'Increasing Returns, Path Dependence and the Study of Politics'. *American Political Science Review*, 94: 251–67.

RADAELLI, C. M. (ed.) 2004. 'Markets and Regulatory Competition in Europe'. Special Issue of *Journal of Public Policy*, 24/1.

RHODES, R. A. W. 1988. *Beyond Westminster and Whitehall*. London: Allen and Unwin.

ROSE, R. 1963. 'The Modernity of Tradition'. In L. Pye and S. Verba (eds.), *Political Culture and Political Development*. Princeton, NJ: Princeton University Press.

—— and DAVIES, P. 1993. *Inheritance in Public Policy: Change without Choice in Britain*. New Haven, Conn.: Yale University Press.

SCHARPF, F. W. 1997. *Games Real Actors Play: Actor-Center Institutionalism in Policy Research*. Boulder, Colo.: Westview.

SCOTT, G. 2000. 'Public Management Reform and the Lessons from Experience in New Zealand'. *International Public Management Journal*, 3/1: 67–78.

SELDON, A., and KAVANAGH, D. 2005. *The Blair Effect, 2001–2005*. Cambridge: Cambridge University Press.

SHEPSLE, K. A. 1989. 'Studying Institutions: Some Lessons from the Rational Choice Approach'. *Journal of Theoretical Politics*, 1/2: 131–47.

SMITH, M. J. 1998. 'Reconceptualizing the British State: Theoretical and Empirical Challenges to Central Government'. *Public Administration*, 76: 45–72.

—— 1999. *The Core Executive in Britain*. London: Macmillan.

STEINMO, S., THELEN, K. A., and LONGSTRETH, F. 1992. *Structuring Politics: Historical Institutionalism in Comparative Analysis*. Cambridge: Cambridge University Press.

TORFING. J. 2001. 'Path Dependent Danish Welfare Reforms: The Contribution of New Institutionalism to Understanding Evolutionary Change'. *Scandinavian Political Studies*, 24: 277–309.

TRENCH, A. 2001. *The State of the Nations, 2001*. London: Academic.

TSEBELIS, G. 2002. *Veto Players: How Political Institutions Work*. Princeton, NJ: Princeton University Press.

—— and GARRETT, G. 1996. 'An Institutional Critique of Intergovernmentalism'. *International Organization*, 50: 269–99.

WEAVER, R. K., and ROCKMAN, B. A. 1994. *Do Institutions Matter? Government Capabilities in the United States and Abroad*. Washington, DC: Brookings Institution.

WHEARE, K. C. 1947. *Federal Government*. Oxford: Oxford University Press.

—— 1955. *Government by Committee*. Oxford: Oxford University Press.

—— 1960. *The Constitutional Structure of the Commonwealth*. Oxford: Oxford University Press.

—— 1963. *Legislatures*. Oxford: Oxford University Press.

WILSON, G. 2001. 'The Whitehall Programme'. *Government and Opposition*, 36: 440–4.

CHAPTER 5

....

RATIONAL CHOICE

....

KEITH DOWDING

5.1 RATIONAL CHOICE METHODOLOGY

....

RATIONAL choice is understood very broadly in this chapter. I assume any article
informed by the idea that we best explain political institutions, processes, events, or
outcomes by assuming that actors respond rationally to their environment counts
as rational choice. 'Rational' here is a technical term meaning actors' behaviour
is predictable by the principles of revealed preference theory under certainty; that
is, their ordinal preferences are reflexive, complete, and transitive; and for cardi-
nal preferences abide by the continuity assumption. All this really means is that
we assume we understand what actors are doing and 'rationally reconstruct' their
behaviour to reveal their maximand. Many models of rational choice assume 'self-
interest' meaning that for the purpose of analysis the actors optimize as defined by
their role. Thus party leaders are thought to act so as to maximize the number of
votes their party receives; consumers try to buy the best goods at the lowest price; and
environmentalists maximize the least damage to the environment given their other
aims. Because so few people understand the technicalities of rational choice theory
and because rational choice can be highly mathematical, there are many misinformed
criticisms and the technique is often considered controversial, though few of the
items I consider here would be considered controversial *because* they are informed
by the rational choice approach, even if others might take issue with their substantive
conclusions.[1]

---

[1] Green and Shapiro (1994) is one of the better misinformed critiques; for response, Friedman (1995)
and Cox (1999).

5.2 WHY SO LITTLE LITERATURE?

Despite the broad understanding of rational choice there is not a great deal to review, hence part of this chapter considers obvious areas of British politics that rational choice could examine. Why is there so little literature? One reason is there are few British political scientists trained in the relevant techniques. The 1960s department at Essex University that could have provided the powerhouse for graduates in rational choice dissipated by the late 1970s as the leading lights pursued higher salaries and better research facilities at US universities.[2] Today Essex still has some of the UK's leading rational choice political scientists, with the LSE and Oxford providing other homes for small viable groups, but most other universities only provide shelter for the odd rational choice advocate much as they once did for Marxists in the 1970s and 1980s. This fact also explains the peculiar 'British quality' to rational choice writing, which tended to be less technical and empirical than its US counterpart (Ward 1996; see Dowding and King 1995 for some examples) though some young academics, notably at the three universities mentioned, are proving their technical competence with important articles.

North and Weingast's (1989) classic article is an exception demonstrating a rule. They argue that the Glorious Revolution of 1688 and the fundamental redesign of the governmental and fiscal arrangements of seventeenth-century England allowed government to commit credibly to non-predation and protect property rights allowing the growth of capital markets and of Britain as a world power. The central role of parliament alongside the Crown and an independent judiciary limited the Crown's ability unilaterally to alter agreements. Thus the Crown could credibly commit to repaying loans allowing the development of capital markets, nascent industry, and strong armed forces (see also Stasavage 2002; 2003). The commitment problem is central to the development of the modern state re-emerging in discussions surrounding central bank independence, where Gordon Brown ensured the credibility of Labour's commitment to high growth and low inflation with his first act as Chancellor of the Exchequer in 1997 (King 2001; 2005). Why is North and Weingast an exception demonstrating a rule? It is exceptional because of the relative paucity of literature on British politics informed by rational choice theory. And it demonstrates a rule, since what there is tends to be historical and based more on analytic narrative than hard data: though in this review I show that this 'rule' is now being broken as rational choice analysis of British political institutions is starting to come of age.

A second reason for the paucity of literature is the general structure of the British political system, which provides less obvious scope for interesting strategic modelling. Strong parliamentary party discipline leaves the British legislature less open to the strategic manoeuvring that occurs with weaker parties or multi-party systems. Many

---

[2] In modern times rational choice began with Arrow (1951/1963) and Downs (1957). Essex in the late 1960s was a world leader. See Dewan, Dowding, and Shepsle (2009) for a review of some of the most important articles in the field.

of the important formal results are driven by the strategic possibilities of multidimensional issue-space and legislative organization to structure more stable equilibriums. The weakness of the British parliament makes its internal organization inherently less interesting. Potential parliamentary disequilibrium is solved by one party dominating between elections. Parliamentary oversight of executive functions is also less important in the UK where the core executive has traditionally been hierarchical with the minister directly accountable to parliament. All in all this means that the standard models of rational choice have less obvious applicability to central areas of British politics. And the secrecy surrounding the central state makes data-driven empirical analysis problematic. However, in recent years attention has been given to the central organs of the state—Cabinet relations, ministerial responsibility, and agency problems within the civil service. And rational choice models have been widely applied to voting behaviour and the electoral party system; and to local government and service provision. Furthermore in recent years a stronger awareness of historical processes has led rational choice writers to examine the past.

5.3 ELECTORAL POLITICS

The dominant theme of British psephology has been (the breakdown of) class voting and how the economy affects voter choice. Class dealignment has made more apparent the economic effects upon government popularity as voters rationally weigh up their party differential and decide whether retrospectively to punish governments for past economic failure.

Early models applied the political-business cycle to explaining economic crisis in the UK (Nordhaus 1975). Governments were thought to manipulate the economy to ensure an upturn prior to an election only to face inflationary problems immediately afterwards. A great deal of econometrics has never conclusively demonstrated the political-business cycle though its existence might depend upon institutional factors (Schultz 1995). The general forecasting of election results on macroeconomic variables began with Goodhart and Bhansali (1970) and following them others predicted government popularity using objective economic indicators (Pissarides 1980). Others have examined specific economic effects on voting, Johnson, Lynch, and Walker (2005) suggesting that British government's fixation on the level of income tax is misplaced electorally. The most comprehensive and successful forecaster has been David Sanders (1991; 1996; 2000; 2003; 2005), who uses a 'core' model of governing party popularity using a lagged endogenous variable specification to map objective economic (largely) variables onto subjective perspectives including a set of 'events' which shock the core model. His earlier models concentrate on lagged interest rates (though unemployment was important in the 1970s); more recently he favours an inductive approach of specifying models which predict past popularity extended to forecasting the near future. There remains no specific theory or political economy of government popularity.

Analysis of party competition from a rational choice perspective has an august history. Anthony Downs (1957) used the UK as an example in (perhaps the first) classic of rational choice theory. He suggests electoral politics in a single dimension lead the parties to the centre. The account can be underpinned by Black's (1948) median voter theorem (MVT) demonstrating that single-peaked preferences and a single dimension ensure the median voter is a unique majority winner. Certainly, the failures of Labour in the 1970s and 1980s can be seen as a result of losing the middle ground as they moved leftwards, and the strategy of New Labour has been to regain that centre ground (Hindmoor 2004). However the Conservatives hardly mapped out a centrist policy stance in the 1970s and 1980s, but rather won through Labour's incoherence. Dunleavy and Ward's (1981; Dunleavy 1991) story of preference shaping where government shifts the political spectrum through policy initiatives might be used to explain the ideological relocation of the median voter.

The Downsian story applied to British politics seems to have entered the consciousness of political leaders but its assumptions are simple, and more complex models produce very different predictions. Whilst a class dimension might allow for an approximation to a single ideological dimension, other issues achieve valence and the multiplicity of issues concerning people mean the MVT single-peaked assumption may not always hold. Probabilistic voting models (Coughlin 1990) and uncertainty over policy positions predict non-convergence (Roemer 2001). Analyses have shown the parties have not consistently moved towards the centre ground to win elections (Robertson 1976; Budge 1994), although whether they adopt complex strategies or simply follow a random walk is not clear (Burt 1997). Recent work combining valence and issue dimensions applying to the UK is found in Adams, Merril, and Grofman (2005: ch. 9) which shows how 'rival' approaches can be represented within the rational choice canon, whilst Kang (2004) uses British data to explain abstention and protest voting in a parties quality-satisficing framework.

5.4 POLITICAL PARTIES

Whilst rational choice theory views parties as vote, office, or policy seeking within competitive settings, there is relatively little work that examines their function within a political system. Parties can be viewed as organizations reducing the cost of collective action and transactions costs in governmental and electoral arenas (Muller 2004). As arbiters of ideology (Downs 1957; Hinich and Munger 1994) parties help solve commitment problems ensuring leaders do not renege on their promises to the electorate once in power. Dewan and Myatt (2007a) show leaders can overcome coordination barriers and give a sense of direction so clarifying a party's position helping instrumental voters in plurality elections coordinate their votes. Other recent formal work on leadership suggests leaders buy their support by distributing private benefits to members of the winning coalition (Bueno de Mesquita et al. 2005). The changing funding nature of the Labour Party helps explain both recent malfeasance and its lack of interest in altering industrial policies inherited from the Conservative administration.

Quinn's (2005) book examines organizational change in the Labour Party explaining the strengthening position of the Labour leader through democratic change. His focus is on how office-seeking politicians transformed the organizational structure to bring control for electoral gain. He demonstrates how organizational changes did not always operate as their supporters thought they might. It can be nicely juxtaposed to Tsebelis's (1990: ch. 5) nested games explanation of why Labour Party activists committed political suicide in the 1980s. Hindmoor (2004) uses a post-Downsian model to explain the success of New Labour, not only in capturing the middle ground but also in persuading the media and public that their policies are centrist.

Motivated by the collective action problem, Whiteley, Seyd, and collaborators (Seyd and Whiteley 2002; Whiteley, Seyd, and Richardson 1994) examine incentives motivating political activists in the main British political parties taking a broad though critical look at political-economic motivations. However, they do not locate their work in broader literature on governing organizational structures, nor examine the role of organizations in shaping the motivations of activists. There is much still to learn about British political parties and the party system from a rational choice perspective.

5.5 CABINET STUDIES

Constitutional law, descriptive analyses, and the relative power of the prime minister once dominated core executive studies. Given the obvious strategic nature of cabinet relations formal techniques should be well placed to examine such power dependencies and develop testable hypotheses about cabinet and core executive relations. The first stage of any such analysis is the mapping of the relationships. Little work, beyond simple line figures, has gone into such a mapping. Dunleavy (1995) has applied a weighted score to ministers in terms of their membership and chairmanship of cabinet committees but without strategic analysis it gives little insight into more general power relations; nevertheless; it provides a first step at quantitatively examining the structure of the innermost core executive. The strategic interrelationships have been little studied, perhaps due to the general secrecy surrounding central government structures, and the difficulties of gaining hard data on those relationships (though see Steunenberg 2005).

For all the welter of anecdotal and historical evidence surrounding the relationship between the prime minister and ministers, or between ministers and departments, there is little that is truly systematic beyond analytic narratives. Cox's (1987) examination of the development of the cabinet is suggestive but the general thrust of cabinet studies remains descriptive. However, the relationships between individual and collective ministerial responsibility are now being formally analysed. Kam (2000) argues that holding ministers solely accountable for departments makes sense as it enables ministers to control senior civil servants more easily than if there were more direct parliamentary scrutiny of those civil servants. Dewan and Myatt (2007*b*) game-theoretically model the relationship between individual and collective cabinet responsibility. Protecting cabinet colleagues has obvious individual advantages when one finds oneself under close scrutiny, but there are costs to such protection. Ministers may have to resign, not so much for what they have done, but because too many colleagues have been protected in the near past. If policy activism is correlated with the propensity to be publicly criticized and if a prime minister wants policy activism, then ministers need protection. Dewan and Myatt demonstrate that such protection enhances ministerial value meaning that tainted ministers will not be as active as untainted ones. Prime ministers do not want to appoint ministers who attract scandal or criticism, but on the other hand they do not want ministers who simply sit on their hands. A balance between risk and stability is required. Berlinski, Dewan, and Dowding (2007) have started to chart the hazard function of ministers. Controlling for the contingencies associated with the particular personalities and problems found with individual prime ministers they find experience is not rewarded in the long run, with ministers who have served the prime minister in a previous government having a higher hazard than those without such experience; older ministers also have a higher hazard, though full cabinet ministers are less at risk than more junior colleagues. Alt (1975) notes that British ministers seem less experienced than those in other countries, and the structure of single-party government might causes the oft-bemoaned feature of their relatively short careers and inexperience (Rose 1971; 1987; Headey 1974). However, the more direct accountability found in the British system as opposed to the strategic nature of coalitional governments suggests the opposite. Shorter terms might make for greater accountability. Indridason and Kam (2008) show that cabinet reshuffles reduce agency loss and moral hazard facing ministers and that efficiency can be enhanced with greater prime ministerial control.

For individual accountability Dewan and Dowding (2005) discover a corrective effect where, contrary to popular belief, individual ministerial resignations *enhance* government popularity. It is the scandals that are bad for government popularity, resignations (more than) correct for such falls. Such corrections would not take place if ministers always resigned when in difficulty. In order for the public to believe prime ministers sack bad ministers and protect good ones they must act strategically with an eye on the long term even when a scandal seems to be damaging the government. If there are short-run advantages to sacking ministers in trouble, long-run advantages reassure the public that the prime minister only gets rid of the most inefficient. Better ministers must be protected so the less efficient ones or those too damaged can be sacked with impunity.

Stories told by politicians and insiders teem with strategic considerations, but little has been formally modelled. The distinction between individual and collective responsibility is much discussed, but what is the *function* of each? Who benefits from individual and who from collective responsibility? Collective responsibility developed in the late nineteenth century in order to rein in criticisms of ministers by other ministers. It enabled the prime minister to gain control over the government and keep talented but warring ministers within the cabinet. Is this its only function? What do ministers gain from collective responsibility? Blondel and Manning (2002) suggest that the collegiality of cabinet government as opposed to hierarchical systems reduces agency problems, and that idea needs closer scrutiny.

5.6 CORE EXECUTIVE

Continuing reforms of core executive organization provide an ideal subject for study. Relationships between the prime minister, different departments, and especially the Treasury and other departments could be analysed using Tsebelis's (2002) veto-player analysis. The problem for scholars of British politics using such techniques is the relative secrecy of British government. Only in retrospect as government papers become available might we discover the importance of agenda-setting powers—and for example why recent prime ministers have seemingly acted so early in the policy process—and just how powerful PMs and the Treasury are as agenda setters and veto players. Steunenberg (2005) applies such analysis to the budgetary decisions suggesting departments are not as weak as might be imagined; the prime minister is a crucial actor and transactions costs increase departmental discretion. McLean and Nou (2006) provide an analytic narrative around veto-player theory to explain the failure of land tax reform between 1909 and 1914. Similar techniques could be utilized in other areas of policy analysis.

Political economy models have been applied rather simply to the civil service using a selected and rather dated band of models. Dunleavy's (1991) transaction costs bureau-shaping model was developed with the British civil service specifically in mind. It has been intensively utilized and criticized (Dowding 1995; James 1995; 2003; John 1998; Pollitt, Birchall, and Putnam 1998; Marsh, Smith, and Richards 2000; Dowding and James 2004), and unlike other models is concerned with what goes on inside bureaucracies rather than relationships between bureaucrats and politicians. Niskanen's (1971) early principal–agent budget-maximizing model has been extensively critiqued in the British context (Dunsire and Hood 1989; Dunleavy 1991; Dowding 1995). Its restrictive assumptions give it only limited applicability. More mainstream modern principal–agent models have hardly been touched upon in the British context. The amount of discretion allowed bureaucrats is contained within the framing of legislation. The more detailed the legislation, the less discretion bureaucrats are allowed. The standard line is that politicians write less detailed legislation giving bureaucrats more discretion according to:

(a) the more risky the legislative intent (the less informed politicians are about the precise outcomes of their legislative intent); and
(b) the more stable the governing coalition (the more sure that they will stay in power for a long period of time).

Legislation and executive directives could be coded to see whether uncertainty affects the degree of discretion, and whether governments with smaller majorities and less certain futures push legislation that is harder to unravel or give less discretion to agencies.

Rational choice teaches us that the degree and type of monitoring depends on the strength of government's policy preferences. If legislation is an electoral response to public demands government is happy to allow 'fire alarm' monitoring where failures are brought to government attention by the public or pressure groups. If legislation is designed to secure the policy preferences of the politicians themselves they are more likely to follow a 'police patrol' monitoring regime, putting in place regular procedures to ensure their wishes are executed. The latter form of monitoring is more costly than the first. Again careful coding and quantitative analysis could tease out whether the monitoring of policies that are publicly demanded does have a different character from that closer to politicians' own preferences. Is the regulatory state a result of the stronger policy preferences of professional politicians?

With the proliferation of agencies there are many applications for examining the subtle differences that might be found in the nature of contracts between agencies and departments. Surprisingly little quantitative work has been conducted to see whether the types of goods and services provided by different agencies correlate with perceived contractual success or failure as suggested in transactions costs economics (Williamson 1996). Targets are another area where modelling could be applied. Setting targets for agencies, health trusts, local governments, schools, universities, or civil servants gives obvious gaming opportunities (Hood 2002). That targets distort policies is well known. In the British audit era where targets proliferate there should be a host of examples of such gaming. A theoretically comprehensive account of how incentives affect gaming activity as well as empirical studies examining the distortion of policy instruments would be compelling. We could do with a Horn (1995) or Huber and Shipan (2002) analysis devoted to the civil service–politician relationship in the UK, as well as analysis of core department–agency relationships more broadly. Miller's (1992) work on organizational structures and the efficiencies of hierarchies against contractual relations might also prove illuminating. Examining the culture and authority relations within public organizations (Kreps 1990) and comparing these with modern contractual relations might help us see more clearly the different types of public-sector failure. The role of information and the signalling games played between actors would be a key feature of any such analysis. One aspect missing from the economic literature on principal–agent problems that political science might be well placed to examine is the role of authority. Political science sees authority as a two-way relationship where those above can give authoritative commands, but in order to command respect and gain efficiency, should also listen to the problems of those below.

5.7 PARLIAMENT

The British parliament offers less scope for strategic analysis than stronger less coherent legislatures. Analysis of parliament in the nineteenth century is more advanced, making use of Aydelotte (1970) and the greater interest of a legislature before strong parties. Of particular interest, of course, has been the ructions around the repeal of the Corn Laws (Schondhardt-Bailey 1994). Cheryl Schondhart-Bailey's (2006) significant book examines the interplay of economic factors and ideas from the voting records, constituency interests, and speeches of MPs during the free trade discussions in the nineteenth-century parliament. Using new empirical techniques and strong data she argues that the generation and interplay of ideas play an important role in structuring changes well beyond economic models based purely upon self-interested material benefits. The Corn Laws are also one of McLean's (2001) cases in a book applying rational choice to British political history, though here his analytic narrative is focused upon the art of manipulation and Riker's (1986) heresthetic politicians. Heresthetics is the art and science of political manipulation. McLean's masterful book shows how some leaders have manipulated issue dimensionality and underlying cyclical majorities to transform political situations, and, sometimes successfully, build new long-term alliances at various important historical junctures. This book is the paradigm example of British rational choice analytic narrative.

More recent parliaments are dominated by parties, so the voting records of parliament are concerned with backbench revolts. There are no general theories of revolts beyond the personal characteristics of MPs (Cowley 2002; Cowley and Norton 1999; Norton 1978; 1980; Benedetto and Hix 2005) but perhaps, in the British context, there is not much more to say. Spirling and McLean (2007) demonstrate the problems of using an optimal classification system of voting records from binary data such as Poole (2005) in a strong party system such as Westminster to try to classify voting patterns. The problem is that whilst government rebels will be voting sincerely, the Opposition are likely to be voting strategically with the result that left-wing rebels such as Tony Benn and Dennis Skinner appear to the right of the Labour Cabinet in a second dimension.

The strategic interaction of the Lords and Commons has been under-studied. The relative weakness of the committee system also leaves little room for analysis of parliamentary oversight of the executive in comparison with many other nations.[3] What might be considered are the strategic possibilities afforded by amending in committee and in the Lords especially in the context of timing when the parliamentary year draws to a close. Another neglected area is the analysis of legislative careers. Diermeier, Keane, and Mirlo (2005) attempt to quantify the career returns of members of Congress. Dynamically modelling career decisions they assess the re-election chances for members of Congress, estimating the effect of Congressional experience on income—from both the public and the private sector. Whilst it is notoriously difficult to analyse such counterfactuals, a similar analysis in the British context would be fascinating. One might hypothesize that the monetary value of a parliamentary career is negative for those who do not make it into cabinet, or high in the shadow cabinet, but surprises might be in store. There might well be different findings for those from, say, backgrounds in law to those with backgrounds in public service—such as teachers or university lecturers. This might teach us something about the changing social composition of parliament and also add both empirical and analytic bite to King's (1981) professionalization of politics thesis.

5.8 LOCAL GOVERNMENT

The large literature on fiscal federalism is little utilized in studying the political economy of local government in the UK. Theories of the effects of intergovernmental grants, notably the flypaper effect, where higher tier grants to lower tiers increase spending by the income elasticity of demand (see Cullis and Jones 1992: 307–20), are constrained by restrictions central government has placed upon local government's tax-raising powers. Not only does the UK not have a federal system, it barely has differential fiscal units, making potential welfare gains from 'competing' authorities problematic. Where there are economies of scale in production, differential size of providers might produce allocative efficiencies. This has led to theories concerning the optimum size of local authorities using club theory (Buchanan 1965; Musgrave and Musgrave 1989) and Tiebout competition. Testing these ideas has proved problematic (Dowding, John, and Biggs 1994) and increasingly so as government gives way to governance, and the numbers and responsibilities of collective-good providers multiply. Exiting behaviour in the UK has been demonstrated (John, Dowding, and Biggs 1995: Dowding and John 1996) and capitalization occurs especially for schools (Cheshire and Sheppard 1998; 2003). Dowding and Mergoupis (2003) claim Tiebout is better tested in the UK than the US despite the lack of tax-raising powers of local

---

[3] Or is that true? Where is the comparative analysis of oversight effectiveness?

authorities because there is a lower mix of single- and multi-purpose providers, with larger non-overlapping authorities whose management and service practices vary less due to national standards allowing for more controlled analysis. For the first time they bring together the three parts of the Tiebout framework: (a) preference revelation (the demand side); (b) competition among local authorities (the supply side); and (c) the combination of the two, leading to superior allocation outcomes (the equilibrium side). Their evidence suggests that English local authorities are smaller than optimal size.[4]

Exiting might have consequences for political activity or voice (Hirschman 1970; Dowding et al. 2000) and survey evidence suggests that collective voice is greater where exit is impossible (Dowding and John 2008, who also challenge the normative foundations of the Labour's government's choice agenda—Dowding and John 2009). One of the difficulties of measuring local government performance is the poor quality of the UK's objective indicators (Boyne 1997; Jacobs and Goddard 2007; McLean, Haubrich, and Guitierrez-Romero 2007), making comparison with subjective survey assessments problematic. Quite how people make assessments—by comparison with other authorities or the private sector or relative gains from past services—is not clear; nor how performance really affects political success. Some progress has been made recently by Besley and Preston (2005). Using electoral and performance data on English local authorities, they examine how patterns of districting affect electoral incentives by making jurisdictions marginal or safe for incumbents. They argue that where the incumbents need to capture the swing voters we should expect to see greater efficiency in government. Competition will enhance governmental effectiveness. Using Audit Commission data on valence issues—that is, policies where virtually every voter would concur on what constitutes improvement—they show that patterns of bias within districting seem to have effects on local government performance.

More traditional analyses try to judge policy differences between ideologically opposed parties. The effects of party control on services and especially tax levels have been extensively examined in the UK. In a survey of the literature Boyne (1998b: ch. 3) concludes that party competition seems to have little or no effect on local policies probably reflecting the incentives and constraints on local politicians from national policies. Ward and John (1999) develop an English pork barrel model where national government targets marginal Westminster constituencies by using local government expenditures and John, Ward, and Dowding (2004) and John and Ward (2005) suggest that some competitive funding under the single regeneration budget was indeed targeted to ministerial constituencies in some regions. Ward and John (2008) spatially model the competitive bidding process and show that in efficient equilibriums many bids will not be under competitive pressure because preferred bids will be so far from the ideal points of erstwhile competitors that competitors would sooner not win the bid. This supports the John, Dowding, and Ward (2004) finding that there were no efficiency gains made through the competitive process in successive rounds of the

---

[4] Kay and Marsh (2007) provide a critique of applying Tiebout in the UK. Dowding (2008) responds.

single regeneration budget nor were the most deprived communities rewarded. These results suggest government attempts to increase efficiency through competition have failed.

Earlier attempts to drive efficiency through competition via privatization and contracting-out demonstrated that the nature of the product determined success. Where writing contracts is easy—such as refuse collection or the provision of passports—competition and contracts ('framework agreements') drove efficiency gains; where contracts are difficult to specify and police, efficiency gains were minimal (Hoopes 1997; Boyne 1998a; 1998b). More generally where privatization led to genuine competition efficiency gains were made, but where private monopolies replaced public ones no significant gains were made (Martin and Parker 1997; Parker 2004).

5.9 CONCLUSION

The relative paucity of rational choice analysis is being addressed by a new set of scholars. It is more difficult to apply off-the-shelf models of the US Congress or legislative–executive relations to the UK than it is to the European Union or presidential systems, and the large literature on coalitional politics is almost irrelevant to Britain. Nevertheless there are areas where rational choice has provided great insights, historically to key features of the British state, to local government and local–central relations, in voting studies, the core executive, and more recently new sets of ideas applied to cabinet studies and the relationship between parliament and the executive. Rational choice theory is not a dominant mode of analysis in Britain, but there is much that can be usefully studied through the rational choice lens.

REFERENCES

ADAMS, J. F., MERILL III, S., and GROFMAN, B. 2005. *A Unified Theory of Party Competition.* Cambridge: Cambridge University Press.

ALT, J. E. 1975. 'Continuity, Turnover, and Experience in the British Cabinet, 1868–1970'. In V. Herman and J. E. Alt (eds.), *Cabinet Studies: A Reader.* Houndmills: Macmillan.

ARROW, K. J. 1951/1963. *Social Choice and Individual Values.* New Haven, Conn.: Yale University Press.

AYDELOTTE, W. O. 1970. *Study 521 (Codebook) British House of Commons 1841–1847.* Iowa City: Regional Social Science Data Archive of Iowa.

BENNEDETTO, G., and HIX, S. 2007. 'The Rejected, the Dejected and the Ejected: Explaining Government Rebels in the 2001–2005 British House of Commons'. *Comparative Political Studies*, 40: 755–81.

BERLINSKI, S., DEWAN, T., and DOWDING, K. 2007. 'The Length of Ministerial Tenure in the UK, 1945–1997'. *British Journal of Political Science*, 37: 245–62.

BESLEY, T., and PRESTON, I. 2005. *Electoral Bias and Policy Choice: Theory and Evidence*. LSE, manuscript.

BLACK, D. 1948. 'On the Rationale of Group Decision-making'. *Journal of Political Economy*, 56: 23–34.

BLONDEL, J., and MANNING, N. 2002. 'Do Ministers Do What they Say? Ministerial Unreliability, Collegiality and Hierarchical Government'. *Political Studies*, 50: 455–76.

BOYNE, G. 1997. 'Comparing the Performance of Local Authorities: An Evaluation of the Audit Commission Indicators'. *Local Government Studies*, 23: 17–43.

—— 1998*a*. 'Competitive Tendering in Local Government: A Review of Theory and Evidence'. *Public Administration*, 76: 695–715.

—— 1998*b*. *Public Choice Theory and Local Government*. London: Macmillan.

BUCHANAN, J. M. 1965. 'An Economic Theory of Clubs'. *Economica*, 32: 1–14.

BUDGE, I. 1994. 'A New Spatial Theory of Party Competition: Uncertainty, Ideology and Policy Equilibria Viewed Temporally and Comparatively'. *British Journal of Political Science*, 24: 443–67.

BUENO DE MESQUITA, B., SMITH, A., SIVERSON, R. M., and MORROW, J. D. 2005. *The Logic of Political Survival*. Cambridge, Mass.: MIT Press.

BURT, G. 1997. 'Party Policy: Decision Rule or Chance? A Note on Budge's New Spatial Model of Party Competition'. *British Journal of Political Science*, 27: 647–58.

CHESHIRE, P., and SHEPPARD, S. 1998. 'Estimating Demand for Housing, Land and Neighbourhood Characteristics'. *Oxford Bulletin of Economics and Statistics*, 60: 357–82.

—— —— 2003. 'Capitalizing on the Value of Free Schools: The Impact of Constraints on Supply and Uncertainty'. Paper to European Regional Science Society; http://www.ersa.org/ersaconfs/ersa03/cdrom/papers/8.pdf.

COUGHLIN, P. 1990. 'Candidate Uncertainty and Electoral Equilibria'. In J. Enelow and M. J. Hinich (eds.), *Advances in the Spatial Theory of Voting*. Cambridge: Cambridge University Press.

COWLEY, P. 2002. *Revolts and Rebellions: Parliamentary Voting under Blair*. London: Politico's.

—— and NORTON, P. 1999. 'Rebels and Rebellions: Conservative MPs in the 1992 Parliament'. *British Journal of Politics and International Relations*, 1: 84–105.

COX, G. W. 1987. *The Efficient Secret*. Cambridge: Cambridge University Press.

—— 1999. 'The Empirical Content of Rational Choice Theory: A Reply to Green and Shapiro'. *Journal of Theoretical Politics*, 11: 147–69.

CULLIS, J., and JONES, P. 1992. *Public Finance and Public Choice: Analytical Perspectives*. London: McGraw-Hill.

DEWAN, T., and DOWDING, K. 2005. 'The Corrective Effect of Ministerial Resignations on Government Popularity'. *American Journal of Political Science*, 49: 46–56.

—— —— and SHEPSLE, K. 2009. 'Rational Choice Classics in Political Science'. In T. Dewan, K. Dowding, and K. Shepsle (eds.), *Rational Choice Politics*, vol. i: *Social Choice Equilibrium and Electoral Systems*. London: Routledge.

—— and MYATT, D. P. 2007*a*. 'Leading the Party: Coordination, Direction, and Communication'. *American Political Science Review*, 1001: 827–45.

—— —— 2007*b*. 'Scandal, Protection, and Recovery in Political Cabinets'. *American Political Science Review*, 101: 63–78.

DIERMEIER, D., KEANE, M., and MERLO, A. 2005. 'A Political Economy Model of Congressional Careers'. *American Economic Review*, 95: 347–73.

DOWDING, K. 1995. *The Civil Service*. London: Routledge.

—— 2008. 'A Pandemonium of Confusions: Kay and Marsh on Tiebout'. *New Political Economy*, 13: 335–48.

DOWDING, K., and JAMES, O. 2004. 'Analysing Bureau-Shaping Models: Comments on Marsh, Smith and Richards'. *British Journal of Political Science*, 34: 183–9.

——and JOHN, P. 1996. 'Exiting Behavior under Tiebout Conditions: Towards a Predictive Model'. *Public Choice*, 88: 393–406.

——— 2008. 'The Three Exit, Three Voice and Loyalty Model: A Test with Survey Data on Local Services'. *Political Studies*, 56/2: 288–311.

——— 2009. 'The Value of Choice in Public Policy'. *Public Administration*, 56: 288–311.

———and BIGGS, S. 1994. 'Tiebout: A Survey of the Empirical Literature'. *Urban Studies*, 31: 767–97.

———MERGOUPIS, T., and VUGT, M. V. 2000. 'Exit, Voice and Loyalty: Analytic and Empirical Developments'. *European Journal of Political Research*, 37: 469–95.

——and KING, D. S. (eds.) 1995. *Preferences, Institutions, and Rational Choice*. Oxford: Oxford University Press.

——and MERGOUPIS, T. 2003. 'Fragmentation, Fiscal Mobility and Efficiency'. *Journal of Politics*, 65: 1190–207.

DOWNS, A. 1957. *An Economic Theory of Democracy*. New York: Harper and Row.

DUNLEAVY, P. 1991. *Bureaucracy, Democracy and Public Choice*. Hemel Hempstead: Harvester Wheatsheaf.

——1995. 'Estimating the Distribution of Positional Influence in Cabinet Committees under Major'. In R. A. W. Rhodes and P. Dunleavy (eds.), *Prime Minister, Cabinet and Core Executive*. Houndmills: Macmillan.

——and WARD, H. 1981. 'Exogenous Voter Preferences and Parties with State Power: Some Internal Problems of Economic Theories of Party Competition'. *British Journal of Political Science*, 11: 351–80.

DUNSIRE, A., and HOOD, C. 1989. *Cutback Management in Public Bureaucracies*. Cambridge: Cambridge University Press.

FRIEDMAN, J. (ed.) 1995. *Critical Review: Special Issue Rational Choice Theory*, 9/1–2.

GOODHART, C. A. E., and BHANSALI, R. J. 1970. 'Political Economy'. *Political Studies*, 18: 43–106.

GREEN, D. P., and SHAPIRO, I. 1994. *Pathologies of Rational Choice Theory*. New Haven, Conn.: Yale University Press.

HEADEY, B. 1974. *British Cabinet Ministers*. London: Allen and Unwin.

HINDMOOR, A. 2004. *New Labour at the Centre*. Oxford: Oxford University Press.

HINICH, M. J., and MUNGER, M. C. 1994. *Ideology and the Theory of Political Choice*. Ann Arbor: University of Michigan Press.

HIRSCHMAN, A. O. 1970. *Exit, Voice and Loyalty*. Cambridge, Mass.: Harvard University Press.

HOOD, C. 2002. 'The Risk Game and Blame Game'. *Government and Opposition*, 31: 15–37.

HOOPES, S. 1997. *Oil Privatization, Public Choice and International Forces*. London: Macmillan.

HORN, M. J. 1995. *The Political Economy of Public Administration*. Cambridge: Cambridge University Press.

HUBER, J. D., and SHIPAN, C. R. 2002. *Deliberate Discretion? The Institutional Foundations of Bureaucratic Autonomy*. Cambridge: Cambridge University Press.

INDRIDASON, I. H., and KAM, C. 2008. 'Cabinet Shuffles and Ministerial Drift'. *British Journal of Political Science*, 38: 621–56.

JACOBS, R., and GODDARD, M. 2007. 'How Do Performance Indicators Add Up? An Examination of Composite Indicators in Public Services'. *Public Management and Money*, 27: 103–10.

JAMES, O. 1995. 'Explaining the Next Steps in the Department of Social Security: The Bureau-Shaping Model of Central State Organization'. *Political Studies*, 43: 614–29.

—— 2003. *The Executive Agency Revolution in Whitehall.* Houndmills: Palgrave Macmillan.

JOHN, P. 1998. *Analysing Public Policy.* London: Pinter.

—— DOWDING, K., and BIGGS, S. 1995. 'Residential Mobility in London: A Micro-level Test of the Behavioural Assumptions of the Tiebout Model'. *British Journal of Political Science*, 25: 379–97.

—— and WARD, H. 2005. 'How Competitive is Competitive Bidding? The Case of the Single Regeneration Budget Program'. *Journal of Public Administration Research and Theory*, 15: 71–87.

—————— and DOWDING, K. 2004. 'The Bidding Game: Competitive Funding Regimes and the Political Targeting of Urban Programme Schemes'. *British Journal of Political Science*, 33: 405–28.

JOHNSON, P., LYNCH, F., and WALKER, J. G. 2005. 'Income Tax and Elections in Britain 1950–2001'. *Electoral Studies*, 24: 383–408.

KAM, C. 2000. 'Not Just Parliamentary "Cowboys and Indians": Ministerial Responsibility and Bureaucratic Drift'. *Governance*, 13: 365–92.

KANG, W.-T. 2004. 'Protest Voting and Abstention under Plurality Rule Elections: An Alternative Public Choice Approach'. *Journal of Theoretical Politics*, 16: 79–102.

KAY, A., and MARSH, A. 2007. 'The Methodology of the Public Choice Research Programme: The Case of "Voting with Feet" '. *New Political Economy*, 12: 167–83.

KING, A. 1981. 'The Rise of the Career Politician in the UK'. *British Journal of Political Science*, 11: 249–85.

KING, M. R. 2001. 'New Lady of Threadneedle Street'. *Central Banking*, 11: 82–91.

—— 2005. 'Epistemic Communities and the Diffusion of Ideas: Central Bank Independence in the United Kingdom'. *West European Politics*, 28: 94–123.

KREPS, D. M. 1990. 'Corporate Culture and Economic Theory'. In J. E. Alt and K. Shepsle (eds.), *Perspectives on Positive Political Economy.* Cambridge: Cambridge University Press.

McLEAN, I. 2001. *Rational Choice and British Politics.* Oxford: Oxford University Press.

—— HAUBRICH, D., and GUITIERREZ-ROMERO, R. 2007. 'The Perils and Pitfalls of Performance Measurement: The CPA Regime for Local Authorities'. *Public Managment and Money*, 27: 111–17.

—— and NOU, J. 2006. 'Why Should We Be Beggars with the Ballot in Our Hand? Veto Players and the Failure of Land Taxation in the United Kingdom, 1909–14'. *British Journal of Political Science*, 36: 575–91.

MARSH, D., SMITH, M. J., and RICHARDS, D. 2000. 'Bureaucrats, Politicians and Reform in Whitehall: Analysing the Bureau-Shaping Model'. *British Journal of Political Science*, 30: 461–82.

MARTIN, S., and PARKER, D. 1997. *The Impact of Privatization.* London: Routledge.

MILLER, G. J. 1992. *Managerial Dilemmas.* Cambridge: Cambridge University Press.

MULLER, W. C. 2004. 'Political Parties in Parliamentary Democracies: Making Delegation and Accountability Work'. *European Journal of Political Research*, 37: 309–33.

MUSGRAVE, R. A., and MUSGRAVE, P. B. 1989. *Public Finance in Theory and Practice.* New York: McGraw-Hill.

NISKANEN, W. A. 1971. *Bureaucracy and Representative Government.* Chicago: Aldine Press.

NORDHAUS, W. D. 1975. 'The Political Business Cycle'. *Review of Economic Studies*, 42: 169–90.

NORTH, D. C., and WEINGAST, B. R. 1989. 'Constitutions and Commitment: The Evolution of Institutions Governing Public Choice in Seventeenth-Century England'. *Journal of Economic History*, 49: 803–32.

NORTON, P. 1978. *Conservative Dissidents.* London: Temple Smith.

NORTON, P. 1980. *Dissension in the House of Commons, 1974–1979*. Oxford: Clarendon Press.

PARKER, D. 2004. 'The UK's Privatization Experiment: The Passage of Time Permits a Sober Assessment'. CESfio Working Paper 1126.

PISSARIDES, C. 1980. 'British Government Popularity and Economic Performance'. *Economic Journal*, 90: 569–81.

POLLITT, C., BIRCHALL, J., and PUTNAM, K. 1998. *Decentralizing Public Service Management*. London: Macmillan.

POOLE, K. T. 2005. *Spatial Models of Parliamentary Voting*. New York: Cambridge University Press.

QUINN, T. 2005. *Modernising the Labour Party*. Houndmills: Palgrave Macmillan.

RIKER, W. H. 1986. *The Art of Political Manipulation*. New Haven, Conn.: Yale University Press.

ROBERTSON, D. 1976. *A Theory of Party Competition*. London: Wiley.

ROEMER, J. E. 2001. *Political Competition*. Cambridge: Cambridge University Press.

ROSE, R. 1971. 'The Making of Cabinet Ministers'. *British Journal of Political Science*, 1: 394–414.

—— 1987. *Ministers and Ministries*. Oxford: Clarendon Press.

SANDERS, D. 1991. 'Government Popularity and the Next General Election'. *Political Quarterly*, 62: 235–61.

—— 1996. 'Economic Performance, Management Competence and the Outcome of the Next General Election'. *Political Studies*, 44: 203–31.

—— 2000. 'The Real Economy and the Perceived Economy in Popularity Functions: How Much Do Voters Need to Know? A Study of British Data, 1974–97'. *Electoral Studies*, 19: 275–94.

—— 2003. 'Party Identification, Economic Perceptions and Voting in British General Elections, 1974–97'. *Electoral Studies*, 22: 239–63.

—— 2005. 'The Political Economy of Party Support, 1997–2004: Forecasts for the 2005 General Election'. *Journal of Elections, Public Opinion and Parties*, 15: 47–71.

SCHONHARDT-BAILEY, C. 1994. 'Linking Constituency Interests of Legislative Voting Behaviour: The Role of District Economic and Electoral Composition in the Repeal of the Corn Laws'. *Parliamentary History*, 13: 86–118.

—— 2006. *Interests, Ideas and Institutions: Repeal of the Corn Laws Re-told*. Boston: MIT Press.

SCHULTZ, K. A. 1995. 'Politics of the Business Cycle'. *British Journal of Political Science*, 25: 79–99.

SEYD, P., and WHITELEY, P. 2002. *New Labour's Grassroots*. Basingstoke: Palgrave Macmillan.

SPIRLING, A., and MCLEAN, I. 2007. 'UK OC OK? Interpreting Optimal Classification Scores for the UK House of Commons'. *Political Analysis*, 15: 86–97.

STASAVAGE, D. 2002. 'Credible Commitment in Early Modern Europe: North and Weingast Revisited'. *Journal of Law, Economics and Organization*, 18: 155–86.

—— 2003. *Public Debt and the Birth of the Democratic State*. Cambridge: Cambridge University Press.

STEUNENBERG, B. 2005. 'The Interaction between Departments and the Treasury: A Model of Budgetary Decision Making in the UK'. Manuscript; http://www.publicadministration. leidenuniv.nl/content_docs/steunenberg/budgetary_decision_making_uk_2005.pdf.

TSEBELIS, G. 1990. *Nested Games*. Berkeley: University of California Press.

—— 2002. *Veto Players*. Princeton, NJ: Princeton University Press.

WARD, H. 1996. 'The Fetishisation of Falsification: The Debate on Rational Choice'. *New Political Economy*, 1: 283–96.

—— and JOHN, P. 1999. 'Targeting Benefits for Electoral Gain: Constituency Marginality and the Distribution of Grants to English Local Authorities'. *Political Studies*, 47: 32–52.

—— —— 2008. 'A Spatial Model of Competitive Bidding for Government Grants: Why Efficiency Gains Are Limited'. *Journal of Theoretical Politics*, 20/1: 47–66.

WHITELEY, P., SEYD, P., and RICHARDSON, J. 1994. *True Blues*. Oxford: Clarendon Press.

WILLIAMSON, O. E. 1996. *The Mechanisms of Governance*. New York: Oxford University Press.

CHAPTER 6

BEHAVIOURALISM

ROBERT JOHNS

BEHAVIOURALISM is often regarded as synonymous with Americanization. However, this is not a chapter about American invasion or about the British discipline's successful resistance against that threat. Adcock et al. caution that 'assumptions about the exceptionalism of Britain and America have obscured, for historians of each, the transatlantic exchanges that have informed the development of their traditions of inquiry' (2007b: 7). And indeed American and British behaviouralism differ little, predictably since many behaviouralist researchers of British politics were from (or at least trained in) the USA. Nonetheless, aspects of the British context have shaped the timing, extent, and substantive focus of behaviouralist research. Thus, although British behaviouralism is not highly distinctive, the British *experience* of behaviouralism is more so.

Behaviouralism is often regarded as a 1950s revolutionary movement, a sharp break with what had gone before. Some also refer to a 'post-behavioural revolution', with powerful critical forces reshaping the movement in the early 1970s. It is a considerable exaggeration to refer either to behaviouralism or (especially) post-behaviouralism as revolutionary. Still, this over-dramatic view of the approach's history helps to provide a structure for the chapter. First, I define and specify three key features of ('early') behaviouralism. Then the focus sharpens onto the various reasons why, and ways in which, the British experience of behaviouralism was distinctive. The third section concerns the notion of post-behaviouralism, supposedly a new version emerging in response to potent criticisms of the approach. While the extent of change has been overstated, the post-behaviouralist critique highlights several criteria for evaluating behaviouralist research. Fourth, I apply those criteria to behaviouralism in Britain, and pick out some of its notable contributions to our understanding of British politics. To conclude, I mention possible ways to enhance that contribution further.

6.1 What is Behaviouralism?

Broadly defined, behaviouralism is a positivist and systematic approach to the study of political behaviour. In this section, I examine the three key elements within that definition.

The most prominent—and controversial—aspect of behaviouralism is its philosophy of social science. Presthus describes this as 'the acceptance of logical positivism as an epistemological system', and characterizes positivism as follows: 'Facts, publicly verifiable and sensually perceived, are regarded as the only valid basis of truth or reality' (1965: 19). Logical positivists furthered an empiricist tradition originating with Hume, and advocated in social science by Comte. They insisted on a distinction between descriptive statements and value judgements. Since only descriptive statements could be verified by observation, only they were held to be meaningful and suitable for political analysis (Elcock 1976: 11–12; Kavanagh 1983: ch. 1). Popper's critique of logical positivism led to falsifiability replacing verifiability as the key scientific credential, but the emphasis on observation remained. Few political behaviouralists stated positivist precepts as starkly as Presthus, but the demand that claims about the political world must be empirically verifiable is the core of behaviouralism.

Perhaps, then, it seems odd that a driving force behind behaviouralism was a feeling that American political science had become dominated by atheoretical description or 'hyperfactualism' (Easton 1953: ch. 2; Dryzek 2006). However, the call was not for theory *instead of* empirical observation; rather, theory was needed to *organize* empirical data and highlight the patterns therein. Theory thus becomes 'a language for recording exhibited regularities' (Hay 2002a: 29). Although derived inductively, such 'empirical theory' (Sanders 2002: 47) can then be used deductively to generate hypotheses for subsequent empirical testing. This 'iterated interplay of theory and empirical research lay at the heart of the behavioralist vision' (Adcock 2007: 189), and reflects the commitment to ensuring that theoretical propositions are subject to possible falsification. Pure empirical theory is unattainable: at the core of any (social) scientific theory are basic definitions and assumptions that are not falsifiable (Lakatos 1971). Nevertheless, Sanders argues, the theory itself is still falsifiable if it yields testable propositions, thus allowing researchers 'to specify the conditions under which they would know that the theory was "incorrect"' (2002: 50). The importance of falsifiability, and the difficulty of testing general assumptions as opposed to specific predictions, helps to explain why most behaviouralists swiftly abandoned the search for a grand theory of political behaviour (cf. Easton 1953).

The second key feature of behaviouralism is the commitment to observable behaviour as the dependent variable in political analysis. This was driven partly by impatience, growing during the inter-war years, with a perceived preoccupation with formal structures and institutions (Kavanagh 1983: 1). Behaviouralists were more interested in 'what do the actors involved actually do and how can we best explain why they do it?' (Sanders 2002: 45). Their motives were epistemological as well as substantive. Behaviour—at least, some behaviour—was *observable*, a point of obvious significance given the positivist agenda. The questions posed by Sanders were paramount for behaviouralists, not necessarily (or not only) because they were most interesting or important, but because hypothesized answers could be tested empirically.

This perspective owes much to behaviourists in psychology (e.g. Watson 1913) who rejected as unscientific those explanations of behaviour based on introspection or on non-observable phenomena like thought or consciousness. However, as discussed below, behaviouralists in political science were never as stringent. Rather than dismissing psychological phenomena (personalities, motivations, intentions, and so on) as unobservable, behaviouralists sought to measure them, typically via surveys. These variables were as important as the more immediately observable political behaviour (Butler 1958: 17). Thus, it was as much behaviouralism's substantive focus—on the mental states and processes underlying behaviour—as its epistemological underpinnings that linked the approach to psychology.[1]

The third core element of the approach, the commitment to 'scientific' methods, is probably the most important. Behaviouralism is as much about *how* as about *what* to study (Kavanagh 1983: xiii). Given the obvious difficulties of applying methods from physical sciences to politics, behaviouralists modified the standards for 'scientific' research, the key signifiers being 'systematic' and 'rigorous' (Adcock 2007: 180; Kavanagh 1983: 10). Of course, these terms are wide open to interpretation (and, as Mackenzie (1971: 25–6) remarks, no political scientist was ever committed to unsystematic research). For Adcock, 'being systematic entailed self-reflection about and refinement of the methods used to gather and analyze information and, where possible, using techniques that yield quantitative data and analyze it statistically' (2007: 191). The first element is uncontroversial, with general agreement that behaviouralism encouraged reflection about methods (Mackenzie 1967: 75; Adcock 2007: 180). The second element, about quantitative methods, needs further discussion.

There is no necessary connection between behaviouralism and quantitative methods (Sanders 2002: 47; Adcock 2007: 191), since qualitative analysis can be systematic and replicable. In practice, though, the behaviouralism–quantification link is strong (Presthus 1965: 19; Blondel 1981: 67). The main reason lies in behaviouralists' commitment to using 'all the relevant empirical evidence rather than a limited set of illustrative supporting examples' (Sanders 2002: 47). This entails quantities of data that are more easily analyzed quantitatively. Moreover, some projects are practicable only with representative samples, and inference from samples to populations is inextricably bound up with quantitative methods. For Butler, 'the Gallup poll and its successors constitute the greatest technical innovation in the study of political behaviour in this century' (1958: 61). This is one of several mid-century developments facilitating behaviouralism, including exponential increases in computer processing speed, advances in multivariate statistics, and the development of quantitative content analysis (Miller 1999: 223). More recent advances extend the list: computer-assisted

---

[1] Wallas had long ago asserted human nature as the crucial element in political behaviour, complaining that, while 'the study of human nature by the psychologists has ... advanced enormously ... it has advanced without affecting ... the study of politics' (1908: 14).

interviewing; the establishment of data archives; huge comparative data collection projects; and a proliferation of training opportunities in quantitative methods. Behaviouralism was driven by the excitement generated by such innovations (Adcock 2007: 187) and in this sense was a revolution in methods more than ideas.

6.2 A British Behaviouralism?

While it has roots elsewhere too (including Britain, courtesy of Graham Wallas), behaviouralism was definitely born in the USA. And whether it is obesity, an interest rate rise, or a new TV drama, Britain usually follows America's lead. There is no reason to suppose otherwise in political science: America accounts for three-quarters of the world's political scientists (Marsh and Savigny 2004), and many leading US scholars have worked in Europe, directly exporting current agendas and—crucially— methods. Yet Britain does not passively accept US output, whether cultural, economic, or academic. Here, I discuss barriers to behaviouralism in British political science, and then consider whether these have left Britain with a distinctive experience, even a different version, of the approach.

6.2.1 Barriers to Behaviouralism in Britain

If behaviouralism in the USA is depicted as a radical disjuncture, then British resistance might be straightforwardly explained by an anti-revolutionary intellectual culture (Bogdanor 1999: 149). Goldsmith and Grant describe the British approach to political science as 'one that resists the wholesale importation of orthodoxies into the discipline, be it 1950s behaviouralism or 1990s rational choice' (2006: 3). However, despite widespread reference to a 'behavioural revolution', there was no dramatic break with the past. Dryzek argues that 'most of the changes involved shifts in emphasis rather than radical novelty' (2006: 490), Dahl (1961a) describes behaviouralism as a 'protest' rather than a revolution, and some of the loudest protesters bemoan the failure to achieve sweeping change (Eulau 1981; Wahlke 1979).[2] Hence an explanation of British opposition goes beyond general conservative inclinations, relating instead to the theoretical and practical specifics of behaviouralism (Kenny 2007: 178–9).

One barrier is in the long-standing eclecticism of political studies in Britain, and especially the persistence of two currents of research—idealism and Marxism—whose proponents reject the behaviouralist agenda (Bevir and Rhodes 2007). Pre-eminent idealist Michael Oakeshott had long dismissed any notion that political knowledge

---

[2] According to Eulau, the notion of a radical revolution has been propped up by 'the latter-day myth that there were ever so bitter and raucous confrontations between "behavioralists" and "antibehavioralists" '; in fact, he argues, the intellectual combat was 'quite genteel and measured' (1981: xi). Disciplinary histories suggesting otherwise often lack references to the supposed belligerence (e.g. Goodin and Klingemann 1996: 10–11).

was obtainable anywhere other than from history (Hayward 1999: 30; Kenny 2007: 166), and later writers in that tradition were fiercely critical of behaviouralism (Green-leaf 1983; Johnson 1989). Meanwhile, Marxists dismissed behaviouralists' claims to value-freedom, pointing to the movement's roots in liberal pluralism and emphasiz-ing its neglect of economics (Bevir and Rhodes 2007: 248). In short, there was strong opposition to behaviouralism from British-based scholars writing in traditions that were (and remain) important in the British discipline.

It was not only idealists and Marxists who denied the possibility of value-freedom. According to Kavanagh (2007: 114), all of the 'Founding Fathers'—those scholars, including G. D. H. Cole, Harold Laski, Ramsay Muir, and the Finer brothers, who did most to shape the study of politics in Britain—would have rejected the notion. Further, as they fathered the modernist empiricism that is a dominant strand in the British discipline (Kavanagh 2007; Bevir and Rhodes 2007), anti-scientism can be seen to have pervaded even those subfields sharing behaviouralism's commitment to empirical observation.[3] For Bogdanor, 'if there is a central tendency to the disci-pline as it has developed in Britain in the twentieth century, it lies in the aversion to positivism, understood as the doctrine that the model of the natural sciences constitutes the only valid form of knowledge' (1999: 150). There was also 'scepticism about model building' (Kavanagh 2007: 97) and an 'aversion to over-arching theory [and] to general laws' (Bogdanor 1999: 149).

To some extent, the critics were reacting to a caricature of behaviouralism, or at least to some of the movement's grander ambitions that were quickly scaled down. As argued below, US behaviouralists were not bent on uncovering immutable laws of politics, and few harboured hopes of building a general theory of political behaviour. However, many British political scientists were sceptical even about the possibility of modest generalizations. Their doubts were as often empirical as philosophical, the objection being that the real world was too complex and unpredictable for the kind of general tendencies or regularities sought by behaviouralists to hold (Butler 1958: 18–19; Miller 1999: 228–9; Finer 1980). Exceptions to rules would abound, explicable only with the attention to (historical) context that distinguished the work of the 'Founding Fathers' and is widely seen as central to the British approach (Bogdanor 1999; Kavanagh 2007; Kenny 2007: 178–9).

Methodological aspects of behaviouralism also caused concern. Mackenzie asso-ciates the movement with 'a rather silly emphasis on introducing quantitative meth-ods at all costs' (1967: 18), and there remain widespread misgivings about quantifying key political concepts (e.g. Byrne 1998; Ragin 2000). More broadly, Crick (1962) and Johnson (1989) strongly criticized a perceived obsession with methodological rigour rather than substantive importance. Bevir and Rhodes (2007: 234) argue that scepticism about methodological fussiness and quantification are important aspects of the self-image of British political science.

---

[3] The symbolic expressions of these attitudes are familiar: Britain has a Political Studies and not a Political Science Association, and there are only two departments of 'Political Science' in the entire country (Hayward 1999; Goldsmith and Grant 2006).

A limited appetite for quantitative methods exacerbated supply-side constraints on behaviouralism in Britain. Many relevant technological and institutional developments happened later. British universities were slow to provide the kind of methods training available at, say, Michigan in the USA (Kavanagh 2007: 115), and few departments appointed more than a token quantitative specialist (Crick 1980: 300). In its first decade, the British discipline's house journal, *Political Studies*, published few behaviouralist articles and little methodological discussion (Kenny 2007: 170–1). And it was some time before academics obtained the funds required for behaviouralism's methodological exemplar, a national sample survey (Miller 1999: 237–9).

6.2.2 What was Different about British Behaviouralism?

Here I consider four ways in which the British experience of behaviouralism might have differed: timing (when did behaviouralism arrive?); quantity (how much did it pervade the discipline?); substantive scope (in which subfields did it take hold?); and, most importantly, nature (was British behaviouralism different?).

Behaviouralism certainly arrived later in Britain (Hayward 1999; Kavanagh 2007). When Mackenzie refers to 'the controversy over the "behavioural movement" which divided American political scientists in the 1950s' (1971: 29), he implies that even the debate over behaviouralism, let alone the approach itself, was then remote from Britain. Just two British scholars (Wallas and Laski) are cited in *The American Voter* (Campbell et al. 1960), illustrating the then marginal relevance of behaviouralism to British political science—and vice versa (Miller 1999: 226). However, Crick's (1961) forceful attack on 'The American Science of Politics' indicates that it was becoming harder to ignore, and in Britain behaviouralism started to gather momentum. The late 1960s saw several relevant developments: new departments at Essex and Strathclyde embracing behaviouralism (Kavanagh 2007: 116); the first national election survey (Butler and Stokes 1969); the instituting of the Essex methods summer school and the UK Data Archive; and the establishment of the ECPR in a bid to ' "Americanize" European political science—beginning with British political science' (Blondel 1997: 117). The timing and impact of the new movement is summarized by Kavanagh: 'the efforts of the [pre-behaviouralist] interwar generation did much to define the character and development of political science in Britain for the first two decades of the post-1945 period, *although not much beyond that*' (2007: 115, emphasis added).

Its delayed arrival meant that initially behaviouralism was something of a minority pursuit in Britain (Kenny 2007: 170–1; Hayward 1991: 96). And the eclecticism of the British discipline ensured that it remained one among several strands of research (Mackenzie 1971: 34; Kenny 2007). Bogdanor (1999) picks seven representatives of major trends in British political science, and the only behaviouralist, the American Richard Rose, has worked mainly on wider comparative studies. No British behaviouralists are cited in Almond's (1996) 'History of the Discipline'. Turning to more systematic evidence of the limited inroads made by behaviouralism, the PSA's surveys of British political scientists consistently show that only around one in ten mention 'political behaviour' as a principal research interest (Goldsmith and Grant 2006). Admittedly, some of those citing, say, 'comparative politics' may take a behaviouralist approach. Still, the rarity of self-identification as a scholar of political behaviour is telling, and contrasts sharply with the results of Marsh and Savigny's (2004) analysis of the disciplinary orientations of articles published in leading UK and US journals. In both countries, behaviouralist articles comprised around two-thirds of all those published between 1975 and 1979, and around half of those published between 1997 and 2002. These are probably overestimates, given the small number of other categories and hence the likely classification as behaviouralist of articles that Bevir and Rhodes (2007) might call 'modernist empiricist'. But here the absolute values matter less than the comparison, which shows that behaviouralism is (and indeed was by the late 1970s) as dominant in British as in American journals (contra Marsh and Savigny 2004: 164). Hence, notwithstanding the enduring pluralism of British political science, behaviouralism has become a prominent strand.

The question of the approach's reach through British political science can also be addressed by comparing subfields. The major manifestation of behaviouralism is 'a developed body of research devoted to the empirical study of mass political behaviour' (Kenny 2007: 169–70). The approach has totally dominated the study of voting behaviour (e.g. Butler and Stokes 1969; Heath, Jowell, and Curtice 1985; Clarke et al. 2004), and predominated in the study of political participation (e.g. Parry, Moyser, and Day 1992; Pattie, Seyd, and Whiteley 2004). Such dominance, established once a generation of scholars trained in behaviouralist methods had entered the profession, has not wavered since. The statistical techniques are more sophisticated but the basic approach has remained the same and monopolizes those subfields. Behaviouralism's imprint on most of the rest of British political science is, however, much less deep (e.g. Smith 2000).[4] To some extent this is inevitable, behaviouralism (like any approach) being better suited to some areas than others. Yet much pioneering American behaviouralist research was in subfields little touched by the approach in Britain (e.g. Kaplan 1957; Dahl 1961b; Miller and Stokes 1963). The contrast makes sense given earlier arguments. However resistant to positivist scientism, the British discipline still experienced the technological progress that drove behaviouralism. Predictably, then, the approach is largely confined to that area—mass behaviour—whose horizons were expanded furthest by such advances.[5] This segregation of behaviouralism has left it largely impervious to trends and disputes elsewhere in British politics. Insofar as there has been controversy about epistemology and method in the British discipline (which is not really very far[6]), the debates have neither involved nor particularly

---

[4] The major exception is Budge's studies of parties' programmes and strategic behaviour (e.g. Laver and Budge 1992).

[5] Hayward (1991) offers another explanation: stringent rules plus a culture of secrecy in British government mean that important behavioural data are often unavailable to researchers.

[6] Save for the sporadic outbreaks of debate over various brands of institutionalism, and the accompanying arguments about structure and agency.

threatened behaviouralists, who remained as peripheral to the mainstream as they were dominant in their subfields.

Finally, there is the question of whether British behaviouralism was qualitatively different. Crucial here is the distinction between behaviouralism and modernist empiricism, the latter a broader category of work sharing the commitment to empirical observation and classification but stopping short of the scientism and hypothesis testing of behaviouralism (Adcock, Bevir, and Stimson 2007b; Bevir and Rhodes 2007). Kenny (2007) suggests that, insofar as a distinctively British political science emerged in the post-war period, it was modernist empiricist, based on a fusion—promoted by Mackenzie, Finer, and Samuel Beer—between a traditionally British historical (Whiggish) empiricism and the new American behaviouralist thinking and methods. There is wide agreement that 'homeopathic doses' of behaviouralism boosted the rigour of modernist empiricism in Britain (Hayward 1991: 104; Mackenzie 1967: 19; Kenny 2007: 168).[7] Equally, many argue that British behaviouralism was distinguished—and enhanced—by association with the historical empiricism that dominated the pre-behavioural era. Kenny (2007) cites the collaboration between British electoral historian David Butler and American behaviouralist Donald Stokes as a particularly productive instance of the fusion mentioned above. Given that their book *Political Change in Britain* is probably the key founding work of British behaviouralism, the tone was set for a more nuanced, more historical brand of the approach. Indeed Miller praises British electoral research for 'the balance between theory, history, awareness of contingency and sensitivity to context on the one hand, and abstract analysis on the other' (1999: 255; see also Bogdanor 1999). Similarly, Hay (2002b) commends British behaviouralists for their willingness to consider institutional as well as historical context.

This credit is due, but the implied criticism of US studies is unwarranted. Most American studies of voting and participation were just as grounded in history and context (and for that matter theory) as the British equivalents (e.g. Key 1949; Dahl 1961b; Almond and Verba 1963; Burnham 1965).[8] Furthermore, while some prominent American behaviouralists sought 'deep-seated "laws" of social behaviour' (Campbell et al. 1960: 36–7), many others—notably V. O. Key (1958)—were just as sceptical as their British counterparts, favouring only modest and context-specific generalizations. In sum, the key difference between America and Britain lies in the *amount* of behaviouralism as opposed to modernist empiricism, the latter more clearly and widely predominant in Britain (Bevir and Rhodes 2007). There is little evidence that British behaviouralism is distinctive, not because it lacks the subtlety and sensitivity to context with which it has been credited, but because American behaviouralism

---

[7] Hayward suggests that the adoption of certain behaviouralist characteristics and methods was 'a classic case of dynamic conservatism: changing enough so as to keep things basically the same' (1999: 31), in this case to maintain the dominance of the less scientized brand of empiricism.

[8] Adcock (2007: 183–4) dismisses as a misconception the notion that the behaviouralist movement 'turned the discipline away from history'. A similar story—of behaviouralists misrepresented as ignoring or dismissing an entire strand of research—can be told with respect to institutions (Dryzek 2006: 490; Dunleavy 1996: 281).

was never as unsubtle or unequivocal as some implicitly comparative treatments have suggested.

6.3 'POST-BEHAVIOURALISM'

According to Almond, the prevailing view of the discipline's history is 'that we are now in a 'post-positivist, post-scientific, post-behavioral stage' (1996: 81). The 'postbehavioral era' was heralded by Graham and Carey (1972) in a sustained attack on positivist, supposedly 'value-free' political science. Exactly as with behaviouralism, there is a danger of overstating both the impact and the novelty of post-behaviouralism.[9] Both denote the attitudes and objectives of a movement within political science, not a radical reorientation of the discipline. Moreover, many post-behaviouralist criticisms had been rehearsed ever since the first stirrings of a behaviouralist movement. Nonetheless, there is a perception that such criticism intensified in the late 1960s (Dryzek 2006: 489), and that behaviouralists responded to the complaints (Gunnell 1983; Sanders 2002). Geertz recommends that, 'if you want to understand what a science is, you should look in the first instance not at its theories and findings, and certainly not at what its apologists say about it; you should look at what the practitioners of it do' (1973: 5). In this section, then, I examine four lines of post-behavioural criticism, in each case assessing whether behaviouralist researchers *do* things differently as a result.

The first line of criticism concerns the objects rather than the methods of behaviouralist study. By 1962 Crick was lamenting the tendency 'to make the criteria for research and study not political importance, but various notions of methodological impeccability' (190). The raised political temperature in the 1960s meant that such detachment seemed still more misguided, and in the US triggered the formation of the 'Caucus for a New Political Science', which demanded that the discipline prioritize commitment and relevance over science (Dryzek 2006: 490–1). Such criticism—of behaviouralism as an apolitical and hence somewhat irrelevant enterprise—was central to Graham and Carey's (1972) arguments. Eulau, less sympathetic to the Caucus cause, describes post-behaviouralism as 'a near-hysteric response to political frustration engendered by the disconcerting and shocking events of the late sixties and early seventies' (1981: viii).

While few dismissed it so scornfully, behaviouralists have generally paid little heed to this criticism. The same charge—too much science and too little politics—is still levelled at the discipline, notably by Ricci (1984) who described it as the 'tragedy of political science'. It might be thought that behaviouralists are entitled to disregard this complaint: those regarding another research agenda as more pertinent should follow it, leaving behaviouralists free to pursue their usual concerns. That argument hinges

---

[9] As Eulau bluntly puts it, 'there never was a "postbehavioral revolution" because there had never been a "behavioral revolution" in political science in the first place' (1981: viii).

on the acceptance of pluralism in methods of study. If some important phenomena are not readily susceptible to empirical observation and testing, and behaviouralists dismiss research based on any other method, then the discipline as they envisage it is inevitably less politically relevant. Hay credits post-behaviouralists with the recognition that other (especially normative) traditions have a role, suggesting that behaviouralists are 'far more prepared than once they were to accept an academic division of labour within political analysis' (2002a: 43; also Sanders 2002: 51). However, without references to these doctrinaire behaviouralists of yesteryear, it is difficult to gauge whether such acceptance is new, and hence whether it can be attributed to the impact of post-behaviouralist critique. This may be a case of limited impact exaggerated by a caricatured view of early behaviouralism.

A second line of criticism is based on the mistaken belief that behaviouralists rejected as non-observable those psychological variables crucial to understanding *why* people behave as they do (Mackenzie 1971: 25). Instead, it was anti-positivists who warned that scientific laws of human behaviour could not include intentions, motivations, and values, because statements like 'X did p because of q' or 'X identifies with p' are too difficult to falsify (Quine 1960; MacIntyre 1985: ch. 7). Behaviouralists have from the outset not only incorporated but built their work on such variables. Prominent examples include the civic culture (Almond and Verba 1963) and party identification (Campbell et al. 1960).[10] The dependent variables—party choice, turnout, legislative voting—were behavioural, unsurprisingly since observable behaviour is the end of the causal chain of human engagement with politics: belief $\rightarrow$ attitude $\rightarrow$ intention $\rightarrow$ behaviour (Fishbein and Ajzen 1975). But far from rejecting those prior variables as unscientific, behaviouralists are distinguished by the attempt to measure them systematically. Any resulting loss of scientific rigour was deemed a price worth paying for extra explanatory leverage.

Little has changed in the post-behavioural era, with numerous important behaviouralist works based on psychological phenomena (e.g. Inglehart 1977; Zaller 1992; Green, Palmqvist, and Schickler 2002). Moreover, insofar as the treatment of such variables was deemed inadequate, the problems persist. Achen (1992) castigates electoral behaviouralists for treating demographics as explanatory rather than exploring the causal paths along which their effects operate. Dunleavy argues that researchers largely ignore 'the known limitations of pre-coded survey questions in uncovering people's complex meanings' (1996: 286). And any atomistic method (quantitative or qualitative) struggles to capture underlying societal ideas and norms, which influence behaviour whether or not consciously internalized (Hay 2002a: 45; Berman 1998: 16).

Again, then, the impact of post-behaviouralist critique is negligible, and exaggerated only through a misreading of early behaviouralism. For Goodin and Klingemann, 'contemporary political science is decidedly substantially post-positivist, in that it certainly has taken lessons of the hermeneutic critique substantially on

[10] Given the pre-eminence of attitudinal variables in the hugely influential Michigan model, it is not obvious what Susser is referring to when asserting that 'in voting studies...there is a clear tendency toward reduction to such empirically distinct factors such as age, sex, income and education in establishing a voter's profile' (1974: 277). No citations are provided.

board ... Subjective aspects of political life, the internal mental life of political actors, meanings and beliefs and intentions and values—all these are now central to political analysis across the board' (1996: 22). Were these aspects previously peripheral to behaviouralism? Are they noticeably more central than before? The answer to both questions is no.

In any case, this addresses only part of the hermeneutic critique. There is also the subjectivity of the observer to consider, if anything a more fundamental barrier to a science of political behaviour (Taylor 1967; Marsh and Furlong 2002). This third line of post-behaviouralist critique was readily acknowledged by behaviouralists. Decades ago Elcock reported that 'there are few nowadays who accept Max Weber's belief that ultimately a value-free social science will develop' (1976: 20). More recently Sanders asserts that 'modern behaviouralists ... roundly reject the notion that theory and observation are independent' (2002: 54). The key question, though, is whether this postmodernist turn in behaviouralists' thinking is reflected in their research practices. The short answer is that it is not. Indeed it is difficult to see how it could be, given the continued centrality of empirical observation in (post-)behaviouralism (Sanders 2002). Such observation is futile unless the data generated are assumed to be at least partly independent of the subjectivity of the observer (Marsh and Furlong 2002: 24–6). Otherwise, testing theories against data becomes an abstract exercise, detached from the real world that is supposed to be under observation.

The implication is that behaviouralists have paid only lip service to this aspect of post-positivist critique. But there was no obvious alternative. Such fundamental epistemological objections could not be addressed by fine-tuning behaviouralist research practice. Bevir and Rhodes suggest that an appropriate reaction to the 'lethal' philosophical attack on positivism would be for 'a broad interpretive or constructivist church to *replace* modernist empiricism' (2007: 257, emphasis added). Dunleavy advocates a similar overhaul, urging students of political behaviour to follow the example of other social science disciplines in which 'postmodernist criticisms have been taken on board as part of an overall process of constructive disciplinary self-renewal' (1996: 291).

The final line of post-behaviouralist critique also owes something to a 'postmodern turn'. Goodin and Klingemann identify 'a retreat away from generality and toward particularity, away from universality and toward situatedness, in the explanatory accounts we offer for political phenomena' (1996: 22). This retreat was prompted by the same concern with the exception argued above to be central to the discipline in Britain. The corollary is distrust of a predictive science of politics. MacIntyre (1985: ch. 8) specifies various sources of unpredictability in social science, concluding that generalizations about political behaviour cannot approach law-like status, being inevitably subject to plentiful counter-examples.

Once more, it is easy to exaggerate the impact of post-behaviouralism. Behaviouralists were never as committed to mechanical laws and predictions as latter-day accounts (e.g. Miller 1999; Hay 2002b) suggest. As Taagepera (2007) laments, genuine prediction was never really on the political science agenda. The summit of behaviouralist ambition was usually 'postdiction' (as delivered by techniques like regression): 'post hoc rationalizations in the form of prediction of events that have already occurred' (Hay 2002b: 9). Behaviouralists would agree with Finer that politics is a science not because of its predictive accuracy, but because 'it can offer reasons and causes from events once those events have happened' (1980: 361).

This more limited ambition—the systematic search for empirical regularities in political behaviour—remains at the heart of behaviouralism (Miller 1999: 223; Hay 2002a: 43–4). The aim has been to apply that approach to the complexity and contingency that confounds prediction. Consider Butler's verdict on the finding that many middle-class voters turned against Labour between 1945 and 1950: 'on its own, it remains merely an interesting fact. It only assumes major significance in the light of an explanation of the period that must perforce be based on qualitative observation and even intuition' (1958: 63). Behaviouralists would disagree, seeking instead to measure perceptions of those key variables—Labour's class image, ideological position, and performance in government—that may explain the observed swing. This approach is expressly designed to deliver just what Hay asks of a new British political science: 'detailed and measured assessments of the conditions of such outcomes' (2002b: 9).

So post-behaviouralism differs little from its earlier incarnation. The criticisms above have undermined the philosophical basis of behaviouralism, and highlighted constraints on its explanatory and predictive power, but they have left its research practices largely unchanged. And, since behaviouralism is above all a way of doing political science, that is the crucial point. The post-behavioural critique is important not because it drastically reformed the approach, but because it draws attention to criteria—sensitivity to context and heterogeneity, consideration of meanings, and awareness of methodological limitations—by which behaviouralist research can be judged. In the next section, I use these criteria to evaluate 'modern' British behaviouralism.

6.4 BEHAVIOURALISM AND BRITISH POLITICAL SCIENCE

This section begins with that evaluation of behaviouralist studies in British political science. Then I assess the contribution of the behavioural approach to our understanding of British politics. As noted, British behaviouralists have focused mainly on electoral behaviour and political participation, and here I pay particular attention to major recent studies on those topics, Clarke et al. (2004) on voting and Pattie, Seyd, and Whiteley (2004) on participation. While both are quite recent, they are fairly representative of an approach that, again as noted above, has at root changed little since its rise to prominence.

6.4.1 Evaluating Behaviouralism in Britain

'Central to virtually all political behaviour research, and still virtually unchallenged in 1990s studies, has been the search for the *single best decision algorithm* with which to characterize the alignments and behaviour of an entire electorate' (Dunleavy 1996: 279, emphasis in original). Dunleavy thus implies that British behaviouralism scores badly on the first criterion for evaluation, namely sensitivity to heterogeneity. The continued commitment to full-sample multivariate regressions to predict party choice (Clarke et al. 2004) and political participation (Pattie, Seyd, and Whiteley 2004) at best downplays difference, and at worst encourages the implausible assumption that everyone decides how to vote and whether to participate in the same way. Bartle (2005) highlights political awareness as one source of heterogeneity, demonstrating that leadership effects on party choice are stronger among the less aware. Partisanship is another obvious source: strong identifiers and non-identifiers will almost by definition approach party choice in wholly different ways, yet are almost always lumped together in analysis, allowing partisanship to operate as a prior but not a moderating variable.

An honourable exception to this neglect of heterogeneity is the extensive literature on variations across geographical context. This began with a focus on social class, Miller (1977) tracking the changing relationship between constituencies' class composition and election results, and Butler and Stokes (1969) analysing contextual variations in the individual-level relationship between class and party choice. More recently, Johnston and Pattie (2006) have undertaken more wide-ranging research into the geography of electoral behaviour. Researchers studying participation have also been mindful of context. Parry, Moyser, and Day (1992) supplement survey data with an in-depth study of participation in six diverse localities, while Pattie, Seyd, and Whiteley (2004) adopt a quantitative approach to assessing community-level variations in citizenship. Multi-level models facilitate such analyses, thereby responding to Dunleavy's objection to homogenizing methods.

The second yardstick for evaluation is the attention paid to what Goodin and Klingemann (1996: 22) call the 'internal mental life' of political actors. It has been established that behaviouralists have always incorporated psychological variables into models of behaviour, and recent major British studies give prominence to such phenomena as party identification, emotions, altruism, national identity, and social trust (Clarke et al. 2004; Pattie, Seyd, and Whiteley 2004). Even so, British electoral researchers have been rebuked for a failure to consider—and measure—those aspects of 'internal mental life' that *explain* the impact of demographic variables on political behaviour. Again, class is central to the debate. As Scarbrough puts it: 'in conceptual terms class voting remains a "black box": socio-structural inputs, behavioural outputs, but only glimpses of what converts the one into the other' (2000: 399; see also Achen 1992). Butler and Stokes (1969) are largely exempt from this criticism, having paid considerable attention to what voters understood by class. Since then, though, Scarbrough's point holds, remarkably given the centrality of class in British electoral research (e.g. Sarlvik and Crewe 1983; Heath, Jowell, and Curtice 1985). A parallel 'black box' argument can be made about education in models of participation (e.g. Parry, Moyser, and Day 1992; Pattie, Seyd, and Whiteley 2004: 138–9).

Even rudimentary perception variables would shine some light into these black boxes. However, a more sophisticated treatment of hermeneutics is difficult with the usual behaviouralist methods. Hence the area of meanings and interpretations is one wherein 'behavioural electoral research has simply not dared to tread ... it is very hard to envisage how the responses to such questions—given the difficulty of measuring those responses systematically—could ever be incorporated into formal analysis' (Sanders 2002: 53). Blondel suggests that the quantification of such variables 'does depend in part on an "act of faith"' (1981: 163). This perspective is unhelpful. The quality—that is, the reliability and validity—of measurement is not a matter of faith; the onus is on the researcher to demonstrate it. Awareness of methodological limitations, the third criterion for evaluating behaviouralism, is not about defeatism; it is about being open about how—and how well—difficult variables are measured, and of striving to maximize the quality of that measurement.

Such openness is well illustrated by Clarke et al. (2004) and Pattie, Seyd, and Whiteley (2004), who report exactly what they did and how they did it, enabling readers to evaluate and potentially to replicate their analysis. In terms of ensuring quality of measurement, the record is somewhat less impressive. British contributions are thin on the ground in the large literatures on the measurement of, for example, post-materialism, political sophistication, or social capital. Party identification is an exception, long-standing controversy over this key variable triggering both qualitative (Bartle 2003) and experimental work (Sanders, Burton, and Kneeshaw 2002), part of what should be an ongoing methodological programme.

Question design research, though plainly worthwhile, will not overcome the broader problems with survey methods. Dunleavy argues that behaviouralists tend simply to ignore the approach's decontextualizing of behaviour, its inherent atomism, and the inevitable 'losses of understanding involved in reducing people's complex meanings to dots and dashes on computer disk' (1996: 283). And indeed, amid a mass of methodological detail, neither Clarke et al. (2004) nor Pattie, Seyd, and Whiteley (2004) mount any defence of their use of (only) the survey method.[11] A related concern is the reluctance to include open-ended questions, especially about reasons for behaviour. If the aim is to understand why political actors behave as they do, there is a strong case—despite coding costs and problems of introspection—for inviting respondents to give their own accounts (Butler 1958: 64–5).[12]

The final issue is the danger of 'hyper-empiricism', ever present with the huge samples and long questionnaires typical of behaviouralism. Pattie, Seyd, and Whiteley

[11] Since both volumes are based on very well-funded research programmes, alternative approaches would have been feasible. The point here is not that such alternatives *should* have been deployed; rather, it is telling that the authors clearly regarded it as more or less self-evident that the national sample survey was an appropriate and sufficient tool for the task.

[12] It is instructive that Sanders describes a key question for behaviouralists as: 'how can *we* best explain why they do it?' (2002: 45, emphasis added). *We* and *they* are liable to generate different types of explanation, and validity is likely to be maximized by considering both.

(2004: 58–73) cross-tabulate twelve aspects of citizenship with eight background variables, resulting in 1,044 cell entries. (Even the table summarizing these data is hard to follow.) Later they report a series of multivariate regressions predicting citizenship attitudes and behaviour (2004: 173–82). The welter of numbers is overwhelming and tends to obscure substantive significance. The authors carefully compare coefficients across analyses, but ignore probably the most important feature of the regressions, namely the very low R^2 values (only surpassing 0.2 in huge composite models). This is not unusual, given the difficulty in surveys of accounting for highly situational behaviour. Still, insofar as the goal here was to explain (or 'postdict') participation, then the behaviouralists' stock approach has not been a success. This point is lost in a flurry of data.

6.4.2 The Behaviouralist Contribution in Britain

Having just sounded a critical note, it is fitting to begin here with Miller's (1999: 253) reminder that virtually everything we know about elections and public opinion in Britain has been learned courtesy of behaviouralism. The approach has, as he also notes, failed at 'uncovering important mechanical "laws of nature" in politics', but then it was not intended to do so. Instead 'careful research proved better at limiting or destroying grand assertions than inventing them' (1999: 254).[13] Rather than reviewing the entire contribution—impossible in many times the space available—I want to re-emphasize that behaviouralism is less about finding universal laws, and more about testing common conjectures against systematic evidence. So I discuss three popular but evidence-light propositions about British politics that have been refuted, or at least modified, by behaviouralist research.

6.4.2.1 'It was *The Sun* Wot Won it'

This claim, made on the newspaper's front page two days after the 1992 election, encapsulated the widespread belief that a decisive late swing to the Conservatives was the result of stridently partisan coverage in the Conservative-supporting tabloids, principally the *Sun* (Linton 1992). The key issue was whether the two phenomena—press coverage and late swing—were causally linked, a question that obliged behaviouralists to go beyond the usual cross-sectional survey. Using long-term panel data, Miller (1991) had already shown that in 1987 the swing to the Conservatives among *Sun* readers took place before the official campaign. Curtice and Semetko (1994) drew the same conclusion about 1992: while the *Sun*—and other newspapers—solidified Conservative support in the long run-up to the election, its intensified campaign coverage had little impact on vote intentions. Newton and Brynin (2001) took an alternative approach, focusing on 'cross-readers', those whose partisanship conflicts

---

[13] Which is of course what would be expected from a Popperian research tradition.

with that of their newspaper. They reached the same verdict: 'if the *Sun* did indeed help to win it in 1992 it was probably because of its steady drum-beat of support over the preceding years, not because it decided to throw its full weight behind the Conservatives in the last week of the campaign' (2001: 280). This maintained a tradition of behaviouralist research puncturing inflated claims about media influence on British voting behaviour (Blumler and McQuail 1968).

6.4.2.2 *It was the Falklands that Won it*

'Most political commentators have argued or assumed that the Tories' sweeping victory in the 1983 general election was at least partly due to a "Falklands factor"— the surge of support for the government associated with the Falklands war of 1982' (Denver and Hands 1992: 243). This was based partly on the common supposition that military success benefits incumbents, but also on timing: government popularity turned so sharply upward so soon after the conflict that to doubt causality seemed perverse. Academic calculations of the war's impact were based on estimating models with a range of independent variables, one of them a Falklands term, to account for these trends in government popularity. Early studies vindicated the popular view, the war being credited with boosts to government popularity of between seven (Clarke, Stewart, and Zuk 1986) and sixteen (Dunleavy and Husbands 1985) percentage points. The consensus was shattered by Sanders, Ward, and Marsh (1987), who showed that the trend in Conservative support—both before and after the war— could be accounted for by aggregate economic expectations (whose upturn could be explained by objective economic indicators rather than post-Falklands triumphal optimism).

This conclusion was strongly challenged on methodological grounds, relating to time lags, functional forms, and model specifications, and debate ensued (Norpoth 1987; Clarke, Mishler, and Whiteley 1990; Sanders, Ward, and Marsh 1990). Hence this cannot be regarded as a simple case of a popular myth exploded. Nonetheless, later contributions to this literature are characterized by more modest estimates of the Falklands effect, and by closer attention to other (principally economic) factors. So this is another instance of behaviouralist analysis undermining a common but over-simplistic explanation of voters' behaviour.

6.4.2.3 *Turnout and Political Engagement*

In the 2001 British general election turnout plummeted to 59 per cent, its lowest level since 1918. This was widely interpreted as indicating deep disillusionment with the British political system, if not a full-blown crisis of democracy (see Bromley, Curtice, and Seyd 2004). The reasoning was broadly as follows: if turning out to vote betokens some sort of commitment to the system, virtually unprecedented levels of abstention must imply a worrying weakening of such commitment.

Compared to the Falklands analyses, the behaviouralist research debunking this thesis was fairly straightforward (Clarke et al. 2004: chs. 8–9).[14] It began with the demonstration that much of the dynamics in turnout can be explained by two contextual factors: the closeness of the race and the perceived gap (in terms of ideology or policy) between the parties. Hence, in 2001, much of the plunge in turnout could be attributed to the fact that the parties were close but the race was anything but. The second element was the revelation (via simple time series of attitudinal indicators) that interest in politics, caring about election results, political efficacy (internal and external), and willingness to participate had been fairly stable not only since the early 1990s—when turnout (in 1992) was 77 percent—but even since the 1960s (Clarke et al. 2004: 284–9). Plainly these static independent variables could not explain dynamics in the dependent variable.

The tendencies to infer causality and to simplify explanations are common biases in human judgement. Behaviouralism offers the possibility of subjecting these intuitively plausible popular beliefs to systematic test. This is useful beyond academia. After all, the policy consequences of the 'mass disillusionment' interpretation of 59 per cent turnout are very different from those implied by the account in Clarke et al. (2004). And the discovery that few voters were affected by the heat of the *Sun*'s coverage in 1992 paints a brighter picture of democracy than was widely envisioned. An important task for behaviouralists is to convey such results to wider audiences.

6.5 Conclusion

Behaviouralism is political science, but inexact science, and in practice behaviouralists were always less rigidly positivist, and less grand in ambition, than is often assumed. Systematic empirical observation is the crux not because it is value neutral, because everything is perfectly measurable, or because precise prediction is feasible. Rather, it allows for the incremental build-up of ordered knowledge. The approach has changed little over time, and differs little between Britain and the USA. However fierce the philosophical attack on positivism, it did little to change the methods used by behaviouralists. An ingrained empiricism meant that they saw no alternative; at least, none that could satisfactorily address the 'how would you know if you were wrong?' question. Through full reporting of methods and results, behaviouralists gave their readers the opportunity to judge whether they were wrong. As well as generating their own propositions about political behaviour—limited and modest rather than universal and grand, but still important—behaviouralist researchers have also tested, and often refuted, many popular hypotheses about British politics.

---

[14] Some observers managed without it. Even before the election, Anthony King (2001) commented that the parties need 'just provide the voters with a closely fought election at which a great deal is at stake and, make no mistake, they will again turn out in their droves'.

There is nevertheless considerable scope for development. The crucial difficulty is that variables offering real explanatory purchase are, for interpretivists, exactly those meanings and reflections that are beyond the reach of behaviouralists. To argue convincingly otherwise, behaviouralists need to command the alternative language— heuristics, impressions, self-perceptions—of psychology (see Kinder 1998). In the USA, political psychology is an established subfield; in Britain, political scientists are only beginning to consider seriously the way in which actors receive, process, and store information. The same focus on cognitive psychology is the key to improving measurement of those genuinely explanatory variables. Since the survey— fielded increasingly often over the Internet—seems likely to remain the workhorse of behaviouralist research, insights into question answering from cognitive science (Tourangeau, Rips, and Rasinski 2000), and the techniques for cognitive pre-testing of questionnaires (Willis 2005), are very valuable.

But behaviouralists should also move beyond the survey. Declining response rates—especially among certain groups—seriously weaken the sample survey's claim to represent public opinion (Brehm 1993). This is much less problematic for exper- imental research, and probably the biggest advantage of the Internet mode is that it enables a range of experimental designs. These demonstrate causality in a way that cross-sections and correlations cannot (Druckman et al. 2006). Meanwhile, the rou- tine merging of individual-level survey data with aggregate information has enhanced behaviouralism's sensitivity to context. Finally, Dunleavy heralds new text-search technologies, which allow researchers to conduct many semi-structured interviews and then to 'analytically surface what influences people's alignments and attitudes by a process of post-hoc interrogation of their full text' (1996: 286). At the very least, this should be done with a subset of respondents from the main sample. Alterna- tively, the main themes discerned from quantitative analysis could then be explored qualitatively. Such triangulation and iterative interaction between quantitative and qualitative methods is widely advocated (e.g. Creswell 2003). Behaviouralists' unwill- ingness even to include open-ended questions in surveys signifies how far they have still to move in that direction. This intransigence is misguided, because combining methods offers depth of understanding, currently behaviouralism's weak point, while maintaining the systematic and replicable measurement that is its strength.

References

ACHEN, C. 1992. 'Social Psychology, Demographic Variables, and Linear Regression: Breaking the Iron Triangle in Voting Research'. *Political Behavior*, 14: 195–211.

ADCOCK, R. 2007. 'Interpreting Behavioralism'. Pp. 180–208 in Adcock, Bevir, and Stimson 2007a.

——BEVIR, M., and STIMSON, S. C. (eds.) 2007a. *Modern Political Science: Anglo-American Exchanges since 1880*. Princeton, NJ: Princeton University Press.

——————2007b. 'A History of Political Science: How? What? Why? Pp. 1–17 in Adcock, Bevir, and Stimson 2007a.

ALMOND, G. 1996. 'Political Science: The History of the Discipline'. Pp. 50–96 in Goodin and Klingemann 1996.

—— and VERBA, S. 1963. *The Civic Culture*. Princeton, NJ: Princeton University Press.

BARTLE, J. 2003. 'Measuring Party Identification: An Exploratory Study with Focus Groups'. *Electoral Studies*, 22: 217–37.

—— 2005. 'Homogenous Models and Heterogeneous Voters'. *Political Studies*, 53: 653–75.

BERMAN, S. 1998. *The Social Democratic Moment*. Cambridge, Mass.: Harvard University Press.

BEVIR, M., and RHODES, R. A. W. 2007. 'Political Science in Britain'. Pp. 234–58 in Adcock, Bevir, and Stimson 2007a.

BLONDEL, J. 1981. *The Discipline of Politics*. London: Butterworth.

—— 1997. 'Amateurs into Professionals'. Ch. 11 in H. Daalder (ed.), *Comparative European Politics*. London: Pinter.

BLUMLER, J. G., and McQUAIL, D. 1968. *Television and Politics*. London: Faber and Faber.

BOGDANOR, V. 1999. 'Comparative Politics'. Pp. 147–80 in Hayward, Barry, and Brown 1999.

BREHM, J. 1993. *The Phantom Respondents*. Ann Arbor: University of Michigan Press.

BROMLEY, C., CURTICE, J., and SEYD, P. 2004. 'Is Britain Facing a Crisis of Democracy?' CREST Working Paper no. 106.

BURNHAM, W. D. 1965. 'The Changing Shape of the American Political Universe'. *American Political Science Review*, 59: 7–28.

BUTLER, D. 1958. *The Study of Political Behaviour*. London: Hutchinson University Library.

—— and STOKES, D. 1969. *Political Change in Britain*. London: Macmillan.

BYRNE, D. S. 1998. *Complexity Theory and the Social Sciences*. London: Routledge.

CAMPBELL, A., CONVERSE, P. E., MILLER, W. E., and STOKES, D. 1960. *The American Voter*. New York: Wiley.

CLARKE, H. D., MISHLER, W., and WHITELEY, P. 1990. 'Recapturing the Falklands: Models of Conservative popularity, 1979–83'. *British Journal of Political Science*, 20: 63–81.

—— SANDERS, D., STEWART, M. C., and WHITELEY, P. 2004. *Political Choice in Britain*. Oxford: Oxford University Press.

—— STEWART, M. C., and ZUK, G. 1986. 'Politics, Economics and Party Popularity in Britain, 1979–83'. *Electoral Studies*, 5: 123–41.

CRESWELL, R. J. W. 2003. *Research Design*. Thousand Oaks, Calif.: Sage.

CRICK, B. 1961. *The American Science of Politics*. Berkeley: University of California Press.

—— 1962. *In Defense of Politics*. Chicago: University of Chicago Press.

—— 1980. 'The British Way'. *Government and Opposition*, 15: 297–307.

CURTICE, J., and SEMETKO, H. A. 1994. 'Does it Matter what the Papers Say?' Pp. 43–64 in A. F. Heath, R. Jowell, and John Curtice (eds.), *Labour's Last Chance?* Aldershot: Dartmouth.

DAHL, R. 1961a. 'The Behavioral Approach in Political Science: Epitaph to a Monument to a Successful Protest'. *American Political Science Review*, 55: 763–72.

—— 1961b. *Who Governs?* New Haven, Conn.: Yale University Press.

DENVER, D., and HANDS, G. 1992. *Issues and Controversies in British Electoral Behaviour*. Hemel Hempstead: Harvester Wheatsheaf.

DRUCKMAN, J. N., GREEN, D. P., KUKLINSKI, J. H., and LUPIA, A. 2006. 'The Growth and Development of Experimental Research in Political Science'. *American Political Science Review*, 100: 627–35.

DRYZEK, J. S. 2006. 'Revolutions without Enemies: Key Transformations in Political Science'. *American Political Science Review*, 100: 487–92.

DUNLEAVY, P. 1996. 'Political Behavior: Institutional and Experiential Approaches'. Pp. 276–93 in Goodin and Klingemann 1996.

——and HUSBANDS, C. T. 1985. *British Democracy at the Crossroads*. London: Allen and Unwin.

EASTON, D. 1953. *The Political System*. New York: Knopf.

ELCOCK, H. 1976. *Political Behaviour*. London: Methuen.

EULAU, H. 1963. *The Behavioral Persuasion in Politics*. New York: Random House.

——1981. 'Foreword: On Revolutions that Never Were'. Pp. vii–xv in S. J. Long (ed.), *The Handbook of Political Behavior*, vol. i. New York: Plenum Press.

FINER, S. 1980. 'Political Science: An Idiosyncratic Retrospect of a Putative Discipline'. *Government and Opposition*, 15: 346–63.

FISHBEIN, M., and AJZEN, I. 1975. *Belief, Attitude, Intention, and Behavior*. Reading, Mass.: Addison-Wesley.

GEERTZ, C. 1973. *The Interpretation of Cultures*. New York: Basic.

GOLDSMITH, M., and GRANT, W. 2006. 'British Political Science in the New Millennium'. Presented at epsNet Plenary Conference, Budapest, 16–17 June.

GOODIN, R. E., and KLINGEMANN, H.-D. (eds.) 1996. *A New Handbook of Political Science*. Oxford: Oxford University Press.

GRAHAM, G. J., and CAREY, G. W. 1972. *The Post-Behavioral Era*. New York: David McKay.

GREEN, D. P., PALMQVIST, B., and SCHICKLER, E. 2002. *Partisan Hearts and Minds*. New Haven, Conn.: Yale University Press.

GREENLEAF, W. H. 1983. *The British Political Tradition*, vol. i. London: Methuen.

GUNNELL, J. G. 1983. 'Political Theory: The Evolution of a Sub-field'. Pp. 3–45 in A. W. Finifter (ed.), *Political Science: The State of the Discipline*. Washington, DC: APSA.

HAY, C. 2002*a*. *Political Analysis*. Basingstoke: Palgrave Macmillan.

——(ed.) 2002*b*. *British Politics Today*. Oxford: Polity.

HAYWARD, J. 1991. 'Cultural and Contextual Constraints upon the Development of Political Science in Great Britain'. Pp. 93–107 in D. Easton, J. G. Gunnell, and L. Graziano (eds.), *The Development of Political Science*. London: Routledge.

——1999. 'British Approaches to Politics: The Dawn of a Self-deprecating Discipline'. Pp. 1–36 in Hayward, Barry, and Brown 1999.

——BARRY, B., and BROWN, A. (eds.) 1999. *The British Study of Politics in the Twentieth Century*. Oxford: Oxford University Press.

HEATH, A., JOWELL, R., and CURTICE, J. 1985. *How Britain Votes*. Oxford: Pergamon.

INGLEHART, R. 1977. *The Silent Revolution*. Princeton, NJ: Princeton University Press.

JOHNSON, N. 1989. *The Limits of Political Science*. Oxford: Clarendon.

JOHNSTON, R. J., and PATTIE, C. J. 2006. *Putting Voters in their Place*. Oxford: Oxford University Press.

KAPLAN, M. A. 1957. *System and Process in International Politics*. New York: Wiley.

KAVANAGH, D. 1983. *Political Science and Political Behaviour*. London: Allen and Unwin.

——2007. 'The Emergence of an Embryonic Discipline: British Politics without Political Scientists'. Pp. 97–118 in Adcock, Bevir, and Stimson 2007*a*.

KENNY, M. 2007. 'Birth of a Discipline: Interpreting British Political Studies in the 1950s and 1960s'. Pp. 158–79 in Adcock, Bevir, and Stimson 2007*a*.

KEY, V. O. 1949. *Southern Politics in State and Nation*. New York: Knopf.

——1958. 'The State of the Discipline'. *American Political Science Review*, 52: 961–71.

KINDER, D. R. 1998. 'Opinion and Action in the Realm of Politics'. In D. T. Gilbert, S. T. Fiske, and G. Lindzey (eds.), *The Handbook of Social Psychology*, vol. ii (4th edn.). New York: McGraw-Hill.

KING, A. 2001. 'Why a Poor Turnout Points to a Democracy in Good Health'. *Daily Telegraph*, 17 May.

LAKATOS, I. 1971. 'Falsification and the Methodology of Scientific Research Programmes'. Pp. 91–196 in I. Lakatos and A. Musgrave (eds.), *Criticism and the Growth of Knowledge*. Cambridge: Cambridge University Press.

LAVER, M., and BUDGE, I. (eds.) 1992. *Party Policy and Government Coalitions*. London: Macmillan.

LINTON, M. 1992. 'Was it *The Sun* wot won it?' 7th *Guardian* Lecture, Nuffield College, Oxford, 30 October.

MacINTYRE, A. 1985. *After Virtue*. London: Duckworth.

MACKENZIE, W. J. M. 1967. *Politics and Social Science*. Harmondsworth: Penguin.

—— 1971. *The Study of Political Science Today*. London: Macmillan.

MARSH, D., and FURLONG, P. 2002. 'A Skin not a Sweater: Ontology and Epistemology in Political Science'. Pp. 17–44 in D. Marsh and G. Stoker (eds.), *Theory and Methods in Political Science*. Basingstoke: Palgrave Macmillan.

—— and SAVIGNY, H. 2004. 'Political Science as a Broad Church: The Search for a Pluralist Discipline'. *Politics*, 24: 155–68.

MILLER, W. E., and STOKES, D. E. 1963. 'Constituency Influence in Congress'. *American Political Science Review*, 57: 45–56.

MILLER, W. L. 1977. *Electoral Dynamics in Britain since 1918*. London: Macmillan.

—— 1991. *Media and Voters*. Oxford: Clarendon.

—— 1999. 'Electoral Systems, Elections, Public Opinion'. Pp. 223–55 in Hayward, Barry, and Brown 1999.

NEWTON, K., and BRYNIN, M. 2001. 'The National Press and Party Voting in the UK'. *Political Studies*, 49: 265–85.

NORPOTH, H. 1987. 'Guns and Butter and Government Popularity in Britain'. *American Political Science Review*, 81: 949–59.

PARRY, G., MOYSER, M., and DAY, N. 1992. *Political Participation and Democracy in Britain*. Cambridge: Cambridge University Press.

PATTIE, C. J., SEYD, P., and WHITELEY, P. F. 2004. *Citizenship in Britain: Values, Participation and Democracy*. Cambridge: Cambridge University Press.

PRESTHUS, R. V. 1965. *Behavioral Approaches to Public Administration*. Tuscaloosa: University of Alabama Press.

QUINE, W. V. O. 1960. *Word and Object*. Cambridge: Cambridge University Press.

RAGIN, C. C. 2000. *Fuzzy Set Social Science*. Chicago: Chicago University Press.

RICCI, D. 1984. *The Tragedy of Political Science*. New Haven, Conn.: Yale University Press.

SANDERS, D. 2002. 'Behaviouralism'. Pp. 45–64 in D. Marsh and G. Stoker (eds.), *Theory and Methods in Political Science*. Basingstoke: Palgrave Macmillan.

—— BURTON, J., and KNEESHAW, J. 2002. 'Identifying the True Identifiers: A Question Wording Experiment'. *Party Politics*, 8: 193–205.

—— WARD, H., and MARSH, D. 1987. 'Governmental Popularity and the Falklands War: A Reassessment'. *British Journal of Political Science*, 17: 281–313.

—— —— —— 1990. 'A Reply to Clarke, Mishler and Whiteley'. *British Journal of Political Science*, 20: 83–90.

SARLVIK, B., and CREWE, I. 1983. *Decade of Dealignment*. Cambridge: Cambridge University Press.

SCARBROUGH, E. 2000. 'The British Election Study and Electoral Research'. *Political Studies*, 48: 391–414.

SMITH, S. 2000. 'The Discipline of International Relations: Still an American Social Science?' *British Journal of Politics and International Relations*, 2: 374–402.

SUSSER, B. 1974. 'The Behavioural Ideology: A Review and a Retrospect'. *Political Studies*, 22: 271–88.

TAAGEPERA, R. 2007. 'Predictive versus Postdictive Models'. *European Political Science*, 6: 114–23.

TAYLOR, C. 1967. 'Neutrality in Political Science'. Pp. 25–57 in P. Laslett and W. G. Runciman (eds.), *Philosophy, Politics, Society*. Oxford: Blackwell.

TOURANGEAU, R., RIPS, L. J., and RASINSKI, K. 2000. *The Psychology of Survey Response*. New York: Cambridge University Press.

WAHLKE, J. C. 1979. 'Pre-behavioralism in Political Science'. *American Political Science Review*, 73: 9–31.

WALLAS, G. 1908. *Human Nature in Politics*. London: Constable.

WATSON, J. B. 1913. 'Psychology as the Behaviorist Views it'. *Psychological Review*, 20: 158–77.

WILLIS, G. B. 2005. *Cognitive Interviewing: A Tool for Improving Questionnaire Design*. Thousand Oaks, Calif.: Sage.

ZALLER, J. R. 1992. *The Nature and Origins of Mass Opinion*. Cambridge: Cambridge University Press.

SECTION THREE: CRITICAL PERSPECTIVES

CHAPTER 7

....

ANTI-FOUNDATIONALISM

....

MARK BEVIR

LET us get one point out of the way at the beginning: anti-foundationalism is an epistemological doctrine not a critical approach to politics. Anti-foundationalism is a doctrine in the philosophy of knowledge. In most versions it asserts that none of our knowledge is absolutely certain. In some versions it asserts more specifically and more controversially that we cannot provide knowledge with secure foundations in either pure experiences or pure reason. I will argue, moreover, that we would be wrong, especially if we are anti-foundationalists, to assume that epistemological doctrines ever lead directly to particular approaches to political science. Anti-foundationalism could be compatible with a wide range of political sciences—from rational choice to ethnography—and an equally wide range of ideologies—from conservatism to socialism.

There is something strange about an epistemological concept being used to define an approach to British politics. This sense of strangeness dissipates, however, if we allow that the connection between anti-foundationalism and critical approaches to politics is a historically contingent one. Hence, after briefly reviewing anti-foundational philosophy and its relation to political science, this chapter will provide a historical narrative of the contingent ways in which anti-foundationalism has been brought to the study of British politics from within critical, socialist traditions.

Thanks to Alan Finlayson, Mike Kenny, and Anna-Marie Smith for helpful comments on this chapter.

7.1 WHAT IS ANTI-FOUNDATIONALISM?

To begin, I want further to spell out the relationship of anti-foundationalism to political science. An anti-foundational epistemology has several implications for social philosophy. I will begin by briefly mentioning some of the less contentious implications, although even these might be subject to some debate. Thereafter I will explain why anti-foundational philosophy is compatible with diverse approaches to political science, and, to end this section, I will consider the implications of my analysis of anti-foundationalism for its place in the study of British politics.

7.1.1 Anti-foundationalism and Philosophy

The term 'anti-foundationalism' is of recent popularity. It is used to refer to any epistemology that rejects appeals to a basic ground or foundation of knowledge in either pure experience or pure reason. Anti-foundational epistemologies thus include many that pre-date the recent spread of the term itself. Examples of anti-foundationalism include not only postmodernists and post-structuralists but also many analytic philosophers who follow the pragmatists, W. V. O. Quine, or Ludwig Wittgenstein.[1] It has even been argued that the high positivists of the Vienna Circle were anti-foundationalists (Uebel 1996). So, contrary to what many political scientists appear to believe, anti-foundationalism is not an obscure, outlandish doctrine to be easily dismissed as a ridiculous rejection of the idea of an external world. Anti-foundationalism is a commonplace among philosophers, and it is surely time political scientists developed enough philosophical literacy to understand it and consider its implications.

The most obvious implications of anti-foundationalism are perhaps meaning holism and anti-representationalism.[2] Given that we cannot have pure experiences, our concepts and propositions cannot refer to the world in splendid isolation. Concepts cannot directly represent objects in the world since our experiences of those objects must in part be ones that we construct using our prior theories. Hence anti-foundationalists conclude that concepts, meanings, and beliefs do not have a one-to-one correspondence with objects in the world, but rather form webs. Although anti-foundationalists have defended many different epistemologies, from pragmatism to radical scepticism, many of them conclude that we cannot justify isolated propositions; rather, any justification of a knowledge claim must be one that applies to a web of beliefs or research programme. It is these kinds of epistemological

---

[1] For a useful (if unsatisfactory) account of anti-foundationalism as temporarily having triumphed in a perennial philosophical debate, see Rockmore and Singer (1992).

[2] The philosophical implications of anti-foundationalism are debatable, especially in their details. I have mentioned only those about which there is considerable agreement. Yet, in discussing why anti-foundationalism implies various other positions, I inevitably hint at my personal analysis of the logical connections involved. For details see Bevir (1999).

ideas that inspire anti-foundational critiques of the positivism and naive empiricism found in much political science.

Anti-foundationalism, with its meaning holism, has implications for social ontol ogy. Meaning holism implies that our concepts are not simply given to us by the world as it is; rather, we build them in by drawing on our prior theories in an attempt to categorize, explain, and narrate our experiences. Hence anti-foundationalists typically uphold social constructivism: they argue that we make the beliefs and concepts on which we act and thus the social world in which we live. This social constructivism asserts not only that we make the social world through our actions, but also that our actions reflect beliefs, concepts, languages, and discourses that themselves are social constructs. It is this constructivist ontology that inspires anti-foundational critiques of the reified and essentialist concepts found in much political science.

Meaning holism feeds into anti-foundational analyses of social explanation. It undermines reductionist attempts to explain actions by reference to allegedly objective social facts without reference to the relevant beliefs or meanings. The crucial argument here is that because people's beliefs form holistic webs, and because their experiences are laden with their prior beliefs, therefore we cannot assume that people in any given social location will come to hold certain beliefs or assume certain interests. To the contrary, their beliefs, including their view of their interests, will depend on their prior theories. Hence anti-foundationalists conclude that social explanation consists not of reducing actions to social facts but of the interpretation of meanings in the context of webs of belief, discourses, or cultural practices.

Social constructivism also feeds into anti-foundational analyses of social explanation. It undercuts a scientism in which social explanation appears as a quest for ahistorical causal links. The crucial argument here is that because beliefs and concepts, and so actions and practices, are historically contingent social constructs, therefore we cannot adequately explain them in terms of a trans-historical correlation or mechanism. Human norms and practices are not natural or rational responses to given circumstances. Hence many anti-foundationalists conclude that social explanation contains an inherently historicist moment: even those concepts and practices that seem most natural to us need to be explained as products of a contingent history.

7.1.2 Anti-foundationalism and Political Science

Approaches to political science are peculiar entities. What political scientists identify as an approach is usually a jumble of philosophy, methods, and topics. So, for example, behaviouralism combined positivist philosophy with new statistical methods and the study of the political behaviour of individuals and groups. Yet the philosophy, methods, and topics do not entail one another. They do not logically have to go together. So, for example, several political scientists study group and network behaviour without using any statistical techniques, and even political scientists who use statistical techniques to explore voting behaviour now often do so without adhering to a positivist philosophy.

To understand the implications of anti-foundationalism for political science, we should distinguish between philosophy, method, and topics. Anti-foundationalism supports a social philosophy characterized by holism, constructivism, interpretivism, and historicism. This social philosophy provides a stark contrast to the lukewarm positivism of much political science. It is clear, in that respect, that anti-foundationalism offers a major challenge to political scientists to clarify and defend the philosophical assumptions that inform their work. Yet, to challenge political scientists to rethink their philosophical assumptions is not necessarily to require them to reject their favoured methods or topics. Anti-foundationalism cautions political scientists how to reflect on the data they generate; it does not tell them that they must or must not use particular techniques to generate data on particular issues.

I am suggesting that an anti-foundational philosophy does not require or preclude particular methods or topics in political science. Anti-foundationalism itself should lead us to recognize that there is just such a conceptual gap between a social philosophy and an approach to political science. Meaning holism implies that our beliefs or concepts form a web. Hence it is possible that political scientists could reconcile anti-foundational philosophy with any given method by suitably modifying their other beliefs or concepts. Political scientists can make their favoured techniques of data generation compatible with anti-foundationalism by modifying their other beliefs so as to suggest that the data they generate are not only saturated with their prior theories but also data about holistic and constructed webs of meaning to be explained by interpretations that include a historical moment. Foundationalists might insist on particular techniques on the grounds that some techniques generate pure facts while others do not. Anti-foundationalists, in contrast, should allow that all kinds of techniques generate theory-laden data that we can accept or challenge in narratives.

Anti-foundationalists might choose to undertake critical studies that reveal the historical contingency and partiality of beliefs that present themselves as naturally given or inherently rational. Equally, one might imagine anti-foundationalists relying on large-scale surveys to generate data from which to postulate certain beliefs for which they then offer a historical explanation. Or one might imagine them using formal models to explore the outcomes that arise from actions based on particular beliefs and desires, and even then postulating particular beliefs and desires on the grounds that doing so best explains certain observed outcomes. No doubt any anti-foundationalists who used behavioural or rational choice approaches to political science would have to allow that the stories they told were provisional ones that related actions and practices to socially constructed webs of meaning. But there is no reason why their provisional stories should not rely heavily on surveys, statistical analysis, or formal models to generate data.

It is worth adding here that anti-foundationalism might even prove compatible with only slightly modified versions of the forms of explanation that are associated with behaviouralism, institutionalism, and rational choice. Anti-foundationalism is, of course, incompatible with a naive belief in the validity of explanations that treat data as pure facts to be explained in ways that reify practices so as to treat them as natural, fixed, or inherently rational. However, political scientists might accept an anti-foundational analysis of social explanation while offering ad hoc or pragmatic justifications for explanations couched in terms of reified concepts. Perhaps they might argue that such simplified explanations are more able to generate policy-relevant knowledge than are nuanced accounts of historical contingency and diversity: they might defend aggregate, formal correlations between poverty and race, gender, marital status, and education on the grounds that these help the state to develop policies that alleviate poverty. Equally, of course, anti-foundationalists might respond by arguing that the dangers and exclusions of having power and policy based on essentialist concepts and formal explanations always outweigh the benefits of acting on simplified correlations or models, or they might argue that other approaches to policy formation are capable of generating similar or more substantial benefits. For now, the important point is that anti-foundationalism itself does not appear conclusively to resolve such arguments in a way that rules out all possible uses of reified or essentialist concepts in formal correlations and models.

7.1.3   Varieties of Anti-foundationalism

In principle anti-foundationalism could be combined with all sorts of approaches to political science. Hence we cannot explain the impact of anti-foundationalism on the study of British politics by appealing to purportedly intrinsic conceptual links between an anti-foundational epistemology and a particular approach to the study of politics. To the contrary, the links between anti-foundationalism and approaches to political science must themselves be contingent historical ones. To explain the impact of anti-foundationalism on the study of British politics, we thus have to explore the particular historical traditions against the background of which political scientists have turned to anti-foundationalism. Indeed anti-foundational approaches to British politics owe as much to the persistence of concepts, concerns, and topics from various historical traditions as they do to purportedly logical consequences of an anti-foundationalist epistemology.

While anti-foundationalism in principle could be combined with all kinds of approaches to British politics, it in practice is associated more or less exclusively with political scientists inspired by critical, socialist traditions of inquiry. We might identify three types of anti-foundationalism in the study of British politics. Each arose against the background of a different critical socialist tradition and absorbed a different type of anti-foundationalism. Table 7.1 provides an overview. Governmentality theory arose against the background of socialist theories of social control, and it absorbed a focus on regimes of power/knowledge. Post-Marxists combined Saussurean linguistics with a socialist concept of hegemony. Social humanists infused postanalytic themes into the New Left's concern with culture, agency, and resistance.

Table 7.1 Varieties of anti-foundationalism

	Governmentality	Post-Marxism	Social humanism
Socialist background			
(i) Thinker(s)	(i) Louis Althusser	(i) Antonio Gramsci	(i) New Left—Raymond Williams and E. P. Thompson
(ii) Key concept	(ii) Social control	(ii) Hegemony	(ii) Radical cultures and traditions
Anti-foundational background			
(i) Thinker/Theory	(i) Michel Foucault	(i) Post-structuralism	(i) Diffuse postanalytic themes
(ii) Key concept	(ii) Power/knowledge	(ii) Semiotic code—relations among signifiers	(ii) Agency situated in cultural practices
Prominent topics	Technical discourses as ways of making subjects through public policy	Collective identities—especially those of gender, race, and sexuality	Governance, with an emphasis on ideologies and resistance
Examples	(i) Rose (1999) (ii) Barry, Osborne, and Rose (1996b)	(i) Laclau and Mouffe (1985) (ii) Smith (1994)	(i) Hall (1983) (ii) Bevir and Trentmann (2007)

My aim in distinguishing these three traditions is to offer an admittedly simplified account of broad movements in the study of British politics. I have divided anti-foundational approaches according to intellectual background because my aim is to provide a historical narrative of the contingent ways in which anti-foundationalism has entered into the study of British politics. Let me stress, then, that these three traditions are not separate from one another. To the contrary, themes often flow from one to the other, and anti-foundationalists often combine themes from different traditions. To offer one example: Stuart Hall's work combined the New Left's emphasis on the sociology of culture with a concept of hegemony quite a while before Ernesto Laclau and Chantal Mouffe combined the concept of hegemony with a post-structuralism linked to Saussurean linguistics (Hall, Lumley, and McLennan 1978; Laclau and Mouffe 1985). To offer a more personal example: my work on New Labour instantiates a social humanist concern with ideologies and agency, but one of its main focuses is on how discourses from the social sciences have impacted on public policy to create a new governmentality (Bevir 2005). Bearing such caveats in mind, let us look at the three anti-foundational approaches to British politics. In each case, we will trace a historical movement from an early socialist background (Althusser, Gramsci, the New Left), through the appearance of anti-foundational themes (Foucault, Laclau and Mouffe, Hall), on to the studies of British politics they have inspired.

7.2 GOVERNMENTALITY

Governmentality theory derives from the writings of Michel Foucault. It has been applied to British society and politics mainly by the so-called Anglo-Foucauldians. The early Anglo-Foucauldians typically had been attracted to the work of Louis Althusser, and, more generally, to Marxist theories of social control. Foucault's work reproduced many tropes from social control theory (Resch 1992; Stedman Jones 1996). He deployed structuralist and post-structuralist ideas to imply that distinctions such as those between madness and sanity or sickness and health were products of particular epistemes or discourses rather than neutral or rational ways of capturing reality (Foucault 1989; 1973). He suggested that the function of institutions such as asylums and clinics was not the scientific and humanitarian promotion of health, but rather social control and the normalization of deviant individuals. Governmentality theory applies a similar approach to explore modern power.

7.2.1 Foucault on Modern Power

Foucault defines governmentality as the conduct of conduct (Foucault 1991). He traces it back to the emergence of the 'art of government' in the middle of the sixteenth century. Before that time, writers, notably Machiavelli in *The Prince*, had adopted a monarchical notion of sovereign power: princes stood apart from their territory, having a fragile relationship to it, so that ruling consisted of identifying and forestalling threats to their rule. Then, in the middle of the sixteenth century, anti-Machiavellian theorists of the art of government began to focus on the conduct of conduct. These theorists explored questions about how to act on individuals so as to influence, limit, correct, and determine their behaviour, whether in terms of the state, the economy, the family, or the soul. They concerned themselves with the activities and relationships in a given society, not the one relationship between a prince and his territory. In doing so, Foucault argues, they set the scene for the rise of modern governmentality.

   In Foucault's account, modern governmentality combines sovereignty with bio-power and pastoral power (Foucault 1977; 1978–85). The anti-Machiavellian concept of the conduct of conduct implied a downward continuity from the well-organized state to an efficient economy and well-run families. In the seventeenth century, this downward continuity was associated with a broad concept of 'police' that embraced all attempts to exert disciplinary political power over people and their activities, including schooling, work, family life, and consumption. In the eighteenth century, populations were constructed as a social object liable to death rates, epidemics, and patterns of growth, and the extension of policing to populations gave rise to what Foucault describes as bio-power; that is, new techniques of discipline that aimed to increase the health, longevity, and productivity of the population.

The final stream that feeds into Foucault's analysis of modern power is a pastoral one. Foucault traces pastoral techniques of government back to practices that developed in the Church. Pastoral power requires individuals to internalize various ideals and norms so that they both regard an external body as concerned with their good and strive to regulate themselves in accord with the dictates of that external body. For Foucault, the secularization of pastoral power involved the state replacing the spiritual end of salvation with worldly ends such as health and well-being. When people accept such ends, they examine, confess, and transform their own behaviour in accord with the regime of bio-power.

7.2.2 The Anglo-Foucauldians

Anglo-Foucauldians often deny that Foucault provided a theory that constitutes the best way of understanding politics. They take him instead to have sketched out a mode and field of inquiry. The mode of inquiry (or method) is genealogy. The aim is to provide cultural histories of discourses that inform current practices so as to reveal their contingency and undermine any suggestion of their being neutral, humanitarian, or scientific. Anglo-Foucauldians describe themselves as offering critical genealogies of problems set by the present. Nikolas Rose writes, 'rather than conceiving of our present as an epoch or a state of affairs, it is more useful, in my own view, to view the present as a series of problems and questions, an actuality to be acted upon and within by genealogical investigation, to be made amenable to action by the action of thought' (Rose 1999: 11). Typically the Anglo-Foucauldians suggest that the purpose of genealogy is to open up new possibilities, and even new ways of being. They dismiss the idea of promoting a particular way of being as tarnished by the utopian dream of eliminating all forms of power/knowledge. They argue that through genealogies, 'the received fixedness and inevitability of the present is destabilized, shown as just sufficiently fragile as to let in a little glimpse of freedom—as a practice of difference— through its fractures' (Barry, Osborne, and Rose 1996a: 5).

The Anglo-Foucauldians' field of inquiry (or empirical domain) directs us away from an excessive focus on the state towards a study of the diverse processes by which subjects are normalized so as to sustain a pattern of rule. This field of inquiry covers all the diffuse ways in which government and social power impact upon individuals, groups, and populations. It draws our attention to the ways in which conduct is shaped to certain ends by discourses and practices. As Rose explains, 'the state now appears simply as one element—whose functionality is historically specific and contextually variable—in multiple circuits of power, connecting a diversity of authorities and forces, within a whole variety of complex assemblages' (Rose 1999: 5).

The concept of the state as just one element in circuits of power might sound very similar to a much elder literature on policy networks. Yet, the Anglo-Foucauldians depart significantly from this literature precisely because their interest lies not with the study of formal institutions but with genealogies of discourses that inform contemporary practices. Anglo-Foucauldians are interested in how apparently neutral, scientific discourses serve to establish particular forms of subjectivity. They might focus on the ways in which expert discourses about education, health, risk, and insurance feed into public policies that then establish normal patterns of behaviour. Or they might focus on the ways in which statistical analysis and formal modelling provide new ways of measuring and analysing populations and thereby governing people.

7.2.3 Liberal Governmentalities

Foucault's essay on governmentality was first made available in English in 1978. It appeared in a collection of essays, *The Foucault Effect: Studies in Governmentality*, edited by Graham Burchell, Colin Gordon, and Peter Miller. *The Foucault Effect* also includes essays exploring governmentality written by French and Italian scholars as well as some Anglo-Foucauldians. The essays define the mode and field of inquiry associated with governmentality, but they do not particularly focus on themes germane to British politics. Nearly twenty years later, there appeared another collection of essays, *Foucault and Political Reason: Liberalism, Neo-Liberalism and Rationalities of Government*, edited by Andrew Barry, Thomas Osborne, and Rose. This collection, with its Anglophone cast of contributors, illustrates themes that characterize a governmentality approach to British politics.

The subtitle of *Foucault and Political Reason* captures one such emphasis. Anglo-Foucauldians conceive of liberalism in terms of a series of political technologies that arose from the nineteenth century through the welfare state and on to the neoliberalism of the Thatcher years.[3] Governmentality theorists portray nineteenth-century liberalism as a political rationality that arose out of worries about extensive policing. In this view, liberalism appears less as a rejection of state intervention and more as a positive political rationality by which to manage complex interactions in society and the economy. Liberalism seeks to produce certain outcomes through dynamics in society and the economy themselves rather than by state activity.

Governmentality theorists discuss the rise of the welfare state in relation to changing problematics of liberalism. In their view, modern industrial society gave rise to new social problems with which liberalism had to contend. Liberalism tried to guarantee the security of the economy and the state, in other words, by addressing social problems through an array of new technologies that collectively constituted the welfare state. For governmentality theorists, public housing, unemployment insurance, and public health are understood as technologies of power that serve to normalize subjects.

The governmentality theorists' account of liberalism sets the scene for their understanding of neoliberalism and contemporary British politics. On the one hand, neoliberalism appears as a critique of welfare state liberalism: it promotes rationalities

---

[3] For Foucault's own discussion of liberalism, especially German post-war liberalism and the Chicago School, see Foucault (2004), and for comment Lemke (2001).

in society and the economy, especially technologies of the market, on the grounds that welfare systems, trade protection, state planning, and Keynesian intervention are unproductive interferences with market relations. On the other hand, neoliberalism appears as a range of governmental technologies that actively foster competitive market relations so as to shift responsibility to the individual while increasing social efficiency: under neoliberalism 'it was the responsibility of political government to *actively* create the conditions within which entrepreneurial and competitive conduct is possible' (Barry, Osborne, and Rose 1996a: 10).

7.2.4 Making Subjects

The governmentality theorists have also extended Foucault's concern with the ways in which apparently neutral, scientific discourses establish particular forms of subjectivity. Indeed, they often conceive of liberalism, welfare state liberalism, and neoliberalism as composed of policies that seek to normalize subjects by drawing on technical discourses from disciplines such as medicine, social science, statistics, and public health. Rose's work on the self, freedom, and psychology provides a more general exploration of contemporary forms of subjectivity (Rose 1999; and also Rose 1989; 1998). Rose argues that the shift from liberalism through welfare liberalism and on to neoliberalism saw the morals and psyche of the individual replace larger units as the main objects of governing rationalities. In his account, early nineteenth-century liberalism, guided by classical political economy, did not seek to manage individual morality so much as to guarantee the security of economic relations. Yet, Rose adds, in the middle of the nineteenth century, liberal governments began to regulate the morals of certain segments of the population. Distinct institutions, such as the poorhouse, appeared to discipline and correct people who had particular pathologies of character.

For Rose, an even more dramatic change occurred with the rise of the welfare state. He argues that early in the twentieth century, statistics, which had been used mainly to calculate national incomes, began to be used to analyse and govern characteristics of the population. In his view, an emerging discourse of 'social' issues focused on problems that afflicted large portions of the population, and a new governmentality arose to prevent these problems spreading further. The welfare state and Keynesianism appear, in Rose's account, as technologies by which experts attempt to govern subjects so as to manage pathologies made visible by new social statistics.

Rose also suggests that neoliberal governmentality constructs and enforces a particular subjectivity. He associates advanced liberalism with an individualization of responsibility. Whereas the welfare state embodies a collectivist ethos, individuals are now constructed as responsible for their own conduct. Neoliberalism promotes freedom, understood as personal choice, at the same time as it deploys psychology to create new forms of control. Psychological technologies increasingly affect how individuals think about almost every aspect of their lives, including sexual relations, work, health, and consumption choices. For Rose, then, advanced liberalism is a form of governmentality in which individuals discipline themselves to use their freedom to make responsible choices. Individuals are expected to analyse themselves and to improve all aspects of their lives in ways that benefit themselves, their community, and the state.

7.3 POST-MARXISM

The post-Marxists, Ernesto Laclau and Chantal Mouffe, are influenced less by the structuralist Marxism of Althusser than by Gramsci's concept of hegemony. Mind you, they modify, and arguably even overturn, Gramsci's humanism by infusing it with the concepts of language and mind developed by structuralists such as Ferdinand de Saussure and Claude Levi-Strauss and then reworked by post-structuralists such as Jacques Derrida and Jacques Lacan. In *Hegemony and Socialist Strategy*, Laclau and Mouffe analyse discourses primarily in terms of the quasi-structural properties of signs. They trace the relations and properties of signs and discourses not to class or other social conflicts but to a quasi-structural psychology associated with Lacan.

7.3.1 Laclau and Mouffe

Laclau and Mouffe set out to rework Marxism in order to dissociate it from foundationalism and essentialism. They reject theories that privilege the economic (rather than the ideological) and social class (rather than discursively constructed identities). In doing so, they redefine hegemony to evoke a submerged strand of left-wing thought that resisted essentialism. Gramsci used hegemony to refer to class domination through ideology: a class could establish an ideological hegemony such that its dominance rested on moral consensus. Gramsci implied, in particular, that bourgeois hegemony explains why the workers consent to capitalism and so why there has not been a revolution. Laclau and Mouffe, in contrast, use the concept of hegemony not just to think about the role of ideologies in a capitalist system defined by its means and relations of production, but also actively to dismiss social theories based on economic and class analysis. In their view, 'the search for a "true" working class and its limits is a false problem, and as such lacks any theoretical or political relevance' (Laclau and Mouffe 1985: 84).

Once Laclau and Mouffe empty Gramsci's concept of hegemony of its Marxist content, they can suggest that historically it has acted as what Derrida calls a supplement. Hegemony has acted as a concept with which to deal with evidence that does not accord with a privileging of the economic base over the ideological superstructure; that is, cases in which the identity of a class does not correspond to its objective social location. Laclau and Mouffe define their project, echoing Derrida's strategy of conceptual inversion, as one of making their concept of hegemony central rather marginal.

Laclau and Mouffe hope that by rethinking Marxist theory, they will redefine the strategy of the left. They argue that the reduction of ideology to class consciousness and thus objective social facts inspires a totalitarianism associated with the belief that Marxist parties can act as a vanguard of the workers. Leninism, they explain, promotes 'political leadership within a class alliance' (Laclau and Mouffe 1985: 55). Leninism legitimates an authoritarian Party or state by suggesting that the Party or state purses the objective class interests of the workers. In contrast, the post-Marxist concept of hegemony is meant to draw attention to the need to provide 'intellectual and moral' leadership to construct subject positions, identities, and discourses. Laclau and Mouffe even write, 'political subjects are not—strictly speaking—classes, but complex "collective wills" ' (Laclau and Mouffe 1985: 67). Hence they conclude that the left should renounce Leninist vanguardism in favour of a historically specific, grassroots struggle.

7.3.2 Discourse Theory

The debt Laclau and Mouffe owe structuralist theories of language appears again in their use of the word discourse as an alternative for ideology. The concept 'discourse' is, after all, less tied to ideas of class and social location than is the concept 'ideology'. Post-Marxists approach a discursive formation as 'a configuration, which in certain contexts of exteriority can be *signified* as a totality' (Laclau and Mouffe 1985: 106). Their language and approach stem from Saussurean linguistics. Saussure argued that the relationship of a signified (or concept) to a signifier (or word) is arbitrary (Saussure 1966). Any signifier can evoke any signified provided only that it differs from other signifiers. Hence the value of any signifier derives solely from relations of difference in a system of signs. Post-structuralists, such as Derrida, are often taken to have argued that the relation between concepts and reality is similarly arbitrary: our concepts too can be understood not as referring to the world but solely in terms of the relations of difference among them within a discourse.

A Saussurean legacy appears in three prominent features of Laclau and Mouffe's concept of discourse. First, Laclau and Mouffe dismiss concerns with the relationship of discourses to a putative extra-discursive reality, such as that of class struggle. Sometimes they imply that the world, including class antagonisms, is a product of discourses. At other times they appear to allow for an extra-discursive reality while contending that only signs in existing discourses can be comprehended. Either way, they rule out attempts to understand discourses as either reflections of or responses to the world. Second, Laclau and Mouffe stress the constitutive role of relations of difference within and between discourses. They imply, for example, that in any given discourse, a binary structure governs concepts of identity such that identities are necessarily defined in opposition to an excluded other. Third, Laclau and Mouffe are dismissive of human agency: they argue that discourses fix or limit what individuals say and do, and they analyse discourses in terms of the structural relations among the signs of which they are composed rather than the use of language by agents.

Laclau and Mouffe tie their concept of discourse not to pre-discursive social facts but to Lacan's psychoanalytic theory. In their account, the subject (or individual) desires 'fullness', conceived as psychological stability based on the integration of the self with the other. Yet, this desire for fullness is thwarted structurally by a primordial 'lack' since there is always doubt as to whether the 'other' has recognized the self. This 'lack' then leads to the other getting blamed for blocked identity. This psychoanalytic theory implies that a quasi-structural antagonism between self and other is integral to the very process of identity formation. Laclau and Mouffe argue that this quasi-structural logic also applies to discourses. On the one hand, discourses exhibit a logic of equivalence in that they try both to integrate many views into one world-view and to stress commonalities in contrast to another, but, on the other hand, they thus exhibit a logic of difference in that they are constituted by an antagonism to the other—an antagonism that always limits the extent to which they can achieve integration. The interplay between equivalence and difference in discourses constitutes hegemonic struggles. So, Laclau and Mouffe argue that a hegemonic discourse increases its bloc of control through the logic of equivalence but its ability to do so is limited by a logic of difference that precludes its achieving full closure and so creates a space for counter-hegemonic discourses to emerge.

7.3.3 Racial Identities

After Laclau and Mouffe wrote *Hegemony and Socialist Strategy*, Laclau concentrated on redefining and defending their approach to discourse analysis, while Mouffe attempted to link their approach to a normative theory of agonistic democracy (Laclau 1990; Butler, Laclau, and Zizek 2000; Mouffe 1993; 2000). The job of applying their work to specific discourses has fallen mainly to students of Laclau from the University of Essex (Howarth, Norval, and Stavrakakis 2000; Howarth and Torfing 2005).[4]

Many attempts to apply post-Marxism have concentrated on discourses connected with identities of gender and race. Post-Marxists argue that subject positions are the constructs of contingent discourses, rather than natural or biological givens. In their view, the subject positions that a discourse creates derive not from pre-discursive social relations or biological facts but from political strategies and the structural relations between concepts in discourses. The appearance of normality that attaches to some subject positions is merely an effect of the hegemonic status of the relevant discourse.

---

[4] Laclau's students have also written books introducing his theory (Howarth 2000; Smith 1998; Torfing 1999).

One attempt to apply post-Marxism to British politics is Anna-Marie Smith's *New Right Discourse on Race and Sexuality*. In the 1950s, Enoch Powell opposed the retreat from imperial power on the grounds that Empire was integral to British identity. Then, once decolonization seemed inevitable, he promoted a new British identity distinct from Empire. Smith writes, 'by representing the Empire as accidental and external, Powell was able to claim that Britishness had remained essentially the same through the imperialist period and would not be significantly altered by decolonization' (Smith 1994: 132). Powellism arose as a discourse of a 'pure' British identity defined against a menacing alien identity. Race was its 'nodal point'. It needed to create an 'other' if it were to postulate some internal space destroyed by decolonization. Hence Powellism reconceived black populations as aliens. Black immigrants represented a disorderly and dangerous other threatening Britain. What is more, Smith adds, Powellism constructed black immigrants as predatory, masculine subjects. In Powell's famous 'rivers of blood' speech, for example, he read from the letter of a 'white woman old-age pensioner' portraying her as the victim of a black invasion that was taking over the once 'respectable' street on which she lived. The influx of blacks had made her a prisoner in her own home. No one came to her aid.

In Smith's account, Powellism exhibits the logics of equivalence and difference that post-Marxists associate with hegemonic discourses. Powellism claimed inclusiveness—a centrist position against 'excessive' immigration—even as it excluded groups. More particularly, Smith identifies several devices by which Powellism pursued equivalence. Powell claimed to represent the interests of both whites and blacks: he 'invoked the image of black supporters...to de-racialize his consistently racist discourse'. Powellism also left a place for the 'good assimilable black' even as it railed against the 'dangerous black invader' (Smith 1994: 140). Powell did not assert that blacks are inherently 'prone to wrong-doing' so much as claim that the immigration of unassimilated individuals leads to social problems, tensions, and violence.

7.3.4 Governance and Policy

Post-Marxists have focused on discursive identities associated with gender and race. There is less work addressed to topics such as parliament, political parties, policy networks, and local politics. One exception is Stephen Griggs and David Howarth's analysis of the campaign against a second runway at Manchester Airport (Griggs and Howarth 2000). In exploring this case study, Griggs and Howarth ask: how did the local village residents and direct action protestors overcome their collective action problem? As post-Marxists, they take the problem of collective action to be less about individual rationality than creating a shared identity through discourse. In the Manchester case, they point to three bases for the creation of such a discourse. First, there was a group identity in that all were affected by the environmental costs of the runway. Second, there was a social network and political entrepreneurs. There was a strong conservationist tradition in the villages and the leaders of the relevant associations had the support of professional people in meeting the costs of the campaign. Third, the campaign forged new political identities aligning 'the Vegans and the Volvos'. According to Griggs and Howarth, this alignment worked because the pro-runway campaign used heavy-handed tactics and stigmatized residents and protestors alike, and because the media linked residents and eco-warriors as fighting a common foe. But, Griggs and Howarth continue, the alignment of the Vegans and the Volvos proved temporary. The protestors lost. The eco-warriors, after being evicted, moved on to the next protest site. The residents split over whether to mount a national-level campaign or to concentrate on the public inquiry. The local authority offered an environmental mitigation package and pursued their case with 'ruthless efficiency.'

7.4 SOCIAL HUMANISM

It is interesting to compare Smith's study of race in Britain with one written some ten years earlier—Paul Gilroy's *There Ain't No Black in the Union Jack*.[5] Both studies concentrate on meanings, and both are inspired by socialist traditions. Yet, whereas Smith's title gives pride of place to 'discourse', Gilroy's subtitle proclaims his study to be one of 'culture and politics', and whereas Smith draws on Laclau and Mouffe with their quasi-structuralist theories of language and psychology, Gilroy adopts a historical and even 'materialist theory of culture'. For Gilroy, culture is both a product of agency and the inherited life-world of agents. His extensive use of black music (reggae and hip hop) suggested that subaltern agents might forge cultures of resistance to a dominant ideology.

Gilroy's concerns with agency, culture, resistance, and history all reflect the influence of the New Left on another tradition of anti-foundationalism. Governmentality theory and post-Marxism draw on structuralism and post-structuralism with their dismissal of subjects, agency, and humanism (Bevir, Hargis, and Rushing 2007). In contrast, the New Left, including E. P. Thompson and Raymond Williams, espoused a humanist Marxism that emphasized the processes by which agents and classes made cultures, especially cultures that resisted capitalism (Thompson 1978).

---

[5] It is well worth pointing out that one legacy of the New Left and cultural studies is an extensive and important literature in post-colonial studies. The combination of an anti-foundational focus on meanings with a post-colonial focus on transnational flows seriously challenges the almost ubiquitous persistence of assumptions about the nation state in the study of British politics—arguably including the very idea of a 'handbook of British Politics'. Tariq Modood's chapter in this volume provides one approach to race. Good examples of the studies of race and transnationalism associated with cultural studies include Centre for Contemporary Cultural Studies (1982) and Gilroy (1993).

7.4.1 The New Left

The New Left preceded Laclau and Mouffe in attempting to liberate Marxism from authoritarian politics and economic determinism. Many members of the New Left responded to the Soviet invasion of Hungary, and knowledge of the brutalities of Stalinism, by leaving the Communist Party and championing an indigenous tradition of radical cultural and moral criticism (Dworkin 1997; Kenny 1995). Historians such as Thompson and Christopher Hill reconstructed a popular tradition of resistance from the Peasant's Revolt through the London Corresponding Society to Chartism (Hill 1965; Thompson 1981; and more recently Stedman Jones 1983). Literary critics such as Williams and Richard Hoggart reconstructed working-class auto-didacticism, and a tradition of literature from the romantics to George Orwell in which the concept of culture challenged capitalism (Williams 1958; Hoggart 1957).

Williams provided arguably the most influential theory of culture from within the New Left. He appealed to culture as a way of explaining aspects of social and political life that did not fit with economic reductionism. He suggested that post-war economic prosperity had dampened the class struggle in a way that made culture an ever more pertinent counter to capitalist values. In doing so, he transformed the concept of culture. Whereas culture had often been associated almost exclusively with high culture, he conceived of mass culture as a site of political dissent and struggle. In *The Long Revolution*, for example, he argued that political battles were being fought out in the world of art and ideas (Williams 1961). He rejected the idea that the economic base determines the cultural superstructure. In his view, the impossibility of dominant groups entirely controlling social processes means that there is always space for subordinate groups to contest ruling ideologies.

7.4.2 Cultural Studies

While Williams and Thompson made culture and agency prominent concepts in the New Left, the emergence of cultural studies owed much to Stuart Hall and his work from 1968 to 1979 as Director of the Centre for Contemporary Cultural Studies at the University of Birmingham. Indeed, the relationship of the New Left to cultural studies was sometimes problematic. On the one hand, there is no denying the importance of the New Left as personal and intellectual influences on a younger generation who pursued critical approaches to the study of culture. Thompson's approach to a history from below inspired numerous explorations of the lived experience of subordinated groups—women, racial minorities, gays and lesbians, and peasants, as well as the working class. On the other hand, however, the New Left often remained at least loosely tied to an orthodox socialist historiography that privileged the economy, production, and class relations (Bevir and Trentmann 2002a). Students of race, such as Hall, and gender, such as Angela McRobbie, sometimes found themselves fighting against the privileging of idealized white male working-class cultures from which the racism and sexism had been written out.[6]

Hall followed the New Left in conceiving of culture as a form of expression that is manifest not only in high art but also in the everyday life of subordinated groups. But, in the late 1960s, an encounter with anti-foundationalism and post-structuralism led him to modify the New Left's notion of lived experience.[7] Williams, and especially Thompson, tended to describe cultures of resistance as responses to experiences of the brutal realities of capitalism. In contrast, Hall now paid more attention to the way in which ideological traditions constructed people's experiences (Hall and Jefferson 1993). The point was not to return to the old view that ideologies represented a false consciousness that hid the reality of the class struggle. The point was, rather, to insist on the importance of ideology as a site of struggle for social change. Other authors have recently explored the ways in which even capitalism and markets have been constructed in part through cultures of resistance (Bevir and Trentmann 2002b; 2004).

To bridge the gap between culturalism and anti-foundationalism, Hall turned to Gramsci's concept of hegemony. For Hall, hegemony is a specific process of ideological struggle—a process that he understands in terms of a humanist historicism rather than the quasi-structural psychology adopted by Laclau and Mouffe (Hall 1988; 1986). Culture thus appears as a site of hegemonic control and struggle: it reinforces present power relations while allowing space for dissent and resistance. Popular culture can reinforce hegemonic ideas and identities, notably by representing them as, say, natural, inexorable, or rational. But popular culture can also be a site of resistance by subordinated groups. Indeed, Hall's concern with agency and resistance spills over into an emphasis on the consumption as well as the production of culture. Subordinate groups can resist cultural discourses and symbols by consuming them in ways that draw on local patterns of dissent.

7.4.3 Thatcherism and After

Social humanists characteristically explore ruling ideologies and resistance to them. The most obvious examples have been studies of Thatcherism and New Labour. In the 1980s, Hall offered an account of Thatcherism as a hegemonic project characterized by 'authoritarian populism'. In his view, Labour attempted to be both a working-class party and a responsible caretaker of a capitalist economy. When the

---

[6] Much gender theory is anti-foundational. For a detailed discussion of feminism see Vicky Randall's contribution to this volume.

[7] Hall identifies with an 'eclecticism' that has little concern for coherence. Typically, he flirts with a range of fashionable Marxist terms—from the Althusserian 'articulation' to signification—inserting them into a broadly constructivist and yet sociological approach to ideologies and cultures of resistance. His lingering debt to the New Left appears in his constant return to agency, practice, resistance, and (in my view rather problematically) modernist sociological categories. Compare Proctor (2004).

economy declined, Labour tried to sustain its caretaker role by adopting corporatist management strategies. It thereby weakened its connection with the workers. The failings of the left thus set the scene for Thatcherism. Thatcherism aligned the neglected workers with anti-collectivism as an alternative solution to the problems of the economy. It presented neoliberal ideas as the common sense of the British people. Hall explains, 'the essence of the British people was identified with self-reliance and personal responsibility, as against the image of the over-taxed individual, enervated by welfare state "coddling" ' (Hall 1983: 29; and also see Hall 1988). This right-wing populism combined themes from a tradition of 'organic Toryism—nation, family, duty, authority, standards, traditionalism—with the aggressive themes of a revived neoliberalism—self-interest, competitive individualism, anti-statism' (Hall 1983: 29). However, Hall adds, Thatcherism governed through authoritarianism. It brought an 'intensification of state control over every sphere of economic life', the decline of democratic institutions, and even the curtailment of formal liberties. The tensions between Thatcherism's populism and its authoritarianism provided a space in which the left might recoup its ideological losses.

No doubt New Labour likes to think it recouped these losses. Social humanists generally disagree. Hall himself portrays New Labour as little more than a continuation of neoliberalism. He argues that New Labour is a hybrid regime, combining a dominant neoliberalism with a subordinate social democratic notion of active government, and able to hold these two discourses together only through the constant use of 'spin' (Hall 2003). Younger social humanists, in contrast, have been more attentive to the ways in which New Labour has transformed both social democratic and neoliberal traditions. Some suggest that New Labour has given up on grand ideological visions of a transformed society, and turned instead to modernization in accord with social theories that purport to analyse inexorable changes in the world (Finlayson 2003). Others argue, in addition, that the social theories on which New Labour most relies are communitarianism and new institutionalism (Bevir 2005; also see Moss and O'Loughlin 2005). They suggest that New Labour's policies deploy these theories in an attempt to transform state and society.

7.4.4 Governance and Resistance

Social humanists have explored the ideologies associated with political parties. They have also studied other traditions of governance and cultures of resistance. Social humanists decentre governance. They show how several different traditions contribute to the construction of the complex patterns of rule found in contemporary Britain.[8] Even when governments promote policies inspired by a given discourse, the formation and implementation of these policies involves diverse actors who imbue the policies with different content against the background of other traditions. These

---

[8] The literature includes Bevir and Rhodes (2003; 2006); Clark and Gains (2007); Clarke and Newman (1997); Dudley (2003); Morrell (2006); Newman (2001); and for comparative studies Bevir, Rhodes, and Weller (2003).

actors, whether intentionally or inadvertently, draw on diverse cultures to resist the governing narratives.

Dissent and resistance are, of course, found far beyond Westminster and Whitehall. Social humanists such as Thompson and Williams argued, as we have seen, that citizens are situated agents who can and do draw upon local cultures to express scepticism and resistance to governing discourses. More recently, social humanists have explored resistance among street-level bureaucrats and citizens. Several chapters in a volume on *Governance, Consumption, and Citizenship*, which I co-edited with Frank Trentmann, show how social movements, street-level bureaucrats, and citizens have actively developed their own beliefs and narratives of 'choice' in explicit contrast to government narratives. John Clarke argues, for example, that the meanings of choice are contextually bounded not universal, and that service providers and citizens alike are sceptical about official discourses (Clarke 2007). His interviews in policy areas such as policing and health reveal a resistance to the appropriateness of 'consumer' and 'choice' as identities and activities. Service providers and service users alike believe that the idea of choice sits uneasily alongside values such as equity. Citizens resist the language of choice and shopping as inappropriate for policing and health care.

Social humanists emphasize the contingent, diverse, and contested nature of governance. In doing so, they imply that governmentality theorists and post-Marxists adopt too monolithic an analysis of discourses such as neoliberalism. Governmentality theorists, with their debt to ideas of social control, focus almost exclusively on official discourses and policies, paying little attention to how these are received or enacted at local levels. In contrast, social humanists, with their debt to the idea of traditions of resistance, explore the diverse ways in which street-level bureaucrats and citizens articulate and practise consumption and citizenship in their everyday lives, often in ways that challenge government narratives. The focus thus shifts from the discourse of policy-makers to the fractured and diverse processes by which discourses and policies are translated into actions.

7.5 CONCLUSION

Anti-foundationalism is an epistemological position that has implications for ontology and social explanation. While in principle it is compatible with all kinds of approaches to political science, in practice it has been absorbed by a range of overlapping critical, socialist theories. On the one hand, the different socialist traditions do much to explain the different concepts and topics associated with the Anglo-Foucauldians, post-Marxists, and social humanists. Yet, on the other hand, we would do well to recognize that, whatever their differences, anti-foundationalists have developed a broadly shared research programme. That research programme contains at least the following four themes:

- A commitment to studying *meanings* (beliefs, discourses, and traditions) as constitutive of social and political practices.
- A belief in the *contingency* and contestability of meanings, and so an opposition to claims that a culture, web of beliefs, or practice is natural, inexorable, or inherently rational.
- A commitment to *historical* explanations of meanings, where historicity conveys contingency thereby undercutting appeals to formal models, fixed institutions, or reified social patterns.
- A use of historical *critiques* to reveal the contingency of webs of belief, which understand themselves as natural, inexorable, or inherently rational.

So, anti-foundationalists portray British government as a historically specific and contestable endeavour. They highlight the importance of exploring the changing meanings that constitute British economic, political, social, and cultural practices in broader post-imperial, European, and other transnational settings. They encourage studies of changing patterns of governance and conceptions of politics, notably in relation to how practices of statecraft are conceived in relation to their objects of intervention. They encourage studies of how society and its discontents have been understood, especially in the context of traditions of social thought and protest and their role in framing patterns of sociality, inequality, and resistance. And they encourage studies of the role of the cultural domain in these transformations and the separation of culture as a discrete realm with its own institutions, forms, and conventions.

The anti-foundationalists' emphasis on meanings, contingency, historical narratives, and critique opens up the study of British politics. Anti-foundationalists have initiated dialogues between British politics and historiography, cultural studies, and post-colonial studies. In addition, they have posed theoretical and interpretive challenges for other students of British politics. They have challenged a lingering, lukewarm positivism that tries to hide questions of meaning and contingency behind appeals to social facts, institutions, structures, and correlations. If other political scientists take up this challenge, the benefits would include greater philosophical sophistication and recognition of new research topics.

REFERENCES

BARRY, A., OSBORNE, T., and ROSE, N. 1996a. 'Introduction'. Pp. 1–18 in Barry, Osborne, and Rose 1996b.
——— (eds.) 1996b. *Foucault and Political Reason*. London: UCL Press.
BEVIR, M. 1999. *The Logic of the History of Ideas*. Cambridge: Cambridge University Press.
——— 2005. *New Labour: A Critique*. London: Routledge.

—— Hargis, J., and Rushing, S. (eds.) 2007. *Histories of Postmodernism*. New York: Routledge.

—— and Rhodes, R. 2003. *Interpreting British Governance*. London: Routledge.

—— —— 2006. *Governance Stories*. London: Routledge.

—— —— and Weller, P. (eds.) 2003. *Traditions of Governance: History and Diversity*, special issue of *Public Administration*, 81/1.

—— and Trentmann, F. 2002a. 'Critique within Capitalism: Historiographical Problems, Theoretical Perspectives'. Pp. 1–25 in Bevir and Trentmann 2002b.

—— —— (eds.) 2002b. *Critiques of Capital in Modern Britain and America: Transatlantic Exchanges 1800 to the Present Day*. Basingstoke: Palgrave Macmillan.

—— —— (eds.) 2004. *Markets in Historical Contexts: Ideas and Politics in the Modern World*. Cambridge: Cambridge University Press.

—— —— (eds.) 2007. *Governance, Consumers, and Citizens: Agency and Resistance in Contemporary Politics*. Basingstoke: Palgrave Macmillan.

Burchell, G., Gordon, C., and Miller, P. (eds.) 1991. *The Foucault Effect: Studies in Governmentality*. London: Harvester Wheatsheaf.

Butler, J., Laclau, E., and Zizek, S. 2000. *Contingency, Hegemony, and Universality*. London: Verso.

Centre for Contemporary Cultural Studies 1982. *The Empire Strikes Back: Race and Racism in 70s Britain*. London: Hutchinson.

Clark, K., and Gains, F. (eds.) 2007. *Constructing Delivery: Implementation as an Interpretive Process*, special issue of *Critical Policy Analysis*, 1/2.

Clarke, J. 2007. ' "It's Not Like Shopping": Citizens, Consumers and the Reform of Public Services'. In Bevir and Trentmann 2007.

—— and Newman, J. 1997. *The Managerial State: Power, Politics, and Ideology in the Remaking of Social Welfare*. London: Sage.

—— —— Smith, N., Vidler, E., and Westmarland, L. 2007. *Creating Citizen-Consumers: Changing Publics and Changing Public Services*. London: Sage.

Dudley, G. 2003. 'Ideas, Bargaining and Flexible Policy Communities: Policy Change and the Case of the Oxford Transport Strategy'. *Public Administration*, 81: 433–58.

Dworkin, D. 1997. *Cultural Marxism in Postwar Britain: History, the New Left, and the Origins of Cultural Studies*. Durham, NC: Duke University Press.

Finlayson, A. 2003. *Making Sense of New Labour*. London: Lawrence and Wishart.

Foucault, M. 1973. *Birth of the Clinic: An Archaeology of Medical Perception*. London: Tavistock.

—— 1977. *Discipline and Punish: The Birth of the Prison*. Harmondsworth: Penguin.

—— 1978–85. *The History of Sexuality*, vol. i: *An Introduction*, vol. ii: *The Use of Pleasure*, and vol. iii: *The Care of the Self*, trans. R. Hurley. New York: Pantheon.

—— 1989. *Madness and Civilization: A History of Insanity in the Age of Reason*. London: Routledge.

—— 1991. 'Governmentality'. Pp. 87–104 in Burchell, Gordon, and Miller 1991.

—— 2004. *Naissance de la biopolitique: cours au Collège de France (1978–1979)*. Paris: Galimard.

Gilroy, P. 1987. *There Ain't No Black in the Union Jack: The Cultural Politics of Race and Nation*. London: Hutchinson.

—— 1993. *The Black Atlantic: Modernity and Double Consciousness*. Cambridge, Mass.: Harvard University Press.

Griggs, S., and Howarth, D. 2000. 'New Environmental Movements and Direct Action Protests: The Campaign against Manchester Airport's Second Runway'. In Howarth, Norval, and Stavrakakis 2000.

HALL, S. 1983. 'The Great Moving Right Show'. In S. Hall and M. Jacques (eds.), *The Politics of Thatcherism*. London: Lawrence and Wishart.

——1986. 'Cultural Studies: Two Paradigms'. In R. Collins (ed.), *Media, Culture and Society*. Londo: Sage.

——1988. *The Hard Road to Renewal: Thatcherism and the Crisis of the Left*. London: Verso.

——2003. 'New Labour's Double Shuffle'. *Soundings*, 24: 10–24.

——and JEFFERSON, T. (eds.) 1993. *Resistance through Rituals: Youth Subcultures in Post-war Britain*. London: Routledge.

——LUMLEY, B., and McLENNAN, B. 1978. 'Politics and Ideology: Gramsci'. In *On Ideology*, Centre for Contemporary Cultural Studies. London: Hutchison.

HILL, C. 1965. *Intellectual Origins of the English Revolution*. Oxford: Clarendon Press.

HOGGART, R. 1957. *The Uses of Literacy: Aspects of Working Class Life*. London: Chatto and Windus.

HOWARTH, D. 2000. *Discourse*. Buckingham: Open University Press.

——NORVAL, A., and STAVRAKAKIS, Y. (eds.) 2000. *Discourse Theory and Political Analysis: Identities, Hegemonies, and Social Change*. Manchester: Manchester University Press.

——and TORFING, J. (eds.) 2005. *Discourse Theory in European Politics: Identity, Policy and Government*. Basingstoke: Palgrave.

KENNY, M. 1995. *The First New Left*. London: Lawrence and Wishart.

LACLAU, E. 1990. *New Reflections on the Revolution of Our Time*. London: Verso.

——and MOUFFE, C. 1985. *Hegemony and Socialist Strategy: Towards a Radical Democratic Politics*. New York: Verso.

LEMKE, T. 2001. ' "The Birth of Bio-Politics": Michel Foucault's Lecture at the Collège de France on Neo-Liberal Governmentality'. *Economy and Society*, 30: 190–207.

MORRELL, K. 2006. 'Policy as Narrative: New Labour's Reform of the National Health Service'. *Public Administration*, 84: 367–85.

MOSS, G., and O'LOUGHLIN, B. 2005. 'New Labour's Information Age Policy Programme: An Ideology Analysis'. *Journal of Political Ideologies*, 10: 165–83.

MOUFFE, C. 1993. *The Return of the Political*. London: Verso.

——2000. *The Democratic Paradox*. London: Verso.

NEWMAN, J. 2001. *Modernising Governance: New Labour, Policy, and Society*. London: Sage.

PROCTOR, J. 2004. *Stuart Hall*. London: Routledge.

RESCH, R. 1992. *Althusser and the Renewal of Marxist Social Theory*. Berkeley: University of California Press.

ROCKMORE, T., and SINGER, B. (eds.) 1992. *Anti-Foundationalism: Old and New*. Philadelphia: Temple University Press.

ROSE, N. 1989. *Governing the Soul: The Shaping of the Private Self*. London: Routledge.

——1998. *Inventing Ourselves: Psychology, Power, and Personhood*. Cambridge: Cambridge University Press.

——1999. *Powers of Freedom: Reframing Political Thought*. Cambridge: Cambridge University Press.

SAUSSURE, F. 1966. *Course in General Linguistics*, ed. C. Bally and A. Sechehaye, trans. W. Baskin. New York: McGraw-Hill.

SMITH, A.-M. 1994. *New Right Discourse on Race and Sexuality: Britain, 1968–1990*. Cambridge: Cambridge University Press.

——1998. *Laclau and Mouffe: The Radical Democratic Imaginary*. London: Routledge.

STEDMAN JONES, G. 1983. 'Rethinking Chartism'. In *Languages of Class*. Cambridge: Cambridge University Press.

—— 1996. 'The Determinist Fix: Some Obstacles to the Further Development of the Linguistic Approach to History in the 1990s'. *History Workshop*, 42: 19–35.

THOMPSON, E. 1978. 'The Poverty of Theory: Or an Orrey of Errors'. In *The Poverty of Theory and Other Essays*. London: Merlin.

—— 1981. *The Making of the English Working Class*. London: Harmondsworth.

TORFING, J. 1999. *New Theories of Discourse: Laclau, Mouffe, and Zizek*. Oxford: Blackwell.

UEBEL, T. 1996. 'Anti-Foundationalism and the Vienna Circle's Revolution in Philosophy'. *British Journal of the Philosophy of Science*, 47: 415–40.

WILLIAMS, R. 1958. *Culture and Society*. London: Chatto and Windus.

—— 1961. *The Long Revolution*. London: Chatto and Windus.

CHAPTER 8

FEMINISM

VICKY RANDALL

8.1 INTRODUCTION

FEMINISM as it reformed and regalvanized from the late 1960s was a revolutionary or 'transformative' political movement. It opposed and criticized practically everything about the then status quo. Feminism in the intervening four decades has undoubtedly impacted, in both intended and unintended ways, on British society and politics. It has also made itself felt within the 'academy'.

This chapter is concerned with the extent and manner in which feminism as a critical perspective has informed scholarly analyses of British politics. Identifying and assessing this impact is no easy task; it is complicated by the broader consequences of feminism as a movement for British politics itself, and by the diversity of forms of feminist thinking. The main conclusion must be that feminism has had a considerable impact, especially in terms of subject matter but also in modifying normative and conceptual understandings. Even so its overall influence has been limited in some significant respects, which have to do with features of feminist discourse itself and possibly also with the predominant character of 'the political science of British politics'.

The chapter begins with an account of British feminism as an evolving dialogue. It assesses the impact of feminism on the study of British politics, in comparison with its impact in other areas of social science and the humanities, and even as compared with other fields of politics such as international relations. It then goes on to examine that impact in greater detail, under the heads of normative thrust, epistemology, subject matter, concepts, and methods.

8.2 Feminism in Britain

The heyday of second-wave feminism as an activist political movement in Britain was in the 1970s and early 80s. From the start it was subject to internal division and bitter arguments, so that it has always been difficult to generalize about what feminists stand for. The very term implies an identification with women, or 'woman', and generally feminism is prompted by some resentment of injustice towards women and a demand for change, but beyond this differences open up concerning the nature and causes of injustice, the desired end-state, strategies, and so forth. In the early days, three strands of feminism were generally identified.

The most distinctively new strand was Radical feminism which put the division and opposition between men and women before anything else. Whilst in some sense extreme, and in the long term unsustainable, this approach played an essential role in legitimizing and clearing intellectual space for examining men–women relationships without having immediately to factor in class, race, culture, and so forth. It highlighted the political character of the supposedly private sphere (the 'personal') and advanced the notion of 'patriarchy', or the system of male rule. It also catalysed the emergence of a series of key issues for women—abortion, rape, domestic violence, incest, pornography.

Over time a new more 'cultural' form of Radical feminism emerged which positively celebrated women's difference from men. This more pro-woman version, though less directly political, also generated new concepts and questions for political analysis, especially to the extent it gave rise to a specific philosophic strand of 'standpoint feminism', discussed below.

'Liberal' feminism had roots in eighteenth-century Enlightenment thinking but by the late twentieth century reflected a kind of pragmatic or commonsense approach. It tended to take the existing social and political framework as given and look for ways of improving women's position within it. But it also evolved, particularly in response to emerging issues and criticism from within the movement, for instance taking on board the arguments for positive discrimination (Radcliffe-Richards 1980), and developing the critique of the public–private distinction.

Third was Marxist, later socialist, feminism, which initially sought to accommodate feminism to a Marxist capitalism-focused framework but later sought a more balanced combination. In the process, socialist feminists came to make the by now widely adopted distinction between 'sex'—the biologically given—and 'gender' or the social construction of masculinity and femininity built upon it. Socialist feminism also contributed some of the most thoughtful early analysis of the relationship between gender and the state (see for instance McIntosh 1978). There is a recent tendency to erase socialist feminism as a distinct approach but we should underestimate neither its past contribution to feminist thinking nor, as Lynne Segal (1999) emphasizes, its continuing relevance.

Feminism as movement and as ideas has changed almost beyond recognition since this time. To some extent practical politics and thought have changed in parallel.

First and probably inevitably has been a tendency over time towards increasing diversification and fragmentation. Sparked especially by black women's critique of the racism of white feminism, but also by conflicts over sexuality, this took the form in particular of an intensifying politics of identity in which it became very difficult for any group of feminists to claim to be speaking for others, let alone some universal category of 'women'. At a more pragmatic level the way through this has often been seen as a 'politics of coalition', 'transversalism'[1] or contingent solidarity between differently identified women's groups. Intellectually however it strengthened the appeal of post-structural approaches. Post-structural feminism, to be discussed further below, is of course primarily concentrated in the academy, but does constitute a major new development in feminist thinking—assuming we accept that it is possible to be both post-structuralist and feminist.

The second trend has been the increasing assimilation of feminist activists and much of the feminist agenda into the political mainstream. One trigger was the advent of Thatcherism, prompting many socialist feminists to join the Labour Party and engage in more conventional forms of politics. With this incidentally went a reappraisal of earlier rather monolithic conceptions of the state, and a growing interest in women's political representation. Such feminist integration received a further boost with the advent of the New Labour government in 1997.

As an autonomous movement, however, British feminism is by now much depleted. Political activism persists, as in the Fawcett Society, the women's refuge movement, and the Women's Environmental Network, and even the thriving 'F-word' website launched in 2001 and successfully targeting young British feminists.

For some feminists these developments amount to 'deradicalization'; to some other observers and even self-styled feminists like Ros Coward (1999) they signal that we are entering a 'post-feminist' era (a suggestion, however, that would seem clearly refuted by the Equal Opportunities Commission's latest report (2007)[2]). At any rate such changes have made it more difficult to specify a clear feminist political agenda. By the same token they make it more difficult to identify and evaluate a specific 'impact of feminism'.

8.3 FEMINISM WITHIN THE ACADEMY

Feminism as a movement has inevitably altered British society; it has seeped into our culture and more directly impacted on the nature of British politics. But in examining its impact on the study of British politics, we need also to consider feminism as a critical perspective within the academy. Whilst feminism has had a

---

[1] For a discussion of this term see Yuval-Davis (2006).
[2] See *Sex and Power: Who Runs Britain 2007?* which details women's under-representation in the senior ranks of key institutional arenas: 'Progress is painfully slow and at risk of going into reverse'.

Table 8.1 Percentage of female staff in politics departments in Britain

Year	2002	2007
All female staff (as percentage of total staff)	24.2	27.0
Female professors (as percentage of total professors)	11.5	12.5

considerable impact on scholarship altogether, the form and intensity of that impact has varied between subject areas and disciplines. Perhaps understandably it has been greatest in fields like sociology and literature. When it comes to politics, we may first need to make a distinction between the study of politics and political science as a discipline. The study of politics—but this begs the question to be taken up shortly of what we mean by politics—especially where it has been undertaken from a sociological disciplinary perspective may well be more obviously influenced by feminism than is political science. Additionally, within the broad field of political studies, political theory and especially international relations seem to have been more influenced by feminism than empirical, including country-based, political studies.

To the extent this is true for the study of British politics, I suggest it is for a combination of reasons. Although feminism is innately political, it brings a normative and conceptual perspective on politics that runs counter to conventional understandings. Traditionally mainstream political activity has seemed a very masculine world in which neither feminist nor feminine notions have much place. Partly reflecting this, perhaps, political science as a profession has been extremely 'male-dominated' (as compared say with sociology or history). The numbers and proportion of women within the discipline have only slowly been increasing (see Table 8.1[3]). Within the senior ranks progress has been still slower.

Of course there is no reason to suppose that individual female political scientists will necessarily be feminist or that male political scientists will not—although it must be said that most research into women/gender and politics in Britain is undertaken by women (Childs and Krook 2006). However the demographics are significant for what they say about the likely culture and power structure of political science as a profession.

Beyond this there may be further factors concerning the character of political science in Britain. There is no consensus on this matter. One view is that political science in general and specifically in Britain is extremely pluralistic in terms of approaches and methodologies (Goodin and Klingemann 1995). Furthermore Hay (2001: 11) has recently claimed that the trend in the study of British politics is towards 'A broadening and re-specification of the legitimate terrain of political analysis and

[3] I am extremely grateful to Richard Topf for these figures. The available data—based on respondents to a survey—incidentally show that female staff are on average considerably younger than male staff: nearly 73 per cent of women but only 60 per cent of men were born in 1960 or later. This does suggest that one factor in women's under-representation in the professorial ranks may be the age distribution.

a growing recognition of extrapolitical variables (such as cultural and/or economic factors)'. Others such as Marsh and Savigny (2004: 155) argue that 'political science, particularly US political science, is still dominated by a positivist epistemology and, particularly, by behaviouralist and rational choice approaches that are underpinned by that positivism' and point to specific 'positivist gatekeepers' such as key journals. Far from diminishing within British political science, some believe these traits are strengthening (Aspinall 2006). To the extent that such fears are well founded, they imply a disciplinary framework not highly receptive to feminist influences. It is perhaps significant that the major impact of feminist ideas in international relations coincided with a strong 'post-positivist' turn and explicit ensuing debate about basic theoretical assumptions (see Steans 2003).

8.4 FEMINISM AND THE STUDY OF BRITISH POLITICS

We can now examine more closely feminism's impact on the study of British politics. As already noted feminism's influence has occurred in many different ways, including changes in British politics as the object of study, but the emphasis here is more on the impact of feminist analysis and thought. In assessing the impact, there is an inevitable tension between a sense of what possibly feminism could contribute and what it actually has contributed. Gauging the potential impact is further complicated by the way in which feminism has been a constantly evolving dialogue rather than one unified coherent position. Even so there are ways in which its implications—normative, conceptual, ontological—could be far-reaching. To provide a coherent account, I consider feminism's impact under five heads— normative thrust, epistemology with particular reference to a feminist standpoint, subject matter, conceptual frameworks, and methods. In each case I discuss what feminism has contributed, the limits to that contribution, and related to this the extent to which its insights have been incorporated into the mainstream of British politics scholarship.

8.4.1 Normative Thrust

Feminism's many, often quarrelsome voices share a strongly normative tone and demand change. We could then expect feminism to provide the basis first for a critical assessment of developments in British politics and second for an effective critique of the way that British politics is studied. Without doubt over time the tone of analyses of British politics has become much less overtly sexist, though this partly reflects wider cultural diffusion of many feminist assumptions, together with the stronger female presence within the country's political elite. But feminism has had less obviously transformative effects than in cognate fields of study.

Initially feminist perspectives informed a telling critique of the 'sexist' masculine lens through which British politics was studied. This lens either ignored women, subsumed them in supposedly gender-neutral generalizations such as 'mankind', considered them only in relation to significant male others, or, finally, portrayed them in terms of traditional and unexamined stereotypes.

Subsequently feminism was the basis for cogent critiques of organizing concepts in (British) political analysis such as the public–private divide and citizenship (see below). Feminist perspectives also contributed to a significant critique of both the 'male breadwinner' British welfare state and its analysis in the mainstream litera-ture, although much of this was undertaken by sociologists (for a valuable overview see Lewis 1997). All these have to some extent been taken up in the mainstream literature.

Despite having to satisfy the discipline's expectations of empirical rigour at the same time as negotiating the increasing diversities both of women and of feminism, feminist-inspired assessments of a whole range of aspects of British politics have if anything grown in number and sophistication in recent years. Authors have found ways of indicating and formulating their basic value orientation. In assessing policy and institutions, they have used expressions like 'woman-friendly', 'gender equality',[4] and 'gender justice' as normative anchor points. A current example is the edited volume (Annersley, Gains, and Rummery 2007), entitled *Women and New Labour*, in which Wilson (2007) notes that all the contributing authors, despite using differently labelled yardsticks, share a common underlying set of values.

Alternatively they have implicitly responded to charges of overgeneralization by relating their assessment to a specific category of women. The journal *Critical Social Policy*, for instance, recently carried two articles assessing the implications of policy for mothers: Carol Smart (2004) discusses the implications of a growing concern with 'father's rights' and Ruth Lister (2006) the implications of New Labour's otherwise laudable preoccupation with child welfare.

Valuable as such feminist criticism has been, it has tended to be somewhat piece-meal. There has been no comprehensive critique of the British (masculine) state and politics, such as might be derived either from a Radical feminist or a standpoint feminist (discussed in the next section) position, comparable to feminist state analysis in International Relations. As suggested earlier, this may reflect the more general dif-ficulty facing radical critique in the study of British politics. Ideological perspectives such as feminism are perceived to lack credibility because of their prior commitment to a particular value position, and because their claims about non-decisions, the concealed faces of power, and so forth seem to fly in the face of common sense and

---

[4] As used for instance by Lewis and Campbell (2007) in their appraisal of New Labour's work/family balance policies.

are open to the charge of non-falsifiability. And yet to the extent that 'Sex class is so deep as to be invisible',[5] meaning male power and authority are normalized and naturalized, it is often difficult to detect and expose with standard political science tools.

8.4.2 Epistemology

Normative perspective obviously overlaps with epistemology. In fact the greater part of feminist-influenced scholarly analysis of British politics has assumed a conventional epistemology; that is, a fairly unreflective empiricism. Nonetheless it is necessary to consider two other kinds of epistemological stance in this connection, standpoint feminism and (feminist) postmodernism.

Standpoint feminism can be seen as logically rooted in cultural feminism, although Hartsock (1983), who provided its most sustained and political formulation, was originally a Marxist. Echoing the idea of the privileged consciousness of the proletariat, she suggested women, as a historically oppressed category, potentially had a superior understanding of reality, combining the received masculine account with the insights of their own distinctive position and experience of production, especially their contribution to subsistence and their role in child-rearing. As in the Marxist formulation, women could not arrive at this privileged understanding on their own; it would need to be refined through a feminist prism. However the resulting feminist standpoint could be a powerful analytical tool.

Hartsock's suggestions rapidly came under fire for generalizing about women's experience, for appearing to confirm socially conservative gender stereotypes, and for 'essentialism', and in later versions she watered this strong thesis down (Hartsock 1998). Yet, for all the problems with the idea of a feminist standpoint, it has been seen, within the field of International Relations, by writers like Ann Tickner (1988) as offering the basis for a powerful critique both of Realism and of militarized conceptions of the state. Such a perspective has also been evident in the field of British politics as in attempts, discussed further below, to ascertain whether women in politics do indeed speak 'in a different voice', or identify with 'an ethic of care'. But arguably scholars could have proceeded further down a road which, whatever its scientific shortcomings, promises to open up the field imaginatively and expand the range of questions and hypotheses brought to bear.

Whilst standpoint feminism could be seen as the one distinctively feminist epistemology, reflecting a particular feminist ontology, postmodernism[6] emerged independently of feminism and to a very mixed feminist reception. It has also incidentally inspired some of the most devastating criticisms of standpoint feminism. Many feminists have been drawn to postmodernism for reasons including the way it problematizes and delegitimizes traditional masculine discourses; its sensitivity

[5] The opening sentence of Shulamith Firestone's pioneering *Dialectic of Sex* (1970).
[6] For convenience sake I am using this as the generic term but it is understood here to include post-structuralism, post-Marxism, and discourse analysis.

to aspects of discourse construction which are of great relevance in thinking about gender relations; the way it appears to provide a solution, conceptually at least, to the political challenge of female diversity; and more specifically the Foucauldian focus on the micro-politics of resistance resonating with feminist interrogation of the public–private divide. However to the extent it calls into question the subject 'woman' and the meta-narrative of feminism itself (Butler 1992), postmodernism is a two-edged sword.

In practice thoroughgoing postmodernist feminist approaches have not been extensively adopted in studies of British politics, certainly not in those based in empirical political science, but drawn on more selectively. So for instance Pringle and Watson (1990) used post-Marxist insights to question monolithic conceptions of the patriarchal state and to demonstrate the constructed and contingent character of 'women's interests'. More recently Karen Bird (2005) has analysed 'discourses' of 'woman', 'man', and 'gender' in her analysis of House of Commons debates in New Labour's first term, while (sociologists) Ball and Charles (2006) develop the notion of discursive opportunity in analysing gendered policy-making in the Welsh Assembly.

8.4.3 Subject Matter

Perhaps feminism's major achievement in regard to British politics as a field of study has been to dramatically expand its subject matter. Initially this often involved ensuring that women were acknowledged as a distinct category in political analysis, rather than ignored or subsumed. Some of its more radical feminist detractors dismissed such activity as 'adding women in' but this was always, and continues to be, necessary, and in any case almost inevitably leads on to more searching questions about reasons for the patterns observed.

A substantial literature by now describes and analyses sex differences in rates and forms of political participation, especially voting. Rosie Campbell (2006) pursues the question of a British voting 'gender-gap', including an analysis of data from the 2005 general election. Numerous studies have also focused on women's access to and experience in the House of Commons, with the emphasis shifting from explaining women's relative absence to assessing the consequences of women's growing presence or 'feminization' for the content and normative assumptions of policy, and for styles of political behaviour (as in Childs 2004). Other studies examine women's experience in political parties, local government, and so forth. The continuing need to bring women into the picture is illustrated in Lowndes's (2004) criticism of typically gender-silent discussions of the fashionable concept of 'social capital' in the local British context.

With the growing recognition of diversity and its attendant responsibilities within British feminism, feminist-inspired studies have also analysed the experience and concerns of specific categories of previously marginalized women—or at least women marginalized as far as the study of politics is concerned. Brown (2006) for instance considers the complexities of British Muslim female identity and rights, whilst Afshar,

Aitken, and Franks (2005) explore the strategies of a group of Muslim women in West Yorkshire negotiating competing claims and pressures of their community, rising Islamophobia, and forms of feminism. Phillips and Dustin (2004) provide a critique of recent UK policy on forced marriages.

But in addition feminism has helped to bring a range of new issues, formerly perceived to be essentially private or social, onto the public political agenda, and thence into the purview of policy studies, such as domestic violence (see for instance Abrar, Lovenduski, and Margetts 2000), abortion, and childcare (Randall 2000). With the development of 'women's policy machinery', itself an outgrowth of feminist activism, there has been considerable research interest in experiences of 'state feminism', including latterly bodies such as the Women and Equality Unit in Whitehall (see for instance Squires and Wickham-Jones 2004; Breitenbach et al. 2002).

A broadly feminist perspective has further inspired an impressive literature exploring gender aspects of New Labour politics and policy. Thus Russell (2005) provides a perceptive analysis of the gender politics of Labour Party 'modernization'. The contributors to *Women and New Labour* (Annersley, Gains, and Rummery 2006) offer a wide-ranging assessment of the extent and consequences, for women and for gender more broadly, of 'feminization' under Blair. Some of this literature is not, incidentally, political science strictly understood. For instance McRobbie (2000), who discusses the implications both for women and for feminism of the 'Third Way', is a cultural theorist, while Lewis and Campbell (2007) who assess Labour's work/family balance policies work in the field of social policy.

If then feminism has enormously raised the visibility of women as a relevant category of British political analysis and has helped to introduce major new policy areas and even institutional forms into the subject's purview, even so there is a sense in which much of this research agenda is not mainstreamed. That is, if feminist scholars were not deliberately continuing to raise these issues, it remains questionable whether they would be raised. It's worth noting, in this context, Annersley, Gains, and Rummery's (2007: 12) comment on writings about policy and politics under New Labour: 'One notable aspect of this whole genre is, with a couple of exceptions—the discussion of the Women's Policy Unity by Flinders (2002) and Squires and Wickham-Jones (2004)—the *lack* of attention paid to gender or gender issues'.

8.4.4 Concepts

Turning next to the conceptual frameworks within which British politics is analysed, feminism, especially Radical feminism, clearly has considerable implications for the way that politics itself is conceptualized. In addition feminist critiques and debates potentially contribute to the elaboration of some central ideas such as citizenship, and in particular representation. British feminist academics have played their part in introducing these feminist themes and critiques into the study of British politics, although the extent to which such ideas have been absorbed and applied within the mainstream of research is at the least uneven.

Feminism has raised crucial questions about the scope of politics. For the early Radical feminists a central concern was to demonstrate that politics—defined above all as power relationships between men and women—was not confined to a specific formalized public sphere but coextensive with society and the family. Indeed there was sometimes the sense that the foundation of (sex) politics lay in the family and the 'personal': not only were the roots or determinants of conventionally understood politics to be found there but this domestic or 'private' level was intrinsically political and worthy of study.

Such a broad understanding of the scope of politics obviously challenges traditional notions of the proper field of concern for political studies. Although Radical feminists were hardly the first to argue that politics was about power relationships, it was their focus on relationships between men and women that indicated spheres largely disregarded within the discipline of politics, though recognized as appropriate for sociologists, social historians, and psychologists. To that extent a feminist critique implicitly calls into question the discipline's sense of its own boundaries, almost its self-image.

In practice the impact of this alternative conception of the scope of politics has been more complex. The notion of the politics of everyday life, not only due to feminism, has become part of popular culture. Within academia also, particularly sociology, studies have explored the 'politics' of gender relationships in homely and intimate settings. To take a couple of recent instances, the feminist political theorist Valerie Bryson (2007), drawing in part on British survey data, reflects upon the gendered politics of time. McRobbie (2007) considers the current widespread incidence of different forms of young women's self-harm in relation to what she terms a 'post-feminist melancholia' or the loss of a feminist discourse through which to address their discontents. Political scientists, including those who would describe themselves as feminist, have been less inclined to follow through on this perception in terms of their own research focus, generally preferring to concentrate on 'mainstream' political processes. So whilst there is much greater acceptance amongst students of politics these days of the idea that politics is potentially everywhere, in practice it has not made that much difference to the study of British politics, in the sense of who, discipline-wise, does what. It does mean that, as already suggested, some of the most interesting feminist analysis of politics, broadly understood, in Britain has been undertaken by practitioners of other disciplines such as sociology.

Closely linked to the question of the scope of politics has been that of a public–private divide. Radical and socialist feminists critiqued what they saw as a 'liberal' insistence on distinct public and private spheres as an ideological, patriarchal construct. Some Radical feminists seemed to want to dispense with the notion altogether. To the extent that notions of public and private, however oppressive, have had practical force, feminists in academia have largely preferred to hold on to the distinction as an organizing idea but apply it critically. Okin (1991), herself an American liberal feminist political theorist, has provided the best dissection of the confusions and inconsistencies in the way notions of public and private have been construed in different contexts. She also, incidentally, stresses the need to hold on to the idea of privacy as something positive for women as for men. Mary McIntosh (1978) showed how the notion of a sovereign private sphere has been used historically to justify the British state's non-interference in domestic violence. Exploring the articulation and consequences of a public–private distinction has continued to prove a fruitful conceptual approach for feminist analysis. To cite a recent example, Fidelma Ashe (2006) shows how traditional assumptions in Northern Ireland about women's place in the private domestic sphere have both constrained and provided symbolic opportunities for the McCartney sisters' campaign to bring their brother's killer(s) to justice.

One further aspect of conceptions of the scope of politics concerns the forms of politics that are studied. Given feminism's history as a social movement, feminist political scientists were for a long time drawn to approaches that included all kinds of informal, local, 'grass-roots' or anti-system activism (see for instance Lovenduski and Randall 1993). There was also specific interest in the interface of the formal and informal, as in Gail Stedward's thoughtful analysis of the ambiguous location of women's aid in Scotland, as a kind of 'thresholder' organization, neither inside nor outside processes of government (1987). However, as noted above and as well described by McKay (2004: 100), with the relative decline of movement feminism and the parallel increase in women's political representation within parliament and other arenas, there has been a clear shift of focus to formal political representation, which she suggests now constitutes 'the most identifiable area of concentrated work by feminist political scientists in British politics'.

In addition to questioning conventional understandings of the scope of politics, feminists, again especially Radical feminists, depicted mainstream political institutions and processes as patriarchal; that is, male-dominated and dedicated to male interests and accordingly exhibiting a series of supposedly repugnant masculine traits. Such an intuition to some degree underlies the whole research endeavour of 'gendering', or providing a gendered account of, British state institutions (Lovenduski 1998). A forthcoming workshop will include a session on organizational cultures, with specific reference to changes in the masculinist political culture of our legislative assemblies.[7]

As we have seen, one response to the masculine character of politics has been to hypothesize an alternative, women's contribution, which may or may not require, amongst others things, a certain critical mass of women to become apparent. Women might, for instance, bring a different style to politics. In her study of the New Labour intake of women MPs (2004: ch. 10), Childs found that a majority of them believed—and this belief strengthened between first and second interviews in 1997 and 2000 respectively—that they did tend to share a feminized style, which included being less combative, less vociferous, more inclined to adopt a down-to-earth language, hard-working, and preferring to operate informally and 'behind the scenes'. Women might also bring distinctive values. Thus drawing on the suggestions of standpoint feminism, that women are associated with a distinctive ethic of care, in contrast to more masculine rights-based notions of justice, McKay (2001) in her

---

[7] Workshop on 'Engendering Politics and Devolution' at Warwick University, Feb. 2008.

study of Scottish women councillors investigated the extent to which they articulated a distinctive 'vocabulary of care'.

Such explorations do by implication tell us about the masculine traits of mainstream politics. But few studies of British politics have as yet engaged more directly with the notion of 'masculinity'. An early and valuable exception was Cockburn's study (1991), investigating forms of resistance to equal opportunities initiatives in local and national government offices and in trade unions, which evoked a range of 'masculinities', their interrelationships, and the consequences of these dynamics for gender relations. Another is the article by Bird (2005) already cited, on the House of Commons. But otherwise there has been little attempt, by political scientists of whatever sex (or gender), to apply or develop in the context of British politics the frameworks of writers like Australian sociologist Robert Connell (1996). His broadly social constructivist conception of masculinity, or masculinities, and hypothesis concerning the existence of hegemonic forms alongside subordinate forms, have stimulated tremendous debate (Connell and Messerschmidt 2005) as well as feeding into a spate of sociological and historical writing. But for British politics most analysis of this kind seems to stop short at around 1945—a partial exception being writing on social policy responses to 'masculinity' or the 'problem of men' (for instance Popay, Hearn, and Edwards 1998; Scourfield and Drakeford 2002).

Beyond its contribution to broad understandings of the meaning and nature of politics, as these pertain specifically to British politics, feminism has helped to inspire critiques and reworkings of some central political concepts. One of these is citizenship, where feminist scholars, predominantly political theorists, have not only demonstrated the extent to which earlier conceptions, notably Marshall's, were gendered but have been central to subsequent debates around the term (as recounted in Squires 1999). But a further important feminist-inspired intervention has been into our understandings of 'representation'. Feminist political theorist Anne Phillips (1998), partly responding to Pitkin's earlier sceptical account of descriptive, as opposed to substantive, representation, introduced the idea, or at least the hypothesis, of a 'politics of presence'. This has been taken up eagerly for instance by Puwar (2004) and Childs (2004) in their research into the experience of women MPs, whilst Campbell (2006) analyses British electoral survey data in order to examine how far women do appear to have distinct 'interests' or concerns requiring an effective women's presence in the House of Commons.

8.4.5 Methods

Finally and more briefly we need to consider methods-related issues, both the impact of feminism on methods and the impact of the prevailing methods regime on feminism's influence. This links back to the issues raised earlier about possibilities for adopting a normative approach and conceptual innovation. Feminist political scientists, partly in response to the methodological preferences of the discipline, have perhaps been insufficiently adventurous in the range of methods they have applied.

Within social science more broadly, feminists have discussed the necessity and possibility of a distinctive feminist method.[8] One particular concern, about the power relationship between researcher and researched, has resonated little in the context of research into British politics. Another, partly related, question is about giving voice to women. The early movement prioritized this as an important aspect of consciousness raising. In these post-postmodern days it is more difficult to believe in the simple authenticity of women's voices or that they are entirely unmediated by broader cultural discourses. Nonetheless in-depth interviews with women, in the movement or within mainstream political institutions, have been a significant and fruitful dimension of feminist political research (Childs and Krook 2006).

In general, however, feminists studying British politics have neither adopted distinctive feminist methods nor restricted themselves to using any particular subset of available methods—Krook and Squires (2006) characterize this as a healthy 'methodological eclecticism'. Even so, issues of method should perhaps be of concern. To the extent that there is a growing preoccupation with method in the study of British politics, and that particular methods of research and analysis, notably quantitative and rational choice approaches, command most prestige, these are not necessarily inimical to feminist-inspired research. Quantitative methods in particular have much to contribute, for instance in testing and adjusting received wisdom, and there is by now a substantial body of quantitative work analysing gender differences in voting behaviour, opinions, political knowledge, and political preferences (as in Frazer and MacDonald 2003; Campbell 2006). At the same time other kinds of method have been regarded more suspiciously in the profession. Childs and Krook (2006) suggest this even applies to elite interviewing, but it is much more the case with forms of participant observation and other kinds of ethnographic approach, although these can be extremely revealing (participant observation was one method employed in Cockburn's study cited earlier).

The direct contribution of feminist perspectives to methodological approaches in the study of British politics, then, has been limited. To the extent that those pursuing a feminist-inspired research agenda are methodologically eclectic, this may be helpful in diffusing awareness and accessibility of their work. However the methodological priorities of mainstream British political studies may also limit the ways in which feminist research questions can be posed and investigated.

8.5 Conclusion

Despite—even in some ways because—of its internal conflicts and debates, feminism as a perspective has tremendous relevance for politics and specifically British politics.

---

[8] For a fuller account of the question of a feminist method see Randall (1991).

In practice, too, and in tandem with developments in the sphere of politics itself, it has significantly impacted on the study of British politics, not simply through an expansion of its subject matter and the greater accuracy with which women's involvement in politics is reported, but through more fundamental questions it has raised. Such questions especially concern definitions of politics, and the nature and interrelationship of public and private, but also relate to central analytical concepts such as representation. In other respects its impact has been more muffled: the strong normative challenge, questioning of the standpoint from which politics is 'objectively' related, exploring the manifestations and constructions of masculinity within and through the state are all potential contributions of feminism which could have been taken further in the context of the study of British politics.

Feminism continues to inspire scholarly research into many different aspects of British politics, and indeed seems to have enjoyed a recent surge with the emergence of a new generation of scholars. Nor is publication of this research 'ghettoized' in particular journals (Childs and Krook 2006: 19). McKay (2004) suggests that gender and politics is by now a well-established subfield of the discipline. Even so there is a sense in which on the one hand feminist-inspired research is constrained both by debates internal to the feminist movement and by the character and methodological inclinations of British political science and on the other 'mainstream research contin- ues not to engage fully with feminist analyses' (Childs and Krook 2006: 20).

References

Afshar, H., Aitken, R., and Franks, M. 2005. 'Feminisms, Islamophobia and Identities'. *Political Studies*, 53: 262–83.

Annesley, C., Gains, F., and Rummery, K. (eds.) 2007. *Women and New Labour*. Bristol: Policy Press.

Arbrar, S., Lovenduski, J., and Margetts, H. 2000. 'Feminist Ideas and Domestic Violence Policy Change'. *Political Studies*, 48: 239–62.

Ashe, F. 2006. 'The McCartney Sisters' Search for Justice: Gender and Political Protest in Northern Ireland'. *Politics*, 26/3: 161–7.

Aspinall, M. 2006. 'Studying the British'. *Politics*, 26/1: 3–10.

Ball, W., and Charles, N. 2006. 'Feminist Social Movements and Policy Change: Devolution, Childcare and Domestic Violence Policies in Wales'. *Women's Studies International Forum*, 29: 172–83.

Bird, K. 2005. 'Gendering Parliamentary Questions'. *British Journal of Politics and International Relations*, 7: 353–70.

Breitenbach, E., et al. (eds.) 2002. *The Changing Politics of Gender: Equality in Britain*. London: Palgrave.

Brown, K. 2006. 'Realising Muslim Women's Rights: The Role of Islamic Identity among British Muslim Women'. *Women's Studies International Forum*, 29: 417–30.

Bryson, V. 2007. *Gender and the Politics of Time*. Bristol: Policy Press.

Butler, J. 1992. 'Contingent Foundations: Feminism and the Question of "Postmodernism"'. In J. Butler and J. Scott (eds.), *Feminists Theorize the Political*. London: Routledge.

CAMPBELL, R. 2006. *Gender and the Vote in Britain: Beyond the Gender Gap?* Colchester: ECPR Press.

CHILDS, S. 2004. *New Labour's Women MPs.* London: Routledge.

—— and KROOK, M. L. 2006. 'Gender and Politics: The State of the Art'. *Politics*, 26/1: 18–28.

COCKBURN, C. 1991. *In the Way of Women: Men's Resistance to Sex Equality in Organizations.* Princeton, NJ: Princeton University Press.

CONNELL, R. W. 1996. *Masculinities.* Cambridge: Polity.

—— and MESSERSCHMIDT, J. 2005. 'Hegemonic Masculinity: Rethinking the Concept'. *Gender and Society*, 19/5: 829–59.

COWARD, R. 1999. *Sacred Cows: Is Feminism Relevant to the New Millenium?* London: HarperCollins.

EOC 2007. *Sex and Power: Who Runs Britain 2007?* London: EOC.

FIRESTONE, S. 1970. *The Dialectic of Sex.* St Albans: Paladin.

FLINDERS, M. 2002. 'Governance in Whitehall'. *Public Administration*, 8/1: 51–75.

FRAZER, E., and MACDONALD, K. 2003. 'Sex Differences in Political Knowledge in Britain'. *Political Studies*, 51: 67–83.

GOODIN, R., and KLINGEMANN, H. D. 1995. 'Political Science: The Discipline'. Ch. 1 in R. Goodin and H. D. Klingemann (eds.), *A New Handbook of Political Science.* Oxford: Oxford University Press.

HARTSOCK, N. 1983. 'The Feminist Standpoint: Developing the Ground for a Specifically Feminist Historical Materialism'. In S. Harding and M. B. Hintikka (eds.), *Discovering Reality.* Dordrecht: Reidel.

—— 1998. 'The Feminist Standpoint Revisited'. In N. Hartsock, *The Feminist Standpoint Revisited and Other Essays.* Boulder, Colo.: Westview.

HAY, C. 2001. 'British Politics Today: Towards a New Political Science of British Politics?' In *Introduction to British Politics Today.* Cambridge: Polity.

KROOK, M. L., and SQUIRES, J. 2006. 'Gender Quotas in British Politics: Multiple Approaches and Methods in Feminist Research'. *British Politics*, 1: 44–66.

LEWIS, J. 1997. 'Gender and Welfare Regimes: Further Thoughts'. *Social Politics*, 4/2: 160–77.

—— and CAMPBELL, M. 2007. 'UK Work/Family Balance: Policies and Gender Equality 1997–2005'. *Social Politics*, 14/1: 4–30.

LISTER, R. 2006. 'Children (but not Women) First: New Labour, Child Welfare and Gender'. *Critical Social Policy*, 26: 315–35.

LOVENDUSKI, J. 1998. 'Gendering Research in Political Science'. *Annual Review of Political Science*, 1: 333–56.

—— and RANDALL, V. 1993. *Contemporary Feminist Politics.* Oxford: Oxford University Press.

LOWNDES, V. 2004. 'Getting on or Getting by? Women, Social Capital and Political Participation'. *British Journal of Politics and International Relations*, 6/1: 45–64.

McINTOSH, M. 1978. 'The State and the Oppression of Women'. In A. Kuhn and A. Wolpe (eds.), *Feminism and Materialism.* London: Routledge.

McKAY, F. 2001. *Love and Politics.* London: Continuum.

—— 2004. 'Gender and Political Representation in the UK: The State of the "Discipline"'. *British Journal of Politics and International Relations*, 6/1: 99–120.

McROBBIE, A. 2000. 'Feminism and the Third Way'. *Feminist Review*, 64: 97–113.

—— 2007. 'Illegible Rage: Young Women's Post-Feminist Disorders'. Lecture given at the Gender Institute, London School of Economics, January 2007. Accessible at: www.lse.ac.uk/collections/LSEPublicLecturesAndEvents/.

MARSH, D., and SAVIGNY, H. 2004. 'Political Science as a Broad Church: The Search for a Pluralist Discipline'. *Politics*, 24/3: 155–68.

OKIN, S. M. 1991. 'Gender, the Public and the Private'. In D. Held (ed.), *Political Theory Today*. Cambridge: Polity.

PHILLIPS, A. 1998. *The Politics of Presence*. Oxford: Oxford University Press.

—— and DUSTIN, M. 2004. 'UK Initiatives on Forced Marriage: Regulation, Dialogue and Exit'. *Political Studies*, 52: 531–51.

POPAY, J., HEARN, J., and EDWARDS, J. (eds.) 1998. *Men, Gender Divisions and Welfare*. London: Routledge.

PRINGLE, R., and WATSON, S. 1990. 'Women's Interests and the Post-structuralist State. In M. Barrett and A. Phillips (eds.), *Destabilizing Theory*. Cambridge: Polity.

PUWAR, N. 2004. 'Thinking about Making a Difference'. *British Journal of Politics and International Relations*, 6/1: 65–80.

RADCLIFFE-RICHARDS, J. 1980. *The Sceptical Feminist: A Philosophical Inquiry*. London: Routledge and Kegan Paul.

RANDALL, V. 1991. 'Feminism and Political Analysis'. *Political Studies*, 39: 513–32.

—— 2000. *The Politics of Child Daycare in Britain*. Oxford: Oxford University Press.

RUSSELL, M. 2005. 'Women in the Party: The Quiet Revolution'. In M. Russell, *The Building of New Labour: The Politics of a Party Organization*. London: Palgrave.

SCOURFIELD, J., and DRAKEFORD, M. 2002. 'New Labour and the "Problem of Men"'. *Critical Social Policy*, 22/4: 619–40.

SEGAL, L. 1999. *Why Feminism?* Cambridge: Polity.

SMART, C. 2004. 'Equal Shares: Rights for Fathers or Recognition for Children?' *Critical Social Policy*, 24: 484–503.

SQUIRES, J. 1999. *Gender in Political Theory*. Cambridge: Polity.

—— and WICKHAM-JONES, M. 2004. 'New Labour, Gender Mainstreaming and the Women and Equality Unit'. *British Journal of Politics and International Relations*, 6/1: 81–98.

STEANS, J. 2003. 'Emerging from the Margins: Feminist Encounters with the "Mainstream" of International Relations'. *British Journal of Politics and International Relations*, 5/3: 428–54.

STEDWARD, G. 1987. 'Entry into the System: A Case Study of Women in Scotland'. In J. Richardson and G. Jordan (eds.), *Government and Pressure Groups in Britain*. Oxford: Clarendon Press.

TICKNER, J. A. 1988. 'Hans Morgenthau's Principles of Political Realism: A Feminist Reformulation'. *Millennium*, 17/3: 429–40.

WILSON, A. R. 2007. 'Theoretical Underpinnings: Women, Gender, Feminizing and Politics'. In C. Annesley, F. Gains, and K. Rummery (eds.), *Women and New Labour*. Bristol: Policy Press.

YUVAL-DAVIS, N. 2006. 'Human/Women's Rights and Feminist Transversal Politics'. In M. M. Ferree and A. M. Tripp (eds.), *Transnational Feminisms: Women's Global Activism and Human Rights*. New York: New York University Press.

CHAPTER 9

....

THE
OAKESHOTTIANS

....

PAUL KELLY

ALTHOUGH a historian of science would find the idea of a national variant of a natural science a puzzling notion, in the social sciences the idea of a national tradition or style is far from a curiosity, however perplexing it may be to those who defend the hard scientific credentials of the social sciences. Yet in the study of politics the idea of national traditions and styles is far from puzzling, and indeed is used as a common subject of enquiry (Hayward, Barry, and Brown 1999: Stapleton 1994). The study of politics in Britain in the post-war world has been shaped by a dialectic between two main approaches; one, an attempt at scientific professionalization that draws upon developments in American political science, and another which draws on a complex of humanistic disciplines such as history, philosophy, and law. This characterization of the development of British political science is somewhat crude, but nevertheless serviceable for our purposes, as it explains the importance of the English historian, philosopher, and sceptical political theorist Michael Oakeshott (1901–90) on the shaping of the subject and profession of political science in Britain.

The Oakeshottians who are the focus of this chapter are not a single self-identifying group of scholars, like the Straussians in American political science, and it would be highly misleading to compare Oakeshott's influence with that of Leo Strauss. Yet Oakeshott certainly attracted many followers within the growing profession and had an impact on the character and ethos of many British politics departments through his humanistic approach to the study of politics. This group of scholars includes such figures as Elie Kedourie and Ken Minogue at LSE, W. H. Greenleaf at Swansea, Bhikhu Parekh and Noel O'Sullivan at Hull, Preston King at Sheffield and elsewhere, and Robert Eccleshall at Belfast. Each pursued careers in areas close to Oakeshott's own research interests in history and political thought, yet they could not be described as an organized group, but were rather a series of strong individual personalities in the profession inspired by Oakeshott's strong personality and example. But Oakeshott was also a major influence on figures who practised a style and approach to the study of politics that has had an influence beyond Oakeshott's own immediate field of interest, namely political philosophy and the history of political thought. And many in this latter group, which includes figures as diverse as Bernard Crick (a colleague as opposed to a student of Oakeshott) and Vincent Wright, but especially their students, many of whom are now dispersed throughout the profession, would perhaps not recognize themselves as directly following in Oakeshottian tradition or approach. In fields such as British politics, European politics, and public administration and policy, an Oakeshottian influence and approach can be detected, just as much as in political philosophy and the history of political thought. In many ways this Oakeshottian approach draws together themes and styles of thinking about politics that have a much more venerable lineage than simply Oakeshott's own teaching or publications from the 1940s through to the 1980s. That said, in tracing the lineaments of this Oakeshottian approach, I will argue that Oakeshott himself brought together many of these styles, methods, interests, and objects of inquiry into a unique synthesis that has undoubtedly affected the British study of politics.

The chapter will begin with a brief overview of Oakeshott's life and career, followed by a section which outlines the three main components of his philosophy of history and politics. The next section will turn from the abstraction and scepticism of his peculiar variant of philosophical idealism to his inaugural lecture at LSE on 'Political Education'. This important essay provides a distillation of Oakeshott's philosophical ideas and their implication for the study of politics. It is this important lecture along with another essay, 'The Study of "Politics" in a University', also published in *Rationalism in Politics* (Oakeshott 1962: 330–3) which shaped the Oakeshottian legacy within British political studies. The remaining sections will focus on areas of the study of politics in which the Oakeshottian impact has been greatest. Some of these subjects were addressed directly by Oakeshott in his major writings, but others still retain distinct signs of his approach to the study of politics set out in 'Political Education'. These sections will cover the political ideas and ideology, the study of government and public administration, the study of nationalism, and more controversially his impact on new fields such as the political theory of multiculturalism. The chapter will conclude with an assessment of the Oakeshottian legacy. Though always a small and never an organized group or faction, the Oakeshottian approach continues to exercise an important influence on the character of British political science.

9.1 LIFE AND CAREER

Michael Oakeshott was an idealist political philosopher, historian of political ideas, sceptical student of politics, and Professor at LSE, where he helped shape a generation of scholars of politics. Born in Chelsfield in Kent, the son of a Fabian socialist and civil servant in the Inland Revenue, Oakeshott became the most sophisticated exponent of a distinctively British anti-rationalist style of thinking about politics. His writings, lecturing, and personality provided a strong influence on the way in which the study of politics in Britain has been conducted since the mid-1940s, and despite his own scepticism of such things he remains one of the very few British scholars of politics who can be said to have established that most un-Oakeshottian of legacies, an 'ism'.

After an unconventional (for his class) and happy education at the coeducational St George's School, Harpendon, Oakeshott went up to Gonville and Caius, Cambridge in 1919 to read Political Science under the History tripos. Then as now Cambridge had no political science department, a fact which reflects the prejudices of one of the dominant Cambridge figures at the turn of twentieth century, the historian F. W. Maitland, who claimed that political science is either 'history or humbug'. The founder of politics teaching at Cambridge, Sir John Seeley, had hoped that the History Tripos would provide the education necessary for the domestic and Imperial ruling elite. In fact the study of politics at the time Oakeshott arrived at Cambridge comprised a form of descriptive comparative institutionalism, with a large dose of institutional history and a crude form of inductivism as the basis for its claim to the mantle of a science. He provides a disparaging description of this form of political science as a vocational education in 'The Study of "Politics" in a University' (Oakeshott 1962: 323). Oakeshott nevertheless excelled in his studies and achieved a First in both parts of the Tripos. In 1923–4 he travelled to Marburg and Tübingen to study theology, and in 1925 won a Fellowship at Gonville and Caius.

Oakeshott's philosophical and theological interests are reflected in a series of early essays and reviews and culminated in his first major publication, *Experience and its Modes*, in 1933. In this important work Oakeshott established his philosophical credentials and developed an idealist philosophy of experience that drew on the tradition of T. H. Green. F. H. Bradley, Bernard Bosanquet, and J. E. M. MacTaggart. Although the book received a favourable review from R. G. Collingwood, Oakeshott's philosophical idealism put him outside the mainstream of philosophy, which under the impact of the Cambridge Trinity of Bertrand Russell, G. E. Moore, and Ludwig Wittgenstein had taken an empiricist and logical atomist turn. One implication of this logical empiricist direction in philosophy was the abandonment of substantive moral and political philosophy and the philosophy of history by the English speaking philosophical mainstream for nearly half a century.

Oakeshott's philosophical idealism was not a complete obstacle to his career as it created an affinity with his friend and colleague Sir Ernest Barker, who from 1927 became the first Professor of Political Science at Cambridge. Barker had been schooled under the influence of Green and philosophical idealism whilst a student at Oxford. During the 1930s Oakeshott and Barker introduced a much greater emphasis on the study of political philosophy within the History Tripos, which even included Oakeshott lecturing on Marx at Cambridge in 1938, something no one else had done despite the presence of prominent Marxist scholars such as the economist Maurice Dobb.

After war service in intelligence, Oakeshott returned to Cambridge before taking up a Fellowship at Nuffield College, Oxford, having been passed over to succeed Barker by Denis Brogan. Oakeshott's time at Oxford was cut short by the surprise offer of the Chair in Political Science at LSE in 1950, following the death of Harold Laski. Laski and his predecessor Graham Wallas were part of the Fabian and social democratic tradition that had founded the LSE: Oakeshott's appointment to the Chair marked an abrupt break in that tradition, at least in the field of political science.[1]

Oakeshott's arrival at LSE was marked by his famous inaugural lecture on 'Political Education' where he set out a manifesto for the study of politics in the British universities in the post-war world. He devoted himself to administering the department of Government and transforming the teaching of politics at LSE and continued to have an impact on the wider development of the study of politics in Britain as one of the founders of the Political Studies Association (Chester 1975: 152–3). During this period he published relatively little, with his main book *Rationalism in Politics* (Oakeshott 1962) being a collection of essays written between the 1940s and early 1960s. Oakeshott's real impact was through his appointments at LSE and the placement of students elsewhere, and also through his teaching; first through his undergraduate lectures on the history of political thought, taught over two years, and secondly from the mid-1960s through the famous M.Sc. seminar on the History of Political Thought. A number of departments at other universities such as Swansea, Durham, Sheffield, and Hull acquired an Oakeshottian 'ethos', but his impact extended much more widely and less formally in Britain and the Commonwealth.

Oakeshott shied away from the direct supervision of Ph.D. students but influenced a large part of the profession of the 1950s, 1960s, and 1970s through his lectures and the M.Sc. seminar. He retired from the school in 1969 but continued to attend the M.Sc. seminar until 1980. During his retirement the fruits of work carried out during his tenure of the Chair saw publication with *On Human Conduct* (Oakeshott 1975) and *On History* (Oakeshott 1983), enhancing his reputation as a major political philosopher and philosopher of history. Since his death in 1990 a number of lectures and collected essays have been published as interest in his ideas and influence continues to grow amongst scholars who had no direct contact with him whilst alive.

9.2 OAKESHOTT'S IDEALIST PHILOSOPHY AND THE UNDERSTANDING OF POLITICS

Oakeshott's first major philosophical book placed him firmly in the idealist tradition of Green and Bradley and outside the logical atomist and analytical tradition

---

[1] The Webb's Fabian vision for the School had already begun to give way to a more independent and academic vision of the social sciences in the late 1920s and early 1930s where LSE professors such as Friedrich Hayek and Lionel Robbins provided opposition to Keynes' *General Theory* and the policy of Keynesian demand management (Dahrendorf 1995).

that was emerging with Russell, Moore, and Wittgenstein. *Experience and Its Modes* continues the idealist attack on the idea of unmediated experience as the basis for knowledge and consciousness of the world. Although a discussion of the intricacies of Oakeshott's idealism would take us beyond the scope the of this chapter, it is important to note the view of one of Oakeshott's closest and most careful students, W. H. Greenleaf's claim that an understanding of Oakeshott's idealism is central to an understanding of his conception of the nature and point of politics (Greenleaf 1968: 93–124). There is indeed an important connection between his philosophical idealism and his sceptical and limited view of philosophy and the study and practice of politics, although it would be a mistake to see his political writings as a simple implication of his metaphysics.

The central tenet of idealism is the denial of a pre-given or unmediated experience as the basis for knowledge. Traditional empiricist theories of knowledge and science assume the idea of a world of facts which are prior to experience and which experience and perception then accumulates into complex bodies of knowledge. Idealists deny this approach to philosophy and claim that all experience is situated and mediated by traditions of enquiry or the theoretical structures with which we approach the world. One consequence of this is that the task of philosophy is not to get behind these theoretical structures to the world as it is in itself, for this is impossible. Instead philosophy is concerned with rendering that manifold of experience coherent. We cannot, therefore, sort true from false claims about the world by comparing them to the world as it really is: we must search for truth in terms of the coherence of a world of experience. One of Oakeshott's central tasks of *Experience and Its Modes* (Oakeshott 1933) is to distinguish the languages we use to render that world of experience coherent. These languages or modes of experience are discrete perspectives of the whole of experience and for Oakeshott there are three main modes, history, science, and practice. Later Oakeshott introduces a fourth mode, namely poetry, which includes the whole of artistic experience.

Each of these modes of experience is complete unto itself, but it persists with others. No one mode is superior to others nor can one mode of experience completely displace other modes of experience. This plurality of experience is irreducible. From this simple idea Oakeshott develops a complex approach to the understanding of politics and the possibility of political science in the rest of his writings. We can, however, already identify a number of features that shape his distinctive approach to understanding politics as both an activity and an object of enquiry.

In the first instance, Oakeshott challenges the essential tenets of a naturalistic political science. The aspiration to a fully scientific understanding of politics reduces the whole of human experience to one mode or language of explanation. This is unsatisfactory for a number of reasons, not least that it ignores the claims of other modes of experience which continually infect a strictly natural scientific approach to politics. But more importantly than simply involving a category mistake, the naturalistic approach assumes a stable object of enquiry (such as a single human nature or fixed institutions) which might make sense in the case of chemical analysis when one is studying the properties to carbon, but does not make sense in the study of politics, as is shown by the malleability of the object of enquiry when considered from the point of view of history.

Oakeshott and his followers are sceptical about the prospects of a naturalistic science of politics, but they are also sceptical about other approaches to the study of politics such as Marxism that derive from similar category mistakes. This also explains the hostility most Oakeshottians show to Marxism as both a tool of political analysis and a political theory.

One immediate consequence of the rejection of a science of politics based on the methods of the natural sciences is a rejection of rationalistic political reform and government, or the application of scientific methods to the solution of political problems. This view of the task of political science was at the heart of the Fabian vision of the LSE and it is relentlessly attacked in Oakeshott's criticism of rationalism in politics. In contrast to the claims of the rationalist, Oakeshott argues that the world of politics is essentially a world of ideas and the task of the student is to make sense of it. Yet the student is no more privileged than the participant in the way in which he or she does this. The defence of the study of politics as a humanistic discipline leaves no room for technical expertise or method over judgement. Oakeshott's anti-rationalism manifests itself in a scepticism of any social scientific techniques for explaining the hidden truths or causal mechanisms behind the practice of politics. His scepticism of methodology is also found in his criticism of the 'methodology of the history of ideas' popularized by Cambridge scholars such as Quentin Skinner and John Dunn in the 1960s. Although this Cambridge methodology also developed as part of a reaction against the dominance of naturalistic political science, its adoption of a 'methodology' in place of a genuinely hermeneutic approach to historical enquiry attracted the particular criticism of both Oakeshott and many of his students.

Consequently the scholar is not the possessor of special knowledge or expertise that can be lent to the politician to make his practice more effective or successful. His scepticism of technical expertise extends to the practice of politics itself, as there is no expertise to be had, politics has no point beyond the contingent points offered by a particular tradition. This Oakeshottian vision of politics is nicely captured in Minogue's *Politics: A Very Short Introduction* (Minogue 1995).

Another example of a category mistake exposed by Oakeshott's philosophical framework is the prescriptivism of much contemporary political philosophy. If there is no end to which politics is directed then there cannot be a privileged perspective from which they can criticize moral and political principles. The mode of practical experience is engaged moral life and this includes the activity of doing politics. But within that mode of experience there are internal rules, conventions, and ways of doing things. Changing or defending those rules and conventions is the business of political or ethical agents and not of some disinterested field of enquiry. So the introduction of the mode of practice into the study of politics raises an important question of academic authority. How does the special knowledge of the academic give rise to political or moral authority? Oakeshott's conclusion is that it does not and the assumption that a scholar's knowledge gives her the authority to prescribe how we should live is a crude and dangerous mistake. Consequently, although Oakeshott was a major scholar of political thought and many of his most famous students followed him in this field (such as Minogue, Parekh, King, O'Sullivan, Greenleaf), Oakeshott set himself against the development of prescriptive theory by Isaiah Berlin, H. L. A. Hart, and Brian Barry in the 1960s and 1970s. Prescriptive normative theory was merely a category mistake and political practice masquerading as special knowledge. Philosophy itself cannot help us avoid this mistake, for as we have seen philosophy is merely concerned with the higher-order task of rendering that experience coherent as it does not give rise to any substantive knowledge or access to moral truths. Thus the study of politics and of political theory has to be rooted in the practices of particular political traditions. This is an idea that has come to have a greater impact on politics and political theory in light of the communitarian and multiculturalist response to rationalist enlightenment liberalism and the dominance of the normative liberalism of John Rawls (for an Oakeshottian inspired critique of Anglo-American normative political theory, see Gray 1989).

It is through a combination of political scepticism and communitarianism that Oakeshott distinguishes himself as a conservative and provides the basis for the recovery of a conservative voice in political theory. Whilst Hayek shies away from the title of 'conservative' (Hayek 1960: 397–414), Oakeshott is more comfortable especially in the essay 'On being Conservative'. Through his influence the conservative voice in political philosophy is preserved into the early twentieth century, yet that conservative voice remains distinctive. Despite being invited to the Conservative Philosophy Group in the 1970s and his thought being associated with the renewal of political conservatism under Margaret Thatcher, Oakeshott's conservatism remained a philosophical disposition rather than an ideological commitment. He rejects the ideological approach to politics, even including the ideology of anti-ideology that was espoused by Hayek. Consequently he can be associated, in only the most loose and general sense, with the development of the 'new right' in the late 1970s.

9.3 'POLITICAL EDUCATION' AND 'THE STUDY OF "POLITICS" IN A UNIVERSITY'

Oakeshott's general philosophical approach to politics is given concrete form in two important essays, 'Political Education' and 'The Study of "Politics" in a University'. The former was his inaugural lecture at LSE in 1951 and both are published in *Rationalism in Politics* (Oakeshott 1962). Both directly address the question of what scholars in politics departments should study and what politics departments are for. 'Political

Education' is a subtle but iconoclastic essay. Its tone is modest and on the surface respectful, but it smashes the legacy of both of Oakeshott's forebears at LSE, Graham Wallas and Harold Laski, the twin pillars of the Fabian tradition of political science. Against Wallas, Oakeshott challenges the idea of an empirical science of politics, and against Laski he dismisses the intellectual respectability of the study of politics with an ideological purpose. He also offers his own conception of politics as a historical or humanistic study of distinct traditions of activity.

Graham Wallas had advocated the idea of a naturalistic science of politics based on a study of political behaviour and human psychology. Yet Oakeshott challenges this idea because of its crude naturalism and empiricism, drawing on his idealist philosophy. He begins his critique by claiming that politics as an academic study is concerned with 'The general arrangements of a set of people whom choice or chance have brought together' (Oakeshott 1962: 112). As such he emphasizes the contingency of the activity of politics and therefore rejects its universal character. Furthermore, it cannot be an empirical study as there is no unmediated object of experience to be studied. Even the idea of political behaviour depends upon some conception of the activity of politics. As we shall see, this does not mean that Oakeshott denies that we should study the political behaviour of voters, parties, and elections. Instead he makes the more fundamental claim that in order to identify political behaviour we already need a conception of the activity in which it occurs, so that we can distinguish it from other kinds of behaviour. Consequently, the study of politics must engage with the presupposition of how we identify political activity in the first place. His conclusion is that this is a historical construction, consequently the master language of the study of politics is a historical and not a scientific one (Oakeshott 1962: 130).

Does this suggest that Oakeshott was sceptical about the need for distinct departments of politics with their own sub-disciplinary identity? Some commentators and followers of Oakeshott do regard him as sceptical about the role and value of the sub-discipline, favouring instead the Maitland preference for history over 'humbug'. Yet this sceptical case is overstated and also misunderstands his peculiar conservative temperament. The emergence of a sub-disciplinary identity had already taken place, so for Oakeshott the question is not whether there should or should not be politics departments. Instead the real task is to pursue the intimations of this activity and respond to these, rather than try to impose a rationalistic plan on these new departments or alternatively to engage in a kind of nostalgic rationalism that would prefer to return the study of politics to history departments. The study of politics in British universities is a distinctive activity and the task before Oakeshott in these two important essays is to survey and characterize that activity.

The other main target of 'Political Education' is the idea of political science with a single ideological purpose and here his target is Laski. The problem posed by Laski is different to that posed by Wallas. Wallas wanted to subsume political experience under the mode of science, whereas Laski wanted to subsume it under the mode of practice: both involve category mistakes but each is different. This critique of Laski's approach identifies one of the more persistent themes of the Oakeshottians, namely the criticism of what they take to be the reduction of politics to ideology (see Minogue 1985; Manning 1980).

An ideology is an abridgement or simplification of a tradition of politics into a number of distinct principles or values. In ordinary political discourse such abridgements are unavoidable and a necessary part of the practical activity of doing politics. Conceiving of British politics as a struggle between the forces of progress and the forces of reaction or conservatism is fair enough for a politician whose task is to promote his values and beliefs. But this is where the category mistake of Laski's ideological politics arises. Any ideology will be a contingent and partisan abridgement of a complex tradition of politics. Whilst this might be acceptable and containable in the realm of practical activity, in the sphere of the academic study of politics it is both inadequate and dangerous. It is inadequate because it assumes the primacy of a single ideological perspective as a basis for understanding political activity and behaviour, yet this is incoherent as all ideologies are abridgements of traditions of political activity. We cannot distinguish between these ideological perspectives by identifying which contains the truth because of their nature all ideologies are partial abridgements of a tradition of practice and cannot ever be the final truth. Once again to conceive of the object of political inquiry as ideological is a category mistake. That said, the study of 'ideologies' or the different abridgements of political traditions is an important part of the study of politics. This study must distinguish itself from ideological commitment or advocacy as that would collapse the distinction between a historical mode of experience in understanding a political tradition and a practical mode of activity which is doing politics. Laski failed to maintain the proper distinction between political activity and the study of politics. The study of politics must therefore confine itself to the study of traditions of the activity of politics. And it is for this reason that Oakeshott and his followers were unsympathetic to the development of prescriptive normative political theory as this forms the basis of a rationalist and ideological approach to politics, by conceiving of political activity under the heading of freedom or social justice.

In opposition to these two distortions of the proper study of politics Oakeshott suggests that the task of political study remains fundamentally historical, and is concerned with the pursuit of intimations of a political tradition. The proper study of politics therefore involves the study of political ideas in which conceptions of political activity are presented and analysed, but also the study of the structures and institutional practices.

This critique of a naturalistic science of politics or the subordination of politics to normative political theory as well as the bold manifesto for a more nuanced historical approach to the study of politics is further fleshed out and qualified in 'The Study of "Politics" in a University'. In this essay Oakeshott is responding to the development of the study of politics in the British university system and once again he urges caution and defends an approach to the study of politics that looks remarkably similar to that he received at Cambridge in the 1920s. The essential qualifications in this paper concern the acceptance of both a level of vocational study and the technical study of political behaviour within the study of politics. The study of politics can indeed be of value to those who wish to pursue careers in politics and government and, therefore, a level of technical sophistication in the analysis of political behaviour and institutions is appropriate. So the study of politics is not simply the historical examination of traditions. But Oakeshott, nevertheless, wishes to keep this technical specialization in its place. Technical tools of analysis remain tools, and as such they are only of use to those who have an appropriate understanding of traditions of political activity. Of further interest is the qualification he makes of a claim in 'Political Education' concerning the propriety of studying more than one tradition of political activity. Oakeshott remains committed to the value of comparative government (historically conceived) and of comparative historical institutionalism, but he cautions about the potential expansion of 'traditions' studied as a response to the state of current affairs. In particular he was especially concerned about the development of the large-scale study of Russian politics at many British universities during the cold war, and the recruitment of a disproportionate number of 'Russianists' or 'Sovietologists' to service this study. Against this trend Oakeshott urged the need to be selective in the choice of historical political traditions and to avoid the fashion of pursuing an 'area studies' approach which fails to concentrate on mature political traditions. For example, Oakeshott did not believe that the USSR embodied a political tradition at all; at best it is a kind of despotism which does not have a politics to study. This is not the expression of a narrow Eurocentrism but follows from his concept of what political activity is. Again the absence of a proper historical sense had the potential of expanding beyond limit the boundaries of what could count as the study of politics at the expense of rendering the subject of study incoherent. For all of Oakeshott's attempts to deflate the claims of ideological politics to dominate all other aspects of human experience, he remained committed to the idea that political education was important and its subject matter could be rendered coherent.

9.4 THE STUDY OF POLITICS 1: POLITICAL PHILOSOPHY AND POLITICAL THEORY

Despite the broad concerns of 'Political Education' and 'The Study of "Politics" in a University', Oakeshott's greatest impact has been on the field of political theory and the study of political ideas. All of his closest students have been scholars of political thinkers or of contemporary political philosophy (see Minogue, Parekh, King, O'Sullivan, Kedourie, Greenleaf). Yet in this field an Oakeshottian tradition is difficult to distinguish as it is largely sceptical and reactive. Although Oakeshottians are committed to the idea of history as the primary language of political studies, they have rejected the reduction of philosophy to history as advocated by many contemporary historicists. So although sensitive to the minutiae of historical traditions of political discourse, they were also hostile to the alternative Cambridge tradition of linguistic contextualism that is associated with J. G. A Pocock, Quentin Skinner, and John Dunn. These Cambridge thinkers reduced the claims of philosophy to historically contingent utterances and therefore deny the possibility of genuine philosophical claims. Oakeshott's whole enterprise leaves philosophy above history and politics, and challenges the idea of a reductive historicism. Thus although Oakeshottian and 'Cambridge' scholars have both been attentive to the historical contexts of political thought and discourse, the Oakeshottians have rejected the idea of a single method-ology of historical enquiry and the idea implicit in linguistic contextualism that all political thought is conducted in the practical mode. For Oakeshott and his followers, great political philosophers, such as Thomas Hobbes, are indeed philosophers and not merely politicians and pamphleteers.

The one area of political theory where Oakeshott has had the least impact was in the field of normative political theory. In Britain this field originated in the work of H. L. A. Hart and Brian Barry, but since the 1970s it has proceeded under the long shadow of John Rawls and other American liberal political philosophers. Many Oakeshottian scholars have tended to be sceptical towards this style of thought, seeing Rawlsian liberal political theory as another ideological version of politics and, therefore, committing a category mistake. Yet it would be too simplistic to suggest that Oakeshott was wholly dismissive of normative political theory. His essays in *Rationalism in Politics* leave little scope for normative political theory, yet by the time he published the essays that comprised *On Human Conduct*, it was clear that his view was more complex. His careful distinction between civil and enterprise associations provides an interesting and peculiarly liberal analysis of the modern state. When his defence of civil association is coupled with the communitarianism implicit in his idealist vision of politics, it is clear that Oakeshott provides an alternative to the constructivist approach to political theory exemplified by Rawls. With the exception of John Gray and Noel O'Sullivan, few Oakeshott-inspired scholars have been inclined to develop this line of thought, and whether it proves a viable research project remains to be seen. Yet it does challenge the simplistic assumption that Oakeshott was hostile to normative political theory as such.

9.5 THE STUDY OF POLITICS 2: POLITICAL TRADITIONS

Perhaps the most faithful example of an Oakeshottian approach to the study of poli-tics is provided by W. H. Greenleaf's massive four-volume (technically three but the third is in two substantial parts) *The British Political Tradition*. Greenleaf had already established himself as a historian of seventeenth-century political thought and was the head of department at Swansea, one of the more self-consciously Oakeshottian departments. Yet as we have seen, the Oakeshottian approach to political theory had transformed it into a historical activity much more closely connected with the history of traditions of political activity. Greenleaf's massive study of the British Tradition provides a survey of the language of politics in Britain from the 1830s until the present. This language is structured using the categories of libertarianism and collectivism which Greenleaf claims are the two main ideas that animate political argument and debate. This ideological heritage is traced through a vast literature that includes political theory and pamphlet literature, but also the institutional changes and developments in local and central government, parliament, and the civil service. This vast literature covers the whole range of British politics with the exception of foreign policy and relations which was supposed to be the subject of the final and as yet unpublished volume.[2] Yet Greenleaf's austerel Oakeshottian work is not the only attempt to study politics along Oakeshottian lines. The complex interweaving of political ideas, ideological analysis, and institutionalism is also well exemplified in Bernard Crick's approach to the study of British politics. One can see the legacy of this Oakeshottian approach in the example of Vincent Wright and the field of comparative politics and historical institutionalism.

Wright began as a student in the Government Department at LSE, where he fell under the influence of Oakeshott's sceptical approach to politics. After doctoral studies in Paris and brief period at Newcastle he joined the staff at LSE teaching in the field of public administration with a research interest in the history of French public administration. He moved to Nuffield College, Oxford, in 1977 where he continued to develop his own distinctively historical and sceptical approach to comparative politics and public administration. Unlike Greenleaf whose interest in the British political tradition is heavily shaped by an interest in British political theory and ideas, Wright's scholarship is more traditionally historical. His *The Government and Politics of France* (Wright 1978) is in many ways as authentically an Oakeshottian work as Greenleaf's. It reflects a fundamentally historical approach to politics; a strong emphasis on the value and distinctiveness of national traditions; as well as a sceptical awareness of the limits of more scientific approaches to the study of politics. Like Oakeshott he does not eschew the value of the tools of political analysis from other approaches to the study of politics, but remains sceptical about the ability to reduce the study of politics to the language of a naturalistic political science.

Wright's influence and that of other scholars like him is an example of the more resilient legacy of Oakeshott's understanding of the study of politics. It is perhaps obscured by the more obviously Oakeshottian concern with political theory by his closest colleagues. Yet Oakeshott was committed to the proper study of the historical traditions of modern politics. As the example of Wright illustrates, this commitment inspired and influenced many students of politics who passed through the

---

[2] Whether this final volume will ever appear is an open question, but Greenleaf has certainly done a considerable amount of work on the potential volume, according to his friends and former students.

LSE in the 1950s and 1960s who were not particularly interested in the study of political philosophy, but also demonstrates the way that legacy is passed on through many other departments and institutions including Nuffield College, Oxford, during Wright's time. Wright's own students, who are now widely dispersed throughout the profession in Britain, continue to pursue the careful comparison of national traditions along with a detailed study of the historical contingency of national administrative institutions and their cultures. Although acknowledging a great debt to Wright himself, few would immediately acknowledge the Oakeshottian roots of this approach.

9.6 NATIONALISM, MULTICULTURALISM, AND IDENTITY

Perhaps the most curious manifestation of an Oakeshottian voice in contemporary political analysis is in the field of identity politics and multiculturalism in the writings of Bhikhu Parekh and Tariq Modood (Parekh 2000; Kelly 2001; Barry 2001; Modood 2007). That this should be surprising is due to the opposition of Oakeshott to prescriptive political theory as a category mistake, but also because in respect of another manifestation of identity politics, namely nationalism, two of Oakeshott's students, Kedourie and Minogue, wrote scathing dismissals of nationalist ideology. Kedourie's critique is the most forthright, claiming that nationalism is a fiction invented by intellectuals and another example of *trahison des clercs* (Kedourie 1966). However, Oakeshott's sensitivity to the intimations of traditions of political activity has been precisely the idea used by Parekh and Modood in setting out the conditions of fair accommodation into the dominant culture of British society by minority ethnic and cultural groups.

Parekh's interest in the theory and politics of multiculturalism and related issues of 'Britishness' derives in part from his involvement in the commission for racial equality, but also reflects his Oakeshottian background. *Rethinking Multiculturalism* (Parekh 2000) consists of an Oakeshottian rejection of the tradition of monistic political liberalism on the grounds of its abstraction and false impartiality. This approach when applied to the terms of minority group integration imposes a set of arbitrary principles and values on different cultural groups whilst claiming that they are universally applicable and justifiable. However, this abstract universalism is a chimera and another example of rationalistic ideologies distorting living traditions of politics. In place of this discredited normative strategy Parekh suggests that minority cultural accommodation should involve a debate about the operative public values of the majority society. In effect, Parekh's account of operative public values is a version of Oakeshott's intimations of our tradition of political activity. Modood, who is also indirectly connected to the Oakeshottian tradition as a student at Swansea during the time of Greenleaf, has also recently adopted an Oakeshottian approach to conceiving of the society into which minority groups must integrate as a living and contingent historical tradition. For Modood, the lesson derived from Oakeshott is not the creation of a new ideology of multiculturalism, which he sees in Parekh's theory; instead Modood sees the fact of multiculturalism as part of British political society. It is part of the tradition of our activity and therefore attempts to impose coercively a monocultural or stipulative account of Britishness is itself a form of ideological abridgement. In this sense Modood's politics of citizenship is a warning against a similar concern with the conditions of British identity defended in Bernard Crick's work on citizen identity, becoming merely another ideological abridgement of the British tradition of politics.

9.7 OAKESHOTTIANISM IN CONTEMPORARY POLITICAL ANALYSIS

Oakeshott's influence on British politics and political analysis is complex and subtle. He was, according to Noel Annan, a 'deviant' in respect of the political commitments and sympathies of what Annan called 'Our Age' (Annan 1990). For Annan, who was an establishment liberal and university administrator, Oakeshott was a deviant in two ways: his political conservatism and his position as a critic outside the mainstream of his disciplinary developments. In respect to both positions Oakeshott's deviance can be overstated. Whilst his own sympathies were conservative he had only a very indirect influence on the conservative revival in British politics. His impact on the resurgence of an ideologically confident conservatism during the 1970s and 1980s was as much personal, through his close associations with writers and commentators such as Shirley Letwin (mother of Oliver Letwin, a prominent Conservative MP), historian of conservatism and political thought as well as close friend of Margaret Thatcher, as it was theoretical. Oakeshott attended the Conservative Philosophy Group, but by all accounts his contributions were small. By the time of the rise of Thatcherism, Oakeshott had already returned to a more strictly philosophical approach to political ideas through his development of the idea of civil association in *On Human Conduct*. This was a complex and sophisticated book that generated some perplexity on publication, yet it is a crude caricature to see this as an inspiration for Thatcherism or the New Right.

The second of Annan's charges is that Oakeshott remained an outsider in the academy. It is certainly true that Oakeshott did not become an establishment figure like Isaiah Berlin, and as the fortunes of political conservatism rose, the academic legacy of Oakeshottianism appears to have declined as the character of departments changed. The LSE, through which Oakeshott had managed to shape a generation of academics, no longer produced Oakeshottians in a recognizable form. By the time Brian Barry occupied the Graham Wallas Chair at LSE in 1986 most of Oakeshott's students were in the latter part of their careers or in retirement. Barry's tenure of the Chair marked a return to the naturalistic aspiration to political science with a normative purpose that had been the aspiration of Wallas at the Chair's inception. It seemed in effect a repudiation of the Oakeshottian approach, and indeed it was. Yet it would be wrong to see Oakeshottianism as merely a temporary block on the way to a fully naturalistic science of politics. In many respects Oakeshottianism was indeed a sceptical reaction to trends in the social sciences and the British university system, and as such it could not survive as a positive tradition or school. But it would be a mistake to see Oakeshott's conception of political studies in doctrinal terms. He did not lead an 'insurgent' group nor did the Oakeshottians have a distinct manifesto. As we have seen, their influence was just as strongly felt in comparative institutionalism as it was in political theory or the history of ideas. Whilst there remain self-consciously Oakeshottian scholars in Britain and the USA, many are younger scholars who are interested in Oakeshott's political and historical thought in the same way that others are interested in John Rawls or Ronald Dworkin. A certain mystique has grown up around Oakeshott the man, as he avoided both the cult of personality and the organization of a faction, yet his ability to attract fierce and sometimes partisan loyalty appears to have achieved precisely that. Annan's judgement is partly a reflection of Oakeshott's being part of the opposition team: a team that looked sceptically at the accomplishments of the likes of Annan's hero Isaiah Berlin, of whom Oakeshott had a rather low opinion. Yet if one probes a bit deeper beneath Annan's *ad hominem* assessment we can see Oakeshott's legacy in a different light.

The challenge to simplistic normativism amongst many British political theorists and a concern with the pursuit of intimations within national traditions of politics, administration, and governance remains central to the study of politics in many British universities. Oakeshott was not the only prominent figure in the emergence of post-war British political studies who objected to social scientific naturalism and who saw the study of politics as being primarily rooted in a historical mode of experience. He drew on a tradition of thinking about political studies that was shared with Sir Ernest Barker amongst others and which goes back to the emergence of the subject in the late nineteenth century. In the field of international relations Martin Wight played a similar role. However, Oakeshott's distinctiveness was that he succeeded in providing (in a way that Barker or Wight could not) one of the most sophisticated expressions of that rejection of philosophical naturalism with its reduction of a humanistic study of political activity to the model of the natural sciences. For students coming of age in the 1940s to 1960s that philosophical restatement of the study of politics on the intellectual map remained unchallenged in Britain. Later generations of students have proved less sympathetic and subsequently turned to continental critical theory or hermeneutics for a similar philosophical foundation to their conception of non-naturalistic political science, but without the attendant conservatism. Yet Oakeshott's philosophical politics remains a serious challenge to the aspirations of scientific and philosophical naturalism in the social sciences in a way that has not been matched by the Cambridge School, or Marxist and postmodernist critics. And the continued presence of an Oakeshottian voice amongst many students of politics who are uninterested in the philosophical provenance of their academic practice refutes Annan's view that Oakeshott and the Oakeshottian voice was a deviation from the proper development of the subject, however much Oakeshott might have enjoyed cultivating the status of an outsider.

REFERENCES

ANNAN, N. 1990. *Our Age: Portrait of a Generation*. London: Weidenfeld and Nicolson.

BARRY, B. 2001. 'The Muddles of Multiculturalism'. *New Left Review*, 8: 49–71.

CHARVET, J. 1982. *Feminism*. London: Dent Everyman.

CHESTER, N. 1975. 'Political Studies in Britain: Recollections and Comments'. *Political Studies*, 23: 151–64.

CRICK, B. 1959. *The American Science of Politics*. London: Routledge.

——1989. 'My LSE'. Pp. 93–105 in *Essays on Politics and Literature*. Edinburgh: Edinburgh University Press.

DAHRENDORF, R. 1995. *The LSE*. Oxford: Oxford University Press.

GRAY, J. 1989. *Liberalisms: Essays in Political Philosophy*. London: Routledge.

GREENLEAF, W. H. 1968. *Oakeshott's Philosophical Politics*. London: Longmans.

——1968. 'Idealism, Modern Philosophy and Politics'. Pp. 93–124 in King and Parekh 1968.

——1983a. *The British Political Tradition*, vol. i: *The Rise of Collectivism*. London: Methuen.

——1983b. *The British Political Tradition*, vol. ii: *The Ideological Heritage*. London: Methuen.

——1987. *The British Political Tradition*, vol. iii (parts 1 and 2): *A Much Governed Nation*. London: Methuen.

HAYEK, F. A. 1960. *The Constitution of Liberty*. London: Routledge.

HAYWARD, J., BARRY, B., and BROWN, A. (eds.) 1999. *The British Study of Politics in the Twentieth Century*. Oxford: British Academy.

KEDOURIE, E. 1966. *Nationalism*. London: HarperCollins.

KELLY, P. 2001. 'Parekh and the Dangers of "Oakeshottian" Multiculturalism'. *Political Quarterly*, 72: 428–36.

KING, P., and PAREKH, B. (eds.) 1968. *Politics and Experience: Essays Presented to Michael Oakeshott*. Cambridge: Cambridge University Press.

MANNING, D. 1968. *The Mind of Jeremy Bentham*. London: Pall Mall.

——1976. *Liberalism*. London: Dent Everyman.

——1980. *The Form of Ideology*. London: Allen and Unwin.

MINOGUE, K. 1969. *Nationalism*. London: Methuen.

——1985. *Alien Powers: The Pure Theory of Ideology*. London: Weidenfeld and Nicolson.

——1995. *Politics: A Very Short Introduction*. Oxford: Oxford University Press.

MODOOD, T. 2007. *Multiculturalism*. Cambridge: Polity.

OAKESHOTT, M. 1933. *Experience and its Modes*. Cambridge: Cambridge University Press.

OAKESHOTT, M. 1962. *Rationalism in Politics*. London: Methuen.

—— 1975. *On Human Conduct*. Oxford: Oxford University Press.

—— 1983. *On History and Other Essays*. Oxford: Basil Blackwell.

PAREKH, B. 2000. *Rethinking Multiculturalism*. Basingstoke: Palgrave.

STAPLETON, J. 1994. *Englishness and the Study of Politics*. Cambridge: Cambridge University Press.

WRIGHT, V. 1978. *The Government and Politics of France*. London: Routledge.

SECTION FOUR: MODES OF POLITICAL WRITING

CHAPTER 10

POLITICAL JOURNALISM

PETER RIDDELL

JOURNALISM has always played a central role in political debate in Britain, but an inherently ambiguous one. Despite changes in patterns of ownership and technology, the underlying relationship, and its associated paradoxes, have not altered. On the one hand, there has been a combination of mutual dependency and constant conflict in trying to find out what governments and politicians do not want disclosed. On the other hand, journalists and their editors and owners have often not been content with observing and informing on political developments; they have also sought to influence the policy outcomes and the careers of politicians, as players in the Westminster game.

This chapter will discuss the nature, and results, of these relationships in the changing framework in which the media operates, covering the transition over a century from when the printed press enjoyed a monopoly, via the slow growth to dominance of radio, and then television, to a world of almost infinite diversity with not only multiple television channels, but also the Internet, blogging, and text messages. It is a transition from a hierarchical and largely oligopolistic structure to an infinitely diverse and potentially democratic one.

For most of the period, really until the last decade of the twentieth century, political journalism was dominated by a relatively few newspaper and broadcasting outlets which concentrated mainly on Westminster. They were interpreting and seeking to influence the world of high politics. The political culture in which they operated was an elite one, in which both journalists and politicians were insiders. The world outside Westminster, out of doors as the Victorians called it, seldom intruded. Journalists, editors, and proprietors were part of the small world about which they wrote and broadcasted. There was little sense of distance. This has not meant that the press has automatically sided with the party in power. Far from it. For much of the time, a significant section of the press has been sharply critical of the Prime Minister of the day and the party in power. But this has often been on behalf of the out-group and within the terms of the Westminster power game.

The very adversarial nature of politics, and the competition between media outlets, has encouraged disclosure. All papers like to trumpet their exclusives. Despite protests about a continuing culture of secrecy, the workings of government have been opened up since the 1960s. Attitudes in Whitehall have changed, and changed before the Freedom of Information Act forced the disclosure of many background documents. For instance, not only does the public know about the line-up of the arguments over entry into the euro, thanks to an active press, but the Treasury also released volumes of supporting evidence in summer 2003 to back up the decision to defer entry indefinitely. By contrast, debates on exchange rate policy were held in total secret in the 1960s.

But these disclosures have commonly been within a narrow definition of news. The frequent focus has been on the fate and reputation of ministers and leading politicians rather than necessarily of policies. Moreover, the insider political culture has occasionally worked against disclosure. For instance, until the 1980s, details of the private lives of politicians—their drinking habits, their adulteries and homosexuality (illegal until 1967)—were generally kept out of the press, even when widely known within the political world. As Jeremy Tunstall records (1996: 243–4), one of the biggest ever peacetime cover-ups occurred in June 1953 when Winston Churchill, in his final premiership (and then aged 78), had a stroke. 'Lords Camrose, Beaverbrook, and Bracken (owners of the *Daily Telegraph*, *Daily Express*, and *Financial Times*) were summoned to Chartwell by Churchill's private secretary; and a press statement was released which concealed the seriousness of the Prime Minister's illness.' Not only would such a situation have been inconceivable today, but the private lives not just of political leaders but also of backbench MPs, and even senior public appointees, are regarded as fair game by both the red-top and middle-market tabloids—and even more by some of the populist muck-raking websites.

Anyone who thinks close relations between the media and political leaders only developed in the Thatcher and Blair eras just needs to look back to the mid-nineteenth century when Delane, the editor of *The Times*, used to go riding with leading politicians such as Palmerston. The mixture of mutual dependency and political and financial advantage which still runs through media/political relationships was vividly illustrated in August 1855 when Delane and Palmerston met. As Oliver Woods and James Bishop record (1983: 87–8):

> Palmerston, the new Prime Minister, had been *The Times*'s bete noire for over two decades, but he had been helped to his position by Delane's attacks on Aberdeen's Government and he badly needed Delane's continued support if his own Government was to prosper. Delane wanted a new contact at the top. In August there was a meeting between the two, and the alliance was sealed by a curious letter in *The Times* of 10 October signed by 'A Constant Reader'. . . . Queen Victoria was so disgusted by the Crimean article

[attacking the conduct of the war] and particularly by the attack on the reigning house of Prussia that she wrote to Palmerston asking 'whether it is right that the Editor, the Proprietor and the Writers of such execrable publications ought to be honoured and constant guests of the Ministers of the Crown?'

That episode epitomizes many of the characteristics of the journalist/politician relationship: the hope by the editor of obtaining privileged insider information to scoop rivals, and the hope of a leading politician for press support. Since the mid-nineteenth century, there have been plenty of examples of proprietors, editors, and journalists becoming closely involved with leading politicians in the hope of mutual advantage: from Gladstone's 'Hawarden kite' on Irish Home Rule in 1885; via Lloyd George's complicated manoeuvrings with the press barons during and after the First World War; Neville Chamberlain's courting of Geoffrey Dawson, the editor of *The Times*, to back his appeasement policy and to suppress alternative views; to Harold Wilson's love/hate relationship with the press; and then Margaret Thatcher's close links with the right-wing press during the 1980s. There was a mutual interest between the Thatcher government and proprietors like Rupert Murdoch and Lord Rothermere in weakening the trade unions, cutting taxes, and promoting deregulation. The proprietors, and their papers, backed her. Yet, as I wrote (1994: 6–8) about her memoirs:

> Margaret Thatcher received a more consistently favourable, and at times fanatically loyal, press than any recent Prime Minister, and certainly than her successor. Yet she almost entirely ignores these supporters in the 914 pages of her *Downing Street Years*. The *Sun* never rises on these pages, nor does the *Daily Telegraph*. Sir David English, Kelvin Mackenzie, Sir Nicholas Lloyd and even Rupert Murdoch might never have existed. That is curiously ungrateful given what they did to sustain her in power.

Yet even if politicians are reluctant publicly to acknowledge the relationship, it exists. The vivid diaries of Piers Morgan, editor of two tabloids, the *News of the World* and the *Daily Mirror* from 1994 to 2004, record how almost every other week he was either meeting or having a meal with Tony Blair and other senior members of his government. He was on first-name terms with them. Whatever the politicians privately thought of the erratic and often hostile Morgan, they were keen to try and win him over, to persuade him about their viewpoint. Morgan writes (2005: 233) how on 3 August 1999, he went to Chequers for the first time for tea with Blair—'we got the full-blown charm offensive for two hours, with Blair even pouring the tea'. The same process of courting has been even more true of Paul Dacre, the Savonarola of his day as editor of the moralistic *Daily Mail*, arbiter of prejudices to Middle England, or so he supposes. He was briefly courted by Blair and on a longer-term basis by both Gordon Brown and David Blunkett.

The Brown/Dacre links continued after the change of Prime Minister in June 2007. The editor of the *Daily Mail* was invited to Chequers. The closeness between the Prime Minister and the editor was essentially personal, a shared puritan personal outlook and commitment to success through hard work. And just as Labour MPs and activists were unhappy, so were many *Daily Mail* journalists eager to put the boot into the Brown government (as they did despite their editor).

Blair and Alastair Campbell, his chief press adviser and spokesman from 1994 until 2004, pursued a deliberate campaign of winning over Rupert Murdoch, both in opposition and in government, in the hope of obtaining the backing of the *Sun*, as they did ahead of Labour's victory in the 1997 general election. The closeness of the relationship is brought out in the diaries of Lance Price, who worked for Campbell during Labour's first term. Price notes (2005: 13) in an entry for Wednesday 24 June 1998 how: 'This morning the *Sun* did a heavy number on the single currency with a pic of TB asking "Is This the Most Dangerous Man in Britain?" And in the past week both Murdoch and the new editor of the *Sun*, David Yelland, were in Number Ten for dinner—not something we've been advertising'. Even more striking are the many references to Murdoch in Alastair Campbell's own diaries, which appeared within a fortnight of Blair's departure from 10 Downing Street. Throughout Blair is portrayed as eager to court and win the approval of Murdoch, and, in particular, the backing of the *Sun*. Campbell argues (Campbell and Stott 2007: 160–2) that Blair's article on the eve of the 1997 election giving an impression of caution over Europe and the euro was crucial in persuading Murdoch. In January 1999 (ibid. 363), Blair is annoyed at the hostility to the EU of Murdoch and his chief advisers, and Campbell says: 'It was faintly obscene that we even had to worry about what they thought, but we had to do what we could to get a better debate going on Europe'. The desire to keep on the right side of Murdoch probably led to a toning down of Blair's instinctive pro-Europeanism and was one amongst a number of factors leading to his decision in April 2004 to promise a referendum on the then EU constitution. It was a Murdoch/Blair relationship rather than a Murdoch/Labour one. Nonetheless, Murdoch also maintained a relationship with Brown, both as Chancellor and then, after June 2007, as Prime Minister. Murdoch appreciated Brown's global viewpoint, and his desire to move away from a European trading bloc approach.

Blair and Campbell only courted Murdoch and other proprietors and editors because they believed they mattered and could influence the political debate and the attitudes of voters. While their motives were the same as Palmerston, Lloyd George, and Wilson, the techniques used have changed considerably (as discussed in Tunstall 1970; 1996; Franklin 2004; and by Nicholas Jones in his accounts of how 10 Downing Street tries to influence the news agenda, notably 2002; 2006). We have had media monitoring units, communications strategies, a Strategic Communications Unit, grids about the timing of announcements, and the daily battle to dominate the news agenda. There is, however, a great danger of succumbing to the mythology of 'spin', propagated either by media advisers or by its 'victims' in the media (the role Nicholas Jones often adopts). The techniques may be different from the past, but the motives are the same. And the results are often less dramatic than assumed. For all the alleged skills of Alastair Campbell in 'spin', Tony Blair faced a hostile press for most of his time as Prime Minister, provoking his 'feral beasts' speech discussed below.

Until the 1920s, the written press enjoyed a monopoly in the provision of political news and they remained the dominant force until the late 1950s since the BBC was limited by statute and by ethos in both what it could report and how it reported news. The key characteristic of the British press was, and is, that it is national. Ever since the arrival of the railways and the abolition of the stamp tax in the 1850s, it has been possible to read a copy of a London edited paper virtually everywhere in Britain. Welsh and Scottish papers have continued to have leading roles in political debate, partly reflecting their distinctive political cultures which have been sustained by legislative devolution in the late 1990s. Many of the English provincial papers had a significant national influence on politics in the nineteenth and early twentieth centuries but have suffered declines in circulation, particularly since the 1980s, leaving the London edited nationals as the dominant voice in political debate in England. However, while daily morning and evening papers in the big cities are in serious decline, local weeklies are surviving and the *Metro* freesheets (financed by advertising) have generally been very successful. The 1,300 local and regional papers still matter within their circulation areas. In both the 2001 and 2005 general elections, Labour, and then the Conservatives, targeted such local papers, as well as women's magazines and the ethnic press, in order to bypass the more partisan national press. Local candidates, and challengers, spent a lot of effort getting their message into such papers, which are widely read precisely for their local focus, including on local candidates rather than national parties.

The reach of the national newspapers has been considerable. The circulation of daily newspapers peaked in the early 1950s at more than 16.6 million, dominated by the strongly pro-Conservative *Daily Express* and the equally strongly pro-Labour *Daily Mirror*, both with daily sales of well over 4 million. Since each paper was read by several people, this meant that the vast majority of the adult population saw a daily paper in this period. Total daily circulation began to decline from the early 1960s onwards, at first gradually, then more rapidly in the 1990s and 2000s. Daily sales went below 14 million at the end of the 1980s and dropped sharply from over 13 million to around 11.5 million between the 1997 and 2001 elections. In 2007, total circulation of the daily newspapers was less than 11 million. This amounts to a loss of more than a third in daily sales in half a century. This decline varies between market sectors, being much worse for the daily and Sunday red-tops. The 'qualities' have sought, with mixed success, to resist decline through DVDs and other promotions, as well as discounted sales to subscription buyers.

The British press has also been fiercely partisan, at least at a national level, though often less so locally (where *Metros* and other freesheets have taken a more impartial stance for marketing reasons). Before 1914 some papers even received direct subsidies from parties and wealthy politicians, and the *Daily Herald* was partly backed by the TUC until the 1960s. A majority of papers, particularly at the mass-selling tabloid end of the market, have strongly supported one party or the other. According to the analysis by David Butler and Gareth Butler (2000: 537), the total circulation of Conservative-supporting papers during the 1950s was roughly half the total, and with around two-fifths of the sales by Labour-supporting papers (the *Daily Mirror* and the partly TUC-financed *Daily Herald*). The remaining tenth of the circulation came from Liberal supporting papers, the *News Chronicle* and the then *Manchester Guardian*. At this period, there was a close correlation between the relative share of

Conservative circulation and the party's share of the vote in general elections. But the Labour Party tended to perform between six and nine points better than the sales share of the two Labour-supporting papers. And the Liberals always underperformed the relative sales of their newspaper allies in the 1950s.

The picture changed in the 1960s, both with the death of the *News Chronicle* in 1960 and its absorption into the *Daily Mail* and the transformation of the *Daily Herald* into the *Sun* in 1964, and its takeover by Rupert Murdoch's News International in 1969. In time, this dramatically changed the balance of partisanship. The percentage of total sales accounted for by Conservative-supporting papers rose steadily in the 1970s, hitting a peak of 78 per cent in the Thatcher landslide election victory of 1983. By the contrast, the relative share of Labour-supporting newspapers declined steadily, to only just over 30 per cent during the 1970s and a low point of 22 per cent in 1983. Support for the Labour Party also dropped sharply in this period, touching a low of 28 per cent in 1983. By contrast with the 1950s, the Liberals, and then in 1983 and 1987 the Social Democratic/Liberal Alliance, were under-represented in the press.

A big change occurred in 1997 when the Conservatives were swept from power by Tony Blair, and the party won just 31 per cent of votes cast. Then, Conservative-supporting papers accounted for just 34 per cent of total circulation. By contrast, Labour-supporting papers accounted for 60 per cent of total sales, and the party won 43 per cent of the total vote. The switch was almost entirely explained by Rupert Murdoch's decision to swing the *Sun* behind Tony Blair. In sales terms, there was a swing of more than 32 per cent from Conservative to Labour between 1992 and 1997, at the same time as there was a 10 per cent swing among voters themselves. These trends were broadly maintained over the following two elections when Conservative-supporting papers had 29 and 37 per cent of total sales in 2001 and 2005 respectively, while Labour-supporting ones had 71 and 54 per cent respectively (see Butler and Butler 2006: 274). The changes between the 1997 and later elections are largely explained by the switch to, and away from, Labour by the *Daily Express*, while *The Times* backed Labour in both 2001 and 2005. Although pro-Labour support was at its peak in 2001, the most significant shift occurred between 1992 and 1997, when Labour won power.

But these shifts do not mean that the press was itself responsible for changes in voting behaviour: 'It's the *Sun* wot won it' was claimed after the unexpected Conservative victory in the 1992 election. Some studies have suggested that the *Sun* and other tabloids made a difference in the final week of the campaign, but mistakes made by Neil Kinnock, the Labour leader, could have been as important. Moreover, the line of causation can as plausibly be seen in the opposite direction with newspapers, particularly the tabloids, following their readers rather than leading them. That was certainly true of the *Sun*'s decision to back Tony Blair at the 1997 election. Polling evidence shows *Sun* readers had moved heavily against the Conservatives much earlier in response to the party's bitter divisions over Europe and a rise in taxes. The eventual switch of political support was much more a case of a newspaper fitting in with a majority of its readers' views than of a proprietor determining voters.

The pro-Conservative bias of the press in the 1960s did not stop Harold Wilson from winning elections. It is important to distinguish between various degrees of pro-Labour, or often pro-Blair, support. The *Daily Mirror*, for instance, remained a pro-Labour paper throughout the Blair years, but, as the Piers Morgan diaries (2005) record, was often fiercely critical of the government, notably over the Iraq War.

Television and radio have become much more important as a source of political news and in shaping public views than the written press since the 1960s. In the 1960s and 1970s, the national political conversation was conducted through the main television evening news bulletins. But the position has become more diverse since the early 1980s as a result of a series of Broadcasting Acts, which have led to gradual deregulation and the proliferation of outlets. First, there was the arrival of Channel 4 in 1982, and then cable and satellite news from 1989. This led to the creation of round-the-clock news channels in Sky News and BBC News 24, matching CNN and later Fox and other channels in the USA. This meant that the combined viewing share of BBC and ITV, including BBC2 and Channel 4, fell from 100 per cent in the late 1980s to less than 75 per cent by 2004.

The main broadcasters are statutorily forbidden from backing one party or another, and have elaborate rules on balance. Until the arrival of ITV in 1955, the BBC's political coverage was anodyne. A more assertive, adversarial, and, at times, aggressive style developed from the 1960s onwards. Together with the changes in newspapers noted above, and the arrival of the Internet, the narrow, heavily regulated, and essentially parternalistic media culture of the middle of the century had disappeared by the mid-to-late 1990s. So far, the Murdoch-controlled Sky has not adopted the stridently conservative partisan style of Fox, its American counterpart in the News Corporation empire.

The influence of newspapers and television has been debated at length. David Denver (1992: 99) has argued that the impact is complicated and indirect thanks to selective exposure (that is, many people avoiding politics altogether in the press or on television); selective perception (existing values editing out information so that people accept what they want to believe and ignore what they do not); and selective retention (so that people remember only what they want to remember). This is what is known as the reinforcement through filter effect. The media may reinforce attitudes and, perhaps most important of all, affect the agenda of the political debate by highlighting issues such as the number of asylum seekers, violent crime, and Europe. The strong Euro-scepticism, indeed Euro-phobia, of the *Daily Mail*, *Sun*, and *Daily Telegraph* from the early 1990s onwards probably had a cumulative impact on voters' views of the European Union. This stridency made political leaders very reluctant to reach new European agreements which might prove to be very unpopular with voters, particularly when there was the implicit threat that proprietors like Rupert Murdoch might withdraw their general support from the governing party.

The rise of television altered the way in which political journalism worked. This has been much less to do with partisanship as such than with deference to the established political order. The world of the fourteen-day rule, banning discussion of issues due to come before Parliament over the following fourteen days, was Westminster centred. Sir Winston Churchill defended the rule shortly before he left 10 Downing Street in 1955 on the grounds that 'it would be shocking to have debates in the House forestalled, time after time, by expressions of opinion by persons who had the status or responsibility of MPs on this new robot organization of television and BBC broadcasting' (as discussed in Cockerell 1988: 50–1). The rule was only abandoned in 1956 with the arrival of ITV and the Suez Crisis.

In this period, senior politicians regarded most political journalists as social, and intellectual, inferiors rather than as equals from a similar educational and social background. Writing about the early 1950s, Anthony Seldon argued (1981: 51) that 'Many of the journalists themselves, compared to their successors a decade later, were comparatively docile and deferential to establishment figures'. That picture is underlined by the classic analysis of lobby correspondents in the late 1960s by Jeremy Tunstall (1970: 33–7): 'the broad picture of the majority of Lobby men coming from middle and lower-middle class backgrounds is supported by the occupations of their fathers, which were mainly within the clerical and white collar range, with a sprinkling of manual workers at one end and professionals at the other'. The median age for finishing education of these correspondents was seventeen. A few had left school at fifteen; two-thirds had gone to a grammar school and just a quarter had been to university. Until 1950, university graduates made up only a tiny minority of entrants to British journalism, including political writers. This is not surprising since only a small minority of the population, even only 6 per cent by 1960, went into full-time higher education. There was, and is, no formal training for political journalists: socialization is informal and on the job. Political correspondents, in particular, have tended to spend a large part of their careers in this role rather than moving on or up a hierarchy.

The rapid expansion of higher education from the 1960s onwards has meant that all but a handful of senior political correspondents in their late fifties now have a university education, a majority at either Oxford or Cambridge. Their backgrounds are very similar to those of the politicians they cover, in both cases from either the public- or private-sector professional middle classes. There are several examples of journalists turned politician and politicians turned journalist, a permeable divide. Similarly, in many cases, journalists and politicians have known each other from university days, so there is no sense of deference. Indeed, in many cases, the relationship has been turned round with MPs envious of the prominence and higher salaries of leading journalists, particularly on television. Fewer younger political journalists have spent time on provincial papers and more have entered nationals via graduate trainee schemes, and there are many more women political correspondents (who hardly existed in the period covered by Tunstall's 1970 book). Women political journalists have formed a group which lunches collectively from time to time with leading politicians, including, but not exclusively, female ones. The Tunstall study has not been updated, but Ian Hargreaves (2003: 122–3) quotes research showing that a British working journalist is as likely to be a woman as a man; more than two-thirds are aged under forty; only 4 per cent are from ethnic minority groups; just 3 per cent of new entrants have parents who were unskilled or semi-skilled; 98 per cent are graduates and are relatively low paid (earning an average of £22,500 in 2002). Political journalists are more likely to be male (despite the growing numbers of female correspondents), older (certainly among political editors and senior correspondents), and even in 2002 to have earned at least twice the average, and in many cases much more.

The similarities of background between many correspondents and the politicians they cover risks reinforcing the image of a closed Westminster world. Even so, this is now much more open than in the 1950s, when not only was the BBC muzzled, but the politicians could also be sure of having their views fully and faithfully reported in the pages of the newspapers. The broadsheets all carried full-page gallery reports of what was said on the floor of the House of Commons. The amount of space devoted to these reports began to decline in the late 1970s and had disappeared entirely by the end of the 1980s. In 1992, Jack Straw, then a member of Labour's Shadow Cabinet, organized a study of the quantity of press reporting of Parliament over a sixty-year period. This highlighted the extent of the decline in gallery coverage. In *The Times*, the daily coverage of Parliament varied between 450 and 1,050 lines on a series of sample dates between the early 1930s and the late 1980s, and was often nearer the upper end. In the *Guardian*, the average was between 300 and 700 lines. But by 1992, fewer than 100 lines a day were dedicated to the proceedings of Parliament in either of these papers (for more details see Straw 1993). However, the public now has direct access to what is said on the floor of the Commons and the Lords via the Parliamentary website, so that many more people follow debates than in the past.

There are two main reasons for this change. First, the decline in newspaper circulations noted above had increased competitive pressures and put a premium on both space and articles which executives believed would attract new, and younger, readers. Second, the Commons chamber was no longer the centre of political debate. This was partly because of the greater importance of television and radio: ministers, opposition spokesmen, and leading backbenchers would far rather have a prime spot on the *Today* programme on BBC Radio 4 in the morning than open a Commons debate. Moreover, power and debate had shifted away from the Commons chamber not just to the broadcasting studios but also to select committees within Westminster and, more importantly, to European institutions, to the judiciary, to devolved legislatures and assemblies, and to semi-independent regulators. The proceedings of Parliament became part of broader political stories. The decline in gallery report has been matched by the increased prominence given to sketches, or witty colour pieces, by star writers on papers. The disappearance of gallery coverage coincided with the arrival of television cameras in the Commons chamber in 1989. Its main effect, paradoxically, was indirect since the creation of extensive television studios at 4 Millbank, a few minutes' walk from the main Palace of Westminster, made it much easier for MPs to give interviews.

These gallery reports have been superseded by more wide-ranging political stories on the key events of the day. These were, and are, written by lobby correspondents, a much misunderstood term for journalists based at Westminster, on a list kept by the Commons authorities, largely for security reasons since attacks by Fenian groups in the 1880s. They are allowed access to parts of the Palace of Westminster, notably the members' lobby outside the Commons chamber and adjoining areas, denied to members of the public.

The most contentious, and misunderstood, aspect of the lobby system is the twice daily briefings (once on Friday) conducted by the Prime Minister's chief press spokesman. As Jeremy Tunstall has noted (1996: 257): 'These daily briefings probably do not generate more than one-fifth of the stories and take up much less than one-fifth of the working time of a team of lobby journalists'. Most of the daily briefings are about the Prime Minister's engagements and comments on the events of the day.

The main criticism is that lobby journalists become too close to their sources. This turns on the unattributable basis of conversations. A politician will talk on so-called lobby terms; that is, his or her identity will not be revealed. This leads to some absurd circumlocutions. Is a senior minister a member of the Cabinet? Is a friend of X minister X himself, or his or her special adviser, or a friendly backbencher? This cannot only be confusing but can also lead to lazy and inaccurate journalism. But unattributable conversations are an inescapable part of political journalism, as of all other kinds of journalism. To insist as some high-minded critics do that all quotations in political stories should be attributed is naive and would unquestionably deprive readers and listeners of their understanding of what is happening in politics. From time to time, newspapers such as the new *Independent* in 1986, and then the *Guardian*, have boycotted the lobby briefings, or have said they will no longer carry unattributable quotations, claims easily contradicted by looking at their papers. The real issue is not the use of unattributable quotations, but their accuracy and reliability. (These issues are well discussed in the account of parliamentary reporting by Andrew Sparrow, a political correspondent himself (2003).)

A more pertinent question is whether political coverage is too Westminster centred—too concerned with parliamentary politics and not enough with what is happening in town and country halls, let alone in the devolved legislatures in Edinburgh, Cardiff, and Belfast. That remains a valid criticism. However, the down-grading of political coverage has been matched by an increase in specialist reporting by non-Westminster based journalists on home affairs, education, health, defence, etc. The political editors of the main papers are no longer as important as they once were. Yet comparing the lengthier stories of the 1950s and 1960s with the shorter ones of the 1990s onwards, the balance sheet is not all negative. There is now a greater willingness to probe behind the words of the official spokesman, while the absence of deference has meant that more is known about internal government discussions.

However, coverage has become more personality and scandal driven. Hard cases, and scandals (alleged or real), make good stories, not analysis or a sense of perspective and proportion. Policy and analysis are seen as boring. Major bills will be discussed only when they are introduced—and then more often by a specialist correspondent rather than by a political journalist. This shift has worked against parties like the Liberal Democrats, or even smaller groups, and individual backbench MPs. More recent moves away from a broadsheet to a tabloid or compact format have reinforced these trends. Instead of a choice of stories on a front page, there is now just one, which is presented more vividly and sharply. But secondary stories suffer and competitive pressures and declining sales have meant more of an emphasis on health and consumer interest rather than political stories.

These trends—the decline in gallery/straight reporting, the decline in deference, the squeeze on political news—have fuelled an adversarial, cynical attitude, an exaggerated populism of 'they are in it for themselves' and 'they are all liars' variety. That has been linked to the rise of the celebrity journalist, often a columnist or broadcasting interviewer, who is not only better known and paid than most elected politicians but is also seen as having a higher public standing, not least by himself or herself. These changes place a premium on attracting audiences: strong opinions and ranting are preferred over analysis and detachment. This is less about partisanship in the traditional sense of a newspaper backing one party or another than of a well-known columnist becoming a partisan figure, in effect a player in the political world.

The growing numbers of by-lined columnists and correspondents, particularly from the 1960s onwards, has had a major influence on the political debate. Via their close, daily contacts with leading ministers and Opposition spokesmen, they have been able to offer superior and more up-to-date insights into the working of the political system than the vast majority of political scientists. If distinguished political scientists such as David Butler, Robert Mackenzie, Anthony King, and Dennis Kavanagh were able to bridge the academic/political divide in the second half of the twentieth century, they were increasingly rivalled by columnists such as David Watt, Hugo Young, and Peter Jenkins as authors of the first draft of history. The latter three, who all died in their prime, were highly influential on the centre and social democratic left and in the elite worlds of Whitehall. They had access which no political scientist could rival. However, from the 1990s onwards, the most influential journalists were on the centre-right and among broadcasters, such as Trevor Kavanagh of the *Sun* (because of the paper he wrote for) and BBC political editors such as Andrew Marr and Nick Robinson. Newspaper columnists tended to be more committed rather than detached, arguing, often cogently, from a clear ideological viewpoint: Polly Toynbee of the *Guardian* or Matthew D'Ancona of the *Sunday Telegraph* and the *Spectator*.

John Lloyd (2004) has forcefully argued that the media are no longer functioning as an inquiring check on the excesses of the political class. Instead, they have become an alternative establishment, dedicated to a theatrical distrust of both individual MPs and of politicians as a class. The counter-view is that political journalism exists to challenge the political world rather than to be responsible or civic. But it is questionable whether many journalists, and media outlets, any longer perform that role. From a different perspective, Peter Oborne (1999; 2007) has discussed the growth of an exclusive media class, as the counterpart and collaborator of a political class, increasingly privileged and detached from the ordinary voter.

Arguments about the role of the press and political journalists boiled to the surface in the second half of the Blair government, notably over the Iraq War. The complicated saga of the open conflict between 10 Downing Street and the BBC over Andrew Gilligan's reports over weapons of mass destruction, the death of the government scientist David Kelly, the subsequent report by Lord Hutton, and the resignations of both the chairman and director-general of the BBC have been fully discussed elsewhere (from one side in Campbell and Stott 2007: 711–54; in Raymond Kuhn's chapter in Seldon 2007: 123–42; in Lord Hutton's report, 2004; and in Oborne 2007: 147–8, 173–4). Without going into all the detail, the affair highlighted the issue of 'spin', tarnished the reputation of Alastair Campbell, and led to lengthy soul-searching at the BBC itself. Before these controversies had erupted, an official committee had been established under Bob Phillis, a distinguished former BBC executive and then chief executive of Guardian Media, to examine the three-way breakdown in trust between government and politicians, the media, and the general public. The report (Phillis 2004: 7) concluded that this had led to popular disillusionment and voter disengagement. In particular, the aggressive approach of Labour and 'increased use of selective briefing of media outlets, in which government information was seen to be being used to political advantage, led to a reaction from the media that has produced a far more adversarial relationship with government'. The result was some organizational changes within Whitehall but little change in the fundamental relationship.

Consequently, on the eve of his departure from 10 Downing Street, Tony Blair gave a major lecture (2007: 476–87) solely about relations with the press, which attracted most attention for just one phrase about the media hunting in a pack and being like a 'a feral beast'. He related this to five complaints: first, 'scandal or controversy beats ordinary reporting hands down'; second, 'attacking motive is far more potent than attacking judgement'; third, 'the fear of missing out means that today's media, more than ever before, hunts in a pack'; fourth, 'rather than just report news, even if sensational or controversial, the new technique is commentary on the news being as, if not more, important than the news itself'; and, fifth, 'the confusion of news and commentary'. The speech divided opinion, largely reflecting the views held about Mr Blair in the first place. Many felt that Mr Blair was an unconvincing media commentator in view of what he and his advisers had themselves done. They were blamed both for day-to-day 'spin' and for changes in regulation which encouraged more competitive and 'feral' media practices. Nonetheless, most of Mr Blair's charges stand up even if some are exaggerated and are the by-product of a vigorous press. The same themes were taken by Alastair Campbell (2008) in the Cudlipp Lecture when he attacked the media's failure to distinguish between speculation and information, or between the important and the trivial; the incestuous way in which television, radio, and newspapers retell each other's stories without further verification; the focus on getting the story first rather than getting it right; and 'the language of extremes' in which most news is framed. Again, most, even sympathetic commentators argued that Campbell was hardly the right person to make the critique since he had been guilty of many of the sins about which he now complained. Gordon Brown came to office determined to be more open, cutting down the size of the Downing Street media operation, and telling Parliament first about government announcements rather than trailing/leaking stories first in the media (his own frequent past approach). These good intentions only lasted into the autumn of 2007. Although there were many Commons statements, the practice of pre-briefing revived, and, after a general reappraisal of his Downing Street operation, the media planning side was strengthened, along lines very similar to the Blair era.

Many long-standing assumptions about political journalism have been challenged by the rise of the Internet since the 1990s. According to research commissioned by the Carnegie Corporation of New York (cited in Riddell 2006: 70), among eighteen to thirty-four-year-old Americans, the Internet beats newspapers by 49 to 9 per cent in providing news 'only when I want it' and by 29 to 4 per cent in being up to date. Only on trustworthiness is there a virtual tie. There are now a multitude of political websites, some of which set out deliberately to challenge the mainstream press, proclaiming that they are outside the journalistic establishment (though, in practice, their sources come from within the world of Westminster). They range from the anarchistic and muck-racking like Guido Fawkes, to a forum for Conservative Party news and developments such as ConservativeHome. The latter supplements the much reduced coverage in most newspapers and has become essential reading for anyone following the Conservative Party. There is a close mutual relationship between conventional journalists and bloggers as each feeds off the other. Many leading print and broadcast journalists are themselves active and influential bloggers. Moreover, the most successful sites are those run by mainstream media groups, notably the BBC and the Guardian, followed by *The Times* and the *Sun*. Many newspapers are integrating their print and online operations so that political journalists can expect both to blog and write for the paper. This is leading to changes in approach: between the immediate, often fast written, blog or post and the more reflective piece in the paper. The extent of these changes is only beginning to be seen.

Blogging has the virtue of being democratic, rather than elitist, and personal and individual. It broadens accountability in that most news stories, features, and columns in the main papers are posted online where readers can blog. So the initial story initiates a discussion. But the very unchecked spontaneity of blogging—its inherent lack of discipline and constraint—is also its central weakness. Blogging can easily descend into the spreading of unreliable and untested assertions, and ignorant and ill-informed prejudices. There is no intermediary, no editing function, apart from the blocking out of the most obviously defamatory or obscene. The comments on the main political sites reveal a world of bigoted and highly partisan obsessives who often do not have a clue what they are talking about. That is pub gossip, not journalism. So, while political blogging is, in theory, democratic, it is in practice often dominated by activists and enthusiasts. Debate may be widened but not the provision of information and analysis. Bloggers can provide instant, on-the-spot reports—and photographs via mobile phones. But they cannot, by definition, provide a rounded picture which can only come through the collective enterprise of conventional journalism.

Nonetheless, the Internet can, and should, supplement conventional newspaper and broadcast journalism. For newspapers, at any rate, it will soon become secondary whether a story or feature is communicated via paper or online, or even by text message on a Blackberry or a mobile phone. Media groups will become brands which communicate in a multitude of different ways. Moreover, official news can be made available more cheaply and widely via the Internet. This applies not just to government publications but also to the Hansard reports on the proceedings of Parliament.

If the Internet is, at its best, an opportunity to broaden political debate away from the traditional elite-talking-to-the-elite model, and to ensure that readers are better served and informed, some traditional journalistic virtues need to be reasserted. The lines between partisan politics and journalism need to be clearer. The party line is the enemy of vigorous, independent journalism. Yet, for all the valid criticisms of partisanship, and an excessive emphasis on personalities, splits, and triviality, the public has the opportunity in at least some parts of the national media, and increasingly the Internet, to become better informed about the main issues of the day, and the background arguments, than in the closed political and media worlds of the 1940s and 1950s.

References

BLAIR, T. 2007. 'Feral Beasts', speech to Reuters Institute, London, 12 June 2007; collected with commentaries in *Political Quarterly*, 78/4 (Oct.–Dec.): 471–99.

BUTLER, D., and BUTLER, G. 2000. *Twentieth-century British Political Facts 1900–2000*. London: Macmillan.

—————— 2006. *British Political Facts Since 1979*. London: Palgrave Macmillan.

CAMPBELL, A. 2008. Cudlipp Lecture, Monday, 29 Jan.

—— and STOTT, R. (eds.) 2007. *The Blair Years: Extracts from* The Alastair Campbell Diaries. London: Hutchinson.

COCKERELL, M. 1988. *Live from Number 10: The Inside Story of Prime Ministers and Television*. London: Faber and Faber.

DENVER, D. 1992. *Elections and Voting Behaviour*. London: Harvester Wheatsheaf.

FRANKLIN, R. 2004. *Packaging Politics: Political Communications in Britain's Media Democracy*. London: Hodder Arnold.

HARGREAVES, I. 2003. *Journalism: A Very Short Introduction*. Oxford: Oxford University Press.

HUTTON, LORD 2004. *Report of the Inquiry into the Circumstances Surrounding the Death of Dr David Kelly CMG by Lord Hutton*. House of Commons paper 247. London: Stationery Office.

JONES, N. 2002. *The Control Freaks: How New Labour Gets its Own Way*. London: Politico's.

—— 2006. *Trading Information*. London: Politico's.

LLOYD, J. 2004. *What the Media Are Doing to Our Politics*. London: Constable.

MORGAN, P. 2005. *The Insider: The Private Diaries of a Scandalous Decade*. London: Ebury Press.

OBORNE, P. 1999. *Alastair Campbell: New Labour and the Rise of the Media Class*. London: Aurum.

—— 2007. *The Triumph of the Political Class*. London: Simon and Schuster.

PHILLIS, R. 2004. *An Independent Review of Government Communications*. London: Stationery Office.

PRICE, L. 2005. *The Spin Doctor's Diary: Inside Number 10 with New Labour*. London: Hodder and Stoughton.

RIDDELL, P. 1994. 'Not a Word of Thanks from Lady Thatcher'. *British Journalism Review*, 5/1.

——1998. 'Members and Millbank: The Media and Parliament'. Pp. 8–18 in J. Seaton (ed.), *Politics and the Media: Harlots and Prerogatives at the Turn of the Millennium*. Oxford: Blackwell.

——2006. 'The Rise of the Ranters: Saving Political Journalism'. In J. Lloyd and J. Seaton (eds.), *What Can Be Done? Making the Media and Politics Better*. Oxford: Blackwell.

SELDON, A. 1981. *Churchill's Indian Summer: The Conservative Government 1951–55*. London: Hodder and Stoughton.

——(ed.) 2007. *Blair's Britain, 1997–2007*. Cambridge: Cambridge University Press.

SPARROW, A. 2003. *Obscure Scribblers: A History of Parliamentary Reporting*. London: Politico's.

STRAW, J. 1993. 'Democracy on the Spike'. *British Journalism Review*, 4/4.

TUNSTALL, J. 1970. *The Westminster Lobby Correspondents: A Sociological Study of National Political Journalism*. London: Routledge and Kegan Paul.

——1996. *Newspaper Power: The New National Press in Britain*. Oxford: Clarendon Press.

WOODS, O., and BISHOP, J. 1983. *The Story of The Times*. London: Michael Joseph.

CHAPTER 11

BIOGRAPHY

DAVID MARQUAND

IN Britain, at least, the relationship between political biography and the academic study of politics varies between the distantly tolerant and the mildly suspicious. Perhaps because politics as an academic discipline had a remarkably slow birth in Britain, and for much of its history had a lower status than many other social sciences, British political science has always been heterogeneous, eclectic, and untidy and has successfully resisted capture by any single orthodoxy. In the early days of the politics profession, what was misleadingly called 'behaviourism' was fashionable, at least among its young Turks. But behaviourism never drove out older institutional and historical approaches and, in any case, the fashion did not last. In the turbulent 1960s and 1970s, Marxist approaches enjoyed a certain vogue, but they too never dominated the discipline. The same has been true of rational choice and its derivatives in our own day. In the crooks and crannies of the politics profession, minority species, which might have perished in a more uniform and tightly organized discipline, have survived and even prospered—biographers among them.

The late Ben Pimlott is perhaps the most glittering case in point. He held a Chair in Politics before becoming Warden of Goldsmith's College, London, and was elected a Fellow of the British Academy, where he belonged to the Politics section. He had gained a doctorate with a careful study of the Labour Left in the 1930s, but he made his reputation with a masterly, and exceptionally well received, biography of Hugh Dalton. He then went on to write biographies of Harold Wilson and the present Queen. Another example is Bernard Crick, a distinguished political theorist who held chairs at the Universities of Sheffield and London, and wrote a best-selling biography of George Orwell. Anthony Wright, now a Labour MP but before his election a political scientist at Birmingham University, has published studies of G. D. H. Cole and R. H. Tawney which are, at least in part, biographical in approach. The best biography of Harold Laski was written by Michael Newman, Professor of Politics at

London Metropolitan University, who has also published a biography of the Marxist political theorist, Ralph Miliband. David McLellan held a politics post at the University of Kent when he published his acclaimed biography of Marx. The present writer was appointed to a Politics Chair at Salford University, largely on the strength of a biography of Ramsay MacDonald.

But though biographers have found homes in the academic discipline of Politics, and have even flourished within it, their numbers have been comparatively small. The ranks of academic biographers have swollen substantially in recent years (a point I shall return to later), but most of them have been historians, not political scientists. And though some political scientists have published political or intellectual biographies, sometimes of high quality, political science *as a discipline* has made little use of their labours, and has had little or nothing to say about the light that biography might throw on the life of politics or on the great questions which students of politics have addressed or might profitably come to address. By the same token, political scientist biographers have rarely tried to apply insights gained from their academic study of politics to their biographical writings.

There is an oddity in all this which deserves more attention than it appears to have received. Political life is, after all, lived by individual people, not by sociological abstractions or economic categories. When Mrs Thatcher famously said there was no such thing as society, but only individuals and their families, she was making a political point designed to discomfit her ideological opponents and give heart to her supporters. But, though her aphorism shocked (and was almost certainly intended to shock) the *bien pensant* liberal-left, it embodied a truth which students of politics, irrespective of their ideological affiliations, ignore at their peril. There is a sense in which there is indeed no such thing as society—and, for that matter, no such thing as class, or party, or nation, or the Treasury, or the Foreign Office, or the Cabinet. Terms like 'the Treasury view', 'the Cabinet's decision', 'the British position', or the 'working-class demand' are convenient shorthand for messy and indeterminate realities, procured by complex interactions between different and sometimes divergent political actors. Decisions are not taken by institutions; they are taken by individuals who belong to institutions. (Anyone who doubts that should read Stephen Roskill's massive and masterly biography of Maurice Hankey (Roskill 1970–4), the first and still the longest-lasting Cabinet Secretary and the effective creator of the Cabinet Office.) The individuals concerned are, of course, constrained in a host of ways by the institutions to which they belong and the values and assumptions which those institutions embody and transmit. But different individuals react to these constraints in different ways.

Even that stern determinist and unbending materialist, Karl Marx, conceded that 'men make their own history', albeit with the caveat that, since the circumstances they encounter are inherited from the past, they cannot make it 'just as they please' (Marx 1951: 225). 'The Eighteenth Brumaire of Louis Bonaparte', from which these famous phrases come, is a mordant study of the interplay between the personal character of Louis Napoleon, an 'adventurer blown in from abroad, raised on the shield by a drunken soldiery', and the social and economic forces with which he had to deal. The tacit premise on which the essay is based is that Louis Napoleon's *coup d'état* was (unsurprisingly) made by none other than Louis Napoleon—and that in making it he made a difference to the balance of social forces in France and the fate of the French. Some contemporary political scientists have followed where Marx led. Ivor Crewe's and Anthony King's study of the SDP (1995) is not a biography, but it contains penetrating analyses of the roles of Roy Jenkins, Shirley Williams, and David Owen in the party's rise and fall and of their motives, assumptions, strengths, and weaknesses; and it shows that the complex interactions between these and others helped to determine the party's fate. Andrew Gamble's now classic account (1988) of the Thatcher revolution leaves the reader in no doubt that Thatcher herself was a prime mover in the story: that a history of the Thatcher years that ignored her extraordinary combination of will, courage, guile, and rhetorical skill would be *Hamlet* without the Prince of Denmark. But Crewe, King, and Gamble have had all too few imitators.

11.1 LIFE WITHOUT THEORY?

A further oddity is that political biography is very much an Anglo-American speciality. Distinguished political biographies have, of course, appeared in Continental Europe. One thinks of Jean Lacouture's biographies of Leon Blum and Charles de Gaulle, for example, to say nothing of Franz Mehring's classic biography of Karl Marx (Lacouture 1977: 1990–1; Mehring 2003). But the tradition of writing about politics in a biographical mode is far stronger in this country and the United States than on the Continent, perhaps reflecting a certain suspicion of high theory endemic in the English-speaking world. (It was not for nothing that Disraeli extolled biography as 'life without theory'.) British and American politicians are not, of course, ideology free, but they are—or at least pretend to be—ideology light, and they inhabit a culture that purports to value robust and down-to-earth common sense more than theoretical speculation. Lord Salisbury's disdain for Iain Macleod on the grounds that he was 'too clever by half' might have been echoed in the United States, but it is hard to imagine a French or German politician saying anything of the sort. Outside the academy, British and American readers have shared Disraeli's assumption that the biographer's 'life without theory' is somehow more real, because less clever, than straightforward history. Non-academic writers have tended to follow suit.

Against that background, I want to trace the evolution of political biography, particularly in Britain, over the last century and a half. The story begins with the vast, intimidating, so-called 'tombstone' biographies of the Victorians and their early twentieth-century successors. The most famous examples are probably the biography of Disraeli by the distinguished *Times* journalists, William Monypenny and George

Buckle; the biographies of Gladstone and Cobden by the Liberal politician and man of letters John Morley; Lady Gwendolen Cecil's biography of her father, the great Lord Salisbury (a much grander figure than the Salisbury who sneered at Ian Macleod); and the biography of Joseph Chamberlain started by the famous *Observer* editor, J. L. Garvin, and completed by the Tory imperialist, L. S. Amery. These were massive, in some cases multi-volume works, enriched with copious quotations from Hansard, from speeches outside Parliament, from letters, and (where they were available) from diaries.

Private lives were treated very decorously, if at all. The working assumption of the authors was that the private lives of public men were irrelevant to their public roles. Their public lives were treated with commensurate respect, partly because the authors shared the political attitudes of their subjects, but much more because, in what was both a highly deferential and an intensely political culture, political activity seemed supremely worthwhile and political leadership inherently praiseworthy. Political biography had, in fact, a celebratory as well as an explanatory function. Biographers wrote (and were expected to write) in the spirit of Ecclesiasticus: 'Let us now praise famous men'. (Sometimes, praise was laid on with a trowel. 'How delicate, how decent is the English biography', wrote Carlyle, 'bless its mealy mouth' (quoted in Pimlott 1995: 153).)

The First World War, with its savage bloodletting, its endless succession of unsuccessful offensives, its bovine military incompetence, and its shameless profiteering and jockeying for promotion, led to a change of mood, among biographers as well as elsewhere. In May 1918, Lytton Strachey's iconoclastic, subversive, and best-selling *Eminent Victorians* swept into the world of the tombstone biographers like a tornado into an enclosed garden. It was not really a biography at all; it was a collection of biographical essays, elegant, short, brilliantly written, and wonderfully funny. It was also a manifesto, even a declaration of war. 'The art of biography', Strachey wrote in the preface, had 'fallen on evil times in England'.

> Those two fat volumes, with which it is our custom to commemorate the dead—who does not know them, with their ill-digested masses of material, their slipshod style, their tone of tedious panegyric, their lamentable lack of selection, of detachment, of design? They are as familiar as the *cortège* of the undertaker, and wear the same air of slow, funeral barbarism. One is tempted to suppose, of some of them, that they were composed by that functionary, as the final item of his job.   (Strachey 1979: 22)

Eminent Victorians was a best-seller. Unlike many best-sellers, it left an enduring mark on the public culture. It epitomized and, at the same time, reinforced a post-war mood of scepticism, verging on cynicism, about the pretensions of the famous, particularly if they were Victorians. The great—great men of action, above all—were inherently suspect. The task of the biographer was to get behind the façade of pompous respectability and probe the hidden weaknesses it concealed. Celebration was out, mocking scepticism was in. Strachey's Cambridge friend, John Maynard Keynes, followed the same approach in his famous depiction of the leading figures at the 1919 Paris Peace Conference. Woodrow Wilson was an 'old Presbyterian', so stubborn and unimaginative that it was impossible to 'de-bamboozle' him once he had been bamboozled. Clemenceau felt about France what Pericles had felt about Athens, 'unique value in her'. He had 'one illusion—France; and one disillusion—mankind' (Keynes 1951: 11–31). Lloyd George, the arch-bamboozler, was a 'syren', a 'goat-footed bard', a 'half-human visitor to our age from the hag-ridden magic and enchanted woods of Celtic antiquity'—cynical, inconstant, and with no discernible principles (ibid. 35).

Strachey and Keynes did not dispute the tombstone biographers' assumption that history revolved around individuals; famously, Keynes thought ideas (produced, of necessity, by individuals) ruled the world. But, in another Strachey phrase, they saw the individuals they wrote about as 'specimens', rescued from the distant depths of the past, to be examined with 'careful curiosity' rather than admiration, or even sympathy (Strachey 1979: 21). Theirs was biography in the spirit of the Cambridge Apostles, among whom they were numbered; and they shared the Apostles' disdain for the vulgarity and crudity of public life, and their emphasis on unflinching private honesty as a supreme good.

11.2 A New Golden Age?

Strachey and Keynes had few imitators—not least because they were both superb stylists, with a mastery of epigram that few could equal. Partly because of their writings, however—and much more because of the mood these encapsulated—tombstone biographers became an endangered species. The mammoth lives of Chamberlain and Disraeli which had been started before 1914 continued on their stately paths after 1918, but they were exceptional. For a generation or so after the First World War, biographers mostly wrote short.

The last forty years, however, have seen an intriguing, though only partial, return to the biographical fashions of the nineteenth century. Increasingly, biography writing has been colonized by scholars, operating in an academic mode, most of them professional historians, as I mentioned above, though with a small admixture of political scientists. (Not all the scholars concerned have been professional academics, however.) With varying degrees of success, the biographers of our day have tried to combine rigorous scholarship with literary grace. As well as the private papers of their subjects, they have used a wide range of archival sources, including other private collections and the voluminous public records in the National Archives. Wherever possible, they have also relied heavily on interviews with survivors. Unlike their nineteenth-century predecessors they have sought to exhume their subjects' private lives as well as their public roles. The result is a new golden age of political (and for that matter intellectual) biography, of remarkable intellectual fertility and literary quality. Biographies are now indispensable sources for the study of recent political and intellectual history; and in many cases they are a pleasure to read.

Ian Kershaw's two volumes on Hitler; Alan Bullock's three volumes on Ernest Bevin; Alistair Horne's two volumes on Harold Macmillan; John Campbell's two volumes on Margaret Thatcher; Roy Foster's two volumes on Yeats; and Robert Skidelsky's magnificent three volumes on Keynes are all great history as well as great biography, rivalling the old tombstone biographies of the nineteenth century in length, but far surpassing them in insight, depth, and scholarship. Substantial single-volume biographies—Philip Williams on Hugh Gaitskell; Robert Rhodes James on Eden; Kenneth Morgan on James Callaghan; José Harris on Beveridge; Robert Blake on Bonar Law and Disraeli; Simon Heffer on Enoch Powell; and V. S. Lyons on Parnell—tell the same story. Seemingly, Disraeli has been vindicated. 'Life without theory' has never been more popular outside the academy or more respected within it.

Yet, on closer inspection, the latest version of 'life without theory' is not as new as it seems. As Ben Pimlott has argued, today's political biographers nearly all follow a set of conventions—implicit, rather than explicit, in characteristic British fashion—different from those of their tombstone predecessors in the nineteenth century, but almost as constraining (Pimlott 1995: 149–61). For example, it has become almost *de rigueur* for biographers to discuss the private lives of their subjects (and particularly their sexual lives), even if the evidence is scanty or if the exercise reveals nothing of value; it is not difficult to see why this convention should have taken root in our prurient age of 'kiss and tell'. But, to put it at its lowest, it is not self-evident that the tacit assumptions underpinning it hold water. According to Pimlott, 'public and private facts clearly cannot be put in separate boxes. Real life accepts no such partition' (Pimlott 1995: 158). But, in truth, 'real life', whatever that might be, *does* accept that partition, and it is a symptom of morbidity when it ceases to do so.

The sexual life of my dentist is a matter of complete indifference to me. All I want from him is to care properly for my teeth. In times gone by the sexual lives of Prime Ministers were viewed with comparable indifference. Everyone in the political world knew that Lloyd George's private secretary was also his lover, but no one lost sleep over it, and the fact was not revealed in the public prints. (To be sure, open scandal in the divorce courts could, and sometimes did, destroy public figures: Charles Stewart Parnell, the leader of the Irish Home Rule party, and Sir Charles Dilke, the radical Liberal, are obvious examples. But the political world was extraordinarily good at avoiding open scandal.) The working assumption of today's biographers seems to be that our knowledge of Lloyd George's sexual proclivities yields a fuller or deeper or somehow more valid understanding of his political life than was available to the public of his day, but no one has explained why this should be so. Or take the case of Ernest Bevin. Bullock's magisterial biography has virtually nothing to say about Bevin's private life, presumably because he could find no evidence about it. Suppose someone discovers that Bevin was, in fact, having an affair with one of his secretaries. The discovery would add to the gaiety of nations, but would it really make Bevin's foreign policy more comprehensible?

This leads on to a wider point. Today, almost all biographers are happy to acknowl-edge errors of judgement on their subjects' part, and some are also prepared to acknowledge flaws of character. But though the celebratory mode of the nineteenth century has died out, its modern successor is essentially exculpatory. (Biographies of monsters like Hitler and Stalin are, of course, exceptions.) All too often, today's biographers behave rather like defence counsels in an imaginary court of history, deftly admitting their client's faults in order to disarm hostile criticism, and abusing the plaintiff's attorneys whenever they get the chance to do so. It is not difficult to see why. Biography writing is an art, not a science; it depends on feeling and intuition as well as on scholarship and analytical skill. Biographers become intimate with their subjects, particularly if the biography is substantial and the trail of paper and interviews long. Often the biographer knows more about the subject than did any single contemporary. Of course, intimacy does not necessarily breed affection; in principle, at least, it might breed contempt or even hatred. Intimacy and indifference, however, are mutually incompatible.

After prolonged immersion in the sayings and doings of another person, even if the person concerned is dead, an emotional relationship of some kind is almost inevitable, and it is usually one of sympathy, even if not of affection or admiration. If the subject has been subject to attack—and few have not—the sympathetic biogra-pher is apt to slide into the role of partisan defender, almost without realizing what is happening. By the same token, necessary and healthy sympathy for the subject often breeds unnecessary and unhealthy hostility towards the subject's rivals and enemies. Roy Jenkins's scrupulously fair-minded biography of Asquith was marred, he conceded himself, by unfair denigration of Lloyd George (private information); I now think that my own biography of Ramsay MacDonald did not do justice to Arthur Henderson, MacDonald's chief adversary in the battle over spending cuts that destroyed the second Labour government.

To use a hackneyed, but indispensable comparison, biographers are like portrait painters. They have to try to uncover the soul of the sitter—knowing, of course, that they can never do so completely. They have to do their best to see the world through their subjects' eyes. In some measure, at least, they have to feel what their subjects felt, or at least convince the reader that they have done so. This means that their approach to the transactions in which their subjects were involved is bound to differ from the straightforward historian's or social scientist's approach. Their task is not primarily to offer an 'objective' analysis and explanation of what happened. It is to explain—subjectively, as it were—how and why their subjects came to act *and feel* as they did. Of course, good biographers perform both tasks, at least to some degree. The third volume of Robert Skidelsky's biography of Keynes contains the best accounts I know, both of the long and complex negotiations that led to the Bretton Woods agreement in 1944, and of the shorter and less happy negotiations over the American Loan to Britain in 1945. But inevitably (and rightly) the focus is on Keynes. Skidelsky throws a massive flood of light on these tangled episodes, but his *purpose* is to show the reader (and 'show' is the right word, not 'tell') what Keynes thought and did. Biographies may, and often do, help us to unravel complex past events. But that is a bonus. The spotlight is trained on one single actor, who may not be the most important one from the historian's or political scientist's point of view. As the old saw had it, biography is, in the end, 'about chaps'—and nowadays, to some degree, about chapesses. Everything else is secondary.

11.3 THE SMELL OF BLOOD

By a fortunate paradox, therein lies biography's chief contribution to political understanding. A focus on individual 'chaps' helps to bring political transactions to life, in a way that more 'scientific' approaches cannot do. A good biographer helps us to smell the blood on the floor in moments of crisis, and to feel the swirling emotions that crisis generates, and is generated by. Reading Blake's biography, we gasp at the breathtaking *chutzpah* with which Disraeli voiced the resentment and sense of betrayal of the Tory country gentleman during the battles over the repeal of the Corn Laws in 1846, destroying the Conservative Prime Minister, Sir Robert Peel, in the process, and transforming himself from marginal political gadfly into front-rank politician. F. S. L. Lyons paints an unforgettable picture of the turbulent, self-destructive emotions that led Parnell into a doomed battle with a majority of the Irish Home Rule party after the revelation of his adultery with Kitty O'Shea, and of the terrible series of meetings in a House of Commons committee room where the Irish party tore itself to pieces. Ben Pimlott tears off the mask of stentorian self-confidence that concealed Dalton's inner insecurities from the world (and perhaps from himself), and in doing so helps us to understand why, despite great apparent qualifications for the post, his Chancellorship of the Exchequer was a story of political weakness, wishful thinking, and ultimate self-destruction.

Straightforward historians, and still more straightforward political scientists, are apt to concentrate too much on structure and not enough on agency. When they do focus on agency, they are apt to overemphasize the role of reason, logic, and calculation and to underemphasize the role of feeling. This is not to say that rational calculation plays no part in political life; patently, it plays a large part. But no one who hopes to understand political decision-making should forget Hume's famous dictum that reason is the slave of the passions. In times of crisis or perceived crisis, that slavery is particularly prominent. Then, above all, the light of reason burns low. Particularly when the decision is difficult or in some way critical, above all when it has existential significance for those involved (as important political decisions nearly always do), rational calculation—careful assessment of the odds, balancing the pros and cons—can only take the decision-maker so far. At the moment of truth, when the die has to be cast, the decision-maker must jump more or less blindly into the unknown, and that final jump can rarely be explained in purely rational terms. The sudden leap from cogitation to decision, in conditions of uncertainty and peril, is, in essence, a leap of faith which has more in common with a religious experience than with the petty transactions of day-to-day politics.

Afterwards, reason may take over again; but it does so *post facto*. By then Hume's 'passions' have prevailed and the balance of forces which rational calculation has to reckon with has changed for good or ill. Retrospectively, observers are apt to say that the decision-maker was always likely to take the decision she actually took, but that is wisdom after the event. In his history of twentieth-century France, Rod Kedward writes that resistance to the German occupation and the Vichy regime in the unoccupied zone was often a 'reflex response. A haphazard encounter was frequently the defining moment.' And he adds that there was 'no photo-fit resister, no ideal type, no model'; only biographies could 'do justice to the individuals involved' (Kedward 2005: 274–82).

Much the same applies, albeit in a different way, to the decisions of political life. One example is Ramsay MacDonald's handling of the financial and political crisis of August 1931. His minority Labour government was deadlocked over spending cuts to halt an accelerating run on sterling. After two weeks of havering, it was clear that it would have to resign. All the evidence suggests that MacDonald's initial reaction was to resign with it, but that, at the urging of the King, he changed his mind at the last moment, and decided to form a National Government instead. The results included a crushing Labour defeat at the subsequent general election, and almost a decade of Conservative hegemony. Many Labour people jumped to the conclusion that MacDonald had planned all along to betray his party. Many more came to believe that his conduct stemmed from deep-seated weaknesses of character and/or a long-standing lack of socialist faith.

But this was hindsight; and, as so often, hindsight was delusive. The truth is that MacDonald was torn. He faced in one direction at one moment, and in the opposite direction at another. Almost certainly he did not know what he was going to do until shortly before he did it. And by the same token, the King's urging—though not haphazard in any normal sense—played a similar role to that of the 'haphazard encounters' that Kedward describes in his paragraphs on the French resistance. We cannot know what went through MacDonald's mind at the crucial moment, but it is hard to believe that rational calculation played much part in it. After he made his leap of faith, events swept him and the Labour Party on, towards a split that no one had wanted or expected at the beginning. Not surprisingly, Labour people looking back at the whole episode once the split had taken place were apt to assume that the confused prelude, the leap of decision, and the bitter aftermath formed a consistent pattern. But consistency was imposed after the event.

There are plenty of other examples. The Falklands War of 1982 was the making of Margaret Thatcher. Before the war she had been one of the most unpopular Prime Ministers in recent British history, but it transformed her into an icon of reborn patriotic pride. Yet before Argentina seized the Falkland Islands in 1982 she had shown no interest in them, and had done nothing to convince the Argentine government that Britain would use force to prevent them from falling under Argentine rule. On the eve of the Argentine invasion it looked as if Britain would be forced to acquiesce: the military chiefs thought it impossible to retake the islands by force, and the Foreign Office wanted to lower the temperature. Then came a haphazard encounter, in the shape of the unscheduled arrival of the First Sea Lord, Sir Henry Leach, at a meeting in Mrs Thatcher's room in the House of Commons. Leach insisted that the navy could assemble a task force capable of recapturing the islands if the government had the necessary political will. Thatcher was persuaded; took her leap into the unknown; made a belligerent Commons speech announcing it; and within days the first elements of a British task force were under way. It was an extraordinary gamble. Rational calculation would have counselled against it, but passion prevailed. Thereafter, events swept on; and Thatcher won the 1983 election with a crushing majority.

Blair's decision to fight alongside the Americans in the Iraq War was also a gamble, as subsequent events have shown. We do not know when he made his leap, and there is no evidence of a decisive haphazard encounter. Arguably, the moment of truth came long before the war—conceivably in his Chicago speech of April 1999 when he singled out Saddam Hussein and Slobodan Milosevic as uniquely evil men; perhaps in the immediate aftermath of 9/11; perhaps early in 2002. But there is little doubt that there *was* a moment of truth and no doubt at all that, once Blair had made his leap into the unknown, rational calculation was subordinate to passion. Gladstone's decision to embrace Irish Home Rule followed a long, somewhat confused period of ratiocination—about the Irish Question itself; about the party politics involved and, not least, about the need, as he saw it, to deflect radical liberalism from the social issues pushed by the rising star of the Liberal left, Joseph Chamberlain. But by the time Gladstone took his decision, passion was in charge. A visitor to his house at Hawarden in the winter of 1885–6 found him:

> so excited when he talked about Ireland, it was quite frightening. He ended the conversation by saying 'Well it has come to this, we must give them [the Irish] a *great deal* or *nothing*.' And I answered with some warmth 'then *nothing*.' Upon which he pushed back his chair with his eyes glaring at me like a cat's, he called to his wife that it was time to go out.   (Quoted in Shannon 1999: 392)

Once again, events then swept on. Gladstone introduced his Home Rule Bill with one of the most powerful speeches ever heard in the House of Commons. The Liberal Party was hopelessly split; the Home Rule Bill was lost; and the broadly liberal hegemony which had prevailed for most of the time since 1832 Reform Act gave way to a twenty-year period of Conservative hegemony.

11.4 FRIENDS AND ENEMIES?

In all this there is more than a hint of Carl Schmitt's famous insight that the crucial political relationship is that of 'friend' to 'enemy', indeed that politics is *about* the identification of friends and enemies (Schmitt 1996). In all the examples I have cited, the leap into the unknown was closely associated with that process—a process which often became one of unmasking false friends as real enemies. For Ramsay MacDonald in August 1931, the enemy was the TUC, whose indifference to the possible consequences of the sterling crisis and refusal to recognize that spending cuts were needed to overcome it stiffened his determination to fight for the cuts, and may have helped to make him receptive to the King's urgings. For Thatcher, the chief enemy was, of course, the Argentine regime, but lesser enemies included the appeasers in the Foreign Office and the faint-hearts in the Defence Department. For Blair, the enemy was Saddam Hussein, who became the local, Middle Eastern incarnation of the forces of darkness at work in the world. For Gladstone, the enemies included the selfish and ignoble upper classes, the mean and partisan Conservatives who refused to see that it was their duty to cooperate in righting Ireland's historic wrongs, and, as the Liberal split intensified, the anti-Home Rule rebels in his own ranks who refused to follow him in what became a crusade for political righteousness. In all these cases, the enemies were not just personally obnoxious; once the leap of decision was made, and the adrenaline (aka the passions) started to flow, the struggle against them took on the exalted character of a battle of right against wrong.

There is no reason to think that biographers are intrinsically better at disentangling passions from reason, or at analysing the effects of Schmitt's friend–enemy distinction, than anyone else. Nor do they have some special insight into the nature and significance of the passions involved, or the mysterious processes through which friends and enemies are identified, in any particular case. But because it focuses on particular individuals at particular moments, biography as a *genre* does draw attention to the role of non- or supra-rational factors at play in the eye of the decision-making storm. It reminds us of the centrality of emotion in decision-making; and it helps us to understand what happens when decisions are taken. In doing so, it underlines the role of contingency in political life, and reminds us that the accidents of personality must never be left out of the account.

11.5 Biography and Charisma

Biography also helps to sensitize us to the crucial role that leadership, and particularly charismatic leadership, plays in political life. Weber, the inventor of the notion, famously believed that charismatic authority was, as he put it, 'outside the realm of everyday routine and the profane sphere'. As such it was utterly different both from traditional and from rational-bureaucratic authority. Where traditional authority was bound by precedents handed down from the past, and bureaucratic authority by 'intellectually analysable rules', charismatic authority repudiated the past and was inherently irrational. It was, in fact, 'a specifically revolutionary force'. While it lasted, charismatic authority swept all before it, by virtue of the 'devotion and trust' that the leader inspired in his followers. But these lasted only so long as the followers believed in his 'charismatic inspiration' (Weber 1964: 358–63).

Charismatic leadership in the full Weberian sense is rare in democratic regimes; indeed, it is hard to see how it could be squared with democratic norms. But De Gaulle came close to it in the later stages of the Second World War and during and immediately after the fall of the Fourth Republic. So did Churchill in the terrible, magnificent summer of 1940; and so did Franklin Roosevelt in the depths of the Depression. Gladstone had more than a touch of the charismatic leader about him, particularly in his philippics against the so-called 'Bulgarian Horrors' in the 1870s, and in his campaign for Irish Home Rule after his conversion to that cause in 1886. In both cases he believed—in true charismatic fashion—that he had been 'called' by a higher power to eschew the retirement he thought he longed for, and to fight for a righteous cause that only he could champion effectively. And in both cases his extraordinary combination of self-belief, forensic force, and rhetorical power enabled him to communicate with his followers on a plane beyond mere quotidian reason. According to H. C. G. Matthew, the editor of Gladstone's diaries, whose introductions to successive volumes are a tour de force of biographical writing, a typical Gladstone speech to a Liberal audience 'was both a rationalistic transfer of opinion and the focal point of an emotional rally'; Gladstone, he added, was a 'mesmeric figure' (Matthew 1995: 298–9).

During the First World War, when he became the chief standard-bearer of the tiny and much-vilified anti-war camp, Ramsay McDonald also drew his authority from personal charisma rather than from bureaucratic or traditional sources. He had resigned from the chairmanship of the Labour Party when the war broke out, in protest against its decision to vote for war credits. He had no bureaucratic support, and cut himself off from the traditional power centres both of the country and of the Labour movement. But he was sustained by the devotion of a tiny band of disciples for whom he was a heroic figure. Listening to a MacDonald speech, wrote one of them later, 'we trembled and exulted' (quoted in Marquand 1977: 244). Lloyd George, with his blithe indifference to precedent and his contempt for official forms, was a classic case of a charismatic leader in democratic clothes, certainly in the last two years of the First World War and to some extent in the early years of his peacetime Coalition.

Weber's insights still resonate. Like all British Prime Ministers, Margaret Thatcher and Tony Blair both enjoyed a degree of Weber's traditional authority and also of its bureaucratic counterpart. They controlled a large government machine, operating on classic bureaucratic lines, and they stood at the apex of a traditional state whose roots lay deep in the past. But unlike all other post-war Prime Ministers their hold on their followers and their fellow citizens also derived, in large part, from a form of Weberian charismatic authority, supra-rational if not exactly irrational, and in certain senses, at least, revolutionary. Both defied convention; both spurned 'intellectually analysable' rules of procedure and conduct; both sought to cut through the established structures of party and bureaucracy to make direct contact with a (largely imaginary) 'people'. Above all, both had a magic about them which none of their colleagues could equal, and which won them the 'devotion and trust' that Weber saw as one of the chief signs of charismatic authority. In two respects, above all, they fitted the Weberian charismatic model remarkably well. Though they could command conventional bureaucratic support from the official machine, they made no secret of their disdain for the ordinary bureaucracy, and depended far more on close-knit groups of personal followers. And both fell when their charisma wore out. Thatcher was brutally deposed in extraordinarily painful circumstances that left a gaping wound in the Conservative Party that lasted for a decade and a half. Blair avoided her fate, but when he told his 2006 party conference, through gritted teeth, that that would be his last conference speech as leader, everyone knew that he had jumped only to avoid being pushed.

There may be a lesson here, which conventional commentators have been slow to draw. Thatcher and Blair held office for a total of twenty-one years out of the twenty-eight since Thatcher first crossed the threshold of No. 10 Downing Street. The reign of John Major, one of the least charismatic Prime Ministers of modern times, was not only comparatively short, it was also miserable and chaotic. In quieter times he might have done well, but he was incapable of navigating the turbulent currents of a rapidly changing society in a globalizing world. This suggests that, in times of confusion, when party loyalties are fluid and party identities evanescent, when established authority of all kinds is suspect, and when the traditional bonds of social class are increasingly fragmented, leadership has to be charismatic, at least in some degree, if it is to succeed. And that, in turn, suggests that we are likely to experience more charismatic leadership in future than we did in the comparatively stable years after 1945.

Charismatic leadership is—or at least ought to be—fertile soil for political biographers. It is, by definition, individual. Charismatic leaders all have something in common, but no two charismatic leaders are exactly alike. The sources of their charisma and the mysterious, supra-rational ties that bind their followers to them are individual too. Here, above all, the empathy, intuitions, and imagination of good political biographers could helpfully redress the balance of conventional political science.

REFERENCES

CREWE, I., and KING, A. 1995. *SDP: The Birth, Life and Death of the Social Democratic Party*. Oxford: Oxford University Press.

KEDWARD, R. 2005. *La Vie en bleu: France and the French since 1900*. London: Allen Lane, Penguin.

LACOUTURE, J. 1977. *Léon Blum*. Paris: Éditions du Seuil.

—— 1990–1. *Charles de Gaulle* (English translation), 2 vols. London: Collins Harvill.

MARQUAND, D. 1977. *Ramsay MacDonald*. London: Jonathan Cape.

MARX, K. 1951. 'The Eighteenth Brumaire of Louis Bonaparte'. In K. Marx and F. Engels, *Selected Works*, vol. i. Moscow: Foreign Languages Publishing House.

MEHRING, F. 2003. *Karl Marx: The Story of his Life*. London: Routledge.

PIMLOTT, B. 1995. *Frustrate their Knavish Tricks: Writings on Biography, History and Politics*. London: HarperCollins.

ROSKILL, S. 1970–4. *Hankey: Man of Secrets*, 3 vols. London: Collins.

SCHMITT, C. 1996. *The Concept of the Political*. Chicago: University of Chicago Press.

SHANNON, R. 1999. *Gladstone: Heroic Minister, 1865–1898*, London: Allen Lane, Penguin.

STRACHEY, L. 1979. *Eminent Victorians*. London: Chatto and Windus.

WEBER, M. 1964. *The Theory of Social and Economic Organization*, ed. T. Parsons. New York: Free Press.

CHAPTER 12

THE NOVEL

BERNARD CRICK

LITTLE has been written in Britain on the relationship between literary culture and the study of politics. Beyond glancing quotations (E. M. Forster's 'only connect' is the favourite), too little use of is made of literary sources even in analytical let alone empirical studies. But the novel can both stimulate the imagination (consider Popper on how hypotheses are imaginative leaps beyond existing theories) and broaden the contexts of inquiries and speculations.

The matter is complex and could range wider. This writer once imagined that if one set a class of good students an essay on 'Literature and Politics' at least a dozen themes might follow—among them: the antipathy of the two concepts; writers and political commitment; the influence of politics on writers and vice versa; censorship and free expression; what constitutes good and bad political writing (*vide* Orwell, 'Above all I wanted to make political writing into an art'); and Lukacs's argument that the novel exemplifies bourgeois elitism. Today this point might be put in populist, postmodern mode—anything goes if enough people like it. But it is at least a half-truth. The novel was, indeed, a novel institution of bourgeois society; but originally, of course—as in Cervantes, Defoe, Rousseau, and Rowlandson—a critique of aristocratic values.

12.1 OPENING WINDOWS: THEORIZING

Stefan Collini's subtly titled *Absent Minds: Intellectuals in Britain* can point us in that direction—as Professor of Intellectual History *and* English Literature at Cambridge. Whether academics of all kinds are also intellectuals largely depends on their literary culture, in which the novel is still salient despite the recent growth, mainly in populist mode, of studies of political film and theatre. But while there are many dual honours courses in Politics and English, they are more often arms-length alliances than integration. Few dual honours courses have a Collini-like intellectual intelligence behind them, or the old idea (not to be rejected as, indeed, elitist) of a liberal education.

Those who in an Arendtian sense *think* (Arendt 1958) usually grow up learning about the wide world through novels: the world is people and places, it is experiences (like sex; nothing like sex—as a young boy I read bad novels to try to find out about sex); and novels rehearse moral, social, and political dilemmas. If popular behaviour and consciousness is influenced by the arts at all, most directly it is by cinema and television. The serious novel is the preserve of intellectuals—those who try with an independent integrity to understand, preserve, or change a culture, conscious of the interplay between tradition, creativity, and modernity. In this dialectic all complex novels mirror or influence to some extent the context of political beliefs, behaviour, and morality. This is rarely so with popular novels and thrillers which simply use unreflectively a political background for a story-line, just as they might sport or travel, however well painted such backcloths—inside No. 10 or the Chief Whip's office. Our political science can do that better.

Novels of greater complexity can both broaden the imagination of political scientists and raise for the reader many of the ethical dilemmas that political philosophers discuss so well—among themselves, with few exceptions (Crick 2000). Novels can more easily raise dilemmas or themes which are often neglected in political studies. For one thing, the novel does not respect disciplinary borders. One could look, for instance, at Conrad's *Nostromo* (1904) as part of political history, economic history, the sociology of political movements, or in philosophy as the ethics of divided loyalties between persons and causes. Novels, however, have to be taken as a whole, bringing all these things together, before one can usefully use them for disciplinary understanding. But a relevant quotation in a Politics lecture or book can often stimulate the listener's or reader's imagination. This small pedagogic point can be as fruitful as formal theoretical discussions. Political insights will occur in novels that are not themselves primarily political.

This chapter arbitrarily limits itself to British and Irish novels in the last century. A transatlantic or a Commonwealth canvas would demand a book not a mere chapter. But a chapter can make the case that reading novels should be part of the mentality of the student of politics; and then to point to some instances which have both literary merit and political interest. I make this necessary if parochial limitation fully aware that many American novels, such as those by Philip Roth or John Updike, or those of the South African J. M. Coetzee, are often more rich and explicit carriers of social and political dilemmas than are typically found in the English novel. Many Irish, Scottish, and novels by new Britons tend to be more political. Illustrations, however, are but illustrations, stimulants to thought about wider issues, not professing impossibly full knowledge of a field nor settling rather than opening up dilemmas inherent to political life.

An obituary by Jonathan Bate (2007) of the literary critic Tony Nuttall said that he was 'receptive to new ways of thinking but always committed to a classically humanist view of literature as a means of helping thoughtful people to make sense of reality'. Part of reality is always political. But making sense of it is not always found in the self-consciously 'political novel', those which are deliberately persuasive and polemical— E. M. Forster's 'world of telegrams and anger'. Often the contrary is the case. Like 'political theatre', most self-consciously political novels distort and simplify. For them, protagonists solve big problems or if defeated then defeat is a personal tragedy with 'the system' to blame; dilemmas vanish and painful compromises between values and interests are never allowed to be a moral virtue—as in Kant's ethics of practical reason. The 'crooked timber of humanity' is hammered straight. J. A. Morris, a professor of English, in his *Writers and Politics in Modern Britain*, gave far more value to books that would engage, challenge, or just interest political and moral philosophers than to what he nicely called the 'hardcore political novels' supposed to be his remit as editor of a comparative series on '*the* political novel'. Rather, he examined politics *in* the novel or *in* the poem. An incidental minor theme or political incident in any complex work of art can often be more thought provoking than the more famous clamour of, say, propagandizing for socialism or, nowadays, against environmental despoliation. Morris invoked Sartre's argument that a novelist must have an implicit commitment to freedom to be able to empathize with and to portray plausibly social and personal diversities. Echoing Sartre he asked, 'where is the great totalitarian novel?' (Sartre 1948). 'Fine lyric poetry', however, writes Morris, has come 'from enemies of freedom, like Ezra Pound or Stefan George', or from writers hostile to civil humanism, like T. S. Eliot or W. B. Yeats in some of his moods or modes (Morris 1977: 30–42).

I wrote in a review of the series:

> ... the novel is a unique carrier of ideas of freedom and of a republican or political culture. If political philosophy in its academic mode remains esoteric, even to the educated reader and citizen, and has lost its public role, the novel often carries this tradition of speculation about types of political justice and the nature and limits of freedom. Where else can one look to for graphic portrayals of moral dilemmas in general and of conflicts of ethical principle and political prudence, or of the individual and conscience against the state? (Crick 1980)

But that is perhaps only half the point, even if one that political theorists rarely acknowledge explicitly. For among Collini's or Berlin's 'general intellectuals' or Morris's 'educated readers' the dilemmas of political philosophy may *only* be found in the novel. The other half-point is that reading novels may stimulate the imagination of both political theorists and political scientists and lead them into broader contexts of society and human motivations.

12.2 TWO NOVELISTS THEORIZE

Susan Sontag once put the same point more generally: 'A novelist, then, is someone who takes you on a journey. Through space. Through time. A novelist leads the reader over a gap, makes something go where it was not'. She pointed to what the non-stop diet of snippets of stories in the media can do to us:

> By presenting us with a limitless number of nonstop stories, the narratives that the media relate—the consumption of which has so dramatically cut into the time the educated public once devoted to reading—offer a lesson in amorality and detachment that is antithetical to the one embodied by the enterprise of the novel.
>
> In storytelling as practiced by the novelist, there is always an ethical component. This ethical component is not the truth, as opposed to the falsity of the chronicle. It is the model of completeness, of felt intensity, of enlightenment supplied by the story, and its resolution—which is the opposite of the model of obtuseness, of non-understanding, of passive dismay, and the consequent numbing of feeling, offered by our media disseminated glut of unending stories.   (Sontag 2007: 33)

But 'completeness' to her is not just 'felt intensity'. Enlightenment must take place in a social context that is in itself part of the ethical dilemmas of the characters in a novel.

Milan Kundera has shown how the two main storylines in what he sees as Tolstoy's greatest novel, *Anna Karenina*, Anna's adultery and Levin's attaining spiritual and personal tranquility, exist in an ever-present but lightly stressed political background which moves to the fore after her suicide. Vronsky in despair goes off to seek death in the war against the Turks while Levin mocks the pan-Slav hysteria of the volunteers marching off to war. 'Tolstoy', says Kundera, 'has obeyed the fundamental propensity of the art of the novel. For narration as it exists since the dawn of time became the novel when the author was no longer content with a mere "story" but opened windows onto the world that stretched all around' (Kundera 2007).

12.3 THEMES AND BOOKS FOR THE CURRICULA

Having stated a case to read complex novels to see 'the world . . . stretched all around', let me now suggest some themes and associated novels particularly supportive of political studies. Many of the novels will already be 'on the list' in 'Politics and the Novel' options or in joint 'Politics and Literature' courses, now far more common than a generation ago. But simply to hop from one book to another, like in old-fashioned History of Political Thought courses, is unlikely to add much to understanding unless tied to themes.

12.3.1 The First World War

It is a truth universally acknowledged that the incidence of the First World War had a more lasting effect on both literary imagination and popular memory than did the even more world-shaking Second World War (Fuselli 1977; Hynes 1990). My mother and her generation, young adults in the First World War, though they mostly 'did their bit' in 1939–45, had no doubt which was *the* war. The cult of the dead appeared everywhere *entre deux guerres*: lists of the dead in stone, new memorial halls, limbless men in wheelchairs on the touchlines of football matches; and the traffic did stop at 11 a.m. each Armistice Day. *My mother's cousin, Primrose League and Earl Hague poppy day organizer, saw the Second World War as profaning the memory of 'the Glorious Dead'. She ignored it, so did my father—old soldier and Chamberlain pacifist.*

Many are surprised that most of today's English novelists writing about war (unlike American novelists) go back to 1914 not 1939, say Pat Barker in her masterly trilogy *Regeneration* (1991–5) and Sebastian Faulks' *Birdsong* (1994) (a title catching the irony of love of nature even amid the slaughter of the Somme). Perhaps this disjunction between the two World Wars is because novelists who are drawn to consider extreme conditions—how men could habituate themselves under command in abnegation of any free will to the slaughter and suffering of the trenches—these novelists find the horror of seemingly complete irrationality in the disproportion between the causes and motivations of the two wars. The consequences of defeat in 1914–18 would have been less when compared with facing Nazism, and yet 'the war' for British novelists has more often referred to the conflict that began in 1914. No major British novels describe the Second World War or the Holocaust. William Golding's experience of war may have given his novels a far more intense awareness of evil than even Catholics like Graham Greene, Evelyn Waugh, and Muriel Spark. But one does not have to be a Christian, only to have lived in the last century, to say that the myth of 'the fallen state of man' has descriptive power lacking in liberal theories and assumptions of progress. Perhaps only the very closing section of Ian McEwen's *Atonement* (2001), on the shambles of the retreat to Dunkirk and the meaningless contingency of death in war, comes near to the intensity of those novels set in the First World War that force us to think about the limitations of humanity.

Ford Madox Ford survived the trenches to write the four books of *Parade's End* (1924–8), one of the acknowledged masterpieces of the twentieth-century novel in English in both content and technique.[1] The content both of characters and contingent events has a Tolstoyian depth and sweep. And the technique was innovative, for while he uses the authorial voice, he does so sparingly; most of the narrative is carried by fragmentary colloquial dialogue of misunderstanding between people of different classes and assumptions. His two main characters—Christopher Tiejens, Tory of Tories, and Valentine Wannop the suffragette ('Miss Wannop had not met a Cambridge Tory man before')—are half the time only half-listening to the other, thinking of something else, and even when only half-listening often misunderstanding. He accurately reproduces the oral experience of overheard speech. Yet from scraps of seemingly inconsequential talk, banalities, and English understatement can come

---

[1] Malcolm Bradbury calls it 'the central modern novel of the 1920s', Anthony Burgess 'the finest novel about the First World War', and Samuel Hynes 'the greatest war novel ever written by an Englishman'. Quoted by Max Saunder (1982: xiv).

depth-charges exploding half-hidden psychological and political crises (as Harold Pinter was to do in his plays). We get three narratives: the Tory ultra-individualist (say Tory anarchist) hating but enduring the vulgarity and harshness of a society growingly dominated by money values and compulsive obsessions with 'getting on'; Miss Wannop's dislike of his principles but growing respect for his integrity and tolerance; and what happens when Tiejens joins the army as a field officer in the trenches, proudly refusing to use wealth and connections to join 'Staff'. Ford Madox Ford had himself done time in the trenches and been invalided out with shell-shock in 1917.

So here is a novel testifying realistically and poignantly to the tragedy and chaos of war, not the heroism and glory, as did the soldier poets of immortal memory— Owen, Blunden, Sassoon, Gurney, Edward Thomas, Reid, and Rosenberg. Tiejens can inwardly detest most people's manners and ambitions but be outwardly tolerant, even punctiliously helpful to unwanted people, because he is a complete relativist. I called Michael Oakeshott a 'Tory anarchist' some years before meeting Christopher Tiejens. Through the confused perceptions and eccentric behaviour of Tiejens, the novelist shows Edwardian England and the cult of the gentleman being slowly disorientated and then dismembered by the war.

Pat Barker, in her *Regeneration* trilogy, owes something to *Parade's End*. She herself says of her trilogy that it was 'trying to tell about parts of the war that don't get into the official record'. One of those parts is the perspective of northern working-class women, so Sarah Lumb and her friends; and another is of her boyfriend, Billie Prior, who comes up from the ranks, uneasily and unhappily, to be an officer. Barker sets down empathetically the thoughts and reactions to war of the semi-articulate and the unreflective. Another neglect in the official record, neglected until recently, was madness (Barham 2004). Some soldiers returned did not return, others returned deranged. The trilogy deals in fictional form with the real William Rivers, the anthropologist and early medical psychiatrist: his anguish at using his new skills at Craiglockhart hospital for officers with 'shell-shock' to get them back into the firing line and probable violent death. Siegfried Sassoon, Robert Graves, and William Owen mix with fictional patients including Billie Prior. Barker handles this 'factoid' form with far greater care for historical truth than so many film and television bio-pics. She even set a little fashion for other 'well-researched' novels by acknowledging sources and advisers (as Ian McEwen in *Saturday* thanks a neuro-surgeon). Political philosophers and students of public policy now encounter professionals in medical ethics. *Saturday* may prepare for such encounters.

The savagery and despair of war appears most strongly in two of the seven obsessive *Chronicle* series—*The Wet Flanders Plain* (1929) and *The Patriot's Progress* (1930)—of a largely forgotten solitary, Henry Williamson (1895–1977). He is forgotten except as the author of the ever-popular *Tarka the Otter*, and not as the naive hero-worshipper of Hitler and Mosley Blackshirt. He had actually taken part in the legendary, sponta-neous Christmas truce of 1914, which agonized him to think what could have followed from it but didn't. Perhaps these imaginings pushed him to political extremes and made him expert and knowing as a portrayer of extremes.

12.3.2 Nostalgia and Time: Town and Country

Through nearly all the Great War novels and poetry, the obverse occurs of the steel and mud hell of the trenches: images of the green and pleasant land of the English countryside. The British, the English markedly, have an extraordinary love of the countryside, the background of so many novels in the vein of Thomas Hardy's Wessex, let alone the utopianism of William Morris's *News from Nowhere* where the Upper Thames becomes the New Jerusalem. The belief that the countryside was 'the real England' has long had political implications. The aristocracy and the well-off commercial and professional classes had both a town house and a place in the country. Edinburgh's New Town was an exception. In the early 1900s the garden suburb was invented: well-spaced houses built with purely ornamental gardens and restrictions on further and different development. Even where there were no controls, the inter-war semi-detached had its own front and back garden, even amid ribbon development. The urban terrace had gone. Students of public administration usually take for granted this strange phenomenon, almost unknown elsewhere, which was plainly not simply a response to new technologies like the suburban railways and the motor car, but rather an emotional rejection, from a deep-rooted national mindset, of the more rational building style, of the urban terrace. William Morris with the Red House was not wholly to blame. His neo-medievalism was itself a reaction to the downside of Britain's great and leading industrial revolution. When Blair in 1997 called for modernization there was a widespread ambivalence about the term itself, unnoticed by him and almost inexplicable if one was not steeped in English novels. The ideal of gentlemanly conduct and love of the countryside went hand in glove. But Machiavelli had been serious in a completely contrary belief: that the countryside was the haunt of the useless *gentiluomini* who hated the republicanism of civic culture. The *campagna* was the haunt of superstition. Most political theorists today have lost these thoughts. Only the environmentalists take them up as if new.

English pastoralism was not necessarily political Conservatism, even though the oeuvre of Shropshire novels by Mary Webb (1881–1927) only became famous when, just after her death, Stanley Baldwin praised her as 'a neglected genius'. Hampstead Garden Suburb, Letchworth, and Bourneville were built by and for men and women of progressive principles, usually political Liberals. Both D. H. Lawrence in his early novels and Orwell in *Coming up for Air* (1939) had radicalism in their heads with progress and emancipation from poverty to be gained via the city, the workshop, and science; but in their hearts was nostalgia for the image of an ever 'unspoiled countryside'. Lawrence's way was to turn his back on anything urban and escape to the hills of Tuscany and then the Mexican desert. But to Orwell the good life was to be found in alternation between town and countryside—'town and country' even before post-war Town and Country Planning and the greenbelt. 'Winston Smith' imagined a 'Golden country . . . A landscape I've seen somewhere in a dream.' Orwell's friend Cyril Connolly called him 'a revolutionary in love with the nineteen-hundreds'. But even the urbane Connolly habitually lugged his fat frame down to country house weekends. That was the social round of bucolic nostalgia of the upper-middle and the professional classes; and for the others there was the weekend family drive in the Morris, Ford, or Austin, to the seaside, the South Downs, the Pennines, or the Trossachs. And for the absolutely others this was done en masse in tight formation on bicycles. After all the nastiness in novels about the city (say George Gissing's *New Grub Street*), country life finally reconciles differences of class as in E. M. Forster's *Howard's End*. Popular novelists still commonly set their amatory plots in rural settings, what they and their readers think to be *the real* England. Stella Gibbon's *Cold Comfort Farm* brilliantly sent up such literature—but with a teasing affection. (The film made us even possessive or preservationist, not disowning, towards the Starkadders). And bodices don't get ripped in sordid city bed-sits—that was for crime, soft-porn novels, and *Brighton Rock*. But Stella Gibbon would not have cared to mock Laurie Lee's phenomenally popular *Cider with Rosie* (1959), nor the once almost equally popular rural short stories of A. E. Coppard (1878–1957) such as his *Adam and Eve and Pinch Me* (1921). The third book of Laurie Lee's memoirs, recounting his time in the International Brigade, had poor sales.

Oakeshott was right. We are more influenced by tradition than by bouts of abstract reasoning; but there are more rival traditions than were dreamt of in his philosophy. 'Merry England' was a radical myth. Today second-home lovers of the countryside are rapidly driving out the old country dwellers; myth engenders political and social problems.

So the theme of time in the novel is worth considering. Joseph Conrad's *The Secret Agent* (1910) is a narrative of anarchism, terrorism, and personal betrayals. Students of terrorism and political extremism will find it familiar, and his *Nostromo* is a profound meditation on conflicts of loyalty. But why was the target for the secret agent's terrorist bomb, of all places, the Greenwich Observatory? Just as his *Heart of Darkness* shows the depths of man's cruelty to man, perhaps the targeting of the observatory may show anarchist philosophy attempting to turn back the very key to modernity—the new universal and standardized. It meant that every working human could then be called to account precisely.[2] Both political theorists and sociologists have written little about the nature of time, although like historians we are pretty free and inventive about giving names and dates to arbitrary chronological 'eras'. Many demand a change in values, but no one theorizes how long it takes for values to change, if at all, through policy and legislation. Generation novels at least give us some sense of this.

12.4 CLASS AND THE POWERS THAT BE

Once upon a time it was all Marxist or quasi-Marxist theory about social class, but where did we actually learn, if at all, any complex sense of the nuances of habit,

---

[2] I thank Professor Randall Stevenson for this thought, the joint editor of *The Edinburgh Companion to Twentieth Century Literatures in English* (Edinburgh University Press, 2006).

conventions, and behaviour, beyond the class in which we grew up and the others? From observation and experience, certainly—some of us learnt more, some of us less; but surely also from reading novels which opened windows on other people, other experiences, and other places. Admittedly some misunderstandings can arise due to time-lag. We know we are in historical time when reading Dickens, George Eliot, Trollope, or Hardy. But Soviet intellectuals in their ideological fix on time really did think that Dickens told of our present. I once talked in 1986 to a young Black ANC gay activist on trial who asked me to send messages of comradely support to the British miners whom he believed were still living as D. H. Lawrence described in *Sons and Lovers*, among books sent to him by Peter Tatchell. But H. G. Wells's *Kipps* (1905) and his *Mr Polly* (1910) had once opened the eyes of our middle and upper-middle class to how their lower-middle class lived. His *Anna Veronica* may have gained more understanding of the justice of female emancipation than what Beatrice Webb in exasperation called 'the screaming sisterhood' of the platforms. Orwell, following Wells, in his pre-war novels *Keep the Aspidistra Flying* (1936) and *Coming up for Air* (1939) saw the lower-middle class as the key factor for the future. Would they go for Socialism or for Fascism? He was expressing a once common view of those activists of the Labour movement, those whose only university was the free public library.

Another missing dimension from academic study has been the most famous former stereotype of Britishness—the image and cult of the gentleman. Paternalism indeed, but civilizing and restraining compared to the ethos of most other European elites, albeit many came to adopt superficial aspects of that code. A good final-year essay might 'Compare and contrast the political background and assumptions of *The Forsyte Saga* with *A la recherche du temps perdu*'. The cult of the gentleman was one of manners, not of birth, and it enabled a social mobility—say Kornhauser's 'penetrable elites'—and provided a code that was binding even on high aristocracy. Henry Cockburn recalled in *Memorials of His Time* an Edinburgh old lady remarking: 'the Prince is no gentleman'. It was a code of mutual trust of great importance in the history of the old Conservative Party, but seldom if ever explored in the literature. The gentlemen paternalists began to lose control of the party, opening the door for the Thatcherite suburban free-market *arrivistes*, when Macmillan assumed that he could always accept a gentleman's word, even at second hand. But Jack Profumo was not a gentleman. He lied to the chief whip.

A major theme of Anthony Powell's irony in his twelve-volume *A Dance to the Music of Time* (1951–75) is the decline of gentlemanly values. John Le Carré chronicles the declining moral code of the English political establishment, somewhat as C. P. Snow attempted, except with ever-increasing anger. His books are far more than spy novels. Each of his recent books have been darker than its predecessor. George Smiley after *Tinker, Tailor, Soldier, Spy* (1974) came to agonize in *Smiley's People* (1979) (though good fellows all) about using dirty tricks to entrap Karla (the old Machiavellian, Jesuit, and republican dilemmas never go away, of whether the ends can justify the means). But the good national purpose is still clear when facing a totalitarian enemy. By *A Perfect Spy* (1986), however, Magnus Pym, MI6 and diplomat (and son of a con man), loses this sense of purpose and ends up out of weakness and friendliness working for both sides. He ends all his contradictions by suicide. (E. M. Forster did say, 'I would rather betray my country than my friend'). But by the time of the *Tailor of Panama* (1996), the *Constant Gardener* (2001), and the ironically titled *Absolute Friends* (2003) (a tale of absolute betrayal by British and American agents in collusion), the establishment is portrayed as sleazy and corrupt. Justin Quayle, the constant gardener (again that symbol of 'real England'), trusts his superiors when seeking to find who killed his wife. But they have been complicit to cover up, even to his death, collusion with a multinational's fatal drug trials on African guinea pigs. Then in the *Mission Song* (2006) a gifted African translator is tricked by his MI6 employers into helping destroy his mother's own people. Presumably in case some readers of spy stories were put off by the new dark Le Carré (his imagery is somewhat more disturbing than John Osborne's Archie Rice, 'Don't laugh too loud. It's a very old house'), the publishers of *The Constant Gardner* put on the jacket David Martin of the *FT* saying 'A vintage Le Carré thriller'; but also A. N. Wilson in the *Daily Mail*: 'Full of righteous fire to offset its desperate prognosis'—a prognosis of what our governing elites have become. Le Carré is not an entertaining satirist. He means it.

Still talking of gentlemen, Kazuo Ishiguro's *The Remains of the Day* (1989) is a masterpiece on the English class system before 1939, the inhibition of personal relationships involved upstairs and downstairs in an allegorical great house; then came the shattering of both its code and ownership by the war. In Ishiguro's case (not so fond of gentlemen) the shattering destroys the pre-war delusions—the gentleman had patronized the British Union of Fascists and his subservient butler saw no fault until too late.

The rise of a Leicestershire Grammar School boy to become a gentleman via Cambridge and 'the corridors of power' is the main thread of C. P. Snow's fifteen-volume *Strangers and Brothers*—and gentlemen, we learn, can fall out. Here the novel is most clearly written as social and political history. Snow fell out of fashion, the novels were of unequal quality, and few of us could see it all through. Left-wing reviewers scorned his attempted objectivity and literary critics mocked his old-fashioned narrative style. For the student of politics perhaps the most interesting are *The Light and the Dark* (1962), a picture of the build-up of fear of catastrophe in the late 1930s and then of the deep uncertainties in the early years of the war. *The Masters* (1951) certainly, but to be read less for the storyline of academic politics than for the dynamics of drawn-out committee decisions in general; and similarly *The Corridors of Power* (1964). It is interesting to note that in the mid-1990s Iain Crichton Smith called on Scottish novelists 'to imagine themselves in the corridors of power' as a means to raise national consciousness. But are *The Masters* and *The Corridors of Power* on any Pub. Admin. reading list? The late and great W. A. Robson had read them appreciatively but would never have put novels on his reading lists, friend though he was of Leonard Woolf, joint editors of the *Political Quarterly*. But perhaps Snow's early novel *George Passant* (1940) was his best. The character of Passant, a provincial solicitor and an eccentric but idealistic socialist, marvellously embodies the ethos and dilemmas of old Labour in the Thirties. And to note in passing that the good 'working class novel of the 1930s' was something more people thought should exist rather than actually existed. Minor and banal works figured in Communist propaganda, praised for their passion and political correctness. But better descriptions of working-class life in the mode of social realism ('let the facts speak for themselves') came from such 'an intellectual of bourgeois origin', as even Grassic Gibbon was called for his pains with his *Grey Granite* (1934), the third part of his trilogy *A Scots Quair*.[3]

12.5 POWER AND THE REASON OF STATE

William Golding's *Lord of the Flies* (1954) was his first novel, only rivalled by Orwell's *Animal Farm* (1945) as most young pupils' first immersion in political thought. For it raises in a terrifying way how legitimate authority can degenerate into absolute power, the plausibility of *libido dominandi* and of reversion to barbarism if we are removed from conventional society. Young readers may distance it as 'just a story' rather than a dark parable of human nature. But the very title has a double resonance: the existential terror of King Lear—'As flies to wanton boys are we to the gods. They kill us for their sport'; but it also suggests Satan or Beelzebub—in Hebrew *Baalzuv* or lord of the fly. Golding does not believe in Satan but he has seen Satanic forces— the war, the bombing of cities, the Holocaust. And the story suggests that thoughtless acceptance of even seemingly benign rule can allow descent into savagery. 'We have got to have rules and obey them, after all we are not savages. We're English and the English are the best at everything'. The island can be as familiar to us as Hobbes's state of nature, but Golding had seen *bellum omnes contra omnes* as the two World Wars, not as civil war and speculative anthropology. He came out of the fire of the Second World War with his work marked and himself marked for life:

> Before the Second World War I believed in the perfectibility of social man; that a correct structure of society would produce goodwill; and that therefore you could remove all social ills by a reorganization of society...but after the war I did not because I was unable to. I had discovered what one man could do to another....I must say that anyone who moved through those years without understanding that man produces evil as a bee produces honey must have been blind or wrong in the head.   (Golding 1965)

Political thinkers might challenge this view (for the political view of the world is one of possibilities not of foreclosures), but they would have to understand it first wherever it occurs at its strongest—not wait for an article in a learned journal to

---

[3] See Cunningham (1988), Bergonzi (1978), and Hynes (1976), none of whom find political novels to match the poetry, essays, or memoirs. Cunningham's study makes Stephen Ingle's interesting *Socialist Thought in Imagination Literature* (Ingle 1979) appear mistaken in considering socialist writings apart from other mutually interactive non- or anti-socialist political writings.

critique. Titles in the early issues of *Political Studies* and even the post-war issues of *Political Quarterly* carry none of this *Weltschmerz*—un-British, unprofessional.

Golding's *Rites of Passage* (1980) and its two sequels (published entire as *To the Ends of the Earth* (1991)), are parables of *staatsraison* exhibiting once again the abandonment of his pre-war scientist's faith in a rational and progressive society. The uncouth autocratic Captain Anderson—no respecter of persons—and his officers keep the decrepit ship-of-the-line afloat so that his mixed bag of self-concerned and unwanted passengers can reach their promised land of the convict settlements of Australia. Such ironies run deep but there is also the horror—the handy common seamen can rape the ineffectual Revd James Colley to madness and death, but with no one caring to inquire too closely what happened. Justice could cause worse trouble for all. The closed order of a ship is, of course, symbolic of the state: liberty and justice yield to arbitrary order for the sake of survival. The fear of anarchy and bleak despair if conventions are not followed permeates both cabins and quarter-deck. Nonetheless, Golding told his Nobel prize audience that as a genre 'The novel stands between us and the hardening concept of statistical man' (Golding 1984: 8).

Lord of the Flies may have had less influence on political opinions than *Animal Farm* but it is more profound philosophically. We can lament the failure of the animals' revolution as preached and prophesied by Old Major—but not despair of progress, for it might have succeeded. Contingencies can work both ways. Orwell's pessimism was of a different kind than Golding's. 'All revolutions are failures', he said, 'but not all are the same kind of failure'. Original intentions may never be fulfilled, but some betterment is always possible.[4]

Nineteen Eighty-Four (1949) is misread if seen as bleak despair and prophecy, and misplaced in courses on 'Utopias and Dystopias' alongside Aldous Huxley's *Brave New World*; for it is Swiftian satire—savage satire of grotesque exaggeration (like the cartoons of Scarfe). Students of Politics seldom study modes of satire as political weapons and their effects. Satire as distinct from cynicism measures against a humane and hopeful standard. The satirist knows there is something better. The cynic (as in so much so-called satire today) mocks not only the abusers of power but all we silly, simple souls who think that things can be made better. If read as a satire, the famous ending of *Nineteen Eighty-Four*, 'He loved Big Brother', becomes ironical. Consider what Big Brother had got, not a newly reconstructed party superman but a pathetic broken everyman whose 'gin-scented tears trickled down the side of his nose'. And it was not 'The End', for there follows the Appendix on Newspeak which admits that the difficulty of translating 'Shakespeare, Milton, Swift, Byron, Dickens and some others' has led to the postponement of the final adoption of Newspeak 'for so late a date as 2050'. The hope for humanity is that the language of great writing cannot be controlled.

Political theorists can relate to his satire of total power, so well written that we might incautiously think the author really believed with the insane O'Brien that 'If

---

[4] 'Socialism is not perfectionist, perhaps not even hedonistic. Socialists don't claim to be able to make the world perfect: they claim to be able to make it better' (Orwell 1943 and Anderson 2006: 74).

you want a picture of the future, imagine a boot smashing on a human face—for ever'.[5] But amid the several themes of the satire consider Julia's job and that she worked among:

> a whole chain of separate departments dealing with proletarian literature, music, drama and entertainment generally. Here were produced rubbishy newspapers containing almost nothing except sport, crime and astrology, sensational five-cent novelettes, films oozing with sex and sentimental songs which were composed entirely by mechanical means on a special kind of kaleidoscope known as a versificator.

But such debauching was no part of either Nazi or Communist practice. Imaginatively Orwell had reinvented and applied to his own society the high theory of Frankfurt School Marxism: capitalism controls the masses not by physical force but by cultural degradation. We now casually call it dumbing down and hesitate to see it as systematic.

12.6 EMPIRE AND THE DOG THAT DID NOT BARK

Whoever wishes to understand the human relationships between the British and the native inhabitants of the Empire can find a rich literature. But it is inspired not by the sometimes too easy assumptions of guilt found in the anti-imperialist polemics, but rather by difficulties of understanding and moral dilemmas of living with radically different cultures and assumptions. E. M. Forster's *Passage to India* (1924) is still the supreme example of this, masterful in its empathy for the nuances of mutual misunderstanding and the gradations of British prejudice. *Burmese Days* (1934) is arguably Orwell's best novel. The hopelessness of the main character faced by the racism of his colleagues and the decency of the Indian doctor is yet put alongside portrayal of a very corrupt Burmese. Orwell later said that it took him many years to realize that the oppressed are not always right. Leonard Woolf's first novel *The Village in the Jungle* (1913), happily reprinted in 2005, is a tale of the lives of poor villagers as if wholly in their own terms. Woolf also knew that to change the world one must first understand it, as when later he was secretary in the 1930s of both the Fabian Society's and the Labour Party's colonial committees. And no academic account of the ending of the Indian Empire could not but benefit from the narrative of the last days in Paul Scott's 'The Raj Quartet'—*The Jewel in the Crown* (1966), followed by *The Day of the*

---

[5] Said Acton, 'All power corrupts and absolute power corrupts absolutely'. But surely Orwell means us to think that the vision of absolute power has destroyed O'Brien's sanity, that he is truly mad when he tells Winston Smith in the torture chamber that 'We control matter because we control the mind.... The stars ... we could reach them if we wanted to.... The earth is the centre of the universe. The sun and the stars go round it'.

Scorpion, *The Towers of Silence*, and *A Division of Spoils*. The quartet was, however, a minority taste, too political and seemingly purely descriptive for the taste of literary critics (as if always defending literature against politics in reaction to the myth of the 1930s). It had big sales only after the television series, *The Jewel in the Crown*. Then Scott reached the audience for whom Wells and Orwell had written.

But there was a dog that did not bark despite nearly all of us in the post-war left believing that dispossessed Anglo-Indians, the Sahibs and the 'heaven born' coming home, would be a strong reactionary force in British politics. Few if any novels try to chronicle the imperial mindset long after real power had gone. Theatre, television, and radio satirists made a hearty meal of Thatcher's and Blair's desire to 'put the "great" back into Great Britain' (through the delusion of the 'special relationship'). But no British novelists have bitten on this big bait, except in incidental allusions. No modern Ford Madox Ford has appeared. Nor has any one novel tackled directly the British identity question in the way that American novelists will tackle 'the American way' or 'Americanism' head on, and at length (Roth 1997; 2004; Updike 1996). The national grand narrative is not the way of English novelists (as perhaps only Anthony Burgess attempted in his portentous *Earthly Powers*); their way has been more typically a modest walk along 'The Guermantes Way', the interplay of character, memory, manners, and circumstance, the imperatives and hesitations of psychologies; even if sometimes with political and social background.

12.7 WHAT HAVE WE TODAY?

Many contemporary novelists touch on political questions, as background or incidents—Peter Ackroyd, Monica Ali, Martin Amis, Julian Barnes, William Boyd, Hanif Kureishi, Doris Lessing, Blake Morrison, Salman Rushdie, Zadie Smith, Graham Swift . . . Swift's *Waterland* (1983) notably carries constant echoes of both World Wars amid the contingencies of his characters' lives. Tom Crick ends his days as an unsuccessful teacher, adding to his misery by discussing with his boys the likelihood of atomic world war. There is the brilliant satiric subplot in Ian McEwan's *Amsterdam* of the ambitious editor of a national newspaper grasping greedily at an exclusive on a Foreign Secretary's infidelity but overthrown by his blindness or indifference to the pain of friends; or the picture in McEwan's *Saturday* of the uncouth violence of the city streets suddenly bursting into the living room of a professional and intellectual household. Both are superb descriptions of contemporary political and social concerns, but these are only incidental to personal relationships. In raising these problems, which are all over the media anyway, they take us no further in considering the master question of political thought—what is justice? There are no resolutions that make us ask even whether the price of progress is worth paying—as with Golding's autocratic captain who keeps his rotten ship afloat and on course by any means. No one could read Paul Scott's less well-written *Raj Quartet* without having to think through—and out of—stereotypes of imperialism good, bad, or simply historical. Scott agonizingly considers and reconsiders the loss of indigenous native traditions as against the gains of an alien modernity.

Alan Hollinghurst in the *Line of Beauty* (2004) reveals the psychology and society of his gay protagonist and of the womanizing Tory minister whose household he enters, witnessing his fall; but again, purely descriptive, or at least commendably non-judgemental, albeit sometimes mere descriptive can open up questions for political theory. Blake Morrison's *South of the River* (2007) follows five characters through the first years of the Blair era. A shrewd reviewer said 'Morrison is never so crude as to venture a direct statement [about the Blair project]. In any case this is not an overtly political book, merely one about a group of people at the mercy of events over which they have no control. Or perhaps that makes it a political book after all' (Taylor 2007). John Banville's *The Untouchable* is a semi-fictionalized life of Anthony Blunt, a profound picture of treachery through sociability, and perhaps an Irish author's irony about the English establishment.

Another chapter would be needed for Ireland, north and south, with their indissoluble interconnections with mainland British culture and politics. There were vivid description of the politics of the streets in the Troubles, from Liam O'Flaherty's *The Informer* to Eoin McNamee's *Resurrection Man;* and the original father of all 'threat to the nation' political thrillers was Erskine Childers' *The Riddle of the Sands* (1902). But more illuminating on conflicting loyalties and moral dilemmas today are such as Bernard MacLaverty's *Cal* (1983), Glenn Paterson's *The International, That Which Was* (1999), Brian Moore's *Lies of Silence* (1990) especially (Hughes 1991; Longley, Hughes, and O'Rawe 2003). A seemingly purely descriptive account of how low-life characters on the streets saw the Troubles, drawn with Dickensian gusto, is Robert McLiam Wilson's *Eureka Street* (1998).[6] Yet another typical bombing:

> Several of the shocked onlookers sat staring dumbly at the excrement and tissue and blood, incapable of comprehending how political this was. One naive fireman, upon retrieving what seemed to be a portion of a severed head, naively believed this to have been a sadistic act. A woman with a bloody face who comforted her young son near the bookshop had no real conception of the historical imperatives leading to such an event.

Such 'pure description' is moral irony of a truly Swiftian kind.

Andrew O'Hara's *Our Fathers* is not merely a good source for understanding aspects of Scottish identity but also raises again the oldest theme of political philosophy, the means/ends dilemma. The father of the central character was once a hero of the Glasgow working class for what he did for council housing and urgent slum clearance. But in old age recriminations burst upon him for the short-cuts and backhanders needed to get it done quickly; even if he himself lives simply and poor in one of the crumbling tower blocks consequent to his methods. The author's tone is an understanding sadness. The ever-popular Muriel Spark's *The Prime of Miss Jean Brodie* (1961) deserves rereading not just as a Scottish comedy of manners but as a

---

[6] I thank Dr Eamonn Hughes of Queen's University Belfast for help with these references.

study in the mistaken use of authority, and how unchallenged authority can make deadly mistakes (the girl's dead brother was on *the other side* in Spain).

One last example. National identity is now much debated. But much of the debate both in the press and in the academy is either polemical or full of muddled abstractions. For personal identities can be manifold and national identities cannot be expressed in precise definitions, certainly not quantifiable; politicians who try to do this make fools of themselves (Aughey 2007; Crick 2008). National identities are to be understood by the experience of simply living in a country perceptively and interactively and by reading both those histories and novels which convey the variety and complexity of beliefs, feelings, sentiments, prejudices, and traditions (in Burkeian and Oakshottian senses). Such novels can help the student of politics reveal what are often the inarticulate presuppositions with which we understand or narrow experience.

12.8 IN CONCLUSION

Many teachers of English Literature and literary critics are a priori suspicious and even censorious of any use of literature for political argument, study, or reflection. This is mistaken, as if to keep novels from all but English Literature graduates. Novels are for all who care. And they can miss a point on which we began: that the novel is 'a unique carrier of ideas of freedom and of a republican or political culture' (Crick 1980). Relationships between English Literature and Political Science can never be definitively theorized. Dual honours courses can lie side by side pleasantly enough and are perhaps the better for not being obsessed with theory and methodology but simply with mutual recognition of disciplinary difference, each a good part of a liberal education. Sometimes it is better not to formulate relationships too precisely or explicitly. Social relationships are always contingent and always changing, adjusting, modifying in different ways. Formal courses on 'Politics and the Novel' or even on 'The Political Novels' may be a small part of a curriculum but can be of disproportionate interest and importance.

REFERENCES

ANDERSON, P. 2006. *Orwell in Tribune*. Petersfield: Politico's.
ARENDT, H. 1958. *The Human Condition*. Cambridge: Cambridge University Press.
AUGHEY, A. 2007. *The Politics of Englishness*. Manchester: Manchester University Press.
BARHAM, P. 2004. *Forgotten Lunatics of the Great War*. London: Yale University Press.
BATE, J. 2007. 'Obituary: Tony Nuttall'. *Guardian*, 27 March.

BERGONZI, B. 1978. *Reading the Thirties*. London: Macmillan.

COLLINI, S. 2006. *Absent Minds: Intellectuals in Britain*. Oxford: Oxford University Press.

CRICK, B. 1980. 'Writers and Politics'. *Critical Quarterly*, 22/2: 63–73.

——1989. 'Literature and Politics'. Pp. 1–19 in B. Crick, *Essays on Politics and Literature*. Edinburgh: Edinburgh University Press.

——2000. 'The Decline of Political Thinking'. Pp. 169–90 in B. Crick, *Essays on Citizenship*. London: Continuum.

——2008. 'The Four Nations: Interrelations'. *Political Quarterly*, 79/1: 71–91.

CUNNINGHAM, V. 1988. *British Writers of the Thirties*. Oxford: Oxford University Press.

FUSELLI, P. 1977. *The Great War and Modern Memory*. Oxford: Oxford University Press.

GOLDING, W. 1965. 'The Fable'. In *The Hot Gates, and Other Occasional Pieces*. London: Faber and Faber.

——1984. Nobel Prize Lecture. Leamington Spa: Sixth Chamber.

HUGHES, E. (ed.) 1991. *Northern Ireland Culture and Politics 1960–90*. Milton Keynes: Open University Press.

HYNES, S. 1976. *The Auden Generation*. London: Bodley Head.

——1990. *A War Imagined: The First World War and English Culture*. London: Bodley Head.

INGLE, S. 1979. *Socialist Thought in Imagination Literature*. London: Macmillan.

KUNDERA, M. 2007. *The Curtain*. London: Faber and Faber.

LONGLEY, E., HUGHES, E., and O'RAWE, D. (eds.) 2003. *Ireland (Ulster) Scotland: Concepts, Contexts, Comparisons*. (Belfast Studies in Language, Culture and Politics 5). Belfast: Clo Ollscoll na Banriona.

MORRIS, J. A. 1977. *Writers and Politics in Modern Britain (1880–1950)*. London: Hodder and Stoughton.

ORWELL, G. 1943. 'As I Please'. *Tribune*, 24 Dec.

——1984. *Nineteen Eighty-Four with a critical introduction and annotations by Bernard Crick*. Oxford: Clarendon Press.

ROTH, P. 1997. *American Pastoral*. London: Jonathan Cape.

——2004. *The Plot against America*. London: Jonathan Cape.

SARTRE, J.-P. 1948. *Qu'est-ce que la literature?* Paris: Gallimard; trans. 1951 as *What is Literature?* London: Methuen.

SAUNDER, M. 1982. 'Introduction'. *Parade's End*. London: Penguin Classics.

SONTAG, S. 2007. *At the Same Time*. London: Hamish Hamilton.

TAYLOR, D. 2007. 'The State We're In'. *Guardian*, 7 Apr.

UPDIKE, J. 1996. *In the Beauty of the Lilies*. London: Hamish Hamilton.

Primary texts: Dates of first publication

BARKER, PAT *Regeneration* (1992)

BURGESS, ANTHONY *Earthly Powers* (1980)

CHILDERS, ERSKINE *The Riddle of the Sands* (1902)

COCKBURN, HENRY *Memorials of His Time* (1856)

CONRAD, JOSEPH *Heart of Darkness* (1902)

CONRAD, JOSEPH *Nostromo* (1904)

CONRAD, JOSEPH *The Secret Agent* (1910)

COPPARD, A. E. *Adam and Eve and Pinch Me* (1921)

FAULKS, SEBASTIAN *Birdsong* (1994)

FORD, FORD MADOX *Parade's End* 4 vols. (1924–8)

FORSTER, E. M. *Passage to India* (1924)

GOLDING, WILLIAM *Lord of the Flies* (1954)

GOLDING, WILLIAM *Rites of Passage* (1980)
GOLDING, WILLIAM *To the Ends of the Earth* (1991)
GIBBON, LEWIS GRASSIC *A Scots Quair* 3 vols. (1932–4)
HOLLINGHURST, ALAN *Line of Beauty* (2004)
HUXLEY, ALDOUS *Brave New World* (1932)
ISHIGURO, KAZUO *The Remains of the Day* (1989)
LE CARRÉ, JOHN *A Perfect Spy* (1986)
LE CARRÉ, JOHN *Absolute Friends* (2003)
LE CARRÉ, JOHN *Mission Song* (2006)
LE CARRÉ, JOHN *Smiley's People* (1979)
LE CARRÉ, JOHN *Tailor of Panama* (1996)
LE CARRÉ, JOHN *The Constant Gardener* (2001)
LE CARRÉ, JOHN *Tinker, Tailor, Soldier, Spy* (1974)
LEE, LAURIE *Cider with Rosie* (1959)
McEWAN, IAN *Amsterdam* (1999)
McEWEN, IAN *Atonement* (2001)
McEWEN, IAN *Saturday* (2005)
MOORE, BRIAN *Lies of Silence* (1999)
MORRIS, WILLIAM *News from Nowhere* (1890)
MORRISON, BLAKE *South of the River* (2007)
O'HARA, ANDREW *Our Fathers* (1998)
ORWELL, GEORGE *Animal Farm* (1945)
ORWELL, GEORGE *Burmese Days* (1934)
ORWELL, GEORGE *Coming up for Air* (1939)
ORWELL, GEORGE *Keep the Aspidistra Flying* (1936)
ORWELL, GEORGE *Nineteen Eighty-Four* (1949)
POWELL, ANTHONY *A Dance to the Music of Time* (1951–75)
SCOTT, PAUL *The Raj Quartet* (1968–74)
SNOW, C. P. *George Passant* (1940)
SNOW, C. P. *The Masters* (1951)
SNOW, C. P. *The Light and the Dark* (1962)
SNOW, C. P. *The Corridors of Power* (1964)
SNOW, C. P. *Strangers and Brothers* (1972)
SPARK, MURIEL *The Prime of Miss Jean Brodie* (1961)
SWIFT, GRAHAM *Waterland* (1983)
WELLS, H. G. *Kipps* (1905)
WELLS, H. G. *Mr Polly* (1910)
WILLIAMSON, HENRY *The Wet Flanders Plain* (1929)
WILLIAMSON, HENRY *The Patriot's Progress* (1930)
WILSON, ROBERT McLIAM *Eureka Street* (1998)
WOOLF, LEONARD *The Village in the Jungle* (1913)

PART II

INSTITUTIONS

SECTION FIVE: DEMOCRACY

CHAPTER 13

PARLIAMENT

ALEXANDRA KELSO

13.1 INTRODUCTION

A frequent refrain in the contemporary study of British legislative politics is that 'parliament matters' (Judge 1993; Norton 1993; 2005). The fact that scholars of parliament have had to so clearly state as much is indicative of the twilight world into which parliamentary research has at times slipped. Gone are the days of those political writers such as Sidney Low (1906), Joseph Redlich (1908), Lawrence Lowell (1912), and Harold Laski (1938) who 'posed grand questions' and explained parliament 'within the context of wider political forces and ideas' (Judge 1993: 1). The behavioural revolution of the 1960s relegated parliamentary analysis to the lowest division of political science studies, and the post-parliamentary literature of the 1970s, encompassing theories of political communities and networks, questioned the role of parliament as a relevant political institution, and threw into doubt the merits of studying it at all. More recently, the governance literature of the 1990s largely omitted parliament from its analyses.

Such dismissal of parliament is both short-sighted and fundamentally flawed, because it is only by commanding a parliamentary majority that state power can be accessed and exercised. As Ralph Miliband (1961) acknowledged, societal change can only be pursued and secured by parliamentary means: there is no legitimate alternative for those who seek state transformation. However, this does not mean that parliament's utility extends *only* to its existence as a forum for legitimate government. Such a 'big picture' approach, while usefully drawing our eye to the landscape on which British politics takes place, can also have the disadvantage of blinding us to the detail in the foreground. In this respect, parliamentary procedure is not only for the anoraks: the fact that government itself seeks to adapt the rules of the parliamentary game more often than it seeks to flaunt them is indicative of their centrality to understanding what parliament is about and the nature of its relationship to the executive to which it plays host. It is through parliamentary procedure that the relationship between government and parliament is mediated and constantly redefined. Consequently, there is a need for a deeper understanding of parliament at the detailed level of its existence, at the level where procedures, rules, and norms come into play. Parliament is a more interesting and influential institution than its detractors suggest, and is becoming increasingly specialized, thorough, and sophisticated in the work it undertakes. Observers misunderstand parliament's institutional impact when they dismiss it as 'weak' and 'irrelevant', which are the favoured words for such repudiation. In 1976, Anthony King sought to move discussion beyond the simple executive–legislative dichotomy, by emphasizing the intra-party, opposition, and non-party modes of operation which delineate identities inside parliament. The 'multiple personality' parliament that King described still exists today, and appreciating its multiplicities and complexities is imperative. Now, however, a similar kind of reorientation is required, a reorientation which rejects banal statements about parliamentary impotence, and which refocuses analysis on the significant ways in which parliament has undergone, and continues to undergo, a process of institutional adaptation and development which has ramifications for the role it plays within the British political system.

13.2 PARLIAMENT AND PARLIAMENTARY GOVERNMENT

Controversially, and unfashionably, one of the most useful ways to contextualize the study of parliament is by way of the Westminster Model. This model has been criticized on the basis that it fails to provide an accurate account of how politics actually works in Britain, with sceptics instead promoting the descriptive capacity of the governance approaches (see Rhodes 1997 for a definitive account). Yet, the Westminster Model continues to act as a legitimizing mythology, which justifies the style of government practised in Britain, and which, crucially, is a reflection of how political actors themselves perceive the political system (Richards and Smith 2002: 48). The Westminster Model is indispensable because it helps us to understand how power is legitimized. Underpinning the Westminster Model is the concept of parliamentary sovereignty, a doctrine that was authoritatively defined by A.V. Dicey in 1885 as meaning that there is no higher authority than parliament, and no legal restraint on the capacity of parliament to do whatever it wishes (Dicey 1885). Parliamentary sovereignty is dependent on parliament being representative of the broader political nation from which its members are drawn, thereby facilitating political accountability

(Gamble 1990: 406). Although parliament is legally sovereign, the political reality is quite different. Goldsworthy (1999: 190) explains that British constitutional thought has accommodated a parliament that is considered 'both legally sovereign and subject to customary restraints'. Parliament may be legally all-powerful, but popular sovereignty and popular accountability nevertheless restrain what parliament can do. In Jennings's (1957: 8) classic example, 'the fact that no government could secure powers to kill all blue-eyed babies is not due to any legal limitations in the powers of parliament but to the fact that both the government and the House of Commons derive their authority from the people'.

Although parliamentary sovereignty is the fundamental principle of the Westminster Model and of British politics, what actually operates in practice is, of course, executive sovereignty. The executive is sovereign at Westminster because of the single-member plurality electoral system, which rewards the largest party with the prize of government and access to state power far in excess of what it may proportionally be entitled to. The winner-takes-all system ensures that parliamentary sovereignty is utilized by the executive to deliver strong and responsible government in accordance with the Westminster Model. Modern British parliamentary government is predicated on the basis of a system of rule that is both representative and responsible (Birch 1964), facilitated by the practice of executive sovereignty and by the convention of ministerial responsibility for and accountability to parliament for executive actions. Parliamentary government constrains the exercise of power by ensuring that the executive is 'directly and constitutionally responsible to the legislature' (Rush 2005: 3). By fusing powers in this way, and by inextricably linking executive and legislature together, British parliamentary government means government through parliament, not government by parliament. In theory, the ministerial responsibility convention is the oil in the engine of parliamentary government, ensuring that ministers have to account to parliament for what they do, and be held accountable by parliament in turn. However, in practice, the convention has been inverted by ministers so as to control their relationship with parliament and enable them to dictate the terms of accountability and responsibility (Judge 1993: 152). Consequently, much depends on ministerial integrity and government cooperation for the convention of ministerial responsibility to parliament to work (Woodhouse 2004: 235). In the final analysis, the convention provides ministers with significant parliamentary hegemony (Flinders 2000: 79).

If parliament facilitates executive sovereignty and ministerial dominance at Westminster, then it is through party that strong, responsible, and accountable government is secured. The party system 'can best be understood in terms of its relationship with parliament as the institutional embodiment of the principles of representation, consent and legitimate government' (Judge 1993: 68). Party and partisanship structure the internal dynamics of parliament, and thereby weave the practice of strong government into the parliamentary fabric. The traditional two-party adversary system at Westminster shapes the internal workings of parliament, and provides for the 'institutionalisation of parliamentary government into government and opposition' (Rush 2005: 23).

Parliament is, first and foremost, an institution of representation, rather than an institution of democracy. The Westminster parliament was born and evolved as a representative institution, and its role was to provide a forum for the political nation (however it has been conceived through history) to secure a redress of their grievances by the executive. The emphasis has always been on government rather than parliament in the British state tradition (Judge 1993: 1). It is therefore mistaken to claim that Westminster is the historic source of parliamentary democracy in Britain: democracy and democratic structures have been a very modern addition to the Westminster complexion. The key moment for the development of parliamentary democracy did not come until 1867, when the Second Reform Act increased the size of the electorate, and compelled the political parties to organize for an age of nascent democratic politics. Parliament has adapted to the democratization of the British state over time, but its continuing characteristic is as an institution of representation, not of democracy. Parliamentary government has always been representative government, and latterly party government, but only recently has parliamentary government also tried to coexist alongside parliamentary democracy. The resulting tension inherent in the distinctively different imperatives between parliamentary government and parliamentary democracy have been a defining feature of British politics ever since.

13.3 THE ROLES OF PARLIAMENT

The fundamental role of parliament is as an institution of legitimation. Parliamentary government is the institutional embodiment of representative government in the British state, and is utilized to justify the use of political power. As Judge (1999: 15) explains, 'representative government in Britain has traditionally been conceived, and functioned, as a means of legitimating executive power through the condition of responsiveness'. Parliament provides legitimation to the executive because it is the representative embodiment of the political nation, and because it performs crucial legislative and scrutiny functions within the British political system.

The most basic tool of parliamentary deliberation—the debate—is the foundation for all legislative and scrutiny work. Most parliamentary time is taken up with debate of various kinds, and so many are the demands made on debate time in the House of Commons, that a parallel chamber—Westminster Hall—has convened since 1999 in order to meet these needs. There are, however, limitations to the debate structure, the most commonly cited of which is that lengthy parliamentary debates are unsuitable in the contemporary context of British politics. In this respect, the occasions when parliamentary debates do have resonance with the public—such as in September 2002 over the decision to go to war in Iraq—are undoubtedly outweighed by the vast majority of those about which the public hears nothing. Yet, the limitations of the debate structure and format have in the past been catalysts for adapting parliamentary procedure. In turn, the way that parliament performs its various roles is frequently subject to examination and reform, the aim of which is to 'improve' how parliament functions, with competing accounts providing different definitions of what 'improvement' might look like.

Crucially, arguments about how to 'improve' parliament are couched in an understanding of the very different functions performed by each of the two Houses of Parliament. While we can of course point to parliament as a formal political institution, the idea of there being a holistic parliamentary identity is at best theoretical. The House of Commons and the House of Lords are very different political creatures. The democratization of the British state during the nineteenth century cemented the House of Commons' claim to be the more important of the two chambers because it was bestowed with democratic legitimacy. The House of Lords has been able to make no such claim. Its historical role as a hereditary chamber left it devoid of democratic credentials. The second chamber has had a significant appointed element since the 1958 Life Peerages Act, and since the 1999 House of Lords Act, which removed the vast bulk of the hereditary peers, its membership has been predominantly appointed. As a consequence, while the House of Lords has legislative, scrutiny, and deliberative functions, as does the House of Commons, it performs them in different ways and for subtly different purposes.

13.4 PARLIAMENT AND LEGISLATION

Parliament has an important legislative function, but in the context of an executive which possesses the power of legislative initiative. Frequently described as a 'reactive' or 'arena' legislature, parliament's legislative role involves it scrutinizing legislative proposals made by government and assenting to them, thereby legitimating government actions and enabling its policies to become law. Parliament's legislative role has always been geared towards legitimating government legislation, and has never been about developing the capacity of parliament to legislate as an institution independent of government (Judge 2005: 44). Between the 1997–8 and 2005–6 sessions, government, in non-election years,[1] had an average legislative success rate of 95 per cent. By contrast, the success rate of legislation initiated by individual MPs was considerably lower, at just 7.5 per cent during the same years.[2]

However, parliamentary assent to government legislation is not assent given in ignorance. The legitimation process is predicated on the existence of parliamentary

---

[1] Non-election years are excluded because, when a general election is called, all remaining legislation falls, so to include such years distorts the figure, because the lower success rate is not only due to any parliamentary impact or influence.

[2] This figure includes all private members' bills: Ballot Bills, Presentation Bills under Standing Order No. 57, Ten Minute Rule Bills under Standing Order No. 23, and Lord's Private Members' Bills.

legislative procedures which expose government legislation to the oxygen of scrutiny, to the possibility of parliamentary amendment, and, in the final analysis, to the potential of parliament to refuse to give assent. Legislation makes its way to the statute books through an often lengthy process, involving several different stages of debate and examination, which afford both government and parliament the opportunity to make changes. It is widely recognized, however, that most substantive change to government legislation is actually the result of government ministers themselves introducing alterations during the legislative process. Parliament has, at best, a 'sporadic' impact on government bills, and both the principle and the detail of legislation is normally accepted (Norton 2005: 93).

Nonetheless, to then assume that parliament has a meaningless impact on government legislation would be mistaken. Parliament can and does affect government legislation, and often in significant ways that are counter to what government would have preferred. Dissension in the House of Commons does take place, and often (Norton 1975; 1980). Analysis of legislation during the Labour parliaments of 1997–2001 and 2001–5 suggests many ways in which parliament is able to change and influence government bills (Cowley 2002; 2005). Parliament's impact is most pronounced in securing change, not in defeating government legislation: indeed, the Labour government first elected in 1997 was not defeated in the House of Commons until November 2005. The relative rarity of government legislation being defeated by the House of Commons is not a testament to the weakness of the House, as some critics claim, but rather a testament to the fact that its role is not to consistently defeat government legislation in the first place. To assume that the strength of the House of Commons is derived from its ability to defeat the government in legislative divisions is to fundamentally misunderstand its role within the political system.

However, it is worthwhile making an important distinction here. When the House of Commons does succeed in making significant changes, it is not necessarily the result of the House as an institution, so much as it is the result of the government's own backbenchers voting against its proposals. Opposition parties, by definition and as a consequence of their minority numbers, can only defeat government legislation when a sufficient number of government backbenchers join them in the division lobbies. Backbench rebellion has, in the last decade, been on the increase (Cowley 2005). Nonetheless, most government MPs, most of the time, will be in agreement with executive proposals as a result of the obvious fact that they share the same party outlook (Cowley 2002; 2005). However, backbench rebellion need not result in a government defeat to have an impact, and even the mere threat of a substantial rebellion can result in changes being made to legislation. Government legislation is therefore most subject to change as a result of the activities of backbench members of the governing party. Parliament remains central to facilitating these activities, which take place in the institutional context of Westminster and the attendant procedural context in which government must operate in order to govern.

Consequently, procedural efficiency has always been a particular concern for government, which has, over time, altered parliamentary procedure to make it easier to secure its legislation. For example, legislative standing committees were cemented in the early 1900s through the work of the Procedure Committee, to create a forum in which government business would overwhelmingly take precedence (HC 89, 1906; Seaward and Silk 2004: 158). The Procedure Committee also played a key role in 1932 (HC 129, 1932), in response to the economic catastrophe enveloping Britain and the apparent institutional failure that accompanied it, and again between 1945 and 1946 (HC 9, 1945; HC 58, 1946; HC 189, 1946), in response to the need to rebuild Britain after six years of war. In both instances, the government aimed to refashion parliamentary procedure in order to minimize the energy expended on the legislative process and maximize the speed with which its legislative proposals became law (Kelso 2009). And in both cases, new procedural mechanisms emerged that fulfilled these governmental aims, with the development of the guillotine—which forced an end to standing committee proceedings regardless of whether legislation had been fully examined—undoubtedly the most significant and contentious tool to be honed in the post-war period (Walkland 1979: 269).

Procedure has changed to improve not only the likelihood that government legislation will be secured, but to enhance the predictability of *when* it will be secured (Kelso 2009). The most recent manifestation of this is the introduction of programming motions under the Labour government from 1997, secured through the specially appointed Modernization Committee (HC 190, 1997; HC 589, 2000; HC 382, 2001; HC 1168, 2002; HC 1222, 2003). Programming motions are designed, in theory, to provide for more even consideration of government legislation, and to enable the government to know with more certainty when its bills will complete each stage of the legislative process. However, the development of programme motions since 1997 has been controversial, prompting debate about whether they have reduced the House of Commons' capacity for proper scrutiny (Kelso 2007a: 149–51). In one respect, the expansion of programming, accompanied by an increase in the use of delegated legislation and statutory instruments (House of Commons Library 2007), which are often either exempt from parliamentary scrutiny or too numerous for proper legislative scrutiny to apply, points to the continuing and extended dominance of the executive at Westminster. Yet, simultaneously, there have also been innovations in the way that the Commons approaches legislative scrutiny, which require more attention than they have received thus far. Pre-legislative scrutiny has been only partially utilized in the Commons, but the recent expansion in its use may well yield benefits from a scrutiny perspective. A more interesting development which will require more scholarly attention as it unfolds is that of the redesign of Commons standing committees, to enable them to take evidence and hold hearings in the context of the bills they scrutinize. These changes are likely, over time, to give more teeth to the legislative scrutiny process, and perhaps enhance the Commons' influence over government legislation, primarily because they will lead to the sort of institutional capacity building that parliament has so far lacked.

The House of Lords also performs a crucial legislative role, which has become more pronounced since the 1999 House of Lords Act. The functions of the House of Lords are intimately linked to broader debates about, and processes of, second chamber reform. The hereditary composition of the second chamber was integral to justifying the constraint of the legislative capacity of the House of Lords during the twentieth century. Its powers to veto legislation were removed by the 1911 Parliament Act, and replaced with a suspensory veto whereby a bill that had been passed by the Commons in three successive sessions could receive Royal Assent without Lords approval, with this being further reduced to just two sessions by the 1949 Parliament Act. Yet the most important aspect of the legislative role of the House of Lords is not that it has lost its powers of veto, but that it has, over the last sixty years, greatly consolidated its ability to engage with useful, and consequential, legislative scrutiny (Walters 2004: 212).

The Conservative bias in the pre-1999 House of Lords led successive Labour governments to claim the House treated Labour legislation with a hostility that was not visited upon Conservative legislation. For example, the Labour government suffered a total of 343 defeats on division in the House of Lords between 1974 and 1979, while the Conservative government of 1979 to 1983 suffered just 45 defeats (House of Commons Library 2006). As a result, the Labour Party had a long-standing commitment to remove the hereditary peers before coming to office in 1997 (Dorey 2006). Yet, almost a decade after the 1999 House of Lords Act removed the vast majority of the hereditary peers, the chamber remained a largely appointed body, albeit with the Conservative bias removed. Nonetheless, the semi-reformed membership of the Lords has had a significant legislative impact: there is emerging evidence that the remaining appointed peers consider their chamber to be more legitimate than in the past, and that this gives them greater latitude to challenge the government to think again about its legislation (Russell and Sciara 2006a). In one respect, the peers are not actually any more democratically legitimate—after all, they remain appointed, and the basis for this perceived enhanced legitimacy is theoretically shaky (Kelso 2006). Yet, the House of Lords has inflicted significant defeats on government legislation since 1999. There were 245 defeats on division in the 2001–5 parliament, up from 108 in the 1997–2001 parliament, with legislative battles over terrorism being particularly hard fought (Cowley and Stuart 2003). Since 1999, only 40 per cent of Lords defeats have been fully reversed in the House of Commons, meaning that the second chamber is reasonably successful in securing policy change (Russell and Sciara 2006b: 318). The pre-reform House of Lords was always credited as subjecting government legislation to far better scrutiny than it received in the House of Commons. The present chamber still lays claim to this accolade, but in the context of a standard of legislative scrutiny that is perhaps not only more rigorous, but also of greater consequence too.

13.5 PARLIAMENT AND SCRUTINY

One of the most significant parliamentary debates heard at the start of the twenty-first century concerns the nature and meaning of Westminster scrutiny of the executive. Strong government in the British political system is rooted in the understanding that it will also be responsible government, and submit itself to systematic parliamentary scrutiny. Yet, as Weir and Beetham (1999: 372) note, the idea of responsible government worked in practice 'because governments were willing to *let* it work' (emphasis added). A key tenet of the liberal theory of the constitution is that government ministers are answerable to parliament for the actions of their ministries (Birch 1964: 140; Judge 1993: 135). Yet the logic of the doctrine has in practice been inverted, in order to preserve the idea of the minister as the key link in the accountability chain, 'precipitating a secret and closed process of decision making' (Judge 1993: 152). Debates concerning the role and meaning of parliamentary scrutiny of the executive have largely been in terms of dealing with that inversion, and about attempting to find new mechanisms and strategies designed to enable parliament to scrutinize the actions of government and determine where responsibility lies for policy- and decision-making.

At various points during the twentieth century, academics and parliamentarians examined how a committee system could be designed and used to impart structure and coherence to parliamentary scrutiny of the executive. In 1931, for example, the House of Commons Procedure Committee took extensive evidence in the course of its inquiry into the functioning of parliament, some of which explored the respective merits of creating new parliamentary machinery specifically dedicated to the task of scrutinizing the executive (HC 161, 1931). In the 1960s, the House of Commons took action under the direction of then Leader of the House, Richard Crossman, and instituted six committees to examine specific areas of government work. This came on the heels of much academic complaint about the way parliament conducted its scrutiny task, from the likes of Bromhead (1959), Crick (1964), Hanson (1964), Ryle (1965), and Wiseman (1959). But it was not until 1979 that a fully structured committee system was created, with individual committees organized on the basis that they would each scrutinize the activities of single government departments. The House of Commons departmental select committee system, recommended by the Procedure Committee in 1978 (HC 588, 1978) and secured by the reforming Leader of the House, Norman St John-Stevas, was a significant step forward for the integrity of parliamentary scrutiny (Jogerst 1993). Yet, despite the move towards scrutiny specialization, the new system lacked powers to compel ministers and their advisers to appear before committees, and was unable to force departments to disclose information, thus restraining parliament's investigatory capacity (Judge 1989; 1992).

The institutional constraints placed upon the select committees at their inception has been a rallying point for parliamentary reformers ever since. Development of the select committee system has, for the last thirty years, been perceived as integral to checking the strong executive that lies at the heart of the British political system, and recommendations have come from parties and think tanks (Conservative Party 2000; Hansard Society 2001) and from the select committees themselves (HC 300, 2000; HC 748, 2000; HC 321, 2001; HC 224, 2001). Significant efforts to secure reform in 2002, led by yet another reform-minded Leader of the House, Robin Cook, enjoyed partial success. Some changes, such as instituting core tasks for select committees and paying their chairpeople, were approved by the House of Commons. Significantly, proposals to remove the power of selecting committee members from the party whips were unsuccessful. This has long been a central complaint about how select committees operate and how they conduct their scrutiny of government. For critics, it is a fundamental mistake to allow those who are key members of the government—the party whips—to have the power to choose those MPs who then preside over the scrutiny of the executive. Removal of the whips from this process would impact on powers of patronage and the parameters of control exercised by the executive over the legislature (Kelso 2003: 70). The executive mentality in operation at Westminster is geared towards preserving executive strength and constraining parliamentary scrutiny, not creating conditions in which such scrutiny can be better performed. Yet, the more subtle point is that changes to the ways that party whips engaged with the process of choosing MPs to sit on select committees did take place within the parties themselves at this time. In this respect, change happened at the party level, even if it did have the impact of weakening the case for change at the parliamentary level (Flinders 2007: 190). Once more, the complex role of party at Westminster is usefully underlined.

It is entirely possible continually to revisit parliament's scrutiny structures and never be fully satisfied with how they operate. And, because of this, it is easy to overlook the useful scrutiny work with which parliament engages, and through which it attempts to hold government to account. The issue is one of perspective, and of properly understanding parliament's role within the political system. Just as parliament's legislative role is to examine government legislation and give assent, rather than persistently defeat it, parliament's scrutiny role is to subject government policy, administration, and expenditure to examination and make recommendations and criticisms, not to continually demand policy and administrative reversals. As the select committee system has bedded down institutionally over the past three decades, its ability to engage in worthwhile scrutiny that shines a spotlight on government work has improved.

In the 2001–5 parliament, for example, the departmental select committee system published around 530 reports scrutinizing government activities, following inquiries which were based on around 390 separate evidence sessions with many thousands of individuals, ranging from government ministers to agency chief executives, from academic specialists to affected citizens. When the work of the non-departmentally aligned select committees is included—Environmental Audit, Public Accounts, Public Administration, and Regulatory Reform—the number of reports increases to over 840, and the number of evidence sessions to almost 550. The work rate of the select committees has grown over the years as they have become more comfortable with the parameters of their role, and aided by the decision in 2002 for committees to have core tasks around which they organized their programme of work.

The sheer volume of materials emanating from the select committees is relevant in terms of them fulfilling their task of exposing government activities to the oxygen of publicity. The fact that select committees can hold public evidence gathering sessions is an important part of the process of obtaining a range of views about public policy and placing them in the public domain. In addition, select committees can, and often do, return to the same topic of inquiry repeatedly if they have concerns that a policy is not working as planned, and that government has not taken on board their concerns. A good example of this is the Child Support Agency, created in 1991 but plagued with problems ever since, prompting the relevant select committees to return to the issue on several occasions (Norton 2005: 104), even after the government announced plans finally to abolish the Agency (HC 219, 2007). The ability of the select committees to return to key policy areas, and develop expertise through the evidence they collect, is integral to how they conduct their scrutiny tasks.

Despite the volume of reports published, however, it is ultimately up to government to decide whether or not to accept select committee recommendations and advice. In the early years of the select committee system, governments paid scant attention to what they said, and the persistent failure of government to respond to their reports was viewed as undermining their entire existence. Yet, this too has changed over time, if only slowly. In the 2001–5 parliament, government provided around 320 replies to select committee reports, and the speed with which these replies emerge has improved, largely due to the doggedness of the select committees themselves in pursuing them.

Crucially, however, the executive undoubtedly retains the advantage with respect to the terms in which it engages with the committees. Select committees cannot compel ministers, civil servants, or special advisers to give evidence to them. While ministers do not normally refuse to attend, there have been particular problems in securing evidence and cooperation from civil servants and ministers and the attendance of government special advisers, which is problematic for the select committees in their task of trying to understand how decision-making works in central government and who is in practice responsible for decisions taken. This was particularly the case in the course of the Foreign Affairs Select Committee investigation into the decision to go to war in Iraq. That committee did not receive the same level of cooperation from government enjoyed by others, such as the Hutton Inquiry, which secured evidence from individuals and the submission of papers that were refused to the Foreign Affairs committee (HC 813, 2003; HC 440, 2004). In 2005, the Public Administration Committee was refused its request to take evidence from the Prime Minister's Strategy Adviser, Lord Birt, as part of its inquiry into long-term strategy and planning in government (HC 690, 2005).

These are by no means isolated examples. However, while highlighting the constraints, we must not overlook the positive developments. For example, in 2002, the Prime Minister agreed to appear before the Liaison Select Committee (the committee on which all the select committee chairmen sit) twice a year. This decision is unprecedented in the history of parliamentary scrutiny, and affords the Liaison Committee the opportunity to scrutinize the Prime Minister for almost three hours at a time on specific areas of government policy. There have been teething problems with this new format, not only in terms of organization and style, but also in terms of mapping out the kind of scrutiny with which it should engage, but, given time, this new form of scrutiny may become a key part of parliament's scrutiny toolbox. Another crucial development is that, despite parliamentary complaints about lack of access to information about the decision to go to war in Iraq, the fact remains that parliament was afforded a debate and vote on that decision prior to the war. This is a significant development, and one that has now set a precedent in terms of future parliamentary authorization for war and the overseas engagement of military personnel, and in so doing has cemented the role of parliament as the pre-eminent forum for debates of national importance (Giddings 2005: 198).

Scrutiny of the executive is also an integral function of the House of Lords, and one which, like its legislative role, has been framed in the context of the reform of its composition. The appearance of life peers in the House after 1958 greatly aided the work of the second chamber, by incorporating experienced individuals who came from a range of professional backgrounds, and who brought expertise to the job. Just as the House of Commons recognized the merits of specialization when it came to executive scrutiny, so too did the House of Lords. Rather than replicate the departmentally based committee system adopted in the Commons, the Lords first focused its attention on two cross-cutting areas which the lower chamber had traditionally neglected: European matters, and science and technology. The Lords developed expertise in these areas, drawing on the knowledge and experience of its life peers, and developed an approach to scrutiny that came to be greatly respected (Shell 1992). Over time, the House of Lords has so expanded its European scrutiny work that it is now conducted through eight different committees. The second chamber has also consolidated its work in those areas that the Commons has overlooked by establishing select committees on the constitution, delegated powers, economic affairs, statutory instruments, and regulators. The scrutiny work of the House of Lords derives its authority from the expertise and professional backgrounds of those engaged with its committees, with many of the life peers able to draw on their extensive careers outside parliament to inform the scrutiny process. Despite continuing to attract criticism for being unelected and undemocratic, the House of Lords nevertheless performs crucial scrutiny functions that complement the work done by the Commons by examining those areas for which the lower chamber fails to find time.

13.6 PARLIAMENT AND DEMOCRACY

It is perhaps ironic that the House of Lords is, on the one hand, condemned for its undemocratic composition, and, on the other hand, applauded for the important contribution it makes to the broad work of parliament. In the past four decades, the apparent contradiction between the absence of democratic legitimacy and the abundance of functional legitimacy in the House of Lords has framed the second chamber reform debate, with the controversy revolving around the extent to which input and output legitimacy can be better balanced. Charged with finding a new basis for the composition of the House of Lords, MPs have been torn about how to reconcile the aim of preserving the expertise found in the chamber, which enables it to be so adept at discharging its duties, while also reconstituting it on a more democratic basis. The common assumption is that a move towards a democratically elected second chamber is incompatible with the aim of maintaining a chamber of expertise, because those who possess such expertise would be unlikely to seek election to the House. In this view, an elected second chamber would simply expand the professional political class, and expand the power of the parties in the House of Lords, at the expense of ensuring parliamentary functions are performed properly. These concerns are hinged around the fundamental requirement that a reformed second chamber does not challenge the supremacy of the first chamber, a situation which opponents of an elected second chamber argue would arise if the House of Lords was reorganized along democratic lines.

Since the Labour Party committed to second chamber reform in its 1997 election manifesto, discussions have been underpinned by a professed desire to make the chamber more democratic, more representative, and more legitimate. Yet the conceptual confusion surrounding these terms has muddied the reform waters, and the government largely failed to make a coherent case for how the chamber can simultaneously be made more democratic, representative, and legitimate (Kelso 2006). A more democratic chamber is not necessarily also more representative, and vice versa. Such difficulties underline the party political considerations associated with second chamber reform. Opposition desires to embarrass the government were in part responsible in February 2003 for the failure of the House of Commons to support one of the seven reform options presented to it (McLean, Spirling, and Russell 2003), undoubtedly aided by unease amongst MPs about what impact a democratic second chamber would have on their own House. Perhaps surprisingly, MPs overcame these doubts in March 2007, when they approved proposals for both a wholly elected and an 80 per cent elected second chamber. A desire to at least attempt to move the reform debate forward figured heavily in this outcome, given the paralysis over the issue since the hereditary peers were expelled in 1999. Whether this decision will in fact accelerate second chamber reform is another question altogether: the House of Lords voted, entirely unsurprisingly, for a wholly appointed chamber on the basis that this is the only way to preserve its functional integrity and distinctiveness. Quite how these opposing views can be reconciled, and a specific and feasible scheme for reform devised, remains to be seen.

The debate over whether the House of Lords should have an elected composition is just one aspect of parliament's adaptation to the gradual democratization of the British state. The trustee basis of representative government, its impact in delimiting public participation in decision-making, along with the repercussions of the winner-takes-all electoral system, all underpin a public discourse of dissatisfaction with how democracy works in Britain, and, by extension, exasperation with parliament's performance of its broad democratic roles. In the autumn 2007 Eurobarometer survey, for example, just 34 per cent of respondents said they trusted the Westminster parliament (Eurobarometer 68, 2007). Parliament has not been without advice about how it can better perform its democratic functions. The Power Inquiry (2006) into the state of British democracy advocated a reinvigoration of parliament by creating structures and processes which facilitated a more participatory form of democracy, such as, for example, the ability of citizens to initiate legislation. More circumspect reports have focused on how parliament performs specific democratic functions, such as that of communicating parliamentary democracy to the public (Hansard Society 2005). Concerns about electoral disengagement, highlighted by the low turnout at the 2001 and 2005 general elections—to 59.4 per cent and 61.4 per cent respectively, down from 71.4 per cent in 1997—have prompted parliament to examine how it engages with the public. Various Commons select committees have explored the quality of the relationship between parliament and the public, and how it might be enhanced (HC 1065, 2002; HC 368, 2004). Recent changes derived from this exploration have included new select committee consultation mechanisms and experiments using the internet to facilitate engagement, which are all small adaptations that may cumulatively amount to important change over time (Kelso 2007*b*).

13.7 CONCLUSIONS

The conclusion to some arguments in favour of reinvigorating politics and democracy in Britain is that parliament needs to be more powerful in terms of how it holds the government to account, challenges its legislative proposals, and examines its policies, expenditure, and administration. From this perspective, there needs to be a greater emphasis on parliamentary democracy, rather than parliamentary government. It is easy, perhaps, to look back to some lost golden age of parliament, when its powers were more formidable than at present. To do so, however, is to look back to a time that never existed. There have been ebbs and flows to parliament's relationship with the executive, to be sure. However, parliament is presently more 'powerful' than it has been for some time: it is flexing its legislative and scrutiny muscles in new and increasingly interesting ways. Yet, in the final analysis, we simply miss the whole point about parliament if we equate its relevance with its powers. As Judge (1993: 2) explains, 'the importance of parliament does not derive from its "powers" but from the very process of representation and the legitimation of government and governmental outputs flowing from that process'.

That is not to say there are not problems with how parliament fulfils its functions. There are issues to do with its representational capacity, particularly if one prioritizes the need for a legislature to be somehow microcosmically representative of the population on whose behalf it acts. Too much legislative scrutiny falls to the second chamber because the first chamber does not find time to do a thorough job. Parliamentary scrutiny of administration and expenditure is improving, but problems remain, particularly with regards to executive constraints on scrutiny capacity and capability. There are, in addition, broader issues to consider with respect to parliament's role in British politics. In particular, the idea of parliamentary sovereignty has always been coloured by our understanding of the practice of executive sovereignty, but the whole notion of sovereignty is even more deeply questioned at the start of the twenty-first century. The meaning of national sovereignty in the context of membership of the European Union has long exercised political and legal theorists, but Westminster sovereignty in the context of devolution in the UK has added an additional facet to the puzzle, a facet which prompts questioning about the long-term role of the UK parliament. Contemporary discussions about the need to address the consequences of asymmetric devolution are essentially questions about the continued role of the Westminster parliament in an era of multi-level governance.

Complex issues such as these, which are the consequence of the continued development of the British state, are not easily squared away. Nonetheless, as things presently stand, there is no national institutional forum other than parliament from which the executive can derive its legitimacy and through which the public can be represented. Consequently, parliament remains integral to the structural underpinnings of the British political system, not just because it is constantly evolving in the context of modern representative democracy, and not just because it is progressively honing its ability to hold the government to legislative and administrative account, but because, in the final analysis, it alone provides legitimate access to the instruments of state power.

References

BIRCH, A. H. 1964. *Representative and Responsible Government*. London: George Allen and Unwin.

BROMHEAD, P. A. 1959. 'How Should Parliament be Reformed?' *Political Quarterly*, 30/3: 272–82.

CONSERVATIVE PARTY 2000. *Strengthening Parliament: The Report of the Commission to Strengthen Parliament*. London: Conservative Party.

COWLEY, P. 2002. *Revolts and Rebellions*. London: Politico's.

—— 2005. *The Rebels*. London: Politico's.

—— and STUART, M. 2003 'Parliament: More Revolts, More Reform'. *Parliamentary Affairs*, 56/2: 188–204.

CRICK, B. 1964. *The Reform of Parliament*. London: Weidenfeld and Nicolson.

DICEY, A. V. 1885. *Introduction to the Study of Law and the Constitution*. London: Macmillan.

DOREY, P. 2006. '1949, 1969, 1999: The Labour Party and House of Lords Reform'. *Parliamentary Affairs*, 59/4: 599–620.

EUROBAROMETER 68 2007. *Public Opinion in the European Union: First Results*. Brussels: European Commission.

FLINDERS, M. 2000. 'The Enduring Centrality of Individual Ministerial Responsibility within the British Constitution'. *Journal of Legislative Studies*, 9/3: 73–92.

—— 2007. 'Analysing Reform: The House of Commons, 2001–5'. *Political Studies*, 55/1: 174–200.

GAMBLE, A. 1990. 'Theories of British Politics'. *Political Studies*, 38/1: 404–20.

GIDDINGS, P. 2005. 'To War or not to War: That is the Question'. In P. Giddings (ed.), *The Future of Parliament*. London: Palgrave.

GOLDSWORTHY, J. 1999. *The Sovereignty of Parliament*. Oxford: Oxford University Press.

HANSARD SOCIETY 2001. *The Challenge for Parliament: Making Government Accountable*. London: Vacher Dod.

—— 2005. *Members Only? Parliament in the Public Eye*. London: Vacher Dod.

HANSON, A. H. 1964. 'The Purpose of Parliament'. *Parliamentary Affairs*, 17/3: 279–95.

HC 9. 1945. *First Report from the Select Committee on Procedure*. London: HMSO.

—— 58. 1946. *Second Report from the Select Committee on Procedure*. London: HMSO.

—— 89. 1906. *First Report from the Select Committee on House of Commons Procedure*. London: HMSO.

—— 129. 1932. *Report from the Select Committee on Procedure*. London: HMSO.

—— 161. 1931. *Special Report from the Select Committee on Procedure on Public Business*. London: HMSO.

—— 189. 1946. *Third Report from the Select Committee on Procedure*. London: HMSO.

—— 190. 1997. *The Legislative Process*, First Report from the Select Committee on Modernisation of the House of Commons. London: HMSO.

—— 219. 2007. *Child Support Reform*, Fourth Report from the Work and Pensions Committee. London: HMSO.

—— 224. 2001. *Select Committees*, First Report from the Select Committee on Modernisation of the House of Commons. London: HMSO.

—— 300. 2000. *Shifting the Balance: Select Committees and the Executive*, First Report from the Liaison Select Committee. London: HMSO.

—— 321. 2001. *Shifting the Balance: Unfinished Business*, First Report from the Liaison Select Committee. London: HMSO.

—— 368. 2004. *Connecting Parliament with the Public*, First Report from the Select Committee on Modernisation of the House of Commons. London: HMSO.

—— 382. 2001. *Programming of Legislation*, First Report from the Select Committee on Modernisation of the House of Commons. London: HMSO.

—— 440. 2004. *Implications for the Work of the House and its Committees of the Government's Lack of Co-operation with the Foreign Affairs Committee's Inquiry into the Decision to go to War in Iraq*. London: HMSO.

—— 588. 1978. *First Report from the Select Committee on Procedure*. London: HMSO.

—— 589. 2000. *Programming of Legislation and Timing of Votes*, Second Report from the Select Committee on Modernisation of the House of Commons. HMSO: London.

—— 690. 2005. *The Attendance of the Prime Minister's Strategy Adviser before the Public Administration Select Committee*, First Special Report from the Public Administration Committee. London: HMSO.

—— 748. 2000. *Independence or Control?* Second Report from the Liaison Select Committee. London: HMSO.

—— 813. 2003. *The Decision to go to War in Iraq*, Ninth Report from the Foreign Affairs Select Committee. London: HMSO.

—— 1065. 2002. *Digital Technology: Working for Parliament and the Public*, Report from the House of Commons Information Committee. London: HMSO.

—— 1168. 2002. *Modernisation of the House of Commons: A Reform Programme*, Second Report from the Select Committee on Modernisation of the House of Commons. London: HMSO.

—— 1222. 2003. *Programming of Bills*, First Report from the Select Committee on Modernisation of the House of Commons. London: HMSO.

HOUSE OF COMMONS LIBRARY 2006. *Government Defeats in the House of Lords*. London: House of Commons.

——2007. *Acts and Statutory Instruments: Volume of UK Legislation 1950 to 2006*. London: House of Commons.

JENNINGS, I. 1957. *Parliament*. Cambridge: Cambridge University Press.

JOGERST, M. 1993. *Reform in the House of Commons: The Select Committee System*. Lexington: University Press of Kentucky.

JUDGE, D. 1989. 'Parliament in the 1980s'. *Political Quarterly*, 60/4: 400–12.

——1992. 'The "Effectiveness" of the Post-1979 Select Committee System: The Verdict of the 1990 Procedure Committee'. *Political Quarterly*, 63/1: 91–100.

——1993. *The Parliamentary State*. London: Sage.

——1999. *Representation: Theory and Practice in Britain*. London: Routledge.

——2005. *Political Institutions in the United Kingdom*. Oxford: Oxford University Press.

KELSO, A. 2003. 'Where were the Massed Ranks of Parliamentary Reformers? "Attitudinal" and "Contextual" Approaches to Parliamentary Reform'. *Journal of Legislative Studies*, 9/1: 57–76.

——2006. 'Reforming the House of Lords: Navigating Representation, Democracy and Legitimacy at Westminster'. *Parliamentary Affairs*, 59/4: 563–81.

——2007a. 'The House of Commons Modernisation Committee: Who Needs It?' *British Journal of Politics and International Relations*, 9/1: 138–57.

——2007b. 'Parliament and Political Disengagement: Neither Waving nor Drowning'. *Political Quarterly*, 78/3: 364–73.

——2009. *Parliamentary Reform at Westminster*. Manchester: Manchester University Press.

KING, A. 1976. 'Modes of Executive–Legislative Relations: Great Britain, France and West Germany'. *Legislative Studies Quarterly*, 1/1: 11–34.

LASKI, H. 1938. *Parliamentary Government in England*. London: George Allen and Unwin.

LOW, S. 1906. *The Governance of England*. London: T. Fisher Unwin.

LOWELL, A. L. 1912. *The Government of England*, vols. i and ii. New York: Macmillan.

MCLEAN, I., SPIRLING, A., and RUSSELL, M. 2003. 'None of the Above: The UK House of Commons Votes on Reforming the House of Lords, February 2003'. *Political Quarterly*, 74/3: 298–310.

MILIBAND, R. 1961. *Parliamentary Socialism*. London: Allen and Unwin.

NORTON, P. 1975. *Dissension in the House of Commons 1945–74*. London: Macmillan.

——1980. *Dissension in the House of Commons 1975–1979*. Oxford: Clarendon Press.

——1993. *Does Parliament Matter?* London: Harvester Wheatsheaf.

——2005. *Parliament in British Politics*. London: Palgrave.

POWER INQUIRY 2006. *Power to the People: The Report of the Power Inquiry into Britain's Democracy*. London: Power Inquiry.

REDLICH, J. 1908. *The Procedure of the House of Commons*, vols. i–iii. London: Constable.

RHODES, R. A. W. 1997. *Understanding Governance*. London: Open University Press.

RICHARDS, D., and SMITH, M. J. 2002. *Governance and Public Policy in the UK*. Oxford: Oxford University Press.

ROGERS, R., and WALTERS, R. 2006. *How Parliament Works*. London: Longman.

RUSH, M. 2005. *Parliament Today*. Manchester: Manchester University Press.

RUSSELL, M., and SCIARA, M. 2006a. 'Legitimacy and Bicameral Strength: A Case Study of the House of Lords'. Presented to the 2006 PSA Parliaments and Legislatures Specialist Group Conference, University of Sheffield.

————2006b. 'Why Does the Government Get Defeated in the House of Lords? The Lords, the Party System and British Politics'. *British Politics*, 2/3: 299–322.

RYLE, M. 1965. 'Committees of the House of Commons'. *Political Quarterly*, 36/3: 295–308.

SEAWARD, P., and SILK, P. 2004. 'The House of Commons'. In V. Bogdanor (ed.), *The British Constitution in the Twentieth Century*. Oxford: Oxford University Press.

SHELL, D. 1992. 'The European Communities Committee'. In D. Shell and D. Beamish (eds.), *The House of Lords at Work*. Oxford: Clarendon Press.

WALKLAND, S. 1979. 'Government Legislation in the House of Commons'. In S. A. Walkland (ed.), *The House of Commons in the Twentieth Century*. Oxford: Clarendon Press.

WALTERS, R. 2004. 'The House of Lords'. In V. Bogdanor (ed.), *The British Constitution in the Twentieth Century*. Oxford: Oxford University Press.

WEIR, S., and BEETHAM, D. 1999. *Political Power and Democratic Control in Britain*. London: Routledge.

WISEMAN, H. V. 1959. 'Parliamentary Reform'. *Parliamentary Affairs*, 12/2: 240–54.

WOODHOUSE, D. 2004. 'Ministerial Responsibility'. In V. Bogdanor (ed.), *The British Constitution in the Twentieth Century*. Oxford: Oxford University Press.

CHAPTER 14

CONSTITUTIONALISM

ADAM TOMKINS

14.1 INTRODUCTION

THIS chapter outlines the nature of the British constitution, explaining its unusual 'unwritten' form (14.2), and giving an account of its main substantive components (14.3). It considers a range of challenges which the contemporary constitution faces (14.4) and argues throughout that the constitution is currently undergoing a profound transformation from being a largely parliamentary or political constitution to being a mainly legal or juridical order in which the courts will play a markedly expanded role, unprecedented in British constitutional history.

14.2 QUESTIONS OF FORM

14.2.1 The Unwritten Constitution and Its Consequences

The British constitution is unusual. Almost every country in the world has a written constitution: a single, codified constitutional text that is superior both to government and to all other law. The United Kingdom is one of only a handful of countries that are commonly said not to have a written constitution. Of the others, Israel has a series of Basic Laws which have a quasi-constitutional status and a committee of its Knesset (legislative assembly) is currently working on a draft constitution; and New Zealand has a Constitution Act (1986) which outlines the functions of the main institutions of state. The United Kingdom has no equivalent of either Israel's Basic Laws or New Zealand's Constitution Act.

It does, however, have several sources (mainly Acts of Parliament) which may be viewed as being fundamental to the constitution. These range from the thirteenth-century compact between King John and his Barons known as Magna Carta, the first great attempt to limit the powers of the monarchy through the force of law (Tomkins 2003: 40–1; Holt 1992) to the Human Rights Act 1998, branded as Britain's 'bill of rights', incorporating most of the European Convention on Human Rights into domestic UK law. The Bill of Rights 1689 (on the relationship between the Crown and the Houses of Parliament), the Act of Settlement 1701 (ditto), the various Acts of Union (with Scotland in 1707, with Ireland in 1800), the Parliament Act 1911 (on the relationship between the two Houses of Parliament—Commons and Lords), the European Communities Act 1972 (on the roles played by European Union law within the UK), and the devolution legislation (most especially, perhaps, the Scotland Act 1998) may likewise be branded as elemental to the constitution.

There is, however, from a formal point of view, nothing special about any of these Acts of Parliament. As the law currently stands, parliament could amend or repeal any provision of any of these Acts at any time and for any reason just as it may amend or repeal any provision of legislation dealing with any other, non-constitutional subject. This is an aspect of what is generally (if somewhat misleadingly) known as the doctrine of the sovereignty of parliament. As it was classically expressed by A. V. Dicey (Dicey 1885: 40), parliament may 'make or unmake any law whatever'. At least from a legal point of view there is nothing entrenched about the British constitution. This, it may be thought, is one of the principal consequences of not having a binding constitutional text—of there being no written constitution (Finer, Bogdanor, and Rudden 1995: 40). Of course, a written constitution would not necessarily have to be formally entrenched—it is perfectly possible to conceive of such a constitution containing a provision to the effect that 'Any provision of this Constitution may be changed by simple majority vote in the House of Representatives' or even 'Any provision of this Constitution may be changed by the Supreme Court'. Most of the world's written constitutions, however, do not contain provisions such as these, at any rate not expressly, and are presented as if they enjoy at least some degree of entrenchment.

That the British constitution is not legally entrenched does not mean that it is particularly fluid or even flexible in practice. Indeed, there is much about the constitutional order that has remained largely unchanged for decades, even centuries, as the dates of the older Acts of Parliament cited above testify. The fundamental relationship between the Crown and parliament—the most divisive secular issue of all British politics in the seventeenth century, let us not forget—has remained constant since the early eighteenth century (this is not the same as the Crown's relationship with the government of the day, which has changed significantly over the last 300 years, as executive power has shifted from the monarchy to ministers). The relationship between the House of Lords and the House of Commons has remained more or less stable since 1911 (Walters 2003) and does not appear to have been much altered by the partial reform to the composition of the upper house effected by the House of Lords Act 1999, even if the House of Lords has used the reforms of 1999 as a basis for becoming more assertive as a scrutineer of the government's legislative proposals (Hazell 2007: 10). That Britain has a Cabinet system of government with a Prime Minister at its head, and which is responsible to parliament, has been true since at least the time of Pitt the Younger in the 1780s and perhaps since Walpole in the 1720s, even if the nature of the Cabinet and its relationship with the Prime Minister have changed since the eighteenth century (Jennings 1936; Birch 1964; Mackintosh 1977). On the other hand, recent years have witnessed a flurry of constitutional change, as the Labour governments of Tony Blair and Gordon Brown have made constitutional reform a centrepiece of their policy (British constitutionalism and New Labour is discussed further, below).

Cabinet government, the office of Prime Minister, and the practice of ministerial responsibility to parliament are features of the British constitution that owe little or nothing to law, *stricto sensu*. They are creatures of what we call constitutional convention (Marshall 1984). This, it may be thought, is a second consequence of the absence of a written constitution: namely, that the constitutional order relies as heavily on non-legal or conventional sources as it does on formal law. On closer examination, however, it becomes clear that written constitutions only rarely approach being complete codes and that many countries with written constitutions rely on conventions or constitutional practice to supplement the formal text (Barendt 1998: 40).

Constitutional lawyers are generally happy to recognize that constitutional conventions are as binding on constitutional actors as are constitutional laws. The difference lies not in the mandatory nature of the rules, but in the identity of the enforcer. Laws are enforced by courts, whereas conventions are enforced politically. Usually, this means through parliament. Thus, if (in breach of convention) the monarch appointed as Prime Minister someone other than the leader of the political party with majority support in the House of Commons, no one could sue the monarch in the courts—the monarch has broken no law. But, even though it is not illegal, such behaviour would be unconstitutional and there would surely be a political reaction. What, precisely, that reaction would consist of is impossible to predict, but it could plausibly range from a mere expression of parliamentary disquiet to legislation abolishing the monarchy altogether, with an array of intermediate options.

Other conventions are routinely enforced by parliament. It is a constitutional convention, for example, that ministers are collectively and individually responsible to parliament for government policy. These conventions, among other matters, require ministers to account to parliament for the policies, decisions, and actions of their departments. Any failure so to account will be addressed by parliament. Sometimes the sanction will be that the minister is called to give a full account, or to correct an inadvertent error in an earlier account, or to apologize for a mistake. On other occasions more serious consequences follow from a breach of the conventions, the ultimate punishment being a forced resignation (Woodhouse 1994; Flinders 2002; Tomkins 2003: ch 5).

14.2.2 From the Political to the Legal Constitution?

That core elements of the British constitution are policed by political institutions such as parliament rather than by legal institutions such as the courts is one of the most significant facets of British constitutionalism (Griffith 1979; Tomkins 2005). In recent years it has become widely disliked, as numerous constitutional commentators have become exasperated by what they see as the constitution being subjected to the vagaries—and oftentimes the self-serving vagaries—of party politics (Mount 1992; Barnett 1997; Weir and Beetham 1999). The 1990s were notorious, for example, for ministers in John Major's Cabinet seeking to rewrite the rules of ministerial responsibility in their favour so as to avoid having to take responsibility for their mistakes or for their failures to keep parliament properly informed of government policy (the full story is told in Tomkins 1998: ch. 1). This led several commentators to go so far as to take the view that '[t]he doctrine of ministerial responsibility has been significantly weakened over the last ten years or so, so that it can no longer be said . . . that it is a fundamental doctrine of the constitution' (Jowell and Oliver 2000: viii; see also Barendt 1998: 116). However, this was a premature obituary and, since 1997, the practice of ministerial responsibility has recovered considerably (Woodhouse 2002; Tomkins 2003: ch. 5).

What may be overlooked in the rush to condemn the British constitution's reliance on political methods of enforcement is that judicial methods of enforcement are likewise subject to vagaries. In the British context, for example, a once vibrant administrative law of judicial review fell almost into desuetude for a prolonged period in the mid-twentieth century, only to be revived slowly and for the most part uncertainly by a cadre of enthusiastic judges in the 1960s and 1980s. Only since the mid-1990s has judicial review really come to the fore of British constitutionalism (Jowell 2003). In the United States, to take a second example, the Supreme Court rather suddenly relied on the commerce clause of the US constitution to strike down Congressional legislation in *US v Lopez* 514 US 549 (1995) after not having previously used that clause for this purpose since 1937. After *Lopez*, the Court's new-found interest in federalism became one the hallmarks of the Rehnquist Court's constitutional jurisprudence—not something that could have been said of the Supreme Court at any time in the previous half century (Young 2004). Turning from political and parliamentary means of accountability and scrutiny to legal and judicial means is less likely to secure the results of consistent 'constitutional justice' (see Allan 2001) than its advocates tend to assume (Poole 2002; Goldsworthy 2003; Tomkins 2005: ch. 1).

Nonetheless, a move away from relying principally on political institutions and methods of accountability, towards relying more strongly on legal institutions and methods of accountability, is one of the hallmarks of the British constitutional experience in the period since the early 1990s (Tomkins 2003: ch. 1). This move can be seen both in the behaviour of constitutional actors (especially, but not only, the courts), as well as in the arguments of constitutional commentators (e.g. Barendt 1998; Allan 2001; Oliver 2003; Dyzenhaus 2006). This move, from a privileging of political constitutionalism in Britain to a privileging of legal constitutionalism, will be a central theme of this chapter. Before we go any further it may be as well to summarize what is meant by it (with the proviso that what follows in the remainder of this paragraph will be expanded upon as this chapter proceeds). The move from political to legal constitutionalism involves, and may be taken as shorthand for, four related developments:

- A denial of the potency of and a loss of faith in political accountability and ministerial responsibility (see e.g. Jowell and Oliver 2000).
- A strengthening of the rule of law and a furthering of the constitutional roles of the courts. This development manifests itself in a variety of ways, such as: extending the reach of the rule of law to embrace formerly political and non-justiciable issues (as in *R v Home Secretary, ex parte Fire Brigades Union* [1995] 2 AC 513; see Tomkins 2003: ch. 1; and *A v Home Secretary* [2005] 2 AC 68; see Turpin and Tomkins 2007: ch. 11); creating new species of common law constitutional rights (as in *R v Home Secretary, ex parte Leech* [1994] QB 198 and *R v Home Secretary, ex parte Simms* [2000] 2 AC 115; see Tomkins 2003: ch. 6); enacting new constitutional rights through legislation (as in the Human Rights Act 1998, on which see below).
- A doubting of the continued appropriateness of the sovereignty of parliament (as in *Jackson v Attorney General* [2006] 1 AC 262, on which see below).
- Leading to a general sense that there are few clear limits to the constitutional roles of the courts (Barak 2006).

One of the consequences of the move from political to legal constitutionalism is that the unusual nature of the British constitution, which formerly distinguished it from the constitutional norm both elsewhere in the Commonwealth and in Europe, is being diluted. The advance of the legal constitution is far from unique to Britain: indeed, in many respects, Britain is playing catch-up, as it takes inspiration from the US Supreme Court, the Supreme Court of Canada, the European Court of Justice, and the European Court of Human Rights, among others (Beatty 2004). Recent scholarship in comparative constitutional law shows the considerable extent to which the globalization of juridical norms in public law is leading constitutional and supreme courts across the world to talk more and more with each other, to cite each other's decisions as authorities, and often even to adopt remarkably similar modes of reasoning and solutions to the disputes that come before them (Beatty 2004; Anderson 2005; Choudhry 2006; although cf. Lasser 2004; Goldsworthy 2006). The juridification of constitutionalism in Britain is an experience it has in common with countries as diverse as Canada, South Africa, Israel, Poland, Hungary, and New Zealand, among many others (Hirschl 2004).

14.3 CONSTITUTIONAL CONTENT

Defining the constitution broadly, we might say that it includes all *the rules, conventions, and practices that describe or regulate the organisation, powers, and operation of government and the relations between private persons and public authorities* (cf. Turpin and Tomkins 2007: 4). Adopting such a definition, what are the core components of the British constitution? The following six features of the constitution may be regarded as central: (a) that the United Kingdom is a constitutional monarchy; (b) the doctrine of the sovereignty of parliament; (c) the doctrine of the rule of law and its recently expanded consequences; (d) the uncertain status of the separation of powers; (e) the doctrine of responsible government; and (f) the changing relationship between central and devolved (regional) government. Each of these will now be examined in turn.

14.3.1 Constitutional Monarchy

Several core features of the British constitution are very, very old. In the previous section reference was made to Magna Carta and to the Bill of Rights of 1689, for example. The principal concern of both these instruments, and of the political turmoil that gave birth to them, was how the powers of the Crown could be substantively limited and subjected to constitutional account. Powers previously possessed and, it was thought, abused by the Crown were either taken away altogether or subjected to parliamentary oversight. Thus, Magna Carta sought to guarantee, in a provision that still remains law, that 'no freeman shall be taken or imprisoned...or exiled...but by...the law of the land', as it limited the powers of the Crown to raise various forms of revenue through taxation and other means. Likewise, the Bill of Rights outlawed what it called 'the pretended power of suspending the laws' and 'the pretended power of dispensing with the laws' as they had been exercised by James II. To this day it is to the Bill of Rights that we owe the fact that the government may levy no tax or charge on the British people other than with parliamentary assent.

Today it is not the monarch him- or herself whose powers the constitution is principally concerned to limit: it is the powers derived from the Crown and exercised by government ministers which are the focus of attention. Herein lies the contemporary constitutional significance of Britain being a monarchy: not in the powers and influence of the Queen and her family, considerable though they remain (Bogdanor 1995), but in the powers exercised in the name of, and on behalf of, the Crown by the government (Brazier 1997; Daintith and Page 1999). While it is clearly the case that ministers have at their disposal a vast array of statutory powers—powers conferred on the government by parliament in legislation—they continue to enjoy, in addition, a range of prerogative powers, powers which parliament has not conferred through the legislative process, but which are derived directly from the Crown. These include the power to declare war, the power to deploy the armed forces, the power to make treaties, powers concerned with the conduct of diplomacy, powers to appoint peers and to confer honours, and powers concerned with the organization of the civil service, as well as a range of others.

Recent years have witnessed extensive parliamentary disquiet about the range and scope of these powers and about the limited extent to which their exercise has been subjected to adequate parliamentary oversight. In the early 1990s the focal point was the government's treaty-making power, a power which became particularly controversial in the context of the Maastricht Treaty on European Union, divisions over which consumed the Conservative Party for much of the decade (Rawlings 1994). The government's prerogative power to claim 'public interest immunity', a power that enables the government to withhold evidence from civil and criminal trials where, in the government's view, the public interest so requires, was equally controversial in the context of covering up the extent to which British arms manufacturers had, with the support of the security and secret intelligence services, traded with Saddam Hussein's Iraq (Tomkins 1998: ch. 5). More recently it has been around the government's power to wage war that the deepest parliamentary concerns have crystallized—as a result, of course, of the controversies surrounding the Iraq War (House of Lords Constitution Committee 2006).

Within a week of becoming Prime Minister, Gordon Brown in July 2007 published a Green Paper on constitutional reform, *The Governance of Britain* (Cm 7170), a highlight of which was an immediate undertaking to qualify a number of the government's prerogative powers. Thus, the power to deploy the armed forces abroad will be subject to a new parliamentary resolution (to the effect that a positive parliamentary vote will normally be required before troops can be sent into combat overseas); the power to ratify treaties will be placed on a statutory footing; the power to recommend to the Queen that parliament be dissolved will be subject to a new constitutional convention (to the effect that a positive vote in the House of Commons will normally be required before such a recommendation may be made); and the power to request that the Speaker should recall the House of Commons during a recess, formerly unique to the government, will be shared with backbench MPs. As such, they are but the latest chapter in what is Britain's oldest constitutional story: namely, the ongoing struggle to subject the Crown and its government to constitutional account through parliament (Tomkins 2003: ch. 2).

None of this means that Britain will cease to be a constitutional monarchy. *The Governance of Britain* stressed that the government had no intention to reform or revise any of the prerogative powers which continue to be exercised by the monarch herself. But, if carried out, the proposed reforms will strengthen the forces of parliamentary constitutionalism as they seek to scrutinize and to hold to account the powers that the government of the day continues to derive from the Crown.

14.3.2 The Sovereignty of Parliament

Most of the time British government is characterized not in terms of conflict between Crown and parliament but as cooperation between them. It is when cooperation ceases that ordinary government becomes impossible, as Charles I found in 1642 and as James II found in 1688. What the events of the 1640s and 1680s reveal is that when conflict between Crown and parliament replaces cooperation, parliament has the constitutional strength to win the argument: since 1689 (indeed, since 1660) we have, for the most part, experienced government by the Crown and its ministers on parliamentary terms, and not parliamentary government on the Crown's terms (Tomkins 2005). While the Crown has on several occasions and through various means tried to subvert the order established in 1642, 1660, and 1688–9, it has not (yet?) been successful in the long term—the eighteenth-century corruption of placemen and pensions, for example, was not a prominent feature by the time Walter Bagehot penned the most famous celebration of Britain's parliamentary constitution in the 1860s (Bagehot 1867). The much more recent rising up of Labour backbenchers against numerous of the Blair government's policies in the 2001–5 parliament is, perhaps, another example of parliament refusing to be cowed by the Crown's ministers (Cowley 2005).

As regards cooperation between Crown and parliament, its most important instantiation is through an Act of Parliament. An Act of Parliament is the formal agreement of the House of Commons, the House of Lords, and the Crown to a legislative proposal (a Bill). An Act of Parliament is the highest form of law known to the English legal system. (Some doubts have been expressed as to whether the same is true in Scots law, but the issue has not arisen for judicial determination and there is a strong argument to be made that the same position holds in Scots law as in the law of England and Wales (Tomkins 2004).) This placing of Acts of Parliament at the apex of the legal order is what is meant by the sovereignty of parliament (Goldsworthy 1999). We saw above that Dicey stated that parliament may make or unmake any law whatever. He went on to state that 'no person or body is recognised by the law . . . as having a right to override or set aside the legislation of Parliament' (Dicey 1885: 40). Thus, it will be seen that it is not parliament that is sovereign under this doctrine, but *Acts of* Parliament, or rather Acts of the *Crown-in-Parliament*. That is to say, Acts which have been formally assented to by both parliament and the Crown, acting together. Acts of Parliament cannot be made by parliament without the Crown, and nor can they be made by the Crown without parliament. They can, exceptionally, be made by the House of Commons and the Crown acting together, without the assent of the House of Lords, but the circumstances in which this is possible, and the procedures required to be followed in such cases, are circumscribed in legislation (Parliament Acts 1911, 1949).

Several challenges have been made in recent years to the doctrine and practice of the sovereignty of parliament. A number of these will be considered later in this chapter.

14.3.3 The Rule of Law

Whereas the sovereignty of parliament is the legal doctrine that governs the relationship between the courts and parliament (providing that the courts have no power to override or set aside parliament's legislation), the rule of law is the legal doctrine that governs the relationship between the courts and the government, or executive. It provides that the government may do nothing without legal authority. The classic exposition of this principle dates from a case decided in 1765: *Entick v Carrington* (1765) 19 St Tr 1029. Entick was a pamphleteer critical of the government. Carrington was instructed by the Earl of Halifax, one of His Majesty's principal secretaries of state, to enter Entick's house, to search his house, to seize his papers, and to arrest him. This Carrington did. Entick sued Carrington for trespass and was successful, the court ruling that a mere warrant in the name of the secretary of state could not excuse liability for trespass. Only a law could excuse liability, and the instructions of a secretary of state were not law. For the trespass to have been lawful it would have had to have been authorized by legislation. If parliament legislates to empower a minister to issue instructions to the police, or to the security and secret intelligence services, to the effect that an individual's papers are to be seized, or that an individual is to be kept under surveillance, a minister issuing such instructions will not be acting contrary to the rule of law in the *Entick v Carrington* sense, as he will be acting with legal authority. In *Entick v Carrington*, Halifax had no such legal authority and the rule of law was therefore breached.

Since the middle of the nineteenth century the courts have developed a body of legal principles that may be seen as having developed the rule of law into a more sophisticated web of rules that the government—and public authorities generally—must follow in their decision-making. Thus, public authorities must act fairly, they must not be biased in their decision-making, they must afford certain parties rights to be heard before decisions are made which affect their interests, they must not misapply the law that regulates their discretion, they must act reasonably, and, at least when human rights are affected by their decisions, they must act proportionately. These rules have been developed by the courts through the case law of judicial review such that Britain now has as modern a system of administrative law as has long been common across continental Europe (the leading treatises on administrative law are Craig 2003 and Wade and Forsyth 2004). Thus, to return for a moment to *Entick v Carrington*, today's parliament has passed a raft of legislation empowering ministers to authorize the police and the security and secret intelligence services to intercept people's communications or to place certain persons under 'control orders' (see, e.g., Regulation of Investigatory Powers Act 2000, s. 5; and Prevention of Terrorism Act 2005, s. 2). In the exercise of these powers, both the ministers and the police and security officers involved must act fairly, reasonably, and proportionately. If they do not their actions may be quashed by a court on a claim for judicial review.

The modern law of judicial review has been developed by the courts—it is an example of the constitution evolving through the common law. More recently parliament has also intervened in an attempt to give impetus to the rule of law, passing legislation that further develops the ability of the courts to control government decision-making. The most important example is the Human Rights Act 1998, considered in more detail later in this chapter. Taken together, the law of judicial review and the Human Rights Act play a leading role in the move from political to legal constitutionalism.

14.3.4 The Separation of Powers

While constitutional monarchy, the sovereignty of parliament, and the rule of law are all core components of British constitutionalism, for the separation of powers that claim cannot be so boldly made. But what appears to be happening is that the separation of powers is growing in constitutional significance in the United Kingdom.

It is clear that the British constitution is not *based on* the eighteenth-century model of the separation of powers that, for example, the US constitution is structured around. This model posits that the state should be divided into three powers or 'branches', separate but equal in terms both of function and personnel. The three branches are the legislature, the executive, and the judiciary, each of which 'checks' or 'balances' the other two (Vile 1998). Even though the British constitution is not based on this model, much of the model is reflected in British constitutional practice (Munro 1999: ch. 9). We do have an identifiably different legislature, executive, and judiciary. But there are numerous overlaps between the branches that would be unconstitutional in the United States. All government ministers are required to be drawn from one or other of the Houses of Parliament, for example. Until the relevant provisions of the Constitutional Reform Act 2005 come into force (in October 2009) the highest court of appeal in the United Kingdom will remain the Appellate Committee of the House of Lords, one of the Houses of Parliament, and all the members of that court continue simultaneously to be members of the legislature, even if they are no longer as active in a legislative capacity as until recently they were. Once the relevant provisions of the 2005 Act come into force the United Kingdom will have a new Supreme Court, which will replace the Appellate Committee of the House of Lords.

The Constitutional Reform Act 2005 is a significant measure. In particular, it contains important measures concerning the independence of the judiciary. It radically curtails the powers of the Lord Chancellor, moving that office more clearly into the executive branch and away from the judicial, and making the Lord Chief Justice the new head of the judiciary in England and Wales. It revises procedures governing the appointment of judges, limiting the direct input of the government and establishing a new Judicial Appointments Commission. In all of these respects, it is clear that one of the animating motives behind the Act was to give clearer expression in the structure of the British constitution to the separation of powers (Windlesham 2005; 2006). In particular, the Act has sought more sharply to demarcate the judiciary from the other two branches—the legislature and the executive. At the same time, the courts have themselves been concerned to underscore the same demarcation. Numerous recent House of Lords cases have emphasized the importance of having the judiciary determine points of law, free of executive influence (for example in the sentencing field, where the Home Secretary's powers to influence the length of sentence served by those imprisoned for 'life' have been effectively transferred to the courts; for the case law, see Turpin and Tomkins 2007: 106–12). The thrust of the case law, as of the 2005 Act, is once more to bolster the ongoing move from the political to the legal in British constitutionalism.

To the extent that the separation of powers has become recognized as a legally enforceable principle, however, such recognition remains partial. The legislative/executive distinction remains blurred, to say the least. Bagehot famously wrote that 'The efficient secret of the...Constitution may be described as the close union, the nearly complete fusion of the executive and legislative powers' (Bagehot 1867). Even if this would be unlikely now to be celebrated as unabashedly as did Bagehot, it is difficult to argue that we have moved substantially on from the picture Bagehot painted. When, for example, in 2006 the government introduced its Legislative and Regulatory Reform Bill, critics objected that the Bill would transfer an unacceptable degree of legislative power from parliament to ministers (the government sought in the Bill to find ways to make it easier for provisions in legislation to be removed where they were deemed to impose an unnecessary regulatory burden). During the passage of the Bill the government was required to concede a range of restrictions, curtailing the extent to which ministers could effectively legislate without parliament. The Bill was passed, however, albeit in amended form, and notwithstanding the amendments the Bill still represents a substantial increase in ministerial powers to amend and repeal provisions of primary legislation. Were the Legislative and Regulatory Reform Act 2006 to be challenged in court on the basis that it violates the principle of the separation of powers, a judge would have to rule, as the law currently stands, that the separation of powers must be read subject to the terms of the Act, and not the other way around.

14.3.5 Responsible Government

We saw above that the relationship between the Crown and its ministers, on the one hand, and parliament, on the other, is the central dynamic at the core of British constitutionalism. We have also seen that, in today's constitution, this dynamic is institutionalized through the conventions of ministerial responsibility: all government ministers are collectively and individually responsible to parliament for government policy and for the policies, decisions, and actions of government departments. Nothing needs to be added to these observations here, other than to underline their centrality to British constitutionalism. No account of the British constitution would be accurate, or even useful, without a full appreciation of the importance of the practice of responsible government (Birch 1964; Marshall 1984; Flinders 2002; Woodhouse 2002; Tomkins 2003: ch 5).

14.3.6 Devolution and the Union State

It used to be generally said that the United Kingdom had a unitary constitution rather than a federal one. More recently the view has come to the fore that the United Kingdom has a *union* constitution that is neither straightforwardly unitary nor systematically federal in character (Walker 2000; Tierney 2006). Clearly, the United Kingdom is not a federation. The country is not divided into regions of equal political power and none of the internal political divisions that exist within the United Kingdom is immune from being altered or repealed by parliament: there is no system of regional entrenchment against central (parliamentary) incursion. On the other hand, to conceive of British government solely in terms of the central institutions of Westminster and Whitehall, along with some moderate input from local government councils, would be to miss what has become one of the most interesting dimensions of British politics: namely, the 'British question' itself—and the divergent approaches that are commonly taken to that question in England, Scotland, Wales, and Northern Ireland.

From a legal point of view the United Kingdom is clearly a union. The very legislation by which the kingdom was united reveals as much: the Acts *of Union* with Scotland (1707) and Ireland (1800). The United Kingdom is a union of three legal systems—those of England and Wales, Scotland, and Northern Ireland. There have always been differences of law, including differences of constitutional law, between these three legal systems. Scots law is different from English law as regards the Crown, for example (Tomkins 2006), and, as we saw above, several Scots lawyers have expressed doubts as to the applicability in Scotland of what a Lord President of the Court of Session, no less, described as the 'distinctively English principle' of the sovereignty of parliament (see Tomkins 2004: 213). The constitutional differences between the constituent elements of the United Kingdom pre-date devolution but they have, no doubt, been greatly augmented by devolution.

Under the various devolution statutes that have been passed since 1998 Scotland has its own parliament and executive, Wales has its own assembly and (since 2006) also a Welsh Assembly Government, and Northern Ireland has its own assembly and power-sharing (i.e. cross-party) executive. In addition, since 2000 London has had a new strategic authority (the Greater London Authority) and mayor, as well as its range of local ('Borough') councils, although whether these arrangements should be classed as either regional government or as a species of devolution is contested. The remainder of England has no regional or devolved institutions, either legislative or executive (a proposal to create an elected regional assembly for the North-East region was comprehensively rejected in a referendum in 2004). (On devolution generally, see Turpin and Tomkins 2007: ch 4; Trench 2004; 2005; and Hazell and Rawlings 2005).

Even though it is frequently referred to as a 'settlement', devolution is not a one-off reform. In the famous words of Ron Davies, Secretary of State for Wales in Tony Blair's first Cabinet, devolution is 'a process, not an event' (Rawlings 2003: 10). How settled that process turns out to be, and what the process will lead to, is far from clear. In its first decade devolution was relatively smooth only in Scotland. In Wales, the devolution package had to be renegotiated as dissatisfaction grew that less was on offer (and less achievable) there than in Scotland. The result was the Government of Wales Act 2006, which replaced the Government of Wales Act 1998 with staggered tiers of devolution, some already in effect but others dependent on positive outcomes in future possible referendums. In Northern Ireland, devolution was suspended in October 2002, not to return until the Spring of 2007. For much of the period since 1998 the politics of Northern Ireland continued to be dominated by security issues but, at the time of writing, the agreement of the DUP and Sinn Fein to share devolved power appears to be holding. How long these new Welsh and Northern Irish arrangements remain in place is impossible even to guess at.

At the beginning of its second decade devolution is looking less smooth in Scotland. During the first two terms of the Scottish parliament (1999–2003, 2003–7) the Labour Party was in government in London and was the lead party in the Scottish Executive, in coalition in Edinburgh with the Liberal Democrats. This period was marked by such a high degree of goodwill and by such a strong desire that devolution should work and be seen to work smoothly that even the semi-formal institutions of intergovernmental relations (such as the Joint Ministerial Committee) were not required to meet (Trench 2005). Such devolution disputes as there were between the British government and the Scottish Executive were resolved privately and informally. No such dispute has yet reached the courts. Within Scotland there was a widespread sense that, notwithstanding the shocking expense of the new Scottish parliament building, the devolutionary scheme of the Scotland Act 1998 had successfully solved the problems of Scottish governance which it had been designed to address (Turpin and Tomkins 2007: ch. 4).

This changed abruptly in May 2007, when the Labour/Liberal Democrat coalition was defeated in the Scottish parliamentary elections. As in 1999 and 2003, no one party secured a majority of seats in the Scottish parliament but, for the first time, the Scottish National Party (SNP) emerged in 2007 as the largest single party, albeit by only a single seat. Since 2007 it has formed a minority administration, with Alex Salmond as First Minister. Above all else, of course, the SNP is committed to independence for Scotland. Within three months of taking office, the new Scottish Executive published a discussion paper on Scotland's constitutional future, in which options, first, for a further devolution of legislative and executive powers and, second, for a move towards independence were outlined (*Choosing Scotland's Future: A National Conversation*).

At the same time the Conservative opposition in Westminster has grown increasingly vocal about the defects—from an English point of view—of Scottish devolution. The principal problem as the Conservatives see it is the unfairness implicit in a system that allows MPs from Scottish constituencies to vote on English matters when MPs from English constituencies cannot vote on Scottish matters where they are devolved to Holyrood. This is the famous 'West Lothian Question'. Labour's answer to it— that devolution would be granted to English regions on demand, just as it had been granted to Scotland—was effectively negatived by the 2004 referendum in northeast England. The Conservatives have suggested that a better answer, 'English votes for English laws', may be to exclude Scottish MPs from voting on purely English matters, but both the workability and constitutional desirability of this must surely be doubted. For one thing, discovering what a purely English matter is would not always be straightforward; for another the majority of MPs may not support the same policies (or party, or even government) as the majority of MPs minus those from Scottish constituencies.

As a result of these developments, the future of Scottish devolution—and, indeed, the future of the Union—has become more uncertain and treacherous to predict. In the coming years we are likely to learn considerably more about whether devolution is the glue that holds the Union together (which was always Labour's intention) or whether it provides precisely the platform that the Nationalists need to make more convincing the case for independence. We may also find out whether the Conservatives (with precious little electoral support in Scotland and Wales) remain a unionist party, or whether they are on the way to becoming an English national party. Whichever way you look at it, at the time of writing, devolution (in particular, Scottish devolution) is the great unknown in British constitutionalism.

14.4 CONTEMPORARY CHALLENGES TO BRITISH CONSTITUTIONALISM

The constitutional challenges that may be posed by devolution are for the future (albeit, perhaps, the near future). Challenges posed from other quarters are more established. Two such are outlined in this section: 'Europe' and New Labour's constitutional reforms. These challenges are not to be underestimated. Indeed, we shall see that their combined effect is to place into question every one of the six core features of British constitutionalism outlined in the previous section (see further below).

14.4.1 'Europe'

'Europe' refers to two separate creations: the first is the European Union (EU); the second is the European Convention on Human Rights (ECHR). Both have had a considerable impact on British constitutionalism, but their respective impacts vary and should not be confused with one another. Let us start with the EU. The United Kingdom joined what is now the EU in 1972. Britain's membership of the EU has had a profound impact on British government. A significant proportion of British legislation is now enacted in consequence of European law. Much ministerial time is taken up with European business—especially in the domains of trade, agriculture, social policy, and, increasingly, also in security, crime, and counter-terrorism policy. But Britain's membership of the EU has also had a significant impact on constitutional law and, in particular, on the doctrine of the sovereignty of parliament. Under EU law, clashes between national law and European law will, in general, be resolved in favour of the latter. The European Court of Justice made this clear in a series of judgments handed down before the United Kingdom joined the EU (principally *Van Gend en Loos* in 1963 and *Costa v ENEL* in 1964: see Turpin and Tomkins 2007: ch. 5).

The sovereignty of parliament, it will be recalled, means that parliament may make or unmake any law whatever. What if parliament now wants to make a law which is contrary to EU law? It is clear that, were this to happen, the European Commission would have standing to bring the United Kingdom before the European Court of Justice and that the Court would be able to rule that the UK had violated EU law. If the United Kingdom refused to amend or repeal its offending legislation, the UK could be fined (Articles 226–8 EC). More interestingly for present purposes are the possibilities that may be open to *British* courts in the event of litigation seeking to challenge an Act of Parliament deemed to be contrary to EU law. Conventionally, no such challenge could hope to succeed—parliament may pass any law whatever, including, presumably, a law that was contrary to EU law. However, under the terms of Britain's entry into the EU, domestic courts were given the jurisdiction to apply and enforce EU law (in addition to the powers to apply and enforce domestic law which they already possessed). And, as we have seen, EU law considers that conflicts between national and European law should generally be resolved in favour of the latter.

One of the remarkable features of the EU's first half-century is how rarely problems such as these occur in practice. Across all the member states there seems to have been an extraordinary desire among both political and legal elites to make the EU work, and to allow it to work as smoothly as possible. Member states have not sought to enact legislation which they know or suspect to be contrary to European law. In part, this may be because member state governments continue to play a lead role in the making of European law, through the legislative functions of the Council of Ministers. In part, though, it stems from a deep political sense that it is in the national interest for the EU to operate successfully. In the British example, there has to date been only one case in which the UK courts were required to confront the tension between the supremacy of EU law and the sovereignty of parliament. The case is called *Factortame*.

Factortame concerned a challenge to provisions of the Merchant Shipping Act 1988 that had been designed to protect British fishing interests. Spanish-owned fishing vessels were disadvantaged by the statutory scheme and they brought proceedings in the domestic courts arguing that it was contrary to Community law. The Divisional Court in London referred the case to the European Court of Justice for a preliminary ruling on the points of Community law, that arose in the case. Meanwhile, the applicants claimed interim relief—a remedy the effect of which would be to suspend the operation of the relevant provisions of the Merchant Shipping Act pending the final resolution of the case. The House of Lords initially held that the applicants could have no such interim relief, as the remedy they sought (an interim injunction against the Crown) was, for technical reasons, not available *in English law (R v Transport Secretary, ex parte Factortame (No 1)* [1990] 2 AC 85). However, it was not their interests in English law, but their rights under Community law, that the applicants were seeking to protect. The question arose, therefore, as to whether the applicants were *as a matter of Community law* entitled to interim relief. This question the House of Lords referred to the European Court of Justice. After receiving that Court's answer, the House of Lords ruled that the applicants were entitled, as a matter of Community law, to a remedy the effect of which was to suspend the operation of certain provisions of the Merchant Shipping Act. The House of Lords, exercising its jurisdiction to apply and enforce Community law, then granted the remedy (*R v Transport Secretary, ex parte Factortame (No 2)* [1991] 1 AC 603). This was the first time since the early seventeenth century that a court in England had granted a remedy the effect of which was to suspend part of an Act of Parliament.

Does this mean that the sovereignty of parliament is dead? Surely no: parliament retains the power to pass legislation that would withdraw the United Kingdom from the European Union. Short of this nuclear option, parliament also retains the power to pass legislation that includes a provision along the following lines: 'This Act shall be construed and shall have effect notwithstanding any provision to the contrary in European Union law'. Whether such a provision would be effective to guarantee that a future House of Lords (or Supreme Court) would not be able in the context of that legislation to repeat the result obtained by the applicants in *Factortame* remains to be seen. Thus far, it has not been attempted. It is clear that such a provision would be contrary to European law and that the Commission would sue the UK in the European Court of Justice were such a provision to be relied upon in the UK. But whether the UK courts would be able to overturn it in the light of the sovereignty of parliament is one of those constitutional imponderables that we will not know the answer to until it happens.

What is clear is that, regardless of whether the *law* of the sovereignty of parliament has changed as a result of Britain's membership of the EU, the political context within which sovereignty operates has changed beyond recognition from the context that prevailed at the end of the nineteenth century, when Dicey was writing (for further argument on these matters, see Craig 1991; Tomkins 2003: ch. 4; Turpin and Tomkins 2007: ch. 5). What is also clear is that disquiet about the doctrine of the sovereignty of parliament is not confined to the EU context. In a House of Lords case decided in 2005, which had nothing to do with EU law, Lord Steyn opined for example that 'The classic account given by Dicey of the doctrine of the sovereignty of Parliament...can now be seen to be out of place in the modern United Kingdom' and Lord Hope stated that while our constitution is 'dominated' by the sovereignty of parliament, 'parliamentary sovereignty is no longer, if ever it was, absolute' (*Jackson v Attorney General* [2006] 1 AC 262; see further Turpin and Tomkins 2007: 66–76, 327–35). If parliament is not sovereign, we may ask, then who is? The implication of these *dicta* from *Jackson* is that a number of judges are preparing themselves to rewrite the law of sovereignty—so that no longer will parliament be able to 'make or unmake any law whatever', but only such laws as the courts hold to be lawful, or constitutional. The move, encountered numerous times in this chapter, from the political constitution to the legal constitution, has begun to encroach, it seems, even upon a matter as fundamental as the sovereignty of parliament.

14.4.2 New Labour and the British Constitution

The second great source of European influence on British constitutionalism is the European Convention on Human Rights (ECHR), a treaty drawn up under the auspices not of the EU but of the Council of Europe (and enforced not by the European Court of Justice in Luxembourg but by the European Court of Human Rights in Strasbourg). While the United Kingdom has been bound by the terms of the ECHR, as a matter of international law, since the treaty's inception, Convention rights have been enforceable in domestic law (i.e. in proceedings before the UK's own courts) only since the Human Rights Act 1998. This Act significantly enlarged the power of the judiciary to impugn both government decisions and statutes where they are argued to be in violation of Convention rights. While the courts cannot *quash* provisions of an Act of Parliament on this ground, under the Human Rights Act, section 4, they may make a 'declaration of incompatibility', a new remedy by which the court declares that a statutory provision is incompatible with Convention rights, inviting government and parliament to consider whether, in the light of such a judgment, the provision should remain law. By contrast, government actions and decisions that are found to be contrary to Convention rights may be quashed by the courts: section 6.

From the point of view of British constitutionalism, what is most significant about the Human Rights Act is the extent to which it further underscores the shift from political to legal constitutionalism. Under the model of the ECHR and the HRA it is no longer principally to parliament and to political institutions that we should look in the quest to hold the government to constitutional account, but to the courts. Parliament continues to have a role—ministers must declare to parliament that the Bills they propose are compatible with Convention rights (Human Rights Act 1998, section 19) and the Joint Committee on Human Rights, which amongst other tasks monitors legislation for human rights compliance, has played an important role in the law-making process in recent years. But the importance of parliament's role has diminished in comparison with that of the courts.

A telling example comes from the counter-terrorism field. Under the model of the Human Rights Act we must now look to the courts for an authoritative opinion on whether the government's counter-terrorism strategies are compatible with the Convention rights to liberty, to a fair trial, and to freedom of expression, whereas we would formerly have looked principally to parliament to provide a crucible in which the policies of the government could be tested against the public interest in informed debate and detailed select committee scrutiny. When in December 2003 a cross-party committee of parliamentarians published a report that was damning in its criticism of numerous aspects of the Anti-terrorism, Crime and Security Act 2001, it caused barely a ripple (Privy Counsellor Review Committee 2003). But when, twelve months later, an eight-to-one majority of the law lords granted a declaration that one particular aspect of the legislation was incompatible with Convention rights, there was an enormous fuss in the media, in parliament, and in the law reviews (*A v Home Secretary* [2005] 2 AC 68; see Turpin and Tomkins 2007: 762–72). Whether the result—the Prevention of Terrorism Act 2005 and its extraordinary regime of 'control orders'—was what the law lords had in mind as the desired outcome is a different question. The point here is not to rehearse the various merits and demerits of the legislative schemes, but to notice what the enormous difference in reaction between the parliamentary report on the one hand and the law lords' judgment on the other suggests about how far British constitutionalism has shifted from being primarily a political constitution to being primarily a legal one.

The Human Rights Act 1998 is one of a number of measures introduced by the New Labour governments of Tony Blair and Gordon Brown to reform the British constitution. Along with the devolutionary arrangements made for Scotland, Wales, and Northern Ireland (see above), the House of Lords Act 1999 (which removed all but ninety-two of the hereditary peers from the House of Lords), the Freedom of Information Act 2000, the Constitutional Reform Act 2005 (see above), and the various commitments to further reform made in the 2007 Green Paper, *The Governance of Britain* (see above), these reforms amount to a substantial degree of rapid constitutional change (Foley 1999; King 2001; Oliver 2003; Johnson 2004). Immediately, however, two caveats must be entered: first, not everything has changed. The powers of the monarchy, the electoral system for elections to the House of Commons, the UK's legal relationship with the EU (and, for that matter, with the Commonwealth), and the relationship between central and local government are all the same now as they were before New Labour came into office. Secondly, it would be a serious error to imagine that the British constitution lay dormant or unchanged in the decades before 1997. Harold Wilson's race relations and sex discrimination legislation; Ted Heath's bringing the UK into the EU; and Margaret Thatcher's and John Major's reforms to the civil service, privatization programmes, and array of legislation on civil liberties all amounted to significant constitutional reform (Turpin and Tomkins 2007: 21–4). But, as Matthew Flinders has argued, not all constitutional change is of the same order. Flinders distinguishes between 'cosmetic', 'moderate', and 'fundamental' reform (Flinders 2005: 61–2). From a constitutional point of view, if not from a socio-economic perspective, British constitutional reform in the half-century before 1997 was generally cosmetic or moderate (the exception being Britain's accession to the EU in 1972). Since 1997, by contrast, it is at least arguable that much of what the government has sought to reform constitutionally has been more fundamental.

This is true at least of the Human Rights Act and of the devolution legislation. As we have seen, the shift from political to legal constitutionalism, to which the Human Rights Act makes a substantial contribution, is the deepest structural change in British constitutionalism in our time. It is of the same order of magnitude as the shift from divine right to parliamentary monarchy in the seventeenth century and as that from the parliamentary government Walter Bagehot so brilliantly captured (Bagehot 1867) to the party government of the twentieth and twenty-first centuries. Equally, the creation (or re-creation) of new sites of political and governmental authority in Edinburgh, Cardiff, and Belfast, combined with the ways in which the proportional electoral systems employed there have qualified the extent to which those new sites of authority are able merely to ape the institutions of Westminster and Whitehall, is a constitutional innovation the full consequences of which have yet to be worked out and which, indeed, are currently unforeseeable.

In other respects, however, it may be that there is rather less to New Labour's constitutional reforms than its keenest advocates would have us believe. Since 1999 there has been much talk but precious little action on reforming the obviously unde-mocratic House of Lords (Hazell 2007: 9–12); the Freedom of Information Act 2000 was a half-hearted affair and has delivered only a fraction of the 'open government' that had been promised in the government's 1997 Green Paper, *Your Right to Know* (Cm 3818; see Austin 2004); since 1998 there has been no movement at all on the issue of electoral reform for elections to the House of Commons; and government attempts to control the House of Commons have been as central to the Whips' mission as ever, albeit that, quite remarkably, the Commons has begun to stand up to government pressure in a variety of ways and, moreover, with some success, both in terms of its scrutiny of legislation (Cowley 2005) and in terms of resisting government attempts to interfere with the composition and work of parliamentary select committees (Flinders 2007; Power 2007). For all the recent emphasis on change and 'modernization' there has been a great deal of politics as usual. In a compelling analysis, Matthew Flinders has argued that, notwithstanding the importance of a number of New Labour's constitutional reforms, there has been no 'far-reaching shift in the nature of [British] democracy', which remains firmly majoritarian rather than consensual in character (Flinders 2005: 63; cf. Mair 2000: 34). All of this said, however, and as our discussion of Scottish devolution suggests, Flinders is wise to point out that even if New Labour's constitutional reforms have been 'less significant than might have been expected', they *might* yet 'set in train a critical momentum and dynamic that may . . . force at some point an explicit reconsideration of the structure and power relationships within Britain' (Flinders 2005: 90).

Three further facets of New Labour's constitutional reform policies should be noted in conclusion. First, while constitutional reform may well be one of the princi-pal achievements for which Tony Blair's period as Prime Minister is remembered, Mr Blair himself was famously uninterested in constitutional reform and had, in terms of the way he conducted politics on a day-to-day basis, strong centralizing and controlling instincts which ran counter to the most important constitutional reforms his governments introduced. David Marquand coined the term 'the Blair paradox' to summarize this peculiar state of affairs (e.g. Marquand 2000). It aptly captures Mr Blair's mixed legacy on constitutional questions. Secondly, it would be better if we spoke in terms of New Labour's constitutional reforms (in the plural), rather than of constitutional reform as a single entity. This is because, as numerous commentators have pointed out, there has been no overall plan (Foley 1999; Oliver 2003: 3; Hazell 2007: 18–19; Turpin and Tomkins 2007: 24). The various constitutional reforms have been advocated by different interest groups, for different reasons, to respond to different perceived weaknesses in the old constitutional order: consider, for example, the diverse pre-histories of devolution, human rights legislation, and freedom of information (Foley 1999: chs. 3–4).

Finally, it should be observed that a number of New Labour's constitutional reforms (and a number of consequences that flow from them) are matters of apparently increasing political contention. The main parties are divided, for example, on House of Lords reform, on whether Scottish MPs in Westminster should vote on Bills that pertain only to England and Wales, and on whether the Human Rights Act should be replaced with a 'British' Bill of Rights, which draws lines between liberty and security differently from how the *European* Convention on Human Rights does it. In 2001 Mark Evans wrote that 'Hitherto the literature on constitutionalism in Britain has been circumscribed by the apolitical nature of its constitutional politics. For much of this last century the UK constitution has remained apolitical' (Evans 2001: 414). With an SNP administration in power in Edinburgh, a Labour government in London that is dependent for its majority on MPs representing Scottish constituencies, and a Conservative Opposition that is increasingly vocal both about 'English votes for English laws' and about certain judicial decisions concerned with the Human Rights Act, the picture Evans painted at the beginning of the decade may well need substantial revision before its end.

14.5 CONCLUSION

If we revisit the six core features of British constitutionalism outlined above, we will see: (a) that the centrality of the Crown/parliament dynamic is lessening in favour of the dynamic between parliamentary government on the one hand and the courts on the other; (b) that the doctrine of the sovereignty of parliament is under great pressure and may be weakening; (c) that the rule of law is growing in reach and in significance; (d) that the separation of powers is gaining greater constitutional importance, especially in terms of demarcating the judiciary from the institutions of parliamentary government; (e) that the focus of responsible government is shifting from parliament to the courts of law; and (f) that the Union, especially the Union between England and Scotland, is the great unknown, the factor with at least the potential to be the fly in the ointment.

The present time is one of rapid and in many cases significant constitutional change in Britain, change which in some instances the Blair/Brown New Labour governments have either caused (devolution) or contributed to (the Human Rights Act and the turn from political to legal constitutionalism) but which in other instances stems from different sources not altogether within the government's control (the common law; the EU). This chapter commenced with the observation that the British constitution is unusual. We live in an era of political and legal harmonization, of common denominators, and of a globalization that shows little respect for exceptionalism, even in matters constitutional (Goldsworthy 2003; Beatty 2004; Hirschl 2004; Anderson 2005; Choudhry 2006). While the various continuities and ongoing traditions of the British constitution should be neither overlooked nor underestimated, the underlying dynamic of much of the constitutional reform examined here—namely, the turn from political to legal constitutionalism—is far from unique to the UK and is, indeed, widely experienced throughout the common law world and elsewhere. If current trends continue, claims as to the unusual nature of the British constitution may not long survive.

REFERENCES

ALLAN, T. R. S. 2001. *Constitutional Justice: A Liberal Theory of the Rule of Law*. Oxford: Oxford University Press.

ANDERSON, G. 2005. *Constitutional Rights after Globalization*. Oxford: Hart.

AUSTIN, R. 2004. 'The Freedom of Information Act 2000: A Sheep in Wolf's Clothing?' Pp. 401–15 in J. Jowell and D. Oliver (eds.), *The Changing Constitution*, 5th edn. Oxford: Oxford University Press.

BAGEHOT, W. 1867. *The English Constitution*. (Modern scholarly editions available from Oxford University Press (ed. M. Taylor, 2001) and Cambridge University Press (ed. P. Smith, 2001).)

BARAK, A. 2006. *The Judge in a Democracy*. Princeton, NJ: Princeton University Press.

BARENDT, E. 1998. *An Introduction to Constitutional Law*. Oxford: Oxford University Press.

BARNETT, A. 1997. *This Time: Our Constitutional Revolution*. London: Vintage.

BEATTY, D. 2004. *The Ultimate Rule of Law*. Oxford: Oxford University Press.

BIRCH, A. H. 1964. *Representative and Responsible Government*. London: Allen and Unwin.

BOGDANOR, V. 1995. *The Monarchy and the Constitution*. Oxford: Clarendon Press.

BRAZIER, R. 1997. *Ministers of the Crown*. Oxford: Clarendon Press.

CHOUDHRY, S. (ed.) 2006. *The Migration of Constitutional Ideas*. Cambridge: Cambridge University Press.

COWLEY, P. 2005. *The Rebels: How Blair Mislaid his Majority*. London: Politico's.

CRAIG, P. 1991. 'Sovereignty of the United Kingdom Parliament after *Factortame*'. *Yearbook of European Law*, 11: 221–55.

—— 2003. *Administrative Law*, 5th edn. London: Sweet and Maxwell.

DAINTITH, T., and PAGE, A. 1999. *The Executive in the Constitution*. Oxford: Oxford University Press.

DICEY, A. V. 1885. *An Introduction to the Study of the Law of the Constitution*. London: Macmillan.

DYZENHAUS, D. 2006. *The Constitution of Law*. Cambridge: Cambridge University Press.

EVANS, M. 2001. 'Studying the New Constitutionalism: Bringing Political Science Back In'. *British Journal of Politics and International Relations*, 3: 413–26.

FINER, S. E., BOGDANOR, V., and RUDDEN, B. 1995. *Comparing Constitutions*. Oxford: Clarendon Press.

FLINDERS, M. 2002. 'Shifting the Balance? Parliament, the Executive and the British Constitution'. *Political Studies*, 50: 23–42.

—— 2005. 'Majoritarian Democracy in Britain: New Labour and the Constitution'. *West European Politics*, 28: 61–93.

FLINDERS, M. 2007. 'Analysing Reform: The House of Commons, 2001–05'. *Political Studies*, 55: 174–200.

FOLEY, M. 1999. *The Politics of the British Constitution*. Manchester: Manchester University Press.

GOLDSWORTHY, J. 1999. *The Sovereignty of Parliament: History and Philosophy*. Oxford: Clarendon Press.

—— 2003. 'Homogenizing Constitutions'. *Oxford Journal of Legal Studies*, 23: 483–505.

—— (ed.) 2006. *Interpreting Constitutions*. Oxford: Oxford University Press.

GRIFFITH, J. A. G. 1979. 'The Political Constitution'. *Modern Law Review*, 42: 1–21.

HAZELL, R. 2007. 'The Continuing Dynamism of Constitutional Reform'. *Parliamentary Affairs*, 60: 3–25.

—— and RAWLINGS, R. (eds.) 2005. *Devolution, Law-Making and the Constitution*. Exeter: Imprint Academic.

HIRSCHL, R. 2004. *Towards Juristocracy: The Origins and Consequences of the New Constitution-alism*. Cambridge, Mass.: Harvard University Press.

HOLT, J. C. 1992. *Magna Carta*, 2nd edn. Cambridge: Cambridge University Press.

HOUSE OF LORDS CONSTITUTION COMMITTEE 2006. *Waging War: Parliament's Role and Responsibility*. HL 236 of 2005–6. (See also government response: Cm 6923.)

JENNINGS, I. 1936. *Cabinet Government*. Cambridge: Cambridge University Press.

JOHNSON, N. 2004. *Reshaping the British Constitution*. Basingstoke: Palgrave Macmillan.

JOWELL, J. 2003. 'Administrative Law'. Pp. 373–400 in V. Bogdanor (ed.), *The British Constitution in the Twentieth Century*. Oxford: Oxford University Press.

—— and OLIVER, D. (eds.) 2000. *The Changing Constitution*, 4th edn. Oxford: Oxford University Press. (See also 5th edn., 2004.)

KING, A. 2001. *Does the United Kingdom still have a Constitution?* London: Sweet and Maxwell.

LASSER, M. 2004. *Judicial Deliberations*. Oxford: Oxford University Press.

MACKINTOSH, J. P. 1977. *The British Cabinet*, 3rd edn. London: Stevens.

MAIR, P. 2000. 'Partyless Democracy: Solving the Paradox of New Labour'. *New Left Review*, 2: 21–35.

MARQUAND, D. 2000. 'Revisiting the Blair Paradox'. *New Left Review*, 3: 73–9.

MARSHALL, G. 1984. *Constitutional Conventions*. Oxford: Clarendon Press.

MOUNT, F. 1992. *The British Constitution Now*. London: Heinemann.

MUNRO, C. 1999. *Studies in Constitutional Law*, 2nd edn. London: Butterworths.

OLIVER, D. 2003. *Constitutional Reform in the UK*. Oxford: Oxford University Press.

PIMLOTT, B. 2001. *The Queen: Elizabeth II and the Monarchy*. London: HarperCollins.

POOLE, T. 2002. 'Dogmatic Liberalism? T. R. S. Allan and the Common Law Constitution'. *Modern Law Review*, 65: 463–75.

POWER, G. 2007. 'The Politics of Parliamentary Reform: Lessons from the House of Commons (2001–05)'. *Parliamentary Affairs*, 60: 492–509.

PRIVY COUNSELLOR REVIEW COMMITTEE 2003. *Report on the Anti-terrorism, Crime and Security Act 2001*. HC 100 of 2003–4.

RAWLINGS, R. 1994. 'Legal Politics: The United Kingdom and Ratification of the Treaty on European Union'. *Public Law*, 254–78 (part 1); 367–91 (part 2).

—— 2003. *Delineating Wales*. Cardiff: University of Wales Press.

TIERNEY, S. 2006. 'Scotland and the Union State'. Pp. 25–44 in A. McHarg and T. Mullen (eds.), *Public Law in Scotland*. Edinburgh: Avizandum.

TOMKINS, A. 1998. *The Constitution after Scott: Government Unwrapped*. Oxford: Clarendon Press.

—— 2003. *Public Law*. Oxford: Oxford University Press.

—— 2004. 'The Constitutional Law in *MacCormick v Lord Advocate*'. *Juridical Review*, 3: 213–24.

—— 2005. *Our Republican Constitution*. Oxford: Hart.

—— 2006. 'The Crown in Scots Law'. Pp. 262–80 in A. McHarg and T. Mullen (eds.), *Public Law in Scotland*. Edinburgh: Avizandum.

TRENCH, A. (ed.) 2004. *Has Devolution Made a Difference?* Exeter: Imprint Academic.

—— (ed.) 2005. *The Dynamics of Devolution*. Exeter: Imprint Academic.

TURPIN, C., and TOMKINS, A. 2007. *British Government and the Constitution*, 6th edn. Cambridge: Cambridge University Press.

VILE, M. J. C. 1998. *Constitutionalism and the Separation of Powers*, 2nd edn. Indianapolis: Liberty Fund.

WADE, H. W. R., and FORSYTH, C. 2004. *Administrative Law*, 9th edn. Oxford: Oxford University Press.

WALKER, N. 2000. 'Beyond the Unitary Conception of the United Kingdom Constitution?' *Public Law*, Autumn: 384–404.

WALTERS, R. 2003. 'The House of Lords'. Pp. 189–235 in V. Bogdanor (ed.), *The British Constitution in the Twentieth Century*. Oxford: Oxford University Press.

WEIR, S., and BEETHAM, D. 1999. *Political Power and Democratic Control in Britain*. London: Routledge.

WINDLESHAM, LORD 2005. 'The Constitutional Reform Act 2005: Ministers, Judges and Constitutional Change'. *Public Law*, Winter: 806–23.

—— 2006. 'The Constitutional Reform Act 2005: The Politics of Constitutional Reform'. *Public Law*, Spring: 35–57.

WOODHOUSE, D. 1994. *Ministers and Parliament: Accountability in Theory and Practice*. Oxford: Clarendon Press.

—— 2002. 'The Reconstruction of Constitutional Accountability'. *Public Law*, 73–90.

YOUNG, E. 2004. 'The Rehnquist Court's Two Federalisms'. *Texas Law Review*, 83: 1–165.

CHAPTER 15

···

JUDICIARY

···

KEITH EWING

15.1 INTRODUCTION

···

Taff Vale *Railway Co Ltd v Amalgamated Society of Railway Servants* [1901] AC 426 is one of the most famous court decisions in British legal and political history, not least because of its decisive contribution to the formation of what is now the Labour Party (Pelling 1965). In seeking an immediate reversal of the decision—which sorely limited the right to strike—the TUC turned to a number of friends, including Sir Robert Reid QC who helped draft a Bill which would deal not only with *Taff Vale*, but with a number of other hostile court decisions as well. Following the Liberal landslide in 1906, Reid was to become Lord Chancellor, and to play an active part in the Cabinet proceedings in arguing for a legislative solution favoured by the TUC rather than the diluted measure proposed by some of his colleagues. As Lord Chancellor, it fell to Reid (by now Lord Loreburn) to pilot the full strength Bill through the House of Lords, introducing it at Second Reading, and carrying it through the later stages, in the process rejecting a number of restrictive amendments. Within two years of enactment, however, a small dispute in South Shields left the Court of Appeal, providing the first opportunity for the Law Lords to consider the Trade Disputes Act 1906 (*Conway v Wade* [1909] AC 606). Such was the promiscuous nature of the British political system that an unusually large Bench of seven judges was presided over by none other than Lord Loreburn, who now had the curious task of interpreting and applying his own Bill in a judicial forum. The other members of the court included Lord James of Hereford, with whom Lord Loreburn had clashed during the parliamentary debates on the Bill, Lord James apparently 'furious' with the opposition in the Lords for failing more vigorously to attack it. Further conflict was however avoided, with Lord Loreburn running up the white flag in what looks like a failure of government nerve in the face of stinging criticism of the 1906 Act by the Court of Appeal and the legal establishment generally. Written on the white flag were a number of hitherto unanticipated qualifications, designed to limit the Act's apparently unequivocal scope, qualifications which were to cause problems in the years to follow (Ewing 2007b).

It would be hard to find a better example of judicial involvement in the political process, or political involvement in the judicial process. In a single incident we have all three branches of government wrapped up in one man. Yet it would also be hard to find a better illustration of how much has changed in 100 years. The events surrounding *Conway v Wade* [1909] AC 606 are a reminder of how things were, not how things are. However, while the position has thus changed profoundly in many different ways, and while judges are no longer as politically engaged as this episode reveals their predecessors to have been, it does not follow that the judicial role has ceased to have a political dimension, for one of a number of reasons. In the first place, the judicial process may be said to be a *political process* because of its nature as a deliberative exercise, which involves the making of decisions, informed in part (sometimes explicitly, sometimes implicitly) by considerations of public policy, which lead to the formulation of rules (and principles) of general application, in the course of which—some would add—it is likely that the 'very general ideological orientation of judges will come into play' (Robertson 1998: 21). In candid moments, judges themselves will openly acknowledge that they have a 'law making function' (*National Westminster Bank plc v Spectrum Plus Ltd* [2005] UKHL 41, at para [32]), with Lord Goff earlier acknowledging judicially that 'the common law is a living system of law, reacting to new events and new ideas, and so capable of providing the citizens of this country with a system of practical justice relevant to the times in which they live': *Kleinwort Benson Ltd v Lincoln City Council* [1999] 2 AC 349, at p 377. There is, however, another sense in which we can refer to the 'courts as political agencies and judges as political actors' (Shapiro and Stone Sweet 2002: 21). Here the focus is not on the judicial process and its outputs, but on its *political impacts and effects*, as a restraint on other branches of government. So although it may be disputed that the legal process is a political process, there is likely to be a ready consensus around the idea that judges place 'limits on law-making behaviour' (Stone Sweet 2000: 1), and limits on the exercise of powers conferred by law.

Until recently, however, there has been less scope for British judges to behave in these ways than for their counterparts in other jurisdictions (though as we shall see this does not mean that there has been no such scope). Indeed, it has been suggested that one reason why judges and courts have been so little studied by political scientists in the United Kingdom is that they have 'never been seen as important institutions' (Robertson 1998: 4), perhaps wrongly perceived to have had little power. In a system of parliamentary sovereignty the judges were firmly subordinate to the legislature, even if by the power of interpretation they could from time to time frustrate the intention of parliament. It is true that the common law gave the judges a great deal of rule-making authority (Robertson 1998), but this authority and this role have gradually diminished as more and more fields of activity in the public and private spheres are governed by the statutes of what has been a sovereign parliament. In recent years, however, much has changed and the role of the courts has expanded, as a result of EU membership and the introduction of measures such as the Human Rights Act (HRA), with British judges now having a greater opportunity to play a part in the judicialization of politics that we see elsewhere in the world (Stone Sweet 2000). This expansion of the role of the courts and the extension of what may be referred to as judicial power bring with it questions about the effectiveness, legitimacy, and accountability of that power. These are the three themes that will be pursued in this chapter, as we consider the implications of the shifting balance of the constitution described by Tomkins (2009), away from what some refer to as the 'political' constitution (Griffith 1979), in the direction of what others might now refer to as the 'legal' constitution. This account will address in particular the implications of the Human Rights Act 1998 and the Constitutional Reform Act 2005, but before addressing these matters, it is necessary to say something about the evolving principles which are the foundations of the judicial role in the British system of government. It will be argued that the story of the 'judicialization' of British politics is to some extent a story of paradox and contradiction, in which outstanding questions remain on each of the three issues of effectiveness, legitimacy, and accountability.

15.2 POLITICS AND THE RULE OF LAW

In an important lecture delivered in October 2007, the senior Law Lord claimed that 'the predominant characteristics of our constitutional settlement in the United Kingdom today' include 'our commitment to the rule of law' and our 'recognition of the Queen in Parliament as the supreme law-making authority in the country' (Bingham 2007). The main point of the lecture was to address the concerns expressed by 'respected and authoritative voices [who] now question whether parliamentary sovereignty can co-exist with the rule of law', an issue that has taken a significant new twist in recent years. One difficulty with this debate about the rule of law, however, is the indeterminacy of the term, with Craig (2007) referring to 'considerable diversity of opinion as to the meaning of the rule of law'. Indeed, according to the House of Lords Constitution Committee, 'the rule of law remains a complex and in some respects uncertain concept' (House of Lords 2007). This is despite the fact that the principle is now to be found in the Constitutional Reform Act 2005, as something the Lord Chancellor is legally obliged to uphold, though the term (and therefore the nature of the obligation) is not defined. Traditional views of the rule of law would emphasize requirements such as (i) the government should have legal authority for its actions, (ii) the law should be clear, prospective, and predictable, so that citizens can conduct their lives in accordance with the law, and (iii) violations of the law should be determined only after a fair trial before independent judges (Raz 1977). There has, however, been a tendency in recent years to seek to inflate our understanding of the rule of law, not just among legal scholars and philosophers (Allan 2001; Dworkin 1986), but also amongst judges and politicians. Lord Bingham, for example, spoke of the rule of law as including core human rights (such as those to be found in the European Convention on Human Rights) and went so far as to argue that 'democracy lies at the heart of the concept of the rule of law' (Bingham 2007), without defining what democracy means for this purpose.

The 'concept of the rule of law' was a source of judicial power and a source of conflict between judges and politicians throughout the twentieth century. In the 1920s Lord Hewart—then Lord Chief Justice—famously railed against the 'New Despotism' of the emerging welfare state, concerned that so much statutory power was being delegated to ministers, and that so much adjudication was being delegated to administrative tribunals. Although contemporary scholars such as Laski (1923) and Jennings (1932) welcomed what they saw as the administrative state and administrative discretion, Hewart saw only what he pejoratively referred to as 'administrative law' and 'administrative lawlessness'. However, many public lawyers would see it as one of the great achievements of the courts in the twentieth century that the rule of law and administrative law have become synonyms rather than antonyms, as the courts moved to 'keep the powers of government within their legal bounds, so as to protect the citizen against their abuse' (Wade and Forsyth 2004: 5). Thus, while 'Parliament as the legislature is sovereign' (ibid.), there is no such thing as a statutory power which is excluded from judicial review. Moreover, in what can be seen as the symbiotic link between the rule of law and the sovereignty of parliament, the courts have insisted that ministers must apply an Act of Parliament consistently with its policy and objects, but that 'the policy and objects of the Act must be determined by construing the Act as a whole, and construction is always a matter of law for the courts': *Padfield v Minister of Agriculture* [1968] AC 997. However, construction is not a science, and as Labour local authorities intermittently and the Labour government in the 1970s were just as famously to discover, it is an activity that could be exercised narrowly to construe powers and frustrate the ambitions of councillors and ministers seeking to extend controversial programmes and empower regulatory bodies (Griffith 1991). Indeed, Lord Atkinson's famous broadside against Poplarism as promoting 'eccentric principles of socialist philanthropy' remains one of the great lines of twentieth-century English jurisprudence: *Roberts v Hopwood* [1925] AC 578 (Fennell 1986).

The other major area where the rule of law brought governments and parliament into conflict with the judges in the twentieth century is around the question of trade union activity. Trade unions in the United Kingdom historically had no statutory rights, but—since 1906—relied instead on statutory immunity from common law liability. From what Stone Sweet (2000) referred to as the 'insular domain' of labour law, the immunities were no more than a legal form designed to establish a freedom, which in other countries was established by a right, in some cases constitutionally protected. From the 'insular domain' of public law, however, the immunities were seen as being 'in entire contradiction of those doctrines of personal freedom and equality before the law which have hitherto been its main aim and object' (*Conway v Wade* [1908] 2 KB 845, at p 854 (Farwell LJ)). This tension between these two domains became more acute in the 1970s when trade union immunities were restored to their 1906 position, at a time when there was some concern about the economic and political status of trade unions and their close constitutional relations with government (Ewing 2000*a*). The new immunities were strongly criticized by the Court of Appeal in a handful of cases in which Lord Denning presided, and were the subject of very narrow interpretations, designed to restrict their scope, in a manner which did not sit easily with the apparent intention of parliament (Wedderburn of Charlton 1980). According to Lord Denning, in a lecture given on the eve of the 1979 general election, 'the greatest threat to the rule of law is posed by big trade unions', adding that 'one of the biggest problems is how to restrain the misuse or abuse of [their] power' (Denning 1983: 321). However, although the House of Lords found the same legislation 'intrinsically repugnant to anyone who has spent his life in the practice of the law or the administration of justice', the sovereignty of parliament was to prevail. According to Lord Diplock, 'it is not for judges to invent fancied ambiguities as an excuse for failing to give effect to its plain meaning because they themselves consider that the consequences of doing so would be inexpedient, or even unjust or immoral': *Duport Steels Ltd v Sirs* [1980] ICR 161.

These two examples illustrate in different ways how legislation may be constrained by judicial perceptions about the rule of law, which may operate to confine the scope of the legislation, and with it the intention of parliament. Yet in what may be an inevitable consequence of these developments, there has recently been a qualitative change in the sense that the judges are now contemplating the possibility that the rule of law may trump rather than simply mediate parliamentary sovereignty. This means that the courts would not only 'interpret' legislation consistently with the 'rule of law', but refuse to apply legislation that failed to comply with it, a power which Lord Denning said he wished the courts had had at the time when his dispute with the government over trade union law was at boiling point (Denning 1982). This claim of the courts that the rule of law rather than the sovereignty of parliament must take priority would greatly extend the boundaries of judicial power, all the more so in view of the indeterminate nature and apparently unconstrained scope of the rule of law as a constitutional principle. Nevertheless, this is a claim to be found in the extra-judicial writings of some judges (Woolf 1995; Laws 1995; 1996), and more significantly in the speeches of some of the Law Lords in *R (Jackson) v Attorney General* [2005] UKHL 56 in which the Countryside Alliance unsuccessfully challenged the legality of the Hunting Act 2004. The Act had reached the statute book by invoking the Parliament Acts 1911–49, and the Alliance contended (i) that the latter of these Acts was invalid, and (ii) that anything passed as a result of having invoked it was also invalid. But although the action failed, the case is notable for important statements by three different members of the House of Lords. According to Lord Hope, 'the rule of law enforced by the courts is the controlling principle upon which our constitution is based'; while in the same case, Lady Hale said that the courts will 'treat with particular suspicion (and might even reject) any attempt to subvert the rule of law by removing governmental action affecting the right of the individual from all judicial powers' (though Lady Hale has since questioned extra-judicially whether the judges really want the power to strike down legislation: Ewing and Tham (2008)).

What thus appears to be taking place here is an attempt to shift the relationship between the rule of law and parliamentary sovereignty, with at least some judges asserting the superior claims of the former over the latter. Indeed, according to Lord Hope in the *Countryside Alliance* case, 'it is no longer right to say that [parliament's] freedom to legislate admits of no qualification'. This challenge to the sovereignty of parliament is very significant from a constitutional point of view, and is potentially also very significant as a result of the relationship between the judges and the other branches of government, not only in view of the open and indeterminate scope of the rule of law as a principle, but in view also of the controversial way in which it has been applied to political circumstances and events in the past. Nevertheless, in an influential piece supportive of these developments, it has been argued that 'it is no longer self evident, or judicially accepted, that a legislature in a modern democracy should be able with impunity to violate the strictures of the rule of law', although it has also been acknowledged that 'it may take some time, provocative legislation and considerable judicial courage for the courts to assert the primacy of the Rule of Law over Parliamentary Sovereignty' (Jowell 2007: 23). It is unclear what kind of legislation would provoke such a response from the courts, though also in the *Countryside Alliance* case, Lord Steyn referred to 'exceptional circumstances involving an attempt to abolish judicial review, or the authority of the courts' as possibly being 'a constitutional fundamental which even a complaisant House of Commons cannot abolish'. These developments have not, however, gone unchallenged, with one academic commentator claiming forcefully that they are 'unargued and unsound', 'historically false', and 'jurisprudentially absurd' (Ekins 2007). In less 'ascerbic' terms, but perhaps more significantly, the senior Law Lord was heard to say extra-judicially that he could not 'accept that [his] colleagues' observations are correct', in a strong defence of the principle of parliamentary sovereignty, which draws heavily on the work of Goldsworthy (1999; Bingham 2007). But it is unclear where many of the other Law Lords sit in this debate.

15.3 THE EFFECTIVENESS OF JUDICIAL REVIEW

It is too early properly to assess the nature and implications of these very significant developments, or the extent to which they reflect a major tilting of the balance between the three branches of government. But a claim has been staked, at a time when other initiatives have been taken to confirm that 'ours is a society governed by the rule of law' (Irvine 2004: 324). Principal amongst these initiatives is the Human Rights Act, though it is not to be assumed that the 'rule of law' was invented as a British constitutional principle by the HRA (Tomkins 2009). Such developments are consistent with the view that '[p]arliamentary supremacy, understood by most students of European politics to be a principle of European politics, has lost its vitality', even if it may be premature to 'declare it dead' (Stone Sweet 2000: 1), at least in the United Kingdom. In the latter jurisdiction there remains a school of thought prepared to challenge the legitimacy of judicial review of legislation on democratic grounds, and claim that it 'does not comport with the respect and honour normally accorded to ordinary men and women in the context of a theory of rights' (Waldron 1993: 51), though Waldron has been understood recently to have introduced an element of conditionality, at least in the context of political systems with weak and ineffective parliamentary scrutiny (Waldron 2005). However, much of the work in opposition to 'rights' rather than 'democracy' was developed by the left at a time of greater ideological conflict between the main political parties (Campbell 1983), and at a time when the judges were seen to be an obstacle to progressive legislation (a view which Lord Denning did little to dispel during his dispute with the government about trade union legislation in the 1970s). But much has changed, and in an era of free markets and globalization, social democracy has been in retreat, at least in the Anglo-Saxon world. So although a principled and persuasive republican case can still be made against judicial supremacy (Goldsworthy 1999; Tomkins 2005; Bellamy 2007), the political context within which opposition to judicial scrutiny was developed is disappearing, and it may be more difficult in the current climate to sustain the argument that the courts will frustrate progressive policies.

Thus, whereas in the past there was thus a fear by some that the courts would (and did) *frustrate* the operation of social and economic rights established by parliament, now there is a hope by others that the judges will *protect* established civil and political rights. In a manner that could only have been predicted with great difficulty, these latter rights are also being threatened by globalization, as governments seek to protect their borders from the free movement of people (Rawlings 2005), and deal with the consequences of what is apocalyptically dubbed the global 'war on terror' (Gearty 2007). So far as the effectiveness of judicial review in such circumstances is concerned, one problem relates to the contradictory position adopted by judges who claim or assert power (in the manner described above), when they seem simultaneously reluctant to use the powers they already have. A great deal of restraint is to be seen in the approach of the courts to the Human Rights Act in the development of what Gearty (2004) refers to in his elegant study as 'the principles of human rights adjudication'. Thus, we have Lord Hope expressing the view in *R v DPP, ex p Kebeline* [2000] 2 AC 326, at p 381, that the courts should 'defer, on democratic grounds, to the considered opinion of the elected body as to where the balance is to be struck between the rights of the individual and the needs of society'. These comments were to find an echo in the speech of Lord Nolan in the *Alconbury* case where referring to the planning system he said that 'to substitute for the Secretary of State an independent and impartial body with no central electoral accountability would not only be a recipe for chaos: it would be profoundly undemocratic': *R (Alconbury Developments Ltd) v Environment Secretary* [2001] UKHL 23; [2003] 2 AC 295, at para [60]. The point is also illustrated by a second challenge by the Countryside Alliance to the Hunting Act 2004, this time on the ground that the measures in question violated a number of Convention rights. In rejecting these challenges, Lord Bingham said that 'The democratic process is liable to be subverted if, on a question of moral and political judgment, opponents of [legislation] achieve through the courts what they could not achieve in Parliament': *R (Countryside Alliance) v Attorney General* [2007] UKHL 52.

It is perhaps inevitable that cautious principles will lead to cautious decisions with significant implications for the relationship between the judiciary and the other branches of government. In light of the foregoing 'principles of adjudication', it is thus not surprising that one leading public lawyer should express scepticism about the vigour with which the courts have protected human rights, claiming that '[d]espite the notoriety of one or two apparently progressive decisions under the Human Rights Act...a close examination of the case law reveals that little has been achieved by way of increased judicial protection of civil liberties' (Tomkins 2008). Although this is a view that would be challenged by those who are less critical of the judicial role, it is nevertheless the case that the statutory restrictions on personal and political freedom continue to expand, with a list of measures—introduced since the Human Rights Act was passed—including the Terrorism Act 2000, the Regulation of Investigatory Powers Act 2000, the Anti-terrorism, Crime and Security Act 2001, the Civil Contingencies Act 2004, the Prevention of Terrorism Act 2005, the Serious Organized Crime and Police Act 2005, the Identity Cards Act 2006, and the Terrorism Act 2006, to name but eight. Although—as Tomkins (2008) acknowledges—the judicial traffic is by no means all one way, at the same time a disappointing litany of decisions continues to grow, as the House of Lords (i) condemns torture but erects evidentiary barriers that make it difficult to establish that torture has been used (*A v Home Secretary (No 2)* [2006] 1 All ER 575); (ii) condemns indefinite detention without trial but permits control orders where people can be subject to house arrest for up to sixteen hours a day (*Home Secretary v JJ (FC)* [2007] UKHL 45); and (iii) permits the retention of the DNA of people who have not been convicted of any offence, at a time of growing concern about state interference in the private lives of citizens (*R(S) v South Yorkshire Chief Constable* [2004] 1 WLR 2196). These and other cases suggest that while we have no reason in the present political climate to be over-anxious about the courts challenging progressive legislation, we have no reason either to be over-confident that they will defend civil and political rights from erosion.

It does not follow, however, that the executive wins *all* of the cases in judicial review, even if it does win *most* of the cases (Steyn 2005). For evidence to the contrary it is necessary to look no further than the momentous decision of the House of Lords in *A v Home Secretary* [2005] 2 AC 68—arguably the most significant judicial decision— at least in the field of public law—since *Entick v Carrington* (1765) 19 St Tr 1030. In the *A* case where unusually a Bench of nine judges was assembled (though a bench of nine was also assembled for the *Jackson* case as well), the House of Lords held by a majority of 8 : 1 that legislation authorizing the indefinite detention without trial of foreign terrorist suspects was a breach of article 5 of the European Convention on Human Rights (ECHR), which protects the right to liberty. The House of Lords further held that the government's derogation from the Convention—made in order to pass the legislation—was also unlawful, in the sense that it went beyond what was 'strictly required by the exigencies of the situation', as demanded by article 15 of the ECHR. According to Lord Bingham, 'If the threat presented to the security of the United Kingdom by UK nationals suspected of being Al-Qaeda terrorists or their supporters could be addressed without infringing their right to personal liberty, it is not shown why similar measures could not adequately address the threat presented by foreign nationals'. In so holding—and in sharp contrast to earlier cases involving national security—Lord Bingham rejected the argument that 'matters of the kind in issue here fall within the discretionary area of judgment properly belonging to the democratic organs of the state'. Thus making a declaration that the legislation in question was incompatible with Convention rights, the House of Lords in *A* also addressed questions about the democratic legitimacy of judicial activism. In a sharp rebuff to counsel for the government who had raised these questions, Lord Bingham said that it was 'wrong to stigmatise judicial decision-making as in some way undemocratic': the courts do not have the power to strike down an Act of Parliament leaving it to the government to decide how to proceed.

As already suggested, this was an extraordinary decision, all the more striking for being the only occasion at the time of writing the House of Lords had declared incompatible an Act of Parliament enacted since the HRA came into force (House of Lords 2007). This alone may help to reinforce the view that the courts are extremely cautious in their use of the HRA, while *A* also reveals other limits relating to the process of judicial review, even when the judges are at their boldest. Thus, the *A* case reveals the process to be inefficient, in the sense that the Anti-terrorism, Crime and Security Act was passed at the end of 2001, and the decision of the House of Lords was not reached until the end of 2004, with a number of people all the while detained in breach of their human rights. The *A* case also reveals the process to be inconclusive, in the sense that the Lords' decision did not lead to the release of any of those who had been detained in breach of their Convention rights. Indeed, what the affair revealed is that the judges are playing in a game they cannot win. The detained individuals remained in custody until new legislation—the Terrorism Act 2005—was introduced giving the Home Secretary the power to detain many of them at home by way of control orders, a form of de facto indefinite detention that was claimed to be worse for some than the indefinite detention in Belmarsh and elsewhere. Although control orders appeared not to be as intrusive as internment and are also subject to challenge in the courts (*Home Secretary v JJ (FC)* [2007] UKHL 45), the government had already moved some paces ahead of the judges by deciding that some of those subject to control orders could be returned to indefinite detention in prison. This was done under immigration powers, pending the deportation of the individuals concerned to states with whom memorandums of understanding were to be concluded, the memorandums being designed to prevent the torture of the detainees once they are retuned (Ewing 2008). It is the futility of litigation in these circumstances that reinforces doubts about the effectiveness of judicial review and strengthens the argument that it is to a reform of parliamentary procedure that human rights activists should be directing their attention (Ewing 2007*b*), particularly if deference to parliament is (not improperly) to be a guiding principle of adjudication.

15.4 THE LEGITIMACY OF JUDICIAL REVIEW

We are thus presented with the curious paradox of the judges claiming and seeking more power over representative institutions, but often deferring to the legitimacy of these same institutions because of their representative nature. Nevertheless, the extension of judicial power into the political sphere—however gingerly in some cases—has reinforced the need for legitimacy on the part of those who exercise it. The issue of judicial legitimacy is most intractable in jurisdictions where the courts (the unelected branch) have the power to strike down legislation (acts of the elected branch) (Bellamy 2007). But although perhaps not as intractable, issues of legitimacy are nevertheless real in other jurisdictions by virtue of the political nature and impact of the judicial role. These issues arise in the United Kingdom where the courts are empowered only to declare legislation incompatible with Convention rights without striking it down, though the urgency of the issue will grow if constitutional foundations change in the manner suggested by some judges in *Jackson*. In the meantime, important steps in the direction of greater legitimacy are to be found in the Constitutional Reform Act 2005, which may be said to address three fundamental preconditions of judicial power and its extension. These are respectively (i) merit, in the sense of professional competence and ability; (ii) independence from the government and political parties; and (iii) the need for a body of men and women sufficiently representative or diverse to command the respect and confidence of all sections of the community. It is important to emphasize that none of these principles was invented by the Constitutional Reform Act 2005, any more than the rule of law was invented by the Human Rights Act. Nevertheless, just as the latter has put lawyers and judges into politics, so in equal measure the former has tried in different ways to take lawyers and judges out of politics. The Constitutional Reform Act 2005 thus confirms changes to the role of the Lord Chancellor who no longer takes the judicial oath and so no longer sits as a judge; provides for the creation of the Supreme Court of the United Kingdom, and disqualifies senior judges from membership of the House of Lords; and creates the new machinery for the appointment of judges through the Judicial Appointments Commission (Windlesham 2005; Woodhouse 2007).

In terms of the government's apparent objectives relating to enhanced legitimacy (as set out in the Constitutional Reform Act), these have only been partially met. Although there is no concern about judicial appointments being made on merit, the goal of institutional independence in terms of a clear separation of function has not been fully achieved. Thus, institutional links between the judiciary and the other branches of government will continue to exist despite the changes introduced by the Constitutional Reform Act 2005, and will do so because the practical benefits of these links outweigh the challenge to principle which they present. It is admittedly a unique feature of the British system of government (at least among major developed democracies) that the Law Lords are also members of the legislature, and that they took part—albeit intermittently—in the legislative business of the House. There are good reasons why judges should not sit in legislative assemblies, not the least being that those who make the law should not also have responsibility for interpreting it: this is the rule of man, not the rule of law. On the other hand, however, judges are seen to make a positive contribution to the work of the legislature, with a number of important pieces of legislation that would otherwise be neglected being due in part to the legislative activity of the Law Lords (Ewing 2000b; Hope 2007). It is also the case that much of the technical scrutiny work of the House of Lords in its legislative capacity was enhanced by the presence of the Law Lords, particularly in relation to the scrutiny of EU business (Wakeham 2000). It is thus thought to be important that the judiciary institutionally should continue to be represented in the House of Lords, even if it is appropriate that serving judges individually should no longer sit in a legislative capacity, with Supreme Court justices to be forbidden by the Constitutional Reform Act 2005 from having a seat in the Lords. The government has consequently given an undertaking that a new convention will be created whereby Supreme Court justices will be made members of the House of Lords on their retirement, ensuring that there will continue to be ongoing 'judicial' input in the work of the House (Hope 2007).

By some way a more contentious qualification of principle relates to the ongoing relationship between the executive and the judiciary, which in crucial respects will be unaffected by the Constitutional Reform Act 2005. Judges have often been called upon to exercise various executive functions on behalf of the government. These functions are of two kinds: the first are standing commitments to act as commissioners to supervise the operation of regulatory regimes (such as those dealing with the interception of communications on the one hand, and the activities of the security services on the other); and the second are ad hoc commitments to investigate controversial events (such as the circumstances surrounding the death of the government scientist Dr David Kelly in 2004: Hutton 2004; 2006), and chairing royal commissions and departmental committees (Beatson 2005). Neither activity is free from difficulty, in the sense that both draw judges individually into controversial political issues, such as the question whether intercept evidence should be used in criminal proceedings (Thomas 2007). There is also the 'equally serious danger' to 'the appearance of impartiality when judges with inside experience of reviewing intelligence matters [obtained by chairing committees or conducting reviews] subsequently sit to hear cases involving questions of national security' (Lustgarten and Leigh 1994: 490). Lustgarten and Leigh (ibid.) identified four major national security cases where senior judges involved in the cases had been involved (sometimes quite recently) in conducting national security work on behalf of the government, including Lord Radcliffe who had completed a review of security procedures in the civil service, Lord Denning who had conducted the inquiry into the Profumo affair, and Lord Diplock who had conducted a review of telephone tapping procedures. There are no indications that the use of judges in either of these ways will stop, and although the practice now is to use retired judges as interception and security service commissioners, the continued use of serving judges to conduct inquiries was signalled by the Inquiries Act 2005, albeit with greater formal input of senior judges in the making of such appointments by ministers.

Despite these reservations, the symbolic value of removing the senior judiciary to a new building on the other side of Parliament Square is not to be underestimated. In addition, by making judges more visible such a move may also serve to make them subject to greater scrutiny by the press and others, to which we return. However, the expansion of the judicial role invites questions not just about where judges are located or where they sit, but how they are recruited and who they are. In this respect, the Constitutional Reform Act 2005 makes another overdue change with the creation not only of the permanent Judicial Appointments Commission with lay and judicial membership, but also the ad hoc Supreme Court Selection Commission, this too with lay representation. But although these procedures dilute (they do not remove) the role of the executive in judicial appointments, they do not fully meet the need of the government's third objective for what has been variously described as a 'representative', 'reflective', or 'diverse' judiciary. This would perhaps matter less if there was a 'right answer' to every legal question which a suitably qualified Herculean judge could work out in every case, subject to correction by the higher courts. But there is not, and adjudication is about experience and judgement (Judicial Appointments Commission 2007), in a context in which the judicial role is expanding. It is in that context in particular that the argument can be made that a diverse range of experiences should be represented on the Bench, so that legal rules develop in accordance with as wide a collective judicial experience as possible. This is quite apart from any other consideration that in a democratic society no rule-making institution should be closed to any member of the community by irrelevant or irrational or insurmountable entry requirements. The scale of the challenge, however, is revealed by the fact on 1 October 2005, 'only one member of the House of Lords was female, all the heads of division were men, only two of 33 Court of Appeal judges were female, and all but six of the 106 High Court judges were men' (Bradley and Ewing 2006: 388). Only one member of these three courts was a member of an ethnic minority (ibid.).

A 'representative' judiciary is not necessarily the same as a 'diverse' judiciary, if by representative it is meant one that has a renewable and accountable electoral mandate. The idea of election to judicial office was decisively rejected by Laski in his pioneering work on the judiciary (as an idea for which 'there is nothing to be said'), mainly because of the 'vital fact that the qualifications for judicial office are not such as an undifferentiated public can properly assess' (Laski 1932: 165). However, not all political scientists have given up on the election route, with Miliband (1994: 79) arguing that there 'is no good reason why electors should not be able to choose judges on the basis of their stated attitude to...questions with a bearing on their function'. But this appears by some way to be a minority position, and it is not to be overlooked that judicial elections in those jurisdictions where they are required (as in some US states) have encountered the same problems encountered in other elections, notably in relation to campaign finance (Schotland 2001; Streb 2007). If by representative it is meant that the judiciary collectively should reflect the make-up of society and its diversity, then for reasons already considered, there is a strong case for a representative bench. Indeed, this has been accepted as a desirable principle for the magistracy for some time (Bradley and Ewing 2006: 388), and it has now been accepted—at least to some extent—by the government in relation to the senior judiciary. It is not clear, however, how the new appointment procedure will significantly affect the position, for although the JAC is required to have regard to 'the need to encourage diversity in the range of persons available for selection for appointments', this is subject to an overriding statutory objective which is to promote selection 'solely' on the ground of merit. The Act may thus have only a marginal effect if—as is likely—there are deeper problems beyond the control of the JAC which prevent under-represented groups from securing the necessary qualifications for appointment in the first place, whether for reasons of poor educational opportunities, difficulty in gaining access to the legal profession, or difficulty in prospering within it, for reasons which include its working practices.

15.5 JUDICIAL REVIEW AND JUDICIAL ACCOUNTABILITY

The government's attempts to enhance the legitimacy of the judiciary have thus been only partially successful, and fall short of a 'deep clean' separation of functions or a 'deep clean' reform of the appointment process (to the extent that diversity is an issue of legitimacy). Indeed, initial press reaction to the impact of these latter procedures has been negative and hostile, on the ground that the procedures have made no impact on the question of diversity in appointment (*Guardian*, 28 January 2008), with the first ten judges appointed under the new procedure being from the same mould as the last ten judges appointed under the old procedure. Nevertheless, the enhanced legitimacy which the Constitutional Reform Act both confers and presages (albeit to a more limited extent than may be desirable) makes even more paradoxical the general reluctance of the courts to be more assertive in the use of their powers than has been suggested above. But as also already suggested, the exercise (or non-exercise) of power does not only raise questions of legitimacy, the extension of power also raises questions of accountability, even if that power is not currently being exercised to the full. It is thus perhaps inevitable that the expansion of judicial power should give rise to emerging questions about judicial accountability, an issue that arises in various forms. Because of the nature of the role they perform, however, it is unlikely that judges could be made subject to the same forms of accountability as the legislature (to the people in elections) or the executive (in the form of ministerial responsibility to parliament). But it is arguable nevertheless that those who exercise power over others should be subject to levels of transparency, accountability, and scrutiny to the fullest extent consistent with their functions. There are of course a number of accountability mechanisms which already apply to judges (Malleson 1999), but these appear weak and relatively underdeveloped compared to the accountability mechanisms affecting other public officials (whether elected or unelected), and at a time of expanding judicial power it is an issue on which perhaps inadequate energy has been expended.

So far as judges are concerned, the areas of accountability are likely to arise first at the stage of appointment, with a possible role for parliament in the confirmation of judicial appointments. Here the aim is to obtain information about the people who are about to occupy high judicial office and the attitudes and experiences they are likely to bring to their work. This was paradoxically much less of an issue in the past than it is now, partly because judges in the past had a much higher political profile before they were appointed. Laski has shown that '[o]ut of 139 judges appointed [between 1832 and 1906], 80 were members of the House of Commons at the time of their nomination; 11 others had been candidates for Parliament', and that of the 80, '63 were appointed by their own party while in office' (Laski 1932: 168–9). By the late twentieth century, however, 'being an active member of a political party seems to be neither a qualification nor a disqualification for appointment' (Griffith 1991: 29), with a study of the modern judiciary able to find only three judges of the High Court or above who had been parliamentary candidates before being appointed to the judiciary (and it seems that none had been a member of parliament) (McKay 2000). Yet, although the Ministry of Justice (2007) has raised the question of parliamentary confirmation hearings before at least some judicial appointments take effect, the government's intentions about this are said to be unclear (House of Lords 2007). There does not appear to be much appetite on the part of the judges for such hearings (Phillips of Matravers 2007), which the House of Lords Constitution Committee thought would be 'an innovation with very profound implications for the independence of the judiciary and the new judicial appointments system' without explaining why (House of Lords 2007). Bald claims of this nature are not a convincing reason for refusing to adopt confirmation hearings, which were used in relation to the appointment of Mr Justice Rothstein to the Supreme Court of Canada in 2006 (House of Lords 2007), relevant because Canada is a Westminster democracy which by the preamble to its constitution inherited British constitutional traditions.

The second area where the issue of accountability arises is in the context of the judicial process, that is to say in terms of the way in which courts and judges make their decisions. So in addition to greater accountability about *who* occupies judicial office, the issue here is about greater accountability in terms of the way they operate and *how* decisions are made once they have taken office. It is true that—save in exceptional circumstances—courts normally sit in public, that legal arguments are normally presented in public, and that a reasoned decision is typically issued by each of the judges in a case. These stages, however, are only part of the decision-making process—the first and third stages, with the crucial second stage being hidden behind a secret veil, which is only rarely pierced (only twice in the last ten years), and then only in relation to the House of Lords. Between the argument and the reason is the stage at which the decision is made once the arguments have been concluded. Questions arise here as follows: what informs the decision of the judge or judges in a difficult case? To what extent do the judges consult with others when drafting their judgements, and with whom do they consult for this purpose? In the case of the Court of Appeal and the House of Lords, how much—if any—collaboration and lobbying goes on between judges as they prepare their decisions in cases that by definition are likely to be controversial? Who are the key players in any such activity and why? Pioneering insights into some of these questions were provided by Paterson (1982), who discovered that the 'Law Lords not infrequently attempt to persuade their colleagues to share their view of the facts and the law in an appeal, particularly if its outcome is finely balanced'. Equally valuable work more recently by Robertson (1998) and Dickson (2007) suggests, however, that the practice may have changed since Paterson's research was conducted. More information is required, for although there is unlikely to be a strong case that any part of this stage in the judicial process should be conducted in public, there may nevertheless be an equally strong case for a fuller account of how the decision-making process operates than is currently available.

A third—and equally difficult—area of accountability relates to judicial performance. At the present time judges are not required to account for their decisions, not even in relation to leading cases, which Lord Goff has described to include 'the decisions which mark the principal stages in th[e] development [of the common law]' (*Kleinwort Benson Ltd v Lincoln City Council* [1999] 2 AC 349, at p 377), which may have major implications for the rules which govern people's lives or by which public bodies are governed. The very idea of accountability in this sense raises questions relating to judicial independence about which lawyers are peculiarly sensitive (Ratushny 2002), and it has been said that:

> Our system has operated on the basis that judges will listen to the arguments both ways and give a reasoned decision; they should be careful to approach issues of law with an open mind and not allow their own prejudices to influence them. This is a counsel of perfection, but generally it works. Accountability, up to the top level, is via appeals up the court system. And if the government or Parliament should disagree with a legal principle developed by the courts, then in our system it is open to them to secure the passage of legislation to change the rule.   (Oliver 2003: 542)

Although a balance has to be struck between accountability and independence, it is not clear whether responses of this nature do full justice to the seriousness of the issues raised. It is not clear why judges—who are prepared to give public lectures—should not be invited to give an account of their work in a parliamentary forum, for example to explain the purpose and implications of any major changes over the common law, including the rules by which they develop themselves to hold government to account (Ewing 2000*b*). The point was well put by Bogdanor (2006), who proposed:

> that judges while not being answerable to Parliament, will nevertheless answer to Parliament. They would as it were, be cross-examined on their lectures and articles in law journals, on their judicial philosophy, by a Select Committee. They would be cross examined by the representatives of the people in Parliament. Judges are in my opinion right to publicise their views, for senior judges are teachers in the field of human rights and civil liberties. But they should not object to discussing these views in a parliamentary forum, in the cause of greater public understanding.

It is already the case that an intriguing relationship is evolving between the judges and parliament, as judges accept invitations to present evidence to select committees. This is a process which the House of Lords Constitution Committee seems prepared to encourage, concluding that 'select committees can play a central part in enabling the role and proper concerns of the judiciary to be better understood by the public at large, and in helping the judiciary to remain accountable to the people via their representatives in Parliament' (House of Lords 2007). Greater accountability of some kind appears now to be accepted by the judges, albeit accountability in the 'explanatory' rather than the 'sacrificial' sense, recognizing also that such accountability must not trespass on the other work the judges are employed to do or on their independence. In the evolving constitutional landscape, there is a great deal to discuss, with senior judges now engaged in a debate *inter se* about the very foundations on which the British constitution is based, and another debate about the extent to which the courts should defer to democratic institutions (Steyn 2005), from both of which the people—whether directly or indirectly through their representatives in parliament—are largely excluded. Given the remarkably wide scope of judicial power under the HRA, the associated power of the courts to determine how far and in what circumstances this power will be fully exercised, and the differences between judges on how these questions are to be approached, there is a case for more public engagement by the judges about the exercise of public power vested in them. Although it is unclear whether the judges are prepared to go this far, such accountability would give some substance to 'the idea that modern constitutionalism should be understood in terms of a constitutional dialogue between courts, legislatures and executives' (Hickman 2005: 306). Yet while this is 'rapidly becoming common currency across the common law world' (ibid.), it is not yet clear that the dialogue metaphor—itself the subject of refinement and revision—fully addresses the concerns of those who remain sceptical of the democratic foundations of the judicialization project, or indeed if it can ever do so.

15.6 CONCLUSION

As we have seen, judicial power appears formally to be expanding in a number of ways. It is notable that this should be taking place in a period when deep political differences between the main political parties are diminishing, and more work is required to find an explanation for this. It may, however, represent an important symbol of what appears to be an ideological victory of liberalism over collectivism, and of liberty over equality. But whatever the explanation, we see the apparent assumption of power by the courts to determine the legal base of the British constitution and the weight to be given to fundamental constitutional principles. Indeed, the *Jackson* case raises the most fundamental question of any democracy, namely (i) who is the guardian of the constitution; and (ii) who is to make that decision about who is the guardian? In both cases, the choice is currently between parliament and the courts, and in both cases the answer (and its implications) is perhaps not as clear in 2008 as it was in 1998. Secondly, there is the power to hold government to account, with the judges having campaigned openly for the incorporation of the ECHR into domestic law, and now better able not only to restrain executive action but also to influence the substance of legislation as well. An important feature of this power, however, is the ability of the judges themselves to develop their own principles of adjudication, as well as the power to determine how these principles are to be applied in the different categories of case coming before them. Thirdly, there is the power of selection, with judges now much more formally engaged in the process of recruitment to the Bench. It is true that judges sit on the various appointment commissions with other lawyers who are not judges and non-lawyers alike. Although this will dilute the influence of judges in recruitment and selection, the operation of these commissions and the relative influence of judicial and other members in decision-making will be an important subject for investigation.

With the position of the courts and judges now expanding, questions arise about the effectiveness, legitimacy, and accountability of judicial review. So far as the effectiveness of the process is concerned, the approach of the judges is contradictory, at times deferential in its tone, and always reactive in the sense that the courts can only operate at some paces behind the other branches of government. This raises questions about whether more effective strategies for the protection of human rights need to be explored given the limited institutional capacity of the courts. So far as legitimacy is concerned, this will become a more pressing issue if the judges are to take the step of trumping parliamentary sovereignty with the rule of law as suggested by some members of the House of Lords in *Jackson*. In the meantime, much of what the Constitutional Reform Act 2005 provides had already been implemented, to the extent that the Lord Chancellor had already relinquished his role as Speaker of the House of Lords and his right to take the judicial oath, while the Law Lords have already given up sitting in the House of Lords for legislative business. Moreover, the creation of the Judicial Appointments Commission is unlikely to make a huge difference to the substance of judicial appointments or to ensure a significantly higher level of diversity on the Bench. Yet it is important that the courts with increased powers (albeit powers yet to be fully utilized) are seen to be more fully representative of the population over which they will exercise greater authority, and important also that they should be responsive to that population (in the way suggested by Lord Goff in relation to the common law). This is not to suggest that the independence of the judiciary should be compromised, but to acknowledge that there is an issue of judicial accountability, which is made more urgent by the evolving role of the courts. As judges have become more powerful and as their independence is better protected, channels of accountability for the exercise of that power (as opposed to questions of conduct) have not been addressed to the same extent.

It is true that the compelling need for judicial independence creates institutional and intellectual barriers to the idea of judicial accountability. But in a democracy it is difficult to justify political power without political accountability, and the fact that political power is exercised in a judicial context may only with difficulty justify an immunity from accountability for the bearers of that power. If it is not possible for judicial power to be used in a responsive and accountable manner, then we have even further cause to be sceptical of the judicialization project. This presupposes—of course—that the judicial role is political, which takes us back to where we started at the beginning of this chapter. For while the open, universal, and unequivocal acceptance of the judicial function as political is a striking feature of political science scholarship (Laski 1932; Robertson 1998; Stone Sweet 2000), judges and lawyers are more hesitant and may be unlikely to see their role in these terms, tending to argue that the courts are the independent branch of government, and by strong implication the apolitical branch of government (Steyn 2005). Nevertheless, it is not clear that '[judicial] independence necessarily involves neutrality' and at least one school of legal thought would argue that '[j]udges are part of the machinery of authority within the State and as such cannot avoid the making of political decisions' (Griffith 1991: 272). This is a school of thought with a long pedigree (Jennings 1936), and a perspective that long pre-dates instruments such as the Human Rights Act. Indeed, the incorporation of the latter makes it more difficult to deny that the judicial process is a political one, with many of the provisions of the ECHR sounding 'like the statement of a political conflict, purporting to be a resolution of it' (Griffith 1979: 16). Yet the final paradox is that while the judges are now invited more closely to scrutinize political decisions, it is difficult to anticipate a judicial decision with more dramatic political consequences than that delivered over 100 years ago in *Taff Vale Railway Co Ltd v Amalgamated Society of Railway Servants* [1901] AC 426.

REFERENCES

ALLAN, T. R. S. 2001. *Constitutional Justice: A Liberal Theory of the Rule of Law*. Oxford: Oxford University Press.

BEATSON, J. 2005. 'Should Judges Conduct Public Enquiries?' 121 *Law Quarterly Review* 221.

BELLAMY, R. 2007. *Political Constitutionalism*. Cambridge: Cambridge University Press.

BINGHAM, LORD 2007. 'The Rule of Law and the Sovereignty of Parliament'. Commemoration Oration, King's College London, 31 Oct.: www.kcl.ac.uk/content/1/c6/01/45/18/TheRuleofLawandtheSovereigntyofParliament.pdf.

BOGDANOR, V. 2006. 'Parliament and the Judiciary: The Problem of Accountability'. Sunningdale Accountability Lecture, 9 Feb.: www.ukpac.org/sunningdale.htm.

BRADLEY, A. W., and EWING, K. D. 2006. *Constitutional and Administrative Law*, 14th edn. Harlow: Longman.

CAMPBELL, T. 1983. *The Left and Rights*. London: Routledge.

CRAIG, P. 2007. 'The Rule of Law'. House of Lords Constitution Committee, Relations between the Executive, the Judiciary and Parliament, Report, HL 151 (2006–7), App. 5.

DENNING, LORD 1982. *What Next in the Law?* London: Oxford University Press.

——1983. *The Closing Chapter*. London: Oxford University Press.

DICKSON, B. 2007. 'The Processing of Appeals in the House of Lords'. 123 *Law Quarterly Review* 571.

DWORKIN, R. 1986. *Law's Empire*. London: Belknap Press.

EKINS, R. 2007. 'Acts of Parliament and the Parliament Acts'. 123 *Law Quarterly Review* 91.

EWING, K. D. 2000a. 'The Politics of the British Constitution'. [2000] *Public Law* 405.

——2000b. 'A Theory of Democratic Adjudication: Towards a Representative, Accountable and Independent Judiciary'. 28 *Alberta Law Review* 708.

——(ed.) 2007a. *The Right to Strike: From the Trade Disputes Act 1906 to the Trade Union Freedom Bill 2006*. London: Institute of Employment Rights.

——2007b. 'Parliamentary Protection of Human Rights'. In K. Ziegler, D. Baranger, and A. W. Bradley (eds.), *Constitutionalism and the Role of Parliaments*. Oxford: Oxford University Press.

——2008. 'The Political Constitution of Emergency Powers: A Comment'. *International Journal of Law in Context*, 39.

——and THAM, J.-C. 2008. 'The Continuing Futility of the Human Rights Act.' [2008] *Public Law* 668.

FENNELL, P. 1986. '*Roberts v Hopwood*: The Rule against Socialism'. 13 *Journal of Law and Society* 401.

GEARTY, C. 2004. *Principles of Human Rights Adjudication*. Oxford: Oxford University Press.

——2007. *Civil Liberties*. Oxford: Oxford University Press.

GOLDSWORTHY, J. 1999. *The Sovereignty of Parliament*. Oxford: Oxford University Press.

GRIFFITH, J. A. G. 1979. 'The Political Constitution'. 42 *Modern Law Review* 1.

——1991. *The Politics of the Judiciary*, 4th edn. London: Fontana.

HICKMAN, T. 2005. 'Constitutional Dialogue, Constitutional Theories and the Human Rights Act 1998'. [2005] *Public Law* 306.

HOPE, LORD 2007. 'Voices from the Past: The Law Lords' Contribution to the Legislative Process'. 123 *Law Quarterly Review* 547.

HOUSE OF LORDS CONSTITUTION COMMITTEE 2007. 'Relations between the Executive, the Judiciary and Parliament: Report'. HL 151 (2006–7).

HUTTON, LORD 2004. *Investigation into the Circumstances Surrounding the Death of Dr David Kelly*. London: HMSO.

——2006. 'The Media Reaction to the Hutton Report'. [2006] *Public Law* 807.

IRVINE, LORD 2004. 'The Impact of the Human Rights Act'. [2004] *Public Law* 308.

JENNINGS, W. I. 1932. 'The Report on Ministers' Powers'. 10 *Public Administration* 333.

——1936. 'The Courts and Administrative Law: The Experience of English Housing Legislation'. 49 *Harvard Law Review* 426.

JOWELL, J. 2007. 'The Rule of Law Today'. Ch. 1 in J. Jowell and D. Oliver (eds.), *The Changing Constitution*, 6th edn. Oxford: Oxford University Press.

JUDICIAL APPOINTMENTS COMMISSION 2007. *Annual Report 2006–7*, IIC 632, 2006–7.

LASKI, H. J. 1923. 'The Growth of Administrative Discretion'. 1 *Journal of Public Administration* 92.

——1932. *Studies in Law and Politics*. London: Yale University Press.

LAWS, SIR J. 1995. 'Law and Democracy'. [1995] *Public Law* 72.

——1996. 'The Constitution: Morals and Rights'. [1996] *Public Law* 622.

LUSTGARTEN, L., and LEIGH, I. 1994. *In from the Cold*. Oxford: Oxford University Press.

McKAY, S. 2000. 'The British Judiciary'. In K. D. Ewing (ed.), *Human Rights at Work*. London: Institute of Employment Rights.

MALLESON, K. 1999. *The New Judiciary: The Effects of Expansion and Activism* London: Ashgate.

MILIBAND, R. 1994. *Socialism for a Sceptical Age*. London: Verso.

MINISTRY OF JUSTICE 2007. *The Governance of Britain: Judicial Appointments*, CP 25/07.

OLIVER, D. 2003. *Constitutional Reform*. Oxford: Oxford University Press.

PATERSON, A. 1982. *The Law Lords*. London: Palgrave Macmillan.

PELLING, H. 1965. *Origins of the Labour Party*, 2nd edn. Oxford: Oxford University Press.

PHILLIPS OF MATRAVERS, LORD 2007. 'Judicial Independence'. Commonwealth Law Conference, Nairobi, Kenya, 12 Sept: www.judiciary.gov.uk/docs/speeches/lcj_kenya_clc_120907.pdf.

RATUSHNY, E. 2002. 'Confirmation Hearings for Supreme Court of Canada Appointments: *Not* a Good Idea!' In P. Thibault et al. (eds.), *Essays in Honour of Gérald-A. Beaudoin: The Challenges of Constitutionalism*. Cowansville: Éditions Y. Blais.

RAWLINGS, R. 2005. 'Review, Revenge and Retreat'. 68 *Modern Law Review* 378.

RAZ, J. 1977. 'The Rule of Law and its Virtue'. 93 *Law Quarterly Review* 195.

ROBERTSON, D. 1998. *Judicial Discretion in the House of Lords*. Oxford: Oxford University Press.

SCHOTLAND, R. 2001. 'Campaign Finance in Judicial Elections'. 34 *Loyola Law Review* 1489.

SHAPIRO, M., and STONE SWEET, A. 2002. *On Law, Politics and Judicialisation*. Oxford: Oxford University Press.

STEYN, LORD 2005. 'Deference: A Tangled Story'. [2005] *Public Law* 346.

STONE SWEET, A. 2000. *Governing with Judges*. Oxford: Oxford University Press.

STREB, M. J. (ed.) 2007 *Running for Judge: The Rising Political, Financial and Legal Stakes of Judicial Elections*. New York: New York University Press.

THOMAS, SIR S. 2007. 'Report of the Interception of Communications Commissioner for 2005–2006'. HC 315 (2006–7).

TOMKINS, A. 2005. *Our Republican Constitution*. Oxford: Oxford University Press.

——2008. 'The Rule of Law in Blair's Britain'. *University of Queensland Law Journal*, Dec.

——2009. 'Constitutionalism'. In M. Flinders, A. Gamble, C. Hay, and M. Kenny (eds.), *Oxford Handbook of British Politics*. Oxford: Oxford University Press.

WADE, H. W. R., and FORSYTH, C. 2004. *Administrative Law*, 9th edn. Oxford: Oxford University Press.

WAKEHAM, LORD 2000. *A House for the Future: Report of the Royal Commission on the Reform of the House of Lords*. Cm 4534.

WALDRON, J. 1993. 'A Right-Based Critique of Constitutional Rights'. *Oxford Journal of Legal Studies* 13.

WALDRON, J. 2005. 'Compared to What? Judicial Activism and New Zealand's Parliament'. [2005] *New Zealand Law Journal* 441.

WEDDERBURN OF CHARLTON, LORD 1980. 'Industrial Relations and the Courts'. 9 *Industrial Law Journal* 65.

WINDLESHAM, LORD 2005. 'The Constitutional Reform Act 2005: Ministers, Judges and Constitutional Change'. [2005] *Public Law* 806 (Part 1).

WOODHOUSE, D. 2007. 'The Constitutional Reform Act 2005: Defending Judicial Independence the English Way'. 5 *International Journal of Constitutional Law* 153.

WOOLF, LORD 1995. 'Droit Public: English Style'. *Public Law* 57–8.

CHAPTER 16

....

THE PARTY SYSTEM

....

PETER MAIR

16.1 INTRODUCTION

....

THIS chapter deals with the nature and dynamic of the British party system and
looks at how it shapes up when viewed from a comparative perspective. The British
party system is one of the oldest in the world, and at a certain level it still remains
one of the most stable and predictable party systems. At the same time, the two
individual parties that lie at the core of this system have become substantially weaker
in recent years, while the system itself faces challenges from the alternative structures
of competition in what is an increasingly multi-level polity. The British party system
is in this sense increasingly vulnerable, and possibly stands at the cusp of a dramatic
change. That said, in the British case perhaps more than in all others, any change at all
is likely to be seen as dramatic, in that the system itself has now endured far beyond
the normal life expectancy of most party systems.

One of the most obvious indicators of the enduring strength of the British party
system is its capacity to resist the entry and challenge of new political parties. This is
a problem that now besets many of the established parties in neighbouring European
polities, and in the following pages I will look briefly at this particular feature of the
British case, and at what it tells us about the character of the party system. I then
go on to look at how we might conceive of party systems more generally, and how
they might best be understood. I then come back to the British case and identify the
factors that have helped to ensure its resilience. Finally, I look at the problems that are
now beginning to face both the parties and the system and assess the scope for party
system change.

16.2 The Challenge of New Parties

During the 1990s, in the large majority of West European polities, new political parties achieved a record share of the vote. These new parties did not always espouse a new politics, as such. Some were genuinely new, of course, including some of the new left and green parties, on the one hand, and the newly mobilized parties of the populist right, on the other, and a number of these parties did climb to new heights in a number of European polities. In other countries the successful formations were new only in a chronological sense, however, being recently formed parties that mobilized on programmes which were not very much different from some of their older and more established competitors. This growth in new party support was part of a broader array of political changes in the 1990s that were also visible at a number of different levels: turnout levels in Europe fell to their lowest levels ever during the 1990s, while levels of electoral volatility—the degree of aggregate change from one election to the next—reached a post-war peak.[1]

But even if the direction of change proved common to the large majority of polities, the actual levels did vary from one system to the next, and it was at the level of aggregate support for new political parties that the contrasts proved most marked. During the 1990s, new parties won close to two-thirds of the vote in Italy. In the Netherlands, they accounted for almost half the vote, in France for more than 40 per cent, and in Belgium and Denmark for close to 25 per cent. In the United Kingdom, however, and quite exceptionally, they accounted for little over 2 per cent of the vote.

So why should British politics prove so difficult for new parties to gain a foothold? The easy answer, and most common answer to be found in the comparative literature, points to the influence of the traditional electoral system: plurality or simple-majority elections in single-member districts discriminate against small parties and favour large parties, and hence they also discriminate against untried or new parties. As Duverger (1954: 205) put it, in what has come to be regarded as almost a law-like generalization, 'The simple-majority single-ballot system encourages a two-party system ...'. A proportional electoral system, by contrast, could be expected to favour smaller parties and new parties, and hence the Dutch electoral system, for example, a system that has been defined as 'extreme' proportional representation (Daalder 1975), and that has just one national electoral district and an effective threshold equivalent to the share of the vote required to win just one parliamentary seat, should place almost no obstacles in the way of new competitors. Nor does it. Indeed, in sharp contrast to the British system, the Dutch system is very hospitable to new political parties, and such parties won an average of almost 46 per cent of the vote in the 1990s, a figure twenty times that in the UK.

But while this may be the easy answer, it is not necessarily the most plausible one. Let us stay with the Dutch–British contrast for the moment. In the Netherlands,

---

[1] Detailed figures on many of these developments are reported in Gallagher, Laver, and Mair (2005).

as has been noted, the threshold for access to parliament is the equivalent of the vote required to win just one seat in the lower chamber (*Tweede Kamer*). In other words, a party can win a seat in parliament if it wins the equivalent of 1/150, or 0.67 per cent, of the total national vote. This is reckoned to be the lowest threshold in Europe, making the Dutch parliament the easiest for a small party to enter. In the 2003 Dutch election, for example, the newly formed Party for the Animals, a small party promoting protection of animal rights, won just less that 48,000 votes, which was the equivalent of 0.5 per cent of the national poll, and narrowly failed to win a seat. In 2006, following a much more effective campaign, and building on the endorsement of a number of high-profile celebrities, it polled close to 180,000 votes, 1.8 per cent of the total, and won two seats in parliament.

The United Kingdom stands in sharp contrast to this. In the United Kingdom, following Lijphart's formula, the notional effective threshold can be estimated at 35 per cent, which is the middle point between 20 per cent of the constituency vote—anything less than that and it is extremely unlikely that a party can win a seat—and 50 per cent (+1), which is the minimum figure required to *guarantee* winning a seat. This effective threshold is some fifty times greater than that in the Netherlands (Lijphart 1994: 21, 25–30).

On the other hand, while the UK threshold is applicable within each single district, the Dutch threshold applies to the country as a whole. Thus while a Dutch party must win 0.67 per cent of the *national* vote in order to take a single seat, a British party need win only 35 per cent of the *constituency* vote, which, given the enormous size of the House of Commons—one of the biggest parliaments in the democratic world—is the equivalent of 0.05 per cent of the national vote. This threshold is therefore only a small fraction of that in the Netherlands. Other things being equal, a small party, or a new party, should therefore find that it is actually easier to win parliamentary representation in the UK than in the Netherlands, in that a relatively smaller share of the (national) vote needs to be won over, albeit concentrated in a single area. In 2005, for example, the Ulster Unionist party won a seat on the back of 127,144 votes—some 0.47 per cent of the total votes cast in the election. George Galloway's new Respect party won a seat with just 68,094 votes—0.25 per cent of the total. And the single candidate standing on behalf of the campaign to save Kidderminster hospital won a seat with just 18,739 votes—0.07 per cent of the total, which is about 10 per cent of the very low Dutch threshold.

These figures are not really comparable, of course, and only those parties in the UK that have a regionally concentrated or locally embedded vote can really benefit from this fortuitous district effect. This was true for the Kidderminster hospital candidate most obviously, but it was also true for George Galloway in Bethnal Green and for the Ulster Unionists in Northern Ireland. In the Dutch case, the threshold might be notionally much higher, but in principle it should be easier to meet that threshold by gathering votes throughout the nation than by being confined to a single small district.

But while this argument is valid, it also takes us one step beyond the electoral system, and introduces new, party-dependent variables. This is a very important qualification, since, following this reasoning, it is not the electoral system as such which works against small parties or new parties in the UK, but rather it is the *combined* effect of the electoral system, on the one hand, and the character of the parties involved, and the party system itself, on the other. That is, the electoral system discriminates against new or small parties, but only when the parties involved are not local or regional parties. Indeed, for these latter sorts of parties, the first-past-the-post electoral system can prove advantageous.

What we see here, then, are also *party system* effects, in which small parties—and new parties—are also discouraged by the constraining effect of a so-called *strong* or well-structured party system. As Sartori (1986: 55) puts it, 'the effects of electoral systems cannot be assessed without assessing at the same time the manipulative properties of the party system as such'. And the manipulative effects in the British party system are very clear: most of the competition revolves around two major parties that compete in the first place to win seats in Westminster, and in the second place to win control of government. When citizens go to the polls, therefore, they are not only choosing among parties—in which case they might give rein to all sorts of expressive preferences—but they are also choosing between potential governments, and this narrows options and excludes other considerations. In this sense, a major reason why British politics is hostile to new or small parties is because these parties don't count in the competition for executive office. It is for this reason that the UK is able to maintain a very strong, well-structured, and simple party system at the national level.

16.3 UNDERSTANDING PARTY SYSTEMS

It is probably fair to say that, within the contemporary literature, the notion of party systems is relatively under-theorized (Wolinetz 2006; Bardi and Mair 2008). Indeed, since the late 1970s, a period in which the literature dealing with the theory and classification of party systems seemed to explode, there has been virtually no further development in thinking on the subject. This waning of scholarly interest in party systems as systems has also led to a decline in the attention being paid to the problems of how party systems hold together, and of what makes them more or less resilient. With less interest being devoted to party systems as such, there is less attention being focused on the understanding of differences between 'strong' and 'weak' party systems. As indicated above, this was the distinction originally used by Sartori in his attempt to reframe Duverger's laws on the impact of electoral systems on party systems.[2] It also coincides closely with Lipset and Rokkan's (1967) distinction between 'frozen' and 'unfrozen' party systems, and with Mainwaring and Scully's (1995) contrast between 'institutionalized' and 'inchoate' party systems. Each

---

[2] See especially Sartori (1968), where he also speaks of 'structured' and 'unstructured' party systems.

of these approaches seeks to grade party systems in terms of their strength or their resistance to change, whether this change be measured in electoral terms, or through the mobilization of new parties, or whatever. Strong party systems are equivalent to 'stable' party systems or 'institutionalized' party systems or 'frozen' party systems; the terms may differ, but the sense is clearly the same.

As Sartori (1976: 43–4) defined it, a party system is the system of interactions between political parties that results from their mutual competition or cooperation. At a minimum, he adds, this requires that the system 'displays properties that do not belong to a separate consideration of its component elements'—that is, the party system is more than the sum of the parties—and that it involves 'bounded, patterned and self-maintaining interdependencies'. For a party system to exist, therefore, there must be more than one party involved and the interactions between the parties must be familiar and reasonably predictable. Parties that exist alongside one another, but that do not interact in any structured or patterned fashion, should better be thought of as a 'set of parties' rather than as a system of parties (Bardi and Mair 2008). Moreover, given the variety of different arenas where parties compete in any given polity—electoral, legislative, and governmental, as well as national, subnational, and supranational—it is also probably misleading to speak of their being just one party system in every polity. Rather, as Dunleavy (2005) has emphasized in the British case, and as Bardi and Mair (2008) have argued more generally, different party systems can coexist with one another and might eventually even compete with one another. This qualification notwithstanding, the focus in this chapter will be on the Westminster party system in particular.

Although scholars have paid relatively scant attention to how a party system might be defined, they have made a considerable effort over the years to distinguish between different types of party system. The most conventional approach is based simply on the number of parties in competition, and the most common distinction involved here, which goes back to Duverger (1954), is that between two-party systems, on the one hand, and multi- (i.e. more than two) party systems, on the other. The British case has always been singled out as the prototypical two-party system, and prior to the emergence of the new democracies of southern and eastern Europe during the 'Third Wave' of democratization, it was also one of the very few genuine two-party systems in the world.

The most important attempt to move away from the idea of classifying party systems on the basis of the number of relevant parties in competition was made by Sartori (1976: 117–323), who combined a measure of the number of parties in a polity with a separate measure of the ideological distance that divided them. Sartori's typology focused explicitly on the interactions between the parties—what he called the 'mechanics' of the system—and he showed how the format of the system, that is, the number of parties, contained 'mechanical predispositions', that is, how it could influence the ideological distance. When lots of parties were in competition, he argued, the ideological distance could become extremely polarized. When fewer parties were in competition, the ideological distance was quite limited. Employing both variables, Sartori went on to identify three distinct types of party system: two-party systems, which were characterized by a limited format and a small ideological distance, and which were typified most clearly by the UK; systems of moderate pluralism, which were characterized by a relatively small number of parties and a limited ideological distance (e.g. Denmark or Germany); and systems of polarized pluralism, which were characterized by a large number of parties and a large ideological distance (e.g. Weimar Germany or post-war Italy).

Sartori also identified a fourth type of party system, which he defined as a 'predominant-party system'. This is a system in which one particular party wins a winning majority of parliamentary seats over a run of three or four elections and hence dominates the polity over an extended period. At the time Sartori was writing, the most obvious examples of such predominant parties were Fianna Fáil in Ireland, the Social Democrats in Sweden, the Liberal Democrats in Japan, and the Congress Party in India. In recent years, however, it has been possible to add the UK to this list. The Conservatives won effective majorities across a run of four elections between 1979 and 1992, and Labour has so far won effective majorities through a run of three elections. Following Sartori's typology, therefore, the British case has moved from being a two-party system to being a predominant-party system, with first the Conservatives at the helm, and then Labour. However, given that this predominant position has transferred from one party to another, a shift which is unprecedented in any other system, and given that it might yet move back again in the future, the British case could also be regarded as an exceptional example of *alternating predominance*. Since this pattern dates back to 1979, it has therefore now endured for almost as long as the more traditional two-party pattern that lasted from 1945 to the mid-1970s.

In the case of predominant-party systems, but also two-party systems and any other competitive party system, the 'core' of the system (Smith 1989) is constituted by the competition for executive office. It is this which structures the party system in the first place, and hence helps it to become institutionalized. Two-party systems, for example, are referred to as such not because only two parties present themselves to the voters—indeed, this is rarely if ever the case—but rather because only two parties matter when it comes to forming a government, be this in a presidential or a parliamentary system. In multi-party systems, by contrast, there are more than two parties that enjoy potential access to executive office. Even within the more complex classification developed by Sartori, it is the competition for office that proves most important. Sartori's moderate pluralism, for example, involves competition between alternative coalition governments, whereas polarized pluralism involves a pattern in which a centre party or parties is more or less permanently in office, and in which one or more extreme parties are permanently excluded from government.

It follows from this that party systems might also be understood not just in terms of some all-embracing classification, within which the question of the numbers of parties in competition obviously plays an important role, but also in terms of contrasting patterns of government formation (Mair 1997: 199–223). Three related criteria are important here. The first concerns the *pattern of alternation in government*, where systems in which there is a regular process of wholesale alternation, in which incumbents are wholly replaced by former non-incumbents, may be separated from those in which alternation is often only partial. Systems in which two alternative parties (or coalitions) alternate with one another, such as the UK, may therefore be distinguished from those in which one or more parties leaves office, while another remains, albeit often with a new coalition partner, such as in Belgium. The second criterion which is relevant here is *familiarity*, with systems in which government is always contested by the same parties or sets of parties being contrasted with those in which patterns of government formation prove more innovative or promiscuous. The third criterion involves the degree of *access of new parties* to executive office. New parties have always found it relatively easy to join innovative government coalitions in the Netherlands, for example. In the UK, by contrast, since at least 1945, no party other than the Conservatives or Labour has ever governed.

Putting these three criteria together allows us to locate party systems along a notional continuum according to the degree to which the structure of competition is open or closed. At one extreme lie the wholly closed systems, where alternation in government is always wholesale, where government formation processes are wholly familiar, and where new or third parties are always excluded. At the other extreme, it is difficult to speak of a party system at all: there is no discernible pattern in how governments alternate, the potential alternatives themselves are unfamiliar and may never have governed before, and access to office is, in principle, open to all. To travel from this latter extreme to the other is therefore to witness the progressive closure of the structure of competition, which is simply another way of saying that the sheer systemness of the party system increases. Party systems as systems are strongest and are most institutionalized when the structure of competition is closed. They are weakest, and almost non-existent, when this structure is wholly open. Following these terms, we can safely state that even though the parties themselves may be weakening, the United Kingdom at Westminster level has one of the strongest party systems in the world.

16.4 BRITAIN: WEAK PARTIES IN A STRONG PARTY SYSTEM

As can be seen from Table 16.1, the electoral domination of the two largest parties has been declining somewhat erratically since the beginning of the 1970s.[3] In 1970, Labour and Conservative together polled almost 90 per cent of the vote, a figure

---

[3] Valuable overviews of the development of the British party system(s) since the 1970s are to be found in the standard work by Webb (2000), and the more recent analyses by Dunleavy (2005) and Lynch and Garner (2005). Finer (1980) remains a classic.

Table 16.1 UK general election results since 1945

	Conservative		Labour		Liberal Democrat		Others		Turnout %
	Vote %	Seats	Vote %	Seats	Vote %	Seats	Vote %	Seats	
1945	39.8	231	48.3	393	9.1	12	2.7	22	72.8
1950	43.5	299	46.1	315	9.1	9	1.3	2	83.9
1951	48.0	321	48.8	295	2.5	6	0.7	3	82.6
1955	49.7	345	46.4	277	2.7	6	1.1	2	76.8
1959	49.4	365	43.8	258	5.9	6	0.9	1	78.7
1964	43.4	304	44.1	317	11.2	9	1.3	0	77.1
1966	41.9	253	47.9	363	8.5	12	1.7	2	75.8
1970	46.4	330	43.0	287	7.5	6	3.1	7	72.0
1974F	37.8	297	37.1	301	19.3	14	5.8	23	78.8
1974O	35.8	277	39.2	319	18.3	13	6.7	26	72.8
1979	43.9	339	37.0	269	13.8	11	5.3	16	76.0
1983	42.4	397	27.6	209	25.4	23	4.6	21	72.7
1987	42.3	376	30.8	229	22.6	22	4.4	23	75.3
1992	41.9	336	34.4	271	17.8	20	5.8	24	77.7
1997	30.7	165	43.3	419	16.8	46	9.3	29	71.5
2001	31.7	166	40.7	412	18.3	52	9.3	28	59.4
2005	32.4	198	35.2	355	22.0	62	10.4	30	61.4

Source: Webb (2000: 6), updated with figures from the *European Journal of Political Research*, Political Data Yearbook.

which crashed dramatically four years later as a result of the sudden growth of the Liberal and Nationalist parties. After that, the big two climbed back up and then fell again, more steadily so after 1992: the two parties polled 76.3 per cent of the vote in that year, falling to 74 per cent in 1997, to 72.4 per cent in 2001, and to just 67.6 per cent—scarcely more than two-thirds—in 2005. Given that turnout also tended to decline across this period, the fall from electoral grace appears even more striking (Figure 16.1). Together, and despite their then ups and downs, the two parties won the votes of an average of some 60 per cent of the electorate during the 1970s. During the 1980s, this figure had fallen to just less than 55 per cent, and fell even further to 43 per cent in 2001 and to 42 per cent in 2005. In electoral terms, at least, these parties are neither strong nor thriving.

The story is very different with respect to representation in Westminster. In the 1970s, the two parties won close to 95 per cent of the seats in parliament, and even allowing for the recent Liberal Democrat successes, they still command just over 85 per cent of the seats. In government, of course, they share 100 per cent control, albeit in alternation with one another (see also below). Within the electorate, in short, and hence on the ground, the two parties have experienced a large-scale erosion of support; within the national institutions, they remain hugely dominant, and it is there that we find the key to the persistence and strength of the traditional British party system (see also Blau 2008).

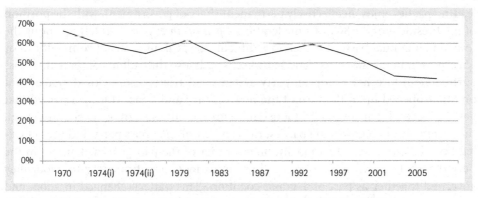

Fig. 16.1 Labour and Conservative share of electorate, 1970–2005

Source: Webb (2000: 6), updated with figures from the *European Journal of Political Research*, Political Data Yearbook.

The United Kingdom currently maintains one of the most closed party systems in Europe. That is, and following the criteria specified above, it is a system in which alternation is exclusively wholesale; in which no new parties have ever gained access to executive office at national level; and in which there has been no change in the governing formulas on offer since 1945. These figures are summarized in Table 16.2, which also includes comparable data for the other long-standing democracies in Europe and which serves to emphasize the outlying position of the UK. The British system is characterized by relatively few changes in the partisan composition of government, in that control of the executive has passed directly from one party to another on only six occasions since 1950—Austria and Switzerland are the only polities to experience fewer such changes of government in this fifty-year period. It is the only system which has never experienced partial alternation in government. In the UK, exceptionally among these democracies, governments always change in their entirety. It is, as noted above, hostile to the entry of new parties into government, and in this it shares the same position as Austria, Luxembourg, and Norway. Indeed, in the British case, the only time we can record a new party in government after 1950, and hence also the only time we can record an innovative government, is in 1951, when the Conservatives first entered office in the period in question. But this is a new experience only in the formal sense of the term, and results from the need to fix the comparative data within a given time period. Even allowing for this, however, the UK again shares the lowest ranking position with Austria and Switzerland, and it is this small group that now constitutes the most closed of Europe's party systems.

Yet even within this group, the United Kingdom is an extreme case.[4] Switzerland is a closed party system by virtue of the so-called magic formula, in which the four

---

[4] One system that is not included here, being measurable from the 1960s on, is Malta, which also maintains a very closed party system, perhaps even more closed than the British system. There are just two parties, Labour and Nationalist, which together account for close to 100 per cent of votes and for all parliamentary seats and which are scarcely ever challenged by third parties. These two parties monopolize government, and compete intensely for the votes of a fully mobilized electorate (turnout regularly exceeds 95 per cent) while alternating with one another on the basis of very small margins of victory (Hirczy de Miño 1995).

leading parties enjoy an effectively permanent share of government, with the position of the President of the Swiss Confederation—*primus inter pares*—rotating among the four on an annual basis. It is therefore difficult to speak in terms of competition for government in the Swiss case, and in this sense it is also difficult to compare the Swiss party system to other European party systems. Austria is also a closed system, but one that opened up at the turn of the new century and hence during a period that lies just beyond that covered by these data. Throughout most of the post-war period, there were just two governing parties, the centre-right People's party and the centre-left Social Democrats. Occasionally, one or other of the pair governed alone (in the period 1966 to 1983); more often, as in 1949 to 1966, and from 1987 to 2000, they governed together as part of a 'grand coalition'. This pattern changed in 2000, and the party system thereby opened somewhat, with the advent to office of a coalition between the People's Party and the far right Freedomites, led by Jörg Haider.[5] This government was re-elected in 2002, and was replaced by a revived version of the grand coalition at the beginning of 2007. In the Austrian case, in short, three parties have been involved in the government formation process, and they have governed in different combinations, leaving the party system more open than might be suggested by the simple figures in Table 16.2.

The contrast between more open and more closed party systems, in which the British case emerges as among the most closed in Europe, also pertains to the relative stability of the systems in question, and that of the individual parties that constitute these systems. In general terms, there are three distinct factors that promote the stabilization of party systems. In the first place, and most obviously, a party system is stabilized when the wider institutional order of which it is part is also stable. This is one of the most obvious lessons that have been learned from the so-called 'neo-institutional' literature. A party system, as Jepperson (1991: 151) notes of any given institution, 'is less likely to be vulnerable to intervention if it is more embedded in a framework of [other] institutions' (see Mair 2001). In the British case, of course, this wider order has proved remarkably resilient, at least prior to the first Blair government (Flinders 2005). Nor have there been substantial changes to the system of elections to Westminster or to other institutional frameworks that might have a direct bearing on how the parties compete. To be sure, and especially since 1997, there have been relevant and substantial changes to levels other than the national—such as the establishment of devolved government in Scotland and Wales, and the adoption of a more proportional voting formula in both these regions as well as for elections to the European Parliament—but these need have little *direct* impact on the competition for government at Westminster, and, as noted above, it is from that arena that the party system derives its identity. I will return to this question later in the chapter.

The second element that stabilizes a party system and helps fix it into place is the cleavage structure on which the parties are based, a feature that is also seen in the

---

[5] Prior to its far-right turn under Haider, the then Freedom Party had once shared government with the Social Democrats, from 1983 to 1987. See Müller (2000).

Table 16.2 Patterns of alternation in government, 1950–2000

	N changes in partisan composition of govt.	Mean level of alternation (%)	N (%) govts. incorporating new parties[a]	N (%) innovative govts.[b]	Total duration of innovative governments (%)[c]
Austria	4	55.0	1 (25.0)	1 (25.0)	16.8
Belgium	20	39.7	4 (20.0)	9 (45.0)	36.2
Denmark	17	60.8	3 (17.6)	8 (47.1)	32.6
Finland	31	35.5	7 (22.6)	21 (67.7)	66.3
Germany	9	61.2	3 (33.3)	8 (88.9)	28.7
Iceland	14	56.6	3 (21.4)	6 (42.9)	30.8
Ireland	13	85.6	3 (23.1)	6 (46.2)	32.7
Italy	31	31.2	3 (9.7)	12 (38.7)	33.8
Luxembourg	8	50.9	1 (12.5)	3 (37.5)	25.5
Netherlands	11	46.1	3 (27.3)	7 (63.6)	37.0
Norway	12	94.9	1 (8.5)	4 (33.3)	9.9
Sweden	9	73.6	3 (33.3)	5 (55.6)	16.4
Switzerland	2	21.5	0 (0)	1 (50.0)	2.0
UK	6	100.0	1 (16.7)	1 (16.7)	6.9

[a] The very first change of government in the period normally implies the advent to office of a new party, even if that party was governing prior to 1950. Since the first change of a Swiss government occurred when the Socialist Party was dropped from the four-party coalition in 1953, hence creating an innovative three-party coalition, while the second (and last) change occurred when the party was brought back on board in 1959, the score in this column is exceptionally 0.

[b] The first new government to hold office in the period is, by definition, one that has never held office (in the period) before, it is then also, by definition, innovative.

[c] Time in office as percentage of fifty-year time span. Innovative governments are deemed innovative until they are either replaced or re-elected, whichever comes sooner.

Sources: Author's calculations from data in Woldendorp, Keman, and Budge (2000) and Müller and Strøm (2000); these data are also discussed in Mair (2007; 2008).

persistence of mass electoral identities. The cleavage structure is not itself part of the party system (Smith 1989), but by helping to close the electoral market it can stabilize the key parties in place, and this may act to stabilize the patterns of party competition and hence the party system. Given the long-enduring class basis of British politics, this was particularly important in the British case, although its weight has clearly reduced in recent years. The decline in party membership, the generally lower levels of party identification, and the erosion of party organizational embeddedness within the wider society have all signalled a loosening of the traditional collective identities that formally sustained both major parties in the UK. Social change has also contributed substantially to the decline in electoral alignments, and this has helped contribute to a more volatile and fragmented electorate, although in this regard the UK, even in relatively recent elections, remains one of the more stable European polities. Finally, class identities will also have been undermined by the cross-party convergence across the mainstream since the late 1990s. The centrist and essentially non-partisan policies pursued by the Blair government in the domestic sphere—and the return to the same centre by a Conservative Party that had failed repeatedly at the polls—have left little room for the clustering of new or even revised competing identities, and hence have done little to maintain two-partism as a meaningful set of political alternatives.[6]

The structure of party competition, which is the third element that stabilizes a party system, and which also helps define the system in the first place, is therefore of crucial importance in the British case. Indeed, it is on this anchor that British two-party politics increasingly depends. Parties in general have performed two crucial functions in the development of democratic systems—a representative function, on the one hand, whereby they give voice to the citizenry, or to their particular constituency among the citizenry; and a procedural or governing function, on the other, whereby, when in office, they assume responsibility for steering the state. Voters have also responded to parties in two ways: through an expressive vote, on the one hand, whereby they signal to the party their preferences in terms of policy, ideology, or culture; and through an instrumental vote, on the other hand, whereby they signal a preference in the choice of governments (Rose and McAllister 1992: 115). Translated into party functions and then into the patterns set by party systems, this connects closely to a distinction once drawn by Rokkan (1970: 93): 'In some countries elections have had the character of an effective choice among alternative teams of governors, in others they have simply served to express segmental loyalties and to ensure the right of each segment to some representation, even if only a single portfolio, in a coalition cabinet'.

One of the great strengths of the British party system over the years has been its capacity to combine both of these functions into one, and hence both types of voting into one. Because of the strong and relatively unidimensional cleavage structure, voting in Britain always had a powerful expressive character. The parties differed in terms of ideology and policy, and they represented relatively distinct groups of voters. In addition, and because of the way competition for executive office was structured, voting also had a highly instrumental character. In choosing the party of cleavage preference, one also chose the government—or at least the party which would ideally win untrammelled control of government. Most British voters were therefore unlikely to be forced to choose between voting expressively and voting instrumentally: two class parties and the prospect of wholesale alternation in government fused both elements together and hence sustained a very stable and coherent party system.

As the class cleavage has waned, however, the anchors of the British party system have come to depend more heavily on the structure of party competition alone. In other words, the two parties continue to dominate the competition for government not because they represent the two most important sets of policy alternatives, or because they offer the principle poles of ideological attraction, but simply because they continue to be seen—by themselves and by others—as the only real options. No

---

[6] A process which Polly Toynbee (*Guardian*, 12 Oct. 2007) has analogized to trends in food and music as 'fusion politics'. See also the insightful essay by Runciman (2006).

other party has governed Britain before, and hence no other party is invested with credibly offering a strategic alternative. No coalition government has ruled Britain since 1945, and hence no other party is seen as being in a position to win office, even in partnership with one or other of the two main players. Each of the two parties may offer an alternative to the other, but there is nothing in living political memory that can offer an alternative to both. In this case, to adapt Schattschneider's famous axiom (1960: 66), it is the definition of the governing alternatives that proves the supreme instrument of power, and hence it is the party system—at least in the governing arena—that protects and promotes the position of the two leading parties, rather than the other way around.

16.5 THE SCOPE FOR PARTY SYSTEM CHANGE

Although the party system in the UK is now so firmly ensconced that it is difficult to see how it might be undermined, a number of factors are beginning to come into play that might well force cracks in its foundations. These factors relate to the three elements identified above as contributing to party system stability—the wider institutional environment, the cleavage structure, and the structure of competition itself—and in each case they challenge one or more of these elements. Let us begin with the structure of competition. In principle, as long as the electoral and parliamentary numbers permit, this should be the most robust component. The governing alternatives are defined by the parties and their leaders, and as Schattschneider (1960: 60–74) also reminds us, it is usually in the interests of those who are at the core of the main political conflict, that is, it is in the interests of *both* sides of the conflict, to prevent that conflict being displaced by another. In other words, neither the Labour nor the Conservative leaders would seem to have any interest in encouraging others to enter the game. Both sides want British politics to continue to revolve around the Conservative–Labour divide. On the other hand, short-term leadership ambitions can often overrule longer-term party interests, and even in the wake of the massive Labour victory in 1997, it seemed that Tony Blair was considering offering a junior coalition partnership to the Liberal Democrats. In the event, the offer came to nothing, although the idea was revived once again when Gordon Brown made overtures to individual Liberal Democrat leaders to join his government when he became Prime Minister in 2007. Had the Liberal Democrats joined Labour in government, and had Britain experienced an innovative coalition cabinet, the structure of competition would clearly have been opened. The same result would follow any future offer by the Conservatives to share power with the Liberal Democrats. Neither of these shifts might be in the long-term party interest of either the Conservatives or Labour, but given that predominance alternates, and that each party has now spent long periods in quite fruitless opposition, a coalition with the Liberal

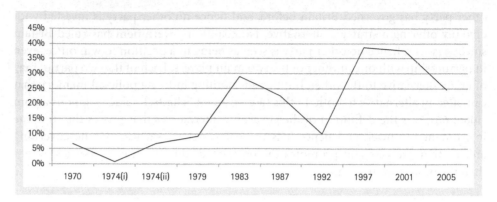

Fig. 16.2 Absolute difference in Labour and Conservative seat shares, 1970–2005

Source: Webb (2000: 6), updated with figures from the *European Journal of Political Research*, Political Data Yearbook.

Democrats might be viewed by either as offering a feasible strategy. This would certainly break open the traditional two-party system, particularly as the system itself is now so dependent on the patterns of competition within the national governing arena.

The second factor which could come into play is the steadily weakening position of the two parties themselves. As noted above, the two parties now command a substantially reduced electorate. Both have lost substantial numbers of members, and no longer enjoy a major presence on the ground. Levels of popular trust in parties have sunk to record lows, and traditional mass politics has become characterized by widespread disengagement. In an effort to maintain their position at the centre of the political stage, the parties are obliged to fight much harder, to compete more vociferously, to manage news more effectively, and to build what have become virtually permanent electoral campaigns. All of this costs a great deal in terms of human, financial, and organizational resources, and it is precisely this which is now lacking due to the parties' declining membership bases and reduced popular legitimacy. The result is that the parties often find themselves turning to large private donors, so risking accusations of private corruption, or drawing money and resources from the state, so risking accusations of public corruption. This weakens the parties further, and eventually risks electoral and parliamentary meltdown. One early indication of this problem is the evident lack of balance in the two-party system itself. This is not only reflected in the shift from alternating government to alternating predominance, but is also to be seen in the widening gap that separates the two parties in Westminster. Whereas election victories in the early post-war decades were measured in scores of seats, contemporary victories are measured in hundreds (Figure 16.2). The party that wins, be it the Conservatives in the 1980s or Labour in the late 1990s, now often wins big, while the party that loses now often loses very badly. Unless this will be countered by a hung parliament, this trend will put further strain on the two-party system, since instead of moving in parallel, the two parties are now skewing ever more widely away from one another.

The third factor that is relevant here is perhaps the most telling, and has been extensively highlighted by Dunleavy (2005). Since the constitutional reforms initiated under the Blair government, party competition has taken a variety of different forms within the different arenas of the UK polity. The Westminster arena itself has remained effectively untouched. But devolution to Scotland and Wales, with the granting of a powerful executive authority to the former; the restoration of devolved government in Northern Ireland; and the adoption of a reformed and much more proportional electoral system for European elections, has led to a fragmentation in forms of party competition. At the European level, for example, where no real structure of competition prevails, in that there is no executive government at stake, the two main parties polled less than 50 per cent of the vote at the most recent election of 2004, with the traditional third-placed party, the Liberal Democrats, being outpolled by the United Kingdom Independence Party. The British Greens also won representation in the European Parliament in 2004, as did Scottish and Welsh Nationalists and three Northern Irish parties. This is a European-level party system—or at least a European-level set of parties—that bears little relation to the balance in the Westminster system. Structures of competition also vary in the devolved parliaments, each of which differs from Westminster in being elected through a form of proportional representation. In Scotland, four main parties compete, with the Scottish National Party emerging as the most successful in the 2007 election, and forming a minority single-party government. Prior to 2007, government in Scotland took the form of a coalition between Labour and the Liberal Democrats. Four parties also compete in Wales, and in 2007 the government was formed by a coalition of Labour and Plaid Cymru, replacing a former coalition of Labour and the Liberal Democrats. In both polities, therefore, there exists a mode of election and a structure of party competition which bears little relation to those of the Westminster system. Taking Britain as a whole, argues Dunleavy (2005: 504), there are now several 'over-lapping party systems with up to five or six parties serious contenders for elected office and five or six parties with distinct ideological positions'. In Northern Ireland, meanwhile, there is a wholly separate party system now dominated by Sinn Fein and the Democratic Unionist Party, currently sharing government together, with absolutely no representation from any of the main mainland parties.[7]

In itself, such fragmentation is not exceptional. In federal and decentralized polities more generally, there are often pronounced incongruities between the party system at the central national level, on the one hand, and those which exist within the devolved or regional level units, on the other (Chhibber and Kollman 2004; Thorlakson 2006; Bardi and Mair 2008). Moreover, in many polities, this multiplicity of party systems can be maintained without the emergence of any serious tensions. In the British case, however, these alternative party systems may yet serve to undermine the traditional resilience and stability of Westminster two-partism. There are two factors involved here. The first is institutional, in that the development of alternative structures of

---

[7] Indeed, this is one of the most evident undemocratic oddities in Europe, with the UK being the only polity where the main contenders for government office refuse to contest elections in one of the parts of the territory they hope to rule.

competition in the different electoral arenas of the UK polity has left the Westminster system in an increasingly isolated and necessarily self-sufficient position. In other words, two-party politics at Westminster is no longer being reinforced or reproduced so widely in the other institutions of the political system, and is no longer being universally sustained by parallel patterns of competition. The two-party system now lacks a robust institutional foundation. The second factor is electoral or behavioural, for, as Dunleavy (2005) emphasizes, the existence of different party systems in the other arenas, the differing range of parties in competition, and the impact of different electoral systems in shaping voter preferences, have now combined to induce other ways of looking at the political contest. As noted above, the stabilization and strength of a party system has much to do with its familiarity and predictability in the eyes of the voters. Politics is defined by the pattern of party competition, and it is defined in a particular and often enduring way. To put it another way, one of the main reasons why British politics continues to be about Labour versus Conservative is that it always has been believed to be about Labour versus Conservative. There has been no other alternative. Now that new party systems and electoral systems have developed beyond Westminster, however, this familiarity and predictability is no longer so self-evident or so constantly reinforced. Voters can now split their ballots between parties, even within the same election; they can think in terms of competing coalitions and rankings of preferences, and they can opt for parties other than the two major protagonists without feeling that their votes will be wasted. In short, voters are now offered new ways of looking at politics. These attitudes are unlikely to remain confined with the individual arenas, and will almost certainly spill over into the Westminster system. In this sense, albeit perhaps quite slowly and unevenly—initially, the impact is likely to be strongest in Scotland and Wales—the behavioural foundations of the two-party system at Westminster might also be undermined.

16.6 CONCLUSION

It has become increasingly evident that the foundation on which the British parties and their system rest has become very vulnerable. The class cleavage has weakened, programmatic differences have become less relevant, and only their status as governors or potential governors remains capable of keeping the major parties in place. In other words, the parties have been reduced to a dependence on their own structure of competition. At the same time, the relevance of this structure of competition is also being challenged on other grounds. The system based on the two major parties and the alternative they offer to one another has now been overtaken in the devolved polities of Scotland and Wales, as well as in the wider European electoral arena. In Northern Ireland, of course, as part of a conscious strategy on the part of both major parties, the mainland British party system never held sway. The result is that the two-party system that the parties both create and depend upon is being isolated ever more effectively within the confines of Westminster, with little purchase beyond the core institutions. It is also an increasingly imbalanced system, with a long stretch of alternating predominance undermining the very equilibrium that helped to make sense of two-party competition.

On the surface, the British party system is one of the oldest, strongest, and most stable of the party systems in Europe. In reality, it has become both vulnerable and brittle, such that even a relatively small shock could lead to a substantial change. Where that shock might come from is more open to question. It might be provoked by further constitutional change, with a strengthening of devolution feeding back into a change in the terms of reference for Westminster elections. It might be provoked by a shift in the strategy of one or other of the leading protagonists, with the loss of majority status leading to the entry of the Liberal Democrats into government as a junior coalition partner. What looks unlikely, however, is that a change will be provoked by a challenge from the ground up, and so far no new party has emerged on the horizon that might credibly mount a sea-changing electoral campaign. Indeed, the last time such a challenge was mounted—when the Social Democrats came close to beating Labour in the mid-1980s—the new party quickly collapsed into an anti-climactic merger with the Liberals. Perhaps the Liberal Democrats themselves might yet mount such a challenge, although they have been waiting outside the corridors of power for so long now it seems difficult to imagine that they might eventually succeed in opening the door and coming in. But the Liberal Democrats may not need to mount a major challenge from the ground. If they can succeed in entering government as a non-threatening junior coalition partner, even with their current electoral following, then they will succeed in changing the game of British politics at its very core. The post-war British party system has always been about the choice between Labour and the Conservatives as the only governing options. Should this set of terms of reference change, everything else will be up for grabs.

References

BARDI, L., and MAIR, P. 2008. 'The Parameters of Party Systems'. *Party Politics*, 14/2: 147–66.

BLAU, A. 2008. 'The Effective Number of Parties at Four Scales: Votes, Seats, Legislative Power and Cabinet Power'. *Party Politics*, 14/2: 167–87.

CHHIBBER, P. K., and KOLLMAN, K. 2004. *The Formation of National Party Systems: Federalism and Party Competition in Canada, Great Britain, India and the United States*. Princeton, NJ: Princeton University Press.

DAALDER, H. 1975. 'Extreme Proportional Representation: The Dutch Experience'. Pp. 223–48 in S. E. Finer (ed.), *Adversary Politics and Electoral Reform*. London: Anthony Wigram.

DUNLEAVY, P. 2005. 'Facing up to Multi-Party Politics: How Partisan Dealignment and PR Voting Have Fundamentally Changed Britain's Party Systems'. *Parliamentary Affairs*, 58/3: 503–32.

DUVERGER, M. 1954. *Political Parties*. London: Methuen.

FINER, S. E. 1980. *The Changing British Party System, 1945–79*. Washington, DC: American Enterprise Institute.

FLINDERS, M. 2005. 'Majoritarian Democracy in Britain'. *West European Politics*, 28/1: 61–93.

GALLAGHER, M., LAVER, M., and MAIR, P. 2005. *Representative Government in Modern Europe: Institutions, Parties, and Governments*, 4th edn. New York: McGraw-Hill.

HIRCZY DE MIÑO, W. 1995. 'Explaining Near-Universal Turnout: The Case of Malta'. *European Journal of Political Research*, 27/2: 255–72.

JEPPERSON, R. L. 1991. 'Institutions, Institutional Effects, and Institutionalization'. Pp. 63–82 in W. W. Powell and P. J. Dimaggio (eds.), *The New Institutionalism in Organizational Analysis*. Chicago: University of Chicago Press.

LIJPHART, A. 1994. *Electoral Systems and Party Systems*. Oxford: Oxford University Press.

LIPSET, S. M., and ROKKAN, S. 1967. 'Introduction'. In S. M. Lipset and S. Rokkan (eds.), *Party Systems and Voter Alignments*. New York: Free Press.

LYNCH, P., and GARNER, R. 2005. 'The Changing Party System'. *Parliamentary Affairs*, 58/3: 533–54.

MAINWARING, S., and SCULLY, T. R. (eds.) 1995. *Building Democratic Institutions: Party Systems in Latin America*. Stanford, Calif.: Stanford University Press.

MAIR, P. 1997. 'Party Systems and Structures of Competition'. Pp. 83–106 in L. LeDuc, R. G. Niemi, and P. Norris (eds.), *Comparing Democracies: Elections and Voting in Comparative Perspective*. London: Sage.

——2001. 'The Freezing Hypothesis: An Evaluation'. Pp. 27–44 in L. Karvonen and S. Kuhnle (eds.), *Party Systems and Voter Alignments Revisited*. London: Routledge.

——2007. 'Party Systems and Alternation in Government, 1950–2000: Innovation and Institutionalisation'. Pp. 135–53 in S. Gloppen and L. Rakner (eds.), *Globalisation and Democratisation: Challenges for Political Parties*. Bergen: Fagbokforlaget.

——2008. 'Electoral Volatility and the Dutch Party System'. *Acta Politica*, 43/2–3: 235–53.

MÜLLER, W. C. 2000. 'Austria: Tight Coalitions and Stable Government'. Pp. 86–125 in W. C. Müller and K. Strøm (eds.), *Coalition Governments in Western Europe*. Oxford: Oxford University Press.

——and STRØM, K. (eds.) 2000. *Coalition Governments in Western Europe*. Oxford: Oxford University Press.

ROKKAN, S. 1970. *Citizens, Elections, Parties*. Oslo: Universitetsforlaget.

ROSE, R., and MCALLISTER, I. 1992. 'Expressive Versus Instrumental Voting'. Pp. 114–40 in D. Kavanagh (ed.), *Electoral Politics*. Oxford: Oxford University Press.

RUNCIMAN, W. G. 2006. 'What Happened to the Labour Party?' *London Review of Books*, 22 June: 17–21.

SARTORI, G. 1968. 'Political Development and Political Engineering'. *Public Policy*, 17: 261–98.

——1976. *Parties and Party Systems: A Framework for Analysis*. Cambridge: Cambridge University Press.

——1986. 'The Influence of Electoral Systems: Faulty Laws or Faulty Method?' Pp. 43–68 in B. Grofman and A. Lijphart (eds.), *Electoral Laws and their Political Consequnces*. New York: Agathon.

SCHATTSCHNEIDER, E. E. 1960. *The Semisovereign People*. New York: Holt, Rinehart and Winston.

SMITH, G. 1989. 'A System Perspective on Party System Change'. *Journal of Theoretical Politics*, 1/3: 349–63.

THORLAKSON, L. 2006. 'Party Systems in Multi-level Contexts'. Pp. 37–52 in D. Hough and C. Jeffery (eds.), *Devolution and Electoral Politics*. Manchester: Manchester University Press.

WEBB, P. D. 2000. *The Modern British Party System*. London: Sage.

WOLDENDORP, J., KEMAN, H., and BUDGE, I. 2000. *Party Government in 43 Societies*. Dordrecht: Kluwer.

WOLINETZ, S. 2006. 'Party Systems and Party System Types'. In R. S. Katz and W. Crotty (eds.), *Handbook on Political Parties*. London: Sage.

SECTION SIX: GOVERNANCE

CHAPTER 17

DELEGATION

MATTHEW FLINDERS

DELEGATION involves the (re)distribution of power within and beyond a political system. It is therefore a central concept within political analysis. Delegation can take many forms but this chapter focuses on *functional* delegation at the national level, which commonly takes the form of arm's-length agencies, independent administrative authorities, non-majoritarian institutions—'fringe bodies, quangos and all that' (Chester 1979). Despite a long-standing history of delegation within the governance of Britain the study of delegation has never formed a central component of political studies. Indeed, delegation provides a classic example of Downs's (1972) 'issue-attention cycle' within twentieth-century British politics. During the 1950s, 1970s, and 1990s delegation and its consequences became the topic of sudden and intense political and scholarly debate but, though still largely unresolved, the attention quickly faded. As a result, very little is known about the institutional structure of the state beyond ministerial departments and our understanding of what might be termed the *politics* of delegation remains arguably narrow and underdeveloped, particularly compared with the analytical frameworks, theories, and methods that have been developed in the United States and Continental Europe. Consequently, this chapter is focused around two core arguments:

1. In order to achieve a more balanced and sophisticated appreciation of the *politics of delegation* (defined as the secondary consequences of delegating functions and most commonly focused on the themes of control, accountability, and patronage) within British political studies there is a need to recognize and challenge the normative and conceptual influences of the Westminster Model as the main ideational framework for the study of British politics and government.
2. The dominant rationality in favour of widespread delegation portrays this process as a neutral element of 'good governance'. In arguing for the

politicization of delegation this chapter seeks to reveal the underlying assumptions and principles beneath this process and thereby locate the logic of delegation firmly within the parameters of public contestation.

The first argument is therefore concerned with illustrating how dominant ideas about the British political system have had direct consequences for: the institutional focus of political studies; the theories and methods used; and the interpretive values held by scholars. The dominant ideational framework acts as a form of intellectual bounded-rationality which has restricted analytical development and awareness. The second argument is more concerned about what is *missing* from the study of delegation within British politics. It suggests that a focus on the consequences of delegation (i.e. the *politics* of delegation) has distracted scholarly attention from a number of macro-political themes and issues of which delegation is a central element. As such, it locates the logic of delegation within critical debates regarding depoliticization, state capacity, and increasing levels of political apathy amongst the public and in so doing appeals for the *politicization* of delegation.

This chapter is divided into four sections and begins by identifying three dominant traditions in the study of delegation and how these traditions affect the deployment of theories and methods. This allows an argument to be sustained regarding what has been distinctive about how delegation has been studied in Britain. In order to explain the origins of this distinctiveness the second section examines the historical disparity between constitutional *theory* and constitutional *practice*. This disparity has led to the construction of a dense labyrinthine tier of delegated governance that has evolved through an ad hoc and unprincipled process of administrative sedimentation and accretion. The third section delayers the British state into its constituent elements in order to distinguish specific forms of delegation and the existence of gradations of autonomy. Having charted the topography of the British state the chapter seeks to present a very specific argument about both the logic of delegation and how delegation has been studied in the fourth and final section. Whereas the vast majority of studies have focused on the secondary consequences of delegation—what I term the *politics* of delegation—in terms of the analysis of accountability frameworks, control mechanisms, and powers of patronage this chapter concludes with a plea for the *politicization* of delegation. This entails a more profound reflection on the *causes* rather than the *effects* of delegation, an awareness that delegation is not a neutral tool of good governance, and a desire to locate delegation back within the sphere of public contestation.

17.1 TRADITIONS IN THE STUDY OF DELEGATION

In order to demonstrate the distinctiveness of a particular object, approach, or method it is necessary to provide some reference points or markers against which judgements concerning idiosyncratic qualities can be made. This section seeks to review the wider literature on delegation and through this process identifies three dominant approaches or traditions in the study of delegation (Table 17.1). Although seeking to specify dominant approaches in this manner risks exaggerating the degree of epistemological and methodological coherency that actually exists, it is possible to argue that a constellation of values and assumptions can be identified in each case.

17.1.1 Tradition 1 (T1)

As Pollack (2002) argues American scholars have played a leading role in terms of the theory and methods employed to understand delegation. Not only does this reflect their long historical tradition of governing through semi-independent agencies and the existence of robust systems of public law and legislative oversight but it also reveals the influence of rational choice theory from the 1970s and the role it played in popularizing specific assumptions, theories, frameworks, and methods. By the end of the nineteenth century the topography of the American state was littered with hybrid bodies which had been established to overcome a number of obstacles faced by traditional public bureaucracies (see Koppell 2003). During the first half of the twentieth century the study of delegation adopted a predominantly case study-based methodology and frequently involved highly normative observations regarding control and accountability (e.g. Guild 1920; Friedrich 1940; Cushman 1941; Seidman 1952).

During the second half of the twentieth century the theories, methods, and assumptions underpinning the study of delegation within this tradition altered significantly under the influence of public choice theory. The view of individuals as rational, self-interested utility maximizers facilitated the construction of models, notably principal–agent theory, from which explanations could be deduced and predictions made of the behaviour of actors (Niskanen 1971). American scholars devised a number of methods to test hypotheses (i.e. a deductive approach) about the existence and influence of presidential and congressional controls over the sphere of delegated governance and it is possible to trace a flow of studies involving gradual theoretical and methodological maturation in response to empirical research (e.g. Weingast and Moran 1983; Moe 1987; Wood 1988; Ferejohn and Shipan 1990).

The 1990s witnessed a further step-change in the theory and study of delegation, as the focus of analysis moved from the behaviour of agents to the delegation stage itself where principals make strategic decisions about the need to delegate and how to balance independence and control. This approach remained rooted in rational choice theory and principal–agent modelling but now sought to gain an improved insight into the conditions under which principals will delegate functions and allocate discretion through the application of a transaction-cost analysis (i.e. the net benefits of delegation minus the administrative and oversight mechanisms established to prevent shirking) (see Huber and Shipan 2000; Epstein and O'Halloran 1999). The transaction-cost approach to delegation was also accompanied by an increased emphasis on the analysis of 'hard' data and a move away from the case study approach

Table 17.1 The study of delegation: three dominant traditions

Tradition	T1	T2	T3
Reluctant epithet	'Americanist'	'Europeanist'	'British'
Normative foundation	Rational Choice & Public Choice Theory Principal–Agent Theory	Principal–Agent Theory (combined in recent work with 'richer' approaches such as historical institutionalism or institutional isomorphism)	Normative Political Theory
Ontology	Foundationalist	Foundationalist	Anti-foundationalist (?)
Epistemology	Positivist	Realist	Critical Realist (?)
Methodology	Quantitative	Blended. Statistical survey evidence complemented by case study analysis and interview material	Qualitative. Descriptive case studies and semi-structured elite interviews. Some superficial survey evidence and analysis
Disciplinary tradition	Scientific management	Public law	History/philosophy
Approach	Deductive	Deductive	Inductive
Thematic priority	Control	Control	Accountability/Patronage
Arguments for	• Provides a rigorous approach with the capacity to analyse a range of variables and their interrelationships across a number of actors. • Tight research design.	• Ability to combine structural-instrumental perspectives with those emphasizing cultural, functional, and external factors.	• Combines a detailed account of the governance of delegation with the capacity to detect the nature and importance of both formal and informal relationships. • This style of approach is accessible to a non-academic audience.
Arguments against	• Quantitative methods and deductive approaches lack the capacity or flexibility to reflect the iterative nature of delegated relationships. • This style of approach is not accessible to a non-academic audience. • Overly concerned with formal mechanisms of delegation and control. • Data driven.	• Underplays political dimensions.	• Little more than 'rich description' or political journalism. • Often insular with little methodological capacity for comparative analysis. • Case studies offer 'low leverage'. • Historically unable to locate delegation within broader socio-political developments. • Polemic anti-delegation stance.
Example text	Epstein & O'Halloran (1999)	Van Thiel (2002)	Barker (1982)
Example journal	*Constitutional Political Economy*	*Public Administration*	*Parliamentary Affairs*

which was increasingly viewed as a 'soft' (i.e. overly descriptive and lacking in theoretical rigour) form of research (see Huber and Shipan 2000: 35).

Overall, T1 consists of five core elements: allegiance to a broadly positivist approach to political analysis; a commitment to deductive logic and reasoning; a preference for quantitative analysis and large-n surveys; a focus on formal mechanisms of delegation and control; and an attempt to discourage normative democratic theory within studies in favour of a more neutral 'scientific' approach to delegation.

17.1.2 Tradition 2 (T2)

Although T2 has borrowed heavily in terms of theory and methods from its colleagues across the Atlantic, it is possible to identify three major differences in terms of its empirical focus, epistemological basis, and research methods. Empirically this approach is targeted on a quite different constitutional terrain as scholars within this school are seeking to understand the nature and consequences of delegation either within or between mainland European parliamentary democracies or inside the evolving architecture of the European Union (EU) (e.g. Huber 2000). In essence, the depth and precision of analysis achieved by T1 reflects the fact that it has been developed and refined around a very specific constitutional configuration and although this may be transferable to other systems with broadly similar characteristics, such as the institutions of the EU (Pollack 2003), its sharpness and precision are dulled by the incorporation of a wider set of dependent variables. Moreover, many of the specific official data-sets that made certain methodological techniques possible in the USA are not available in other countries, thereby closing off certain analytical choices.

Second, although the scholars who operate within this approach are broadly committed to a deductive approach, accept principal–agent theory as a valuable frame of reference, and are skilled in quantitative methodological techniques, they are less committed to the positivist zeal which is implicitly or explicitly ingrained within T1. Although rational choice theory is influential its application is tempered by the need to develop theories and approaches to the study of delegation that can accommodate institutional complexity while also reflecting the existence of informal or 'soft' mechanisms of autonomy and control. For these reasons (and thirdly) T2 is characterized by a pluralistic approach to methodology combining sophisticated large-n quantitative analysis *alongside* a number of detailed case studies and elite interviews, which is frequently missing from studies within T1 and T3 (Van Thiel 2001). Elgie (2006: 211) defends this methodological approach by stating 'there are distinct advantages to an approach that combines large-N and case studies…findings are likely to be more robust if they are based on information from different types of investigation rather than only one. It is the accumulation of evidence across the different types of study that matters as no single piece of information proves or disproves any of the hypotheses advanced'.

Moreover, scholars within this tradition have also sought to accommodate the tension between breadth and depth by adopting a common and reasonably effective research design in which a number of country profiles are located within introductory and concluding sections which provide and then reflect on a thematic or theoretical framework of analysis (see, for example, OECD 2001; Pollitt and Talbot 2004; Pollitt et al. 2004). In this context Thatcher and Stone Sweet's (2003) *The Politics of Delegation*, Bergman, Muller, and Strom's *Delegation and Accountability in Parliamentary Democracies* (2003), and Braun and Gilardi's (2006) *Delegation in Contemporary Democracies* represent arguably the most advanced or state-of-the-art studies within this tradition. What these studies provide is a greater level of theoretical and methodological depth than had hitherto been present within T2. Conceptually and methodologically this involves a willingness to adapt or complement functional principal–agent approaches with 'richer' explanations: 'the politics of delegation calls for analyses going well beyond simple functional logics, involving how actors' interests are defined, policy is made and enforced and the legitimacy of government is conceived' (Thatcher and Stone Sweet 2003: 20). Institutionally this approach frequently utilizes the notion of 'chains of delegation' to fit not only within the complexity of parliamentary democracies but also emerging models of multi-level governance.

The advantage of T2 exists at a number of levels. From a normative perspective it avoids the overly positivist pretensions of T1 while also rejecting the highly normative anti-delegatory thrust of T3. Empirically it offers the capacity to achieve a detailed and consistent comparative analysis that can reveal cross-national patterns and trajectories and methodologically its pluralistic approach sensitizes analysis to the existence of formal and informal modes of control as well as the complex interplay between agency, context, and structure.

17.1.3 Tradition 3 (T3)

T3 is distinctive because is has proved largely resilient to the influence of the positivist and rational choice determined approaches that have been dominant for some time within T1 and increasingly influential in T2. In this regard it imports its own assumptions, theories, and methods into the study of delegation which are in themselves derived from a well-documented 'British approach' to the study of politics that is imbued with an enduring 'anti-scientific' sentiment (Hayward, Barry, and Brown 1999). T3 has therefore been infused from its inception by ambivalence towards explicit deductive modelling and conceived as more of a cooperative enterprise between practitioners and academics characterized by: an inductive approach; little sophisticated modelling or hypothesis generation; a preference for qualitative methodologies (notably case studies and semi-structured elite interviews); a tendency to locate analyses within normative democratic theory; and an insular, almost parochial, focus on delegation in Britain.

The study of delegation aimed to demystify the institutions and processes of politics and government in a manner which eschewed 'scientific' posturing and was suspicious of importing theories or frameworks from overseas. This approach was epitomized in seminal texts like Finer's *Primer of Public Administration* (1950). The

British approach was, and to some degree remains, somewhat complacent, smug even, in that it suggests that the British political tradition with its emphasis on flexibility and 'muddling through' could placate the challenges of modern governance in a way that other countries could not. This atheoretical descriptive-prescriptive normatively laden approach is found within the majority of twentieth-century studies that focused on tracing the changing contours of the state (e.g. Cushman 1941; Bunbury 1944; Anderson 1946; Street 1950; Friedman 1951; Willson 1955; Chester and Willson 1957; Parris 1969; Jordan 1976; Chester 1979), examined the issue of control and coordination (e.g. Robson 1936; Hanson 1954; Schaffer 1956; Hanson 1969), focused on accountability (e.g. Finer 1940; Daniel 1960; Chapman 1973; Barker 1982) and ministerial patronage (e.g. Jennings 1938; Finer 1952; Richards 1963; Goldston 1977; Doig 1978). Of particular significance in terms of distinctiveness is T3's highly normative foundation. Almost without exception scholars within this tradition have adopted an anti-delegation stance and a *critical-descriptive-prescriptive* style of writing in which issues are raised, examples provided, and recommendations for reform made. Quasi-autonomous bodies are interpreted as a 'bad' thing. Indeed the 'quango debate' has been curiously one-sided, which led Hogwood (1995: 227) to conclude 'the only shared value seems to be that quangos are rather shameful'.

Towards the end of the twentieth century two new strands emerged within T3. First, the *politics* of delegation became a central element of the 'governance turn' to the degree that it was suddenly located within a concerted drive towards a more theoretically driven and methodologically rigorous approach. Through its emphasis on central strategic capacity, the steering of complex networks and fuzzy forms of accountability governance theory provided a framework, discourse, and approach to delegation which posed distinctive questions about the 'unravelling' of the state (Hooghe and Marks 2003). The second strand involved a challenge to the normative foundation of T3 and particularly its assumption that delegation and democracy were incompatible. Indeed, according to work within this strand delegation may offer an as yet unrealized democratic potential by opening up new arenas of democratic engagement and mechanisms of accountability (see Marquand and Harden 1999). These two strands merged to promote the study of 'delegated' or 'distributed' public governance which were not new terms for well-trodden issues but marked a distinct approach to the study of delegation based around a number of themes. Central among these was an acceptance of delegation as a central feature of modern state projects, an awareness of the role of delegation above and below the nation state and encouraging a deeper and more analytically refined appreciation of delegation than the overly descriptive and frequently normatively charged accounts that had dominated T3 for much of the twentieth century (e.g. Flinders 2004).

The impact, however, of these two strands should not be exaggerated. Although governance theory marked an influential and highly distinct alteration in understandings of the state, it did not reflect an attempt to promote the theories and methods of studying delegation that were pivotal within T1 and T2. If anything it marked a further shift away from rational choice-inspired deductive modelling and quantitative techniques (e.g. Bevir and Rhodes 2005). Older traditions had been adapted rather than repudiated. Moreover, traditions, styles, and cultures are notoriously difficult to alter and despite the influence of governance theory and the work of proponents advocating a less normative foundation for analyses, the 1980s and 1990s saw the publication of a number of influential scholarly texts that were clearly written and located squarely in the T3 tradition (e.g. Barker 1982; Weir and Hall 1994; Skelcher 1998).

As with any typological endeavour it is possible to suggest that Table 17.1 could and/or should be further refined by the addition of more traditions or sub-strands and yet the aim here has been to put down a number of markers or reference points on an otherwise uncharted conceptual terrain. Clearly not *all* the scholars within a specific geographic terrain are operating within the parameters of a single tradition. The work of a number of scholars with an attachment to the London School of Economics, notably Dunleavy (1991), Dowding (1995), and James (2003), has sought to import elements of T1 and T2 into British political studies. The approach of Dowding (see, for example, 2001) is noteworthy for its explicit critique of T3's qualitative and 'un-scientific' approach. Conversely, several American scholars have recently produced highly influential studies of delegation which appear more closely attached to T3 than T1 in terms of theory and methods (e.g. Carpenter 2001; Koppell 2003). However, at a relatively broad level it is possible to justify a typology exhibiting three specific traditions and propose a relatively clear relationship between them and research in the USA, mainland Europe, and Britain respectively. It is in this vein that Pollack (2002) seeks to draw out a specifically 'Americanist' and 'Europeanist' approach to the study of delegation. The critical element of this threefold typology is its attempt to draw out a particularly distinct British tradition from that of its European neighbours. Moreover, although it is possible to identify a degree of convergence between T1 and T2 as the Europeanists 'learn from the Americanists (again)' (see Pollack 2002), as exemplified in the work of Yesilkagit (2004), T3 appears peculiarly resilient to external influences. The significance of these traditions in the context of this chapter stems from the fact that dominant approaches inculcate certain values, not just regarding the nature of knowledge in the social sciences but specific ideas and beliefs regarding the object of analysis and how it should be studied. In order to understand the distinctive qualities of T3 it is necessary to understand British constitutional history and theory.

17.2 BRITISH CONSTITUTIONAL HISTORY AND THEORY

As the embryonic British state evolved from the sixteenth century onwards, the delegation of functions to Crown-appointed independent boards and commissions represented the dominant administrative model as it offered a number of administrative (continuity, expertise, flexibility, etc.) and political (increased sphere of patronage, limited accountability, etc.) benefits (Willson 1955). However, during the nineteenth century, particularly after the 1832 Reform Act, the changing constitutional relationships between the Crown, executive, and parliament created an environment in which delegation became the topic of intense controversy. The House of Commons felt empowered by the extension of franchise and demanded an increased capacity to scrutinize the state; while the executive sought to reduce the patronage of the Crown and develop a more professional, efficient, and coherent public service. These political objectives dovetailed with the writing of constitutional theorists like Bentham, Mill, and Bagehot who were advocating the benefits of 'single seatedness' through the theory of the ministerial department and convention of individual ministerial department to parliament (see Schaffer 1956).

The very small size of departments at this time—the Home Office consisted of just one chief clerk and ten civil servants—made the idea of enforcing the *personal* responsibility of ministers for all that happened in their department a reasonable notion. The mid to late decades of the nineteenth century were also a period that preceded the development of professional political parties, meaning that MPs were generally independent and the executive's control of the procedures and timetable of the House not yet established. As Maitland's (1908) *Constitutional History of England* recounts, this was a period in which the House of Commons really did 'make or unmake' departments and ministers had few opportunities to engage in blame-games or seek the protection of a dominant and loyal party caucus. The balance of power between the executive and parliament during the second half of the nineteenth century meant that Bagehot's constitutional 'buckle' (i.e. the theory of the ministerial department and the convention of ministerial responsibility) was interpreted as achieving a workable balance between *representative* and *responsible* government (Birch 1964). Consequently, while robust public law systems were being designed and implemented in the USA and within continental European polities, in Britain ministerial responsibility became entrenched as the legitimating foundation of the constitution. Bureaucratic discretion and delegation were legitimate because they existed under the auspices of a ministerial department whose political head could be held to account by the legislature.

However, as Parris's *Constitutional Bureaucracy* (1969) illustrates, although the idea of the ministerial department was upheld in *theory* it was not in *practice*. Irrespective of the political and scholarly discourse promoting the ministerial department, throughout the second half of the nineteenth century functions and responsibilities continued to be delegated to independent boards. As the responsibilities of the state increased during the twentieth century so did the scale of delegation and the degree to which ministerial departments became the visible tip of a huge administrative iceberg of which by far the largest part existed below the visible waterline and parliamentary scrutiny. The First World War led to the creation of ten new ministerial departments and over 160 independent boards and commissions. The Report of the 1918 [Haldane] Committee on the Machinery of Government (Cmd. 9230) canonized the ideal of the ministerial department and stressed that it was highly undesirable to create independent boards beyond the departmental model 'immune from ordinary parliamentary criticism' and beyond direct ministerial control, but apart from restating the constitutional theory the report did very little to dissuade ministers from 'hiving-off' tasks. Street (1950: 158) noted, 'Generally speaking...the sentence of the Haldane Committee was not carried out...in the decades that followed when there was a proliferation of quasi-government bodies'. A fact not overlooked by Jennings (1938: 42):

> The greatest potential danger is neither in the central government nor in local government, but in the numerous independent statutory authorities, which are springing up like mushrooms under recent legislation...[the greatest danger] lies in the development of new governmental institutions outside the system of democratic control.

The Westminster Model (WM) was, therefore, forged during a critical period of constitutional history in which the issue of delegation had come to the fore. As such, it became (and to some degree still remains) the dominant ideational framework that shapes the beliefs, assumptions, and understandings of politicians, officials, scholars, and the public. And yet in many ways right from its nineteenth-century origins it failed to confront the existence and implications of delegation. Instead it sought to design a framework that could mask or obscure the existence of widespread delegation by loosely accommodating it within the parameters of ministerial responsibility. As the size, scale, and complexity of delegation increased, the constitutional elasticity of this doctrine became increasingly stretched and the constitutional fault-lines that had always existed became wider. The core concern of twentieth-century British politico-administrative history has been how to accommodate an increasingly long and complex chain of delegation within a credible model of ministerial responsibility. However one consequence of this failure explicitly to acknowledge the challenge of delegation in the nineteenth century was that the philosophy of British public administration has never provided an explicit set of rules, procedures, or principles concerning the delegation of functions away from ministers. In many ways it could not, as the principles of the British constitution—outlined in political speeches, constitutional conventions, and scholarly textbooks—clearly emphasized the location of functions within ministerial departments. The dominant ideational framework therefore prevented, or at least discouraged, any explicit acknowledgement of the widespread use of delegation. As a result the British state evolved through a piecemeal and largely unplanned process in which departments hived off functions to quasi-autonomous bodies with little references to the broader consequences of this process or the bureaucratic structure as a whole. The sphere of delegated governance simply augmented through a process described as 'incoherent arbitrariness' by Parris (1969) and 'mad empiricism' by Hood, Dunsire, and Thompson (1978).

The role of ideas therefore affected the manner in which delegation was implemented by the state. Delegation took place 'off-stage' in constitutional terms and the obvious fact that the process, although necessary in practical terms, could not easily be accommodated within a theory of the state focused on departments meant that there were few incentives for officials or ministers to overly expose this process to parliamentary or public attention. As a result comprehensive data on the number of delegated public bodies, their role, staff, formal organizational status, etc. has never been maintained within the core executive. The link between constitutional *theory*, the *use* of delegation, and the *study* of delegation therefore takes three forms. First, delegation has not traditionally been a major topic of study when compared to the level and extent of analyses in the USA and Continental Europe. Second, the lack of available or reliable data restricted the capacity of those studies that were conducted as scholars were required to undertake major scoping studies in order to map out the topography of the state and identify certain variable or reference points around which the later analysis could be based. However, the 'incoherent arbitrariness' that these studies tended to uncover, combined with the intensely frustrating and time-consuming nature of research in the field, tended to defeat even the most tenacious scholars and reduce them to making the most tentative conclusions regarding accountability and control. Finally, the WM also cast a more insidious and far-reaching shadow over the study of delegation through its promotion of unrealizable constitutional expectations regarding the personal capacity of ministers plus rather narrow understandings of accountability and legitimacy.

Indeed, the narrative and discourse of the British political tradition became shaped by an understanding of *legitimate* government (i.e. ministerial departments) which not only formed the exception rather than the rule in practical structural terms but also failed to acknowledge that certain constitutional principles could be upheld through a range of methods. When viewed against the *specific* precepts of the WM sponsored bodies could hardly be viewed as anything but 'illegitimate' in democratic terms. The dominance of this model within the study of British politics during the twentieth century explains the normative anti-delegation foundation of the majority of studies ('T3 above). In many ways the WM provided a form of 'bounded rationality' which defined the parameters of 'legitimate' political action, thereby influencing and restricting the interpretation of modes of governance that did not conform to this model. This created an acute problem for forms of public governance which embraced alternative forms of accountability (managerial, market, professional, public, etc.) or legitimacy (expertise, experience, objectivity, professionalism, efficiency). As the chain of delegation grew longer and more complex throughout the twentieth century, so the capacity of the convention of ministerial responsibility to legitimate state action became more tenuous, to the point at which the constitutional elasticity of the convention appeared overstretched. However, dominant ideas, cultures, and traditions—the ideational framework—are notoriously resistant to change; not least because they generally support or serve to legitimate the existing distribution of power within a polity and, as such, those benefiting from this arrangement are unlikely to support change.

During the twentieth century, as the balance of power shifted markedly from the legislature to the executive, the convention of ministerial responsibility became corrupted by the 'negative executive mentality' from a mechanism through which parliament could control the executive and scrutinize the administration to a tool through which the executive could restrict the flow of information to parliament and legitimate the rejection of reforms designed to empower the legislature vis-à-vis the bureaucracy. And yet the convention was always designed to act as a way of balancing the competing demands of operational capacity, principally the ability to focus on the core tasks without distraction, against democratic accountability. As Bagehot (1867/1963: 190–1) emphasized:

> The incessant tyranny of Parliament over the public offices is prevented and can only be prevented by the appointment of a parliamentary head, connected by close ties with the present Ministry and the ruling party in Parliament. The Parliamentary head is a protecting machine.

The issue of proportionality between democratic accountability and economic efficiency is clearly then a long-standing theme within the study and practice of delegation. But before examining this theme in more detail, it is necessary to chart the contours of the state and particularly the topography of delegated governance.

17.3 THE RUSSIAN DOLL MODEL

As the previous section argued, although delegation is very much the rule rather than the exception in British governance, its use has been shrouded by constitutional mythology and an administrative culture that did little to forge coherent and transparent structures. Understanding the structure of the British state in terms of what bodies actually exist, let alone the underlying principles that shape the process of delegation, is incredibly difficult and there exists a considerable lineage of academic, official, and parliamentary inquiries that have largely failed in their attempts to chart the topography of the state with any certainty (for a review see HC 209, 1999).

Unlike in the USA no comprehensive Directory of Government exists, different departments employ different definitions, and the Cabinet Office lacks the capacity proactively to monitor delegation across government or verify departmental returns. The House of Commons' Public Administration Select Committee (PASC) reports have repeatedly called for delegation to be operationalized within a more transparent and coherent governance framework (e.g. HC 209, 1999; HC 367, 2001; HC 165, 2003; see also HL 55, 1998). But these have received little support from an executive that has few incentives to alter the dominant mode of governance. As noted above, the historical lack of available data on the exact number, role, status, management, personnel, functions, etc. of sponsored bodies meant that British scholars had little choice but to either focus on specific case studies or dedicate the greater part of their resources to a mapping exercise. Irrespective of the method employed, research has also been impeded by a cultural predisposition within the civil service that is

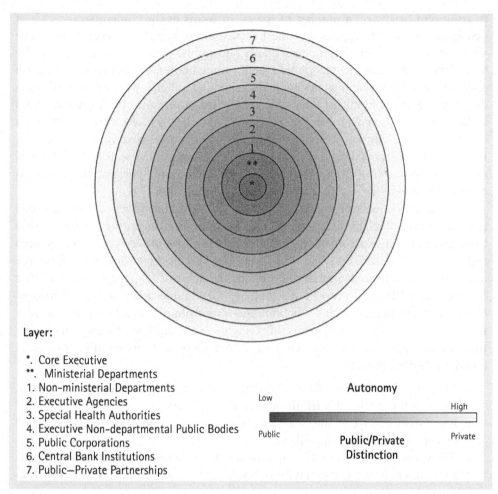

Layer:

*. Core Executive
**. Ministerial Departments
1. Non-ministerial Departments
2. Executive Agencies
3. Special Health Authorities
4. Executive Non-departmental Public Bodies
5. Public Corporations
6. Central Bank Institutions
7. Public–Private Partnerships

Autonomy

Low

High

Public

Public/Private
Distinction

Private

Fig. 17.1 The Russian Doll Model

suspicious of external requests for information, defensive in terms of its default status, and responds to a political dynamic which seeks to keep the 'quango count down'. However, Flinders (2008) provides the information through which it is possible to delayer the British state into its component levels based upon organizational forms that are each designed to enjoy a different level or degree of delegation. The British state is, therefore, best characterized as a series of nested layers, like a Russian doll, with relatively small departments at the core and a series of fairly distinct layers working outwards.

The Russian Doll Model (RDM) is an organizing perspective that provides a framework through which a complex set of interrelated issues or variables can be observed and to some degree understood. Although it is sufficient here to note the existence of these layers, instead of providing a detailed account of each one's specific characteristics (legal, funding, political, constitutional, etc.), it is necessary to comment briefly on a number of issues. In terms of the contemporary *scale* of delegation the RDM suggests that the British state is in fact a delegated state. The six layers between ministerial departments and public–private partnerships on the boundary of the state include 339 delegated public bodies, employing over 800,000 staff with a combined annual budget in excess of £80 billion—75 per cent of which is direct government funding (Table 17.2). Delegated governance therefore consumes at least one-third, and probably nearer a half (see below), of central government expenditure and employs around three-quarters of central government personnel. However, the degree of delegation is much higher in some policy sectors. For example, over 80 per cent of the Department for Culture, Media and Sport's annual budget is disseminated to its 'family' of sixty-three sponsored bodies.

One of the benefits of the Russian Doll Model is that it reflects, on a broad basis, a number of relatively uncontroversial assumptions concerning the relationship between organizational form and autonomy. It also allows observers to track 'quango drift' (Greve, Flinders, and Van Thiel 1999) as specific functions move from the centre outwards through a variety of organizational forms (e.g. the Forensic Science Service). The RDM also reveals the existence of 'double-delegation' as sponsored bodies delegate further specific functions and responsibilities to other bodies or enter into complex public–private partnerships (Figure 17.2). Another advantage of viewing the state as a series of concentric circles is that it allows us to map out jurisdictional and definitional boundaries:

1. The official British (or minimalist) definition of a 'quango' refers to just Layer 4, whereas the maximalist definition includes all layers.
2. Employees in Layers 1 and 2 are civil servants and appointments are regulated by the Civil Service Commission.
3. The Commissioner for Public Appointments regulates *ministerial* appointments to bodies in layers 3, 4, 5, and those bodies in layer 7 that are classified as within the public sector.

Table 17.2 Delegated governance, 2007

Layer	Number	Staff	Government funding, £m	Total gross annual expd., £m
1. Non-ministerial Departments	29	160,928	1,958	2,383
2. Executive Agencies	75	283,648	18,136	25,676
3. Special Health Authorities	12	17,951	561	2,662
4. Executive NDPBs	199	93,416	31,667	36,751
5. Public Corporations	23	270,814	4,007	19,412
6. Independent Central Bank	1	2,000	0	230
Totals	339	828,757	56,329	87,114

Note: Not including the devolved administrations.

4. The annual publication *Public Bodies* contains information on layers 3, 4, 5,

5. The Cabinet Office's guidelines on openness relate to layers 3, 4, 5.

There are, however, three reasons why the RDM risks imposing a false sense of rationality and coherence on an innately incoherent and irrational structure. First, the above suggestion that the sphere of delegated governance is significantly larger than that indicated by Table 17.2 stems from the fact that many delegated public bodies 'simply exist' without any formal organizational status and are therefore not included within the various publications and databases from which this table was constructed. This would include organizations like the Carbon Trust, Energy Savings Trust, Adventure Activities Licensing Authority, and Social Care Institute for Excellence that are sponsored by a ministerial department, receive public funding, and fulfil a public task and yet for reasons that remain unclear they exist and operate 'off-stage' in constitutional terms. The RDM therefore fails to reflect the administrative hinterland beyond the formal layers of delegation. It was an awareness of this issue that led PASC to recommend in July 2003 that the Cabinet Office undertake a fundamental review of *all* sponsored bodies and particularly those bodies operating beyond the formal classifications as ' "other bodies" in departmental corners, no doubt doing good and necessary work, but not very transparent and accountable' (HC 165, 2003: para. 36). The government accepted this recommendation but over four years later the review remains unpublished.

Another issue with the RDM is that it veils the existence of great confusion within the layers in terms of functional distribution. There is no clear logic in terms of why certain functions have been delegated to Layer 1 in some situations but Layer 4 in others. The official review of Next Steps agencies in 2002 could find no rationale within the distribution of tasks to Layers 2, 3, and 4; while research into PPPs has highlighted a lack of consistency across departments in terms of which services are put out to tender (Flinders 2005). There is also little consistency in terms of which functions are delegated to Layers 1–7 as opposed to being established as independent parliamentary bodies or independent professional self-regulatory bodies. The government's plans to establish the House of Lords Appointments Commission, for example, as an independent parliamentary body modelled on the Electoral Commission appears inconsistent with its rejection of parliamentary demands that the Office of the Commissioner for Public Appointments and the Judicial Appointments Commission also be designated *parliamentary* rather than *governmental* bodies.

Finally, the RDM suggests a hierarchical pattern in which all public bodies operate within the parameters of a ministerial department and can therefore be captured, however precariously, within the legitimating confines of ministerial responsibility. However in some cases delegation is based within a framework of *multiple* (as opposed to *individual*) ministerial responsibility. The Office of Communication (Layer 5) and Design Council (Layer 4), for example, operate under the *joint* responsibility of the Department for Trade and Industry and Department for Culture, Media and Sport.

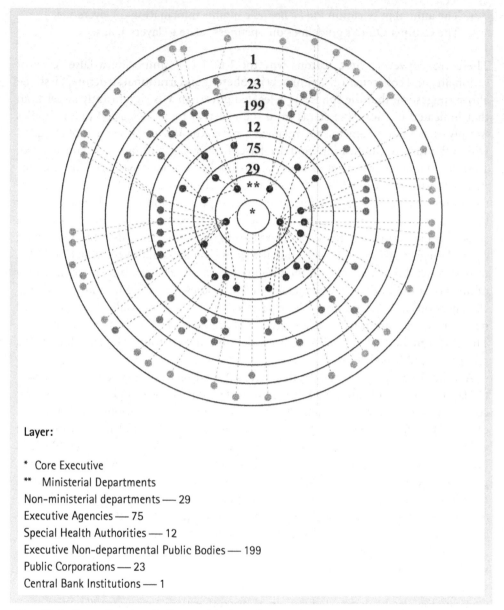

Layer:

*   Core Executive
**   Ministerial Departments
Non-ministerial departments — 29
Executive Agencies — 75
Special Health Authorities — 12
Executive Non-departmental Public Bodies — 199
Public Corporations — 23
Central Bank Institutions — 1

Fig. 17.2 From Russian Doll to spider's web

The sphere of delegated governance is, in short, far more complex than the RDM suggests and might more appropriately be described as involving a series of vertical and horizontal linkages resembling a spider's web (see Figure 17.2). Nevertheless, the RDM does demonstrate the existence of gradations of delegation each of which raise specific questions about control, accountability, and patronage—in short, the *politics* of delegation. So far this chapter has argued that the study of delegation within British political studies is characterized by a number of features which both set it apart from its American and Continental European counterparts and have their origins in a very specific and critical debate that took place concerning delegation in the nineteenth century. The outcome of this debate was a normative theory of the state that was tied to a specific organizational form which did much to both conceal the continuing and widespread use of delegation as a central tool of statecraft and establish an anti-delegation perspective within political analysis. Consequently many debates concerning delegation are couched in crude, over-simplistic, and frequently false terms. However instead of seeking to review and revise a number of relatively well-trodden debates about delegation in the British context (accountability, patronage, control, etc.) the next section focuses on what is missing from the study of delegation and argues for a shift in the analytical focus of British scholars away from the *politics* of delegation and towards the *politicization* of delegation.

17.4 THE POLITICIZATION OF DELEGATION

The modern state could not function without delegation. The delegation of functions and responsibilities to sponsored bodies operating with a significant degree of autonomy arguably empowers governments to address a wide range of social issues simultaneously without having to be involved with the minutiae of day-to-day socio-political interactions. Delegation therefore provides a structural and esoteric capacity beyond the cognitive and physical limits of politicians. However, it also creates a number of political dilemmas concerning internal control, external accountability, and appointments. In terms of understanding these dilemmas the tradition that has been prevalent within British political studies—one that tends to eschew explicit theoretical frameworks; adopts a highly normative foundational position; and remains tightly wedded to the precepts of the WM (Section 17.1)—has arguably led to rather simplistic, crude, and often polemical interpretations becoming prevalent. This chapter has sought to tease apart this issue by illustrating the influence of the WM in terms of theories and methods (17.2), and the delayering the British state in order to reveal the scale and complexity of delegated governance (17.3). However, in focusing on the *politics* of delegation, it is possible to suggest that scholars have overlooked the existence of a number of broader macro-political themes which, taken together, demonstrate the need for the *politicization* of delegation. The logic of delegation itself, rather than its consequences, needs to be the focus of critical political analysis in order to push the process back within the sphere of public contestation. The logic of delegation appears almost beyond dispute: it has become an 'essentially *un*contested' concept—to invert Gallie's (1956) phrase—within contemporary conceptions of good governance. Global institutions, such as the International Monetary Fund and World Bank, advocate large-scale delegation and hiving-off as a central aspect of building state capacity, maximizing efficiency, and ensuring market confidence. The 'new governance agenda' within the EU is also tied to the creation of a number of quasi-autonomous agencies (see Thatcher 2002). The logic of delegation has become so embedded that Marcussen (2006) argues in some policy areas it has become 'apoliticized', as anyone challenging the notion risks being immediately labelled irrational. And yet the benefits of delegation remain far from uncontested. The work of Van Thiel (2004), James (2003), and McNamara (2002), to provide just a few examples, questions the link between delegation and superior economic outcomes. This leads Peters and Pierre (2004) to suggest that the 'Faustian bargain'—a decline in democratic clarity in return for economic benefits— is delivering very little.

Consequently, the *politicization* of delegation emphasizes the existence of contingency. National politicians do enjoy choices in relation to *whether* to delegate specific services, in *which* form delegation should take place, *how* a proportionate balance should be achieved between independence and control, *when* to intervene, and at *what point* to reinstitute direct ministerial control. These choices take on added emphasis when it is appreciated that delegation creates its own epistemic momentum through a process of deskilling. As the number of functions and responsibilities delegated to sponsored bodies and PPPs operating at the periphery of the state increase, so the latter undermines its own intellectual capacity; thereby creating information asymmetries that weaken its bargaining position, reduce its holistic knowledge base and institutional memory, which, taken together, further decreases confidence in the direct delivery capacity of the state. As more functions 'drift' across the spectrum of autonomy and PPPs become a mainstream governance tool rather than an instrument of last resort for failing services, the intellectual evisceration of the state may become acute. And yet there has been very little reasoned debate on this process or whether a residual number of core functions and responsibilities should be maintained beyond the grasp of delegatory forces (see Brown 2003). Delegation is therefore linked to a loss of confidence in politics, the state, and the potential for collective action; as well as the decline of the public sphere (Marquand 2004) and concern regarding the development of 'post-democracy' (Crouch 2004).

Furthermore, although Ranciere (1995: 19) suggests that 'Depoliticization is the oldest task of politics', the belief that numerous functions and responsibilities should be delegated well beyond the direct control of elected politicians has become particularly influential since the election of Labour in 1997 (Burnham 2001; Buller and Flinders 2005):

> What governs our approach is a clear desire to place power where it should be: increasingly not with politicians, but with those best fitted in different ways to deploy it. This depoliticizing of key decision-making is a vital element in bringing power closer to the people.   (Secretary of State for Constitutional Affairs 2003)

Depoliticization, however, represents an acutely pessimistic response to the challenges of modern British governance. It delegates power not to the people, through transparent structures and procedures, but creates arenas of fugitive power operating largely beyond the realm of political deliberation. The tactics and tools of depoliticization conspire to narrow the realm of conventional politics while locating the drivers for this process beyond the control of national politicians (Buller and Flinders 2006). Hay (2007) therefore isolates depoliticization as a key variable in explaining contemporary levels of public disenchantment with politics. To call for the *politicization* of delegation is therefore to work within the parameters of Habermas's (1996: 62) work on depoliticization and the public sphere: 'the depoliticization of the mass of the population and the decline of the public realm as a political institution are components of a system of domination that tends to exclude practical questions from public discussion'. It is repositioning the existence of *choice* regarding delegation, and thereby a more optimistic view on the potentialities of collective action, within the sphere of public contestation with which this chapter has been principally concerned.

REFERENCES

ANDERSON, J. 1946. 'The Machinery of Government'. *Public Administration*, 24: 147–56.

BAGEHOT, W. 1867/1963. *The English Constitution*. London: Penguin.

BARKER, A. (ed). 1982. *Quangos in Britain*. London: Macmillan.

BERGMAN, T., MULLER, W., and STROM, K. 2003. *Delegation and Accountability in Parliamentary Democracies*. Oxford: Oxford University Press.

BEVIR, M., and RHODES, R. 2005. *Governance Stories*. London: Routledge.

BIRCH, A. 1964. *Representative and Responsible Government*. London: Unwin.

BRAUN, D., and GILARDI, F. (eds.) 2006. *Delegation in Contemporary Democracies*. London: Routledge.

BROWN, G. 2003. *A Modern Agenda for Prosperity and Social Reform*. London: Cass Business School.

BULLER, J., and FLINDERS, M. 2005. 'The Domestic Origins of Depoliticization'. *British Journal of Politics and International Relations*, 7: 526–44.

——— 2006. 'Depoliticization: Principles, Tactics and Tools'. *British Politics*, 1: 293–319.

BUNBURY, H. 1944. 'The Public Corporation'. *Public Administration*, 22: 137–42.

BURNHAM, P. 2001. 'New Labour and the Politics of Depoliticization'. *British Journal of Politics and International Relations*, 3: 127–49.

CARPENTER, D. 2001. *The Forging of Bureaucratic Autonomy*. Princeton, NJ: Princeton University Press.

CHAPMAN, R. 1973. 'The Vehicle and General Affair'. *Public Administration*, 51: 273–90.

CHESTER, D., and WILLSON, F. M. G. 1957. *The Organization of British Central Government 1914–1956*. London: Allen and Unwin.

CHESTER, N. 1979. 'Fringe Bodies, Quangos and All That'. *Public Administration*, 57: 51–5.

CMD. 9230. 1918. *Report of the Machinery of Government Committee*. London: HMSO.

CROUCH, C. 2004. *Post-Democracy*. Cambridge: Polity.

CUSHMAN, R. 1941. *The Independent Regulatory Commissions*. London: Oxford University Press.

DANIEL, G. 1960. 'Public Accountability of the Nationalised Industries'. *Public Administration*, 38: 27–35.

DOIG, A. 1978. 'Public Bodies and Ministerial Patronage'. *Parliamentary Affairs*, 30: 86–94.

DOWDING, K. 1995. *The Civil Service*. London: Routledge.

——2001. 'There Must be End to Confusion'. *British Journal of Politics and International Relations*, 49: 89–105.

DOWNS, A. 1972. 'Up and Down with Ecology: The Issue-Attention Cycle'. *Public Interest*, 28: 38–50.

DUNLEAVY, P. 1991. *Democracy, Bureaucracy and Public Choice*. Hemel Hempstead: Harvester Wheatsheaf.

ELGIE, R. 2006. 'Why Do Governments Delegate Authority to Quasi-Autonomous Agencies?' *Governance*, 19: 207–27.

EPSTEIN, D., and O'HALLORAN, S. 1999. *Delegating Powers*. New York: Cambridge University Press.

FEREJOHN, J., and SHIPAN, C. 1990. 'Congressional Influence on the Bureaucracy'. *Journal of Law, Economics and Organization*, 6: 1–19.

FINER, H. 1940. 'Administrative Responsibility in Democratic Government'. *Public Administration Review*, 1: 335–50.

FINER, S. 1950. *A Primer of Public Administration*. London: Muller.

——1952. 'Patronage and the Public Service'. *Public Administration*, 30: 329–60.

FLINDERS, M. 2004. 'Distributed Public Governance in Britain'. *Public Administration*, 82: 883–909.

——2005. 'The Politics of Public–Private Partnerships'. *British Journal of Politics and International Relations*, 7: 543–67.

——2008. *Delegated Governance and the British State: Walking without Order*. Oxford: Oxford University Press.

FRIEDMAN, W. 1951. 'The Legal Status and Organization of the Public Corporation'. *Law and Contemporary Problems*, 16: 576–93.

FRIEDRICH, C. 1940. 'Public Policy and the Nature of Administrative Responsibility'. *Public Administration Review*, 1: 3–24.

GALLIE, W. B. 1956. 'Essentially Contested Concepts'. *Proceedings of the Aristotelian Society*, 56: 167–98.

GOLDSTON, R. 1977. 'Patronage in British Government'. *Parliamentary Affairs*, 30: 80–97.

GREVE, C., FLINDERS, M., and VAN THIEL, S. 1999. 'Quangos: What's in a Name?' *Governance*, 12: 129–47.

GUILD, F. 1920. 'Special Municipal Corporation'. *American Political Science Review*, 14: 286–91.

HABERMAS, J. 1996. 'The Scientization of Politics and Public Opinion'. In W. Outhwaite (ed.), *The Habermas Reader*. London: Polity.

HANSON, A. 1954. 'Labour and the Public Corporation'. *Public Administration*, 32: 203–9.

——1969. 'Ministers and Boards'. *Public Administration*, 47: 65–75.

HAY, C. 2007. *Why We Hate Politics*. Cambridge: Polity.

HAYWARD, J., BARRY, B., and BROWN, A. (eds.) 1999. *The British Study of Politics in the Twentieth Century*. Oxford: Oxford University Press.

HC 165. 2003. *Government by Appointment*. Fourth Report of the Public Administration Select Committee. Session 2002–3.

——209. 1999. *Quangos*. Sixth Report of the Select Committee on Public Administration. Session 1998–9.

——367. 2001. *Mapping the Quango State*. Fifth Report of the Select Committee on Public Administration. Session 2000–1.

HL 55. 1998. Report of the Public Service Committee. Session 1997–8.

HOGWOOD, B. 1995. 'The Growth of Quangos'. In F. Ridley and D. Wilson (eds.), *The Quango Debate*. Oxford: Oxford University Press.

HOOD, C., DUNSIRE, A., and THOMPSON, S. 1978. 'So You Think You Know What Government Departments Are...?' *Public Administration Bulletin*, 27: 20–32.

HOOGHE, L., and MARKS, G. 2003. 'Unravelling the Central State, but How?' *American Political Science Review*, 97: 233–43.

HUBER, J. 2000. 'Delegation to Civil Servants in Parliamentary Democracies'. *European Journal of Political Research*, 37: 397–413.

—— and SHIPAN, C. 2000. 'The Costs of Control'. *Legislative Studies Quarterly*, 25: 25–52.

JAMES, O. 2003. *The Executive Agency Revolution in Whitehall*. Basingstoke: Palgrave.

JENNINGS, I. 1938. 'Corruption and the Public Service'. *Public Administration*, 9: 31–46.

JORDAN, G. 1976. 'Hiving Off and Departmental Agencies'. *Public Administration Bulletin*, 21: 37–52.

KOPPELL, J. 2003. *The Politics of Quasi-Government*. Cambridge: Cambridge University Press.

MCNAMARA, K. 2002. 'Rational Fictions'. Pp. 47–77 in M. Thatcher and A. Stone Sweet (eds.), *The Politics of Delegation: West European Politics*, 25: 47–77.

MAITLAND, F. 1908. *Constitutional History of England*. Cambridge: Cambridge University Press.

MARCUSSEN, M. 2006. 'Institutional Transformation?' In T. Christensen and P. Laegried (eds.), *Autonomy and Regulation*. London: Edward Elgar.

MARQUAND, D. 2004. *Decline of the Public*. Cambridge: Polity.

—— and HARDEN, I. 1999. *How to Make Quangos Democratic*. London: Charter 88.

MOE, T. 1987. 'An Assessment of the Positive Theory of Congressional Dominance'. *Legislative Studies Quarterly*, 12: 475–520.

NISKANEN, W. 1971. *Bureaucracy and Representative Government*. Chicago: Aldine.

OECD 2001. *Distributed Public Governance*. London: OECD.

PARRIS, H. 1969. *Constitutional Bureaucracy*. London: Allen and Unwin.

PETERS, G., and PIERRE, J. 2004. 'Multi-level Governance and Democracy: A Faustian Bargain'. Pp. 75–90 in I. Bache and M. Flinders (eds.), *Multi-level Governance*. Oxford: Oxford University Press.

POLLACK, M. 2002. 'Learning from the Americanists (Again)'. *West European Politics*, 25: 200–19.

—— 2003. *The Engines of European Integration*. Oxford: Oxford University Press.

POLLITT, C., and TALBOT, C. (eds.) 2004. *Unbundled Government*. London: Taylor and Francis.

—— —— SMULLEN, A., and CAULFIELD, J. (eds.) 2004. *Agencies*. Basingstoke: Palgrave.

RANCIERE, J. 1995. *On the Shores of Politics*. London: Verso.

RICHARDS, P. 1963. *Patronage in British Government*. London: Allen and Unwin.

ROBSON, W. 1936. 'The Public Service'. *Political Quarterly*, 7: 179–93.

SCHAFFER, B. 1956. 'A Consideration of Non-Ministerial Organization in Central Government'. Unpublished Ph.D., London University.

SECRETARY OF STATE FOR CONSTITUTIONAL AFFAIRS 2003. Speech to the Institute for Public Policy Research, London.

SEIDMAN, H. 1952. 'The Theory of the Autonomous Government Corporation'. *Public Administration Review*, 12: 89–96.

SKELCHER, C. 1998. *The Appointed State*. Buckingham: Oxford University Press.

STREET, A. 1950. 'Quasi-Government Bodies since 1918'. In G. Campion (ed.), *British Government since 1918*. London: George Allen.

THATCHER, M. 2002. 'Regulation after Delegation'. *Journal of European Public Policy*, 9: 954–9.

—— and STONE SWEET, A. (eds.) 2003. *The Politics of Delegation*. London: Frank Cass.

Van Thiel, S. 2001. *Quangos: Trends, Causes, Consequences*. London: Ashgate.

—— 2004. 'Why Politicians Prefer Quasi-Autonomous Organizations'. *Journal of Theoretical Politics*, 16: 175–201.

Weingast, B., and Moran, M. 1983. 'Bureaucratic Discretion or Congressional Control?' *Journal of Political Economy*, 91: 765–800.

Weir, S., and Hall, W. 1994. *EGO-Trip*. London: Charter 88.

Willson, F. 1955. 'Ministries and Boards'. *Public Administration*, 33: 43–58.

Wood, B. 1988. 'Principals, Bureaucrats and Responsiveness in Clean Air Enforcement'. *American Political Science Review*, 82: 213–34.

Yesilkagit, K. 2004. 'Bureaucratic Autonomy, Organizational Culture and Habituation'. *Administration and Society*, 36: 528–52.

CHAPTER 18

REGULATION

MICHAEL MORAN

18.1 INTRODUCTION: 'REGULATION' AND 'BRITISH' REGULATION

IN the study and the practice of British politics 'regulation' is a comparatively new term, but it describes a long-established activity. This very novelty, we shall see, is itself illuminating about the nature of regulation in modern British politics. 'Regulation' is defined in many ways, but at its core lies the notion that social behaviour is governed by rules administered by an institution or institutions (Ogus 1994 for discussion). We thus distinguish those areas of social life that are regulated from those that are the subject of spontaneous social coordination (as in some market exchanges, private recreations, and some personal relationships.) Like many definitions this is serviceable but does not bear too close an interrogation. The notion that the market, for instance, is an arena of spontaneous social organization is hard to sustain; on the contrary, all the evidence is that functioning markets depend on the creation of a framework of rules—of a system of regulation, in other words. But identifying regulation in the terms defined here immediately alerts us to regulation and its variations, and helps us begin to understand the peculiarities of 'British' regulation; for different modes of regulation indeed do differentiate how different markets have been ruled in Britain at different times.

Two important kinds of variation in regulation are immediately obvious: in the nature of the rules, and in the nature of the power wielded by regulating institutions. Much regulation in British politics was not recognized as such because it involved

I am grateful for the valuable comments of two anonymous referees, and of the editors, on my first draft of this contribution.

rules that were not legally enforceable—thus the rules often looked like spontaneous manifestations of social coordination. The regulating institutions were often private bodies, like trade associations, clubs, or corporations. If we think about this comparatively we are, in other words, looking at a distinctive British approach: distinctive from the reliance on law that has characterized the United States; and on formally organized public institutions that characterized the national systems that pioneered the foundation of what has now become the European Union.

These historical forms in Britain were commonly labelled 'self-regulation'. Self-regulation legitimized the exercise of considerable social power by private interests. A legitimizing ideology pictured self-regulation as superior to modes of regulation that relied on the creation of legally enforceable rules administered by a public body and backed by legal sanctions. The legitimizing ideology pictured self-regulation as more flexible in the face of problems, and as more responsive and capable of swift adaptation. The ideology sanctioned the exercise of power by private interests, notably in important markets, especially in the wake of the rise of a democratic, interventionist state in Britain.

One way to think of this historically established system is as a variant of the strategy of 'depoliticization' explored by a number of scholars (for instance Burnham 2001; Buller and Flinders 2005; Hay 2007.) But while these scholars picture depoliticization as a response to a great crisis of Keynesian political economy, my argument is that alongside the 'depoliticization' of the 1980s and 1990s there was simultaneously occurring a process by which hitherto depoliticized domains were being invaded by partisan political argument and by high politics. The case studies below of financial regulation, the government of education, and the government of medicine are offered as exemplars of this.

This new politicization is a product of the crisis of the old dominant system of self-regulation. For nearly a generation this dominant system of regulation has been in turmoil and retreat, and is being replaced by systems of regulation that rely on the command of law and on enforcement by public bodies.

The chapter is about that crisis in the historical system: about the extent to which it has been replaced by arrangements based more on the command of law; and about the limits that are being experienced by this command system. I show at the end that the turn to command is in key respects both unexpected and dysfunctional; it arises from the unavailing struggle of social actors to cope with crisis. A key implication of the chapter is that agency has mattered less in these developments than accident, unanticipated consequences, and blind fate.

18.2 The Crisis of Self-regulation

Although there is a prehistory of regulation in Britain going back at least to Tudor times (Ogus 1992), the dominant historical pattern of regulation in the United

Kingdom is fundamentally the product of the critical timing of the development of industrialism, on the one hand, and of democracy on the other. Britain, famously, was the first industrial society, and thus the first society that had to face the problems of how to cope with the consequences of fully developed industrialism. The timing of the industrial revolution meant that these problems were coped with in a society that had neither a tradition of extensive state intervention in economic life, nor a democratic political system or culture. The kind of regulation that became commonplace in the twentieth century, and that was pioneered in the greatest modern 'regulatory state', the United States—one where powerful statutory agencies regulated economic interests under the pressures of democratic politics—was therefore in an almost literal sense unthinkable in Britain.

The coincidence helps account for the particular shape of the British regulatory system. The middle decades of the nineteenth century, when society had to cope with the full brunt of industrialism, was the key epoch. There was laid down a pattern of industrial, financial, and professional regulation that endured for much of the twentieth century. It had three features. First, in the case of industrial regulation it was marked by a distinctively cooperative style, which emphasized the importance of implementing any statutory based rules with the cooperation of those affected, especially when they were businesses (Carson 1970; 1974; 1979; Ashby and Anderson 1981). Second, in critical areas of economic regulation the state shied away from any direct involvement at all, relying on the self-policing of markets. The most important instances of this were in the financial markets, notably those in the City of London, and in the new financial professions such as accounting and auditing that developed to service these markets. The predominance of self-policing in the financial markets reflected the longer-established power position of the City of London, dating back even before the rise of industrialism, to the end of the seventeenth century (Moran 1986; 1991). Third, the nineteenth century saw a wave of innovation in professional regulation, often in professions like medicine whose emergence reflected the elaboration of the division of labour under industrialism (Perkin 1990). The predominant form of regulation in these professions, even when there was some statutory framework, emphasized self-policing. In a case like medicine, for instance, the state established a framework in the 1858 Medical Act, endowing the General Medical Council, as it became, with powers to govern the profession, but for a century it simply took no interest in how those powers were exercised (Berlant 1975).

These three features, though not unknown in other industrial societies, nevertheless in combination marked Britain out among the leading capitalist nations. The stress on cooperative, consensual regulation in which the adversarial rules of law and the courts were marginalized, marked out the United Kingdom from the United States, where there developed a culture of high legalistic adversarialism in regulatory relationships (Vogel 1986; Kagan 2001; Kagan and Axelrad 2001). In the larger capitalist nations of Europe the tradition of cooperative regulation was indeed well established, but in cultures that had two distinctive features compared with the UK: in some states, of which France is the prime example, there existed a long tradition of centralized state-controlled and sponsored systems of regulation; in more decentralized cases, of which the Rhineland systems are good examples, there existed traditions supporting the development of public law institutions. In the latter, self-regulation was practised, but within a much more explicit and closely controlled legal framework than in the case of the UK.

In short, the historically established system of regulation in the UK was conditioned by three features: by the fact that it developed its predominant institutions and cultures before the rise of democratic politics; by the fact that it appeared in advance of any state institutions that had significant interventionist ambitions, or the bureaucratic resources to back those ambitions; and by the fact that cooperation with, and deference to, corporate and professional elites defined its dominant style.

The emergence of three linked political phenomena in the early decades of the twentieth century presented a considerable challenge to these arrangements: the First World War transformed the state, equipping it with interventionist ambitions and resources; as a result of the War the party system consolidated into an adversarial contest between a Conservative Party aligned to corporate and professional elites, and a Labour Party which was more hostile to those elites; and the emergence of an interventionist, mildly radical Labour Party was itself the product of the fuller development of formal democracy, signified by the extension of near universal adult suffrage in 1918. These developments were highly dangerous for the established regulatory system, a danger that briefly crystallized as a 'revolutionary moment' in 1919, when a ripple from the great European revolutionary storm emanating from Russian Bolshevism briefly caused a tremor in the UK.

This threat to the established regulatory order was met in two ways. First, a variety of organizational responses sought to ensure that the institutions of self-regulation would be protected from what was now, potentially, a threatening democratic state. Second, this institutional protection was reinforced by ideological protection: an ideology of regulation developed that pictured self-regulation, notably the British variety, as uniquely well adapted to the complex tasks of control in an advanced industrial society. To this was commonly added a picture of British 'common sense' and flexibility, by way of contrast with the supposedly more rigid, legalistic ways of foreigners. The City of London was a great pioneer in this process: it reorganized itself under the guidance of the Bank of England in the immediate aftermath of the Great War; and it elaborated the ideology of self-regulation when faced with challenges, on occasions like the great inquiries into its functioning, such as that conducted by the Macmillan Committee, which reported in 1931 (Macmillan 1931; Moran 2007). The City was a great pioneer because its huge power and prestige allowed it to lay down the ideological template for British self-regulation. Indeed some other key regulatory elites, such as in the accounting and auditing professions, and key parts of the law like commercial law, were effectively part of the City's service sector.

Though there were incremental changes in many areas of regulation over the half-century after the close of the Great War, the institutions of self-regulation, and the ideology legitimizing the system, showed remarkable resilience. In areas like professional regulation, the regulation of the university elite, or the regulation of the

City elite, someone who had fallen asleep in 1920 and woken in 1970 would have recognized a remarkably similar institutional world. By contrast, a Rip Van Winkle who fell asleep in 1970 and woke at the turn of the new millennium would have been baffled by the extent of regulatory change. In the intervening thirty years the system of self-regulation had been refashioned under the impact of virtually continuous crisis. This crisis was caused by features that were engrained in the established arrangements. These ingrained features can be summarized as economic, cultural, and political.

Economically, self-regulation of markets needed some source of authority, and since the point of self-regulation was to make it autonomous of the democratic state, it could not borrow that authority too directly from the state. Self-regulation, to work, needed to offer privileges to those agreeing to abide by the rules of the self-regulatory system—and, by extension, needed sanctions against those who broke the rules. The result was that the system of self-regulation across the British economy was bound in with a system of cartels and restrictive practices—in service and product markets, and in markets for professional services. Insiders benefited from the cartels and restrictive practices; the price of benefiting was willingness to obey the rules of the self-regulatory club.

Culturally, the creation of the hegemonic ideology of self-regulation had been a considerable, and highly successful, exercise in mystification. But for mystification to endure, the ideology required constant maintenance, to validate the claim that 'flexible' self-regulation was a superior form of control (superior for instance to closer legal controls that would be the product of democratic politics). Self-regulation was designed to provide protection against the institutions and cultures of liberal democracy; but of course it could not abolish liberal democracy, and it had to live with a certain level of scrutiny from liberal democratic institutions. A critical issue, it turned out, was how it could manage 'scandals'—something to which we return in a moment.

This cultural vulnerability was obviously connected to the third ingrained feature, the political. Surrounding self-regulation for most of the twentieth century was the turbulence of democratic politics, a system of politics that provided obvious incentives to politicians to propose the extension of democratic controls over self-regulated domains, especially when 'scandals'—failures in the competence of the self-regulatory system—were revealed.

The presence of these three ingrained features meant that the system of self-regulation, even before it entered its decades of crisis, was anything but stable. Building a mesh of cartels in a market economy was always a tricky business. Restrictive practices and cartels were constantly being undermined by the competitive ambitions of market actors, notably of aggressive new entrants who had not been socialized into appropriately British ways; that was a constant story of the life of the City of London from the 1950s to the 1970s (Kynaston 2001). Scandals were common, and could only be contained if a convincing case could be made that they were exceptional, or if their full magnitude could be concealed; neither task was easy in a society with a comparatively free media and a culture of open debate. Finally, the political project at the heart of self-regulation—to protect corporate and professional elites from democratic control—was often threatened by the response of democratic politicians to revealed scandals and to the costs of cartels and restrictive practices. These pressures, always hard to control, simply became unmanageable in the closing decades of the twentieth century, when there occurred a great crisis of self-regulation.

The *symptoms* of this crisis could be seen in an intensification of the problems that, we have seen, were ingrained in the established system. In the economy, there had been an incremental growth in the force and effectiveness of competition policy, dating back to as long ago as the passage of the Act abolishing Resale Price Maintenance in 1964. But the dam really burst under the impact of the market liberalization reforms of the 1980s. In the middle of the decade the single most important instance of a self-regulatory system linked to restrictive practices, in the financial markets of the City of London, was swept away in the trading reforms usually summarized as the 'Big Bang' of 1986. The volume of scandals rose sharply across a wide range of the most prestigious regulatory systems: the regulation of solicitors entered a period of virtually perpetual scandal; the self-regulatory system in medicine failed very publicly to respond, notably to well-publicized cases of maltreatment of patients by doctors; the Lloyds insurance market—at the core of the City establishment—was revealed to be both crooked and imprudent (see Clarke 1981; 1986; 1990; 2000). The consequence of these scandals was that, from the 1970s on, a key part of the self-regulatory historical compact—that the democratic state would keep out of self-regulatory domains—was breached. Law, medicine, the City markets, the universities: all saw state-sponsored reorganization and intervention. The state also began actively to reshape such statutory institutions of regulation as existed, many largely undisturbed since the nineteenth century, and to create a new wave of bodies to regulate hitherto autonomous areas of social life. (For details, see later.)

The collapse of cartels, the taint of scandal, and the increasing intrusion of the democratic state are described as only *symptoms* here precisely because they arose from two more fundamental factors. The first is well known. The great crisis of the British economy in the mid-1970s, itself a product of a wider crisis of the global capitalist economy which terminated the 'thirty glorious years' of economic growth, produced a radical policy response. The most immediate manifestation was the great Thatcherite revolution in ownership and market organization of the 1980s, which attacked the foundations of many of the cartels that had been central to the self-regulatory system. But as we shall see in the next section the great changes did not stop with the end of Mrs Thatcher's extraordinary premiership; her revolution inaugurated a change of direction that has since continued relentlessly. The second fundamental cause helps explain why change has indeed been so relentless, and has happened independently of any particular human agent. As I have argued above, the 'traditional' style of self-regulation fulfilled an important function—it protected important elites from democratic institutions. The transformation of much self-regulation in the last thirty years is a sign of the collapse of this system of protection. How and why the collapse came about is a central theme of the next section.

18.3 THE TRANSFORMATION OF SELF-REGULATION

The British system of self-regulation was extraordinarily pervasive, and charting its changes comprehensively would demand more space than is available here. I try to convey the changes by focusing on three key cases: financial regulation; the regulation of the school system; and the regulation of medicine. The importance of the first of these is virtually self-evident: the regulation of the City was the paradigmatic model for the self-regulatory system. The regulation of the school system is selected because it shows an extraordinary surge in overt central control in an area of the welfare state that had for most of the twentieth century simply been handed over to self-regulation by a single profession, teachers. The regulation of doctors I choose because the pattern of self-regulation here was both the most developed and the most influential, for professions that organized after the doctors.

18.3.1 The Transformation of Financial Regulation

The transformation of financial regulation is traceable back to the 1970s when a systemic crisis in banking forced abandonment of a private, informal system of prudential banking regulation administered by the Bank of England, and its replacement by a statutory system (see Moran 1986). But the really great changes took place in two subsequent giant steps. The first occurred in the Financial Services Act 1986, a law that was partly prompted by a series of frauds and collapses among financial investment firms, and partly by pressures from modernizers in the state bureaucracy and the biggest firms, who wanted more effective controls to position the City as a key location in the global financial services industry. (Vogel 1996: 93–117 is authoritative.)

It accompanied, and was a corollary of, one of the most important state-directed episodes in economic modernization: the 'Big Bang', which deregulated City markets with the aim of securing London's place as a leading world financial centre. The 1986 regulatory legislation which accompanied the change in market practices is significant because it saw a large step in the direction of a hierarchical system of state-backed controls, while nevertheless trying to retain the language, and some of the institutions, of self-regulation. It systematically organized all the main markets into a hierarchy of self-regulatory organizations (SROs). These self-regulatory organizations gained monopoly control over the markets—that is, membership, and obedience to their rules, was a condition of entry. In turn their own rules and internal government were subjected to oversight by an overarching self-regulatory organization, the Securities and Investments Board, which in effect licensed the individual SROs. All this greatly increased the degree to which the self-regulatory system was codified: the SROs of necessity acquired rule books, and these rule books over time became more detailed and more elaborate, and of course acquired legal force. The Securities and Investments Board spoke the language of self-regulation, and as a gesture towards independence was constituted as a corporate body financed by a levy on the industry. But the power it wielded over the SROs was based on statute: its own constitution was prescribed in law, its leading officers were publicly appointed, and it was required to report to parliament and to the central state in Whitehall. (Reid 1988 tells the whole story.)

Scandals greatly damaged ideological mystification because they continually posed the awkward question: if self-regulation is so superior why is it so prone to scandal? The reforms in the City now further damaged ideological mystification because they posed the awkward question: if flexibility is the great virtue of self-regulation why is the self-regulation system moving so decisively in the direction of formality? Indeed, even this remarkable advance in the direction of a state-designed hierarchy in financial self-regulation did not endure. The passage of the 1986 Financial Services Act was followed by more than a decade of instability in financial regulation: periodic regulatory crises and scandals, and internal struggles within the financial services industry, as scandal and failure pushed the regulatory authorities towards more controls, while supporters of traditional light-touch self-regulation tried to preserve as much as possible of the old order. That struggle has culminated for the moment in the changes associated with the passage into law of the Financial Services and Markets Act of 2000. The Act completes in a radical way the transformation of self-regulation begun in 1986. Some vestiges of the old forms of self-regulation, admitted, do still remain. The new institution charged with implementing the Act, the Financial Services Authority, is a company limited by guarantee financed by a levy on the industry, thus conferring 'ownership' on the regulated themselves. But this is a weak echo of the voice of the old world of self-regulation. The Authority (originally established in advance of the law in 1997, but deriving its powers from the statute of 2000) has some claim to be the most impressively empowered financial services regulator in any leading world financial centre. If, for instance, we compare the system usually taken as the model of tight legal control, the United States, we find a striking contrast: all the powers over the full range of markets and institutions concentrated into the hands of the FSA in London are in the case of the US dispersed among a wide range of regulatory bodies at state and federal level. The FSA in effect licences all institutions and products, and does so by virtue of power conferred by statute. It has thus displaced the Bank of England from any significant role in prudential regulation of markets or institutions. Authorization, standard setting, supervision, and enforcement: all come within its range. The creation of the Authority amounts to the diffusion into the financial markets of a major recent institutional innovation in the British system, the specialized regulatory agency empowered by law. (Other important examples include the regulation of food safety and the regulation of human fertility.) As a regulatory agency, the Authority has a radically different relationship with the central state from that enjoyed by the old institutions of City regulation and by the Bank of England. The Treasury appoints its Board, it reports annually to the Treasury and the House of Commons, and it is required to give evidence to the Commons' Treasury Select Committee.

To summarize: in just about fifteen years from the middle of the 1980s self-regulation of financial markets was transformed. There were radical changes along at least three dimensions: a sharp increase in state surveillance; a growth in the volume and complexity of rules, including legally prescribed rules; and the development of a comprehensive hierarchy of controls operated by a single, legally empowered regulator. That regulator in turn, equipped with great legal powers, an increasingly assertive sense of regulatory mission, and subject to powerful popular pressures to respond to cases of regulatory failure, is emerging as a major actor in both the regulatory politics of the markets and the bureaucratic politics of the central state. What is more, even this command system is not stable. The Northern Rock crisis of 2007—involving the first public run on a bank since the nineteenth century—will certainly prompt a reconstruction of the system, and almost certainly yet another step-change up in the system of command.

It is of course the case that the actual practice of financial regulation has not thus far been notably draconian—the Northern Rock crisis suggests that much of the old culture of cooperation and consensus survives. Financial regulation has certainly been nothing like as severe as the new schools' inspection agencies described below. In the next main section of the chapter I explore the reasons for these limits on the fuller development of a command regulatory system.

18.3.2 The Transformation of the Regulation of Schools

The core of the traditional system of regulation in school education lay in the school inspection system. This is a revealing case because it shows that self-regulation could exist even in parts of the welfare state that were overwhelmingly publicly funded. It was a domain where a largely autonomous teaching profession, layers of government below the level of the metropolitan, and bits of the central state itself inhabited a 'secret garden' of regulation. (The phrase is from Hood et al. 1999: 139.) This was a world where the 'British' style of informal, cooperative regulation was deeply embedded, and where the scrutinizing gaze of the state had all but disappeared: the Secretary of State at the beginning of the present upheavals once estimated that under the old system it would take central inspectors 200 years to complete inspection of all schools (cited in Hood et al. 1999: 147). It was a domain where, despite the fact that the teachers were a client profession of the state, they had won an operational autonomy that compared well with the autonomy of traditionally 'self-regulated' liberal professions.

Much of this was turned upside down following the passage of the Education Reform Act (1988) and the Education (Schools) Act of 1992. The formation of OFSTED as the state body concerned with the regulation of standards in education in 1992 heralded a significantly different regulatory approach. (Gray and Wilcox 1995: 133–48 summarize the history of this transformation.) Gone was the Arnoldian conception of the schools inspector as a kind of gentle encourager of the dissemination of high culture; in its place was a ferocious insistence on the inspector as the driver of standards in the name of national efficiency. In OFSTED was created an institution that in culture and working practices was far removed from the main interests that had supported the old cooperative system. At the same time there was a marked increase in the formal organization and institutional density of the regulatory system. In place of the fairly simple, small regulatory community that had joined an educational elite and a mandarin elite there now developed a large, overlapping, and often competing range of regulatory bodies. In addition to OFSTED there also now existed: individual local authorities, the kingpins of the historically displaced system, who still nevertheless retained significant roles; a Funding Agency for Schools; a Schools Curriculum and Assessments Authority; and several others, including 'all purpose' regulators like the Audit Commission and the National Audit Office who intervened unpredictably in the regulatory system (Hood et al. 1999: 143–4). At the same time there developed a marked shift in regulatory style, especially after the appointment of a new Chief Inspector of Schools in 1995, towards a more adversarial and judgemental system. This was in turn associated with a move to more explicit, quantitatively expressed regulatory standards, notably in the use of standardized attainment tests and targets, and a policy of 'naming and shaming' those who failed to meet targets. (Pring 2001 documents this intensification.)

The return of a new Labour administration in 1997, though it ultimately displaced some individuals, changed little. The Labour government was convinced both that educational standards were an electorally sensitive issue, and that fostering human capital and the skill base were the keys to international competitiveness. Thus the pressure to achieve targets was if anything intensified.

In summary: in the space of less than a decade a cooperative, enclosed, informal regulatory world had been broken open. Micro-management of the school system from the centre was now so great that ministers were forming views even on such detail as particular methods of teaching skills like reading. In the course of the 1990s the country acquired one of the most ambitious schemes of school inspection in the world. Wilcox and Gray's summary catches the ambitions of all this:

> the system of inspection inaugurated by the 1992 Act represented an unprecedented attempt to apply a universal model of inspection of ambitious frequency and comprehensiveness, carried out by independent inspectors drawn from a wide range of backgrounds and operating on a competitive commercial basis. We doubt if any more ambitious programme of school-by-school evaluation and review has ever been mounted anywhere in the world.   (Wilcox and Gray 1996: 2)

18.3.3 The Regulation of Medicine

A long historical consensus about the shape and structure of self-regulation in this domain dated back to the Medical Act of 1858, which established the ancestor of the General Medical Council as the centrepiece of a system of autonomous self-regulation. That consensus started to fall apart in the late 1960s. The most important signs of this were open revolt by sections of the profession against the authority of the General Medical Council, followed by the first extensive public inquiry ever— by the Merrison Committee—in the early 1970s. (Stacey 1992: 29–44 for the revolt; Merrison 1975 for the report.) Although Merrison's language faithfully reflected the ideology of club government, intoning the traditional defence of the flexibility of self-regulation, the mere existence of the Committee was a hugely damaging development. The hearings and the report inevitably undermined one of the key requirements of traditional self-regulation: it converted the tacit and the private into the explicit and the public. More damaging still, Merrison produced no stable regulatory settlement. No new consensus capable of returning control of the regulatory institutions to the professional elite has been possible in the intervening years. A symptom of this is that for almost a generation now we have lived through constant reform of the structure, powers, and culture of the General Medical Council.

One reason for this continuing instability is that there have been recurrent scandals about the behaviour of doctors, forcing constant changes in both the content of regulations and the structure of the GMC itself. One of the most striking features of these scandalous cases is the gap they revealed between the conception of professional standards that guided the General Medical Council's own workings and what an increasingly assertive lay public thought were appropriate standards. Thus a number of highly publicized cases of callousness, incompetence, and neglect were admitted by all, professionals and non-professionals alike, to be quite unacceptable—but could not be deemed unprofessional given the GMC's narrow conception of professional misconduct. Here was a particularly stark instance of the encounter between the nineteenth-century culture of self-regulation and the expectations of a modern democratic culture. (Smith 1989 on these cases.) It graphically demonstrates that 'scandals' were accidents waiting to happen in the system of self-regulation: they grew out of the incongruence between a nineteenth-century oligarchic regulatory culture and a modern democratic culture. There was consequently increasing legislative intervention in the regulatory affairs of the profession, including intervention to reshape the composition of the regulatory institution itself (Stacey 1992: 51–85).

Behind all this lies the collapse of the compact that doctors successfully negotiated with the state at the foundation of the NHS, a compact memorably summarized in Klein's phrase 'the politics of the double bed': the compact assigned control of the practice of medicine, and of the everyday allocation of resources, to medical professionals, and confined the state to the role of deciding the absolute level of resources to be allocated to the Service (Klein 1990). It thus 'modernized' the nineteenth-century bargain between the state and profession in such as a way as to protect the autonomy of the profession. But after the great economic crisis of the 1970s, and the rise of a state increasingly concerned to squeeze maximum efficiency out of welfare state professionals, the Faustian character of that bargain became increasingly apparent. Doctors found themselves the object of increasingly detailed public intervention in their working practices. (Harrison, Hunter, and Pollitt 1990 on the growth of all this.) Thus the particular turmoil in the regulatory institutions was compounded by a wider breakdown of the political bargain between the profession and the state. As Salter put it in 2001, in the wake of a spate of crises in medical authority: 'Medical regulation, as much as medical self-regulation, is now centre stage in the politics of the National Health Service and the profession can expect to be subject to the full range of devices at the disposal of this particular theatre' (Salter 2001: 871).

In summary: the regulation of the medical profession is now subjected to unprecedented, and growing, public debate, increasing intervention in the daily professional activities of physicians, and increasing oversight by the central state.

18.4 THE LIMITS OF COMMAND REGULATION

The shift to command regulation across the British system is in many ways a surprising development. It contradicts expectations aroused by at least three distinct points of view. First, it contradicts the everyday 'commonsense' picture of the last quarter-century as an era of liberalization. Second, it flies in the face of perhaps the commonest picture of the modern regulatory state, which pictures it as an exercise in comparatively light-touch 'steering', by comparison with the more interventionist practices of the three decades or so after the end of the Second World War. (The most influential account is by Majone 1991; 1996; 1999.) Most serious of all, it runs counter to the expectations generated by much of the influential modern literature on governance, which pictures command and control as too blunt an instrument to regulate complex modern societies, and which invokes an image of 'governance' precisely to suggest that there are powerful functional reasons for a shift to regulation through more flexible means: through distributed networks and through the development of systems of reflexive regulation, in which the emphasis is, precisely, on reflexivity in the regulatory process (see for instance Rhodes 1997; 2006).

The importance of 'governance' is not an illusion. 'Thick descriptive' studies of the regulation of some of the most complex social and technological processes—for instance the regulation of safety in high-technology industrial processes—show a recurrent pattern of reflexive regulation that departs drastically from the command system (Gunningham and Rees 1997; Gunningham, Grabosky, and Sinclair 1998; Gunningham and Johnstone 1999). More generally, the field of environmental regulation shows a similar widespread pattern of reflexive regulation. The impact of the European Union has been important in this process, for while it has obliged the constitutionalization and formalization of many British self-regulatory domains, it has also worked through the delegation of many regulatory responsibilities to the lowest possible institutional levels—which in practice has meant the objects of regulation themselves (Weale et al. 2000). Nor has international influence been confined to the European Union. The globalization of economic life has re-created supranationally many of the features of economic and professional self-regulation: two important examples are the wide range of technical standard-setting bodies and the rise of self-regulation in global financial markets and allied sectors, like accounting and auditing (Braithwaite and Drahos 2000).

These developments indicate that the spread of command and control regulation domestically in the UK is anything but a functional response to the demands of high administrative or technical complexity. It is the product of a crisis of an old social order—that order created in pre-democratic Britain, and then adapted, institutionally and ideologically, to meet the threat of democratic institutions. The collapse of that regulatory order led to an era of chaotic struggle for control over regulatory processes, virtually perpetual reconstruction of the systems that succeeded the old order—and a set of changes driven by chaos, crisis, and fate rather than human agency.

The history of chaos and reconstruction continues for, broadly, four reasons: the invasion of regulatory domains by adversary politics; the struggles by the regulated to evade and reshape regulatory controls; the limits of command regulation in coping with complex social processes; and the inability of nationally based command systems to control processes that, increasingly, are happening on a global scale. I examine each of these in turn.

Traditional self-regulation provided a protection from adversary politics by 'depoliticizing' regulatory domains—removing them from the sphere of democratic politics. The collapse of those insulating devices has exposed much regulation to competitive adversarialism: politicians in government and opposition, drawn into the details of regulation, have substantial career incentives to intervene and to micromanage. The process has been seen most clearly in the regulation of key domains of the welfare state, like education and health: controls over hitherto autonomous professions have grown as competing political parties have sought to direct professionals to deliver performance targets whose achievement is the very centre of the party adversarial battle. The competitive struggle in an adversarial culture helps explain why there is so little stability in the new regulatory worlds; the investment that ministers have in taking credit, or avoiding blame, for performance helps explain the ubiquity of micro-management.

But the transformation of self- regulation has not been made in a consensual way. On the contrary, the transformation of regulation among public sector elites was done in the face of powerful opposition from those who controlled the old self-regulatory system. The result has been to create cycles of strategic games in which McBarnet and Whelan's 'creative compliance' has been a dominant feature of the games (McBarnet and Whelan 1991; 1999). The forms of creative compliance include capture of the regulatory process, typified by the capture of the Research Assessment Exercise, in the name of peer review, by academic elites in the universities; manipulation of performance indicators so as serve the interests of the monitored, rather than to measure the underlying value which the indicator was originally designed to measure—a perennial problem in the management of the health service; or the distortion of social processes so as to ensure compliance with the target rather than to ensure achievement of the goal which the target is designed to reach, as when teachers teach just to pass tests.

These problems are only exemplars of familiar 'limits to control' problems (Hood 1976; 1998) but they are especially acute in the UK case because of the circumstances surrounding the reconstruction of the regulatory system; a reconstruction that was driven by elites in the core executive responding to the great British economic crisis, and determined to reshape the institutions that were believed to be part of the cause of the crisis. This history has guaranteed adversarialism, where the regulated have seen the new order as one to be circumvented or subverted.

One of the puzzles of the shift to command away from the old system of self-regulation was that it contradicted expectations from an established body of theory: those governance theories that pictured many modern social processes as so complex that their control could only be pursued through the creation of cooperative networks that relied heavily on voluntary coordination and cooperation. In particular regulatory domains these are exemplified by control processes in some very high-technology domains: as we noted earlier, the regulation of safety in the most advanced process industries, and environmental regulation when applied to the most high-technology industrial domains. The phenomenon of high complexity suggests that attempts to impose command regulation on many social domains will simply fail.

Finally, the limits to the command system are set by external forces, and not only those already referred to in the European Union. The globalization of economic processes has created a world of business self-regulation that has substantially escaped national economic controls. A key profession in the control of modern economic life, accounting, now largely has its standards determined by the International Accounting Standards Board, a body substantially under the control of the largest globally organized firms (Braithwaite and Drahos 2000 for the global web of regulatory bodies). More generally, there exists a world of standard setting across a wide range of industries that occurs in internationally organized institutions, often under industry control.

18.5 REGULATION: FROM A SILENT TO A CONTESTED PART OF THE CONSTITUTION

Regulation, an activity little considered until comparatively recently, turns out to be a clue to the history of British political development and to the state of contemporary British government. It was, to adapt Foley's (1989) graphic phrase, one of the silences of the constitution: barely considered as a distinct activity because the institutions and the ideologies of self-regulation ensured that control was organized out of democratic politics, into the hands of economic and professional elites. The function of silence was precisely to protect key elites from democratic control. The big story of the last three decades is the collapse of that particular constitutional settlement, partly because successive policy failures culminated in the great crisis of the British economy and polity in the 1970s, and partly because cultural and social changes made it increasingly difficult to preserve an ideology that excluded democratic control from key areas of economic and social life.

The collapse was followed by a decisive shift to command modes of regulation, but there has been no new stable constitutional settlement. Instead, the UK has lived through a period of regulatory chaos and constant institutional innovation. No new consensus has been forged to succeed the consensus that undoubtedly existed about the old self-regulatory system. The command revolution in regulation over the last thirty years has for the most part been a revolution from the top, or perhaps more accurately from the centre of the core executive, imposed on unwilling economic and professional elites who have, in the absence of a consensus, responded with opportunistic modes of resistance and circumvention. The command revolution has been attempted in circumstances where there are powerful functional pressures, and powerful economic interests, pressing for a different regulatory style—one that stresses flexibility, reflexiveness, and the delegation of regulatory authority to powerful private economic interests. One of the ironies of the British regulatory revolution is that it destroyed industrial self-regulation nationally in the very era when a new burst of globalization reconstructed precisely such a system in the global economy.

REFERENCES

ASHBY, E., and ANDERSON, M. 1981. *The Politics of Clean Air*. Oxford: Clarendon Press.

BERLANT, J. 1975. *Profession and Monopoly: A Study of Medicine in the United States and Great Britain*. Berkeley: University of California Press.

BRAITHWAITE, J., and DRAHOS, P. 2000. *Global Business Regulation*. Cambridge: Cambridge University Press.

BULLER, J., and FLINDERS, M. 2005. 'The Domestic Origins of Depoliticisation in the Area of British Economic Policy'. *British Journal of Politics and International Relations*, 7/4: 526–43.

BURNHAM, P. 2001. 'New Labour and the Politics of Depoliticisation'. *British Journal of Politics and International Relations*, 3/2: 127–49.

CARSON, W. G. 1970. 'Some Sociological Aspects of Strict Liability and the Enforcement of Factory Legislation'. *Modern Law Review*, 33/4: 396–412.

—— 1974. 'Symbolic and Instrumental Dimensions of Early Factory Legislation: A Case Study in the Social Origins of Criminal Law'. Pp. 107–38 in R. Hood (ed.), *Crime, Criminology and Public Policy: Essays in Honour of Sir Leon Radzinowicz*. London: Heinemann.

—— 1979. 'The Conventionalization of Early Factory Crime'. *International Journal for the Sociology of Law*, 7/1: 37–60.

CLARKE, M. 1981. *Fallen Idols: Elites and the Search for the Acceptable Face of Capitalism*. London: Junction.

—— 1986. *Regulating the City*. Milton Keynes: Open University Press.

—— 1990. *Business Crime: Its Nature and Control*. Cambridge: Polity.

—— 2000. *Regulation: The Social Control of Business between Law and Politics*. Basingstoke: Macmillan.

FOLEY, M. 1989. *The Silence of Constitutions: Gaps, 'Abeyances' and Political Temperament in the Maintenance of Government*. London: Routledge.

GRAY, J., and WILCOX, B. 1995. *'Good School, Bad School': Evaluating Performance and Encouraging Improvement*. Buckingham: Open University Press.

GUNNINGHAM, N., GRABOSKY, P., and SINCLAIR, D. 1998. *Smart Regulation: Designing Environmental Policy.* Oxford: Clarendon Press.

—— and JOHNSTONE, R. 1999. *Regulating Workplace Safety: Systems and Sanctions.* Oxford: Oxford University Press.

—— and REES, J. 1997. 'Industry Self-Regulation: An Institutional Perspective'. *Law and Policy,* 19/4: 363–414.

HARRISON, S., HUNTER, D., and POLLITT, C. 1990. *The Dynamics of British Health Policy.* London: Routledge.

HAY, C. 2007. *Why We Hate Politics.* Cambridge: Polity.

HOOD, C. 1976. *The Limits of Administration.* London: Wiley.

—— 1998. *The Art of the State: Culture, Rhetoric, and Public Management.* Oxford: Clarendon Press.

—— SCOTT, C., JAMES, O., JONES, G., and TRAVERS, T. 1999. *Regulation inside Government: Waste-Watchers, Quality Police, and Sleaze-Busters.* Oxford: Oxford University Press.

KAGAN, R. 2001. *Adversarial Legalism: The American Way of Law.* Cambridge, Mass.: Harvard University Press.

—— and AXELRAD, L. (eds.) 2001. *Regulatory Encounters: Multinational Corporations and American Adversarial Legalism.* Berkeley: University of California Press.

KLEIN, R. 1990. 'The State and the Profession: The Politics of the Double Bed'. *British Medical Journal,* 301 (3 Oct.): 700–2.

KYNASTON, D. 2001. *The City of London, IV: A Club No More 1945–2000.* London: Chatto and Windus.

OGUS, A. 1992. 'Regulatory Law: Lessons from the Past'. *Legal Studies,* 12/1: 1–19.

—— 1994. *Regulation: Legal Form and Economic Theory.* Oxford: Clarendon Press.

McBARNET, D., and WHELAN, C. 1991. 'The Elusive Spirit of the Law: Formalism and the Struggle for Legal Control'. *Modern Law Review,* 54/6: 848–73.

—— —— 1999. 'Challenging the Regulators: Strategies for Resisting Control'. Pp. 67–77 in C. McCrudden (ed.), *Regulation and Deregulation: Policy and Practice in the Utilities and Financial Services Industries.* Oxford: Oxford University Press.

MACMILLAN, LORD (chair) 1931. *Committee on Finance and Industry Report.* Cmnd. 3897. London: HMSO. 1969 reprint.

MAJONE, G. 1991. 'Cross-National Sources of Regulatory Policymaking in Europe and the United States'. *Journal of Public Policy,* 11/1: 79–109.

—— 1996. *Regulating Europe.* London: Routledge.

—— 1999. 'The Regulatory State and its Legitimacy Problems'. *West European Politics,* 22/1: 1–24.

MERRISON, A. W. 1975. *Report of the Committee of Inquiry into the Regulation of the Medical Profession.* Cmnd. 6018.

MORAN, M. 1986. *The Politics of Banking.* London: Macmillan.

—— 1991. *The Politics of the Financial Services Revolution.* London: Macmillan.

—— 2007. *The British Regulatory State: High Modernism and Hyper-innovation,* 2nd edn. Oxford: Oxford University Press.

PERKIN, H. 1990. *The Rise of Professional Society: England since 1880.* London: Routledge.

PRING, R. 2001. 'Managing the Professions: The Case of Teachers'. *Political Quarterly,* 72/3: 278–90.

REID, M. 1982. *The Secondary Banking Crisis 1973–5.* London: Macmillan.

—— 1988. *All Change in the City: The Revolution in Britain's Financial Sector.* Basingstoke: Macmillan.

RHODES, R. A. W. 1997. *Understanding Governance: Policy Networks, Governance, Reflexivity and Accountability*. Buckingham: Open University Press.

—— 2006. 'Policy Network Analysis'. Pp. 425–47 in M. Moran, M. Rein, and R. E. Goodin (eds.), *Oxford Handbook of Public Policy*. Oxford: Oxford University Press.

SALTER, B. 2001. 'Who Rules? The New Politics of Medical Regulation'. *Social Science and Medicine*, 52: 871–83.

SMITH, R. 1989. 'Discipline 1: The Hordes at the Gate'. *British Medical Journal*, 298 (3 June): 1502–5.

STACEY, M. 1992. *Regulating British Medicine: The General Medical Council*. Chichester: Wiley.

VOGEL, D. 1986. *National Styles of Regulation: Environmental Policy in Great Britain and the United States*. Ithaca, NY: Cornell University Press.

VOGEL, S. 1996. *Freer Markets, More Rules: Regulatory Reform in Advanced Industrial Countries*. Ithaca, NY: Cornell University Press.

WEALE, A., PRIDHAM, G., CINI, M., KONSTADAKOPULOS, D., PORTER, M., and FLYNN, B. 2000. *Environmental Governance in Europe: An Ever Closer Ecological Union*. Oxford: Oxford University Press.

WILCOX, B., and GRAY, J. 1996. *Inspecting Schools*. Buckingham: Open University Press.

CHAPTER 19

CENTRAL STATE

OLIVER JAMES

THE central state is an important topic within the study of British politics. Studying the topic includes analysis of the resources of members of the executive, the relationship between senior public servants and their political masters, and the methods for coordinating across and between departments and other associated public bodies. Instead of reviewing the vast body of work that now exists on the British central state this chapter locates a discussion of these topics within a broader argument about the theories and methods through which these themes and issues should be studied and understood. It achieves this by seeking to draw out and consider the contribution of the 'interpretivist' approach in the study of British politics. The central argument of this chapter is that although this approach might be accepted as a 'rhetorical device' for provoking greater reflection about the tools of political analysis it offers little when compared to the insights of mainstream approaches. Moreover the unnecessarily pessimistic assumptions about the possibilities of empirical knowledge vis-à-vis the central state stand in stark contrast to the insights and lessons of other approaches.

In order to develop this line of argument this chapter is divided into four sections. The first section examines the conflict between interpretivists and mainstream researchers about the purpose of research and the role of theory, method, and evidence in the context of the British central state. It argues that the potential significance of the interpretivist critique is reduced because it is directed more at quantitative political science than the qualitative political science and political history approaches that currently dominate mainstream research in this context. The second section locates this debate within the context of the vaunted transition from *government* to *governance*. In this regard the interpretivist approach arguably contributes very little, and indeed overlaps in many places, with mainstream historical, qualitative, or quantitative approaches. In order to drill down still further the third section examines recent 'third wave' governance-theoretic research and provides greater precision by examining six specific research agendas in this field. These are: power in policy-making networks; multi-level governance; core executive studies, prime ministerial power; central departments and the administrative/politics interface; and the central state beyond departments. The final section returns to the core argument and locates the study of the central state within a number of broader themes and issues.

19.1 THE POLITICS MAINSTREAM AND ITS INTERPRETIVIST CRITICS

The debate between 'interpretivists', especially as reflected in the work of Bevir and Rhodes (hereafter B&R), and different strands of what can be described as mainstream politics research on the central state raises fundamental issues about the purpose of research and the role of theory, method, and evidence. Discussion of these issues can be frustrating for those seeking answers to seemingly straightforward questions about, for example, the relationship between different departments in making policy, the influence of the prime minister relative to other ministers, or why ministers resign from their posts. However, the debates are unavoidable because they, in part, determine the answers to these questions, whether answers are possible, and even whether they are seen as appropriate questions to ask.

Contemporary mainstream research is varied but can, in broad terms, be summarized as being of three main approaches: political history, and quantitative and qualitative versions of political science. The categories are not fully mutually exclusive or exhaustive of all work on the central state but the mainstream dominates research on this topic.[1] The approaches are summarized in Table 19.1 with illustrative examples. Contemporary political history tends to pursue understanding of specific cases or events using an idiographic method with limited development of empirical generalization or general theory. Political science is split between qualitative work which tends to examine a small number of cases with little formalization of theory, and quantitative political science which tends to use a large number of cases and sometimes entails formal specification of theoretical models. Political science tends to be interested in attempting empirical generalization and causal explanation,

---

[1] There are also debates between interpretivism and 'critical realist' perspectives beyond the mainstream (McAnulla 2006; Marsh 2008). The politics literature on the central state cannot be comprehensively referenced in a short chapter, for specific topics: on governance see Rhodes (1997), Richards and Smith (2002); on the core executive see Smith (1999), Marsh, Smith, and Richards (2001); on multi-level governance see Bache and Flinders (2004); on the civil service see Dowding (1995a), Hood and Lodge (2006); on research traditions see Bevir and Rhodes (2003). Other disciplines also address the central state, particularly economics, history, and sociology.

Table 19.1 Mainstream politics research on the central state and its interpretivist critics

	Contemporary political history	Qualitative political science	Quantitative political science	Interpretivism (Bevir and Rhodes 2003)
Main purpose of research	Understanding specific cases sometimes including causal explanation	Limited empirical generalization, sometimes causal explanation, prediction and knowledge to enable intervention	Broad empirical generalization, sometimes causal explanation, prediction and knowledge to enable intervention	Understanding the meanings, beliefs, and preferences of actors, and the relation between traditions, beliefs, and dilemmas
Role of theory	Limited role for general theory	Explicit theory, usually non-formal	Explicit theory, often formal	Programmatic role of the non-formal theory of tradition, beliefs, and dilemmas
Orientation to empirical work including research methods and the role of evidence	Empirically oriented with diversity of approach, often uses individual case studies with an idiographic method	Empirically oriented with diversity of approach, often uses small-n studies, use of a wide range of methods for data collection and analysis	Empirically oriented with a conventional approach to observational studies of a large n and statistical testing of hypotheses drawn from theory	Anti-'positivist', anti-'modern empirical', rejection of 'objectified' social facts, varied methods but interpretivism in practice involves small-n studies, ethnographic techniques, and an emphasis on first person accounts
Illustrative examples	Hennessy (1986; 1989), Theakston (1997)	Rhodes (1997), Marsh, Smith, and Richards (2001), James (2003), Bache and Flinders (2004)	Alt (1975), Berlinski, Derwan, and Dowding (2005)	Bevir and Rhodes (2003; 2006a; 2006b). Hybrids: Richards (2007); Clarke and Gains (2007)

examining the reasons why events occur, with quantitative work often being more explicitly focused on these tasks. In a typical quantitative observational study, the average causal effects of a set of independent variables on a dependent variable are estimated in a model which 'controls' to isolate the effect of each variable of interest. This approach, in many respects, attempts to be analogous to experimental designs that attempt to isolate causal effects by comparing treatment and control groups, a form of design that is difficult to implement in the central state. Quantitative empirical research conventionally includes statistical tests of hypotheses drawn from theory, with the tests incorporating assumptions about the data-generating process giving rise to the observations. Political science work is sometimes engaged in the prediction of outcomes, and knowledge about causes could in principle be used to suggest interventions to change outcomes.[2]

The interpretivist approach is suggested as having broad applicability to politics, including the central state, and several varieties of interpretivism exist (Hay 2002: 205–6; Bevir and Rhodes 2003: 20–4; Finlayson 2004). However, the most extensive statement of the interpretivist approach in the context of the British central state is set out in *Interpreting British Governance* (Bevir and Rhodes 2003) and related work (Bevir and Rhodes 2006a; 2006b; Rhodes 2007). The interpretivist approach has been suggested as increasingly influential (Kerr and Kettell 2006: 13; Marsh 2008: 251) and has been adopted, at least in part, by other authors (Clarke and Gains 2007; Richards 2007). B&R state their view that 'Interpretive approaches begin from the insight that to understand actions, practice and institutions, we need to grasp the relevant meanings, the beliefs and preferences of the people involved' (Bevir and Rhodes 2003: 1). This contention appears similar in many respects to the long-standing tradition of hermeneutics, broadly defined as the theory of understanding entailing interpreting texts and actions. B&R refer to this work as one of the 'varieties of interpretation' (Bevir and Rhodes 2003: 20–4). Most researchers in the politics mainstream would agree that examining beliefs and preferences is at least part of what they do, so this aspect of B&R's analysis does not seem particularly controversial (Dowding 2004: 136).

A more significant dispute arising from B&R's focus on interpreting 'interpreta-tions' leads them to criticize what they see as 'empiricist' and 'positivist' approaches used in political science. Some authors suggest that a key contribution of B&R's work has been to 'highlight the inadequacy of "positivist" and "modern empiri-cist" approaches that have dominated postwar British political science' (McAnulla 2006: 113). Mainstream political scientists tend to want to evaluate rival accounts by appeal to evidence that can be used to assist the process of choosing between them. However, B&R suggest using a 'normative standard embedded in a prac-tice of criticising and comparing rival accounts of "agreed facts"' to avoid both the pitfalls of 'postitivism' and the relativistic position of judging accounts merely

---

[2] Much mainstream politics research on the central state could also be described as public administration research because it examines organizations, especially research that is intended to improve their design and operation which, it is suggested, should be key aims of public administration (Evans 2006).

by a standard of knowledge of what a community 'happens to agree on'. They claim that this standard should originate in 'anti-foundationalism' (Bevir and Rhodes 2003: 39).

For many mainstream authors, particularly but not exclusively from quantitative political science, this 'anti-foundational' approach does not appear to give sufficient emphasis to the role of evaluating theory by direct appeals to evidence about the social world. Dowding (2004: 140) insists that 'When I engage in political science I am attempting to discover truths about political institutions and processes. I try to explain what is "really happening".' From this perspective, it appears difficult for B&R to be guided by normative standards in assessing evidence that stand outside of the particular 'community' or 'conversation' that agrees the facts (Bevir and Rhodes 2003: 39). However, the political science and interpretivist positions may not be as incompatible as they appear on this issue. Dowding (2004: 140) suggests that B&R mislabel the political science approach as 'positivist', a position which is something of a strawman and not subscribed to by most practitioners. This argument can be extended. As part of a quantitative political science research programme that discovers 'truths' it is necessary to make statements that do not rest solely on empirical evaluation in order to evaluate hypotheses, and this may potentially be an area of agreement. For example, the evaluation of different theories through their rival hypotheses in a particular empirical setting is conducted in the context of background assumptions. If evidence comes to light that does not conform with a hypothesis, it could be that an aspect of the associated theory is wrong or some of the background assumptions are violated. For example a breakdown in the means of measurement could be producing the apparently inconsistent evidence. Assumptions about measurement, and other background assumptions, might in principle be open to empirical evaluation in a similar way to hypotheses, but just not all at the same time. Much political science, at least in practice if not always explicitly, recognizes these issues and is not as vulnerable to the standard criticism of being based on simple-minded 'positivism' as B&R suggest.

Interpretivists further argue that political science has become too involved in attempts to develop general theoretical models and to identify patterns across cases that form regularities governing social life (Bevir and Rhodes 2003: 17–20). They dislike the approach of testing general hypotheses derived from theory using multiple cases, and attempts to undertake 'causal' explanation using such general theory, which also suggests hostility to attempting prediction or intervening on the basis of such knowledge. Instead, B&R seek to identify the conditional and volitional relationships between beliefs, preferences, intention, and actions. In the context of the British state, B&R identify 'narratives' of different 'governance traditions' at the aggregate level. They also seek to identify the meanings of actors at the level of individuals (Bevir and Rhodes 2003: 145–69, 170–94). The beliefs of individuals sit within the broader traditions, defined as an initial influence on people that colours their later actions if their agency has not led them to change it (Bevir and Rhodes 2003: 33), that are part of their social context. Traditions are loose structures that do not necessarily limit later actions, which partly differentiates their approach from accounts suggesting traditions have a greater role in constraining actions, notably Greenleaf (1983). B&R argue that dilemmas arise for individuals or institutions when a new idea stands in opposition to existing beliefs or practices and forces a reconsideration of these existing beliefs and associated traditions. Dilemmas come from ideas that people hold to be true rather than as a result of 'allegedly objective pressures in the world' (Bevir and Rhodes 2003: 36).

It has been noted, as a criticism of B&R's approach by authors of otherwise different viewpoints, that the concept of 'tradition' is not easily separable from the beliefs of actors, and is certainly not an independent variable that could be used in an explanation of beliefs (Dowding 2004; Hay 2004; Finlayson 2004). B&R respond that 'our interpretive approach is rooted in a philosophical analysis of the human sciences that rejects the methodological rigour they urge on us. Our philosophical analysis suggests that because people are not autonomous, they gain their beliefs against the background of an inherited tradition' (Bevir and Rhodes 2004: 159). They also note that 'when human sciences try to specify them [belief and tradition] they are misled by a spurious concept of scientific rigour into adopting a form of explanation that is inappropriate for human action' (Bevir and Rhodes 2004: 159). Perhaps the greatest clash is between interpretivists and quantitative political scientists that use a large number of cases to establish associations or even average causal effects of variables through multivariate models, often used as analogues to the idea of experiments with controls. B&R are particularly concerned that quantitative operationalization of variables neglects the contingent nature of relationships and risks objectification by obscuring the different meanings that actors have in relation to an apparently simple concept and the approach may involve the researcher imposing their definition of meaning on subjects (Bevir and Rhodes 2004: 157).

The clash over causal explanation also occurs with qualitative political science and political history research that engages in causal explanation. Hay (2004: 144–9) advocates a social constructivist approach to examine ideas as the causes of policy-makers' actions, giving the example of how belief in the ideas of globalization has limited the social and economic policy ambitions of some social democratic governments. This kind of approach might present the possibility that government policy would be changed if the ideas about globalization were changed, other things remaining equal. The interpretivist approach seems very pessimistic about the prospects for the study of politics in this regard, limiting the usefulness of their approach for people interested in questions such as how actors' interests or ideas are causal influences on policy outcomes, or those interested in intervention informed by systematic knowledge about causal relations in the central state. This lack of ambition seems an unnecessary restriction of research activity to those not convinced by their philosophical arguments.

Whilst B&R claim to be open to a variety of methods, they particularly advocate the use of qualitative methods based on anthropological and historical approaches including 'thick description' which dominate the practice of interpretivist research by these authors. The identification of aggregates such as traditions is mainly based on their categorization of academic and policy documents, with individuals' beliefs established mostly by interviews, observation of action, and examination of the statements of practitioners. However, the significance of B&R's critique is reduced because existing qualitative interview-based research methods have been proposed on the grounds that they allow consideration of central state agents' understandings and their historical context (Marsh, Richards, and Smith 2004: 190). Biographical methods have long been used to examine the beliefs and actions of key individuals in this context (Theakston 1997). In practice, interpretivists give particular prominence to first-person accounts in the identification of narratives, especially through use of interview material and other statements by politicians and civil servants. This method seems to neglect insights from the mainstream, where most authors are concerned about error or deliberate misrepresentation by respondents. B&R recognize these potential problems but do not widely practise techniques that are commonly suggested for addressing them, such as systematic triangulation of statements with action and other sources to assess consistency (Dowding and James 2004).

19.2 GOVERNANCE AND GOVERNANCE NARRATIVES

Despite differences in the purpose of research and the role of theory and method, both mainstream and interpretivist authors share an interest in the substantive topic of governance and the central state, although much is included under this label. This interest can be roughly characterized as occurring in three waves of research. The first wave identified a general trend towards 'governance' as a critique of the traditional 'Westminster model' as a way of thinking about the British state (Rhodes 1997; Smith 1998; Richards and Smith 2002). The 'Westminster model' includes plurality rule elections, single-party government, cabinet responsibility, executive control of the state machine including the use of Crown powers, ministerial responsibility, a neutral career civil service, a semi-closed elite policy system, and central state dominance in the hierarchy of the UK administrative system. The Whitehall model refers particularly to the executive and administrative elements of the broader model and reflects an elitist conception of power, with the capacity to steer Britain's strategic policy primarily located in the upper echelons of the governmental machine. Governments' authority rests on commanding a majority in the House of Commons and the associated capacity to pass laws following due process. The executive's dominance is occasionally tempered by parliament's role in legitimating their policies with occasional rebellions that are especially salient in the case of small government majorities and of course are seen as having a non-activist role.

The first-wave perspective on governance was developed by one of the main current proponents of interpretivism without any explicit mention of the later approach, notably in *Understanding Governance* (Rhodes 1997). The governance perspective suggested the growing importance of networks of policy actors, the role of information and persuasion as well as legislation, and the fluidity of pub-lic/private and domestic/international boundaries. This perspective better reflected the contemporary variation in the state's relationship with civil society and other state actors in different forms of network for the making and implementa-tion of policy than did the Westminster model. The contrast between unstable, open issue networks and more stable, closed policy communities was a particu-lar focus of interest (see Marsh and Rhodes 1992). In general, networks reflect a more open, interdependent governance relationship compared to the command-and-control-oriented form of Whitehall 'government' in the Westminster model (Rhodes 1997; Richards and Smith 2002). The changing nature of the state's rela-tions with other entities was said to involve a 'hollowing out' of capacity (Rhodes 1997) such that many of its activities are now only conducted jointly with pri-vate or international actors, reducing its ability to influence outcomes, especially in economic and industrial policy, though the increasing penetration of market forces.

Despite the progress made in the first wave of governance research, B&R argue that an interpretivist approach is necessary to enable the practice of 'a shift from government of a unitary state to governance in and by networks' to be critically assessed by 'unpacking the relevant beliefs' of people involved in this practice and exploring 'why they arose' (Bevir and Rhodes 2003: 1). Other authors observe that 'If we are in the midst of a shift from top-down "command and control" to a looser framework of "governance", then the time of interpretivism may well have arrived' (Finlayson 2004: 129). Interpretivists call for a 'decentred' approach 'to think about governance in relation to diverse narratives, traditions and dilemmas' (Bevir and Rhodes 2003: 62). They set out their 'governance narrative' for the central state including a prominent application to 'Thatcherism' for a period in which much central state reform occurred. B&R identify 'narratives of governance', bundling authors under the 'narrative traditions' of 'Tory', 'Liberal', 'Whig', and 'Socialist' which influence the narratives of Thatcherism (Bevir and Rhodes 2003: 108–18). The traditions are suggested as encountering 'dilemmas', forcing changes to beliefs and reshaping of the traditions. For example, they note the dilemma of 'state overload' and a tension between a Thatcherite project to impose reform through state authority and simultaneously to increase the scope of markets in the public services which, in some respects, reduced central state capacity (Bevir and Rhodes 2003: 120).

However, the interpretivist account of 'governance' seems not to add nearly as much to the literature compared to the first wave's identification of the move from government to 'governance'. In some respects it even appears only partially con-sistent with the stated aims of the interpretivist project. In particular, for those concerned to avoid over-generalization, B&R's 'decentred' approach in practice appears to involve very broad-brush characterizations of traditions. B&R acknowl-edge that the authors they survey don't fit in single categories and that their list of traditions is not exhaustive, particularly noting the case for a 'Marxist' tradition that they do not develop (Bevir and Rhodes 2003: 123 n. 1). So the practice of interpretivist research would seem likely to alarm those anxious to elaborate fully the beliefs and intentions of the large number of different authors writing on this topic. B&R do not articulate criteria that would enable consensus to be built on how far the process of adding narratives should be taken. In the extreme case, a narrative for each author would not seem unreasonable, yet this is very far from the approach that they adopt. B&R could be seen as being guilty of the violation that they accuse quantitative political science of being prone to in forcing categories on the subjects of research that those subjects would not accept or possibly even recognize.

To take an example of B&R's packaging of traditions, Andrew Gamble's (1988) influential interpretation of Thatcherism sits uneasily in the socialist tradition that B&R describe as entailing 'structural explanations focused on economics factors and class with its critique of capitalism'. Gamble suggests Thatcherism as a combination of traditional Conservative thinking and a revived neoliberalism, as reflected in the populist project of the 'free economy and the strong state'. Gamble's account appears subtle, drawing on several 'traditions' and not simply reflecting one of the 'differences in emphasis' within the socialist tradition that B&R acknowledge (Bevir and Rhodes 2003: 115–16). Similarly, there is little explicit justification for the selection of four specific 'dilemmas' of Thatcherism (welfare dependency, state overload, inflation, globalization) for detailed attention from the long list of possible dilemmas that might be claimed to exist. For example, an additional dilemma of technological change might note how developments in information systems could facilitate quasi-markets or collaborative forms of government in 'digital-era governance' (Dunleavy et al. 2006), but it could also act as a spur to new forms of bureaucracy based on standardized procedures for information gathering and processing. However, such a dilemma, whilst seeming eminently plausible, is absent from B&R's account. McAnulla (2006: 126) makes a similar point in suggesting the irony that the dilemmas identified by B&R in their account appear to be treated as 'givens', or are at least not obviously the subject of contestation, but they are highly contested within the literature on Thatcherism.

The second wave of governance research is a label covering a range of work, but defined by shared characteristics of broadly agreeing with the changes described by the label governance but criticizing some of the first-wave work. The changes were not as marked as some of the proponents of governance suggested, notably because the central state was fragmented historically. The initial governance perspective also neglected the significance of trends to strengthen central state structures. The core parts of government developed new capacities for control in recent years (Holliday 2000). The central state has retained, and at times increased, influence over the resources of the nation, with government spending fluctuating as a proportion of UK GDP between about 37 per cent and almost 50 per cent in recent years, and currently hovering around 42 per cent. However, the influence of the state is not confined to ownership and funding. The regulatory state using public authority to influence otherwise private activities has grown and changed its form (Moran 2002). In addition, central government has increasingly been recognized as having a regulatory means of influence over the public sector through standard setting, monitoring, and enforcement (Hood et al. 1999; Hood, James, and Scott 2000). The most recent wave of governance research is discussed in the next section.

19.3 Disaggregating Governance

The third wave of research on governance shares the view that governance needs to be disaggregated into specific topics and its operation is contingent on a variety of factors, particularly policy sector, timing, and the institutions and actors of the central state and other bodies involved. Institutions of the central state, as reasonably stable patterns of behaviour or formal organizations, play an important role, and the formal institutions are summarized in Figure 19.1. Most current work is from within mainstream politics rather than B&R's interpretivist approach. The literature is large and space allows only a partial analysis, so six key topics are surveyed to illustrate the current and potential contributions of interpretivists and mainstream approaches. The topics are: power in policy-making networks, multi-level governance, the core executive, presidentialization of the prime ministership, departments and politician–civil servant relationships, and the central state beyond departments.

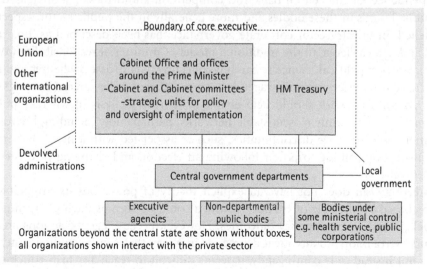

Fig. 19.1 The central state

19.3.1 Power in Policy-making Networks

Much mainstream governance literature uses a broadly liberal democratic characterization of the state that goes beyond the traditional focus on formal institutions to locate state structures in explicit theories of political power. The concept of state power invoked dates back at least to Weber (1948) with the view that states are human communities that claim sovereignty, including the monopoly of the use of legitimate physical force, within territorial boundaries (Hay and Lister 2006). The use of policy networks including central state actors in explanations of policy outcomes has been criticized for using networks as a metaphor for redescribing relationships rather than explaining variation in policy outcomes using a model incorporating variation in the structure of the networks (Dowding 1995b). A partial response to this criticism has been the development of the resource dependence model which emphasizes that actors in policy domains need to agree to work together because they do not have the necessary resources to ignore others, and that bargaining relations between them are often positive sum, providing an incentive to cooperate (Rhodes 1997). In contrast, the 'asymmetric power' model gives more emphasis to the inequality of power relations in policy-making. In particular, it notes that the central government has influence at the centre of policy networks but is itself segmented and is uneven in its external influence. The central state faces structured inequality of societal actors' ability to advance their interests, exchange relationships with actors on which it depends for information and cooperation to develop and implement policies (Smith, Marsh, and Richards 2001).

The increased use of institutions, at least partly independent from ministers, has been noted as involving depoliticization of some aspects of policy (Burnham 2001; Flinders and Buller 2006; Wilks 2007). This trend remodels policy networks to reduce the salience of links between administrators and ministers and has included greater independence for the central bank and competition authorities. The increased use of public boards in these bodies and more generally in the public sector, especially modelled on private-sector corporate governance, has been described as 'boardisation' and is a challenge to the traditional model of ministerial responsibility (Wilks 2007). Current political science research is collecting data to assess whether and how government ministers set policy agendas across different policy areas (Jennings and John 2007). This work should help enable systematic analysis of whether policy-making involves mainly closed, stable networks, perhaps now including boards, or whether there are large discontinuities, such as associated with a new government administration coming to power following an election and changing priorities for the central state.

Interpretivism does not have an explicit theory of power but its implicit view seems based on the role of traditions, which could be seen as having an influence on beliefs and, in turn, policy outcomes. However, because agents' actions are not bound by traditions to any great degree, or in a way that can be studied systematically but instead only contingently, it seems difficult to reach any firm conclusions about the influence of particular traditions. The view of power, insofar as it rests on traditions which don't constrain, seems naive from a politics perspective which has long recognized important systematic inequalities in actors' involvement in policy-making (Marsh 2008). Mainstream political history, which address many of the concerns about generalization and the difficulties of broad theorizing raised by B&R, are similarly more attentive to issues of power in their accounts of the central state than are interpretivists (Hennessy 1986; 1989).

19.3.2 Multi-level Governance

The multi-level governance perspective, developed within the mainstream of political science, places emphasis on the structure of power relations in which the central state sits. It suggests that networks of policy-making operate with strong hierarchical elements. The multiple levels of supranational, central state, and local and regional state in this hierarchy are suggested as being particularly important. The European Union increasingly involves the British central state working both in intergovernmental decision-making between member states and in relations with a supranational level (Bache and Flinders 2004; Flinders 2002; 2004). The process of Europeanization has influenced the whole political system in which the central state is located, influencing the politics of interest group orientation and policy development and making it much less narrowly focused on the domestic level (Featherstone and Radaelli 2003). This trend is apparent across the full range of policy sectors but is particularly evident in trade, agriculture, and the environment. In some circumstances, the central state is increasingly bypassed with regions and devolved administrations having direct links, especially in the case of funds for regional economic assistance. However, the structure of interaction with the EU in many areas of policy reflects the departmental organization of Whitehall, so the earlier institutional structures have had some influence on contemporary multi-level systems (Bulmer and Burch 1998).

Devolution has made the multi-level governance perspective even more relevant. The British state, as the main part of the UK state incorporating Northern Ireland, has always had historical territorial administrative structures for Wales and Scotland. Devolution has created devolved powers for Scotland and Northern Ireland, with Wales making secondary legislation, within a UK state exercising reserved powers. All parts of the UK remain dependent on spending decisions made centrally but the developed administrations have differing degrees of discretion on their use. The formal arrangements for policy coordination across the UK include a Joint Ministerial Committee and concordats for the UK. It is mainly on issues involving the EU that the more formal structures are systematically used. However, this situation might alter under governments of different parties and as the devolved administrations develop more distinctive administrative and political trajectories (Rhodes et al. 2005). Conflict because of perceived unfairness may eventually lead to a depoliticized method for the allocation of spending which might remove it from the direct control of central state politicians (McLean 2005).

19.3.3 The Core Executive

Mainstream political science governance research rejects the Westminster model that places cabinet government at the centre of the political executive. Much historical debate concerned the relationship between Cabinet and the Prime Minister. However, the core executive (Dunleavy and Rhodes 1990; Rhodes 1995) has come to be recognized as a better description of contemporary arrangements for central coordination of state activity, with a network of actors around the Cabinet Office, de facto Prime Minister's Office, and the Treasury setting strategic priorities, coordinating and directing the broader executive system. The spending allocation process, cabinet committee system, and policy review units are tools used by these organizations for coordination and direction. Some definitions of the core executive include central government departments because of their role in policy development and because some ministers in these bodies are involved in core executive institutions, for example sitting in cabinet (Smith 1999). However, the dominant approach is to maintain a distinction between the 'core' parts of central government that are primarily strategic and the departmental parts which tend to have more narrowly focused sector-specific remits.

The core executive has attempted to strengthen its capacity for steering, in part to counter the centrifugal pressures of policy-making being conducted in networks specific to distinct policy sectors. There are increased resources in the centre of the government machine and more regularized networks focused on the heart of the system (Burch and Holliday 1996: 106; Hay and Richards 2000). An additional 'tool of governance' for core executive monitoring, direction, and coordination of government activities is the regime of Public Service Agreement (PSA) performance measures and targets (James 2004). The system is run by the Treasury with the involvement of offices around the Prime Minister. Secretaries of State or other ministers are individually responsible for reporting performance against PSA targets, and individual civil servants are made champions of particular targets or sets of targets. The PSA documents are published and, as well as their use within government, are available to enhance parliamentary and public scrutiny of government activity. However, the targets vary in specificity, with those for foreign affairs and defence being vague whilst those for public services are relatively precise, although, even in this latter case, assessing performance against targets has been complicated by the many changes to targets that have been made. There have been few consequences for ministers who have failed to meet targets, although the resignation of the Secretary of State for Education in 2002 was partly the result of promises she made to meet targets that were subsequently not achieved. The core executive has further exercised its strategic role through the coordination of policy and services using a range of tools.

These efforts to 'join up' government to improve policies that cut across departmental and other institutional boundaries have included staff transfers, joint budgets, joint working arrangements, and joint target regimes (Flinders 2002; Richards and Smith 2002; James 2004).

In contrast to this research, the interpretivist approach appears to reject the possibility of core executive tools of governance. Rhodes argues that 'A decentred approach undercuts the idea of network steering as a set of tools by which we can manage governance. If governance is constructed differently, contingently and continuously, we cannot have a tool kit for managing it' (Rhodes 2007: 1257). This statement seems to establish before research is undertaken that the tools won't work, whereas the mainstream research discussed above has found that the tools work in some contexts but not in others. For example, joint targets shared by departments to promote joined-up working have met with success where it has been backed up with extra funding to incentivize collaboration, but has been less successful in its absence where traditional departmental interests have acted as a barrier.

19.3.4 Prime Minister and the Presidentialization Thesis

Mainstream research has a consensus that the power of the institution of Prime Minister is influenced by the political, social, and economic context and its use by the office holder. The contemporary literature developed in part as a critique of earlier research that over-emphasizes the influence of the personality of individual Prime Ministers. The commonly noted power resources of the institution of Prime Minister include the ability to appoint and dismiss ministers, and power to chair cabinet meetings, manage government business, and oversee the machinery of government. Cabinet is generally thought of to be less influential as a collective decision-making body than in the past and the Prime Minister's central position on cabinet committees and appointments to these committees are an important source of influence. The Prime Minister is also able to use small ad hoc meetings, including bilateral meetings with ministers, to bypass broader collective discussion. The Prime Minister's position as party leader is both a strength and a potential weakness because it allows control through patronage and party machinery but also facilitates removal by means other than a general election (Hennessy 1986; Smith 1999; Kavanagh and Seldon 2000; Heffernan 2003).

The increased use of personal leadership, including direct appeals through the media and the growing dominance of leaders within parties, especially at time of election, has been termed the 'presidentialization' of the prime ministerial post (Foley 2000). This term affords more importance to the post than is recognized in the Westminster model and has particularly developed because the media presentation of central state policy has become increasingly centralized on the Prime Minister, with systems for scheduling news releases in a coordinated manner and for responding to incidents. However, the willingness and capacity of Prime Ministers to use their media resources in a 'presidential' fashion varies, perhaps reaching recent highpoints in the case of Margaret Thatcher around the 1983 election and in the emphasis given to Blair in Labour's campaigning in the run-up to the 1997 election and in the popular mandate he claimed this approach subsequently gave him personally in government. It has been argued that Blair's personal leadership was particularly important to his party electorally in this period as part of the Labour Party's project to construct and capture the 'centre' ground of British politics (Hindmoor 2004: 188–200).

Beyond the use of the media, the degree of president-like influence depends on many factors, especially Prime Ministers' ability to control their parliamentary majority and government ministers, especially cabinet ministers (Heffernan 2003; 2005a; 2005b). The notion of a presidential Prime Minister sits uneasily with collective elements of the senior political elite which are still evident, despite full cabinet meetings largely being symbolic affairs. In particular, the Chancellor of the Exchequer is a post within cabinet that is well placed to challenge Prime Ministers' authority because of the Treasury's important financial, economic, and public expenditure roles, and ministers with substantial power bases in the governing party are also influential (Heclo and Wildavsky 1974; Thain and Wright 1995; Heffernan 2005a; 2005b). Research on presidentialization from within mainstream political science is increasingly defining presidentialization more explicitly from the framework of comparative politics research on heads of government. To do so notes that using the term 'president' in the British context can mislead as much as illuminate, and, whilst there are similarities between Prime Ministers and Presidents as chief executives, the different constitutional positions and roles in policy-making systems need more careful attention (Heffernan 2005b).

Intrepretivist work on presidentialization has focused on the way practitioners understand the relationship between the Prime Minister and other actors, identifying 'tales' of presidentialization when Blair was Prime Minister. They argue that presidentialization tales acted as a 'smokescreen' because Blair was locked into a complex pattern of domestic and international dependence reflecting contemporary governance. The views of presidentialization are themselves interpreted through different traditions of the Westminster model, notably Tory, Whig, and Socialist (Bevir and Rhodes 2006a). However, there seem to be multiple narratives that could be constructed and no way of telling why these three are to be preferred to other possibilities. Bevir and Rhodes's more general interest in presidentialization seems centred on Blair's personal control of the policy agenda and the achievement of his preferred policy outcomes. A political science version of this project might systematically map out what Blair wanted and how far he managed to achieve his aims across the full range of policy sectors, with careful attention to variation across sectors. It would then move on to identifying and assessing the barriers to him getting what he wanted. Of course, the secrecy of the central sate is a possible obstacle to such research, although interpretivists are more optimistic than most about the possibilities of gaining access (Rhodes 2007: 1256).

19.3.5   The Central Departments and Politician–Civil Servant Relations

The mainstream notes the role of departments in networks and their particular importance for sectoral policy-making, unless the core executive takes a particular interest in that sector; interpretivists seem broadly to concur with this analysis. Traditionally the relationship between the Prime Minister and ministers in cabinet have formed the main focus of mainstream inquiry, but the activities of departmental ministers and junior ministers has received increasing attention (Heady 1974; Rose 1987; Smith, Marsh, and Richards 2001; Dewan and Dowding 2005). Departments, each headed by a minister, use Crown and statutory powers and operate within a doctrine of ministerial responsibility for initiating policies and accounting for them. The exercise of routine processes, for example statutory instruments under powers delegated to departments, has received increasing attention (Page 2001). The different departmental 'cultures' that develop over time influence the conduct of policy-making (Smith, Marsh, and Richards 2001).

Mainstream research has long noted that individual ministerial responsibility is a constitutional convention which, in the sense of resignation for errors made by departments, has rarely been observed in practice. Similarly, collective ministerial responsibility has rarely brought about resignation, although it is more influential as an internal disciplining device to encourage commitment to shared policy goals. Most work on ministerial resignations uses a political history approach; political science study of ministerial tenure is relatively recent (but for an exception see Alt 1975). A 'corrective' effect of ministerial resignation on public support for the government following unpopularity created by resignation issues has been found (Dewan and Dowding 2005). There is evidence of prime ministerial 'styles' of firing ministers, and ministers with an Oxbridge educational background and more senior ministers have greater durability. In particular, ministers of cabinet rank are able to survive longer than those outside cabinet (Berlinski, Dewan, and Dowding 2007). This work is particularly notable because of the relative scarcity of quantitative research on the central state. The conflict between interpretivists and the mainstream is at its most severe over the status of this work, with interpretivists alleging the independent variables used in such modelling are unjustified 'objectifications' that do not focus on the beliefs of actors. However, it could be argued that a variable such as educational background is a proxy for beliefs that are associated with particular backgrounds. If such proxies were to be accepted as being of some interest, the dispute with interpretivists would then seem to be about whether the relationships found in multivariate modelling are valid. The regression coefficients reflect average effects or associations and are generalizations about effects across cases of the kind interpretivists claim should be avoided. However, narratives also seem to be generalizations of a kind in the extent to which they bundle multiple authors into particular traditions. The objections from within an interpretivist account are not however limited to these points.

Mainstream politics work has examined the relationship between the political and administrative elites in central government, focusing on the appointment of officials, their tenure, promotion and removal, and behaviour, including influence over policy outcomes. These issues have often been bundled together in the topic of whether the civil service is in some sense 'politicized' or whether it embodies neutral competence, or 'speaks truth to power', in the policy-making process. Interest has focused on how the cadre of career civil servants' position has been affected by increasing appointments from outside, especially in the cases of executive agency chief executives, outside entrants to policy ranks, and special advisers. The consensus is that policy advice now comes from a wider range of sources and senior civil servants are generally less influential than in the 'village' model of Whitehall of thirty years ago (Heclo and Wildavsky 1974). The changes have been described as the 'end of the Whitehall model' for the relationship between senior civil servants and ministers (Campbell and Wilson 1995) or a change in the 'public service bargain' (Hood and Lodge 2006). In this latter perspective, civil servants have greater incentivization through performance pay and through top pay levels that are higher multiples of average salaries than has traditionally been the case. The formal competencies stress capacity for both policy development and implementation, although there has been increased emphasis on officials' role in 'delivery' of policy. There has been a bifurcation in loyalty and responsibility, with some increased emphasis on public reporting and resignation for poor performance amongst agency chief executives but continued protection of position for the policy elite in departments. There continues to be a 'partnership' bargain between politicians and senior officials in policy-making where the longevity of civil servants and their access to information networks can still give them great influence in the policy process.

Interpretivism has perhaps had its widest application in relation to this topic, where it follows in a long tradition of interview- and observation-based studies of the senior civil service dating back to Heclo and Wildavsky (1974). Interpretivist work has suggested the importance of policy-setting by ministers and constitutional propriety of officials in the justifications for action offered by these actors. However, it has also been noted that these conventions can break down at times of crisis (Richards and Smith 2004). The governance stories offered by interpretivists similarly note the conventions practised by elite actors in the central state, but also point out that they don't operate at all times (Bevir and Rhodes 2006b; Richards 2007).

19.3.6 The Central State Beyond Departments

Mainstream politics research has identified the influence of the central state well beyond central departments in networks of government. This influence is exercised through the use of executive agencies, a host of non-departmental public bodies, and through central state steering of local government, the health service, public corporations, devolved administrations, and a range of contractors. Closest to departments are executive agencies, organizational units set up over the past two decades to have management freedoms, operating semi-detached from departments to enable them to focus on the task at hand. The agencies operate in an accountability framework of policy aims and resources set by the department, with a chief executive responsible for overall performance of the agency. The ideas were influenced by an Anglo-American business corporate governance model of the multi-divisional organization in which specialist units are given freedom to manage within a framework of focused accountability and budget for each unit (James 2001). The structures are supposed to enhance management capacity but maintain ministers' strategic direction, and about 60 per cent of civil servants work in agencies.

The agency creation initiative in part reflected 'bureau-shaping' strategies of senior officials who sought to protect their role in policy-making by passing on responsibility for management to chief executives rather than reduce their policy role (Dunleavy 1991; James 2003: 41–69). The performance of services handled by individual agencies has been improved in many cases, but agencies have increased 'horizontal' organizational fragmentation; performance target regimes led some agencies to focus on their own activities regardless of negative spillover effects on the broader state system. Agency structures also contributed to 'vertical' fragmentation between 'policy' handled by departments and 'operations' handled by agencies, resulting in some policies being developed with insufficient regard to issues of implementation (James 2003: 109–24). The bureaucratic networks around agencies have come increasingly to affect the way policy is developed and implemented in the central state (Gains 2003).

The use of partly independent quasi-autonomous public bodies, or 'distributed public governance', has grown in recent decades (Flinders 2004). Central state influence comes through finance, manipulation of organizational structures, and the use of authority, often embodied in regulation. Appointments to over 70,000 posts are under the control of central government departments (Skelcher 1998). The central state also makes extensive use of contracts with private firms. These arrangements have become more complex, involving relational contracting and public–private partnerships which have been especially used for new infrastructure projects (Grimshaw, Vincent, and Willmott 2005). Some recent research influenced by interpretivism has begun to examine implementation systems, but in a way which also draws on the more mainstream governance literature on complex networks (Clarke and Gains 2007).

The need to steer and coordinate complex networks has led central government to develop systems of regulation for the public sector. Research on regulation of government notes the common themes involved in audit, inspection, and oversight of public bodies and the growth of this activity in recent years. In the early 1990s, regulators of government spent about £770m on their own activities, with subsequent growth bringing this total closer to £1,000m by 2000 (Hood et al. 1999: 23; Hood, James, and Scott 2000). The growth of regulation seems to reflect a public-interest view of regulation, with less attention paid to the counter-productive aspects of the system compared to the regulation of business where public-interest models of regulation have long been questioned, especially the compliance costs of regulation (Hood et al. 1999; James 2000). Associated with regulatory systems have been target regimes, especially for public services. Recently, there is increased recognition that these systems place burdens and can encourage 'gaming' behaviour by those subject to them, and other unintended consequences (Boyne, Day, and Walker 2002; James 2004; Bevan and Hood 2006). However, central government has been reluctant to dismantle regulatory and target systems because of the apparent capacity it provides to exert influence far beyond Whitehall.

19.4 CONCLUSION

The interpretivist contribution to knowledge about the central state does not compare favourably with that gained from mainstream approaches. The potential of interpretivism is not promising either: it seems driven by a philosophical project that has unnecessarily pessimistic conclusions for the possibility of empirical generalization and causal explanation as undertaken by the mainstream. The interpretivists' programmatic theory based on the relationship between beliefs, traditions, and dilemmas seems unnecessarily constraining and does not adequately address the key disciplinary interests of power, conflict, and the role of organizational structures and networks. The 'first-wave' analysis of governance was initially developed without any reference to the interpretivist approach and still sets the broad framework for current research.

The vibrant current 'third-wave' research on governance is mostly within the mainstream and has contributed knowledge about important substantive topics, as discussed in the Section 19.3 above. The debate between the mainstream and interpretivists risks crowding out discussion of important issues of theory and method. Discussion of theory might particularly centre on how the British central state sheds light on theory in comparative politics, and how research can be less parochial. Whilst some authors claim the core executive in Britain is weak, compared to executives in many other states it appears strong. There are relatively few veto-points to block governments that want to bring about policy change (Tsebelis 2002). The discussion of multi-level governance could similarly be situated more explicitly in comparative work on varieties of federal system, such as whether the central state is becoming part of a federal EU system or a multi-level system with a more complex allocation of jurisdictions (Hooghe and Marks 2003).

In terms of method, the complementarities of quantitative and qualitative approaches are only beginning to be fully explored, mainly because of the scarcity of quantitative work until recently and a lack of dialogue between researchers using different methods. Systematic gathering of data about the central state to produce measures for well-worn concepts is likely to be a major contribution to research in the coming years. However, quantitative researchers require valid variables and qualitative work has much to offer, and warn against, in this regard. Some of the protagonists in the current debate about interpretivism admit to their use of 'rhetorical devices' with the aim of 'provoking new ways of seeing British government' (Rhodes 2007: 1258). In the sense of generating debate, they have been successful. We now need careful development of theory and its empirical implications, and systematic collection and analysis of evidence, rather than grand summary statements of developments or attempts to change the whole approach to the study of the central state.

REFERENCES

ALT, J. E. 1975. 'Continuity, Turnover and Experience in the British Cabinet, 1868–1970'. Pp. 33–54 in V. Herman and J. E. Alt (eds.), *Cabinet Studies: A Reader*. London: Macmillan.

BACHE, I., and FLINDERS, M. 2004. *Multi-Level Governance*. Oxford: Oxford University Press.

BERLINSKI, S., DEWAN, T., and DOWDING, K. M. 2007. 'The Length of Ministerial Tenure in the UK 1945–1997'. *British Journal of Political Science*, 37/2: 245–62.

BEVAN, R. G., and HOOD, C. 2006. 'What's Measured is What Matters: Targets and Gaming in Healthcare in the English Public Health Care System'. *Public Administration*, 84/3: 517–38.

BEVIR, M., and RHODES, R. A. W. 2003. *Interpreting British Governance*. London: Routledge.

——— 2004. 'Interpretation as Method, Explanation and Critique'. *British Journal of Politics and International Relations*, 6/2: 156–64.

——— 2006a. 'Prime Ministers, Presidentialism and Westminster Smokescreens'. *Political Studies*, 54: 671–90.

——— 2006b. *Governance Stories*. London: Routledge.

BOYNE, G. A., DAY, P., and WALKER, R. 2002. 'The Evaluation of Public Service Inspection: A Theoretical Framework'. *Urban Studies*, 39: 1197–212.

BULMER, S., and BURCH, M. 1998. 'Organising for Europe: Whitehall, the British State and the European Union'. *Public Administration*, 76: 601–28.

BURCH, M., and HOLLIDAY, I. 1996. *The British Cabinet System*. London: Prentice Hall, Harvester Wheatsheaf.

——— 2004. 'The Blair Government and the Core Executive'. *Government and Opposition*, 39/1: 1–21.

BURNHAM, P. 2001. 'New Labour and the Politics of Depoliticisation'. *British Journal of Politics and International Relations*, 3/2: 127–49.

CAMPBELL, C., and WILSON, G. K. 1995. *The End of Whitehall: Death of a Paradigm?* Oxford: Blackwell.

CLARKE, K., and GAINS, F. 2007. 'Constructing Delivery: Implementation as an Interpretive Process'. *Critical Policy Analysis*, 1/2: 133–8.

DEWAN, T., and DOWDING, K. 2005. 'The Corrective Effect of Ministerial Resignations on Government Popularity'. *American Journal of Political Science*, 49: 46–56.

DOWDING, K. M., 1995a. *The Civil Service*. London: Routledge.

——— 1995b. 'Model or Metaphor? A Critical Review of the Policy Network Approach'. *Political Studies*, 43: 136–58.

——— 2004. 'Interpretation, Truth and Investigation: Comments on Bevir and Rhodes'. *British Journal of Politics and International Relations*, 6/2: 136–42.

Dowding, K. M., and James, O. 2004. 'Analysing Bureau-Shaping Models: Comments on Marsh, Smith and Richards: Notes and Comments'. *British Journal of Political Science*, 34/1: 183–9.

Dunleavy, P. 1991. *Democracy, Bureaucracy and Public Choice*. Hemel Hempstead: Harvester Wheatsheaf.

——Margets, H., Bastow, S., and Tinkler, J. 2006. 'New Public Management is Dead: Long Live Digital-Era Governance'. *Journal of Public Administration Research and Theory*, 16: 467–94.

——and Rhodes, R. A. W. 1990. 'Core Executive Studies in Britain'. *Public Administration*, 68/1: 3–28.

Evans, M. 2006. 'The Art of Prescription: Theory and Practice in Public Administration Research'. *Public Policy and Administration*, 84/2: 479–515.

Featherstone, K., and Radaelli, C. M. (eds.) 2003. *The Politics of Europeanisation*. Oxford: Oxford University Press.

Finlayson, A. 2004. 'Meaning and Politics: Assessing Bevir and Rhodes'. *British Journal of Politics and International Relations*, 6/2: 149–56.

Flinders, M. 2002. 'Governance in Whitehall'. *Public Administration*, 80/1: 51–75.

——2004. 'Distributed Public Governance in Britain'. *Public Administration*, 82/4: 883–909.

——and Buller, J. 2006. 'Depoliticisation: Principles, Tactics and Tools'. *British Politics*, 1/3: 1–26.

Foley, M. 2000. *The British Presidency*. Manchester: Manchester University Press.

Gains, F. 2003. 'Executive Agencies in Government: The Impact of Bureaucratic Networks on Policy Outcomes'. *Journal of Public Policy*, 23/1: 55–79.

Gamble, A. 1988. *The Free Economy and the Strong State*. London: Macmillan.

Greenleaf, W. H. 1983. *The British Political Tradition*, vols. i and ii. London: Methuen.

Grimshaw, D., Vincent, S., and Willmott, H. 2005. 'Going Privately: Outsourcing and Partnerships in UK Public Services'. *Public Administration*, 80/3: 475–502.

Hay, C. 2002. *Political Analysis: A Critical Introduction*. Basingstoke: Palgrave.

——2004. 'Taking Ideas Seriously in Explanatory Political Analysis'. *British Journal of Politics and International Relations*, 6/2: 142–9.

——and Lister, M. 2006. 'Introduction: Theories of the State'. Pp. 1–20 in *The State: Theories and Issues*. Basingstoke: Palgrave Macmillan.

——and Richards, D. 2000. 'The Tangled Webs of Westminster and Whitehall: The Discourse, Strategy and Practice of Networking within the British Core Executive'. *Public Administration*, 78/1: 1–28.

Heady, B. 1974. *British Cabinet Ministers*. London: Allen and Unwin.

Heclo, H., and Wildavsky, A. 1974. *The Private Government of Public Money*. London: Macmillan.

Heffernan, R. 2003. 'Prime Ministerial Predominance? Core Executive Politics in the UK'. *British Journal of Politics and International Relations*, 5: 347–72.

——2005a. 'Exploring (and Explaining) the British Prime Minister'. *British Journal of Politics and International Relations*, 7/4: 605–20.

——2005b. 'Why the Prime Minister Cannot be President: Comparing Institutional Imperatives in Britain and America'. *Parliamentary Affairs*, 58/4: 53–70.

Hennessy, P. 1986. *Cabinet*. Oxford: Basil Blackwell.

——1989. *Whitehall*. London: Fontana.

Hindmoor, A. 2004 *New Labour at the Centre*. Oxford: Oxford University Press.

Holliday, I. 2000. 'Is the British State Hollowing Out?' *Political Quarterly*, 71/2: 167–76.

HOOD, C. C., JAMES, O., and SCOTT, C. 2000. 'Regulation in Government: Has it Increased, Is it Increasing, Should it be Diminished?' *Public Administration*, 78/2: 283–304.

—— and LODGE, M. 2006. *Public Service Bargains*. Oxford: Oxford University Press.

—— SCOTT, C. W., JAMES, O., JONES, G. W., and TRAVERS, T. 1999. *Regulation inside Government*. Oxford: Oxford University Press.

HOOGHE, L., and MARKS, G. 2003. 'Unravelling the Central State, but How? Types of Multi-level Governance'. *American Political Science Review*, 97/2: 233–43.

JAMES, O. 2000. 'Regulation inside Government: Public Interest Justifications and Regulatory Failures'. *Public Administration*, 78/2: 327–43.

—— 2001. 'Business Models and the Transfer of Business-Like Central Government Agencies'. *Governance*, 14/2: 233–52.

—— 2003. *The Executive Agency Revolution in Whitehall: Public Interest versus Bureau-Shaping Perspectives*. Basingstoke: Palgrave Macmillan.

—— 2004. 'The UK Core Executive's Use of Public Service Agreements as a Tool of Governance'. *Public Administration*, 82/2: 397–418.

JENNINGS, W., and JOHN, P. 2007. *Punctuations and Turning Points in British Politics? The Policy Agenda of the Queens' Speech, 1940–2005*. Mimeo.

KAVANAGH, D., and SELDON, A. 2000. *The Powers behind the Prime Minister: The Hidden Influence of Number Ten*. London: HarperCollins.

KERR, P., and KETTELL, S. 2006. 'In Defence of British Politics: The Past, Present and Future of the Discipline'. *British Politics*, 1/1: 3–25.

McANULLA, S. 2006. 'Challenging the New Interpretivist Approach: Towards a Critical Realist Alternative'. *British Politics*, 1: 113–38.

McLEAN, I. 2005. *The Fiscal Crisis of the United Kingdom*. Basingstoke: Palgrave.

MARSH, D. 2008. 'Understanding British Government: Analysing Competing Models'. *British Journal of Politics and International Relations*, 10/2: 251–68.

—— and RHODES, R. A. W. 1992. *Policy Networks in British Government*. Oxford: Oxford University Press.

—— RICHARDS, D., and SMITH, M. 2004. 'Understanding and Explaining Civil Service Reform: A Reply to Dowding and James'. *British Journal of Political Science*, 34/1: 183–9.

—— SMITH, M. J., and RICHARDS, D. 2001. *Changing Patterns of Governance: Reinventing Whitehall*. Basingstoke: Palgrave Macmillan.

MORAN, M. 2002. *The British Regulatory State*. Oxford: Clarendon Press.

PAGE, E. C. 2001. *Governing by Numbers: Delegated Legislation and Everyday Policy-Making*. Oxford: Hart.

RHODES, R. A. W. 1995. 'Introducing the Core Executive'. In R. A. W. Rhodes and P. J. Dunleavy (eds.), *Prime Minister, Cabinet and Core Executive*. London: Macmillan.

—— 1997. *Understanding Governance*. Buckingham: Open University Press.

—— 2007. 'Understanding Governance: Ten Years On'. *Organizational Studies*, 28/8: 1243–64.

—— CARMICHAEL, P., McMILLAN, J., and MASSEY, A. 2005. *Decentralizing the Civil Service*. Buckingham: Open University Press.

RICHARDS, D. 2007. *New Labour and the Civil Service: Reconstituting the Westminster Model*. Basingstoke: Palgrave.

—— and SMITH, M. 2002. *Governance and Public Policy in the United Kingdom*. Oxford: Oxford University Press.

—— 2004. 'Interpreting the World of Political Elites'. *Public Administration*, 82/4: 777–800.

ROSE, R. 1987. *Ministers and Ministries*. Oxford: Clarendon Press.

SKELCHER, C. 1998. *The Appointed State: Quasi-governmental Organisations and Democracy*. Buckingham: Open University Press.

SMITH, M. J. 1998. 'Reconceptualising the British State: Theoretical and Empirical Challenges to Central Government'. *Public Administration*, 76/20: 45–72.

—— 1999. *The Core Executive*. Basingstoke: Palgrave Macmillan.

—— MARSH, D., and RICHARDS, D. 2001. *The Changing Role of Central Government Departments*. Basingstoke: Macmillan.

THAIN, C., and WRIGHT, M. 1995. *The Treasury and Whitehall*. Oxford: Oxford University Press.

THEAKSTON, K. 1997. 'Comparative Biography and Leadership in Whitehall'. *Public Administration*, 75/2: 651–67.

TSEBELIS, G. 2002. *Veto Players: How Political Institutions Work*. Princeton, NJ: Princeton University Press.

WEBER, M. 1948. *Writings of Max Weber*. London: Routledge.

WILKS, S. R. M. 2007. 'Boardization and Corporate Governance in the UK as a Response to Depoliticization and Failing Accountability'. *Public Policy and Administration*, 22/4: 443–60.

CHAPTER 20

LOBBYING

GRANT JORDAN

20.1 GOVERNANCE: THE INSIDER POLICY-MAKING FORM

THOMAS (in McGrath 2005: preface) suggests that 'lobbyists work to influence government decisions to the benefit of their group or client, usually through direct contact with politicians and civil servants'.[1] While this accurately summarizes the 'heroic' self-image of the lobbyist, in 'humdrum' reality most lobbyists spend little time in face-to-face contact with decision-makers: the bulk of activity involves generating press cuttings and summaries of relevant documents for clients. In offering a low key version of lobbying, this chapter is suggesting that it has functional utility within modern polyarchies. British lobbying is best seen as typically attempting to modify public policy in specialist policy debates through persuasion and information rather than pressurizing politicians (never mind doing so improperly). Indeed a more fully developed version of the argument undermines the famous Westminster/majoritarian model of democracy as set out by Lijphart (1984).

Of course Lijphart (1984: 16) immediately qualified his dramatic 'top down' image. He said, 'In Britain, majority rule does not entail majority tyranny'. In a further reservation he noted, 'the simple picture of an omnipotent one-party cabinet using its parliamentary majority to carry out the mandate it has received from voters is, and has always been false and misleading...In fact it has long been recognised that in Britain and other democracies many organised groups compete for influence, and

---

[1] For an account of Euro lobbying see special issue of *Journal of European Public Policy*, 14/3 (2007); Mahoney (2008). The European dimension increases 'venue shopping (Baumgartner and Jones 1993) whereby groups can seek the most receptive channel.

that they tend to check and balance not only each other but also the political parties and the government'. He commended the idea of 'the *illusion* of governmental authority' (citing Keehn 1978). But qualifications are less potent than myths: unintentionally Lijphart reinforced the misleading 'pictures in our heads' (Lippman 1922). Arguably a proper appreciation of lobbying needs an acceptance of a complex 'insider politics' process where consent of affected interests is valued, interests are seen as possessing invaluable information—and capacities for policy delivery. Lobbying in this reading is part of a bargaining style of governance.

In rejecting the press 'lobbyist-as-devil' notion, this chapter connects to discussion of a particular *insider* style of policy-making (Maloney, Jordan, and McLaughlin 1994; Grant 1978; May and Nugent 1982; Page 1999; Jordan and Maloney 1997; Page 2001). Maloney, Jordan, and McLaughlin (1994: 19) say:

> The image of an insider group has to be related to the practice of policy making being made in consultation between sections of the bureaucracy and clientelistic interests...On many occasions policy making civil servants are likely to be scanning the horizon for groups who may be able to aid them in policy formulation...The policy relevant group can simplify the policy making task.

Interaction of this type is the context of lobbying. In this perspective there is an exchange-based pattern of transactions (*over time*[2]) in low-publicity policy-making venues whereby policy-makers (often officials) grant access and influence in return for political support and policy advice. Koeppl (2001) in a survey of EU Heads and Deputy Heads of Commission found that 73.3 per cent considered written material from lobbyists useful, and only 17.7 per cent were 'negative' to lobbying; 67.5 per cent thought strong lobbies were 'necessary' in Brussels.

If politics is about the public, parliament, and politicians then lobbying is democratically suspect in altering outcomes in self-regarding ways, but if instead (more realistically) it is seen as being about civil servants, clients, consultation, and consensus, then it is part of a messy pattern of information sharing. On their website (February 2007) Citigate Public Affairs quote a British government minister: 'If I do something that damages your business because I didn't know it would, that's your fault, not mine'. So lobbying is about making every effort to get advantage out of government—or a least to minimize the disadvantage.

Lobbying, as used here, is a type of *competitive* 'insider' persuasion that follows certain conventions and rules. In the USA Browne (1990: 500) describes this exchange/transactional perspective:

> the services of various interest-group suppliers (and their policymaker consumers) constitute worthwhile goods that are the basis for exchanges, or transactions, that facilitate policy-making...organized interests...must have something recognizable to market within some one or more relevant networks of decision making.

---

[2] The time dimension constrains behaviour. Lobbying (for professionals) is iterative and therefore reputation must be protected.

This exchange is about helping policy-makers (principally officials) to get their policies 'right'. Truman (1951: 333) identified this ability to supply information as 'One important factor among the informal determinants of access'. He said, 'Any politician . . . is obliged to make decisions that are guided in part by the relevant knowledge that is available to him . . . Access is likely to be available to groups somewhat in proportion to their ability to met this need'.

In contrast to the negative press interpretation, this conception of lobbying emphasizes trust. Finer (1958: 34) quoted the director of a national trade association claiming that departmental recognition:

> depends primarily on the statesmanlike way in which the association handles its problems and on the confidence inspired by the staff in their dealings with government officials . . . government officials will trust the staff sufficiently to inform and consult them on matters which are still highly confidential . . .

Berry (1984: 119–22) in the USA also related effective lobbying to reputation and expertise. He argued, 'Credibility Comes First . . . honesty is not so much a matter of virtue as it is of necessity'. He continued, 'Create a Dependency . . . The optimal role for a lobbyist to play is that of trusted source of information whom policy makers can call on when they need hard-to-find data'.

Lobbying in a friendly 'reading' is about *competing* supplies of arguments for policy-makers to referee. Analogously, capitalism is defended by proponents as a competitive process to supply goods efficiently at lowest cost, but individual capitalists want to suppress competition and drive prices up. So too in lobbying: for 'sellers' the best lobbying situation is where there is one-sided access and no counter-argument. This is what the customer of the professional lobbyist wants, but this has none of the *system benefits* that competition provides. Of course lobbyists have a vested interest in permitting clients to assume that for money they can 'fix' things, but useful lobbying is generally about ensuring arguments are considered rather than buying decisions. Given the heightened scrutiny of lobbying, and popular suspicion, politicians are unlikely to want to be identified with causes that cannot be reconciled to their constituents' interests.

The ambition of the lobbyist is thus about improving the legislative or regulatory environment for a policy participant. Stigler (1971) argued much regulation is industry stimulated (as opposed to being a burden on the regulated). This leads to a 'standard profit-seeking model of lobbying' (Grier, Munger, and Roberts 1994; Hansen and Mitchell 2000) that sees the level of lobbying as a response of group size and resource; the impact of government on the firm or group; and the concentration of the sector. Accordingly lobbying is a predictable activity and its insider form can also be predicted as this is the cost-effective route. While there are 'multiple venues' (Baumgartner and Jones 1993), openings, and opportunity structures for lobbyists, the payoffs at lowest cost encourage technical resolution with officials either in Whitehall or in EU Directorates.[3] Relevant to this idea of low-cost lobbying is the

---

[3] Burrell (in McGrath 2005: 309) notes, 'Remember that civil servants matter . . . The sorts of issues on which we are likely to be lobbying will be points of detail rather than of national principle, and

major theme in the literature as to whether lobbyists actually talk to sympathizers (Bauer, Pool, and Dexter 1963) or seek to persuade opponents. In line with the argument so far accepted conventional wisdom says, 'The principal effect of lobbying is not conversion but reinforcement' (Matthews 1960: 191). In other words lobbying is usually about the undramatic success of helping predisposed policy-makers carry weight rather than securing dramatic policy U-turns. The 'trick' is not to make policy-makers contradict their first instincts, but to portray what the lobbyist wants as compatible with general policy. Disappointingly for cynics, the focus of most real-life lobbying is policy improvement. Elizabeth Drew quoted a leading lobbyist in the USA: 'You got to understand what motivates the politician. Dummies, even in this town, think that politicians just want to be re elected. Well [when I talk about public policy with these legislators], I'm talking merits [of policy] with most of them' (cited in Mansbridge 1990: 13). Most lobbyists—successful or otherwise—are attempting to advance *their* interpretation in policy debates. That these debates are often esoteric and non-public reflects the necessary detail associated with insider policy-making rather than some conspiratorial exclusion.

20.2 FOCUSING ON A DEFINITION

While the Thomas definition at the head of this chapter is a good start, as with most social science terms 'lobbying' lacks an agreed meaning. Gerring (2001: 38) notes the temptation to 'just to get on with it' in social science, but he concludes to the contrary that a 'blithely empirical approach' undermines the possibility of an accumulation of knowledge.[4]

The lack of a generally regarded definition permits substantial difference in scope of discussion of authors. A major study by Baumgartner and colleagues looks at US lobbying (http://lobby.la.psu.edu) (see also Baumgartner et al. 2009). They construct a list of those active (1,264) on a random sample of 98 issues. In their research design lobbying is not seen as confined to contract lobbyists, but captures all those engaging in registered lobbying. (Such an approach allows generalization from typical rather than unusually newsworthy cases.) Citizen groups were most frequently found to be active (26 per cent), while trade and business were represented by 22 per cent of mentions (though a further 15 per cent of cases were businesses operating on their own account). Professional associations were 11 per cent. Lobbying (policy influencing) is thus wider than the activity of lobbyists (for-hire specialists).

politicians tend to rely on their officials for the detail…99 times out of 100 the Minister will be accepting the recommendation made by officials'.

[4] A Special Issue of *Parliamentary Affairs*, 51/4 (1998), considers definitional issues and ethical and regulatory dimensions.

The full population of bodies relevant to policy change has been labelled 'pressure participants' (Jordan, Halpin, and Maloney 2004) and 'interest organizations' (Gray and Lowery 1996). Such labels subsume corporations, interest groups, parts of government, agencies, and local governments, etc. But not all of their policy-influencing activities would (conventionally) be regarded as lobbying. A mass protest might be counted as 'policy-influencing' but not necessarily as 'lobbying'. This broad definition of lobbyist is similar to that in the draft Report on Lobbying (2007/2115INI) published in February 2008 by the EU Committee on Constitutional Affairs (Stubb Report). It argued that its use:

> 7. Agrees with the Commission's definition of lobbying as 'activities carried out with the objective of influencing the policy formulation and decision-making processes of the European institutions...;
>
> 8. Emphasises that all actors falling within that definition should be considered as lobbyists and treated in the same way: professional lobbyists, companies' in-house lobbyists, NGOs, think-tanks, trade associations, trade unions and employers' organisations and lawyers when their purpose is to influence policy rather than case-law;...

A common, but much narrower, conception of lobbying restricts the use to the operations of for-hire, commercial, paid lobbyists who act for different clients on a fee basis. But as indicated in Figure 20.1 below, lobbying, as understood here, is done by a variety of pressure participants (A and B) as well as C. They also pursue a range of strategies (D–F), with the implication that some policy activities (such as G) are not included as lobbying.

20.3 TYPES OF LOBBYIST

Various types of lobbying participant can be identified—from those acting on their own-account, to those involved in collective action intervention, to commercial/contract organizations. The first category (A) refers to organizations or even individuals pursuing their own political ends. Included in this *own-account* type would be a corporation employing specialist government affairs staff. Grantham and Seymour-Ure (in Rush 1990) note that, 'Many large firms...have their own professional staff with specific responsibility for governmental and parliamentary relations'. Another own-account variant is the non-corporate civil society organization that might become active to avoid the adverse impacts of policy. Thus in 2006 the Camphill Rudolf Steiner School in Aberdeen ran a slick campaign against the proposed Aberdeen Western Peripheral Route (WPR), and indeed they also hired a lobbying company (DLA Piper based in Edinburgh).

Intra-government organizations can themselves be seen as engaging in own-account lobbying. Mitchell (Jordan 1991: 3) claimed, 'Government itself is a lobby...it

Means of policy modification:
<meaning shades into public relations—shades into 'grass roots' and protest>

Effective actors:	D Framing	E Information supply	F Political pressure	G Illegal persuasion Non–lobbying change
A. Own–account policy participants (i.e. political pressure as ancillary activity) a. Individual b. Corporate (inc. government affairs staff) c. Civil society organization d. 'Governmental' organization	i	ii	iii	iv non-lobbying
B. Interest group (i.e. organized to exert political pressure as a main function) a. Self–interested sectional grouping b. Cause group	v	vi	vii	viii non-lobbying
C. 'Third party'/commercial/ for–hire/contract lobbying consultancy	ix	x	xi	xii non-lobbying

Fig. 20.1 Range of 'lobbying' meanings

has to persuade, lobby for its objectives'. The public sector itself recruits lobbyists: an Ordnance Survey advertisement in January 2007 sought a Head of Public Affairs to 'manage a team that focuses on influencing across complex executive and legislative systems'. Therefore in *some* broad uses of the term lobbying, government can be seen as the agent as well as the target.

A second broad category of lobbyists (B) are *collective* organizations. The Greenbelt Alliance involved in the Aberdeen WPR battle differed from the Camphill example in that the latter was acting on its own account (and lobbying was a subordinate organizational goal) whereas the Alliance was set up expressly to lobby for a multi-organizational coalition, and lobbying was its primary purpose. Grantham and Seymour-Ure's quotation above actually runs on, 'Most of the larger and better-organized charities and pressure groups, too, employ a parliamentary liaison officer... as do the majority of trade associations'.

In this milieu groups develop research capacities and seek negotiating relationships. For example, the Federation of Small Businesses' website says that 'its lobbying arm... applies pressure on MPs, Government and Whitehall, lobbies politicians in their constituencies and puts the FSB viewpoint over to the media'. Relevantly for this general argument, the chairman's introduction made the point that 'Lobbying is not an exact science and sometimes it is difficult to present definitive achievements, particularly when we are involved in the stages when Government is looking at ideas, well ahead of the legislative process'.

The weight of press coverage connects lobbying with for-hire agencies (C), but most lobbying is done in-house for corporations (A) or by collective groups (B). In the USA, Heinz et al. (1993: 67) noted that for each professional in a law firm or lobbying consultancy there might be a four to one preponderance towards those working for in-house set-ups (corporate or collective body). So, in summary, lobbying in this chapter is wider than simply 'what *paid* lobbyists do', but it does not accept that *all* policy-making influences should be included under the lobbying umbrella.

Lobbying here *is a broad process modifying public policy by information-based inter-action between groups and organizations* and government. This use expands 'lobbying' from a narrow (press) focus on misdeeds by paid (commercial) lobbyists to instead see it as *policy-influencing behaviour*, and hence a key component of governance. Lobbying is not *any* attempt to alter policy, but is seen as (frequently 'information-based') transactions between policy-makers and affected interests. Other activities— direct action and law breaking (even non-violent)—may seek to influence policy, but 'lobbying' would usually not stretch to cover such activities.

The normal currency in the lobbying process is policy relevant information. Thus on retail shopping the British Retail Consortium data on high street sales, or its Business Crime survey, are accepted as indispensable by policy-makers. The policy-making units of government are usually small and not unusually the relevant groups may have more expertise than government itself.

Most lobbying thus relates to information supply. In practice, for those involved in lobbying it is usually necessary to talk the language of 'public good'. Naturally when approaching MPs or ministers, for example, companies will tend to talk about 'jobs for constituents' rather than 'profits for shareholders'. The best kind of lobbying resource might depend on the venue. Technical detail might be the best leverage with civil servants, but arguments such as public opinion might be more effective with politicians.

Much of the interaction between government and pressure participants is about joint (win:win) working to remedy problems in particular policy niches (E), but lobbying organizations might also apply political pressure (F)—especially if more technical 'conversations' are failing. Or the press could be briefed; public opinion mobilized, etc. (D). Changing the 'frame' (often through a media campaign) has consequential policy outcomes. The rise in support among MPs for a nuclear energy option may be linked to campaigning by the Nuclear Industry Association (*Public Affairs*, 23 October 2006: 21). Successful reframing, it has to be stressed, is an unusual political occurrence. Such 'framing' activities might be labelled public relations rather than lobbying: there are permeable boundaries between the terms.

In the literature there are discussions of *'grass-roots lobbying'* (also 'outside' or indirect lobbying) where the public (usually constituents) are mobilized to put pressure on politicians to secure policy changes (see Kollman 1998). This is seen here as at most 'non-core' to the phenomenon of lobbying. Nonetheless when Japanese recording tape manufacturers wanted to stop a levy in the UK on tapes to protect artists' copyright, their lobbyist used two main tools. They reframed the 'levy' as a 'tax' (even less popular) and they found allies that maybe had greater priority with UK politicians—consumers groups, educationalists, and above all the blind. The Royal National Institute for the Blind used their members as a resource—organizing what they termed a 'white sticks and dogs' lobby of Parliament—which caused disruption as intended. As a result the Department of Trade and Industry had 5,368 representations against and 235 in favour. (Significantly the lobbyist describing this concluded that unlike in the US this kind of grass-roots campaign was 'the exception that proves the rule' (Burrell in McGrath 2005: 306).)

Insider lobbying has as its core formalized consultation between interests and government (of course there are also multiple ad hoc contacts that are not part of the consultative map). Critics of the practice claim consultation is simply cosmetic. However in the broad range of public policy, party principles are a poor guide to decision. Where government has no ideological 'guide', they try to massage problems away by working out something broadly acceptable with the policy community of affected interests. In other words the scope of policy covered by the Lijphart sort of Westminster majoritarian characteristics is empirically limited.

This account has tried to stress that lobbying is the role of many sorts of policy advocates—not simply the paid consultant. Lobbying now has three trade bodies[5] that represent, and to an extent self-regulate, it—but the focus on the first two at least is the for-hire elements: Association of Professional Political Consultants (APPC), Public Relations Consultants Association (PRCA), Chartered Institute for Public Relations—Government Affairs Group (CIPR GAG). Milner (2006a; 2006b) uses registration data with the APPC to sketch the growth and coverage of the industry in the UK. In December 2006 it had thirty-eight member firms and claimed to represent over 80 per cent of the for-hire sector by turnover.

The CIPR estimate that there are 48,000 individuals involved in broadly defined PR with around 14,000 of those involved in governmental affairs (Parvin 2007: 10). Parvin notes that, 'The common consensus within the industry is that the in-house sector is growing and becoming more professional'. Parvin (2007: 16) also notes that the Trade Association Forum claims there are about 3,000 trade associations in the UK, around 600 of whom lobby in a 'meaningful way'. And around 100 have 'major full-time staff and government affairs teams'. (The Stubb report on EU lobbying (see above) suggested, 'At the moment it is estimated that there are about 15000 lobbyists and 2500 lobby organisations in Brussels. Counting permanent visitors' badges and "express"-badges there are approximately 5000 lobbyists operating in the European Parliament'.)

---

[5] The Association for Scottish Public Affairs has forty-one members.

20.4 THE DEVELOPMENT OF
PROFESSIONAL PERSUASION

Congress attempted to regulate lobbying in the USA in 1927 (Crawford 1939: 1). However the UK discussion is comparatively recent:[6] Jordan's (1991: 14) edited volume was aimed 'at stimulating more notice of the activity of commercial lobbyists in Britain'. Grantham and Seymour-Ure[7] start their chapter (in Rush 1990: 45), 'In the early 1970s it was still considered vaguely unethical and probably pointless for someone wishing to influence ministers, officials, or Members of Parliament to hire a professional political consultant'. However, embryonic lobbying certainly existed in Britain in the 1950s and 1960s. The Association of Professional Policy Consultants' history of lobbying on their website credits the first professional consultancy to Commander Christopher Powell around 1928. Souza (1998: 248) describes Powell as essentially a parliamentary draftsman: his niche was in large part Private (and Private Members') Bills where political parties had no interest and technical work was still needed.

By 1976, in connection with the nationalization of Aircraft and Shipbuilding Industries Act, the Bristol Channel Ship Repairers Ltd was able to hire International News Service to lobby. By then—unlike Powell's approach which was based on procedural expertise—new players were literally hiring MPs. This 'payments for questions' stimulated controversy—peaking in the court cases in 1999 and 2000 between Neil Hamilton MP and Mohamed Al Fayed (see below)— and the paid role of MPs has declined in the past decade as a result of press attention. Press stories however consistently emerge, stopping the matter disappearing off the agenda. In October 2007 the *Guardian* was reporting that former Labour MP Lord Hoyle was paid a 'consultancy' fee by Whitehall Advisers, for arranging a lobbyist's introduction 'to say hello' to the new defence minister, Lord Drayson. (See also the *Sunday Times*, 25 January 2009, 'Revealed: Labour Lords Change Laws for Cash'.)

Thus despite the fact that given the 'post-parliamentary' nature of most policy-making, effective lobbying tends to be with officials rather than MPs, there is continuing 'sensationalist' interest in lobbying and parliament. Reflecting this press attention, in June 2007 the Public Administration Committee of the House of Commons launched (yet another) parliamentary inquiry (PAC 2009). The invitation to submit evidence noted, 'In the intervening years, lobbying has been at the centre of political scandals. The cash for questions affair, amongst others, tarnished the word with the stain of sleaze. The industry responded by introducing an element of self-regulation and encouraging professionalization of its work, but lobbying is still viewed with suspicion in some quarters'. The PAC inquiry aimed to (re-)consider topics such as the need for external regulation of the industry. The Committee considered issues such as 'cash for access' and the funding of All Party Groups by lobby firms.

---

[6] US sources include Nownes (2006); Birnbaum (1993); West and Loomis (1999); Thomas (2004); Hansen (1991); Dexter (1969).

[7] They give extensive examples.

20.5 BUSINESS BIAS?

Much attention in the literature is paid to lobbying by business—largely on the assumption that there is an inherent pro-business bias. But Lindblom's (1977) central argument was that businesses' core power was the ability to make or withdraw investment; this is not the sort of influence that the term 'lobbying' signals. While the assumption that business power is widely accepted, Heinz et al. (1993: 381) argue that government affairs departments are a 'response to uncertainty': business acting not out of strength but vulnerability. Businesses may lobby—because they are affected *adversely* by policy. Milner (2006a: 14) shows that the number of casinos lobbying in the UK more than doubled between 2001 and 2004 (from four to ten). This was a response to government putting supercasinos on the agenda rather than the power of casinos in promoting the topic. Lobbying is thus often reactive: cost avoidance response to regulation or a proposed EU Directive.

A further common assumption is that a united business community is bound to be successful; however, Smith (2000) ingeniously shows that themes that unify business are ideological and partisan and generate intense attention from the media and mobilize public attention. As a consequence, perversely, a united business community is unlikely to get its own way! West and Loomis (1999: 228) suggest that the Golden Rule is that, 'he who has the gold makes the rules'. But at the end of the (long) day, 'weaker' interests may prevail; race matters get addressed, smoking gets banned, and car safety regulated.

20.6 LOBBYING AS CORRUPTION: OR THE CORRUPTION OF LOBBYING? THE UNATTRACTIVE SIDE OF UK LOBBYING?

Arguably the press coverage of controversies reveals the 'corruption of lobbying' rather than that lobbying is inherently corrupt. The UK literature mostly divides into 'lobbying *cookbooks*' of the 'how to do it' type—stressing the respectability of the practice. Such books are compatible with the insider perspective. These include Thomson and John (2006); Moloney (1996); Miller (2000); and Connelly (1992). Perhaps surprisingly, few follow up Eckstein (1960) to show *how* group/governmental interaction produced particular outcomes (Jordan 1992).

On the other hand there are the 'lobbyist as *crook books*'—books of the 'What They Should *Not* Have Been Caught Doing' nature. While the cookbooks present lobbying as a Democratic Contribution, the crook books record it as a Democratic Challenge: for example, three fairly recent UK books share the title *Sleaze* (Leigh and

Vulliamy 1997; Ridley and Doig 1995; Baston 2000). (Also see Cook 1995; Dale and Fawkes 2006; Palast 2002). Souza's *So You Want to be a Lobbyist* (1998) sounds like the cookbook type—and has much of the content of the second type.

Under the tide of crook books, the lobbying industry/trade/profession in the UK has a constant battle to defend its legitimacy from critics. *The Directory of Political Lobbying 2002–3* (Johnson 2002: 1) notes it contains entrants who themselves assert 'we prefer not to think of ourselves as lobbyists'. Johnson says, 'The associations with "underhand" or undemocratic practices is perhaps part of the reason companies are eschewing the title "political lobbying".' Distinctions *can* be teased out but the terms 'government affairs' or 'public affairs' seems to be cosmetic attempts at rebranding. Even those within the industry seem obliged to claim that they have just 'stopped beating their wives'. Thomson and John (2006: 1) begin their guide by conceding, 'The lobbying industry is, to put it mildly, not viewed favourably…'

Milner (2006*a*: 1) says, 'whether I refer to an individual as lobbyist, political consultant, public affairs practitioner, or by some other name makes no difference…As a lobbyist brought up in the shadow of liberation politics, I think it is time to reclaim the language'. This ambition has yet to succeed. The 'tainted' reputation of the lobbyist is of course professionally dysfunctional. Precisely because they have a reputation for succeeding, business lobbyists may find resistance. Parvin's study (2007: 24–9) found that all the lobbyists interviewed and twenty-two out of twenty-five journalists interviewed thought lobbying was a 'legitimate part of the political process'. But twenty-three of the thirty-one lobbyists and sixteen of the twenty-five journalists thought the public did not trust lobbyists.

In the USA too the term has had adverse associations (indeed probably worse), most spectacularly involving Jack Abramoff in 2006. As early as *Trist v Child* (1875) the Supreme Court declined to oblige payment to a lobbyist on the grounds that such a contract was contrary to 'sound policy and good morals'. They added: 'If any of the great corporations of the country were to hire adventurers who make markets of themselves in this way, to procure passage of a general law with a view to the promotion of their private interests, the moral sense of every right minded man would instinctively denounce the employer and the employed as steeped in corruption and the employment as infamous' (quoted in Crawford 1939: 2). (For the current US position re the Lobbying Disclosure Act, 1995, and dramatic increases in the past decade, see Petersen 2007.)

While this account seeks to downplay corruption and to stress the insider approach, it has to be acknowledged that cases repeatedly challenge this complacency. In 1998 Enron made three payments to the Labour Party of a total of £27,500. At the Labour Party conference that year it sponsored a 'gala' dinner for £15,000 and three weeks later a takeover bid for Wessex Water was 'nodded through' without reference to the Monopolies Commission. The government abandoned a moratorium on gas-fired power stations in time for Enron to build a plant in Teesside and then Isle of Grain (based on extract from Wheen, 2004 edn., www.Riskoffreedom.com, 10 Jan. 2007). The issue is one of causality. Did the policy changes come because of the funding—was it all coincidence—or did the access brought by money give the Enron lobbyists the opportunity to make a convincing 'public interest' case?

20.6.1 1994: Cash for Questions

Rumours that MPs were being paid to ask questions were tested by an investigative journalist working for the *Sunday Times*, who found four Conservatives out of
ten agreed to a request (Cook 1995: 136; Dixon 1996: 32; Parris 1997). Also in 1994
the classic case of 'brown envelope lobbying' emerged. This concerned Tim Smith
and Neil Hamilton (then MPs) and the businessman Mohamed Al Fayed. Al Fayed
had two important personal agendas to pursue. One was the securing of a British
passport and another was in relation to a business battle. He thought that a paid
relationship with Members of Parliament would be of use in these projects. Hamilton
was recruited by Ian Greer Associates in 1985 (Leigh and Vulliamy 1997: 4). Fayed
was quoted by Leigh and Vulliamy (1997: 64) as saying that Greer had advised him,
'you need to rent an MP just like you rent a London taxi'. Less than dignified though
this mercenary exploitation of parliamentary status may have been, its importance
may be overestimated. As Parris noted (1997: 367), 'What did Fayed's money buy? An
oddity of the whole affair is that the money was paid not to ministers, who may have
the power to change things, but to backbenchers: lobby fodder'. The money went to
neither the dignified nor the efficient.

20.6.2 1997: Ecclestone and All that

Trying to exploit the Conservative Party's association with sleaze in March 1997,
Tony Blair asserted, 'We have got to be whiter than white if we are to rebuild trust
in government'. By that time the Labour Party had already (January 1997) received
a £1m donation from Bernie Ecclestone, head of Formula One motor racing. On
taking office Labour proposed a ban on all sports sponsorship by tobacco companies;
but coincidentally, or otherwise, Formula One was to be temporarily exempt. The
bureaucratic argument in favour of this exemption was that Formula One could
withdraw from any country that was unsupportive. However the exception raised the
implication of a possible connection between the gift and policy—and on the advice
of the chair of the Committee on Standards in Public Life, the money was repaid. As
Baston suggests (2000: 201), the furtive way the matter was handled made it appear
that there was something being hidden—but perhaps it was reliance on a former
Conservative donor, and the subtext that cash from unions was now less important,
that was being concealed.

20.6.3 1998: Cash for Access

Famously in June 1988 Derek Draper, former New Labour ministerial assistant, reinvented as a commercial lobbyist, claimed to an undercover investigative *Observer*
journalist, 'There are seventeen people that count, and to say that I am intimate
with all of them is the understatement of the century...I can have tea with Geoffrey

Robinson [Paymaster General]. I can have tea with Ed Balls [Gordon Brown's economic advisor.]'. Draper claimed that he secured access for Powergen to talk to the Treasury about a previously rejected merger. Another lobbyist, Karl Milner, who had also been a Treasury adviser to Gordon Brown, claimed to Greg Palast, 'We have many friends in government...They like to run things past us some days in advance, to get our view, to let them know if they have anything to be worried about, maybe suggest some changes' (Palast 2002). Of course here may well be (understandable if unattractive) over-claiming by the industry to attract fees.

20.6.4 1999: Devolved Draper?

Similar 'over-claiming' came from Kevin Reid, son of the then Scottish Secretary, Dr John Reid. He too fell for undercover reporting and claimed, 'Three or four of the [Scottish Executive's] special advisers are close personal friends of mine...I know the Secretary of State very well because he's my father...' (Schlesinger, Miller, and Dinan 2001: 227). Schlesinger, Miller, and Dinan (2001: 228) say, 'Beattie Media's consultants claimed that they could use ministers...to "make things easier" for their clients'. They noted that the Scottish First Minister, Jack McConnell, had previously been employed by Beattie Media. They remarked, 'In one of the...more candid and damaging passages in *The Observer's* evidence, Alex Bass remarked, "We appointed Jack McConnell...to head up our public affairs consultancy, in the certain knowledge that Jack would get a safe seat from the Labour Party, and in the hope and expectation that he would also get a Cabinet position..."'.

It is important to underline that the British cases are not of ministers or civil servants making decisions for personal advantage ('Cash for Questions' was exceptional, if petty). Usually in the UK questionable money goes to the party. In the USA it is candidates that need election funding. Prudent US lobbyists will finance both major candidates in a race (perhaps not equally) just to be sure they have backed the winner. And the lobbyist might well not be the instigator; the candidate's fundraiser might be making the first call. In the UK local campaign spending is tightly regulated, so political parties in the UK are a better target: parties, not candidates, need campaign funds.

20.7 THE REVOLVING DOOR

Many lobbying firms 'recyle' used politicians or officials, but there is perennial suspicion of what might be termed post-governmental employment—not simply with lobbying consultancies, but also any interest where government experience suggests useful access. The 'retread' of officials may give employing organizations disproportionate influence. These career moves are superintended by the Standing Advisory Committee (on Business Appointments.) The most common restriction they impose refers to lobbying. There is usually a short period to 'sanitize' relations.

20.8 THE CONTENT OF LOBBYING

Despite reservations prompted by the kind of examples reviewed above, this chapter generally sees lobbying in positive terms and accordingly queries whether the headline problem cases *are* lobbying or whether instead they represent its *abuse*. 'Rule-breaking behaviour' has to be distinguished from legitimate lobbying activities, but the bulk of the existing literature focuses not on lobbying, but the perversion of it. This is as if football reports in the press only discussed managers, agents, and financial irregularity in transfers without actually reporting the matches.

Lobbying is often, indeed typically, about matters that are important to specific companies or sectors, but might appear as esoteric to the broad public. A specific example in 2004–6 was an interpretation by the Scottish Environment Protection Authority (SEPA) that Scottish Power could not use waste-derived fuel (WDF) in Longannet power station as this breeched the 2003 Waste Incineration Regulations which implemented Directive 75/442/EEC (as amended) and Directive 2000/76/EC. The core issue was whether WDF was *combusted* in a power station or *incinerated*. To those uninvolved the distinction appears pedantic, but for Scottish Water to have their dried by-product from screening outflows defined as a cheap fuel rather than waste (the burning of which was tightly controlled) was economically important. To resolve this a judicial review was instituted in 2005 against the SEPA opinion [2005 CSOH 67] and lobbying in Brussels via the 'trade body', Water UK, was used in 2006. Political ideology does not help resolve such issues.

So much lobbying is about securing technical changes by arguments on their merits. This does not mean that lobbying is thereby peripheral and minor. Freeman (1965: 33) argued that:

> Many of the decisions reached in subsystems, though they be considered minor or detailed or insignificant...are collectively the stuff of which a large share of our total public policy is made...their cumulative importance as well as their specific importance...cannot be disregarded.

The press ridiculed a rift between the EU and China over textile imports in 2006 as the 'bra wars'. But the emergence of interests like the European Branded Footwear Coalition showed how (apparent) minutia was vital to those with a stake. Definitional discussions of 'low fat' in foodstuffs may appear abstruse, but European labelling proposals have generated intense politics (*Marketing*, 24 May 2006: 17). In line with Truman, Schlozman and Tierney (1986: 396) argue, 'Organizations whose political ends are narrow and technical are more likely to be influential than those whose goals are more encompassing'. But they (1986: 311) also point out, 'such influence should not be dismissed as negligible'.

20.9 LOBBYING AND CONTESTATION: PUBLIC GOOD FROM SELF-INTERESTED ADVOCACY?

The provision of 'contestation' through lobbying may contribute to worthwhile polyarchy. Indeed is not simply associated with the self-interested. Parvin (2007: 13) cites, for example, Friends of the Earth claiming credit for helping 'secure the Kyoto protocol . . . [and] in getting eight Acts of Parliament passed in eight years through an effective programme of "persuading" MPs, "convincing" Parliament and "influencing" decisions'. Parvin (2007: 14) cites government-funded NGOs lobbying government to change policy or lobbying in support of government objectives such as smoking reduction.

While in 2006 the administrative support to All Party Parliamentary Groups by lobbyists was treated as a scandal by the media,[8] Parvin shows (2007: 15) far more APGs received support from trade organizations, charities, and not-for-profit bodies than from private-sector lobbyists. His report said that only 20 per cent of MPs believed 'companies are generally more adept at lobbying than charities/pressure groups'.

In summary there are two broad benchmarks against which lobbying may be judged. The *Ivory Tower* interpretation sees policy as best made by disinterested politicians and civil servants searching for some common good. Such a belief reflects a long-standing suspicion of self-interest as a basis for political participation. The lobbyist in this light is seen as distorting a high-minded search for public policy. The second, *Insider Politics* approach sees public policy as emerging from untidy pluralist interactions between governing personnel and affected interests. Accepting the second interpretation—that the activities of lobbyists are part of a useful pattern of group/government negotiation—substantially undermines textbook distinctions between majoritarian and consensual democracies.

By the first benchmark lobbying is some dangerous distortion of democracy, but in the second it becomes de facto a contribution to a sort of *ersatz democracy* (see Mueller 1999). In discussing the 2006 'controversy' over the funding and support of All Party Groups in parliament by outside interests, Peter Riddell noted, 'All party groups are defensible . . . Naturally, also, most groups argue for more public money or help for the interest concerned. That is the stuff of politics. Nor is there anything

---

[8] House of Commons Committee on Standards and Privileges, *Lobbying and All Party Groups*, 9th Report 2005–6, HC 1145.

inherently wrong about outside interests, whether commercial or voluntary, seeking to influence Parliament. Lobbying has developed a pejorative image, but it is a necessary, even desirable part of pluralist democracy for outside groups to argue their case' (*The Times*, 13 January 2006).

So lobbying is less controversial in the UK political system if the processes are accepted as being based on a search for consensus by policy-makers. Policy improvement comes through the complaints of those losing out—and a readiness by government to take comments on board. Austin Mitchell MP (in Jordan 1991: 3) referred to lobbying as 'tugs at the sleeve of power'. Lobbying in this understanding is a (functionally useful) facet of the bargaining networks that characterize policy-making in modern states.

REFERENCES

BASTON, L. 2000. *Sleaze*. London: Channel 4 Books.

BAUER, R., POOL, I. DE S., and DEXTER, L. 1963. *American Business and Public Policy*. New York: Atherton Press.

BAUMGARTNER, F., and JONES, B. 1993. *Agendas and Instability*. Chicago: University of Chicago Press.

——— BERRY J., HOJNACKI, M., KIMBALL D., and LEECH, B. 2009. *Lobbying and Policy Change*. Chicago: University of Chicago Press.

BERRY, J. 1984. *The Interest Group Society*. Boston: Little, Brown.

BIRNBAUM, J. 1993. *The Lobbyists*. New York: Times Books.

BROWNE, W. 1990. 'Organized Interests and their Issue Niches'. *Journal of Politics*, 52/2: 477–509.

CONNELLY, P. 1992. *Dealing with Whitehall*. London: Century Business.

COOK, J. 1995. *The Sleaze File*. London: Bloomsbury.

CRAWFORD, K. 1939. *The Pressure Boys*. New York: Messner.

DALE, I., and FAWKES, G. 2006. *The Little Red Book of New Labour Sleaze*. London: Politico's Media.

DEXTER, L. 1969. *How Organizations Are Represented in Washington*. Indianapolis: Bobbs Merrill.

DIXON, P. 1996. *Truth about Westminster*. Eastbourne: Kingsway.

ECKSTEIN, H. 1960. *Pressure Group Politics*. Stanford, Calif.: Stanford University Press.

FINER, S. 1958. *Anonymous Empire*. London: Pall Mall.

FREEMAN, J. 1965. *The Political Process*. New York: Random House.

GERRING, J. 2001. *Social Science Methodology*. New York: Cambridge University Press.

GRANT, W. 1978. 'Insider Groups, Outsider Groups and Interest Group Strategies'. University of Warwick Department of Politics Working Paper No. 1.

GRAY, V., and LOWERY, D. 1996. 'A Niche Theory of Representation'. *Journal of Politics*, 58/1: 91–111.

GRIER, K., MUNGER, M., and ROBERTS, B. 1994. 'The Determinants of Industry Political Activity'. *American Political Science Review*, 88/4: 911–26.

HANSEN, M. 1991. *Gaining Access*. Chicago: University of Chicago Press.

HANSEN, W., and MITCHELL, N. 2000. 'Disaggregating and Explaining Corporate Political Activity'. *American Political Science Review*, 94/4: 891–904.

HEINZ, J., LAUMANN, E., NELSON, R., and SALISBURY, R. 1993. *The Hollow Core*. Cambridge, Mass.: Harvard University Press.

JOHNSON, J. 2002. *Directory of Political Lobbying 2002–2003*. London: Politico's.

JORDAN, G. (ed.) 1991. *The Commercial Lobbyists*. Aberdeen: Aberdeen University Press.

—— 1992. *Engineers and Professional Self Regulation*. Oxford: Clarendon Press.

—— HALPIN, D., and MALONEY, W. 2004. 'Defining Interests: Disambiguation and the Need for New Distinctions'. *British Journal of Politics and International Relations*, 6: 1–18.

—— and MALONEY, W. 1997. 'Accounting for Subgovernments'. *Administration and Society*, 29/5: 557–83.

KEEHN, N. 1978. 'GB: The Illusion of Governmental Authority'. *World Politics*, 30/4: 538–62.

KOEPPL, P. 2001. 'The Acceptance, Relevance and Dominance of Lobbying the EU Commission'. *Journal of Public Affairs*, 1/1: 69–80.

KOLLMAN, K. 1998. *Outside Lobbying*. Princeton, NJ: Princeton University Press.

LEIGH, D., and VULLIAMY, E. 1997. *Sleaze*. London: Fourth Estate.

LIJPHART, A. 1984. *Democracies*. London: Yale University Press.

LINDBLOM, C. *Politics and Markets*. New York: Basic Books.

LIPPMAN, W. 1922. *Public Opinion*. New York: Harcourt, Brace & Co.

MCGRATH, C. 2005. *Lobbying in Washington, London and Brussels*. Lampeter: Edwin Mellen Press.

MAHONEY, C. 2008. *Brussels versus the Beltway: Advocacy in the United States and the European Union*. Washington, DC: Georgetown University Press.

MALONEY, W., JORDAN, G., and MCLAUGHLIN, A. 1994. 'Interest Groups and Public Policy'. *Journal of Public Policy*, 14/1: 17–38.

MANSBRIDGE, J. (ed.) 1990. *Beyond Self Interest*. Chicago: University of Chicago Press.

MATTHEWS, D. 1960. *US Senators and their World*. Chapel Hill: University of North Carolina Press.

MAY, T., and NUGENT, T. 1982. 'Insiders, Outsiders and Thresholders'. PSA conference.

MILBRATH, L. 1963. *The Washington Lobbyists*. Chicago: Rand McNally.

MILLER, C. 2000. *Politico's Guide to Political Lobbying*. London: Politico's.

MILNER K. 2006*a*. *The Growth of Consultancy Lobbying Firms in the UK*. Leeds: Leeds Business School.

—— 2006*b*. *Why the Public Sector Needs to Hire Lobbyists*. Leeds: Leeds Business School.

MOLONEY, K. 1996. *Lobbyists for Hire*. Aldershot: Dartmouth.

MUELLER, J. 1999. *Capitalism, Democracy and Ralph's Pretty Good Grocery*. Princeton, NJ: Princeton University Press.

NOWNES, A. 2006. *Total Lobbying*. New York: Cambridge University Press.

PAC 2009. *Public Administration Committee First Report, Lobbying: Access and Influence in Whitehall*. Session 2008–9, HC 36.1 and 11.

PAGE, E. 1999. 'The Insider/Outsider Distinction'. *British Journal of Politics and International Relations*, 1/2: 205–14.

—— 2001. *Governing by Numbers: Delegated Legislation and Everyday Policy Making*. London: Hart.

PALAST, G. 2002. *The Best Democracy that Money Can Buy*. London: Pluto Press.

PARRIS, M. 1997. *Great Parliamentary Scandals*. London: Robson Books.

PARVIN, P. 2007. *Friend or Foe? Lobbying in British Democracy*. London: Hansard Society.

PETERSEN, R. E. 2007. *Lobbying Disclosure: Themes and Issues*. 110th Congress, CRS Report, 12 January.

RIDLEY, F., and DOIG, A. (eds.) 1995. *Sleaze*. Oxford: Oxford University Press.

RUSH, M. (ed.) 1990. *Parliament and Pressure Politics*. Oxford: Oxford University Press.

SCHLESINGER, P., MILLER, D., and DINAN, W. 2001. *Open Scotland*. Edinburgh: Polygon.

SCHLOZMAN, K., and TIERNEY, J. 1986. *Organized Interests and American Democracy*. New York: Harper and Row.

SMITH, M. 2000. *American Business and Political Power*. Chicago: University of Chicago Press.

SOUZA, C. 1998. *So You Want to Be a Lobbyist?* London: Politico's.

STIGLER, G. 1971. 'The Theory of Economic Regulation'. *Bell Journal of Economics and Management Science*, 2/1: 3–21.

THOMAS, C. 2004. *Research Guide to US and International Interest Groups*. Westport, Conn.: Praeger.

THOMSON, S., and JOHN, S. 2006. *Public Affairs in Practice: A Practical Guide to Lobbying*. London: Kogan Page.

TRUMAN, D. 1951. *The Governmental Process*. New York: Knopf.

WEST, D., and LOOMIS, B. 1999. *The Sound of Money*. New York: Norton.

WHEEN, F. 2004. *How Mumbo-Jumbo Conquered the World*. London: Fourth Estate.

Section Seven: Territory

CHAPTER 21

....

DEVOLUTION IN THE UK

....

CHARLIE JEFFERY

21.1 INTRODUCTION: DEVOLUTION AND THE UNION STATE

....

A decade on, devolution appears to be producing the kind of transformative impact on UK politics that many anticipated at its launch (Hazell 1999). Arrangements for government in the four nations remain deeply contested. In May 2007 Scotland elected a (minority) Scottish National Party government committed in principle to Scottish independence. In August 2007 it published a historic White Paper on Scotland's constitutional options, which prompted an intense cross-party debate on additional powers the parliament might seek. In Wales the nationalist Plaid Cymru entered government in coalition with Labour in 2007, with the two parties agreeing a plan for a referendum on further-reaching devolution by 2011.

And by 2007, a new and vigorous debate about the government of England had also flared up. Prompted mainly by Conservative commentators, this did not focus on the aborted Labour agenda of English regionalization but rather perceptions of inequity in the post-devolution Anglo-Scottish relationship. One outcome appears to be a firming up of the Conservative Party's commitment to reform the way Westminster deals with English business as a consequence of devolution outside England.

Only on Northern Ireland is there broad satisfaction with the devolution arrangements following the resumption of devolution after a five-year hiatus in 2007. The curious government of opposites formed by the Democratic Unionists and Sinn Fein has managed to relaunch devolution in a deliberately low-key manner which has—so far at least—avoided the polarizing constitutional debates which disabled its predecessors. Few would bet, though, that the government of Northern Ireland has achieved enduring stability.

The territorial politics of post-devolution UK remain, in other words, in flux. This contribution reviews some of the main themes in post-devolution research. It takes its cue from a range of accounts which call attention to the historical context within which the current reforms have unfolded (e.g. Bogdanor 2001; McLean and McMillan 2005; Mitchell 2009). A common thread is that post-1997 dynamics are not simply the result of a 'process' (Davies 1999) set off in the late 1990s. This contribution presents devolution instead as the *latest attempt*—shaped by continuities extending back over centuries—at accommodating distinctive Northern Irish, Scottish, and Welsh political communities alongside the numerically and economically dominant English in a single state structure.

Mitchell (2003; 2006*a*) in particular has drawn attention to the peculiar and persistent problems of territorial politics in the UK's 'union state' (Rokkan and Urwin 1982). The UK is the product of the series of unions struck between England and the other UK nations, each under quite different conditions over four centuries (the annexation of Wales by England from 1536, the treaty of union of Scotland with England to form Great Britain in 1707, and the union of Great Britain with Ireland made in 1800 and remade, with the partition of the rest from the six counties of Northern Ireland, in 1922). Union states are not unitary; to use contemporary language, they are asymmetrical. They allow for administrative differentiation of some matters in some parts of the state, though typically have 'administrative standardisation' across 'most of the territory' of the state (Rokkan and Urwin 1982: 11).

By 1997 the UK union state tradition of administrative differentiation was embodied in UK central government offices for Scotland, Wales, and Northern Ireland, Cabinet-level departments with responsibilities for policy implementation in their respective nations. There was no equivalent territorial department for England. The devolution reforms transferred most of the responsibilities formerly exercised by the territorial departments to devolved legislatures established by new electoral processes. UK central government retained responsibility for a residual mix of UK-wide and English functions. Beyond the introduction of a Greater London Authority with limited administrative powers, there has been no significant devolution of powers from UK government to England-wide or English regional authorities. England remains, by and large, a territory of 'administrative standardisation'.

This latest iteration of the union state tradition carries forward a number of path dependencies. Foremost is that devolution was not approached as a comprehensive, integrated reform of the UK state, but as a series of disconnected responses to changing, and different, demands about how the unions of Scotland and Wales with England and Northern Ireland with Great Britain should be renewed. It has been a project of the parts, not the whole, with reforms drawn up by different ministries, reflecting different territorial circumstances, and using different institutional templates. This has two implications. First, the trajectories of territorial politics in each of the four nations of the UK have been highly self-contained. Second, and conversely, there has been little attempt to understand and manage the combination of extensive devolution outside England and continued centralization within England as an integrated system of government.

This contribution follows the logic of these features of the union state tradition. The next section explores central themes in devolution research on the four nations of the UK. The third section then draws out a number of overarching, UK-wide problems which arise from the failure to conceive of devolution as an integrated set of reforms to the UK state. The contribution argues that this disconnected approach to the UK's territorial constitution, while consistent with the traditions of the union state, is inherently unstable now that the UK has several governments rather than one, each with competing mandates. Democratic devolution opens up new potentials for the political mobilization of territorial cleavage. The contribution concludes by setting out a number of scenarios which may emerge as the UK grapples with this new territorial politics.

21.2 DISCONNECTED DEVOLUTIONS: THE DYNAMICS OF POLITICAL CHANGE IN THE FOUR NATIONS

Devolution happened for different reasons in different places. In Scotland the debate on devolution was reinvigorated by the accumulated dissatisfactions of being governed from 1979–97 by a Conservative Party which had been for decades a dwindling force in Scotland. In Wales there was a less vigorous version of the same debate. In Northern Ireland devolution was one component of a strategy of pacification of conflict in a divided society. In England regional devolution was about bringing better coordination to the delivery of central government services and (especially in the north) boosting regional economies.

Mirroring the patchwork quality of the devolution reforms, post-devolution scholarship has largely been differentiated by UK nation. Though there has been some work comparing Scotland and Wales (e.g. Taylor and Thomson 1999; Bradbury 2006a; Wyn Jones and Scully 2006) and on Anglo-Scottish relationships (Miller 2005; Devine 2008), three- or four-nation treatments are rare.[1] Northern Ireland often gets bracketed out as *sui generis* and England for not having 'real' devolution. The result is a growing stock of single-nation studies, including systematic accounts of territorial political systems (Keating 2005; Rawlings 2003; Sandford 2005; Travers 2004; Tonge 2005), a number of edited collections (Carmichael, Knox, and Osborne 2007; Chaney, Hall, and Pithouse 2001; Hazell 2006; Wright 2000; Tomaney and Mawson 2002; Wilford 2001), and a burgeoning collection of contributions to scholarly journals

---

[1] The *State of the Nations* series is a welcome exception: Hazell (2000; 2003); Trench (2001; 2004; 2005a).

and other outlets.[2] It is not feasible in this framework to give a full account of these works. Instead the following draws out shared themes of constitutional structure and political process in research on the four nations.

21.2.1 Evolving Constitutional Debates

21.2.1.1 *Wales*

A first theme concerns the durability of the institutional arrangements established in each of the four nations. Wales has seen most change. Unlike in Scotland Welsh devolution was not prefigured by a vigorous debate on devolution spearheaded by a broad-based campaign. Its institutional form emerged much more as the result of negotiations between pro- and anti-devolution factions within the Welsh Labour Party. The result was a compromise at a low common denominator: the National Assembly had a form of devolution based on secondary legislative empowerments scattered over hundreds of Westminster statutes, as previously exercised by the UK Welsh Office; and—with pointed analogies to local government practice—it had no formal separation of government and opposition. This 'strange anatomy' (Rawlings 2003: 85) of Welsh devolution was difficult to understand—even for insiders—and to operate. What followed, unsurprisingly, has been an 'uninterrupted . . . constitutional debate' (Rawlings 2003: 85), involving:

- An Operational Review of the Assembly in 2001–2, which led to a de facto move to a government–opposition model.
- A Commission on the Powers and Electoral Arrangements of the Assembly chaired by Lord Richard from 2002 to 2004, which proposed, *inter alia*, a staged move to full, primary legislative powers, with interim measures to widen the Assembly's autonomy under secondary legislative powers.
- A White Paper in 2005, followed by the 2006 Government of Wales Act which significantly widened the Assembly's secondary powers and allowed for a later move to full legislative powers, subject to a referendum.
- A commitment by the 2007 Labour–Plaid Cymru coalition to hold a referendum on full legislative powers by 2011.
- The establishment in 2008 of an 'All Wales Convention' to prepare the ground for the proposed referendum.

This constitutional saga is indicative of the fragmented approach of the union state to its territorial politics. The compromises in the mid-1990s were not part of any overarching vision of how to run a devolved nation as part of a modernized union, but rather what could be sold to a reluctant Welsh Labour Party. When played out in practice these compromises were unsustainable. It would be difficult to find any academic analysis which argues that the original form of Welsh devolution was fit for

---

[2] The Economic and Social Research Council's programme on Devolution and Constitutional Change alone produced around 500 publications.

purpose.[3] Responses to the current halfway house are barely more positive (Trench 2005*c*; Miers, Patchett, and Rawlings 2005). All the time there has been a backdrop of public opinion in which full legislative devolution has been more popular than the Assembly model of secondary legislative powers (Wyn Jones and Scully 2008: 68). Welsh devolution in other words appears hobbled by the narrowness of perspective the Welsh Labour Party brought to the question of renewing the Welsh relationship with the UK.

21.2.1.2 *Scotland*

By contrast well over a decade's campaigning from the early 1980s produced a template for devolution which had broad support in Scotland. Even so public opinion has also consistently been behind further-reaching devolution, including more powers to raise revenues in Scotland to fund the responsibilities of the Scottish Parliament (Curtice 2006: 107). What Scots do not endorse is Scottish independence, with support stable at around 30 per cent since 1999 and falling recently (Curtice 2008*a*: 40).

Against that background the SNP's 2007 White Paper is intriguing. It sets out the SNP's preference for independence and its commitment to hold an independence referendum by 2011. That appears unlikely given the opposition to a referendum of Labour, the Conservatives, and the Liberal Democrats, who together hold a unionist majority in the Scottish parliament. But the White Paper also recognizes what now appears to be a consensus among the unionist parties (and the general public) for further devolution within the UK (Scottish Executive 2007: 5–6). Though the unionist parties have refused to join the 'National Conversation' on Scotland's constitutional future announced in the White Paper, they have set up their own Devolution Commission to explore possible adjustments to the devolution settlement. The establishment of the Commission makes more likely some measure of further-reaching devolution in the short term. Significantly the SNP has welcomed the Commission. There is perhaps a sense in this, and in the general tenor of thinking in the White Paper, of SNP recognition that independence is not an absolute and that there may ultimately be little practical distinction between enhanced devolution within the UK and notional independence in a British Isles/European Union setting.

21.2.1.3 *Northern Ireland*

In Northern Ireland there is less of an institutional dynamic at play. At heart this reflects the intricacies of the Belfast Agreement painstakingly negotiated in 1998 and the refusal of some of the parties to it—most importantly Sinn Fein—to revisit it. It does not mean there is consensus on the adequacy of the Agreement as a basis for stable government. Debate has focused on its 'consociational' properties. Consociational political systems have features designed to manage conflict in divided

---

[3] See, for example, the library of evidence submitted to the Richard Commission; at http://www. richardcommission.gov.uk/content/template.asp?ID=/content/evidence/index.asp.

societies through a mix of power sharing and protections for the autonomy of distinct communities (Lijphart 1977). Many of the features of Northern Ireland devolution follow consociational models.

The repeated early suspensions of the Assembly then the long suspension from 2002 to 2007 were a clear enough sign that consociation in Northern Ireland was not working. The debate is about whether there is a fix, either as recalcitrants in power sharing come on board (as the DUP under Ian Paisley in the end did), or through tweaking the institutions of consociation (McGarry and O'Leary 2007: 70–8), or whether there is a more fundamental problem. Wilson (2007), for example, has argued that the competing, ethno-national constitutional visions in Northern Ireland (union with the UK versus the reunification of Ireland) leave little room for the sense of shared territorial commitment, normally to a single state, that successful consociations typically have. Without that shared commitment power-sharing rules may run the danger of polarizing divisions rather than bridging them. The challenge for Wilson is to move 'beyond consociationalism' to a new, 'post-ethnic' or 'cosmopolitan' agenda that establishes a sense of shared commitment to the territory of Northern Ireland (Wilson 2007: 26–8).

The connections these theoretical debates have with everyday concerns in Northern Ireland are ambiguous. There is a strong pattern of spatial division of Protestant and Catholic communities—in housing, schooling, recreation, and so on—especially in parts of Belfast (Shirlow and Murtagh 2006). Yet alongside that polarization of everyday life there is also evidence of growth in (aspirations to) mixed communities.[4] There are similar ambiguities in data on constitutional preference. Given a choice in principle, over 80 per cent of Protestants consistently prefer continued membership of the UK, while around half of Catholics consistently prefer reunification with the Republic of Ireland (Mac Ginty 2006: 35). At that level there is clearly no consociational commitment to a shared territory. But given the current options, *in practice*, of either the Northern Ireland Assembly or Westminster having 'most influence over how Northern Ireland is run' support for the Assembly far outweighs Westminster in *both* communities. Devolution has also been the majority constitutional preference in Northern Ireland from 2003 on (Mac Ginty 2006: 37–9).[5] These data suggest that a pragmatic desire for a functioning local politics is now the cross-community default option in Northern Ireland. There may, in that case, be a solid platform for power-sharing devolution.

21.2.1.4 *England*

Questions of government structure within England remain open ended. Labour was unable to build a general agreement on the purposes of policy on the English

---

[4] Compare the 'Community Relations' sections in the Northern Ireland Life and Times Survey, e.g. for 2003 (http://www.ark.ac.uk/nilt/2003/Community_Relations/index.html) and 2006 (http://www.ark.ac.uk/nilt/2006/Community_Relations/index.html).

[5] See also http://www.ark.ac.uk/nilt/2005/Political_Attitudes/FUTURENI.html and http://www.ark.ac.uk/nilt/2006/Political_Attitudes/FUTURENI.html for later survey waves.

regions (cf. Sandford 2005: 16, 98–100) nor, as a result, on the institutions needed to carry out that policy, with some favouring beefed-up central government agencies in the regions, and others elected regional assemblies. No single voice in government was able to combine or prioritize these different views into an agenda shared across government, beyond a long-standing commitment to establish a London-wide authority. The only consistent advocate of elected regional assemblies, John Prescott, was widely considered an ineffective minister. This gave other Whitehall departments opportunities to block significant transfers of responsibility to the regional level. So when the Draft Regional Assemblies Bill did appear in 2004—a full seven years after the initial manifesto commitment in 1997—it foresaw elected regional assemblies with very modest powers largely cobbled together from different parts of Prescott's own department. This unconvincing institutional recipe was convincingly rejected in the North-East as 'just another expensive talking shop' (Rallings and Thrasher 2006).

But by removing elected regional government from the agenda for the foreseeable future, the North-Easterners helped open up scope for a different English debate on the balance of the UK constitution; that is, on the appropriate arrangements for governing the English territory *as a whole*. That debate intensified with the prospect of the Scottish MP Gordon Brown becoming UK Prime Minister, which some Conservative commentators used to revive the 'West Lothian Question' about inequities of representation of the Scots and the English after devolution. Subsequently Conservative commitment to excluding Scottish MPs from decisions on England-only business appears to have firmed up.

As in Northern Ireland, it is not clear that the English have much connection to these debates about new ways to govern them. A majority of the English remain happy with the status quo of direct rule by Westminster with at most 20 per cent or so supportive of regional assemblies and 20 per cent or so of a separate English parliament (Curtice 2008*b*). Unlike the Scots, Welsh, and Northern Irish, the English think that Westminster *should* have most influence over them. There is, though, some evidence that concerns about Anglo-Scottish inequity have resonance. A clear majority of the English feel that Scottish MPs should no longer be able to vote on English business at Westminster. There are also concerns that the Scots, after devolution, have undue advantages over the English on public spending and the economic benefits of shared UK membership (Curtice 2006: 105–7). None of this has yet proved politically salient. But there is clearly a correlation with Conservative concerns about the unresolved 'English question' which could become a basis for political mobilization of Anglo-Scottish cleavage.

That potential illustrates one of the problems that the characteristically disconnected UK approach to territorial politics may bring: a policy, such as Scottish devolution, which makes sense in its own terms, and addresses a distinctive Scottish problem, may have a 'displacement' effect which challenges the legitimacy of governing arrangements in some other part of the UK (Mitchell 2006*b*). But equally any change in how English business is handled at Westminster might be expected, in turn, to raise further grievances about different statuses of membership of the UK parliament. Similarly, if Scotland won fuller fiscal autonomy or some other asymmetric development of devolution, the effect might be to prompt demands for emulation in Northern Ireland or Wales. The union state tradition of disconnected rather than overarching territorial reform might, in other words, be expected to continue to throw up unintended spillovers that prompt further waves of reform.

21.2.2 Political Dynamics in the Four Nations

The devolution reforms were intended to enable the UK's nations to address collective problems in their own ways. Given the lack of systemic integration between those reforms, it is no surprise that politics has become more diverse across the four nations. Tracking and characterizing that diversity has been one of the main preoccupations of post-devolution scholarship, with particular focal points on voting behaviour and party systems, and policy process and outcomes.

21.2.2.1 *Scotland and Wales*

Devolved elections in Scotland and Wales have been a rich testing ground for the assumption that devolved elections are 'second order' (Reif and Schmitt 1980); that is, shaped by Westminster-level rather than devolved issues. The evidence so far is mixed, though some voters appear to make systematic distinctions between electoral arenas, not least in a trade-off which sees 'differential voting' as Labour voters at Westminster elections switch to Scottish and Welsh Nationalists in devolved elections (Wyn Jones and Scully 2006). This pattern was one of the reasons behind the entry of the SNP and Plaid Cymru into devolved government in 2007. Another was the effect of broadly proportional electoral systems which have limited the scope for single-party government and made possible new minority and coalition government formations.

One result has been a more left-leaning and cooperative dynamic of party competition than at Westminster. This is one reason that policy in Scotland in particular has diverged in places from the Westminster pattern; on a number of landmark issues (tuition fees, proportional representation in local elections) difference from Westminster arose from cross-party negotiations in coalition building from 1999 to 2007. Another cause of policy divergence is differences in policy process in Scotland and Wales, though neither have fully realized the optimistic rhetoric of a 'new politics', more open and inclusive than the 'old' politics at Westminster that accompanied devolution (McAllister 2000; Mitchell 2000). That rhetoric was always overblown and naive. In Wales what emerged instead was a new form of regional centralism with a Labour-dominated Assembly appearing to privilege (Labour-dominated) public-sector producer interests (cf. Greer 2004: 157; Morgan and Upton 2005: 79).

In Scotland the commitment to a 'new' politics had greater heft. It was an aspiration carried through from the 1990s devolution campaign and has had direct impact on the way the Scottish parliament works (Arter 2003), and on gender balance in the parliament (Mackay 2004). Elsewhere on the new politics balance sheet, though, an experiment with a civic forum as a platform for input by civil society organizations into the policy process failed, with funding withdrawn in 2005. And a tendency under Labour to nurture corporatist relationships with public-sector interests, notably in higher education (Keating 2005: 180) and health care (Greer 2004: 72)—itself project-ing forward pre-devolution patterns—has been confirmed under the SNP govern-ment since 2007.

Policy processes in both Wales and Scotland are, in sum, distinctive as compared with those at UK level. They are marked by left-leaning party competition, cross-party cooperation, and policy communities in part opened up to new influences, in part to capture by public-sector interests. The result has been a set of policy outcomes which stand to the left of (both Conservative and Labour) Westminster orthodoxy. There has been less openness to market-like principles and private finance in the delivery of public services, and a preference for universalism. The Welsh First Minister, Rhodri Morgan, produced the rhetorical flourish of 'clear red water' between Welsh and 'new' Labour to describe all this. Similarly, Keating (2007: 282) has described Scotland as 'an enclave of social democracy'. McEwen (2006) and others (Béland and Lecours 2005) have developed terminologies of 'welfare nationalism'. All may well understate continuing commonalities with England. Nonetheless there are clearly differences of emphasis in the balance of market and state in Wales and Scotland as compared to norms at Westminster.

21.2.2.2 *Northern Ireland*

Little of the foregoing applies in the case of Northern Ireland. Elections and party competition in Northern Ireland are unique. None of the Britain-wide par-ties currently contest elections in Northern Ireland; instead there are parallel, community-based party systems. The DUP competes with the Ulster Unionists and other unionist splinter groups for Protestant/Unionist votes, while Sinn Fein and the Social Democratic and Labour Party compete for Catholic/Nationalist votes. What has been striking has been the polarization of voting behaviour within these communities over the post-devolution era (Table 21.1).

Table 21.1 Electoral polarization in Northern Ireland, 1997–2005 (%)

Election	DUP	UUP	SDLP	Sinn Fein	'Centrist' (UUP+SDLP)	'Polarised' (DUP+SF)
Westminster 1997	13.6	32.7	24.1	16.1	56.8	29.7
NI Assembly 1998	18.0	21.3	21.9	17.6	43.2	35.6
Westminster 2001	22.5	26.8	20.9	21.7	47.7	44.2
NI Assembly 2003	25.7	22.7	16.9	23.5	39.6	49.2
Westminster 2005	33.7	17.7	17.5	24.3	35.2	58.0
NI Assembly 2007	30.1	14.9	15.2	26.2	30.1	56.3

Percentage are of first preference votes.

This pattern of polarization is a steady one, unaffected by whether the contest is for the Assembly or Westminster. There is no debate in Northern Ireland about first- and second-order elections; all elections appear to carry the same resonance, marked by existential concerns—political violence, policing and security, fundamental constitutional choices—absent elsewhere in the UK.

This polarization may appear problematic given the need under the Belfast Agreement for cross-party cooperation in power-sharing government. Patterson and Kaufman (2007: 94) for example argue that the shift of support from moderate UUP to the more trenchant unionism of the DUP reflects a long-term realignment of the unionist activist base that renders the elite accommodation required for power-sharing difficult. Dowds and Linn (2005) offer a more optimistic perspective. They show that by 2003 there had been notable shifts in the characteristics of DUP supporters, with rising agreement that on the need for compromise and 'a dramatic rise in support for a system of power-sharing within Northern Ireland—from 35% to 71%' (Dowds and Linn (2005: 5–6). In other words it does not necessarily follow that in making polarized choices voters expect polarized representation. The migration from the centre to the DUP and Sinn Fein may be less about polarization than a commitment to power sharing on condition of robust defence of community interests.

The absence of devolution over the period 2002–7 (and the stuttering progress of devolution before 2002) means that the impact of devolution on policy process and outcomes has so far been limited, with the partial exception of areas like equality policy and human rights which intersect with the more existential agendas of Northern Irish politics (Dickson and Osborne 2007). Otherwise there has been a strong trend of continuity, tempered by an incipient pattern of suspicion while devolution was in operation that devolved ministers were favouring their own ethnic community within briefs like health (Greer 2006: 115) and education (Osborne 2006: 71–4). Relaunched devolution in its 2007 guise may also be open to suspicions about this kind of ethnic patronage.

21.2.2.3 *England*

Even though the elected assembly track of English regionalization failed, the English regions have seen a set of administrative reforms which have established new, or expanded, regional governance structures over the last ten years. Sandford (2005) argues that these disparate initiatives together have a systemic quality involving semi-formalized networks of regional 'stakeholders' in local government, the private and voluntary sectors which have carved out some scope for influencing central government policies in the regions. Others, notably Pearce and Ayres (2006; 2007), are more sceptical about any sense of 'system', noting that new regional networks compete with more firmly established central–local policy relationships, often causing new coordination problems. They have in practice little grip on the centre, typically acting in response to top-down prompts rather than feeding in new ideas, and they lack the legitimacy—and clout—that elected tiers of government can claim. More generally there is little sense that Whitehall has real interest in differentiated policy responses in the English regions; at best it sees the regional scale as a convenient one for delivering standard policies across England (House of Commons 2003: 67).

The only exception in this is London, where the Greater London Authority is now firmly established as a body capable of using modest powers to bring about significant change, for example in transport policy (Travers 2004: 190–1) or the vigorous lobbying that contributed to the success of the 2012 Olympics bid. It is also a body which appears to have the support of Londoners (Margetts and Dunleavy 2005). But London also—perversely, for all its claims to 'global city' status—is one of the most insular parts of the UK, consumed in its own specificities as an urban region. It is not likely to act as a catalyst for reform elsewhere in England. This leaves England, London aside, as a territory with a highly centralized system of government producing essentially uniform public policies at a time when elsewhere in the UK further-reaching devolution reforms and growing policy divergence from England are in prospect.

21.3 A 'SYSTEM' OF POST-DEVOLUTION GOVERNMENT IN THE UK?

That mix of devolution and divergence outside England and centralization and uniformity in England is an uneasy one. Though it projects forward the union state tradition—part differentiation, mainly standardization—it has added a new ingredient: democratic process. Former incarnations of the union state were (excepting Northern Ireland from 1922 to 1972) governed by a single, union-wide government able to trade off territorial interests within a framework of collective decision-making. Now, the new democratic processes in Scotland, Wales, and Northern Ireland have transformed the old *intra*-governmental framework for accommodating different territorial interests into a new setting. Different governments composed of different parties can now use devolved powers to pursue different policy agendas (or, indeed, seek further powers). Meanwhile the UK government has used its undiluted power in England to drive on marketizing reforms in the public services, amplifying the already centrifugal dynamic that has resulted from devolution.

What has been perhaps most remarkable about UK devolution is the absence of thought put by government into managing that dynamic. Though devolution is logically about enabling more difference, just how much difference is possible, or manageable within a common state? What limits need to be set, and how might they be policed? These questions have bothered political scientists—especially those with interests in comparative territorial politics—since the launch of devolution, and produced two broad and interconnected themes in research. The first has focused on the need for some kind of renewed statement of purpose of the union, post-devolution. A second has argued for a denser and more formal web of institutional linkages between devolved and UK institutions. Both are about reconceiving the meaning and operation of the union state in its new circumstances.

21.3.1 What is the Union For?

Though there is a *sui generis* tenor to much work on UK devolution, some, notably Jeffery (2002; 2005a; 2006; Hough and Jeffery 2006), stress that the UK is by no means alone in addressing new circumstances. Over the last thirty years there have been extensive reforms to regional institutional structures in Belgium, Spain, and Italy and protracted debates (though few actual reforms) on the institutional configuration of federalism in Canada, Germany, Austria, and Switzerland. These reform debates have articulated competing judgements about what is right and just in the balance of meeting state-wide objectives versus territorial claims to distinctiveness and autonomy. In Germany strong decentralist pressures from the wealthy south have challenged, though not (yet) transformed, the legacy of post-war commitments to state-wide 'uniformity of living conditions'. In Canada and Belgium centrifugal pressures based in distinctive identity (Quebec, Flanders) and declining interregional solidarity (Alberta, Flanders) have opened up scope for the pursuit of regional objectives, but are still bound by enduring state-wide commitments to Canadian 'social union' and a Belgium-wide understanding of social security. In Italy, Austria, and Switzerland themes of autonomy, identity, and desolidarization have also played into debates on rebalancing the central state and the component units. In all of these places, through state-wide debate, some general notion of the (changing) common purposes of shared statehood, and a sense of the state-wide 'rules of the game', needed to achieve those common purposes have emerged, even if they remain for some contested and unsatisfactory.

That sense of a state-wide common purpose is largely absent in a post-devolution UK marked by disconnected devolution reforms and divergent territorial politics. That absence led Hazell and O'Leary (1999: 42) to set out a clear challenge for the UK government on the purposes of union back in 1999: 'The trick will be to identify and understand what items need to be held in common throughout the kingdom as constants of UK citizenship; and what items can be allowed to vary'. Others since have explored similar themes. T. H. Marshall's (1950/1992) concept of social citizenship has become a catalyst for research on how far the supposedly territory-blind benefits of the welfare state are compromised by, or reconcilable with, devolution (Banting 2006; Jeffery 2006; Mitchell 2006a; Wincott 2006). Others have used concepts of (pan-UK) 'territorial justice' to explore the potential roles of UK-level government in limiting territorial economic disparities (Adams, Robinson, and Vigor 2003: 213–19).

The UK government has not exactly risen to these challenges. Tony Blair rarely spoke about devolution after its introduction in 1999, and never in any depth. Only Gordon Brown, Blair's successor as Prime Minister, has shown a sustained interest. In part that has been interpreted as an opportunistic attempt to reaffirm his credentials as a Scot to be UK Prime Minister in the post-devolution state, not least in his series of speeches on 'Britishness'. But his interest is in other respects an enduring one. Brown had already posed the question of how state-wide welfare objectives could be combined with devolution in his doctoral thesis back in 1981 (Mitchell 2006a: 163). By 1999 Brown claimed to have the answer by emphasizing how core components of the post-war welfare state remained 'British' despite devolution:

> Today when people talk about the National Health Service whether in Scotland, Wales or England people think of the British National Health Service ... And its most powerful driving idea is that every citizen of Britain has an equal right to treatment regardless of wealth, position or race and, indeed, can secure treatment in any part of Britain ... When we pool and share our resources and when the stronger help the weak it makes us all stronger.   (Brown 1999)

Brown's claims about the strength of common, Britain-wide beliefs—which he also extended to education and labour market policies—are in one sense well founded. Despite divergent post-devolution policy agendas, there are at best marginal differences in the values that the English, Northern Irish, Scots, and Welsh hold on the balance of market and state, or on preferences on some of the headline issues which have seen territorial policy variation since devolution like free personal care for the elderly or tuition fees. And most people across the UK appear to dislike the idea that policy standards might diverge from place to place as a result of devolution (Jeffery 2006: 78–80).

Yet while Brown's claims may resonate with public opinion, they are wrong empirically and getting more wrong as time passes. In practice, because of the administrative differentiation of the union state, health and other public policies have probably never been delivered in ways consistent with Britain-wide uniformities of public opinion (Wincott 2006: 176–8). The divergences of devolved governments from the policies of the UK government acting for England have added significantly to that historical legacy: Greer (2007: 159) concludes that devolution has 'already had an impact on the meaning and rights associated with citizenship in the UK'; Jeffery (2006: 90) that social citizenship has become less UK-wide and increasingly 'territorialised'; and Morgan (2006: 201) that the UK 'fails to meet ... any ... reasonable definition of territorial justice'.

21.3.2 Reconfiguring the Union

The thrust of these conclusions is that the notion of 'union' is losing substance since devolution. Such conclusions are not—as is sometimes suggested—arguments for a recentralization of the UK, or for uniform, pan-UK policy provision. Rather they point to a concern to express better and more explicitly how the balance of devolved autonomy with continuing, pan-UK objectives is understood and achieved (Jeffery 2005b). Yet post-devolution UK lacks a framework for pursuing specific territorial interests and reconciling them with those of the union as a whole. Analysis on what the union would need in order to reconcile union and devolution has largely followed two tracks: arrangements for financing devolved government; and intergovernmental relations.

Work on territorial finance, though often cloaked in the rationalist language of economics, often reflects different perspectives on the nature and desirability of union (cf. Jeffery and Scott 2007). Proponents of a needs-based system of fiscal equalization (Bell and Christie 2001; McLean and McMillan 2005: 237–8) generally articulate UK-wide concerns about interregional equity. Proponents of greater devolved fiscal autonomy (almost wholly focused on Scotland) generally have in mind some kind of loosening of the Scottish–UK relationship (Hallward and MacDonald 2006). In Scotland these issues of equalization versus autonomy are central to the debates of both the SNP's National Conversation and the unionist parties' Devolution Commission. There are also stirrings of debate in Wales (about the impact of alternatives to the current system) and Northern Ireland (about cross-border tax competition with the Republic of Ireland). What is missing—yet entirely consistent with the fragmented approach in the UK to managing union—is policy debate in UK government about UK-wide objectives in the structure of territorial finance.

There is a similar picture in the field of intergovernmental relations. The system of intergovernmental coordination that evolved in the first years of devolution was, in essence, a simple projection forward of procedures for discussing territorial concerns within UK government before devolution. As such it was informal, behind the scenes, ad hoc, and normally carried out by civil servants working in a context of collegiality and goodwill. The question persistently raised by devolution research is whether that largely pre-devolution practice is 'fit for purpose' (Jeffery 2007). The general consensus is that it is not, or more precisely that it was workable if the same party led governments both at UK level and in Scotland and Wales, but that as soon as that congruence was broken informality and goodwill would be insufficient. The point was well made in the very first recommendation of the very first official inquiry on devolution (by the House of Lords Constitution Committee, then chaired by Lord Norton): 'We recommend that further use be made of the formal mechanisms of intergovernmental relations, even if they seem to many of those presently involved as excessive ... Such mechanisms are likely to become increasingly important when governments of different political persuasions have to deal with each other' (House of Lords 2002: 5).

The 2007 elections have brought 'governments of different persuasions'. Predictably enough the response has been renewed arguments for beefing up current, but under-used institutional linkages between UK and devolved governments, like the Joint Ministerial Committee (JMC). There is a question mark, though, over whether this kind of institutional tweaking would be sufficient. There are two concerns. First, effective institutional coordination mechanisms arguably need a normative under-pinning, a sense of the underlying rules of the game in balancing state-wide and territorial interests. Yet post-devolution UK lacks a sense of what it, as a whole as well as part by part, is for. The failure of Gordon Brown to acknowledge the contradiction between his arguments about the benefits of sharing welfare risk on a UK-wide scale and the erosion in practice of UK-wide commonalities is striking. It is indicative of a mindset in UK central government which remains curiously unchanged since and by devolution. That mindset sees devolution as a minor tweak to the UK constitution. It has been entrenched by the piecemeal approach to the devolution reforms which have fragmented any sense of a 'bigger picture' of reform across the UK.

21.3.3 The Problem of England

This rigidity of thinking at the centre has been facilitated, second, by the preponderance of England—where indeed nothing much has changed—in the business of Westminster and Whitehall. England is devolution's big problem. It dominates the perspective of the UK centre, which has so far failed not just to decentralize within England, but also to disentangle its England-only and wider UK roles (Lodge and Mitchell 2006: 98–102). This creates a number of problems. Because England is such a big component of the UK (85 per cent or so of population and GDP), what happens there can have significant spillover consequences outside England. Because England-only and UK-wide roles are so entangled, that potential for spillover is often not recognized (McLean and McMillan 2005: 219) and at times wilfully ignored (cf. Aron 2007). And because it is simultaneously the government for England, the UK's government appears ill-suited to the arbiter role that central governments typically play in the management of competing territorial interests. There is an obvious risk that the UK-wide roles of government become captured by English territorial interests and as a result sharpen incipient territorial cleavages, in particular that between England and Scotland.

21.4 Perspectives

This, needless to say, is not a promising basis for the effective accommodation of distinctive territorial interests in different parts of the union. It is, though, a logical outcome of a reform process since 1997 which has taken forward the union state tradition of patchwork reform into the new territory of democratic devolution. That patchwork approach on the one hand has failed to stabilize the constitutional structure of devolution; on the other it has opened up new territorial political processes which have evolved discretely and are becoming increasingly diverse. The scope for the UK centre to hold the ring is compromised by its failure to renew itself for the post-devolution era and by its continuing preoccupation with England. As a result (Anglo-)UK and devolved politics by and large talk past one another.

While there is general agreement that this disconnection of centre and parts could work, more or less as a policy of benign neglect (cf. Bradbury 2006b: 579), while Labour dominated government in Westminster, Scotland, and Cardiff, less is agreed about what might unfold now that the era of 'Labour all round' is over. Broadly speaking three scenarios have been identified:

1. Continuity of current arrangements, with minor incremental adaptations on the usual disconnected, nation-by-nation pattern (Trench 2005b: 264–5).
2. A more thoroughgoing reform aimed at a more general and union-wide rebalancing of the post-devolution constitution, but still with a recognizable lineage to the reforms of 1997–9, including further-reaching autonomy in Scotland and Wales, a fuller distinction of English and UK business in Westminster and Whitehall, a needs-based system of fiscal equalization and some element of fiscal autonomy for the devolved administrations, and a more systematic approach to intergovernmental coordination (Trench 2005b: 264–8).
3. A move by Scotland to a new constitutional status, either as a special status nation within the UK, or as an independent state outside the UK. McLean offers two accounts of such a move (McLean 2001: 444–6). The first (his 'Quebec scenario') envisages a process led, from Scotland, by an SNP continuing to push for independence. The second (his 'Slovak scenario') envisages an English (most likely Conservative) calling of the SNP's bluff in a backlash against the apparent privileges of the Scots in the post-devolution state.

The most likely of these scenarios is the second. A more thoroughgoing rebalancing of the devolution arrangements appears feasible as discussions on reform in Wales and, in particular, Scotland unfold. Though the SNP's National Conversation and the unionist Devolution Commission are running in parallel, and have competing ultimate objectives of independence versus union, there is a large common ground shared by all the significant parties in Scotland around pushing the devolution arrangements further. Much depends, though, on the willingness in Westminster and Whitehall, whether under Gordon Brown or perhaps, after the next UK election, David Cameron, to accept—or, better, understand—the rationale for further reform. The third scenario is still a distant one, though in the absence of a systematic rethinking of current arrangements it may, whether through Scottish or English agency, or simply intransigence at Westminster, zoom rapidly into focus. What is clear is that the status quo—scenario one—is not much of an option. The scale of the dysfunctions of the current arrangements, and their as yet unchecked centrifugal logic, suggests that muddling through will not be enough. In one way or another the UK faces a protracted debate about how—and whether—it can continue to accommodate its multinational heritage within a shared state.

References

ADAMS, J., ROBINSON, P., and VIGOR, A. 2003. *A New Regional Policy for the UK*. London: IPPR.
ARON, M. 2007. 'EU Business: Reviews of Engagement with Europe and of EU Office'. Internal memorandum of the Scottish Executive.

ARTER, D. 2003. *The Scottish Parliament: A Scandinavian-Style Assembly?* London: Frank Cass.

BANTING, K. 2006. 'Social Citizenship and Federalism: Is the Federal Welfare State a Contradiction in Terms?' Pp. 44–66 in S. Greer (ed.), *Territory, Democracy and Justice.* London: Palgrave Macmillan.

BÉLAND, D., and LECOURS, A. 2005. 'The Politics of Territorial Solidarity: Nationalism and Social Policy Reform'. *Comparative Political Studies*, 38: 676–703.

BELL, D., and CHRISTIE, A. 2001. 'Finance—The Barnett Formula: Nobody's Child?' Pp. 135–52 in A. Trench (ed.), *The State of the Nations 2001: The Second Year of Devolution in the United Kingdom.* Thorverton: Imprint Academic.

BOGDANOR, V. 2001. *Devolution in the United Kingdom*, updated edition. Oxford: Oxford University Press.

BRADBURY, J. 2006a. 'British Political Parties and Devolution: Adapting to Multi-Level Politics in Scotland and Wales'. Pp. 214–47 in D. Hough and C. Jeffery (ed.), *Devolution and Electoral Politics.* Manchester: Manchester University Press.

—— 2006b. 'Territory and Power Revisited: Theorising Territorial Politics in the United Kingdom after Devolution'. *Political Studies*, 54: 559–82.

BROWN, G. 1999. Speech at the Smith Institute, 15 April.

CARMICHAEL, P., KNOX, C., and OSBORNE, R. 2007. *Devolution and Constitutional Change in Northern Ireland.* Manchester: Manchester University Press.

CHANEY, P., HALL, T., and PITHOUSE, A. (eds.) 2001. *New Governance—New Democracy? Post-Devolution Wales.* Cardiff: University of Wales Press.

CURTICE, J. 2006. 'A Stronger or Weaker Union? Public Reactions to Asymmetric Devolution in the United Kingdom'. *Publius: The Journal of Federalism*, 36: 95–114.

—— 2008a. 'Public Attitudes and Elections'. Pp. 39–60 in C. Jeffery (ed.), *Scotland Devolution Monitoring Report.* January. https://www.ucl.ac.uk/constitution-unit/research/devolution/MonReps/Scotland_Jan08.pdf.

—— 2008b. 'Has England had Enough? Public Opinion and the Future of the Union'. Evidence presented to the House of Commons Justice Committee, 28 March.

DAVIES, R. 1999. 'Devolution: A Process not an Event'. *Gregynog Papers*, 2/2.

DEVINE, T. (ed.) 2008. *Scotland and the Union: 1707–2007.* Edinburgh: Edinburgh University Press.

DICKSON. B., and OSBORNE, R. D. 2007. 'The Impact of the Human Rights Act in Northern Ireland'. Pp. 201–22 in J. Morison, K. McEvoy, and G. Anthony (eds.), *Judges, Transition, and Human Rights.* Oxford: Oxford University Press.

DOWDS, L., and LINN, B. 2005. 'The Changing Face of Unionism: Evidence from Public Attitude Surveys'. Devolution Briefings No. 32 at http://www.devolution.ac.uk/pdfdata/Briefing%2032%20Dowds.pdf.

GREER, S. 2004. *Territorial Politics and Health Policy: UK Health Policy in Comparative Perspective.* Manchester: Manchester University Press.

—— 2006. 'The Politics of Health Policy Divergence'. Pp. 98–120 in J. Adams and K. Schmuecker (eds.), *Devolution in Practice 2006.* London: IPPR.

—— 2007. 'The Fragile Divergence Machine: Citizenship, Policy Divergence and Devolution'. Pp. 136–59 in A. Trench (ed.), *Devolution and Power.* Manchester: Manchester University Press.

HALLWARD, P., and MACDONALD, R. 2006. 'The Economic Case for Scottish Fiscal Autonomy: With or Without Independence'. At http://policyinstitute.info/resource/2007/10/macdonaldapr06.pdf.

HAZELL, R. 1999. 'The Shape of Things to Come: What Will the UK Constitution Look Like in the Early 21st Century'. Pp. 7–20 in R. Hazell (ed.), *Constitutional Futures: A History of the Next Ten Years*. Oxford: Oxford University Press.

—— (ed.) 2000. *The State and the Nation: The First Year of Devolution in the United Kingdom*. Thorverton: Imprint Academic.

—— (ed.) 2003. *The State of the Nations 2003: The Third Year of Devolution in the United Kingdom*. Thorverton: Imprint Academic.

—— (ed.) 2006. *The English Question*. Manchester: Manchester University Press.

—— and O'LEARY, B. 1999. 'A Rolling Programme of Devolution: Slippery Slope of Safeguard of the Union'. Pp. 21–46 in R. Hazell (ed.), *Constitutional Futures: A History of the Next Ten Years*. Oxford: Oxford University Press.

HOUGH, D., and JEFFERY, C. 2006. *Devolution and Electoral Politics*. Manchester: Manchester University Press.

HOUSE OF COMMONS 2003. *ODPM: Housing, Planning, Local Government and the Regions Committee: Reducing Regional Disparities in Prosperity*. Ninth Report of Session 2002–3. HC 492-I. London: Stationery Office.

HOUSE OF LORDS 2002. Select Committee on the Constitution Session 2002–3, 2nd Report, *Devolution: Inter-Institutional Relations in the United Kingdom*, HL Paper 28. London: Stationery Office.

JEFFERY, C. 2002. 'Uniformity and Diversity in Policy Provision: Insights from the US, Germany and Canada'. Pp. 176–97 in J. Adams and P. Robinson (eds.), *Devolution in Practice: Public Policy Differences within the UK*. London: IPPR.

—— 2005a. 'Devolution and the European Union: Trajectories and Futures'. Pp. 179–98 in A. Trench (ed.), *The Dynamics of Devolution: The State of the Nations 2005*. Thorverton: Imprint Academic.

—— 2005b. 'Devolution and Divergence: Public Attitudes and Institutional Logics'. Pp. 10–28 in J. Adams and K. Schmuecker (eds.), *Devolution in Practice 2006: Public Policy Differences within the UK*. London: IPPR.

—— 2006. 'Devolution and Social Citizenship: Which Society, Whose Citizenship?' Pp. 67–91 in S. Greer (ed.), *Territory, Democracy and Justice*. London: Palgrave Macmillan.

—— 2007. 'The Unfinished Business of Devolution: Seven Open Questions'. *Public Policy and Administration*, 22: 92–108.

—— and SCOTT, A. 2007. *Scotland's Economy: The Fiscal Debate*. Edinburgh: Scottish Council for Development and Industry.

KEATING, M. 2005. *The Government of Scotland: Public Policy Making after Devolution*. Edinburgh: Edinburgh University Press.

—— 2007. 'A Scottish Social Democracy?' Pp. 281–7 in M. Keating (ed.), *Scottish Social Democracy: Progressive Ideas for Public Policy*. Brussels: Peter Lang.

LIJPHART, A. 1977. *Democracy in Plural Societies: A Comparative Exploration*. New Haven, Conn. Yale University Press.

LODGE, G., and MITCHELL, J. 2006. 'Whitehall and the Government of England'. Pp. 96–118 in R. Hazell (ed.), *The English Question*. Manchester: Manchester University Press.

McALLISTER, L. 2000. 'The New Politics in Wales: Rhetoric and Reality?' *Parliamentary Affairs*, 53: 591–604.

McEWEN, N. 2006. *Nationalism and the State: Welfare and Identity in Scotland and Quebec*. Brussels: PIE-Peter Lang.

McGARRY, J., and O'LEARY, B. 2007. 'Stabilising the Northern Ireland Agreement'. Pp. 62–82 in P. Carmichael, C. Knox, and R. Osborne (eds.), *Devolution and Constitutional Change in Northern Ireland*. Manchester: Manchester University Press.

MAC GINTY, R. 2006. 'Public Attitudes to Constitutional Options in the Context of Devolution'. Pp. 31–46 in P. Carmichael, C. Knox, and R. Osborne (eds.), *Devolution and Constitutional Change in Northern Ireland*. Manchester: Manchester University Press.

MACKAY, F. 2004. 'Gender and Political Representation in the UK: The State of the "Discipline"'. *British Journal of Politics and International Relations*, 6/1: 101–22.

MCLEAN, I. 2001. 'The National Question'. Pp. 429–48 in A. Seldon (ed.), *The Blair Effect: The Blair Government 1997–2001*. London: Little, Brown.

——and MCMILLAN, A. 2005. *State of the Union: Unionism and the Alternatives in the United Kingdom since 1707*. Oxford: Oxford University Press.

MARGETTS, H., and DUNLEAVY, P. 2005. 'The 2004 GLA London Elections Study: Devolution Briefings No. 33'. At http://www.devolution.ac.uk/pdfdata/Briefing%2033%20-%20Margetts.pdf.

MARSHALL, T. 1950/1992. 'Citizenship and Social Class'. Pp. 3–51 in T. Marshall and T. Bottomore (eds.), *Citizenship and Social Class*. London: Pluto Press.

MIERS, D., PATCHETT, K., and RAWLINGS, R. 2005. White Paper 'Better Governance for Wales': Submission To Welsh Affairs Committee. At http://www.publications.parliament. uk/pa/cm200506/cmselect/cmwelaf/551/5101804.htm.

MILLER, W. (ed.) 2005. *Anglo-Scottish Relations from 1900 to Devolution*. Oxford: British Academy/Oxford University Press.

MITCHELL, J. 2000. 'New Parliament, New Politics in Scotland'. *Parliamentary Affairs*, 53: 605–21.

——2003. *Governing Scotland: The Invention of Administrative Devolution*. Basingstoke: Palgrave Macmillan.

——2006a. 'Evolution and Devolution: Citizenship, Institutions and Public Policy'. *Publius: The Journal of Federalism*, 36: 153–68.

——2006b. 'Devolution's Unfinished Business'. *Political Quarterly*, 77: 465–74.

——2009. *Devolution in the United Kingdom*. Manchester: Manchester University Press.

MORGAN, K. 2006. 'Devolution and Development: Territorial Justice and the North–South Divide'. *Publius: The Journal of Federalism*, 36: 189–206.

——and UPTON, S. 2005. 'Culling the Quangos'. Pp. 78–99 in J. Osmond (ed.), *Welsh Politics Comes of Age: Responses to the Richard Commission*. Cardiff: Institute of Welsh Affairs.

OSBORNE, R. 2006. 'Devolution and Divergence in Education Policy: The Northern Ireland Case'. Pp. 70–5 in J. Adams and K. Schmuecker (eds.), *Devolution in Practice 2006*. London: IPPR.

PATTERSON, H., and KAUFMAN, E. 2007. 'From Deference to Defiance: Popular Unionism and the Decline of Elite Accommodation in Northern Ireland'. Pp. 83–95 in P. Carmichael, C. Knox, and R. Osborne (eds.), *Devolution and Constitutional Change in Northern Ireland*. Manchester: Manchester University Press.

PEARCE, G., and AYRES, S. 2006. 'Emerging Patterns of Governance in the English Regions: The Role of Regional Assemblies'. *Regional Studies*, 41: 1–14.

——2007. 'New Patterns of Governance in the English Region: Assessing their Implications for Spatial Planning'. *Environment and Planning C: Government and Policy*, 24: 909–27.

RALLINGS, C., and THRASHER, M. 2006. ' "Just Another Expensive Talking Shop": Public Attitudes and the 2004 Regional Assembly Referendum in the North East of England'. *Regional Studies*, 40: 927–36.

RAWLINGS, R. 2003. *Delineating Wales: Constitutional, Legal and Administrative Aspects of National Devolution*. Cardiff: University of Wales Press.

REIF, K., and SCHMITT, H. 1980. 'Nine Second-Order National Elections: A Conceptual Frame-work for the Analysis of European Election Results'. *European Journal of Political Research*, 8: 3–44.

ROKKAN, S., and URWIN, D. 1982. *The Politics of Territorial Identity*. London: Sage.

SANDFORD, M. 2005. *The New Governance of the English Regions*. Basingstoke: Palgrave Macmillan.

SCOTTISH EXECUTIVE 2007. *Choosing Scotland's Future: A National Conversation*. Edinburgh: Scottish Executive.

SHIRLOW, P., and MURTAGH, B. 2006. *Belfast: Segregation, Violence and the City*. London: Pluto Press.

TAYLOR, B., and THOMSON, K. 1999. *Scotland and Wales: Nations Again*. Cardiff: University of Wales Press.

TOMANEY, J., and MAWSON, J. 2002. *England: The State of the Regions*. Bristol: Policy Press.

TONGE, J. 2005. *The New Northern Irish Politics?* Basingstoke: Palgrave Macmillan.

TRAVERS, T. 2004. *The Politics of London: Governing an Ungovernable City*. Basingstoke: Palgrave Macmillan.

TRENCH, A. (ed.) 2001. *The State of the Nations 2001: The Second Year of Devolution in the United Kingdom*. Thorverton: Imprint Academic.

—— (ed.) 2004. *Has Devolution Made a Difference? The State of the Nations 2004*. Thorverton: Imprint Academic.

—— (ed.) 2005a. *The Dynamics of Devolution: The State of the Nations 2005*. Thorverton: Imprint Academic.

—— 2005b. 'Conclusion: The Future of Devolution'. Pp. 253–68 in A. Trench (ed.), *The Dynamics of Devolution: The State of the Nations 2005*. Thorverton: Imprint Academic.

—— 2005c. 'Better Governance for Wales: An Analysis of the White Paper on Devolution for Wales'. Devolution Policy Papers, No. 13. At http://www.devolution.ac.uk/Policy_Papers.htm.

WILFORD, R. 2001. *Aspects of the Belfast Agreement*. Oxford: Oxford University Press.

WILSON, R. 2007. 'Constitutional Innovation since 1972: Where Next?' Pp. 16–30 in P. Carmichael, C. Knox, and R. Osborne (eds.), *Devolution and Constitutional Change in Northern Ireland*. Manchester: Manchester University Press.

WINCOTT, D. 2006. 'Social Policy and Social Citizenship: Britain's Welfare States'. *Publius: The Journal of Federalism*, 36: 169–88.

WRIGHT, A. (ed.) 2000. *Scotland: The Challenge of Devolution*. Aldershot: Ashgate.

WYN JONES, R., and SCULLY, R. 2006. 'Devolution and Electoral Politics in Wales and Scotland'. *Publius: The Journal of Federalism*, 36: 115–34.

—— 2008. 'Wales Devolution'. Monitoring Report January 2008. At https://www.ucl.ac.uk/constitution-unit/research/devolution/MonReps/Wales_Jan08.pdf.

CHAPTER 22

LOCALISM

JONATHAN DAVIES

We must ceaselessly remember that the monistic theory of the state was born in an age of crisis and that each period of its revivification has synchronised with some momentous event which has signalised a change in the distribution of political power.

(Laski 1919: 563)

22.1 INTRODUCTION

POLITICAL power in Britain is 'ruthlessly centralised' (Travers 2007). The doctrine of parliamentary sovereignty means that, formally, local government exists on sufferance and it is not entirely fanciful to suggest that it could be abolished. Nicholas Ridley (1998), as Secretary of State for the Environment, aspired to a world of residual local authorities meeting once per year to award service contracts to business. While promising 'an enhanced role and new powers' for compliant authorities, newly elected Prime Minister Tony Blair stated that local government must 'deliver the policies for which this government was elected', or he would 'have to look to other partners to take on your role' (1998: 22). Both perspectives reflect the nadir or the 'immiseration' of British local government at the end of the twentieth century (White 2005: 76).

Many thanks to Professor David Wilson, colleagues at the Local Government Centre at Warwick, my lead editor Matt Flinders, and anonymous referees for excellent advice on earlier drafts.

However, recent years have seen a change of tone. Ministers argue that government cannot micro-manage local politics. Then Secretary of State at the Department of Communities and Local Government (DCLG), Ruth Kelly, wrote in her preface to the 2006 Local Government White Paper that improvements to public services since 1997 had been 'driven largely from the centre'. However, 'we must have the courage at the centre to let go' because the country faces challenges that are too complex for 'all solutions to be imposed' (DCLG 2006: 4). This devolutionary *Zeitgeist* makes the 'new localism' a pertinent theme in contemporary political analysis.

This chapter assesses the nature and significance of the localist turn, set in a theoretical and historical context. It explains two salient contradictions in New Labour's localism: its simultaneous appeals to market entrepreneurialism and conservative communitarianism and the fact that despite the rhetoric of localism, political centralism has increased (see Davies 2008). This trend exemplifies the 'Blair Paradox'. How is it, asks Flinders (2005: 87), that a government ostensibly committed to devolving power can 'be seen, at the same time, as having a strong centralizing and controlling approach to governing'? The answer suggested here is that both anomalies arise from the contradictions of neoliberal governance (Harvey 2005). The coincidence of liberalism and communitarianism and localist rhetoric and centralizing practice is therefore no coincidence. Each entails the other. This argument contrasts with the perspective on localism developed by Gerry Stoker (2002; 2004), which depicts governing as a chaotic, somewhat fragile process, replete with tensions and is sceptical towards structure-centred explanation.

The first part of the chapter focuses on conceptual issues. It begins by considering the normative foundations of localism and centralism. It then looks at how different conceptions of power have influenced the study of localism. The second part of the chapter then explores the emergence of contemporary localism, before proceeding to examine the New Labour approach since 1997. The final section explains the Blair Paradox in terms of contradictions within neoliberalism.

22.2 WHY LOCALISM?

Like much contemporary political thought, localism of a kind can be traced back to Aristotle who, in Crick's words, argued that: 'if a tyrant was to be secure, he must destroy all intermediary groups, because however unpolitical they were, it was participation in such social groups that created *mutual trust* between individuals, without which any opposition to tyranny…is futile' (2002: 497). Later, Alexis de Tocqueville (1994: 61) also argued that liberty demands the presence of intermediate groups, including municipal institutions, which 'constitute the strength of free nations'. These ideas inspired nineteenth-century liberal municipalists who preached

Britain's civic gospel (see further below). Localist principles were also salient among the foundations of modern British conservatism. According to Edmund Burke:

> ... we begin our public affections in our families ... We pass on to our neighborhoods, and our habitual provincial connection. These are inns and resting places. Such divisions of our country as have been formed by habit, and not by the sudden jerk of authority, were so many little images of the great country in which the heart found something which it could fill.   (Cited in Carlson 2006: 1)

It was 'through this natural chain of loyalties, resting on spontaneous, organic units tied to place, that the good society emerged' (ibid.). For Burke, social institutions must be built from the bottom up and thus, famously, the 'small platoon' must be the 'pillar of the state' (Crick 2002: 497). Gordon Brown often associates himself with these conservative ideas (e.g. 2000):

> There is a strong case for saying that in the age of enlightenment, Britain invented the modern idea of civic society ... eventually incorporating what Edmund Burke defined as little platoons ... ideas we would today recognise as being at the heart not only of the voluntary sector but of a strong society. Call it community, call it civic patriotism, call it the giving age, or call it the new active citizenship, call it the great British society—it is Britain becoming Britain again.

Writing in the centre-left journal *Renewal*, Davies and Crabtree express misgivings about the appropriation of conservative communitarianism to the extent, they suggest, that Labour and Conservative policies 'often look spookily similar' (2004: 42). However, as argued below, the way that New Labour performs the synthesis draws attention to the limits of contemporary localism and the central contradiction explored in this chapter: while appealing to bottom-up conceptions of community and locality, New Labour practises authoritarian centralism, as did its Conservative predecessors (Gamble 1994).

The persistence of centralism has prompted scholars to revisit the case for localism. Chandler (2008: 358) develops an ethical justification premised on the notion that 'as individuals should be free to follow their beliefs, provided these do not harm others, then communities with self regarding interests should also be free to pursue their ideas'. He concludes that such a justification would 'establish a much clearer rationale for determining the structure and functions of differing tiers of community within and including the state' (2008: 370). In prescriptive vein, Copus (2006) suggests a new constitutional settlement to enshrine the powers of local government. His model of a federalized UK based on strong local government is thought provoking. These developments are welcome, but require elucidation, not least in confronting the opposing case for centralism.

The case for centralized authority can be sourced to Plato's *Republic* and his conception of the ideal city-state governed by philosophers. Platonic thinking may be reflected in what John Stewart (2000: 95–6) calls the 'elite contempt' for local government with which he charges Blair, Thatcher, and forebears back to Mill, who despite asserting the importance of local government, commented:

The local representative bodies and their officers are almost certain to be of a much lower grade of intelligence and knowledge than Parliament and the national executive (and) they are watched by, and accountable to, an inferior public opinion.

(1975: 375; cited in Chandler 2008: 360)

In contrast, journalist David Walker makes a principled case for the strong centre, arguing that 'the case against devolving powers and responsibilities rests on a profound commitment and its name is equity'. He warns that the price of greater local autonomy would be 'inequality, under provision and capriciousness' (2002: 5). The condition of municipal socialism, he claims, is 'strong, redistributive central government' (2002: 7). He further argues that countries 'notable for their focus upon grants equalisation ... their strong social democratic heritage and remarkably fair distributions' include Denmark, Finland, Norway, and Sweden (2002: 8). Only national governments have the capacity to regulate markets, or direct resources from rich to poor (2002: 9). Walker presents contemporary localism as the conceit of socialists who, uneasy with New Labour, find themselves occupying the terrain of the right. He urges socialists to re-embrace centralism, nevertheless conceding that target-based performance management has gone too far.

Walker's argument has merit, up to a point. It is true, for example, that the typical localist, unlike advocates of states' rights in the USA, would stop well short of allowing localities to expel immigrants or abolish business taxes. However, he inexplicably dismisses the proposition that centralized decisions on tax are compatible with devolved decisions on spending. He argues: 'At this point in the argument some localists turn round and demand a grants system that somehow combines equity at the national level with freedom for local or regional spenders', asserting that 'True devolution must mean devolving decisions on tax as well as spend' (Walker 2002: 21). From the perspective of de Tocqueville or Burke, this might be true; but from a socialist perspective, it confuses state accountability with public accountability. Walker overlooks, for example, the fact that Denmark is not only more equitable than Britain, but also one of the most decentralized systems in Europe (Mouritzen 2007). The Danish system is not immune from criticism; but here, equalization and decentralization coexist. So, why is it not plausible that the centre should redistribute resources between individuals and places and that, simultaneously, accountability for the requisite share should reside locally where citizen-taxpayers can hold an elected local authority accountable?

A socialist case for localism might therefore begin with three propositions. First, neoliberalizing centralism undermines both equality and liberty. Second, the centralized procurement of resources under a progressive government is compatible with devolved decisions on spending. Third, there is no prima-facie reason to believe that local representatives are not as competent to make political decisions about localities as are national representatives to make decisions about countries. Nevertheless, the practical challenge for localists of any political disposition remains: how can meaningful devolution occur in political conditions that seem to auger further neoliberal centralism?

22.3 STUDYING LOCALISM: PERSPECTIVES ON POWER

One of the difficulties inherent in evaluating New Labour's localist credentials lies in establishing a common mode of assessment. A perspective on political power, although not always explicit, invariably lies at the heart of contemporary debates. These debates are partly about what individual scholars think the relationship is, and should be, between centre and locality; but they are also inherently methodological in that when trying to ascertain what the relationship is, scholars make distinctive assumptions about power: essentially, whether the greater problem is the mobilization and coordination of fragmented governing resources, or domination.

In UK political science, Rhodes's (1997) view that governance by network is pervasive has gained the 'semblance of orthodoxy', constituting what Marinetto calls the 'Anglo-governance school' (2003: 593). Network governance entails negotiated, 'non-hierarchical exchanges between systems of governing at different institutional levels' (Pierre and Stoker 2002: 30) in a world characterized by growing complexity and interdependence between many actors. Taking this heterarchical view of fragmented power draws attention to the contingently assembled and fragile nature of governing capacity, or 'power to' (Stone 1989). It demands that attention be paid to resource mobilization, coalition building, and leadership, key themes in the New Labour agenda. It tends to promote a generative model of political interaction, where constructive efforts can be mobilized towards a putative common, or public, interest. This outlook does not deny the persistence of power inequalities and competing interests but in some hands, it resonates with Talcott Parsons's (1963) conception of power as a positive sum game, where the total amount of power in society is increased by cooperation, predicated on a tacit foundational consensus.

Similar assumptions underpin the government's emphasis on building cross-sector partnerships comprising the public, market, voluntary, and community sectors. For Blair, there are now 'all sorts of players on the local pitch jostling for position where previously the council was the main game in town' (1998: 10), necessitating a partnership approach. The condition for effective partnership is that ideological conflicts are subordinated and that all parties focus on the problem of mobilizing and coordinating resources in pursuit of agreed objectives, in the process overcoming public service fragmentation.

However, this approach is criticized by scholars who argue that concentrating on resource mobilization and coordination elides a central problem, reflected in contemporary central–local relations: power and wealth, have become more concentrated, not less (e.g. Harvey 2005). For Skelcher, Mathur, and Smith (2005: 586) 'technical expertise is privileged' in local governing networks 'and decisions proceed through a rational process little impacted by the political world'. Davies (2007: 787) concludes that local governance is subject to a process of 'creeping managerialism', where both local political autonomy and community voices are increasingly sacrificed to top-down, technocratic modes of service delivery.

Underpinning these studies is a more or less overt concern with power as domination (Lukes 1974).

This debate, essentially a structure–agency controversy, resonates with that over urban regime theory and the politics of its leading international proponent, Clarence Stone (1989). Stone's central claim, simply, is that local politics matters. Like the Anglo-governance school, he argues that localities are politically differentiated, governing resources are dispersed, and therefore studying the production and execution of local governance is of profound importance. However, Stone's critics argue that socio-economic structures play a stronger role in determining local politics than he allows, particularly in the context of continuing socio-economic polarization (Imbroscio 2003).

The dilemma is, as Stone puts it (2004: 39), whether one studies systems and the reproduction of local institutions within them, or the ways in which localities generate different governing capabilities. One way of resolving the dilemma is to dissolve the analytical distinction between 'power to' and 'power over'. Stone himself points to such a solution, when he asserts that 'power to' 'spills over into a kind of domination' (1989: 229). Practically, this means focusing on the conditions in which localities mobilize and coordinate governing resources. If partnership generates new governing capacity, to what ends is it deployed, for whom, and at the expense of what alternative interests, agendas, and capacities? Questions posed this way put 'power over' at the centre of the inquiry, but in a manner requiring local research and without denying the possibility of local differentiation.

The argument developed below is that 'power over' is deeply entwined in 'new localist' attempts to mobilize governing resources in the UK. However, asserting this does not entail the claim that central governments, or for that matter global capital, exercise perfect, unmediated control over local politics. On the contrary, it is argued that while local authorities are politically quiescent, the fact that they are often unable to deliver in accordance with central government objectives signifies a failure of neoliberalism, for which the UK government has vainly attempted to compensate with further centralizing measures. The discussion now turns to the politics of contemporary localism, set briefly in its historical context.

22.4 OLD LOCALISM(S)

What White (2005: 79) calls 'very old localism indeed' (also Powell 2004) originated in the nineteenth century with the proliferation of undemocratic single-purpose statutory authorities. However, as Stewart (2000) demonstrates, nineteenth-century localism was visionary. The 'civic gospel' in Birmingham was proclaimed by the Reverend George Dawson (cited in Stewart 2000: 28). Municipalism, he proclaimed, would lead to:

the discovery that perhaps a strong and able Town Council might do almost as much to improve the conditions of life in the town as Parliament itself. I have called it a 'discovery', for it had all the freshness and charm—it created all the enthusiasm—of a good discovery. One of its first effects was to invest the Council with a new attractiveness and dignity ... The speakers, instead of discussing small questions of administration and of economy, dwelt with growing enthusiasm on what a great and prosperous town like Birmingham might do for its people. They spoke of sweeping away streets in which it was not possible to live a healthy and decent life ... of providing gardens and parks and music; or erecting baths and free libraries, an art gallery and a museum ... Sometimes an adventurous orator would excite his audience by dwelling on the glories of Florence ... in the middle ages, and suggest that Birmingham, too, might become the home of a noble literature and art.

This inspiring passage, drawing inspiration from de Tocqueville's liberal municipalism, heralded the rebirth of social optimism amidst the squalor of Victorian England. It calls local government to action, demanding political debate on a grand scale. In today's inestimably wealthier society, it remains a benchmark against which to compare and contrast the scope and ambition of contemporary localism. At the same time, it is important to understand that the civic doctrine remained 'illusory': precisely because of the 'special political rights' accorded to property then (Palmowski 2002: 381), and forcefully asserted now under neoliberalism.

Historians disagree about the origins of contemporary centralism, but it probably has multiple sources. Some scholars argue that the poor law of 1834 was of 'seminal importance' in 'establishing the principle of state regulation over the locality' or alternatively that Lloyd George's social reforms unleashed an unprecedented level of central involvement in local politics (Palmowski 2002: 383). However, White's (2005) story of the decline of local democracy pinpoints 1930 to 1948 as the heyday of localism. He argues that 'Whole spheres of public life were owned and managed locally that are now seen as entirely the province of national government or the private sector' (2005: 75), including most education services, control of the emergency services, electricity production, and health. White argues that the present era of centralization commenced in the late 1940s with the development of the welfare state, but gained fresh impetus with the neoliberal ascendancy after the mid-1970s. Certainly, the period between 1945 and 1979 appears 'localist' by comparison with today. Local government was relatively free to spend and provided public services directly to citizens as part of the post-war welfare state. Thus, the following discussion of contemporary localism situates it in the analysis of centralizing trends since the 1970s.

22.5 THE ORIGINS OF TWENTY-FIRST CENTURY LOCALISM

The concept of 'new localism' emerged in political science in the late 1980s and early 1990s alongside the 'new urban politics' (Goetz and Clarke 1993) in the USA and the post-Thatcher localist turn in the UK. US scholars at the time were beginning to grapple with the challenge posed to localities by economic globalization and the perceived hyper-mobility of capital. The literatures of the 1980s and 1990s depicted increased capital mobility as forcing cities to adopt ever more entrepreneurial policies (Hall and Hubbard 1996). The concern for American urbanists was what, if anything, localities might do to protect redistributionist goals, given the pressure on cities (aggravated by anti-collectivist national governments) to indulge the appetites of footloose capital.

In the UK, however, the soubriquet 'new localism' was closely linked to the study of central–local relations. It emerged in the early 1990s in response to a thaw following the political battles of the 1980s, around municipal socialism. In 1984, the UK government introduced rate capping to control local spending. Some councils, notably Lambeth, Liverpool, and Sheffield, resisted (Boddy and Fudge 1984). However, by 1986, the short-lived movement was defeated and bastions of the left, like the Greater London Council, were on the way to abolition. For the remainder of the 1980s, local government was excluded from key decisions, notably about development. Thus, the concerns of the 'new urban politics' spread to Britain but by different means. Whereas in the USA most city governments were disposed to pursue market-led growth anyway (Imbroscio 2003), a prominent minority in the UK had to be forced. Throughout the 1980s, the Tories tried to create an entrepreneurial culture in local government: by allowing unemployment to rise, rate capping, compulsory competitive tendering for public services, and giving business a substantial say in local development. Lawless (1994: 1304) argued that the late 1980s represented the 'high tide of anti-collectivism towards the cities'.

However, by 1990, the government was calling for a 'spirit of co-operation, of partnership' between central and local government and business (Lawless 1994: 1304). This policy shift was based partly on the government's confidence that it had quelled the resistance of Labour local authorities. At the same time, the marginalization of local government was also being criticized and business-led development perceived to be failing within the Tory party itself (Le Gales and Mawson 1995: 222). The overthrow of Mrs Thatcher and her replacement by John Major as PM in November 1990 created the space for a change of direction. Major reappointed Michael Heseltine as Secretary of State at the Department of the Environment, his second tenure there. Heseltine instigated a 'partnership' approach with local government. In 1991, he introduced City Challenge, a regeneration programme calling on local authorities and others to form partnerships and bid for funding in competition with other partnerships. This approach, symbolizing the outbreak of peace between central and local government, was called 'new localism' by Murray Stewart (1994) and Stuart Wilks-Heeg (1996). However, Wilks-Heeg noted that while it partially rehabilitated local government, the new localism did so 'within a highly competitive and managerialist framework over which central government retains considerable control' (1996: 1271). Contributors to the 1992–7 ESRC Local Governance Programme took similar views (Stoker 1999; 2000). Their findings pointed to the emergence not of the autonomous governing networks heralded by Rhodes, but the perpetuation of hierarchical modes of governance. Morgan, Rees, and Garmise (1999: 196) memorably dismissed the notion that governance is increasingly about horizontal networks as a 'fatal conceit'.

22.6 NEW LABOUR'S NEW LOCALISM

The new localist turn occurred when, arguably, local government was at its lowest ebb since universal suffrage. White argues that now, 'English local government seems largely residual and exiguous to the central state machine' (2005: 76). Today's local government is beholden to the centre for some 75 per cent of its revenues (DCLG 2007a: 3) and has limited control over the remaining 25 per cent raised through the Council Tax. As Ruth Kelly's foreword to the 2006 White Paper conceded, New Labour continued the centralizing trend. The White Paper acknowledged that 80 per cent of local government reporting was to the centre, only 20 per cent to local citizens (DCLG 2006: 117). To ensure that local authorities prioritized national targets, New Labour established an elaborate system of audit and inspection. The Comprehensive Performance Assessment (CPA) framework, established in 2002, ranked local authorities from 'poor' to 'excellent'. Depending on its ranking, a local authority could expect more or less coercive intervention by agents of the centre. The 'best' authorities would receive what the government called 'earned autonomy'. Attaining 'excellence' would entitle them to 'freedoms and flexibilities'. However, exemptions from reporting and planning obligations were few and offered little by way of political freedom (Ellison and Ellison 2006: 34). Reform seemed to connote slower centralization, not devolution. The watchword of the day, 'earned autonomy', was of a piece with the centralizing dynamic of the time. Ultimately, the very concept implied central control, turning the authority's attention away from meeting the needs of local citizens towards meeting the demands of government (Lowndes 2002: 140).

However, Ruth Kelly argued that there had been 'good reason' for New Labour's top-down approach (DCLG 2006: 4):

> In 1997 this Government, after decades of under-investment, inherited public services and institutions which were not always fit for purpose. We responded with massive investment and by setting a strong direction nationally. Combined with the hard work and commitment of local government and others, this has led to radical improvements. But, for these improvements to continue, we must have the courage at the centre to let go.

This passage contains several messages. First, reflecting 'elite contempt', it says that in 1997 local government was anachronistic and could not be trusted to 'modernize' public services. Second, it hints at the government's view that a critical, information rich, and individualized public will not tolerate high public spending without commensurate improvements in performance. Third, it suggests that centralism has worked, but has had its day. Local government is now fit for purpose and can be trusted, indeed must be trusted, to drive improvement.

Stoker argues that New Labour now faces a choice between two modes of multi-level governance. The first, constrained discretion, entails localized management of a political agenda set by the centre (2005: 166), as happens now. The second model, advocated by Stoker, sees local government as a strategic community leader with considerable autonomy in determining goals and speaking for communities (2005: 162). Local government should be trusted with fomenting debate, encouraging the development of shared aspirations and ensuring that resources are mobilized and coordinated to achieve them. This approach is not unlike the 'coordinative' role with which Sharpe (1970: 166) tasked local government: 'coherently adjusting public services and linking them to local knowledge and a participatory environment—which could not be fulfilled simply by out-stationed field agencies'. Stoker's (2004: 117) definition of the new localism reflects this vision. It is 'a strategy aimed at devolving power and resources away from central control and towards front-line managers, local democratic structures and local consumers and communities, within an agreed framework of national minimum standards and policy priorities'.

However, despite its recency, the concept of 'new localism' remains fluid, depicted variously in the language of 'earned autonomy' and 'constrained discretion' (Stoker 2004: 5) and more recently 'double devolution' and 'place-shaping'. 'Double devolution' was favoured during David Miliband's brief tenure as Secretary of State at DCLG. He commented (Miliband 2006):

> I call it 'double devolution'—not just devolution that takes power from central government and gives it to local government, but power that goes from local government down to local people, providing a critical role for individuals and neighbourhoods, often through the voluntary sector.

For Miliband, the new localism was less about the relationship between central and local government than that between government and citizens called upon to play an active role in shaping the future. As Alan Milburn (2006) commented, writing in the *Guardian* on the same day as Miliband's above-quoted speech, the government must 'redistribute *power* so that *responsibility* for meeting the challenge of economic, demographic, environmental, social and cultural change is shared between citizens, states and communities' (emphasis added). This double-edged comment highlights a perennial question about civil renewal. How far is it about community empowerment (enabling) or social engineering (domination)? It is argued below that in facing the contradictions posed by neoliberal strategy, the UK government has deployed a coercive variant of conservative communitarianism, but with limited effect.

After the appointment of Ruth Kelly in May 2006, 'place-shaping' superseded 'double devolution', forming the conceptual spine of Sir Michael Lyons' inquiry into the structure and functions of local government. For Lyons (2007: 3), place-shaping is about community leadership, entailing a 'wider strategic role for local government' making 'creative use of powers and influence to promote the general well-being of a community and its citizens'.

These discursive manoeuvres, occurring over a short timescale, may be significant. They are suggestive of a government constantly adapting rhetoric and policy in response to events, but in doing so attempting to navigate a consistent political course. New Labour's three local government white papers lend support to this interpretation. Each reveals the paradox of a government pledging decentralization, but continuing to centralize. To illustrate, the discussion draws on Davies (2008).

22.7 RHETORIC AND REALITY: THREE LOCAL GOVERNMENT WHITE PAPERS

In 1997, New Labour proclaimed a new era for local government. It announced a central–local partnership and established an institution of that name under the 'Framework for Partnership' agreement. The first White Paper (DETR 1998), warning local government to rise to the challenge of modernization, nevertheless adopted the tone of partnership. The Local Government Association welcomed it as a move away from 'a centralised and over-prescriptive approach'. Even Blair's notorious (above-quoted) threat to sweep aside recalcitrant local authorities did not quell optimism that the revival of local government was imminent. With the publication of a second White Paper (DTLR 2001), however, the Secretary of State for Transport, Local Government and the Regions, Stephen Byers, conceded that centralizing trends had persisted. His *mea culpa* reiterated the pledge made in 1998:

> I want to tackle the trend towards excessive central prescription and interference, which dominated central local relations in the 1980s and 90s. We are reversing that approach. The White Paper marks a pronounced step away from centralisation. . . . It is truly about local government. It is a significant shift away from local administration. Based on a belief that we don't need to control everything, and a recognition that local authorities are often in the best position to respond to local needs and aspirations.   (DTLR 2001*b*)

Reviewing this second New Labour White Paper, however, Lowndes detected the opposite: the intensification of managerialism at the expense of local democracy, artfully disguised in democratic language (2002: 144) and constituting a 'new centralism' (2002: 136). If anything, the government's second term was more centralizing than the first, with the imposition of performance management mechanisms like CPA and the seeming subordination of 'community led' partnerships to intensive audit and micro-management. As Wright et al. put it in a scathing evaluation of the New Deal for Communities regeneration programme (2006: 347), 'if NDC is a community-led programme, it is community led in the sense that government decides how the community will be involved, why they will be involved, what they will do and how they will do it'. Such is the tenor of many commentaries about partnership (e.g. Skelcher, Mathur, and Smith 2005; Geddes 2006).

In this light, Kelly's introduction to the 2006 Local Government White Paper, quoted above, provokes a sense of déjà vu and the content of the paper suggests that it is no more devolutionary than its predecessors were. The first striking feature is the proselytizing tone, suffused in a breathless 'change' narrative, interpolated with exhortations on unexceptional local authorities to catch up with 'the best', who are 'already' doing it in response to what the government has 'already' done. Reflecting the government's globalization mania, it comments excitedly 'the world has moved on apace. The speed of change, often driven by global forces, can be startling . . .' (DCLG 2006: 154). Or, 'such is the pace of change that we cannot afford to be complacent' (2006: 25). In response, 'the best' local authorities are 'already' delivering transformed services, but 'we need to increase the pace of change' (2006: 26). The trade-off for fewer national targets is that 'the pace of public service improvements will quicken' (2006: 117) and local government will be judged on the 'pace of improvement' (2006: 126). Thus, the world is changing, people are changing, and local government needs to change, emulating 'the best' in the sector, which is 'already' changing but must nevertheless change again, change faster, and change continuously. The demand for increasingly frantic 'change' is a prima-facie case of control-freakery.

The direction of 'change' is, in turn, heavily prescribed. Public services must be further 'personalized' in an ever-wider 'partnership' with the private sector. Councils:

> will have to challenge traditional methods of delivery, root out waste, keep all council activity under review and work with other public bodies to share assets, systems, data, skills and knowledge more effectively. . . . Ambitious efficiency gains will therefore be required as part of the 2007 Comprehensive Spending Review.   (DCLG 2006: 12)

Personalization or 'choice' is another controversial feature of government policy. Advocates contend that it is a vehicle to deliver the services that 'modern consumers expect and demand' (DCLG 2006: 22). Critics, however, see it as a synonym for destructive competition between public services. They argue that like empowerment 'personalization' is a synonym for 'responsibility' because it demands active engagement by citizens, who will be judged if their choices do not deliver the requisite outcomes (Clarke 2005). Personalization, improvement, and efficiency are also predicates of competitiveness. Local authorities, expected to 'drive down costs' as a matter of course (DCLG 2006: 135), are urged to create new markets and expose new areas of work to 'competition and contestability' (2006: 121/135). This proselytizing tone sets the neoliberal agenda in stone. It offers no space for political difference or dissidence, central criteria of political freedom.

The government's response to the modest reforms proposed by the Lyons Inquiry (2007) further illustrates its reluctance to localize. It dismissed cautiously progressive proposals to extend council tax bandings together with the long awaited property revaluation. Lyons' recommendation that council tax capping should be abolished was also dismissed. Local Government Minister at the time, Phil Woolas, argued that the government 'does not consider that its powers to cap council tax increases necessarily need to be seen as weakening the freedom and accountability of local government to its electorate' (DCLG 2007b). Yet, capping is a powerful emblem of the neoliberal centralizing tradition and together with New Labour's fetish for markets, perhaps the most potent symbol of continuity with the Thatcher era. Control over local spending is, as Travers (2007) argued, an issue of constitutional importance, one upon which the political autonomy of local government depends.

Thus, while local political and managerial leaders may be equipped with a wider range of instruments for mobilizing governing resources, the political direction and institutional mechanisms for local governance have been further prescribed by the three white papers. The new localism is predicated not on any commitment to enhanced local democracy, or local political autonomy (Pratchett 2004), but on the acknowledgement that central political and managerial control have limited effectiveness. Greater flexibility is about enhancing reflexive management; the ability of local actors to select from myriad creative governing responses of their own making in response to local circumstances, but commensurate with the neoliberal agenda. These are the politics of 'constrained discretion', the common thread running through episodic developments in the government's agenda.

22.8 UNDERSTANDING THE BLAIR PARADOX

The trends depicted above have led some scholars to impute a lack of coherence to the government's approach. Early on, for example, Sullivan identified the tensions between ideas such as community leadership, improved public management, and building social capital (2001: 1), noting that different localities used them in a variable mix (2001: 20–1). Stoker sees manoeuvres and inconsistencies as characteristic of the inability of central government to exercise effective control over local authorities, try as it might. He argues that New Labour's strategy follows from its fatalistic world-view, seeing all systems as capricious (Stoker 2002: 419). '[A]t the top of New Labour there is a widespread but not universal culture of paranoia that sees enemies all around' (2002: 432). Fatalism anticipates governance failure. Thus, stymied by the rubber levers of power and recognizing that the prospect of effective control is limited, New Labour devised a lottery approach to policy to shake up and create uncertainty among local authorities unwilling or incapable of adapting to the modernization agenda. This strategy, 'incoherence with a purpose', created instability and the impression of 'control-freakery gone mad' (Stoker 2004: 74–5). Although the time has come to move beyond this approach, the upside was that uncertainty generated space and impetus for local innovation (Stoker 2004: 69).

To a degree, Stoker's perspective chimes with this account. The lottery approach could explain, for example, rapid changes in governmental discourses of localism. It also suggests reasons why a government with limited effective power continuously churns out top-down initiatives in an almost desperate attempt to reinvigorate local government. However, the approach developed here differs in two particulars. First, it argues that the capriciousness inherent in contemporary local governance is the consequence not of complexity and differentiation, but of contradictions integral to the neoliberal strategy pursued by New Labour. Second, apparent tensions in government policy, specifically those between individualism and communitarianism and centralism and localism, arise from the attempt to manage the effects of these contradictions. Hence, it is possible to make sense of the new localism as an instance of the Blair Paradox, through a unifying explanation centered on the dysfunctionality of neoliberalism.

The distinctive characteristic of actually existing neoliberalism is the unintended synthesis of liberalism and authoritarianism (Harvey 2005). The basic principle of economic liberalism is that economic dynamism is possible only in relatively unfettered markets, regulated by minimal states. However, extending the market has caused a 'paradoxical' increase in state intervention (Jessop 2002: 454). Apologists, says Jessop, claim that after a brief transitional period, the state will retreat to the light-touch supervisory role. Jessop rejects this argument asserting that the strong state is, in fact, the precondition of the 'free' economy (see also Gamble 1994).

Thus, neoliberalism is liberalism gone wrong. However, why should centralization be the necessary unintended consequence of liberalization? First, liberalizing governments are faced with the continuing, if weakening, legacy of post-war 'welfarism', still significantly embedded in the public and professional consciousness despite the thirty-year long neoliberal assault (e.g. Park et al. 2003). Technocratic managerialism, attempting to place local policy beyond politics (Skelcher, Mathur, and Smith 2005), is one response to this continuing challenge (see also Geddes 2006). Second, they have to manage the polarizing and exclusionary effects of liberalization marked, for example, by ever-increasing inequality and concomitant upward pressure on public expenditure (e.g. Dorling et al. 2007). As Harvey (2005) put it, the social instability generated by neoliberalization is thoroughly dysfunctional for economic growth and profitability. The rollback of socialist aspirations has not opened the door to the spontaneous regeneration of a responsible, entrepreneurial citizenry; on the contrary, it has created fractured, damaged, and unhappy societies. Third, neoliberal doctrine demands that greater value be extracted from every public pound, placing downward pressure on expenditure but requiring robust management to deter free riders, driving it up again.

Each of these factors predicts centralization. To maintain social cohesion, liberalizing states have turned to coercive mechanisms and unifying doctrines of community and active citizenship which, in the case of New Labour, encompass appeals to individual responsibility, family, community, and nation. In its attempt to reinvent community, New Labour has imported Burke's vision of 'small platoons' in corrupted form, as an authoritarian injunction upon citizens ripped from their moorings by casino capitalism. In the Burkean view, communities of this kind are 'artificial collectives', denuding small platoons of their vitality and thus making governmental intervention inherently self-defeating (Saunders 1993: 78). This approach portends what Lupton and Fuller (2007) call the 'new disempowerment' of communities, achieved through a 'deep substratum of coerced co-operations and collaborations'

(Harvey 2000: 181). Thus, neoliberalism is repressive, 'denying the very freedoms that it is supposed to uphold' (Harvey 2005: 69).

In this context, the instability caused by simultaneous depoliticizing, economizing, liberalizing, and remoralizing creates frantic demand for constant 'change' and 'improvement' alongside attempts to clamp down on costs. It explains simultaneously the breathless and moralistic tone of the White Paper, the proliferation of top-down initiatives, and attempts to generate the reflexive, creative governance envisioned in the new localism. It also explains rapid shifts in localist discourse and apparent tensions between different goods; first 'constrained discretion' and performance, then 'double devolution' and responsible communities, and now 'place-shaping' and strong leadership to enforce 'community cohesion'. This strategy is indeed philosophically incoherent. However, it is minimally incoherent in that it poses less of a direct challenge to market individualism than, say, major tax hikes upon income and wealth to fund redistribution.

Thus, political centralization is a corollary of New Labour politics, no less than it was for Margaret Thatcher's Conservatives and is likely to remain so until the political economy of the UK is transformed. It is the unwanted but indispensable governmental response to social instability unleashed by deregulation, the extension of the market realm, rising inequality, and the consequent 'decline of the public' (Marquand 2004). This contradiction has manifested in the new localism from the outset and there is no reason to think that it will soon be resolved.

22.9 CONCLUSION

Hazel Blears (2008), current Secretary of State at DCLG, recognizes that control-freakery is a hard habit to break:

> I want to make sure that whenever we're confronting a new problem ... I want to think about what mechanisms we can put in place to make sure that our first reaction isn't new regulation, but to ask how we can learn from, and work with, town halls and their partners.

Blears is sincere. However, should mechanisms be introduced, they would probably be ineffective. New Labour's commitment to capitalist globalization, and the consequences thereof, generates tensions and contradictions apparent in the government's evolving and adaptable approach to localism. In the face of localist rhetoric, ongoing centralization is the government's response to the antinomies of liberalization. The imposition of conservative communitarianism, one instance of ongoing centralization, attempts to enhance public adaptability in a manner minimally compromising to the free market agenda. To the extent that citizens remain wayward, either because of the centrifugal effects of liberalization, or because of their political intransigence, it is likely that the juxtaposition of political centralization and localist rhetoric will continue. Clarke and Newman (2007: 754) discovered that citizens tend to reject the consumerist assumptions driving the government's personalization agenda and conclude that 'passive dissent' of this kind matters for New Labour. The New Labour project demands that citizens and communities be active and entrepreneurial, asserting that no 'modern' nation can thrive without them. Unless the citizenry is effectively 'remoralized' (Etzioni 1997), capable of adapting spontaneously to the vicissitudes of the risk society, then further liberalization will lead to further social instability, followed by further centralization. Elsewhere, I describe this scenario as New Labour's 'dialectical bind' (Davies 2005: 327). Localism remains a neoliberal conceit.

This analysis suggests that it is possible, by conceptualizing 'localism' as a problem in political economy, to develop an overarching explanation for the apparent political incoherence in New Labour politics, thus offering a solution to the Blair Paradox. However, the discussion poses significant research questions for scholars of localism. First, how much localism of what kind is appropriate in pursuit of what political ends? Scholars might do well to rethink this question in light of Dawson's civic gospel, but remember why it failed. Under what political circumstances, then, might modern localists aspire to such a vision, if it is appropriate? However, the second and pivotal question is from where the necessary political agency will come. The essence of the argument is that localism is incompatible with neoliberalism, specifically with the New Labour variant. This problem takes us back to the question of whether and when distinctive local politics are feasible. Stone himself (2004: 39) acknowledged that the challenge facing regime theorists is to demonstrate that any progressive regimes 'can maintain viability within the current international political economy'. Progressive localists must demonstrate, in other words, what localities can contribute to challenging neoliberalism. If it is true that centralization is, paradoxically, a symptom of the failure of control, then how might localities take advantage of that in order to construct alternative modes of governing? There is significant opposition to the neoliberal agenda at the local scale, suggesting that nascent alternatives may be found in dissident politics. Yet, to be minimally effective, dissidents would have to be able to exercise 'power over' to the extent necessary for maintaining effective barriers against neoliberal state intervention. The fate of municipal socialism in the 1980s suggests that such an approach in one locality, or even a significant number of localities, would not be effective for long. Thus, if the coercive strategies of dissident movements are to be effective locally in the long term, they will have to assert themselves on the national and perhaps the international stages in an attempt to replace neoliberal capitalism.

This analysis, finally, suggests that the conundrum of localism will continue to tax us across the descriptive, explanatory, and normative domains. How much localism do we actually have, of what kind, and why? What form of localism is appropriate? What are the barriers to localism? Under what contemporary circumstances, if any, does it flourish? There is sufficient scope in these questions to occupy enthusiastic scholars, practitioners, and activists for many years. Studying localism throws up myriad challenges; but it is richly rewarding to those who do it.

REFERENCES

BLAIR, T. 1998. *Leading the Way: A New Vision for Local Government*. London: Institute for Public Policy Research.

BLEARS, H. 2008. 'A New Deal for Local Devolution?' Speech at the New Local Government Network Annual Conference, 22 January. At http://www.communities.gov.uk/speeches/corporate/localdevolution; accessed 24 Jan. 2008.

BODDY, M., and FUDGE, C. (eds.) 1984. *Local Socialism*. Basingstoke: Macmillan.

BROWN, G. 2000. 'Speech by the Chancellor of the Exchequer, Gordon Brown MP and the NCVO Annual Conference'. HM Treasury. At http://www.hm-treasury.gov.uk. 9 Feb.

CARLSON, A. 2006. 'Localism'. *New Pantagruel*, 2/3: 1–2. Online journal at http://www.newpantagruel.com/issues/2.3/localism.php; accessed 2 Jan. 2008.

CHANDLER, J. 2008. 'Liberal Justifications for Local Government in Britain: The Triumph of Expediency over Ethics'. *Political Studies*, 56/2: 355–73.

CLARKE, J. 2005. 'New Labour's Citizens: Activated, Empowered, Responsibilized, Abandoned?' *Critical Social Policy*, 25/4: 447–63.

—— and NEWMAN, J. 2007. 'What's in a Name? New Labour's Citizen-Consumers and the Remaking of Public Services'. *Cultural Studies*, 21/4–5: 738–57.

COPUS, C. 2006. 'British Local Government: A Case for a New Constitutional Settlement'. *Public Policy and Administration*, 21/2: 4–21.

CRICK, B. 2002. 'Education for Citizenship: The Citizenship Order'. *Parliamentary Affairs*, 55/3: 488–504.

DAVIES, J. S. 2005. 'Local Governance and the Dialectics of Hierarchy, *Market* and Network'. *Policy Studies*, 26/3: 311–35.

—— 2007. 'The Limits of Partnership: An Exit-Action Strategy for Local Democratic Inclusion'. *Political Studies*, 55/4: 779–800.

—— 2008. 'Double Devolution or Double Dealing? The Local Government White Paper and the Lyons Review'. *Local Government Studies*, 34/1: 3–22.

DAVIES, W., and CRABTREE, J. 2004. 'Invisible Villages: Technolocalism and Community Renewal'. *Renewal*, 12/1: 40–7.

DCLG 2006. *Strong and Prosperous Communities: The Local Government White Paper*. London: HMSO. Cm. 6939.

—— 2007a. *Key Facts and Trends: Local Government Finance in England*. http://www.local.odpm.gov.uk/finance/stats/lgfs/2007/index.htm; accessed 18 Sept. 2007.

—— 2007b. 'Government Welcomes Lyons Report'. News Release 2007/0052. 21 Mar.

DETR 1998. *Modern Local Government: In Touch with the People*. London: HMSO. Cm. 4014.

DORLING, D., RIGBY, J., WHEELER, B., BALLAS, D., THOMAS, B., FAHMY, E., GORDON, D., and LUPTON, R. 2007. *Poverty, Wealth and Place in Britain, 1968–2005*. York: Joseph Rowntree Foundation.

DTLR 2001a. *Strong Local Leadership, Quality Local Services*. London: HMSO. Cm. 5237.

—— 2001b. 'Byers Sets out Vision for Stronger Local Government with New Freedoms to Deliver Better Quality Services'. News Release 2001/0535: 11 Dec.

ELLISON, N., and ELLISON, S. 2006. 'Creating "Opportunity for All"? New Labour, New Localism and the Opportunity Society'. *Social Policy and Society*, 5/3: 327–36.

ETZIONI A. 1997. *The New Golden Rule: Community and Morality in a Democratic Society*. London: Profile Books.

FLINDERS, M. 2005. 'Majoritarian Democracy in Britain: New Labour and the Constitution'. *Western European Politics*, 28/1: 62–94.

GAMBLE, A. 1994. *The Free Economy and the Strong State*, 2nd edn. Basingstoke: Macmillan.

GEDDES, M. 2006. 'Partnership and the Limits to Local Governance in England: Institutionalist Analysis and Neo-liberalism'. *International Journal of Urban and Regional Research*, 30/1: 76–97.

GOETZ, E. G., and CLARKE, S. E. (eds.) 1993. *The New Localism: Comparative Urban Politics in a Global Era*. Newbury Park, Calif.: Sage.

HALL, T., and HUBBARD, P. 1996. 'The Entrepreneurial City: New Urban Politics, New Urban Geographies?' *Progress in Human Geography*, 20/2: 153–74.

HARVEY, D. 2000. *Spaces of Hope*. Edinburgh: Edinburgh University Press.

—— 2005. *A Brief History of Neoliberalism*. Oxford: Oxford University Press.

IMBROSCIO, D. L. 2003. 'Overcoming the Neglect of Economics in Urban Regime Theory'. *Journal of Urban Affairs*, 25/3: 271–84.

JESSOP, B. 2002. 'Liberalism, Neoliberalism, and Urban Governance: A State-Theoretical Perspective'. *Antipode*, 34/3: 452–72.

LASKI, H. 1919. 'The Pluralistic State'. *Philosophical Review*, 28/6: 562–75.

LAWLESS, P. 1994. 'Partnership in Urban Regeneration in the UK: The Sheffield Central Area Study'. *Urban Studies*, 31/8: 1303–24.

LE GALES, P., and MAWSON, J. 1995. 'Contracts versus Competitive Bidding: Rationalizing Urban Policy Programmes in England and France'. *Journal of European Public Policy*, 2/2: 205–41.

LOWNDES, V. 2002. 'Between Rhetoric and Reality: Does the 2001 White Paper Reverse the Centralising Trend in Britain?' *Local Government Studies*, 28/3: 135–47.

LUKES, S. S. 1974. *Power: A Radical View*. London: Macmillan.

LUPTON, R., and FULLER, C. 2007. 'Mixed Communities: A New Approach to Spatially-Concentrated Poverty in England'. Mimeo, University of Warwick.

LYONS, M. 2007. *Place-Shaping: A Shared Ambition for the Future of Local Government. Executive Summary*. London: Stationery Office.

MARINETTO, M. 2003. 'Governing beyond the Centre: A Critique of the Anglo-governance School'. *Political Studies*, 51/3: 592–608.

MARQUAND, D. 2004. *The Decline of the Public*. Cambridge: Polity.

MILBURN, A. 2006. 'We Can't let the Right be the Voice of the "Me Generation"'. *Guardian*, 21 February.

MILIBAND, D. 2006. 'Empowerment not Abandonment'. Speech to the National Council of Voluntary Organisations annual conference. 21 February.

MORGAN, K., REES, G., and GARMISE, S. 1999. 'Networking for Local Economic Development'. Pp. 181–96 in G. Stoker (ed.), *The New Management of British Local Governance*. Basingstoke: Macmillan.

MOURITZEN, P. E. 2007. *Reforming Local Government in Denmark: How and Why?* Centre for Local Innovation, Diputacio de Barcelona.

PALMOWSKI, J. 2002. 'Liberalism and Local Government in Late 19th Century Germany and England'. *Historical Journal*, 45/2: 381–409.

PARK, A., CURTICE, J., THOMSON, K., JARVIS, L., and BROMLEY, C. 2003. *British Social Attitudes: The 20th Report*. London: Sage.

PARSONS, T. 1963. 'On the Concept of Political Power'. *Proceedings of the American Philosophical Society*, 107/3: 232–62.

PIERRE, J., and STOKER, G. 2002. 'Toward Multi-level Governance'. Pp. 29–46 in P. Dunleavy, A. Gamble, R. Heffernan, I. Holliday, and G. Peele (eds.), *Developments in British Politics 6*. Basingstoke: Palgrave.

POWELL, M. 2004. 'In Search of the Old and New Localism'. Presented at ESPAnet Conference, Oxford, 9–11 September.

PRATCHETT, L. 2004. 'Local Autonomy, Local Democracy and the New Localism'. *Political Studies*, 52/2: 358–75.

RHODES, R. A. W. 1997. *Understanding Governance: Policy Networks, Governance, Reflexivity and Accountability*. Buckingham: Open University Press.

RIDLEY, N. 1998. *The Local Right*. London: Centre for Policy Studies.

SAUNDERS, P. 1993. 'Citizenship in a Liberal Society'. Pp. 57–90 in B. Turner (ed.), *Citizenship and Social Theory*. London: Sage.

SHARPE, L. J. 1970. 'Theories and Values of Local Government'. *Political Studies*, 18/2: 153–74.

SKELCHER, C., MATHUR, N., and SMITH, M. 2005. 'The Public Governance of Collaborative Spaces: Discourse, Design and Democracy'. *Public Administration*, 83/3: 573–96.

STEWART, J. 2000. *The Nature of British Local Government*. Basingstoke: Macmillan.

STEWART, M. 1994. 'Between Whitehall and Town Hall: The Realignment of Urban Regeneration Policy in England'. *Policy and Politics*, 22/2: 133–45.

STOKER, G. (ed.) 1999. *The New Management of British Local Governance*. Basingstoke: Macmillan.

—— (ed.) 2000. *The New Politics of British Local Governance*. Basingstoke: Macmillan.

—— 2002. 'Life is a Lottery: New Labour's Strategy for the Reform of Devolved Governance'. *Public Administration*, 80/3: 417–34.

—— 2004. *Transforming Local Governance: From Thatcherism to New Labour*. Basingstoke: Palgrave.

—— 2005. 'Joined-up Government for Local and Regional Institutions'. Pp. 156–74 in V. Bogdanor (ed.), *Joined up Government*. Oxford: Oxford University Press.

STONE, C. N. 1989. *Regime Politics: Governing Atlanta*. Lawrence: University Press of Kansas.

—— 2004. 'Rejoinder: Multiple Imperatives, or Some Thoughts about Governance in a Loosely Coupled but Stratified Society'. *Journal of Urban Affairs*, 26/1: 35–42.

SULLIVAN, H. 2001. 'Modernisation, Democratisation and Community Governance'. *Local Government Studies*, 27/3: 1–24.

TOCQUEVILLE, A. DE 1994. *Democracy in America*, vol. i. New York: Knopf.

TRAVERS, T. 2007. 'Loss of Nerve over Lyons'. www.publicfinance.co.uk, 30 Mar.; available at http://www.cipfa.org.uk/publicfinance/opinion_details.cfm?News_id¹/430265 (accessed 6 Apr. 2007).

WALKER, D. 2002. *In Praise of Centralism: A Critique of New Localism*. London: Catalyst.

WHITE, J. 2005. 'From Herbert Morrison to Command and Control: The Decline of Local Democracy and its Effect on Public Services'. *History Workshop Journal*, 59: 73–82.

WILKS-HEEG, S. 1996. 'Urban Experiments Limited Revisited: Urban Policy Comes Full Circle?' *Urban Studies*, 33/8: 1263–80.

WRIGHT, J. S. F., PARRY, J., MATHERS, J., JONES, S., and ORFORD, J. 2006. 'Assessing the Participatory Potential of Britain's New Deal for Communities'. *Policy Studies*, 27/4: 347–61.

CHAPTER 23

....

EUROPEAN DEVOLUTION

....

MICHAEL KEATING

23.1 DEVOLUTION AS A CONCEPT

....

DEVOLUTION is a peculiarly British term introduced in the nineteenth century to
resolve a problem that is characteristically (but not uniquely) British.[1] This is how
to reconcile national diversity with unity, and how to grant territorial autonomy
while retaining a unitary state. The recipe, from Gladstone's first Irish Home Rule
bill in 1886 to the Scottish, Welsh, and Northern Irish settlements of 1998, is to set
up self-governing bodies for the constituent nations and regions, while insisting
that the sovereignty of the Westminster parliament is unabridged. Westminster in
theory retains the right to change the settlement unilaterally and even to abolish
the devolved institutions altogether. It is this that chiefly distinguishes devolution
from federalism, in which there are constitutional limitations on both levels of
government and the centre cannot change the system without the consent of the
constituent parts. While this distinction is vital for the British political parties, which
can thus claim to be defending the unity of the state, in practice it is much less
clear. The devolved institutions were established by referendum, implying an element
of self-determination for the constituent nations of the United Kingdom, and the
constitutional conventions that limit Westminster government will likely extend to
respecting their prerogatives. While in theory not as strong as federalism, devolution
is recognized as a 'constitutional' matter, on a par with membership of the European

[1] It is also typical of the case that in the very first sentence we encounter a terminological problem.
The state in question is the United Kingdom but, lacking an adjective for it, I have followed the
convention of using 'British'.

Union and different from local government, which can be and has been reorganized regularly by fiat of Westminster (and now of the devolved Scottish Parliament). On the other hand, in its weaker forms, devolution can appear as little more than an extension of municipal local government. Rather than drawing a sharp distinction among federalism, devolution, and local government, it makes sense to see devolution as an intermediate form of territorial self-government, covering a fairly broad spectrum and overlapping with federalism at one end and municipal government at the other.

Defined in this loose way, the term devolution can be applied more widely in Europe to the emerging level of government between the centre and the municipal level. Often this is referred to as the regional level, but this term is not acceptable to stateless nations like Scotland and Wales and its meaning can vary according to what criteria are applied. So the term 'meso' has been used as a more neutral and encompassing term (Sharpe 1993). Such a level of government has now emerged in all the large states of the European Union (France, Italy, Spain, the United Kingdom, and Poland) as well as in Belgium and, in a rather attenuated form, Hungary and the Czech Republic. Germany is excluded since it is a mature federation in which the *Länder* were entrenched at the time of the constitution. Belgium is also officially a federation, but can be included in the devolution category since powers were transferred over time by the centre in a process that is still evolving.

23.2 WHY DEVOLUTION?

Devolution is a response to the spatial rescaling of economic and social systems (Brenner 2004; Keating 1998); to shifting responsibilities of government and the need for new governing instruments; and to pressures for territorial autonomy. The different forms it has taken in various countries reflect these varied influences.

One common theme concerns state modernization and development policies. In the 1960s, European states engaged in spatial planning and regional development policies intended to integrate national markets, encourage more even development, and improve the performance of underdeveloped or declining regions. The logic of such policies was economic, to stimulate depressed regions and integrate them into the national economy so as to enhance overall performance; social, as the spatial expression of the welfare state; and political, to boost support for the state and for governing parties in regions where this might be problematic. The package has subsequently been labelled 'spatial Keynesianism', a territorial counterpart to the managed national economy. These policies tended to be centralized and based on a mixture of financial incentives to investors and infrastructure provision. In order to implement regional policies and encourage more self-sustaining development, governments also put in place planning machinery at the regional level and systems for consultation and participation by local actors, from business, trade unions, farmers, and local government. These forms of regional coordination and concertation were a mixed success, since the participants were caught between their role as implementers of central policy and representatives of distinct regional interests. They also tended to lack powers and control over resources. At the same time, governments strengthened their own presence in the regions with regional offices, coordination among departments, and deconcentration of powers to field offices. The British equivalents were the Regional Economic Planning Councils and Boards set up by the Labour government in 1964 in England and, in a slightly different way (and without the 'regional' title), Scotland and Wales.

Since the 1980s, this type of centralized regional policy has given way to decentralized forms, drawing on new understandings of how regional development works. In the new thinking, what matters are not traditional factor endowments like natural resources, or proximity to markets, but rather soft factors like research and development, entrepreneurship, and the existence of networks of innovation. These are not amenable to old policies such as grants and infrastructure programmes but depend on institutional and cultural elements in the regional society (Cooke and Morgan 1998). Each region is recognized as having its own characteristics and opportunities and regions are seen as being in competition with each other for markets, technology, and investment. There is a confusion in some versions of this argument, since the insistence that regions are competing is often combined with the assurance that they can all win the competition, but there is no doubt that this has affected governments' views on territorial government. Centralized regional policy managed from above has declined and more responsibilities have been transferred to the regions themselves.

Since the late 1980s, the regional level has featured in programmes for welfare state reform (Fererra 2006; McEwen and Moreno 2005). Resources may be allocated more effectively at a regional level, where local priorities can be worked out. In a more critical vein, it has been suggested that governments have also sought to decentralize difficult decisions about welfare state retrenchment and unpopular service cuts in a 'decentralization of penury' (Mény and Wright 1985). There is some evidence of governments transferring rationing to the regional level, for example in the Italian health service, but there is a lot of variation across cases so that it is difficult to make generalizations. Regional devolution may also serve reform by breaking systems of clientelism based on the centre–locality nexus and the ability of local politicians to extract resources from the centre. In the case of Belgium, one motive was to end the wasteful practice of having to match every expenditure in one part of the country with a similar programme in the other part, irrespective of need or demand. Of course, it may also result in reproducing clientelism at the regional level.

There has been a strong push for local autonomy in the name of democratization and pluralism. In European countries where the French Jacobin tradition is strong, democracy was traditionally seen as requiring centralization in order that the democratic will of the people should not be frustrated by partial interests. This tradition has been weakening over recent decades, with the rediscovery of older ideas of locality and community. Social democratic parties, in particular, moved away from centralized models based on the need to control the commanding heights of the economy and redistribute resources from the centre, rediscovering older strands of regionalism and localism in their ideology and practice. From the 1960s, new social movements often took up regionalism as a challenge to existing power structures and as a space not already colonized by the old political parties.

Autonomy, however, is not of concern only to the local and regional level. Governments have a natural tendency to centralize power and functions but then discover that centralization can be self-defeating since it overwhelms the centre with detail and subjects it to the pressure of local demands. Better control can be achieved by decentralizing detail and implementation, maintaining a strategic capacity at the top. So the French decentralization process of the 1980s can be seen as much as a way of re-establishing the autonomy of the centre from local influences as of freeing the localities themselves. This concept of 'central autonomy' was captured in the British case in the work of Jim Bulpitt (1983), who argued that state elites had managed a 'dual polity' in which high politics were kept at the centre, while day-to-day management was entrusted to local collaborators.

There is a growing recognition of cultural and national diversity, a point of obvious relevance to the United Kingdom. Belgium has long been characterized by a linguistic division and practices of consociationalism and power sharing at national level. From the 1960s, this began to give way to a territorial division of power, with the drawing of fixed territorial boundaries for the language communities (except in Brussels) and a gradual transfer of power to regional governments and communities until by 1993 the country had officially become a federation (Brassinne 1994; Fitzmaurice 1996). In Spain, the transition to democracy called for new approaches to the nationalities question, which was addressed through territorial devolution, first to the historic nationalities of Catalonia, the Basque Country, and Galicia, but spreading rapidly to the rest of the country (Aja 2003). Following the Second World War, Italy gave autonomy to four special status regions, the islands of Sicily and Sardinia and the border regions of Val d'Aosta and Trentino–Alto Adige, to which in 1961 was added Friuli-Venezia-Giulia. France has been less willing to concede autonomy to cultural or historical regions and even drew its regional boundaries so as to divide historic territories or amalgamate them with others. Brittany was truncated, Normandy divided in two, French Catalonia merged with part of Languedoc, and the Basques not acknowledged. Only Corsica was given special treatment, but even this was limited in comparison with the status of Scotland and Wales after 1999. Countries in central and eastern Europe have been very reluctant to institute regions corresponding to nationality or ethnic boundaries or historic territories like Silesia or Bohemia. The main problems of national integration there concern national minorities, who are not always territorially concentrated, or not in regions that would make sense from a functional point of view.

European integration has been widely credited with stimulating regionalism, especially since the 1980s, although the matter is in practice rather complex. The European single market has increased the competition among regions for markets, technology, and investment, as has the opening of global markets more generally. The new models of economic development, with their emphasis on institutions and networks, appear to give an advantage to those regions that are better organized and hence have stimulated the search for new forms of government. The attitude of the European Union itself is more ambivalent. Since 1988 there has been an elaborate set of regional development policies under the umbrella of the Structural Funds and competition among states, regional actors, and the European Commission as to who will control them (Hooghe and Keating 1994). The Commission's interest, however, is limited to ensuring that the mechanisms are in place to manage the funds and that these respect various partnership principles. It has never, contrary to a widely held opinion, stipulated that states must establish regional governments. On the contrary, the Structural Funds are organized around functional programmes and operate at a variety of territorial levels. Indeed in the case of the new Member States that entered the Union in 2004, the Commission insisted that Structural Funds should be managed by the central state and not regionalized (Keating 2003; Hughes, Sasse, and Gordon 2004).

Europe has also had an influence on the workings of regional government once it is established. Since many of the competences devolved to regions are shared by the EU as well, the effect has been to recentralize power within the state as it is central government that is represented in the Council of Ministers and the committee structure around the Commission. In response to this, regions have sought a greater role in EU matters (see below).

The result of these developments has been a linking of the themes of regional devolution and regional integration as two forces that are transforming the state from below and from above. Regionalist and minority nationalist movements have latched on to this, seeing Europe as something that might weaken the state framework and provide a new political and institutional space for their own aspirations (Lynch 1996; Keating 2004). For some, like the Scottish National Party, Europe provides a new framework for national independence, looking after some of the externalities that had plagued independence proposals in the past. Others, like the Catalan Convergència i Unió, many Basque nationalists, and (most of the time) Plaid Cymru, have gone beyond this, arguing that Europe makes the traditional concept of independence redundant. This 'post-sovereigntist' (Keating 2001) position has been taken up by some minorities in central and eastern Europe as well, although the model of the unitary nation state has a strong hold in countries that have only recently recovered full sovereignty.

23.3 MODELS OF DEVOLVED GOVERNMENT

Devolution, as noted above, is a mechanism for reconciling territorial autonomy with the unitary state. It is not a single defined form of government but covers a range of forms between the unitary and the federal state (Mény 1982; Le Galès and Lesquesne 1997). In some cases, there is symmetry, with all parts of the country being treated the same, while in others special status is given to some territories. Asymmetry is often used in unitary states to accommodate demands in one part of the country while keeping the rest of the state together as before. Despite the complaints made about this in the United Kingdom by anti-devolution commentators, it is not an uncommon arrangement. The special status Italian regions have existed since the 1940s and even the French have conceded a distinct law for Corsica, albeit not without controversy. In other cases, however, the state has sought to limit asymmetry in the interests of preserving the unity of the state, especially where the self-governing territories are substantial in size and population and economically important to the state. The Spanish constitution is in principle symmetrical, providing that all autonomous communities can achieve the same status, but there are different ways of getting there, effectively preserving asymmetries for a long time. Nationalists in Catalonia and the Basque Country have sought to maintain these differences (the *hecho diferencial*) while central government has sought more uniformity in a tactic known as *cafe para todos* (coffee all round). The Basque Country and Navarre have a very distinct fiscal regime. Belgium is in practice asymmetrical. Power is devolved to three regions (Flanders, Wallonia, and Brussels) and to three language communities (the Flemish, the French, and the German). In Flanders, the regional and language institutions have been merged, with some special arrangements for the Flemish speakers in Brussels, while elsewhere they have remained separate.

The process of devolution also varies. In some cases, it is imposed from above, as in France or Italy, where the state laid down the general scheme and the boundaries. In Spain, on the other hand, the initiative must come from the regions themselves, who propose boundaries and a range of powers within the limits of those provided in the constitution. Some of these turned out to be historic regions, others were provinces raised to the status of regions. Two paths to autonomy were laid down in the constitution, one leading to full powers immediately while the other involved a gradual transfer of responsibilities over a period of years. The first was intended for the historic nationalities who were allowed to proceed down this road immediately on the grounds that they had voted autonomy statutes under the Second Republic in the 1930s. Other regions wishing to take this route had to go through a complicated referendum process and the only one to succeed was Andalusia. It is also the regions themselves who take the initiative in reforming their statutes of autonomy, and since 2005 there has been a wave of new statutes to replace those negotiated during the transition. In Belgium the regular constitutional changes are negotiated by political parties who nowadays are confined to the two linguistic communities so that, while the regional governments themselves are not the main protagonists, regional interests are.

Since devolution is a general term covering a range of constitutional arrangements, it is difficult to break it down into specific models, yet we can discern two broad types. The first is functional devolution, which consists in setting up bodies with specific and limited powers. Here the central state dominates and the regional level cooperates with it and implements central policies. This is often accompanied by forms of socio-economic representation, with the social partners (business, unions, the voluntary sector) expected to cooperate in carrying out central strategies. One form consists of agencies nominated by government, alongside some consultative machinery in order to incorporate relevant social interests such as the business community. As noted above, such arrangements were common in the 1950s and 1960s when states were pursuing regional development policies in an essentially centralizing framework. The most elaborate were in France, where the CODER (Commissions de Développement Économique Régional) represented local government and the so-called *forces vives*, or dynamic sectors of civil society. Complementing these were regional prefects, responsible for coordinating the work of government departments in the field. This model was influential in the British arrangements introduced after 1964 and was introduced into Hungary in the 1990s. After 1997 it was reintroduced into England. It has proved unstable everywhere and has either evolved into elected regional government (as in France and Italy) or relapsed into centralization (as in England after 1979 and again in 2007 with the abolition of the regional assemblies). Now that the move to regional government in England has again been halted, it is not clear how the regional development machinery will evolve but it seems unlikely to grow in strength.

The world of agencies, indirectly elected authorities, and partnerships of various sorts is an example of the phenomenon known as 'governance'—insofar as that word has an agreed meaning. This is not the place to get into the vexed debate about governance, but one widely shared meaning is a form of governing with no clear hierarchy or division of roles and where policy-making takes place in networks rather than parties, executives, and legislatures. There is surprisingly little in the literature about the politics of such devolved 'governance' or about policy-making and who wins and who loses. Discussion tends to be dominated by the language of governance, networks, and the search for consensus, rather than the clash of interests and ideas. One reason may be that academics follow governments' own reasoning, when setting up such systems and then attempting to depoliticize regional development by presenting it as a technical problem and one on which distinct interests can easily agree since the aim is positive-sum development. Yet this might often be a mere cover for dominance by the business community together with the technical bureaucracy.

In practice, governing arrangements under functional devolution are rife with clashes of interest, between central government and local representatives, between business interests and social movements, and between pro-development and environmental concerns. There is also a tension between the bottom-up impetus that inspires the presence of local actors, and the continued retention of power in the hands of the centre. It is the inability to handle this form of conflict that has undermined functional and non-elected forms of regional regulation, in England and elsewhere, and prompted a move, either back to centralization as in England, or forward to elected government. If this is so, then the general move to elected regional councils represents a move from governance to government in its more traditional sense.

Election brings in a wider range of social and economic interests, including those who may challenge the business community. It politicizes policy-making and broadens the policy agenda from questions of development in the narrow sense to issues of distribution and who gains and who loses from any particular development project. Even after direct election, however, regional government may remain functionally limited, as in the case of France, where regions are essentially responsible for planning and investment programming rather than for pursuing distinct public policies. The same has largely been true of Italian regions. Polish regions, too, are essentially functional bodies, despite being directly elected. Italian regions, directly elected since 1970, were dominated by health spending and, until the reforms of the 1990s, had little control over its distribution, passing most of it on to the local health agencies.

A more expansive form of devolution is both elected and multi-functional, so amounting to regional government in the full sense. Such is the system in Spain, Belgium, and in the devolved territories of the United Kingdom. Italy has been moving in this direction, with the transfer of more powers to the regions and a higher political profile for them. Such elected governments have the planning and development role of the previous type, but add welfare state services such as education, social services, and housing. They may also take on a wider political role in articulating local views on national issues and innovating across policy fields. Elected status, broad functional reach, and the general role in representing the territory bring in a wider range of social and political interests, allowing the region to become a political arena in its own right (Keating 1997). In its stronger forms, this can come close to a federal system, as many observers have noted of Spain (Moreno 1997; Aja 2003). Regions also have a key role as intermediaries, between central and local government and between state and civil society even in cases, such as France, in which their statutory responsibilities are limited (Négrier and Jouve 1998).

Students of federalism have recently come to make a distinction between federations in which the constituent units are merely territorial or functional, and those in which they represent distinct historic, cultural, or national communities (Karmis and Norman 2005). The same applies to devolved systems. This is not a legal or strictly constitutional distinction, but it is an important political principle. Where meso governments correspond to strong collective identities and devolution is used to keep multinational states together, then there is a great sensitivity to symbolic matters as well as the division of powers. The United Kingdom has in many ways explicitly accepted that it is a multinational union, recognizing the four nations in symbolic ways and giving each a distinct constitution. For many years, indeed, the strongest argument advanced by opponents of devolution was precisely that the state is multinational and that therefore devolved assemblies would assume for themselves the right of self-determination and probably secede (Dicey 1912; Wilson 1970). The same fear is present in Spain, where parties in Madrid have generally been adamant that there is a single Spanish nation and that the historic nationalities have no special political status. After 2004, however, the Socialist government of José Luís Rodriguez Zapatero has adopted the concept of the plurinational state, in which a diversity of ways of being Spanish are recognized, so bringing Spain into line with the United Kingdom. On the other hand, the Spanish parliament refused to accept the wording of the revised statute of autonomy for Catalonia, stating that Catalonia was a nation. Instead, it produced a tortuous preamble to the effect that the Catalan parliament considered Catalonia to be a nation. A more serious dispute arose in the Basque Country at the time of the transition over the *fueros*, or traditional privileges of the Basque provinces, which Basque nationalists insist on as historic rights not owing their existence to the constitution (Herrero de Miñon 1998). Eventually a compromise was found, in an appendix to the constitution in which recognition is given to the historic rights without accepting them as superior to the constitution itself. France has resolutely resisted this idea and an apparently innocuous clause in Corsica's statute of autonomy referring to the 'Corsican people' was struck down by the constitutional court.

23.4 THE DIVISION OF POWERS

Powers are distributed between central and devolved governments in a variety of ways. A classic distinction in federal systems, as to whether the lower units have a general competence or merely assigned powers, arises here. French, Italian, and Polish regions have assigned powers, hence their continuing 'functional' basis. In Spain, the constitution lists powers that must be retained by the state, powers that must be devolved to the autonomous communities, and powers that may be devolved. There is also a confusing clause allowing other state functions to be transferred. In Belgium, the central parliament decides which functions to transfer to the regions and communities. Although the federal constitution supposedly leaves the state with only assigned functions, leaving the residual powers to the lower level, it has not been possible to realize this since it is necessary to decide for each power whether the regions or the language communities will be the beneficiary. In Scotland and Northern Ireland, only the reserved functions are specified, giving them a wider range of competences than any other devolved governments in Europe, while Wales has only specified powers.

In much of the literature, especially in Continental Europe, a distinction is made between devolved regions with legislative powers and those that merely have administrative functions. There is some value in this distinction at the extremes, but at the margin it is often difficult to draw. So Italian regions have legislative powers while the National Assembly for Wales until 2006 had only executive and secondary legislative powers. Yet in Italy matters are subject to legislation that in the United Kingdom would be dealt with by orders in council or executive action, so that it does not follow that Italian regions had more scope than did Wales. Spanish autonomous communities have legislative powers but they work within framework laws that limit their policy choices, while the Scottish parliament works under no such restriction and can repeal any law that does not fall within the reserved powers. Westminster continues to insist on the right to legislate in Scotland within devolved fields although there is a convention that it will seek the assent of the Scottish parliament first. If this consent is not forthcoming, Westminster might insist on legislating anyway, but the Scottish parliament could just repeal the law the next day. French regions do not have legislative powers but constitutional reforms in 2004 did move some little way in this direction. A pan-European association, the Regions with Legislative Powers, was established in the early 2000s, in view of the negotiations on the new European constitutional treaty, but membership was in practice more a matter of political standing than of a rigorous distinction between regions with legislative powers and those without.

Governments have been reluctant to concede tax-raising powers to devolved levels, preferring to occupy the main tax fields themselves and to transfer resources downwards according to various formulas. They have also tended to transfer money for specific services, often with detailed regulations on its use. Over time, however, they have moved to block transfers and allowed regional governments to raise more of their own revenue. This is because of the difficulties of maintaining detailed control from the centre and a realization that they were taking the political blame for raising taxes and allowing regions to gain the credit for providing the services. Fiscal devolution can thus paradoxically strengthen the autonomy of the centre. So in all cases there is now a mixture of locally raised taxation and transfers from the centre, based on relative wealth so as to achieve a degree of equalization. In Spain and Belgium, devolved authorities now have a share of national taxation in addition to a range of smaller taxes of their own. Italian regions collect the national health service levy which counts as own revenue. French regions do not have access to national taxation but collect some local taxes.

There has also been pressure from below, especially from better-off regions, to decide on levels of service and taxation and to reduce intergovernmental transfers. Typically the wealthy regions start off by insisting that they do not want to reduce redistribution to their poorer neighbours, merely to make it explicit and quantifiable. The effect, however, is to politicize the issue of equalization and allow politicians to complain about cross-subsidization and unequal burdens. This has become a significant issue in Belgium, where Flanders complains about subsidizing Wallonia; in Italy, where the northern regions complain about subsidizing the south; and in Spain where Catalonia insists that its contribution to the rest of Spain is excessive. It would be a mistake, however, to conclude that decentralization necessarily leads to a reduction in territorial equity. Centralized systems, where resources are distributed on a functional basis, often conceal large territorial disparities, which devolution reveals. This may then create pressure for more explicit fiscal equalization, as has happened in the United Kingdom.

23.5 INTERGOVERNMENTAL RELATIONS

In any system of devolution, there is a sphere of matters reserved to the centre, a sphere devolved to the regions, and a large area of shared and overlapping responsibilities. This puts a premium on intergovernmental cooperation and all the systems under consideration have a set of mechanisms to discuss common issues and resolve conflicts. In Spain there are sectoral conferences over a range of matters. Italy has a State–Regions conference. Belgium has a series of ministerial conferences and a national conciliation committee. France does not have a similar mechanism. Liaison with the state is the responsibility of the regional prefects who are supposed to be the sole channel of communication with the centre, but in practice there are numerous links with sectoral ministries in Paris. In all cases, indeed, political mechanisms for resolving intergovernmental disputes and coordinating policy are more important than formal conferences. In Spain, Belgium, and to some extent Italy[2] the political parties are the key device for coordination. In France, personal networks, a long-standing feature of French politics, play the main role. Local and regional politicians continue to hold national mandates and prefects will take care to keep the main local notables on side. The technical bureaucracy, present at all levels, also serves to sustain continuity and common ideas on problems and policies.

Devolution, as was noted at the beginning, is a way of reconciling the unity of the state with the transfer of powers to its component parts short of full federation. There are various ways in which the prerogatives of the regions are safeguarded and protected from arbitrary intervention. In Spain and Belgium the regions feature in the constitution and their powers cannot be reduced unilaterally by central government. There are override clauses in Spain, but these are clearly intended only for drastic circumstances and subject to the jurisdiction of the Constitutional Court. During the 1980s there was a lot of litigation as the boundaries of devolved and reserved matters were set, but since then disputes have tended to be resolved politically (Aja 2003). Italian regions also feature in the constitution, although they were not actually set up until more than twenty years later and received their powers slowly over a long period. Efforts to entrench them more strongly in the constitution have foundered in recent years on party politics as successive governments have rejected the proposals introduced by their predecessors. In Belgium the regions and communities have

---

[2] In Italy, the parties were of critical importance before the collapse of the party system in the early 1990s.

strong constitutional protection, although the fact that national governments are now made up of coalitions of regional-based parties means that they are not seriously threatened. French regions had no constitutional status until 2004 and owed their existence to ordinary legislation.

In all the European cases, a devolved level of regional government has been inserted into an existing system containing central and local government. While there have been many proposals to abolish existing tiers of provincial, departmental, or county government, this has never happened. Consequently, devolved regions have had to compete with existing territorial governments for political profile and functional competences. This has seriously weakened regional governments in France and Italy, where the prerogatives of the department/province and of the municipalities are guaranteed by law and constitution and these serve as power bases for important politicians. In Belgium and Spain, on the other hand, the meso level is predominant and has become the main territorial power base.

Another key area of intergovernmental relations concerns links to European decision-making. In the Treaty of European Union (Maastricht Treaty), regions gained a consultative forum, the Committee of the Regions, and the right to participate in the Council of Ministers where their own national law permits it (Jeffery 2000). In these cases, regions must speak for the state as a whole and not just for themselves, so maintaining the unity of the state in its external dimension. French and Polish regions have no place in determining national policy on European matters. They are present in the Committee of the Regions but not in the Council of Ministers. In Spain and Belgium there are provisions for regions (and Belgian communities) to be consulted on European matters and to participate in the Council. The strongest position is in Belgium, where regions and communities have a right to participate and even to lead the Belgian delegation where regional or community matters are at stake. In Spain since 2006 there is provision for regional participation in a predetermined set of fields, but the predominant power remains with the centre, as is still the case in the United Kingdom; a weaker arrangement exists in Italy.

23.6 THE UNITED KINGDOM IN COMPARISON

The United Kingdom is an extreme example of attempts to reconcile the unitary state with the devolution of power, with a mixture of forms of government across the state and even within its component parts. The United Kingdom is more asymmetrical than any of the other cases, with no effort at uniformity save the covering clause that it is all subject to parliamentary supremacy. This reflects the weakness in British constitutional tradition of the concept of the state and the idea that it is a 'union' rather than a single entity, yet the constitutional implications of this have never really been worked out. It is the most explicitly multinational of the devolution settlements, giving the constituent units a symbolic recognition as nations well beyond that conceded elsewhere. Yet on the other hand, it insists that the devolved bodies are creatures of statute, emanations of the will of parliament, and have no entrenched or sovereign rights of their own. This creates tensions in constitutional interpretation similar to those that have arisen in Spain as to whether the rights of the nations are original or not (Keating 2001; Tierney 2004). Opinion in Scotland continues to see Scotland as possessed of elements of sovereign rights and the union as the result of negotiation and agreement; Westminster doctrine disagrees.

Scotland possesses a high degree of legislative devolution with the full set of parliamentary, executive, and administrative institutions and a broad set of responsibilities as a general-purpose government. Its relationship with the United Kingdom is a quasi-federal one, like the Spanish autonomous communities. The same might be said for Northern Ireland, although the provision for it to secede and join the Republic of Ireland is unique in Europe. Wales has a system of executive devolution, which might be compared to the weaker Spanish autonomous communities, before the full transfer of powers. It is, like them, an evolving system in which legislative competences are being acquired gradually. England was left with a system of functional regionalism rather similar to that of the period 1964–79 or to France before the election of regional councils in 1986. The failed devolution proposals, rejected in the North-East in 2004, would have brought English regions more in line with post-1986 France; now it is headed to centralization.

As elsewhere, intergovernmental relations in the United Kingdom are informal, with political channels predominating over official committees. There has, in contrast to Spain, been very little litigation although that might change given a difference in political control at the two levels. Fiscal powers for devolved governments are also weak although there is a debate about this and it is likely that the United Kingdom will follow other European states in giving more fiscal responsibility to the lower levels.

The devolution settlement in the United Kingdom is, as Charlie Jeffery notes in this volume, unstable. It is not unique in this. Belgium for the last thirty years has been on a path of constitutional reform that leads to periodic adjustments of the territorial balance. Regions in Spain are engaged in a path of competition for more competences, so that whatever is conceded to the historic nationalities is demanded by the others (Moreno 1997). In the United Kingdom, the English regions have not, as many expected, reacted similarly to Scottish and Welsh devolution, but Scotland and Wales will certainly gain more powers, so that asymmetries are likely to increase. This makes the United Kingdom an extreme example of the spatial rescaling that is taking place across Europe more generally, as the territorial, social, cultural, economic, and jurisdictional boundaries of the polity correspond ever less (Keating 2001; Bartolini 2005). The devolution formula has its limits and, at some point, the pretence that we have a unitary state merely lending authority to devolved governments, but retaining ultimate power and sovereignty, will be exposed as a constitutional fiction. Reinventing the old unitary state, or even the symmetrical federation of the nineteenth and twentieth centuries, however, is unlikely to be possible; while secession commands little support among the regions and stateless nations of Europe. It is probable, then, that devolution will give way to a looser and even more asymmetrical form of confederation, nested in a broader European order (Keating 2001).

REFERENCES

AJA, E. 2003. *El estado autonómico: federalismo y hechos diferenciales*. Madrid: Alianza.

BARTOLINI, S. 2005. *Restructuring Europe*. Oxford: Oxford University Press.

BRASSINNE, J. 1994. *La Belgique fédérale*. Brussels: CRISP.

BRENNER, N. 2004. *New State Spaces: Urban Governance and the Rescaling of Statehood*. Oxford: Oxford University Press.

BULPITT, J. 1983. *Territory and Power in the United Kingdom: An Interpretation*. Manchester: Manchester University Press.

COOKE, P., and MORGAN, K. 1998. *The Associational Economy: Firms, Regions, and Innovation*. Oxford: Oxford University Press.

DICEY, A. V. 1912. *A Leap in the Dark: A Criticism of the Principles of Home Rule as Illustrated by the Bill of 1893*, 3rd edn. London: John Murray.

FERRERA, M. 2006. *The New Boundaries of Welfare*. Oxford: Oxford University Press.

FITZMAURICE, J. 1996. *The Politics of Belgium: A Unique Federalism*. London: Hurst.

HERRERO DE MIÑON, M. 1998. *Derechos históricos y constitución*. Madrid: Tecnos.

HOOGHE, L., and KEATING, M. 1994. 'The Politics of EU Regional Policy'. *Journal of European Public Policy*, 1/3: 368–93.

HUGHES, J., SASSE, G., and GORDON, C. 2004. *Europeanization and Regionalization in the EU's Enlargement to Central and Eastern Europe*. London: Palgrave.

JEFFERY, C. 2000. 'Sub-National Mobilization and European Integration'. *Journal of Common Market Studies*, 38/1: 1–24.

KARMIS, D., and NORMAN, W. 2005. 'The Revival of Federalism in Normative Political Theory'. In D. Karmis and W. Norman (eds.), *Theories of Federalism: A Reader*. London: Palgrave.

KEATING, M. 1997. 'Les Régions constituent-elles un niveau de gouvernement en Europe?' In P. Le Galès and C. Lesquesne (eds.), *Les Paradoxes des régions en Europe*. Paris: La Découverte.

——1998. *The New Regionalism in Western Europe: Territorial Restructuring and Political Change*. Cheltenham: Edward Elgar.

——2001. *Plurinational Democracy: Stateless Nations in a Post-Sovereignty Era*. Oxford: Oxford University Press.

——2003. 'Regionalization in Central and Eastern Europe: The Diffusion of a Western Model?' In M. Keating and J. Hughes (eds.), *The Regional Challenge in Central and Eastern Europe: Territorial Restructuring and European Integration*. Brussels: Presses Interuniversitaires Européenes/Peter Lang.

——2004. 'European Integration and the Nationalities Question'. *Politics and Society*, 31/1: 367–88.

LE GALÈS, P., and LESQUESNE, C. (eds.) 1997. *Les Paradoxes des régions en Europe*. Paris: La Découverte.

LYNCH, P. 1996. *Minority Nationalism and European Integration*. Cardiff: University of Wales Press.

McEWEN, N., and MORENO, L. (eds.) 2005. *The Territorial Politics of Welfare*. London: Routledge.

MÉNY, Y. (ed.) 1982. *Dix ans de régionalisme en Europe: bilan et perspectives*. Paris: Cujas.

——and WRIGHT, V. (eds.) 1985. *Centre–Periphery Relations in Western Europe*. London: Allen and Unwin.

MORENO, L. 1997. *La federalización de España: poder politico y territorio*. Madrid: Siglo Veintiuno.

NÉGRIER, E., and JOUVE, B. (eds.) 1998. *Que gouvernent les régions d'Europe? Échanges politiques et mobilisations*. Paris: L'Harmattan.

SHARPE, L. J. (ed.) 1993. *The Rise of Meso Government in Europe*. London: Sage.

TIERNEY, S. 2004. *Constitutional Law and National Pluralism*. Oxford: Oxford University Press.

WILSON, C. 1970. 'Note of Dissent'. In *Scotland's Government: Report of the Scottish Constitutional Committee*. Edinburgh: Scottish Constitutional Committee.

PART III

IDENTITIES

SECTION EIGHT: IDENTIFICATION

CHAPTER 24

POLITICAL PARTIES

RICHARD HEFFERNAN

THE three dominant British political parties, Labour, the Conservatives, and the Liberal Democrats, can trace their inheritance back to the latter part of the nineteenth century and beyond. Of contemporary minor parties, setting aside the Scottish and Welsh nationalists, only the UK Independence Party has been created in the past ten years. Other smaller parties, among them the Greens and the far-right BNP, lay claim to long established peripheral political traditions. Parties—and the party system within which they operate—clearly reflect the history within which politics has been forged. They are impacted by—and sometimes shape—the environmental contexts within which party politics is enacted. There are four such environmental contexts:

- the institutional environment (constitutional imperatives, the political system, the electoral rules);
- electoral environment (party system, the electoral strength, status and standing of parties; modes of electioneering);
- ideational environment (ideological appeal and relevance); and
- socio-economic environment (economic successes or failures; social, cultural, and demographic changes).

These contexts frame the boundaries within which parties operate. The first environment, the institutional, is invariably fixed. Constitutional imperatives change, if at all, usually only at the margin. Britain's parliamentary system has been significantly reworked, not least in terms of European Union membership since 1973 and Scottish and Welsh devolution since 1999 but, emergent forms of multi-level governance notwithstanding, many features of the Westminster–Whitehall model remain in place. The second environment, the electoral, essentially pickled in aspic by the two-party system between 1945 and 1970, has become increasingly volatile since 1974. The last two environmental contexts, the ideational and the socio-economic, both of which help determine the set of policy approaches considered permissible or achievable, significantly impact all parties by affecting their programmatic objectives. Party programmes, influenced by the ideational environment, reflect their current ideological orientation. This orientation, while reflecting the party's historical form as being of either left or right, progressive or conservative, is subject to periodic renewal, most likely in response to electoral realities and the demands imposed by socio-economic and cultural factors.

Party actions, reflecting often complex intra- and inter-party processes, owe much to electoral outcomes and likely electoral outcomes. These reflect the realities of the prevailing party system. Such a party system, the 'particular pattern of competitive and cooperative interactions displayed by a given set of political parties' (Webb 2000: 1), determines the given set of parties in play at any one time. Britain's party system, like others a product of historical processes (Lipset and Rokkan 1967; Rose and Unwin 1970; Mair 1989), has undergone significant changes in recent years, something reflecting long-standing electoral trends and the demise of the old left–right programmatic differences reflected in the old Labour–Conservative dichotomy. British parties, in keeping with counterparts elsewhere, have additionally undergone an organizational metamorphosis in the past fifty or so years. Parties tend now to be 'electoral professional' (Panebianco 1988) and no longer possess a mass membership base. Today's 'catch-all parties', no longer over-dependent on certain occupational or demographic groups, seek support from all sections of society and are increasingly directed by a predominant party leadership. As a result, subject to the mediating environments listed above, the party's programmatic appeal and electioneering strategy are all—now more than ever—heavily influenced by the party leadership, with the party leader as Prime Minister or would-be Prime Minister playing a central role.

24.1 PARTIES AND THE BRITISH PARLIAMENTARY SYSTEM

British parties reflect the constitutional norms of parliamentary politics. Their modus operandi echoes centralizing tendencies inherent within Britain's majoritarian, unitary state (Lijphart 1999) which imposes the following key imperatives:

- a unitary state which, even if it has ceded power and authority upwards, downwards, and outwards to the market, agencies, quangos, devolved governments,

and international institutions, still exerts a considerable influence over government outputs;
- a dominant executive form, namely, so far, single-party government, something
  facilitated by the single-member plurality electoral system; and
- asymmetrical executive–legislative relations where the party-led executive,
  granted a workable Commons majority, can significantly lead (if never peremptorily command) a reactive asymmetrical bicameral legislature.

A comparison of parliamentary, unitary Britain with the presidential, federal United
States shows how institutional imperatives impact party form. In the USA the party's
presidential candidate does not direct the policy stance on which federal legislative
candidates seek election and has no say over the local platforms offered by state
candidates. In Britain, however, it is the party leader—the Prime Minister or the
prime ministerial candidate and their staffs—who, in consultation with other key
party figures, draws up the manifesto presented to the electorate. The structures of US
parties, organized at state and federal levels, divided at the federal level into legislative
branch (therein subdivided into House and Senate) and executive branch, reflect the
horizontal and vertical separation of powers created by its presidential and federal
regime. British political parties, even when an unintended consequence of Scottish
and Welsh devolution has been to partly 'semi-federalise' the Scottish and Welsh
components of the national parties (Laffin and Shaw 2007), largely reflect a British
majoritarian impulse not to separate power.

In Britain electors tend to vote for a party candidate in support of the party's
national political image, programmatic stance, and, increasingly some say, in support
of its candidate for Prime Minister. While a US President might have congressional
coat-tails—and may influence mid-term congressional elections—Senators and Con-
gressmen usually get themselves elected with only some help—usually financial—
from their state and 'national' party. In Britain election to the House of Commons
owes much to an MP's party affiliation and little to an MP's personal attributes. A
sizeable national swing, such as the one that swept away the Conservatives in 1997,
will unseat the able and the wretched MP, the loyal and the rebellious. In the USA,
election to Congress owes more to the individual attributes of the candidate, his or
her policy stances, the predilections of his or her state or district, than it does to their
party affiliation.

Single-party government, hitherto the British norm since 1945, save Labour's
minority administrations of 1974 and 1977–9 and the whittling away of John Major's
majority after 1993, reflects the fact that the single-member plurality system (SMPS)
invariably grants the party with the largest minority of votes a majority of Commons seats. British MPs see themselves as being Labour, Conservative, or Liberal
Democrat MPs. Their service in the Commons is refracted through their party
affiliation. Loyalty to the party line, even when not particularly married to ability,
is rewarded; rebellion, even allied to ability, is not. In spite of recent fractious-
ness among Labour MPs (Cowley 2005), the parliamentary party remains the key
support mechanism for the Prime Minister and his or her government, particularly

when the government delivers significant public goods such as electoral popularity and political success. MPs toe the party line for a number of reasons, foremost among them policy agreement, partisan disposition, and self-interest. The majority party inevitably prioritizes supplying and supporting the government over trying to check and balance it. Of course, MPs are not rubber stamps. Not all always reply 'how high' when asked to jump by their party whip. Leaders have to negotiate with MPs, sometimes cajole or coerce them into supporting government policy, other times plead with them to do so, and have sometimes to back down, accept unwelcome amendments, or make concessions to win support (Cowley 2005; Norton 2005).

It is through its parliamentary party that the British government is granted control over the legislature. Party dependence works both ways, however, because, in addition to being able to lead their parliamentary party, party leaders have only the leasehold of their party leadership, not the freehold. As John Major observed, 'Every leader is leader only with the support of his party' (Major 1999: 626). Both Margaret Thatcher (peremptorily and brutally) and Tony Blair (gradually and politely) left Downing Street when a critical mass of their MPs no longer wanted them to stay. For Prime Ministers and their governments the party is both an exemplary resource and a significant constraint. It can be the seed of weakness, but, for the more powerful leader, it is more likely a source of authority. Parties, being a leadership (collegial) resource, not only the leader's (personalized) resource, are the tool of the leadership elite as a whole. They remain 'coalitions of the willing' and, in partisan terms, being opponents of their competitors, define themselves by being mechanisms to elect a party government, not simply propel the party leader into office as Prime Minister.

Partisanship, despite significant (sometimes stark) intra-party differences, remains the glue binding parties together. The 1981 split within the Parliamentary Labour Party aside, when some 10 per cent of Labour MPs defected to form the SDP (Crewe and King 1995), British parliamentary parties, the occasional individual defection aside, remain hardy, robust institutions. This is why the importance of the party face in the present-day House of Commons—and in British politics more generally—cannot be overestimated. The likelihood of a minority of MPs voting against their party whip is growing (Cowley 2005), but, ministerial concession to and compromise with rebels and would-be rebels aside, long a feature of the parliamentary process, such rebels rarely defeat the government. The Blair government lost only 4 out of 3,089 divisions in ten years and even the most rebellious Labour MP still voted with the Labour whip some 90 per cent of the time. In Britain, as elsewhere in Europe, what is referred to as parliamentary democracy might be seen as being a party democracy (Muller and Strom 1999). The parliamentary imperative at the heart of the British constitution helps frame the 'behaviour of parties, the preferences of their leaders, and the conditions which affect the formation of governments in politics with distinct institutional structures' (Montero and Gunther 2002: 13), something which makes it the dominant institutional environment with which parties engage.

24.2 PARTIES, VOTERS, AND ELECTIONS

The electoral environment, not least the party system it shapes, exerts the greatest short-term impact on parties and distinguishes major from minor parties (Kirchheimer 1966; Sartori 1976; Mair 1983). Two-party alternation in government has been the post-1945 norm but there have been 'four different party systems during the twentieth century, from 1906 to 1914, from 1918 to 1931, from 1935 to 1970 and from 1974 to 1997' (Bogdanor 2004: 718). Before 1945, excepting 1906–10, 1922–3, 1924–9, and 1935–40, coalition or minority government was the dominant pattern. After 1945, setting aside the peculiarities of Northern Ireland, the party system has taken the following forms:

- the 1945–70 period, the classic era of two-party majoritarianism, characterized by the fact that Labour and the Conservatives won an average of 90.3 per cent of the vote between them;
- the 1970–97 period, perhaps best described as the emergence of a 'two-party-plus others' system as the dominance of Labour and the Conservatives was challenged by the emergence of the third party, the Liberal Democrats (and their predecessor parties, the Liberals and the SDP), and also by the growth of nationalist parties in Scotland and Wales; and
- the post-1997 period, which has seen the final demise of the two-party system and its fragmentation into a 'three party plus others' system and the emergence of distinct party systems in elections to the Scottish parliament and the Welsh and London assemblies. Whereas 96.8 per cent of voters supported either Labour or the Conservatives on a turnout of 82.5 per cent in 1951 only 67.6 per cent of voters did so in 2005 when turnout had fallen to 61.2 per cent. The emergence of a multi-party system at Westminster (and, so far, a coalition government in Whitehall) remains stymied, however, by Britain's plurality electoral system.

This reworked party system, even when Labour and the Conservatives still seemingly alternate as single-party governments, reflects far reaching changes in electoral alignments (Ware 1996). It also reflects the emergence of what Webb describes as 'latent moderate pluralism' (2000). Previously electors associated themselves 'psychologically with one or other of the parties, and this identification ha[d] predictable relationships with their perceptions, evaluations and actions' (Campbell et al. 1960: 90; Butler and Stokes 1974). Since the 1970s, partisan dealignment meant that, as party identification fell and issue voting increased, parties found themselves adrift from their past electoral mooring (Denver 2004; Clarke et al. 2004). British voters now far less identify with a party and, as witnessed in the dramatic decline in turnout from 77.7 per cent in 1992 to 59.4 per cent in 2001 (against the background of a post-war average of 75 per cent), they are less likely to vote. Voting electors are now far more conditional in their support. As Denver suggests, 'the transition from an aligned and socialised electorate to a dealigned and judgemental electorate...has underpinned electoral developments in Britain over the past half century' (Denver 2004: 124). As a result, parties operate within an unstable and unreliable electoral marketplace. The Conservative share of the vote ranged between 41.4 and 49.3 and Labour's between 49.4 and 43.9 per cent in the elections held from 1945 to 1970, but the Conservative share was between 44.9 and 30.7 per cent and Labour's between 44.3 and 28.3 per cent in the elections between 1974 and 2005. Whereas a 46.4 per cent share of the vote gave the Conservatives a Commons majority of 31 in 1970 it took only a 35.3 per cent share to give Labour a majority of 66 in 2005.

When electoral ties of attachment become looser, electoral behaviour becomes more volatile. Dunleavy argues that more proportional elections in London, Scotland, Wales, and for the European parliament means voters now 'support a multiplicity of parties and are disillusioned with the grip of an artificially maintained "two-party" politics' (Dunleavy 2005: 503). As a result, he suggests, multi-party politics in Britain and its constituent nations has now become a reality (2005; 2006). Yet, while voters might cast their votes slightly wider than Labour, the Conservatives, and the Liberal Democrats in second-order elections to the Scottish parliament, Welsh assembly, and the much less important European parliament, the three major parties still together won 90.7 per cent in 2001 and 89.7 per cent in 2005 in elections to the House of Commons. All three parties currently hold between them 95.5 per cent of Commons seats. Voters for the House of Commons might no longer want to vote only Labour or Conservative (something that has been happening since 1974), but they do not yet remotely vote in significant numbers for parties beyond the Liberal Democrats and the SNP and Plaid Cyrmu in Scotland and Wales. At Westminster the old two-party system no longer exists (the Liberal Democrats, while presently unable to form a government on their own, are surely now an unshakeable electoral fixture) but in Whitehall the two-party 'plus others' system presently persists. It persists, thanks to SMPS, in terms of Commons seat share and by making it almost certain that—short of a hung parliament—only Labour or the Conservatives can secure the necessary sufficient support to form a single-party government. This, despite changes in the party system beyond Westminster, is the reality with which parties presently grapple. It will surely remain the reality until swept away in a hung parliament when (assumedly) the Liberal Democrats can leverage electoral reform from either Labour or the Conservatives as the price for entering a coalition.

Modern parties are presently affected by two specific electoral environmental changes reflecting the unconditionality with which general election voters cast their ballots:

- emergent changes in established electorates of belonging, from which parties draw support, something reflected in declining levels of party identification; and
- the rise of judgemental voting, which obliges parties to pay ever closer attention to leaders, images, and issues. Parties have to—or perceive they have to—compete with one another for vote, and office, by convincing an ever more sceptical electorate that they have a more attractive set of leading politicians and policies than their opponents (Denver 2004; Clarke et al. 2004).

Social structural change prompts changes in the electoral alignments upon which parties draw. Such alignments have been further altered by the rise of issue-based competition and changes in the value orientations of parties and their electors. Now, in light of low turnouts and a declining vote share, parties recognize the contingent nature of their electoral support. In such circumstances, particularly amid the rise of issue voting (Clarke et al. 2004; Evans and Norris 1999), party competition has become more, not less, important. As a result, party image and appeal, not least that of its leadership, has been placed at the heart of a party's electioneering strategy.

24.3 PARTY LEADERSHIP PRE-EMINENCE AS MODERN ORGANIZATIONAL FORM

British parties, while unitary actors, contain sub-groups, factions, and fractions. They have, at times quite starkly, been fractiously divided into left and right, moderates and radicals, as evidenced by infighting within the Labour Party in 1951–5 and 1979–85 and the Conservatives' division over Europe in 1992–5. Parties are not always congenial places. Churchill famously reminded an ambitious MP that in the House of Commons he 'faced his opponents on the other side of the House, but sat surrounded by enemies on his own side'. Intra-party differences, especially when parties underperform or are in crisis, are the stuff of the Westminster village. Yet, irrespective of such recurrent division, parties, perpetually divided into leaders and led, have long been hierarchical in form, more often than not publicly united in purpose (despite the presence of off-stage bickering), something reflecting the majoritarian British political tradition.

A party leader, serving at the sufferance of their parliamentary party, who is able to use their resources wisely, make concessions when necessary, and deliver the goods the party seeks, will possess considerable authority. As McKenzie famously noted in the 1950s, party leaders take note of the obstacle of party opinion, but the distribution of power within parties has long been skewed in their favour. As a result, 'Effective decision making authority will reside with the leadership groups thrown up by the parliamentary parties (of whom much the most important individual is the party leader), and they will exercise this authority so long as they retain the confidence of their parliamentary parties' (McKenzie 1964: 635). The conundrum McKenzie drew attention to is that parties, nominally internally democratic, are in practice run by their parliamentary elite. All party leaders, Conservative and Labour alike, have been perceived to dominate (if never to totally command) their parties. Today, such is the degree of leadership predominance, the party in government (and the party frontbench in opposition), being both forms of the 'party in public office', has become ever more visible and significant.

This leadership predominance owes much, in keeping with their continental counterparts, to British parties having metamorphosed from old-style pre-democratic 'cadre' parties, large membership-based 'mass bureaucratic' parties, to today's 'catch-all' 'electoral professional' parties (Kirchheimer 1966; Daalder and Mair 1983; Panebianco 1988; Muller and Strom 1999). Organizational change is a one-way street; parties first take on one form and then another. Such change, while linear, 'is suggestive: models of parties are "ideal types" that do not always neatly correspond to real-world political parties. Instead, most parties contain a mix of characteristics of different types, although usually one or another is sufficiently pronounced as to allow the analyst to characterise parties as loose enough to one or the other as to be placed within the typology' (Montero and Gunther 2002: 21–2). Today British parties are 'electoral professional', elite driven, top-down organizations, best described as 'modern cadre parties'. An electoral professional party has the following characteristics:

- professionals with expertise in electoral mobilization are in charge of election campaigning;
- weak vertical ties to social groups and broader appeals to the 'opinion electorate';
- the pre-eminence of public representatives and personalized leadership;
- financing through interest groups and public funds; and
- an emphasis on issues and leadership (Panebianco 1988: 264).

Recent party reforms, including some forms of plebiscitory democracy seeking member approval of leadership initiatives, enable parliamentary leaders to form policy, particularly when established forms of party democracy, based on the annual conference or the party executive, are downgraded. Obviously, 'the often disorganised and atomised mass membership of the party . . . is likely to prove more deferential to the party leadership and more willing to endorse its proposals. It is in this sense that the empowerment of the party on the ground remains compatible with, and may actually serve as a strategy for, the privileging of the party in public office' (Katz and Mair 2002: 129). Party leaders have 'the power of the drafter and the agenda setter, it fixes the basic parameters of political acceptability. Wants and demands that are deemed unacceptable will be suppressed or deflected via the numerous gateways operated by official gatekeepers' (Shaw 2004: 61). Parties may thus be said to have been 'hollowed out' as extra-parliamentary parties; while able to elect (or help elect) the party leader from a shortlist presented to them by the parliamentary party when there is a vacancy, they make little contribution to policy formation other than by occasionally endorsing—and thereby legitimating—the agenda of the party leadership.

There is, in addition to the standing divide between the parliamentary party and the extra-parliamentary party, division within the parliamentary party, between senior frontbenchers, other frontbenchers, and backbenchers. Parliamentary parties, believing that political leadership is the key 'medium of political discourse and information' (Foley 2000: 230), build themselves around party leaders. In modern politics the leader is, in Foley's illuminating phrase, 'stretched' (ibid.) away from other MPs. This usually empowers the party leader, but may also disempower him or her; being praised in good times means he or she is disproportionately blamed in bad times. Leadership does not, however, make the Prime Minister a 'president' (Foley 2000; 2004; Poguntke and Webb 2005) because, by being an authoritative Prime

Minister, the party leader is more influential by being a parliamentary chief executive (Heffernan 2005). Authoritative and popular leaders (exemplified by Tony Blair at his peak) centralize their control over 'the location and distribution of effective decision making authority within the party' (Janda 1980: 108). Such changes in the party's organizational form, 'motivated by the desire to enhance the policy making autonomy of the leadership' (Webb 2004: 29), mean that the tight control of policy formulation, campaign strategy, and the management of finance and party administration are now key leadership prerogatives which are (at best) only delegated to a party apparatus which is firmly under the control of (or in sync with) the party leadership, not other frontbench MPs (and certainly not those on the backbenches). Tony Blair and his allies (alongside Gordon Brown and his) ran New Labour after 1994, in the words of Blair's strategist, Philip Gould, by replacing 'competing existing structures with a single chain of command leading directly to the leader of the party . . . [and by having] one ultimate source of campaigning authority . . . the leader' (Gould 1998: 240–2).

The centrality of the party leader–Prime Minister owes much to the ongoing personalization of politics, something considerably reinforced by the centrality of the news media in the practice of politics. The personalization of politics is, in itself, nothing new. The Conservative 1945 manifesto was entitled 'Mr Churchill's Declaration of Policy' and leaders such as Churchill, not to mention Gladstone, Disraeli, Lloyd George, and Thatcher, at times bestrode their political scene. In contemporary politics, however, personalization has reached unimagined heights. Party leaders, ever eager to be empowered, less constrained by the party mechanism, use the media to agenda-set within their own parties. A leader is empowered when the news media report him or her as successful and popular, but naturally disempowered when reported as a failure and liability. Leaders use the news media not only to advantage their party, but to advantage themselves, particularly by raising their public profile and demonstrating their indispensability. This further encourages the party's electoral professional propensities, particularly when leader-centric parties use the media to showcase leading politicians, and so serves to further 'hollow out' the political party.

There are, naturally, intra-party limits on the degree of autonomy the party leadership may command. Party disunity is largely dependent upon the ideational differences at stake, but the degree to which disunity divides the party is largely dependent upon the leeway granted the party's 'dominant coalition' (now reflecting the interest of the leadership) to lead the party in its chosen direction. Such leeway, should the leadership's grip on the party be reinforced by it being popular and successful, is forthcoming more often than not. Still, (fewer) formal and (many more) informal limits ensure that even the most powerful party leaders merely lead, never command, their party. Leaders are, at best, authoritative and powerful, never omnipotent. All know they may one day be replaced. Harold Wilson, when asked who would replace him should he be knocked down by a bus, replied 'probably the person driving the bus'. Margaret Thatcher was brought down in 1990 by her parliamentary party, not the electorate. Iain Duncan Smith was unseated by a formal vote of no confidence by MPs in 2003, and the public declaration of twenty-five Liberal Democrat MPs that they would not serve on a frontbench led by Charles Kennedy required Kennedy to stand down in 2006. Even Tony Blair, who wanted to serve a full third term as Prime Minister, was obliged by party MPs (largely supporters of his Chancellor, Gordon Brown) to leave office earlier than he wished even when doing so by a timetable of his making.

The widening of the franchise to elect the party leader beyond the parliamentary party, a reform first fought for by the extra-parliamentary Labour left, has served to strengthen, not weaken, the party leader. Formal leadership challenges are extremely rare, with only three in the Labour Party (two of those, in 1961 and 1988, having no remote chance of success) and five in the Conservative Party since 1945. Leaders depart of their own volition, usually following electoral defeat or through ill-health. The wider electoral franchise makes it more difficult for a vote of no confidence in the leader to be organized and it creates high nomination barriers deterring would-be challengers. These impose high eviction costs which help make leaders more secure in office, not less (Quinn 2005). Leaders have to be reasonably successful, be popular, and avoid scandal to remain secure in office. They must take careful note of what their party will tolerate and carry sufficient of their parliamentary party—and a base within the wider party—with them. Leaders have, above all, carefully to manage their senior parliamentary colleagues, as Tony Blair's relationship with Gordon Brown demonstrates (Seldon 2004; 2007; Peston 2005).

24.4 MEMBERS, MONEY, AND MODES OF CAMPAIGNING

The state regulation of British parties, previously 'treated as if their constitutional significance was akin to that of golf or tennis clubs' (Bogdanor 2004: 717–18), has increased, not decreased, in the past ten years. Parties, thanks to the Registration of Political Parties Act 1998, and the Political Parties, Elections and Referendums Act 2000, are now legally obliged to be increasingly transparent, not least in terms of their sources of funding. Such regulation is likely to increase in the future. Limits are likely to be applied to the type of monies parties can raise (any donation over £5,000 has now to be declared) and the ways in which they spend money. Election expenditure is now capped at £20 million—in the campaign itself—and this rule is likely to be tightened and could be extended to cover the period running up to an election.

24.4.1 Members

Some 98.5 per cent of the British population do not belong to a political party (Gamble and Wright 2002: 123). Younger, better-educated citizens are less likely to have a party attachment or to join a political party. The handful of new members tend to be inactive and to let their membership lapse. Labour Party membership, rising briefly under Tony Blair in 1994–7, has been falling for thirty years. From a claimed membership of 265,000 in 1994 Labour membership increased to 405,000 in 1997, but then more than halved after 1997. In 2002 Labour claimed a membership of 248,294 and 177,000 in 2007. In 2007 only 53 per cent cast a postal ballot in the deputy leadership election and, while Labour claims some 3,006,216 levy-paying union members and 43,405 people belonging to other affiliated organizations, less than 300,000 participated in that election. The Conservatives had 2,805,032 members in 1952 but only 247,394 in 2006. Where some 256,797 Conservative members cast ballots in the leadership election in 2001, only 198,844 did so in 2005. Some 52,036 Liberal Democrat members voted in the ballot electing Ming Campbell leader in 2006, but only 41,465 cast votes in 2007 when electing Nick Clegg. Of minor British parties the Greens claimed a membership of 7,000 and UKIP some 18,000 in 2006.

The decline in party membership owes something to the post-1960s rise of pressure groups and the rise of social movements, new emergent forms of group-based politics organized around identity and individualism. Such 'new' political issues have little in common with the traditional left–right economic issues that previously delineated the partisan boundaries between the two major parties (Inglehart 1990; Dalton 2002). Political cynicism, something encouraged by the personalization of politics, the media's propensity to prioritize the reportage of bad news and scandal, and by unmet expectations by parties when in government, surely also plays some part in falling membership.

Party leaders, while valuing party members as a source of legitimacy, financial backing, and campaigning muscle, are seemingly resigned to membership decline. Many would probably prefer their party to be backed by observant supporters (not participating members, who have to be both serviced and managed) who could cheer the leadership, be hit on for money, and be mobilized at election time. With declining membership comes the professionalization of the party ranks. The thinning ranks of 'amateur' party members can be increasingly distinguished from the 'professional' party members; young, ambitious would-be politicians, many working as party officials, special advisers, or parliamentary staffers or else employed in think tanks, trade unions, or the growing number of political consultancies. It is the latter who increasingly people party structures. The professionalization of MPs, where middle-class, university-educated career politicians carve out a niche in public life before becoming MPs, is not only a modern fact of the parliamentary scene, but a key feature of the modern political party.

24.4.2 Money

Party funding has long proved a thorny problem. Parliamentary salaries and allowances, variously paid to MPs, MEPs, MSPs, and AMs, provide a considerable indirect financial benefit to parties with elected public representatives. Officials, often the public face of the party, are the party's representative in the constituency as well as the constituency's representative in parliament. Public funding, not least the Short money paid to opposition parties represented in parliament, has since the mid-1970s played a key role in facilitating the work of opposition parties. With the collapse of their subscription-based membership base (and with expensive professional election campaigns becoming the rule) parties have had to resort to fundraising from new sources. For instance, of some £66 million donated to Labour between 2001 and 2005, 64 per cent was provided by trade unions, but some 25 per cent was drawn from thirty-seven wealthy individuals. Large donations from wealthy individuals (including Lord Sainsbury, Blair's one-time science minister, who donated some £16 million between 1995 and 2005) have been the mainstay of Labour's finances since 1997. The same is true for the Conservatives.

Fundraising has become imperative as election costs have soared, not least in terms of the need to facilitate the permanent campaigning that parties now undertake. Labour's income of £26.9 million in 2003, £29.3 million in 2004, and £35.3 million in 2005 was set against expenditure of £24.3 million in 2003, £32.1 million in 2004, and £49.8 million in the election year of 2005. Some 80 per cent of Labour's expenditure might have been spent on day-to-day running costs, but elections impose considerable financial pressures. Labour spent £10,945,119 on its 2001 election campaign and £17,939,617 in 2005; the Conservatives spent £12,751,813 and £17,852,240 and the Liberal Democrats £1,361,377 and £4,324,574. The present system of party funding is clearly broken and reform, perhaps by introduction of some form of state funding, paid for by the taxpayer, appears now to be a very real possibility.

24.4.3 Modes of Campaigning

Parties endlessly strive to secure positive public attention. Previously parties had 'tended to have greater control over the political agenda, in that they controlled a substantial component of the means of political communications. Nowadays, however, they are forced to confront a much greater diversity of agenda setters' (Mair, Muller, and Plasser 2004: 7). Such additional agenda setters, the news media and its ever expanding 'commentariat', as well as social movements, interest and pressure groups, mean parties have now to mount 'permanent' election campaigns particularly when, in the age of devolution, they have more elections to contest than ever before. General elections have now largely been nationalized, but local candidate-based activism, which may make some difference to party strength, by both raising electoral turnout and improving party performance, while in decline, still plays some positive role in local vote gathering (Denver, Hands, and MacAlllister 2004; Pattie and Johnston 2003). Local electioneering is, however, increasingly dominated by the national campaign. Election campaigns, usually containing a combination of positive and negative modes of electioneering, are almost entirely organized by a party headquarters reporting to the leader and his or her key staffers. Such campaigns, focused on news media-based public relations strategies, require parties to be 'on message' and possess coherent, presentable policies and reliable, trustworthy leaders (Wring 2004; Foley 2000; Norris et al. 1999; Scammell 1995).

Such a permanent election campaign requires modern electioneering to be expensively fought out by communicating indirectly with electors by means of the news media. Spin and marketing, pursued by a combination of public staged events (press conferences and keynote speeches) and private events (discreet contacts between leading politicians, their trusted proxies, and well-connected journalists and news executives) are now the parties' indispensable weapons. The relentless attention of the twenty-four-hour news media spotlight, further reinforced by modern 'catch-all' leader-centred electioneering, is just one further phenomenon to enhance the persona of the party leader. It is reinforced by leader-centric parties taking care to ensure that a unified message, careful product development, effective communication, and news management is made integral to everything that they do.

24.5 THE PROGRAMMATIC CONFIGURATION OF BRITISH POLITICAL PARTIES

Parties are influenced by—but also influence—their socio-economic and ideational environments. The first is the rule, the second the exception. Exceptions happen, however, as Labour helped make the political weather after 1945 and the Conservatives did likewise after 1979. In programmatic terms parties are often as reactive as they are proactive. They are more likely to adopt incremental measures to crisis manage as to pursue carefully constructed plans. They are often more shaped by the world around them than they shape that world. As ever, while 'prescription precedes response' (Mair, Muller, and Plasser 2004: 9), parties 'inherit before they choose' and, while making choices available to electors, they reflect (as well as sometimes shape) the imperatives of the prevailing 'policy Zeitgeist'.

Parties, while still possessing certain ideational proclivities, have moved away from established points in the political spectrum. Being engaged in a catch-all quest for votes influences the programmatic appeals parties make, reinforcing a wider post-ideological engagement reflecting new and different electoral—and political— demands. Labour no longer advocates Keynesian demand management and the nationalized public corporation (such policies being, to different extents and purposes, common to governments of all parties between 1945 and 1979). Instead, alongside the Conservatives, it accepts the fact that excessive old-style statism had become an economic and social problem (Kavanagh 1990; 1997; Gamble 1994). Following the collapse in public support for high rates of direct personal taxation, expanded public ownership, and the maintenance of trade union privilege, Labour, bested by the Thatcher- and Major-led Conservatives after 1979, felt electorally obliged to abandon such measures. As Labour's electoral heartland shrank as male manual employment in manufacturing industries declined, the Thatcherite Conservatives fashioned a reliable base among skilled manual workers (the C1s and C2s) in the 1980s. This, in addition to the successes of 'actually existing Thatcherism', helped prompt the internal party reassessment that led Tony Blair, building on reforms engineered under Neil

Kinnock, to further reformulate the Labour Party to appeal to electors to Labour's right after 1994.

The socio-economic left–right divide previously found at the heart of party politics no longer has significant purchase. Parties, because they pose the same existential threat to the other's office-seeking ambitions, compete with each other as vigorously as ever, but the programmatic divide between them is no longer that between divergent left and right. While Labour instinctively prefers more state intervention and the Conservatives less, both parties, together with the Liberal Democrats, pursue social reforms by championing wealth creation, promoting business, and encouraging entrepreneurship. 'New' Labour differs from 'Old' Labour in that it no longer wants to control the market through an old-style social democratic, quasi-corporatist state. The Cameron-led Conservatives differ from old-style Thatcherites by aligning themselves with notions of personal identity and preference, collective interest, and by championing public services. Labour under Blair and Brown has not simply offered a modernized form of Thatcherism, just as the Conservatives after 1951 never became socialists. Parties continue to make a difference. Labour's constitutional reform agenda, including devolution for Scotland and Wales, the passing of the Human Rights Act, and reform of the House of Lords, are obvious examples of where a change of party government ushered in a change of direction. The minimum wage, increasing child benefit, and the use of indirect (and direct, at least in the form of increased National Insurance contributions) tax revenues to redistribute resources to the working poor and fund increased expenditure on public services mark a departure from the previous Tory agenda. Yet ideological differences between the parties have been transformed. This is clearly demonstrated by Labour's embrace of the post-Thatcherite market economy since 1987. The parties are not starkly divided on government's role as a guardian of the public welfare. Nor do they differ radically on the need for the state to empower, free, and liberalize the market economy (to re-regulate it when necessary) rather than control and restrict it.

Party politics have become increasingly inclusive, not least in terms of embracing women's participation and representation (Childs 2004; Lovenduski 2005). Politics more generally increasingly focuses on issues which transcend the age-old left–right spectrum within which politics was traditionally framed. Europe, terrorism, civil liberties, immigration and asylum, a liberal interventionist foreign policy, and identity politics involving gender, racial, and sexual equality, the dominant issues of the day, do not easily fit into the old political categories and may now be said to lack one common and definitive party home.

24.6 PARTY CHANGE AMID PARTY CONTINUITY

Political parties are able, when necessary, to remodel themselves in line with changing electoral and ideational contexts. Electoral professional British parties retain some element of the old, mass-party form. Such remnants, not least its parliamentary party, the need to have an extra-parliamentary membership of sorts, and an electoral base can limit the autonomy of leading cadres. Labour, for instance, may vote-seek well beyond its traditional class base, but it retains links with the trade unions (even if this link is not especially valued at the highest levels of the party) and remains financially dependent on union largesse. Labour's electoral base, significantly broadened under Tony Blair, remains reliant on Labour heartlands. The same can be said of the Conservatives. Labour's DNA requires the party to draw electoral strength from leftist, progressive voters who oppose the Conservative Party and instinctively want Labour to push leftwards not rightwards. The opposite still applies to the Conservatives, especially in regard to its right-leaning electoral base.

Parties increasingly see policy competence, not political ideology, as the key to electoral success. Today all party leaders perceive the need to be pragmatic, flexible, and electoralist. They seek three related objectives: First, to increase their autonomy over both the parliamentary and the extra-parliamentary party; second, to professionalize and whenever possible personalize their party's mode of campaigning; and third, to win elections and thereafter enact public policies. Parties have a set of stated and identified objectives reflecting the interplay of a threefold set of party goals; office seeking, vote seeking, and policy seeking (Muller and Strom 1999; Harmel and Janda 1994). These three goals are obviously interrelated in that parties need votes to secure office in order to enact policy. For Britain's two largest parties, Labour and the Conservatives, vote seeking is essentially the same as office seeking, while smaller parties, including the third party, the Liberal Democrats, vote seek in Westminster elections with little expectation, short of electoral reform or a hung parliament, of attaining governmental office. Party goals can and do conflict with one another. This is particularly so if, say, a policy-seeking stance is seen to damage a party's office-seeking objective. In which case the party will have then to alter its stance and decide which party goal it will prioritize.

Electoral professional parties are said automatically to prioritize vote seeking (Wolinetz 2002), but party change, when defined as an alteration in the predominant party goal embraced by the party, is often a response to a considerable—and repeated—exogenous shock or series of shocks (Katz and Mair 2002; Strom 1989; 1990; Muller and Strom 1999). Such shocks, political parties being at root vote or office maximizers, are invariably electoral in form (Harmel and Janda 1982; 1994). Thus Labour shifted programmatically leftward after 1979 in response to what it perceived as being the policy and electoral failures of the Wilson and Callaghan governments. Here, Labour, or at least its activists, briefly backed by affiliated trade unions, sought to prioritize policy seeking over office seeking (or they may have believed that only leftist policy seeking would enable Labour to successfully office-seek). Gradually, however, after the election defeats of 1983, 1987, and 1992, Labour became acutely aware that its policy-seeking profile (however moderated it had been between 1983 and 1987) was a major obstacle to its electoral success; it began therefore to prioritize office seeking over policy seeking. It therefore 'modernized' itself, altering its programmatic objectives (Hay 1999; Heffernan 2001). The same phenomenon may be glimpsed at work today in the Conservatives' programmatic reorientation under David Cameron in the wake of Conservative defeats in 1997, 2001, and 2005.

Party change, then, is best measured in changing party form and function, ideology, and strategy. It is best understood as resulting from the interrelationship of two distinctive phenomena:

- inter-party politics, the changing ways in which the parties engage with each other within the electoral arena and the programmatic appeals with which they do so; and
- intra-party politics, the means over time by which the party in public office, specifically the parliamentary leadership, has been granted ever greater privileges over the wider party at large.

Party change is expressed in programmatic and organizational change and is usually prompted by key changes in the electoral and ideational environments the party inhabits. Again, as the Conservatives demonstrated after 1945, Labour dramatically—if gradually—demonstrated after 1983, and the Conservatives, it would seem, are presently demonstrating after 2001 and 2005, a major party that loses consecutive elections will, eventually, alter its programmatic appeal and image—as well as choose new leaders—to chase electoral success. Parties will inevitably prioritize office seeking over policy seeking when past forms of policy seeking are deemed to have inhibited successful office seeking. As argued above, electoral defeats are the most effective external shock requiring a party response. Such electoral shocks are the catalyst for party change, particularly when they are sharp and especially when they are repeated. Parties, even those that famously pride electoral office, can be slow to respond or react to unfavourable change in their electoral environment. Like the brontosaurus, they process any external stimuli slowly. If likened to the proverbial ship, they can take an age to alter their course. The degree to which a party can alter its predominant goal and modernize its programmatic appeal—the ease with which it may change—is largely dependent upon the freedom of manoeuvre its leadership, the party grouping best placed to effect change, is granted. Electoral professional, catch-all parties are more likely to enable British parliamentary leaders to pursue the party reforms considered necessary.

24.7 CONCLUSION

The comparative literature on political parties is vast (Muller and Strom 1999; Gunther, Moreno, and Linz 2002; Dalton and Wattenberg 2002). The literature on individual British political parties is robust, specifically in terms of party case studies, with Labour, unsurprisingly, the focus of much recent research (Russell 2005; Coates

2005; Quinn 2004; Cronin 2004; Wring 2004; Fielding 2002; Heffernan 2001; Shaw 1994; 2007). However, recent studies of the party role in wider analyses of election outcomes aside (Butler and Kavanagh 1997; 2002; Kavanagh and Butler 2005; Bartle and King 2005; King 2002; Norris 2001), the literature on comparative work across British political parties is thinner. Webb (2000) is still the recent outstanding leader in the field, alongside others (Ware 1996; Maor 1997), while McKenzie (1964), essentially now a historical work, remains relevant. Comparative work beyond the case study tends—with exceptions (Webb 2000)—to be largely confined to studies where British parties are compared, not to each other, but to other national counterparts (Diamond and Gunther 2001; Mair, Muller, and Plasser 2004).

Individual case study, focusing on policy and electoral politics rather than organizational form, is the way research on British parties has tended to be framed. Such studies, tending to follow the dominant party of the moment, significantly advance our understanding of party form and function. British parties, further changes to the party system notwithstanding, remain essential to the working of representative democracy. The two major parties, when they form the single-party Westminster government, are granted extraordinary powers to direct public affairs. Party leaders in government may have to manage their MPs and ministers, note the anticipated reaction of the electorate, suffer the critical scrutiny of the news media, and deal with the relentless hostility of opposition leaders, but politics remains, for good or ill, an elite-driven, party-based activity. Tony Blair claimed, when leader of the opposition, that John Major 'followed' his party while he, Blair, 'led' his. In modern British party politics such a model, leading from the front, running against your party's traditions, and being seen to take 'tough' decisions is considered by many the definitive objective of party leadership. This leadership model is, in spite of the formidable forces and structures that assail present-day political leaders, the defining characteristic of today's electoral professional, office-seeking British political parties.

References

BARTLE, J., and KING, A. 2005. *Britain at the Polls 2005*. London: Chatham House.

BOGDANOR, V. 2004. 'The Constitution and the Party System in the Twentieth Century'. *Parliamentary Affairs*, 57/4: 717–33.

BUTLER, D., and KAVANAGH, D. 1997. *The British General Election of 1997*. Basingstoke: Palgrave.

—— —— 2002. *The British General Election of 2001*. Basingstoke: Palgrave.

—— and STOKES, D. 1974. *Political Change in Britain*. London: Macmillan.

CAMPBELL, A., CONVERSE, P., MILLER, W. E., and STOKES, D. 1960. *The American Voter*. New York: Wiley.

CLARKE, H., SANDERS, D., STEWART, M., and WHITELEY, P. (eds.) 2004. *Political Choice in Britain*. Oxford: Oxford University Press.

CHILDS, S. 2004. *New Labour's New Women MPs: Women Representing Women*. London: Routledge.

COATES, D. 2005. *Prolonged Labour: The Slow Birth of New Labour in Britain*. London: Palgrave Macmillan.

COWLEY, P. 2005. *The Rebels*. London: Politico's.

CREWE, I., and KING, A. 1995. *SDP: The Birth, Life, and Death of the Social Democratic Party*. Oxford: Oxford University Press.

CRONIN, J. 2004. *New Labour's Pasts*. London: Longman.

DAALDER, H., and MAIR, P. (eds.) 1983. *Western European Party Systems*. London: Sage.

DALTON, R. J. 2002. *Citizen Politics*. New York: Chatham House.

—— and WATTENBERG, M. 2002. *Parties without Partisans*. Oxford: Oxford University Press.

DENVER, D. 2004. *Elections and Voters in Britain*. London: Palgrave Macmillan.

—— HANDS, G., and MACALLISTER, I. 2004. 'The Electoral Impact of Constituency Campaigning in Britain, 1992–2001'. *Political Studies*, 52/2: 289–306.

DIAMOND, L., and GUNTHER, R. (eds.) 2001. *Political Parties and Democracy*. Baltimore: Johns Hopkins University Press.

DUNLEAVY, P. 2005. 'Facing up to Multi-party Politics'. *Parliamentary Affairs*, 58: 503–32.

—— 2006. 'The Westminster Model and the Distinctiveness of British Politics'. In P. Dunleavy, R. Heffernan, P. Cowley, and C. Hay (eds.), *Developments in British Politics 8*. London: Palgrave Macmillan.

EVANS, G., and NORRIS, P. 1999. *Critical Elections: British Parties and Voters in Long Term Perspective*. London: Sage.

FIELDING, S. 2002. *The Labour Party: Continuity and Change in the Making of New Labour*. London: Palgrave Macmillan.

FOLEY, M. 2000. *The British Presidency*. Manchester: Manchester University Press.

—— 2004. 'Presidential Attribution as an Agency of Prime Ministerial Critique in a Parliamentary Democracy'. *British Journal of Politics and International Relations*, 6: 292–311.

GAMBLE, A. 1994. *The Free Economy and the Strong State: The Politics of Thatcherism*. London: Macmillan.

—— and WRIGHT, T. 2002. 'Commentary: Is The Party Over?' *Political Quarterly*, 73/2: 123–4.

GOULD, P. 1998. *The Unfinished Revolution: How the Modernisers Saved the Labour Party*. London: Little, Brown.

GUNTHER, R., MONTERO, J. R., and LINZ, J. (eds.) 2002. *Political Parties: Old Concepts and New Challenges*. Oxford: Oxford University Press.

HARMEL, R., and JANDA, K. 1982. *Parties and their Environments*. New York: Longman.

—— —— 1994. 'An Integrated Theory of Party Goals and Party Change'. *Journal of Theoretical Politics*, 6/3: 259–87.

HAY, C. 1999. *The Political Economy of New Labour: Labouring under False Pretences*. Manchester: Manchester University Press.

HEFFERNAN, R. 2001. *New Labour and Thatcherism: Political Change in Britain*. London: Palgrave.

—— 2005. 'Why the Prime Minister Cannot be a President: Comparing Institutional Imperatives in Britain and America'. *Parliamentary Affairs*, 58: 53–70.

HOUSE OF COMMONS CONSTITUTIONAL AFFAIRS COMMITTEE 2006. *Party Funding*. London: TSO.

INGLEHART, I. 1990. *Culture Shift in Advanced Industrial Society*. Princeton, NJ: Princeton University Press.

JANDA, K. 1980. 'A Comparative Analysis of Party Organization: The United States, Europe, and the World'. In W. J. Crotty (ed.), *The Party Symbol: Readings on Political Parties*. San Francisco: W. H. Freeman.

KATZ, R., and MAIR, P. 2002. 'The Ascendancy of the Party in Public Office: Party Organisational Change in Twentieth Century Democracies'. In R. Gunther, J. R. Montero, and J. Linz (eds.), *Political Parties: Old Concepts and New Challenges*. Oxford: Oxford University Press.

KAVANAGH, D. 1990. *Thatcherism and British Politics*. Oxford: Oxford University Press.

——1997. *The Reordering of British Politics*. Oxford: Oxford University Press.

——and BUTLER, D. 2005, *The British General Election of 2005*. Basingstoke: Palgrave.

KING, A. 2002. *Britain at the Polls 2001*. London: Chatham House.

KIRCHHEIMER, O. 1966. 'The Transformation of Western Party Systems'. In J. LaPalombara and M. Weiner (eds.), *Political Parties and Political Development*. Princeton, NJ: Princeton University Press.

LAFFIN, M., and SHAW, E. 2007. 'British Devolution and the Labour Party: How a National Party Adapts to Devolution'. *British Journal of Politics and International Relations*, 9/1: 55–72.

LIJPHART, A, 1999. *Patterns of Democracy: Government Forms and Performance in Thirty-Six Countries*. New Haven, Conn.: Yale University Press.

LIPSET, S. M., and ROKKAN, S. 1967. 'Cleavage Structures, Party Systems and Voter Alignments'. In S. M. Lipset and S. Rokkan (eds.), *Party Systems and Voter Alignments: Cross National Perspectives*. New York: Free Press.

LOVENDUSKI, J. 2005. *Feminizing Politics*. Cambridge: Polity.

McKENZIE, R. T. 1964. *British Political Parties*. London: Heinemann.

MAIR, P. 1983. 'Adaptation and Control: Toward and Understanding of Party and Party System Change'. In H. Daalder and P. Mair (eds.), *Western European Party Systems*. London: Sage.

——1989. 'The Problem of Party System Change'. *Journal of Theoretical Politics*, 1: 251–76.

——MULLER, W. C., and PLASSER, F. 2004. *Political Parties and Electoral Change*. London: Sage.

MAJOR, J. 1999. *John Major: The Autobiography*. London: HarperCollins.

MAOR, M. 1997. *Political Parties and Party Systems*. London: Routledge.

MONTERO, J. R., and GUNTHER, R. 2002. 'Introduction: Reviewing and Reassessing Parties'. In R. Gunther, J. R. Montero, and J. Linz (eds.), *Political Parties: Old Concepts and New Challenges*. Oxford: Oxford University Press.

MULLER, W. C., and STROM, K. (eds.) 1999. *Policy, Office or Votes? How Political Parties in Western Europe Make Hard Decisions*. Cambridge: Cambridge University Press.

NORRIS, P. 2001. *Britain Votes 2001*. Oxford: Oxford University Press.

——CURTICE, J., SANDERS, D., SCAMMELL, M., and SEMETKI, H. 1999. *On Message: Communicating the Campaign*. London: Sage.

NORTON, P. 2005. *Parliament in British Politics*. London: Palgrave Macmillan.

PANEBIANCO, A. 1988. *Political Parties: Organisation and Power*. Cambridge: Cambridge University Press.

PATTIE, C. J., and JOHNSTON, R. J. 2003. 'Local Battles in a National Landslide: Constituency Campaigning at the 2001 British General Election'. *Political Geography*, 22/4: 381–414.

PESTON, P. 2005. *Brown's Britain*. London: Short Books.

POGUNTKE, T., and WEBB, P. (eds.) 2005. *The Presidentialization of Politics: A Comparative Study of Modern Democracies*. Oxford: Oxford University Press.

QUINN, T. 2004. *Modernising the Labour Party: Organisational Change since 1983*. London: Palgrave Macmillan.

——2005. 'Electing the Leader: The British Labour Party's Electoral College'. *British Journal of Politics and International Relations*, 6: 333–52.

ROSE, R., and UNWIN, D. 1970. 'Persistence and Change in Western Party Systems, 1945–1969'. *Political Studies*, 18: 287–319.

Russell, M. 2005. *Building New Labour: The Politics of Party Organization*. London: Palgrave Macmillan.

Sartori, G. 1976. *Parties and Party Systems: A Framework for Analysis*. Cambridge: Cambridge University Press.

Scammell, M. 1995. *Designer Politics: How Elections are Won*. London: Macmillan.

Seldon, A. 2004. *Blair*. London: Free Press.

—— 2007. *Blair Unbound*. London: Simon and Schuster.

Shaw, E. 1994. *The Labour Party since 1979: Crisis and Transformation*. London: Routledge.

—— 2004. 'The Control Freaks? New Labour and the Party'. In S. Ludlam and M. J. Smith (eds.), *Governing as New Labour: Policy and Politics under Blair*. London: Palgrave Macmillan.

—— 2007. *Losing Labour's Soul: New Labour and the Blair Government, 1997–2007*. London: Routledge.

Strom, K. 1989. 'Interparty Competition in Advanced Democracies'. *Journal of Theoretical Politics*, 1: 277–300.

—— 1990. 'A Behavioural Theory of Competitive Political Parties'. *American Journal of Political Science*, 34/2: 565–98.

Ware, A. 1996. *Political Parties and Party Systems*. Oxford: Oxford University Press.

Webb, P. 2000. *The Modern British Party System*. London: Sage.

—— 2004. 'Party Responses to the Changing Electoral Market in Britain'. In P. Mair, W. C. Muller, and F. Plasser (eds.), *Political Parties and Electoral Change*. London: Sage.

Wolinetz, S. 2002. 'Beyond the Catch-All Party: Approaches to the Study of Parties and Party Organization in Contemporary Democracies'. In R. Gunther, J. R. Montero, and J. Linz (eds.), *Political Parties: Old Concepts and New Challenges*. Oxford: Oxford University Press.

Wring, D. 2004. *The Politics of Marketing the Labour Party*. London: Palgrave.

CHAPTER 25

....

VOTING
AND IDENTITY

....

CHARLES PATTIE
RON JOHNSTON

IDENTITY looms large in modern political theory and society. Individuals identify with particular groups based on their ethnicity, religion, gender, sexuality, or other markers. Translating these identities into political choices is not straightforward, however: people sharing the same identity may draw different political conclusions and they may hold several identities simultaneously, creating cross-cutting political positions. These complications notwithstanding, identity politics suggests a move away from assumptions of dispassionate rational political calculation based on interests (Kenny 2004; Parekh 2008).

What do identity politics imply for analyses of British elections and voting? Two quite different responses are possible. The first emphasizes the emergence of a multicultural Britain in the late twentieth and early twenty-first centuries, in which the politics of identity plays a growing role in elections. Paradoxically, however, the second (and dominant) perspective in the empirical political science literature suggests quite the opposite trajectory, from an electoral politics dominated by identity to one dominated by rational action. This chapter traces that shift in academic understandings of British voting.

25.1 IDENTITY VOTING: THE ALIGNED ELECTORATE

From the 1950s to the 1970s, the dominant academic paradigm on voting behaviour stressed the importance of electoral alignments, long-standing and stable links between voters and parties. Voting was seen as an expressive, not a deliberative, act. Most voters would support the same party in election after election, and hence parties could count on a 'normal vote', especially when abstention rates were low, as was the case until the 1990s. Parties mobilized as many core supporters as possible and fought for the support of the relatively small group of uncommitted 'floating' voters who might decide elections by changing their preferred party between contests. Explanations of alignment drew primarily on two different theoretical traditions: partisan identification and social cleavages.

25.1.1 Partisan Identification

Partisan identification, pioneered in 1950s America (Campbell et al. 1960), stresses individual voters' psychological attachments, initially formed in childhood, as parents socialize their children into supporting a particular party. As children grow into adulthood, their inherited party identification strengthens over time, forming a psychological heuristic through which they judge aspects of their political environment. Republican identifiers will be positively predisposed to Republican politicians, and Democrat identifiers to Democrat candidates. Voters may occasionally deviate from their party identification with Democrat identifiers occasionally supporting Republicans and vice-versa. But in the long term partisans return to voting for the party they identify with.

British voters in the 1960s reported strong attachments to particular parties (Butler and Stokes 1969). In 1964, for instance, around 95 per cent of respondents to the British Election Study (BES) identified with a named political party: 45 per cent identified 'very strongly' with it, and a further 39 per cent identified with it 'fairly strongly' (Table 25.1). And they voted accordingly. The stronger their identification with a party the more likely they were to turn out at an election: 40 per cent of the very small group of individuals who identified with no party abstained in 1964, compared to (for instance) just 7 per cent of very strong Conservative identifiers. And the stronger an individual's identification with a party, the more likely he or she was to vote for it. Around 90 per cent of 'very strong' Conservative or Labour identifiers voted for their respective party. But this dropped to two-thirds of those who were weak Conservatives, and 60 per cent of those who were weak Labour supporters. A similar pattern held for those who identified with the Liberals, though overall loyalty rates for this party were lower than for the 'big two', not least as the Liberals fielded candidates in only 365 of the 630 constituencies at the 1964 election: some Liberal identifiers had no Liberal candidate to vote for in 1964.

Table 25.1 Partisan identification, 1964

Party identification	% identifiers (column percentages)	Vote 1964 (row percentages)				
		Abstained	Conservative	Labour	Liberal	Other
Very strong Conservative	19.3	7.4	90.2	1.5	0.9	0.0
Fairly strong Conservative	16.2	12.0	82.3	2.1	3.2	0.4
Not very strong Conservative	4.2	14.9	67.6	9.5	8.1	0.0
Very strong Labour	21.8	5.8	1.3	92.1	0.3	0.6
Fairly strong Labour	16.4	6.3	2.1	88.9	2.8	0.0
Not very strong Labour	4.8	34.1	1.2	59.8	4.9	0.0
Very strong Liberal	3.8	5.9	14.7	11.8	67.6	0.0
Fairly strong Liberal	5.9	8.7	19.4	17.5	54.4	1.0
Not very strong Liberal	2.1	20.0	20.0	11.4	48.6	0.0
Very strong other	0.0	0.0	0.0	0.0	0.0	0.0
Fairly strong other	0.1	0.0	50.0	50.0	0.0	0.0
Not very strong other	0.0	0.0	0.0	0.0	0.0	0.0
No party identification	5.4	40.2	17.2	26.4	16.1	0.0

Source: 1964 British Election Study.

25.1.2 Social Cleavages

The identities enacted in voting were not simply psychological, however. Major social cleavages also produced long-standing patterns of party support. Lipset and Rokkan (1967) traced the salient mid-twentieth century European political cleavages to two waves of radical nineteenth-century social change. The national revolution resulted in divisions between centre and periphery in the new states and (in Catholic Europe at least) between church and state. The industrial revolution produced divisions between agriculture and industry and between bourgeoisie and workers. Parties crystallized around each cleavage, representing one side or the other. Centre–periphery cleavages stimulated separatist and regionalist parties in peripheral areas; conflicts between Christian Democrat and secularist parties represented the church–state cleavage; peasant parties and/or parties representing the old landed aristocracy arose from the agriculture–industry divide (e.g. Cox 1970); and the bourgeoisie–worker divide was colonized by parties of the right and left (particularly, in the latter case, socialist and social democratic parties). Which cleavage came to dominate in a particular national context, Lipset and Rokkan argued, depended on which was most active when the franchise extended to most adult males. Once established, the major parties on either side of the cleavage became institutionalized, allowing them to continue even if the initial tensions stimulating the cleavage had ameliorated.

In Great Britain, the class cleavage dominated the twentieth century. The late nineteenth-century extension of the franchise to most adult males created a large new group of voters, the urban working class, and by the start of the twentieth century, a new party, Labour, emerged from the trade union movement explicitly to represent them. The Conservatives became the party of the middle classes and of business interests. While around two-thirds of BES respondents in the main middle-class groups voted Conservative in 1964, only between a quarter and a fifth of voters in the manual working-class groups did so (Table 25.2). Conversely, while over half of manual workers voted Labour, only about 16 per cent of the middle classes did so. In a class-divided society, 'class [was] the basis of British party politics; all else [was] embellishment and detail' (Pulzer 1967: 98).

25.1.3 The Exceptions

A fully aligned electorate, in which people always voted in line with their partisan and/or class identities, would produce stable election results. Electoral change would be relatively glacial, as older voters died and were replaced by the young. But this clearly does not fit the experience of fluctuating party support over time, or the regular turnover of governments. Even when electoral alignments are strong, some citizens are floating voters, with weak attachments to any party, and open to being swayed one way or the other in any given election. It is no accident that the 1950s and 1960s in the UK were marked both by strong partisan attachments and by broad ideological consensus between Labour and the Conservatives: with their bases secured by voter alignment, the parties appealed to the small number of Downsian median floating voters for the extra votes needed to win.

A significant minority of voters in 1964 chose parties other than the one they identified with, or (even more so) might be thought of as their 'natural' class party (Tables 25.1 and 25.2); such minorities were central to British election results for much of the twentieth century. Had the class cleavage been absolute, an in-built manual working-class majority in the electorate would have delivered Labour victory in most elections before the 1980s (in 1964, around 60 per cent of the electorate were in manual working-class households: Table 25.2). The electoral dilemma for the

Table 25.2 Household class and voting, 1964

Social class	% in class (column percentages)	Vote 1964 (row percentages)				
		Abstained	Conservative	Labour	Liberal	Other
Higher managerial (A)	5.8	5.2	68.0	15.5	10.3	1.0
Intermediate managerial (B)	8.7	5.4	64.2	16.9	12.8	0.7
Clerical and supervisory (C1)	23.7	9.9	51.2	22.8	15.3	0.7
Skilled manual (C2)	37.9	12.6	25.7	54.1	7.6	0.0
Semi & unskilled manual (DE)	24.0	14.6	21.4	58.4	5.4	0.2

Source: 1964 British Election Study.

Conservatives throughout the period was how a party drawing largely on middle-class support could win power given an electorate dominated by the manual working class.

Clearly, the Conservatives solved their dilemma, becoming by far the most success-ful electoral force in twentieth-century British politics (Seldon 1994). Their ability to win support from a significant minority of working-class voters reflected partly on support from forms of social identity other than class. In a few areas (such as west-central Scotland and Liverpool) with large Irish Roman Catholic communities, the politics of Irish nationalism produced a unionist backlash from working-class Protestants, which the Conservatives capitalized on. A more widespread factor was social deference among some working-class voters, identifying the Conservative Party elite as a natural ruling class, notably in rural areas (McKenzie and Silver 1968; Jessop 1974; Newby 1979). But some working-class Conservatives were driven by pragmatic evaluations, voting Conservative based on their positive evaluations of the party's performance in government (McKenzie and Silver 1968).

No less striking were middle-class Labour voters. Social mobility played a part: 58 per cent of the Labour-voting middle classes in the 1964 BES sample had fathers who were manual workers, compared to just 44 per cent of all middle-class respondents, and only 39 per cent of those who voted Conservative. For some, then, Labour voting reflected an older identification, drawing from childhood socialization. But cross-cutting identities were also involved. The growth of Britain's welfare state after 1945 meant many depended on the state for either or both of major services and employ-ment (including, within the middle class, a growing number of public-sector man-agers and professionals). This created the basis for a new set of politicized identities (Dunleavy 1979; Dunleavy and Husbands 1983). Those identifying (as either service consumers or employees) with the public sector were more likely to vote Labour than those who identified with the private sector.

These cross-cutting sectoral identities partly account for middle-class Labour vot-ing. At the October 1974 election, for instance, BES data reveal that while 14 per cent of private-sector professional and managerial workers voted Labour, this almost doubled to 26 per cent among public-sector professionals. The corollary held too: 50 per cent of private sector professional and managerial workers voted Tory, compared to just 30 per cent in the public sector. Cross-cutting sectoral cleavages appeared as a result of variations in housing tenure; 59 per cent of manual workers who rented their home from the public sector voted Labour in October 1974, but only 42 per cent of those who were homeowners (12 and 27 per cent respectively voted Conservative).

Social identities influenced British voting in the 1960s and the early 1970s, there-fore, but in complex ways. While some identities reinforced each other politically (middle-class private-sector workers, for instance), others pulled in opposite direc-tions (as for working-class homeowners). But economic restructuring in the 1970s and 1980s saw the steep decline of traditional manual industrial jobs and the growth of the white-collar service sector. In 1951 65 per cent of the working population were in working-class jobs: by 1991, just 38 per cent were (Heath, Jowell, and Curtice 2001: 13).

At the same time, more Britons aspired to middle-class lifestyles and home ownership grew rapidly in all social classes—around two-thirds of all households were owner-occupiers in 1997. The implications were very different for Britain's largest two parties. For the Conservatives, embourgoisement promised electoral ascendancy (a vision they exploited in the 1980s, through policies such as the right to buy council houses). For Labour, the decline of the traditional working class raised the spectre of permanent consignment to the electoral wilderness (Hobsbawm 1981; Franklin 1985; Crewe 1988; Heath, Jowell, and Curtice 2001). Labour's challenge at the end of the twentieth century was similar to that facing the Conservatives at the century's start: extending its appeal beyond the dwindling manual working class was central to New Labour, for instance.

25.2 DEALIGNMENT: AWAY FROM IDENTITY VOTING?

But class and partisan alignments were not unchanging. From the mid-1970s, dealignment took hold (Crewe, Särlvik, and Alt 1977; Särlvik and Crewe 1983; Franklin 1985; Heath, Jowell, and Curtice 1985; Crewe 1986; Clarke et al. 2004; Sanders 1998). The weakening of class alignment is illustrated by decade-on-decade trends in the Alford index, which subtracts the percentage of non-manual workers who vote Labour from the percentage of manual workers who do so. Where the class cleavage is absolute, all manual workers will vote Labour, and no non-manual workers will do so, producing an index of 100. Where there are no class differences in voting, the index is 0. The UK's Alford index has dropped in every decade since the 1960s (Figure 25.1). Whereas in 1964, 63 per cent of voters voted for their 'natural' class party, by 2005 only 41 per cent did so—the lowest share of any election between those dates.

Voters' psychological identification with political parties has dropped steeply too. Whereas in the 1960s around 45 per cent of BES respondents identified very strongly with a political party, only 11 per cent on average did so in the 2000s (Figure 25.2). At the same time, the proportion identifying weakly or not at all with a party increased. Whereas in the 1960s, only around 6 per cent of voters on average identified with no party and a further 10 per cent were weak identifiers, by the 2000s these positions were shared by 14 per cent and 35 per cent respectively.

The origins of dealignment lie in the deep 1970s recession. Neither Labour nor Conservative governments could resolve the crisis (King 1975). Public confidence in political parties fell. Between 1970 and 1974, partisanship decreased abruptly in all age cohorts, and did not subsequently recover (Abramson 1992). Subsequently, the rebirth of the Liberal Party, the creation of the SDP in 1981, and its Alliance with the Liberals for the 1983 and 1987 general elections provided an alternative focus for voters relatively alienated from the two main parties (Crewe and King 1995; Rose and

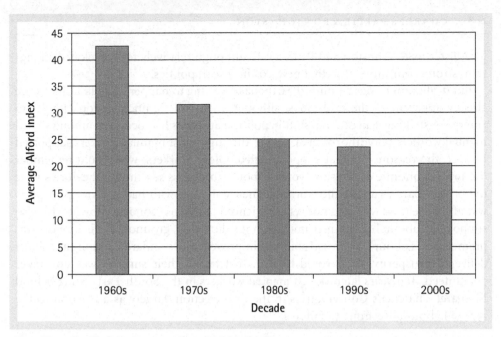

Fig. 25.1 Declining class voting, 1960s–2000s

Source: British Election Studies 1964–2005.

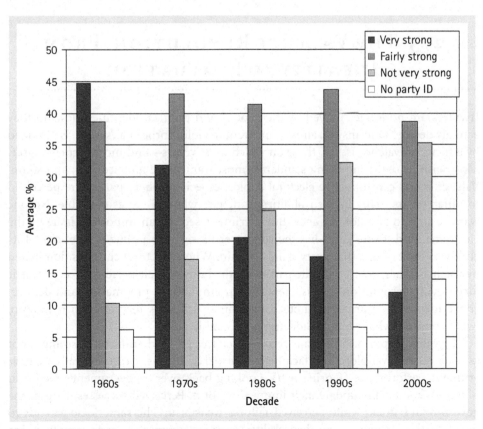

Fig. 25.2 Weakening partisanship, 1960s–2000s

Source: British Election Studies 1964–2005.

McAllister 1986; Johnston and Pattie 1988), although relatively few developed a long-term strong commitment to that new axis in British politics.

But dealignment was a political earthquake waiting to happen. The faultlines were already apparent in the mid-1960s, although their full significance took longer to emerge. A striking generational shift in political attitudes had occurred among skilled manual workers (Goldthorpe et al. 1968). Although most manual workers supported Labour, the reasons for that support varied. Older workers, who could remember the 1930s economic depression, voted Labour from class sentiment: the Tories were the bosses' party, Labour the workers'. Their children, who had grown up in post-war affluence (and who had not yet experienced the 1970s economic downturn), also supported Labour, but on instrumental, not solidaristic, grounds. Their support was premised on Labour's promised ability to improve living standards. As long as Labour delivered prosperity, they would back it. If it failed, their support was no longer guaranteed. Ten years later, skilled manual workers in the South-East swung behind Margaret Thatcher's Conservatives in the 1979 election, largely as a reaction to the 1974–9 Labour government's failures.

25.3 THE VALENCE REVOLUTION: FROM IDENTITY TO EVALUATION

If voters are no longer moved by their social and political identities, how do they actually decide? One answer, already apparent in Goldthorpe et al.'s work, is provided by a focus on valence issues, those on which most voters—and most parties—agree. Most wish to see rising living standards; most want peace and security; and so on. Valence issues can influence electoral choice, especially where parties are perceived to differ substantially in their abilities to deliver what all see as desirable. No one wants crime to rise, for instance. But if crime is seen as an important issue by the electorate, and if one party has the edge over its rivals in public perceptions of its ability to fight crime, that party stands to gain. Where electoral choice is dominated by valence issues, voters evaluate parties on the basis of their performance, not their ideology. In recognition of this, New Labour emphasized pragmatism and delivery above ideological purity: to quote Tony Blair in Labour's 1997 election manifesto, 'what counts is what works' (Giddens 1998; Gamble 2005).

The valence approach radically reconceptualizes party identification, seeing it not as long-term psychological attachment to a party, but as a running tally of government performance (Fiorina 1981). Looking back over a government's record in office, voters steadily update their impressions of it. Perceived successes increase the government's stock, while perceived failures weaken it. The same logic extends to other parties, depending on their ability to project themselves as fit for office. Far from representing a stable long-term outlook, party identification should move in keeping with the ups and downs of the political business cycle.

Empirical evidence backs this up. Many studies use the economy as a shorthand measure for government performance (Lewis-Beck 1988; Lewis-Beck and Paldam 2000). Most voters have neither time nor expertise to monitor all the different fields of government activity and hence will not update their running evaluations of government performance in the light of each twist and turn of public policy. However, all are affected by the state of the economy and most hold the government at least partly responsible for it; indeed more tend to blame governments for poor economic performance than credit them when things are going well (Alt 1979; Brug, Eijk, and Franklin 2007).

These feelings influence party support (MacKuen, Erikson, and Stimson 1989; 1992; Erikson, MacKuen, and Stimson 1998; 2000). The worse voters feel the economy performed in the past, or the more pessimistic they are about its future prospects, the lower is partisan identification with the main party of government, and the higher identification with the opposition. Conversely, the more positive voters are about past economic performance, or the more optimistic they are about the future, the higher their identification with the government, and the lower that with the opposition.

Party support in Britain is influenced by such valence issues. As early as the late 1960s, analyses of monthly trends in government support found that it tracked changes in the economy (Goodhart and Bansali 1970): as unemployment and/or inflation rose, the government's support dropped (and as they fell support increased). More recent analyses have examined voters' economic perceptions. The best-known example is the 'Essex model', which analyses monthly trends in government popularity as a two-step process (Sanders, Ward, and Marsh 1987). First, economic conditions (unemployment rates, inflation rates, and so on) influence voters' expectations about the future. If the economy is doing well, voters become more optimistic about their own future financial prospects; when it is doing badly, they become more pessimistic. The second stage is to model monthly trends in government popularity. In the 'classic' Essex model, this is a function of just two factors: the government's popularity in the preceding month (sudden changes in government popularity are rare); and aggregate personal economic expectations (the more optimistic voters feel about how affluent they will be in the future, the more support the government gets).

The model was first used to claim that Mrs Thatcher's landslide re-election in 1983 was caused not by victory in the Falklands but by economic recovery after the deep recession of the early 1980s (Sanders, Ward, and Marsh 1987; though see e.g. Clarke, Mishler, and Whiteley 1990). A notable success for the model was its use to predict accurately the outcome of the 1992 election eighteen months before the event. That contest was widely expected to be very close. But, as Sanders (1991) predicted, the government won re-election on a barely changed vote share (albeit with a substantially reduced parliamentary majority) thanks to policies aimed at economic recovery introduced sufficiently in advance of the election.

Economic voting has become a new orthodoxy in British voting studies and in British party thinking alike. Ironically, however, in some respects the 1992 election represented a high-water mark for straightforward applications of the theory in the UK. Strikingly, the Conservatives, having won re-election in 1992 as Britain emerged from a recession, went on to their worst election defeat of modern times in 1997, even though the economy was relatively strong (and had been for several years). The Labour government elected in 1997 was re-elected twice in part on its economic record, having presided over one of the longest periods of continued economic growth in recent British history. And yet, throughout the period between 1997 and 2005 (and in sharp contradistinction to the years of Conservative government between 1979 and 1997), monthly trends in government popularity did not track personal economic expectations at all (Sanders 2005). The core relationship which underpinned the Essex model in the 1980s and early 1990s broke down over the subsequent decade.

But valence is not restricted simply to economic performance. For instance, the attribution of responsibility is important. Voters may feel the economy is strong, but judge that this is despite the government's policies, rather than because of them. Linked to this, a reputation for competence is a valuable political asset; a reputation for incompetence is a fast track to defeat. The Conservatives lost in 1997 despite an economic boom because the 1992 ERM crisis badly damaged public perceptions of their economic competence. Up until late 1992, the Conservatives invariably out-polled Labour as the party most likely to handle the economy well. The party had recently taken Britain into the European Exchange Rate Mechanism (ERM), arguing this was essential for the future economic well-being of the country. But in September 1992, market pressure forced the government to abandon ERM membership, a dramatic policy failure. The Conservatives lost their long-established lead on economic competence, and hence the 1997 election (Sanders 1999). Labour picked up this accolade and its ownership of the issue was strengthened first by Tony Blair's New Labour project and then, *a fortiori*, after 1997 by Gordon Brown's reputation as a competent Chancellor presiding over a prolonged economic boom (Clarke et al. 2004; Sanders 2006).

Similarly, perceptions of party leaders have come under renewed scrutiny (e.g. Bartle and Crewe 2002; Clarke and Stewart 1992; 1995; Clarke, Stewart, and Whiteley 1997; 1998; Clarke et al. 2004). Leadership is a valence issue in that few if any would wish to elect a Prime Minister with no leadership skills. Perceptions of leadership competence have independent effects on party choice, even after controlling for factors such as underlying party identification and evaluations of the economy. Leaders matter, and can be an electoral asset for their party (as Blair was for Labour in 1997) or a liability (as, arguably, Gordon Brown rapidly became in early 2008). Other valence issues of importance in influencing party choice include voters' evaluations of competence in handling major public services such as the NHS and education, benefits such as pensions, and public problems such as crime and security (Clarke et al. 2004; Johnston and Pattie 2001).

Table 25.3 Modelling voting at the 2005 general election: multinomial logit

	Vote (versus voted Labour)			Chi-square[a]
	Conservative	Liberal Democrat	Other	
Constant	0.54	0.80	2.10	
Identity and demographics				
Respondent age group	0.22**	0.15**	0.15*	17.95
Respondent class	−0.22**	−0.11*	0.03	17.47
Respondent education	0.05	0.08	−0.02	1.17
Respondent gender	−0.26	−0.27	−0.79**	10.22
Respondent party identification (comparison = other party ID)				488.66
No party ID	0.19	−0.40	−2.33**	
Labour identifier	−1.94**	−2.02**	−3.22**	
Conservative identifier	2.03**	−0.53	−1.68**	
Lib Dem identifier	−0.38	0.82*	−1.75**	
Political ideology				
Tax and spend scale	−0.11*	0.04	−0.08	10.14
Left–right scale	0.21**	0.02	0.11	11.89
Valence issues				
Personal economic expectations	−0.55**	−0.15	−0.11	20.08
Feelings about Tony Blair	−0.42**	−0.37**	−0.42**	169.24
Feelings about Michael Howard	0.37**	0.01	0.03	58.15
Feelings about Charles Kennedy	0.03	0.23**	0.07	30.38
Model improvement		1902.48		
Model significance		0.00		
% correctly classified		74.6		
Nagelkerke R^2		0.74		
N		1757		

* Significant at $p = 0.05$; ** significant at $p = 0.01$.
[a] This column gives the difference in −2 log likelihood between the final model and a model omitting the indicated variable.
Source: 2005 British Election Study.

How do identity and valence issues stack up as explanations of contemporary voting? We illustrate this in a multinomial logit model of voting at the 2005 general election, controlling for a range of demographic, identity-based, ideological, and valence measures (Table 25.3). Data are drawn from the 2005 BES panel survey, which interviewed a national sample of voters around a month before the election took place, reinterviewing them immediately after the election. The independent variables in the model are all taken from the pre-election wave of interviews, and hence are not contaminated by voters' knowledge of the election results, and are less likely than are measures derived from post-election surveys to be affected by their eventual vote choices. The demographic and identity measures are:

- Age, coded into 7 age bands: 18–24-year-olds; 25–34-year-olds; 35–44-year-olds; 45–54-year-olds; 55–9-year-olds; 60–4-year-olds; and those aged 65 or over. The higher the score, the older the individual;

- Class: professionals and managers coded 1; skilled non-manual workers 2; the self-employed 3; manual workers in supervisory roles 4; manual workers 5; and others 6;
- Highest educational qualification: those with no formal qualifications are coded 1; school-leaving qualifications are coded 2; post-school qualifications short of degree level are coded 3; and university-level qualifications are coded 4;
- Gender, coded 1 for women, 0 for men; and
- Party identification, coded 0 for those who identify with no party, 1 for Labour identifiers, 2 for Conservatives, 3 for Liberal Democrats, and 4 for those who identify with some other party.

Political ideology is measured using responses to two scales:

- Tax–spend: an 11-point scale, ranging from those whose preference is to cut taxes, even if this means cutting public spending (coded 0) to those who want to raise public spending, even if this means raising taxes (coded 10); and
- Left–right: another 11 point scale, this time anchored at one end by those who self-identify with the left of the political spectrum (coded 0) and at the other with those who identify with the right (coded 10).

Four valence issues are included, one reflecting economic evaluations and the others evaluations of the party leaders. They are:

- Personal economic expectations, ranging from those who expected, on the eve of the 2005 general election, that their personal economic circumstances would get much worse over the next year (coded 1) to those who felt they would get much better (coded 5); and
- Three variables measuring feelings towards the three main party leaders in 2005: Tony Blair for Labour; Michael Howard for the Conservatives; and Charles Kennedy for the Liberal Democrats. Each is coded on an 11-point scale, where 0 indicates that the respondent strongly dislikes that particular leader and 10 indicates that they strongly like them.

The model contrasts voters for the Conservatives, Liberal Democrats, and other parties (primarily the Scottish and Welsh nationalists but also minor parties) against those who voted Labour. Identity, ideology, and valence all affect vote choice. Conservative and Liberal Democrat voters in 2005 were rather older than Labour voters (as were voters for other parties), and less likely to be working class. Prior party identification was important: compared to those with no party identification, Labour identifiers were much less likely to vote for other parties than they were to vote Labour; Conservative identifiers were much more likely to vote Conservative (but less likely to vote 'other') than they were to vote Labour; and Liberal Democrat identifiers were more likely to vote Lib Dem, and less likely to vote 'other' than to vote Labour. Left–right ideology differentiated between Labour and Conservative voters: the latter were more likely to favour tax cuts and place themselves on the right of the political spectrum than were Labour voters. Valence also mattered. Choice between the two most likely parties of government, Labour and Conservative, was influenced by personal economic expectations: the better-off individuals expected to be in the future the less likely they were to vote for the Conservative opposition rather than for the incumbent Labour government. Party leader evaluations mattered too. The more negative voters felt about Tony Blair, other things being equal, the less likely they were to vote Labour rather than to vote for another party. The more positive people felt about Michael Howard, the more likely they were to vote Conservative rather than Labour, with positive feelings about Charles Kennedy raising the chances of voting Liberal Democrat rather than Labour.

Party identification was the single most important factor in accounting for vote choice, though the next most important was the valence measures (Table 25.3, final column). Political identity still matters. However, if (as Fiorina and others suggest) party identification is a running tally of party performance evaluations, then it is a summary of valence, not a measure of long-term identity. To find out, we model pre-election party identifications as a function of the other variables employed in the analysis of 2005 vote choice.

Table 25.4 Modelling party identification at the 2005 general election: multinomial logit

	Party identification (versus no party ID)				Chi-square[a]
	Labour	Conservative	Liberal Democrat	Other	
Constant	−3.12	−4.59	−5.29	−0.84	
Identity and demographics					
Respondent age group	0.16**	0.11**	0.14**	0.08	20.38
Respondent class	0.07	−0.17**	0.03	−0.04	27.60
Respondent education	0.06	−0.01	0.10	0.03	1.81
Respondent gender	−0.13	−0.02	−0.10	−0.21	1.60
Political ideology					
Tax and spend scale	0.21**	0.01	0.17**	0.10	47.74
Left-right scale	−1.04*	0.53**	−0.08	−0.24**	212.48
Valence issues					
Personal economic expectations	0.21*	0.16	0.10	−0.11	11.44
Feelings about Tony Blair	0.42**	−0.15**	0.02	−0.01	477.55
Feelings about Michael Howard	−0.16**	0.54**	0.05	−0.01	338.06
Feelings about Charles Kennedy	−0.04	−0.13**	0.51**	0.19**	231.81
Model improvement		1892.02			
Model significance		0.00			
% correctly classified		60.8			
Nagelkerke R^2		0.60			
N		2260			

* Significant at $p = 0.05$; ** significant at $p = 0.01$.
[a] This column gives the difference in −2 log likelihood between the final model and a model omitting the indicated variable.

Source: 2005 British Election Study.

The likelihood of identifying with a major party increased with age, the only demographic factor to have a general effect (Table 25.4). There was a class dimension in identification with the Conservatives: the more working class a person, the less likely he or she was to identify with the Conservatives in 2005 compared to identifying with no party at all. But this does not suggest a return of class voting: no equivalent effect was found for Labour identification. That aside, the main factors underlying respondents' party identifications were ideological and valence based. The relative ideological positions of voters for each party match the parties' own relative positions (Budge 1999). The more left-wing an individual on each of the ideology scales, the more likely he or she was to identify with Labour. Conservative identifiers were relatively right-wing on the left–right self-placement scale (those identifying with the minor parties were relatively to the left on this scale), and Liberal Democrat identifiers were relatively to the left on the tax and spend scale. Turning to valence measures, the more confident respondents felt about their personal economic prospects in the future, the more likely they were to identify with Labour (though this had no bearing on identification with other parties). And positive feelings towards a party leader resulted in a greater probability of identifying with his party, and a lesser probability of identifying with his rivals' parties. The final column in the table shows that by far the major factors underlying party identification were political ideology and feelings towards the party leaders. Partisanship is influenced by valence issues.

25.4 ELECTORAL PARTICIPATION

The rise of valence as an explanation of voting in Britain has coincided with the growth of concern over falling electoral turnout. Whereas in the 1950s, around 80 per cent of British voters regularly took part in general elections, only around 60 per cent did so in the 2000s, raising anxieties over the representativeness of election results. To some extent, the shift from identity to valence politics outlined above is implicated in turnout decline. As we have seen, turnout is highest among those with the strongest party identifications. Even in 2005, only 9 per cent of very strong identifiers abstained, compared to 42 per cent of those with no partisan identification, figures very similar to those quoted above for 1964. But, of course, far fewer voters were strong partisans, and far more were non-partisan at the later election than the earlier. As fewer voters over time identify strongly with political parties, and more identify with no party at all, electoral participation falls (Heath 2007).

Political failure in the 1970s was one of the triggers of partisan dealignment. Similar concerns regarding growing public disenchantment with politics are now widespread (e.g. Mulgan 1994; Stoker 2006; Hay 2007). So has the shift from identity to valence politics been inimical for electoral participation? The picture is somewhat more

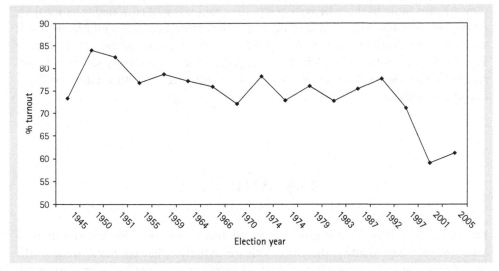

Fig. 25.3 Turnout at British general elections since 1945

complex than this suggests, however: there is both good and bad news for those concerned by rising abstention.

First, the good news: it is too often forgotten that abstention was relatively low at most post-war British general elections (Figure 25.3). It was only in 2001 and 2005 that turnout fell below the normal post-war range. One of the best predictors of electoral turnout between the 1950s and late 1990s was the closeness of the election: the tighter the contest, the higher the turnout (Heath and Taylor 1999; Pattie and Johnston 2001). Even the low turnout of 1997, much commented on at the time, was completely explicable when the size of Labour's pre-election lead over the Conservatives and the perceived ideological closeness of the two main parties at that election are taken into account. The decline of identity politics and the rise of valence pre-date by some decades the rapid rise in abstention since 1997.

Furthermore, the relationship between competitiveness and turnout (also observable at the level of individual constituencies: Denver and Hands 1997; Johnston and Pattie 2006) implies that the rational, evaluative mindset at the heart of valence politics can actually encourage participation. Electors are more likely to vote when their participation is more likely to make a difference than when the result is a certainty. A Labour victory was almost guaranteed at each British general election between 1997 and 2005, hardly conditions conducive to high turnouts. From this perspective, a return to more competitive elections should generate a rise in turnout—especially if the major parties are perceived as offering distinctive programmes. In any case, the evidence on growing political disenchantment is ambiguous. Politicians are distrusted and disliked but levels of public interest in politics have not changed dramatically for decades (Clarke et al. 2004).

There is bad news too, however. Abstention is not randomly distributed across the electorate: non-voters are not only less likely to be strong partisans than voters, they are also more likely to be younger, poorer, and less well educated (Denver 1995; Pattie and Johnston 2001; Clarke et al. 2004). Abstention becomes an ingrained habit too: the more elections individuals abstain from, the more likely they are to abstain again in future contests (Franklin 2004). Rising abstention among younger voters at recent elections suggests fewer electors in future will have the voting habit, hardly an encouraging sign.

25.5 AND YET

British electoral behaviour is now influenced much more by valence issues than by class and partisan identity, therefore. Valence matters: what counts is what works (or at least, what is perceived to work). However, this is not quite the last word. Recent research has questioned valence politics. Evans and Andersen (2006) argue voters view the economy through the lens of their party preferences, not vice versa. If I support the party in power, I am more likely to think the economy is performing well: if I don't approve of the governing party, however, I am more likely to think the economy is performing badly. Their analysis of BES panel data between 1992 and 1997 demonstrates that once prior support for the (incumbent) Conservatives is taken into account, economic evaluations played no role in explaining party choice.

If true, this reinstates the importance of political identity and suggests the effects of valence issues are overstated. However, trends in economic evaluations follow trends in the real economy in sensible ways, irrespective of party support (Lewis-Beck 2006). While some voters do evaluate valence issues in the light of their party preferences, others do not—and it is these swing voters who have the potential to shape election results. Comparative research on economic voting in Europe suggests that economic conditions affect elections through their impacts on party preferences, and in particular on the likelihood of individuals voting for particular parties (Brug, Eijk, and Franklin 2007). A worsening economy may make voters a little less likely to vote for one party and a little more likely to vote for another—but if that pushes enough voters from one camp to the other, it will affect the election result, even if most voters stay with their original preference. Valence still matters.

A further complication lies in the conceptualization of identity. The discussion so far has examined class and partisanship. However, the impetus for the recent upsurge of interest in identity politics comes from the recognition that Britain is a multicultural society (Kenny 2004; Parekh 2008). What are the electoral implications?

Surveys from the 1970s to the 1990s routinely showed that between around 70 per cent and 85 per cent of Black and Minority Ethnic (BME) voters supported Labour (Saggar 1998). Ironically, this fact, and the assumption that BME voters tend to be most concentrated in safe Labour seats, has limited academic (and political party) interest in their party choices. The accepted wisdom has been that the BME vote is unlikely to change and hence of little interest. Where the parties have, in the past, taken an interest, they have tended to assume BME voters are interested primarily in terms of racism and race relations (Saggar 1998: 27).

However, these are serious misjudgements. First, much of the reason for Labour's success here reflects the socio-economic marginalization of many in BME communities—Labour's traditional role as the party of the economic underdog assists it. But more importantly, treating the BME vote as a fixed bloc underestimates the diversity of interests and ideals within the BME 'community'. A very clear indication of this came in the 2007 general election, when Labour saw its vote fall dramatically in previous strongholds with relatively large proportions of Muslim voters, in most places largely as a consequence of the Liberal Democrats' campaign against the government's controversial stance on the Iraq War (Norris and Wlezien 2005). Perhaps the most dramatic example was in Bethnal Green and Bow, however; in a seat with many voters of Bengali Muslim origin, the incumbent Labour MP was defeated by the anti-Iraq War Respect Party candidate, George Galloway.

Does BME voting mark a return of identity politics in the electoral arena? The jury remains out on the wider case of BME support for Labour. As noted above, some of the reasons for this support rest on social and economic factors, not identity. The recent defection of Muslim voters from Labour is more complex, however. It seems clear that individuals' Muslim identifications were important: the war in Iraq was all too readily presented as a war against Islam. However, there is also a valence perspective. Iraq represents one of the most controversial, and arguably least successful, postwar British foreign policy initiatives. What could be more 'valence' than to punish a government for such a (perceived) failure?

25.6 IDENTITY AND VOTING WITHIN THE UK

Throughout this chapter we have discussed the British electorate as a whole. Over recent decades, however, the sense of British identity has declined, particularly among younger generations, and is being replaced by stronger identification with the constituent nations of the UK (Tilley and Heath 2007). This has contributed to cleavages around national identity in Scotland, Wales, and Northern Ireland.

One of those cleavage systems is longer established than the others. Since the creation of Northern Ireland in 1922, voting at all elections there—including UK general elections as well those as to the devolved Assembly—has been based on the province's main identity divide, between parties which strongly advocate retention of the union of Northern Ireland with Great Britain (most importantly the Ulster

Unionist and Democratic Unionist parties) and those (notably the Social Democratic and Labour Party and Sinn Féin) which advocate union of Northern Ireland with the Republic of Ireland. This cleavage is very strongly associated with Northern Ireland's major religious divide: Protestants overwhelmingly support the unionist parties whereas Roman Catholics similarly are associated with the nationalist and republican parties (Tonge 2005).

The 1970s saw a resurgence of nationalist sentiment in Scotland and Wales. Both the Scottish National Party (SNP) and Plaid Cymru have sought to mobilize support throughout their relevant country, but have had more success with some groups and in some areas than others. Reflecting the importance of language for Welsh nationalism, Plaid Cymru have found most support among Welsh-speaking voters in north-west Wales but has struggled in largely monoglot English-speaking South Wales, where Labour traditionally dominates (Balsom, Madgwick, and Van Echelon 1983; Wyn Jones, Scully, and Tristran 2002). However, following devolution, Plaid made some inroads into those South Wales Labour heartlands in Assembly elections, appealing increasingly to voters disaffected with New Labour (Wyn Jones and Scully 2006). At the 2007 Assembly election, Plaid came a strong second to Labour in such iconic Labour seats as Caerphilly, Rhondda, Cynon Valley, and Neath.

Unlike Wales, Scotland enjoyed a significant degree of autonomy within the United Kingdom since Union in 1707. That notwithstanding, for much of the nineteenth and twentieth centuries most Scots supported the Union and Scottish independence was the preserve of the political fringes (Colley 1992; Bennie, Brand, and Mitchell 1997). But from the late 1960s onwards, however, electoral support for the SNP grew significantly, following economic decline and the discovery of significant oil reserves in the North Sea. The former helped weaken support for the Union while the latter provided the promise of an economically viable independent Scotland. By the 1974 elections, around a quarter of Scottish voters supported the SNP.

National identity is associated with party choice in Scotland and Wales—though it is complicated somewhat by the many-faceted nature of identity (Bennie, Brand, and Mitchell 1997; Brown et al. 1999; Paterson et al. 2001). There is no simple binary divide in Scotland between those who consider themselves Scots and those who identify with Britain: most Scots feel both British and Scottish. While a quarter of respondents to the 2007 Scottish Election Study felt completely Scottish, over 60 per cent felt both Scottish and British; 7 per cent felt completely British (the remainder had some other national identity: Table 25.5). Voting in the 2007 Scottish parliament election (as in previous elections in Scotland) followed national identity. Whereas half of those who felt wholly Scottish voted SNP, only 7 per cent of those who felt wholly British did so. The groups most likely to vote Labour, meanwhile, were those who felt both British and Scottish. And the more British (and hence less Scottish) voters felt, the more likely they were to vote Conservative.

As with BME voting, however, voting in Scotland, Wales, and Northern Ireland is not just about identity. Valence matters too. For instance, a substantial surge in support for the SNP at the 2007 Scottish parliament election ended Labour's long dominance of Scottish politics. The SNP emerged (narrowly) as the largest party

Table 25.5 National identity and the regional vote at the 2007 Scottish parliament election

	% national identity (column percentages)	% regional vote (row percentages)					
		Abstain	Conservative	Labour	Lib Dem	SNP	Other
Scottish not British	25.1	19.6	1.6	12.1	4.0	50.8	11.8
More Scottish than British	30.0	22.0	5.9	18.0	8.4	29.3	16.4
Equally British and Scottish	25.9	17.5	15.3	25.7	12.7	15.1	13.8
More British than Scottish	5.4	25.0	25.0	23.8	8.8	5.0	12.5
British not Scottish	7.4	24.1	22.2	10.2	18.5	7.4	17.6
Other	6.4	27.4	16.8	10.5	9.5	14.7	21.1

Source: 2007 Scottish Election Study.

in Holyrood, with a third of the vote and forty-seven MSPs. However, this did not mark a sudden increase in the proportion of the electorate espousing a Scottish identity: the proportions in 2007 were very similar to responses ten years earlier, when the SNP won only 22 per cent of the Scottish vote in the 1997 UK general election. But a major contributor to the SNP surge was growing dissatisfaction with the record of the Labour-controlled Scottish Executive (Johns et al. 2009). The new SNP-led Executive will, in its turn, undoubtedly be judged on its performance.

25.7 CONCLUSIONS

British voting studies have moved against the grain, leaving behind an interest in identity as other areas of politics embrace it. The cases of BME and nationalist voting notwithstanding, the new accepted wisdom in the field is that identity is now much less important than evaluations of government performance. Indeed, valence issues have always (or at least as far back as good survey evidence will stretch—to the early 1960s) been important in UK elections (Clarke et al. 2004). Voters weigh up what they see before them and vote, or abstain, accordingly. Delivery and success are rewarded; failure is punished. To that extent, British elections still fulfil the role implied for them in standard democratic theory: they hold Britain's governments to account.

REFERENCES

ABRAMSON, P. R. 1992. 'Of Time and Partisan Instability in Britain'. *British Journal of Political Science*, 22: 381–95.

ALT, F. J. 1979. *The Politics of Economic Decline*. Cambridge: Cambridge University Press.

BALSOM, D., MADGWICK, P. J., and VAN ECHELON, D. 1983. 'The Red and the Green: Patterns of Partisan Choice in Wales'. *British Journal of Political Science*, 13: 299–325.

BARTLE, J., and CREWE, I. 2002. 'The Impact of Party Leaders in Britain: Strong Assumptions, Weak Evidence'. In A. King (ed.), *Leaders' Personalities and the Outcomes of Democratic Elections*. Oxford: Oxford University Press.

BENNIE, L., BRAND, J., and MITCHELL, J. 1997. *How Scotland Votes: Scottish Parties and Elections*. Manchester: Manchester University Press.

BROWN, A., MCCRONE, D., PATERSON, L., and SURRIDGE, P. 1999. *The Scottish Electorate: The 1997 General Election and Beyond*. Basingstoke: Macmillan.

BRUG, W. VAN DER, EIJK, C. VAN DER, and FRANKLIN, M. 2007. *The Economy and the Vote: Economic Conditions and Elections in Fifteen Countries*. Cambridge: Cambridge University Press.

BUDGE, I. 1999. 'Party Policy and Ideology: Reversing the 1950s?' In G. Evans and P. Norris (eds.), *Critical Elections: British Parties and Elections in Long-Term Perspective*. London: Sage.

BUTLER, D., and STOKES, D. 1969. *Political Change in Britain: Forces Shaping Electoral Choice*. London: Macmillan.

CAMPBELL, A., CONVERSE, P., MILLER, W., and STOKES, D. 1960. *The American Voter*. New York: John Wiley and Sons.

CLARKE, H. D., MISHLER, W., and WHITELEY, P. 1990. 'Recapturing the Falklands: Models of Conservative Popularity, 1979–1983'. *British Journal of Political Science*, 20: 63–81.

—— and STEWART, M. C. 1992. 'The (Un)importance of Party Leaders: Leader Images and Party Choice in the 1987 British Election'. *Journal of Politics*, 54: 447–70.

—— —— 1995. 'Economic Evaluations, Prime Ministerial Approval, and Governing Party Support: Rival Models Reconsidered'. *British Journal of Political Science*, 25: 145–70.

—— —— and WHITELEY, P. F. 1997. 'Tory Trends: Party Identification and the Dynamics of Conservative Support since 1992'. *British Journal of Political Science*, 27: 299–331.

—— —— —— 1998. 'New Models for New Labour: The Political Economy of Labour Party Support, January 1992–April 1997'. *American Political Science Review*, 92: 559–75.

—— SANDERS, D., STEWART, M. C., and WHITELEY, P. 2004. *Political Choice in Britain*. Oxford: Oxford University Press.

COLLEY, L. 1992. *Britons: Forging the Nation 1707–1837*. New Haven, Conn.: Yale University Press.

COX, K. R. 1970. 'Geography, Social Contexts and Voting Behavior in Wales, 1861–1951'. Pp. 117–59 in E. Allardt and S. Rokkan (eds.), *Mass Politics*. New York: Free Press.

CREWE, I. 1986. 'On the Death and Resurrection of Class Voting: Some Comments on How Britain Votes'. *Political Studies*, 35: 620–38.

—— 1988. 'Has the Electorate Become Thatcherite?' In R. Skidelsky (ed.), *Thatcherism*. London: Chatto and Windus.

—— and KING, A. 1995. *SDP: The Birth, Life, and Death of the Social Democratic Party*. Oxford: Oxford University Press.

—— SÄRLVIK, B., and ALT, J. 1977. 'Partisan Dealignment in Britain, 1964–1974'. *British Journal of Political Science*, 7: 129–90.

DENVER, D. 1995. 'Non-voting in Britain'. In J. Font and R. Virós (eds.), *Electoral Participation in Europe*. Barcelona: Institut de Ciènces Polítiques I Socials.

—— and HANDS, G. 1997. 'Turnout'. In P. Norris and N. T. Gavin (eds.), *Britain Votes 1997*. Oxford: Oxford University Press.

DUNLEAVY, P. 1979. 'The Urban Basis of Political Alignment: Social Class, Domestic Property Ownership and State Intervention in Consumption Processes'. *British Journal of Political Science*, 9: 409–43.

—— and HUSBANDS, C. 1983. *British Democracy at the Crossroads: Voting and Party Competition in the 1980s*. London: George Allen and Unwin.

ERIKSON, R. S., MacKUEN, M. B., and STIMSON, J. A. 1998. 'What Moves Macropartisanship? A Response to Green, Palmquist and Schickler'. *American Poltiical Science Review*, 92: 901–12.

—— —— —— 2000. 'Bankers or Peasants Revisited: Economic Expectations and Presidential Approval'. *Electoral Studies*, 19: 295–312.

EVANS, G., and ANDERSEN, R. 2006. 'The Political Conditioning of Economic Perceptions'. *Journal of Politics*, 68: 194–207.

FRANKLIN, M. 1985. *The Decline of Class Voting in Britain*. Oxford: Oxford University Press.

—— 2004. *Voter Turnout and the Dynamics of Electoral Competition in Established Democracies since 1945*. Cambridge: Cambridge University Press.

FIORINA, M. 1981. *Retrospective Voting in American National Elections*. New Haven, Conn.: Yale University Press.

GAMBLE, A. 2005. 'The Meaning of the Third Way'. In A. Seldon and D. Kavanagh (eds.), *The Blair Effect, 2001–5*. Cambridge: Cambridge University Press.

GIDDENS, A. 1998. *The Third Way: The Renewal of Social Democracy*. Cambridge: Polity.

GOLDTHORPE, J., LOCKWOOD, D., BECHHOFER, F., and PLATT, J. 1968. *The Affluent Worker: Political Attitudes and Behaviour*. Cambridge: Cambridge University Press.

GOODHART, C. A. E., and BANSALI, R. J. 1970. 'Political Economy'. *Political Studies*, 18: 43–106.

HAY, C. 2007. *Why We Hate Politics*. Cambridge: Polity.

HEATH, A., JOWELL, R., and CURTICE, J. 1985. *How Britain Votes*. Oxford: Pergamon Press.

—— —— —— 2001. *The Rise of New Labour: Party Policies and Voter Choices*. Oxford: Oxford University Press.

—— and TAYLOR, B. 1999. 'New Sources of Abstention?' In G. Evans and P. Norris (eds.), *Critical Elections: British Parties and Voters in Long-Term Perspective*. London: Sage.

HEATH, O. 2007. 'Explaining Turnout Decline in Britain, 1964–2005: Party Identification and the Political Context'. *Political Behaviour*, 29: 493–516.

HOBSBAWM, E. 1981. *The Forward March of Labour Halted?* London: Verso.

JESSOP, B. 1974. *Traditionalism, Conservatism and British Political Culture*. London: Allen and Unwin.

JOHNS, R., MITCHELL, J., DENVER, D., and PATTIE, C. 2009. 'Valence Politics in Scotland: Towards an Explanation of the 2007 Election'. *Political Studies*, 57: 207–33.

JOHNSTON, R. J., and PATTIE, C. J. 1988. 'Are We Really All Alliance Nowadays? Discriminating by Discriminant Analysis'. *Electoral Studies*, 7: 27–32.

—— —— 2001. 'Dimensions of Retrospective Voting: Economic Performance, Public Service Standards and Conservative Party Support at the 1997 British General Election'. *Party Politics*, 7: 469–90.

—— —— 2006. *Putting Voters in their Place: Geography and Elections in Great Britain*. Oxford: Oxford University Press.

KENNY, M. 2004. *The Politics of Identity: Liberal Theory and the Dilemmas of Difference*. Cambridge: Polity.

KING, A. 1975. 'Overload: Problems of Governing in the 1970s'. *Political Studies*, 23: 284–96.

LEWIS-BECK, M. 1988. *Economics and Elections: The Major Western Democracies*. Ann Arbor: University of Michigan Press.

LEWIS-BECK, M. 2006. 'Does Economics Still Matter? Econometrics and the Vote'. *Journal of Politics*, 68: 208–12.

—— and PALDAM, M. 2000. 'Economic Voting: An Introduction'. *Electoral Studies*, 19: 113–21.

LIPSET, S. M., and ROKKAN, S. E. 1967. 'Cleavage Structures, Party Systems and Voter Alignments'. Pp. 3–64 in S. M. Lipset and S. E. Rokkan (eds.), *Party Systems and Voter Alignments*. New York: Free Press.

MCKENZIE, R., and SILVER, A. 1968. *Angels in Marble: Working Class Conservatives in Urban England*. London: Heinemann.

MACKUEN, M. B., ERIKSON, R. S., and STIMSON, J. A. 1989. 'Macropartisanship'. *American Political Science Review*, 83: 1125–42.

—— —— 1992. 'Peasants or Bankers? The American Electorate and the US Economy'. *American Political Science Review*, 86: 597–611.

MULGAN, G. 1994. *Politics in an Antipolitical Age*. Cambridge: Polity.

NEWBY, H. 1979. *The Deferential Worker: A Study of Farm Workers in East Anglia*. Harmondsworth: Penguin.

NORRIS, P., and WLEZIEN, C. 2005. 'The Third Blair Victory: How and Why'. *Parliamentary Affairs*, 58: 657–83.

PAREKH, B. 2008. *A New Politics of Identity: Political Principles for an Interdependent World*. Basingstoke: Palgrave Macmillan.

PATERSON, L., BROWN, A., CURTICE, J., HINDS, K., MCCRONE, D., PARK, A., SPROSTON, K., and SURRIDGE, P. 2001. *New Scotland, New Politics?* Edinburgh: Polygon.

PATTIE, C. J., and JOHNSTON, R. J. 2001. 'A Low Turnout Landslide: Abstention at the British General Election of 1997'. *Political Studies*, 49: 286–305.

PULZER, P. G. J. 1967. *Political Representation and Elections in Britain*. London: George Allen and Unwin.

ROSE, R., and MCALLISTER, I. 1986. *Voters Begin to Choose: From Closed-Class to Open Elections in Britain*. London: Sage.

SAGGAR, S. 1998. 'Analyzing Race and Elections in British Politics: Some Conceptual and Theoretical Issues'. In S. Saggar (ed.), *Race and British Electoral Politics*. London: UCL Press.

SANDERS, D. 1991. 'Government Popularity and the Next General Election'. *Political Quarterly*, 62: 235–61.

—— 1998. 'The New Electoral Battleground'. In A. King (ed.), *New Labour Triumphs: Britain at the Polls*. Chatham, NJ: Chatham House Press.

—— 1999. 'Conservative Incompetence, Labour Responsibility and the Feelgood Factor: Why the Economy Failed to Save the Conservatives in 1997'. *Electoral Studies*, 18: 251–70.

—— 2005. 'Popularity Function Forecast for the 2005 UK General Election'. *British Journal of Politics and International Relations*, 7: 174–90.

—— 2006. 'Reflections on the 2005 General Election: Can the Tories Win Next Time?' *British Politics*, 1: 170–94.

—— WARD, H., and MARSH, D. 1987. 'Government Popularity and the Falklands War: A Reassessment'. *British Journal of Political Science*, 17: 281–313.

SÄRLVIK, B., and CREWE, I. 1983. *Decade of Dealignment: The Conservative Victory of 1979 and Electoral Trends in the 1979*. Cambridge: Cambridge University Press.

SELDON, A. 1994. 'Conservative Century'. Pp. 17–65 in A. Seldon and S. Ball (eds.), *Conservative Century: The Conservative Party since 1900*. Oxford: Oxford University Press.

STOKER, G. 2006. *Why Politics Matters: Making Democracy Work*. Basingstoke: Palgrave Macmillan.

TILLEY, J., and HEATH, A. 2007. 'The Decline of British National Pride'. *British Journal of Sociology*, 58: 661–78.

TONGE, J. 2005. 'Northern Ireland: Meltdown of the Moderates or the Redistribution of Moderation?' In A. Geddes and J. Tonge (eds.), *Britain Decides: the UJ General Election 2005*. Basingstoke: Palgrave Macmillan.

WYN JONES, R., and SCULLY, R. 2006. 'Devolution and Electoral Politics in Scotland and Wales'. *Publius: The Journal of Federalism*, 36: 115–34.

—————— and TRISTRAN, D. 2002. 'Why Do the Conservatives Always Do (Even) Worse in Wales?' Pp. 229–45 in L. Bennie, C. Rallings, J. Tonge, and P. Webb (eds.), *British Elections and Parties Review 12*. London: Frank Cass.

CHAPTER 26

ETHNICITY AND RELIGION

TARIQ MODOOD

THE settlement in Britain of new population groups from outside Europe (principally from the Caribbean, South Asia, and Africa) has made manifest certain kinds of racisms in Britain, and anti-discrimination laws and policies began to be put into place from the 1960s. These laws and policies, initially influenced by contemporary thinking and practice in relation to anti-black racism in the US, assumed till recently that the dominant post-immigration issue was 'colour-racism' (Rex and Moore 1967; CCCS 1982; Sivanandan 1985; Gilroy 1987). This perspective was epigrammatically expressed by the writer Salman Rushdie: 'Britain is now two entirely different worlds and the one you inherit is determined by the colour of your skin' (Rushdie 1982). An alternative view would be that the new populations are best understood as a racialized ethno-religious diversity, though this has only become apparent as the settlements have matured and the minorities have become political actors. The accounting of this perspectival change, and the understanding of ethno-religious minority politics today, requires reviewing the breaking-up of the assumptions of the earlier period.

Till late 2003, it was lawful, except in Northern Ireland, to discriminate against religious minorities unless they were recognized as ethnic groups within the meaning of the law. The latter was the case with Jews and Sikhs but the courts did not accept that Muslims are an ethnic group and so it was possible, for example, to deny a Muslim a job qua Muslim. In such a circumstance, Muslims only had some limited indirect legal protection qua members of ethnic groups such as Pakistanis, Arabs, and so on. It was only in 2003, nearly four decades since legislation on 'race', that an offence of religious discrimination was created, though even then it was confined to employment until 2007. Even before issues of international terrorism and foreign affairs intruded into domestic matters, religion in the form of Muslim politics was becoming central to minority–majority relations. No mainstream politician ever desired, let alone anticipated, this. So, how has it happened? While initially unremarked upon, the long-standing exclusive focus on race and ethnicity, and the exclusion of Muslims but not Jews and Sikhs, came to be a source of resentment amongst some Muslims. At the same time the analyses, campaigns, policies, and legislation associated with racial and ethnic equality and diversity were the principal source of precedence and legitimacy as Muslim activists began to make political claims upon British society and the polity. In short, one of the principal ways of seeing the emergence and development of ethno-religious equality is in terms of a grievance of exclusion from the existing equality framework and its utilization in order to extend it to address the felt exclusion and to develop and seek public recognition for a minority subjectivity ignored by liberal legislators.

26.1 THE RISE AND FALL OF POLITICAL BLACKNESS

The initial development of anti-racism in Britain followed the American pattern, and indeed was directly influenced by American personalities and events. Just as in the USA the colour-blind humanism of Martin Luther King Jnr. came to be mixed with an emphasis on black pride, black autonomy, and black nationalism as typified by Malcolm X, so also in the UK (both these inspirational leaders visited Britain). The minorities' politics, the cutting-edge anti-racism that developed in Britain in the 1970s and early 1980s, first in radical activism and ultra-left corpuscles then, following the Brixton riots of 1981, in some local government, trade unions, radical public-sector professional associations, and the Labour Party, was based on a concept of political blackness. The British population was divided into two groups, black and white. The former consisted of all those people who were potential victims of colour racism, though in both theory and practice they were assumed disproportionately to have the characteristics of the African-Caribbean population (Modood 1994). Thus a fundamental problem for political blackness came from an internal ambivalence, namely whether blackness as a political identity was sufficiently distinct from and could mobilize without blackness as an ethnic pride movement of people of African descent. This black identity movement, in a growing climate of opinion favourable to identity politics of various kinds, was successful in shifting the terms of the debate from colour-blind individualistic assimilation to questions about how white British society had to change to accommodate new groups. But its success in imposing or making a singular identity upon or out of a (unlike black America or South Africa) diverse ethnic minority population was temporary or illusory. What it did was pave the way to a plural ethnic assertiveness, as South Asian groups, including Muslims, borrowed the logic of ethnic pride and tried to catch up with the success of a newly legitimized black public identity. Indeed, it is best to see this development of racial explicitness and positive blackness as part of a wider socio-political climate which is not confined to race and culture or non-white minorities. Feminism, gay pride, Quebecois nationalism, and the revival of Scottishness are some prominent examples of these new identity movements which have come to be an important feature in many countries, especially those in which class politics has declined.

This political movement has played an important part in opening up the question of 'race' in Britain and has come to define the identity of many people (especially at its height in the mid to late 1980s). Whether at any point this political identity was embraced by the majority of South Asians or Muslims is an open question (I personally think not: Modood 1994). Two things however are clear. Firstly, this identity was embraced by some Asian political activists in the 1980s, especially those whose activism was concerned with mainstream British society rather than the organization of communities of Asian descent. Secondly, from the late 1980s onwards, if not earlier, most Asians were emphasizing a more particular ethnic or religious identity rather than this all-inclusive non-whiteness. Several factors were at play here. For example, time, numbers, and confidence. As the Asian communities became more settled and thought of themselves less as sojourners, as they put down familial and community roots, and as some Asian groups, especially African Asians, began to acquire a prosperity and respectability that most Asians sought, they began to express their 'own' identities rather than the borrowed identity of blackness, with its inescapable African-Caribbean resonances. Movements outside the UK were relevant (for example, the Sikh battle for Khalistan, the growth of Hindu cultural nationalism, the rise of Islamism in various parts of the world). Additionally, a certain multicultural climate played an important part in encouraging people to define and publicly project themselves in terms of authenticity, 'difference', and victimhood and gave them the confidence to reject opposing arguments (such as that newly settled groups should be seen and not heard; that when in Rome do as the Romans do).

A key measure/indicator of racial discrimination and inequality has been numerical under-representation in prestigious jobs, public office, etc. Hence people have had to be (self-)classified and counted, and so group labels, and arguments about which labels are authentic, have become a common feature of certain political discourses. Over the years it has also become apparent that by these inequality measures it is Asian Muslims, and not African-Caribbeans, as policy-makers had originally expected, who have emerged as the most disadvantaged and poorest groups in the country (Modood et al. 1997). To many Muslim activists the misplacing of Muslims into 'race' categories and the belatedness with which the severe disadvantages of the Pakistanis and Bangladeshis came to be recognized by policy-makers meant, at best, that race relations were an inappropriate policy niche for Muslims (UKACIA 1993) and, at worst, that it was seen as a conspiracy to prevent the emergence of a specifically Muslim socio-political formation (Muslim Parliament 1992).

26.2 OUT OF RACE: ETHNICITY
AND MUSLIM HONOUR

So, in relation to both identity issues and socio-economic disadvantage, a white–black analysis of Britain was becoming unsatisfactory and being challenged by some of those for whom the designation 'black' was meant to be self-illuminating and emancipatory. Indeed, political blackness was unravelling at a grass-roots level at the very time that it was becoming hegemonic as a race relations discourse in British public life (the 1980s; see Modood 1994).[1] Two important events also show the ways in which practical action in relation to 'colour' was being ethno-religionized.

One was a religion-based political campaign which ran alongside, perhaps even preceded, political blackness and which had a significant effect in shaping the practice of racial equality. In the 1960s on a number of occasions Sikhs found themselves in conflict with employers, such as bus companies, who disallowed the wearing of the turban as contravening uniform requirements (Singh 2005). Sikhs responded by organizing strikes, demonstrations, street processions, appealing to their MPs, and so on and the general pattern of resolutions consisted of employers allowing the turban but within stipulated uniform colour schemes. Sikhs also fought a national campaign against section 32 of the Road Traffic Act (1972), which enforced the requirement of protective head gear when travelling on a motor-cycle. They achieved an amendment in the Motor-Cycle Crash Helmets (Religious Exemption) Act (1976) which declared that it 'shall not apply to followers of the Sikh religion while he is wearing a turban' (quoted in Poulter 1998: 297). An interesting feature of these campaigns was that they were mainly Sikh-only affairs: Sikhs did not attempt to mobilize other minorities and the campaigns were not integrated into a general anti-discrimination struggle. Moreover, the concessions that the Sikhs were granted were understood in terms of respect for religious conscience or duty. However, their most important victory intersected with the evolving racial equality framework. The 1976 Race Relations Act, borrowing from American legislation, widened the concept of discrimination by introducing the concept of 'indirect discrimination', while at the same time defining a 'racial group' by reference to 'colour, race, nationality or ethnic or national origins'. When a Sikh schoolboy was sent home by his headmaster for refusing to conform to the school uniform regulations by not taking off his turban, a case of racial discrimination was filed. The dispute went all the way to the House of Lords, who decided that racial discrimination had taken place. The school's uniform policy made no reference to any racial groups but it indirectly, even if unintentionally, had a greater adverse impact on Sikhs than on other groups and so was indirect discrimination if it could be shown that Sikhs were a racial group. The Lords recognized that

---

[1] The single most notable achievement for political blackness and its high-water mark was getting five Black Sections candidates selected for safe or winnable Labour seats in 1986–7, four of whom got elected as MPs in the general election of 1987. On an alternative reading the arrival of political blackness in local government and Westminster marked its 'degradation' and an 'end of anti-racism' (Sivanandan 1985; Gilroy 1990; Ali 1991; and James Hampshire, this volume).

the Sikhs were a religious group but argued they were also an 'ethnic group' and therefore a racial group in law (*Mandala v Lee*, 1982). In their opinion there were two essential characteristics of an ethnic group: a long shared history and a cultural tradition of one's own. Arguing however that other characteristics were also relevant, they included: a common geographical origin, or descent from a small number of common ancestors; a common language; a common literature; a common religion; being either a minority or a majority within a larger community. Interestingly, no other religious group has subsequently been recognized as an ethnic group (Muslims and Rastafarians have failed the legal test), and Jews have never had to prove that they are a race, the idea being taken to be self-evident by parliament, the courts, and public opinion. Nevertheless, in this landmark judgment the legal idea of racial equality was extended into the domain of the rights of ethno-religious groups.

Another notable conflict in which racial equality, ethnicity, and religion came to be combined and set an important precedent was 'the Honeyford Affair' (Halstead 1988). Ray Honeyford was headteacher of a Bradford local authority school in which the majority of pupils were of Pakistani descent and Muslim. In a series of articles in 1983–4 in a national right-wing journal, the *Salisbury Review*, he argued that the education of children such as those in his school was being retarded by the cultural and religious practices of their parents, which prevented Pakistani ethnicity children, especially girls, from gaining rapid proficiency in English, from participating in the full curriculum (e.g. in sport, dance, and drama), from socializing with whites, and from succeeding fully in British education and society. He was particularly critical of what he said was the widespread practice of Pakistani parents taking or sending their children to Pakistan for weeks or months at a time, disregarding the duty to observe the school calendar. These comments—many of which were indeed the concerns of educationalists—were presented in an extremely critical, generalizing way that portrayed Pakistani working-class culture and aspects of Islam in a negative way and were augmented by comments about Pakistan as 'obstinately backward', plagued by 'corruption at every level', and the 'heroin capital of the world' (Honeyford 1984). The articles were judged as racist by white anti-racists, locally and nationally, and some secular Asian activists, who initiated a call for Honeyford's resignation, which soon came to be supported by most of the parents and the leading local Muslim organizations, including the Bradford Council of Mosques. The Bradford Pakistani community were stirred up by so much public airing of unflattering comments about them, exacerbated by the distribution of Urdu translations of Honeyford's views by his opponents (Samad 1992: 513). This community, largely of peasant Kashmiri background, culturally conservative, and obedient to their clan and religious leaders, began to stand up for itself against what it perceived to be insults to its culture and to its religious restrictions, especially as they applied to gender and sexuality. Left-wing anti-racists therefore came to mobilize conservative Pakistanis on the issue of community honour and in due course the alliance was successful and Honeyford was pressured into early retirement. The wider and longer-term effect of the alliance and of other local developments of the time was to develop the Pakistani community, especially the mosque leadership, as a political force in Bradford, at the expense of white anti-racists and others rooted in a secular, multi-ethnic coalition, as the former considerably outnumbered the latter (Samad 1992).

Both the turban campaigns, conducted through self-organizations and outside the frame of 'race' but concluding with significant effect upon the meaning of racial equality, and the defence of Pakistani community honour, initially roused by anti-racists but leading to the empowerment and emboldening of an ethno-religious leadership, were, then, actions which showed that Asian religious communities were emerging as political actors within the race landscape and were capable of winning battles. The single event that most dramatically illustrated the emergence of these new forms of ethno-religious actors—with again Bradford a scene of action, and damaged honour a cause of mobilization—was the battle over the novel, *The Satanic Verses* (*SV*), that broke out in 1988–9, with Muslims protesting its portrayal of the Prophet Muhammad and other revered figures. This time the secular anti-racists were virtually absent from the conflict, for while many were sensible to the racial stereotyping and divisions it was causing, they were unhappy that it was fuelled by religious anger. Above all they saw it as a case in which freedom of speech should not be compromised, but reluctant to join in the chorus against Muslims they mainly kept a low profile. On the Muslim side, however, it generated an impassioned activism and mobilization on a scale greater than any previous national campaign against racism (Modood 1990; 2005). Many 'lapsed' or 'passive' Muslims (Muslims, especially, the non-religious, for whom hitherto their Muslim background was not particularly important) (re)discovered a new community solidarity and public identity. This is movingly described by the author Rana Kabbani, whose *Letter to Christendom* begins with a description of herself as 'a woman who had been a sort of underground Muslim before she was forced into the open by the Salman Rushdie affair' (Kabbani 1989: ix). What was striking was that when the public rage against Muslims was at its most intense, Muslims neither sought nor were offered any special solidarity by any non-white minority (even less so than was the case with the Sikh campaigns). It was in fact some white liberal Anglicans that tried to moderate the hostility against the angry Muslims, and it was inter-faith forums rather than political-black organizations that tried to create space where Muslims could state their case without being vilified.[2] Political blackness—seen up to then as the key formation in the politics of post-immigration ethnicity—was seen as irrelevant to an issue which many Muslims insisted was fundamental to defining the kind of 'respect' or 'civility' appropriate to a peaceful multicultural society, that is to say, to the political constitution of 'difference' in Britain (Modood 2005). The *SV* affair, then, divided anti-racists and egalitarians, giving rise to organizations like Women Against Fundamentalists, an offshoot of Southall Black Sisters, who turned up at Muslim demonstrations to publicly express their support for Rushdie. Other egalitarians tried to assimilate Muslim concerns into the equality movement and to some extent this division has

---

[2] The large Fourth Survey found that nominal Christians and those without a religion were more likely to say they were prejudiced against Muslims than those Christians who said their religion was of importance to them (Modood et al. 1997: 134).

since become a feature within the broad politics of 'multiculturalism' in Britain (for an attempt at reconciliation, see Phillips 2007).

26.3 PRIMARY IDENTITIES

This politics, which has meant not just a recognition of a new religious diversity in Britain but a new or renewed policy importance for religion, is based on a sociological fact. Namely, the religion of one's family is the most important source of self-identity amongst South Asian origin people, especially Muslims. The Fourth National Survey of Ethnic Minorities, a large, nationally representative survey conducted in 1994, found that rather than skin colour, which was prominent in the self-descriptions of Caribbeans, it was religion that was prominent in the self-descriptions of South Asians (Modood et al. 1997). This owes as much to a sense of community as to personal faith, but the identification and prioritization of religion is far from just a nominal one. Very few South Asians marry across religious boundaries (indeed the 2001 Census records only 5 per cent of them as even having married someone outside the Asian group, the lowest intermarriage figure of all ethnic groups: ONS 2005). Moreover, most South Asians expect that their children will be inducted into their religion. When a third of Britons were saying they do not have a religion, nearly all South Asians said they have one, and 90 per cent said that religion was of personal importance to them (compared to 13 per cent of whites). While about a quarter of whites attended a place of worship once a month or more, over half of Hindus and seven out of ten Sikhs did so once a month or more, and nearly two-thirds of Muslims attended at least once a week (much higher amongst men than women, for whom congregational worship is not a duty). Even among the young expressions of commitment were exceptionally high: more than a third of Indians and African Asians, and two-thirds of Pakistani and Bangladeshi 16–34-year-olds said that religion was very important, to how they led their lives compared to 5 per cent of whites (though nearly a fifth of Caribbeans took this view). An analysis by logistic regression showed that the longer an individual was resident in Britain (as a proportion of their life) the less likely they were to think religion was very important but the older they were the more likely; yet for all ethnic minority groups the young were less likely to think religion was very important to them (Modood et al. 1997: 305–8). There is some evidence to suggest that a decade later this may no longer be the case, at least for young Muslims. A Channel 4 GfK NOP survey done in Spring 2006 found that 79 per cent of Muslim 16–34-year-olds said that religion was very important to the way they lived their life, slightly more than their elders; and on a number of questions the young were tending to be more 'Islamic' or more 'radical' than their elders (GfK NOP 2006; see also Mirza, Senthilkumaran, and Ja'far 2007, where this generational contrast is even stronger).

There are two important points to make here about these identities, especially Muslim. Firstly, they cannot be characterized as belonging to private life and irrelevant to public policies and resources. For example, half of the Muslims interviewed in the Fourth Survey said that there should be state funding for Muslim schools. Secondly, religious and ethnic identities were not simply an expression of behaviour, of participation in distinctive cultural practices. For, across the generations and in relation to time spent in Britain, there was a noticeable decline in participation in the cultural practices (language, dress, attendance at place of worship, and so on) that go with a particular identity. Yet the decrease in self-identification with a group label (black, Muslim, etc.) was relatively small. That is to say, there are, for example, people in Britain who say of themselves that they are Sikh or Muslim but who may not be at all religious. So, if there is a sense in which 'race' and ethnicity has been 'religionized', it is also the case that for some religion has been ethnicized.

In one sense, there is nothing new or peculiar about the above identification/behaviour distinction (it is common in South Asia and many other parts of the world). In another sense, it marks a new conception of ethno-religious identities. For what we are not talking about are passive or fading identities. That would be to overlook the pride with which they may be asserted, the intensity with which they may be debated, and their capacity to generate community activism and political campaigns. People may still feel passionate about the public recognition and resourcing of aspects of their community identity, even though as individuals they may not wish that resource for themselves. So, for example, the demand for public funding of Muslim schools has been a source of Muslim grievance, with some non-religious as well as religious Muslims highlighting the injustice of a system that funds Christian and Jewish, but not Muslim, schools. Yet in the Fourth Survey only half of those Muslims who supported funding of Muslim schools said that if they had the choice they would prefer to send their own child to a Muslim school; once again, the young were not much less likely to want the funding but were much less likely to want to take up the option for their own (future) children (though young Muslims preferring the option has increased considerably over time; see GfK 2006). Muslim purists might disparage these ambivalences but in fact the success of some Muslim campaigns has partly depended on the political support of the non-fully-religious Muslims, on the extensive as well as the intensive mobilization of the Muslim community. Hence, it would be wrong to think of the non-fully-religious Muslims as only token or 'symbolic' Muslims (Rex 1996: para. 4.13).

26.4 EXPANDING RACIAL EQUALITY TO INCLUDE RELIGIOUS EQUALITY

With the emergence of Muslim political agency through the *SV* affair, the lead national moderate organization, UK Action Committee on Islamic Affairs

(UKACIA), which later broadened out into the Muslim Council of Britain (MCB, founded in 1998), emerged as the most representative, or at least the most effective, grouping of mainstream Muslim organizations and came to be accepted as such by the government and other bodies. It became the chosen interlocutor and as domestic and international crises affecting British Muslims became more frequent and rose up the political agenda it came to have more regular access to senior, up to the very top, policy-makers across Whitehall than any other organization representing a minority, religious, ethnic, or racial, singly or collectively. The MCB's pre-eminence began to suffer from the mid-2000s, as it grew increasingly critical of the invasion of Iraq and of the so-called 'war on terror'. The government started accusing it of failing to clearly and decisively reject extremism and sought alternative Muslim interlocutors.[3] From the early 1990s to that point, UKACIA/MCB lobbied primarily on four issues (UKACIA 1993 and MCB website). The first was mobilizing and getting a Muslim religious community voice, not subsumed under an Asian or black one, heard in the corridors of national and local power, and that UKACIA/MCB should be the voice of that community. Secondly, getting legislation on religious discrimination and incitement to religious hatred. Thirdly, getting socio-economic policies targeted on the severe disadvantage of Bangladeshis, Pakistanis, and other Muslim groups. Finally, getting the state to recognize and resource some Islamic schools.

The legal system, we have noted, left Muslims particularly vulnerable because, while discrimination against yarmulke-wearing Jews and turban-wearing Sikhs was deemed to be unlawful *racial* discrimination, Muslims, unlike these other faith communities, were not deemed to be a racial or ethnic group. Nor were they protected by the legislation against religious discrimination that did exist in one part of the UK: being explicitly designed to protect Catholics, it covers only Northern Ireland. Similarly, incitement to religious hatred was unlawful only in Northern Ireland, while the offence of incitement to racial hatred, which extended protection to certain forms of anti-Jewish literature, did not apply to anti-Muslim literature. After some years of arguing that there was insufficient evidence of religious discrimination, the hand of the British government was forced by Article 13 of the EU Amsterdam Treaty (1999), which includes religious discrimination in the list of the forms of discrimination that all member states are expected to eliminate. Accordingly, the British government, following a European Commission directive that it played a key role in drafting and that many member states have been slow to implement, outlawed religious discrimination in employment, with effect from December 2003. This however, was only a partial 'catching-up' with the existing anti-discrimination provisions in relation to race and gender. While religious discrimination was extended to cover the provision of goods and services in 2007, there is still no duty upon the public sector to take proactive steps to promote religious equality as was created in respect of racial equality by the Race Relations Act (Amendment) Act 2000 and as also exists in relation to gender

---

[3] The government played an active role in encouraging the formation and promotion of alternative national Muslim organizations on the grounds that they were more moderate and representative, especially the Sufi Muslim Council and the British Muslim Forum. With the realization that no single Muslim organization was fully reflective of non-jihadi Muslims, the government seems to have readmitted the MCB back into the fold but now only as part of a plurality.

and disability. Moreover, the government seems unwilling to remedy this within a proposed Single Equalities Act, which is meant to bring together, and at least to some extent 'equalize', the various and differential anti-discrimination legislation that the recent Commission on Equalities and Human Rights has been created to implement.

Muslims, at the time of the *SV* affair, having failed to get the courts to interpret the existing statute on blasphemy to cover offences beyond what Christians hold sacred, came to demand an offence of incitement to religious hatred, mirroring the existing one of incitement to racial hatred. The government inserted such a clause in the post-9/11 security legislation in order to conciliate Muslims, who among others were opposed to the new powers of surveillance, arrest, and detention. As it happened, most of the latter was made law, but the provision on incitement to religious hatred was defeated in parliament. The government continued to have difficulties getting support for such legislation, not least from their own supporters, inside parliament and outside it, where it especially provoked resistance from comedians, intellectuals, and secularists, who feared that satire and criticism of religion was at risk, being mindful of not just Muslim campaigns but a recent case in Birmingham where Sikh protests against the play *Bezhti* had led to some violence and the cessation of further performances (on the latter, Grillo 2007; more generally Meer 2008: 71–80). Finally, parliament passed a bill in early 2006 to protect against incitement to religious hatred. Yet it was only passed after members of both houses of parliament, supported by much of the liberal intelligentsia, forced the government to accept amendments that weakened its initial proposals. Unlike the incitement to religious hatred offence in Northern Ireland, and the incitement to racial hatred offence in the UK, mere offensiveness was not an offence, and moreover the incitement must require the *intention* to stir up hatred. Nevertheless, a controversy shortly after this bill was passed showed that the media was coming voluntarily to restrain itself. This was the case of the Danish Muhammad cartoons, the cartoons being reprinted in several leading European newspapers but not by any major organ in Britain, suggesting there was a greater understanding in Britain about anti-Muslim racism and about not giving gratuitous offence to Muslims than in some other European countries (for a debate reflecting several sides of the issue and how they have divided liberals, see Modood et al. 2006).

There is no prospect at present of religious equality catching up with the importance that employers and other organizations give to sex or race. A potentially significant victory, however, was made when the government agreed to include a religion question in the 2001 Census. This was the first time this question had been included since the inception of the Census in 1851 and was largely unpopular outside the politically active religionists, among whom Muslims were foremost. Nevertheless, it has the potential to pave the way for widespread 'religious monitoring' in the way that the inclusion of an ethnic question in 1991 had led to the more routine use of 'ethnic monitoring'.

In relation to the severity of the disadvantages suffered by Pakistanis and Bangladeshis, the evidence was so overwhelming (the key study was Modood et al. 1997) that the government, especially New Labour, came quickly to accept it and the need to act in relation to it. Most of this was done within the government's general socio-economic policies, e.g. the improvements in the household incomes of the working poor and of poor families with children have been particularly beneficial to deprived communities like the Asian Muslims. Moreover, on most measures of socio-economic disadvantage the government collected and analysed data by ethnic group, and not just by using the undifferentiated 'Asian' figure but by disaggregating Indians (who are relatively well off) from the Pakistanis and Bangladeshis. On some occasions the government came explicitly to target resources and effort at specific ethnic groups. When this was done, for example, in relation to improving educational attainment levels, Bangladeshis and Pakistanis were invariably selected.

Turning to the issue of faith schools, in England over a third of state-maintained primary and a sixth of secondary schools are in fact run by a religious group, though all have had to deliver a centrally determined national curriculum since it was introduced in the 1980s. Some Muslims have been campaigning for certain private Muslim schools to be incorporated into the state sector on the same basis as enjoyed by thousands of Anglican and Catholic schools and some Methodist and Jewish schools. Initially, neither multiculturalists (Swann 1985) nor the Conservative governments were supportive, but New Labour reversed this policy shortly after coming to power and to date eight Muslim schools exist within the state sector (as well as a Sikh and a Seventh Day Adventist school). Some secularists are unhappy about this (and public opinion since 9/11 has shifted in their direction as a consequence of anxiety about Muslim segregation and extremism).[4] As it is politically difficult to fund religious schools in general and simply deny funding to Muslim schools, some who accept the argument for treating all religions equally believe this should be achieved by the state withdrawing its funding from all religious schools. Most Muslim spokepersons reject this form of equality in which the privileged lose something but the underprivileged gain nothing. More specifically, the issue between 'equalizing upwards' and 'equalizing downwards' here is about the legitimacy of religion as a public institutional presence, something clearly important to most Muslims.

These policy demands no doubt seem odd within the terms of, say, the French or US 'wall of separation'. But it is clear that they virtually mirror existing anti-discrimination policy provisions in the UK. In any case, it is important to be clear that in the French case, the issue is not simply secularism but a minority-blindness that repudiates 'race' and ethnicity, no less than religion (Scott 2007). The giving up of pre-French identities and assimilation into French culture is thought to go hand in hand with the acceptance of French citizenship. If for some reason assimilation is not fully embraced—perhaps because some people want to retain pride in their Algerian ancestry, or want to maintain ethnic solidarity in the face of current stigmatization and discrimination—then their claim to be French and equal citizens is jeopardized. In any case, the French approach of ignoring racial, ethnic, and religious identities does not mean that they, or the related problems of exclusion, alienation, and fragmentation, vanish.

For any strong secularist, the single most important issue is to maintain a gap between the state and organized religion. Certainly, this is how secularism is

---

[4] On the lack of association between Muslim state schools and extremism, see Meer (2007).

understood in the USA, where churches can be very powerful political actors but the constitution has a strong 'no establishment clause'. By this measure, it is not at all clear that France is developing a less secularist position than Britain. Britain has two 'established' churches, the Church of Scotland and the Church of England, but it is the latter that most people have in mind when they speak of 'establishment'. In the late 1980s and early 1990s some secular progressives began to argue that the emergence of a multi-faith society meant it was no longer appropriate for the state to privilege one faith, and the Church of England ought to be disestablished (the Liberal Democrats passed such a motion at their 1990 conference; see also WAF 1990 and IPPR 1991). Few members of religious minorities initially joined this discussion and so the secular multiculturalists were taken to be speaking for the marginal religious minorities. Yet, when the latter did join this debate, spokespersons of a number of non-Christian religious minorities actually argued for the importance of maintaining a symbolic and substantive link between religion and the state (Modood et al. 1997). Indeed, somewhat surprisingly, religious minorities, including Muslims who, as we have seen, have been very assertive across a broad front, have not challenged the Anglican privileges or 'establishment' or even the conception that Britain is/ought to be a Christian country (Modood et al. 1997). The minorities seem to prefer an incremental pluralization of the religion–state linkages, rather than their abolition. This is what is implicit in the demand for including Muslim and Sikh schools within the state sector. It is also echoed in the recommendations of the Royal Commission on the Reform of the House of Lords (2000). It argued that the number of Anglican bishops in the Lords should be reduced from twenty-six to sixteen and that they should be joined by five representatives of other Christian denominations in England, five seats should be allocated to other Christian denominations in the rest of the UK, and a further five should be used to include the presence of non-Christians. These recommendations have not been accepted but it is interesting that governments have felt the need to create multi-faith consultative bodies. The Conservatives created an Inner Cities Religious Council in 1992, chaired by a junior minister, which was replaced in 2006 by a body with a much broader remit, the Faith Communities Consultative Council. Moreover, the new Department of Communities and Local Governments, which is represented in the Cabinet, has a division devoted to faith communities. It is notable that most of the Muslim goals described in this section have had formal inter-faith support and sometimes would not have been possible without active cross-faith support (e.g. the religion question in the Census; see Sherrif 2003).[5]

In having an active policy of deepening state–religion linkages Britain is not unusual. Most West European countries are accommodating religious minorities or

---

[5] Other than Muslims themselves, a leading actor in bringing Muslim concerns and racial equality thinking into contact with each other has been the Runnymede Trust, recognizing Islamophobia as one of the chief forms of racism today when it set up its Commission on Islamophobia (Runnymede Trust 1997; 2004). Talk of Muslim identity used to be rejected by racial egalitarians as an irrelevance ('religious not political') and as divisive, but in the last few years Muslim organizations like the Muslim Council of Britain (MCB) and Forum Against Islamophobia and Racism (FAIR) have co-organized events and demonstrations with groups such as the National Assembly of Black People, and are often supported by the Commission for Racial Equality, and especially the Mayor of London.

at least Muslims; from an EU perspective the British focus on religion/Muslims is normal; it is the focus on American-style race that is peculiar (this is partly because most 'non-whites' in Continental Europe are Muslims and mainly from places where the idea of 'blackness' was not prominent). As early as 1974 the Belgian state decided to include Islam within its Council of Religions as a full member, and Muslims in the Netherlands have long had state-funded religious schools and television channels as a progressive step in that country's traditional way of institutionally dealing with organized religion, namely 'pillarization'.[6] Similarly, a 'Muslim community' is becoming recognized by public authorities in Germany by appealing to the historic German idea of a 'religious society' (*Religionsgesellschaft*) and initiating the 'Islam Conference', a regular governmental dialogue with Muslims led by the Interior Minister. Again, a series of French Interior Ministers have taken a number of steps to 'normalize' Islam in France by creating an official French Islam under the authority of the state in ways that make it identical to other faiths. Those who think that French *laïcité* consists of a wall of separation between the state and church are badly mistaken. The French state has formal institutional and financial connections with the Catholic and Protestant churches, the Jewish Consistory, and now a Council of the Muslim Faith (Bowen 2007; for more on various European cases see Modood and Kastoryano 2006 and Cesari 2004).

The British approach has in some ways been less statist and corporatist in its accommodation of Islam and the other newly present faiths than its continental neighbours. It has also been more liberal. This can be illustrated by reference to one of the most illiberal cases, the French ban on the wearing of the Muslim headscarf, the *hijab* (and other 'ostentatious' religious symbols) in French state schools in February 2005. This was shortly followed by a proposed ban in the Netherlands; admittedly it related to the more controversial face-veil, the *niqab*, but this time it applied to all public places. In contrast, the *hijab* hardly attracts any controversy in Britain. The *niqab* has been an object of a fierce and intense debate, launched by the senior governmental figure, Jack Straw MP, but he was careful to insist that he was not advocating the use of the law but was voluntarily requesting that Muslim women remove the *niqab* when speaking to him at his surgery (Straw 2006).

In certain ways the minority politics described in this chapter has been joined by foreign policy and security concerns from around the time of the terrorist attacks of 9/11, and especially after the invasion of Iraq in 2003 and the London bombings of 7/7.[7] But that the Muslim equality agenda has got as far as it has is because of the liberal and pragmatic political culture of this country on matters of religion, as opposed to a more thoroughgoing secularism that requires the state to control religion. A more fundamental ideological reason is that Muslims utilized and extended

---

[6] This principle that recognized that Protestants and Catholics had a right to state resources and some publicly funded autonomous institutions officially ended in 1960. It is, however, still considered a 'relevant framework for the development of a model that grants certain collective rights to religious groups' (Sunier and von Luijeren 2002) in such matters as state funding of Islamic schools. So, the accommodation of Muslims is being achieved through a combination of mild pillarization and Dutch minority policies.

[7] Though this has certainly not led to the 'death' of multiculturalism that so many have discerned in the events following 9/11 and 7/7 (Modood 2007; Meer and Modood 2009).

previously existing arguments and policies in relation to racial and multicultural equality. By emphasizing discrimination in educational and economic opportunities, political representation and the media, and 'Muslim-blindness' in the provision of health, care, and social services, and arguing for remedies which mirror existing legislation and policies in relation to sexual and racial equality, most politically active Muslims in respect of domestic issues have, at least in the period discussed in this chapter, adjusted to and become part of British political culture in general and British multiculturalist politics in particular. Indeed, it could be said that they achieved a significant measure of political integration. Most of this progress has taken place under a Labour administration. Cynics have argued that the success of the Muslim agenda is because the government has had to placate Muslim anti-Iraq War anger. A more long-term analysis, as offered here, shows that Labour's attentiveness to that agenda precedes the war or even 9/11. As part of its effort to advance racial and religious equality, the government has consciously, although sometimes grudgingly, pursued policies that did not exist before 1997—such as the funding of Muslim schools, the creation of Muslim peers, legislation to prevent religious discrimination and hatred, and the introduction of the religion question in the 2001 Census. It is true that many Muslim activists have walked away from the Labour Party and many more others feel betrayed by the Iraq War and feel victimized by the anti-terrorism measures, and so have worked, for example, in the 2005 general election, to punish the party. Yet in the long term I expect Asian Muslims, like Irish Catholics before them, to become integral to a working-class party; it will be upwardly mobile groups such as Hindus who will disperse across parties, as Jews have done.

REFERENCES

ALI, Y. 1991. 'Echoes of Empire: Towards a Politics of Representation'. In *Enterprise and Heritage: Cross Currents of National Culture*. London: Routledge.

BOWEN, J. 2007. *Why the French Don't Like Headscarves: Islam, the State, and Public Space*. Oxford: Princeton University Press.

CCCS (Centre for Contemporary Cultural Studies) 1982. *The Empire Strikes Back: Race and Racism in 70s Britain*. London: Hutchinson.

CESARI, J. 2004. *When Islam and Democracy Meet*. New York: Palgrave.

GILROY, P. 1987. *There Ain't no Black in the Union Jack: The Cultural Politics of Race and Nation*. London: Heinemann.

——1990. 'The End of Anti-Racism'. *New Community*, 17: 71–83.

GfK NOP SOCIAL RESEARCH 2006. 'Attitudes to Living in Britain: A Survey of Muslim Opinion'. 1 Sept.: 37–8. At http://www.gfknop.co.uk/content/news/news/Channel4_MuslimsBritain_toplinefindings.pdf.

GRILLO, R. 2007. 'Licence To Offend? The Behzti Affair'. *Ethnicities*, 7/1: 5–29.

HALSTEAD, J. 1988. *Education, Justice and Cultural Diversity: An Examination of the Honeyford Affair, 1984–85*. London: Falmer Press.

HONEYFORD, R. 1984. 'Education and Race: An Alternative View'. *Salisbury Review*, Winter/ 9: 292.

IPPR (Institute of Public Policy Research) 1991. *The Constitution of the United Kingdom.* London: IPPR.

Kabbani, R. 1989. *Letter to Christendom.* London: Virago.

Meer, N. 2007. 'Muslim Schools in Britain: Challenging Mobilisations or Logical Developments?' *Asia-Pacific Journal of Education,* 27/1: 55–71.

——2008. 'The Politics of Voluntary and Involuntary Identities: Are Muslims in Britain an Ethnic, Racial or Religious Minority?' *Patterns of Prejudice,* 42 /1: 61–81.

——and Modood, T. 2009. 'The Multicultural State We Are In: Muslims, "Multiculture" and the "Civic Re-balancing" of British Multiculturalism'. *Political Studies.*

Mirza, M., Senthilkumaran, A., and Ja'far, Z. 2007. *Living Apart Together: British Muslims and the Paradox of Multiculturalism.* London: Policy Exchange.

Modood, T. 1990. 'British Asian Muslims and the Rushdie Affair'. *Political Quarterly,* 61/2: 43–160 (also in J. Donald and A. Rattansi (eds.), *Race, Culture and Difference.* London: Sage).

——1994. 'Political Blackness and British Asians'. *Sociology,* 28/4: 859–86.

——2005. *Multicultural Politics: Racism, Ethnicity and Muslims in Britain.* Minneapolis: University of Minnesota Press.

——2007. *Multiculturalism: A Civic Idea.* Cambridge: Polity.

——Berthoud, R., Lakey, J., Nazroo, J., Smith, P., Virdee, S., and Beishon, S. 1997. *Ethnic Minorities in Britain: Diversity and Disadvantage.* London: Policy Studies Institute.

Modood, T., Hansen, R., Bleich, E., O'Leary, B., and Carens, J. 2006. 'The Danish Cartoon Affair: Free Speech, Racism, Islamism, and Integration'. *International Migration,* 44/5: 3–57.

——and Kastoryano, R. 2006. 'Secularism and the Accommodation of Muslims in Europe'. In T. Modood, A. Triandafyllidou, and R. Zapata-Barrero (eds.), *Multiculturalism, Muslims and Citizenship: A European Approach.* London: Routledge.

Muslim Parliament of Great Britain 1992. *Race Relations and Muslims in Great Britain: A Discussion Paper.* London: Muslim Parliament.

ONS (Office of National Statistics) 2005. 'Ethnicity & Identity Inter-ethnic Marriage'. http://www.statistics.gov.uk/cci/.

Phillips, A. 2007. *Multiculturalism without Culture.* Princeton, NJ: Princeton University Press.

Poulter, S. 1998. *Ethnicity, Law, and Human Rights: The English Experience.* Oxford: Clarendon Press.

Rex, J. 1996. 'National Identity in the Democratic Multi-Cultural State'. *Sociological Research Online,* 1/2. http://www.socresonline.org.uk/socresonline/1/2/1.html.

——and Moore, R. 1967. *Race, Community, and Conflict.* Oxford: Oxford University Press.

Runnymede Trust Commission on British Muslims and Islamophobia 1997. *Islamophobia: A Challenge to Us All.* London: Runnymede Trust.

——2004. *Islamophobia: Issues, Challenges and Action.* Stoke-on-Trent: Trentham Books.

Rushdie, S. 1982. 'The New Empire within Britain'. *New Society,* 9 Dec.

Samad, Y. 1992. 'Book Burning and Race Relations: Political Mobilisation of Bradford Muslims'. *New Community,* 18/4: 507–19.

Scott, J. W. 2007. *Politics of the Veil.* Princeton, NJ: Princeton University Press.

Sherrif, J. 2003. 'Campaigning for Religion Question in the 2001 Census'. Muslim Council of Britain website: http://www.mcb.org.uk/downloads/census2001.pdf; accessed 31 Jan. 2008.

Singh, G. 2005. 'British Multiculturalism and Sikhs'. *Sikh Formations,* 1/2: 157–73.

Sivanandan. A. 1985. 'RAT and the Degradation of the Black Struggle'. *Race and Class,* 26/4: 1–33.

Straw, J. 2006. 'Straw in Plea to Muslim Women: Take off your Veils'. *Lancashire Evening Telegraph,* 5 Oct. http://www.lancashireeveningtelegraph.co.uk.

Sunier, T., and von Luijeren, M. 2002. 'Islam in the Netherlands'. Pp. 144–58 in Y. Haddad (ed.), *Muslims in the West: From Sojourners to Citizens*. New York: Oxford University Press.

Swann, Lord 1985. *Education for All: Final Report of the Committee of Inquiry into the Education of Children from Ethnic Minority Groups*. Cmnd. 9453. London: HMSO.

UKACIA (UK Action Committee on Islamic Affairs) 1993. *Muslims and the Law in Multi-faith Britain: Need for Reform*. London: UKACIA.

Women Against Fundamentalism (WAF) 1992. 'Founding Statement'. *Women Against Fundamentalism Journal*, 1/1.

SECTION NINE: NATIONAL IDENTITIES

CHAPTER 27

ENGLAND

JULIA STAPLETON

A key difficulty in interpreting England and Englishness is the subconscious level of national life—both British and English—they appear to have occupied, until recently at least. Alone among nations, England has conspicuously lacked any literary and political 'fathers' and an organized democratic movement to pursue national goals. While there is a long tradition of commentary on all things English by foreign observers, the English people have shown little interest in themselves as a collectivity, still less in overt displays of their nationhood. As G. K. Chesterton wrote in 1935, the English have never been among the 'singing or marching' nations, their national identity being far more reclusive (Chesterton 1935: 206). This was once the occasion of quiet pride, malcontents such as Chesterton apart, which the English enjoyed relatively free of challenge (Barker 1928: 194; Dicey 1905: 463; Chesterton 1907). However, with the decline of empire after the Second World War and the future of the United Kingdom in increasing question, the unobtrusiveness of English nationhood has become the focus of much hostility. England has been castigated for its failure to follow a 'normal', essentially egalitarian path of nation building; it has served the needs of a British 'imperialist' state instead and has still to accomplish a full transition to 'postcolonial' status (Nairn 1977; Haseler 1996; Gardiner 2004).

Against the critics, this chapter emphasizes the complex and shifting nature of England and Englishness as powerful and not always unarticulated focuses of loyalty, attachment, and shared identity. Not least, this is due to England's historic entanglements with, but also distance from, empire, the United Kingdom, and, most recently, devolved nations within the latter. The chapter begins by analysing different

I am most grateful to Arthur Aughey for sharing his expertise and providing helpful comments on earlier drafts of this chapter.

interpretations of England's position within the wider unit of Britain from which all these other entanglements flowed. Further, it addresses the 'civilizational perspective' on English national *character* in the eighteenth and nineteenth centuries that inhibited the development of a sense of innate English difference from other European nations. The second section explores the deep well of patriotism that 'England' has engendered since at least the mid-nineteenth century, but still firmly within the 'civilizational perspective'. It illustrates this pivotal form of national consciousness and identity in the Edwardian writings of G. K. Chesterton. The third section considers the English shadow that was cast across understandings of Britain in the inter-war period, but also continuing contestation of England itself among popular writers on both the left and the right. The fourth section situates Enoch Powell's conception of Englishness in the wake of mass immigration within well-established traditions of English Conservatism, liberalism, and patriotism. The fifth section analyses recent charges of shallowness, bigotry, and insularity levelled against the English people as the cracks in their imperialist and British façade have become increasingly apparent. In response, the chapter emphasizes a national culture rich in appreciation of the value of 'conversation' in both politics and society across national and other divides. As the chapter concludes, this is a quality that has underpinned England's central British role, without which both Englishness and the United Kingdom are inconceivable.

27.1 The Place of England and 'the English People' Before 1900

At the outset, it is necessary to clarify the place of England within the wider British state: the United Kingdom of Great Britain and Ireland, or Northern Ireland after 1922. While the other component nations generally maintained dual national identities when they were absorbed into Britain, albeit with considerable cross-currents well into the twentieth century, the English were far more self-effacing. They regarded themselves—in public, at least—as primarily British. Indeed, invisibility was the price that had to be paid for ascendancy in terms of population, wealth, and power within the Union and empire more widely (Crick 1991: 92; Kumar 2003: 36–7).

However, 'silence' in these circumstances in no way spelt absence. The identity *of* England may have been vigorously contested on behalf of different classes, religions, and regions but until recently an overarching identity *with* England was largely taken for granted, and not just in the modern period. As a recent commentator, Robert Colls, has suggested English identities long pre-dated the eclipse of empire since the late nineteenth century (Colls 2005). This Krishan Kumar considers 'the moment' of English nationalism, when the cover of its 'missionary' nature was blown (Kumar 2003). At the same time, while the 'consciousness' of Britain was English, and readily accepted as such among England's partners in the Union (Grainger 1986: 53), this was not a reflection of English dominance; rather, as Arthur Aughey has maintained, it reflected English humility in sacrificing its nationality to the interests of a wider whole. England was *primus inter pares*, the key force for integration within Britain before the experience of 'disintegration' in the post-war period. This role cohered around the 'English ideology' of liberty that flowed through the channels of English culture and politics in the nineteenth century and cut across the Whig–Tory divide (Aughey 2006: 47–8). While soiled at times by 'colonialist' attitudes such as those of Lord Salisbury in relation to the 'Hottentot' Irish, these could not be described as characteristically English.

Integral to the self-abnegation underlying the English ideology was the 'civilizational' perspective that ruled out any conception of nationhood, particularly English nationhood, in terms of innate racial difference. This had deep roots in late eighteenth-century patriotism. In a path-breaking study, Peter Mandler has argued that patriotism in this period took 'resonant symbols of state and majesty' for its focus in the war with France, not images of a distinctive people. This was true of both loyalist and oppositional propaganda (Mandler 2006: 16). The famed 'John Bull' of the 1790s was more in evidence at the level of foreign commentary on the English, at least in the hearty, freedom-loving form of this figure (Langford 2000: 11). In Radical propaganda of the time, much concern is evinced instead for the 'active population of the island', the 'general interest' that suffered by war, and the gaining of due representation of 'the people' in the councils of state (Robinson 1798: 241). It could not be otherwise given the continuing and dominant sense of 'heterogeneity' celebrated in Defoe's famous poem of 1700, 'The True-Born Englishman' (1865). This was a figure bred 'mongrel-like' from Scots, Picts, Britons, Romans, and Danes. Unquestionably, England stood for 'Britain' among both the inhabitants of, and the visitors to, the British Isles, although the English have always been loath to lose themselves entirely in a British identity (Langford 2000: 13; Chesterton 1918; Baldwin 1926: 1).

As confidence among elites in the political capacities of the people rose after 1832, the idea of an English 'national character' that would lay the basis of a sense of shared nationhood came into its own. Even then, however, national loyalty and pride remained firmly fixed on the institutions of church and state, thereby dampening down the fires of nationalist—interpreted as democratic—passion that would lead to a steep civilizational descent (Mandler 2006: 21–6, 52–3). Most significantly, the concept of English national character was freely deployed by the Radical opposition to further the universalist (certainly British) ideals of freedom, constitutionalism, and humanity in the reform of parliament, the slave trade, factory law, and the removal of religious disabilities (Cunningham 1981). This was consistent with the lack of any sense of national myth or legend relating to a homogeneous people and agreement on a national history (Hilton 2006: 482–7). The civilizational line of thought posited England as exceptional *and* exemplary, highly distinctive in its successful path of political and economic development but by that very fact a model for other nations to emulate (Aughey 2007: ch. 2).

27.2 ENGLISH PATRIOTISM IN LATE VICTORIAN AND EDWARDIAN BRITAIN: G. K. CHESTERTON

Much of England, 'civilizational' style, cohered around a Protestantism that coloured considerably the terms in which an exemplary 'national character' was drawn. Nowhere is this better expressed than in Thomas Jones Barker's engraving, *The Bible: The Secret of England's Greatness* (1864), in which Queen Victoria presents a copy of the bible to one of her African subjects. But while the Protestant religion had been a seminal bond of 'Britishness' following the Act of Union with Scotland in 1707, it developed its own, peculiarly English inflections in the course of the nineteenth century (Mandler 2006: 33–4; Walton 2002: 520). This was evident in the competing claims that Anglicanism and Nonconformism made on an *English* 'national tradition' after 1850 in their search for cultural legitimacy beyond associations with the state (Burns 2006; Leighton 2008). At the same time, English identity crystallized in the English language and an evolving conception of 'national literature' (Collini 1991: 354).

The convergence of religion, language, and literature in defining a national culture specific to England towards the end of the nineteenth century mirrored the development of new and more resonant invocations of English nationhood than that of a shared national character. These centred on the notion of an English 'soul' and 'spirit', engendering a strong sense of national pride and belonging among its people. They are consistent with a new understanding of the English as a 'breed'. They are certainly evident in the imperialist poetry and prose of the *fin de siècle*, for example that of W. E. Henley and Rudyard Kipling (Henley 1896; Kipling 1896: 53; 1920). But they could also be wielded *against* imperialism, not least by the socialist left. Its rousing song, 'England Arise', was composed in 1886 by the writer and poet Edward Carpenter to project a purer, non-imperialist ideal of 'Britain', at the level of conquest and subjugation at any rate (Geoghegan 2003: 510–11, 515, 519).

As Paul Readman has shown, the national self-consciousness of the English at the turn of the twentieth century was especially enhanced by increasing interest in, and celebration of, a specifically *English* past at a popular, local level. Here, also, a sense of detachment from empire was evident. It found expression in centenary celebrations—particularly the millenary of Alfred the Great in 1901—pageantry, tourism, and the preservationist movement (Readman 2005; 2001*b*). Moreover, while stopping well short of political nationalism, a firm sense of English national identity and its imperatives influenced party politics in Edwardian Britain (Readman 2001*a*; 2001*c*). The permutations of this movement and its legacy are especially apparent if we consider one of its most articulate spokesmen, the poet, journalist, and literary critic, G. K. Chesterton.

Born in 1874, Chesterton embraced patriotism as the handmaid of Liberalism and literature, although untainted by imperialist ambitions. As a keen opponent of the Boer War, he affirmed the 'sanctity' of the individual and individual things, nations included (Chesterton 1905: 56, 61). This was a far cry from the old, 'thin' language of 'national character', not least in opposing the political establishment. His alternative set an especially high premium on small nations, the victims of imperialism, chief among which he counted Ireland, the Boer nation, *and* England. Condemning the 'deaf and raucous Jingoism' that passed for patriotism in the aftermath of the Boer War, Chesterton emphasized how a military and economic preoccupation with colonies had obscured the more vital spiritual achievements in the empire's 'head and heart' (Chesterton 1901: 167). Not surprisingly, he mocked the sham patriotism of 'Empire Day'. This was inaugurated in 1904 as a result of the efforts of Lord Meath to raise the imperial consciousness of the nation's youth in particular. Empire Day amounted, in Chesterton's view, merely to a 'jerry-built jubilee' (Chesterton 1908).

What did 'Britain' mean to Chesterton as a prominent 'Little Englander'? In one of his weekly columns for the *Illustrated London News* he referred to Britain merely as a 'group' of nations. England was clearly the dominant player within this group, although it had paid a heavy price in terms of the obscurity it had been made to endure as a result. The Scots had played a lesser although still significant role in maintaining the Union, and he paid full tribute to the strengths of their culture (Chesterton 1918). For Ireland, Chesterton had nothing but sympathy as the sharp end of English imperialism (Chesterton 1904). For Wales, by contrast, Chesterton expressed only blank incomprehension, an attitude he thought was typical of the English generally (Chesterton 1911). Still, for all his regret about the suppression of its identity, Chesterton was no advocate of national self-determination for England (Chesterton 1910; 1918).

Despite Chesterton's rejection of empire, recent critics have perceived in his conception of the English nation only a groundswell of resistance to the forces of progress (Wright 2005). However, in doing so, they have missed his modernism and radicalism, not least in identifying the 'true' English people of the twentieth century. For Chesterton, as for E. M. Forster, these were no longer the upper middle classes who for too long had created a false image of the English, especially abroad, as cold, taciturn, and cosmopolitan in all their tastes and interests (Stapleton 2006: 346–7; Baldick 2004: 318). The English were epitomized instead in an array of menial but non-industrial and mainly urban occupations: cabmen, railway porters, navvies, dustmen, and crossing-sweepers (Chesterton 1910). These were the heirs of an older, essentially oppressed England that he immortalized in his poem, 'The Secret People', of 1907 (Chesterton 1907). The revolutionary hopes he entertained of his fellow countrymen there is hard to square with a softer paean he wrote a year later (Chesterton 1908).

He referred to the 'profoundly poetical character of the English, that quality of mixed feelings and emotional hesitation which makes the cloudy pictures of Constable or the vague rhythms of Keats'. But this very different register retained in full the political motive of the poem. With so sensitive a side to the national character, imperialism could not be other than alien to the English people now, as in the time of Alfred the Great. The British Empire was the product instead of plutocratic influences that had become the bane of England, an echo of the American dichotomy between Main Street and Wall Street (Chesterton 1910). Chief among these influences was the Jewish financier and businessman. Chesterton proceeded to tighten the boundaries of English belonging in ways that excluded the Jews. In doing so he was by no means exceptional among his contemporaries; anti-Semitism was rife on the Edwardian left (Geogehegan 2003: 522; Walton 2002: 525) as well as being a key force in the emergence of a radical right in these years (Villis 2006). Moreover, he disclaimed all belief in the 'majority of Jews' being 'tyrants' and 'traitors' (Chesterton 1911), even though his language at times suggested otherwise.

27.3 INTER-WAR REFLECTIONS ON ENGLAND AND ENGLAND-BRITAIN

Patriotism in England was at a low ebb in the immediate aftermath of the First World War, discredited by its association with militarism, chauvinism, and the carnage of the trenches (Grainger 1986: 329–61). Instead, this period witnessed concerted attempts to popularize the notion of citizenship—with Britain as its focus—through a variety of campaign groups which enjoyed elite support (Stapleton 2005a: 162–9). While shrill imperialist enthusiasms receded, the Unionist cause bore up well in the face of both world wars, the development of business and trade union networks, and common cultural institutions such as the British Broadcasting Corporation (Ward 2005). The classicist and Liberal Ernest Barker was typical of this movement, the author of a spate of books and articles on themes such as 'national character', nationality, and democracy, education, and citizenship. The concept of 'civic nationalism' is integral to Barker's view of Britain as an inclusive nation rooted in contract and the ideal of 'neighbourliness' rather than 'thick' ethnic ties (Stapleton 1994: ch. 4; Kearney 2000: 22). Like the Conservative Prime Minister, Stanley Baldwin, he was at pains to emphasize the Union as a partnership of equal nations, even if for Barker, at any rate, recognition of Ulster proved more problematic, certainly in the days of the debate over Home Rule (Barker 1928: 131; Baldwin 1926: 237–58; Barker 1913; Ward Smith 2001).

Yet Barker—again like Baldwin—could never disguise his English identity and sympathies. His 'civic' ideal of Britain as a 'quasi-nation'—unlike, for example,

Austro-Hungary—was made very largely in an image of English nationhood as both solid and yet unusually capacious (Barker 1928: 131; Stapleton 1994: 120–5, ch. 7; Williamson 1999: 251). His homage to England in the afterglow of victory in the Second World War represented English national consciousness at its most intense, reflective, and proud. He wrote of the flexibility and adaptability of the English, who never indulged in the kind of *Weltschmerz* to which other nations were prone (Barker 1947: 558). So exalted a view of the English was unlikely to escape Scottish censorship even in its pre-nationalist days (Mandler 2006: 205).

The inter-war projection of Britain as largely English emphasized that England itself was by no means a lost cause beyond its Edwardian prime. In the 1930s *English* patriotism was championed in the journalistic writings and popular histories of Arthur Bryant (Stapleton 2005*b*); also in the work of the equally popular chronicler of 'the King's England', Arthur Mee (Smith 1986). The celebration by these writers of an England rich in character and history was rooted in a wider interest in the landscape, increasingly accessible with the advent of mass motoring. This was in no way anti-modern, its central concern being the maintenance of order against development that was 'unplanned' (Daniels 1993: 220). Moreover, the inter-war imagination readily embraced the north as well as the late Victorian and Edwardian idyll of 'the south country' (Howkins 1986) as unimpeachably English. J. B. Priestley immortalized the music-hall culture of northern English towns as the quintessence of Englishness in his *English Journey* of 1932 (Waters 1994). This work had many commonalities with Orwell's famous essay, *The Lion and the Unicorn* (1941). Here, Orwell outlined a 'New England' emerging in the centres of light industry which would preserve all that was best in the old (Clarke 2006: 104). Both Priestley and Orwell offset the Marxist, inter-nationalist left which regarded nationalism and patriotism—relating to their own country, at least—as forces of reaction rather than progress (Grainger 1986: 338–9).

27.4 ENGLISHNESS ON THE DEFENSIVE

However, such socialist champions of England and Englishness were more influential outside than within the left in British politics and culture (Forster 1950). The distancing of the left from Orwell, at least, was true even of those who were to develop an interest in the 'peculiarities of the English' for their own purposes after the Second World War, in defiance of the greater New Left, for example E. P. Thompson (Thompson 1965: 22; Kenny 1995: 181). Beyond Thompson, the antagonism of the intellectual left towards all things English acquired new force in the post-war era. In the late 1970s the Scottish nationalist writer, Tom Nairn, forecast 'the break-up of Britain', an outcome that was delayed only by the tardiness of the English in recognizing their separate nationhood. Lacking the 'mature' national consciousness of the French in 1789, England merely shored up a creaking *ancien régime* centred on Britain.

Nairn's main target was Enoch Powell, whose staunch defence of an Anglocentric ideal of Britain in the face of mass immigration he regarded as 'destiny-fantasy' propelled by 'domestic racism'. Nairn likened Powell's views to a 'stale fungus', the legacy of a ruling class that had lost its grip on 'social realities' (Nairn 1977: 287); that is, the 'materialist' course of history.

However, Nairn missed the particular idiom in which Powell was seeking to address the upsurge of *English* nationalism in the face of mass immigration. Recent research has shown that this long pre-dated his views on English national identity in the 1960s. It was rooted in the integral links he drew between democracy, the free market, and a homogeneous national culture while he was still an imperialist contemplating the problems of Indian self-government in the 1940s (Brooke 2007). Nairn also missed the oppositional character of the Conservatism Powell deployed in the immigration debate, notwithstanding his liberal cast of mind; it leant back towards Bolingbroke (Foote 2006: ch. 6) and had clear echoes, too, of Disraeli, or rather the 'Disraeli myth'. The latter invoked a unique bond between the Tory party and the English-British people as a whole. The people were the guardians of the rights enshrined in the constitution, rights that were emphatically individual not communal. They had the greatest vested interests in the upholding of these rights, which the Tory party alone served and ignored at its peril (Powell 1966).

Roger Scruton has argued that Powell's mistake lay not in misjudging the scale and impact of immigration but rather the emotional receptiveness of his fellow compatriots to another myth: that of an ancient and heroic national past centred on England, one that was bathed in a warm Arthurian glow (Powell 1969: 254–7). But was Powell speaking 'into a [nationalist] void' that would inevitably be filled by racism and xenophobia (Scruton 2006b)? This seems somewhat exaggerated, even if a patriotism focused on England as well as England-Britain, and reinforced through literature and history of the kind that has been explored above, was losing momentum in the 1960s, especially among elites (Stapleton 2005b: ch.13).

27.5 ENGLAND AS A 'MODERN' NATION

The precise character of English nationalism in this assumed climate of 'absence' has continued to exercise a range of commentators. This is particularly so in the last decade when the question of England and Englishness has moved to the forefront of debate. With the implosion of empire, economic decline, a crumbling British façade in the wake of devolution, and associated concerns about England's 'democratic deficit', the English have come under increasing pressure to define, or rather redefine, themselves. There is widespread anxiety about 'who' exactly the English people now are and in particular what has become of their self-restraint. Was it perhaps the case, wondered Jeremy Paxman, that the vehemence of English nationalism on the football terraces in recent years and general loss of decorum in other ways is linked to the decline of well-established, distinctively English codes of conduct? He replied in the negative. 'England enters the third millennium not in a dark suit but in an exuberant variety of guises, owing everything and nothing to the past' (Paxman 1998: 255). There, the rough and smooth combined freely, as in the present.

This assurance notwithstanding, Europe is widely regarded as the best context within which the English may rediscover themselves, their 'best selves', that is. It has been argued that constructive engagement with Europe would help them to overcome their inveterate Euroscepticism (Smith 2006) and bigotry (Brown 2001; 2005). They would become less insular and menacing as a result (Ascherson 2000), less prey to exploitation by the extreme right. Positive attitudes to Europe would also enable the English to rise above what is perceived as the 'ethnic' and class-based nature of their nationalism hitherto in favour of a new (or is it not an old?) and more inclusive 'civic' variety (Lee 2006: 59). The idea that English sympathies should be cultivated simultaneously with those of Europe unites such disparate commentators as Stephen Haseler, Edwin Jones, and Mark Leonard. Their common assumption is that Europe offers England the only prospect of cultural, spiritual, and institutional renewal (Aughey 2007: ch. 9).

Even when Europe is rejected as the new framework for an England increasingly deprived of its former British trappings, the emphasis on the need for English identity to change, and change radically, remains. Thus, at the time of the millennium, the historian David Starkey urged England to look outward rather than inward, forward rather than backward, for its new sense of identity—in short, to economic and cultural success in a global world. He views Englishness, old style, as essentially a minority identity, the flag of St George sported only by 'taxis and the white-van-driving classes' (Starkey 1999).

Common to many such writers is a belief that England, appropriately reimagined, holds the key to a new, 'post-nationalist' era (Starkey 1999) or alternatively the 'nationalism of the future'. For Paxman, this would be 'modest, individualistic, ironic, solipsistic, concerned as much with cities and regions as with counties and countries'; in other words, all the separate ingredients of Englishness but without its aggregate weight crystallized in the state, 'anthems and flags' (Paxman 1998: 265–60). Kumar, too, is anxious that England should avoid regressing to old-fashioned nationalism. Like others, he looks optimistically to wider organizations like the European Union, as 'but one theatre in which the nations', England especially, 'can suppress their rivalries and antagonisms for the greater good of all' (Kumar 2006: 10).

Evident in all these perspectives is a concern that the English people should travel as lightly as possible on the identity front lest the old superiority complex resurface in new, more popular and virulent forms. However, bids to attenuate the sense of English nationhood have not passed unchallenged, not least by those who emphasize diversity rather than homogeneity as the hallmark of Englishness. This note has been struck recently by a historian on the left, Robert Colls. In *The Identity of England* he emphasizes the multi-layered and dynamic nature of English national identity in the past. In his view, the identity of England was never an exclusively 'top-down' affair; it was crafted instead by a mass of ordinary people besides, at different times and in different forms at any one time, often in defiance of elites. The pluralistic nature of England reflected in its range of identit*ies* augured well for the adaptation necessitated by recent political and cultural change. However, the erosion of the old *primus inter pares*—Crown-in-Parliament—remains for Colls a clear challenge to the maintenance of Englishness in all its diversity. The 'conversation' and 'trust' once fostered by a polity of this nature were mainstays of English nationhood, old style, and key to an overarching sense of unity-in-difference. The recovery of a working partnership between state and nation offers for Colls the only prospect of democratic inclusion in a globalized world (Colls 2002: conclusion).

The 'national' character of English liberty and its centrality to English nationhood has also been invoked on the right. Roger Scruton has done so against widespread criticism of the sea of English flags on display at home and abroad in two World Cups as evidence of the shallowness of English nationalism. For Scruton, sport provides an outlet for legitimate national emotions that have been denied any other expression in multicultural Britain (Scruton 2004). What Scruton has termed the 'forbidding of England', or 'oikophobia', is simply the outcome of a perverse antipathy to national success on the part of elites, both political and intellectual, not least the success of England in securing widespread loyalty and allegiance (Scruton 2006a: 36). He emphasizes the role of England as the cultural and ethical backbone of Britain, the 'soul' inside Britain's 'body' (Scruton 2001: 73; 2006a: 21). The implication is clear that the Union was made possible by the essentially English form of 'corporateness' whereby strangers learned to live with other strangers without violating their freedom and integrity. This form of incorporation furnished a sense of identity and restraint that underlay the permanence and stability of Britain.

For Scruton, England is a seamless national whole in which the character of its people, language, culture, institutions, climate, and landscape were interpenetrated by the same values and ethos. These were further underwritten by the English church (Scruton 2001: 85). Order, unity, accommodation, and settlement were the watchwords of English national life, no matter how much driven by an ultimate concern on the part of its members to keep themselves to themselves. In this analysis of the English psyche, Scruton echoed the work of the conservative philosopher, Michael Oakeshott. Famously, Oakeshott cited Schopenhauer's fable of the porcupines in articulating what was evidently for him a uniquely English way of avoiding the claustrophobia engendered by 'communities'. It did so while maximizing human interaction and enjoyment of the individuality of others (Eccleshall 1992: 182, 184; Oakeshott 1947: 489–90). Scruton also echoed the work of foreign commentators, similarly impressed by the tendency among the English for 'social feelings' to take the form, 'not so much of respect for the community, as of respect for the individuality of others' (Dibelius 1922: 147). Integration through 'conversation' between the members of society is once again the key to understanding Englishness; its influence has been identified in literary genres such as the eighteenth-century essay (Ackroyd 2002: 317–18) as well as in political institutions.

Conceiving experience, character, and habitat as integral to a common Englishness, Scruton nonetheless sought to legitimize a particular version of English identity: one that privileged the landed estates and hereditary titles now all but abolished in the wake of New Labour. Corrupted by prosperity, modern England had become plagued by sexual and other forms of deviancy, leaving traditional values such as patriotism and liberty, and 'the land' on which they drew, at a large discount (Scruton 2001: 247). In one respect, his English perspective touches that of radicals such as Richard Weight; both offer anti-establishment views of England as existing in an advanced state of neglect among elites who should have known better. For Weight this was to discount a vibrant *popular* culture, one which was by no means insular. His concern is to release England from the suffocating effects of 'Britain' and Britishness, but without giving up on the United Kingdom entirely. His assumption is that only the left could have drawn out a 'democratic narrative' of (English) nationalism in readiness for a post-Union world; sadly, the historic opportunity was missed (Weight 2002: 726).

Not all apostles of Conservative Englishness have been driven to such extremes of anxiety as Scruton. Simon Heffer, for example, like Weight, sees more resilience in England thus despoiled, and more potential for a future that would reflect its own inner light. But—unlike Weight—it would be outside Europe, outside Britain, and beyond the destructive reach of multiculturalism (Heffer 1999). Nevertheless, both paradigms of Conservative Englishness—and radical Englishness—are distinct from responses to English nationhood among a section of the contemporary left which elevates common citizenship above nationhood. This seeks to substitute rights and duties enshrined in new constitutional documents for inherited sympathies and outlooks, and against the background of a 'standardized' account of national history around which all the different communities in Britain might rally (Colley 2006). While some in this camp are uneasy about the loss of a once powerful connection between rights, benefits, duties, and *national* societies, they retain an emphasis on contract rather than sentiment as the basis of a renewed sense of *British* citizenship, one that is noticeably free of its erstwhile English core (Goodhart 2006).

In the search for rational rather than emotional bases of loyalty *in* rather than *to* England-Britain, regions have assumed a new importance. Both the Labour government in its 2002 White Paper, *Your Region, Your Choice*, and the European Union following the Maastricht Treaty have attempted to break up old national boundaries and allegiances by creating new administrative areas (Johnston 2002; Copping and Kite 2006; Aughey 2007: ch. 8). For Labour, 'Regional Assemblies' and concomitant bureaucracies have been advanced as a solution to the 'English problem' in the wake of devolution, with a good deal of support from opponents of the perceived power wielded in the United Kingdom by 'monocultural', Anglo-British England (Bryant 2006: 232). However, the policy has encountered considerable obstacles, not least the rejection by electorates of proposals to regionalize local government through the creation of a new super-tier. The 'cussedness' of the English has been much in evidence in resisting such change. But so, too, has attachment to something regarded as 'real' and fundamental—English nationhood. This is in the face of persistent attempts to divide, weaken, and deprive it of an effective voice (Heffer 2006).

27.6 CONCLUSION

Ultimately, the issue of the future of England and Englishness falls on sympathies, allegiances, and identities which have hardened in a cultural and political environment increasingly hostile to their expression, certainly in forms which miss the 'egalitarian' mark. As a result of devolution, in particular, there has been a considerable decline among the English of a primary British identity and a corresponding increase in primary English identities. According to the *British Social Attitudes* (January 2007) report, 63 per cent of English correspondents identified with Britain in 1992 but just 48 per cent do so now; and while 31 per cent claimed an English identity in 1992, 40 per cent did so fifteen years later (Heath, Martin, and Elgenius 2007: 11). This enhanced affiliation with England is reflected in substantial opposition to Scottish MPs voting on English and Welsh legislation at Westminster: 62 per cent according to an ICM poll in December 2007, although this figure seems stable (Curtice 2007). The travails of devolution have generated new English lobby groups such as the English Democrats and Campaign for an English Parliament. Both are at pains to dissociate themselves from racism and focus instead on the enhancement of democratic rights in Britain, although insisting on England's separate national identity.

The *British Social Attitudes* report (2007) also reveals that England, like Britain, fails to engender any sense of community among those who identify with these nations comparable to that of Scotland and Wales, or even Europe (Heath, Martin, and Elgenius 2007: 16). However, as we have seen, the homogeneity of the English nation is often projected in terms of a desire for liberty that seeks to maximize the distance between individuals, at a public level at least. This perspective does not 'exclude' other loyalties and identities but values the conditions—conversational in character—in which they can be accommodated, subject to acceptance of the conditions themselves. Rarely has Englishness been articulated in the triumphalist terms of a master race; and only then as a call to vigilance, an expression of insecurity rather than complacency (Kipling 1920). When English voices have shown leanings towards exclusion of one kind or another, they have been brought up short. Chesterton faced a barracking by critics who found his anti-Semitism unworthy both of his own values, and those of England more widely (Anon. 1936: 894).

We have seen that Englishness has served different causes—political, cultural, and religious—at different times and in different contexts. However, it has retained a clear centre of cultural gravity, not least in a unifying *patriotism* which—at its height in the Second World War, and despite inevitable fissures—few other nations could rival (Stapleton 2001: 197, 201 n. 39; Rose 2003). The continuing power of English patriotism to move and inspire at higher levels than mere bigotry and racism is evident, not just in sporting events such as the Ashes in 2005 but in literature (Ackroyd 2002) and popular culture, too (Ashley 2006; Bragg 2006). Whether the sense of English nationhood can provide the basis for a sovereign English state in the event of Scottish independence and the disintegration of the Union is uncertain. This is especially so given that for the English—no less than the Scots—the Union is 'a part of what they have been and are' (Pocock 2000: 48). Equally uncertain is the likelihood that either the weaker or the stronger identities now being proposed for the English people can match the levels of responsiveness that England-in-Britain elicited in the past, and continues to command in the present (Curtice 2007).

REFERENCES

ACKROYD, P. 2002. *Albion: The Origins of the English Imagination*. London: Chatto and Windus.

ANON. 1936. 'G. K. Chesterton: Child and Man. The Making of an Optimist'. *Times Literary Supplement*, 7 Nov.: 893–4.

ASCHERSON, N. 2000. 'On with the Pooling and Merging'. *London Review of Books*, 17 Feb.

ASHLEY, P. 2006. *Unmitigated England: A Country Lost and Found*. London: Adelphi.

AUGHEY, A. 2006. 'Challenges to English Identity'. Pp. 45–63 in R. Hazell (ed.), *The English Question*. Manchester: Manchester University Press.

——2007. *The Politics of Englishness*. Manchester: Manchester University Press.

BALDICK, C. 2004. *The Oxford English Literary History*, vol. x: *1910–1940: The Modern Movement*. Oxford: Oxford University Press.

BALDWIN, S. 1926, *On England: And Other Addresses*. London: Philip Allan.

BARKER, E. 1913. 'Lord Hugh Cecil and Sovereignty: Old and New Theories'. *The Times*, 12 Mar.: 8b.

——1927. *National Character: And the Factors in its Formation*. London: Methuen.

——(ed.) 1947. *The Character of England*. Oxford: Clarendon Press.

BRAGG, B. 2006. *The Progressive Patriot: A Search for Belonging*. London: Bantam.

BROOKE, P. 2007. 'India, Post-Imperialism and the Origins of Enoch Powell's "Rivers of Blood" Speech'. *Historical Journal*, 50: 669–87.

BROWN, Y. A. 2001. 'After Multiculturalism'. Pp. 47–56 in B. Crick (ed.), *Citizens: Towards a Citizenship Culture*. Oxford: Blackwell.

——2005. 'England oh England'. *Independent*, 12 Sept.

BRYANT, C. G. A. 2006. *The Nations of Britain*. Oxford: Oxford University Press.

BURNS, A. 2006. 'The Authority of the Church'. Pp. 179–200 in P. Mandler (ed.), *Liberty and Authority in Victorian Britain*. Oxford: Oxford University Press.

CHESTERTON, G. K. 1901. 'In Defense of Patriotism'. Pp. 163–72 in *The Defendant*. London: Dent.

——1904. 'The Folly of Union'. *Daily News*, 11 June: 6.

——1905. 'The Poetic Quality of Liberalism'. *Independent Review*, Feb.: 53–61.

——1907. 'The Secret People'. *The Neolith*, 1: 1–2.

——1908. 'Our Notebook'. *Illustrated London News*, 30 May: 778.

——1910. 'Our Notebook'. *Illustrated London News*, 26 Nov.: 816.

——1911. 'Our Notebook'. *Illustrated London News*, 2 Sept.: 353.

——1918. 'Our Notebook'. *Illustrated London News*, 14 Sept.: 290.

——1935. 'The Shy-Bird'. Pp. 205–14 in D. Collins (ed.), *A Handful of Authors*. London: Sheed and Ward, 1953.

CLARKE, B. 2006. 'Orwell and Englishness'. *Review of English Studies*, NS 57: 84–105.

COLLEY, L. 2006. 'British Values, Whatever they are, won't Hold us Together'. *Guardian*, 18 May.

COLLINI, S. 1991. *Public Moralists: Political Thought and Intellectual Life in Britain, 1850–1930.* Oxford: Clarendon Press.

COLLS, R. 2002. *Identity of England.* Oxford: Oxford University Press.

—— 2005. Review of K. Kumar, 'The Making of English National Identity'. *Sociological Review,* 53: 581–3.

COPPING, J., and KITE, M. 2006. 'New EU Map Makes Kent Part of Same "Nation" as France'. *Sunday Telegraph,* 3 Sept.

CRICK, B. (ed.) 1991. *National Identities: The Constitution of the United Kingdom.* Oxford: Blackwell.

CUNNINGHAM, H. 1981. 'The Language of Patriotism, 1750–1914'. *History Workshop Journal,* 12: 8–33.

CURTICE, J. 2007. 'How Long Will the English–Scots Union Last?' *Sunday Telegraph,* 9 Dec.

DANIELS, S. 1993. *Fields of Vision: Landscape Imagery and National Identity in England and the United States.* Cambridge: Polity.

DEFOE, D. 1865. *Works,* vol. v. London: Bohm.

DIBELIUS, W. 1922. *England.* London: Jonathan Cape, 1930.

DICEY, A. V. 1905. *Lectures on the Relation between Law and Public Opinion during the Nineteenth Century.* London: Macmillan, 1940.

ECCLESHALL, R. E. 1992. 'Michael Oakeshott and Sceptical Conservatism'. Pp. 173–96 in L. Tivey and A. Wright (eds.), *Political Thought since 1945: Philosophy, Science, Ideology.* Aldershot: Edward Elgar.

FOOTE, G. 2006. *The Republican Transformation of Modern Britain.* London: Macmillan.

FORSTER, E. M. 1950. 'George Orwell'. Pp. 69–72 in *Two Cheers for Democracy.* Harmondsworth: Penguin, 1951.

GARDINER, M. 2004. 'A Light to the World: British Devolution and Colonial Vision'. *Interventions,* 6: 264–81.

GEOGHEGAN, V. 2003. 'Edward Carpenter's England Revisited'. *History of Political Thought,* 24: 509–27.

GOODHART, D. 2006. 'National Anxieties'. *Prospect,* June.

GRAINGER, J. H. 1986. *Patriotisms: Britain, 1900–1940.* London: Routledge.

HASELER, S. 1996. *The English Tribe: Identity, Nation and Europe.* Basingstoke: Macmillan.

HAZELL, R. (ed.) 2006. *The English Question.* Manchester: Manchester University Press.

HEATH, A., MARTIN, J., and ELGENIUS, G. 2007. 'Who Do We Think We Are: The Decline of Traditional Social Identities'. Pp. 1–34 in A. Park et al. (eds.), *British Social Attitudes: The 23rd Report—Perspectives on a Changing Society.* London: Sage.

HEFFER, S. 1999. *Nor Shall my Sword: The Reinvention of England.* London: Weidenfeld and Nicolson.

—— 2006. 'The English Will be Heard, by George'. *Daily Telegraph,* 22 Apr.

HENLEY, W. E. 1896. 'What Have I Done for You'. Pp. 253–4 in *Poems.* London: David Nutt, 1898, 1907.

HILTON, B. 2006. *A Mad, Bad, and Dangerous People: England, 1783–1846.* Oxford: Oxford University Press.

HOWKINS, A. 1986. 'The Discovery of Rural England'. Pp. 62–88 in R. Colls and P. Dodd (eds.), *Englishness: Politics and Culture.* London: Croom Helm.

JOHNSTON, P. 2002. 'Labour's Balkanised England: Will it All End in More Tiers?' *Daily Telegraph,* 10 May.

KEARNEY, H. 2000. 'The Importance of Being British'. *Political Quarterly,* 71: 15–25.

KENNY, M. 1995. *The First New Left: British Intellectuals after Stalin.* London: Lawrence and Wishart.

KIPLING, R. 1896. 'The Native-Born'. In *The Seven Seas*. London: Methuen.

—— 1920. 'England and the English'. Speech to the Royal Society of St George, www.theenglandproject.net/documents.

KUMAR, K. 2003. *The Making of English National Identity*. Cambridge: Cambridge University Press.

—— 2006. 'Empire and English Nationalism'. *Nations and Nationalism*, 12: 1–13.

LANGFORD, P. 2000. *Englishness Identified: Manners and Character, 1650–1850*. Oxford: Oxford University Press.

LEE, S. 2006. 'Englishness in the Political Imagination: Past, Present and Future Approaches'. *Identity, Self and Symbolism*, 1: 34–69.

LEIGHTON, D. P. 2008. 'T. H. Green and the Dissidence of Dissent: On Religion and National Character in Nineteenth-Century England'. *Parliamentary History Yearbook Trust*, 27/1: 43–56.

MANDLER, P. 2006, *The English National Character: The History of an Idea from Edmund Burke to Tony Blair*. London: Yale University Press.

NAIRN, T. 1977. *The Break-up of Britain: Crisis and Neo-Nationalism*. London: Verso.

OAKESHOTT, M. 1947. 'Contemporary British Politics'. *Cambridge Journal*, 1: 474–90.

PAXMAN, J. 1998. *The English: A Portrait of a People*. London: Michael Joseph.

POCOCK, J. G. A. 2000. 'Gaberlunzie's Return'. *New Left Review*, 2nd ser. 5: 41–52.

POWELL, J. E. 1966. 'Legend and Living Force'. Review of R. Blake, *Disraeli* (London: Eyre and Spottiswoode). *Sunday Times*, 23 Oct.: 45.

—— 1969. *Freedom and Reality*, ed. J. Wood. London: Batsford.

READMAN, P. 2001*a*. 'The Conservative Party, Patriotism, and British Politics: The Case of the General Election of 1900'. *Journal of British Studies*, 40: 107–45.

—— 2001*b*. 'Landscape Preservation, "Advertising Disfigurement", and English National Identity *c*.1890–1914'. *Rural History*, 12/1: 61–83.

—— 2001*c*. 'The Liberal Party and Patriotism in Early Twentieth Century Britain'. *Twentieth Century British History*, 12: 269–302.

—— 2005. 'The Place of the Past in English Culture *c*.1890–1914'. *Past and Present*, 186: 147–200.

ROBINSON, A. 1798. *A View of the Causes and Consequences of English Wars from the Invasion of this Country by Julius Caesar to the Present Time*. London: J. Johnston.

ROSE, S. 2003. *Which People's War? National Identity and Citizenship in Britain, 1939–1945*. Oxford: Oxford University Press.

SCRUTON, R. 2001. *England: An Elegy*. London: Pimlico.

—— 2004. 'Why Shoudn't We Fly the English Flag'. *Daily Mail*, 11 June.

—— 2006*a*. *England and the Need for Nations*. London: Civitas.

—— 2006*b*. 'Should he have Spoken?' *New Criterion*, Sept.

SMITH, A. D. 2006. ' "Set in the Silver Sea": English National Identity and European Integration'. *Nations and Nationalism*, 12: 433–52.

SMITH, D. 1986. 'Englishness and the Liberal Inheritance after 1886'. Pp. 254–82 in R. Colls and P. Dodd (eds.), *Englishness: Politics and Culture*. London: Croom Helm.

STAPLETON, J. 1994. *Englishness and the Study of Politics: The Social and Political Thought of Ernest Barker*. Cambridge: Cambridge University Press.

—— 2001. *Political Intellectuals and Public Identities in Britain since 1850*. Manchester: Manchester University Press.

—— 2005*a*. 'Citizenship versus Patriotism in Twentieth-Century England'. *Historical Journal*, 48: 151–78.

—— 2005*b*. *Sir Arthur Bryant and National History in Twentieth-Century Britain*. Lanham, Md.: Lexington Books.

STAPLETON, J. 2006. 'The England of G. K. Chesterton'. *Chesterton Review*, 23: 339–55.

STARKEY, D. 1999. 'Chronicle of the Future'. *Sunday Times Online Forum*, 21 Feb.

THOMPSON, E. P. 1965. 'Outside the Whale'. Pp. 1–34 in *The Poverty of Theory*. London: Merlin Press, 1978.

VILLIS, T. 2006. *Reaction and the Avant-Garde: The Revolt against Liberal Democracy in Early Twentieth-Century Britain*. London: Tauris.

WALTON, J. K. 2002. 'Britishness'. Pp. 517–31 in C. Wrigley (ed.), *A Companion to Early Twentieth-Century Britain*. Oxford: Historical Association/Blackwell.

WARD, P. 2005. *Unionism in the United Kingdom, 1918–1974*. Basingstoke: Palgrave Macmillan.

WARD-SMITH, G. 2001. 'Baldwin and Scotland: More than Englishness'. *Contemporary British History*, 15/1: 61–82.

WATERS, C. 1994. 'J. B. Priestley (1894–1984): Englishness and the Politics of Nostalgia'. Pp. 209–28 in S. Pedersen and P. Mandler (eds.), *After the Victorians: Private Conscience and Public Duty in Modern Britain*. London: Routledge.

WEIGHT, R. 2002. *Patriots: National Identity in Britain, 1940–2000*. London: Macmillan.

WILLIAMSON, P. 1999. *Stanley Baldwin: Conservative Leadership and National Values*. Cambridge: Cambridge University Press.

WRIGHT, P. 2005. 'Last Orders'. *Guardian Review*, 9 Apr.: 4–6.

CHAPTER 28

IRELAND

RICHARD ENGLISH

28.1 INTRODUCTION

THE clash of rival Irish national identities has been one of the most significant features of UK history, embodying vital dynamics of modern world politics: contested state legitimacy; the clash between state and nation amid rival national identities; the intersection of ethnicity, religion, and nationalism; and the use of political violence to pursue competing nationalist goals. This chapter will begin by defining some crucial terms. It will then discuss rival Irish national identities within the modern UK, organized rival nationalisms in Northern Ireland, and some related complexities of British national identity.

28.2 DEFINITIONS

The terms 'nation', 'national identity', and 'nationalism' all require precise definition. Drawing on the work of Anthony Smith, a nation will here be defined as 'a named human population sharing an historic territory, common myths and historical memories, a mass, public culture, a common economy and common legal rights and duties for all members'; and the fundamental features of national identity will be taken as:

1. a historic territory, or homeland;
2. common myths and historical memories;
3. a common, mass public culture;

4. common legal rights and duties for all members; and

5. a common economy with territorial mobility for members (Smith 1991: 14).

In line with my own research findings (English 2006), nationalism will be defined as involving a particular interweaving of the politics of community, struggle, and power. At root, community suits human nature and our deepest human instincts: we want survival, self-protection, safety, and security and we possess a group instinct; social by nature, we want to belong to a stable, coherent, and effective community which will meet psychological needs (regarding purpose, self-esteem, meaning) as well as material and practical ones. The shared features of nationalist community (drawn variously from territory, people, descent, culture, history, ethical superiority, and exclusivism) are important here as possible means of communication. And such national community offers rewards that are more capacious and powerful than those offered by rival versions of group identity.

This community identification is only part of the nationalist story and explanation: collective struggle is also vital, whether for national sovereignty, unity, independence, material benefits, cultural status, or group and individual advancement. Each of these goals possesses its obvious appeal, but there can be allure also in the rewards of struggle as such. And this collective mobilization turns on questions of power: power as a goal (the establishment, legitimation, possession, and consolidation of power, often in the form of a nation-based, sovereign, and self-determining state), and also power as something by means of which you secure and guarantee the goods which you pursue as a nationalist.

28.3 RIVAL IRISH NATIONAL IDENTITIES WITHIN THE MODERN UK

Irish national identities have expressed themselves meaningfully in modern Britain in a range of ways, some of them comfortable within that setting, others sharply at odds with it (Hickman 2000). But the weightiest Irish national identities within recent UK politics have unquestionably been expressed within Northern Ireland. This was particularly true during the post-1960s Ulster conflict, the story of which has been told frequently (Tonge 2006; English 2004; Wood 2006). The politics of identity have become variously salient in recent decades in democratic societies (Kenny 2004); in Northern Ireland it is emphatically *national* identities which have been the vitally determining ones.

The contested nature of national identity remains abundantly clear in contemporary Northern Ireland. Asked about nationality in the early twenty-first century (and allowed to select as many or as few labels as applied), Northern Irish responses were as follows: 45 per cent British; 30 per cent Irish; 27 per cent Northern Irish; 9 per cent

Ulster; 11 per cent choosing other labels (Gilland and Kennedy 2003: 99). And divided national allegiances were clear too in the period immediately preceding the onset of late twentieth-century political violence. Richard Rose's important 1968 questionnaire survey valuably examined attitudes under the old Stormont Belfast regime. Regarding national identities, Rose (1971: 208) found a profound overlap between religious and national allegiance, as the following figures demonstrate:

Protestants: 39 per cent British, 32 per cent Ulster, 20 per cent Irish;
Catholics: 76 per cent Irish, 15 per cent British, 5 per cent Ulster.

Two important points might be noted, however, concerning these pre-Troubles percentages. First, the number of Northern Irish Protestants at that stage happy to describe themselves as Irish (20 per cent) was comparatively high. This situation changed during the subsequent conflict, as the concept of Irishness became more clearly and frequently defined in terms of Irish nationalism and Irish republicanism. In the era of Provisional Irish Republican Army (IRA) violence in pursuit of a non-British, independent, Gaelic Ireland, favoured almost exclusively by Irish Catholics, it became more difficult for Ulster Protestants to entertain an Irish self-image. By 1986 only 3 per cent of Northern Irish Protestants described themselves as Irish, and this figure remained stable through to the end of the century (English 2006: 396).

Second, there were important complexities behind the stark figures of 1960s declared national identity. When asked, for example, whether people in England, or people in the Republic of Ireland (or people in Northern Ireland from the opposite religious group), were 'much different' or 'about the same' as people in Northern Ireland (or people in Northern Ireland from one's own religious group) the answers were revealing. Rose's survey found that, among Northern Irish Protestants, 29 per cent thought English people about the same, 45 per cent thought people from the Republic of Ireland about the same, while far more—67 per cent—thought Northern Irish Catholics to be about the same. Among Catholics a similar pattern emerged: 30 per cent thought English people to be about the same, 44 per cent thought this of people from the Republic of Ireland, while 81 per cent thought Northern Irish Protestants to be about the same (Rose 1971: 214, 486, 496). Even at the dawn of the Troubles, therefore, each religious group (Catholic and Protestant) thought the other Northern Irish group to be much closer in similarity to itself than were the populations of either England or the Republic of Ireland. A very striking feature of Northern Irish identity was then, as it has remained, its distinctiveness within either a UK or an all-Ireland framework of identity.

Richard Rose did note that, 'A resident of Ulster has a wealth of identities to choose from' (Rose 1971: 205), and in more recent times some have even pointed to a supposed erosion of the dominance of national identity among the various options available in Northern Ireland. It has, for example, been claimed that national identities in Northern Ireland have become subverted by European (especially European Union) developments and by other transnational (economic, social, political, cultural) challenges to the dominance of the nation state and its associated sovereignty (McCall 1999). Certainly, the accession of the UK and the Republic of Ireland to the then European Economic Community in 1973 did set in train developments of great significance—politically, economically, and culturally. But it would be unwise to overstate the subversive effect of European identity on and in Northern Ireland. Asked their views in 2002, even on something as mechanical as the effect of participation in the EU, only 48 per cent of people in Northern Ireland endorsed the quite modest view that 'Participation has been useful' (McGowan and O'Connor 2004: 35). In Northern Ireland, identity has largely been defined *within* the rival national blocs, and the enduringly dominant self-image of most Northern Irish people has been that associated with their respective, rival national identities.

Irish nationalist identity in Northern Ireland has been complicated by its relationship to two states: the UK (within which northern nationalists have existed, but from which many have withheld loyalty and allegiance), and the neighbouring Republic of Ireland (to which many nationalists would have preferred the north to be united, in an independent Irish republic). Thus, from the outset of Northern Ireland in the 1920s, northern nationalism involved the sustenance of an alternative politics and culture: a national identity durably at odds with the formal identity of the state. This involved a sense of territory, properly (in nationalist eyes) extending beyond the boundaries of Northern Ireland itself. In the words of Sinn Fein's Gerry Adams, 'Ireland is historically, culturally and geographically one single unit. The partition of Ireland...divides Ireland into two artificial statelets' (Adams 1986: 88). This was a view long held by Irish nationalists north and south, and it was a position reinforced by the various pillars of national identity for northern nationalists: Catholic hierarchy, nationalist newspapers, and nationalist politicians.

Northern nationalists shared powerful myths and memories: of their own position as an Irish Catholic minority within a British and Protestant state; of long-term nationalist victimhood at the hands of England or Britain over the centuries; of historical heroes and villains and iconic moments of past national identity. There was a strong and shared mass public culture, focusing partly on the Catholic Church and faith. Denominational organization, belief, and practice offered undoubted rewards tied to Irish national identity as, without state power, the Catholic nationalist community witnessed a powerful interweaving of national identity with confessional allegiance. The northern nationalist press was full of Catholic Church matters, and the idea that Catholicism was central to Irish national identity long remained axiomatic (Elliott 2000: 450).

Catholicism was accompanied by other cultural inheritances and practices, Gaelic sport and music among them, and the sense of shared and compelling duty to such cultural traditions was pronounced (English 2006: 358–9). Shared duties of a different kind were assumed in the northern nationalist pursuit of communal redress of grievance: in campaigning for civil rights in the 1960s, national rights during the Troubles, and the politics of equality during the peace process. Taken together, these various elements constituted an alternative Irish nationalist political culture in Northern Ireland from the outset of the state: here was an effective counter-life within the UK, embodied in an Irish nationalist community possessing a distinctive structure and national identity of its own.

Some of this remained relatively constant, an example being the cross-class aspect of such confessionally based national culture. There was, and remains, far more of a shared political identity between Catholic nationalists of various classes than between, for example, the Catholic-nationalist and Protestant-unionist working classes in Northern Ireland. But some aspects of this national identity have proved more fluid. It was long merely assumed by Irish nationalists that the Irish nation was coextensive with the island of Ireland, and that unionists were Irish people existing in a state of false consciousness which would evaporate once Britain decided to withdraw from Ireland. But even members of the Provisional republican movement have now publicly conceded that this view was inadequate (English 2004: 312–13). And the political context has changed for nationalists also. The 1985 Anglo-Irish Agreement between the UK and Ireland gave institutional blessing, for example, to the legitimacy of Irish national identity within the UK, and recognized the need for an Irish dimension which incorporated a role for the Republic of Ireland in the politics and culture of the north.

It would be wrong to see Irish national identity and British unionist identity in Northern Ireland as mirror images of one another. They are not. Whether one examines churches, schools, paramilitary groups, political parties, or even the two states with a role in Ulster, it is the asymmetry which is striking. But there has existed, in competition with northern nationalist identity, a unionist British identity representative of the majority of the people in Northern Ireland. It too has had a notion of territory, involving for some a marked attachment to the north-east of Ireland itself, and for all a strong sense that the appropriate unit of attachment was the UK rather than an all-island, non-British identity. Unionists had a long, historic commitment to their territory; they also shared common myths and historical memories, including the shared sense of vulnerability to Irish nationalist subversion and attack, and also a positive identification with the manifold achievements of British culture, of economic, scientific, and other intellectual accomplishment, and of the contribution of Ulster unionists and Protestants to these historical riches. British national identity among unionists had its mass public culture, too: Protestant churches provided one means of achieving this, as did the monarchy, the Orange Order, various sporting allegiances, and a wide range of civil society mechanisms. Duties were profound: of loyalty to the state, to other members of the community, and to the law and order needed (and often threatened) in Northern Ireland since the 1920s.

Ulster unionist British identity derived cohesion from its recognition of the dangers posed by Irish nationalist assertion, whether in the form of the growing minority of nationalists within Northern Ireland itself, or in terms of the Irish nationalist state to the south (which long claimed jurisdiction over the six counties of Northern Ireland). Unionist identities have often been characterized as incoherent, owing to their various layers. But there is nothing inherently peculiar about layered identity as such, and during the early years of Northern Ireland's existence, unionists could understandably see themselves as simultaneously Northern Irish, British, Irish, and Imperial. The last two of these layers have now been lost (Irishness effectively having been assumed by nationalists, and the empire having died). But the concentric circles of contemporary unionist identity (for some Northern Ireland, Britain/UK, Europe) need not be mutually incompatible. Moreover, some unionists have identified their own national culture with an Anglo-American, liberal-democratic tradition (McCartney 2001; Trimble 2001), pointing towards features of unionist identity which should, at least, be recognizably valid to many observers.

Some other key points might be made regarding unionist national identity. One concerns the resilience of Britishness, despite the politics of decline. The extent and the avoidability of British decline have often been exaggerated (English and Kenny 2000), but there is no doubt that relative British decline has been a defining feature of modern UK politics. This has had an eroding effect on aspects of Ulster unionist Britishness: as noted, the empire has passed away; Protestantism has become less central to contemporary British life than many Northern Irish unionists would like; the monarchy has been transformed; and the death of industrial power has diminished the economic weight of unionist Ulster. Yet British national identity among Ulster Protestants remains extraordinarily resilient despite all this, and the commitment to retaining the union of Northern Ireland and Great Britain remains almost unanimous among Ulster Protestants. It is not that all Catholics oppose the union, recent evidence suggesting that 33 per cent of Northern Irish Catholics favour its retention (Irwin 2002: 202). But the unanimity of Protestant opinion on the subject does point again to the profound overlap in Northern Ireland between confessional background and political identity (English 2006: 555).

That religion is important to Ulster unionist national identity is unarguable (Bruce 1994: 18, 30), but other aspects of that identity might be more open to debate. The frequent suggestion of triumphalist superiority within unionist culture (often enough associated with the Northern Irish politics of parades) (Bryan 2000; Kaufmann 2007) might perhaps better be read as the swagger born of constant insecurity. This certainly emerges from some important studies of loyalism (Nelson 1984; Bruce 1994). And the notion of monolithic unionist identity should also be questioned. Scholars have long noted divisions within the unionist community over identity, such work dating back at least as far as Jennifer Todd's 1987 argument that there existed two main ideological traditions within Northern Irish unionism: Ulster loyalism (primarily attached to a northern Protestant community, secondarily attached to the British state, and seeing religion and politics as inextricably linked); and Ulster British ideology (primarily attached to the community of Greater Britain, secondarily defined by a Northern Irish regional patriotism, and characterized by liberal political values) (Todd 1987). Some would question the durability of this dichotomous reading (Farrington 2006), pointing out that many actually existing unionists would seem to have lived in both camps. But, as intra-unionist divisions during the peace process period have demonstrated, unionist political identity has been fissiparous rather than monolithic.

28.4 ORGANIZED RIVAL NATIONALISMS IN NORTHERN IRELAND

The most forceful expression of rival Northern Irish national identities has been found in the respective organized nationalisms of nationalists and unionists. Some would dispute the treatment of unionism under the label of nationalism at all, but it seems to me that we can valuably analyse the dynamics of Northern Irish unionist politics through the lenses of our reading of the phenomenon of nationalism.

Unionists in Northern Ireland have been preoccupied with questions of survival, self-protection, safety, and security, having been under actual threat since the revolutionary period from which Northern Ireland was born, through to the recent Troubles. Within this context, the importance of communal organization and strength has been clear, as have various bases of coherent, durable group identity and organization. Unionist politics have focused on the various component parts so often found in nationalist movements: territory, people, shared descent and culture and history, and a belief in the distinctive value of one's own community and the boundaries which mark it out from its competitors. Unionists have been involved in repeated, organized struggle: to avoid Irish Home Rule in the era prior to the foundation of Northern Ireland; to defend the existence and identity of their Northern Irish state and government between 1921 and the introduction of Direct Rule from Westminster in 1972; and to protect life and unionist interests against republican and nationalist assault during the bloody decades of the late twentieth century. The attempt to guarantee the future of the union with Great Britain reflected a complex theme so often central to organized nationalist struggle: the focus on national sovereignty, on the unity held necessary to achieve this, on the freedom which this sovereignty involves, and on the material benefits to be derived from such freedom. All of these elements were to be found in the organized politics of Northern Irish unionists.

And crucial to all of this was the question of power. If a nation-based state was one which reflected your own national identity, culture, and community, then your interests were held to be safer. Hence the unionist zeal to preserve their own government in Belfast, for one of the paradoxes of modern unionism has been its mistrust of London governments. The most famous of all latter-day unionists, the resolutely anti-republican Ian Paisley, even admitted in the 1990s 'something that is very repugnant to me, but it's become a reality, that people have more faith in the statements of the IRA than they have in the statements of the British government' (quoted in English 2004: 268).

The unionist approach towards the battles of national identity has been a somewhat defensive one, in a context in which threatened and actual change have tended to move history in an Irish nationalist rather than an Ulster unionist direction. How has this worked in practice? During recent decades unionist Ulster has overwhelmingly expressed itself in formal-political terms through two main parties, the Democratic Unionist party (DUP) and the Ulster Unionist party (UUP). The latter, known for many years as the Official Unionist party, provided the governing party of Northern Ireland between 1921 and 1972 (Walker 2004). During these years the party was deeply committed both to retaining the union between Northern Ireland and Great Britain and also to defending the existence and powers of the Belfast parliament. The UUP has, since the 1960s, been at times sharply divided between more reformist and more conservatively traditional wings: this was evident in rival responses within the party to the civil rights movement of the 1960s, to the 1973–4 experiment in power sharing with northern nationalists, and, more recently, to the 1998 Belfast Agreement. Traditionally, the UUP was the larger and more popular of the two main unionist parties. But its position has slipped dramatically in recent years, as is evident from its performance in UK general elections from 1983, 1992, 2001, and 2005: in 1983 the UUP won 34 per cent of the vote and eleven seats; in 1992 it obtained 35 per cent of the vote and nine seats; in 2001 it managed 27 per cent of the vote and seven seats; but in 2005 it won 18 per cent of the vote and only one seat. The party endorsed the 1998 Belfast Agreement, and when unionist opinion turned against that deal in subsequent years—with unionists thinking its implementation heavily to have favoured Irish nationalists—the UUP paid an electoral price, being eclipsed by the long-anti-Agreement DUP.

The UUP had throughout its political life focused on maintaining UK sovereignty over Northern Ireland. As such, it had deeply opposed the 1985 Anglo-Irish Agreement which introduced a formal role for the Republic of Ireland in the affairs of the north: though happy enough at the prospect of economic cooperation with the Republic, the party held that there was no proper political role for Dublin in the politics of Northern Ireland. Indeed, much UUP opinion in the later 1980s had favoured full integration into the UK, namely the integration of Northern Ireland into the UK on exactly the same basis as any other part of the state.

In the 1990s peace process, elements within the party eventually came to accept that some north–south, cross-border Irish dimension would be required as part of a successful deal ending the Ulster conflict. But well into the 1990s there remained a hostility towards a Dublin role in Northern Irish political decision-making. Under the leadership of David Trimble in the 1990s (Godson 2004), the party played a major part in negotiating and supporting the Good Friday Agreement. This marked a recognition of some key realities in Northern Ireland's organized war of national identities: neither the Protestant nor the Catholic community could expect to enjoy a large enough majority to enable it to win the war of rival nationalisms (the 2001 Northern Ireland Census showed a population comprising 53 per cent Protestant, 44 per cent Catholic, 3 per cent other) (English 2004: 389). Moreover, some form of power-sharing arrangement had long been seen by London as the proper basis for devolved power in Belfast and so a compromise—such as that of 1998—made much sense. For when Direct Rule had been introduced in 1972, the UUP had been diminished in importance from a governing party to a significant but ultimately powerless party of protest; the realities of power now necessitated a different kind of struggle.

Eventually, this seemed the case even to the most famously anti-republican unionist of all, Ian Paisley, whose DUP in 2007 participated in a power-sharing government with their Sinn Fein enemies. By that stage the DUP had emerged as the dominant party of Northern Irish unionism, but this process had taken a very long time in coming to fruition. The DUP had been founded in 1971 by Revd Ian Paisley and Desmond Boal, the two men sharing a hostility towards the reformist instincts of some Ulster unionists at that time. The party, which Paisley himself led from the outset, was to represent a non-violent but hardline unionism: it was long opposed to any concessions to republican or nationalist constitutional demands, and it was staunchly keen to defend the union with Great Britain. The DUP's sense of struggle has been sharp, and it traditionally called for an uncompromisingly hard line against the IRA, towards whom it held successive London governments to have been far too lenient.

Paisley's party, rather than paramilitary-related loyalist political parties, was the means of organized expression for hardline unionist electoral instinct. The DUP sustainedly obtained electoral success: in the 1979 UK general election it won 10 per cent of the vote; in the 1983 UK general election it obtained 20 per cent of the vote; and by the time of the 2005 UK general election—when the DUP's popularity had risen as unionist hostility to the Good Friday Agreement had grown—the party's success was even more marked, with the DUP winning 34 per cent of the vote and establishing itself as the dominant Northern Irish unionist party.

Issues of power were central to this brand of unionism, hence the party's long hostility towards power sharing with Irish nationalists. But culture also played a significant role, especially in the form of religion. Ian Paisley's Free Presbyterian Church (which he had founded in 1951) has by no means been coextensive with his political party (the latter drawing on a far larger constituency), but there has been a strongly Protestant dimension to some of Paisley's arguments and stances. Though often helpful to Catholic constituents, Paisley himself has at times been publicly hostile towards the Roman Catholic Church and sceptical about Protestant–Catholic ecumenism. For him, unionist struggle has been, in part, about defending a politics interwoven with Protestant conviction and adherence.

Organized unionist politics have been represented by these two constitutional political parties, but also by violent loyalist paramilitaries whom those parties have long condemned. Groups such as the Ulster Defence Association (UDA) and the Ulster Volunteer Force (UVF) have carried out high levels of fatal violence in pursuit of their own brand of unionist struggle. Violence has been held by them to offer a necessary response to IRA and other republican violence, and to what loyalists have perceived as the inadequate response of the state in dealing with that republican threat. Paradoxically, therefore, loyalist paramilitaries have, in supposed defence of the UK state, challenged that state's Weberian claim to a monopoly of legitimate violence within its boundaries, precisely because they have held the state not to have used that monopoly effectively enough against the state's republican enemies. Between 1966 and 2001 loyalist paramilitaries killed 1,071 people in the Northern Ireland Troubles (Irish republicans killing 2,148 people in the same period, and security forces killing 365) (McKittrick et al. 2001: 1496).

Organized Irish nationalism took a different form from that of unionism, the central dichotomy between its own rival wings being between two well-supported

groups, one of which eschewed and the other of which long pursued political violence. The Social Democratic and Labour Party (SDLP)—Irish nationalist, pro-
European, and constitutionalist in outlook—was founded in 1970 to further the cause
of a united Ireland by consent. It favoured the ending of Irish partition but on the
basis of persuading (rather than violently coercing) a majority of people in Northern
Ireland to take this path. It should be stressed that, despite frequent assumption that
Northern Ireland demonstrates the victory of extremism over moderation, it was this
moderate, constitutional nationalist party which repeatedly gained majority support
among Irish nationalists while the IRA was engaged in violent conflict. In pre-
ceasefire Northern Ireland, the constitutional-nationalist SDLP clearly and repeatedly
defeated the IRA's political party, Sinn Fein, at the polls (English 2006: 383):

General Election 1983	SDLP 17.9 per cent	SF 13.4 per cent
General Election 1987	SDLP 21.1 per cent	SF 11.4 per cent
General Election 1992	SDLP 23.5 per cent	SF 10.0 per cent
District Council Elections 1985	SDLP 17.8 per cent	SF 11.8 per cent
District Council Elections 1989	SDLP 21.0 per cent	SF 11.2 per cent

The SDLP have focused on self-determination as a nationalist right, on power as
something to which Irish nationalists in the north should have access, on the pursuit
of material advantage for the nationalist community, and on pursuing an ultimate
goal of independent, united Irish sovereign statehood. In terms of method, they long
argued that there was no justification for IRA violence, and that such violence merely
accentuated divisions in Ireland. There was much friction with the IRA: a reflection
of the intra-communal tension which often developed in Northern Ireland but which
has been obscured by the inter-communal conflict. In essence, the party's policy has
involved achieving a united Ireland through peaceful, consensual means, although by
no means all party members actually favour a united Ireland, and the party has at
times espoused joint authority.

The SDLP endorsed the 1998 Good Friday Agreement as a valid resolution of the
conflicting interests of the north's competing national traditions. Indeed, much of
what the 1998 deal actually involved (power sharing with a north–south dimension;
respect for two national traditions; shared access by both communities to decision-
making and power, for example) had been SDLP policy for many years (Murray and
Tonge 2005; Aughey 2005: 30). The party had long espoused the politics of power
sharing and the involvement of the London and Dublin governments in Northern
Ireland solutions.

Culture too played its part in this organized nationalist story. Though stressing
peaceful means and a respect for different traditions (unionist as well as nationalist),
the SDLP's support base was always overwhelmingly Catholic. A figure such as John
Hume (one of the party's founder members in 1970, and its leader from 1979 onwards)
repeatedly appealed to Protestants for a shared approach to Northern Ireland, but
remained for most Protestants a figure whose politics held no significant appeal
at all.

He was, however, less despised by Ulster Protestants than were his intra-communal rivals: the Provisional republican movement. The Provisional IRA was founded at the end of 1969 as a break-away faction splitting from the existing IRA. The Provisionals had emerged for a number of interwoven reasons, including a perceived need for the defence of northern Catholic communities under attack in the 1969 sectarian crisis, together with a sense that the existing IRA was focusing too much on left-leaning and quasi-parliamentary politics, rather than on issues such as defence or more militarily-inclined republicanism. From its early days, the new IRA's own version of organized nationalist struggle involved attempted defence, retaliation, and an offensive campaign of violence aimed at undermining and ultimately destroying the Northern Ireland state. The IRA held the north to be irredeemably sectarian and undemocratic; they held that reform of Northern Ireland was futile, and that the only solution to this discriminatory unionist state was its abolition, to be brought about through their own campaign of violence.

That campaign was lengthy, the IRA killing 1,778 people between 1969 and 2000, and as such killing more people than any other group in the Northern Ireland conflict (English 2004: 379). They initially had an expectation of comparatively early victory, and then (from the mid-1970s onwards) saw their struggle as involving a longer nationalist war which would, they anticipated, ultimately break the will of the London government and lead the latter to withdraw from Ireland. IRA thinking was well encapsulated in repeated declarations of the purpose of their violence, as with the following from 1989: 'The IRA strategy is very clear. At some point in the future, due to the pressure of the continuing and sustained armed struggle, the will of the British government to remain in this country will be broken. That is the objective of the armed struggle' (quoted in English 2004: 263).

In practice, the IRA was unable to defend Catholic communities or to force British withdrawal from Northern Ireland. But it long argued the need for Irish self-determination, and became such a major factor in the conflict that its political wing—Sinn Fein—had to play a significant role in any proposed solution. During the 1990s the IRA shifted its mode of struggle considerably. It embarked on ceasefires (in 1994 and then again from 1997 onwards), engaged in dialogue with the Dublin and London regimes, and ultimately decommissioned its weapons and brought an end to its war. By the early twenty-first century it was Sinn Fein, rather than the IRA, which had become the dominant partner in the Provisional republican marriage.

Why did the Provisional movement change from war to peace? First, it came to recognize that its violence was producing not victory, but merely a bloody stalemate; second, it recognized that the politics of ceasefire and peace process would produce definite and more positive results (a higher vote for Sinn Fein, prisoner release, the reform of the north of Ireland); third, it recognized some realities long denied by its traditional thinking (that Northern Ireland rested on economic subvention from Britain and that immediate British withdrawal was therefore not feasible; that the IRA's reading of unionism had underestimated unionists' resolve and their durable centrality to the Northern Irish situation; that the Republic of Ireland was a state legitimate in its own right and far from zealous for a united Ireland).

Thus the IRA eventually retired from the political stage. Some republican aims and elements remained constant: an ultimate goal of a united, independent, sovereign Ireland; a commitment to Irish self-determination; and a Catholic-nationalist base in the north. But much had also changed: the politics of armed struggle had ended; compromise with a British Northern Ireland appeared to offer the best way forward for northern nationalists; and a reformed north in which republicans shared power seemed appropriate.

So while republicans still contested the ultimate legitimacy of the British state in Northern Ireland, they effectively came to acknowledge that the UK would continue to operate in the north for the medium-term future. There were certainly gains in shifting from violent to more constitutional forms of nationalist struggle. With the IRA's 1994 and 1997 ceasefires, and the 1998 Good Friday Agreement and its gradual, jagged implementation, Sinn Fein became not only the dominant wing of the republican movement, but also the dominant voice in northern nationalism. In the 2001 UK general election the SDLP was overtaken by Sinn Fein, with the latter winning four seats to the SDLP's three; in the UK general election of 2005 this process was reinforced, Sinn Fein winning five seats and the SDLP three.

Ironically, therefore, a party which had long denounced parliamentary politics, political compromise (such as power sharing within Northern Ireland), reform rather than the destruction of the Northern Ireland state, and the rights of unionists to remain in the UK, came to dominate northern nationalism on the basis of espousing these views (Murray and Tonge 2005: 239). Sinn Fein might still hold to its ultimate preference for a sovereign and independent united Ireland, but this has become relegated to the long term in practice, and the party became keen to build its support and power base within the two separate Irish states, north and south, and to work in less obviously hostile relation to London or Dublin regimes. A form of political pragmatism has, with Sinn Fein, apparently won out, as intransigent purism waned (Rafter 2005).

The republican movement had therefore evolved dramatically. But throughout these differing phases, the politics of nationalism could be discerned in ways that explain the allure of the movement. Issues of nationalist survival, self-protection, safety, and security were, for example, to the fore at the very birth of the Provisionals in 1969, when one of the impulses behind the new movement lay in its supposed capacity to offer defence when Catholic communities were under loyalist attack. Republicans' sense of durable, coherent community (with a strong sense of inherited and justifying history, or of shared cultures of Gaelicism and Catholicism), offered routes to comforting and effective self-image and national identity. A muscular movement offered leverage in gaining attention for one's grievances, and both the IRA and Sinn Fein have constantly pressed for communal advantage in terms of national recognition for their community and in terms of material economic advantage and advancement. Struggle was shaped to suit a form apparently most effective at any given point: where the early Provisionals saw themselves fitting into a late 1960s and early 1970s Zeitgeist of anti-imperial, colonial-liberationist campaigns, the latter-day

Sinn Fein recognized the futility of ongoing paramilitary stalemate and the value instead of a politics of constitutional progress and struggle.

Power was vital, both as a method (the Provisionals consciously used their violent power in order to maximize their leverage) and as the goal to be pursued: ideally, a sovereign and independent Irish national state run by people who shared republicans' national identity and culture. The foundation for this was the Provisionals' case for the right of Irish national self-determination. This remained a key component of their nationalist argument; it also points towards one of the crucial ways in which rival Irish nationalisms have exemplified the complexities of British national identity.

28.5 THE COMPLEXITIES OF BRITISH NATIONAL IDENTITY

Behind nationalist enthusiasm for one's own national freedom lies the assumption of an international order modelled according to the universal principle of national self-determination. Indeed, nationalism has arguably been a doctrine of self-determination (the power of a people to determine its own politics and government) as much as it has been anything else. Nationalists have defended the right of national majorities within a territory collectively to decide their own political lives and, in doing so, to enjoy freedom from outside control or domination. And both Irish nationalists and Ulster unionists have argued that self-determination supports their case. Traditionally, nationalists have claimed that the unit of self-determination should be the people of Ireland as a single unit, and that this group would favour an independent and united Ireland. Unionists, by contrast, have held that the six-county state of Northern Ireland (or, at times, the UK as a whole) should be the unit. Here we face the paradox of self-determination: the places in which the idea seems most urgently required as the key to unlocking a national problem have often tended to be the very places in which there is least agreement about which 'self' should do the 'determining'. Predictably, each side tends to prefer a 'self' which will 'determine' in its own favour.

The UK's contested legitimacy in Northern Ireland provides here a version of the wider problems currently faced in the United Kingdom regarding self-determination, legitimacy, and separatism. Those nationalists (whether Scottish, Welsh, English, or Irish) who argue for the separation of their own nation from the UK state face the clash between perceived historic rights to self-determination and the complexities of actually-existing opinion and of pragmatic politics and economics. In each of the four constituent parts of the UK there are voices calling for separatism, and there are those on both left and right who consider the dissolution of the UK to be inevitable. But Northern Ireland—for all of its distinctive recent bloodiness—perhaps highlights some broader UK patterns here.

First, although the UK state embodies a less emotionally alluring or fashionable cause than do its centrifugal nationalisms, the reality of popular opinion in Northern Ireland (and perhaps in the other component parts of the UK as well, were a realistic end to the union actually in prospect) favours the UK rather than separatism. This is backed up (in Northern Ireland as in Scotland and Wales) by the further current reality that independence probably lacks economic feasibility. And there does seem to be scope—even in as sharply contested a setting as the north of Ireland—for reconceiving self-determination in ways more subtle and flexible than an automatic recourse to nation-state independence. Here, the Northern Ireland peace process and the 1998 Belfast Agreement perhaps point the way forward regarding other UK devolutionary or separatist challenges. In Ulster, self-determination still lies at the heart of political argument, and its centrality to politics has helped keep Irish nationalists within that process. But self-determination has been doubly reimagined in the Northern Irish context, altering it from its traditional Irish nationalist notion of an all-island vote in favour of Irish unity and independence from Britain. Self-determination is now exercised in the two parts of Ireland, simultaneously but separately, as in the referendums on the Good Friday Agreement in 1998; and the new political structures within the north allow for self-determination in the form of communal-national will on either side within a divided polity: there is emerging in Northern Ireland an effective right of communal veto (for either national group, Irish nationalist or British unionist) over certain political or cultural developments. This has reinforced the situation in which many Irish nationalists in the north have been prepared to accept something far short of sovereign independence from Britain. Their national identity is built into state structures, and their community has protective rights of veto.

This relates to another point: the assumption that Northern Ireland's departure from the UK is somehow inevitable at some stage in the future rests on a related assumption that a united, independent Ireland is a viable prospect. This may be so. But there are reasons for doubting it at present, and for thinking that Irish national identity and British unionist identity might coexist within a UK setting for some while to come. As noted, there existed at the most recent Northern Ireland Census (2001) a majority of people from a Protestant background, the vast majority of whom are unionist in sympathy. Even if one assumed (and one should not) that the 3 per cent designating themselves 'other' were all Catholic, there would still exist some ground to catch up before Catholics constituted a majority of the population of Northern Ireland. Moreover, Protestant hostility towards a united Ireland is more pervasive and intense than is Catholic enthusiasm for such an outcome. In the early twenty-first century, it remains the case that the percentage of Northern Irish Protestants preferring political unification with the rest of Ireland (5 per cent) is far lower than the percentage of Catholics preferring to remain in the UK (21 per cent), and that the percentage of Protestants committed to remaining in the UK (82 per cent) is far higher than the percentage of Catholics committed to unification with the rest of

Ireland (49 per cent). In the early years of the twenty-first century only 24 per cent of Northern Ireland's population actually support Irish unity (Tonge 2006: 7). Tellingly, recent research suggests that only 50 per cent of even SDLP members themselves state that a united Ireland would be the best solution to the Northern Ireland problem (Murray and Tonge 2005: 204). So there would need to be a huge Catholic majority before a northern majority favoured a united Ireland. Moreover, for a variety of economic, cultural, and political reasons, there is no practical enthusiasm in the Republic of Ireland for Irish unity (English 2004: 361–3; 2006: 421–3).

Again, our sense of how benign a phenomenon British national identity is will depend on whether we address it within a UK or a purely British framework. Contrary to some arguments about the supposedly benign quality of nationality and nationalism, it might be argued that the Irish–British relationship as painfully embodied in Northern Ireland—a subject usually ignored in such arguments—demonstrates some of the troubling features of nationality and nationalism on all sides: the painful tension between nation and state; the problem of disaffected and non-accommodated minorities within the UK; the durable importance of religion as a distinguishing marker within national identity; and the possibilities for political violence as an expression of national identity and aspiration.

It might, for example, seem strange for a scholar as rigorous and intelligent as David Miller to stress the beneficent aspects of nationality, and then refuse engagement with that part of the UK in which it has displayed its most cruel nature (Miller 1995: 173). There are glancing references to Northern Ireland in a later, equally valuable work by the same author (Miller 2000), but again there is no attempt here to consider in any detail the problems raised by the Ulster conflict for Miller's philosophical defence of nationality. The word 'crisis' has very often been deployed in relation to aspects of modern British experience (in the literature on decline, for example). But one of the most central crises of the UK state has involved that part of the UK not in Britain: here—in Northern Ireland—there has long been something like a civil war, and its causes and dynamics exemplify the darker side of the complex phenomenon of British national identity and its difficult legacies.

Yet again, in the post-9/11 terrorist crisis, the question of ethno-religious identity and political violence has become awkwardly salient in Britain, with much argument regarding Islam, Islamism, and the British state. One feature of this debate has been its apparent amnesia regarding what we know from the UK's experience of ethno-religious national identity and political violence in Northern Ireland. Indeed, the narrative of post-9/11 UK responses to jihadism has a depressingly familiar sound to anyone who knows the politics of Northern Ireland and the eruption of violence there in the late 1960s and early 1970s. It is clear that some lessons have not been well learned. In the post-9/11 crisis, rushed legislation has undermined important civil liberties without obviously preventing the likelihood of further attacks on the west (Dworkin 2003); imprisonment or internment have been further marred by allegations of mistreatment (including those in Guantanamo Bay and Abu Ghraib), thereby offering a propaganda victory to opponents of the UK and USA; there have been instances (including one in London) in which the wrong person was targeted and killed; and there has been a formal military deployment to respond in war-mode to a terrorist challenge, without adequate development of accurate and precise counter-terrorist intelligence or planning.

In all of this there are echoes of the less successful features of UK response to the IRA threat, and we could and should have learned these lessons in ways that would have offset some damaging post-9/11 policies. In Britain during the 1970s anti-terror legislation was rushed through parliament in the wake of IRA bombs in England; it did not prove especially helpful in combating the IRA, but it did seem at times to make the state look repressive. Internment of many of the wrong people in the early 1970s in Northern Ireland helped to deepen support for the IRA among nationalist communities there, as did mistreatment of prisoners while in custody. Shoot-to-kill allegations in the 1980s—though comparatively rare in number—handed propaganda advantage to the far more murderous opponents of the state. And throughout the Northern Ireland conflict the deployment of formal British Army soldiership was of less value than was the acquisition and preventative deployment of intelligence information in fighting the IRA—a lesson only slowly learned in Northern Ireland, but absolutely central in the fight against terrorism. Conventional military approaches are of far less value in combating the terror threat than are data acquired quietly through intelligence agents and informers within militant groups themselves and their host communities. The latter allowed for the placing of a ceiling on the level of effective IRA operations; and yet the evidence of the Iraq War episode is that insufficient attention has—even after 9/11—been paid to intelligence acquisition, and that more emphasis has been placed on the deployment of formal military power.

And the UK's experience in Northern Ireland demonstrated perhaps the key lesson in dealing with non-state violence: the necessity of avoiding actions or policies around which resistance can mobilize through the mechanism of victimhood. (And the implications of this lesson for the delicate handling of the inter-ethnic dimensions of contemporary British national identity should be very clear.) The 1976–81 Northern Irish war of the prisons allowed the IRA to present itself as the victim—turning a lethal set of prisoners into vulnerable prison-protesters and hunger-strikers in the eyes of world opinion. An avoidable prison stand-off thus injected life into what had—in the mid-1970s—been a rather flagging Irish republican movement.

Overall, one of the most telling lessons from the painful experience of contested national identities in modern Ulster has been that political violence tends to make such problems more famous and more urgent of resolution, while making that resolution itself far more difficult. In Northern Ireland, two communities neighboured one another largely in cold mistrust from the 1920s until the 1960s. The post-1960s violence then rendered trust, compromise, and magnanimity far more difficult still to achieve, and it is tempting to see the political violence of late twentieth-century Northern Ireland less as a necessary means to achieving progress, than as a symptom of that myopic vision (on all sides) which encouraged the futile pursuit of military victory rather than the achievement of messy compromise. Here again there are Ulster pre-echoes for the problems of contemporary British national identity as it relates to the wider international crisis of war and terror. For many and for a long time, political violence was seen in Northern Ireland as offering a means of effecting desirable and necessary change: Irish republicans saw their violence as necessary both to the defence of their community and to the achievement of national liberation; Ulster loyalists considered their violence necessary as a defence against Irish nationalism and as a means of strengthening their place within the UK; the state itself initially relied heavily on military might in its attempt to defeat terrorism and disorder. Yet violence failed to meet the challenge of achieving legitimate accommodation between groups possessing durable but rival national identities. We now know the hideous personal cost of this in Northern Ireland (McKittrick et al. 2001; Myers 2006), and the ultimate futility of conflicts such as that fought out over national identity in late twentieth-century Ulster. Whether we apply these lessons in other arenas of British politics remains to be seen.

REFERENCES

ADAMS, G. 1986. *The Politics of Irish Freedom*. Dingle: Brandon.

AUGHEY, A. 2005. *The Politics of Northern Ireland: Beyond the Belfast Agreement*. London: Routledge.

BRUCE, S. 1994. *The Edge of the Union: The Ulster Loyalist Political Vision*. Oxford: Oxford University Press.

BRYAN, D. 2000. *Orange Parades: The Politics of Ritual, Tradition and Control*. London: Pluto Press.

DWORKIN, R. 2003. 'Terror and the Attack on Civil Liberties'. *New York Review of Books*, 6 Nov.

ELLIOTT, M. 2000. *The Catholics of Ulster: A History*. London: Allen Lane.

ENGLISH, R. 2004. *Armed Struggle: The History of the IRA*. London: Pan Macmillan (1st pub. 2003).

—— 2006. *Irish Freedom: The History of Nationalism in Ireland*. London: Pan Macmillan.

—— and KENNY, M. (eds.) 2000. *Rethinking British Decline*. Basingstoke: Macmillan.

FARRINGTON, C. 2006. *Ulster Unionism and the Peace Process in Northern Ireland*. Basingstoke: Palgrave.

GILLAND, K., and KENNEDY, F. (eds.) 2003. 'Data Yearbook 2002'. *Irish Political Studies*, 17: 1–108.

GODSON, D. 2004. *Himself Alone: David Trimble and the Ordeal of Unionism*. London: HarperCollins.

HICKMAN, M. 2000. 'A New England through Irish Eyes?' Pp. 96–110 in S. Chen and T. Wright (eds.), *The English Question*. London: Fabian Society.

IRWIN, C. 2002. *The People's Peace Process in Northern Ireland*. Basingstoke: Palgrave Macmillan.

KAUFMANN, E. P. 2007. *The Orange Order: A Contemporary Northern Irish History*. Oxford: Oxford University Press.

KENNY, M. 2004. *The Politics of Identity*. Cambridge: Polity.

McCALL, C. 1999. *Identity in Northern Ireland: Communities, Politics and Change*. Basingstoke: Macmillan.

McCARTNEY, R. 2001. *Reflections on Liberty, Democracy and the Union*. Dublin: Maunsel.

McGowan, L., and O'Connor, J. S. 2004. 'Exploring Eurovisions: Awareness and Knowledge of the European Union in Northern Ireland'. *Irish Political Studies*, 19/2: 21–42.

McKittrick, D., Kelters, S., Feeney, B., and Thornton, C. 2001. *Lost Lives: The Stories of the Men, Women and Children Who Died as a Result of the Northern Ireland Troubles*. Edinburgh: Mainstream (1st pub. 1999).

Miller, D. 1995. *On Nationality*. Oxford: Oxford University Press.

——2000. *Citizenship and National Identity*. Cambridge: Polity.

Murray, G., and Tonge, J. 2005. *Sinn Fein and the SDLP: From Alienation to Participation*. Dublin: O'Brien Press.

Myers, K. 2006. *Watching the Door: A Memoir 1971–1978*. Dublin: Lilliput.

Nelson, S. 1984. *Ulster's Uncertain Defenders: Loyalists and the Northern Ireland Conflict*. Belfast: Appletree Press.

Rafter, K. 2005. *Sinn Fein 1905–2005: In the Shadow of Gunmen*. Dublin: Gill and Macmillan.

Rose, R. 1971. *Governing without Consensus: An Irish Perspective*. London: Faber and Faber.

Smith, A. D. 1991. *National Identity*. London: Penguin.

Todd, J. 1987. 'Two Traditions in Unionist Political Culture'. *Irish Political Studies*, 2: 1–26.

Tonge, J. 2006. *Northern Ireland*. Cambridge: Polity.

Trimble, D. 2001. *To Raise up a New Northern Ireland: Articles and Speeches 1998–2000*. Belfast: Belfast Press.

Walker, G. S. 2004. *A History of the Ulster Unionist Party: Protest, Pragmatism and Pessimism*. Manchester: Manchester University Press.

Wood, I. S. 2006. *Crimes of Loyalty: A History of the UDA*. Edinburgh: Edinburgh University Press.

CHAPTER 29

SCOTLAND
AND WALES

CHRISTOPHER HARVIE

29.1 INTRODUCTION: STATISTICS AND STORIES

'SCOTLAND feels more like a different country,' wrote Andrew Marr in his *History of Modern Britain*, 'and London now seems a lot more than 400 miles from Edinburgh'. Devolution, he concluded, did not seem to have renewed the Union, although it hadn't taken an axe to it, 'It is more like two pieces of pizza being gently pulled apart, still together but now connected only by strings of molten cheese' (Marr 2007: 527).[1] The simile is vivid, though it fitted no political science template, save perhaps the tendency to sell policies by stories rather than by statistics. This had intruded itself after the tide had gone out on 'great power' inquests such as Arthur Koestler's *Suicide of a Nation* (1961) or Martin Wiener's *English Culture and the Decline of the Industrial Spirit* (1981). Alan Milward had been more reassuring about the resilience of the greater European states in his *European Rescue of the Nation-State* (1992), but was Britain numbered with the chosen?

Marr was a competent historian, and a Scot with a humanist education and a keen knowledge of poetry, which he shared with the Scottish First Minister, Alex Salmond, who concluded his inaugural campaign speech with a vivid line from Hugh MacDiarmid, 'The present's theirs, But the past an' future's oors'.

Such autonomy had impressed itself on a similar figure in Wales, R. S. Thomas:

---

[1] For an extended treatment of the historical background, see Harvie (2008).

And all the time in Wales, as in Scotland, the essential spirit of our people, 'a spirit profoundly alien to England' hides itself far down in the depths of the personality, overlaid by generations of alien influence, productive of those inhibitions so common in our folk, yet waiting, waiting for the leaders who are great and fearless enough to awaken it to that 'enlargement of national consciousness...'   (Thomas 1946: 102)

This chapter was written by a Nationalist in the Scottish parliament, and revised while keeping a minority government in office. In Wales the upheaval took longer to show, but even a National Assembly 'grand coalition' of Labour and Plaid Cymru failed on 1 May 2008 to secure Labour authority in more than four local authorities. This piece may bear out Heisenberg's thesis that the researcher becomes part of his research and maybe tries to make the topic over-exciting. But though devolution may have spawned an academic cottage industry, the number of academics—latter-day Bryces, Crossmans, or Mackintoshes—in the various chambers is very few.

This is unusual in nationalist politics where, A. J. P. Taylor reminded readers of his *Habsburg Monarchy* (1947), 'Intellectuals had to create their own nationality...led by writers, principally poets and historians'. A professor compiling a linguistic dictionary was more dangerous than meetings passing resolutions. The same Taylor tended to deprecate the other nations in these islands, maybe reinforced by the two figures who brooded over his own career, David Lloyd George and Lord Beaverbrook. They were respectively Welsh and Scots, and sought their destinies in the world-metropolis of London. Lloyd George's masterstroke was to turn the UK's pacific industrial provinces into the world-arsenal which destroyed by attrition the military-industrial complexes of the Central Powers. The consequences haunted Britain thereafter, raising the curtain on the movements and events that take the stage in this chapter (Taylor 1976; 1965).

Contemporary arguments about academic—and other—studies of identity issues in Scotland and Wales have to be measured against the history. This doesn't just involve (1) political science, media, and cultural studies, their concerns and methodologies: a post-1945 development dependent on opinion polling and the resulting data; but (2) historians assessing the *longue durée* of government, economy, and culture in both countries since (3) the mages, improvers, and historians of the Enlightenment (from 'Ossian' MacPherson and Iolo Morganwg on the mystic/fantasy side to the 'steam intellects' of Robert Owen and James and John Stuart Mill) and the— notable but less discussed—sociologists, jurists, and anthropologists of the post-Darwinian period, from J. G. Frazer via Ernest Jones to R. D. Laing and Raymond Williams.[2]

Particularly important were the two 'war-formed' generations (4) who coped with the critical economic depression of 1920–39 through 'administrative devolution'. The experience of articulate politicians, along with public servants and journalists (the likes of Tom Johnston, Walter Elliot, Alec Cairncross, James Griffiths, Thomas Jones) has still to be properly assessed, as has the epoch's 'ideal-typical' presentation in the extended metafiction of such as Lewis Grassic Gibbon (1932–4), Alasdair Gray (1982), Richard Hughes (1961; 1973), and Emyr Humphreys (1974–86).

[2] See the essays in Brown (1996).

This ought to enable us to assess the durability of the 1997–9 settlement (5) in the 'settling in' of the new arrangements, the incidental but radical change brought about (through PR and enhanced women's representation); the absence of the ethos of 'cooperative federalism' within British politics; and the effect of the recent dominance of Scots in Westminster politics on British identity when countered by an emergent but inchoate Englishness. Fitting it into a theoretical typology is another matter.

The Scots and Welsh experience provides a territorial epitome of many of the topics discussed elsewhere in the *Handbook*. How stable is it, in mid-2009? Hence the above framework matters, as does the writer as activist. A debt to the Czech historian Miroslav Hroch (1985) will be noted. His revisionist-Marxist account (a product of the Prague Spring of 1968) of the typology of nationalist movements in the transition to modernity stressed the convergent development of activists derived from academia and culture, concerned with institutions and ethos, and their influence on popular and economic-interventionist movements, moving from discourse to propaganda to mass political organization. Hroch deeply influenced a European Science Foundation inquiry into minority nationalism and ethnic groups, 1850–1940 (Wales figured; Scotland did not), but it was notably remote from political science concerns (Thompson 1991–2).

29.2 THE ACADEMIC FRAME

The distinctiveness that sustained Scottish identity during the Union—culture, dialect, Calvinist religion, education, distinctive media—faces eclipse just as national independence plants itself on the agenda. Welsh acceptance of the National Assembly, after a hairsbreadth result in 1997, may not be enough to save the language. The pillars of Welsh nationality in the 1970s—coal and steel, nonconformity, even rugby—have fallen. Ten per cent of the Scots population were born in England, as were almost 25 per cent of Welsh residents. A Scot is Prime Minister, a Welshman Archbishop of Canterbury. Identity is 'complex and difficult' as Raymond Williams, theorist of Anglophone culture and member of the *Blaid*, would say: denser, more layered, and contradictory than much opinion poll data: often unforthcoming about priorities, not just the ranking of issues, but their involvement with non-political choices, propensity to vote or take civic action, deference to particular authorities. But in both countries the praxis of politics increasingly conditions cultural identity.

This first section foregrounds academic interpretation, but also argues that much of it rests on shaky foundations. Robert Hazell's *Constitutional Futures: A History of the Next Ten Years* (1999) from the influential Constitution Unit, centred on devolution, but cited only two histories: Taylor's *English History* and Linda Colley's *Britons: Forging the Nation, 1688–1837* (1992); both stimulating but under the long Anglo-British shadow cast by the great power epoch. Keith Stringer and Sandy Grant's symposium *Uniting the Kingdom* (1993) which stressed the mutability of intra-British relationships and the variables that determined this didn't figure (Wiener 1981).

History in the Victorian Scots universities, however, was Anglo-British-diplomatic. Scottish politics per se was not part of their traditional 'philosophical first year', although George Davie argued in his *Democratic Intellect* of 1961 that for the Scot as citizen and migrant, philosophy was as important as the farmer's manual of husbandry or the engineer's micrometer. Its ending in the 1960s, ironically, made space for the empirical political discourse which drove autonomy forward. Though Scottish 'philosophy', distinct from the elitism of Oxford and Cambridge, essentially combined flexible modernist theology and logic with an opening to the nascent social sciences. In the hands of gifted Oxbridge-Scot popular educators like James Bryce, John Buchan, and A. D. Lindsay it fed both into the English civic university tradition and into various governmental and academic initiatives of 'Scottish administrative devolution' 1886–1999 (Mitchell 2003). Propelled by a 'civic gospel' in the pre-1914 period when Scots (or Welsh) entrepreneurs would swallow being called 'English' when abroad when there was a bargain to be struck, this became 'national' in response to the post-1921 crisis and the 'middle opinion' groups—the Scottish National Development Council, and so on—responding to it.[3]

This institution-building affected the infant social sciences. In applied economics James Bowie, the pioneer of human resource management, founded the Dundee School of Economics and wrote the first economic case for devolution, *The Future of Scotland*, in 1939. Alec Cairncross edited a comprehensive survey of the Scottish economy in 1953 and became adviser to Harold Macmillan in his regional development phase, 1957–63. Social geography's origins lay with Patrick Geddes and his disciples J. A. Herbertson and Fraser Darling, while social anthropology produced the community studies of James Littlejohn and Ronald Frankenberg. Associated with these were agricultural science under the nutritionist and first head of the World Health Organization Sir John Boyd Orr and regional planning, with pioneer work from the 1940s on by Frank Tindall and Percy Johnson-Marshall, and local electoral studies by R. B. MacCallum, G. S. Pryde, and S. B. Chrimes. Some of these were connected with the *Third Statistical Account of Scotland*, 1950–92, started by the Social Service Council, but lack of resources after the late 1950s slump meant that the detailed work of the early volumes, J. B. Cunnison and J. B. S. Gilfillan's *Glasgow* of 1958 in particular, tailed off badly (Meller 1990).

This had Welsh parallels and precedents, since Glasgow was as influential on Wales as Oxford or the National University until 1914. Sir Henry Jones, the Welsh Hegelian who was Professor of Philosophy at Glasgow, 1894–1922, 'unmistakably the dominant force in the speculative life both of the West of Scotland and of Wales', attracted R. H. Tawney and Thomas Jones as disciples, and influenced Tom Johnston. Tawney's influence on the English left was diffuse, but Tom Jones left his mark on as many Welsh institutions as he could, such as the university involvement in the problems of the mining valleys and regional economic surveys, notably by Hilary Marquand

---

[3] For background see Finlay (2004).

(*A Plan for Wales*) in 1931–7, followed by more theoretical treatments by Brinley Jones and L. J. Williams. Patrick Geddes coined 'Walestown' to describe the urban—though debateably civic—mining valleys, and was invoked in human geography by H. J. Fleure in Aberystwyth, Emrys Evans, and the social anthropologists Alwyn Rees and Iorwerth C. Peate. There were parallel agricultural advances to those in Scotland, associated with Sir George Stapledon at Aberystwyth and an overall interest in conservation and regional planning involving Edgar Chappell and Clough Williams-Ellis as well as the obligatory Thomas Jones.[4]

Biographies matter because personal networks, not regional government, had to cope with economic crisis. 'Recovery' meant the restoration through rearmament of the heavy-industrial status quo. Only in 1939 was the Scottish Office physically located in Scotland, and only in 1964 was it partnered by a Welsh Office. The period around 1960, combining drastic shrinkage of traditional industries with limited light and service industry and educational expansion, was also marked by a *British* distrust of the metropolitan 'establishment', from *Beyond the Fringe* and *Private Eye* to the technocracy of C. P. Snow and Arthur Koestler. This meant that much of the investment in new cultural forms was spun out from the involvement and interest of incomers in recent Scottish or Welsh politics and history which stemmed from Robbins-era university expansion. See the cultural activities of two English settlers: the historian T. C. Smout in Scotland and the art historian Peter Lord in Wales.[5]

Postgraduate study drew on the old English universities, which led after the reforms of the 1870s in research and political influence. But Oxford had traditional links both with Scotland and with Wales, through Balliol and Jesus Colleges. Diceyite parliamentary-sovereignty dogmatism, which underlay assumptions about British political homogeneity, was queried by James Bryce's proto-pluralist ideas, further developed by the likes of the young Harold Laski and A. D. Lindsay in the 1900s, and carried into the present by such Balliol dissenters as Neil MacCormick, John Mackintosh, Arthur Marwick, and Tom Nairn. But Scotland also owed much to Cambridge. Pupils of Peter Laslett and George Kitson Clark such as Smout, Harry Hanham, and Geoffrey Best, contesting the Diceyite tradition and influenced by pluralist ideas, explored middle-class politics and Scottish 'notions' in urban and central administration that favoured autonomous styles.

This paralleled Neo-Marxian ideas in the hands of V. G. Kiernan at Edinburgh and the influence of the Italian radical Antonio Gramsci (Sardinian as well as Communist) on such 'people's remembrancers' as Hamish Henderson in Scotland and Gwyn Alf Williams in Wales, who advanced complex ideas of cultural hegemony against both Conservative Unionism and the dogmatic 'industrial history' of Clydeside or Valleys Communism (Gramsci 1971). There were paradoxes here, between a concern with central British institutions—Mackintosh on Cabinet government, Marwick on class and wartime administration, Angus Calder on imperialism—and a growing discourse

---

[4] The information in this section draws heavily on the entries in the *Oxford Dictionary of National Biography*, 2004, www.oxforddnb.com.

[5] Smout (1969) and Lord (2003; 1999a; 1999b). Both are projects without which the national history would be distorted.

about traditional autonomy and its recovery, which paralleled the European regional revival. Some of this was encapsulated in Gordon Brown's *Red Paper on Scotland*, 1975, influencing practically everyone except (it seemed) the editor.

In Wales the dominance of David Lloyd George and Aneurin Bevan led such politicized scholars as Kenneth O. Morgan and Dai Smith to explore the divided polity in which both dealt—*Y Fro Gymraeg* and 'American South Wales' and deep involvement in the 'high politics' of Fleet Street and Westminster. This met with Wales's greater openness to 'small is beautiful' and ecological ideas—from E. F. Schumacher (1973) and Leopold Kohr (1940)—and their incorporation into the programme of Plaid Cymru in the 1950s and 1960s.

Another factor present in both countries was the influence of their 'Diasporas', particularly on a democracy which met with frustration at home: the migration of such figures as Geddes and his disciples; Welsh trade unionists like Billy Hughes in Australia and John Llewellyn Lewis in the USA; the influence of Scottish elites in the 'old commonwealth'—Andrew Fisher, MacKenzie King—and in the creation of the 'new'—Julius Nyerere, Kenneth Kaunda—was considerable. Besides the influence of colonial self-government on the Home Rule Scottish Covenant movement (1948–51) much cash came back to both countries as academic endowment: from the Dick Bequest to Andrew Carnegie. The 'frontier' side of the Scots-Irish settler tradition, notably in Ulster, quoted by devolutionists in the 1940s, was downplayed by a Labour Party seeking Catholic votes.

29.3 'THE REAL FOUNDATIONS'

The Marxist scholar David Craig used his *Scottish Literature and the Scottish People* (1961) to denounce nationalism as a parochial sort of arrested development. His later book, *The Real Foundations* (1973), dwelt on base–superstructure relations in industrial society. The cognate concept of 'from status to contract' had been promulgated by the Scots jurist Sir Henry Maine in the 1860s, the same decade as the 'nationalizing' manifesto of *Essays on Reform* (1867)—involving James Bryce, A. V. Dicey, Leslie Stephen, and Frederic Harrison. J. S. Mill and H. T. Buckle criticized the deductive metaphysic of the Scots Enlightenment, while Matthew Arnold and Walter Bagehot encapsulated the manoeuvrable qualities of the Anglo-British state in *Culture and Anarchy* and *The English Constitution*.

Interpreted from London, this gave an exaggerated picture of British integration, influenced by paradigms of 'national unity' from a rather exceptional decade which saw the violent unification of Italy, Germany, and the United States. Yet the Scots' continuing distinctiveness had precedents in the contractual quality of Scottish constitutional and religious theory, going back to the success of the country's early-medieval elite in holding together five different ethnic/linguistic groups: Scots, Picts,

Britons, Angles, and Norse. It fed into the Enlightenment 'stadial' sociology of Adam Ferguson (hunter-pastoralist-farmer-merchant) and his 'notions' of social bands and in-groups and out-groups whose influence on Germany would return via Schiller to Carlyle and the 'English social critical tradition' of F. R. Leavis and Raymond Williams (Oz-Salzberger 1995).

The autonomy of industrial Scotland during the Union existed by virtue of the culture of contract. Distinctive manufacturing and trading patterns, dominant in particular global sectors, were while things went well resistant to takeover. The *Glasgow Herald Review of Trade and Industry* was before 1914 a world authority on shipbuilding, while the Glasgow stock exchange set the world price for iron. Typical 'capitalist-rational' bodies, unbound by nationality, were investment trusts, production and trade cartels, shipping conferences, trading banks. These paralleled powerful local corporations, including urban improvement trusts, chambers of commerce, employers' associations, port authorities, railways, and banks, which shared regional self-government with the traditional 'estates' of law, education, local government, and religion.

Demonstrations of nationality of a harmless and heartwarming sort (religion was avoided as being too conflict ridden, protestant harrying protestant) were used to glue this emotionally together: historical and regional associations and ceremonies, and ritualized conflicts, notably over religious patronage and land-ownership, lastingly in games and sports: characterized by Tom Nairn as 'the great Tartan monster' and by the present writer as the balance of 'Red' and 'Black' Scotland. Contractual facility still showed itself as late as 1918 in the Scots Liberal elite's 'incorporation' of the Irish immigrant community through the creation of a separate Catholic schools system: a clever move which cut off the prospects of Sinn Fein, then sweeping Ireland.

A similar divide in Wales was de facto linguistic: economic man's language was English, God's was Welsh. Overemphasis on the former led to Michael Hechter's economistic centre–periphery model of 1975, but the latter was actually enhanced by the industrial experience, and structured in its own favour by the London Welsh. Welsh industry was, however, predominantly extractive, and its politics and sociology—*littoral* trading-cities and mining-settlements—was closer say to South America than to Scotland. Much of the Welsh commercial elite— the Douglas-Pennants, David Davieses, J. A. Thomases, Butes, Bruces, Robertsons, MacLarens, Cawdors—had also extensive Scots interests, and through the linguistic establishment, Cymmrodorion Society, and *crachach* (the Welsh-speaking Cardiff cultural-bureacratic elite) an interest in cultural nationalism (Hume and Rees Pryce 1986).

Military romanticism on the Tory side, Liberal-imperial democracy on the left: both used the history of a very articulate country to place Scotland favourably in the Union, through the assistance of two groups who bridged Gramsci's 'organic' and 'traditional' intellectuals: teachers and journalists. Growing migration, tourism, and cheap literature made for a diffusion of its image as simultaneously industrial and historical-touristic: something pioneered on a smaller scale by Wales in the late eighteenth century and then massively expanded in Scotland through rail and steamer connections and the patronage of the royal family. The Scots' privileges led to the English *ressentiments* Julia Stapleton observes in the period of Chesterton and Belloc.

This cultural and industrial investment was cashed in during the First World War. Lloyd George rose on the brief but devastating tide of Welsh militarism. West-central Scotland, a massive industrial region of coal and ship and railway building (almost wholly catering for civilian customers), was transformed into the Clyde Munitions District, and shifted from peace to war production, 1915–21. It arguably proved decisive in the crisis year of 1917, but the simultaneous collapse of the economy, the Irish Union, and Liberal politics in 1919–22 had two effects.

The pattern of geographical diffusion evident under administrative devolution had hinged on the 'floating commonwealth' of the ports and industrial basins of the western *littoral*. In the 1920s its agenda was formed by precipitate industrial rundown (20 per cent of Scottish workers were unemployed after 1920, 10 per cent emigrated; in the Welsh mining valleys the situation was worse) but also afforded entry to Irish nationalism and Catholic doctrines of subsidiarity, though these were not necessarily co-terminous. These factors both fitted into and contested F. A. Schumpeter's model of 'creatively chaotic' capitalism and gifted management on the part of the British elite. The *mittelstand* element of Scottish entrepreneurialism—in the Victorian period the sponsor of much academic activity—was lamed and replaced by literal migration, notably to the English Midlands and to the security of large 'British' concerns: the 'grouped' railways, ICI (then the paradigm of a Britain-wide company), the banks, the trade union and cooperative movements, and in due course the expansion of the Welfare State, central and local.

This would be countered by the emergence in the mid-1960s of nationalist challenges in both countries: reactions to the weakening of the manufacturing order, unsophisticated 'British homogeneity' dogma, and excessive Oxbridge-driven centralism within Labour. Academic change, in two disproportionately *étatiste* political societies, fed into the civil service, journalism, and the expanding world of regional television, sprung from its BBC shackles by the setting up of the commercial channels in 1955. Such a dialogue/debate wasn't subsequently to be dislodged.

The 1920s weakened the economic-political-religious linkage that had kept an informally quasi-federal Britain together, and broadly left-of-centre. Without the Irish, the centre-left with its vague programme of home rule vanished. Labour ticked the home-rule box but left it at that. Its political-nationalist successors—Plaid Cymru was founded in 1925, the National party of Scotland in 1928—remained weak, movements rather than parties. They shared their impetus with non-party nationality during the 1930s until the 'second wind' fostered by rearmament and the wartime destruction of competitors revived the old order—and indeed kept it going until the 1960s.

Subsequently, industrial traumas were to undermine the strength in both countries of the Labour movement; particularly the collapse of the heavy industries, hammered by a first wave of closures involving ships, railways, and coal around 1960, and reaching its last act with the miners' strike of 1984–5.

The Scottish route out was the more complex, as North Sea oil effectively revived and then 'offshored' much heavy industry, while notions of planned industrial recovery through an Oil Fund were replaced by a privileged public sector financed through the Barnett Formula. Both brought about a pragmatic anti-Tory 'national left' rooted in education and the public sector, with a goal of political autonomy, radicalized by the aforementioned university activism, and for the first time foregrounding women. A new and realistic mapping in Wales was evident in Denis Balsom's 'Three Wales Model' (1981), a reaction to the devolution debacle of 1979, which placed in autonomist hands the same sort of pragmatic approaches later claimed at a British level by New Labour (Harvie 1993*b*; Balsom, in Osmond 1981).

In 1986 the GDP of the Republic of Ireland was still under two-thirds of that of the UK, and in 1990 its record since independence was subjected to ruthless comparisons with other nations of similar size at the hands of Professor Joseph Lee, a contemporary historian who was also a European specialist and, as a Senator for the Universities, a politician. This sort of effective synthesis helped clear the ground for the remarkable recovery of Ireland in the 1990s. This was not to be separated from demographic good fortune—old-style Catholic piety producing large families, followed by a fall to European level, leaving in Lee's words 'lots of well-educated youngsters who won't fall ill for thirty years'. The transfer pricing of multinationals, allocating profit-centres to nations with low corporation tax, also helped, as did the turmoils of the once-dominant Catholic Church, and the feminist movement which gave the country in Mary Robinson an intelligent reformist President who was also high profile. Until the 2009 crash it also gave a new non-English paradigm—'the arc of prosperity'—to the Scots and the Welsh (Day and Rees 1991).

29.4 THE FATE OF THE CULTURES

National definition also involved an exploration and retelling of the past, whose importance increased as protestant religious affiliation declined after the First World War, hit by secularist growth, economic depression, and demographic change. One factor common to both countries was the dominance in the nationalist story of a charismatic individual bridging academic and cultural/linguistic life, a role which went back to the fantasy folklore of James 'Ossian' MacPherson and Iolo Morganwg in the eighteenth century. This had vividly real consequences, through Johan Gottfried Herder and his equation of culture and identity with language, for European nationality. It also repeated itself in the contested period after the industrial driver lost momentum in the 1920s (Hobsbawm 1984).

By then cue and style could be taken from the Irish literary revival by Christopher Murray Grieve 'Hugh MacDiarmid' (1892–1978) in Scotland and John Saunders Lewis (1895–1985) in Wales. Both were founder-members of their respective nationalist parties, whose intellectual impact was considerable if unstraightforward (MacDiarmid borrowed eclectically from left and right; Lewis emphatically from the French Catholic/monarchist tradition). Neither fitted into the regional political establishment (see below) yet so substantial was their intellectual legacy that it continued to work away in academic/cultural life and such institutions as regional broadcasting, journalism, publishing, and the theatre. MacDiarmid wrote in 1928 that his work would take more than a generation to bear fruit, which turned out pretty accurate. This was only partly due to his huge (and variable) output as a poet. He was also determined to play the role of national culture critic, along the lines of the Goncourt brothers in France or Georg Brandes in Scandinavia, in his *Contemporary Scottish Studies*, (1926) aimed at the teaching profession: a crash course in the modern movement in which few of the comfortable certainties of old-style commercial nationalism survived.

Wales had a similar revival but it was more deeply divided between the Dragon's two tongues, and hampered by the conservatism that Saunders Lewis represented. The contested society of the valleys and the cosmopolitan society of the southern port-cities—Eric Linklater, Roald Dahl, and Howard Spring were *all* born near Cardiff—had little in common with the highly structured Cymric world of the Eisteddfod and the waning support it got from a shrinking nonconformity (Smith 1993). The great success was the individual voice and persona of Dylan Thomas, like his contemporary the novelist Gwyn Thomas possessed of a uniquely resonant English which probably arose from being a first-generation speaker; but one who nevertheless projected some of the values of the country—greenish, childlike, radical in an unspecific way—worldwide. That the American radical folk singer Bob Zimmerman followed Welsh practice in taking Dylan as his bardic name emphasizes the facility both countries had in connecting the global icon—Burton, Connery, Rowling—with the local.

Plaid Cymru's 'second wind' could be said to begin with Lewis's radio broadcast 'Tynged y'r Iaith' ('The Fate of the Language') in 1962 even though it was explicitly a rejection of the *Blaid's* parliamentary politics. The year 1961 saw the publication of *The Democratic Intellect* by George Elder Davie, MacDiarmid's friend and disciple, which argued that the concerns of the Scottish enlightenment continued into the nineteenth century and the Scots university establishment, influencing such un-British regionalist thinkers as J. H. Lorimer and Patrick Geddes and, through them, the writers of MacDiarmid's Scottish renaissance. This contribution, coinciding with fundamental economic crisis in the heavy industries, meant that the study of political behaviour inevitably broadened into intellectual, art, and cultural history and social critiques (Humphreys 1983).

The cultural-touristic identity of both countries had already been altered by the relative decline of manufacture in the inter-war years, which placed a premium on the marketing of distinctiveness—from climbing and golf courses to the Edinburgh Festival. In a sense there was a race between the centre, with its ability to integrate regional elites, demonstrated by T. S. Eliot's *Notes towards the Definition of Culture*, 1954, and the nationalists. But the centre was at the mercy of government or the transnational commercial players in Anglophone culture. Backed up with their own political centres, could the 'niche markets' of Wales or Scotland be the more resilient? And did the London centre know, or want to know, what was going on?

29.5 CONTAINMENT AND EXPERIMENT

The economic and nationalist challenges had since the 1920s generated establishment responses which were sympathetic, politically diversionary, but cumulatively devolutionist: see the careers of such Tory intellectuals as John Buchan and Walter Elliot. The former, after rekindling Ramsay MacDonald's home rule enthusiasm, ended with a passion for a democratic multiracial Canada; the latter while Secretary of State organized the Glasgow Empire Exhibition of 1938 and the Scottish Economic Committee and coined 'the democratic intellect' concept, which George Davie elaborated. The Tories drew on the tradition of self-government within the empire, and many of the two million signatories of the Scottish Covenant, 1950, must also have helped them to their biggest-ever Scottish vote in 1955. Their fumbling approach to the heavy industrial slump initially helped Labour, but by 1967 it had to face the challenge of a revived SNP. Also supposed to kick nationalism (at this stage backed by Edward Heath, drawing on such traditions and his own Europhilia) into touch was Harold Wilson's Crowther/ Kilbrandon commission, 1968, but it stimulated academic research and commitment, and created political aftershocks when its report in autumn 1973 coincided with a fresh SNP wave, this time powered by oil. This in turn fed the 'devolutionist response', Gordon Brown's *Red Paper*, 1975, and further academic discourse, funded through the North Sea Oil Panel of the SSRC under Lord Runciman. Arguably the dominance of the 'Scottish question' in the 1970s was Hroch's 'incremental nationalism', obscured an evolving but still inchoate 'Englishness' which initially expressed itself in hostility to the EU and a suspicion of multiculturalism. Scotland was in fact more hostile than England to entry to the European Community in the 1975 referendum (though this was carried against the opposition of the SNP and Labour parties, a fact which gave hope to opponents of devolution). But both there and in Wales the idea of 'independence in Europe' was subsequently to gain momentum, because of the expansion of the EU's regional programmes and the evident dislike of Mrs Thatcher and her backers in the press for the European project (Harvie 1993*a*; Lynch 1996).

Such initiatives meant that, although devolution and the SNP were divided and defeated in 1979, recovery was fairly rapid. Other collaborative projects were coming on stream—large-scale research ventures like the *New History of Scotland*, the *History of Scottish Literature*, etc., as well as political/cultural enterprises as varied as the campaign to save the Royal Bank from takeover (1981) and for the Scottish Poetry Library (1983). This was paralleled in Wales by an even more energetic campaign

(1981–3) to secure the Welsh television channel S4C, which did much to help the autonomy cause to recover from the pit of 1979, and to raise Plaid Cymru's morale sufficiently for it to benefit from the changed political scene after the miners' strike.

Academic–media collaboration, as yet unexplored, underlay multi-media projects like ITV's *Divided Kingdom* (1983), *The Dragon has two Tongues* (1985), and the BBC's ambitious *Scotland 2000* project in 1986–7. (Compare with Metromedia's bestseller obsession—Schama, Starkey, Ferguson, etc.—in the new century). In Scotland an intellectual *ressentiment* encouraged tactical voting at the 1987 elections, reducing Tory MPs from twenty-two to ten, and not long after that came the publication of Scotland's Claim of Right by *bien-pensant* Lib-Lab devolutionists, and the movement for a Scottish Constitutional Convention. This was boosted in November 1988 by a spectacular by-election victory for the SNP's Jim Sillars at Glasgow Govan, although the SNP itself was not represented in the Convention.

The Convention, under the chair of an ecumenical clergyman Canon Kenyon Wright and meeting in the Kirk's Assembly Hall (arguably the churches sought to recover in politics the influence they had been losing since the 1960s), sat from 1989 to 1993, and out of it came the country's *Perestroika* in the form of the proportional representation system of the proposed parliament. The London-based Charter 88 was both inspired by and associated with this, and was paralleled by the 'anti-quango' campaign in Wales (where Conservative support was so low that ministerial appointments went to English MPs and public patronage to tax exiles). In England, however, schemes for democratic regionalism went no further, while Linda Colley's gutsy but dogmatic *Britons* (1992) became an instrument of Gordon Brown's 'Bard of Britain' neo-centralism.

A more visceral explanation—see the silly pages at the end of Simon Schama's *soi-disant History of Britain*, volume iii: 'Why should post-imperial Britain not resemble the happy patchwork of nations which is post-communist Yugoslavia?'[6]—would see nationalist echoes of a cruder sort in the Scottish reception of Mel Gibson's film *Braveheart* in 1986, Hollywood's take on William Wallace. In fact this hokum divided the 'national left' and had no influence on the 1997 election, though the Tartan Army's ludic parody of 'Mad Mac'—face-painting and orange wigs—helped make the World Cup competition held in France in 1998 a carnival rather than a confrontation. The episode might however concentrate the academic mind on the effect of right-wing Australian *ressentiments* on metropolitan Britishness. Rupert Murdoch was the grandson of the Aberdeenshire-born founder of the Free Church of Australia. His papers had backed the SNP in the 1992 election; their change almost in mid-sentence to back New Labour in 1997 could have come straight out of George Orwell's *1984*. The Sun King's strings were false when Holyrood 2007 came round: the melodramatic unionism of the Scottish *Sun* being countered by Murdoch's 'serious' *Sunday Times* espousing the SNP.

---

[6] Schama (2002: 550). Davies (1999) took the break-up line of Nairn, but its arguments stopped at the anecdotal.

29.6 POST-DEVOLUTION

The study of how institutional change 'beds itself in' ought to occupy political scientists more than it has done. Adaptation may simply need time. Sir Robert Calderwood, Chief Executive of Strathclyde Region, reckoned it took from 1974 to 1984 for the Region to 'find itself' in terms of its tasks, relations with subordinate District Councils, and *ésprit de corps*. Yet the wartime munitions programme, the Open University, and indeed the securing of North Sea oil through a massive production-platform and pipe-laying programme after 1970 were effective *because* rapid. These, however, occurred in a country with a substantial and sophisticated manufacturing sector, which had dwindled to near-insignificance by 2007.

The actuality of the new assemblies seemed to prove Calderwood's point—not least because the Holyrood building, four years late and four times over budget, cast a long and gloomy shadow. Factors such as cabinet politics, ministry development, individual influence, relations with local government, etc. are only now, into the third term, being adequately studied, and starting to evict an obsession with opinion polling. On the other hand, some of the incidental consequences of devolution have themselves been important. While only *six* Welsh women were elected to Westminster in the eighty years from 1918 to 1997, the Assembly gained them equal representation, against about 40 per cent representation in Scotland. This has both influenced legislation (see free home-care, smoking bans, anti-drink campaigns) and fed through to the cultural/academic milieu. Perhaps excessively. With kilted 'Bravehearts' continuously subject to the attentions of health and safety rather than the stimulus of innovation and risk-taking, was a nanny state wearing the trousers?

In 2007, perhaps, buildings, symbolism, and function seemed to have reached a fruitful equilibrium at Holyrood and Cardiff Bay, at the iconic centre of explicit cultural capitals which have European roles denied to English provincial cities (Rawlings 2002). But the 'Guggenheim effect' which had brought fame to Bilbao through Frank Gehry's museum proved temporary, and in Glasgow poverty and dereliction required an infrastructure far better funded than what was on offer. Even after ten billions had been spent on the West Coast Railway, and air travel was environmentally suspect, Glasgow remained at least five hours distant from London, twice the time it took a TGV train to connect Paris with Strasbourg. This reflected growing political disjunction. Under First Ministers Donald Dewar, Henry McLeish, and Jack McConnell, there was a continuum of party legitimacy from Downing Street to Holyrood to most of the main Scottish local authorities. But the Lib-Lab coalition could only survive by passing proportional representation for local government, and the elections of 3 May 2007 saw Labour lose control of all but two Scottish councils.

The relations of the devolved governments and the Union state were linked to this, and also raise the peculiar nature of responsibilities within the Cabinet that carried devolution. Post-Granita (the de facto dyarchy, fashioned by Blair and Brown after John Smith's death, which ran Labour 1994–2007) devolution initially appeared to be a 'Tony-and-Gordon thing', with a strong role being played by the Prime Minister's ally Lord Chancellor Irvine, and the English provinces being represented by the supposed bluff good sense of John Prescott. Blair first mishandled Wales, imposing Alun Michael as First Minister in 1999 and seeing him all but defeated in the first election, and then removed in favour of Rhodri Morgan. Prescott then quickly deflated, along with his would-be super-ministry. Gordon Brown had responsibility for Scotland but his relations with First Minister McConnell were poor. If it took him three weeks to contact First Minister Salmond, McConnell admitted that he and the Chancellor had never exchanged a word during his first year in office.[7]

Despite the didactic efforts of the Constitution Unit at University College London, there was no British evolution towards a cooperative-federalist settlement on *Bundesrepublik* lines. (Do politicians, devolved or Westminster, ever read academic studies of themselves, as opposed to the 'docusoaps' of memoirs or the press?) Apart from Northern Ireland, the territorial ministers survived as titles, like the smile of the Cheshire Cat, but their authority quickly dwindled to insignificance. It might have sustained itself, had there been a concerted effort at English regional self-government plus a revival of regional planning of industry. But the first vanished in the defeat of a North of England Assembly in November 2004, and the second never seriously challenged the housing-retail driver, the persistent rhetoric of 'enterprise' being in actuality based on the Chancellor's encouragement of consumer debt. There might have been a common discourse of pluralism and decentralization, of the sort once boosted by Charter 88. Instead, interest in any sort of 'British' reform fell away, and it seemed that even the normal 'national conversation' had fallen to a murmur.

This may be a result of two things. First, the changes in technology and control of the British media which mean that regional versions of 'British' papers contain material, less than 10 per cent of which finds its way to London readers, and the breakdown of the 'regional' structure of ITV; the result being concentration of authority in London, under the aegis of Ofcom as well as the centralism of the BBC. Second, there was the non-functioning of much of the Anglo-Irish Good Friday Agreement, which might have, in the 'Council of the Isles', produced a quasi-federal forum, with longer-lasting and more resilient conferences of ministers and senior civil servants generating both resilient layers of transactions and obligations, and an expert group skilled in navigating them (Blain and Hutchison 2008). Critics of the German state have seen this regional-diplomatic level, clustering round *Land* cabinets and their Berlin or Brussels *Vertretungen* (High Commissions), taking power away from the *Land* MPs. Instead, what Larry Eliott has christened 'the United Kingdom of London', has been rapidly evolving its financial interests since the 'Big Bang' of 1986, showing far more interest in international partnerships with cognate centres than in any sort of regional links. What goes for the Monetary Policy Committee of the Bank of England also goes for Ofcom. The inevitable result has been a steady alienation

---

[7] These have been charted since 2000 by the annual volumes published by the Constitution Unit as *The State of the Nations* (Exeter: Imprint Academic, 2000–); parallel series of analyses can be found in the quarterly *Scottish Affairs* (1993–) (succeeding *The Yearbook of Scottish Politics*, 1976–92) and *Contemporary Wales*, while the Scottish Parliament has its own in-house review, *Holyrood*.

from Westminster in Scotland and Wales despite the initial difficulties of the new parliament and assembly (Elliott 2007).

Paradoxically, there was an accession of power to a Westminster-Scottish elite whose role since 1990 in Conservative as well as Labour cabinets was much greater than it had been in earlier years. Was this because MSPs, coping with the daily grind of court cases and school and housing problems, made their constituency burden easier? Or because the traditional Conservative elite had deserted politics for the far richer pickings of the City? At the time of revising, Spring 2009, the oscillations of power relationships in London and the mounting problems of the British economy, deeply dependent on the housing boom and its role as a driver of economic growth based on retail and somewhat opaque financial services, made the future exceptionally difficult to predict. First Minister Alex Salmond, as the former oil economist of the Royal Bank of Scotland (briefly one of Europe's biggest), was acutely aware that the price of oil in 1999—the peak year of UK North Sea production—had by spring 2008 climbed almost twelvefold, and that this resource was necessary to enable the country's endowment of renewable energy to be tapped.

The Nationalist minority government in Holyrood enjoyed as much as 48 per cent support in the polls by then, although backing for its key aim of independence remained lower. To Salmond this was not a disabling contradiction, given the unpopularity in Scotland of both Westminster parties, and the absence of constitutional alternatives which had long-term credibility. He believed that Scotland could offer Europe a package of alternative energy resources, based on wind, tide, and wave energy, and the use of the North Sea's oil network to bury much Europe's carbon dioxide—at a price. This could only be gained by an accession of authority to Holyrood which amounted to autonomy sufficient to use the remaining oil resources to be used as collateral, and his strategy was to raise the country and his government's profile to a point where this seemed more plausible than any alternative. Good relations with the monarchy, which was persuaded that the *ci-devant* republican Salmond was the very model of a modern Commonwealth premier, a high-quality Council of Economic Advisers mandated to judge performance independently, and the rise of the country's main financial institution, the Royal Bank, to European dominance were important picture cards. But the RBS's eclipse would be as rapid as that of Labour under Gordon Brown.

The Cabinet's Scots could not survive Labour's loss of power. But there was little sign of any compensating Conservative recovery in Scotland. If relations between Holyrood and New Labour were bound to be difficult, the austerities of Chancellor Darling's Consolidated Spending Review implying little growth in the block grant— Andrew Marr's molten strands of cheese being relentlessly stretched—a Tory government in Downing Street and without support in Scotland or any real knowledge of the place could quickly find them impossible.[8]

To return to where we started. Change—both in events and in the institutions which interpret them—tends to be incremental, or the reflex of long cycles, such

---

[8] For a check-list of these see Hassan (2005); Brown (2007); Milward (1992).

as the recurrent patterns of integration and individuation within the nations of the British islands detected in Stringer and Grant's 1993 symposium. This has generally gone unobserved by the centre, where 'high politics' tends to occlude regional concerns, but can be punctuated by moments in which a new situation announces itself uncompromisingly and counsels drastic (though not always reasoned) action. Changes in direction then become stark and unavoidable, though what distinguishes history from the social sciences is what long ago Dicey called the cross-currents and counter-currents of different social forces, and the ability of adaptive individuals in certain circumstances to juggle with them and alter seemingly inevitable outcomes.

If national identity becomes concentrated on political institutions, however, such conflicts are likely to be much more explicit.

REFERENCES

BLAIN, N., and HUTCHISON, D. (eds.) 2008. *The Media in Scotland*. Edinburgh: Edinburgh University Press.

BROWN, R. (ed.) 2007. *Nation in a State*. Edinburgh: Ten Pound Books.

BROWN, T. (ed.) 1996. *Celticism*. Amsterdam: Rodopi.

COLLEY, L. 1992. *Britons: Forging the Nation, 1688–1837*. London: Yale University Press.

DAVIES, N. 1999. *The Isles*. London: Macmillan.

DAY, G., and REES, G. (eds.) 1991. *Regions, Nations and European Integration: Remaking the Celtic Periphery*. Cardiff: University of Wales Press.

ELLIOTT, L. 2007. *Fantasy Island*. London: Constable Robinson.

FINLAY, R. 2004. *Modern Scotland*. London: Profile.

GIBBON, L. G. 1932–4. *A Scots Quair*. London: Jarrolds.

GRAMSCI, A. 1971. 'The Intellectuals'. In *Prison Notebooks*. London: Lawrence and Wishart.

GRAY, A. 1982. *Lanark*. Edinburgh: Canongate.

HARVIE, C. 1993*a*. *Europe and the Welsh Nation*. Aberystwyth: National Library of Wales.

——1993*b*. *Fool's Gold: The Story of North Sea Oil*. London: Hamish Hamilton.

——2008. *A Floating Commonwealth: Politics, Technology, and Culture on Britain's Atlantic Coast, 1860–1930*. Oxford: Oxford University Press.

HASSAN, G. (ed.) 2005. *Scotland 2020*. London: Demos.

HAZELL, R. 1999. *Constitutional Futures: A History of the Next Ten Years*. Oxford: Oxford University Press.

HECHTER, M. 1975. *Internal Colonialism: The Celtic Fringe in British National Development*. London: Routledge.

HOBSBAWM, E. (ed.) 1984. *The Invention of Tradition*. Cambridge: Cambridge University Press.

HROCH, M. 1985. *Social Preconditions of National Revival in Europe*, trans. B. Fowkes. Cambridge: Cambridge University Press (1st pub. 1968).

HUGHES, R. 1961/1973. *The Human Condition*. London: Chatto.

HUME, I., and REES PRYCE, W. T. (eds.) 1986. *The Welsh and their Country*. Llandyssul: Gomer Press.

HUMPHREYS, E. 1974–86. *Land of the Living*. London: Dent.

——1983. *The Taliesin Tradition*. Bridgend: Seren Books.

KOHR, L. 1940. *The Breakdown of Nations*. London: Routledge.

LORD, P. 1999*a*. *The Visual Culture of Wales*, ii: *Industrial Society*. Cardiff: University of Wales Press.

——1999*b*. *The Visual Culture of Wales*, iii: *Imaging the Nation*. Cardiff: University of Wales Press.

——2003. *The Visual Culture of Wales*, i: *The Medieval Vision*. Cardiff: University of Wales Press.

LYNCH, P. 1996. *Minority Nationalism and European Integration*. Cardiff: University of Wales Press.

MARR, A. 2007. *A History of Modern Britain*. London: BBC/Macmillan.

MELLER, H. 1990. *Patrick Geddes: Social Evolutionist and City Planner*. London: Routledge.

MILWARD, A. S. 1992. *The European Rescue of the Nation State*. London: Routledge.

MITCHELL, J. 2003. *Governing Scotland: The Invention of Administrative Devolution*. Basingstoke: Palgrave Macmillan.

OSMOND, J. 1981. *The National Question Again*. Bridgend: Gomer.

OZ-SALZBERGER, F. 1995. *Translating the Enlightenment*. Oxford: Oxford University Press.

RAWLINGS, R. 2002. *Delineating Wales: Constitutional, Legal and Administrative Aspects of National Devolution*. Cardiff: University of Wales Press.

SCHAMA, S. 2002. *History of Britain*, vol. iii. London: BBC.

SCHUMACHER, E. F. 1973. *Small is Beautiful*. London: Abacus.

SMITH, D. 1003. *Aneurin Bevan and the Culture of South Wales*. Cardiff: University of Wales Press.

SMOUT, T. C. 1969. *A History of the Scottish People, 1560–1830*. London: Collins.

——1986. *A Century of the Scottish People, 1830–1950*. London: Collins.

TAYLOR, A. J. P. 1965. *English History*. Oxford: Oxford University Press.

——1976. *The Habsburg Monarchy*. London: Penguin.

THOMAS, R. S. 1946. 'Some Contemporary Scottish Writing'. *Wales*, 23/Autumn.

THOMPSON, M. (ed.) 1991–2. *Comparative Studies on Governments and Non-dominant Ethnic Groups in Europe*, 6 vols. Aldershot: European Science Foundation/New York University/Dartmouth Press.

WIENER, M. 1981. *English Culture and the Decline of the Industrial Spirit*. Cambridge: Cambridge University Press.

SECTION TEN: LOCATION

CHAPTER 30

THE EUROPEAN UNION

JIM BULLER

30.1 INTRODUCTION

TRADITIONALLY, it has been popular to view Britain as an 'awkward' or 'semi-detached' partner in Europe (Charlton 1983; Radice 1992; Denman 1996; George 1998; Young 1998; Gowland and Turner 2000; see also Daddow 2004: 58–113).[1] This reputation in part derives from its negative diplomatic style. Since the European integration process took off in the 1950s, successive governments have continually shown themselves to be inept at playing the 'Community game'. In particular, they have failed to understand that decision-making in Brussels can often be a positive-sum exercise, whereby alliances must be forged and side payments made in order for objectives to be achieved. But semi-detachment is also related to genuine and persistent disagreements over policy substance. The first decade of membership was dominated by a dispute over Britain's contributions to the European budget. Later in the 1980s, Thatcher's more general fears about an emerging federal super-state meant that ministers often found themselves in a minority of one in the EU. Finally, 'awkwardness' is attributed to the repeated failure of British politicians to develop a pro-European discourse when talking about this issue at the domestic level. With no counter-narrative to challenge them, Euro-sceptics have won the battle of political ideas, thus further reinforcing this negative stance.

[1] The author would like to thank participants at a Politics Department seminar, University of York (14 June 2007), as well as an anonymous referee for helpful comments on an earlier draft of this chapter. The usual disclaimers apply.

However, a superficial survey of Britain's relations with the EU since 1997 suggests that change has taken place in this policy sphere. For example, the Blair government has consistently deployed a more cooperative *diplomatic style* at the European level. The discussion below will detail instances where negotiators have forged a range of alliances with different countries over separate issues; even working with France and Germany to drive forward certain initiatives. Furthermore, since 1997, Britain has continually had a constructive impact on the *substance* of EU policy. One example of such influence is in the area of foreign and security affairs, whereby the Blair government played a leading role in bringing about the creation of an EU Rapid Reaction Force. However, the role of British diplomats in supply-side economic policy, and even institutional questions arising from the Constitutional Convention, will also be given attention below. One indication of such change is the fact that scholarship in recent years has begun to focus on the *impact of the EU on British politics and policy*. Indeed, a number of studies have concluded that Whitehall has comfortably adjusted its policies and decision-making practices to EU requirements. This 'Europeanization' process (as it has been called) is the subject of a separate chapter in this volume, and will not be given detailed treatment here (for a comprehensive introduction, see Bache and Jordan 2006; and Featherstone, this volume).

The purpose of this chapter is to both chart and begin to account for this changing relationship between the British government and the EU. Such a task requires three preliminary theoretical observations. The first is that much of the existing literature has focused on continuity rather than change and, as such, appears to be of little help. As already noted, Britain has traditionally been perceived as an 'awkward' partner, and a consistent one at that. While a range of factors are thought to contribute to this persistent semi-detachment, some writers have invoked a 'new institutionalist' approach to focus on the constraining impact of Britain's *particular* institutional setup (see for example Bulmer 1992; George 1992; Armstrong and Bulmer 1996; Dearlove and Saunders 2000: 739–49). Looking particularly at political institutions, these scholars have noted how party divisions and the adversarial political culture within Westminster frustrate the possibility for a more pro-European consensus (Ashford 1992; Wallace 1996; 1997; Aspinwall 2000; 2004; Usherwood 2002). The chance of such collaboration is not helped by the continued Euro-sceptical stance of the British electorate, fuelled by an increasingly Euro-phobic press. Most significantly perhaps is the symbolic importance of sovereignty, which in turn is linked to the centralized nature of the British state (Wallace 1986; Wilks 1996). Even if policy-makers wanted to adopt a more *communautaire* stance towards the EU, this institutional terrain frustrates them from doing so.

Second, if this focus on the constraining properties of institutions has elicited an emphasis on continuity (i.e. 'awkwardness') it seems reasonable to suggest that our account of change should bring a notion of *agency* to the fore. While political actors operate within an institutional environment that will constrain their behaviour at any one moment, there may be occasions where human beings enjoy relative autonomy from such structures. Acting purposively, not only will they reproduce the structures that surround them, in certain circumstances they may be able to redefine and reform that context in such a way as to make it easier for them to realize their objectives in the future (on the structure–agency debate, see Hay 2002: 89–134; McAnulla 2002). It should be said that this theoretical position is not necessarily inconsistent with the new institutionalist approach noted above. However, the possibility that British policy-makers may enjoy space at the domestic level to pursue a more pro-European approach is not one that is discussed frequently in the literature on Britain's relations with the EU. Neither is the feasibility that changes in EU institutions may provide opportunities for British diplomats to achieve their objectives in the European arena.

Finally, it is important to clarify the concept of change as it is understood in this chapter. As Hay has argued, change implies 'contrast between states or moments of a *common* system, institution, relationship entity...' (Hay 1999a: 26) (author's emphasis). To define change in this way is to raise a paradox. Change implies some element of continuity as opposed to the complete transformation of an object, which represents discontinuity (see also Hay 2002: 135–67). Applying Hay's definition to the developments summarized above, it is not being claimed that a transformation has taken place in all elements of Britain's relations with the EU. However, certain shifts can be detected and these have occurred alongside enduring continuities. Since 1997, Whitehall has adopted a more creative political style that has influenced the substance of negotiation in some, but not all, policy areas. But to say that British statesmen are more comfortable in Europe these days is not to imply that the European issue fits more easily into the broader contours of the British polity. As we shall see, the British party system remains as allergic as ever to all matters European.

To fully understand the nature of this change in the British government's relations with the EU, this chapter employs a temporal perspective. It begins by exploring the reason for Britain's awkwardness, concentrating on the period 1987–97. It asserts that this diplomatic tendency cannot just be explained by the constraining properties of Britain's political institutions. Instead, awkwardness at this time was the result of a complex, dialectical relationship between institutions and agency over different territorial levels. More precisely, (a) a renewed process of integration at the European level helped to (b) generate critical *narratives* about the EU and its relationship to the British political system. Held by an increasingly vocal set of *agents* (Conservative Euro-sceptics) these narratives (c) in turn constrained the scope of British foreign policy, helping to produce a heightened sense of awkwardness or semi-detachment under the Major government. The final section of this chapter argues that change after 1997 was the result of a similar interplay of factors, only in reverse. Structural developments at the global level impacted on EU institutions in a way that created opportunities for Whitehall to pursue a more positive statecraft. At the same time, New Labour has been aided in this goal by a more favourable domestic political context.

30.2 Britain as an Awkward Partner, 1987–97

30.2.1 Global Structural Change and the Renewed Process of European Integration

Any understanding of political change needs to be grounded in some kind of historical perspective. That said, the choice of 1987 as the initial temporal base point employed here requires some justification. While Britain has always had a reputation for being a semi-detached partner in the EU, constraints of space dictate a more contemporary focus. Moreover, as Bulpitt (1996: 243–4) has argued, the nature of this domestic–European connection changed significantly from the second half of the 1980s onwards. If British politicians had been 'awkward' before 1987, it was often because they found such a tactic convenient for domestic political purposes. Mrs Thatcher's stance over Britain's budgetary contribution in the first half of the 1980s can be viewed in this light. After 1987, Conservative leaders became 'awkward' not because of the (perceived) electoral advantages, but because they became increasingly worried that developments at the European (and global) level would impact adversely on national politics.

Indeed, one could go further and suggest that 1987–97 represents a period of heightened awkwardness in Britain's relations with the EU. In this context, one could point to Mrs Thatcher's intensifying Euro-phobia: an attitude which troubled enough Conservative MPs that it was thought to be one of the reasons why she had to go as leader in November 1990. Despite his pledge to put Britain 'at the very heart of Europe', Major's opt-out of the Social Chapter and the Single Currency project at Maastricht confirmed this impression of semi-detachment. A number of highly publicized rows over the appointment of a successor to Jacques Delors as President of the European Commission again saw Britain in a minority of one. Indeed, British complaints in 1996 that other EU member states had used the BSE issue to institute protectionist measures against British beef saw Major go one further than Thatcher: he pursued a policy of 'non-cooperation' on all questions requiring a unanimous vote in the Council of Ministers until the ban was lifted (Seldon 1997: 639–53).

As noted above, any understanding of awkwardness must take into account the complex relationship between institutions and human agency as it develops across different territorial levels. The first task in this context is to delineate the structural changes that helped to generate a renewed process of European integration which began to impact on British politics from the second half of the 1980s onwards. It is ironic that origins of this process can be in part traced back to a treaty amendment signed and publicly promoted by Mrs Thatcher herself. The agreement in question was the Single European Act (SEA) (1987) and it gained British support in the mid-1980s largely because it had, as its centrepiece, a programme to remove all non-tariff barriers to the free movement of goods, services, capital, and labour by December

1992. It was perceived in London that this Single Market project would complement the range of neoliberal economic reforms that were being pursued at the domestic level at this time. To achieve this objective, the British delegation had to offer a range of concessions or 'side-payments'. One of these was the inclusion of Article 20 of the SEA which, for the first time, explicitly committed member states to work for the goal of Economic and Monetary Union (EMU). The Thatcher government also had to accept the extension of qualified majority voting (QMV) in all areas pertaining to the completion of the Single Market, including health and safety matters as set out in Article 118a. Thatcher in particular was nervous about offering these concessions, but in the end she accepted the erosion of political sovereignty in the name of free market economics (Buller 2000: 68–118).

Not surprisingly, it was a matter of some controversy within the Conservative Party when the European Commission under Jacques Delors attempted to use the momentum generated by the SEA to propose Economic and Monetary Union (EMU) as the next big Community project. Utilizing tactics often referred to as 'spillover', Delors argued that the Single Market would be incomplete without a Single Currency (the logical endpoint of EMU), and that both the Preamble and Article 20 of the SEA gave the EC legislative authority to develop such a policy. By April 1989, a committee of central bankers headed by Delors had produced a three-stage plan for the eventual realization of EMU (Padoa-Schioppa et al. 1987; Thompson 1996: 108–47). This episode served to heighten the tension and acrimony that was building in Whitehall at this time. Mrs Thatcher suggested that she had been tricked into signing the SEA by a Euro-phile Foreign Office, a charge that officials in King Charles Street furiously denied (compare, for example, Lawson 1992: 888–916; Thatcher 1993: 688–726, 740–2; Howe 1994: 533–41, 573–86).

Just as contentious was an attempt by Delors to exploit this more favourable structural context to develop a 'social dimension' to complement the Single Market project. One initiative encouraged by the Commission in this context was the Social Charter, which set out a range of new minimum rights to be enjoyed by all employees in the EC relating to: trade union organization and collective bargaining; training; information and worker consultation; health and safety; and social security (Grahl and Teague 1990: 209–13). Underpinning this Charter was a broader recognition that the route to a competitive economy was investment in human capital, not simply driving down wages in a 'race to the bottom'. As a way of complementing this goal, Delors also attempted to revive the idea of a 'social dialogue', a Community concept going back to at least the 1960s. The 'social dialogue' represented the idea that the 'social partners' (Union des Confederations de l'Industrie et des Employeurs d'Europe and the European Trade Union Congress) would be given an institutional place within Europe's decision-making framework from which they could drive this social policy agenda forward (Wise and Gibb 1993). The Conservatives responded to both initiatives with horror. Having spent the first half of the 1980s 'rolling back' the powers of the British trade unions, they were in no mood to accept a decision-making mechanism that would allow for renewed worker influence through a European back door (Bale and Buller 1996).

By the early 1990s, not only was this integration process an unwelcome shock, it appeared to be irreversible. One reason momentum was so powerful at this time was because it was *underpinned by a set of related structural developments at the global level*. For example, international financial forces impacted on the European Exchange Rate Mechanism (ERM) (set up in 1979) in a way that reinforced the case for a Single Currency. By the mid-1980s, the Deutschmark had come to dominate the ERM on account of the size and wealth of the German economy. As a result, when the international community agreed to work together in 1986 to manage a devaluation of the dollar (as a result of the Plaza Agreement) this concerted action had the effect of putting upward pressure on the DM. The rising value of the DM in turn had the effect of dragging other European currencies up with it via their connections through the parity grid. Faced with the choice of accepting a significant tightening of monetary policy or rejecting its European obligations, the French government chose the latter course, allowing the franc to fall through the floor of its ERM band. A post-mortem on the crisis carried out in Paris reached two conclusions. First, German (and especially Bundesbank) influence over European monetary policy was too powerful and had to be curbed. Second, the method by which such an objective should be achieved was a furthering of European integration in the area of monetary policy. In January 1988, French finance minister Balladur called for a 'monetary construction of Europe' and, more particularly, for the establishment of a supranational European Central Bank (Dyson and Featherstone 1999: 156–72, 320–6).

Certain shifts in the geopolitical structural environment buttressed this momentum towards EU integration. First, the fall of the Berlin Wall in November 1989 and the collapse of Soviet Communism heralded the possibility of Germany loosening its ties with the EU and turning its attention eastwards. While the cold war may have been a source of much tension in Western Europe, its structures did have the advantage of providing an environment which helped diffuse concerns about renewed German influence in central Europe. Second, the reunification of Germany in 1990, and the style in which this decision was made, did nothing to alleviate these fears. Helmut Kohl announced with no advanced consultation that East and West Germany would be reunited and put forward a ten-point plan for realizing this goal (Sandholtz 1993; but also Moravcsik 1998: 379–417). President Mitterrand's first reaction was to visit East Germany and the Soviet Union to make speeches warning about the pace of reunification and the threat this development posed to the balance of power in Europe. In this context, the attraction of further European integration was again that it might constrain this 'German Gulliver'. This integration process culminated in the signing of the Treaty of European Union at Maastricht in December 1991.

30.2.2 Institutions, Narratives, and the Constraining Impact of Agency on British Statecraft Towards the European Union

Britain's heightened awkwardness during this period cannot just be explained by pointing to the constraining impact of Britain's institutions in the context of the

European integration process. From Major's point of view, what was just as restricting was an increasingly vocal set of political agents (Conservative Euro-sceptics) and the narratives they deployed about this integration process and its relationship to the British political system (Buller 2006). It is of course dangerous to make generalizations about Conservative Euro-sceptic opinion in the 1990s. To do so risks oversimplifying the complex set of motives, concerns, and arguments held by different factions within this group (see, for example, Spicer 1992; Baker, Gamble, and Ludlam 1994; Sowemimo 1996; Forster 2002). However, one belief that Euro-sceptics increasingly came to share (and which differed from earlier periods) was that the EU had become a 'Euro-ratchet' (Bulpitt 1992). In particular, the renewed phase of European integration noted above meant that the institutional terrain of this regional organization was now inexorably biased against the interests of Britain (and the Conservative Party). Indeed, for Euro-sceptics, a powerful Franco-German axis, allied with resurgent Community institutions, made redundant any diplomatic efforts by Britain to frustrate this process.

Various incidents during this period confirmed the veracity of these arguments as far as Euro-sceptics were concerned. For example, one could point to the failed attempt by the Thatcher government to prevent EMU by introducing both the Competing Currencies and Hard Ecu Plans. Both British schemes sketched out a more gradual, evolutionary process whereby the Single Currency *might eventually* emerge as a result of market forces. It was however, the qualified and conditional nature of these proposals which led to their swift rejection by the Commission and other member states (Lawson 1992: 939–42; Stephens 1996: 161–2). More significant perhaps was the Euro-sceptics' perception of events leading to the introduction of the Working Time Directive. When the Commission initially tabled this legislation providing for a maximum forty-eight-hour week, it did so under Article 118a of the SEA, which as already noted related to health and safety matters. While British negotiators contested whether working hours counted as an issue of health and safety, the advantage for Brussels was that all legislation pertaining to Article 118a was subject to qualified majority voting. By June 1993, all attempts by the Major government to veto the Commission's proposals were circumvented, and they passed into law. The Major government took the Commission to the European Court of Justice, arguing that the meaning of Article 118a had been misinterpreted. In November 1996, the Court rejected British claims and allowed the legislation to stand. The story of the Working Time Directive became something of a cause célèbre for the sceptics, confirming in their mind that the EC was biased against Britain.

At the same time, Euro-sceptics warned that the impact of this 'Euro-ratchet' on Britain's political institutions would be disastrous. One popular narrative at this time pointed to the possible deleterious consequences of European integration for British parliamentary sovereignty. For the Euro-sceptics, parliament was both the body that held the executive to account and the arena where the views of the electorate were represented. At the same time, as more and more power over policy was passed up to EC institutions, MPs would find themselves increasingly unable to play this dual role. Such a development was dangerous in itself, but also because of the dominant place that parliament occupied with the British polity more generally. British government was parliamentary government; Westminster was the institution that accorded legit-imacy to what was otherwise a comparatively centralized system of rule. In other words, to ride roughshod over MPs risked undermining the institutional basis of the whole political class (see for example Portillo 1998; Forster 2002).

When we reconstruct the discourse of the Conservative Euro-sceptics in this way, it becomes easier to understand (although not necessarily to accept) why any sign of concessions to Europe on the part of the Major leadership was met with ever louder displays of hostility and indiscipline. It was not just that Euro-sceptics thought this more cooperative diplomacy was mistaken. The desire to put Britain 'at the very heart of Europe' was positively dangerous, and could only mean further pain for the Conservative Party as it became further stretched out on this rack. Indeed, some Euro-sceptics began to suspect that Major was deliberately failing to confront this 'Euro-ratchet' in the hope that Britain would be dragged along surreptitiously. Major's failure to rule out Single Currency membership for the lifetime of the next parliament was viewed in this light. Euro-sceptics suspected a secret plot to abolish sterling 'by stealth'. However, the defining moment in this context appears to have been Major's refusal to use Denmark's rejection of the Maastricht Treaty in June 1992 to halt the ratification process in Britain. In the words of one leading Euro-sceptic: 'it was then that we realised that Major was not one of us' (quoted in Seldon 1997: 294).

Of course, it must not be forgotten that what enhanced the influence of the Euro-sceptics at this time was the material reality of the changing parliamentary situation facing the Conservative Party more generally. The Major government began the 1992–7 parliament with a majority of twenty-one, only to see it reduced to nothing after a string of by-election defeats and defections by Tory MPs to other parties. The emergence of the Referendum Party further strengthened the position of the Euro-sceptics, although its impact at the 1997 election was not as significant as some commentators had expected (Hurd 1997). Interestingly Major sanctioned a series of ever more draconian methods of party management at this time, which only ended up generating perverse results. A decision to withdraw the whip from eight Conservative rebels after they failed to support the government during the passage of the 1995 European Finance Bill only served to wipe out Major's dwindling majority, necessitating an embarrassing reversal months later (Seldon 1997: 511). To conclude, awkward diplomacy during this period reflected a complicated interplay of both institutional and agential factors.

30.3 The 'Normal' Partner: New Labour and the European Union, 1997–2009

The rest of this chapter attempts to document and account for a number of gradual changes that have taken place in Britain's relations with the EU over the last decade or so. It detects a more positive rhetoric (when Labour wants to discuss this policy sphere) and a constructive diplomatic style in negotiations with European partners. At the same time, it asserts that Britain has made a constructive input into the substance of policy in certain areas. As noted earlier, the case for change should not be exaggerated. Whitehall remains isolated from the main body of European opinion on issues such as the Single Currency, border controls, and the Charter of Fundamental Rights (see below). That said, Britain appears to be developing into a 'normal' member of the EU, cooperating successfully in some areas, while fighting its corner on others. Again, an emphasis on the dynamic relationship between institutions and agency over different territorial levels will be employed to help understand this change. This section begins by detailing alterations to the international and European context that have benefited British diplomacy since 1997.

30.3.1 Global Structural Change and the Weakening of EU Integrationist Pressure

If the fall of the Berlin Wall and the collapse of the Soviet Union contributed to pressure for further European integration, these structural developments also set off separate changes that were to have an arguably contradictory impact on the EU from the mid-1990s onwards. The most important development in this context was the enlargement of the EU from the twelve countries represented at Maastricht, to twenty-seven countries in January 2007. Free from the shackles of Communist rule, a number of states in central and eastern Europe began to lodge applications for membership in the anticipation of receiving a number of economic, political, and military benefits (Croft et al. 1999; Fierke and Weiner 1999; Curzon Price and Landau 1999). Although the EU had long articulated a pledge to overcome the 'unnatural' division of the European continent, this pressure for enlargement was met with a mixture of ambivalence and anxiety (Kramer 1993; Friis and Murphy 1999). Applicant states exhibited wide disparities in terms of economic and political development. A number of long-standing national and ethnic rivalries were beginning to emerge as the repressive apparatus of Soviet Communism was gradually removed. Ultimately, enlargement posed fundamental questions concerning the EU's institutions and processes. How, for example, would the Commission and Council of Ministers operate with approximately double the number of states now participating in Union business?

These questions have given rise to a protracted debate over the future institutional structure of the EU, producing an evolving configuration of intergovernmental bargaining at the EU level that has helped to mitigate images of British semi-detachment. Instead, arguments concerning these institutional questions have often revolved around a big-state–small-state split. For large countries, enlargement raised the prospect of a substantial increase in the number of small countries within the EU and, with it, the possibility that those smaller countries would combine together to outvote their larger counterparts on legislation decided by QMV. As a result, bigger states spent the 1990s lobbying for extra representation in the Council of Ministers, as well as a demographic criterion to take the population of each country into account. These proposals caused general anxiety in the capitals of the smaller states, especially when they were accompanied by suggestions for reform of the Commission. France led the way in warning that an enlarged Commission would be over-bureaucratic and unworkable and called on the EU to review whether permanent representation for each government at Brussels was now desirable. Small states opposed these assertions, viewing their permanent representation on the Commission as insurance against domination by the large states. For the most part, Britain has remained relaxed during these discussions, and certainly not in a minority of one.

As well as enlargement, the increased globalization of the international economy is arguably another structural change at the international level that has provided additional opportunities as well as constraints for British policy-makers in Europe. It is true that this new global economy is said to be continually challenging the capacity of nation states to implement a variety of policy goals. Commentators have highlighted how discretionary and interventionist strategies of economic management have been undermined by the global flows of trade and production and finance. However, it should be noted that the 'material reality' of globalization is a matter of fierce debate among academics and politicians alike, with some 'sceptics' doubting the novelty of these developments (see, for example, Held and McGrew 2007). Of particular interest here is the work of some political scientists who have argued that narratives about globalization have had just as important an impact on British politics as the reality of this process. For example, Colin Hay and Matthew Watson have asserted that New Labour has utilized arguments about the constraining nature of this international environment in part to 'lock in' supporters to the neoliberal principles and policies considered crucial for winning elections (Hay and Watson 1999; Hay 1999b; 2001). The discussion below will investigate whether British negotiators have successfully deployed a similar discourse about globalization to change the climate of ideas in Europe.

If a combination of developments at the global and European levels has created some space for more a positive diplomatic approach towards the EU, the Blair government certainly arrived in office promising a more pro-European statecraft. A central feature of this more *communautaire* discourse was acceptance of the globalization thesis sketched out above. Because of these global economic developments, Britain now inhabited a new international community where states were mutually dependent on each other and national objectives were largely determined by intergovernmental collaboration. Understood in these terms, EU membership was something not only to be welcomed, but positively embraced. Blair went further in asserting that a self-confident Britain under a united Labour Party would play a new leadership role in Europe by constructing alliances and forging joint solutions to common problems (see, for example, Giddens 2006; 2007). It is not clear at this time whether this positive message reflected an appreciation that the changing external context (noted above) might provide opportunities for more creative diplomacy. Rather, what distinguished Blair's views in early interviews was a belief that institutions and structures *did not matter*. To achieve one's goals, all that was needed was a clear vision and the requisite political will to drive them through (Young 1997).

There is also evidence to suggest that the Blair government has delivered on this more positive message, at least in certain areas. Take for example, the sphere of foreign and security policy. After years of opposing such a move, British negotiators in 1998 agreed to the abolition of the Western European Union (WEU) as a way of strengthening European political cooperation in this domain. While the WEU's military functions were transferred to NATO, its political role was shifted to the EU, thus enhancing the authority of the newly created post of High Representative. Ministers followed up this concession by playing a formative role in the creation of the European Rapid Reaction Force of 60,000 troops, with a remit to engage in peacekeeping and humanitarian missions (White 2001). It is of course true that Blair's support for the Bush administration's invasion of Iraq (2003) represents a powerful exception to this argument. But what is interesting is how the political fallout from this episode appears already to have disappeared. Despite opposing this action at the time, France and Germany have since joined together with Britain in heading up an EU mission to persuade Iran to halt its uranium enrichment programme. It is worth noting in this context that there is no constitutional provision for such an alliance. Under EU rules, the usual practice is for the current Troika to respond to pressing external issues (Smith 2005).

Similar comments could be made in the area of supply-side economic policy. Since 1997, the Blair government has tried to use arguments about globalization to develop a narrative stressing how important it is for the EU to complete the Single Market programme. According to this argument, the EU (like Britain) now faces the challenge of an increasingly competitive global economy, where patterns of trade and production are shifting towards developing countries such as China and India. If Europe is to succeed against this backdrop, *it has no alternative* but to: continue to ensure that it promotes flexibility and competitiveness in product, capital, and labour markets through the completion of the Single Market; work for the continued liberalization of international trade; implement reform of the Common Agricultural Policy and restructure the priorities of the EU budget towards research and development, skills, and training; become an outward looking 'Global Europe' of independent nation states, cooperating where necessary to confront these challenges head on. Britain, whose economy is described as already possessing many of these traits, is presented as the member state ideally placed to lead the way on these reforms (see, for example, Brown 2005*a*; 2005*b*).

There is evidence that these arguments have had some success influencing the substance of policy in this area, although resistance to this Anglo-Saxon message remains. In 1998 Blair was able to announce at the Cardiff European Council that the British Presidency had negotiated a set of guidelines aimed at promoting a skilled, trained, and adaptable workforce. Heads of government also agreed to set up national action plans to put these guidelines into effect. Labour kept up this pressure in its first term by signing bilateral agreements with Spain and Italy to push for further reforms in this area. These efforts seemed to bear fruit at the Lisbon Summit, where member states promised to transform Europe into the most competitive and dynamic economy in the world by 2010. Although progress towards this goal has been disappointing, British negotiators can at least point to the conversion of the European Commission to its discourse. A recent initiative by Verheugen (Enterprise Commissioner) to cut back unnecessary regulations on European business can be seen in this light (http://europa.eu.int/growthandjobs; Parker and Buck 2005). Agreement on both the Services Directive and the Takeover Directive (both in 2006) would be another example, although both measures were significantly watered down by other member states (Buck 2006a; 2006b).

Finally, the protracted and sometimes acrimonious debate at the EU level over institutional reform has allowed Britain to take advantage of a more fluid pattern of inter-state politics to play a more constructive role in negotiations over the Constitutional Treaty. For example, the Blair government took the lead in proposing reforms strengthening the presidency of the European Council. Currently, the chair of this body has rotated between countries every six months. Under the Constitutional Treaty, future presidents of the European Council will be elected for a two-and-a-half-year term, renewable once. The UK delegation made a similar positive contribution to reforms concerning the presidency of the Council of Ministers. In this case, the Constitutional Treaty also provides for the abolition of the current six-month rotating chair, and replaces it with a system whereby a team of three countries holds the presidency for eighteen months (Duff 2005: 22, 85). It could be added that British negotiators consistently supported suggestions giving national parliaments the right to raise a reasoned objection to any draft EU law within an eight-week period, although it should be noted that EU institutions are not obligated to respond to these concerns by changing their proposals during the decision-making process.

Of course, when the Labour government was uncomfortable about certain provisions in the Constitutional Treaty, it secured the usual range of vetoes and derogations. For example, unanimity was preserved in areas of taxation, social security, and EU budgetary arrangements, whereas Britain has retained its opt-out in areas relating to criminal and justice matters. Furthermore, government lawyers are confident they have secured a form of wording ensuring the Charter of Fundamental Rights can never be utilized to overturn Britain's industrial relations legislation (see also Cm. 6309 2004; Magnette and Nicolaidis 2004; Norman 2005; Church and Phinnemore 2006), although doubts remain about such claims. In June 2005, the Constitutional Treaty was rejected by France and the Netherlands after both governments conducted referendums on this document. The treaty then lay dormant until the summer of 2007 when it was resurrected and renegotiated to become the Lisbon or Reform Treaty. This document was signed by all twenty-seven member states in December 2007.

In summary, Britain has gradually become a more 'normal' member of the EU. This change can be explained in part by charting how related structural developments at the global and European level have created opportunities for a more positive diplomatic approach. However, in developing this more pro-European foreign policy, the Blair and Brown governments have also benefited from a more favourable domestic political context. In particular, the public splits and rows over Europe have, for the moment, disappeared. To make this point is not to suggest these divisions and problems have been resolved. Nor is it to imply that the more cooperative approach detailed above has reversed decades of Euro-scepticism at the domestic level. Instead, what we have witnessed since the mid-1990s is a depoliticization of the European question: a process that again can be accounted for by a mixture of structural and agential factors (see also Oppermann 2008).

30.3.2 The Depoliticization of the European Issue in British Politics

The depoliticization of Europe at the domestic level reflects in part a conscious strategy by political agents at the top of the Blair government. An early example is the way the Single Currency question was handled by Brown as Chancellor of the Exchequer. Through this period, the Treasury argued that entry into the eurozone had to be shown to be clearly and unambiguously in the material interests of the British economy (Balls 2002; Cm. 5776 2003), while at the same time accepting there were no constitutional barriers to Euro membership. To this end, the Treasury developed five economic tests against which any assessment will be judged, with Brown himself as the final arbiter. Many commentators (not to mention Cabinet ministers) now accept that these tests are too broad to produce an incontrovertible verdict on membership (Rollo 2002). This of course is precisely the point: the tests convey an image of academic rigour while at the same time allowing the government (or more accurately the Treasury) to put off what will ultimately be a contentious *political* decision. Of course, it helps that these actions (or non-actions) are commensurate with Britain's institutional terrain as described at the beginning of this chapter. For example, since 1997, MORI has consistently recorded that approximately two-thirds of the British electorate is against joining the Single Currency (www.ipsos-mori.com).

Since becoming Prime Minster, Brown has employed similar tactics in his handling of the Constitutional/Reform Treaty issue. Stepping over the threshold of Number 10 in July 2007, Brown inherited from Blair a troublesome manifesto commitment to provide a referendum on the Constitutional Treaty. However, Brown used this renegotiation process over the summer and autumn of 2007 to argue that the newly labelled Reform Treaty is substantially different from the Constitutional Treaty. As a result, Labour's election pledge can be dropped, leaving this amended document to be ratified via the usual parliamentary methods. It should be said that no government publication has attempted to set out in any detail how these two documents differ, making it difficult to verify the claim that a referendum is now no longer needed (see, for example, Cm. 7174 2007). One attempt by the European Scrutiny Committee to conduct such an exercise accepts that a number of symbolic changes have taken place. Gone is any reference to the 'constitutional concept', while reference to the EU flag and anthem have also been exorcized. That said, the conclusion of the committee is: 'Taken as a whole, the Reform Treaty produces a general framework which is substantially equivalent to the Constitutional Treaty' (HC 1014 2007: 16).

That Brown has been able to get away with these tactics rests in part on a more favourable domestic institutional context, thus taking our discussion full circle. As noted above, the Major government's ever decreasing parliamentary majority boosted the influence of the Euro-sceptics in the 1990s. Since 1997, Blair and Brown have enjoyed the sort of parliamentary majorities that Major could only dream about. With its current majority of sixty-six Labour (helped by the support of the Liberal Democrats) has been able to secure ratification of the Reform Treaty through both Houses of Parliament. However, it is not clear at the time of writing how much political pressure Labour would be under, even if its majority were much smaller. While the Conservatives have been critical of Brown's U-turn, Cameron appears wary of pushing this issue too hard. A demand by Euro-sceptics for a referendum on the Reform Treaty irrespective of the outcome of the parliamentary vote has yet to become official party policy. Cameron is said to be worried that the Conservatives may once again give the appearance of being obsessed by this issue; an obsession that has only damaged their electoral fortunes in the recent past (Eaglesham 2007). At present, a cross-party consensus *not to talk* about the European question now seems to exist in British politics.

30.4 CONCLUSION

It has been argued in this chapter that a subtle change has taken place in the British government's relations with the EU, and that this trend is the result of a complex interplay of institutional and agential factors. The twin pressures of enlargement and globalization have helped to shift the pattern of intergovernmental politics in the EU in such a way that British policy-makers may currently have as good an opportunity as any to play the sort of leadership role that Whitehall has sporadically promised, but failed to deliver on. It is perhaps typical then that faced with such a favourable external context, Britain (in the shape of Gordon Brown) appears to be turning its back on Europe once again. We have already mentioned Brown's formative role in keeping sterling out of the Single Currency since 1997. Whereas Blair employed three aides to advise him on EU matters, Brown now has one foreign policy adviser, who presumably divides his time between Europe and other aspects of external affairs. However, it is Brown's conscious decision to turn up three hours late for the signing of the Reform Treaty that most graphically symbolizes a new sense of semi-detachment in Britain. That said, if there is one message from this chapter, the foreign policy of any one country cannot be reduced to the beliefs and action of one person. Whether this diplomatic style continues under a Brown government remains to be seen (see also O'Donnell and Whitman 2007).

REFERENCES

ARMSTRONG, K., and BULMER, S. 1996. 'United Kingdom'. In D. Rometsch and W. Wessels (eds.), *The European Union and Member States: Towards Institutional Fusion*. Manchester: Manchester University Press.

ASHFORD, N. 1992. 'The Political Parties'. In S. George (ed.), *Britain and the European Community*. Oxford: Clarendon Press.

ASPINWALL, M. 2000. 'Structuring Europe: Powersharing Institutions and British Preferences on European Integration'. *Political Studies*, 48/3: 415–42.

—— 2004. *Re-thinking Britain and Europe*. Manchester: Manchester University Press.

BACHE, I., and JORDAN, A. (eds.) 2006. *The Europeanisation of British Politics*. Basingstoke: Palgrave.

BAKER, D., GAMBLE, A., and LUDLAM, S. 1994. 'The Parliamentary Siege of Maastricht 1993: Conservative Divisions and British Ratification'. *Parliamentary Affairs*, 47/1: 37–60.

BALE, T., and BULLER, J. 1996. 'Casting Doubt on the New Consensus: Conservatives, Labour and the Social Chapter'. *Review of Policy Issues*, 2/1: 59–80.

BALLS, E. 2002. 'Why the Five Economic Tests? The 2002 Cairncross Lecture', 4 Dec.

BROWN, G. 2005a. 'Global Britain, Global Europe: A Presidency Founded on Pro European Realism'. Speech at the Mansion House, London, 22 June.

—— 2005b. 'Global Europe: Full Employment Europe'. www.hm-treasury.gov.uk/093/BF/global_europe_131005.pdf.

BUCK, T. 2006a. 'Brussels hails "Breakthrough" Accord on Services'. *Financial Times*, 31 May.

—— 2006b. 'Setback of EU as Members Opt-Out of Takeover Rules'. *Financial Times*, 2 Mar.

BULLER, J. 2000 *National Statecraft and European Integration: The Conservatives and the European Union, 1979–97*. London: Pinter.

—— 2006. 'Contesting Europeanisation: Agents, Institutions and Narratives in British Monetary Policy'. *West European Politics*, 29/3: 289–409.

BULMER, S. 1992. 'Britain and European Integration: Of Sovereignty, Slow Adaptation and Semi-Detachment'. In S. George (ed.), *Britain and the European Community*. Oxford: Clarendon Press.

BULPITT, J. 1992. 'Conservative Leaders and the Euro-Ratchet: Five Doses of Scepticism'. *Political Quarterly*, 63/3: 258–75.

—— 1996. 'The European Question'. In D. Marquand and A. Seldon (eds.), *The Ideas That Shaped Post-War Britain*. London: Fontana.

CASH, W. 1991. *Against a Federal Europe*. London: Duckworth.

CHARLTON, M. 1983. *The Price of Victory*. London: BBC.

CHURCH, C. H., and PHINNEMORE, D. 2006. *Understanding the European Constitution: An Introduction to the EU Constitutional Treaty*. London: Routledge.

CM. 5776 2003. *UK Membership of the Single Currency: An Assessment of the Five Economic Tests.* London: HM Treasury.

——6309 2004. *White Paper on the Treaty Establishing a Constitution for Europe.* London: Stationery Office.

——7174 2007. *The Reform Treaty: The British Approach to the European Union Intergovernmental Conference, July 2007.* London: HMSO.

CROFT, S., REDMOND, J., WYN REES, G., and WEBBER, M. 1999. *The Enlargement of Europe.* Manchester: Manchester University Press.

CURZON PRICE, V., and LANDAU, A. 1999. 'Introduction: The Enlargement of the European Union: Dealing with Complexity'. In V. Curzon Price, A. Landau, and R. G. Whitman (eds.), *The Enlargement of the European Union.* London: Routledge.

DADDOW, O. J. 2004. *Britain and Europe since 1945: Historiographical Perspectives on Integration.* Manchester: Manchester University Press.

DEARLOVE, J., and SAUNDERS, P. 2000. *Introduction to British Politics*, 3rd edn. Cambridge: Polity.

DENMAN, R. 1996. *Missed Chances: Britain and Europe in the Twentieth Century.* London: Cassell.

DUFF, A. 2005. *The Struggle for Europe's Constitution.* London: I. B. Tauris/Federal Trust.

DYSON, K., and FEATHERSTONE, K. 1999. *The Road to Maastricht.* Oxford: Oxford University Press.

EAGLESHAM, J. 2007. 'Hague Tries to Calm Tory EU Anger'. *Financial Times*, 22 Oct.

FIERKE, K. M., and WEINER, A. 1999. 'Constructing Institutional Interests: EU and NATO Enlargement'. *Journal of European Public Policy*, 6/50: 721–42.

FORSTER, A. 2002. *Euroscepticism in Contemporary British Politics.* London: Routledge.

FRIIS, L., and MURPHY, A. 1999. 'The European Union and Central and Eastern Europe: Governance and Boundaries'. *Journal of Common Market Studies*, 37/2: 211–32.

GEORGE, S. (ed.) 1992. *Britain and the European Community.* Oxford: Clarendon Press.

——1998. *An Awkward Partner*, 3rd edn. Oxford: Oxford University Press.

GIDDENS, A. 2006. *Europe in a Global Age.* Cambridge: Polity.

——2007. *Over to You Mr Brown: How Labour Can Win Again.* Cambridge: Polity.

GOWLAND, D. A., and TURNER, A. 2000. *Reluctant Europeans: Britain and European Integration 1945–1998.* Harlow: Longman.

GRAHL, J., and TEAGUE, P. 1990. *1992—The Big Market: The Future of the European Community.* London: Lawrence and Wishart.

HAY, C. 1999a. 'Continuity and Discontinuity in British Political Development'. In D. Marsh et al. (eds.), *Postwar British Politics in Perspective.* Cambridge: Polity.

——1999b. *The Political Economy of New Labour: Labouring under False Pretences.* Manchester: Manchester University Press.

——2001. 'The Invocation of External Economic Constraint: A Genealogy of the Concept of Globalisation in the Political Economy of the British Labour Party, 1973–2000'. *European Legacy*, 6 /2: 233–49.

——2002. *Political Analysis: A Critical Introduction.* Basingstoke: Palgrave.

——and WATSON, M. 1999. 'Labour's Economic Policy: Studiously Courting Competence'. In G. Taylor (ed.), *The Impact of New Labour.* Basingstoke: Macmillan.

HC 1014 2007. *House of Commons European Scrutiny Committee: European Union Intergovernmental Conference: 35th Report of Session 2006–7.* London: HMSO.

HELD, D., and McGREW A. (eds.) 2007. *Globalization Theory: Approaches and Controversies.* Cambridge: Polity.

HIRST, P., and THOMPSON, G. 1999. *Globalization in Question*, 2nd edn. Cambridge: Polity.

——— 2000. 'Globalization in one Country? The Peculiarities of the British'. *Economy and Society*, 29/3: 335–56.

HOWE, G. 1994. *Conflict of Loyalty*. London: Macmillan.

HURD, D. 1997. 'Directions out of the Wilderness'. *Financial Times*, 3 May.

KRAMER, H. 1993. 'The European Community's Response to the "New Eastern Europe"'. *Journal of Common Market Studies*, 31/2: 213–44.

LAWSON, N. 1992. *The View From Number Eleven*. London: Bantam.

MAGNETTE, P., and NICOLAIDIS, K. 2004. 'The European Convention: Bargaining in the Shadow of Rhetoric'. *West European Politics*, 27/3: 381–404.

MCANULLA, S. 2002. 'Structure and Agency'. In D. Marsh and G. Stoker (eds.), *Theories and Methods in Political Science*, 2nd edn. Basingstoke: Palgrave.

MORAVSCIK, A. 1998. *The Choice for Europe: Social Purpose and State Power from Messina to Maastricht*. New York: Cornell University Press.

NORMAN, P. 2005 *The Accidental Constitution: The Story of the European Convention*, 2nd edn. Brussels: Eurocomment.

O'DONNELL, C. M., and WHITMAN, R. G. 2007. 'European Policy under Gordon Brown: Perspectives on a Future Prime Minister'. *International Affairs*, 83/1: 253–72.

OPPERMANN, K. 2008. 'The Blair Government and Europe: The Policy of Containing the Salience of European Integration'. *British Politics*, 3/2: 156–82.

PADOA-SCHIOPPA, T., et al. 1987. *Efficiency, Stability, and Equity: A Strategy for the Evolution of the Economic System of the European Community*. Oxford: Oxford University Press.

PARKER, G., and BUCK, T. 2005. 'Bonfire of Red Tape Aims to Signal New Era in Brussels'. *Financial Times*, 25 Apr.

PORTILLO, M. 1998. *Democratic Values and the Currency: Occasional Papers 103*. London: Institute for Economic Affairs.

RADICE, G. 1992. *Offshore: Britain and the European Idea*. London: I. B. Tauris.

ROLLO, J. 2002. 'In or Out: The Choice for Britain'. *Journal of Public Policy*, 22/2: 217–29.

SANDHOLTZ, W. 1993. 'Choosing Union: Monetary Politics and Maastricht'. *International Organisation*, 47/1: 1–39,

SELDON, A. 1997. *Major: A Political Life*. London: Weidenfield and Nicolson.

SMITH, J. 2005. 'A Missed Opportunity? New Labour's European Policy 1997–2005'. *International Affairs*, 81/4: 703–21.

SOWEMIMO, M. 1996. 'The Conservative Party and European Integration'. *Party Politics*, 2/1: 77–97.

SPICER, M. 1992. *A Treaty too Far*. London: Fourth Estate.

STEPHENS, P. 1996 *Politics and the Pound*. Basingstoke: Macmillan.

THATCHER, M. 1993. *The Downing Street Years*. London: HarperCollins.

THOMPSON, H. 1996. *The British Conservative Government and the European Exchange Rate Mechanism, 1979–94*. London: Pinter.

USHERWOOD, S. 2002. 'Opposition to the European Union in the UK'. *Government and Opposition*, 37/2: 211–30.

WALLACE, H. 1996. 'Britain out on a Limb'. *Political Quarterly*, 66/1: 46–58.

——— 1997. 'At Odds with Europe'. *Political Studies*, 45/4: 677–88.

WALLACE, W. 1986. 'What Price Independence? Sovereignty and Interdependence in British Politics'. *International Affairs*, 62/3: 367–90.

WHITE, B. 2001. *Understanding European Foreign Policy*. Basingstoke: Palgrave.

WILKS, S. 1996. 'Britain and Europe: An Awkward Partner or an Awkward State?' *Politics*, 16/3: 159–65.

WISE, M., and GIBB, R. 1993. *Single Market to Social Europe: The European Community in the 1990s.* Harlow: Longman.

YOUNG, H. 1997. 'Not a Promised Land'. *Guardian*, 1 May.

——1998. *This Blessed Plot.* Basingstoke: Macmillan.

CHAPTER 31

....

BRITAIN AND AMERICA

....

ANDREW GAMBLE

AMERICA in all its different forms has been a powerful shaper of British politics since its creation more than 200 years ago. As the world's leading power the United States has had special relationships with many countries, but there have been a number of specific aspects of its relationship with Britain which have given the relationship a peculiar intensity. After the end of the Second World War the intensity might have been expected to fade, but following a difficult period in the 1960s and 1970s it appeared to strengthen once again. The climax of this phase was reached when Britain emerged as the leading member of the coalition of the willing formed to conduct liberal wars of intervention after 9/11 in Afghanistan and Iraq (Kampfner 2003; Riddell 2003). Continuing evidence of the closeness of the military and strategic relationships abounds. In March 2007 the Labour government won a vote in the House of Commons to update the Trident missiles and the submarines that carry them at a cost of £20 billion, and later that year it was announced that the RAF base at Menwith Hill which is operated by the Information Operations Squadron of the US Air Force would be adapted to house the communications equipment for a new US missile system designed to intercept hostile missiles.

The relationship has not always been so close. In the first hundred years after the American revolutionary war which prised the colonies loose from Britain, there was considerable hostility, fuelled by Britain's extensive interests in the western hemisphere and the large reserves of anti-British feeling among many Americans as well as new immigrants, particularly those from Ireland. Britain continued to be seen by many Americans as the antithesis of the ideals of the Republic—it was monarchical, aristocratic, imperial, hierarchical, traditional and privileged, anti-egalitarian, and anti-democratic. There was widespread distrust of Britain's intentions and of its worldwide power. The feelings were reciprocated. British governing circles were often contemptuous towards the Americans, and the vulgarity of their new egalitarian social order. There was widespread sympathy for the Confederates in the American civil war, partly because they were landowners and the nearest thing to an aristocracy the United States possessed, and partly because many in the British political class did not want to see the United States emerge as a strong federal Union.

In the last hundred years, however, and particularly after the United States entered the Second World War on Britain's side in 1941, the relationship between the two countries has been close. Winston Churchill who had worked tirelessly to bring the alliance about described it in 1946 as a *special* relationship. By the term 'special relationship' Churchill meant more than just a close military alliance. The two countries also shared common ideals, common language, common institutions, and common racial stock. Churchill had long been an advocate for greater unity between the English-speaking peoples and for an understanding between the main representatives of the Anglo-Saxon race (Churchill 1956). Many of the believers in Anglo-Saxondom looked forward to the day when the two nations would be reunited as one. In his Fulton speech in 1946 Churchill even predicted the achievement of common citizenship between the two nations.

Churchill's idea of the special relationship became part of his broader conception of the role of Britain in the world (Churchill 1948). He pictured Britain in several post-war speeches as being at the centre of three circles—the British Empire and Commonwealth, the English-speaking countries, and united Europe. Britain was involved in all of them, but not defined by any single one. Churchill saw the relationship with America as the priority for Britain in military and strategic terms. The Empire and Commonwealth still inspired greater emotion and affection, but Churchill could already see in 1946 that the Empire was increasingly a matter of the heart rather than the head. Europe was a lower priority, impossible to ignore because it was such a close neighbour, and always a potential threat to Britain's peace and stability, but not a part of an imagined English space in the way that America and the Empire were.

Churchill's bold assertions have met with some scepticism, particularly the idea that there is a continuing special relationship between Britain and the United States. Critics have argued that it was always given much greater importance on the British side than on the American (Watt 1984; Dumbrell 2001; Louis and Bull 1986). Churchill's notion that Britain's role in the world is defined by being at the centre of three circles has also been questioned. This formulation has often been viewed as a delaying tactic, avoiding the need to make difficult decisions about where Britain's priorities lay in the post-war world. Pretending to be important in all three circles meant pretending to an influence and an importance which was no longer possible. On this reading the three circles was a face-saving formula which prevented a hard look at Britain's real position, as Dean Acheson was to point out in December 1962.

Yet despite such criticisms, and despite the marked decline in Britain's capacity and reach in the global system over the last sixty years, Churchill's formulations still point to something important in Britain's relations with the rest of the world. The notions of a special relationship with the United States, and of the three circles of British influence and interest, refuse to disappear. They are periodically revived, and continue to frame debates about identity, foreign policy, and political economy. One of the most recent examples of the perennial strength of these notions in British thinking was Tony Blair's characterization of Britain during the Iraq war as a bridge between Europe and America (Blair 2004). His critics responded by accusing him of having become George Bush's poodle. This preoccupation with America in the British political imagination, both positive and negative, is a sign that the relationship between Britain and the United States is much more than the relationship between two independent and powerful nation states. This is what Churchill understood. To grasp the broader context of the relationship between these states it is necessary to understand how it fits within larger conceptions such as Anglo-America and the Anglosphere.

This chapter argues that the impact of Anglo-America on Britain and British politics has been profound and persistent, and that it is best understood as a transnational political space, an 'imagined community' (Anderson 1991) encompassing both ideals and interests, which has been constructed and sustained through various narratives and embodied in particular institutions. Such transnational political spaces are a key feature of our world, although often less studied than either nation states or the global economy. Such spaces arise particularly around powerful states, but they exist to some extent for all states, since no state is entirely self-contained. Some states because of their history (Britain is an obvious example) are involved in many such transnational spaces, some of them overlapping. For Britain the three most important have been the Empire (with its many subdivisions), Europe, and Anglo-America. Such spaces and the communities of interest and ideals to which they give rise can be a potent source of political identity and political projects. They have certainly been so in the case of Britain and America.

This chapter first outlines the historical development of Anglo-America and reviews different theoretical perspectives for understanding it. It then analyses three key aspects of the relationship—strategic, economic, and ideological—and shows how they have come to define Anglo-America.

31.1 History

Britain and the United States constitute two of the most important states within the transnational space of Anglo-America and their relationship has been pivotal to its development, ever since the thirteen colonies successfully threw off British rule at the end of the eighteenth century. The Declaration of Independence in 1776 plunged Britain into a second civil war, which rehearsed many of the arguments of the first, 140 years earlier, and ended with formal separation of the American colonies from Britain and the creation of a new state, the United States. During the nineteenth century relationships between the two states gradually improved, particularly as there were many common economic interests. British capital poured into the United States to fund the development of its agriculture and its infrastructure, especially its railways (Hobsbawm 1969). The cultural ties between the two states remained close, but the growing power of the United States alarmed British governments. The consolidation of a more centralized federal union across the whole of the North American land mass was opposed by Britain, and this partly explains why Britain maintained a policy of neutrality in the conflict, and was prepared to supply arms to the Confederacy. British radicals, notably Cobden and sections of the working class, gave strong support to the federal government because it was opposed to slavery (Mahin 1999).

In the nineteenth century there was no 'special' relationship between Britain and the United States. That was only to develop after 1880 and particularly in the twentieth century with the emergence of the United States as the world's leading industrial, commercial, financial, and subsequently military power. Britain's position of hegemony in the global order was challenged by the rise of Germany and the United States and forced a major strategic readjustment (Friedberg 1988). The history of the special relationship in the twentieth century is about how that readjustment was made and its consequences. Britain concluded that it could not fight both Germany and America, and also that it could not defeat Germany without the help of the United States. In the course of defeating Germany, however, it became apparent that the British Empire was no longer sustainable on the old basis. Britain no longer had the capacity to sustain its hegemonic role (Barnett 1972; Kindleberger 1973).

Harold Macmillan remarked during the Second World War that Britain was increasingly compelled to play Greece to America's Rome, but as Christopher Hitchens has pointed out, the real relationship was between two Romes—a declining Rome, and a rising Rome (Hitchens 2004). The accommodation that was reached between them was the heart of the special relationship; Britain would acquiesce in the rise of the United States and would encourage the United States to take over its hegemonic role in order to preserve the liberal global order, a fundamental British interest. This peaceful replacement of one hegemonic power by another was unprecedented, and was not accomplished without considerable friction and misunderstandings, but there was no war. Instead Britain became the foremost ally of the United States (Watt 1984).

The process by which Britain surrendered hegemony and the United States assumed it was far from smooth, and was facilitated by the circumstances of the two world wars, which forced Britain to become financially dependent upon the United States. Following the Venezuela incident in 1898 when the United States invoked the Monroe Doctrine to claim that Venezuela lay within its sphere of influence, the British chiefs of staff concluded that Britain did not have the capacity to wage a war simultaneously on the eastern seaboard of the United States and in Europe. The inevitable conclusion was that American power had to be appeased, and if possible co-opted (Adams 2005). Although both nations drew up contingency plans for war with the other, they were never tested. A variety of factors ensured that when the United States became involved as a great power it would be in alliance with Britain rather than opposed to it, but it would be an alliance on American terms.

One important factor in this outcome was that it had long been the settled purpose of influential sections of the political elite in both Britain and the United States. The idea of a Greater Britain (Dilke 1868), of uniting all the disparate sections of English-speaking peoples into a grand confederation, had become popular in the late nineteenth century. Anglo-America was an imagined community with both cultural and racial roots, and cooperation between its leading states was promoted as a matter of prudence in an increasingly threatening and hostile world (Bell 2007). There were dissenters to this vision of Anglo-America. Many British Conservatives wanted above all to sustain the British Empire and feared that alliance with the United States would require the dismantling of that empire; while many Americans were totally opposed to the maintenance of the British Empire and resolutely opposed their government becoming a support for it. The strength of feeling in the United States against being drawn into the quarrels and wars of the old world was responsible for the initial reluctance of the United States government to become involved in either world war.

America's entry in each case proved decisive to the eventual outcome of both wars, but after the First World War the United States was not yet ready to undertake world leadership by organizing its own hegemony (Kindleberger 1973). Instead Britain, as the former hegemon, attempted to reassemble the elements of its former commercial, industrial, financial, and naval supremacy. It failed. Naval supremacy was given up following American insistence at the Washington Naval Conference that Britain should accept parity of its fleet with that of the United States. Financial supremacy was lost following the restoration then final collapse of the gold standard in 1931. Industrial supremacy had been severely eroded before 1914, and while the extent of British industrial decline has been exaggerated, since Britain remained a leader in several key technologies and industries in the military field (Edgerton 2006), it could not recover its former position. Britain retained control of its empire, but by 1939 it was ill-prepared for another major military struggle, and in the early years of the war was close to being overwhelmed.

The entry of the United States into the war in 1941 transformed the prospects for Britain's survival. But it was clear from the outset that this survival was to be on American terms. The close alliance that was forged after 1941 between Britain and the United States saw close collaboration particularly between the military and intelligence establishments of both states, and this continued into the post-war period, and is still in important respects intact today. But the United States fiercely resisted moves by Britain which it judged were aimed mainly at restoring its imperial power, and it also exerted severe financial pressure on Britain, which limited the capacity of Britain to preserve its imperial position after 1945 even had it had the political will to do so. The withdrawal from empire might have been faster than it was had it not been for the advent of the cold war, which persuaded the Americans, now ready and eager to exercise a global hegemonic role, that there should not be a too precipitate withdrawal by Britain from areas which were vulnerable to communist insurgents.

Nevertheless it was clear that after 1945 Britain could no longer claim to be the equal of the United States, although it remained the most important military power in the Western alliance, and until the 1950s the most important economic power as well. The new relationship was symbolically illustrated by the ill-fated Suez invasion of 1956 (Thomas 1970), when the Anglo-French invasion force was first halted, and then withdrawn, having achieved its military objectives, by the use of American financial pressure. Britain did not act independently of the Americans in a major military enterprise again. The Falklands War in 1982 was heavily dependent on American logistical support, and it was highly exceptional. Everywhere else British forces were withdrawn and colonies given their independence. By the time of the return of Hong Kong to China in 1997 the British Empire had been reduced to a few isolated far-flung islands like the Falklands and old fortress colonies like Gibraltar.

Through this period from 1945 to 1990 the special relationship waned, especially after 1956, but it still possessed a reality through the extensive defence and intelligence collaboration between the two states. These were two extremely well-developed Anglo-American communities. It also could be revived from time to time as in the 1980s when Britain under Margaret Thatcher proved the most reliable of all the NATO allies for the United States during the new cold war. But Britain's overall importance as a global power was much less in 1980 than it had been in 1950. It was only one of many allies of the United States, and ties of culture and race were not sufficient to outweigh hard-headed calculations of national interest. Many concluded as a result that the special relationship was now a fiction, perhaps had always been a fiction, a rhetorical device invented by Churchill and used by his successors to disguise the fact of Britain's displacement as a great power.

31.2 THEORY

There have been many explanations in political science and international relations as to why such a close relationship between Britain and America was forged and why it has persisted. From a realist perspective, particularly a Marxist one, it looks counter-intuitive. The abandonment of British power and the British Empire without a serious fight and Britain's apparent voluntary subordination to the United States in the twentieth century does not fit easily with realist assumptions about the nature of power and the international system. Britain did after all contest German claims and German ambitions, but American claims and American ambitions, although just as far-reaching, and certainly detrimental to many British interests, were not treated in the same way. Trotsky's prediction in 1926 that the next imperialist war would be between Britain and the United States proved incorrect, although plausible at the time it was made (Trotsky 1926).

The argument that the two states did not go to war because they shared common interests and common values has to be part of the answer, but it ignores the very sharp conflicts that did occur. There was nothing inevitable about the participation of the United States in the Second World War, and powerful reasons why it should not engage. There were serious disagreements between the two states during the Second World War and after it, the Washington Loan Agreements and the Suez episode being just two examples. The interests of the two states were often divergent (Burnham 1989), and the appeal to common values was not sufficient to heal the rifts.

Liberal realist explanations acknowledge this by giving priority to British security interests in the formation of British state policy (Dumbrell 2001; Dobson 1995). The awareness in the British political class from the beginning of the twentieth century that Britain lacked the capacity to sustain indefinitely its world role and its power meant that the British were continually on the defensive, looking for ways either to contain or to co-opt the rising powers which threatened their interests. This acceptance of the inevitability of the decline in British power informed many of the judgements that were made, and in this context both the appeasement of Germany in the 1930s and the attempt to enlist the United States as an ally during the Second World War and afterwards made perfect sense. In the post-war world the alliance with the United States commanded support in all parties because it was regarded as necessary to secure essential British interests, which included containing the USSR, maintaining peace and stability, and rebuilding a liberal economic order. None of these tasks could have been accomplished by Britain on its own, so from this perspective the embrace of America was perfectly rational on grounds of British national security.

A second perspective offers a structuralist account of the nature of the international state system and the international economy after 1945. The position of superiority which the United States enjoyed gave it a position of unchallenged hegemony (Wallerstein 1996; Gilpin 1987). It had commanding leads in production, finance, and trade, as well as in military capacity. This structural dominance of the United States narrowed the options for all other states. Only the USSR was in a position to challenge the US hegemony rather than accept it, and organize its own sphere of influence in opposition to it. All other states, apart from those which chose to join the Soviet sphere or were forced into it, had to decide what their relationship to the United States should be, the terms on which they could join the American alliance, and what degree of protection and what concessions they could expect. Other writers from this perspective have also pointed to how the US hegemony came to be sustained by common agreement between the political elites in many different states. Kees van der Pijl has argued that this had led to the creation of a transnational political class, with common interests in the preservation of the liberal world order under American leadership, which transcended domestic politics (Van der Pijl 1984).

A third perspective has developed constructivist accounts of how particular discourses have been used to construct entities such as the West and the Anglosphere which permit the subordination of the interests of other nations to the United States (Coker 1997). The British willingness to accept American leadership was made palatable by these discourses of common values and shared purpose. The importance of some of these discourses is undeniable, not least in isolating elements within both main political parties in Britain which might have pressed for a more independent British policy. This was true of the Imperialist wing of the Conservative Party, and the socialist wing of the Labour Party. In both cases the discourse of Atlanticism came to dominate the perspective of the party leaderships. Attempts to cast the United States as the other, the enemy of British identity and interests, have at times been made (Pelling 1956), and continue to be made (Heffer 1998; Benn 2003), but have failed to capture lasting support in the British political class. In British political discourse it is Europe which has much more frequently occupied the position of the other, while positive images of the United States have generally predominated over negative ones. There has always been a persistent current of anti-Americanism, which at times has increased sharply, but the ability of the United States to reinvent itself, and to reassert its moral leadership, has always been high. The association of the United States with great causes such as modernity and progress, freedom, and prosperity has been an important aspect of the voluntary acceptance of US leadership.

31.3 THE STRATEGIC RELATIONSHIP

These three perspectives throw light on the distinct but overlapping relationships—strategic, economic, and ideological—which make up Anglo-America. Security remains at the heart of the relationship between Britain and the United States. In the period since the fall of Communism in the Soviet Union and Eastern Europe and the reunification of Germany there was much talk of a new world order, brought about by the disappearance of the bipolar world which had hitherto existed. The undisputed military predominance of the United States now seemed to make irrelevant any further talk of a special relationship between Britain and the United States, and even inspired speculation that NATO itself might no longer be needed. Both the Bush (senior) and Clinton administrations regarded NATO as playing an important role in maintaining world order, as was shown in the first war against Iraq and the intervention in the Balkans. The close understanding between the British and the Americans was an important factor in both interventions, and Britain demonstrated once again that it was prepared to commit its forces to American missions to an extent which was either not true or not possible for other allies of the United States (Dumbrell 2001).

In that sense the end of the cold war changed little as far as Britain was concerned. British governments in the 1990s remained strongly committed to NATO and therefore to the United States continuing to be the heart of security arrangements in Europe. A senior Labour Cabinet minister, George Robertson, Secretary of State for Defence in the Labour government elected in 1997, moved to be NATO Secretary-General, a sign of the continuing importance of NATO for Britain. The bipartisan support for NATO and the United States as the cornerstone of Britain's defence had been a fixed point of British politics since the 1940s, when the Labour government of Clement Attlee had helped establish NATO. The commitment was briefly called into question, firstly in 1960 when the Labour conference passed a unilateralist motion and then again in the 1980s when Labour moved closer to a unilateralist position in its 1983 manifesto. The 1960 vote was reversed the following year, and after 1983, under first Neil Kinnock (a member of the Campaign for Nuclear Disarmament) and then John Smith and Tony Blair, the Labour Party moved back firmly to its traditional position on the Atlantic Alliance. The support of John Major for the action against Iraq in 1991 and of Tony Blair for the intervention in Kosovo in 1999 were unconditional. Indeed in both cases the British tended to be hawks in the coalition, pressing for tougher action than some in the US administration wanted. The same pattern was evident in the intervention in Afghanistan in 2002 (Kampfner 2003).

Ever since the arrival of the wartime US armies in Britain to prepare for the opening of the second front against Hitler, Britain has also been willing to provide military bases for the Americans. In the last sixty years the United States has not annexed territory as Britain did in building its empire; instead it has established military bases on the sovereign territory of other countries. The novelty of this procedure, particularly so far as leading military powers such as Britain are concerned, is one of the most striking aspects of the exercise of US hegemony in the post-war period. There have been occasional frictions at times over the existence and use of these bases, including in the 1980s the siting of Cruise and Pershing missiles at Greenham Common and the bombing of Libya from American bases in the UK in 1986, but only very rarely have the Americans been obliged to give up a base, or found that their operational freedom has been affected by the existence of these bases in territory over which they do not enjoy formal sovereignty. It has provided them with a number of 'unsinkable aircraft carriers' around the world (Campbell 1984).

The military and intelligence establishments in Britain and America remain very close, there is routine exchange of information, and there have been some notable military collaborations, most recently in Kosovo, Afghanistan, and Iraq. It remains true that this is not a relationship of equals, since by far the greater part of the equipment and the personnel in these conflicts was provided by the United States. Nevertheless the British contribution was particularly important symbolically as far as the Americans were concerned. As a result, to many outsiders Britain and the United States are so closely identified in security matters that they seem almost always to be following the same policy. Anglo-America, or Anglo-Saxondom in the old parlance, here appears indivisible.

With the election of George W. Bush in 2000, the United States appeared determined to pursue a unilateral course in pursuit of US interests, whatever the cost to multilateral treaties and arrangements. This American desire to be much more assertive in imposing solutions, and much less ready to accept concessions in order to get agreement, risked a sharp deterioration in relations not only with Russia and China, but also with the EU and with Japan. Ideologues of the new path justified it in terms of the superiority of the US system and its model of capitalism, and were critical of the shortcomings of other states. The new aggressive tone of US diplomacy posed difficult problems for Britain, because it raised once more in acute form the strategic dilemma of whether Britain should make Europe or Anglo-America its priority (Gamble 2003).

All this was transformed by the events of 9/11 and their aftermath. The pull of Anglo-America was once again amply confirmed, with Britain once more confirmed as the United States' most reliable ally. Tony Blair in particular played a leading role in helping to organize the international coalition for action against terrorism (Diamond 2008). The renewed closeness between Britain and the United States was affirmed in many different ways—Tony Blair acquiring a stature and recognition in the United States which only Thatcher and Churchill had enjoyed before him (Seldon 2007). The crowning symbol of this was the invitation he received to address a joint session of Congress in 2003, a sign of the status he had achieved for Americans. 9/11 showed not only that the heart of the old special relationship in the military and intelligence fields was still intact, but also that Anglo-America remained a key point of reference and determinant of identity for a large section of the political class, not only in Britain but also in the United States, to an extent which is not matched by any other country.

31.4 THE ECONOMIC RELATIONSHIP

At the heart of the economic relationship between Britain and America has been cooperation in promoting a global liberal economic order, and conflict over particular economic interests. The former has taken different forms in the last 200 years, but its most recent manifestation is globalization. From its inception globalization has been predominantly an Anglo-American discourse and an Anglo-American project (Hay and Marsh 1999). It originated in the 1970s following the collapse of the Bretton Woods system. Monetarism emerged as the preferred solution to the problems of accelerating inflation and deepening recession, and was enforced through the international agencies of the global order, particularly the IMF, and backed by the financial markets (Clarke 1987; Glyn 2006; Harvey 2005). Monetarism was not a policy solution that was home-grown in particular countries. It was adopted first by the international agencies and became the new consensus for the governance of the global economy, becoming known as in the 1980s as the Washington Consensus. More recently it has been referred to as disciplinary neoliberalism (Gill 1998), an international framework of rules and institutions beyond the reach of democratic accountability, accepted and adopted by national governments with varying degrees of ideological enthusiasm.

The Reagan/Thatcher partnership consolidated the hold of the new consensus and made it the new common sense throughout Anglo-America. It drew further strength with the collapse of Communism in Europe at the end of the 1980s and the claim that there were no longer any viable alternatives to the liberal capitalist model (Fukuyama 1992). The discourse of globalization has enlarged this idea, implying in some of its more extreme formulations that transnational financial and trade flows have completely overwhelmed all forms of regulation based on territorial order, and that as a result all national governments are obliged to adjust their institutions and policies to those prescribed as the international norm (Ohmae 1995).

There has been resistance to these ideas within Anglo-America itself as well as from many states outside it, but it has not prevented the consolidation of neoliberalism as the dominant framework for discussion of global governance (Wolf 2005). It is not a monolithic doctrine, and there are important variations within it, as there were with earlier dominant discourses; these included the rather ill-named 'post-Washington consensus' of the 1990s and the Third Way pursued by Bill Clinton and Tony Blair. But underpinning all such variations has been an acceptance of the necessity and inevitability of globalization, and the need for appropriate forms of national and international governance to ensure that globalization is allowed to develop unhindered.

Despite the ideological certainties of Thatcher and Reagan, the 1980s were a difficult time for Anglo-America because of the continuing weakness of Britain and the challenges to United States hegemony. One particular form this took was the elaboration of arguments about the developmental state and models of capitalism which pointed to deep-rooted problems in the organization of the Anglo-American model of capitalism and argued that it was being outcompeted by other models, particularly those of Germany, Sweden, and Japan (Coates 2000; Albert 1991).

The basis of this Anglo-American model are the common ideals on liberty of the individual within a framework of the rule of law, which encouraged the development of capitalist enterprise which was fundamentally individualist and at arm's length from government. Although many historical details of this characterization could be challenged, it has helped sustain the dominant Anglo-American preference for the primacy of the market and civil society over the state, and the restriction of the role of the state to an enabling one—removing the barriers to free market exchange and sustaining the institutions which could define and defend individual property rights (Hall and Soskice 2001). Many of the characteristics of the Anglo-American model have stemmed from this approach, in particular its voluntarism and short-termism, as well as the character of its welfare system (Esping-Andersen 1990) and corporate governance (Parkinson, Gamble, and Kelly 2000), and the relative importance of its financial institutions, particularly its stock markets (Hutton 1995).

In the post-1945 global economy different models of capitalism flourished, and different ways of involving the state in the economy. Germany, France, Scandinavia, and Japan all had markedly different institutions to those of Britain and America, and all involved a very different role for the state in defining and promoting the public interest as far as the economy was concerned. Criticism of the Anglo-American model and its shortcomings reached a crescendo in the 1970s and 1980s with the well-publicized difficulties of the British economy in comparison to its main competitors and with the apparent strains within the United States, which led some observers to predict that the United States would be overtaken by the economies of East Asia. The hegemony of Anglo-America might still be pre-eminent in the security field, but it appeared to be under considerable challenge in the economic. Its model was regarded as obsolescent, in danger of being outcompeted (Kennedy 1986).

Many of these conclusions can be seen to have been premature. The resurgence of the American economy and to a lesser extent of the British economy in the 1990s was treated as vindication of the Anglo-American model, and of its particular suitability to the conditions of globalization. Those European and East Asian economies which did relatively less well in the 1990s boom were described as sclerotic and inflexible, unable and unwilling to restructure themselves to meet the challenges of the new global economy. This turn of events made Britain and America the leading proselytizers for globalization, and allowed the British to postpone fuller participation in European integration. The renewed success of the Anglo-American model of capitalism was used by Euro-sceptics to celebrate British links to America, and warn how these could be imperilled by absorption into Europe (Redwood 2001; Holmes 1996).

The globalization discourse in the 1990s became very much an Anglo-American discourse, which was consciously used as a weapon against the opponents of Anglo-America as well as a means of enforcing order through the global economy. It became a new means of hegemonic control. It took some time to emerge and be effective, but the foundations were already laid by the mid-1970s following the collapse of the Bretton Woods system. The new doctrines, such as monetarism, that guided the practices of the international institutions were designed to re-establish the conditions of international financial stability, at whatever cost to domestic spending programmes and domestic employment. The development of neoliberalism as a set of doctrines and discourses took place first of all in the United States and was then imposed or accepted throughout the global economy (Turner 2008; Gray 1998; Harvey 2005). Sometimes the adjustments were painful, as in Britain, in France, in Sweden, and most recently in East Asia. What was striking however in Britain was that having once succumbed to the medicine that was prescribed, the British political class, first Conservative and latterly Labour, became enthusiasts and proselytizers for the new dispensation. Denis Healey, Labour Chancellor in the 1970s, was described as an unbelieving monetarist when he took the first decisive steps to create a monetarist policy regime in the UK, imposing cash limits on public spending and monetary targets. There was nothing unbelieving however about the regime that followed (Maynard 1988; Young 1989).

British politicians became evangelists for neoliberal economic policies and for the superiority of the Anglo-American model. The belief in flexible labour markets, deregulation of business, privatization, low taxes, and minimal state involvement became articles of faith which were pressed on Britain's European partners as offering the best way to create a prosperous and competitive economy. The globalization narrative was used to argue that there was no alternative to the adoption of neoliberal economic policies and the Anglo-American model. Resistance to globalization was futile, it was claimed, because national governments no longer had the power to control global economic forces. States had to either work with globalization or be overwhelmed by it (Hay 1999). All this was to change in 2008.

31.5 THE IDEOLOGICAL RELATIONSHIP

The ideological relationship is the least tangible of the three relationships which help define Anglo-America but it pervades everything, since it provides the discourses which construct all three relationships. Anglo-America is an old ideological community, rooted in both the common language, institutions, and culture, and also in the great conflicts and schisms which shook England, Scotland, Wales, and Ireland in the seventeenth century, and prised the American colonies away from Britain in the eighteenth. The War of Revolution was a civil war within Anglo-America, with substantial minorities in both America and Britain supporting the Revolution or the King. The colonists wished to assert the rights of freeborn Englishmen in America just as radicals like Tom Paine had wanted to do in England (Keane 1995). He found America much more fertile ground. But the ideological argument was the same. For the radicals, George III was a tyrant wherever he ruled, and the overthrow of hereditary title and royal authority in America completed the work which the rebels against Charles I a century before had begun but not finished.

Although the political institutions and traditions of the two countries diverged after independence, a strong English influence remained, both on the institutions themselves and on what later became known as the American Creed (Myrdal 1962; Lieven 2005). The Constitutional Convention sought to draw up a constitution which would reflect the best English practice but avoid its mistakes, and put in safeguards to prevent abuses. It reflected a shared understanding about the nature of politics and the possibilities and limitations of political institutions. The contrast between the parliamentary and presidential systems sometimes hides the common core from which both spring. The President was intended to perform the role of the King in the English constitution, but was hedged around with formal checks and balances so that he could not abuse his position. The history of the American presidency has been in part its attempt to escape from those constraints, while in Britain the Crown has gradually shed its power and been confined to a largely dignified role in the constitution, its powers being usurped by that second monarch in the British system, the Prime Minister. Many incumbents of that office, however, constantly dream of converting their role into a presidency, which helps explain the popularity of *The West Wing* for so many of the inhabitants of the Westminster Village.

What this example illustrates is that both countries have been models for each other at different times in their development. The United States has increasingly moved away from its English roots, and its identity has become much more complex. When Anglo-America is narrowly defined as that part of America which can trace British descent, it is a rapidly shrinking part of the whole (Kaufmann 2004), and some have voiced concern about the loss of a core part of American identity (Huntington 2004). For Britain however the images of America increased their hold through the twentieth century and show no sign of fading. American models in culture, economics, politics, and science still exert a fascination over the British political class and over British citizens which is not equalled by any other country. Like other nations the British exhibit a love–hate attitude towards the Americans, often finding in the country the things they most love as well as the things they most hate. But in the British case there is a particular intensity because of the shared language and the shared political institutions and ideological discourse.

Many of the debates in Anglo-America have always been transatlantic debates. Several prominent commentators in the UK, including Irwin Stelzer, are American, and several in the USA, including Christopher Hitchens, are British. There is a great deal of contact between think-tanks in the two countries, between publishers, and between journals. American themes are very quickly picked up and debated in Britain, and there is a fascination with American politics and the American political process. The attention given by the British media and by British politicians to American politics and American political leaders far outweighs the attention given to elections anywhere else. It has also been the case that the political cycles in the two countries have often, though not always, matched Republicans with Conservatives and Democrats with Labour, leading to some famous pairings, including Attlee/Truman; Macmillan/Eisenhower; Wilson/Johnson; Heath/Nixon; Callaghan/Carter; Thatcher/Reagan; and Blair/Clinton.

Images of America, both positive and negative, have shaped British political debate throughout the period since 1945. America has been the leading pole of attraction and repulsion in British politics, and has greatly influenced the way all issues, including Europe, have been discussed. For both right and left in British politics America has been something to be copied and something to be avoided. British politicians have used different images of America to sharpen their arguments and to define their own political identities. Four images of particular importance have been American democracy, American civil society, American capitalism, and American power.

Positive images of America as a democracy focus on its liberalism, the depth of its civil liberty, its self-acting citizens, the richness of the associational life of its civil society, the decentralized and accountable nature of power, the rule of law, and egalitarianism. Negative images of America as a democracy by contrast emphasize its elitism, the degree of non-participation by particular groups in politics, the exclusion of so many from decision-making, the power of lobbies and special interests, the influence of wealth, the biases of the media, and the resulting narrowness of political debate and political alternatives.

Positive images of America as a civil society stress the opportunities it makes available to all Americans. This is the American Dream, the society of mobility, individuality, openness, and inclusion, the society where everything is possible, where hard work brings reward, and where every citizen can aspire to any position in the society. Negative images of America as a civil society emphasize its conversion into a mass society, characterized by immobility and conformity. Here individualization means atomization and the driving down of standards to a basic minimum.

Positive images of America as a capitalist society celebrate it as the champion of free enterprise, prizing entrepreneurship, voluntary exchange, flexibility, mobility, private property rights, and individual initiative. Everyone has the potential to be a capitalist and a property owner, ensuring their own financial security. The negative image of America as a capitalist society emphasizes instead the concentration and centralization of economic power in the hands of the large corporations, the entrenched inequalities in the distribution of power and wealth, the national and global exploitation of labour, and the commodification of social relations.

Positive images of America as a great power treat it as the leader of the free world, an anti-imperialist, anti-colonial power, the opponent of the imperialism and colonialism of the European powers, the leader of an alliance of democracies to promote national self-determination, democracy, and peace, against powers that seek the destruction of those values, which have included Imperial and Nazi Germany, Soviet Russia, and now radical Islam. The negative image of America as a great power is as a new empire, imposing a world order which disregards international law when it suits American interests to do so, seeking to preserve American primacy with policies which maintain the hugely unequal global distribution of power and wealth.

Enduring themes in Anglo-American ideological discourse with special current resonance have been ideas of nationhood, citizenship, and constitutional government. There have been lively debates over Britishness, multiculturalism, immigration, and constitutional reform in recent decades, and America has again provided positive and negative images and models. Discussion has focused in particular on whether US civic patriotism provides a model for a more active kind of British citizenship, on whether the US experience of migration and integration has lessons for Britain, and whether Britain needs a written constitution and a more formal separation of powers between executive, legislature, and judiciary. Images of America have been deployed on both sides of the argument (Kenny 2004; Johnson 2004; Barnett 1997; Hansen 2000).

31.6 CONCLUSION: BRITAIN, AMERICA, AND EUROPE

Anglo-America is not the only transnational space in which Britain is involved. Europe has become increasingly important in recent decades. The British have been notoriously reluctant to make a wholehearted commitment to EU membership (Young 1998), although the Americans have often pressed them to do so. The transnational spaces of empire and of Anglo-America have been the imagined communities to which the British have clung, while Europe has supplied a long line of hostile others (Catholic Spain, Bourbon and Napoleonic France, and Imperial and Nazi Germany) against which British identity has been defined.

Despite the ever deeper involvement of Britain in the process of European integration, a significant part of the British political class and British public opinion is increasingly Euro-sceptic. In the Conservative Party this Euro-scepticism is not isolationist or protectionist. On the contrary it is globalist—its allegiance is to the liberal world order dominated by the United States, and one of its main complaints about the European Union is that it is too interventionist, too statist, too protectionist. Rejecting a European future for Britain means endorsing an Anglo-American one. Some Conservative Euro-sceptics have even advocated that Britain should leave the EU and join NAFTA instead (Redwood 2001). Throughout the long European debate the opponents of Europe have always been prepared to argue their case in terms of identity, and to emphasize Britain's Anglo-American identity, which is regarded as far superior to the European identity represented by Brussels and the institutions of the EU.

The United States has often played an important role in the European debate. It has always seen great advantages to itself in Britain being a full participating member. US administrations became impatient with British hankering after an independent world role, and strongly urged British governments to join the European Community. They thought that if Britain did so the Community would be stronger and more viable, while at the same time if Britain was at the heart of Europe yet still a loyal ally of the United States this would have advantages in inhibiting moves to which the United States was opposed, such as European defence forces independent of NATO and therefore of American control.

In pursuing these objectives the US rationale is similar to that of British policy in the nineteenth century towards the United States. It is not in America's interest to see a weak and fragmented Europe always prone to the kind of instability and conflict which afflicts the Balkans. But it is also not in America's interest to see Europe develop as a rival superpower which begins to contest American hegemony. If Britain's membership of the EU helps slow down the movement towards the creation of such a superpower, then it is a bonus as far as the United States is concerned. Apart from the devotees of the Anglosphere (Bennett 2004) there is little support in the USA for Britain detaching itself from the EU, and integrating more closely with the United

States. This would have few advantages for the USA and would leave behind an EU which was potentially harder to manage.

Anglo-America will not lose its importance for Britain so long as the United States is still the world's leading power and at the centre of its governance. There is still a question as to whether in the long term Anglo-America can provide a serious alternative to Europe for Britain (Diamond 2008). Many observers assume that Britain will at some point embrace fully the logic of European integration, including joining the euro, while seeking much stronger constitutional guarantees to limit the powers of the European executive. There is no inevitability, however, that Britain will develop in this direction. A part of the British political class and the media remains viscerally attached to Anglo-America and does not hide its distaste for the European Union. Joining the euro has been ruled out for the foreseeable future, and there are still deep British reservations on the creation of a European army, on a common European security policy, and on common borders. Such scepticism makes the British government cling to its relationship with the United States, by supporting its continuing hegemony and proposing that Britain remain a bridge between the two worlds of Anglo-America and Europe. This stance may become increasingly hard to sustain, as the worlds of Europe and America continue to divide. But Anglo-America has always shown a remarkable capacity to renew its hold on the British political imagination, and shows no sign yet of relaxing its grip.

References

ADAMS, I. 2005. *Brothers across the Ocean: British Foreign Policy and the Origins of the Anglo-American Special Relationship 1900–1905.* London: Tauris.

ALBERT, M. 1991. *Capitalisme contre capitalisme.* Paris: Seuil.

ANDERSON, B. 1991. *Imagined Communities.* London: Verso.

BARNETT, A. 1997. *This Time: Our Constitutional Revolution.* London: Vintage.

BARNETT, C. 1972. *The Collapse of British Power.* London: Eyre Methuen.

BELL, D. 2007. *The Idea of Greater Britain: Empire and the Future of World Order 1860–1900.* Princeton, NJ: Princeton University Press.

BENN, T. 2003. *Free Radical: New Century Essays.* London: Continuum.

BENNETT, J. 2004. *The Anglosphere Challenge: Why the English-Speaking Countries will Lead the Way in the Twenty-First Century.* Lanham, Md.: Rowman and Littlefield.

BLAIR, T. 2004. Speech at the Lord Mayor's Banquet, City of London, 15 Nov.

BURNHAM, P. 1989. *The Political Economy of Postwar Reconstruction.* London: Macmillan.

CAMPBELL, D. 1984. *The Unsinkable Aircraft Carrier: American Military Power in Britain.* London: Michael Joseph.

CHURCHILL, W. 1948. *The Sinews of War: Post-War Speeches*, ed. R. Churchill. London: Cassell.

——1956. *A History of the English-Speaking Peoples.* London: Cassell.

CLARKE, S. 1987. *Keynesianism, Monetarism and the Crisis of the State.* Aldershot: Edward Elgar.

COATES, D. 2000. *Models of Capitalism.* Cambridge: Polity.

COKER, C. 1997. *Twilight of the West.* Boulder, Colo.: Westview.

DIAMOND, P. 2008. *Shifting Alliances: Europe, America and the Future of Britain's Global Strategy.* London: Politico's.

DILKE, C. 1868. *Greater Britain.* London: Macmillan.

DOBSON, A. 1995. *Anglo-American Relations in the Twentieth Century: The Politics and Diplomacy of Friendly Superpowers.* London: Routledge.

DUMBRELL, J. 2001. *A Special Relationship: Anglo-American Relations in the Cold War and After.* London: Macmillan.

EDGERTON, D. 2006. *Warfare State: Britain 1920–1970.* Cambridge: Cambridge University Press.

ESPING-ANDERSEN, G. 1990. *The Three Worlds of Welfare Capitalism.* Cambridge: Polity.

FRIEDBERG, A. 1988. *The Weary Titan: Britain and the Experience of Relative Decline 1895–1905.* Princeton, NJ: Princeton University Press.

FUKUYAMA, F. 1992. *The End of History and the Last Man.* London: Hamish Hamilton.

GAMBLE, A. 2003. *Between Europe and America: The Future of British Politics.* London: Palgrave Macmillan.

GILL, S. 1998. 'European Governance and New Constitutionalism: Economic and Monetary Union and Alternatives to Disciplinary Neoliberalism in Europe'. *New Political Economy*, 3/1: 5–26.

GILPIN, R. 1987 *The Political Economy of International Relations.* Princeton, NJ: Princeton University Press.

GLYN, A. 2006. *Capitalism Unleashed: Finance, Globalisation, and Welfare.* Oxford: Oxford University Press.

GRAY, J. 1998. *False Dawn: The Delusions of Global Capitalism.* London: Granta.

HALL, P., and SOSKICE, D. 2001. *Varieties of Capitalism: The Institutional Foundations of Comparative Advantage.* Oxford: Oxford University Press.

HANSEN, R. 2000. *Citizenship and Immigration in Post-War Britain: The Institutional Orgins of a Multicultural Nation.* Oxford: Oxford University Press.

HARVEY, D. 2005. *A Brief History of Neo-liberalism.* Oxford: Oxford University Press.

HAY, C. 1999. *The Political Economy of New Labour.* Manchester: Manchester University Press.

—— and MARSH, D. (eds.) 1999. *Demystifying Globalisation.* New York: St Martin's Press.

HEFFER, S. 1998. *Like the Roman: The Life and Times of Enoch Powell.* London: Weidenfeld.

HITCHENS, C. 2004. *Blood, Class, and Empire: The Enduring Anglo-American Relationship.* New York: Nation Books.

HOBSBAWM, E. 1969. *Industry and Empire: An Economic History of Britain since 1989.* London: Weidenfeld.

HOLMES, M. (ed.) 1996. *The Eurosceptical Reader.* London: Macmillan.

HUNTINGTON, S. 2004. *Who Are We?* London: Simon Schuster.

HUTTON, W. 1995. *The State We're In.* London: Cape.

JOHNSON, N. 2004. *Reshaping the British Constitution: Essays in Interpretation.* London: Palgrave Macmillan.

KAMPFNER, J. 2003. *Blair's Wars: Liberal Imperialism in Action.* London: Free Press.

KAUFMANN, E. 2004. *The Rise and Fall of Anglo-America.* Cambridge, Mass.: Harvard University Press.

KEANE, J. 1995. *Tom Paine: A Political Life.* London: Bloomsbury.

KENNEDY, P. 1986. *The Rise and Fall of the Great Powers.* London: Unwin Hyman.

KENNY, M. 2004. *The Politics of Identity: Liberal Political Theory and the Dilemmas of Difference.* Cambridge: Polity.

KINDLEBERGER, C. 1973. *The World in Depression, 1929–1939.* London: Allen Lane.

LIEVEN, A. 2005. *America Right or Wrong: An Anatomy of American Nationalism.* London: Element.

LOUIS, R., and BULL, H. (eds.) 1986. *The Special Relationship: Anglo-American Relations since 1945*. Oxford: Oxford University Press.

MAHIN, D. 1999. *One War at a Time: The International Diplomacy of the American Civil War.* New York: Brassey.

MAYNARD, G. 1988. *The Economy under Mrs Thatcher*. Oxford: Blackwell.

MYRDAL, G. 1962. *An American Dilemma: The Negro Problem and Modern Democracy*. New York: Harper and Row.

OHMAE, K. 1995. *The End of the Nation-State*. London: HarperCollins.

PARKINSON, J., GAMBLE, A., and KELLY, G. (eds.) 2000. *The Political Economy of the Company*. London: Hart.

PELLING, H. 1956. *America and the British Left from Bright to Bevan*. London: Adam and Charles Black.

PIJL, K. VAN DER 1984. *The Making of an Atlantic Ruling Class*. London: Verso.

REDWOOD, J. 2001. *Stars and Strife: The Coming Conflicts between the USA and the European Union*. London: Palgrave Macmillan.

RIDDELL, P. 2003. *Hug Them Close: Blair, Clinton, Bush and the Special Relationship*. London: Politico's.

SELDON, A. 2007. *Blair Unbound*. London: Simon and Schuster.

SHONFIELD, A. 1965. *Modern Capitalism*. Oxford: Oxford University Press.

THOMAS, H. 1970. *The Suez Affair*. Harmondsworth: Penguin.

TROTSKY, L. 1926. *Where is Britain Going?* London: Allen and Unwin.

TURNER, R. 2008. *Neo-liberal Ideology: History, Concepts and Policies*. Edinburgh: Edinburgh University Press.

WALLERSTEIN, I. 1996. *Historical Capitalism*. London: Verso.

WATT, D. C. 1984 *Succeeding John Bull: America in Britain's Place 1900–1975*. Cambridge: Cambridge University Press.

WOLF, M. 2005. *Why Globalisation Works*. New Haven, Conn.: Yale University Press.

YOUNG, H. 1989. *One of Us: A Biography of Margaret Thatcher*. London: Macmillan.

——1998. *This Blessed Plot: Britain and Europe from Churchill to Blair*. London: Macmillan.

CHAPTER 32

AFTER EMPIRE

JOEL KRIEGER

AT its height during the reign of Queen Victoria (1837–1901), the British Empire encompassed fully one-quarter of the world's population, exerting direct colonial rule over some four dozen countries scattered across the globe. With varying political and constitutional arrangements, Britain presided over a vast mélange of countries and dependent or semi-dependent territories, which were connected by a diverse set of strategic, cultural, and historical links, rather than by allegiance to Crown or mother country (Darwin 1991: 4).

Because the connections between the elements of the empire varied considerably in character and degree, both the spatial and the temporal boundaries of the British Empire cannot be sharply drawn. The first volume of *The Oxford History of the British Empire*, *The Origins of Empire* (Canny 1988), even refuses to identify a commencement date, and the fourth volume, *The Twentieth Century* (Brown and Louis 2001), resists the conventional argument that empires and great powers decline and fall, which of course would require an end date. Instead, Louis claims 'the British Empire experienced a renewal of the colonial mission after both world wars' (Brown and Louis 2001: p. viii). In this way, both revived and transformed, Britain was able to adjust to the radically changed circumstances triggered by decolonization (Brown and Louis 2001: 703). In this post-imperial era the legacies of colonial rule continue to affect Britain profoundly as well as the international order on which the UK continues to exert significant influence, although its sway on former colonial territories is not as great as anticipated (Darwin 1988: 329–30).

How best can we come to terms with the enduring legacies of empire in Britain? P. D. Morgan offers an important methodological starting point. He argues that to understand the British Empire, it is essential to recognize empire as 'an entire interactive system, one vast interconnected world' that integrated the colonizer and the colonized 'into one frame, into a single analytical field,' which was defined by the complex interplay of similarities and differences, intriguing and provoking parallels, shared fates, and interdependent mindsets (Morgan 1999: 68). The same method that Morgan applied to the study of empire can be applied productively to this analysis of the legacies of empire.

In a stunning reversal of Britain's global status and fortunes, the empire fell apart in the half-century of decolonization between the independence of India in 1947 and the return of Hong Kong to China in 1997. Apart from a few scattered dependencies, the sun finally set on the British Empire, but the interconnections lived on and in some ways intensified.

After the demise of empire, Britain remains a cosmopolitan and interconnected world that integrates the descendants of colonizer and colonized not only in a single analytical field but also, more significantly, in close physical and cultural proximity, which produce endless and varied encounters. Morgan's methodological injunction remains, but the focus and scope of this contribution are very different from Morgan's and the many others who have contributed to our understanding of the British Empire.

Caveat lector. This chapter is not intended to contribute to the debate on the British Empire (its causes, how the imperial system operated, why it collapsed, its economic consequences or moral reckoning). Nor is it intended to be a brief history of empire or a broad overview of post-imperial Britain. The analysis of empire is a very different matter from the analysis of the consequences of empire for contemporary British politics. It is one thing to analyse the empire (its causes, modalities, justifications, consequences). Assessing how Britain's past as colonizer shapes contemporary developments is a different matter.

The diverse experiences of empire and loss of empire have profoundly shaped Britain, as the legacies of empire leave their complex, disputed, ambivalent, and constantly evolving stamp on British politics. This chapter analyses the enduring significance of Britain's imperial past for understanding various aspects of contemporary British politics, in particular its effects on British national identity and its role in shaping perspectives on globalization and foreign policy, as those policies attempt to modernize and maximize the UK's continuing role in great power politics. In short, this chapter takes up 'the elusive question of the *effects* of the end of empire on post-colonial Britain', which is not treated in the end of empire debate (Darwin 1991: 5).

32.1 NATIONAL IDENTITY AND THE REVERBERATIONS OF EMPIRE

The UK's imperial past has created diffuse boundaries of inclusion and nation-hood. These have been subject to extensive redefinition during the post-war and post-colonial period, and dislocating effects have continued on the diverse and heterogeneous communities and individuals with complex multi-ethnic and transnational heritages. Ethnicity, intra-UK territorial attachments, and the processes of Europeanization and globalization are complicating national identity. Context-specific identities are being shuffled and left unsettled. As a result, it is becoming increasingly difficult for UK residents automatically to imagine themselves as Britons, people who constitute a resonant national community.

What does constitute 'Britishness'? Has Britain fragmented into smaller communities and scattered individuals living side by side, but not necessarily in amiable proximity? These questions are so difficult to answer categorically because British identities, and degrees of inclusion and exclusion, operate on several conceptual, cultural, and territorial frontiers. These matters are often ambiguous, and they are always subject to political challenges and contested narratives (Cohen 1994).

J. G. A. Pocock, who helped launch the 'four nations or one' historiographical debate, asks what becomes of the definition of national community and 'the identity it offers the individual' when sovereignty is 'modified, fragmented or abandoned' as it was with Britain's entry into the European Union (Pocock 1992: 364). Hugh Kearney questions whether the United Kingdom as a political unit comprises four nations or one—and tries to slide past the conundrum by emphasizing the 'multicultural' as distinct from the 'multinational' history of Britain (Kearney 1991). Stuart Hall notes that in defining themselves, UK residents say they are 'English or Welsh or Indian or Pakistani' (Hall 1992: 291). Britishness becomes lost as people assert separate territorial or ethnic or cultural identities that are based either on nations within the UK or on places of origin or descent outside the UK.

How about English identity as a source of attachment and self-identification? 'The sense of identity of the English is almost as difficult to specify as the name of the state', observes Bernard Crick (1991: 91), reinforcing Hall's argument. He then explains that 'British' is a concept appropriately applied to matters of citizenship and political institutions and emphasizes, 'It is not a cultural term, nor does it apply to any real sense of nation' (Crick 1991: 97). As Crick observes, for the English it is easy to mistake patriotism for nationalism (a 'Britishness' transposed into and experienced as English nationalism). It is important to add, however, that this is a confusion to which ethnic minorities are not prone, especially given the complex interplay between nation and race in rhetorical definitions of Englishness/Britishness and in post-war immigration and nationality policy.

Without digging very deeply into the historical record, it is easy to recognize a potent blurring of lineage, race, and nationality that extends from the mid-seventeenth-century historiography of the Norman invasion in 1066 (foreigners oppressing the 'Anglo-Saxon race') through to Margaret Thatcher's 1982 justification for war against Argentina. ('The people of the Falkland Islands, like the people of the United Kingdom, are an island race' (Miles 1987)). To ethnic minority communities, the patriotic appeals during the Falklands War to a dubious part of the UK political community 8,000 miles away emphasized the exclusion that ethnic minority individuals felt right in the heart of England (Gilroy 1991: 51). Thus, one way of constructing the national community appears to privilege race (the assertion of common 'stock' or ancestry) over place (who actually lives in the UK, ethnic identity aside) (Goulbourne 1991; Jackson and Penrose 1994).

Pooled sovereignty within the European Union, the commingled histories (and historiograhies) of four nations, and the complex interplay of race and nationality have created doubts about British identity that run deep. Britain's imperial past created diffuse boundaries of inclusion and nationhood, which were subject to extensive redefinition during the post-war, post-colonial period, and were dramatized further by 9/11 and 7/7, which have inflamed already strained relations between the dominant white Britons and the Muslim community.

Before anyone talked about globalization, the undeniably global phenomenon of colonial and post-colonial migration transformed people's lives and vastly complicated the national identities of many thousands of new UK residents and citizens from Africa, South Asia, and the Caribbean. Inevitably, experiences of ethnic minorities have been framed by the politics of citizenship and nationality and driven by notions about what ethnic groups 'belong' in Britain (and to what degree).

What constitutes 'Britishness'? This question remains so contentious because British identity, which is framed by degrees of inclusion and exclusion, operates on several conceptual, cultural, and territorial frontiers. The definition of 'Britishness' remains ambiguous, politically malleable, and a source of continuing dispute, especially in an era in which heightened concerns about security raise the stakes about the importance of shared values and a common core identity.

Before 9/11, a counter-hegemonic multicultural narrative of Britain was emerging with considerable force. In this narrative Britain was seen as a multi-ethnic society that benefits from the diversity in its midst. The authors of a high-profile commission report on multi-ethnic Britain (Commission on the Future of Multi-Ethnic Britain (CMEB) 2000), the Parekh Report, captured this sentiment: 'Many communities overlap; all affect and are affected by others. More and more people have multiple identities—they are Welsh Europeans, Pakistani Yorkshirewomen, Glaswegian Muslims, English Jews and black British. Many enjoy this complexity but also experience conflicting loyalties' (CMEB 2000: 10). There was a growing recognition of the reality on the ground of life in a multi-ethnic society, which motivated a powerful counter-hegemonic narrative that emphasized the value of social inclusion, political integration, and diversity, and that raised profound questions about tolerance, justice, and inclusion in contemporary UK society. In a powerful and controversial analysis, the report observed that 'the word "British" will never do on its own.... Britishness as much as Englishness, has systematic, largely unspoken, racial connotations' (CMEB 2000: 38). This narrative of a cosmopolitan liberal, multi-ethnic, and multicultural Britain has suffered intensive backlash, defections, and recriminations.

Against the backdrop of intensified hostility directed at the Muslim community, the period since 9/11 has witnessed a hardening of government policy on asylum, refuge, and immigration, and has placed multiculturalism on the defensive. There is increasing concern across the political spectrum that Britain needs to find a way to deepen the ties of shared political culture and values in order to hold society together as well as to ensure security. By implication, too much attention to racial and ethnic diversity in the UK or to the reverberating implications of colonization and post-colonial immigration on British identity—and the schisms within British identity—may become dangerously destabilizing.

By spring 2004, race, immigration, and asylum issues were even stealing headlines from the war in Iraq. There were charges of widespread fraud in the treatment of East European applications for immigration. Beverly Hughes, the minister in charge of immigration and asylum, resigned in the midst of accusations that she had misled parliament. Official government data revealed record levels of hate crimes in England and Wales. After an episode in which British-born Muslims set fire to the Union Jack in London, debate raged about the validity of 'separateness' among ethnic communities, and the chairman of the Commission for Racial Equality, Trevor Phillips, called for a return to 'core British values' and the abandonment of the government's commitment to building a multicultural society. As Britain experienced increased ethnic tension, polls indicated widespread unease with ethnic diversity. By the start of the election campaign in April 2005, nearly one-quarter (23 per cent) of the British people ranked immigration and asylum as the single most important issue facing the nation—nearly double the percentage who thought health care (13 per cent) was the biggest issue. A strong majority thought that laws on immigration should be tougher (nine out of ten supporters of the Conservatives, but also six out of ten Labour supporters) (MORI 2005). Then came the events of 7 July 2005.

Ever since the London bombings on 7/7, intense scrutiny has focused on the Muslim community, and harassment has increased. According to police, the number of hate crimes primarily affecting Muslims soared 600 per cent in the weeks after the bombings. There were 269 hate-motivated attacks in the three weeks following the bombings, compared to 40 in the same time period in 2004. In October 2006, Jack Straw, a highly visible MP and former Foreign Minister, sparked a controversy and angered Muslim groups when he said that the full facial veil worn by some Muslim women had become a 'visible statement of separation and difference'. He then urged them to remove the veil when they came to see him in his constituency office in Blackburn. Then, in 2007, the Queen knighted Salman Rushdie, whose book, *The Satanic Verses*, had offended many Muslims around the world and forced him into hiding in the face of a formal death threat from Iranian religious leaders. Rushdie's knighthood was widely held to be an affront to the Muslim community in Britain.

There is increasing concern across the political spectrum that Britain needs to find a way to deepen the ties of shared political culture and values in order to hold society together as well as to ensure security, but there is little agreement about the way forward. Is multiculturalism the disease or the cure?

To make sense of the ongoing debate about multiculturalism in the UK, it is useful first to note that 'multiculturalism' is a term that is subject to several interpretations. Three related but distinct multicultural arguments stand out for their seriousness, for their applicability to post-imperial Britain, and for the challenges they pose for British politics and society:

1. With reference to post-immigration and post-colonial Britain and other Western democracies, multiculturalism is a political project to accommodate minorities, advance their political and social integration, narrow socio-economic
   inequalities, reduce colour racism and anti-Muslim cultural racism that foster
   systematic disadvantage, and produce in all citizens a sense of belonging to a
   shared political community (Modood 2005; 2007). Multiculturalism understood
   in this way as an explicit political project reflects the argument and policy recommendations of the Parekh Report including, crucially, its characterization of
   Britain as both 'a community of individuals and a community of communities',
   and needs to reconcile these sometimes conflicting requirements (CMEB 2000:
   48; see Modood 2007: 17).
2. Multiculturalism is also a component of a theory of politics that analyses how
   identities and difference are embedded in and sustained by culture, which is
   understood as systems of beliefs and practices through which individuals and
   groups organize and interpret their lives. This approach requires fundamental
   changes in the role and function of the state to reconcile unity and diversity,
   while 'cherishing plural cultural identities without weakening the shared and
   precious identity of shared citizenship' (Parekh 2000: 342).
3. Multiculturalism is also a politics of recognition, which contends that our identity as individuals and as members of a group, and how we understand our worth
   and fundamental attributes as human beings, are shaped by the recognition
   or non-recognition or distorted recognition of others, which can cause real
   damage and erode prospects for equal citizenship. The demand for recognition
   is especially urgent when it comes from minority groups who disproportionately
   experience misrecognition, are subject to demeaning or distorting characterizations, and have difficulty persuading others to recognize cherished beliefs and
   practices or remedy the maldistribution of resources (Taylor 1994; Fraser and
   Honneth 2003).

It is probably correct to note that multiculturalism is neither the disease nor the
cure. But as outlined in the three versions identified above, multiculturalism captures
a set of challenges that are not uniquely British, but that do pose particular problems
for UK politics. 'Paradoxical as it may seem, the greater and deeper the diversity in
a society, the greater the unity and cohesion it requires to hold itself together and
nurture its diversity', observes Bhiku Parekh. 'A weakly held society feels threatened
by differences and lacks the confidence and the willingness to welcome and live with
them' (Parekh 2000: 196). Parekh's observations capture the contemporary moment
of uncertainty about the future of multi-ethnic Britain and expose vulnerabilities at a
time when deep concerns about security heighten the challenges of unity.

Each of the three versions of multiculturalism identified above—multiculturalism
as a distinct political project, as a contribution to a political theory that requires a
transformed state, and as a demand for the politics of recognition—poses particular
challenges of conceptual clarification, political mobilization, and policy implementation. Moreover, multiculturalism faces the immense obstacle of achieving demands

for equal citizenship, recognition, and redistribution under difficult circumstances, heightened by a sense that Britain must resist becoming what Parekh above, theorizing more generally, characterized as a weakly held society. For multiculturalism to succeed, it must overcome a context that is framed by fluid and contested identities and by mistrust—mistrust that is heightened by legitimate security concerns, which focus on British Muslims, who comprise about one-third of the ethnic minority population in the UK.

Multiculturalism must also succeed on the merits of the case that the legitimate grievances of ethnic minorities in the UK reflect an institutionalized bias that stems from the experience of colonization and decolonization. To succeed, multiculturalism also requires not only remedies for individual claimants, but also the recognition of identify groups as rights-bearing collectivities. This approach cuts against the grain of liberal democracy, especially as it is practised in the UK where, as Modood observes, 'an ethical primacy is given to the individual and individual rights are politically fundamental' (Modood 2007: 6).

Modood is right to present multiculturalism 'as a political project that we might be for or against' (Modood 2007: p. vii). Even so, this characterization understates the specific, perhaps unique, character of multiculturalism. Whatever reservations about multiculturalism may animate opposition to any or all of the three versions noted above, this much is clear: the post-imperial terrain of 'plural Britishness' (Modood 2005: 185–209) represents profound and irreversible facts on the ground. The term 'multiculturalism' may be problematic, and the conditions for success of multiculturalism in any of the versions described remain daunting, but does it make sense any longer to stake out positions for or against multiculturalism as a project of political and social integration? Until Britain achieves a good deal of success in resolving the tension between unity and diversity, the unease about the future of multi-ethnic, multicultural Britain will remain an enduring legacy of empire.

32.2 RETREAT FROM EMPIRE AND THE SEARCH FOR A NEW ROLE

As Cain and Hopkins observe, in assessing the changes Britain has experienced both in the domestic realm and in the country's role in the world in the last fifty years, 'winning the war and losing the empire are the most immediately striking developments in the period' (Cain and Hopkins 2002: 619). War, empire, and the retreat from empire have had profound and continuing reverberations for Britain's foreign policy orientations ever since the Second World War. These developments shape UK foreign policy and perspectives on globalization and humanitarian intervention, and they produce what appears to be a path-dependent determination to assert great power status and preserve a 'special relationship' with the United States, even at the expense of a full commitment to economic integration with and leadership in the European Union. In short, the legacy of empire and the retreat from empire have inspired the search for a new role befitting a former imperial and still ambitious great power.

With the end of the Second World War and the ouster of Winston Churchill, the long-time leader of the most intransigent imperial stalwarts, in the election of July 1945, priorities as well as mindsets began to shift. As A. J. P Taylor famously observed, and as many people in Britain came rather quickly to recognize, 'Imperial greatness was on the way out; the welfare state was on the way in. The British empire declined; the condition of the people improved' (Taylor 1965: 600). A different political order, marked by new, often contradictory, sensibilities about the empire, was emerging and a new post-imperial approach to great power politics came to dominate British foreign policy, despite variations and party squabbles. Although the view that empire produced prosperity was still widely held (not least in the Labour government, by Attlee, Bevin, and Morrison), Britain's imperial power was ebbing quickly. India achieved independence under the Attlee government, and East and West Pakistan were formed. Burma (now Myanmar) achieved independence, became a republic, and quickly departed from the Commonwealth. The Irish Free State became a republic, Ceylon became a dominion. Palestine was abandoned, with the end of British mandate rule (1922–48), the impasse over plans for partition between Jewish and Arab states, and the ensuing war in 1948–9.

The return of the Conservatives in 1951, with Churchill as Prime Minister, produced a schizophrenic period in Britain. The government acquiesced reluctantly to independence movements in Sudan and the Gold Coast, but dug in against them in Cyprus and several other territories. Also under the Conservatives, a series of federations provided interim arrangements in parts of Africa, Asia, and the Caribbean, which ultimately led to independence (Judd 1996). Through the 1950s, diehards still insisted, 'the British Empire could continue to exist if only the Colonial Office, and above all the cabinet, would buck up, show more determination and less defeatism' (Louis 2006: 1). But with Eden's Suez debacle of 1956, and the withdrawal of all troops east of Suez, the ultimate retreat from empire had become a fait accompli.

However reluctantly, Britain retreated from empire more readily than it gave up an imperial mentality in foreign policy, which insisted, at times unrealistically, on a pivotal role for Britain as a global leader. Winston Churchill bequeathed to post-war and post-empire British foreign policy two distinct but more or less compatible orientations that have, with important modifications, remained important guiding principles. He left an indelible image of three interlocking circles of influence— the United States, the Commonwealth, and Europe—with the United Kingdom the link among the three (Hennessy 1993). Even more powerfully, Churchill articulated Britain's evolving foreign policy orientation and profoundly shaped the post-war order in his 1946 'Sinews of Peace' speech in Missouri, a speech in which he symbolically passed the torch of empire to the United States. This speech is most famous for the reference to 'the iron curtain' that helped define the cold war, but it also powerfully constructed the post-war order and the newly emerging hegemonic order in another way. In 'Sinews of Peace', Churchill, in front of Harry Truman, also codified the 'special relationship between the British Commonwealth and Empire and the United States' (Churchill 1946).

Churchill also made explicit the view that bilateral relations between the USA and UK, however essential and mutually productive, must not be used as means to erode the power and effectiveness of critical multilateral institutions, beginning with the United Nations.

The end of empire did not bring the end of great power aspirations, but it did bring new British foreign policy formulations and challenges. 'There was a profound draw-back to [the] three-ring version of Britain's place in the world', noted Peter Hennessy. 'The rest of the world did not share it' (Hennessy 1993: 343). There was also a profound drawback to the special relationship with the United States: it was inevitably a rela-tionship between unequal partners, which has tended to exert a tremendous magnetic pull on British foreign policy, to the relative neglect of European partnerships and broader international influences. This context of post-imperial aspirations and the problem of reconciling the US–UK special relationship with the three-ring vision of Britain's place in the world help explain Britain's continuing global role, leading up to, and including, the war in Iraq.

Tony Blair's role in the Iraq story has to be understood by looking outwards to the pulling force of Washington, and to the quite reasonable judgement that British interests are often served by powerful strategic ties to the United States as the hege-monic power. That said, Blair's decision to join the war in Iraq, despite the readily foreseeable political costs, can be understood at least as well by looking inward, to the premises of past and present British—and in particular, Labour—foreign policy orientations. These orientations present a complex and ambivalent portrait of a party with powerful, and still unresolved, cross-currents of imperial and anti-imperialist orientations.

To be sure, deep currents of internationalism and anti-militarism have historic roots within the Labour Party, from as far back as the International Labour Party (ILP) and the broader socialist foreign policy critique in the inter-war period to the *Keep Left* mobilization after 1945, which called for a 'third force' between Soviet Communism and American capitalism and argued that Britain should take a moral lead in foreign affairs. This position still resonated deeply with the initial New Labour foreign policy approach when Robin Cook was UK foreign secretary. Nevertheless, when Britain faced security threats and the external demands of great power politics, there has been a consistent tendency for the party to rally around flag and country. The support for national war efforts was reaffirmed in party manifestoes issued in the aftermath of the First World War, the Second World War, and the Korean War, in which the party rightly asserted its contributions to wartime success (George 1991: 9). Despite subtle shifts with time and circumstances, Labour's traditional foreign policy comes down to a set of permanent objectives that transcend party preferences: 'self-regarding promotion of national interests, defense of a far-flung imperial and commercial network, and management of a European balance as a condition of

British security—all backed, whenever necessary, by the application of force' (Gordon 1969: 1).

It should be noted as well that Labour foreign policy traditionalists put great stock in massaging the relationship of Prime Ministers and party leaders with American Presidents. Despite sharp differences over the Vietnam War and the refusal to send even a symbolic British force to Vietnam—which put considerable strain on the Atlantic alliance—Harold Wilson worked hard to preserve a close relationship with the United States, and in large part for this reason pumped very significant resources into NATO. James Callaghan was determined to reverse what he perceived as Edward Heath's commitment to Europe, which he held responsible for weakening Britain's ties with the United States. Working to undo the damage to relations with the United States that resulted from Labour's support for unilateral nuclear disarmament through much of the 1980s (until its defeat in the 1987 general election prompted a major policy review), Labour Party leader Neil Kinnock supported the Gulf War in 1991, a development that strengthened the relationship between the Labour Party and the US administration. And in a prelude to Tony Blair's wartime alliance with George W. Bush, after a meeting in Washington with President George H. W. Bush in July 1991, the Labour Party leader, upon his return to London, proclaimed 'there are no differences at all between us in the areas we discussed' (George 1991: 10). Kinnock's testimony is a fitting valedictory to Labour's traditional foreign policy and a presentiment of things to come.

The war in Iraq is the outgrowth of legacies left in the mindsets of contemporary Labour leaders by the world-views of their predecessors, as these mindsets have been shaped by the legacies of empire, understood as a civilizing mission expressed both in support for humanitarian intervention and in support for a robust international role to advance UK interests and influence, both of which may involve the use of force.

Initially Blair, who came to office without a foreign policy portfolio, created the space for productive discussions within the government about foreign policy principles and policy directions. In the first two years of Blair's premiership, the Foreign Minister, Robin Cook, took the lead in framing an ethical foreign policy ('a leading force for good in the world'). This included expansive commitments to human rights, civil liberties, and democracy, and a stronger activist role to strengthen multilateral institutions and advance global development (Hill 2005; Coates, Krieger, and Vickers 2004: 9–21; Lawler 2000).

Before 9/11 New Labour stood for a coherent and progressive foreign policy framework, one that linked globalization to a growing commitment to narrow the development gap. The Kosovo War created the context for Blair's explicit linkage of globalization with foreign and security policy. In a speech delivered in Chicago on the eve of NATO's fiftieth anniversary, Blair argued that isolationism was no longer an option. After all, financial insecurity in Asia destroyed jobs all the way from Chicago to his own constituency in County Durham, and conflict in the Balkans brought refugees to Germany as well as to the United States (Blair 1999).

Blair's 'doctrine of international community' gave new weight to the notion of global interdependence by asserting a responsibility to use military force when necessary to achieve humanitarian objectives and contain catastrophic human rights abuses. This doctrine, as well as Blair's Atlanticist leanings, conditioned his response to 9/11 and subsequently to the war in Iraq.

Instinctively, Tony Blair recognized the need (as he himself put it) to 'stand shoulder to shoulder' with the United States, thus cementing his privileged relationship with George W. Bush and raising his international profile. In the days immediately after the terror attacks of September 2001, Blair played an important role in tamping down fears that 9/11 was demonstrating the validity of Samuel Huntington's 'clash of civilizations' thesis (Huntington 1993). Blair made clear that Al-Qaeda did not represent Islam and expressed his belief in a liberal and multicultural Britain in which the government had no concerns about the allegiance of Muslims (Hill 2005).

But in the days immediately following 9/11, the fateful attraction of the Atlantic alliance, with Blair's distinctive inflections, took an irresistible hold over British foreign policy. At this critical juncture, several elements came together to forge the decision to support the US administration, even when the venue of the war on terror changed from Afghanistan to Iraq:

1. a fear that if the USA were left to fight the war on terror by itself, then unilateralist forces in Washington would be strengthened, and the world would be worse off (Riddell 2003: 289);
2. Blair's conviction that Iraq should be understood, like Kosovo, as an exercise in humanitarian intervention to save Muslims from catastrophic human rights abuses (Blair 2004); and
3. a particular reading of the special relationship.

It seems clear that Blair's interpretation of the special relationship gives it a status above broader multilateral institutions, an interpretation that Churchill rejected (Churchill 1946); it is also much more confining than the position of Harold Wilson, who refused to support the American war in Vietnam, since it appeared to require unqualified support for policies that made the UK a hostage to fortune as it assumed a subordinate role in advancing America's imperial design.

In an equally significant way, the UK's foreign policy and geopolitical orientation has been shaped by New Labour's interpretation of globalization. The New Labour leadership of both Blair and Brown accept globalization as a fact of life: not as a set of transformations to be lamented, but as a set of challenges to be met and mastered through pragmatic and innovative policies. The first critical postulate of New Labour's geopolitical strategy is revealed by this stance on globalization: its commitment to interdependence and its pragmatic acquiescence to a world in which the British state cannot control outcomes. This vision correlated precisely with the early internationalism and multilateralism that framed the initial New Labour reconfiguration of UK foreign policy on ethical lines.

This reading of globalization produces a clear set of foreign policy goals. Britain should harness the forces of globalization and the practical realities of interdependence to advance internationalism, multilateralism, and cooperation in the economic, environmental, and security dimensions of foreign affairs. When necessary, it must advance humanitarian policy through resolute military means that are consonant with the doctrine of international community and advance the strategic goal of enhancing Britain's global power and prestige. Its ethical responsibilities mean that it must also engage the questions of debt reduction and institutional reform that are required to secure the aims of human rights, democratic governance, and security. In Blair's doctrine of international community, the reverberations of empire were unmistakable. The civilizing mission of empire and the right of the metropolitan power to use force against the weaker dependent or failed states were both understood as an exercise of humanitarian intervention.

It is too early to be certain about what Gordon Brown and his foreign policy team will make their priorities and what new inflections they will add to Britain's Atlanticist and imperialist traditions. But two appointments may prove revealing: David Miliband as Foreign Minister and Mark Malloch Brown, former United Nations Deputy Secretary-General under Kofi Annan and a vociferous critic of the UK's role in the war in Iraq, as a minister with broad international responsibilities. Will Brown's foreign policy involve a renewed commitment to institutionalizing the UN's Millennium Development Goals (MDGs) and to advancing a far-reaching international aid-financing agenda? Will it involve sustained efforts to mobilize an international coalition for UN system reform and revitalize the UN's capacity to respond to humanitarian crises? How effectively will it help the Obama administration revitalize multilateral institutions? Will it involve sustained commitment to leadership on climate change? If so, then the world will witness the emergence of a distinctive new role for Britain, one that positively affirms the legacies of empire with robust initiatives to advance development and aid agendas by playing a leading role in important multilateral efforts.

32.3 LEGACIES OF EMPIRE

The legacies of empire come through very clearly in Britain's foreign policy orientations, its approach to globalization, and its continuing commitment to international development goals; and in debates about—and fractures within—Britain's multicultural and multi-ethnic polity.

A recent leader in the *Economist* included this observation: 'Perhaps because of its imperial and trading past, Britain is remarkably at ease with globalisation' (*Economist* 2007: 12). Indeed, under Blair and Brown, globalization has been the glue that holds the model of government together, integrating a domestic commitment to modernization, skill acquisition, and welfare reform, to a determined agenda to enhance British competitiveness. With exports in goods and services accounting for one-quarter of its GDP, Britain is a highly integrated economy (World Bank 2006). The UK's imperial legacy may also be seen also in its natural assumption of leadership in European foreign and security policy, in its advocacy of the use of force for humanitarian purposes, and in its robust commitments to global development agendas.

The 'entire interactive system, one vast interconnected world' (Morgan 1999: 68) that integrated colonizer and colonized in the period of empire began decisively to come apart more than sixty years ago, but the debates about the British Empire show no sign of ebbing. Although the larger debate about the British Empire itself falls outside the scope of this chapter, it is worth noting that one after-effect of the British Empire is the shadow it casts on American politics. In recent years, competing evaluations of the British Empire have been invoked in a powerful shadow fight about an emergent American Empire. The claim that America's post-9/11 geopolitical strategy heralds the birth of a new American Empire has generated a far-reaching debate. Niall Ferguson, one of the leading figures in the empire debate, warns that the United States may not have the determination and staying power to succeed in its global mission. He argues that the British Empire succeeded because many of the best and the brightest were willing to spend their careers and much of their lives in colonial outposts. How many of their American counterparts today will be eager to take on long tours of duty in Kabul or Baghdad? Ferguson exhorts America to throw off its cultural reluctance to 'do Empire' and put its best and brightest into an enduring imperial project (Ferguson 2002; 2003). Ferguson's many critics have challenged his assessment that on balance the empire was beneficial. They object to its tendency to glorify empire by arguing that it was the inescapable path to development and modernization (Porter 2002) and for taking the further highly controversial step of using a retrospective defence of the British Empire as an exhortation for a muscular and unilateralist projection of power by the United States. As this debate makes clear, long after its demise, the British Empire inspires and provokes debates with considerable contemporary resonance.

Perhaps more than for any other former colonial power, the legacy of empire animates a continued civilizing mission for the UK, with all the controversy and cross-cutting motives of compassion, presumption, and pride such a role involves. Indeed, the echoes of eighteenth-century commentaries about the conduct of the British Empire may still be heard in contemporary foreign policy debates. Speaking about the need for conciliation with the United States, rather than war against this much admired colony, Edmund Burke observed in 1775 'the use of force alone is but temporary. It may subdue for a moment, but it does not remove the necessity of subduing again: and a nation is not governed which is perpetually to be conquered' (Burke 1999). Burke provides a timely reminder that the effect of the use of force may be ephemeral. What made that reminder even more timely and compelling was that Burke's remarks were quoted verbatim on the eve of the war in Iraq by Admiral Sir Michael Boyce, Chief of the Defense Staff (CDS) at the time of the 2003 invasion (Boyce 2003).

At the same time, the experiences of colonization and empire are powerfully evoked in contemporary debates about British national identity and the challenges of multiculturalism in post-colonial Britain. Consider the intensity of the backlash against the Parekh Report, the debate unleashed by Jack Straw's well-meaning but incendiary advice that Muslim women who came to his constituency office should remove the full facial veil, and the controversy surrounding Salman Rushdie's knighthood. All these episodes suggest that one abiding legacy of empire is heightened unease about and tension within multi-ethnic and multicultural Britain. There is no end in sight.

The British Empire remains the subject of unremitting ambivalence, passionate debate, and, if anything, increasingly intense reflection more than sixty years after the independence of India signalled the empire's inevitable end. The experience of empire and loss of empire have shaped Britain so profoundly that it is all but impossible to think about Britain present and future without thinking of its imperial past.

As complicated as the history of empire may be, the challenges facing Britain after empire may be simply stated: to achieve a high degree of social and political integration that helps resolve the tension between unity and diversity; and to refocus British foreign policy and the special relationship to advance development goals and strengthen multilateral institutions that will serve enduring British interests and sustain a robust international community.

REFERENCES

BLAIR, T. 1999. 'Doctrine of the International Community'. http://www.globalpolicy.org/globaliz/politics/blair.htm.
——2004. Speech in Sedgefield. http://politics.guardian.co.uk/iraq/story/0,12956,1162991,00.html.
BOYCE, M. 2003. 'Achieving Effect: Annual Chief of Defense Staff Lecture'. RUSI Journal, 148: 11.
BROWN, J. M., and LOUIS, W. R. (eds.) 2001. The Oxford History of the British Empire: The Twentieth Century. Oxford: Oxford University Press.
BURKE, E. 1999. Selected Works of Edmund Burke, vol. i. Indianapolis: Liberty Fund.
CAIN, P. J., and HOPKINS, A. G. (eds.) 2002. British Imperialism, 1688–2000, 2nd edn. Harlow: Longman/Pearson Education.
CANNY, N. (ed.) 1988. The Oxford History of the British Empire: The Origins of Empire. Oxford: Oxford University Press.
CHURCHILL, W. 1946. 'Sinews of Peace (Iron Curtain)'. http://www.winstonchurchill.org/i4a/pages/index.cfm?pageid=429.
COATES, D., KRIEGER, J., with VICKERS, R. 2004. Blair's War. Cambridge: Polity.
COHEN, R. 1994. Frontiers of Identity: The British and Others. London: Longman.
COMMISSION ON THE FUTURE OF MULTI-ETHNIC BRITAIN (CMEB) 2000. The Future of Multi-Ethnic Britain. London: Profile.
CRICK, B. 1991. 'The English and the British'. Pp. 90–104 in B. Crick (ed.), National Identities: The Constitution of the United Kingdom. Oxford: Blackwell.

DARWIN, J. 1988. *Britain and Decolonisation: The Retreat from Empire in the Post-War World.* Houndmills: Palgrave Macmillan.

——1991. *The End of the British Empire: The Historical Debate.* Oxford: Basil Blackwell.

Economist 2007. 'You've Never Had it so Good'. 3 Feb.: 13.

FERGUSON, N. 2002. *Empire.* New York: Basic Books.

——2003. 'The Empire Slinks Back'. *New York Times Magazine*, 27 Apr.

FRASER, N., and HONNETH, A. 2003. *Redistribution or Recognition?* London: Verso.

GEORGE, B. 1991. *The British Labour Party and Defense.* New York: Praeger.

GILROY, P. 1991. *There Ain't No Black in the Union Jack.* Chicago: University of Chicago Press.

GORDON, M. 1969. *Conflict and Consensus in Labour's Foreign Policy: 1914–1965.* Stanford, Calif.: Stanford University Press.

GOULBOURNE, H. 1991. *Ethnicity and Nationalism in Post-Imperial Britain.* Cambridge: Cambridge University Press.

HALL, S. 1992. 'The Question of Cultural Identity'. Pp. 273–325 in S. Hall, D. Held, and T. McGrew (eds.), *Modernity and its Futures.* Cambridge: Polity.

HENNESSY, P. 1993. *Never Again: Britain 1945–1951.* New York: Pantheon.

HILL, C. 2005. 'Putting the World to Rights: Tony Blair's Foreign Policy Mission'. Pp. 384–409 in A. Seldon and D. Kavanagh (eds.), *The Blair Effect 2001–5.* Cambridge: Cambridge University Press.

HUNTINGTON, S. 1993. *The Clash of Civilizations and the Remaking of the World Order.* New York: Simon and Schuster.

JACKSON, P., and PENROSE, J. (eds.) 1994. *Constructions of Race, Place and Nation.* Minneapolis: University of Minnesota Press.

JUDD, D. 1996. *Empire: The British Imperial Experience from 1765 to the Present.* New York: Basic Books.

KEARNEY, H. 1991. 'Four Nations or One?' Pp. 1–6 in B. Crick (ed.), *National Identities: The Constitution of the United Kingdom.* Oxford: Blackwell.

LAWLER, P. 2000. 'New Labour's Foreign Policy'. Pp. 281–99 in D. Coates and P. Lawler (eds.), *New Labour in Power.* Manchester: Manchester University Press.

LOUIS, W. R. 2001. 'Foreword'. Pp. vii–x in Brown and Louis 2001.

——2006. *Ends of British Imperialism.* London: I. B. Tauris.

MILES, R. 1987. 'Recent Marxist Theories of Nationalism and the Issue of Racism'. *British Journal of Sociology*, 38/1: 24–43.

MODOOD, T. 2005. *Multicultural Politics: Racism, Ethnicity and Muslims in Britain.* Edinburgh: Edinburgh University Press.

MODOOD, T. 2007. *Multiculturalism: A Civic Idea.* Cambridge: Polity.

MORGAN, P. D. 1999. 'Encounters between British and "indigenous" Peoples, c.1500–c.1800'. Pp. 42–78 in M. Daunton and R. Halpern (eds.), *Empire and Others: British Encounters with Indigenous Peoples.* Philadelphia: University of Pennsylvania Press.

MORI 2005. 'State of the Nation'. 10 Apr. http://www.mori.com/pubinfo/rmw/state-of-the-nation.shtml.

PAREKH, B. 2000. *Rethinking Multiculturalism.* Cambridge, Mass.: Harvard University Press.

POCOCK, J. G. A. 1992. 'History and Sovereignty: The Historiographical Response to Europeanization in Two British Cultures'. *Journal of British Studies*, 31/4: 358–89.

PORTER, A. 2002. Review article: *Empire.* http://www.history.ac.uk/reviews/paper/porterA.html.

RIDDELL, P. 2003. *Hug Them Close.* London: Politico's.

TAYLOR, A. J. P. 1965. *English History, 1914–1945*. Oxford: Clarendon Press.

TAYLOR, C. 1994. 'The Politics of Recognition'. Pp. 25–73 in A. Gutmann (ed.), *Multiculturalism: Examining the Politics of Recognition*. Princeton, NJ: Princeton University Press.

WILSON, W. 2003. *The Island Race: Englishness, Empire and Gender in the Eighteenth Century*. London: Routledge.

WORLD BANK 2006. World Development Indicators Online. http://go.worldbank.org/RVW6YTLQH0

PART IV

INEQUALITIES

SECTION ELEVEN: SOURCES

CHAPTER 33

··

CLASS

··

FIONA DEVINE

IN the opening decade of the twenty-first century, class still makes the news in Britain. The current concern is that class inequalities are getting worse. This deterioration takes many forms. After decreasing for a while, child poverty is on the rise again. Income inequalities are growing as the pay of the rich soars ahead of everyone else (Brewer et al. 2007). Wealth increasingly determines where you live so that the rich and the poor hardly ever meet (Dorling et al. 2007; Massey 2007). Finally, social mobility—the movement of people between classes—is declining, which undermines the ideals of equal opportunities and meritocracy (Blanden et al. 2004; 2005). All of these trends are seemingly happening under a Labour government which is committed to making Britain a more equal society. Awkward questions are raised about Labour's social policies and their impact on class. Of course, the growing consensus that class inequalities are widening does not mean they are unequivocally getting worse. The evidence in support of these claims is not clear-cut and it will be many years before it can tell us about trends in class inequalities under Labour. By implication, it is not yet obvious whether Labour's social policies have succeeded or failed or, more likely, fallen somewhere in between. The aim of this chapter is to weigh up the evidence on widening class inequalities and to consider how that evidence may be used to assess Labour's ten years in power as it has sought to make Britain a more equal society.

This chapter will consider class with reference to social mobility because it is seen as the key to equal opportunities for all and to the creation of a meritocratic society. A concern with equal opportunities might be described as Labour's modest equalitarian agenda. To this end, it is important to understand social mobility in a

I would like to thank Yaojun Li for his detailed comments on this chapter. I am very grateful to the reviewers and editors for their helpful remarks in improving the final draft.

historical timeframe. The first section focuses on the main patterns and trends in class inequalities in Britain from the 1940s to the 1990s. It will be seen that the 1940s–70s were characterized by much absolute upward mobility although relative mobility chances stayed the same. The 1970s–90s witnessed a slowdown in absolute upward mobility and relative mobility rates remained the same. The second section considers ongoing controversies around class and the growing consensus that social mobility is declining. It will be argued that the evidence is not clear-cut and it remains to be seen whether generations of young people growing up under Labour have less opportunities for social mobility than before. The third section considers Labour's social policies to improve social mobility with specific reference to its education policies. Some progress to reduce class inequalities in educational attainments has been made but it is slow and class differentials in education remain stark. The conclusion will consider the challenges that remain and the difficulties that Labour—indeed, any government in power—confronts in tackling inequalities that have proved so resistant to change.

33.1 CLASS INEQUALITIES 1945–97

Before discussing the statistics, it is important to discuss some definitional issues around class and the categories by which we understand it. This chapter does not consider class in terms of class identities (Heath et al. 2007), how people feel about class inequalities (Pahl et al. 2007), or the cultural dimensions of class (Gayo-Cal et al. 2006). It focuses on class, defined in terms of employment relations, since it draws on national data from official sources and other survey data used by sociologists and economists. It makes reference, for example, to Goldthorpe's class schema, the Registrar-General's socio-economic status classification which was used in official statistics until 2001, and its replacement National Statistics Socio-Economic Classification (NS-SEC) (Rose and Pevalin 2003). This latest classification distinguishes between seven classes although analysis of class inequalities is often based on a distinction between the middle class (high-level non-manual employees) and working class (low-level semi- and unskilled manual workers). People are allocated a class position according to their occupation and other details on their contract of employment. The focus is on the economic dimensions of class and its implications for life chances. Of course, this definition and measurement of class is narrow. Nevertheless, this 'employment aggregate' approach to measuring class is appropriate for understanding national patterns and trends in social mobility (Crompton 2008).

The main patterns and trends in class mobility in Britain since the Second World War can be divided into two periods: (1) the post-war period 'of the long boom' (1940s–1970s) which was characterized by economic stability, high economic growth, low unemployment, and decreasing income inequality; and (2) the mid-1970s to the present day characterized by economic turbulence, lower growth, higher unemployment, and growing income inequality. Our knowledge of the mid-twentieth century comes from the Oxford Mobility Study (OMS) carried out by sociologists at Nuffield College, Oxford. The survey was conducted in the early 1970s and the results published in 1980 (Goldthorpe et al. 1980; 1987; Halsey et al. 1980). Goldthorpe and his colleagues (1987) found there was considerable upward mobility, including long-range mobility, from manual jobs into non-manual professional and managerial careers. There was, in other words, a significant amount of mobility of people from working-class origins moving into middle-class destinations. There was little downward mobility in the opposite direction so the total amount of mobility was high. Goldthorpe et al. (1987) explained these important changes with reference to the changing occupational structure. The growth of high-level professional and managerial jobs had a profound effect on the shape of the class structure and movement between classes. Thus, changes in absolute mobility were the product of structural changes in the shape of the occupational order as the distribution of jobs altered.

While highlighting these momentous changes, however, Goldthorpe and his colleagues (1987) also noted considerable stability in class relations. Relative rates of mobility—where the relative chances of people coming from different classes ending up in the middle classes are compared—had not changed. Middle-class children had a 4:1 chance of securing a middle-class occupation compared with working-class children and they had only a 1:4 chance of falling into a working-class job. They explained this stability with reference to the evolution of the occupational structure. That is to say, the growth of middle-class occupations meant there was 'more room at the top' for everyone. There was space for those of middle-class *and* working-class origins. Thus, changes in the shape of the class structure and patterns of mobility between different classes had not made Britain a more open or meritocratic society. Where people started out very much influenced where they arrived, despite the development of the welfare state, and specifically the introduction of a universal education system free for all after 1944. Attempts at equalitarian reform, such as government legislation to establish formal equality of educational opportunity in the post-war period, failed to establish a more open society. The individual mobility of people moving between classes had not made Britain more equal.

Goldthorpe and his colleagues' research generated much controversy. There was considerable debate over Goldthorpe's class schema and his very wide definition of the middle class—embracing employers, alongside professionals and managers (Penn 1980). Similarly, there was a heated debate on the failure to include women in the survey (Crompton 1980). Subsequent research by Marshall et al. (1988) showed that women had not enjoyed as much upward mobility as men and often experienced downward mobility out of the middle class. Interestingly, these debates did not engage with the substantive findings on social mobility and the policy implications. The first to do so were Marsh and Blackburn (1992) who argued that social policy had made a difference to class differences in access to higher education in the 1960s and 1970s. Without maintenance grants, for example, working-class children would have been unable to go to university and class inequalities would have grown. Later, Saunders

(1995; 1997), preferring to focus on absolute rather than relative mobility, argued Britain is a meritocracy and one based on intelligence. His argument about the pivotal role of intelligence was quickly dismissed (Breen and Goldthorpe 1999; 2001; 2002; Heath et al. 1992; Savage and Egerton 1998). Arguably, whether the focus should be on absolute or relative rates of mobility is an unresolved issue. The difficulties of simultaneously appreciating change (the glass is half full, which is a 'good' story) and continuity (the glass is half empty, which is a 'bad' story) in patterns and trends in social mobility has not gone away.

Turning to the later decades of the twentieth century, the mid-1970s onwards has been characterized by economic turbulence with lower growth rates, mass unemployment, and rising income inequality (Atkinson 1997; Gallie et al. 1998; Heath and Li 2008; Li and Heath 2007). We do not have a survey like the OMS specifically designed to provide an authoritative picture of patterns and trends in social mobility in this later era. That said, sociologists have used the British Election Surveys (BES) because some of the data are very similar—with the addition of women—to the information collected for the OMS (Goldthorpe et al. 1987; Macdonald and Ridge 1988). Drawing on pooled data (1964–97), Heath and Payne (2000) analysed the social mobility of seven cohorts of people born before 1900 to 1959. The new analysis confirms the earlier OMS findings on absolute mobility. The results on relative mobility are somewhat different, however. Heath and Payne found the relative chances of a working-class son securing a middle-class occupation improved relative to middle-class sons. There was a downward trend across the century as the odds dropped from 16.0: 1 for the cohort born pre-1990 to 7.7: 1 for the final birth cohort (1950–9). The same trend, albeit less pronounced, was found among women (see Table 33.1). Britain had become a more open—i.e. equal—society over the twentieth century (although the trend is not always in a progressive direction).

This conclusion, which varies from the earlier findings presented above, has been contested by Goldthorpe. Goldthorpe and Mills (2004) have examined intergenerational class mobility by drawing on the General Household Survey (GHS) between 1973 and 1992. On absolute mobility, the trend towards increasing upward mobility among men had been superseded by a slight decline while the trend towards declining downward social mobility had reversed towards a slight rise. The overall effect on total mobility (upward and downward mobility) is one of 'no change'. Thus, focusing on men, Goldthorpe and Mills (2004: 202–3) concluded 'the generally optimistic picture obtained from the OMS is by now in need of revision. Over the last decades of the twentieth century, the previous rates of total, and especially of upward mobility to rise has been halted and, if anything, it is downward rather than upward mobility that has become more frequent'. For women, they found a steady increase in the rate of upward mobility while downward mobility had decreased or flattened out as more women from middle-class origins secured middle-class destinations than in the past. The substantial upward mobility facilitated by the growth of high-level professional and managerial occupations, which had characterized the 1940s–70s had slowed from the mid-1970s to the mid-1990s—when many low-level service sector jobs were created (McKnight et al. 2005)—and might now even be reversing.

Table 33.1 Symmetrical odds ratios: men and women

	Pre-1900	1900–9	1910–19	1920–9	1930–9	1940–9	1950–9
(a) Men							
Salariat: working class	16.0	10.0	19.0	14.0	10.3	5.6	7.7
Salariat: petty bourgeoisie	5.5	7.0	6.7	9.4	6.8	4.1	7.3
Petty bourgeoisie: working class	9.5	11.0	9.6	8.2	5.8	3.2	4.9
(b) Women							
Salariat: working	–	17.2	15.2	13.4	7.3	10.6	5.8
Salariat: routine non-manual	–	2.1	1.0	1.5	1.7	1.3	0.6
Routine non-manual: working	–	6.5	4.5	1.9	3.3	2.7	3.2

Sample: Men aged 35 and over at the time of the survey and on the GB electoral registers. Retired or economically inactive are assigned to classes on the basis of their last occupation. Economically inactive men (other than retired) are excluded. Women aged 35 and over at the time of the survey and, on the GB electoral registers. Women who have never had a job or who describe themselves as 'looking after the home' are excluded. Women who describe themselves as 'retired' are assigned to classes on the basis of their last occupation.

Source: Heath and Payne (2000), tables 7.12 and 7.13.

Turning to relative mobility, Goldthorpe and Mills (2004; see also Goldthorpe 2007) found that there have been some slight shifts in relative rates of class mobility. Relative chances of upward mobility have improved. While the ratio of middle-class sons securing middle-class occupations relative to working-class sons securing middle-class occupations was 4:1 in the 1970s, this had changed to 3:1 by the 1980s (Goldthorpe 2007: 228). There was more openness in this direction and this applied to women too. However, the relative chances of downward mobility had got worse. While the chances of middle-class sons experiencing downward mobility into working-class jobs compared with working-class sons staying in working-class destinations was 1:4 in the 1970s, this ratio had increased to 1:5 in the 1980s. The effect of these trends on total mobility is to cancel each other out (i.e. a counterbalance effect) leaving no change or even declining openness. Despite slight fluctuations, Goldthorpe and Mills (2004: 222) concluded that the new analysis confirmed the earlier finding of 'the OMS that point to a high degree of temporal stability as a feature of relative rates'. This stability results from the ability of the middle class to maintain its position over time. Formal qualifications are important for entry into professional and managerial positions and they protect people, irrespective of class origins, against downward mobility. This security facilitates stability across people's lives (Gershuny 1993) and across the generations.

The analysis of different data-sets has produced different results and interpretations of social mobility trends from the 1970s onwards. Methodological issues may explain these differences. Leaving these issues aside, Goldthorpe's (1996; Goldthorpe et al. 1987; Erikson and Goldthorpe 1992) argument that advantaged middle-class families mobilize their economic, cultural, and social resources to ensure intergenerational stability has been widely endorsed. The ownership or non-ownership of these resources shapes the opportunities and constraints on participation in higher education, for example. A plethora of qualitative studies have illustrated the ways in which middle-class parents increasingly mobilize their resources, via various strategies and tactics, to ensure their children's success in an education system driven by market principles introduced under Thatcher and Major, and, arguably, pursued further by Blair and Brown (Vincent and Ball 2006; Ball 2003; Butler with Robson 2004; Gewirtz et al. 1995; Power et al. 2003; Devine 2004; Reay et al. 2005). Much of this material suggests that there is considerable middle-class anxiety about educational and occupational success which has fuelled strategic action—moving to gain entry into high-performing schools, buying additional coaching, and so forth—to secure advantages across generations. All of these individual actions at the micro-level have the effect of reproducing advantage across the generations at the macro-level. This is why the class structure can be said to have 'self-maintaining properties'.

While sociologists endorse this view, debate still rages as to why working-class children do not pursue further education and, most especially, higher education. The classic debate over whether economics (money) or culture (values) explains why 'working-class kids get working-class jobs' (Willis 1977) continues to divide opinion. Sociologists like Goldthorpe suggest that economic factors predominate. They influence the choices about schooling—especially the perceived risks of staying on—rather than any 'poverty of aspirations' among working-class children and their parents. Others emphasize the importance of cultural predispositions. Working-class parents and their children do not value educational success because it will not be an important dimension in their working lives. There is surprisingly little contemporary ethnography of working-class children and their parents. The most recent study to enjoy media attention is Evans's (2006) study of white working-class children in London. Not surprisingly, as an anthropologist, she emphasizes the role of culture in the reproduction of disadvantage. There is a disjunction between the home and the school in relation to learning and participation which explains why working-class children do less well than middle-class children in the education system. This implies that the class differential in educational attainment is a key issue and it will be considered with reference to Labour's education policies in due course. Before then, however, attention will turn to current controversies about class inequalities and social mobility since Labour came to power in 1997.

33.2 WORSENING INEQUALITIES 2005–

When Labour came to power in 1997, it inherited 'levels of poverty and inequality unprecedented in post-war history' (Stewart and Hills 2005: 1). Child poverty had more than doubled and income inequalities widened considerably. Unemployment among men and workless households was a major source of these problems (Gregg et al. 1999; Berthoud 2007). Initially very cautious, Labour committed itself to Conservative spending plans between 1997 and 1999. From mid-1999, however, Labour launched a wide-ranging programme of social policies. Indicative of its high priority, a raft of education policies were introduced—reducing class sizes, introducing literacy and numeracy hours, and so forth—to raise standards (McKnight et al. 2005: 47). It sought to reduce child poverty through income support via Working Families Tax Credits (WFTC) and unemployment through a welfare-to-work initiative such as the New Deal for Young People (Stewart and Hills 2005: 10). Child poverty started to decline and income inequality stabilized. Labour's social policies, it seemed, were beginning to work. The news was good. More recently, however, bad news stories have hit the headlines. Social mobility has haltered, or worse, is declining. A consensus has emerged that rather than being a more equal society, Britain is becoming a more unequal society under Labour.

The most important recent evidence of declining social mobility has been collected by economists including Paul Gregg (who is a member of the Council of Economic Advisors at the Treasury), Steve Machin, Jo Blanden, and colleagues attached to the Centre for Economic Performance at the London School of Economics. A research report for the Sutton Trust generated much media commentary (Blanden et al. 2005; see also Machin and Vignoles 2004). As economists, they focus on income mobility (rather than class mobility). They examined changes in intergenerational mobility using longitudinal data from the National Child Development Study (NCDS) which consists of a sample of children born in 1958 (who grew up in the 1960s and 1970s) and the British Cohort Study (BCS) which is a sample of children born in 1970 (who grew up in the 1970s and 1980s). They found that intergenerational mobility had fallen for those sons born in 1970 compared with those born in 1958. (The analysis was not conducted for daughters!) The percentage of sons in the lowest income quartile whose parents were also in the lowest quartile rose from 31 per cent in 1958 to 38 per cent in 1970, while the percentage of sons in the highest income quartile whose parents are also in the highest quartile rose from 35 per cent among the 1958 cohort to 42 per cent among the 1970 cohort (Blanden et al. 2005: 8). In other words, equality of opportunity had declined across the two cohorts of young men.

Blanden and her colleagues argue that the decline in intergenerational mobility is the result of a closer relationship between family income and educational attainment between the 1958 and 1970 cohorts. Drawing on additional data from the British Household Panel Survey (BHPS) to consider a third cohort of children reaching age sixteen in the 1990s, they found that more children (sons and daughters) from both rich and poor families stayed on in further education after sixteen. The proportion of children from the richest income group who went into FE rose from 45 per cent in 1974 to 70 per cent in 1986 and then 86 per cent in the mid-1990s. The equivalent proportions of children from the poorest income group were 21 per cent, 32 per cent, and 61 per cent. Inequality between the two groups rose between the 1970s and 1980s as the participation rates of the richer children surged ahead (a 38 per cent gap) although inequality then fell as the participation rates of poorer children

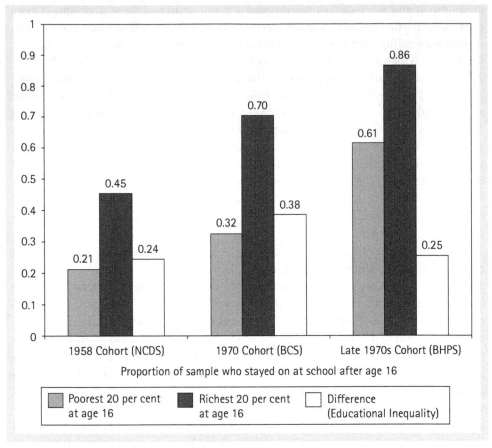

Fig. 33.1 Staying on rates (proportions) by parental income group

Source: Blanden, et al. (2005), Figure 1.

rose substantially in the mid 1980s–90s (a 25 per cent gap) (Blanden et al. 2005: 11). Turning to higher education, and looking at degree completion rates, they found degree attainment rates grew for both the richest 20 per cent and poorest 20 per cent over the 1970s–90s. They noted, however, that the rise in participation across income groups differed considerably in that the proportion of young people from the richest backgrounds increased from 20 per cent to 46 per cent (a 26 per cent increase) while the proportion of young people from the poorest backgrounds increased from 6 per cent to 9 per cent (a 3 per cent increase). Thus, the participation rates between the two groups widened from 14 per cent to 37 per cent over time.

The authors concluded that, 'Our research…implies that the big expansion in university participation has tended to benefit children from affluent families more and thus reinforced immobility across generations' (Blanden et al. 2005: 14). Equally influential work, using the same longitudinal data-sets, for the Joseph Rowntree Foundation has focused on the other end of the spectrum: namely, the persistence of poverty across generations (Blanden and Gibbons 2006). For those teenagers growing

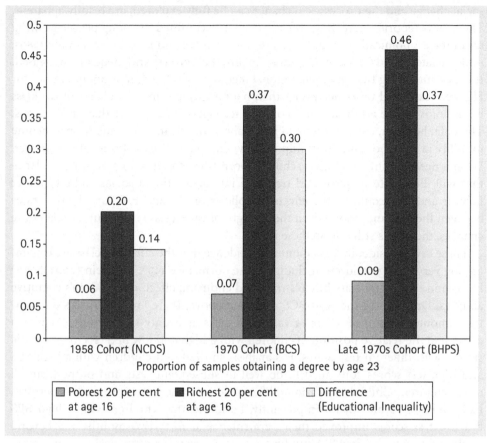

Fig. 33.2 Degree completion by age 23 by parental income group

Source: Blanden et al. (2005), figure 2.

up in the 1970s, the chances of being poor as an adult were double if they were poor as a teenager. For teenagers growing up in the 1980s, the chances of being poor as an adult were four times as likely if they were poor teenagers. In other words, the persistence of poverty strengthened—especially for women—across cohorts (Blanden and Gibbons 2006: 12). Of course, there are numerous factors which explain why poverty persists. They found that general family background disadvantages, especially parental non-employment and low education and other factors such as being out of work, having a partner out of work, having a limited work history, and poverty in itself (as in a lack of money), contributed to the higher risk of poverty (Blanden and Gibbons 2006: 30). Overall, early advantages are associated with later advantageous outcomes while early disadvantages are associated with disadvantageous outcomes. The effects of class background are profound.

   This evidence has contributed to the growing consensus that intergenerational mobility is falling and the view that Labour is failing to reverse these trends. The evidence is very powerful. The strengths of longitudinal research, where economic and social change and the processes of change can be fully explored, are readily apparent. The results reported here, however, are primarily confined to young people growing up in the economically turbulent decades of the 1970s and 1980s. It was in the 1980s, under Thatcher-led Conservative governments, that poverty and inequality increased. It is not surprising that intergenerational inequality declined, that opportunities for HE were exploited by richer rather than poorer groups, and the effects of workless households on the adult outcomes of poor teenagers were greater than in the 1970s. The data, however, cannot tell us so much about trends in intergenerational income mobility in the 1990s and, most importantly, since 1997 when Labour came to power. What is needed is information on children born after 1997. It is this empirical evidence that will illuminate patterns and trends in intergenerational social mobility under Labour and, for example, the effects of policies on FE and HE participation rates between the rich and poor. Given the strength of early class background on later life chances, the jury is still out on these issues.

These caveats aside, there is mounting evidence that the effects of class are evident among very young children, including those born since 1997. Feinstein (2003; 2006) has found that social class has a 'strong and enduring effect' on children's cognitive abilities. Drawing on the 1970 BCS discussed above, there are social class differentials among children tested on a variety of tasks at twenty-two months. Feinstein compared the relative position of children with a high and low SES (socio-economic status) with different test scores. His analysis showed that children with a high SES and high test scores continued to do well in subsequent tests and outperform all other children. Children with low SES and low test scores continued to perform badly relative to all others. Importantly, he found that children with a high SES but low test scores improved their performance at forty-two months and beyond while children with a low SES but high test scores experienced a decline from forty-two months onwards. Feinstein (2006: 415) concluded, 'Thus, there is discontinuity after 22 months but it is heavily socially determined. The advantageous mobility is overwhelmingly for children from advantaged backgrounds, the downward mobility for children from disadvantaged backgrounds'. Indeed, as Figure 33.3 shows, between the ages of five and ten years the high achievers (children who scored in the top quartile (Q) in the index of cognitive development at twenty-two months) from lower-class backgrounds had been overtaken by the poor achievers (in the bottom quartile) from higher-class backgrounds. This happens when children are in school.

Feinstein (2006: 413) rightly emphasizes that class does not determine children's lives since 'relative ability is not fixed'. That said, test results at twenty-two months are a good predictor of GCSE results at sixteen. The effects of class are, again, quite profound. They are now being found among children born in 2000–2. The Millennium Cohort Study (MCS) is a longitudinal survey of 19,000 UK children born in 2001–2 whose parents were interviewed when cohort members were nine months. These children will be followed into adulthood like the NCDS and BCS (Dex and Joshi 2005). The second survey, with the children now aged three, has also established class differences in child development. Using a variety of tests, researchers (George et al. 2007: 97–8) found that the majority of children are of average ability so there is an

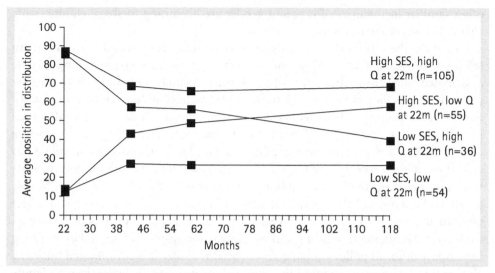

Fig. 33.3 Average rank of test scores at 22, 42, 60, and 120 months by SES of parents and early rank position

Source: Feinstein (2003: 73–98). See also Feinstein (2006: 411).

overlap between middle-class and working-class children. Nevertheless, middle-class children are more likely to score average or above average in tests while working-class children are more likely to be average or below average in performance. The results mirror those of Feinstein. The MCS was designed to capture high concentrations of minority ethnic populations whose presence has grown since 1970. Of note is that children of Pakistani and Bangladeshi parents—invariably in lower rather than higher social classes—underperformed in these tests. The effects of class and race are evident.

The MCS was also designed to over-represent areas of child poverty and slightly higher levels of poverty (26 per cent) were found among the families of the survey than is the case in the total population (22 per cent) in 2003–4 (Ward et al. 2007: 172). Not surprisingly, they found that poverty (with family income below the 60 per cent of the median threshold) affected few middle-class mothers (4.7 per cent) and middle-class fathers (5.4 per cent). It was much more prevalent among working-class mothers and fathers with poverty experienced by between a quarter (24.7 per cent) and a third (35.9 per cent) of working-class families. Not surprisingly, it was very high among all lone parents who did not work (92.3 per cent), fathers and mothers who did not work (85 per cent), and families where the father was not employed although the mother worked (Ward et al. 2007: 176). Differences in poverty rates, therefore, were readily apparent amongst parents of this most recent survey. It should also be noted that poverty was most prevalent among all lone parents (72.1 per cent)—highlighting the effects of changing family demographics over time—and it was high also among Pakistani and Bangladeshi families (67.9 per cent and 67 per cent respectively) (Ward et al. 2007: 173–6). Thus, for 'children of the new century', social class differences and other familiar inequalities of race and gender are beginning to shape children's life chances in ways to which we are accustomed.

Of course, these children were only three years old in 2003–5 and it is too early to tell how they will get on in education and employment. Interesting findings can be anticipated when these children progress through primary school from about now (2005–11) and as they move through the secondary school system (from 2011 to 2016). Some of their primary school years will be under Labour. These children will not go into FE until 2016, nor enter HE until 2018. Labour may have left power long before 2018 (or, if they are in power, they are likely to have lost it in between). It will be this cohort of children who will be most able to tell us whether the Labour governments from 1997 have improved social mobility. Unfortunately, the MCS might not be able to tell us about one of Labour's early intervention policies—Sure Start—and its effect on reducing child poverty since most Sure Start childcare places only came on-stream from 2007. Measuring trends in social mobility is a long-term affair and establishing the impact of social policy on patterns of social mobility is a complicated business. Noting this, and bearing in mind the powerful early effects of class—through family backgrounds—on later life chances, attention will now turn to Labour's policies to improve education for all children.

33.3 EDUCATION POLICY AND POLITICS

Declining social mobility and enduring class inequalities, then, have been quickly associated with Labour in power and the prevailing consensus has put pressure on the government to renew efforts to deliver on policies close to its heart. At the time of writing, the Labour government has been in power for ten years—1997–2007—having allowed for evaluations of some of the policies that are seeking to reduce social exclusion and increase opportunities. The most extensive evaluation of Labour's social policies has been carried out by researchers at the ESRC Centre for Analysis of Social Exclusion (CASE) at the London School of Economics. Led by John Hills, this group of scholars has proffered a sophisticated and balanced assessment of Labour's social policies, their success or otherwise to date, and their prospects for success or not in the future (Hills 2004; Hills et al. 2002; Hills and Stewart 2005; Hills et al. 2007). Not all of Labour's social policies can be considered here, of course, even though many of them are interrelated with, for example, child poverty. Rather, given the importance attached to education for improving social mobility, attention will focus on Labour's education policies, the extent to which policy interventions have been successful in enhancing social mobility and the political implications of this assessment. Of course, all of these issues have to be understood in the wider context of the perpetuation of market principles and an emphasis on choice in public services like education (Ball 2003).

Considerable effort has been devoted to pre-school children (0–4 years) since inter-vention in a child's early years is seen as an effective way of improving educational performance later (Sparkes and Glennerster 2002: 200). This is significant since, in the past, these years were 'treated as almost entirely a private responsibility' (Piachaud and Sutherland 2002: 152). There is recognition of the importance of the family as part of any education policies although, arguably, this is a very difficult area in which governments can intervene. There are a whole host of initiatives associated with the 'early years' agenda which is about the provision of better public services for under-fives. Initiatives have included Sure Start which seeks to help families with children from birth to the age of four in areas where children are at most risk of poverty and exclusion. Launched in 1998, it was operating in 522 neighbourhoods covering 400,000 children including a third of all poor children by 2004. Its educational aim is to promote the cognitive development of poor children so they are better prepared for school and the early attainment gap between poor and rich children is narrowed (Lupton and Power 2005: 121). Other more focused educational policies include the expansion of nursery school provision for three- and four-year-olds and investment in high-quality childcare via the 1998 National Childcare Strategy (Stewart 2005: 148). Considerable investment, therefore, has gone into 'early years' education.

Sufficient time has elapsed for evaluations of these policies to have been under-taken and, to date, the findings are somewhat mixed, indicating that much remains to be done. With regard to Sure Start, an early, modest objective to ensure that all children within its remit have access to good quality play and learning opportunities has been achieved (Power and Willmott 2005: 284; Stewart 2005: 161). The results are not so clear-cut with regard to more challenging educational objectives, however. The national evaluation of Sure Start (Meadows 2005; Belsky et al. 2007) has indi-cated that its beneficial effects (across the board) have been small while it has had some small negative effects too. The verbal abilities of children of young mothers involved in the scheme, for example, were lower than children of mothers in non-Sure Start areas. Another report on the quality of childcare settings of children in the Millennium Cohort Study, while critical of Sure Start where educational objectives compete against other ones, found that high-quality provision—usually group child-care settings—improved literacy skills although much more could be done for maths and science (Mathers et al. 2007). Disadvantaged children, therefore, require high-quality childcare to enhance their cognitive skills. Thus, while considerable effort has gone into the 'early years' agenda, and some objectives realized, much remains to be done—especially for children from poorer class backgrounds.

Turning to primary schools, Labour's twin preoccupations have been to raise educational standards for all while narrowing class differentials in attainment. There have been various policy initiatives including a reduction in class sizes, literacy and numeracy hours, curriculum developments, and so forth. The performance of chil-dren at Key Stage 1 (tests at seven) has improved continuously since 1996. In maths, for example, 89 per cent of boys and 92 per cent of girls reached or exceeded the expected standards through teacher assessment in 2006 (*Social Trends 37* 2007: 32). The class gap in attainment has also narrowed. While the performance of children in maths improved from 94 per cent to 97 per cent between 1997 and 2001 in rich schools (where less than 10 per cent receive free schools meals (FSMs)), it increased from 70 per cent to 82 per cent in poor schools (where over 40 per cent of children receive FSMs) (McKnight et al. 2005: 58). At Key Stage 2 (tests at eleven), 83 per cent of boys and 85 per cent of girls performed at expected levels for science in 2006 (*Social Trends 37* 2007: 32). The class gap in performance is greater at KS2. Nevertheless, the performance of children in maths improved from 79 per cent to 85 per cent between 1997 and 2001 in rich schools while it increased from 37 per cent to 52 per cent in poor schools (McKnight et al. 2005: 58). This gap is considerable but the difference has declined. Labour's policies have been partially successful although targeted initiatives to reduce it are still required.

Various policy initiatives have sought to meet Labour's twin objectives at secondary school level. Some—the targeting of low attaining schools such as the Excellence in Cities (EiC) initiative, the establishment of faith schools and academies, selection procedures, and more choice—have been contentious. The evidence suggests that attainment levels have improved for everyone. Three-quarters of young men and women reached the expected standard for maths in 2005 (74 per cent and 77 per cent respectively) at Key Stage 3 (tests at fourteen) (*Social Trends 37* 2007: 32). The class gap in rich and poor schools, however, is stark. The median share of pupils reaching expected levels in maths at KS3 in rich schools in 2001 was 86 per cent compared with just 14 per cent in poor schools (McKnight et al. 2005: 58). EiC schools have improved the performance of pupils with lower levels of attainment (Machin et al. 2003) so their impact is not insignificant but it is modest given the task at hand. Key Stage 4 (GCSEs at sixteen) results have improved since the mid-1990s with 57 per cent of pupils securing five or more GCSE grades A* to C in 2004–5. Success, however, varies by FSM eligibility. While 61 per cent of all pupils who do not get FSMs secured five grades A*–C, only 33 per cent receiving FSMs did so (*Social Trends 37* 2007: 33). Young people receiving FSMs with the lowest levels of attainment in deprived neighbourhoods need greater support through sustained interventions.

Since the mid-1980s, as we saw, there has been a rise in the number of young people staying on in further education (16–19) (Bynner et al. 1997; Ferri et al. 2003). Over three-quarters (76 per cent) of young people aged sixteen stayed on in 2005 (*Social Trends 37* 2007: 29). Staying-on rates, however, are patterned by class so that young people from middle-class backgrounds have a staying-on rate of 80 per cent compared with 58 per cent of young people from working-class backgrounds. Prior attainment in key stage tests explains this gap although middle-class young people are more likely to do A levels whatever the level of attainment than their working-class equivalents (Jackson et al. 2005). Again, there have been a number of '14–19 reforms' although there has been much disappointment about the failure to take up the recommendations of the Tomlinson Report on academic and vocational routes through FE. In 2004, Labour introduced a weekly cash allowance (up to £30)—Education Maintenance Allowance (EMA)—payable to young people from low-income families who stay in post-compulsory education full time. Direct financial assistance of this kind is anticipated to improve staying-on rates among target groups although whether the policy works will not be known until 2005–6 figures are published.

Finally, as we have seen, a substantial and rapid rise in the number of young people going into higher education (aged 19+) began around 1987 and presently stands at 43 per cent. As part of a widening participation agenda, Labour has set itself a target of 50 per cent of eligible young people attending an HE institution by 2010. The current figure is close but Labour is unlikely to meet this target. The class gap of course remains, as young people from affluent families have taken up the opportunities to go to university at a faster rate than young people from poor families. Of course, in the 1960s and 1970s, means-tested maintenance grants facilitated working-class entry into HE and allowed working-class students to take up the opportunities to go to university as much as middle-class students. In the 1990s, however, the situation was different. Under successive Conservative administrations, means-tested grants were gradually replaced by student loans. Against the background of a crisis in the funding of HE, Labour introduced top-up fees of £1,000 per annum in 1998 which were paid up-front by students or, more likely, their parents (McKnight et al. 2005: 65). There was considerable opposition to this move—not least from Labour backbenchers—who were concerned that both loans and fees would deter young people in low-income families from going to university.

These policies were expected to see a drop in university applications from young people in low-income families because they are debt averse (Callender 2003). Research has show that HE participation is more sensitive to parental income in the 1990s than the 1970s and that the impact of early tuition fees widened the class gap (Galino-Rueda et al. 2004). Further policy changes have taken place, however. In 2005, universities were allowed to vary tuition fees up to a maximum of £3,000 per annum. These fees take the form of an income-contingent loan which is repaid after gradu-ation (McKnight et al. 2005: 65). Again, fears were expressed that higher fees, even as a loan, will deter potential students from low-income families. To date, however, official statistics indicate the introduction of fees has not affected participation rates. The proportion of students from low-income families increased from 25 per cent in 1997–8 to 29 per cent in 2005–6 (HEFCE). Still, controversy surrounds the slow place of change and doubts have been raised about initiatives like *AimHigher* which seeks to raise the aspirations of poor teenagers. The class stratification between HE institutions is also increasingly apparent as working-class young people dominate the post-1992 new universities rather than the long-established old ones (Reay et al. 2005). The recent announcement on the reintroduction of means-tested maintenance grants from 2008—where students will get £3,000 a year if their family income falls below £25,000—has been welcomed. The impact of this new policy on class differentials in HE has yet to be seen.

Overall, Labour governments have made considerable efforts to reduce class inequalities in educational attainment. Some of these policies will take years to have an effect. In time, evaluations of policy can take place which will judge them a success or otherwise. To date, the drive to improve educational attainment in primary schools has seen children from poor homes do better in school than in the past. Some policies, therefore, may be judged successful, albeit partially so, since much remains to be done. Other policies, however, have not broken down the class attainment gap, most notably at secondary school. Differential success rates then influence participation rates in FE and HE. Interventions here have achieved only modest outcomes so far. Sustained efforts are required to reduce class inequalities because the pace of change is modest and slow. Labour is not unaware of the challenges that remain. The political implications of this story are not predictable. Will Labour suffer in an election if it has failed to deliver? The main opposition parties make political capital out of the slow progress to raise the life chances of poor children. Both the Conservatives and Liberal Democrats claim to be the 'party of aspiration'. Many issues feature in a general election, however. Whether Labour's attempt to increase equal opportunities to reduce class inequalities is the key issue on which it is judged remains to be seen.

33.4 CONCLUSION

This chapter has considered class inequalities in the context of contemporary British politics. Particular attention has been paid to patterns and trends in social mobility—the movement of people between classes—as a way of looking at the extent to which Britain is an open society. The focus of attention has been on equal opportunities and meritocracy since they are key parts of Labour's modest egalitarian agenda. The chapter has not spoken of a more radical agenda which might focus on issues of equal outcomes or acknowledge the dark side of meritocracy. This is not to say that these topics do not feature in contemporary political controversies in Britain. Discussions about a more redistributive tax and benefit system, especially when it is the growing income of the rich that is driving the rise in income inequalities, are taking place. Indeed, economists at the Institute for Fiscal Studies have been arguing for some time that Labour's equality agenda can only be achieved if the taxes on the affluent—with annual salaries over £100,000 (when the average is around £23,000)—are raised. The targets on child poverty will not be met otherwise (Brewer et al. 2007). All of these aspects of class inequalities—and how to reduce and eradicate them—shape the political climate in Britain. They will influence how all three main political parties appeal to the electorate in future years.

These issues aside, the chapter has drawn on a wide range of material from official data to theoretically informed empirical research—of the highest quality—by sociologists and economists and specialists in social policy. It is pleasing that Labour's policies have been informed by this academic research. Much of the evidence shows that class inequalities are remarkably durable and resistant to change. The effects of class are felt early in children's lives and shape the subsequent paths they take in life. The influence of families is profound. Given this fact, the task facing Labour—or any political party committed to equality—is enormous. The reproduction of class inequalities across generations is a complex affair and policy interventions have to be equally sophisticated in fashion. To date, policies to alleviate class inequalities have been modest in their effect. Any progress has been gradual and slow. Sustained effort, which includes finding out what really works, is required. Labour can hardly feel satisfied with the progress that has been made so far. Even so, it does not have to be ashamed of its efforts to make Britain a more equal society.

References

ATKINSON, A. B. 1997. 'Bringing Income Distribution in from the Cold'. *Economic Journal*, 107: 297–321.

BALL, S. J. 2003. *Class Strategies and the Education Market Place*. London: Routledge Falmer.

BELSKY, J., et al. 2007. *The National Evaluation of Sure Start: Does Area-based Early Intervention Work?* Bristol: Policy Press.

BERTHOUD, R. 2007. *Work-Rich and Work-Poor: Three Decades of Change*. York: Joseph Rowntree Foundation.

BLANDEN, J., and GIBBONS, S. 2006. *The Persistence of Poverty across Generations: A View from Two British Cohorts*. York: Joseph Rowntree Foundation.

—— et al. 2004. 'Changes in Intergenerational Income Mobility in Britain'. In M. Corak (ed.), *Generational Income Mobility in North America and Europe*. Cambridge: Cambridge University Press.

—— et al. 2005. *Intergenerational Mobility in Europe and North America: A Report Supported by the Sutton Trust*. London: Centre for Economic Performance.

BREEN, R., and GOLDTHORPE, J. H. 1999. 'Class Inequality and Meritocracy: A Critique of Saunders and an Alternative Analysis'. *British Journal of Sociology*, 50: 1–27.

—— —— 2001. 'Class, Mobility and Merit'. *European Sociological Review*, 17: 81–101.

—— —— 2002. 'Merit, Mobility and Method: Another Reply to Saunders'. *British Journal of Sociology*, 53: 575–82.

BREWER, M., et al. 2007. *Poverty and Inequality in the UK: 2007*. London. Institute for Fiscal Studies Briefing Note No. 73.

BUTLER, T., with ROBSON, G. 2004. *London Calling*. Oxford: Berg.

BYNNER, J., et al. 1997. *Twenty-something in the 1990s: Getting on, Getting by, Getting Nowhere*. Aldershot: Ashgate.

CALLENDER, C. 2003. 'Student Financial Support in Higher Education: Access and Exclusion'. In M. Tight (ed.), *Access and Exclusion: International Perspectives on Higher Education Research*. London: Elsevier Science.

CROMPTON, R. 1980. 'Class Mobility in Modern Britain'. *Sociology*, 14: 117–19.

—— 2008. *Class and Stratification: An Introduction to Current Debates*, 3rd edn. Cambridge: Polity.

DEVINE, F. 2004. *Class Practices: How Parents Help their Children Get Good Jobs*. Cambridge: Cambridge University Press.

DEX, S., and JOSHI, H. 2005. *Children of the 21st Century: From Birth to Nine Months*. Bristol: Policy Press.

DORLING, D., et al. 2007. *Poverty, Wealth and Place in Britain, 1968–2005*. York: Joseph Rowntree Foundation.

Evans, G. 2006. *Educational Failure and Working Class White Children in Britain*. Basingstoke: Palgrave.

Erikson, R., and Goldthorpe, J. H. 1992. *The Constant Flux: A Study of Class Mobility in Industrial Societies*. Oxford: Clarendon Press.

Ferri, E., et al. 2003. *Changing Lives, Changing Britain: Three Generations at the Turn of the Century*. London: Institute of Education.

Feinstein, L. 2003. 'Inequality in the Early Cognitive Development of British Children in the 1970 Cohort'. *Economica*, 70/277: 73–97.

—— 2006. 'Social Class and Cognitive Development in Childhood in the UK'. In H. Lauder et al. (eds.), *Education, Globalisation, and Social Change*. Oxford: Oxford University Press.

Galino-Rueda, F., et al. 2004. 'The Widening Socio-economic Gap in UK Higher Education'. Centre for Economics of Education Paper 15, LSE.

Gallie, D., et al. 1998. *Restructuring the Employment Relationship*. Oxford: Clarendon Press.

Gayo-Cal, M., et al. 2006. 'A Cultural Map of the United Kingdom, 2003'. *Cultural Trends*, 15/2–3: 213–38.

George, A., et al. 2007. 'Child Behaviour and Cognitive Development'. In K. Hansen and H. Joshi (eds.), *Millennium Cohort Study: Second Survey*. London: Centre for Longitudinal Studies.

Gershuny, J. 1993. 'Post Industrial Career Structure in Britain'. In G. Esping-Andersen (ed.), *Stratification and Mobility in Post-Industrial Societies*. London: Sage.

Gewirtz, S., et al. 1995. *Markets, Choice and Equity in Education*. Buckingham: Open University Press.

Goldthorpe, J. H. 1996. 'Class Analysis and the Re-orientation of Class Theory: The Case of Persisting Differentials in Educational Attainment'. *British Journal of Sociology*, 47: 481–505.

—— 2007. On *Sociology*, ii: *Illustrations and Retrospect*, 2nd edn. Stanford, Calif.: Stanford University Press.

—— and Mills, C. 2004. 'Trends in Intergenerational Class Mobility in Britain in the Late Twentieth Century'. In R. Breen (ed.), *Social Mobility in Europe*. Oxford: Oxford University Press.

—— et al. 1980. *Social Mobility and Class Structure in Modern Britain*. Oxford: Clarendon Press.

—— et al. 1987. *Social Mobility and Class Structure in Modern Britain*, 2nd edn. Oxford: Clarendon Press.

Gregg, P., et al. 1999. 'The Rise of the Workless Household'. In P. Gregg and J. Wadsworth (eds.), *The State of Working Britain*. Manchester: Manchester University Press.

Halsey, A. H., et al. 1980. *Origins and Destinations*. Oxford: Clarendon Press.

Heath, A., and Li, Y. 2008. 'Period, Life-Cycle and Generational Effects on Ethnic Minority Success in the Labour Market'. *KZfSS*.

—— and Payne, C. 2000. 'Social Mobility'. In A. H. Halsey with J. Webb (eds.), *Twentieth-Century British Social Trends*. Basingstoke: Macmillan.

—— et al. 1992. 'Towards Meritocracy: New Evidence on an Old Problem'. In C. Crouch and A. F. Heath (eds.), *Social Research and Social Reform: Essays in Honour of A. H. Halsey*. Oxford: Oxford University Press.

—— et al. 2007. 'Who Do We Think We Are? The Decline of Traditional Social Identities'. In A. Park et al. (eds.), *British Social Attitudes: The 23rd Report*. London: Sage.

Hills, J. 2004. *Inequality and the State*. Oxford: Oxford University Press.

—— and Stewart, K. 2005. *A More Equal Society? New Labour, Poverty, Inequality and Exclusion*. Bristol: Policy Press.

—— et al. 2002. *Understanding Social Exclusion*. Oxford: Oxford University Press.

—— et al. 2007. *Making Social Policy Work*. Bristol: Policy Press.

JACKSON, M., et al. 2005. 'Education, Employers and Class Mobility'. *Research in Social Stratification and Mobility*, 23: 3–34.

LI, Y., and HEATH, A. 2007. 'Ethnic Minority Men in the British Labour Market (1972–2005)'. *International Journal of Sociology and Social Policy*, 28/5–6: 231–44.

LUPTON, R., and POWER, A. 2005. 'Disadvantaged by Where you Live? New Labour and Neighbourhood Renewal'. In J. Hills and K. Stewart (eds.), *A More Equal Society? New Labour, Poverty, Inequality and Exclusion*. Bristol: Policy Press.

MACDONALD, K. I., and RIDGE, J. 1988. 'Social Mobility'. In A. H. Halsey (ed.), *British Social Trends since 2000*. London: Macmillan.

MACHIN, S., and VIGNOLES, S. 2004. 'Educational Inequality: The Widening Socio-economic Gap'. *Fiscal Studies*, 25: 107–28.

—— et al. 2003. 'Improving Pupil Performance in English Secondary Schools: Excellence in Cities'. *Journal of the European Economic Association*, 2: 396–405.

MCKNIGHT, A., et al. 2005. 'Education, Education, Education . . .: An Assessment of Labour's Success in Tackling Education Inequalities'. In J. Hills and K. Stewart (eds.), *A More Equal Society? New Labour, Poverty, Inequality and Exclusion*. Bristol: Policy Press.

MARSH, C., and BLACKBURN, R. 1992. 'Class Differentials in Access to Higher Education'. In R. Burrows and C. Marsh (eds.), *Consumption and Class, Divisions and Change*. Basingstoke: Macmillan.

MARSHALL, G., et al. 1988. *Social Class in Modern Britain*. London: Hutchinson.

MASSEY, D. 2007. *World City*. Cambridge: Polity.

MATHERS, K., et al. 2007. *Quality of Childcare Settings in the Millennium Cohort Study*. London: HMSO.

MEADOWS, P. 2005. *Implementing Sure Start: First Report on Case Studies*. London: National Institute for Economic and Social Research.

PAHL, R., et al. 2007. *Inequality and Quiescence: A Continuing Conundrum*. Colchester: ISER Working Paper 2007–22.

PENN, R. 1980. 'The Nuffield Class Categorisation'. *Sociology*, 15: 265–71.

PIACHAUD, D., and SUTHERLAND, H. 2002. 'Child Poverty'. In J. Hills et al. (eds.), *Understanding Social Exclusion*. Oxford: Oxford University Press.

POWER, A., and WILLMOTT, H. 2005. 'Bringing up in Poor Neighbourhoods under New Labour'. In J. Hills and K. Stewart (eds.), *A More Equal Society? New Labour, Poverty, Inequality and Exclusion*. Bristol: Policy Press.

POWER, S., et al. 2003. *Education and the Middle Class*. Buckingham: Open University Press.

REAY, D., et al. 2005. *Degrees of Choice*. Stoke: Trentham.

ROSE, D., and PEVALIN, D. (eds.) 2003. *A Researcher's Guide to the National Statistics Socio-economic Classification*. London: Sage.

SAUNDERS, P. 1995. 'Might Britain Be a Meritocracy'. *Sociology*, 29: 23–41.

—— 1997. 'Social Mobility in Britain: An Empirical Investigation of Two Competing Explanations'. *Sociology*, 31: 261–88.

SAVAGE, M., and EGERTON, M. 1998. 'Social Mobility, Individual Ability and the Inheritance of Class Inequality'. *Sociology*, 31: 645–72.

Social Trends 37. 2007. Basingstoke: Palgrave Macmillan/HMSO.

SPARKES, J., and GLENNERSTER, H. 2002. 'Preventing Social Exclusion: Education's Contribution'. In J. Hills et al. (eds.), *Understanding Social Exclusion*. Oxford: Oxford University Press.

STEWART, K. 2005. 'Towards an Equal Start? Addressing Childhood Poverty and Deprivation'. In J. Hills and K. Stewart (eds.), *A More Equal Society? New Labour, Poverty, Inequality and Exclusion*. Bristol: Policy Press.

Stewart, K., and Hills, J. 2005. 'Introduction'. In J. Hills and K. Stewart (eds.), *A More Equal Society? New Labour, Poverty, Inequality and Exclusion*. Bristol: Policy Press.

Vincent, C., and Ball, S. J. 2006. *Childcare, Choice and Class Practices: Middle-Class Parents and their Children*. London: Routledge.

Ward, K., et al. 2007. 'Income and Poverty'. In K. Hansen and H. Joshi (eds.), *Millennium Cohort Study: Second Survey*. London: Centre for Longitudinal Studies.

Willis, P. 1977. *Learning to Labour: Why Working Class Kids Get Working Class Jobs*. Farnborough: Saxon House.

CHAPTER 34

....

RACE

....

JAMES HAMPSHIRE

34.1 INTRODUCTION

....

AT the heart of the politics of race in contemporary Britain lies a paradox. On the one hand, there is abundant evidence of race-based disadvantage in Britain today. Non-white Britons experience significant discrimination, inequalities, and exclusion, and are under-represented in positions of power. As the Commission for Racial Equality puts it in its 2007 legacy report, 'an ethnic minority British born baby is sadly still more likely to go on to receive poor quality education, be paid less, live in substandard housing, be in poor health and be discriminated against in other ways than his or her white contemporaries' (CRE 2007: 1; cf. Modood et al. 1997). Yet at no previous point in modern British history has the legitimacy of racial inequality and discrimination been more widely challenged than today. Since the 1960s, when boarding-house signs reading 'No Irish, No Coloureds, No Dogs' were commonplace, genuine progress has been made to reduce racist discrimination. Such blatant racism is now not only illegal but also morally inconceivable. Britain was one of the first European countries to develop anti-discrimination legislation and its racial equality provisions are among the most extensive in the EU. A powerful anti-racist norm pervades British politics; to challenge this norm is to be cast to the political extremes.[1]

This presents an analytical puzzle as well as a moral quandary. How can the existence of a powerful anti-racist norm in political culture be reconciled with the persistent evidence of racial disadvantage and discrimination in British society? And if the anti-racist norm can apparently coexist with race-based disadvantage, does the norm itself need to be re-examined? Is this a case of rank hypocrisy, a promise

---

[1] Even the British National Party is careful to disavow racism in its public statements.

unfulfilled, or does it reveal something more complex about the nature of race politics today?

To address these questions it is necessary to recognize that the apparent paradoxes surrounding race politics in the early twenty-first century are not unique to Britain. The contradictions of the British situation are part of a wider global 'racial crisis' characterized by the persistence of racially based social structures in the face of a widespread delegitimation of race and racism (Winant 2006: 987). In the aftermath of decolonization, Jim Crow, the Holocaust, and apartheid, race has been undermined as a concept and ordering principle, yet it remains present as an identity, practice, and social structure.

This poses a number of dilemmas, not the least of which is the dilemma of non-racialism versus race consciousness. This dilemma arises because states that espouse a normative commitment to anti-racism yet continue to be characterized by racially structured socio-political orders—and this includes nearly all liberal democratic states—must steer a course between the denial and reproduction of race. The very policies and institutions designed to tackle racism and establish a post-racial society have a tendency to reproduce existing, and even produce new, racial categories. Census questions, anti-discrimination legislation, racial monitoring, and affirmative action programmes all rest on racial classifications. Thus the anti-racist dilemma: a refusal to recognize race may help delegitimize it as a social category, but at the cost of denying the reality of race-based disadvantage; whereas race-based legislation intended to address racial disadvantage risks reproducing the very categories that it seeks to overcome. The political struggles around race in Britain today are caught on the horns of this dilemma.

Whilst all advanced capitalist societies experience racial crisis to one degree or another, its manifestations are shaped by distinct national contexts. Britain experiences the crisis in a different way from, say, France or the United States, whose respective race policies and institutions differ markedly in their approach to the anti-racist dilemma. This chapter argues that Britain's *race relations* policy paradigm embodies this dilemma in an especially acute way. By refusing to institutionalize a pure form of either non-racialism or race consciousness, founders of the race relations paradigm struck a pragmatic balance which in many ways succeeded in tackling racism. But the limitations and inherent tensions of the race relations paradigm have become increasingly apparent as it has failed to eradicate race-based disadvantage.

34.2 THE POLITICS OF RACE MAKING

Race is not a self-evident category of identification or analysis. While the language of race lingers on in both popular and academic discourse, the use of 'race' as a term to distinguish sub-groups of the human species is now almost unanimously rejected by natural scientists and its validity as a category of social analysis is also questioned. Some scholars go so far as to argue that the ordinary language of race has no place at all in social scientific analysis (e.g. Miles 1989; 1993).

For most of the modern period, however, naturalistic ideas about race were taken for granted. The belief that the world's population was divided into discrete races to which behavioural attributes could be ascribed was widespread and deep-seated. Though it came in many guises, the naturalistic understanding of race assigned human beings to discontinuous racial groups, often based on observed phenotypical variation, and then identified moral, social, and political differences with this variation, with biology the determining factor (Banton 2002: 3). On these dubious foundations a myriad of racial theories and typologies were built (see Banton 1998; Hannaford 1996; Malik 1996).

It was not until the middle of the twentieth century that the naturalistic understanding of race was challenged. In the years following the end of the Second World War, abhorrence at the horrors of the Nazi 'racial state' (Burleigh and Wippermann 1991), anti-colonial movements, and cold war politics gave momentum to national and international anti-racist movements. Notwithstanding the fact that the world's most powerful democracy, the United States, remained a racially hierarchical sociopolitical order (see King 1995), from the late 1940s onwards race was denaturalized and an anti-racist norm began to develop across the liberal capitalist states. Ever since this epistemic shift, governments, policy-makers, activists, and social scientists alike have struggled over what to do with the race concept. In the words of Michael Omi and Howard Winant, having repelled the temptation to think of race as 'an *essence*, as something fixed, concrete, and objective', many moved towards the 'opposite temptation: to imagine race as a mere *illusion*, a purely ideological construct which some ideal non-racist social order would eliminate' (Omi and Winant 1994: p. xx).

Today, scholarly work on race operates between the essentialist and illusory poles. Attention is focused on how race is constructed through practical social and political activity. Processes of 'racial formation' (Omi and Winant 1994) or 'race-making' (Banton 2005; see also Murji and Solomos 2005) take place in many spheres of society, ranging from everyday interactions in private spaces to public discourse and social scientific analysis. No single set of actors or institutions has a monopoly on the processes by which race is defined and given meaning. Nevertheless, it is clear that politics, and specifically the state, plays an important role in the formation, maintenance, and dissolution of racial categories and groups. As Michael Banton argues, race making is strongly shaped by official policies and institutions:

> If the legislature prohibits discrimination 'on racial grounds' it will define those grounds and, inevitably, lend authority to a certain conception of race. In a similar fashion, if the government holds a population census and requires members of the public to identify themselves in terms of racial or ethnic origins, this will have an important influence.
>
> (Banton 2002: 17; cf. Banton 2005: 64)

While some states in the past sought to define race for racist ends—e.g. the Nuremberg laws in Nazi Germany, South African apartheid laws, or Jim Crow legislation in the United States—in contemporary liberal democracies the politics of race making occurs primarily through anti-racism initiatives. States committed to anti-racism are drawn into racial definition and categorization as part of their efforts to gather data and develop anti-discrimination policies. As US Supreme Court Justice Harry Blackmun put it in the landmark *Bakke* case: 'in order to get beyond racism, we must first take account of race' (cited in Banton 2002: 3).

Not all states approach anti-racism in the same way, however, and this has important implications for race making. State approaches to anti-racism can be conceptualized in terms of a spectrum, with complete disavowal of the race concept at one end and official recognition at the other (Bleich 2003: 206). At the former, 'colourblind' end of the spectrum, the validity of race is denied, race is not recognized in state institutions or policies, and its use as a basis for legislation is refused. Of contemporary liberal democracies, France most closely approximates this model. At the other end of the spectrum lies a 'race-conscious' approach to anti-racism, in which race is recognized as a valid category of analysis and racial categories are used in legislation. The United States approximates this model.[2]

The politics of anti-racism in Britain operates between these two poles, though it is closer to the American than the French model. On the one hand, and unlike in France, in Britain race is recognized as a valid category of analysis and intervention: there is a developed body of anti-discrimination legislation referring to, and defining, racial groups; official statistics capture racial and ethnic data; and programmes targeted at particular racial groups are mandated. On the other hand, Britain has stopped short of the kind of affirmative action programmes that were developed in the United States from the 1970s (see Skrentny 1996). While some positive action measures are allowed in Britain, quota-based approaches or even accounting for racial background in hiring practices is illegal. Thus British anti-racist policies recognize race, but they refuse to use it as the basis for certain kinds of preferential treatment. This ambivalent attitude is embedded in Britain's race relations policy paradigm.

34.3 THE RACE RELATIONS PARADIGM

The term 'race relations' was first used in Britain in the late 1940s and 1950s by sociologists of the Edinburgh School in their pioneering work on colonial immigrants (e.g. Little 1948; Banton 1955). It was soon adopted by political elites and enshrined in early anti-discrimination legislation, where it has remained to this day.

---

[2] Although it should be noted that race-conscious policies, especially affirmative action programmes, are highly controversial. Moreover, the limits imposed on affirmative action measures by the Supreme Court in *Regents of University of California v Bakke* (1978) and more recently *Gratz v Bollinger* (2003) represent a weakening of race-based university admissions policies, if not an end to the use of race per se (see King 2007).

As an approach to anti-racism, race relations can be usefully analysed as a policy paradigm: 'a framework of ideas and standards that specifies not only the goals of policy and the kind of instruments that can be used to attain them, but also the very nature of the problems they are meant to be addressing' (Hall 1993: 279). Understood in this way, the British race relations policy paradigm has several identifiable features. First, as mentioned above, since the 1960s British politicians have largely accepted race as a valid basis for social analysis and policy intervention; second, the form of racism that has received most policy attention has been *access racism*; and third, racism has been understood primarily in terms of *colour discrimination* (this characterization is adapted from Bleich 2003: 170).

The very idea of race relations logically presupposes the validity of race as a category since it postulates relations between racial groups. It therefore bestows legitimacy on the idea of race. Its reference to relations between racial groups also implies that this is something in need of regulation to prevent conflict or hostility from arising. For these reasons, most academics are now uncomfortable with the term, but it remains widespread in official discourse and popular understanding. For example, all three major pieces of anti-discrimination legislation and subsequent amendments have been named Race Relations Acts (see below). At the same time, policy discourse today often avoids explicit talk of race or racial minorities and refers more often to ethnic minorities. In recent years, the former Commission for *Racial* Equality has been much more likely to talk about *ethnic* minorities in its publications (e.g. CRE 2007).

A good example of the confusion surrounding the concept of race in Britain was the 'ethnic group' question in the 2001 census. In its final version, the question asked respondents to indicate their 'cultural background', before offering a range of categories some of which were defined by skin colour (e.g. white, black), some with reference to nationality (e.g. Chinese, Indian, Pakistani), and some by region (e.g. African, Asian, Caribbean). This muddle of categories reveals just how confused the concept of race has become in British politics. Nevertheless, the wider point is that in its attempt to challenge racism the British state has had to get into the business of defining racial groups. This marks Britain out from other European countries such as France (Bleich 2003: 145) and Germany (Thränhardt 2000), where the term race is either illegitimate or taboo.

The second distinguishing feature of the British race relations paradigm is its focus on *access racism*. Bleich (2003: 9) defines access racism as discrimination in employment, housing, and the provision of goods. It can be distinguished from expressive racism, which consists of verbal or written statements made against individuals or groups, and physical racism, which involves attacks against persons or their property motivated by racial hatred. At the core of the 1965, 1968, and 1976 Race Relations Acts were provisions to tackle racist discrimination in hiring and provision of services, with civil law penalties for discriminators. This is not to say that expressive and physical racism have gone unlegislated: on the contrary, the 1965 Race Relations Act included anti-incitement provisions, which were updated in the 1986 Public Order Act and then most recently in the 2006 Racial and Religious Hatred Act; while the 1998

Crime and Disorder Act enables courts to treat racist motivation as an aggravating factor and impose stiffer sentences and fines. Nevertheless, as Bleich points out, compared to access racism, expressive and physical racism 'have taken a consistently low profile' (Bleich 2003: 52).

Lastly, the race relations paradigm conceptualizes racism primarily in terms of *colour discrimination* (Bleich 2003: 170; cf. Modood 1992). Discrimination on the basis of skin colour has been a concern of anti-racists since the early days of post-war immigration. In the 1950s and 1960s, colonial immigrants were often perceived in homogeneous terms as 'coloured', and later 'black', while racist discrimination and conflict was understood in dichotomous terms: a 'white' indigenous population versus the 'coloured' immigrant minority. Although this obscured the existence of anti-Irish and anti-Semitic attitudes, colour racism was arguably a more prevalent phenomenon and it was certainly the primary concern of the progressives who drafted the early race relations legislation. This is in stark contrast to France and Germany, where the legacy of anti-Semitism and the Holocaust shaped an understanding of racism that is as much about genealogy and ethnicity as skin colour.

The story behind the evolution of the race relations paradigm is complex and told in some detail elsewhere (e.g. Bleich 2003: 35–113; Hampshire 2006; Layton-Henry 1992: 44–70; Saggar 1992; Solomos 2003: 82–94), but two key factors warrant discussion as they help to explain why the paradigm took the shape it did: first, the intertwining of immigration and race relations legislation; and second, the strategic calculations that shaped this legislation.

The politics of race and immigration in Britain are inextricably connected, most obviously in the sense that post-war immigration transformed Britain into a multiracial society, but also in the sense that immigration and race relations legislation were developed as part of an explicit policy package. It is often forgotten by British commentators that this race–immigration nexus is not universal. On the one hand, it marks out Britain from countries where anti-racism was not primarily determined by immigration, for example France, where immigrant integration was a less important influence on early anti-racism initiatives than memories of Vichy, or the United States, where the legacy of slavery and racial segregation were foremost in policymakers' minds. It also distinguishes Britain from the so-called 'guestworker' countries, such as Germany or Austria, where immigration was not initially framed in terms of race, largely because early guestworkers were not perceived to be racially different.

In Britain, 'coloured' immigrants *were* perceived as racially different and the race–immigration linkage was extremely close. Indeed, the race relations paradigm was, in its early years at least, Britain's version of an immigrant integration policy (Favell 2001; Soysal 1995). As significant numbers of non-white immigrants settled in Britain during the 1950s, a handful of progressives within the opposition Labour Party argued that legislation was required to tackle racist discrimination, which was impeding the newcomers' ability to participate in British society (Bleich 2003: 54–7; Hampshire 2006: 318–19). Strongly influenced by the civil rights movement in the United States, organizations such as the Society for Socialist Lawyers and the Campaign Against

Racial Discrimination (CARD) lobbied MPs to pass anti-discrimination legislation. The claims of these progressives fell on largely deaf ears until the 1958 riots in Notting Hill, London, in which mobs of white youths attacked Caribbean immigrants. These events, which were widely reported in the press as 'race riots', persuaded the Labour Party leadership that they should pass anti-discrimination legislation once in government, and a commitment to this end was included in the party's 1964 election manifesto.

After winning that election, the Labour government passed the 1965 Race Relations Act. It faced a bumpy ride through parliament, which partly explains why it was, in hindsight at least, such an astonishingly weak piece of legislation. Whilst the Act outlawed discrimination on the grounds of 'colour, race, or ethnic or national origin' (note the plurality of definitions) in specified public places, it excluded the crucial areas of housing and employment; in addition, the Race Relations Board (RRB) which was established to enforce the Act enjoyed only very limited powers. Despite these major shortcomings, the Act created a legislative beachhead such that it was inevitable that the anti-discrimination provisions would be extended to those spheres where discrimination was most significant. Indeed, this is exactly what happened: in 1968 the Labour government passed a second Race Relations Act which extended the anti-discrimination measures to employment and housing and increased the powers of the RRB; then in 1976 a third Race Relations Act was passed by the Callaghan government. This Act, which remains the foundation of race relations policy today, outlawed indirect discrimination (i.e. treatment that is formally equal but which has a discriminatory effect on a particular racial group), created some limited positive action measures such as targeting of resources to disadvantaged racial groups, and replaced the RRB with the Commission for Racial Equality (CRE), which was given extended powers of formal investigation.

Throughout this period race relations legislation was viewed as one side of a policy package. As successive Labour governments enacted increasingly restrictive immigration legislation—driven by hostile public opinion (Hansen 2000: 14) as well as elite fears about multiracialism (Hampshire 2005; Spencer 1997)—they sought to appease internal and external critics by adopting a more progressive stance on race relations. As Anthony Lester put it in a 1966 internal report on 'Labour's White Problem': 'a restrictive immigration policy would take the issue out of politics and so enable the Government to have a decent policy on race relations' (cited in Hampshire 2006: 323). The package worked the other way round too: it was hoped that by taking a progressive stand on race relations the bitter pill of racially discriminatory immigration legislation would be sugar-coated for the left of the party. Politically, this was a success; but its implications for social relations were more ambiguous. Essentially this is because the illiberal rhetoric and practice of 'tough' immigration policies sits uneasily—and maybe even undermines—the progressive aim of promoting good race relations.

This Janus-face is not so surprising given that the commitment to anti-racism was not popular in the 1960s. Indeed, the race relations legislation was not, as is sometimes supposed, the product of grass-roots mobilization. Rather, it was the result of lobbying by an elite group of policy entrepreneurs who eventually gained the support of the Labour Party leadership due partly to growing evidence of racism and fear of social disorder but also, crucially, due to party political calculations. This is not to deny the moral opposition to racism that motivated many in the party, nor can it obfuscate the fact that every piece of race relations legislation has been passed by a Labour government; but it is to recognize that the admirable cause of racial equality was shaped by strategic considerations.

By the mid-1970s, the institutional architecture of the race relations policy was in place: legislation outlawing direct and indirect discrimination, backed up with civil law measures, and enforced by the CRE. Moreover, the framework of ideas that defines the race relations paradigm was well established: legitimation of the idea of race, a focus on access racism, and an emphasis on colour discrimination. With only minor adjustments, this framework remained in place for the next three decades.

34.4 RACE RELATIONS UNDER STRAIN

While the policy paradigm hardly evolved from the 1970s to the late 1990s, British society was changing apace. This put race relations under considerable strain and its limitations became increasingly apparent through the 1980s and 1990s. Despite considerable successes in reducing racist discrimination and embedding an anti-racist norm in British political culture, race-based disadvantage persisted and in some respects increased during this period. The shortcomings of the race relations paradigm were especially apparent in terms of its failure to secure racial equality and to challenge the deep-seated prejudices that existed in parts of British society. These two shortcomings can be illustrated with reference to political representation and policing, respectively. Firstly, the continued under-representation of black and Asian persons in positions of power, especially among national governing elites, has made it increasingly difficult to argue that anti-discrimination measures alone will ensure equal representation of racial groups. Secondly, a perception of police racism and brutality caused relations between the police and some minority communities to deteriorate rapidly, culminating in riots and urban unrest in the 1980s. I shall discuss each in turn.

The anti-discrimination legislation of the 1960s and 1970s helped secure the black and Asian vote for the Labour Party (Saggar 1998; 2000). It did not, however, succeed in achieving equal representation of minority communities in national level institutions. Indeed, until 1987, when three black and one Asian MP were elected to parliament (Diane Abbott, Paul Boateng, Bernie Grant, and Keith Vaz, all Labour MPs), there were no non-white politicians in the Commons or Lords. The situation has improved only slightly since then: there are now fifteen black or Asian MPs (thirteen Labour, two Conservative), but if minority community representation was proportionate to population size there would be at least fifty-one. Interestingly, the House of Lords, which is largely appointed, fares slightly better: twenty-eight black or Asian Peers (out of a total of 738). Westminster is in no way anomalous. Under-representation stretches well beyond parliament to include many other elite institutions: for example, while ethnic minorities comprise 8 per cent of the British population, in 2007 they accounted for less than 1 per cent of senior judges,[3] and only 2.4 per cent of directors of FTSE 100 companies (CRE 2007: 18)

These figures belie an implicit assumption of the race relations paradigm as it was developed in the 1960s and 1970s, namely that simply by outlawing discrimination—whether direct or indirect—racial equality could be achieved. This assumption, though rarely spelled out, rested on the belief that intentional discrimination, often at the point of hiring or service provision, was the chief obstacle to racial equality in Britain. According to this logic, once legislation was in place to discourage and penalize discrimination, race-based disadvantage would begin to ebb away. As white, black, and Asian people competed on the proverbial level playing field, society would move towards greater levels of equality. This was to ignore the persistence of racism at a societal and institutional level.

What would later be described in the Stephen Lawrence Inquiry Report (see below) as 'institutional racism'—that is, processes, attitudes, and behaviour that amount to racial discrimination through unwitting prejudice, ignorance, and stereotyping—was rife in British society during the 1980s and 1990s. Perhaps witting prejudice was also widespread. Certainly, both were left largely unchallenged by the race relations legislation. Though it is difficult to prove, it seems likely that many white Britons were aware of the racist attitudes and prejudices that persisted below the radar of the evolving anti-racist norm and discrimination legislation. For example, in the sphere of party politics a belief that parts of the electorate would react negatively to the selection of a black or Asian parliamentary candidate factored into the calculative decisions of party elites during this period.

This was especially true of the Conservative Party, which didn't select a non-white parliamentary candidate until 1990. Indeed, when the Conservatives did finally try to address this issue they faced a backlash that appeared to bear out their fears. In 1990 John Taylor, a black barrister, was selected for the safe Conservative seat of Cheltenham, apparently with some intervention by Conservative Party Central Office. A number of local party activists revolted. One local member complained about the 'bloody nigger' that 'central office have foisted...upon us'.[4] Taylor was eventually confirmed as the party's candidate, but he went on to lose the seat in the 1992 election, with a massive swing to the Liberal Democrats. Whether Cheltenham's electorate were rebelling against Taylor or his local party's treatment of him is hard to say.

[3] Judiciary of England and Wales, Statistics—Minority Ethnic Judges in Post, 1 Apr. 2007; http://www.judiciary.gov.uk/keyfacts/statistics/ethnic.htm.

[4] Sheila Rule, 'Tories in Uproar over Black Candidate', New York Times, 6 Dec. 1990. Accessed at http://query.nytimes.com/gst/fullpage.html?res=9C0CE0DC1538F935A35751C1A966958260.

The Taylor incident revealed an ugly seam of racism in the local Conservative Party office of a predominantly white, middle-class constituency. But in some ways the greater obstacle to equal representation was the failure of the Labour Party to make more progress in increasing representation of minority groups. Until the late 1970s, the Labour Party conspicuously failed to incorporate its black and Asian supporters into its ranks (Solomos 2003: 207). While black and Asian voters solidly supported Labour they were poorly represented within it. As the urban unrest of the early 1980s unfolded the party did begin to reflect upon its failings in this area. At the local level, a number of Labour-controlled local authorities initiated race equality policies and anti-racism initiatives. And within the national party a number of black members called for the formation of 'black sections' to increase representation and promote race issues (Shukra 1998: 70–80). This was debated at annual conferences during the 1980s, but resisted by the party leadership who feared it would be divisive. Advocates of black sections were not successful in achieving formal recognition, but they did manage to put the issue of minority representation on the political agenda and contributed towards the election of four non-white MPs in 1987, all of whom had been involved in the black sections movement.

The issue of minority under-representation has not gone away and if anything it has moved to a higher level of contention. From the late 1990s onwards, the possible use of positive action measures, particularly minority shortlists for parliamentary candidates, has been discussed by the Labour Party. Most recently, in February 2008, a report by pressure group Operation Black Vote argued for the creation of minority shortlists in up to eight parliamentary constituencies to ensure that more black and Asian MPs are elected. The report was commissioned and received the endorsement of Labour's Deputy Leader, Harriet Harman, but it remains to be seen whether the government will endorse the proposals (Hinsliff 2008). The central problem is that minority shortlists would require a change in the law as the weak positive action provisions allowed under the 1976 Race Relations Act do not permit such measures. Indeed, quotas or other race-based preferential treatment are illegal under the 1976 Act.

The controversy that would attend such a development was indicated in February 2008 when Keith Vaz MP introduced a 10 Minute Rule Bill to allow for minority shortlists. The brief exchange neatly captured the dilemma of non-racialism versus race consciousness. Presenting his bill, Vaz argued that positive action was necessary to create 'a Parliament that mirrors the society it represents'. Only such a race-conscious measure could ensure that 'the problems of imbalance in representation' were addressed: 'race can be used in a positive way to electrify the political process,' he claimed. The Conservative MP and member of the Campaign Against Political Correctness, Philip Davies, immediately shot back that this was 'good, old-fashioned positive discrimination . . . true equality should mean selecting people on merit irrespective of their racial background'.[5] The Liberal Democrat leader, Nick Clegg, has indicated that he supports the proposal for minority shortlists, but the Conservatives,

---

[5] Hansard, House of Commons, 6 Feb. 2008, cols. 973–7.

whose leader David Cameron has drawn up his own 'A-List' of parliamentary candidates, nevertheless oppose it. At the time of writing it is unclear whether the proposal will be included in the government's promised equalities legislation.

A second problem left untouched by the race relations legislation of the 1960s and 1970s was the issue of police–community relations. This is doubly important both because it was (and remains) a pressing issue in the daily lives of minority communities and because it has resulted in a major revision to the race relations paradigm. Indeed, policing has become one of the most incendiary dimensions of race politics in Britain.

From the early post-war years, black and to a lesser extent Asian immigrants, who often had little choice but to settle in the most deprived areas of urban Britain, were associated with criminality in police reports and media discourse. For example, a Scotland Yard inquiry in the early 1950s into the 'public morals' of 'coloured Commonwealth immigrants' made lurid allegations regarding their involvement in vice and criminality (see Hampshire 2005: 127–32). Following the Notting Hill 'race riots' in 1958, non-white immigration also became associated with social disorder and violence, nowhere more virulently than in Enoch Powell's notorious 1968 'Rivers of Blood' speech. Relations between the police and young Afro-Caribbean males in particular deteriorated during the 1960s and 1970s. The police force persistently denied it was a racist institution, but many young black men experienced harassment, wrongful arrest, and even assault at the hands of the police. In some cities a climate of distrust and hostility developed, and black criminality became a central trope in media discourse (see Gilroy 1987; Hall et al. 1978).

In 1972, the Select Committee on Race Relations and Immigration published a report on *Police/Immigrant Relations* which acknowledged the growing tensions, but apportioned blame equally between police officers and young black men. It accepted that young blacks did face discrimination but argued that it was impossible to 'prove or disprove' claims of harassment or mistreatment (cited in Solomos 2003: 128–9). In this context, it was not especially promising that public authorities, including the police, were excluded from the provisions of the 1976 Race Relations Act.

In 1980–1, tensions between black residents and the police boiled over in a number of British cities. Particularly violent confrontations occurred in the St Paul's area of Bristol, (April 1980), Brixton, London (April 1981), Handsworth, Birmingham (July 1981), and Toxteth, Liverpool (July 1981). As in 1958, these events were widely reported in the mass media as 'race riots'. The images of smouldering buildings, looting, and bloodied policemen provided a major shock to the political system. In response to the Brixton riots, the Conservative government, which had hitherto shown little interest in racial politics or problems of urban alienation, appointed Lord Scarman to conduct an investigation into what had happened and what should be done.

The Scarman Report concluded that the riots could only be understood 'in the context of complex political, social and economic factors which together create a predisposition towards violent protest' (Scarman 1981: para 8.7). Deprivation, unemployment, alienation, and experiences of discrimination produced a combustible atmosphere of resentment which was sparked by particular policing incidents. The report's assessment of the role of police racism was somewhat equivocal: it argued that 'racial discrimination' was a factor behind the unrest, but it denied the existence of 'institutional racism' in the police force.

Scarman's recommendations fell into two groups: measures to improve policing methods and restore black communities' confidence in the police force, and measures to address the 'racial disadvantage' that underpinned the violence. The government accepted many of the former—for example, by introducing new safeguards on police powers of stop and search in the Police and Criminal Evidence Act 1984—but it largely rejected the latter. In particular, Scarman's suggestion that positive action measures were urgently needed to tackle racial disadvantage was not implemented. Given that successive Labour governments had not seen fit to enact substantive positive action measures, it was highly unlikely that a Conservative government committed to free market ideology would endorse such interventionist policies. In any case, the post-Scarman reforms failed to repair police–community relations (Benyon 1984) and violence erupted again in Brixton, Handsworth, and Tottenham in 1985.

In 1999, the failure of race relations legislation and post-Scarman measures to eliminate racism from the police force was starkly revealed by the Macpherson Report into the Metropolitan police's botched investigation of the racist murder of black teenager Stephen Lawrence. Lawrence had been stabbed to death by a gang of white youths whilst standing at a bus stop in Eltham, south London, in April 1993. Following a prolonged campaign by his parents, the Labour government appointed an inquiry into the police investigation under Sir William Macpherson. The Macpherson Report described the investigation as 'a sequence of disasters and disappointments', but more importantly it found there to be 'institutional racism' within the Metropolitan police and indeed policing generally. Institutional racism was defined as:

> the collective failure of an organisation to provide an appropriate and professional service to people because of their colour, culture, or ethnic origin. It can be seen or detected in processes, attitudes and behaviour which amount to discrimination through unwitting prejudice, ignorance, thoughtlessness and racist stereotyping which disadvantage minority ethnic people. (Macpherson 1999: para. 6.34)

Whereas Scarman had refused to accept the idea of institutional racism, Macpherson claimed it was a feature not only of the police, but also 'other agencies including for example those dealing with housing and education' (Macpherson 1999: para. 6.35).

It would be hard to overstate the impact of the Macpherson Report. The Labour government responded immediately with the 2000 Race Relations (Amendment) Act, which extends the 1976 legislation to all public bodies, including the police, and to all private bodies exercising public functions. In addition, the 2000 Act creates a positive duty on public authorities to eliminate unlawful discrimination, promote equality of opportunity, and promote good relations between people of different racial groups. As Hansen argues in this volume, this represents a significant shift from policies focused on process to a concern with outcomes. The statutory duty means that it is no longer sufficient for public authorities to avoid unlawful discrimination; they must also demonstrate that they have in place policies and procedures that promote good race relations.

The 2000 Act, as well as reforms to policing made in response to Macpherson, have undoubtedly improved police–community relations. Nevertheless, some tensions remain. For example, in February 2008, the Flanagan Report on policing recommended that the rules on 'stop and account' (when a person is stopped but not searched) should be relaxed. The Home Secretary has accepted these recommendations and also announced pilot schemes to give the police time-limited powers to stop and search persons without giving a reason. These proposals met with a sceptical response from members of the black community, some of whom believed they marked a return to the hated 'sus' laws (under which a police officer could search someone on suspicion alone) (e.g. Wheatle 2008).

The controversies surrounding political under-representation and police racism serve to illustrate some of the limitations and tensions of the race relations paradigm as it was developed from the 1960s and 1970s. Although it would be churlish to blame the race relations paradigm for the failure to eradicate racism from all spheres of British society, certain assumptions have had a limiting effect on the pursuit of racial equality: the paradigm's focus on access racism and the refusal of stronger positive action measures were both important limitations, as was the decision to exclude public authorities from the original legislation. Furthermore, the tension between race consciousness and non-racialism that lies at the heart of the race relations paradigm can be seen today in debates over positive action measures. Whether the recent calls for minority shortlists are accepted remains to be seen. The outcome will either nudge Britain's anti-racism paradigm closer towards full race consciousness or retain its uneasy balance between the legitimation and denial of race.

34.5 WHITHER RACE RELATIONS?

This chapter began with the observation of a paradox. On the one hand, at no previous point in British political history has anti-racism been more firmly embedded in the legal and political culture than today; on the other, it is clear that racial inequalities, discrimination, and disadvantage persist in British politics and society. It should hopefully be clear by now that this paradox is not the result of hypocrisy or the rank failure of anti-racist policies: the commitment to anti-racism is real and there has been progress in shifting the moral climate. Rather, it is better understood in terms of the inherent limitations of the state's capacity to eradicate racism and the specific limitations of the race relations paradigm. British policy-makers' decision to legitimate race in order to tackle racism, their definition of the problem in terms of (implicitly) conflictual relations between racial groups, and their focus on access racism and colour discrimination are all comprehensible in the British context. But these core features have nevertheless delimited the anti-racist agenda, not always for the good. In particular, the ambivalent stance on race-conscious policies—for example in the ongoing debates over positive action measures—illustrates the difficulty of simultaneously recognizing race as a grounds of disadvantage and refusing to use it as the basis of means to rectify that disadvantage.

Whatever its strengths and weaknesses, the race relations paradigm remained essentially intact at the turn of the twenty-first century. For although there have been some important revisions, notably in the aftermath of the 1999 Macpherson Report, there hasn't been anything like a paradigm shift since the 1960s. Given the extent of social change since that time, the longevity of this policy paradigm is nothing short of remarkable; to draw an analogy, it is as if Keynesian demand management had survived the economic changes of the last half-century.

This is not to say that the race relations policy paradigm is immutable. We have already seen that major events have prompted policy change, and if proponents of minority shortlists win the argument, then 'harder' positive action measures may yet develop in Britain. Moreover, two recent developments, one institutional, the other societal, suggest that the British state's approach to anti-racism is currently undergoing a period of re-evaluation which may yet lead to more fundamental changes to the race relations paradigm.

Firstly, in 2007 a new Equalities and Human Rights Commission (EHRC) was established to supersede the work of the three existing equality commissions, the CRE as well as the Equal Opportunities Commission and the Disability Rights Commission. The new body has taken over the work of these 'legacy commissions' as well as incorporating other aspects of equality related to age, sexual orientation, and religious belief. Although it is too early to tell what this means for race relations, it does suggest that the government is moving away from a distinct approach to race issues, and towards framing them within a wider context of equality and rights. This has caused concern amongst some anti-racist campaigners who believe that racism could be neglected; but for those who have long argued for a shift away from a language of race relations to one of human rights (e.g. Banton 2002: 170 ff.) it may prove a positive step towards a post-racial society. Whether this institutional reform will effect a profound transformation in the state's approach to anti-racism remains to be seen (the legal basis for race relations has not been significantly amended, although the government has promised a single Equality Bill).

The second, and arguably even more significant, shift relates to the changing nature of prejudice and discrimination in British society. As we have seen, race relations were originally conceived in dichotomous terms as relations between a 'white' indigenous population and a homogeneous 'coloured' or 'black' immigrant population, the latter including persons of Caribbean, south Asian, and African descent. While this made sense in the early years of post-war immigration—in which different groups faced similar problems of discrimination and exclusion—it became increasingly untenable as the socio-economic position of immigrant groups was differentiated. Along with events such as the 1989 Rushdie affair, which exposed ideological disagreements between white, black, and Asian groups (themselves increasingly unwieldy cate-gories), this led to a fragmentation of anti-racist coalitions and the decline of 'political blackness' from the 1980s onwards (see Modood, this volume).

Today, this fragmentation is increasing as society becomes more diverse and racism takes on new forms. In particular, the focus on colour discrimination looks increas-ingly restrictive as anti-Muslim attitudes have developed into an important source of prejudice. At first glance it might seem that anti-Muslim attitudes are distinct from racist attitudes—Muslims are after all a religious group. But scholars such as Tariq Modood (2005) argue that Muslims are an increasingly racialized religious group who experience not 'colour' but 'cultural racism': 'a certain culture is attributed to them, is vilified, and is even the ground for discrimination' (Modood 2005: 7). How this relates to colour racism is a vexed issue (see e.g. Hall 2000); and whether labelling it racism is analytically or normatively helpful is also debatable. What cannot be doubted is that there has clearly been an inequality in the law on this question. For whereas Jews and, since 1982, Sikhs are defined as ethnic groups and therefore protected under race relations legislation, Muslims have not enjoyed these protections. As Modood argues in this volume, a feeling of 'grievance of exclusion from the existing equality framework' is a major factor behind the emergence and development of ethno-religious claims.

The government has not responded by defining 'Muslim' as a racial or ethnic group, but rather by extending religious discrimination laws. Religious discrimina-tion in employment was outlawed in 2003, which was then extended to the provision of goods and services in the 2006 Equality Act (which also established the EHRC). There has also been legislation to outlaw religious hate speech. The complex issues raised here go well beyond the scope of this chapter. But even this brief sketch provides a further illustration of how the assumptions embedded in the race relations policy paradigm—in this case colour racism—have struggled to keep pace with the evolving politics of race in contemporary Britain.

REFERENCES

BANTON, M. 1955. *The Coloured Quarter: Negro Immigrants in an English City*. London: Jonathan Cape.

—— 1998. *Racial Theories*, 2nd edn. Cambridge: Cambridge University Press.

—— 2002. *The International Politics of Race*. Cambridge: Polity.

—— 2005. 'Historical and Contemporary Modes of Racialization'. Pp. 51–68 in K. Murji and J. Solomos (eds.), *Racialization: Studies in Theory and Practice*. Oxford: Oxford University Press.

BENYON, J. (ed.) 1984. *Scarman and After*. Oxford: Pergamon.

BLEICH, E. 2003. *Race Politics in Britain and France: Ideas and Policymaking since the 1960s*. Cambridge: Cambridge University Press.

BURLEIGH, M., and WIPPERMANN, W. 1991. *The Racial State: Germany 1933–1945*. Cambridge: Cambridge University Press.

CRE (Commission for Racial Equality) 2007. *A Lot Done, A Lot to Do: Our Vision for an Integrated Britain.* London: Commission for Racial Equality.

FAVELL, A. 2001. *Philosophies of Integration: Immigration and the Idea of Citizenship in Britain and France,* 2nd edn. Basingstoke: Palgrave.

GILROY, P. 1987. *There Ain't No Black in the Union Jack: The Cultural Politics of Race and Nation.* London: Routledge.

HALL, P. 1993. 'Policy Paradigms, Social Learning, and the State: The Case of Economic Policymaking in Britain'. *Comparative Politics,* 25/3: 275–96.

HALL, S. 2000. 'Conclusion: Multicultural Questions'. In B. Hesse (ed.), *Un/settled Multiculturalisms: Diasporas, Entanglements, Transruptions.* London: Zed Books.

——CRITCHER, C., JEFFERSON, T., CLARKE, J., and ROBERT, B. 1978. *Policing the Crisis: Mugging, the State and Law and Order.* London: Macmillan.

HAMPSHIRE, J. 2005. *Citizenship and Belonging: Immigration and the Politics of Demographic Governance.* Basingstoke: Palgrave.

——2006. 'Immigration and Race Relations'. Pp. 309–29 in P. Dorey (ed.), *The Labour Governments, 1964–1970.* London: Routledge.

HANNAFORD, I. 1996. *Race: The History of an Idea in the West.* Baltimore: Johns Hopkins University Press.

HANSEN, R. 2000. *Citizenship and Immigration in Post-war Britain.* Oxford: Oxford University Press.

HINSLIFF, G. 2008. 'Labour Report Backs All-Black Shortlists'. *Observer,* 10 Feb. Accessed at http://www.guardian.co.uk/politics/2008/feb/10/harrietharman.labour.

KING, D. S. 1995. *Separate and Unequal: Black Americans and the US Federal Government.* Oxford: Oxford University Press.

——2007. 'The American State and Social Engineering: Policy Instruments in Affirmative Action'. *Governance,* 20/1: 109–26.

LAYTON-HENRY, Z. 1992. *The Politics of Immigration.* Oxford: Blackwell.

LITTLE, K. 1948. *Negroes in Britain: A Study of Racial Relations in English Society.* London: Kegan Paul.

MACPHERSON, SIR W. 1999. *The Stephen Lawrence Inquiry: Report of an Inquiry by Sir William Macpherson of Cluny.* Cm. 4262–1. London: HMSO.

MALIK, K. 1996. *The Meaning of Race.* Basingstoke: Macmillan.

MILES, R. 1989. *Racism.* London: Routledge.

——1993. *Racism after 'Race Relations'.* London: Routledge.

MODOOD, T. 1992. *Not Easy Being British: Colour, Culture, and Citizenship.* London: Trentham Books.

——2005. *Multicultural Politics: Racism, Ethnicity and Muslims in Britain.* Edinburgh: Edinburgh University Press.

——BERTHOUD, R., LAKEY, J., NAZROO, J., SMITH, P., VIRDEE, S., and BEISHON, S. 1997. *Ethnic Minorities in Britain: Diversity and Disadvantage.* London: Policy Studies Institute.

MURJI, K., and SOLOMOS, J. (eds.) 2005. *Racialization: Studies in Theory and Practice.* Oxford: Oxford University Press.

OMI, M., and WINANT, H. 1994. *Racial Formation in the United States: From the 1960s to the 1990s,* 2nd edn. London: Routledge.

SAGGAR, S. 1992. *Race and Politics in Britain.* New York: Harvester Wheatsheaf.

——(ed.) 1998. *Race and British Electoral Politics.* London: Routledge.

——2000. *Race and Representation: Electoral Politics and Ethnic Pluralism in Britain.* Manchester: Manchester University Press.

SCARMAN, LORD 1981. *The Brixton Disorders 10–12 April 1981: Report of an Inquiry by the Rt Hon. The Lord Scarman OBE*. London: HMSO.

SHUKRA, K. 1998. *The Changing Pattern of Black Politics in Britain*. London: Pluto Press.

SKRENTNY, J. D. 1996. *The Ironies of Affirmative Action: Politics, Culture, and Justice in America*. Chicago: University of Chicago Press.

SOLOMOS, J. 2003. *Race and Racism in Britain*, 3rd edn. Basingstoke: Palgrave.

SOYSAL, Y. 1995. *Limits of Citizenship: Migrants and Postnational Membership in Europe*. Chicago: Chicago University Press.

SPENCER, I. R. G. 1997. *British Immigration Policy since 1939*. London: Routledge.

THRÄNHARDT, D. 2000. 'Conflict, Consensus, and Policy Outcomes: Immigration and Integration in Germany and the Netherlands'. In R. Koopmans and P. Statham (eds.), *Challenging Immigration and Ethnic Relations Policies: Comparative European Perspectives*. Oxford: Oxford University Press.

WHEATLE, A. 2008. 'Authorised to Intimidate'. *Guardian*, 31 Jan. Accessed at http://www.guardian.co.uk/commentisfree/2008/jan/31/politics.race.

WINANT, H. 2006. 'Race and Racism: Towards a Global Future'. *Ethnic and Racial Studies*, 29/5: 986–1003.

CHAPTER 35

··

GENDER

··

FIONA MACKAY

35.1 INTRODUCTION

··

GENDER equality (GE) provides a remarkable case of the institutionalization of new—
previously marginalized—claims, social values, and policy goals into British politics
and governance. Over the last thirty years, in common with most industrialized
democracies, GE has developed into a distinct area of public policy by means of the
introduction of 'blueprint' policies in the form of legal frameworks for equal treatment, specialist women's policy machinery within government, and, from the mid-
1990s onwards, the widespread international diffusion of the Gender Mainstreaming
(GM) policy approach. These, together with the gender quotas, provide striking
examples of international policy and norm diffusion.[1]

My focus is the institutionalized politics of gender equality in Britain: the legal
and governmental architecture, political debates, state–society relations (particularly
the input of feminist gender equality advocates), and policy approaches that have
developed in order to address gender inequalities and to endorse gender equality as a
societal value and a political and public policy goal.

Patterns of inequality between women and men have changed dramatically in the
last thirty years. However, change has happened in complex and uneven ways with
highly differentiated outcomes resulting from the intersection of gender and other
social divisions such as ethnicity, class, disability, and generation. These changes
coexist with intractable and persistent patterns of material and cultural inequality
between men and women.[2] While it is far from settled as to the extent to which states

---

[1] Mazur (2002); Squires (2007). For reasons of space, I leave gender quotas to one side. See
Lovenduski (2005); Krook and Squires (2006).
[2] For current trends, see EOC (2006); Equalities Review (2007).

and their legal and policy instruments are primary agents of social change, especially in increasingly globalized contexts, nonetheless there is compelling evidence that states and governments are implicated in the reproduction of gender inequalities and are also players in any political project of reform (e.g. Sainsbury 1999; Walby 1997; Mazur 2002; O'Connor, Orloff, and Shaver 1999).

The form, function, and goals of GE public policy and politics are contested, and progress has been far from linear. Although always in danger of being bureaucratized and professionalized, the GE 'project' is an 'irredeemably political enterprise' (Forbes 2002: 20), and its development is shaped by wider socio-economic and political conditions and ideational contexts. This makes it a fascinating and distinctive area of scholarly research, crossing the disciplinary boundaries between political studies, social policy, sociology, law, and management (Newman 2002).

In this chapter, after reviewing the contested concepts of gender equality and debates within feminist scholarship, I contrast these complex understandings with the impoverished conceptions of gender and equality in public and political discourse and argue there is a need for a common language of gender. I then draw upon a range of British and comparative literature to survey and contextualize political and institutional developments over three decades. Researchers have raised questions about the nature, extent, and significance of change: has GE gained a place at the heart of government and the centre of the political agenda? Or is it an issue of symbolic rather than substantive significance—still marginal and subordinate to other government objectives? What has driven change and what are the underlying continuities? To what extent do GE policy and processes address substantive issues of inequality? Do recent developments add up to a 'regendering' of British politics?

35.2 WHAT IS GENDER?

Gender is a confusing and contested concept. In much public—and indeed some academic—usage it is taken as a synonym for sex or women (Carver 1996). The British sociologist Ann Oakley is credited with being among the first scholars to introduce the sex/gender distinction, although others see its origins in Simone de Beauvoir's famous axiom, 'One is not born, one becomes a woman'. Sex is taken to refer to the biological, chromosomal, and reproductive differences between women and men; in contrast, gender relates to the social meanings, roles, and expectations attributed to those biological differences. In other words, sex refers to nature and gender to culture. Gender is socially constructed and there is much evidence that the specific meanings, roles, and ideologies surrounding what it means to be a woman or a man vary across time and space (Oakley 1972; 2005). However, enduring patterns of differentiation, dichotomy, and hierarchy can be mapped across cultures, where those bodies, activities, roles, and attributes gendered as 'masculine' are deemed superior to and more human than their 'feminine' counterparts.

The sex/gender distinction was a simple but powerful insight, and has been a key contribution to feminist analysis and to wider social science. Furthermore, by distinguishing between the effects of biology and the effects of culture/society, feminists challenged essentialist accounts that women were naturally and inevitably subordinate to men and exposed the historic and socially constructed nature of women's oppression. This has under-girded a feminist political project of change; if gender is socially constructed, it is amenable to reform or transformation. So, for example, whilst it is a biological fact that (some) women give birth to children, the meaning of motherhood is social constructed. The fact that motherhood means primary—sometimes exclusive—responsibility for domestic labour and unpaid caring responsibilities in many societies results from gender—and its attendant ideologies—not sex differences. Furthermore, the low status assigned to caring work both paid and unpaid is not natural or inevitable, neither are the adverse social and economic consequences of motherhood for many women. Instead, these are the results of the institutionalization of gender inequality within social and economic systems.

Most gender analysis and theory, generated by feminists over the last thirty years, has come within a broadly social constructionist paradigm.[3] Concepts of gender have developed over time from a narrow definition of the cultural constructions of masculinity and femininity, to incorporate insights that gender is a dynamic process—as well as a category—which operates at different levels with material, symbolic, and cultural consequences. Early articulations of gender as rooted in a single social structure and giving rise to two unified categories of 'woman' (and 'man') have been complicated and enriched by pluralized accounts of gender: attentive to the differentiated processes and institutions of patriarchy or gender regimes (Walby 1997; Connell 2002); and alert to the multiple identities and experiences of different groups of women as a result of the intersection of gender with structures such as race, class, disability, sexual orientation, and nationality (Squires 1999). Furthermore, the simple sex/gender distinction has been undermined: by greater awareness of intersexed bodies, which challenges the dimorphic model of biological sex and lends weight to Butler's assertion that discourses of gender construct sex as binary and fixed in order to justify heterosexuality (Butler 1990); and by understandings of the ways in which bodies are shaped by social processes and are simultaneously agents in those processes (Connell 2002).

Gender theory has its roots in feminism and feminist scholars have been largely concerned with women and their unequal status, female ontology, feminine identity, and structures and mechanisms of gender inequality. However, men have come under increasing scrutiny by feminist scholars and by researchers and theorists of masculinities. According to scholars, there are multiple masculinities, which intersect with other social divisions. However, distinction needs to be made between hegemonic and subordinate masculinities: hegemonic masculinity is an ideologically legitimized ideal—and pattern of practices—which requires all men to position themselves in

---

[3] See discussion in Squires (1999: 54–79).

relation to it. Whilst individuals and groups of men may be disadvantaged within the social order, it is argued that men as a group benefit from the 'patriarchal dividend' of economic, social, and cultural advantages that accrues from an unequal gender order (Connell 1995; 2002).

A plethora of gender schemas exist but most accounts see gender operating on at least three levels: subjective and/or interpersonal; institutional and/or social structural; and symbolic. There is also widespread agreement that gender works as a primary way of signifying relationships of power, and as a category through which humans organize their social activity and create and reinforce hierarchy (Harding 1986: 17–18).

Squires notes a difference between constructionist accounts that still retain a material or social base—i.e. where there is a referent to 'real women' however differentiated and culturally specified, and a causal connection between sex and gender—and post-structural accounts which are discursive and loosen or lose altogether the link between sexed bodies and gender. Here the emphasis is on femininity as a linguistic construct, generated discursively and in relation to masculinity (Squires 1999: 59–61). This discursive shift in gender theory is part of a wider challenge to the utility of 'fixed' categories within social science.

35.3 GENDER AND PUBLIC DISCOURSE: MEN ARE FROM MARS AND WOMEN ARE FROM VENUS

The sex/gender distinction and social constructionist explanations of the causes and consequences of women's inequality have had some purchase in wider public discourse. However, these have always coexisted with essentialist accounts and powerful popular discourses, often reinforced by dubious populist science and pop psychology, which renaturalize gender as sex differences hardwired into the genes or ordained by the planets: that, in the words of the best-selling title on personal relationships, 'Men are from Mars and Women are from Venus'. As Oakley has remarked, there is scarcely a week goes by without some new 'discovery' of sex differences reported in the media, often using studies of animal and insect behaviour to infer innate and immutable differences between women and men. Oakley sees this as part of an ongoing backlash against feminism and women in British culture (Oakley 2005: 44).

There are paradoxes: on the one hand, gender is routinely used as a synonym for women and the gender of men is seldom articulated in political discourse. On the other, the move from talking about 'women's rights' and 'women's equality' or 'women's liberation' to 'gender' and 'gender equality' is underpinned by an apparent symmetry—where women and men are seen as potentially equally vulnerable to difference as disadvantage. For example the low numbers of men working in day care is seen as an equivalent gender inequality to the low numbers of women working in engineering, without attention being given to the different meanings and status of the gender gaps in wider context. In other words, gender is used without attention to the underlying structures of asymmetric power relations that are central to the concept.

Leaving aside the question of whether or not there is a backlash, there are impoverished understandings of gender in public discourse; political elites and public alike have difficulties in addressing gender, especially when compared with race, and are prone to misunderstandings and simplistic assumptions. Gender is both open and invisible (as compared with race). Open in the sense that people are comfortable accounting for distinctions as fixed and natural; less visible in the sense that it can be difficult to 'find' gender inequalities on a day-to-day level because 'its hierarchy is made through the often-subtle accumulation of often-small advantages across a host of different institutional spaces—at work, in the family, in school, in religious institutions' (Burns 2005: 138). That 'private ills' may be rooted in patterns of gendered hierarchy and structural differentiation and disadvantage can often only be illuminated by looking at aggregate trends over time and space or by making links between different institutional effects within an overall context.[4]

The gulf between popular and academic understandings and discussions of gender and gender equality has been noted in British, European, and North American contexts; and scholars argue that there is a pressing need to find ways in which complex ideas can be successfully integrated into political discourse, 'common sense', and public policy. This suggests there is a need for 'a common language of gender' (Beckwith 2005). Arguably, despite the theoretical difficulties, the sex/gender distinction remains useful as a holding concept—'as if' it were the case—as it is this explanation of gender which is most readily translatable into political and policy discourses and debates (Oakley 2005: 50). However, at the same time, articulations need to be carefully contextualized as part of a more complex understanding of: how gender is produced and reproduced at interpersonal, institutional, and symbolic levels; how systems of gender intersect with other social structures such as 'race'/ethnicity and class; and how gender provides a lens for analysing power hierarchies in institutions.

35.4 EQUALITY FRAMES AND POLICY DIRECTIONS

Dominant frames and norms with respect to meanings of equality shape and constrain the approaches and strategies that are developed and adopted by governments, employers, and the GE lobby. Much of the work around gender inequality is

---

[4] Burns (2005). Her study addresses the US context, but resonates with public discourses in the UK.

positioned within the overlapping frame of equal opportunities (EO) with concerns and dilemmas about the contested meanings of equality as a value and goal and strategies for change shared with theorists, researchers, and practitioners from other fields of equality, such as race, class, and disability.

Formal, liberal conceptions of equality centre upon the rights of all individuals to equal treatment and rights. The translation into EO policy results in a procedural model, which focuses upon equal opportunities for individuals to compete for scarce resources (jobs, wealth, power, authority). Unequal distributions in outcomes result from merit, rather than prejudice. Radical conceptions of equality are concerned with equality of outcomes amongst social groups, and with the adoption of measures to redress historic and ongoing disadvantage, such as employment and education quotas and other forms of redistribution. Although the term 'equal opportunities' would appear to be most closely tied to liberal minimalist approaches, in practice it is an umbrella term under which liberal and radical aspirations and understandings coexist in tension. It also encompasses more complex conceptions of substantive equality, which seek to challenge underlying norms upon which merit, fairness, and competition are based (Webb 1997: 160).

Moreover the relative strengths and weaknesses of universal and particularist models of equality and citizenship play out in a fundamental debate within feminism about whether women should seek to be treated like men or differently. In other words, GE—if understood as formal equality—may not be the same as the liberation of women, which may require different treatment to meet their specific needs. However both visions underpinning the equality–difference question can be and have been used to subordinate and disadvantage women.

Critics of equality—or 'integrationist'[5]—approaches argue that all too often equality means that masculine-defined values and male-constructed institutions are presented as universally valid models (of knowledge, citizenship, politics, humanity). In other words, that the gender neutral individual is in reality gendered as masculine and therefore those that are not male are disadvantaged from the outset. Difference feminists have thus sought to assert the value of alternative cultural norms and activities, those associated with women, particularly the norm and social practice of care. However such strategies of 'reversal' carry with them the danger of essentializing and reifying gender difference, and ignoring differences amongst women. Claims of feminine virtues can also be used by conservative forces to justify the exclusion of women from the public sphere.

Something of a consensus has emerged in recent years about the need for more complex and contextualized interpretations of equality: an equality that 'requires the recognition and inclusion of difference' (Scott 1998: 48). These ideas move beyond the equality/sameness–difference dilemma in order to challenge the gender neutrality of the standard model and 'displace' the dichotomy by, for example, refusing to frame issues in those terms. As Bacchi notes, 'By posing some new questions about how we think and organise as a society, we open up the possibility of a new and better

---

[5] Squires's typology. See Squires (1999).

vision. The questions we must ask are: why should it matter if women are the same as or different from men? Why is pregnancy constituted a disadvantage in our society? Why does the economic system reward competition and penalise caring?' (Bacchi 1990: p. xvi).

35.5 THE POLICY APPROACHES AND INSTITUTIONAL POLITICS OF GENDER EQUALITY

It is useful to consider the broad trajectories of GE policy approaches within the wider European context. Equalities concepts and strategies—in Britain as elsewhere—are contested, shaped, and promoted through different frames in the context of different political sites and shifting political conditions. Whilst some comparative welfare state scholars are sceptical that the European Union has had a discernible impact on gender equity outcomes (e.g. Ostner and Lewis 1995), nonetheless the European arena is an important site for the development of approaches to GE. Rees has characterized the changing approaches of the EU in the past three decades as 'Tinkering' (1970s), 'Tailoring' (1980s), and 'Transforming' (1990s), with the dominant focus for each decade being respectively, Equal Treatment, Positive Action, and Mainstreaming (Rees 1998). These three approaches are also found in the UK. However, both in the UK and in Europe more generally, there has not been a neat chronological evolution. Earlier approaches have not been discarded—nor have they remained static—but rather they have developed and coexisted and not necessarily in a coherent manner (Breitenbach et al. 2002; Daly 2005).

Equal treatment perspectives are underpinned by ideas of liberal formal equality and are oriented towards non-discrimination legislation. Squires equates this approach with the feminist strategy of integration (Squires 1999). As noted earlier, this characterizes the dominant approach to EO (including GE) in British politics to date. However the principles of equal treatment do not produce equal outcomes. For example, equal treatment legislation had a negligible impact on gender inequalities in pay in the UK and elsewhere (Browne 2007).

Criticisms of the limitations of this approach led to positive action measures by the EU and domestic states. Such initiatives were designed to ameliorate disadvantage from 'deficits' from the norm and create an equal playing field through the provision of, for example, women-only training initiatives. However, positive action approaches can stigmatize and fail to challenge the underlying norms or the standard from which 'women' deviate. Squires equates the positive action approach with the feminist strategy of 'reversal', noting the shared emphasis on women as a group and on gender difference. According to critics, neither Equal Treatment nor Positive Action is sufficient to tackle institutionalized discrimination (Rees 1998).

The gender mainstreaming (GM) approach, which seeks to integrate considerations of gender equality into the process and practice of policy-making and delivery, comprises a remarkable case of global policy diffusion (True and Mintrom 2001). Powerful champions include the EU, who adopted GM in the mid-1990s, and the UN, through its post-Beijing Platform for Action. GM is viewed by supporters as a potentially transformative approach, because of its capacity to 'expose' the hidden differential effects of policies on women and men, and different social groups, and to challenge institutional discrimination. Institutional or structural discrimination occurs when various aspects of work policies, practices, norms, and values and wider social systems combine to disadvantage specific groups. These may be directly discriminatory, for example through workplace cultures that stereotype, devalue, and denigrate women, ethnic minority groups, and the like. However it is more likely to be 'unconscious' and 'unwitting' through uncritical and taken-for-granted ways of thinking and 'doing things round here', and through the collective failure of institutions to recognize and tackle indirect discrimination. Squires views GM as related to the feminist strategy of displacement (in other words the deconstruction of norms and gender dichotomies), but not wholly congruent with it because it does not go far enough. She argues that it does not make sense—in the context of theorizing about intersectionality and diversity—to look at gender in isolation from other forms of equality (Squires 2005).

35.6 GENDER EQUALITY: THE INSTITUTIONAL TERRAIN 1970S–90S

The 1970s saw a raft of anti-discrimination legislation enacted, following on from the path-breaking Race Relations Acts of the 1960s. Landmarks included equal pay and sex discrimination legislation, the strengthening of race relations law, and legislation for Northern Ireland that outlawed religious discrimination in employment. Enforcement machinery was also established, with the Equal Opportunities Commission (EOC) set up as a non-departmental public body—an agency at arm's length from government—to monitor and enforce gender equality legislation in Britain. In addition, Article 119 of the Treaty of Rome (signed by the UK government in 1973), and subsequent equality directives between 1975 and 1978, provided legal foundations for the principle of equal pay for equal work.

The 1970s anti-discrimination legislation in Britain was distinctive in that it was potentially more sophisticated and more wide ranging than its European counterparts, In part, this can be explained by Britain's characteristic position 'between Europe and America' and, consequently, the impact of legacies and influences of different legal and political traditions (Gamble 2005). One example is the Sex Discrimination Act 1975. Influenced by the US experience in race relations, it incorporated the notion of indirect discrimination, which 'at least in principle recognizes that social category membership may be a source of disadvantage or exclusion' (Webb 1997: 162). It also gave extensive enforcement and investigative powers to the EOC. However, the Act eschewed US-style provisions for 'strong' affirmative action in terms of employment or educational quotas in favour of weaker 'positive action'. In addition, there were significant exemptions, especially where compliance with the provisions might have implications for government expenditure (Gregory 1999).

Scholars have pointed to a number of factors to explain why successive Labour governments in the 1970s acted to promote gender equality. These include pressures and demands from organized women's movement groups for equal citizenship, within the context of wider civil rights movements and a political environment of reform and social progressiveness, as well as global and regional pressures by bodies such as the United Nations, who promoted women's rights and their institutionalization through initiatives such as government women's policy machinery from the mid-1970s onwards. Anticipation and subsequent membership of the EEC provided another impetus for change. In other words, developments relate to a range of endogenous and exogenous factors including internationalization, regionalization (in the form of Europeanization), and new social forces (women's movements), within the context of wider social and economic trends.

35.7 1980S AND 1990S: GENDER EQUALITY POLICY IN A COLD CLIMATE

UK equality legislation has been characterized as piecemeal and confusing, reflecting a minimalist, individualistic, and reactive approach. Implementation has been, for the most part, voluntaristic with the onus placed upon aggrieved individuals to take a case through a long and complex process. Critics argue that the limited scope of the legislation explains in part the limited impact it has had on the gendered patterns of employment and issues of pay, occupational segregation, and so on. There are also significant issues with relation to the operation and interpretation of the legislation (Browne 2007).

However, it may also be the case that the full potential of equality legislation was never realized in the unpromising post-1979 political climate.

Almost as soon as gender equality legislation and policy machinery were put in place in Britain, and just as equal opportunities policies and procedures started to be developed and implemented, the economic, political, and institutional terrain underwent a sea-change with the incoming Conservative government of 1979. In general, parties of the right are less amenable to social justice claims, including gender equality, than their left counterparts. In addition, social democratic welfare arrangements are viewed as more conducive to the pursuit of gender equality than are liberal welfare states. Over this period, fundamental shifts occurred in political discourses about welfare, citizenship, and the respective roles of the state and the market, and in thinking about the scope and function of state bureaucracies towards a neoliberal and minimalist model. These trends had important consequences for gender relations and for the development of equalities work, not least the marginalization of such concerns from the mainstream political agenda, and the exacerbation of gender inequalities generated by marketization, deregulation, and other employment policies, welfare state retrenchment, and public spending cuts.

EO and GE initiatives tend to be 'carried' in the sense of the need to coincide or be congruent with other public policy or political objectives. Crudely speaking, claims—or rationales for action—are framed around citizenship and social justice, and the need for a state to retain or regain legitimacy in the eyes of its citizens and external actors, on the one hand; and, on the other, driven by a human capital or 'business' case agenda, concerned with the role of women in economic growth, efficiency, and development. In the cold climate for equalities during the Conservative years, Webb notes the marked shift in the rhetoric of public agencies such as the EOC towards the business case for equalities, 'restricting its agenda much more to employment issues and the use of women as a resource to meet government [employment and efficiency] priorities' (Webb 1997: 162), and eschewing the language of equal rights or gender justice.

Nonetheless, despite the inhospitable neoliberal context and successive central Conservative governments' indifference if not hostility to gender equality claims, some advances were made over this period. A number of commentators account for this modest progress by pointing to the central importance of European institutions in the 1980s and 1990s in promoting and strengthening gender equalities provisions in the UK: a case of 'European law to the rescue' (Gregory 1999: 98–9). In response to the reconfiguration of the British state and the 'uploading' of power and competences to the European level, domestic equality campaigners and feminist activists reoriented to engage at the supra-state level. One form this activism took was of feminists strategically mobilizing through a re-energized EOC to seek redress for gender grievances through European institutions (Lovenduski 1995). The European Commission and the European Court of Justice provided crucial alternative avenues to bring cases to challenge 'the shortcomings of domestic law and to limit the damage caused by neo-liberal economic policies' (Gregory 1999: 98–9). During the Thatcher and Major governments, the impetus for more than 40 per cent of the decisions that promoted gender equality in the areas of women's rights and equal opportunities and pay in employment came from either the European Commission or the European Court of Justice (Bashevkin 1998).

Mobilizing opportunities were also provided by UN initiatives such as CEDAW and the global women's conferences, in the context of the trend towards an internationalization of gender equality policy in the 1990s and beyond. The run-up to the 1995 Beijing Conference and subsequent Platform for Action which governments endorsed provided leverage for women's groups in the UK to press claims on the Conservative government of the day. These provide examples of a 'boomerang' strategy in terms of attempts to influence the supranational level in order to bring pressure to bear on national government.[6]

The British case is distinctive within Europe in that, while the 1980s and 1990s were periods of central national government activity in many countries, demonstrating the state's capacity to institutionalize new demands for equality, in the UK developments were forced upon a reluctant centre by Europe or took place 'under the radar' through local government women's, equal opportunities, and race equality committees and their accompanying specialist units and officers, and similar developments in trade unions—as part of the general oppositional political environment. There has been surprisingly little analysis of the 'local' politics of gender equality over this period and its legacies.[7] These developments have also fallen 'under the radar' of feminist comparative scholarship, which has tended to (over-)emphasize the level of the nation state and the machinery of central government.[8] However the lacunae can also be seen as part of the central state-centric tendencies of British politics scholarship more generally (Kerr and Kettle 2006).

Nonetheless, we must be careful not to over-state the impact of feminist GE advocates or international and sub-state organizations. Governments over this period made only grudging concessions and minimal adjustments after judgments from the European Court of Justice on issues such as equal value, unequal retirement ages, and pregnancy dismissals and rights for part-time workers (Gregory 1999: 98–9). The Conservative government's response to the post-Beijing Platform for action also was minimal: mostly—although not entirely—rhetorical. At local level, municipal women's committees were relatively short lived; most of these initiatives had been abolished or neutralized by the early 1990s, apart from some exceptions, mostly in Scotland.

35.8 GENDER EQUALITY POLITICS IN POST-1997 BRITAIN

The post-1997 period saw an apparent reprioritization of equalities—including gender equality, illustrated by the New Labour government's espoused commitment to gender mainstreaming, the creation of new policy machinery in central and devolved governments, the implementation of new legal duties on public bodies, and an ongoing review of equality legislation. In contrast to the grudging and minimalist approach of the Conservatives, New Labour brought a different approach to Europe in its commitment to sign the Social Chapter of the Maastricht Treaty and to (re-)introduce minimum wage protection, in line with other member states. In addition, there have been some policy gains for women, or groups of women. Taken

---

[6] See Keck and Sikkink (1998).
[7] Though see Breitenbach et al. (2002); Lovenduski and Randall (1993); Edwards (1995).
[8] See e.g. the influential RNGS framework at http://libarts.wsu.edu/polisci/rngs.

together, these developments have provoked the question as to whether or not these developments add up to a substantive change: to what degree has GE become institutionalized and embedded within British politics as a value and policy goal?

Labour fulfilled its commitment to appoint a Minister for Women with Cabinet status. In addition, specialist women's policy machinery was set up inside government for the first time in the form of a Women's Unit (later renamed the Women and Equality Unit). Established in June 1997, the unit was charged with scrutinizing legislation to promote gender equality and the promotion of women friendly policies. Labour also set up a cross-departmental Cabinet subcommittee with the intention of coordinating gender equality work across government. The government's commitment to gender mainstreaming was formalized with the publication of revised Policy Appraisal for Equal Treatment (PAET) guidelines in 1998 (Gregory 1999; Squire and Wickham-Jones 2004). In addition to institutional machinery, policy initiatives with direct or indirect relevance to GE include the introduction of the National Minimum Wage (NMW), the enhancement of the rights and protections of part-time workers, extended maternity leave provision and the introduction of parental leave, expansion of childcare places, Working Tax Credits, pension reform, gender pay reviews in public and private sectors, and new pay scales in the public sector.

However, early assessments of New Labour and its impact on women or on gender equality were typically cautious and sceptical about the extent to which the Labour modernization project offered substantive support for equalities, including GE. The predominant view was that, while New Labour represented a change in terms of its explicit commitment to social justice and democratic renewal, it represented continuity in respect of economic policy, limited public spending, and an attachment to market mechanisms.[9] For commentators such as Coote, gender equality is not a part of New Labour but rather was smuggled in by party feminists and their allies, drawing upon older strands of egalitarianism in the party (Coote 2000).

A recent wide-ranging edited collection evaluates the impact of New Labour on women and on GE. The central contention of the authors—which finds resonance in the wider literature—is that the gender equality agenda remains subordinate to other, sometimes congruent, oft-times contradictory, policy objectives. Whilst Labour has addressed some issues typically described as 'women's concerns', its achievements may be as much 'the unintended consequences of other policy initiatives' than 'the result of purposive strategy' (Annesley, Gains, and Rummery 2007: 3). In part, this relates to a lack of political commitment to—or understanding of—gender equality; and in part, it results from the considerable constraints upon making change happen, ranging from patriarchal ideology to the power dependency and coordination problems inherent in the institutions of policy-making in the UK system.

Turning first to employment-related family policy, New Labour has been more proactive and cross-cutting in its approach than its Conservative predecessors. Under the influence of the Treasury it has directed it 'firmly towards the "adult worker" model and to promote a social investment conceptualisation of childcare services

---

[9] See e.g. Bashevkin (2000); Rake (2001).

and education' (Clarke 2007). According to this analysis, gender inequality has been secondary to other policy drivers such as addressing child poverty through increased parental employment, particularly in the case of lone parents. These efforts have been accompanied by certain measures to rebalance parenting models and encourage men to play a more active role in caring, some prompted by the European Directives on Working Time and Part Time Work. For example, parents of children under the age of six (fathers and mothers) can request a reduction in their working hours (although there is no obligation upon the employer to grant this). Of note also are: the 2002 Employment Act, which introduced a statutory right to two weeks' paternity leave; and since 1999, there have been new limited entitlements to unpaid parental leave and emergency leave by either parent (Clarke 2007: 160, 195). According to Clarke, these developments amount to a 'substantial raft of measures to promote maternal employment, particularly among poor families where lone mothers are concentrated, and, to a lesser extent, to encourage and support greater involvement by fathers in caring for children' (Clarke 2007: 161). However, in practice, the results have been mixed. Despite changes to maternity rights and an unprecedented expansion of childcare provision and support, mothers of pre-school children are still less likely to be in employment than counterparts with children of school age. Overall, although there is recognition in policy documents of the desirability for greater paternal involvement in families, policies to date have predominantly focused upon getting women to conform to the Adult Worker model whilst simultaneously reinforcing their primary care role. There have been substantial increases in the employment of lone mothers, although some argue that, in many cases, paid work does not necessarily lift them out of poverty. It is also the case that childcare provision and maternity and parental leave and benefits remain among the poorest in Europe (Browne 2007: 265).

In terms of equal pay, policy interventions have been characterized as minimal and timid. Policy action to reduce the gender pay gap and improve women's job security conflict with—and are frequently trumped by—other key government policies. Labour governments have refused to acknowledge that their economic, public-sector marketization, and welfare reform policies are each implicated in the gender pay gap, whilst its NMW initiative is situated in the wider context of an unwillingness to address wage inequalities more generally, and has resulted in only minimal improvements to the relative position of low-paid women workers. In 2005, more than half of all female part-time workers were classified as low paid as were a quarter of full-timers (compared with one in seven male full-time workers). As evidence of New Labour's lack of sustained commitment, critics point to the refusal of government to allow the level of the minimum wage to be set by the Low Pay Commission, in a manner similar to the setting of interest rates, and to the government's consistent rejection of mandatory pay audits for private sector employers. By contrast, there has been stronger performance in addressing gender pay inequalities in the public sector, and the newly instituted positive gender duty requires public-sector organizations to prepare action plans. However, these effects are diluted and frustrated by the persistence of outsourcing public services and jobs to the private sector (Grimshaw 2007).

Turning to GM as the approach endorsed by central government for institution-alizing and delivering GE: how has it fared? Scepticism prevails about its impact or efficacy with little evidence to suggest it has achieved its transformatory potential—or even had a substantive effect upon key GE issues. Reporting on an eight-country study, Daly adjudges GM in Britain as 'a highly fragmented endeavour, confined either to a small number of policy domains or to a specific program with a domain and disconnected from general government policy on gender' (Daly 2005: 439). As a largely bureaucratic-technocratic enterprise, it also has had little success to date in democratizing the policy process—in other words, giving voice to grass-roots women's organizations and women and citizens (Squires 2005; 2007)—although the devolved territories have made more progress in this respect (McLaughlin 2007). Furthermore, the Women's Unit—later Women and Equality Unit—responsible for driving mainstreaming initiatives at UK level is adjudged to have been weak, hobbled by confusion over remit, lack of credibility and authority within civil service hierar-chies, and ambivalent support from senior politicians, all adding up to a lack of insti-tutional capacity to act (Durose and Gains 2007; Squires and Wickham-Jones 2004).

Space precludes a detailed discussion of devolution effects on GE and equalities policy. Scotland, Northern Ireland, and Wales have each pursued a generic or multi-strand mainstreaming approach, and promoted positive equality duties and citizen participation—precursors of the emerging UK approach (McLaughlin 2007). Equalities policy has been regarded as having a higher priority in the devolved jurisdictions than at the centre, although no systematic comparative research has yet been undertaken.

35.9 CONCLUSIONS AND NEW DIRECTIONS

There have been fundamental changes to gender relations in Britain since the 1970s, as evidenced by the transformation in the status and roles of women. However, these changes are complex and highly differentiated according to the intersection between gender and ethnicity, class, disability, and generation. The British state has played a role both in reinforcing and reshaping these patterns and distributional imbalances.

There has been significant institutionalization of GE through legislative frame-works, policy machinery, and policy approaches over the last thirty years; a trend that has accelerated in the post-1997 period under successive Labour governments. We can discern processes of internationalization and Europeanization over this period including the 'boomerang' strategies of feminist GE activists; using different levels and sites in order to apply leverage to—or bypass—a recalcitrant central state. Do these changes add up to a fundamental 'regendering' of politics?

Whilst some argue GE has acquired a new centrality to the political agenda, the weight of empirical evidence suggests that GE remains relatively marginal and subor-dinate to other political and objectives. Furthermore, contradictory policy goals and competing understandings of GE serve to dilute or distort the effects of initiatives to reduce inequalities. It is important to note that, in the context of significant constraints, continuities, and competing priorities, New Labour has undertaken a range of measures that has resulted in both modest concrete policy gains and symbolic outcomes. However, there has been little evidence of a politics that 'negotiates the complexities of gender' (Annesley, Gains, and Rummery 2007: 3).

Progress has been uneven and the field is characterized by a series of disconnections: the gap between understandings of gender and equality in theory and in practice; the disconnection between GE values, needs, and goals and the dominant neoliberal political and economic orthodoxy; and, perhaps surprisingly, the disconnection between GE machinery and approaches, such as mainstreaming, and gender equality objectives. These each provide future research directions, as will the theoretical and policy challenges posed by the implementation of new multi-strand or intersectional approaches to equality, and the impact of emerging territorial dynamics of devolution.

The current trajectory in the UK is one of an evolution from gender mainstreaming to equality and diversity mainstreaming as the predominant approach to the management of equalities issues. This follows the logic of the Amsterdam Treaty and subsequent equality directives that recognize and require the management of new strands of inequality. The 2006 Equality Act created a new combined Equality and Human Rights Commission, and positive duties on public bodies to promote Gender Equality and Disability Equality are currently being implemented, together with a strengthened race equality duty. In order to simplify and modernize discrimination law, the government introduced a Single Equality Bill in 2008. The Bill is informed by the findings of the Discrimination Law Review, which recently undertook a fundamental review of the patchwork of discrimination and legislation.

On the one hand, new institutional, legal, and policy developments promise an opportunity for a more coherent legislative approach with similar levels of protection for groups deemed marginalized. A diversity framework and single equality and human rights body makes sense in terms of the recognition of multiple and intersecting dimensions of discrimination; that racism and sexism are intertwined and cannot be understood or remedied separately. These developments are congruent with theoretical efforts to address intersectionality and move beyond category politics. They resonate with models that understand identities articulated through gender, race, class, sexuality, and disability as fluid and interrelated, rather than fixed or essential, and that require new forms of deliberative equality practice (Williams 1992). Squires argues that diversity and equality models of mainstreaming have the potential to provide these sorts of deliberative opportunities and connect them to the policy process (Squires 2005).

On the other hand, the practical obstacles to the implementation of an effective brand of equality and diversity mainstreaming are considerable. To date the record on gender mainstreaming has been far from impressive, with significant gaps between theory and practice; not least because of minimalist understandings of gender by policy-makers in their implementation of gender mainstreaming, and in wider gender equality policy initiatives. Furthermore, the outcomes of the operation of early forms of equality mainstreaming in Northern Ireland, Wales, and Scotland are inconclusive (McLaughlin 2007). In addition, sceptics see the diversity frame as managerial and minimal, masking rather than exposing asymmetries of power, and undermining the solidarities of group politics (Connell 2002: 134).

The Equalities Review, set up to inform a period of intensive institutional change with respect to equalities, has argued that new, more relevant definitions of equality are required, and a political and public consensus on equality. In *Fairness and Freedom*, it sets out a new approach, which draws upon concepts of human rights and human capabilities as a potential way forward.[10] However the signs are that understandings of equality, and resultant policy initiatives, will remain tightly constrained by the still-dominant neoliberal and market logics.

REFERENCES

ANNESLEY, C., GAINS, F., and RUMMERY, K. (eds.) 2007. *Women and New Labour*. Bristol: Policy Press.
BACCHI, C. L. 1990. *Same Difference*. Sydney: Allen and Unwin.
BASHEVKIN, S. 1998. *Women on the Defensive*. Chicago: University of Chicago Press.
—— 2000. 'From Tough Times to Better Times'. *International Political Science Review*, 21/4: 407–24.
BECKWITH, K. 2005. 'A Common Language of Gender?' *Politics and Gender*, 1/1: 128–37.
BREITENBACH, E., BROWN, A., MACKAY, F., and WEBB, J. (eds.) 2002. *The Changing Politics of Gender Equality in Britain*. Basingstoke: Palgrave.
BROWNE, J. 2007. 'The Principle of Equal Treatment and Gender: Theory and Practice'. Pp. 250–79 in J. Browne (ed.), *The Future of Gender*. Cambridge: Cambridge University Press.
BURNS, N. 2005. 'Finding Gender'. *Politics and Gender*, 1/1: 137–41.
BUTLER, J. 1990. *Gender Trouble*. London: Routledge.
CARVER, T. 1996. *Gender is Not a Synonym for Woman*. Boulder, Colo.: Lynn Rienner.
CLARKE, K. 2007. 'New Labour: Family Policy and Gender'. Pp. 155–73 in C. Annesley, F. Gains, and K. Rummery (eds.), *Women and New Labour*. Bristol: Policy Press.
CONNELL, R. W. 1995. *Masculinities*. Cambridge: Polity.
—— 2002. *Gender*. Cambridge: Polity.
COOTE, A. (ed.) 2000. *New Gender Agenda*. London: IPPR.
DALY, M. 2005. 'Gender Mainstreaming in Theory and Practice'. *Social Politics*, 12/3: 433–50.
DUROSE, C., and GAINS, F. 2007. 'Engendering the Machinery of Governance'. Pp. 93–114 in C. Annesley, F. Gains, and K. Rummery (eds.), *Women and New Labour*. Bristol: Policy Press.
EDWARDS, J. 1995. *Local Government Women's Committees*. Aldershot: Avebury.
EOC 2006. *Facts about Women and Men in Great Britain 2006*. Manchester: EOC.
EQUALITIES REVIEW 2007. *Fairness and Freedom: The Final Report of the Equalities Review*. London: HMSO.
FORBES, I. 2002. 'The Political Meanings of the Equal Opportunities Project'. Pp. 20–44 in E. Breitenbach et al. (eds.), *The Changing Politics of Gender Equality in Britain*. Basingstoke: Palgrave.
GAMBLE, A. 2005. *Between Europe and America: The Future of British Politics*. London: Palgrave.
GREGORY, J. 1999. 'Revisiting the Sex Equality Laws'. Pp. 98–118 in S. Walby (ed.), *New Agendas for Women*. Basingstoke: Macmillan.

---

[10] See Robeyns (2007).

GRIMSHAW, D. 2007. 'New Labour Policy and the Gender Pay Gap'. Pp. 133–54 in C. Annesley, F. Gains, and K. Rummery (eds.), *Women and New Labour*. Bristol: Policy Press.

HARDING, S. 1986. *The Science Question in Feminism*. Ithaca, NY: Cornell University Press.

KECK, M., and SIKKINK, K. 1998. *Activists beyond Borders: Advocacy Networks in International Politics*. Ithaca, NY: Cornell University Press.

KERR, P., and KETTLE, S. 2006. 'In Defence of British Politics: The Past, Present and Future of the Discipline'. *British Politics*, 1/1: 3–25.

KROOK, M. L., and SQUIRES, J. 2006. 'Gender Quotas in British Politics'. *British Politics*, 1/1: 44–66.

LOVENDUSKI, J. 1995. 'An Emerging Advocate'. In D. M. Stetson and A. Mazur (eds.), *Comparative State Feminism*. London; Sage.

—— 2005. *Feminizing Politics*. Cambridge: Polity.

—— and RANDALL, V. 1993. *Contemporary Feminist Politics*. Oxford: Oxford University Press.

MAZUR, A. 2002. *Theorizing Feminist Policy*. Oxford: Oxford University Press.

MCLAUGHLIN, E. 2007. 'From Negative to Positive Duties: The Development and Constitutionalization of Equality Provisions in the UK'. *Social Policy and Society*, 6/1: 111–21.

NEWMAN, J. 2002. 'Managerialism, Modernisation and Marginalisation: Equal Oppotunities and Institutional Change'. Pp. 102–23 in E. Breitenbach et al. (eds.), *The Changing Politics of Gender Equality in Britain*. Basingstoke: Palgrave.

OAKLEY, A. 1972. *Sex, Gender and Society*. London: Temple Smith.

—— (ed.) 2005. *The Ann Oakley Reader*. Bristol: Policy Press.

O'CONNOR, J., ORLOFF, A. S., and SHAVER, S. 1999. *States, Markets, Families: Gender, Liberalism and Social Policy in Australia, Canada, Great Britain, and the United States*. Cambridge: Cambridge University Press.

OSTNER, I., and LEWIS, J. 1995. 'Gender and the Evolution of European Social Policies'. Pp. 159–93 in S. Leibfried and P. Pierson (eds.), *European Social Policy: Between Fragmentation and Integration*. Washington, DC: Brookings Institution.

RAKE, K. 2001. 'Gender and New Labour's Social Policies'. *Journal of Social Policy*, 30/2: 209–31.

REES, T. 1998. *Mainstreaming Equality in the European Union*. London: Routledge.

ROBEYNS, I. 2007. 'When Will Society be Gender Just?' Pp. 54–74 in J. Browne (ed.), *The Future of Gender*. Cambridge: Cambridge University Press.

SAINSBURY, D. (ed.) 1999. *Gender and Welfare Regimes*. Oxford: Oxford University Press.

SCOTT, J. 1998. 'Deconstructing Equality-Versus-Difference: Or, the Uses of Post-structuralist Theory for Feminism'. *Feminist Studies*, 14/1: 33–50.

SQUIRES, J. 1999. *Gender in Political Theory*. Cambridge: Polity.

—— 2005. 'Is Mainstreaming Transformative? Theorizing Mainstreaming in the Context of Diversity and Deliberation'. *Social Politics*, 12/3: 366–88.

—— 2007. *The New Politics of Gender Equality*. Basingstoke: Palgrave.

—— and WICKHAM-JONES, M. 2004. 'New Labour, Gender Mainstreaming and the Women and Equality Unit'. *British Journal of Politics and International Relations*, 6/1: 81–98.

TRUE, J., and MINTROM, M. 2001. 'Transnational Networks and Policy Diffusion: The Case of Gender Mainstreaming'. *International Studies Quarterly*, 45: 27–57.

WALBY, S. 1997. *Gender Transformations*. London: Routledge.

WEBB, J. 1997. 'The Politics of Equal Opportunity'. *Gender, Work and Organization*, 4/3: 159–69.

WILLIAMS, F. 1992. 'Somewhere over the Rainbow: Universality and Diversity in Social Policy'. In N. Manning and P. Page (eds.), *Social Policy Review 4*. Canterbury: Social Policy Association.

SECTION TWELVE: MANAGEMENT

CHAPTER 36

AGEING AND GENERATIONAL POLITICS

ALAN WALKER

THIS chapter examines the relationship between ageing and politics, a long neglected topic in political science, and emphasizes its dynamic nature. At the macro-level of politics the liberal portrayal of older people as a deserving group, on which like all Western ones the British welfare state was based, is being challenged. At the meso- and micro-levels of politics, the last decade of the twentieth century saw the growth of grass-roots activity and new structures of local participation. While this account focuses on Britain similar trends may be observed in other European countries (Walker and Naegele 1999). The chapter comprises three sections: a summary of the new politics of ageing with reference to the macro- and meso/micro-levels; a discussion of the limitations of the political influence and potential influence of older people which casts doubt on the popular notion of grey power; and, finally, some reflections on the prospects for generational relations in Britain.

36.1 THE NEW POLITICS OF AGEING

Recent developments in the relationship between ageing and politics have been characterized as the emergence of a new politics of old age (Walker 1998; 1999). In the

I am grateful to Paul Whitely for supplying data from the British Election Study and to the referees for their suggestions.

case of ageing politics, this is overwhelmingly concerned with resource distribution, public identities, and human rights. This necessarily puts the spotlight on public and social policy but does not diminish the importance of the personal identity work that older people undertake everywhere as they negotiate and shape their responses to ageing. Indeed there are important connections between public policy and identities in old age (Hendricks 2004; Walker 1999; 2005). This chapter, however, is concerned with the public issues rather than the personal ones, even when these are political. This reflects Mills' (1970) classic sociological distinction between the 'personal troubles of milieu' and the 'public issues' of social structure. In the public arena there are micro-level political activities undertaken by older people, individually or in groups, to promote their interests. Then there is a range of meso-level organizations and structures that represent their interests in the form of either self-advocacy or representational politics (or a mixture of both). Finally, at the macro-level, there are policies that mainly emanate from the state (including local government)—as well as from corporations, the third or voluntary sector, and intergovernmental organizations (IGOs). In practice there is a maldistribution of power between the different levels. Looking top down the state, the representatives of 'grey capitalism' (Blackburn 2002), and the IGOs constantly make policies that impact hugely on the everyday lives of older people. However, from a bottom-up perspective, the scope for influence through micro- and meso-level participation fluctuates but remains very limited.

What is meant by the 'new' politics of ageing becomes clearer if we consider first the period 1945 to the early 1970s that may be described now as the 'old' politics of ageing. Going back further still, the formative years of the modern politics of ageing are rooted in the campaigns waged in the late nineteenth and early twentieth centuries by older people and organized labour to establish pension systems. These contributed to the introduction of public pensions, with the legislative bricks being laid first in Bismarck's Germany (1889), followed by the UK in 1908. In contrast to the early history of protests and campaigns for public pensions the post-Second World War period was characterized by political passivity. This passivity arose mainly from a rather negative social construction of old age, even though some of the motivations behind this were clearly benevolent.

One key element of this negative social construction was the close identification between older people and the welfare state. Like all welfare states the British one originated, wholly or partly, in the provision for old age and pension systems. They are now the largest item of social expenditure. Welfare states were constructed at a time of relative optimism about tackling need and the prospects for the future funding of benefits. Given their economic situation and difficulty remaining employed, older people were regarded as a deserving cause for welfare spending. This was not entirely good news because it also entailed their social construction as dependent in economic terms and encouraged popular ageist stereotypes of old age as a period of poverty and frailty (Townsend 1981; 1986; Walker 1980). There was certainly a case for action because the poverty rate among older people remained high—one in every three in the late 1960s—despite the introduction of pensions and other measures to assist them.

The other key element in the negative social construction of old age was the fact that older people were largely excluded from the political and policy-making systems by a process of disengagement whereby, on retirement, they no longer participated in formal economic structures and institutions. Thus retirement operated as a process of both social and political exclusion which detached senior citizens from some of the main sources of political consciousness and channels of representation. This exclusion contributed to a popular perception of older people as being politically passive. This then fed into age discriminatory stereotypes that portrayed older people as inactive, acquiescent, family orientated, and, therefore, uninterested in political participation.

The scientific community played its part by contributing social theories that purported to explain the social and political passivity of older people. For example the functionalist sociological theory of 'disengagement' was put forth in the early 1960s. This theory argued that old age consisted of an inevitable and mutual process of disengagement between the ageing individual and other members of society (Cumming and Henry 1961). In accordance with it, most older people would not be expected to be active participants in social and political life. The theory, however, neglected the structural processes, noted above, that in effect were excluding older people from participation (Walker 1980). Of course there were living examples of active senior citizens who contradicted the stereotype, but this does not negate the general social construction.

Other factors also operated to limit the extent of political participation on the part of older people in the early post-war period. In a general political sense old age was less significant than it is today. There were fewer older people; they were less healthy; and retirement still acted as the key regulator of entry into old age. Also, in political terms, age was less salient because attention was directed chiefly at rebuilding the physical infrastructure damaged by the war and constructing the major institutions of the welfare state. Thus, the politics of old age reflected the general politics of the time. Issues of conflict were dominated by traditional class and religious divisions, with corporatism containing policy conflicts within the political system.

During this post-war phase in the politics of old age, pressure groups were established to represent the interests of older people including the two currently dominant ones—Age Concern and Help the Aged. Organizations such as these were not primarily concerned with the political mobilization of the older population. Instead they chiefly spoke on behalf of older people in the policy arena. Thus the politics of old age in this period was characterized by consensus: pressure groups representing older people who bargained for public policy advances within a context of shared understanding. Generally the groups agreed about the possibilities of politics, the (Fabian) assumption of progressive welfare development, and the deservingness of the case they espoused. It is not surprising therefore that this period has been described as the 'bureaucratic lobby' phase (Estes, Biggs, and Phillipson 2003). Today things are quite different.

36.2 THE NEW MACRO-POLITICS OF AGEING

This 'new' (but now deeply entrenched) politics of ageing consists of two distinct but causally related macro- and meso/micro-aspects. At the macro-level politicians and policy-makers began to reject the consensus on which the welfare state was based—in this case that older people were the deserving poor. Instead, they began to question, more openly and frequently than hitherto, the cost of population ageing. The first wave of this critical approach to welfare, particularly the public expenditure implications of pensions and health care, occurred in the mid-1970s following the world oil price shock and the fiscal crisis it contributed to (O'Connor 1977). This was followed by a second wave of criticism in the 1980s when the macro-economic implications of pension system maturation and the financial costs of long-term care were the subjects of (sometimes heated) debate in Britain as well as other countries. The immediate impact of this new approach was the change from wage to price indexation for the basic national insurance pension (BP). The State Earnings Related Pension was also cut substantially, and those still employed were offered tax incentives to take out private pre-funded pensions (Walker 1991; 1993).

Sometimes this new discourse is expressed in terms of generational equity with, invariably, the grossly simplified 'dependency ratio' between older people and those of working age invariably quoted as evidence of impending doom. The fact that this crude dividing line is not an indication of economic contribution because it excludes the active above pension ages and the general tax contributions of older people, the historic decline in the age dependency ratio, and the absence of an optimum relationship in the face of rising productivity, is rarely considered when these ratios are invoked (Walker 1990). Their political power and status belies the flimsy scientific foundations on which these ratios are based. Only in the USA was there a sustained public debate on generational equity that was spurred on by the creation, in 1985, of the pressure group Americans for Generational Equality (AGE) (Quadagno 1989). However, the organization proved to be a front for an anti-welfare ideology and signally failed to dent the support of the general public in the USA for programmes for older people, support which has remained resilient (Marshall, Cook, and Marshall 1993).

Similar discourses concerning the future costs of population ageing emerged later in the other northern European countries, and this has led to modifications to most countries' pension systems. The fact that Britain led the way in Europe, on this front if not any others, is due to the abrupt hegemonic replacement of the last remnants of liberal Butskellism with neoliberal Thatcherism.

The emergence of the neoliberal 'New Right' may be traced to the revision of conservative politics that took place in the 1970s, especially in the UK and USA. This revision intertwined the previously separate strands of liberal belief in a free economy with the conservative belief in a small but strong state (Gamble 1986). Monetarist economics was the practical tool used to implement neoliberal thinking, and this was the justification (or scientific legitimation) for reducing the role of the state in welfare and the privatization of public interest (Walker 1984; 1990). Social policies are always to some extent 'path dependent' in that they reflect a particular country's historical legacy and institutional model. This explains why the UK (and Ireland) adopted neoliberalism more readily than the countries of Continental Europe where a social democratic tradition had been more prevalent. This sea-change in political ideology had a critical impact on the relationship between older people and the welfare state and, therefore, on the politics of ageing.

Over the last twenty years this neoliberal ideology has been globalized by the IGOs—particularly the International Monetary Fund (IMF) and World Bank but more recently the World Trade Organization (WTO) and, to a lesser extent, the Organization for Economic Cooperation and Development (OECD) (Estes and Phillipson 2002; Walker 1990; Walker and Deacon 2003). This global aspect of the macro-level new politics of old age is of increasing importance in determining the nature of provision in old age. Moreover, its power to undermine long-standing public pension and social protection systems is immense as national governments, for various reasons, fall in line with the neoliberal consensus. Back in the 1980s the first signs of the emerging consensus on policies for old age were already visible in two influential OECD (1988a; 1988b) reports. These were followed by others derived from a broadly similar 'burden of ageing' discourse and advocated policy prescriptions that typically involved a reduction in public pay-as-you-go (PAYGO) and private defined benefit pension schemes and an increase in private, defined contribution ones (World Bank 1994; OECD 1998). In other words, an ageing crisis was manufactured as a pretext for welfare retrenchment that would be consistent with the ideological objectives of neoliberals (Minkler and Robertson 1991; Quadagno 1989; Vincent 1996; Walker 1990). The next logical step is the liberalization of the trade in services (including health and social care) under the WTO, which would challenge national government prerogatives to provide free services or to subsidize national not-for-profit providers (Estes and Phillipson 2002; Walker and Deacon 2003). Thus, in Britain and globally, neoliberalism has had a profound effect on the macro-politics of ageing by framing policies that have reduced the extent to which the state guarantees socio-economic security in later life (Estes 2004; Estes, Biggs, and Phillipson 2003). Although beyond the scope of this chapter, population ageing has been described as a grave geopolitical threat (Jackson and Howe 2008).

36.3 THE NEW MESO- AND MICRO-POLITICS OF AGEING

At the meso- and micro-levels the new politics of old age consists of a rapid expansion in direct political involvement on the part of older people (including joining action groups and taking part in demonstrations). Thus the National Pensioners Convention (NPC) was reconstituted in 1992 by an amalgamation of different preexisting grass-roots and trade union groups (with Jack Jones as its first president). The NPC has around 1.5 million affiliated members in the local pensioner action groups that have mushroomed under its aegis (Carter and Nash 1992). Its annual Pensioners Parliament in Blackpool involves more than a thousand delegates. While this growth in grass-roots activity is mirrored in other European countries these new social movements among older people involve relatively few pensioners. Activism is pursued by a minority of persons in all birth cohorts, but many more older persons are now involved than in the previous consensus era and apparently more actively so (Carter and Nash 1992; Walker and Naegele 1999). Furthermore the nature of political participation and representation is changing: there are more examples of direct action by senior citizens, and the new action groups are citizens' organizations composed of older people who want to represent themselves. It is too soon to say how permanent these new social movements will be. Indeed organizational instability is a familiar feature of grass-roots activity, and it is predictable that some will fail, as happened to the political party for older people in Belgium. The impact of these new forms of self-advocacy will be discussed in the next section. But first, how do we explain this transformation in the political participation and representation of older people?

To begin with, the growth in political action by older people is merely a reflection of the global upsurge in social movements spanning almost every element of political life (Jenkins and Klandermans 1995). This may be seen as one facet of the transition from modernity to late modernity. On the one hand, this means the breakdown of the traditional economic and social certainties of modernity. On the other hand, it reflects the opening up of new concepts of citizenship and consumerism and new channels of political action (Harvey 1989). The emergence of new social movements outside of the familiar political institutions (political parties and trade unions) is not surprising given the profound realignments under way in the social and economic orders of the advanced industrial societies.

Secondly, some socio-demographic developments have supported both a heightened political awareness of old age as a political issue and the likelihood that older people will participate actively. Quite simply there are more older people and, therefore, they are more visible than 15–20 years ago in political terms. Also the cohort effects of a healthier and better-educated older population have produced a potentially active pool of people in early old age (the 'third age').

Thirdly, the neoliberal inspired negative changes in the macroeconomic and social policy contexts referred to earlier have had an impact on the radicalization of the politics of old age. The primary focus of the pensioners' campaigns has been government actions; both local and national campaigns have been concerned almost exclusively with cuts in pensions and social services provision and related issues. In Britain the relative inadequacy of welfare for older people has sharpened the grass-roots' response in comparison to the impact of social expenditure cuts in some other European countries such as Germany (Maltby and Rohleder 2008). There may also be a reciprocal relationship between the growth of social policy in the ageing field and the participation of older people. For example, Campbell (2003) points out that in the USA the growth in social security coverage has been accompanied by a parallel rise in the political participation (i.e. voting and campaign contributions) of older people from the 1950s to the 1990s.

Fourthly, the growth of political participation among older people has been encouraged by policy-makers. Most of the participation of older people in daily life takes place at a local level, and this unit of administration is responsible, directly or indirectly, for many of the services that they receive. It is useful, however, to distinguish two different dimensions of participation in decision-making at the local level. On the one hand there is the public policy-making process which determines the general direction of services and the distribution of resources between groups. In contrast, there are policy decisions taken at an interpersonal level, often by bureau-professionals, which concern the delivery of specific services to older people.

As far as the local municipal policy-making process is concerned, the New Labour government came to power pledged to increase the participation of older people. Thus, in 1997, it introduced the Better Government for Older People initiative consisting of fifty pilot projects designed to improve their participation in local authority decision-making. Turning to the second dimension of participation in decision-making at the local level, we are faced with a very complex interplay of personal and professional relationships. The health and social services are key agencies in the construction of dependency in old age (Townsend 1981). Professional groups have been trained to regard themselves as autonomous experts, and this has had the common effect of excluding older people and their family carers from decision-making about the services required to meet their care needs. The last decade has seen the build-up of pressure for increased participation in decisions previously regarded as the sole province of professionals. These are coming, first, from the rise of consumerism (the transition from modernity to late modernity) and the reassertion of individualism. This social change is creating twin pressures for greater choice and for a participating voice. Secondly there are grass-roots pressures from service users and from informal carers. Thirdly there are changes within professions in their orientation and practice that are beginning to question professional autonomy and which are opening up professional practice to user involvement. Together these processes are emphasizing the importance of the participation of older service users and their carers. Although Britain has a relatively paternalistic service tradition, user groups are being established by many local authorities (Cook, Maltby, and Warren 2004), although this does not often represent a radical form of empowerment (Barnes and Walker 1996).

Thus the recent growth in the political participation of older people and the development of what appears to be a new grass-roots politics of old age must be regarded as the consequence of two distinct impulses. From *below* there are undoubtedly pressures on the part of older people seeking a political voice; from *above*, policy-makers have consciously encouraged the involvement of older people.

36.4 THE MYTH OF GREY POWER

To what extent has this political involvement been translated into effective power? The evidence suggests that much of the increase in political participation witnessed in the past decade has not led consistently to influence over events affecting older people. In fact the ideological construction of grey power, often promoted by popular press headlines (especially in the USA), has created a myth that sheer numbers and high voter turnout are all that matters in the battle for political influence (Binstock 2005a; Peterson and Somit 1994; Walker 1991). On the central issues in the UK pensioners' campaigns—the restoration of the earnings link with the BP and a reduction in means-tested support—the New Labour government was immovable. This is despite a 1997 Manifesto pledge that the BP would remain the 'foundation' of retirement income, campaign promises to restore the link and reduce means testing by the Prime Minister and Chancellor, and the establishment of a Pensions Working Party consisting of NPC leaders and Barbara Castle (following the latter's challenge at the 1997 Labour Party Conference). By 1999 the then Secretary of State for Social Security, Alistair Darling, wrote in the following bullish terms to Jack Jones (NPC president):

> You have expressed concern that a consequence of linking the minimum income guarantee to earnings could, in the short term, be to increase the number of today's pensioners dependent on means-tested benefits. I acknowledge that in the short term our approach will increase the numbers on income support. I am unapologetic about this. We believe that the minimum income guarantee is the most effective way to help those most in need.

Although there has been a significant reduction in poverty in old age over the past decade, it remains relatively high: one-fifth of pensioners have incomes below the official poverty line. In fact the only instance of pensioners exercising substantial political influence in recent times was the outrage that accompanied the 75p rise in the BP in 1999 and then it was not only older people who were angry.

The reasons why the apparently latent power of older people has not been mobilized consistently will be discussed later. However, it is important to note here that the ideological construction of grey power sits closely alongside the neoliberal myth of ageing as a burden on society and serves a complementary purpose. Moreover it may be that the various new forms and structures of participation, assembled in the UK and other EU countries over the past twenty years, are masking to some extent the absence of effective political power held by older people. Scientific evidence is required to test this hypothesis, for example comparative studies of influence in different countries and localities. On the positive side, however, there is some evidence that it is possible to overcome the various barriers to organizing the local participation of older people. Several of the BGOP pilot projects reported a successful impact on decision-making. A strong desire for active engagement in the local policy-making process and to have a voice in decisions affecting their lives has been demonstrated even among some of the most difficult groups to involve, such as older women from ethnic minority groups (Cook, Maltby, and Warren 2004). It is clear though that we must be mindful about the limitations of local advisory councils. Also the structures for local citizen participation are invariably the same and, therefore, fail to take on board inequalities between older people. Research demonstrates that participation takes many forms and this suggests that the structures created to facilitate it must be flexible to be fully inclusive.

On balance, the available evidence suggests that grey power is a myth not just in the UK but also in the USA and the rest of Europe (Walker and Naegele 1999), and its popular promotion by policy elites and the media may have more to do with attempts to legitimize neoliberal-inspired policies intended to reduce public spending on older people than any genuine examples of sustained influence over policy at the macro-level (as opposed to providing 'advice' at the local level). Also, while there are continuing examples of the operation of grey power in local politics, these tend to be part of the ebb and flow of pluralism rather than a sign of structured power, for example to change resource distribution in favour of older people.

36.5 BARRIERS TO POLITICAL PARTICIPATION AND INFLUENCE

While few would doubt the importance of the transformation that has taken place in the meso- and micro-politics of old age it is important not to overstate what has happened. So far this change has involved only a minority of older people. This suggests, at least, that the barriers to political participation may be more formidable than has been recognized generally and, perhaps, that there is no sound basis for general political mobilization among older people. There are five main impediments to such participation by older people in specifically age-related politics.

In the first place, contrary to popular perceptions, older people do not necessarily share a common interest by virtue of their age alone which transcends all other interests (Binstock 2000; Street 1999; Walker and Naegele 1999). Thus it is mistaken to regard senior citizens as a homogeneous group which might coalesce around or be attracted by a one-dimensional politics of ageing. In other words, age is only one of several forms of socio-political consciousness such as socio-economic status, race, gender, religion, and locality. This perspective marked a break with the long-standing tendency for social scientists to regard older people as a distinct and homogeneous social group cut off from their *own* status and class position formed at earlier stages of the life cycle (Quadagno 1982; Walker 1981). Although no longer prevalent in social sciences this is still a view held by policy-makers in many different countries and in IGOs (OECD 1994; Walker 1990). As Estes (1982) has argued, a largely classless view of old age has been incorporated into public policy.

In fact, older people are just as deeply divided along social class and other structural lines as younger adults. This means that large organizations such as Age Concern are dealing with a very diverse membership, which can cause difficulties if the organization takes a high-profile stance on an issue, or that the competition between different organizations representing older people may diffuse potential mobilization (Douglas 1995; Binstock 2005a). A fundamental fault line is gender, and not only is this consistently underplayed by policy-makers, but their policies are also crucial in maintaining it (Arber and Ginn 1991; Calasanti and Slevin 2001; Estes et al. 2001; Estes 2004). The process of retirement, not ageing, does impose reduced socio-economic status on a majority of older people. Even so, retirement has a varying impact depending, among other things, on prior socio-economic status. For example invariably there is unequal access to occupational pensions (Reday-Mulvey 2005; World Bank 1994). Women and other groups with incomplete employment and pensions contribution records are particularly disadvantaged in the UK and most other Western countries (Ginn 2003).

Secondly the majority of older people remain relatively powerless politically. Traditionally the main source of working-class political power has been the economic base provided by the workplace and trades union organization. Retirement is often associated with social processes of exclusion that remove older people from their main source of income but also from potential collective political power and sources of socio-political consciousness. After retirement a larger portion of time is spent, on average, engaged in private and individualized home-based activities. Of course the 'Fordist' model of work organization is increasingly inappropriate as a description of the late-modern often individualized world of work (Harvey 1989) but paid employment remains a collective activity for the majority of those in employment.

Thus, in contrast to the mobilization effect of public policy referred to earlier, detachment from paid employment may act as a dampener on political action, which deters some from political activities or creates barriers for others to surmount in order to be active. This is not to say that *interest* in politics and minimum levels of engagement, such as voting, are diminished necessarily. Political interest and engagement have been demonstrated consistently to be positively related to education and income levels (Verba, Schlozman, and Brady 1995). Recently, however, Campbell (2003) has found that interest in social security is high in the USA across all education and income groups. Furthermore social security-specific participation (including writing a letter, making a financial contribution, protesting, and voting) is higher for low-income groups than for the high-income ones. This latter finding is not surprising given that social security comprises 82 per cent of the income of US older people in the lowest quintile and only 18 per cent in the highest. But the 'democratizing' effect of social security's universalism in the USA seems to mirror that of the classic Scandinavian citizenship welfare state (Korpi 1983; Esping-Andersen 1990; Palme 1990). Apart from local campaigns in the UK, for example with regard to transport or access to services, it is the universal BP that has been the main rallying point for British pensioners.

Despite the apparent pressures towards bifurcation, European and US research suggests that differences between younger and older voters in attitudes towards key policy issues are relatively small. This was the conclusion of a unique pan-European study of attitudes (Walker 1993) and of an analysis of the 1996 presidential election in the USA (Binstock 1997). In fact, it is not age as such that determines political attitudes and behaviour; rather it is 'the cleavages that cut across cohorts such as economic, educational, racial and ethnic, gender, and partisan divisions' (Binstock and Day 1996: 364). Of course, it is obvious that some issues, such as pensions, have greater salience for older cohorts.

The observation of a relationship between political efficacy and occupation dates back more than forty years to US research by Almond and Verba (1963). Using a similar approach twenty years later British survey analysis found that propensity for collective action is lowest among the retired and, in contrast to the employed and other groups in the labour market, retired people have a preference for personal over collective action (Young 1984). The explanation for this passivity on the part of older people consisted of a sense of powerlessness or non-competence which, in turn, reflected a lack of real resources with which to gain political influence. There was, predictably, a close association between both socio-economic group and education and subjectively assessed power. Campbell's (2003) US research does not contradict these findings, since her focus was primarily on voting and political knowledge. In other words, minimum levels of participation, high levels of political interest, and low levels of collective action are not necessarily inconsistent.

Older people do demonstrate consistently greater political engagement than younger people in one important respect: voting. Globally older people are more likely than younger ones to turn out in national (general) elections, and this is true for both men and women. Also the gender gap grows with age, which means that older women are more likely than older men to vote in general elections (among those aged sixty-five and over the difference is 3.7 per cent in non-turnout levels: 13.1 per cent for women and 16.8 per cent for men) (Pintor and Gratschew 2002). In both Western Europe and the USA, older people commonly record the highest turnout of all age groups in general elections (Turner, Shields, and Sharp 2001). European data emphasize the higher turnout among older than younger people, even among those aged seventy and over, which averages 90 per cent (International Institute for

Table 36.1 Voting turnout in general elections by age and gender

Age	1970		1983		1997		2001		2005	
	M	F	M	F	M	F	M	F	M	F
18–24	67	66	74	73	56	64	60	46	33	37
25–34	74	77	76	79	67	70	59	56	46	48
35–44	81	84	87	88	77	78	66	74	62	63
45–54	86	85	88	90	83	86	76	81	63	68
55–59	88	86	89	93	90	87	79	82	77	76
60–64	79	84	82	90	87	88	80	80	70	72
65 and over	93	84	86	82	87	85	87	87	71	63

Source: British Election Study, National Centre for Social Research; University of Essex.

Democracy and Electoral Assistance (IDEA) 1999). The USA has seen long-term growth in the portion of votes cast by older people in presidential elections (Binstock 2000). Since 1972 those aged sixty-five and over have comprised a larger share of voters than of those eligible to vote, and this gap has grown over time. The key factor in this rise is the changing turnout rates of different age groups: an increase of 6.5 per cent among those aged sixty-five and over between 1972 and 1996 coupled with reductions in other age groups (e.g. 34.7 per cent among 18–24-year-olds). In the 2004 US presidential election the senior turnout rate was 68 per cent compared with 54 per cent for the electorate as a whole (Binstock 2005b). As Table 36.1 shows, turnout at general elections in the UK is consistently higher among older than younger age groups although the gender imbalance does not match the general Western one.

Thirdly, pensioners often lack formal channels through which to exert political influence. Indeed the UK's political representation system effectively excludes older people from key institutions. For example, one of the major political parties provided an organizational context for pensioners or made special efforts to include them in their machinery. (This contrasts with Germany where political parties have taken steps to try to incorporate them including a network of senior circles at district and regional levels within the Social Democratic Party (Alber 1995).) Similarly, the trade unions have been poor at involving ex-members and in providing continuing membership after labour force exit although some, such as the TGWU, have done this.

Fourthly, there are important physical and mental barriers to political participation in old age. Disability and socially disabling later life-course events, such as widowhood, may further fragment political consciousness and discourage political activity. The experience of ageing itself creates barriers to collective action and political participation for a minority of older people. For those with intellectual or learning disabilities who are now reaching old age for the first time, the ageing process merely confirms their socio-political exclusion (Walker, Walker, and Ryan 1996). Other social structural factors that militate against active political participation include poverty and low incomes, and age, gender, and race discrimination. For instance those suffering social exclusion as a result of poverty face substantial material and psychological barriers to active engagement and are among the least likely to be represented within the formal political system (Scharf, Phillipson, and Smith 2004). This includes a small but significant proportion that live in institutions of various kinds, whose voices are usually the quietest. In addition a large number of older people, particularly women, are actively involved in caring for spouses and others in need and, therefore, may not have the physical energy and mental space to be active on the political scene as well. Despite these obvious barriers there is political activity among low-income groups. Indeed as noted previously, in the US Campbell (2003) found a *higher* level of activity among low-income senior citizens than more affluent ones with regard to social security issues. This is possibly a function of the interaction between the significance of social security to pensioners and the political culture.

Finally there is conservatism. It is not necessarily the case that people become more conservative as they grow older—despite the commonplace nature of that assumption (Hudson 1980). In terms of public opinion, on most issues they differ very little from younger people in both the EU and the USA (Peterson and Somit 1994; Walker 1993). However there is evidence that older people are more conservative in certain respects than younger ones, but the reasons are not related primarily to age. Several key factors have been mentioned already, such as the removal of sources of potential influence and activity. In addition, there is a generational dimension. The present older generations have different reference points from younger people. Many of their formative years occurred between 1935 and 1955, a unique historical period in Europe and the wider world. Although the direction of party allegiance depends to some extent on age cohort effects (Hudson and Strate 1985), when it comes to the strength of such attachments the evidence shows that, in both Western Europe and the USA, there is a uniform tendency for a disproportionate number of older people to hold strong party allegiances, an observation that was first made in the USA (Campbell et al. 1960; see also Binstock 2000; McManus 1996). All of this suggests that older people are *not* more conservative in voting terms, but, rather, they have had a tendency to vote for the party they have always voted for.

36.6 THE PROSPECTS FOR GENERATIONAL RELATIONS

Despite the development of a distinctly new politics of old age, with interrelated macro- and meso/micro-features, it is clear from the previous section that the social and economic foundations for political power and mobilization among older people remain relatively weak. This is not peculiar to old age but a demonstration that age is not, in itself, a sound basis for political consciousness. The relatively new direction of macroeconomic and social policies in the UK and other developed countries is clear. However, based on the available evidence, grey power is more hype than substance. Furthermore the ageing power myth is being reproduced and amplified regularly in support of macro-level neoliberal policy prescriptions: growing numbers of older people are not only swamping those in employment but they are also controlling the political agenda to caricature matters somewhat. One reason for the apparent ease with which this myth gets translated into popular discourses is the virtual absence of scientific research on this topic in either gerontology or political science (Walker 1986).

A prime example of the tendency for hyperbole to fill a scientific vacuum is political discourses on intergenerational relations. Indeed, even when there is some hard evidence in this field, it is commonly discounted in favour of a controversial headline or sound-bite. Looking backwards the occasional references to potential generational strife in the UK and other EU countries have always proved illusory. Research continues to find high levels of solidarity between the generations as demonstrated, at the macro-level, by support for the social contract underpinning public pensions and health care (Walker 1993; Brook, Hall, and Preston 1997; Hills and Lelkes 1999) and, at the micro-level, by the support provided within families (Dench, Ogg, and Thomson 1999). Even in the USA, where a high-profile campaign was waged on this issue in the 1980s, it proved to be groundless (and the campaign a front for an anti-welfare lobby) with continuing high levels of support for social security (for older people) (Marshall, Cook, and Marshall 1993). In practice it has been the younger generation that has attracted most media interest and, in the political arena, the voting habits of older people have not only been neglected but taken for granted.

Contemporary discourses on the 'baby boomer effect' need to be regarded with circumspection in the absence of research evidence which demonstrates any real effects. Of course there are differences between generations: one recent comparison between Germany and the UK concluded that there are more differences between generations within the two countries than between them (Potratz, Gross, and Hilbert 2009). In other words, there are new generations of younger older people (50–74) who, as a result of continuous employment and pension scheme maturation, are more affluent than their forebears and display higher levels of hedonistic consumption and lifestyle. This transition has led to a new emphasis on consumption in the sociology of ageing (Gilleard and Higgs 2000). While there are key differences between the boomers and previous generations, such as their greater affluence, higher levels of education, and socio-political attitudes (especially individualism and liberalism) (Evandrou 1997; Huber and Skidmore 2003), the key political question is: how salient are they? This is a topic calling out for research but, for the moment, the answer must be 'not very'. Existing solidarities remain intact but, in practice, the traditional definitions of 'old age', by arbitrary pension ages, are becoming less and less useful. Moreover, speculation about how the baby boomer generations will behave, a favourite topic for quiet news periods, is invariably misplaced. First of all the boomer generations share some similarities but are also heterogeneous in terms of income and wealth, education, gender, ethnicity, and political consciousness. Secondly such speculations

usually display 'cohort centrism' which overemphasizes the uniqueness of the generation in question and its internal characteristics while downplaying both the structural
context and the ageing process itself (Riley 1992).

Looking forward and without indulging in speculation there are two critical political questions that are likely to influence generational relations and may, possibly,
destabilize them. On the one hand there is the issue of the distribution of resources
between the generations. In the past the welfare state has been managed as an efficient
system of horizontal distribution that has, more or less, retained parity between
generations (thus each generation has got out of the social contract what it put
into it (Hills 1996)). However the neoliberal inspired individualization of welfare
responsibility and reduction in the scope of the welfare state threatens this balance.
Put simply, if younger contributors face the prospect of little or no pension in retirement they may reasonably question their support for older generations. The UK was
very forward in adopting neoliberal policy prescriptions but it has been backward in
realizing the dangers inherent in the individualization of the social. To head off any
potential risks on this score is straightforward in social policy terms, if challenging
politically. It would mean reasserting the social contract and the importance of the
BP, combating child poverty, progressively raising the level of the minimum wage,
encouraging the extension of working life, and ending age discrimination.

On the other hand there is always a chance that politicians will talk the country into
generational conflict. Thus the unrecognized downside of heady political rhetoric
about dependency ratios and the 'burden' of pensions (which implies the burden
of older people) is that it will be taken seriously. The intelligent way to avoid such
dangers is to encourage an open, evidence-based debate about generational relations.
This would emphasize their fundamental importance to society and social cohesion,
encourage generational harmony, and subject all policies to a generational impact
audit (as happens in Austria). Gradually this sort of approach would move towards an
open discussion of generational distribution and, perhaps, even a reform of the social
contract in which all generations can expect equal shares. The idea of a prudential
lifespan account is only one of several possibilities (Daniels 1998).

36.7 CONCLUSION

This chapter has explored the relationship between ageing and politics and emphasized flux at all levels of society. Despite the signs of growing political participation,
it concluded that the barriers to it remain formidable and that the notion of 'grey
power' is far-fetched. The final main section consisted of some reflections on the risks
of generational conflicts and how to avoid them. While the future politics of ageing
and generations is unknown the key reference point is social policy. In other words,

the future politics of ageing and generations depends a great deal on how the politics of welfare develops in the coming decades.

Assuming the continued dominance of the neoliberal consensus, there are likely to be conflicts between the organized pensioners' groups and whichever of the two major political parties is in power. The present Labour government has promised to restore the link between the BP and average earnings but this is not likely to happen until 2012 with no back-dating. This will perpetuate the relatively high proportion of British pensioners on low incomes, compared with many of their European counterparts, and maintain the momentum of campaigning on this front. The collapse of the occupational pension system, which was the main source of affluence in old age and has marked one of the major income divisions among older people for the past thirty years, and the continuing inequality in pension entitlements between men and women, will increase the political focus on the BP. Because of the low level of the BP in comparative terms a concerted policy to extend working life would offset concerns with regard to its sustainability (Aspalter and Walker 2008). It is possible that this sort of strategy would enable the BP to be raised, thereby lifting many older people out of the means-tested pension credit system without running any electoral risks. The other major terrain of conflict is likely to be long-term care because the need for care in advanced old age is rising as a result of longevity and the present means-tested system is intruding increasingly into the sensitive area of property inheritance.

It is likely too that, rather than a conflict between young and old (assuming that politicians realize the dangers in time), greater differences will emerge between those within the older population, as the relatively affluent group in the third age pursues its own hedonistic interest, including full or partial location abroad (Warnes 2006), and the frail and dependent group within the oldest old remains heavily reliant on the welfare state. There will undoubtedly be some further dynamic polarization of interests in this direction but it should not be regarded as a simple fault line because of the diversity of both groups and their common interests, such as the NHS, taxation, and the fact that the main family carers for the fourth age are in the third one. Nonetheless the relatively affluent part of the third age, baby boomers, are likely to continue to redefine early 'old' age in their own image. Whether this development has any political salience, at the moment, is a matter of speculation.

REFERENCES

ALBER, J. 1995. 'The Social Integration of Older People in Germany'. Pp. 111–62 in A. Walker (ed.), *Older People in Europe: Social Integration*. Brussels: EC, DG5.

ALMOND, G. A., and VERBA, S. 1963. *The Civic Culture*. Princeton, NJ: Princeton University Press.

ARBER, S., and GINN, J. 1991. *Gender and Later Life: A Sociological Analysis of Resources and Constraints*. London: Sage.

ASPALTER, C., and WALKER, A. (eds.) 2008. *Securing the Future for Old Age in Europe*. Hong Kong: Casa Verde.

BARNES, M., and WALKER, A. 1996. 'Consumerism versus Empowerment: A Principled Approach to the Involvement of Older Service Users'. *Policy and Politics*, 24/4: 375–93.

BINSTOCK, R. H. 1997. 'The 1996 Election: Older Voters and Implications for Policies on Aging'. *Gerontologist*, 37: 15–19.

—— 2000. 'Older People and Voting Participation: Past and Future'. *Gerontologist*, 40: 18–31.

—— 2005a. 'The Contemporary Politics of Old-Age Policies'. In R. B. Hudson (ed.), *The New Politics of Old Age Policies*. Baltimore: Johns Hopkins University Press.

—— 2005b. 'Older Voters and the 2004 Election'. *Gerontologist*; 46: 382–4.

—— and DAY, C. 1996. 'Aging and Politics'. Pp. 362–87 in R. H. Binstock and L. George (eds.), *Handbook of Aging and Social Sciences*, 4th edn. London: Academic Press.

BLACKBURN, R. 2002. *Banking on Death*. London: Verso.

BROOK, P., HALL, J., and PRESTON, L. 1997. *What Drives Support for Higher Public Spending?* London: Institute for Fiscal Studies.

CALASANTI, T., and SLEVIN, K. 2001. *Gender, Social Inequalities and Aging*. Walnut Creek, Calif.: Alta Mira Press.

CAMPBELL, A. L. 2003. *How Policies Make Citizens: Senior Political Activism and the American Welfare State*. Princeton, NJ: Princeton University Press.

—— CONVERSE, P., MILLER, W., and STOKES, D. 1960. *The American Voter*. New York: Wiley.

CARTER, T., and NASH, C. 1992. *Pensioners Forums: An Active Voice*. Guildford: Pre-Retirement Association.

COOK, J., MALTBY, T., and WARREN, L. 2004. 'A Participatory Approach to Older Women's Quality of Life'. Pp. 149–66 in A. Walker and C. Hennessy (eds.), *Growing Older: Quality of Life in Old Age*. Buckingham: McGraw-Hill.

CUMMING, E., and HENRY, W. E. 1961. *Growing Old: The Process of Disengagement*. New York: Basic Books.

DANIELS, N. 1998. *Am I My Parents' Keeper?* New York: Oxford University Press.

DENCH, D., OGG, J., and THOMSON, K. 1999. 'The Role of Grandparents'. In R. Jowell, J. Curtis, A. Park, and K. Thomson (eds.), *British Social Attitudes*, 16th Report. Aldershot: Ashgate.

DOUGLAS, E. 1995. 'Professional Organisations in Aging: Too Many Doing too Little for too Few'. *Generations*, 19/2: 35–6.

ESPING-ANDERSEN, G. 1990. *The Three Worlds of Welfare Capitalism*. Oxford: Polity.

ESTES, C. L. 1982. 'Austerity and Aging in the US'. *International Journal of Health Services*, 12/4: 573–84.

—— 2004. 'Social Security Privatization and Older Women: A Feminist Political Economy Perspective'. *Journal of Aging Studies*, 18: 9–26.

—— BIGGS, S., and PHILLIPSON, C. 2003. *Social Theory, Social Policy and Ageing: A Critical Introduction*. Maidenhead: Open University Press.

—— and PHILLIPSON, C. 2002. 'The Globalisation of Capital, the Welfare State and Old Age Policy'. *International Journal of Health Services*, 32/2: 279–97.

—— et al. 2001. *Social Policy and Aging*. London: Sage.

EVANDROU, M. (ed.) 1997. *Baby Boomers: Ageing in the 21st Century*. London: Age Concern England.

GAMBLE, A. 1986. *The Free Economy and the Strong State*. Houndmills: Macmillan.

GILLEARD, C., and HIGGS, P. 2000. *Cultures of Ageing*. Harlow: Prentice Hall.

GINN, J. 2003. *Gender, Pensions and the Lifecourse*. Bristol: Policy Press.

HARVEY, D. 1989. *The Condition of Postmodernity*. Oxford: Blackwell.

HENDRICKS, J. 2004. 'Public Policies and Old Age Identity'. *Journal of Aging Studies*, 18: 245–60.

HILLS, J. 1996. 'Does Britain Have a Welfare Generation?' Pp. 56–80 in A. Walker (ed.), *The New Generational Contract*. London: UCL Press.

——and LELKES, O. 1999. *Social Security, Redistribution and Public Opinion*. CASE Brief 14, London School of Economics.

HUBER, J., and SKIDMORE, P. 2003. *The New Old*. London: Demos.

HUDSON, R. B. 1980. 'Old Age Politics in a Period of Change'. Pp. 147–89 in N. G. McCluskey and E. F. Borgatta (eds.), *Aging and Society*. London: Sage.

——and STRATE, J. 1985. 'Aging and Political Systems'. Pp. 554–85 in R. H. Binstock and E. Shanas (eds.), *Handbook of Aging and the Social Sciences*, 2nd edn. New York: Van Nostrand Reinhold.

International Institute for Democracy and Electoral Assistance (IDEA) 1999. *Youth Voter Participation*. Stockholm: International IDEA.

JACKSON, R., and HOWE, N. 2008. *The Graying of the Great Powers*. Washington, DC: Centre for Strategic and International Studies.

JENKINS, J. C., and KLANDERMANS, B. (eds.) 1995. *The Politics of Social Protest*. London: UCL Press.

KORPI, W. 1983. *The Democratic Class Struggle*. London: Routledge.

MacMANUS, S. A. 1996. *Young v. Old: Generational Combat in the 21st Century*. Boulder, Colo.: Westview.

MALTBY, T., and ROHLEDER, C. 2008. 'Societal and Political Participation'. In G. Naegele and A. Walker (eds.), *Ageing and Social Policy in Germany and the UK*. Houndmills: Palgrave.

MARSHALL, V., COOK, F., and MARSHALL J. 1993. 'Conflict over Intergenerational Equity: Rhetoric and Reality in a Comparative Context'. Pp. 119–40 in V. Bengtson and W. A. Achenbaum (eds.), *The Changing Contract across Generations*. New York: Aldine.

MILLS, C. W. 1970. *The Sociological Imagination*. Harmondsworth: Penguin.

MINKLER, M., and ROBERTSON, A. 1991. 'The Ideology of Age/Race Wars: Deconstructing a Social Problem'. *Ageing and Society*, 11: 1–23.

O'CONNOR, J. 1977. *The Fiscal Crisis of the State*. London: St Martin's Press.

OECD (Organization for Economic Cooperation and Development) 1988a. *Reforming Public Pensions*. Paris: OECD.

——1988b. *Ageing Populations: The Social Policy Implications*. Paris: OECD.

——1994. *New Orientations for Social Policy*. Paris: OECD.

——1998. *Maintaining Prosperity in an Ageing Society*. Paris: OECD.

PALME, J. 1990. *Pension Rights in Welfare Capitalism*. Stockholm: Swedish Institute for Social Research.

PETERSON, S., and SOMIT, A. 1994. *Political Behavior of Older Americans*. New York: Garland.

PINTOR, R., and GRATSCHEW, M. 2002. *Voter Turnout since 1945: A Global Report*. Stockholm: International Institute for Democracy and Electoral Assistance.

POTRATZ, W., GROSS, T., and HILBERT, J. 2009. 'The Silver Economy: Purchasing Power and the Quest for Quality of Life'. Pp. 82–105 in A. Walker and G. Naegele (eds.), *Social Policy in Ageing Societies*. Houndmills: Palgrave.

QUADAGNO, J. 1982. *Aging in Early Industrial Society: Work, Family and Social Policy in Nineteenth Century England*. New York: Academic Press.

——1989. 'Generational Equity and the Politics of the Welfare State'. *Politics and Society*, 17: 353–76.

REDAY-MULVEY, G. 2005. *Working beyond 60*. Houndmills: Palgrave.

RILEY, M. 1992. 'Cohort Perspectives'. Pp. 52–65 in E. Borgatta and M. Borgatta (eds.), *The Encyclopedia of Social Sciences*. New York: Macmillan.

SCHARF, T., PHILLIPSON, C., and SMITH, A. E. 2004. 'Poverty and Social Exclusion: Growing Older in Deprived Urban Neighbourhoods'. In A. Walker and C. Hennessy (eds.), *Growing Older: Quality of Life in Old Age*. Buckingham: McGraw-Hill.

STREET, D. 1999. 'Special Interests or Citizens' Rights? "Senior Power," Social Security, and Medicare'. Pp. 109–30 in M. Minkler and C. Estes (eds.), *Critical Gerontology: Perspectives from Political and Moral Economy*. Amityville, NY: Baywood.

TOWNSEND, P. 1981. 'The Structured Dependency of the Elderly: The Creation of Social Policy in the Twentieth Century'. *Ageing and Society*, 1/1: 5–28.

——1986. 'Ageism and Social Policy'. Pp. 15–44 in C. Phillipson and A. Walker (eds.), *Ageing and Social Policy*. Aldershot: Gower.

TURNER, M., SHIELDS, T., and SHARP, D. 2001. 'Changes and Continuities in the Determinants of Older Adults: Voter Turnout 1952–1996'. *Gerontologist*, 41: 805–18.

VERBA, S., SCHLOZMAN, K., and BRADY, H. 1995. *Voice and Equality: Civic Voluntarism in American Politics*. Cambridge, Mass.: Harvard University Press.

VINCENT, J. 1996. 'Who's Afraid of an Ageing Population? Nationalism, the Free Market and the Construction of Old Age as an Issue'. *Critical Social Policy*, 16: 3–26.

WALKER, A. 1980. 'The Social Creation of Poverty and Dependency in Old Age'. *Journal of Social Policy*, 9/1: 45–75.

——1981. 'Towards a Political Economy of Old Age'. *Ageing and Society*, 1/1: 73–94.

——1984. 'The Political Economy of Privatisation'. Pp. 19–44 in J. Le Grand and R. Robinson (eds.), *Privatisation and the Welfare State*. London: Allen and Unwin.

——1986. 'The Politics of Ageing in Britain'. Pp. 30–45 in C. Phillipson, M. Bernard, and P. Strong (eds.), *Dependency and Interdependency in Old Age: Theoretical Perspective and Policy Alternatives*. London: Croom Helm.

——1990. 'The Economic "Burden" of Ageing and the Prospect of Intergenerational Conflict'. *Ageing and Society*, 10/4: 377–96.

——1991. 'Thatcherism and the New Politics of Old Age'. Pp. 19–36 in J. Myles and J. Quadagno (eds.), *States, Labor Markets and the Future of Old Age Policy*. Philadelphia: Temple University Press.

——1993. 'Poverty and Inequality in Old Age'. Pp. 280–303 in J. Bond, P. Coleman, and S. Peace (eds.), *Ageing in Society*, 2nd edn. London: Sage.

——1998. 'Speaking for Themselves: The New Politics of Old Age in Europe'. *Education and Ageing*, 13/1: 5–12.

——1999. 'Public Policy and Theories of Aging: Constructing and Reconstructing Old Age'. Pp. 361–78 in V. Bengston and K. W. Schaie (eds.), *Handbook of Theories of Ageing*. New York: Springer.

——2005. 'The Political Economy of Ageing Revisited: Understanding the Structure/Agency Tension'. In J. Baars, D. Dannefer, C. Phillipson, and A. Walker (eds.), *Aging, Globalisation and Inequality: The New Critical Gerontology*. Amityville, NY: Baywood.

——and DEACON, B. 2003. 'Economic Globalisation and Policies on Ageing'. *Journal of Societal and Social Policy*, 2/2: 1–18.

——and NAEGELE, G. (eds.) 1999. *The Politics of Old Age in Europe*. Buckingham: Open University Press.

——WALKER, C., and RYAN, T. 1996. 'Older People with Learning Difficulties Leaving Institutional Care: A Case of Double Jeopardy'. *Ageing and Society*, 16/2: 1–26.

WARNES, T. 2006. 'Older Foreign Migrants in Europe: Multiple Pathways and Welfare Positions'. Pp. 141–56 in S. O. Daatland and S. Biggs (eds.), *Ageing and Diversity*. Bristol: Policy Press.

WORLD BANK 1994. *Averting the Old Age Crisis*. New York: Oxford University Press.

YOUNG, K. 1984. 'Political Attitudes'. Pp. 11–46 in R. Jowell and D. Airy (eds.), *British Social Attitudes*. Aldershot: Gower.

CHAPTER 37

··

WELFARE REFORM

··

HOWARD GLENNERSTER

'WELFARE reform' was originally an American campaign slogan. In that context it had a restricted meaning—limiting assistance given to lone parents. The term was introduced into British politics by the Blair administration (Cm. 3805 1998, 'The Welfare Reform Green Paper'). It still had a rather restricted meaning, being largely concerned with social security payments to those of working age. Yet changes to the wider British welfare state in the last thirty years have been substantial. It is 'welfare reform' in this broader sense we discuss in this chapter. We begin by briefly reviewing political science writing about British social policy in the immediate post-war era in order to contrast it with the 'new politics of welfare' that some commentators see emerging internationally after the economic crises of the 1970s (Pierson 2001).

We examine how far such a description fits the British case. Our contention is that there is less that is new in British social politics than this literature suggests. We end with a comparison of welfare reform, in its narrower sense, in the USA and the UK to illustrate how different institutional traditions produce different responses to apparently similar social and economic changes.

37.1 THE OLD POLITICS OF WELFARE

···

The incremental growth of the post-war British welfare state first attracted political scientists' attention as a way to illustrate wider arguments.

As interest group politics became a fashionable topic writers turned their attention to social service producer interests—the British Medical Association, teachers' unions, and the construction interests that had helped shape public housing policy, for example (Eckstein 1955; Manzer 1970; Beer 1965; Dunleavy 1981). Later interpretations saw interest group power over the public sector as a cause of Britain's political malaise (Beer 1982).

The new 'politics of budgeting' (Wildavsky 1964) focused on reasons for the incremental growth of public spending, much of it on social policy (Heclo and Wildavsky 1974). However, there were frequent attempts to restrain that growth, especially given Britain's poor economic performance, even if they sometimes failed (Lowe 1989).

Other authors analysed the social policy process. Heclo (1974) produced an influential account of social policy-making in the UK and Sweden emphasizing the role academic and civil service elites played in analysing and responding to new political demands and failings in old institutions—'political learning'. Banting (1979) saw 'intellectual and institutional adaptation' as central. Social structures and poverty had not changed that much in the 1950s and 1960s, he argued, but attitudes to them, driven by changing knowledge and ideology, had.

There was interest in the battle for ideas within the Labour Party. Crosland (1956) sought a complete break with its partially Marxist traditions. He rejected public ownership as an end in itself and claimed that reducing social inequality was the true socialist goal. That was to be achieved in large part through social policy. Miliband (1961; 1969) saw Labour betrayed by such ideas. In the end, the revisionists won. Social policy became central to Labour's electoral appeal. Indeed, it became central to British politics.

Most successful social policy ideas in the post-war period had been Fabian Socialist, or at least Liberal, in origin. The Institute of Economic Affairs, founded in 1955 to advance market solutions and challenge the growth of the state, began to revive thinking about alternatives to the post-war welfare institutions—an end to rent control, more private provision of pensions, health care, and education (Cockett 1995). These ideas made little immediate headway, except on relaxing rent control. The big welfare structures erected between 1944 and 1949 remained intact. Then, the economic turmoil of the 1970s resulted in the UK's humiliating petition for help from the IMF in 1976. This produced a more advantageous climate in which such ideas could take root, just as the Second World War had been advantageous to ideas of state collectivism.

37.2 A NEW POLITICS OF WELFARE?

Pierson (2001) and his fellow contributors' contention was that all welfare states had entered an era of 'permanent austerity' after the 1970s, despite their resilience he had noted in an earlier study (Pierson 1994). Global economic pressures would force changes of three kinds:

- 'Re-commodification' (Esping-Andersen 1990; 1996)—or moves to back to more market-driven welfare entitlements;
- Cost containment—cutting back generous pay-as-you-go state pensions and other cuts;
- Recalibration—reforming institutions to make them more effective in responding to social change.

I shall argue that these predictions do not entirely fit the British case. Where they do, as in the final case, such a process is not new.

37.2.1 Re-commodification?

It is certainly true that in the 1980s, during Mrs Thatcher's administration, a series of initiatives were taken that do fit this description. The more generous wage-related sickness and unemployment benefits, introduced in the 1960s, were repealed. The purpose was to make living on state benefits less attractive and hence prompt an earlier return to work. It is these measures that were picked out in an international study of welfare state reform (Korpi and Palme 2003) to suggest that the UK had moved furthest in a 'de-commodified' direction. In fact, the benefits chosen for illustrative purposes in this study constituted less than 4 per cent of UK social security spending but the story could be said to hold for other benefits too. The more generous wage-related state pension scheme, only added as a supplement to the old post-war pension scheme in the late 1970s, was cut back in the mid-1980s and big tax inducements were given to employees to opt out and join private schemes. The aim, endorsed by the Blair government, was to make private pensions the prime source of income in old age. Most important, the basic state pension, which had been raised in line with earnings since the 1950s, was linked only to prices after the early 1980s. This steadily reduced the basic state pension relative to the incomes of the wider working population. So far, the predictions might be said to hold. However, important elements in recent British social policy have worked in the opposite direction.

The fastest recent (post-1999) increases in spending have been on *universal* services like health and education where access is based on a test of residence not even formal citizenship. The National Health Service's share of GDP rose from 5.8 per cent in 1998 to nearly 9 per cent in 2008—a larger increase than had occurred in the fifty previous years of its existence. Competition-based reforms in health and education derived, in part, from an attempt to make these services more responsive to consumers and less to the interests of producers. Probably the most significant extension of the British welfare state since 1948 has been the wider access to childcare. We discuss these changes later. None fit the rather ugly term 'de-commodification'. None would have been possible without the relative success of the UK economy since the mid-1990s—something that eluded it in the period of the old politics of welfare.

37.2.2 Cuts in Pay-as-you-go State Pensions?

It is certainly true that almost all Continental European pension schemes have been reduced in generosity for *future* recipients during the last decade. In Sweden, Germany, Italy, and even France long negotiations between political parties, unions, and employers have led to major reductions in pension entitlements (Fenge and Werding 2004). The United Kingdom never had had a generous state pension. The brief attempt to build one on a continental model by the 1975 Labour government was dismantled by Mrs Thatcher in the 1980s. State pension income has been the lowest of any major advanced economy (Pensions Commission 2004). The historical reasons for this situation are discussed in the volume by Pemberton, Thane, and Whiteside (2007).

Uniquely, the UK has relied on individuals' *voluntary* membership of occupational and private pension schemes, underpinned by means-tested additions to a very low flat-rate state pension. This whole strategy was predicated on the continued success of occupational pension schemes. But they were beset by some of the same problems that faced generous public schemes in other countries—rising expectation of life, too generous promises given in better times, and high labour costs resulting from the need to fund accumulating pension rights. Private firms began to close their defined benefit pension schemes to new entrants and reduce their contributions to any new defined contribution schemes they offered.

In the absence of improving private provision and with declining public pensions, three-quarters of the population could have expected, by mid-century, to be dependent on means-tested public support (Pensions Commission 2005). This would have made private pension saving even less attractive. An important, and growing, section of the electorate faced a bleak pension future. So, too, did the public finances that would have to pick up the pieces.

Pensions became of major political importance again. The voluntary private market solution favoured by both major parties had failed. Government turned to an old political strategy, largely discarded since Mrs Thatcher's time, a commission of inquiry.

The Pensions Commission (2004; 2005) produced two reports which were highly critical of past policies and contained some of the best policy analysis in any public document since the Second World War. The Commission pointed out that the share of adult life spent in retirement had risen steadily since 1948 and could not go on rising without taxes and pension contributions having to rise steadily too, something no party was advocating. By spelling out the realities it managed to get all political parties to sign up to the proposition that the age at which a full state pension should be received should rise in line with life expectancy. In return the basic state pension should be increased enough to free most people from pension means testing. It did not seek to abandon the UK's post-war path in pension policy, which gave a large role to private funded pensions. But it did increase the role of the state in making them work. All employees would be expected to pay into a national savings scheme if they were not part of a good employer's pension scheme. They could take steps to exclude themselves but if they did not their contributions, together with matching funds required from their employers with state help, would be placed in a personal account held nationally. The holder would choose into which state-approved private scheme his or her funds will be placed. Nearly all of the recommendations were accepted by government (Cm. 6841 2006; Cm. 6975 2006). Legislation to enact them was passed in 2007.

This reform built on the UK's pension past but it was also a major policy innovation. It involved a significant additional role for the state and took substantially more public money—about an extra 1 per cent of the GDP. It also won cross-party support largely lacking since the Second World War in this field of policy. An old political device had been used to build a new policy consensus. The policies of both major parties had collapsed. The alternative—to leave a majority of the deserving and growing elderly population dependent on means-tested handouts—was politically untenable.

The Commission incorporated recent findings from behavioural economics (Choi, Laibson, and Madrian 2004) which showed that most individuals do not act in their own long-term best interests when making financial decisions about the future. However, governments can use inertia to guide them to make advantageous long-term decisions—assuming government gets those default choices right!

Thus, it its true that throughout Europe governments have been adapting their pension schemes to fit demographic and fiscal reality. In every case this has entailed *reducing* the state's previous commitments. In the UK the reverse has happened. Both state spending and the state's role in regulating the private pension market have grown. The Swedish and German reforms do, however, share some of the same elements—raising pension ages in line with growing life expectancy and encouraging, or requiring, private savings to be invested in schemes of the individual's choice. The last element has been taken furthest in the UK reforms.

37.2.3 Recalibration and Response to Social Change?

37.2.3.1 *Family–Work Life Balance*

We have just seen how the British welfare state has had to adapt pension policy to an ageing population and to private market failure. Aside from ageing, one of the most important social changes in British society, as in others, over the past forty years has been the extended roles played by women and the tensions families face in balancing home and work. Yet, for a long time, neither public services nor social policy more generally took much account of this phenomenon. Britain continued to provide minimal childcare facilities while Scandinavian and French governments expanded theirs. Extensive childcare provision had been provided during the Second World War and dismantled immediately after. Such provision had been opposed by trade unions as endangering male jobs and by Conservatives as invading women's natural roles (Blackstone 1971). Schools were open only part of the day and provided no support for working parents. Childcare provision was the responsibility of social services departments in local authorities, education the responsibility of another department. British institutional history seemed set against any significant change. Political attitudes to the family and women's roles were very slow to respond to changing social reality (Lewis 2000). It was a gap New Labour sought to exploit in attracting back women's votes, though it did so very cautiously so as not to offend too many traditionalists. As Lewis and Campbell (2007) have argued, the Labour government, from 1997 on, did introduce a steady stream of incremental changes to existing practice—'policy instruments' as Hall (1993) calls them—which together add up to a significant change of policy direction (Streeck and Thalen 2005). Entry to formal nursery schooling was extended from the age of five to begin at three years old. Earlier and more extensive childcare and family services were provided in poor areas. Then, in 2007, the government embarked on a programme that would provide every child with care or education from eight in the morning to six at night from an early age for those who chose it, mostly based on extended provision attached to schools. This programme was the result of interdepartmental collaboration led by the Treasury (2004). Parental leave was extended and family working time regulations introduced. The overall outcome has been to move the UK much nearer to family policy models established in Scandinavia and France. It amounts to the biggest extension of universal welfare provision since 1948, and a significant response to a major social change.

37.2.3.2 A Widening Gap Between Rich and Poor

Another major social change produced a less successful response—the widening gap that opened up from the late 1970s between the incomes of the top and bottom income groups. During the next quarter of a century the UK moved from being one of the more equal of the advanced economies to one of the most unequal in terms of income, nearly matching the inequality found in the USA. The fundamental causes, shared with other advanced economies, lay in changing technology and the impact of the global economy on the demand for low-skilled labour. But in the UK these causes were exacerbated by the deliberate reductions in social benefits discussed earlier (Hills 2004).

By the mid-1990s inequality rose to near the top of voters' concerns indicated by public opinion polling. No less than 87 per cent of respondents in a national public attitude survey agreed the gap was 'too wide'. This was highest since the early 1980s (Hills 2004: 32–6). New Labour asked to be judged on the extent to which it could reverse these trends (Mandelson 1997). Pledges to abolish child poverty in a generation (Blair 1999) and to reduce pensioner poverty were followed by higher benefits targeted on poor families and the poor elderly. But there were also structural changes to the benefits system that merged the administration of benefits with that of tax collection. This was not helpful to those numerous families whose circumstances changed rapidly (Hills, Smithies, and McKnight 2006).

Though some progress was made in reducing levels of both child and pensioner poverty, overall levels of inequality shifted very little even if they did not go on rising (Hills and Stewart 2005; IFS 2007). Most voters were not prepared to see taxes rise substantially. Where they were prepared to see small increases it was to finance services most people used—health and education—not cash benefits for those out of work (Taylor-Gooby and Hastie 2002). Labour politicians, scared by their experiences in the 1980s, concluded they could not afford to raise the top levels of tax. After a decade in power Labour was unable to show it could reverse the big shift to inequality that had occurred. This raised deep questions about the core case for social democracy advanced by Crosland a half-century before. Not even Sweden has managed to completely stem the widening of income distribution since the 1980s (Brandolini and Smeeding 2007). Though the scale of welfare state redistribution has increased since the Second World War, it has been outpaced by growing inequality in the marketplace (Glennerster 2007: 269–72).

37.2.3.3 *Consumer Interests and the Role of Ideas*

The climate of ideas and the experiences that had influenced the post-Second World War welfare state were changing. The scale of the economic crisis in the 1970s made politicians of both major parties question them as they had not done since the 1940s and early 1950s. Economic crisis was seen not just as a random external shock. The view that the welfare state had been a cause of the UK's economic decline gained ground (Bacon and Eltis 1976). In the wake of the IMF visit the Labour government stabilized public spending and introduced more powerful controls over it (Wright 1980). For the new Conservative government in 1979 high public spending was seen as the *main* culprit—'at the heart of Britain's economic difficulties' (Cmnd. 7746 1979). As the economic crisis passed and new political demands arose public spending constraints eased. But those ideas that challenged the role of the state in delivering welfare services were to have a lasting impact. In preparing for their third election victory in 1987 the Conservatives presented plans to reform schooling, higher education, housing, and, after the election, health and social care for the elderly.

The underlying principle for all these reforms was that consumers should continue to have access to free services, or in the case of the elderly, means-tested ones, but that schools, hospitals, and old people's homes should compete either for an individual's state-financed custom or for that of a local purchasing agency. None of these ideas were new. Many had been trailed, for example, by the Institute of Economic Affairs since the 1960s, drawing heavily on Milton Friedman (1962). Now they were taken seriously, modified, and legislated.

The Institute for Contemporary History in London brought together senior civil servants who had been in post during that period. It was clear from their accounts (Centre for Contemporary British History 2007) that the driving force initially was a desire to find ways of containing their departments' long-term budgets. If the productivity of these services could be improved this would provide some relief to demands for more public expenditure. The reasons for poor performance lay, in part, in the power of providers over users. Such power could be challenged by competition. These ideas were taken up with a different set of motivations by the New Labour government after 1997. Only if services were seen to be delivering quality improvements would voters be prepared to go on voting more money. Improving public service efficiency and shifting more power into the hands of service users also tapped into an old strand of social democratic thought dating from the 1930s which feared that undue producer power exercised in monopoly public services would cripple their efficiency. Competition between public providers was the solution (Durbin 1949; Brooke 1996; Le Grand and Estrin 1989; Le Grand 2003).

Thus, right- and left-wing traditions overlapped enough for these ideas to influence both administrations. How to run welfare services more efficiently, more responsive to users' needs, has became the centre ground on which the main parties are now fighting.

In short, the British welfare state has gone on expanding, though at a slower rate than before 1976, just as most other welfare states have (Castles 2004). Major universal services have been expanded and others extended. The state has expanded its role in providing and regulating pensions while keeping the large role played by private funded schemes. It has responded to some major social changes and not merely remained static in the face of them, as critics argue has happened particularly in the USA (Orloff 2004; Hacker 2005). It has not been able to reverse the trend to greater inequality.

So far, though, none of the policy examples we have cited cover 'welfare reform' in the American sense. A comparison is instructive.

37.3 WELFARE REFORM US AND UK STYLE

37.3.1 The US Case

Until recently, 'welfare' referred to one particular federal programme—Aid for Families with Dependent Children (AFDC). It had originated as a Federal programme in the Roosevelt era as Aid to Dependent Children supporting children in families with no 'breadwinner', normally as a result of widowhood. As a tiny programme for the deserving poor it raised little political interest. The New Deal had established a contributory Federal pension scheme and state-run unemployment insurance but public assistance was left to the states to administer. The southern Democrats would not allow a national safety net that could include blacks (Skocpol 1995: 218–19).

In 1962 as part of Kennedy's poverty programme the scheme gave money to mothers as well as the children. It began to become the target of popular criticism for several reasons:

- The substantial growth in the number of lone parent households.
- 'Welfare mothers' were seen as 'a suspect social class, living apart from middle class norms regarding marriage and child bearing' (Brodkin 2006).

- Though numerically most recipients were not black the common perception was that they were.
- It was a trend many felt had been encouraged by the welfare system (Murray 1984).
- Costs tripled between 1965 and 1970 making the programme a target for any party or President trying to reduce taxes.

Several attempts were made to contain the growth of welfare roles from President Nixon's time on (King 1996). His Family Assistance Plan, essentially a national negative income tax scheme, was defeated in the Senate Finance Committee dominated by southern Democrats who were convinced work incentives would be undermined. Various programmes to encourage work through training and support did get legislated but proved very ineffective. President Carter tried again, giving more emphasis to training and creating public service jobs. But fears about perverse incentives, lack of harsh enough penalties to satisfy the right, and low minimum income guarantees that did not satisfy the left, helped defeat the plan. Above all the old regional divisions between members from the north and the south in Congress persisted (King 1996).

Reagan's administration had also set about reducing claims on welfare first by tightening eligibility rules. The Family Support Act 1988 required states to help mothers into work in a variety of ways such as training, transport, and childcare. However, it was the federal government's strategy of permitting states to try tougher methods, including caps on the time recipients could be on welfare, that really began to move the debate and local practice.

This gave Clinton the chance to turn welfare into a federal campaign issue. He embraced 'welfare reform' in his bid for the centre ground. In his original presidential campaign he used the slogan 'ending welfare as we know it' to distinguish himself from the old 'tax and spend' Democratic Party. Research by liberal academics (Ellwood and Bane 1986) had suggested that mothers, children, and taxpayers would benefit if sufficient inducements could be introduced to get them back into work including adequate childcare, health care, and tax-subsidized low wages. This gave Clinton the intellectual basis for a break with the old Democratic past and gave an opening for some kind of cross-party agreement and agenda change (Weaver 2000). Many American liberals and feminists saw Ellwood's (1988) support for work requirements as a betrayal of poor mothers (Orloff 2001).

However, Clinton's strategy and American ideas clearly influenced Blair and Brown (Deacon 2002). Welfare reform could be used to help distinguish New from 'old' Labour and much of the language and ideas found their way into New Labour policy (King and Wickham-Jones 1999).

37.3.2 The British Case

What was common to both countries was the rise in the scale of lone parenthood and the belief that benefit policy had helped bring this about. The USA and the

UK had more lone parent families than most Western nations and had seen the fastest growth (Kiernan, Land, and Lewis 1998). One of Blair's first acts in 1997 was to adopt Conservative plans to abolish the lone parent premium—a higher benefit introduced by a previous Labour government. He accepted the Conservative case that this was a perverse incentive that encouraged lone parenthood. To abolish it would emphasize the 'new' in New Labour. So far a parallel can be drawn with the US story. Yet, despite the similarity in political slogans and social phenomena, the institutional histories of welfare provision in Britain were very different.

What had emerged after the Second World War in the UK was a nationally administered and financed safety net (National Assistance) which may have been set low but did include all citizens in need and for the most part catered for older people—the deserving poor—not as in the USA, a stigmatized minority. This universally available safety net had always been balanced by a requirement that recipients seek work or face penalties. The 1948 National Assistance Act regulations and those of its successor the Supplementary Benefit Commission were tough. Unemployment Review Officers reviewed the cases of those out of work for six months in the case of older workers and three months for younger people under forty-five. They could call on medical advice. If convinced someone was not seeking work they could prosecute. Such a person could have their benefits reduced, be prosecuted, fined, put on probation or in prison (Cmnd. 6615 1976). Others could be sent to 'Re-establishment Centres' to recover the work habit and train for a new occupation. Thus, conditions had always been applied to the receipt of assistance for most of those of working age. They had become impossible to *enforce* during the years of very high unemployment in the Thatcher era.

By the 1990s the prime political concern in the UK was with high *male* unemployment, especially of young people. Layard (1997), asked to advise the incoming Labour government, argued that what distinguished the UK from its European neighbours was the scale of long-term unemployment. This was not just costly but made it very difficult to control inflation. The reasons lay, it was argued, in the newly lax administration of benefits. This situation had arisen not from any very clear policy design but from the very difficulty of requiring recipients to seek work when there had been large-scale unemployment in the 1980s. Much of the reform effort was thus directed at the long-term unemployed and the young—quite different targets from those of the USA.

In the case of lone parents the tougher strategy was to backfire. The public assistance rules set after the Second World War reflected the view that the child's best interests were served by the mother being at home, whoever she was (Lewis 2002). The idea of forcing women with young children into the labour force affronted much conservative as well as liberal opinion. The proposal to abolish the lone parent premium in the first months of Blair's term caused the biggest Labour backbench revolt since opposition to the IMF-imposed spending cuts in 1976. From then on Blair and Brown trod very carefully. New rules required the parent, usually the mother, to attend a work-related interview as the child neared five and she was advised about paid work possibilities. If job prospects were poor she would be advised about ways to improve her work opportunities—training, considering a different range of jobs, information about job-related benefits, or arrangements for childcare. There were no threats or sanctions, merely advice. Such a parent was assigned a personal adviser like all the other categories of benefit recipients under the reforms. This advice was widely appreciated and the results, though not dramatic, were worth it in cost–benefit terms (McKnight 2000; Gregg and Harkness 2003).

The age at which such interviews were required was steadily reduced and their frequency grew. In Labour's third term the strategy sharpened markedly (Cm. 7130, 2007). From October 2008 lone parents whose youngest child is over twelve were longer entitled to income support. They may become eligible for a Jobseekers Allowance and hence job search requirements. From 2010 that age will fall to seven. Even that will be older than the benefit rules in almost all other OECD countries.

The more positive side of the policy meant that low-income families in work have had those incomes raised by a tax credit partly modelled on the US earned income tax credit scheme and by a minimum wage.

Numbers of lone parents on benefit fell from nearly a million in 1997 to 775,000 in 2007. That was nothing like the halving in welfare roles that had occurred in the USA (Haskins 2006). Much more worrying to the Treasury was the larger and rising numbers of those on long-term sickness benefits (Nickell and Quintini 2002). The government tightened the rules for gaining invalidity benefit, newly named the Employment and Support Allowance. It involves stricter medical tests, help back into work for those who can work, and more money for those who are unable to work again. These changes took effect in 2008.

Waldfogel (2007) has compared the outcomes of the two reform strategies as they affected families. Reductions in child poverty occurred in both countries but to a larger extent in the UK. In the USA such reductions as there were came about as a result of increases in paid work. In the UK the reduction in poverty was primarily the result of higher benefits. In the USA higher lone parent family incomes went very largely in meeting the costs of work—travel, childcare, mothers' clothing—and were not spent on the children. In the UK most of the higher income was spent on child-related features of the family budget—children's clothing, toys, fruit and vegetables, books, and magazines.

Critics argue that US-style welfare reform sprang from a misdiagnosed problem and a false solution foisted on a weak section of the population by powerful economic interests, male politicians, and a racially prejudiced electorate. The lone parent 'problem' was misdiagnosed because the definition of work was limited to the formal labour market. It ignored the crucial contribution of women in producing and educating healthy future citizens (Pateman 2005). Welfare reform ought to involve an as-of-right citizen's income, at least for mothers. This would enable mothers who wished to stay at home to bring up their children if they so wished regardless of their married status. There is limited political support for this view in either country, at least for the present.

37.4 WHAT IS NEW?

We have argued that the history of the past thirty years has not produced an entirely 'new politics' of welfare. It has not been a story of declining expenditure or even of declining state responsibility. Changes have taken place in the nature of state involvement as society has changed. Consumers have become more concerned with quality and responsiveness. This has all made the management of state welfare services more demanding. But a process of political learning, the interaction between ideas generated by academic and political elites, vocal user interests, and the resistance of professional providers have continued. Policy *is* importantly affected by the historical legacy of our institutions, as we can see in the comparison of American and British interpretations of 'welfare reform'.

REFERENCES

BACON, R., and ELTIS, W. 1976. *Britain's Economic Problem: Too Few Producers*. London: Macmillan.

BANTING, K. G. 1979. *Poverty, Politics and Policy: Britain in the 1960s*. London: Macmillan.

BEER, S. H. 1965. *Modern British Politics: A Study in Parties and Pressure Groups*. London: Faber.

—— 1982. *Britain against Itself: The Political Contradictions of Collectivism*. London: Faber.

BLACKSTONE, T. 1971. *A Fair Start: The Provision of Pre-school Education*. London: Allen Lane.

BLAIR, T. 1999. 'Beveridge Revisited: A Welfare State for the 21st Century'. Pp. 7–27 in R. Walker (ed.), *Ending Child Poverty: Popular Welfare in the 21st Century*. Bristol: Policy Press.

BRANDOLINI, A., and SMEEDING, T. M. 2007. 'Inequality Patterns in Western-Type Democracies: Cross-Country Differences and Time Changes'. Luxembourg Income Study Working Paper Series No. 458.

BRODKIN, E. Z. 2006. 'Does Good Politics make for Good Practice? Reflections on Welfare-to-Work in the US'. In G. Marsdon, P. Henman, and C. McDonald (eds.), *Refereed Conference Proceedings: The Politics and Practice of Welfare to Work*. Brisbane: Queensland University. www.uq.edu.au./swah/welfaretowork/Final/conferencepaperBrodkinfinal.pdf.

BROOKE, S. 1996. 'Reassessing a Labour Revisionist'. *Twentieth Century British History*, 7: 27–37.

CASTLES, F. C. 2004. *The Future of the Welfare State: Crisis Myths and Crisis Realities*. Oxford: Oxford University Press.

CENTRE FOR CONTEMPORARY BRITISH HISTORY 2007. *Consumerism and Choice in the Conservative Internal Market 1987–1992*. Oral History Programme. London: London University.

CHOI, J., LAIBSON, D., and MADRIAN, B. 2004. 'For Better for Worse: Default Effects and 401K Savings Behaviour'. Pp. 81–125 in D. Wise (ed.), *Perspectives in the Economics of Ageing*. Chicago: Chicago University Press.

CM. 3805 1998. *A New Contract for Welfare*. London: Stationery Office.

—— 6841 2006. *Security in Retirement: Towards a New Pensions System*. London: Stationery Office.

—— 6975 2006. *Personal Accounts: A New Way to Save*. London: Department for Work and Pensions.

CM. 7130 2007. *In Work Better Off: Next Steps to Full Employment*. London: Department of Work and Pensions.

CMND. 6615 1976. *Supplementary Commission Annual Report 1975*. London: HMSO.

——7746 1979. *The Government's Expenditure Plans 1980–81*. London: HMSO.

COCKETT, R. 1995. *Thinking the Unthinkable: Think Tanks and the Economic Counter Revolution 1931–83*. London: Fontana.

CROSLAND, C. A. R. 1956. *The Future of Socialism*. London: Jonathan Cape.

DEACON, A. 2002. *Perspectives on Welfare*. Buckingham: Open University Press.

DUNLEAVY, P. 1981. *The Politics of Mass Housing 1945–75: A Study of Corporate Power and Professional Influence in the Welfare State*. Oxford: Clarendon Press.

DURBIN, E. F. M. 1949. *Problems of Economic Planning*. London: Routledge and Kegan Paul.

ECKSTEIN, H. 1955. 'The Politics of the British Medical Association'. *Political Quarterly*, 36/4: 345–59.

ELLWOOD, D. T. 1988. *Poor Support: Poverty in the American Family*. New York: Basic Books.

——and BANE, M. J. 1986. 'Slipping into and out of Poverty: The Dynamics of Spells'. *Journal of Human Resources*, 21: 1–23.

ESPING-ANDERSEN, G. 1990. *The Three Worlds of Welfare Capitalism*. Cambridge: Polity.

——1996. *Welfare States in Transition*. Cambridge: Polity.

FENGE, R., and WERDING, M. 2004. 'Ageing and the Tax Implied in Public Pension Schemes: Simulations for OECD Countries'. *Fiscal Studies*, 55: 159–200.

FRIEDMAN, M. 1962. *Capitalism and Freedom*. Chicago: Chicago University Press.

GIORGI, G. 2005. 'The New Deal for Young People Five Years On'. *Fiscal Studies*, 26: 371–83.

GLENNERSTER, H. 2007. *British Social Policy: 1945 to the Present*. Oxford: Blackwell.

GREGG, P., and HARKNESS, S. 2003. 'Welfare Reform and the Employment of Lone Parents'. Pp. 98–115 in R. Dickens, P. Gregg, and J. Wadsworth (eds.), *The Labour Market under New Labour*. London: Palgrave.

HACKER, J. S. 2005. 'Policy Drift: The Hidden Politics of the US Welfare State Retrenchment'. In W. Streeck and K. Thelen (eds.), *Beyond Continuity*. Oxford: Oxford University Press.

HALL, P. 1993. 'Policy Paradigms, Social Learning and the State: The Case of Economic Policy-Making in Britain'. *Comparative Politics*, 25: 275–96.

HASKINS, R. 2006. *Work over Welfare: The Inside Story of the 1996 Welfare Reform Law*. Washington, DC: Brookings Institution.

HECLO, H. 1974. *Modern Social Politics in Britain and Sweden: From Relief to Income Maintenance*. New Haven, Conn.: Yale University Press.

——and WILDAVSKY, A. 1974. *The Private Government of Public Money*. London: Macmillan.

HILLS, J. 2004. *Inequality and the State*. Oxford: Oxford University Press.

INSTITUTE OF FISCAL STUDIES (IFS) 2007. *Poverty and Inequality in Britain: 2007*. IFS Briefing Notes BN 73. London: Institute of Fiscal Studies.

——SMITHIES, R., and MCKNIGHT, A. 2006 *Tracking Income: How Working Families' Incomes Vary Through the Year*. CASEreport 32. London: London School of Economics, CASE.

——and STEWART, K. 2005. *A More Equal Society? New Labour, Poverty and Inequality*. Bristol: Policy Press.

KIERNAN, K., LAND, H., and LEWIS, J. 1998. *Lone Motherhood in Twentieth Century Britain*. Oxford: Oxford University Press.

KING, D. 1995. *Actively Seeking Work*. Chicago: Chicago University Press.

——1996. 'Sectionalism and Policy Formation in the United States: President Carter's Welfare Initiatives'. *British Journal of Political Science*, 26: 337–67.

——and WICKHAM-JONES, M. 1999. 'From Clinton to Blair: The Democratic (Party) Origins of Welfare to Work'. *Political Quarterly*, 70: 62–74.

KORPI, W., and PALME, J. 2003. 'New Politics and Class Politics in the Context of Austerity and Globalisation: Welfare State Regress in 18 Countries, 1975–95'. *American Political Science Review*, 97: 425–46.

LAYARD, R. 1997. 'Preventing Long-Term Unemployment: An Economic Analysis'. Pp. 333–49 in D. J. Snower and G. de la Dehesa (eds.), *Unemployment Policy: Government Options for the Labour Market*. Cambridge: Cambridge University Press.

LE GRAND, J. 2003. *Motivation, Agency, and Public Policy: Of Knights and Knaves, Pawns and Queens*. Oxford: Oxford University Press.

——and ESTRIN, S. 1989. *Market Socialism*. Oxford: Clarendon Press.

LEWIS, J. 2000. 'Family Policy in the Post War Period'. Pp 81–100 in S. Katz, J. Eekaar, and M. Maclean (eds.), *Cross Currents: Family Law and Policy in the US and England*. Oxford: Oxford University Press.

——2002. 'Individualisation, Assumptions about the Existence of an Adult Worker Model and the Shift towards Contractualisation'. In A. Carling, S. Duncan, and R. Edwards (eds.), *Analysing Families*. London: Routledge.

——and CAMPBELL, M. 2007. 'Work/Family Balance Policies in the UK since 1997'. *Journal of Social Policy*, 36: 365–81.

LOWE, R. 1989. 'Resignation at the Treasury: The Social Services Committee and the Failure to Reform the Welfare State'. *Journal of Social Policy*, 18: 505–26.

McKNIGHT, A. 2000. 'Transitions off Income Support: Estimating the Impact of the New Deal for Lone Parents Using Administrative Data'. Pp 51–85 in C. Hasluck, A. McKnight, and P. Elias (eds.), *Evaluation of the New Deal for Lone Parents: Early Lessons—Cost Benefit and Econometric Analysis*. DSS Research Report No. 110. Leeds: Corporate Document Services.

MANDELSON, P. 1977. *Labour's Next Steps: Tackling Social Exclusion*. Fabian Pamphlet 58. London: Fabian Society.

MANZER, R. 1970. *Teachers and Politics*. Manchester: Manchester University Press.

MILIBAND, R. 1961. *Parliamentary Socialism*. London: Allen and Unwin.

——1969. *The State in Capitalist Society*. London: Weidenfeld and Nicolson.

MURRAY, C. 1984. *Losing Ground: American Social Policy 1950–1980*. New York: Basic Books.

NICKELL, S., and QUINTINI, G. 2002. 'The Recent Performance of the UK Labour Market'. *Oxford Review of Economic Policy*, 18: 202–20.

ORLOFF, A. S. 2001. 'Ending the Entitlement of Poor Mothers: Changing Social Policies, Women's Employment and Care Giving in the Contemporary United States'. Pp. 133–59 in N. Hirschman and U. Liebert (eds.), *Women and Welfare: Theory and Practice in the US and Europe*. New Brunswick, NJ: Rutgers Press.

——2004. 'Social Provision and Regulation: Theories of States, Social Policies, and Modernity'. Pp. 190–224 in J. Adams, E. Clemens, and A. S. Orloff (eds.), *Remaking Modernity: Politics, History and Modernity*. Durham, NC: Duke University Press.

PATEMAN, C. 2005. 'Another Way Forward: Welfare Social Reproduction and a Basic Income'. Pp. 34–64 in L. M. Mead and C. Beem (eds.), *Welfare Reform and Political Theory*. New York: Russell Sage.

PEMBERTON, H., THANE, P., and WHITESIDE, N. (eds.) 2007. *Britain's Pension Crisis: History and Policy*. Oxford: Oxford University Press and the British Academy.

PENSIONS COMMISSION 2004. *Pensions: Challenges and Choices. The First Report of the Pensions Commission*. London: Stationery Office.

——2005. *A New Pensions Settlement for the Twenty-First Century: Second Report of the Pensions Commission*. London: Stationery Office.

PIERSON, P. 1994. *Dismantling the Welfare State? Regan, Thatcher and the Politics of Retrenchment*. Cambridge: Cambridge University Press.

PIERSON, P. 2001. 'Coping with Permanent Austerity: Welfare State Restructuring in Affluent Democracies'. Pp. 410–56 in *The New Politics of the Welfare State*. Oxford: Oxford University Press.

SKOCPOL, T. 1995. *Social Policy in the United States*. Princeton, NJ: Princeton University Press.

STREECK, W., and THALEN, K. (eds.) 2005. *Beyond Continuity*. Oxford: Oxford University Press.

TAYLOR-GOOBY, P., and HASTIE, C. 2002. 'Support for State Spending: Has New Labour Got it Right?' Pp. 75–96 in A. Park, J. Curtis, K. Thompson, L. Jarvis, and C. Bromley (eds.), *British Social Attitudes: 19th Report*. London: Sage.

TREASURY, HM 2004. *Choice for Parents: The Best Start for Children: A Ten Year Strategy for Child Care*. London: HM Treasury.

WALDFOGEL, J. 2007. *Welfare Reforms and Child Wellbeing in the US and UK*. CASEpaper No. 126. London: LSE.

WEAVER, R. K. 2000. *Ending Welfare as We Know It*. Washington, DC: Brookings Institution.

WILDAVSKY, A. 1964. *The Politics of the Budgetary Process*. Boston: Little, Brown.

WRIGHT, M. (ed.) 1980. *Public Spending Decisions: Growth and Restraint in the 1970s*. London: Allen and Unwin.

CHAPTER 38

AID AND INTERNATIONAL DEVELOPMENT

OLIVER MORRISSEY

38.1 INTRODUCTION

BRITISH international development policy has witnessed change since the Department for International Development (DFID) was established in 1997, initially under the stewardship of Clare Short as Secretary of State for International Development. International development concerns, in particular reducing poverty, were given a higher profile on the domestic political agenda than had previously been the case, the aid budget was increased significantly, and initiatives in aid policy have been espoused and promoted. Britain has emerged as a donor that is prepared to take a lead on aid policy thinking, and changes in aid policy have distinguished and identified British international development policy since 1997. The changes have not been radical, and often the differences between Britain and other donors or its British predecessor are subtle, relating to how policy is implemented. This chapter argues that nevertheless some of the developments are significant, concentrating on aid because policy implementation is under the direct control of the British government, specifically DFID.

Some benchmarks are needed to identify distinctive elements of policy; while some comparisons are made with its predecessor, the main contrasts in this chapter are drawn between DFID and the World Bank (as representing mainstream development policy). Since the late 1990s the World Bank has promoted aid selectivity, favouring countries that were pursuing policies conducive to economic growth (World Bank 1998). Economic growth was seen as the prerequisite for development and poverty reduction and donors were viewed as having limited influence over the policy choices implemented by recipient countries and limited ability to ensure that aid was spent in the way intended by donors. Thus, donors should select recipients according to the policies they were implementing rather than trying to use aid to influence these policies. Although DFID did not openly disagree with the World Bank aid proposals, nor with the received wisdom on the types of economic policies conducive for growth, aspects of the aid policies implemented by DFID differed from the Bank approach. In particular, there was recognition that growth was not the only means to achieve poverty reduction and that governments with a commitment to tackle poverty could be trusted to use aid sensibly, even if they did not necessarily meet the Bank's selection criteria. One way of characterizing the difference is that DFID policy placed relatively greater emphasis on the needs of poor countries for assistance in their strategy to reduce poverty, whereas the World Bank placed greater emphasis on a growth-led poverty reduction strategy.

This chapter analyses the evolution of British international development policy under DFID, particularly since the early 2000s, as revealed in White Papers and other policy documents, relating these to practice. Unlike earlier studies such as Morrissey, Smith, and Horesh (1992), this is not an analysis of aid policy-making; we do not assess the influence of individual actors or political processes. Rather, by looking at policy statements and actions we infer DFID's intentions and contrast DFID's policy actions with those of other donors. One implication is that we cannot claim to identify why DFID chose particular policy options or actions, or which actors were instrumental in choices (although we offer suggestions in the final section), but we can assess if DFID established an identity in aid policy that distinguished it from other donors.

The structure of the chapter is as follows. The second section provides the historical and global context, sketching the changing position of the international development agency within Whitehall and major developments in global thinking on aid and development policy. The third section briefly reviews the organization of DFID as it relates to aid policy and reviews some trends in aid volumes. In the next two sections DFID policy is contrasted with mainstream thinking (as represented by the World Bank): the fourth section covers aid allocation for poverty reduction, while the fifth addresses the emphasis on partnerships rather than conditionality. Two core arguments are made in these sections. First, whereas the World Bank approach to aid for poverty reduction emphasizes growth and economic policy, DFID policy is closer to an alternative approach that emphasizes spending aid on social sector services that benefit the poor. Second, whereas the World Bank favours increasing aid to countries pursuing approved economic policies (selectivity), DFID has been willing to increase aid to countries showing a commitment to poverty reduction (such as through how they allocate aid and public spending). The following section considers aspects of broader development policy, in particular how Britain has perceived the role of trade relations with developing countries. The final section considers why DFID chose certain approaches and concludes with a discussion of current policy statements that emphasize economic growth and, in certain respects, suggest a shift of British development policy thinking to closer alignment with the mainstream. This raises the question of whether there will be a lasting legacy of DFID policy.

38.2 CONTEXT AND BACKGROUND

As befits a colonial power, Britain has a long history of aid and engagement with developing countries (before and after independence). The notion of providing regular aid to colonies to support development planning dates to the 1930s and was formulated in the first Colonial Development and Welfare Act, 1940 (Morgan 1980*a*). Until the mid-1950s almost all aid was to colonies, was untied so that it could be spent locally, and typically financed infrastructure projects or technical assistance (especially in education). Loans to independent states were tied, so that money would support British exports, and this was extended to aid to colonies from 1962, from when most became independent. During the 1960s almost 90 per cent of bilateral aid went to Commonwealth countries, although this fell to around 65 per cent in the 1970s and 1980s (Morrissey, Smith, and Horesh 1992: 7). Thus, from the establishment of the Ministry for Overseas Development (ODM) in 1964 a major strategic objective of aid was to support British trade (and, to a lesser extent, foreign policy objectives). It is interesting to reflect that it was an incoming Labour government that established the ODM, with a belief that the ministry should be strong to show a commitment to developing countries (Morgan 1980*b*), and that the first minister was Barbara Castle, a strong-willed and popular female politician. History does indeed repeat itself.

British aid policy in the early decades was similar to most other donors: all donors focused on aid for projects and technical assistance, providing profile to the donor even when not actually supporting donor exports. There were differences in the countries to which donors allocated most of their aid, but these reflected foreign policy and/or commercial concerns: the British and French were most concerned with their ex-colonies, the USA was concerned with the 'fight against communism', and the Scandinavians tended to support socialist-oriented regimes such as that in Tanzania. Until the 1970s, the broad focus of most donors was that aid should finance projects to support and promote industrialization-led development, with less emphasis on agriculture and social services (particularly education rather than health). The need to address poverty only came to the fore in 1973, promoted by Robert McNamara as president of the World Bank (Britain followed suit in the 1975 White Paper), but the focus remained on projects (such as rural integrated projects).

A shift in global aid policy began in the early 1980s as the World Bank introduced structural adjustment programmes; aid became overtly conditional—specified economic policy reforms were required as part of the aid programme. Where the World Bank went most bilateral donors followed: even if they did not offer conditional aid themselves, they required developing countries to have an agreement in place with the World Bank. The desirability and effectiveness of conditional lending became hotly contested, critics arguing that the conditions (what came to be known as the 'Washington Consensus'—Williamson 1990) were at best inappropriate and at worst damaging for developing countries while supporters argued that the reforms would work if only countries implemented them. This debate is beyond our scope here (see Mosley, Harrigan, and Toye 1991), but two observations are relevant. First, the Thatcher government in Britain in the 1980s was ideologically committed to the market-oriented principles of adjustment and at the global level British aid policy was in line with the Bank's approach. Second, donors, especially the Bank, tended to attribute any failures to a lack of commitment from developing countries. The lack of political will to implement reform was soon reinterpreted as a problem due to poor governance and a lack of democracy; economic conditionality transformed into political conditionality (see Stokke 1995).

The 1980s also witnessed changes in British aid policy. The ODM had been incorporated into the Foreign and Commonwealth Office (FCO) in 1970 and became the Overseas Development Administration (ODA). The Labour government of 1974–9 again restored the ODA to ministry status, but the Conservatives moved it back into the FCO in 1979. Although individual ministers were successful in giving particular concerns priority (Chris Patten was the first to emphasize environmental concerns and Linda Chalker added emphasis on women), British aid in the 1980s was largely driven by foreign policy and commercial (export) interests, although it delivered neither very well (Morrissey, Smith, and Horesh 1992). The most dramatic change was the decline in the value of aid from 0.48 per cent of GNP in 1978 to 0.31 per cent in 1989, at a time when other donors were maintaining their aid levels (Morrissey, Smith, and Horesh 1992: 90); while the rhetoric supported exporters, less money was available to support these interests.

The formation of the Department for International Development, with Clare Short as Secretary of State for International Development having a seat in Cabinet, to replace the ODA was among the first measures implemented by the Labour government of Tony Blair elected on 1 May 1997. Short not only provided DFID with clear and strong leadership, she was also a powerful advocate of development policy within the government. DFID was soon involved actively in policy formulation and a White Paper (DFID 1997) was produced as early as November 1997 with another three years later (DFID 2000). The 'Short–Blair years' (Morrissey 2005a) saw the emergence of DFID as a leading donor that promoted an approach to international development policy that was often relatively independent from the global donor community. Although Clare Short resigned in 2003 (ultimately over the invasion of Iraq), the impetus she bestowed on DFID was maintained by her successors, Baroness Amos and then Hilary Benn, with another White Paper (DFID 2006). When Gordon Brown became Prime Minister in 2007 Douglas Alexander was appointed as Minister for International Development; the 'Alexander–Brown' years are showing signs of a shift in DFID policy, with increased emphasis being placed on economic growth (see Section 38.7, below).

The various White Papers allow one to trace the evolution of DFID, hence British, policy. The first (DFID 1997) was the incoming government's statement of international development policy, with the aspiration in the title of 'Eliminating World Poverty'. Aid should be guided by the interests of the poor in developing countries, and should be targeted at the poorest countries with the objective of promoting development. However, the broader development policy presented was a rather uncritical acceptance of the benefits of trade and investment liberalization (Morrissey 1998). The second (DFID 2000) had the same title, but with the subtitle 'Making Globalisation Work for the Poor' there was recognition that liberalization need not necessarily benefit poor countries. The emphasis was on what Britain would do to help achieve international development targets, not only as an aid donor but also by exerting influence on other donors and multilateral agencies, in particular regarding trade policy. Developing countries too were given responsibility to show their commitment by adopting poverty reduction strategies. The third White Paper (DFID 2006) had the subtitle 'Making Governance Work for the Poor' and placed greater emphasis on institutions and government in developing countries (with renewed emphasis on the importance of economic growth), with Britain targeting aid on social sectors and human development.

The enhanced political status of international development under New Labour was matched by funding. Gordon Brown, as Chancellor of the Exchequer, showed a commitment to provide funds to support developing countries and reduce poverty, and DFID fared well with the real value of British aid doubling over ten years. In 1998 Britain ranked fifth among bilateral donors in terms of the volume of aid whereas by 2007 it ranked second behind the USA. The orientation of aid policy changed, with much greater emphasis on using aid effectively to reduce poverty in the poorest countries and an increased proportion of aid being focused on poor countries. This orientation can also be seen in the Commission for Africa (2005) and the poverty-reduction commitments agreed at the G8 summit in Gleneagles in June 2005. Although both of these are initiatives associated with the then Prime Minister, Tony Blair, they had DFID involvement and were statements of British international development policy.

38.3 ORGANIZATION AND AID VOLUMES

The establishment of DFID in 1997 gave international development an independent department in Whitehall and a voice at the cabinet; under Clare Short until 2003, this was a clear voice (see Morrissey 2005a for a review of this period). Previously, the core function of the ODA was in effect administering the aid budget; development policy was essentially a mix, often uneasy, between diplomatic interests of the FCO and business priorities of the Department of Trade and Industry (DTI). The relationship with the FCO, which became the Department of Foreign Affairs, may have been made easier when DFID became an independent department. It is likely, however, that the relationship with the DTI became more strained as DFID was strongly committed to not using aid to support British exporters; indeed, the untying of aid so that it was not linked to British exporters was considered an early success of DFID (Morrissey 1998). Interestingly, DFID forged a close relationship with Her Majesty's Treasury (HMT), partly because Gordon Brown as Chancellor of the Exchequer was committed to debt relief and helping the poorest countries (and DFID's budget had been increasing), and partly because HMT established its own International Poverty Reduction Team that worked with DFID on policy issues. International development policy became politically more important because it had a dedicated department, independent of the FCO and DTI and largely aligned with the Treasury.

There was increased focus on policies to promote development and poverty reduction, especially in poor countries, rather than the more traditional focus that could be described as 'spending aid monies'. This change in focus was associated with a shift from viewing the aid agency as responsible for administration to viewing DFID as responsible for delivering development. For DFID, aid should be deployed to promote growth, development, and poverty reduction, and officials had a role to ensure that the effectiveness of British aid could be improved. A practical manifestation of this shift in goal was an increase in the number of young professionals, economists in particular, employed in DFID, and a strengthening of their in-house capacity to research, analyse, and promulgate policy. The process of policy dialogue in which DFID engaged included consultations, workshops, and commissioned papers with academics, NGOs, and the broader development community. Thus, while there was almost no external consultation in preparing DFID (1997), DFID (2000; 2006) involved wide-ranging consultation. Among donor agencies, DFID provided a voice on development and aid policy that was typically informed and often innovative.[1] However, the differences mostly related to the practice of aid delivery and engagement with recipients rather than broad views of what was required to achieve development; the types of economic policies supported by DFID were entirely consistent with those advocated by the World Bank.

The objectives of DFID to promote development led to a focus on building partnerships with recipients and pursuing agreed development targets, negotiated relatively openly with recipient countries. DFID negotiated agreed objectives and targets with recipients, and resulting country strategies were made publicly available. Arguably, DFID interpreted partnership as building a strong relationship based on mutual respect. The approach to partnership was reinforced by the increase in the number of DFID local offices and in the number of DFID employees based overseas (Morrissey 2005a: 165). Although DFID shared the general support for 'economic liberalization' as the route to growth and development, it arguably provided greater flexibility than other donors in how this was applied in agreements with individual

---

[1] For example, the two presentations on policy issues at the OECD-DAC 'Informal Experts Meeting on Aid Effectiveness' in 2001 were by DFID staff and one of these (Beynon 2001) was quite critical of the World Bank approach.

countries. Nevertheless, DFID often attracted criticism, especially from NGOs, for being too closely aligned with World Bank liberalization policies (e.g. promoting privatization of utilities).

DFID inherited an aid budget equivalent to 0.26 per cent of gross national income in 1997 (compared to 0.27 in 1990) and this was increased to 0.32 per cent of gross national income in 2000 (IDC 2002: 30); by 2006 it had risen to 0.51 per cent of gross national income. The policy statements of DFID suggested that aid allocation to the poorest countries should increase most, as these were countries with high poverty, established relationships with Britain, and in need of assistance. This has happened to some extent: there was a noticeable increase in the share of bilateral aid going to low-income countries (at a time when bilateral aid was taking an increasing share of the aid budget, from just over 40 per cent in 2000–1 to over 50 per cent in 2006–7), which accounted for over two-thirds of the total by 2007 (Table 38.1). Table 38.1 also shows that an increasing share was allocated to Africa, especially sub-Saharan Africa (SSA), and Asia, with reductions to Latin America and other regions. While total bilateral aid increased by 47 per cent, aid to Africa increased by over 50 per cent and to Asia by over 60 per cent (largely accounted for by Afghanistan and Iraq).

It is difficult to compare the figures in Table 38.1 directly with earlier years as the regional classifications and precise aid definitions used in published statistics change often. Nevertheless, in 1990–1 some 35 per cent of bilateral (country programme) aid went to Africa, rising to 41 per cent in 1997–8 and 55 per cent in 2000–1 (Morrissey 2005a: 168). The allocation to Africa has fallen slightly as a share of the total since the early 2000s: 42 per cent in 2002–3, 37 per cent in 2003–4, and 44 per cent in 2006–7 (DFID 2008c: 25). The reason is evident in the composition of the ten major aid recipients. In 1998–9 three were in Asia (India, Pakistan, and Bangladesh) and the others were Ghana, Kenya, Malawi, Mozambique, Rwanda, Tanzania, and Uganda (DFID 2001: 159–60). In 2004–5, Pakistan, Kenya, Mozambique, and Rwanda dropped out

Table 38.1 Allocation of bilateral aid, 2002–3 and 2006–7

Bilateral programme	2002–3		2006–7		Change %
	£m	%	£m	%	
Africa	741	42.5	1,135	44.3	53.2
Of which sub-Saharan Africa	703	40.3	1,107	43.2	57.5
Americas	95	5.4	62	2.4	−34.7
Asia	542	31.1	881	34.4	62.5
Total	1,745		2,562		46.8
Low-income countries	1,024	58.7	1,725	67.3	68.5

Notes: Change is over 2002–3 to 2006–7 as percentage of 2002–3 figure. Regional shares are as percentage of bilateral country programme (Total) and do not add up to 100 due to omitted categories.

Source: Statistics on International Development 2002-3–2006-7, available at www.DFID.gov.uk.

of the top ten, replaced by Afghanistan (reconstruction), Ethiopia, Iraq, and Sudan (humanitarian aid). By 2006–7, Ghana and Malawi also dropped out (to positions 11 and 13 respectively) and Congo DR and Nigeria entered (DFID 2008c: 27). The intention of DFID to increase aid to the poorest African countries was somewhat thwarted by political realities determined on a broader political stage: reconstruction aid to Afghanistan, reconstruction and debt relief to Iraq, and debt relief to Nigeria.

The prominence of the first two of these countries highlights another development. Traditionally, challenges to the (policy) autonomy of the aid agency arose regarding the FCO and DTI, but since 9/11 relations with the Ministry of Defence (MoD) have become important. This is a complicated and under-researched area where the division between the aid and defence budgets becomes blurred, where the MoD is sometimes expected to undertake what is effectively an aid agency role, and where DFID staff face the challenge of working in conflict environments. Whilst Afghanistan and Iraq are prominent examples, related issues (especially the last one) arise in many African countries. DFID (following earlier ODA initiatives) showed a strong, and relatively successful, commitment to Mozambique and Rwanda; Sierra Leone is a case where the military played a major role in ending conflict and DFID invested heavily in reconstruction (effectively funding the budget). It remains to be seen if lessons have been learned to apply elsewhere, such as Congo DR.

38.4 AID POLICY: AID AND POVERTY REDUCTION

Aid in its various facets is central to the implementation of development policy. Traditionally, aid effectiveness has been evaluated against impacts on economic performance and in particular on economic growth. Morrissey (2006) characterizes the current state of the debate as being between those who view the glass as half full and those who view it as half empty. The pessimists (half empty) contend that aid is generally not effective in contributing to growth, although countries with good economic policies are able to utilize aid effectively; this is essentially the view promoted by the World Bank (1998) and accepted by many donors and researchers (especially those based in the USA).[2] The optimists (half full) counter that aid is in general effective, independent of policy, but the impact on growth is quite small; this view has no institutional champion but is promoted by many researchers, especially

---

[2] In this context it is generally the World Bank that defines what constitutes 'good policy' and this could broadly be considered as the so-called Washington Consensus, which has been heavily criticized (see Jomo and Fine 2006). As observed above, however, Britain or DFID have never disagreed strongly or openly with these broad economic policy prescriptions.

European, and has to a large extent been accepted by DFID.[3] Recently donors and researchers have placed more emphasis on the impact of aid on poverty reduction, the explicit objective of British aid policy.

Poverty and poverty reduction can be defined and interpreted in many different ways. One approach is to focus on aggregate country measures of income poverty, typically the headcount ratio (the proportion of the population below some income poverty line) or simply the headcount (the number of poor). In this context reducing poverty means reducing the headcount which means increasing incomes (of some of the poor). As there is a strong correlation between economic growth (rising incomes) and poverty reduction (falling headcount), achieving growth is typically advocated as the core strategy to reduce income poverty. An alternative approach focuses, at least conceptually, on a broader definition of poverty accounting for non-income aspects such as health status and access to health services, education, and clean water, for example; in economic language, a common term used would be the welfare of the poor (which includes income, but also includes access to non-pecuniary goods and services that provide utility or benefit).

Associated with the dichotomies outlined above (aid pessimists who tend also to adopt income poverty and aid optimists more prone to think in welfare terms) we characterize two approaches to directing aid towards poverty reduction. The first focuses on the allocation of aid across recipients so as to maximize the reduction in the number of poor and is closely associated with the World Bank. Given the assumptions that donors are unable effectively to target aid on poor households, or to ensure that aid finances pro-poor public spending, and that growth is the only sustainable way to reduce poverty, donors 'can only affect poverty by raising aggregate income' (Collier and Dollar 2002: 1483); proponents of this approach advocate reallocating aid to those recipients where the potential of aid to increase growth is greatest. The second approach focuses on how aid is used, in particular aid-financed government spending: aid can be used to finance particular projects, interventions, or types of government spending, some of which are more likely to benefit (increase the welfare of) the poor than others. Proponents argue that aid used to increase the provision of public goods offers the greatest potential to improve the welfare of the poor (and in doing so can contribute to growth objectives); policy and growth exist in the background and aid is important because it finances government spending or delivers public goods directly.[4]

The first approach can be said to encapsulate a World Bank discourse on aid and poverty reduction that revolves around growth-promoting policies. Contributions in this literature create a discourse by explicitly repeating, or implicitly accepting, a number of propositions: aid is only effective in countries with good policies, good policies are those that promote growth, good policies require good governance, and

---

[3] For example, 'aid helps reduce poverty by increasing economic growth, improving governance and increasing access to public services' (DFID 2006: 12).

[4] The two approaches are not necessarily inconsistent; for example, one can recognize the importance of growth (and that certain policies are conducive to growth) but target aid to finance public goods. In practice, however, the approaches have been presented as being distinct.

growth is a prerequisite for poverty reduction. Collier and Dollar (2001; 2002; 2004) provide a coherent and persuasive strategy for increasing the effectiveness of aid, in contributing to growth and to reducing poverty, based on selective reallocation to countries with better governance and economic policies. Emphasis is on the policies supported and promoted by donors; Poverty Reduction Strategy Papers (PRSPs) are perhaps a dominant current example of this discourse.[5]

This approach can be presented in a four-step argument (Morrissey 2006). First, the amount of aid alone has no effect on growth (World Bank 1998; Burnside and Dollar 2000). Second, aid makes a positive contribution to growth only in those countries with good policy: 'the interaction of aid and policy is good for growth, so that aid enhances the growth effect of policy and good policy increases the growth effect of aid' (Collier and Dollar 2001: 1787–8). Third, attaching policy reform conditionality to aid does not work, i.e. donor leverage does not ensure that governments implement good policies or pro-poor spending. Donors 'are unable to exert significant net influence on policies and institutions, and are unable to by-pass the government in implementing expenditures' (Collier and Dollar 2004: F245). Fourth, and as a consequence, (increased) aid should be given to those recipients already implementing good policies—the selectivity approach.

The Collier and Dollar (especially 2002; hereafter CD) poverty-efficient aid allocation model estimates the allocation of aid across countries that would maximize the number of people lifted out of poverty. This optimization is based on estimates of country parameters for the impact of growth on poverty reduction, and this impact is conditional on policy. Thus, aid should be reallocated to countries with growth-promoting policies, including good governance. 'The general point is that the optimal allocation of aid for a country depends on its level of poverty, the elasticity of poverty with respect to income, and the quality of its policies' (Collier and Dollar 2002: 1489). Other avenues for reducing poverty are precluded given donors assumed inability to target the poor (directly or through public spending) or affect income distribution.

Although the CD approach places considerable emphasis on the importance of good policy, this factor transpires to be of minimal actual importance in determining their poverty-reducing aid allocation. A DFID economist, Beynon (2002), reanalysed the data and showed that even in CD's own model the impact of reallocating aid on the basis of poverty criteria is bigger than reallocating aid according to policy criteria, i.e. the reallocation is driven by the cross-country incidence of poverty rather than by variations in policy. Collier and Dollar (2004: F247) acknowledge this and point out that the 'good policy' criterion effectively operates between countries with similar poverty levels to prevent allocation away from those with fairly good policies (e.g. Uganda) towards others with relatively bad policies (e.g. Sudan).[6] Nevertheless, the implementation of the CD approach implies that donors adopting selectivity (e.g.

---

[5] While one may challenge many aspects of PRSPs, in particular some of the specific economic policies included, one achievement has been to place poverty firmly on the political agenda in poor countries. Booth (2003) provides an informed analysis.

[6] These examples are salient in our context as Uganda (largely because of strong commitment to poverty reduction) and Sudan (for humanitarian reasons) were major recipients of British aid

the USA and Netherlands stated they would do so) should tend to allocate aid in line with recipient scores on policy and governance indicators (Hout 2007a).

As its aid policy developed, DFID diverged from this World Bank approach. As it adopted a somewhat more optimistic view of aid effectiveness, greater emphasis was placed on delivering aid-financed services (what aid was spent on) to promote poverty reduction as compared to the emphasis on economic growth (or more broadly the recipient policy environment in which aid was given). In effect, DFID placed less emphasis on the economic policies a country was pursuing (as long as they were broadly acceptable) and more on the commitment to allocate government spending in ways that contribute to poverty reduction. As a concrete example, DFID was one of the first donors to offer aid in the form of General Budget Support (GBS), effectively trusting that recipients will spend the money appropriately rather than trying to specify how elements of aid should be spent (for a discussion of GBS see Koeberle, Stavreski, and Wallister 2006), and is the donor most supportive of GBS; by 2006–7, some 18 per cent of DFID's bilateral aid was allocated as (general or sector) budget support with the view that this promoted poverty reduction (DFID 2008d).

In the 'public goods approach' to aid, well-being can be interpreted as increased access of the poor to public social services (especially health, education, and sanitation) in addition to increasing the consumption of the poor or reducing income poverty (Gomanee et al. 2005). Aid can improve well-being directly (through donor-managed projects), indirectly through growth (if this is in some sense pro-poor), and indirectly through aid finance for the provision of public goods (especially public expenditure on social sectors). There are two general arguments for (increasing) spending on social sectors. First, it finances the provision of, and therefore increases access to, public goods, which would be underprovided otherwise, and contributes to welfare; to the extent that the latter includes improving the quality of human capital this contributes to growth. Second, there are equity arguments as spending on social sectors is the type of government expenditure most likely to increase aggregate welfare and to benefit the poor. This approach was evident in DFID (2006) with the commitment that 50 per cent of bilateral aid should be allocated to public services for the poor, in particular providing clean water and sanitation and supporting greater access (e.g. eliminating the need to rely on user fees for primary education and health). This is also reflected in DFID's approach to GBS; in general this is provided to countries demonstrating a commitment to social sector spending.

A major concern is that whilst aid can increase the level of social spending, this spending is not very effective in delivering public goods and services (especially in ensuring access for the poor). The available evidence suggests that the efficiency of spending is quite low in poor countries, although there is fairly robust evidence that aid does increase welfare and this effect appears to be greater for low-income than for middle-income countries (Gomanee et al. 2005). The need to address this problem underpins the emphasis on 'making governance work for the poor' in DFID (2006).

throughout the period. Uganda was the first country to draw up a PRSP and was also the first country to which DFID granted general budget support.

Thus, the way in which DFID differs from the 'mainstream' (World Bank) view is in the mechanisms it adopts for aid delivery—GBS and a focus on social spending. In this context, the World Bank tends to the view that donors cannot ensure that recipients will allocate aid to appropriate public spending and are therefore, like many other donors, wary of GBS.

38.5 AID POLICY: SELECTIVITY AND CONDITIONALITY

As developed from the 1980s, conditional lending by the IMF and World Bank, and bilateral donors that followed suit, required recipients to implement specified (initially economic but from the 1990s including democratization and governance) policy reforms in return for being granted aid. The reforms did not have to be fully implemented prior to funds being released, as the practice was to release funds in stages as conditions were met. In principle, this would allow the donor to assess if countries were undertaking the required actions, and to deny resources if they failed to do so. Although conditionality has been central to donor–recipient relationships for more than two decades, as outlined above it has not been demonstrably successful and has attracted criticism (some arguing that it is the conditions that were wrong, others that recipients failed to implement the policy conditions to a significant degree). There is evidence that, over time, countries receiving aid subject to conditionality have implemented reforms so that policy has moved in the direction, although not at the speed, advocated by donors (Morrissey 2004).

The general criticisms of conditionality associated with policy-based lending have led to considerable rethinking of how best to link aid with leverage for policy reform (see Koeberle et al. 2005). Two approaches emerged as front-runners for a new form of conditionality. The first is *selectivity*, mentioned above and as advocated by many in the World Bank and particularly evident in US views, where conditions (in the form of prior actions or indicators, such as for governance or corruption) are used as a means of selecting the most deserving recipients and excluding the least deserving. As indicated above, selectivity is based on the premise that countries with 'better policies' (defined in some way by the donor) will make the best use of aid, therefore (more) aid should be allocated to such countries. The Netherlands is an example of one donor that adopted this approach, although it did not appear to have a significant effect on actual aid allocation (Hout 2007a).

A second alternative approach is 'conditionality with a light touch', where the emphasis is on dialogue with recipients and *monitoring* the use of aid and the complementary policies being implemented to enhance aid effectiveness (Morrissey 2005c). This is the approach adopted by DFID, who placed less emphasis on selectivity and more emphasis on monitoring the use of aid to engage more effectively with recipients with different policy environments (such as fragile states). From the outset, DFID was inclined towards a monitoring with dialogue approach based on partnership rather than selectivity: 'genuine partnership between poorer countries and the donor community are needed if poverty is to be addressed effectively and in a coherent way' (DFID 1997: 37). The obvious concern is how donors can be transparent in demonstrating the way recipient governments can qualify as partners (Maxwell and Riddell 1998). It is not sufficient that partners are revealed *ex post* as being those with whom an aid agreement is signed. There must be a mechanism for announcing in advance how recipients can demonstrate their suitability as partners. What emerged is that recipients, by revealing commitment to poverty reduction through adopting a PRSP (including reasonable economic policies) and allocating increased spending to social sectors, could earn the entitlement to a partnership.

The second White Paper did not use the language of partnership but recognized that development success 'is dependent on developing country leadership but some of the resources needed will have to be provided by the international community' (DFID 2000: 14). If developing countries reveal their commitment to poverty reduction DFID can determine that they are eligible for a partnership agreement. Thus, DFID (2003) has a chapter on 'Partnerships to Reduce Poverty' and budget support is seen as the instrument of partnership to deliver aid in countries that demonstrate their commitment to poverty reduction. To target aid on the poor, emphasis is given especially to health and education spending. This emphasis on aid to finance delivery of social services is evident in DFID (2006), which also places the onus on recipient countries to provide good governance (this is their side of the partnership agreement). In fact, although DFID emphasized partnership rather than selectivity, the effect was quite close to the implications of selectivity. Among the major European donors, Britain was the most selective in the sense of giving most aid to the poorest countries that performed relatively well on governance (Hout 2007b).[7]

The UK government advocated partnership based on the belief 'that it is inappropriate and ineffective for donors to impose policies on developing countries' (DFID 2004: 3). Although this downplays policy conditionality, conditions may be applied to monitor how aid resources are used and whether recipients are attempting to implement agreed policies to achieve agreed objectives. The donor–recipient relationship may include terms and conditions attached to aid, but these should be mutually agreed 'within the framework of the recipient country's own poverty strategy', 'linked to poverty reduction benchmarks', and with provisions for interrupting aid if there is a breakdown in the partnership (DFID 2004: 6).

The differences in approach between DFID and the Bank should not be overstated as the distinction between selectivity and monitoring is often blurred. Although DFID did not promote the selectivity approach as advocated by the World Bank (it did not advocate selection according to a mechanistic rule applied to policy indicators, even

---

[7] This is in part because DFID increased aid to countries that met their side of the partnership agreement, but should not be overstated (Sudan remained among the top recipients because of humanitarian aid; Afghanistan and Iraq emerged as major recipients).

if DFID had such formulae to guide allocations), in practice it was quite selective according to its own criteria (it increased aid to those recipients who abided by partnership commitments). Furthermore, whilst officially the World Bank promoted selectivity, in practice it adopted more flexible, simple, and transparent approaches to conditionality, advocating ownership and partnership and 'an approach based on reputation and results' (Koeberle et al. 2005: 66). However, prior actions (good policies) are still viewed as an important element of conditionality, if only to signal commitment to a particular direction of policy. Although monitoring is seen as important, it is not usually interpreted simply as monitoring the way in which aid is used but rather 'monitoring has typically focused more on compliance with *ex ante* conditionality than on progress, outcomes and poverty impacts' (Koeberle et al. 2005: 74). There is a difference between what DFID has pursued in practice compared to the selectivity proposed by the Bank.

38.6 ECONOMIC DEVELOPMENT POLICY

So far we have focused on DFID's approach to aid policy, an area over which it has direct control, and have argued that it has often taken positions independent of other donors (in particular the World Bank). However, DFID has also expressed British views on broader aspects of economic development policy, especially in the various White Papers. The first White Paper considered international development policy in relation to economic policies, specifically trade, agriculture, and investment (DFID 1997: 58–67), but could be considered rather naive and accepting of prevailing development policy views (i.e. consistent with the Washington Consensus): (trade) liberalization was advocated to 'encourage and assist developing countries to become more fully integrated into the multilateral system ... [and help] developing countries build their own capacity to take advantage of globalisation' (DFID 1997: 58). Statements of this form were more qualified in the second White Paper: 'support for open trade is not to be confused with unregulated trade [and] there are substantial inequities in the existing international trading system' (DFID 2000: 69). In DFID (2000) specific attention was given to the constraints facing poor countries and how donors could help in removing these constraints. British policy was more aware of the realities of the imbalances and inequities in global trade, even if it remained supportive of the principles of economic liberalization and globalization, and these themes are also present in the Commission for Africa (2005). This awareness may reflect the consultation process behind DFID (2000) as a response to views expressed by NGOs and researchers.

The Commission for Africa (2005, especially chapter 8) places considerable emphasis on trade, albeit with a strong focus on increasing exports but neglect of imports (Morrissey 2005*b*), and argues that if African countries are to benefit from more liberal trade regimes, aid is needed to finance investment, support economic policy and institutional reform, and promote an investment environment attractive to the private sector.[8] Aid can also be used to facilitate trade ('aid for trade'), e.g. paying the costs of establishing product standard boards and testing facilities or computerization to improve Customs procedures. This reflects increasing emphasis on the private sector in DFID policies 'on the ground' or in-country. For example, in Ghana and Tanzania, as part of general support and specific measures for trade capacity building, considerable support and emphasis is given to promoting the private sector.

A theme evident in all British development policy statements and initiatives is the importance of a concerted and cooperative global effort. DFID (2000: 95–7) advocated the need to reform the aid practices of the European Commission (crit- icized because aid administration was very inefficient and not focused on poor coun- tries), the World Bank, and the United Nations. Developed countries must all play a role, through liberalizing access to their markets and providing increased funding, but developing countries must also act. Although Britain has limited discretion to implement trade policy towards developing countries (trade policy is negotiated and implemented by the EU, and Britain is only one among the competing interests of member states), it has played a role. Within the EU, one can infer (from the White Papers) that Britain has been a strong advocate for recognizing the interests and needs of developing countries, and this is important to counter the protectionist tendencies of other member states (at the time of writing, President Sarkozy has openly expressed strong French support for protection). It is important that Britain has been and continues to be an advocate, globally and within the EU, of Doha being a genuine development round. Although British support for a pro-development stance on trade policy can be identified this cannot be related to implemented policy, in large part because negotiations are conducted by the EU (but presumably Britain remains influential). Where Britain could implement policy, it supported (through aid) capacity building in developing countries for trade, trade policy-making, and negotiation (e.g. supporting the costs for African countries to send representatives to WTO ministerial meetings).

38.7 BRITISH DEVELOPMENT POLICY IN 2008

The core argument of this chapter is that although the British view of broad economic development policy was not at variance with the mainstream (World Bank) view, DFID aid policy was not so closely in line with the mainstream and this altered the relationship between Britain as a donor and the recipient countries. To a greater

---

[8] The Commission for Africa (2005) argues for a substantial increase in resources, an additional $25 billion per annum in aid to Africa to be achieved by 2010, with a further $25 billion per annum increase by 2015. Such money has yet to materialize.

practical extent than most other donors, DFID followed a partnership approach; recipient countries had an input to the agreed aid programme, and DFID was willing to maintain relationships with countries as long as there was a sustained commitment to growth and poverty reduction. In particular, DFID is often one of the first to commit support to reconstruction, and the most willing to offer General Budget Support.

The feature that distinguished DFID aid policy from the World Bank and other donors was the recognition that poverty reduction could, at least in part, be met by public spending on social sectors and that (some) recipient governments could be trusted to allocate aid-financed public expenditure to these sectors. In essence, this appears to be a belief in the redistributive qualities of public spending, a vestige of Old Labour thinking (perhaps attributable to Clare Short). The commitment to financing government spending to reduce poverty, recognizing that economic growth is not the only way to reduce poverty in conjunction with acceptance that poverty has many dimensions (not all captured by income poverty), was the distinguishing feature of DFID aid policy as compared to most other donors, especially the World Bank. This may not appear to be a radical distinction, but it does imply a relationship with recipient governments guided by partnership more than by conditionality. Although there is no space here for an adequate review, this approach is consistent with much of the British-based research on aid management (e.g. Hubbard 2005) and aid policy or effectiveness; some of the research is cited above, or in DFID (2000; 2006), and others in Morrissey (2006).

Although DFID has been quite successful as an aid agency, this is not to suggest that it has been without critics. In very broad terms, there have been two types of criticisms. On the one hand, many have argued that DFID, and Britain and donors more generally, have not done enough for developing countries (such arguments are particularly associated with NGOs). Despite the promises made in the Commission for Africa (2005) and at the G8 Summit in Gleneagles, aid volumes have not increased since 2005.[9] Indeed, if one strips out debt relief and allocations to Afghanistan and Iraq, aid volumes (and flows to Africa) have actually declined. A related criticism, although it should not be applied specifically to DFID, is that rich countries have not made the appropriate concessions to developing countries in global trade negotiations: the Doha Round is repeatedly facing collapse and the intransigence of the rich countries is a major reason. On the other hand, there are more specific criticisms of DFID (and other donors') practice, such as that they tend to turn a blind eye to corruption despite their rhetoric of good governance (e.g. Hanlon 2004) or that the 'realpolitik' pressures of operating in conflict countries, for which aid bureaucrats are inexperienced, undermine the ability of donors to achieve humanitarian objectives (e.g. Marriage 2006). It is worth noting that the Conservative Party, through the Globalization and Global Poverty Policy Group (2007: 25–45), is not very critical of

---

[9] The 'celebrity development advocates' such as Geldof and Bono have done much to place global poverty reduction on the political agenda, and have played a role in prompting strong commitments by politicians. However, such commitments have rarely translated into action on the ground, and it is difficult to identify practical impacts attributable to the celebrities.

DFID's record: most of the recommendations are to refine and improve what DFID is doing, with no major policy departures.

Recently there has been a shift in focus: while for some ten years DFID concentrated on social spending and poverty reduction policies, now there is a re-emerging view that economic 'growth is the best way to reduce poverty' (DFID 2006: 57). This has been reinforced in the light of 'consistently strong evidence that rapid and sustained growth is the single most important way to reduce poverty' (DFID 2008a: 3). At the time of writing a major initiative relates to funding research on growth that can be applied to inform policy as a core element in the research strategy for 2008–13: 'to take knowledge about what influences growth and apply it to the priorities of developing countries. Our new International Growth Centre will introduce a major new research programme to support individual countries with their growth strategies' (DFID 2008b: 7). Whereas implicit in the approach to aid policy was a view that human development would contribute to growth, the emphasis now is that growth can promote human development. 'There is overwhelming evidence that higher incomes lead to a better quality of life, not least in terms of the Millennium Development Goals on health and education' (DFID 2008a: 9).

This apparent change in emphasis need not imply a change in the way in which aid policy is implemented. The partnership approach underpinning country strategy papers and agreements with recipients will be maintained, as will the tendency to focus aid on providing social services. 'The strong links between growth and human development are often mediated by policy choices and structural factors, such as the priority given to investing in health and education vis-à-vis other potential policy interventions to achieve faster growth' (DFID 2008a: 10). Two major policies emerged under DFID: British trade policy was fully decoupled from aid (a major, early achievement), and aid relationships were guided by varying interpretations of partnership (a strategy agreed between donor and recipient) with aid used primarily to support recipient spending on delivery of public services. In the period since DFID was established, Britain has become one of the most important and influential donors in terms of the volume of aid and aid policy and it is this that represents the international development legacy. DFID may not have altered global discourses on development or the types of economic policies most widely promoted, but it has influenced discussion of how to deliver aid and engage with developing countries. Hopefully, this will be a lasting legacy for improved donor–recipient relationships.

References

BEYNON, J. 2001. 'Policy Implications for Aid Allocations of Recent Research on Aid Effectiveness and Selectivity'. Presented at the 'Joint Development Centre/DAC Experts Seminar on Aid Effectiveness, Selectivity and Poor Performers'. 17 Jan., Paris.
——— 2002. 'Policy Implications for Aid Allocations of Recent Research on Aid Effectiveness and Selectivity'. Pp. 199–264 in B. Mak Avin and S. Schuck (eds.), New Perspectives on Foreign Aid and Economic Development. Westport, Conn.: Praeger.

BOOTH, D. (ed.) 2003. *Fighting Poverty in Africa: Are PRSPs Making a Difference?* London: Overseas Development Institute.

BURNSIDE, C., and DOLLAR, D. 2000. 'Aid, Policies, and Growth'. *American Economic Review*, 90: 847–68.

COLLIER, P., and DOLLAR, D. 2001. 'Can the World Cut Poverty in Half? How Policy Reform and Effective Aid Can Meet International Development Goals'. *World Development*, 29/11: 1787–802.

————2002. 'Aid Allocation and Poverty Reduction'. *European Economic Review*, 46/8: 1475–500.

————2004. 'Development Effectiveness: What have we Learnt?' *Economic Journal*, 114/496: F244–F271.

COMMISSION FOR AFRICA 2005. *Our Common Interest: Report of the Commission for Africa.* London: Commission for Africa.

DFID 1997. *Eliminating World Poverty: A Challenge for the 21st Century.* White Paper on International Development. Cmnd. 3789. London: Stationery Office.

——2000. *Eliminating World Poverty: Making Globalisation Work for the Poor.* White Paper on International Development. London: Stationery Office.

——2001. *DFID Departmental Report 2001.* London: Stationery Office.

——2003. *DFID Departmental Report 2003.* London: Stationery Office.

——2004. *Partnerships for Poverty Reduction: Changing Aid 'Conditionality'.* Draft policy paper, 17 Sept. London: DFID, HMT, and FCO.

——2005. *Trade Matters in the Fight against Poverty.* Policy paper. London: DFID.

——2006. *Eliminating World Poverty: Making Governance Work for the Poor.* White Paper on International Development. London: Stationery Office.

——2008*a*. *Growth: Building Jobs and Prosperity in Developing Countries.* Policy paper. London: DFID.

——2008*b*. *Research Strategy 2008–2013.* London: DFID.

——2008*c*. *Statistics on International Development 2002/03–2006/07.* Available at www.DFID. gov.uk.

——2008*d*. *Poverty Reduction Budget Support.* Policy paper. London: DFID.

GLOBALISATION AND GLOBAL POVERTY POLICY GROUP 2007. *In it Together: The Attack on Global Poverty.* Submission to the Shadow Cabinet. July.

GOMANEE, K., MORRISSEY, O., MOSLEY, P., and VERSCHOOR, A. 2005. 'Aid, Government Expenditure and Aggregate Welfare'. *World Development*, 33/3: 355–70.

HANLON, J. 2004. 'Do Donors Promote Corruption? The Case of Mozambique'. *Third World Quarterly*, 25/4: 747–63.

HOUT, W. 2007*a*. *The Politics of Aid Selectivity: Good Governance Criteria in World Bank, US and Dutch Development Assistance.* London: Routledge.

——2007*b*. 'The Netherlands and Aid Selectivity 1998–2005: The Vicissitudes of a Policy Concept'. Pp. 146–70 in P. Hoebink (ed.), *The Netherlands Yearbook on International Cooperation 2007.* Assen: Van Gorcum.

HUBBARD, M. (ed.) 2005. 'Symposium on Reforming Aid Management'. *Public Administration and Development*, 25/5.

IDC 2002. *Financing for Development: Finding the Money to Eliminate World Poverty*, 2 vols. House of Commons International Development Committee, Fifth Report of Session 2001–2, HC 785–I and II. London: Stationery Office.

JOMO, K. S., and FINE, B. 2006. *The New Development Economics: After the Washington Consensus.* London: Zed Books.

KOEBERLE, S., STAVRESKI, Z., and WALLISTER, J. (eds.) 2006. *Budget Support as More Effective Aid? Recent Experiences and Emerging Lessons.* Washington, DC: World Bank.

KOEBERLE, S., BEDOYA, H., SILARSZKY, P., and VERHEYEN, G. (eds.) 2005. *Conditionality Revisited: Concepts, Experiences and Lessons.* Washington, DC: World Bank.

MARRIAGE, Z. 2006. *Not Breaking the Rules, Not Playing the Game: International Assistance to Countries at War.* London: Hurst and Company.

MAXWELL, S., and RIDDELL, R. 1998. 'Conditionality or Contract: Perspectives on Partnership for Development'. *Journal of International Development,* 10/2: 257–68.

MORGAN, P. 1980a. *The Official History of Colonial Development,* i: *The Origins of British Aid Policy 1924–1945.* London: Macmillan.

—— 1980b. *The Official History of Colonial Development,* iv: *Changes in British Aid Policy 1951–1970.* London: Macmillan.

MORRISSEY, O. 1998. 'ATP is Dead: Long Live Mixed Credits'. *Journal of International Development,* 10/2: 247–56.

—— 2004. 'Conditionality and Aid Effectiveness Re-evaluated'. *World Economy,* 27/2: 153–71.

—— 2005a. 'British Aid Policy in the "Short–Blair" Years'. Pp. 161–83 in P. Hoebink and O. Stokke (eds.), *Perspectives on European Development Co-operation.* London: Routledge (Research EADI Studies in Development).

—— 2005b. 'Imports and Implementation: Neglected Aspects of Trade in the Report of the Commission for Africa'. *Journal of Development Studies,* 41/4: 1133–53.

—— 2005c. 'Alternatives to Conditionality in Policy-Based Lending'. Pp. 237–47 in Koeberle et al. 2005.

—— 2006. 'Aid or Trade, or Aid and Trade?' *Australian Economic Review,* 39/1: 78–88.

—— SMITH, B., and HORESH, E. 1992. *British Aid and International Trade.* Buckingham: Open University Press.

MOSLEY, P., HARRIGAN, J., and TOYE, J. 1991. *Aid and Power: The World Bank and Policy Based Lending.* London: Routledge.

STOKKE, O. (ed.) 1995. *Aid and Political Conditionality.* London: Frank Cass for EADI.

WILLIAMSON, J. 1990. 'What Washington Means by Policy Reform'. In J. Williamson (ed.), *Latin American Adjustment: How Much Has Happened.* Washington, DC: Institute for International Economics.

WORLD BANK 1998. *Assessing Aid: What Works, What Doesn't, and Why.* Washington, DC: Oxford University Press for the World Bank.

SECTION THIRTEEN: CONFLICT

CHAPTER 39

PROTEST

BRIAN DOHERTY

RESEARCH on protest in Britain is divided between two distinct approaches: analysis of protest as a form of political participation and studies of protests as social movements. The micro-level approach of participation surveys is best placed to address the question of who protests; both approaches have something to say about how much protest there is; and social movement research has most to say about how forms of protest have changed and what their impact on politics has been. This chapter will review these questions as they have been applied to protest in Britain. I begin, however, with the question of how to define protest.

39.1 DEFINING PROTEST

In the classic study, *Political Action*, protest is defined as 'unconventional political behavior [which]...does not correspond to the legal and customary regime norms regulating political participation' (Marsh, Barnes, and Kaase 1990: 15). This reflected a consensus in political science in the 1950s and 1960s that it was possible to make a sharp distinction between conventional politics within political institutions and unconventional politics outside them. Underlying this was the view that once citizenship rights had been achieved, protest in democracies should not be necessary and was even, according to mass society theorists, irrational. The *Political Action* study showed that protest potential had risen in the mid-1970s in Western Europe and

I am grateful to Christopher Rootes and the editors of this volume for their advice on the first draft of this chapter.

the USA, particularly amongst the post-industrial and post-material new middle class with higher education, and that protest was not generally linked with revolutionary anti-system beliefs. The subsequent accumulation of evidence (discussed below) that showed protest as an increasingly normal form of political participation in democracies (Meyer and Tarrow 1998; Tarrow 2000; Norris 2002; Dalton 2006; Norris, Walgrave, and van Aelst 2006) made the continued use of unconventional political behaviour to describe protest problematic.

A less pejorative definition developed from the protest events literature, a research method which catalogues reports of protests from the media or other sources (Rucht and Olemacher 1992; Kriesi et al. 1995; Fillieule and Jiménez 2003). A protest event is 'a collective, public action by non-state actors, involving at least three people, and with the expressed purpose of critique or dissent together with societal and/or political demands' (Rootes 2003a: 53). Even this inclusive definition is still open to some questions: for instance, should we exclude protests by individuals (Jasper 1997: 5); and how should we apply terms such as critique, dissent, and societal demands that are clearly open to different interpretations? Nevertheless the definition of protest as collective, public action based on social or political demands does have the advantage of being descriptively neutral, and this is the definition that will be used here.

39.2 HAS PROTEST INCREASED?

Protest has probably increased in Britain in recent decades. There were several unprecedentedly large demonstrations in 2002–5, and in surveys more people report having taken part in protest in recent years than in the past. However, systematic data exist only for the last three decades and there are reasons to be cautious about its validity.

Survey-based research on participation has been the dominant tradition in the analysis of protest in British political science, and whilst it has produced substantial and valuable data (cf. Parry, Moyser, and Day 1992; Jowell et al. 1997; Bromley, Curtice, and Seyd 2001; Pattie, Seyd, and Whiteley 2004), it also has some limitations. The first of these concerns the reliability of the survey findings. Much of the literature is based on surveys of protest potential, but there are problems with using responses to questions that ask respondents about protest actions that they might be willing to take as reliable indicators of the level of actual or potential levels of protest (Rootes 1981; Van Aelst and Walgrave 2001; Blanchard and Fillieule 2006). Topf (1995: 59) argues that rather than allowing prediction of actual behaviour, questions about protest potential should be seen as evidence about what respondents thought that they ought to do. Changes over time in protest potential probably reveal more about changes in the legitimacy of protest than in levels of action.

The obvious alternative is to ask people whether they have actually taken part in protests, but even this is not always convincing, since surveys of actions that people only undertake occasionally are usually seen as less reliable. The UK Citizen Audit carried out in 2000 therefore only asked respondents about actions that they had taken in the previous twelve months. Only 5 per cent had attended a demonstration, the same percentage as in 1984 (Pattie, Seyd, and Whiteley 2004: 81). In contrast, data from several decades of the World Values Survey showed a rise in reported protest participation in Britain over time. The percentage that said they had ever attended a lawful demonstration rose from 6 per cent in the mid-1970s (based on the data in Barnes et al. 1979) to 10 per cent in the early 1980s and 13 per cent in 1999–2001 (Norris, Walgrave, and van Aelst 2006: 295). The same survey showed that 25 per cent of Britons claimed to have taken part in a challenging act (at least one of boycotts, demonstrations, occupations, or an unofficial strike) at least once in their lives (Dalton 2006: 66), but in the Citizen Audit in 2000 30 per cent claimed to have taken part in boycotts in the previous twelve months (Pattie, Seyd, and Whiteley 2004: 81). Although these findings are not necessarily contradictory, given slight variations in questions and timing, there is enough disparity to reinforce the need to be wary about making strong claims based upon them.

Reported rates of participation in demonstrations have increased in Britain in recent decades, but less so than in most other industrialized countries (e.g. *inter alia* France, Italy, the USA, and Germany), which suggests that Britain remains a relative laggard in protest. The consistency in the cross-national increases does lend weight to the claim that demonstration activity has risen; nevertheless the suspicion remains that questions of this kind are vulnerable to unsystematic biases based on the legitimacy of protest in general or of particular protests at any point in time for different social groups (Blanchard and Fillieule 2006).[1] Yet it would be wrong to ignore general population survey data altogether; despite its limitations, it remains the best source that we have about changes in aggregate levels of protest over time, and for cross-national comparisons, but accounts of protest that also draw on other sources are likely to be stronger.

What of the other alternative, the number of protest events? For instance, it would be possible for there to have been more protest events, but fewer people participating in them than in previous decades (and, indeed, this seems to have been the case in Germany since the 1960s; cf. Rucht 2006). Perhaps surprisingly there is no definitive record of how many protests take place in Britain, or most other countries. While social movement researchers have in recent years made extensive use of protest event surveys, which seek to catalogue protests based on reports in published sources, these fall short of a definitive or even a reliable record of how much protest actually occurs. There have been a number of landmark studies in other European countries and the USA but this research method is labour-intensive and so most surveys focus on particular movements, as distinct from all protest (Kriesi et al. 1995; Rootes 2003*a*).

---

[1] Blanchard and Fillieule cite the example of research on AIDS activists in France, where respondents claimed to have taken part in gay rights demonstrations during the 1970s, even though their youth made this impossible (2006: 3).

Only in Germany has a comprehensive survey covering all protest been attempted and this does show a significant rise in the number of reported protests (Rucht 2005). As protest event researchers themselves point out (Rootes 2003a; Fillieule and Jiménez 2003), the main methodological weakness with protest event data, which in Britain are necessarily based on media sources, is that the media do not cover all protests. Editors favour novelty, spectacle, and confrontation, so that many smaller, less dramatic, or less novel protests are not reported. It is even less likely that local events and protests by more radical groups will be reported (Mueller 1997) as are events occurring outside a major protest cycle.[2] Since visibility in the public domain is essential to national impact, analysis of national media coverage can show us which protests achieve prominence, but we cannot be confident that it provides us with a clear measure of how much protest is actually occurring. Its principal value is not in measuring how many protests there are, but in providing indicators of how the most visible protests are changing. The most important instance of this for British protest is the historical longitudinal comparison of protests between 1758 and 1850 by Charles Tilly (1995). This demonstrates the emergence of modern forms of protest such as the rally, the march, and the petition, in which for the first time associations formed for a specific campaign and addressed the national authorities in the name of its citizens—gradually replacing the previously local, and often violent, protests which were aimed at punishing specific moral offenders. Tilly's work on the invention of modern forms of protest in Britain is a major contribution to the understanding of the role of contention in the struggle for democracy as well as a salient reminder of the importance of conflict, disruption, and challenges to elites in the shaping of British politics.

39.3 WHO PROTESTS?

A research technique that offers the possibility of offsetting some of the problems with surveys of protest by the general population is survey research carried out during demonstrations (Favre, Fillieule, and Mayer 1997; Van Aelst and Walgrave 2001; Verhulst and Walgrave 2007; Norris, Walgrave, and van Aelst 2006). It is particularly well suited to gathering information on the kinds of participants who attend demonstrations, allowing comparisons between demonstrators against immigration or for global justice for instance, and also comparisons between demonstrators on the same issue in different countries, as in the case of the 15 February 2003 demonstrations against the Iraq War (Verhulst and Walgrave 2007). There are methodological

---

[2] Doherty, Plows, and Wall (2007) used data from activist sources to analyse environmental direct action in three UK cities, but such sources are not always available and have selection biases of their own.

challenges in carrying out surveys during demonstrations, particularly regarding effective sampling, and this kind of survey tends to underestimate participation by the most radical protesters, who are generally sceptical of surveys or who avoid conventional rallies (Rootes and Saunders 2006; Norris, Walgrave, and van Aelst 2006). However, once these limitations are taken into account, data from demonstrations provide a useful addition to that provided by more general population surveys. It also allows us to test some of the central questions about the motivations of demonstrators more confidently than in general population surveys.

Three main theoretical models have been advanced to explain participation in protest. The first suggests that protest signifies a fundamental disaffection with the political system and that protesters are likely to be mainly anti-system radicals—whether of the right or the left. In this theory, if protest is rising, then the political system is under threat (Gurr 1970; Crozier, Huntington, and Watanuki 1975). A second model suggests that it is those with the most resources who are most likely to act politically. The expansion of education has created a more cognitively skilled and demanding set of critical citizens who use protest instrumentally as a means to advance their interests (Inglehart 1990; Norris 2002). Rather than being anti-system radicals, most protesters are likely to be well integrated into the political system. The third model suggests that protesters vary contextually according to the issue and the organizers (Tilly and Tarrow 2007; Norris, Walgrave, and van Aelst 2006). We might then expect different kinds of protesters to attend a far-right demonstration, a global justice demonstration, and a trade union demonstration and to see a less consistent over-representation among demonstrators of the well-resourced middle class.

The disaffection theory, very popular in media explanations of protest, receives little support from general population surveys (Marsh, Barnes, and Kaase 1990; Norris 2002; Dalton 2006) or from surveys of demonstrations. Surveys of the February 2003 anti-war demonstrations in London and Glasgow and the 2005 Make Poverty History demonstration in Edinburgh (Rootes and Saunders 2006) showed no significant evidence of anti-system sentiment and strong evidence of organizational embeddedness.[3] Protesters are more likely than the general population to vote, and much more likely to be members of political parties, NGOs, and community, charitable, or religious organizations. Over three-quarters of British anti-war protesters in 2003 were active members of a civil or political organization (Verhulst and Walgrave 2007), for instance. It is of course not easy to assess anti-system sentiment using surveys, but the evidence available does seem to refute the view that a rise in participation in demonstrations is linked to either a decline in social capital or a decline in trust in political institutions.

There is more evidence to support resource-based models because protest seems to be disproportionately carried out by those with skills and capacities developed through education and middle-class professions. If these groups are most able to

---

[3] There was also evidence of overlapping involvements with 48 per cent of MPH marchers having also been on an anti-war march and considerable overlapping membership of NGOs, such as Amnesty International, Friends of the Earth, Greenpeace, and Oxfam (Rootes and Saunders 2006: 11).

use protest as a means of influencing government, the inequality in the protest population could have negative consequences for democracy (Dalton 2006: 74). The picture is complex, however, and may vary cross-nationally: an analysis of a wide range of sources on Belgian protesters in the late 1990s (a time of particular political turmoil in Belgium) showed that demonstrators were more representative of the general population than were members of political parties and those who join civic associations; social class was not an accurate predictor of demonstration activism (Norris, Walgrave, and van Aelst 2006: 296), providing support for the contextual model. Cross-national analysis of participants in the February 2003 anti-war demonstrations in Western Europe and the USA showed considerable differences between participants (Verhulst and Walgrave 2007). For instance, in the UK and Netherlands around 50 per cent of the participants were first-time demonstrators, compared to an average in the USA, Spain, Italy, Sweden, Belgium, and Greece of 22 per cent. Within Britain, there were significant differences between anti-war protesters and members of the Countryside Alliance (CA). Participants in the CA at its height in 2002 were overwhelmingly Conservative voters, whereas those on the February 2003 anti-war marches voted for parties of the left; two-thirds of CA members were male, whereas 54 per cent of anti-war marchers were female; CA members were mostly aged over fifty (40 per cent were retired, compared to 7 per cent of anti-war marchers); and around a third of CA members had university-level qualifications (higher than average for the age group but well below the two-thirds of anti-war marchers) (Verhulst and Walgrave 2007; Lusoli and Ward 2003). It seems that while protest is similar to other forms of political participation that go beyond voting in that the well resourced are over-represented, the more that we learn about who protests, the more the evidence also supports contextual explanations.

It is perhaps surprising that so much uncertainty remains about the amount of protest and the motivations of protesters. As we have seen, this is in part because of the absence of a definitive public record of protest events in Britain as in most countries, but despite the need for caution about strong claims based on the various kinds of survey, there have been advances in our knowledge of protest. It is likely that the number of people who protest has increased and clear that protest has diffused socially, so that it is now an option for a wider range of social groups than it was in the 1970s, albeit that critical citizens with more resources and political skills remain predominant.[4] We can say with some confidence that attitudes to protest have changed so that it is now more acceptable in principle to British citizens (cf. Dunleavy et al. 2005). It also seems that this is not a sign of a legitimacy crisis, despite the evidence of declining trust in political institutions and leaders. As protest has become more familiar it has also become less threatening. We have learned to accept contained and non-violent forms of protest as a normal feature of politics, even if most of us never engage in protest ourselves.

---

[4] Also, the decline in working-class trade union membership and the related decline in trade union marches and rallies have reinforced the concentration of protest among middle-class professionals.

39.4 WHEN PROTESTS BECOME SOCIAL MOVEMENTS

What can the study of social movements tell us about protest in Britain? First, it is important to clarify the relationship between protest and social movements: not all protests are part of social movements and not all that social movements do is protest. According to Tilly (2004: 3–4), a social movement combines three elements: (1) sustained collective and public action in support of claims directed at opponents (usually, but not necessarily, the authorities), *a campaign*; (2) the use of some particular forms of action such as demonstrations or marches, petitions, vigils, site occupations, and the formation of special-purpose associations, *a repertoire*; and (3) the autonomous demonstration by participants of worthiness, unity, numbers, and commitment (WUNC).

Some protests are too short-term and lack the unity necessary to sustain a campaign. An example was the fuel protests of September 2000. The blockade of oil depots by around 2,000 farmers and hauliers was spectacularly disruptive, but this was in part because spontaneous action had caught the authorities off guard and those involved were themselves unprepared for the impact of their unplanned protests. The lack of prior joint-campaigning experience among the fuel protesters, who were spread around the country, meant that they lacked the solidarity to be able to sustain their campaign, and quickly fell out over who would lead further action (Doherty et al. 2003).

Protest develops into social movement when it is sustained in the form of a campaign, linking activists in a network based on shared aims that challenge opponents politically. There is nothing inherently anti-hierarchical about a social movement; their organizations are likely to vary—according to the aims of the campaign and the culture of their activists—between informal groups, with considerable investment in participatory processes (as in the case of environmental direct action groups like those who tried to stop road-building in the 1990s), and groups staffed by experts based in a national office who carefully control the protests sanctioned on behalf of their organization (as in the case of Greenpeace). And if these organizations work together in a sustained campaign based upon shared aims, which challenge power holders, then they can be seen as part of the same social movement (in this case the green movement). Nor are social movements the preserve of the left, as movements against immigration and in defence of country sports have shown.

These points are important as correctives to some of the assumptions about movements that were based on the emergence of the new social movements (NSMs) such as second-wave feminism and environmentalism in the 1970s. The arrival of these groups created a debate about whether these were a new kind of left-wing social movement, and distinct from the previous labour or women's suffrage movements, insofar as they had moved away from claims based upon civil and political rights and wages to post-material concerns (Inglehart 1990). The reality was more complex.

Social historians pointed to features in some nineteenth-century movements that had been seen as distinctive to the NSMs (Calhoun 1995), such as the prioritization of creating new identities over seeking to gain state power. More plausible was the claim that NSMs had developed new ideologies that politicized issues such as gender and the environment in innovative ways. Social theorists saw in the ideas of these new radical movements a reaction to, and attempt to engage with, epochal changes in Western society, such as the increased power of knowledge creators (Melucci 1996; Habermas 1987: 392; Touraine 1981), but it was harder to show that their actions or their organizations were distinctively new.

Instead, it seems that what made this seem like a new politics was the shock effect that radical protests by young people from relatively privileged backgrounds had on a settled and consensus-based politics in the post-war era. In many countries the renewal of interest in social movements as subjects of study began in the 1970s, after the major debates that were provoked by the civil rights movement in the USA and the New Left protests of the late 1960s. This was later reinforced by 1970s anti-nuclear protests, militant trade unionism, and the emergence of new social movements. Social movements did not attract the same academic interest in Britain,[5] perhaps because New Left protests in Britain in the late 1960s lacked the epochal drama of those in other countries. Some identified a 'British exceptionalism' in the lack of strong environmental protests in the 1970s and 1980s (Eyerman and Jamison 1991), which they attributed to the influence of class politics and Labour on British movements. This was only partly correct and even then accurate only for a brief period. During the 1970s, new social movements had emerged in Britain to campaign for women's and gay and lesbian liberation, anti-militarism, and environmentalism, but much of their effort was in building movement communities that could demonstrate the feasibility of alternative social relations (Doherty 2002a; Lent 2001). This was more than simply lifestyle politics, but since much of the focus was internal, on changing the lives of participants in the movement, it was not very visible and its protests were mostly local and small scale. British governments had not chosen to expand nuclear energy in the same way as in many other European countries (and had less need to do so because of reserves of coal, oil, and gas) and so the anti-nuclear conflicts which were so influential in radicalizing the environmental movement in many countries were on a much smaller scale in Britain (Rüdig 1990). The return of large-scale social movement protest came as a result of the second cold war of the early 1980s, which revived the Campaign for Nuclear Disarmament (CND) as part of a European peace movement. This coincided with Labour's turn to the left, which created new opportunities for institutional power at local level for many new social movement activists in radical Labour councils and also made a Labour government seem the most likely route to achieving nuclear disarmament in Britain for peace activists. Labour's about-turn on nuclear disarmament after election defeats in 1983 and 1987 and its retreat from 'loony left' commitments on feminism, race, and sexuality in municipal government was a disillusioning experience for many movement activists.

[5] An exception was Frank Parkin's study of CND (1968).

By the time environmental issues rose to the top of the political agenda in the late 1980s, Labour had moved to the right and so the party was no longer an attractive political option for the new younger generation of activists who followed. British exceptionalism was therefore a misperception of British movement politics, dependent on a contingent moment when Labour had seemed briefly attractive to new social movement activists in the early 1980s, and a lack of appreciation of the less visible alternative movement cultures that had developed in the 1970s. More significant for the 1990s generation of activists was the movement against the poll tax. Again, the position taken by the Labour Party was important. The failure of the national party to support the anti-poll tax campaign outside parliament, combined with the obduracy of the Conservative government in the face of the consistent opposition from the majority of public opinion, led anti-poll tax campaigners to argue that their protest was justified by the weakness of British democracy. The withdrawal of the tax and the resignation of Mrs Thatcher were not wholly attributable to the protests, but for a new generation of young environmentalists, they seemed to demonstrate the value of direct action (Rootes 2003b; Wall 1999).

In the 1990s, when environmental protest seemed to be in decline in some other countries, radical and confrontational forms of direct action against roads and airports was on the increase in Britain. Importantly, this movement was not completely divorced from the movements of the 1970s and 1980s. For instance, one of the major innovations of the 1980s direct action wing of the peace movement was the protest camp, the best-known and most influential of which was the women's peace camp at Greenham Common (Roseneil 1999). Environmental direct action protesters chose to establish camps in the 1990s not only as means of occupying a site to protect it, but also as a means of demonstrating their commitment to forms of praxis that prefigured a more egalitarian society. Their ethos was not the same as the radical feminism that developed over time at Greenham, but it is clear that the form and purpose of the camp was a direct inheritance. Thus, even when the aim was not to protect a site from destruction, a camp was the taken-for-granted form of protest, as in the Climate Action camps at Drax power station in 2006 and Heathrow Airport in 2007. The frequency of protest camps in Britain is a feature of the particularity of the repertoire developed by British direct action networks and sustained across a range of movements over several decades. While some forms of protest such as the demonstration have diffused across social and political boundaries, others such as protest camps remain distinctive to particular movements. It is in these networks that we find a sustained tradition of radical critiques of the political system and central features of modernity (Doherty et al. 2003). While their numbers are small, when set against the larger numbers of protesters who are embedded in conventional political activity, their confrontational actions on questions of peace, gender, and the environment have repeatedly provoked substantial debate and attracted significant public support (Dunleavy et al. 2005).

Social movements have shaped British politics since modern forms of political protest were first invented in Britain in the early nineteenth century (Tilly 1995) but despite this the study of social movements has not been as significant a part of political sociology in the UK in either politics or sociology as it has been in the USA or the rest of Europe. This may have begun to change with a number of British scholars emerging who specialize in the study of social movements (cf. Bagguley 2002; Barker, Johnson, and Lavalette 2001; Byrne 1997; Chesters and Welsh 2006; Crossley 2001; Doherty 2002b; Rootes 2003a; Roseneil 1999). As in the USA, however, the study of social movements is stronger in sociology than politics, perhaps because most research in Britain focuses on understanding the culture and motivations of groups who usually position themselves as outsiders and challengers to the political system, whereas political science in Britain remains strongly institutionalist in its focus.

39.5 THE IMPACT OF PROTESTS

If protest has increased, diversified, and normalized and if new social movements continue to emerge, does the apparent expansion in protest itself politics matter if protest itself remains uninfluential?

Analysis of the outcomes of protest, whether episodic or the result of sustained social movement campaigns, is bedevilled by a number of obstacles. First, movements rarely see their demands translated directly into public policy. When this does come about, the number of intervening variables is so substantial that it is very difficult to establish a causal relationship between movement action and policy outcome (Amenta and Caren 2005; Gamson 1990; Giugni 2004a). For instance, Britain has moved further and faster than countries with weak environmental movements to develop policy on climate change, but while there may be a correlation between strength of environmental movement and willingness to act, there are other possible causal factors such as the response of other interest groups, public opinion, competition between the political parties, and international pressures. It would be unconvincing to say that the environmental movement had played no role in policy on climate change, but hard to show that it could claim sole credit.

Most analysts argue that policy impact is facilitated most by splits in elites, which provide the movement with allies within the polity. Indeed, some also argue that splits within the authorities provide the opportunities that encourage protesters to act in the first place (Kriesi 2004). The likelihood of this is dependent on the structure of the state. This can be illustrated by comparisons between France and Britain. Large-scale protests in France such as those against the youth employment legislation in 2006 often provoke splits between the parties of the governing coalition. Movements are also able to put pressure on the French Prime Minister due to his weaker authority in a presidential system. In the UK while governments with small majorities have been vulnerable to backbench rebellions, the dominance of the two major parties and the stronger executive power of the Prime Minister make the British government more protected against the effects of protest. Disruption might cause crises, but it rarely forces changes in government policy, except where there are deep divisions in the governing party, as in the case of the poll tax in 1990.

A further factor is whether the aims of the protest touch on the core interests of the state. Some scholars have argued that peace movements have had relatively little impact on policy precisely because they attack one of the core areas of state policy (Rochon 1990; Kriesi et al. 1995). Nevertheless, while they may fail in their principal demands, it is not necessarily the case that they fail altogether. CND claimed plausibly in the 1980s that it had opened up debates about defence policy on issues such as first use of nuclear weapons that had previously been seen as the preserve of strategic experts.

It can be argued that environmentalism has always lost out in confronting economic growth because capital accumulation is too central to the purpose of the state in capitalist societies, but it is possible that a new state imperative of environmental conservation is emerging around the politics of climate change and the politics of manufactured risks such as GM foods, which offers new opportunities to environmentalists. Dryzek et al. (2003) argue that the prospects for environmental movements taking advantage of this depends on the responsiveness of particular states to environmentalism, and the ability of movements to overcome obstacles by making the right strategic choices. Paradoxically, they argue that relatively open systems that responded early to environmentalism, such as Norway, are not necessarily conducive to the development of the strong environmental movements required to achieve this substantial goal. Movements that lack a radical protest constituency lack the ability to mobilize pressure and also lack the internal movement debates necessary to challenge the orthodoxies of policy. In this reading, the UK environmental movement was strongest in the mid-1990s when the institutionalized environmental groups were combined with a strong environmental direct action protest network.

A second area of impact is the effect that movements have on the participants in protest. It has been estimated that only around 100,000 people are 'really committed political activists' in Britain, in the sense that for them politics is 'a really time-consuming activity' (Moran 2005: 7). If that is the case, those with experience in social movements and protest are likely to constitute a significant section of the politically active, both inside and outside political institutions, and accordingly play a disproportionately influential role in politics. Biographical evidence on New Left activists shows that those who became core activists remained committed to the ideals of their youth and more likely to be involved in political activity than their peers (Giugni 2004b; McAdam 1986). This runs counter to the life-cycle arguments that suggest that radicalism is a passing phase of youth and the popular myth that young radicals always become 'old yuppies'. Activists from one movement often have an influence on other movements (Meyer and Whittier 1994). Small numbers who remain active over time or who have involvement in multiple movements spread repertoires and frames between related movements. An example is the way that feminist ideas influenced subsequent movements even though feminist protest reduced sharply after the mid-1980s (Whittier 2004). It further suggests that as protest movements embed themselves, the number of activists available for episodic remobilization will increase.

The third and probably most enduring impact of protest movements is on culture and values. For some movements the ability to define and express a collective identity is at least a partial success in itself. The women's movement challenged the taken-for-granted conventions of masculinity and femininity that excluded women from effective participation in public life and this entailed transforming the identity of activists themselves. Although the impact of feminism on values and ideas is hard to measure and by no means irreversible, it is clear that feminist arguments have had a significant impact on values, gender roles, and language, as well as on public policy and political institutions in Britain (Bagguley 2002; Walby 1997; Mansbridge 1993). Here again, it is possible to distinguish the impact of a sustained social movement, which diversified into institutionalized and radical sections, from the more superficial effects of short-term, single-issue protest movements.

Most often, the impact of a protest movement falls well short of its declared aims, particularly in the case of the more radical social movements. Nevertheless, it is clear that many movements force responses from government and other opponents in society, have a profound effect on their participants, and have a demonstrable impact on wider culture and values.

39.6 CONCLUSION

There is evidence that protest has increased and participation in protest has spread to new groups in recent decades. When party leaders join protest marches, as the leader of the Conservative Party did at the Countryside March in September 2002 and the Leader of the Liberal Democrats did at the anti-war march of February 2003, this suggests that protests have become normal in British politics. Participation in protest is still unrepresentative and a minority form of action, but attitudes to protest among the wider population have been increasingly positive, reinforcing the view that it is increasingly accepted as a conventional form of political participation. There is little evidence to support the view that protest in Britain is an expression of anti-political sentiment or that people are switching to protest in large numbers from other forms of political participation.

Radical forms of protest remain in the networks of British social movements, which keep alive the knowledge of protest repertoires and remain available for remobilization in new campaigns. Although increasingly engaged in transnational campaigns on global issues, most social movement activism is carried out locally and is still bound by national traditions.

The impacts of protest are difficult to demonstrate precisely, since even when protesters seem to have a substantive impact there are invariably other possible causes. Nevertheless protest has certainly been a consistent feature of the development of

British democracy since the early nineteenth century, and it continues to influence political culture and to shape public spheres of debate.

Suffrage movements from the Chartists to the Suffragettes all played an essential role in democratizing the British state and the consistent history of protest movements having pushed social and political change through disruptive challenges to elites throughout the past two centuries gives the lie to the model of Britain as a deferential civic culture. Since the early nineteenth century there has been a consistent recurrence of conservative concern expressed about the dangers posed by protest (Crozier, Huntington, and Watanuki 1975), or a view that it is self-indulgent and lacks seriousness (Stoker 2006: 88), but, in the centralized and majoritarian political system of Britain, there are good arguments to say that non-violent protest serves as a defence against the excesses of government and in a positive expression of citizenship. Beetham (2003) argues that there is a good case in democratic theory for governments in representative democracy to defer to large protest movements, providing that movements can sustain their action and show that they represent majority opinion on an issue of national importance which has been the subject of sustained public debate. The campaign against the poll tax and the opposition to the invasion of Iraq would both have met these criteria. While the number of critical citizens prepared to engage in protest may still be small, on occasion protesters represent sustained majorities on issues of national significance, which if repeatedly ignored, would be likely to increase alienation from the political process. If that is the case, it is necessary to start to think seriously about how representative democracy might be amended to make it more responsive to protest.

REFERENCES

AMENTA, E., and CAREN, N. 2005. 'The Legislative, Organizational, and Beneficiary Consequences of State-Oriented Challengers'. Pp. 461–88 in D. A. Snow, S. A. Soule, and H. Kriesi (eds.), *The Blackwell Companion to Social Movements*. Oxford: Blackwell.

BAGGULEY, P. 2002. 'Contemporary British Feminism: A Social Movement in Abeyance?' *Social Movement Studies*, 1/2: 169–85.

BARKER, C., JOHNSON, A., and LAVALETTE, M. (eds.) 2001. *Leadership and Social Movements*. Manchester: Manchester University Press.

BARNES, S. H., KAASE, M., ALLERBACK, K. R., FARAH, B., HEUNKS, F., INGLEHART, R., JENNINGS, M. K., KLINGEMANN, H. D., MARSH, A., and ROSENMAYR, L. 1979. *Political Action: Mass Participation in Five Western Democracies*. London: Sage.

BEETHAM, D. 2003. 'Political Participation, Mass Protest and Representative Democracy'. *Parliamentary Affairs*, 56/4: 597–609.

BLANCHARD, P., and FILLIEULE, O. 2006. 'Individual Surveys in Rallies (INSURA): A New Eldorado for Social Movement Research?' Presented at the conference on Crossing Borders, WZB, 5–7 Oct.

BROMLEY, C., CURTICE, J., and SEYD, B. 2001. 'Political Engagement, Trust and Constitutional Reform'. In A. Park, J. Curtice, K. Thomsen, L. Jarvis, and C. Bromley (eds.), *British Social Attitudes: The 18th Report*. London: Sage.

BYRNE, P. 1997. *Social Movements in Britain*. London: Routledge.

CALHOUN, C. 1995. 'New Social Movements of the Early Nineteenth Century'. Pp. 173–215 in M. Traugott (ed.), *Repertoires and Cycles of Collective Action*. Durham, NC: Duke University Press.

CHESTERS, G., and WELSH, I. 2006. *Complexity and Social Movement*. London: Routledge.

CROSSLEY, N. 2001. *Making Sense of Social Movements*. Buckingham: Open University Press.

CROZIER, M., HUNTINGTON, S., and WATANUKI, J. 1975. *The Crisis of Democracy*. New York: New York University Press.

DALTON, R. 2006. *Citizen Politics*, 4th edn. Washington, DC: CQ Press.

DOHERTY, B. 2002a. 'The Revolution in High Lane? Direct Action and Community Politics in Manchester in the 1970s'. *North West Labour History Journal*, 27: 60–4.

—— 2002b. *Ideas and Actions in the Green Movement*. London: Routledge.

—— PLOWS, A., and WALL, D. 2007. 'Environmental Direct Action in Manchester, Oxford and North Wales: A Protest Event Analysis'. *Environmental Politics*, 16/5: 804–24.

—— PATERSON, M., PLOWS, A., and WALL, D. 2003. 'Explaining the Fuel Protests'. *British Journal of Politics and International Relations*, 5/1: 1–23.

DRYZEK, J. S., DOWNES, D., HUNOLD, C., and SCHLOSBERG, D. 2003. *Green States and Social Movements*. Oxford: Oxford University Press.

DUNLEAVY, P., MARGETTS, H., SMITH, T., and WEIR, S. 2005. *Voices of the People*. London: Politico's.

EYERMAN, R., and JAMISON, A. 1991. *Social Movements*. Cambridge: Polity.

FAVRE, P., FILLIEULE, O., and MAYER, N. 1997. 'La Fin d'une étrange lacune de la sociologie des mobilisations: l'étude par sondage des manifestants. Fondaments théoriques et solutions techniques'. *Revue Française de Science Politique*, 47: 3–28.

FILLIEULE, O., and JIMÉNEZ, M. 2003. 'The Methodology of Protest Event Analysis and the Media Politics of Reporting Environmental Protest Events'. Pp. 258–79 in C. Rootes (ed.), *Environmental Protest in Western Europe*. Oxford: Oxford University Press.

GAMSON, W. A. 1990. *The Strategy of Social Protest*, 2nd edn. Belmont, Calif.: Wadsworth.

GIUGNI, M. G. 2004a. *Social Protest and Policy Change: Ecology, Antinuclear and Peace Movements in Comparative Perspective*. Lanham, Md.: Rowman and Littlefield.

—— 2004b. 'Personal and Biographical Consequences'. Pp. 489–507 in D. A. Snow, S. A. Soule, and H. Kriesi (eds.), *The Blackwell Companion to Social Movements*. Oxford: Blackwell.

GURR, T. R. 1970. *Why Men Rebel*. Princeton, NJ: Princeton University Press.

HABERMAS J. 1987. *The Theory of Communicative Action*, vol. ii. Cambridge: Polity.

INGLEHART, R. 1990. *Culture Shift in Advanced Industrial Society*. Princeton, NJ: Princeton University Press.

JASPER, J. 1997. *The Art of Moral Protest*. Chicago: Chicago University Press.

JOWELL, R., CURTICE, J., PARK, A., BROOK, L., and AHRENDT, D. (eds.) 1997. *British Social Attitudes: The 14th Report*. Aldershot: Ashgate.

KRIESI, H. 2004. 'Political Context and Opportunity'. Pp. 67–90 in D. A. Snow, S. A. Soule, and H. Kriesi (eds.), *The Blackwell Companion to Social Movements*. Oxford: Blackwell.

—— KOOPMANS, R., DUYVENDAK, J. W., and GIUGNI, M. G. 1995. *The Politics of New Social Movements in Western Europe*. Minneapolis: University of Minnesota Press.

LENT, A. 2001. *British Social Movements since 1945*. Basingstoke: Palgrave.

LUSOLI, W., and WARD, S. 2003. 'Hunting Protesters: Participation, and Protest Online in the Countryside Alliance'. Presented at the European Consortium for Political Research, Edinburgh, 28 Mar.–2 Apr.

McAdam, D. 1986. 'Recruitment to High Risk Activism: The Case of Freedom Summer'. *American Journal of Sociology*, 92/1: 64–90.

Mansbridge, J. 1993. 'Feminism and Democratic Community'. In J. W. Chapman and I. Shapiro (eds.), *Democratic Community: NOMOS XXXV*. New York: New York University Press.

Marsh, A., Barnes, S. H., and Kaase, M. 1990. *Political Action in Europe and the USA*. Basingstoke: Macmillan.

Melucci, A. 1996. *Challenging Codes*. Cambridge: Cambridge University Press.

Meyer, D. S., and Tarrow, S. (eds.) 1998. *The Social Movement Society*. New York: Rowman and Littlefield.

—— and Whittier, N. 1994. 'Social Movement Spillover'. *Social Problems*, 41/2: 277–98.

Moran, M. 2005. *Politics and Governance in the UK*. Basingstoke: Palgrave.

Mueller, C. 1997. 'Media Measurement Models of Protest Event Data'. *Mobilization*, 2/2: 165–84.

Norris, P. 2002. *Democratic Phoenix: Reinventing Political Activism*. Cambridge: Cambridge University Press.

—— Walgrave, S., and van Aelst, P. 2006. 'Does Protest Signify Dissatisfaction?' Pp. 279–309 in M. Torcal (ed.), *Political Dissatisfaction in Contemporary Democracies*. London: Routledge.

Parkin, F. 1968. *Middle Class Radicalism*. Manchester: Manchester University Press.

Parry, G., Moyser, G., and Day, N. 1992. *Political Participation and Democracy in Britain*. Cambridge: Cambridge University Press.

Pattie, C., Seyd, P., and Whiteley, P. 2004. *Citizenship in Britain: Values, Participation and Democracy*. Cambridge: Cambridge University Press.

Rochon. T. 1990. *Mobilizing for Peace*. Princeton, NJ: Princeton University Press.

Rootes, C. 1981. 'On the Future of Protest Politics in Western Democracies'. *European Journal of Political Research*, 9/4: 421–32.

—— 2003a. 'Britain'. Pp. 20–58 in C. Rootes (ed.), *Environmental Protest in Western Europe*. Oxford: Oxford University Press.

—— 2003b. 'The Resurgence of Protest and the Revitalisation of British Democracy'. Pp. 137–68 in P. Ibarra (ed.), *Social Movements and Democracy*. New York: Palgrave Macmillan.

—— and Saunders, C. 2006. 'The "Movement of Movements" as a "Network of Networks": The Global Justice Movement and the "Make Poverty History March" '. Presented at the ESRC seminar on Social Capital and Social Movements, Nottingham, 8 Dec.

Roseneil, S. 1999. *Common Women, Uncommon Practices: The Queer Feminism of Greenham*. London: Cassell.

Rucht, D. 2006. 'Political Participation in Europe'. Pp. 110–37 in R. Sakwa and A. Stevens (eds.), *Contemporary Europe*, 2nd edn. Basingstoke: Palgrave.

—— and Olemacher, T. 1992. 'Protest Event Data Collection'. In M. Diani and R. Eyerman (eds.), *Studying Collective Action*. London: Sage.

Rüdig, W. 1990. *Anti-Nuclear Movements*. Harlow: Longman.

Stoker, G. 2006. *Why Politics Matters*. Basingstoke: Palgrave.

Tarrow, S. 1998. *Power in Movement*. Cambridge: Cambridge University Press.

—— 2000. 'Mad Cows and Social Activists'. Pp. 270–90 in S. J. Pharr and R. D. Putnam (eds.), *Disaffected Democracies*. Princeton, NJ: Princeton University Press.

—— 2005. *The New Transnational Activism*. Cambridge: Cambridge University Press.

Tilly, C. 1995. *Popular Contention in Britain, 1758–1834*. Cambridge, Mass.: Harvard University Press.

—— 2004. *Social Movements 1768–2004*. Boulder, Colo.: Paradigm.

TILLY, C., and TARROW, S. 2007. *Contentious Politics*. Boulder, Colo.: Paradigm.

TOPF, R. 1995. 'Beyond Electoral Participation'. In D. Fuchs and H. Klingemann (eds.), *Citizens and the State*. Oxford: Oxford University Press.

TOURAINE, A. 1981. *The Voice and the Eye*. Cambridge: Cambridge University Press.

VAN AELST, P., and WALGRAVE, S. 2001. 'Who is that (Wo)man in the Street? From the Normalisation of Protest to the Normalisation of the Protester'. *European Journal of Political Research*, 39: 461–86.

VERHULST, J., and WALGRAVE, S. 2007. 'Protest and Protesters in Advanced Industrial Democracies: The Case of the 15th February Global Anti-War Demonstrations'. Pp. 255–85 in D. Purdue (ed.), *Civil Societies and Social Movements*. London: Routledge.

WALBY, S. 1997. *Gender Transformations*. London: Routledge.

WALL, D. 1999. *Earth First! and the Anti-Roads Movement: Radical Environmentalism and Comparative Social Movements*. London: Routledge.

WHITTIER, N. 2004. 'The Consequences of Social Movements for Each Other'. Pp. 531–51 in D. A. Snow, S. A. Soule, and H. Kriesi (eds.), *The Blackwell Companion to Social Movements*. Oxford: Blackwell.

CHAPTER 40

IMMIGRATION AND CITIZENSHIP

RANDALL HANSEN

SINCE the late nineteenth century, Britain has experienced three waves of immigration. The first was of Europeans, including many Jews fleeing pogroms, from the 1870s until 1905, when the Aliens Act introduced Britain's first immigration control on aliens (non-British subjects). The second occurred from 1948 until 1971, when hundreds of thousands of Commonwealth immigrants took advantage of privileged citizenship laws to migrate to the UK. The third occurred from 1997, when policy change intersected with strong economic growth to create in absolute terms the greatest level of immigration Britain has ever experienced.

In a manner that few people predicted in the 1990s, the latter half of that decade and the one that followed were affected by the politics of immigration. When the Labour government under Tony Blair came to power, it adopted a more open attitude to immigration, which it saw as important to Britain's economic growth and as part of the new, modern vision of the country articulated by New Labour. The government relaxed the previous Conservative government's policy on work permits, and skilled migration began picking up. By 2002 the UK was issuing record numbers of work permits—well over 80,000 were issued each year from 2002 to 2006. From 2004, a dramatic and unprecedented increase in immigration followed from the granting of labour market rights to A8 (2004 EU accession countries minus Malta and Cyprus) nationals. The majority of these migrants were unskilled. By the middle of the 2000s, therefore, skilled and unskilled immigration were running at historic highs.

Economic migration formed one pillar of the post-1997 immigration experience. Asylum seekers formed the second. In the 1980s, Britain was a no-go zone for would-be refugees. While Germany frequently had more than 100,000 applications,

Britain received less than 10,000. This situation changed sharply in the 1990s. Asylum seekers rose to 28,000 in 1993, and then tripled to 100,000 in 2000; for the first time ever, Britain (temporarily) overtook Germany as asylum seekers' main destination in Europe.

These movements provoked contrasting reactions. Despite the high numbers, work permit holders created few difficulties for the UK government. The majority were skilled workers who integrated easily into the City and other professional sectors. Asylum seekers, by contrast, provoked a bitter, tabloid-led public backlash. Partly because they were highly visible—cameras caught asylum seekers nightly jumping onto trains in France bound for the UK—the government was under intense pressure to act. It responded with a clampdown on asylum, driving the numbers back down. Just as the government was getting asylum numbers under control, the arrival (or legalization) of tens of thousands of unskilled workers from Eastern Europe reignited the immigration issue. Much tabloid press reflected old hysterias about immigration—overwhelming numbers, rising crime—but a new twist was added: low-skilled immigration might penalize low-skilled workers, making it worse for the worst-off and making Britain more unequal.

Taking immigration's current salience as its starting point, this chapter provides an overview of immigration, integration, and citizenship in Britain. It proceeds in three steps. First, it provides a brief history of immigration and anti-discrimination legislation in the UK, considers the turn from multiculturalism in the early 2000s, and examines economic immigration. Second, it examines scholarly interpretations of UK immigration policy as they evolved over the post-war period. Finally, it offers an institutional explanation of British immigration policy's trajectory.

Integration is understood in this chapter to mean socio-economic integration—the extent to which ethnic minorities are indistinguishable from the broader population in their economic and educational achievements. The assumption is that the smaller the gap between ethnic minorities' employment, pay, and education, the greater the degree of integration. This socio-economic understanding of integration is distinct from what might be called 'cultural integration', or the degree to which immigrants acquire the broader culture of their new country. The choice is deliberate in that defining integration in terms of culture acquisition is problematic for a number of reasons. There is often little agreement on what constitutes national culture (Scots and Englishmen would likely disagree, as would aristocrats and workers), and 'culture' is not fixed but malleable and ever-developing, not least in response to immigration itself.

40.1 IMMIGRATION POLICY

Immigration policy refers to the complex of measures governing the temporary and permanent migration of people to the UK. It includes policies towards asylum seekers, permanent labour migrants, family members, temporary workers, foreign students, and tourists. The instruments for implementing immigration policy include visas (tourist, entry, student, and family), work permits, grants of permanent residency, and grants of citizenship. Measured by the size of the immigration streams, immigration to Britain has three main components: economic immigration, asylum seekers, and family migrants.

40.1.1 Economic Immigration

In most countries, there is a lively debate about economic immigration, one which tends to polarize. Proponents of economic immigration argue that it offers huge economic benefits, and they tend to cite large net figures to bolster their case. On the basis of very little reliable evidence the Home Office popularized the claim that immigration to the UK was responsible for 0.7 per cent or more of Britain's GDP. Most recently, Home Office officials claimed that immigrants contributed £6–11 billion of the UK economy. As this is larger than the total net contribution of immigrants to the American economy, the figure is doubtful. Similarly, those opposed claim great negative consequences for house prices (much higher) and wages (much lower). Most econometric analysis shows that the truth lies between the extremes: immigration brings a small net positive economic benefit, chiefly in the form of wage depression (Chiswick 2005). It also creates winners and losers. Low-skilled migration reduces the wages of low-skilled workers and increases demand for higher-skilled workers and for capital (Chiswick 2005: 167). High-skilled migration lowers the wages of high-skilled workers but raises the productivity of low-skilled workers and capital (Chiswick 2005: 168). If the high-skilled workers are in science or engineering they may also introduce technological changes that increase the competiveness or productive capacity of the economy (Chiswick 2005: 168). In the UK, the great surge in low-skilled migration since the late 1990s (partly through the asylum system, partly through enlargement) has had predictable effects. The conclusion of a House of Lords inquiry into immigration (headed by Lord Wakeham) that 'The available evidence suggests that immigration has had a small negative impact on the lowest-paid workers in the UK and a small positive impact on the earnings of higher-paid workers' most likely gets it right (BBC 2008).

40.1.2 Economic Immigration Streams

Until 2008, the work permit scheme was the foundation of Britain's economic policy for skilled migrants. As Table 40.1 indicates, the Home Office has issued 65,000–85,000 work permits every year since 2000.

Total arrivals under these categories were 137,035 in 2005 and 145,120 in 2006.

In addition to the work permit scheme, Britain operated its own version of the Canadian points system (which gives people 'points' for language, education, and experience and specifies a minimum number of points that individuals have to

Table 40.1 Admissions of work permit holders and their dependants, excluding EEA nationals, by category and nationality, 2000–4

	United Kingdom					Number of persons	
	2000[a]	2001[a]	2002	2003	2004 (P)[c]	2003 Excluding accession states[d]	2004 Excluding accession states[d]
Employment for 12 months or more	36,290	50,280	51,525	44,480	42,265	40,715	41,360
Employment for less than 12 months[b]	30,785	30,785	34,095	36,870	40,450	33,560	38,490
Dependants of work permit holders	24,970	27,760	34,495	37,830	41,595	37,005	41,490
All categories	92,050	108,825	120,115	119,180	124,310	111,280	121,235
Of which:							
Europe	9,880	10,040	14,090	17,785	15,520	9,890	12,450
Americas	33,855	31,375	31,900	29,250	29,465	29,250	29,465
Africa	9,160	14,100	15,695	14,400	13,860	14,400	13,860
Indian subcontinent	13,915	19,750	22,810	25,580	35,795	25,580	35,795
Rest of Asia	17,960	23,645	26,030	24,935	23,570	24,935	23,570
Oceania	7,175	9,785	9,370	7,070	5,950	7,070	5,950
Other nationalities	105	125	220	160	145	160	145
All nationalities	92,050	108,825	120,115	119,180	124,310	111,280	121,235

[a] A change in procedures may have resulted in some under-recording for the fourth quarter of 2000 and the first quarter of 2001.
[b] Includes the majority of work permit trainees.
[c] Includes nationals of the Czech Republic, Cyprus, Estonia, Hungary, Latvia, Lithuania, Malta, Poland, Slovakia, and Slovenia before 1 May, but excludes them from this date.
[d] Figures in italics exclude nationals of the Czech Republic, Cyprus, Estonia, Hungary, Latvia, Lithuania, Malta, Poland, Slovakia, and Slovenia (countries which became part of the EEA on 1 May 2004) for the whole of 2003 and 2004.
(P) Provisional figures.
Source: Dudley et al. (2005).

achieve): the Highly Skilled Migrant Programme (HSMP). Few people, however, took advantage, and in March 2006 the government took the decision to replace all categories of labour migration with a points-based system, which took effect in 2008. The new system consolidates all tiers of visa applications into five streams: (i) highly skilled workers—scientists, entrepreneurs; (ii) skilled workers with job offers—nurses, teachers, etc.; (iii) low-skilled workers filling temporary shortages; (iv) students; and (v) youth schemes. Points are awarded based on aptitude, experience, age, and level of need in any given sector. The system replaces all existing work permit schemes. The scheme will be implemented for all tiers except tier (iii) over the next few years.

Table 40.2 Grants of Settlement for Family Formation and Reunion, excluding EEA nationals, 2000–4

	United Kingdom					Number of persons	
	2000	2001	2002	2003	2004 (P)	2003 Excluding accession states	2004 Excluding accession states
Husbands	14,495	16,915	15,520	17,380	8,190	17,105	8,140
Wives	24,265	26,835	25,120	30,795	12,925	28,950	12,395
Children	6,870	6,795	6,355	8,955	5,855	8,770	5,805
Parents and grandparents	2,435	1,760	1,750	3,090	1,985	3,070	1,985
Other and other unspecified dependents	5,000	4,570	4,015	5,855	5,945	5,745	5,905
Total family grants	53,065	56,875	52,760	66,075	34,905	63,640	34,230

(P) Provisional figures.

Source: Dudley et al. (2005).

40.1.3 Family Migrants

Because the flow is split into these various streams, it is difficult to determine the exact number of family migrants the UK takes in, but Home Office statistics on settlement (which show how many family members become permanent residents) suggest that some 50,000 to 60,000 family members migrate permanently to Britain every year (Table 40.2).

40.1.4 Asylum Seekers

An asylum seeker is one who is seeking to secure the status of refugee under national and international law. British refugee policy is governed by the United Nations convention relating to the status of refugees and its 1967 protocol, which the UK has signed. The convention defines a refugee as one with a well-founded fear of persecution on the grounds of race, religion, nationality, membership in a particular social group, or political opinion. The convention does not create a right to asylum, but rather creates a duty on states not to return a refugee to a country where he or she would face persecution. In practice, respecting this duty has involved hearing pleas for asylum and determining whether the individual is a genuine refugee, one with a well-founded fear of persecution.

As noted, asylum applicants were very low in the 1980s, and shot up in the late 1990s (see Table 40.3).

In addition to these three categories of migrants, an unknown number of (old) EU workers and their families move to the UK each year. As they have full migration

Table 40.3 Asylum applications in select Western countries, 1985–98 (in thousands)

Year	'85	'92	'93	'94	'95	'96	'97	'98	'99	'00	'01	'02	'03	'04	'05	'06
United Kingdom	6.2	32.3	28.0	42.2	55.0	27.9	32.5	46	71.2	99	91.6	103.08	60.05	40.6	30.46	28

Rounded figures.

Sources: John Salt, *Current Trends in International Migration in Europe*, Strasbourg: Council of Europe (CDMG (99) 10), 1999; *World Refugee Survey* 1999; US Committee for Refugees, Washington, 1999; ECRE Country Reports, 1998, websites: http://www.unhcr.ch/statist/99profiles/can.pdf, http://www.unhcr.ch/statist/rsd220601.pdf, '2000 Global Refugee Trends. Analysis of the 2000 Provisional UNHCR Population Statistics, May 2000': http://www.unhcr.ch/statist/2000provisional/trends.pdf (consulted 19 Sept. 2001); UNHCR, *The State of the World's Refugees 1995: A Humanitarian Agenda* (Oxford: Oxford University Press, 1995), *Asylum Trends and Levels in Industralized Countries 2005* (UNHCR, 2005).

and residence rights, their arrival is not recorded, but anecdotal evidence suggests that the strong British economy lured large numbers of such workers, particularly to the service sector. Britain was also one of only three countries that granted citizens of central and eastern EU members the right to work following the EU enlargement of 1 May 2004.

40.2 ETHNIC DIVERSITY IN THE UNITED KINGDOM

These three types of migration—economic, family, and asylum seeker—have transformed the UK into a highly diverse society. Today, 10 per cent of the population (5.75 million people) has 'community backgrounds' outside the UK (Parekh 2000). Some 5.7 per cent (3.25 million people) has community backgrounds in Africa, the Caribbean, or Asia. Ethnic minorities are concentrated in England's cities, and above all in London: 57 per cent of all African-Caribbean people live in Greater London, as do 82 per cent of all Africans, 49 per cent of Bangladeshis, 42 per cent of Indians, and 29 per cent of Pakistanis. There are also substantial ethnic minority concentrations in the West Midlands (including Birmingham) and in West Yorkshire (including Bradford).

40.3 BRITISH INTEGRATION POLICIES

The core of Britain's integration policy is an anti-discrimination framework gradually developed since the 1960s, always under a Labour government. A Conservative government enacted the first immigration controls on Commonwealth immigration in 1962, and the Labour opposition bitterly denounced the measure as populist and racist. Two years later, the Labour Party was in power, and it quickly recognized that family reunification meant that every pre-1962 migrant would bring to the UK two to four of his family members. It abandoned its previous commitment to open borders and extended immigration controls in 1965 (Hansen 2000: 136–7). At the same time, there had long been pressure from backbenchers (above all, the indefatigable Fenner Brockway) to enact anti-discrimination legislation, and the Home Secretary of the day, Frank Soskice, argued that immigration restrictions would be more palatable to the left wing of his party if accompanied by legislation against racial discrimination. These liberal and illiberal sympathies were synthesized in 1965: labour immigration from the Commonwealth was halved, and race relations legislation was passed. The legislation criminalized the use of threatening, abusive, or insulting written or spoken expressions designed to stir up hatred against others on the grounds of race, colour, or ethnic or national origin. Prohibitions on discrimination were limited to public places (hotels, pubs) and did not include discrimination in employment, the banking and insurance sectors, or the private housing market. Heavily influenced by thinking in the United States and Canada (Bleich 2003: 52–5), discrimination was subject to civil rather than criminal sanction: it was dealt with by conciliation backed up by recourse to the civil courts. The legislation was timid, difficult to enforce, and limited in its application (Bleich 2003: 59).

The 1965 legislation has been extended three times in the last forty years. Roy Jenkins was behind two of these moves. When he became Home Secretary in 1965, he appointed the activist Liberal MP Mark Bonham Carter as the first chair of the new Race Relations Board. Bonham Carter made a condition of his acceptance his ability to push for the legislation's extension (Bleich 2003: 72). Jenkins agreed, and gave him support inside and outside parliament. Reflecting Jenkins's particular concern with discrimination in unemployment (Bleich 2003: 72), the Race Relations Act 1968 extended the prohibition on discrimination to employment, housing, credit, and insurance facilities. The legislation also increased funding for the Race Relations Board and empowered it to investigate independently instances of racial discrimination. It was and would be for a long time the most robust anti-discrimination legislation in Europe.

Although the legislation was an improvement on its ineffective 1965 predecessor, those implementing it faced three difficulties: direct discrimination was difficult to prove, the administrative procedures invoked in cases of suspected discrimination were cumbersome, and the English civil courts were conservative in their judgments. At the same time, the period from 1968 to 1975 was the high point in Enoch Powell's at times demonic campaign against non-white immigration. For many in the Labour Party, backing anti-discrimination legislation was a means to marking the distance between them and 'Powellism' (Bleich 2003: 92).

The 1976 Race Relations Bill addressed all three shortcomings: it allowed individuals to appeal directly to the civil courts or to employment tribunals, it replaced the previous two-tiered structure (a race relations board supported by the Community

Relations Commission) with the Commission for Racial Equality (CRE), and, most ambitiously, it expanded the definition of discrimination to include direct and indirect discrimination. The latter covers requirements or conditions that are formally non-discriminatory but that disproportionately penalize members of a particular racial group. Individuals who believe they have suffered racial discrimination have three months to take the complaint to an industrial tribunal and six months to take it to a county court.[1]

Alongside the civil sanctions against discrimination, the UK has—and always has had—provisions on the incitement to racial hatred, against which criminal charges can be brought. The incitement provisions are invoked in some eighty cases per year.

40.4 THE RACE RELATIONS ACT 2000

A defining moment in the evolution of race relations legislation followed the murder of a black Londoner, Stephen Lawrence, in 1993. Following police bungling and a failure to secure any convictions, Lawrence's family led a polished and dignified campaign on their son's behalf, securing an endorsement from South Africa's Nelson Mandela. The media coverage greatly raised public awareness of hate crimes, and the government responded by appointing a committee of inquiry which recommended sweeping changes in police practice. The Labour government responded with a new Race Relations Act.

Although enacted in response to the failings of the police service, it affected a much broader range of institutions. It extended the 1976 race relations legislation to all public bodies—the police, the universities, the National Health Service—and to all private bodies exercising public functions, with the exception of parliament, the security services, and immigration officers. It also placed a general duty on public authorities to work towards the elimination of unlawful discrimination and to promote equality of opportunity and good relations between people of different racial groups.

40.5 CITIZENSHIP POLICIES

Until very recently, the United Kingdom provided liberal access to a thin citizenship. Though viewed as inclusionary today, citizenship by birth—*jus soli*—has its origins in feudalism (what's born within the realm of the lord belongs to the lord) and imperialism. From the early seventeenth century on, anyone born within the realm of

---

[1] I am grateful to Erik Bleich, Middlebury University, for providing me with these statistics.

the British monarch was a subject of that monarch, and British-subject status was the basis of British nationality right up to 1981. This basic principle was carried over into the age of empire, and all those born within the British Empire were British subjects who enjoyed, in theory, full rights within the UK. This system was reaffirmed in 1948, and it meant that the 500,000 non-white British subjects who entered the UK before 1962 did so not as immigrants but as citizens. The UK ended pure *jus soli* (which no longer exists anywhere in Europe) in 1981, but there has otherwise been a high degree of continuity in citizenship policy. All those born in the UK to permanent residents, citizens, or recognized refugees are citizens at birth. Others may naturalize after three years of marriage to a UK citizen or after six years of residence in the UK. Dual citizenship is fully accepted.

40.6 INTEGRATION OUTCOMES

Since the 1991 Census, the National Office of Statistics has recorded ethnic minority unemployment, income levels, and educational attainments. Overall, the ethnic minority unemployment rate has remained double that of the white population. Unemployment rates are highest in the Bangladeshi community, at 38 per cent, or over nine times the national rate of 4.1 per cent (2001–2 figures). The Pakistani and black communities (both African and Caribbean) also suffer from high unemployment. Only the Chinese and Indian communities enjoy employment levels similar to those of the white population, though both suffer from higher unemployment. Figure 40.1 provides data of unemployment levels among various ethnic groups.

With the exception of Indian men (who earn slightly more on average than white men) and Chinese men, ethnic minorities earn lower wages than whites. In 1998–9, black men earned £1 per hour less on average than white men, whereas Bangladeshi and Pakistani men earned £1.50 less. The average white wage was £9.24 per hour. Assuming a forty-hour work week and fifty-two weeks of work per year, the average white man earned £19,219; the average black man, £17,130; and the average Pakistani/Bangladeshi, man £16,099. Women of all ethnic backgrounds, including white, earned less than men. A broad range of studies have confirmed these patterns of race-based disadvantage.

These economic outcomes do not correlate perfectly with educational achievement. In the tertiary sector, black students start at the age of five at the same broad level as the national average. By the age of ten, they have fallen behind, particularly in mathematics, and black students are far less likely than others to secure five GCSEs (Parekh 2000: 146). Indian students, by contrast, achieve results above the national average, particularly in their GCSEs. At the university level, the results are overall more positive. In terms of entry into university, Indian, Pakistani, and Afro-Caribbean women exceed the national average, as do Indian, Pakistani, and

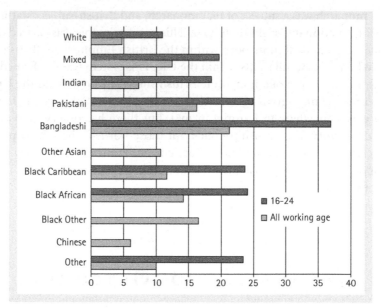

Fig. 40.1 Unemployment rates by ethnic group and age, 2001–2

Source: Annual Local Area Labour Force Survey, Office for National Statistics.

Bangladeshi men (Parekh 2000: 147). They are, however, disproportionately placed at the least prestigious universities: 70 per cent of Afro-Caribbean men and 60 per cent of Indian, Pakistani, and Bangladeshi students study at universities that were once polytechnics (technical schools or community colleges), compared to 35 per cent of the general population (Parekh 2000: 148). These institutions consistently fare worse than older universities when it comes to placing job candidates. Finally, within these averages there is substantial polarization: Bangladeshi and Pakistani students are over-represented among both university entrants and sixteen-year-olds with the poorest qualifications.

Evidence of any race-based gap in achievement is worrying, but two more questions need to be asked. First, to what degree does the gap reflect inadequate human capital (language skills, education), which can be remedied, at least between generations? Second, are these gaps narrowing or increasing over time? Taking into account personal characteristics (skills and education), sociologists working on the first question note the disparity that persists between the chances of ethnic minorities securing employment or higher-level jobs or income and the chances of others doing so; they refer to it as the 'ethnic penalty' (Heath and Yu 2005). It thus includes, but is broader than, the concept of discrimination. Separate studies have concluded that Pakistanis and Bangladeshis (and particularly Pakistani and Bangladeshi women) pay the highest ethnic penalty, while Indians (and particularly Indian men) pay the lowest. Black men and women fall between these two groups. The literature is, however, less clear on why they pay this penalty, simply restating the question. Scholars have suggested that discrimination in hiring and promotion practices accounts for the distinction (Carmichael and Woods 2000; Berthoud 2000). In the 1960s and 1970s, field experiments (which involved having white British, white non-British, and ethnic minority applicants apply for the same job) demonstrated high levels of racial discrimination (Hansen 2000: 226). These have not been repeated, but surveys on perceptions of discrimination suggest that discrimination declined between 1968 and 1974 yet remained constant over the next twenty years (Heath and Yu 2005).

It is certainly plausible that discrimination partially accounts for higher unemployment and lower wages among ethnic minorities, but this explanation cannot easily account for variance in ethnic minority performance. It is not obvious why one group of South Asians (Bangladeshis) would pay a high ethnic penalty while others (Indians) paid a low one. Drawing on Robert Putnam's distinction between bonding social capital (which links members of a social group with each other) and bridging social capital (which links members of a group with the wider society), a recent study has suggested that Pakistanis and Bangladeshis have high bonding but relatively low bridging social capital (Heath and Yu 2005). This would mean that while they have the networks necessary to ensure employment in family businesses and/or the informal economy, they lack the networks that play a decisive role in securing employment and promotion outside the community. The issue can be further explored by considering ethnic minorities' experiences in education and the labour market over time.

40.7 Migrants' Success (and Failure) Over Time

There are no UK data comparing recent migrants' experience with that of earlier generations of migrants (partly because the concern is with racial minorities, migrants or not), but Anthony Heath and Soojin Yu use multivariate analysis to compare the ethnic penalty between first- and second-generation migrants in three areas: access to the salariat, education, and employment (2005). The first generation was born between 1940 and 1959, and most would have been migrants to Britain. The second generation was born between 1960 and 1979, and most would have been born in Britain. Heath and Yu find that while the first generation has enjoyed increased access to the salariat over time, it has failed to close the gap with whites. By contrast, in the second generation, Indians have overtaken whites in access to the salariat, and Pakistanis and Bangladeshis have closed the gap. Given the last two groups' high unemployment levels, this is an important finding. As the statistics suggest, the most notable cross-generational changes have been in education. Whereas the first generation had notably lower education levels than the population at large, the second generation has closed the gap, and Indians have overtaken whites. The authors do not mention it, but this conclusion should be qualified by noting ethnic minorities' concentrations in less prestigious universities. Finally, it is in the area of employment that outcomes are the worst. Although the first generation paid no ethnic penalty in the form of higher unemployment, there is a large one for the second—particularly, as noted, for Pakistanis and Bangladeshis. If the authors' argument about bridging social capital is to hold, it has to be the case that bridging social capital either declined in these groups or became more important than previously in the job market. Both developments are possible, but the authors suggest another explanation: discrimination is class based. For each election from 1974 until 1979, British Election Studies provided the percentage of respondents who felt that 'attempts to give equal opportunities to black people and Asians in Britain have gone too far'. The results show a consistent pattern of greater prejudice among managers and employers in small businesses than among professionals or managers in large organizations. The evidence supports the authors' hypothesis that there is greater discrimination at the lower levels of the labour market than the higher ones, and it might explain why there are continuing ethnic penalties in unemployment but not in access to the salariat. Similarly, as Indians (and Chinese) are over-represented in the salariat while Pakistanis and Bangladeshis are over-represented in manual positions, class-based discrimination would explain the varying ethnic penalties they have paid.

40.8 THE TURN AGAINST MULTICULTURALISM IN THE UK

Following the election of the Labour Party in 1997, 'multiculturalism' became a fashionable term in the UK. Cabinet members used it frequently; the Home Office commissioned reports on the topic and organized conferences around it; and ministers came back from trips to Canada with glowing words for its immigration and multiculturalism policies. Eight years later, the term had almost become a dirty word. The major newspapers ran articles and editorials denouncing the balkanizing effects of multiculturalism, and the Home Office placed the accent once again on integration in, and loyalty to, Britain. To be sure, the realization that three out of four of the July 2005 bombers were born in Britain and had relatively affluent backgrounds was a profound shock to the national psyche; it had an effect comparable to that which the murder of film-maker Theo Van Gogh had on the Netherlands. The rhetorical shift began, however, before this. In the summer of 2001, riots broke out in northern English cities between Asian (that is, of Pakistani, Bengali, or Indian descent) and white youths. Although the rioting Asians were UK citizens, Home Secretary David Blunkett framed the riots as a problem of immigration and integration. Since then, the government has stiffened requirements for citizenship with the goal of ensuring that naturalized migrants are better integrated: a US-style citizenship ceremony with an oath of allegiance to the Queen and the UK was introduced in 2004; and since 2005, naturalizing migrants have had to pass language and citizenship tests. All of these measures were enacted or set in motion before the bombings. Even the Equality and Human Rights Commission (formerly the Commission for Racial Equality, CRE), the official voice of ethnic minority concerns in the UK, has joined the integrationist chorus. In 2004, the CRE's black director, Trevor Phillips, made national headlines by insisting that 'multiculturalism is dead'.

Is it? In the main, these changes amount to a shift in accent or rhetoric rather than policy. The right of ethnic minorities to practice their religion, speak their language, join ethnic associations, and lobby for group-based causes is fundamental to liberal democracy in the UK and elsewhere. To this degree, multiculturalism flows from liberalism: it manifests itself in group-based claims and activities, but these claims and activities derive their logic and justification from individual rights grounded in national constitutions and defended by the courts. Changes have of course occurred. There are more obligations involved in acquiring citizenship, and its acquisition is meant to reflect a meaningful attachment to Britain (which is hardly an unreasonable expectation). That this threatens multiculturalism is doubtful: it is not at all clear that requiring citizens to speak the national language violates multicultural principles; only denying them the right to speak their own language would do that. In contrast with the Canadian government, the UK government has provided no national funds for sustaining different cultures; in contrast with their counterparts in the Netherlands, ethnic minorities in the UK have not been encouraged to organize politically along ethnic lines (indeed, such efforts within the national political parties have been resisted). The government's main flirtation with group-based politics was its highly controversial informal association with the Muslim Council of Britain (the MCB), an organization that claims to speak for all Muslims. The association attracted intense criticism following the MCB's denunciation of homosexuality, equivocal response to terrorism (describing Hamas-inspired suicide bombers as 'freedom fighters'), and refusal to recognize Holocaust Memorial Day.

40.9 BRITISH IMMIGRATION POLICY AND THE STUDY OF POLITICS

With some exceptions (Geddes 1996; Hansen 2000; Shaggar 1998; Studlar 1978; Hampshire 2005), students of politics have played relatively little attention to British immigration history and policy. The claim that immigration is important will secure enthusiastic agreement in departmental meetings or at conferences, but this is rarely followed through with research projects. Given that at certain periods—in the late 1960s, when Enoch Powell was at the peak of his powers, and from 1997 to the present—immigration is central to British political life, this is curious. For whatever reason, immigration has not captured the same level of interest among British political scientists as the Westminster institutions, the country's relationship with Europe, devolution, or economic and social policy. Only recently have comparativists turned their attention to the topic (more on this below).

Part of this inattention reflects the original framing of the issue. To a unique degree in the Western world, British policy-makers have interpreted immigration through the lens of 'race:' immigration created race problems and the goal of public policy was 'good race relations' (meaning an absence of racial problems, namely violent conflict). The first scholars working on the topic—Nicholas Deakin, E. J. B. Rose, and John Rex—were empiricists. The earliest works in this vein offered an essentially pluralist interpretation: the steady rise in non-white Commonwealth immigrants in the 1950s, and the accelerated arrival in the early 1960s, led the Conservative government to end, reluctantly, the right of Commonwealth immigrants to enter (Deakin 1968; 1969; Rose 1969).

By the early 1970s, 'race relations' was becoming an academic industry dominated (like left-wing politics in Britain generally in the 1970s) by Marxism. One early, seminal work applied class analysis to the whole of Europe, including the UK (Castles and Kosack 1974; also see Miles 1982). According to Marxist-functionalist interpretations, immigrants responded to the needs of capitalism (namely a supply of cheap labour), cushioned its crises-tendencies (by bearing the brunt of unemployment), and delayed its inevitably collapse.[2]

Closely related to this literature was a set of arguments that might be grouped together under critical race theory (Carter, Harris, and Joshi 1987; Solomos 1989; Gilroy 1987). The title of Paul Gilroy's book, *There Ain't no Black in the Union Jack*, said it all. The British and their immigration policies were determined to a superlative degree by racism, and British identity itself was thoroughly race-based (or 'racialized'). Betraying their Marxist origins, under some versions of the thesis, the British working class was seen as enlightened and foreigner-friendly until being duped into racism by Labour and Conservative politicians (Foot 1965; Paul 1997).

Like many schools, both the Marxist functionalist and critical race approaches offered important insights. British immigration to the UK was largely market driven, and it was true that British politicians had a tendency to think that 'race' rather than 'racism' was the problem. But in the end they left too little unexplained. Opposition to immigration came too often from those with the greatest interest in capitalism (such as Margaret Thatcher) to accept the Marxist-functionalist story as an explanation of policy (as distinct from an account of how markets move migrants). Similarly, the emphasis of racism could not explain: why immigration policy stayed so liberal for so long (open borders until 1962, and easy movement until 1971); why there was never any serious effort to block family immigration; and why politicians such as Iain

---

[2] Another important argument was offered in an important book by Ira Katznelson (1973), who argued that Britain's integration policy reflected an adoption in the metropole of the colonial strategy of indirect rule: issues of immigration and race were shunted to the periphery (i.e. local government) where they were dealt with in cooperation with local elites.

MacLeod (over the Kenyan Asians), Ted Heath (over the Ugandan Asians), or Roy Jenkins (over anti-discrimination) legislations adopted bold, pro-migrant positions at variance with public opinion. Finally, the claim that the working class was a bastion of liberal opinion talked into racism could not be taken seriously.

From the 1990s, comparativists—mostly in political science, but also in sociology—began to study the UK as one case among others in Europe. Two related trends stood out. First, British immigration policy had shifted from periods of great liberality (the 1950s and 1960s), to great restrictiveness (the 1970s to mid-1990s), back to (relative) liberality again (the mid-1990s to the present). Numbers fluctuated accordingly: high in the 1960s to early 1970s, low in the 1980s, and high again in the last decade. Second, rhetoric on the UK showed similar tendencies: periods of bipartisan consensus keeping immigration out of politics (the mid-1960s, much of the 1970s, 1980s, and early 1990s) were suddenly disrupted by periods of intense bipartisan competition. A number of authors (Freeman 1995; Joppke 1999; Hansen 2000) explained these features with reference to British institutions. The absence of the checks on the executive found in the United States or Germany mean that the UK can maintain for relatively long periods policies that fly in the face of public opinion (open immigration). When governments do restrict, however, those same institutions also mean that they are able to achieve a high degree of restrictiveness.

An institutional account also sheds light on the jarring shifts in rhetoric over immigration. Immigration is a highly divisive issue that tends to split the parties: traditionally, between the free trade/pro-European versus protectionist/little Englander wings of the Conservative Party and the working class/liberal professional wings of Labour. It is also exceptionally hard to respect discourse constraints: as in Germany or the USA, debates about immigration often bring out nativist or xenophobic sentiment in both the parties and the public. For these reasons, the parties often agree informally to leave the issue alone. Yet, at the same time, Britain's system of adversarial government encourages competition over the issue, and both parties and individuals have an incentive to politicize the issue. This is particularly true when numbers are high and when there is little distance between the parties on economic issues (true of the 1960s and of today).

Framed in this way, an institutional account avoids the over-determination of Marxist-functionalist or critical-race interpretations. Institutions encourage certain responses, but leave much room for agency. In the 1960s, Roy Jenkins articulated a vision of an inclusive, tolerant society (partly out of principle, partly because it did him a lot of good with the intellectual wing of the Labour Party). In the 1980s, Thatcher (and some of her ministers, such as Kenneth Baker, Norman Tebbit, and Alan Clark) were particularly hostile to immigration. Finally, in the 1990s, Tony Blair and others in the new Labour government, who were too young to have lived through Enoch Powell and the immigration crises of the 1960s and 1970s, viewed immigration as an issue to be managed in the interest of Britain's economic success. Nonetheless, in several of these cases—Enoch Powell in the 1960s, Thatcher in the late 1970s (when she famously said that the British feared being 'swamped' by people of a different culture), and then-Tory party leader Michael Howard in 2005—used immigration to create political distance between themselves and the opposition. Somewhat paradoxically, British institutions make UK immigration both excessively liberal and excessively illiberal.

REFERENCES

BBC 2008. 'Immigration "Small Benefit" to UK'. 1 Apr.

BERTHOUD, R. 2000. 'Ethnic Employment Penalties in Britain'. *Journal of Ethnic and Migration Studies*, 26/3: 389–416.

BLEICH, E. 2003. *Race Politics in Britain and France: Ideas and Policymaking since the 1960s.* Cambridge: Cambridge University Press.

CASTLES, S., and KOSACK, G. 1974. *Immigrant Workers and Class Structure in Western Europe.* London: Oxford University Press.

CHISWICK, B. 2005. 'The Economic Effects of Migration'. In M. Gibney and R. Hansen (eds.), *Immigration and Asylum from 1900 to the Present.* Santa Barbara, Calif.: ABC-CLIO.

CARMICHAEL, F., and WOODS, R. 2000. 'Ethnic Penalties in Unemployment and Occupational Attainment: Evidence for Britain'. *International Review of Applied Economics*, 14/1: 71–98.

CARTER, B., HARRIS, C., and JOSHI, S. 1987. 'The 1951–55 Conservative Government and the Racialization of Black Immigration'. In W. James and C. Harris (eds.), *Insider Babylon: The Caribbean Diaspora in Britain.* London: Verso.

DEAKIN, N. 1968. 'The Politics of the Commonwealth Immigrants Bill'. *Political Quarterly*, 39: 25–45.

——1969. 'The British Nationality Act of 1968: A Brief Study in the Political Mythology of Race Relations'. *Race and Class*, 11/1: 77–83.

DUDLEY, J., ROUGHTON, M., FIDLER, J., and WOOLLACOTT, S. 2005. *Control of Immigration: Statistics United Kingdom, 2004, Control of Immigration Statistics, 2006.* London: Office for National Statistics.

FOOT, P. 1965. *Immigration and Race in British Politics.* Harmondsworth: Penguin.

FREEMAN, G. P. 1995. 'Modes of Immigration Politics in Liberal Democratic States'. *International Migration Review*, 29/4: 881–902.

GEDDES, A. 1996. *The Politics of Immigration and Race.* London: Baseline.

GILROY, P. 1987. *There Ain't No Black in the Union Jack.* London: Hutchison.

HAMPSHIRE, J. 2005. *Citizenship and Belonging: Immigration and the Politics of Demographic Governance in Post-war Britain.* Houndmills: Palgrave.

HANSEN, R. 2000. *Citizenship and Immigration in Postwar Britain.* Oxford: Oxford University Press.

HEATH, A., and SOOJIN, Y. 2005. 'Explaining Ethnic Minority Disadvantage'. Pp. 187–224 in A. Heath, J. Ermisch, and D. Gallie (eds.), *Understanding Social Change.* London: Proceedings of the British Academy.

JOPPKE, C. 1999. *Immigration and the Nation-State: The United States, Germany, and Great Britain.* Oxford: Oxford University Press.

——2005. 'Citizenship'. In M. Gibney and R. Hansen (eds.), *Immigration and Asylum from 1900 to the Present.* Santa Barbara, Calif.: Clio.

—— 2006. 'Multiculturalism and Immigration: A Comparison of the United States, Germany, and Great Britain'. *Theory and Society*, 254: 449–500.

KATZNELSON, I. 1973. *Black Men, White Cities: Race, Politics, and Migration in the United States, 1900–30, and Britain, 1948–68*. London: Oxford University Press.

MILES, R. 1982. *Racism and Migration Labour*. London: Routledge and Kegan Paul.

PAREKH, B. 2000. *The Future of Multi-Ethnic Britain: The Parekh Report*. London: Profile Books.

PAUL, K. 1997. *Whitewashing Britain*. Ithaca, NY: Cornell University Press.

ROSE, E. J. B. 1969. *Colour and Citizenship: A Report on British Race Relations*. London: Oxford University Press.

SAGGAR, S. 1998. *Race and British Electoral Politics*. London: UCL Press.

SALT, J. 1999. *Current Trends in International Migration in Europe*. Strasbourg: Council of Europe.

SOLOMOS, J. 1989. *Race and Racism in Contemporary Britain*. London: Macmillan.

STUDLAR, D. T. 1978. 'British Public Opinion, Colour Issues, and Enoch Powell: A Longitudinal Analysis'. *British Journal of Political Science*, 4/3: 371–81.

UNHCR 1995. *The State of the World's Refugees 1995: A Humanitarian Agenda*. Oxford: Oxford University Press.

—— 2005. *Asylum Trends and Levels in Industrialized Countries*. Oxford: Oxford University Press.

US COMMITTEE FOR REFUGEES 1999. *World Refugee Survey*. Washington, DC.

CHAPTER 41

....

THE SECURITY STATE

....

RICHARD J. ALDRICH

THIS chapter will examine developments in the UK security state, focusing on the intelligence and security services, together with the Whitehall machinery that connects these agencies with the core executive. It will also consider related aspects of security policing or 'high policing'. It seeks to interpret the major developments that have taken place since the end of the cold war against the background of Europeanization, globalization, and the so-called 'Global War on Terror'. The discussion will address some of the more important legislative changes that have ushered in mechanisms for oversight and a remarkable new culture of regulation. However, before analysing these changes it might be helpful to advance some general propositions. During the last two decades, the UK security state has undergone a major transformation that might be said to have three main aspects.

First, the UK security state has moved from the shadows to centre stage. During the 1980s the very existence of the security services was often denied by a government characterized by obsessive secrecy. The main agent for change here was Europe. Important cases brought before the European Court propelled many countries, including the UK, to avow their agencies, to place them on a firm legal basis, and to institute oversight mechanisms. By the mid-1990s, Whitehall had begun to make virtue of necessity, employing the Central Intelligence Machinery as a flagship of Open Government and employing websites for personnel recruitment. This shift towards a higher public profile accelerated with the debate over intelligence prior to the Iraq War. Thereafter, multiple inquiries into intelligence transformed what had been a gentle limelight into a harsh spotlight. By early 2005, as John Scarlett took up his new post as Chief of the Secret Intelligence Service (MI6) at Vauxhall Cross, his face was well known and his track record was actively debated in the broadsheet press. Hitherto secret parts of government have witnessed unprecedented exposure.

Second, the inhabitants of the security state have ceased to be watchers and have instead become fixers and enforcers. The main driver here has been globalization. Until 1989 (with the exception of Northern Ireland) the cold war had required the secret services to focus largely on the passive observation of a relatively static enemy. However, by the late 1990s, the liberalization of economies, together with the impending expansion of Europe, had increased anxiety about crime. Indeed, across the world organized crime was killing more people than either war or terrorism and was increasingly regarded as a security problem in its own right. This prompted a shift towards intelligence-led policing and towards security agencies that would not only observe but also disrupt harmful activities. This trend was already evident in 1999, but the upsurge in terrorism has completed a transformation of the security agencies.

Third, the security state has expanded remarkably and its boundaries are now uncertain. The size of the UK Security Service (MI5) has broadly doubled, reaching c.4,000 in 2008. Expansion is also taking place in the Metropolitan Police Special Branch—now merged with the anti-terrorist police. MI6 and Government Communications Headquarters (GCHQ) are also growing. In April 2006, they were joined by a new Serious Organized Crime Agency (SOCA) with a strong intelligence component. Moreover, all elements of government are now empowered to conduct 'covert operations'. There are also important public–private partnerships. Increased size has consequences for complexion and character. One of the historic virtues often claimed for the UK security state is that it is small and operates as a genuine community. Senior staff have tended to be long-term professionals rather than political appointees (unlike the United States) and are known to each other. However, the UK's expanded security state poses new challenges in terms of coordination and management.

We also need to pause to consider the analytical frameworks that have been applied to the security state. Conventionally, this area has been conceptualized in terms of 'intelligence', 'surveillance', and 'secrecy'. 'Intelligence' has been defined as a secret activity designed to provide information that makes policy or operations more effective, typically through advanced warning of events. Both Christopher Andrew and James Der Derian have asserted that intelligence is remarkably for its under-theorization (Andrew 2004; Der Derian 1993). It is perhaps more accurate to say that it has been narrowly theorized, with much focus on why surprise attacks often defeat elaborate bureaucracies designed to provide warning. Although limited and profoundly positivist, this work has convincingly shown that intelligence failures rarely occur because of poor intelligence collection. Instead they tend to result from analytical weakness, bureaucratic failure, or poor responses by policy-makers (Betts 2007).

The use of the phrase 'security state' in the domestic context is synonymous with excessive 'surveillance' and odious interference in everyday life (Sidel 2005: 10–14). Ideas of surveillance have proved far more amenable to post-positivist approaches. Theorists have often connected 'surveillance' with Foucauldian ideas of disciplining, or with Gramscian notions of hegemony (Scott-Smith 2002: 9–12). Christopher Dandeker emphasizes the central importance of information gathering on citizens as a facet of modern governance. This extends far beyond security agencies to areas such as public health and the welfare state. Similarly, Giddens has argued that surveillance is key to the mobilizing of administrative power in the modern state (Dandeker 1990; Giddens 1990). Sociologists have tended to place more emphasis on technology and view surveillance as an inescapable manifestation of modernity (Lyons 1994). This latter approach reminds us that surveillance often manifests itself as 'dataveillance' by corporations as well as states. Security activity now involves public–private partnerships that facilitate the data mining of passenger records, or data aggregation using business methods. The UK public has proved surprisingly amenable to surveillance, whether through its customer loyalty cards or CCTV.

Others have argued that the key conceptual prism for those analysing the security state is not information but 'secrecy' (Vincent 1998). Many of the functions of the security state, including gathering information, are not especially distinct from other areas of government, or indeed the private sector—except that they are covered by a cloak of intense secrecy. This opens the door to critical perspectives that suggest that secrecy has less to do with operational efficiency and more to do with hiding unsavoury activities, or evading democratic accountability. Typically, this might mean the surveillance and disruption of fringe groups that are legitimate but inconvenient, such as environmental campaigners. Accordingly, critical writers often use the term 'security state' interchangeably with the 'secret state'. The most sophisticated treatment of the lineage of UK 'secret state' is offered by Peter Hennessy who underlines its long-standing cold war connections with states of emergency and resilience. However, Hennessy argues that the UK secret state represented a proportionate response to the credible threat of Soviet subversion (Hennessy 2000: 18).

Contemporary theorization of the UK security state requires some consideration of ideas of regionalization and globalization. Practitioners and scholars alike have made great play upon the distinction between domestic security surveillance and foreign intelligence, especially in recent legislation. In reality, within areas such as communications interception, the distinction between the domestic and the foreign is breaking down. More importantly, this chapter argues that the UK security state has been placed under contradictory pressures by globalization. On the one hand, its work in policing the underside of globalization—including global terrorism—has required riskier operations by the security agencies and cooperation with unsavoury overseas partners. On the other hand, the rise of global civil society has placed security agencies under increasing scrutiny, one might say even 'counter-surveillance', by an informal network of pressure groups and the media. Europe has also operated as a restraining factor. The most visible manifestation has been the uncertainty about how the UK might simultaneously embrace an American ally that conducts 'extraordinary rendition' while meeting the provisions of the ECHR (Rees and Aldrich 2005: 905–7).

41.1 THE END OF THE COLD WAR

The overall architecture of the UK security state still reflects its heritage. The most venerable component is the police Special Branch whose origins lie in counter-terrorism in the 1880s. The UK's lead security element consists of the Security Service (known as MI5), created in 1909 in response to anxieties about German espionage. Their main cold war opponents were the Soviet Bloc espionage services whose human agents achieved remarkable success in gathering intelligence, albeit their masters proved incapable of making effective use of it in their policy (Andrew and Mitrokhin 1999: 554–5). The cold war and the rise of ideological conflict introduced concomitant anxieties about 'subversion' and this in turn led to the expansion of political policing.

MI5's directive, set out by the Home Secretary, Maxwell Fyfe, in 1952, required them to address the problem of 'subversion', often defined as the undermining of democracy by political, industrial, or violent means. Most of the activities surveilled by the security state constitute a crime under UK law, but subversion does not. In reality the notion of subversion focused on the possibility of instrumental economic disruption. There is now substantial evidence of organized entryism by the far left using flawed union elections during the 1960s. The Special Branch of each constabulary worked with major companies such as car manufacturers to keep known activists off the payroll. Large companies also made extensive use of intelligence gathered by freelance organizations staffed by former intelligence officers. Surveillance of unions probably reached its high point during Margaret Thatcher's confrontations with the miners in the early 1980s. Ironically, the process of curtailing union power eventually turned in on the security state itself with the prolonged GCHQ trade union dispute between 1984 and 1997 (Leigh and Lustgarten 1994: 396–403).

MI5 activity also involved a process of background checks on UK citizens engaged in sensitive government work, referred to as 'vetting'. The volume of individuals vetted was high and included policy-makers in Whitehall, researchers at Aldermaston, and even non-government staff in the arms industry. Vetting was introduced in 1951 under strong American pressure following the discovery of Soviet moles, including the atom spy, Klaus Fuchs. This was one of the last initiatives of the Attlee government. During the 1960s and 1970s fear of Soviet penetration in both Washington and Whitehall was intense. Security measures included background checks on BBC employees who were sometimes debarred from promotion for fringe political activities. If deemed suspect they had a 'Christmas Tree' stamp placed on the cover of their personnel file. Controversially, potential ministers could also be blacklisted. Betty Boothroyd, the former speaker of the Commons, has revealed that MI5 had once asked her to gather information on four Labour MPs. MI5 also maintained files on both Jack Straw and Peter Mandelson as a result of their youthful political activities (*Sunday Times*, 18 Feb. 1996; Barnett 2002: 376–7).

The end of the cold war took the UK's security agencies by surprise. It was not predicted by the UK's main intelligence analysis body, the Joint Intelligence Committee (JIC), nor indeed by the intelligence agencies of its allies. Although this resulted in budgetary cuts of some 25 per cent for the UK security agencies, they did not suffer the sort of psychological crisis that gripped their American counterparts. After 1989, the IRA was still active and spare resources were redirected towards Northern Ireland. In 1992, MI5 were given overall responsibility for intelligence on the IRA on a worldwide basis. Moreover, the need to maintain a watch on extremist groups and to maintain databases to support vetting remained. During the 1990s the focus moved to single-issue groups such as animal rights activists (Leigh and Lustgarten 1991: 613–42).

41.2 NORTHERN IRELAND: THE OTHER LONG WAR

Although the UK security state enjoys a reputation for joined-up government and integration with the core executive, this did not occur in Northern Ireland where six different intelligence and security services spent the first decade of the Troubles tripping over each other. For most of the 1970s there were over 250 deaths each year and it was only in the 1980s that this fell significantly. Gradual penetration of the paramilitaries, together with the deployment of a vast range of surveillance technologies, deterred an increasing proportion of the planned attacks. In part this required the UK to build a large corps of intelligence officers who were skilled in running covert operations, a process which typically takes a decade (Gearty 1991: 123).

The challenge of Northern Ireland was assisted by the development of additional Cabinet Office machinery. Hitherto the role of coordinating the intelligence and security services had fallen to the Cabinet Secretary, reflected most clearly in his chairmanship of the Permanent Secretaries' Committee on the Intelligence Services (PSIS) which reviewed budgets. This role had been greatly enjoyed by Burke Trend in the 1960s, but was becoming increasingly time consuming. In 1968 this role transferred to the newly created post of Intelligence Coordinator in the Cabinet Office. The first incumbent was Dick White (1968–72), former head of MI5 then MI6. His successors were confronted with squabbling agencies in Northern Ireland. Proper order was not imposed on intelligence in the province until the mid-1980s with the creation of six regional Tasking and Coordinating Groups (TCGs) which had full over-sight of all covert operations in a particular area. The current National Intelligence Model employed by the UK police makes use of TCGs and other lessons learned in Ireland.

Although MI5 gradually became the intelligence overseer in the province, the most important institutional effect was the 'Ulsterization' of the British Army. Large military intelligence units were developed and even routine regiments of the line devoted 10 per cent of their strength to plain-clothes surveillance. Special sections such as the Force Research Unit applied ruthless pressure to the paramilitaries through agent penetration. However, this confronted the government with the awk-ward problem of running agents who needed to commit criminal acts to main-tain their cover. They also faced the possibility that violence between the various paramilitaries would result in the loss of key agents who it had taken years to put in place. The desire to avoid this contributed to the alarming collaboration between intelligence and protestant paramilitaries revealed by the Stevens Report in 2004 (Rolston 2006).

A frequent complaint about the security state is that they can facilitate invisible policies that are not subject to democratic scrutiny. This was certainly the case in Northern Ireland. Contrary to Margaret Thatcher's assertions about 'not talking to terrorists', the UK was engaging with the IRA continuously through MI6 officers based in Dublin. Latterly, this eased the way towards a political settlement in Northern Ireland. Declining IRA activity was felt most keenly by MI5. Having taken the lead on Irish terrorism following the end of the cold war, it was now losing another area of core business. To keep it alive, the government took the extraordinary step of handing MI5 some responsibility for intelligence support on organized crime after a process of minimal consultation.

In retrospect, the last spate of IRA activity, which targeted the UK's financial dis-tricts, now looks like the first wave of the future. The attacks on the City of London in 1992 and Canary Wharf in 1996 signalled a new anxiety about strategic terrorism that threatened national infrastructures and economic well-being, and raised worrying questions about resilience. The response also pointed the way towards public–private partnerships in security. A 'Ring of Steel' was thrown up around the City of London reflecting a network of agreements between government agencies, private security companies, and the financial institutions. The latest format is Operation Griffin, which not only helps to train private security operatives employed by the banking houses, but also permits the exchange of intelligence between public and private partners. Some of the communications infrastructure for Griffin is provided by JP Morgan rather than by government networks. 'Griffinization'—the development of public–private security partnerships—has accelerated (London Assembly 2005: 39–42).

41.3 EUROPEANIZATION AND
THE EUROPEAN COURT

Alongside shifting targets, the UK security state has also faced nothing short of a regulatory revolution. The main driver was two cases in the European Court of Human Rights. The first was brought in 1984 by Harriet Harman when an MI5 officer revealed that files were held on her and a colleague. The nub of their argument was that MI5 had no legal standing and lacked proper mechanisms for oversight and accountability. In the Leander case of 1987, the European Court found against the Swedish security service on similar grounds. Like most European states, the UK and Sweden had dealt with its security services by pretending that they did not exist and hoping that its operatives were never caught. Across Europe, states now rushed to put their agencies on the statute books. Despite initial anxiety, a firm legal status and clear guidelines for surveillance have meant that agencies are free to carry out more operations. The legislation has been permissive since the criterion is now 'is it legal?' rather than 'will we get caught'? This outcome was not anticipated, nor indeed welcomed, by civil rights campaigners who had long advocated greater regulation.

The Security Service Act of 1989 and the Intelligence Services Act of 1994 placed the UK's three main agencies on the statute book and gave them formal remits. Additionally the functions of the National Criminal Intelligence Service were covered by the 1997 Police Act. MI5 retained a brief for countering subversion, although the problematic term 'subversion' was no longer employed in the statute. A range of tribunals and commissioners, normally former judges, were created to deal with public complaints arising from operations. The security services introduced staff counsellors to respond to colleagues who had anxieties about their work. Most importantly perhaps, they also conjured into existence what has become the most visible mechanism for UK accountability, the Intelligence and Security Committee.

The UK Intelligence and Security Committee (ISC) resembles a Parliamentary Select Committee. However, it is merely a statutory committee and has not enjoyed the full powers of a select committee, nor is it owned by parliament. Instead its members are selected from parliament by the Prime Minister and report to Downing Street. ISC reports are made public, together with the responses of government, but in a sanitized form, and can be edited by the Prime Minster. In short it is a committee of parliamentarians but it is not of parliament. The ISC initially lacked any research component, rendering it anodyne by comparison with its foreign equivalents. Meanwhile members of genuine UK Parliamentary Select Committees, typically on Home Affairs, have argued that the creation of ISC curtails their own right to introspect into the security agencies. Some have complained that its reports are mere 'audits' and contain only limited reflection or analysis, albeit there is a good working relationship with the agencies. There is little consensus on the effectiveness of the ISC. In July 2007, Gordon Brown's Green Paper on 'The Governance of Britain' undertook to consult on how the ISC could be brought 'as far as possible' into line with that of other select committees, including the restoration of the investigator whose services were abruptly dispensed with in 2004. Similar notions were aired in the 2008 UK National Security Strategy (Gill 1996: 313–31; Glees, Davies, and Morrison 2006; Leigh 2005: 84–9, 93).

Observers have expressed scepticism concerning the modernized security state. Some have argued that the advent of tribunals, commissioners, and counsellors was in part an attempt to keep disaffected intelligence officers away from the unpredictable realm of courts and normal employment tribunals. Only one complaint to any tribunal concerning intelligence and security matters has been upheld since their creation in the mid-1980s. Depending on one's view, this is either very reassuring or else very worrying (HC 314 2007, s. 38). The argument that increased regulation has in reality meant greater opaqueness is most compelling with regard to the new Official Secrets Act of 1989. The original Act had been introduced to parliament in 1911 and passed in an afternoon. Widely criticized down the years by senior judges, including Lord Denning, its last vestige of credibility was destroyed by the failed case against Clive Ponting in 1985 and the *Spycatcher* affair in 1987. The new Act removed the notorious catch-all Section 2, replacing it with offences that related to specific groups of people and information. However, the new Act also went to great lengths to remove the possibility of a 'public interest' defence. Subsequently, 'whistleblowers' such as David Shayler, the dissident MI5 officer, have had to fall back on the ECHR with its relatively weak protection of freedom of expression. Notwithstanding this, whistleblowers continue to trump government lawyers, as underlined by the Catherine Gunn case in 2005 and the Derek Pasquill case in 2007 (Gill 1996: 313–20; Morrison 2006: 51–2).

More important has been the Regulation of Investigatory Powers Act of 2000 (RIPA), which sought to control the use of covert surveillance, agents, informants, and undercover officers by UK authorities. On the face of it, this legislation was marked by the commendable incorporation of parts of the ECHR into its operating principles. Managers are required to show that surveillance was necessary to avoid public harm and that the information could not be obtained by less intrusive means. There are also important references to the proper control of, and safety of, the agents themselves, a category of person who is sometimes recruited under duress and whose rights have historically received precious little respect. RIPA also created an Investigatory Powers Tribunal which superseded the Security Service Tribunal, the Intelligence Services Tribunal, and the Interception Tribunal that had been established between 1985 and 1994. This has the power to quash warrants, destroy records, and award compensation. Importantly, the tribunal can also hear proceedings brought under Section 7 of the Human Rights Act of 1998 against any of the intelligence services.

At the same time, the public were disconcerted to learn just how many government departments were now empowered to use covert surveillance. This included not only the obvious praetorian elements, but all departments of state and even local government. In 2008, Britain's interception of communications commissioner revealed that nearly 800 public bodies, including NHS trusts, were making an average of nearly 1,000 requests a day for communications data, including actual phone taps, mobile phone records, email or web search histories, not to mention old-fashioned snail mail. Empowered bodies also include 474 local councils who made 1,700 requests to access mobile phone records and other private information in the last nine months of 2006. Therefore, while Europe has initiated the UK security state into the new culture of regulation, this was of a facilitating kind (Ash 2008).

41.4 GLOBALIZATION, E-INFRASTRUCTURE, AND ORGANIZED CRIME

The end of the cold war, and to some extent the drawing down of conflicts such as Northern Ireland, reflected broader changes in the international system which relate to 'globalization'. Globalization is most commonly associated with deterritorialization and assertions of the decline of the sovereign state, together with notions about the communications revolution as an accelerator of these processes. For the UK, globalization has perhaps been most significant in economic terms. The UK deregulated faster than most other European states and gained visibly from the expansion of world trade and the financial services industry. This is symbolized by the growth of London as a major financial capital and the emergence of its airport as the world's largest air transport hub. In short, the declinist predictions about the UK were confounded.

Accordingly, during the early 1990s, few in government viewed globalization as anything other than unqualified good. Many had bought into Francis Fukuyama's assertions about a peaceful post-cold war system characterized by economic competition between liberal democracies. A notable exception was Sir Colin McColl, the Chief of MI6. Against the background of the end of the cold war and the decline in domestic terrorism, he reassured his staff that they would not be without work. Far from witnessing 'the end of history', he predicted that, instead, they would soon be busier than ever. During the early 1990s, MI6 created a global issues section. Their working style gradually began to shift from a focus on country stations in capitals around the world to more London staff who responded to problems on a global basis. However, they were unable to dissuade the Treasury from cutting the budgets of the security agencies (Smith 2003: 233, 240).

McColl was right. One of the entities that thrived on globalization was Al-Qaeda, which emerged just as the capacity to address it was being curtailed drastically. Moreover, the 1990s saw the rise of separate but connected challenges, many of which might be described as complex clandestine networks. They included narcotics, money laundering, people trafficking, war-lordism, nuclear proliferation, and the illegal light weapons trade. These problems were accelerated by globalization and overlapped with new civil wars, of which the former Yugoslavia was the most prominent. In Russia, the Balkans, and Central Asia, a range of shadowy figures from the security services were also major players in the criminal underworld.

The common element among these new threats was that many of them operated clandestinely. The UK response was to redirect the security state. One symptom was more intelligence-led policing underlined by the creation of the National Criminal Intelligence Service and eventually a National Intelligence Model that was rolled out to all police services by the end of the decade. By 1998 government was reversing the cuts in the budgets of the security agencies (Rice and Thomas 1997: 14–15). The shift in emphasis was confirmed by a summit at 10 Downing Street in late 1999 attended by MI5, MI6, and GCHQ which authorized a significant diversion of their resources against organized crime. In June 2000, the shocking discovery of fifty-eight Chinese illegal immigrants who had perished in a container lorry at Dover highlighted the seriousness of these issues. They were now reconceptualized as a security problem. In part this reflected the planned expansion of NATO and the European Union, giving the UK an open frontier that extended as far as the Urals (National Criminal Intelligence Service 2000; Barnett 2002: 366–7).

The increase in the power of global markets has been intimately associated with the retreat of the state. In the UK this has manifested itself in terms of deregulation and privatization. The UK's new dependence on financial and service industries has also required concerted attention to critical national infrastructure. In the 1990s, the new priority was to guarantee secure e-commerce. This required a major culture change for the UK security state. Hitherto the security of communications infrastructure had been conceived largely in terms of government agencies. The work-a-day security of government cyphers had been protected by the Communications Electronic Security Group, the defensive arm of GCHQ in Cheltenham. However, during the 1990s there was a growing realization that government would need to roll out the same level of protection to banks and businesses. Moreover, many activities that had been state owned, including the UK's telecom infrastructure itself, had been privatized. Accordingly, by 1997 the Communications Electronic Security Group transformed itself from a secretive entity into a national technical advisory service with a public face, setting standards for encryption and offering support to business on a cost recovery basis. However, its activities have remained controversial, since many question its interest in encouraging the independent growth of truly secure systems.

GCHQ is the intelligence giant in the UK, constituting the largest and most expensive element in the UK security state. Yet despite its size, the exponential increase in global communications traffic, together with new modes of communication, have presented severe challenges. A Treasury-inspired review under Roger Hurn in 1995 revealed that GCHQ was falling behind and needed to undertake significant change. The following year, under the direction of David Omand, much of the old Fordist organizational structure was abandoned. Modelling themselves on leading business corporations, they undertook a management revolution, which resulted in flatter hierarchies, flexible teams, and greater knowledge sharing. Its Mechanical

Engineering Division was entirely privatized. This was followed by a decision to invest in cutting-edge technologies under a programme entitled Signals Intelligence New Systems (SINEWS). Emblematic of this change was the move to a vast new GCHQ building on a PFI basis, completed in 2003 at many times the original estimated cost. However, the world remained stubbornly unpredictable and the new building was soon found to be too small to accommodate the expansion of GCHQ personnel that followed the terrorist attacks of 9/11.

41.5 TERRORISM: AFTER 9/11

During the late 1990s, the UK security state was gradually becoming aware of what some have called the 'new terrorism'. This was characterized by religious motivation and ambitious attacks together with new organizational structures and operations that took advantage of globalization. The physical manifestation of this was the exodus of trained foreign fighters from Afghanistan after the end of the Western-backed war against the Soviet occupation. There was also growing concern about the interaction between terrorism, proliferation, failed states, and organized crime. These trends were addressed by the UK Terrorism Act of 2000 which offered a much wider definition of terrorism which included political, religious, or ideological causes and also covered activities outside the UK. The new act expanded police powers relating to stop, search, and detention and empowered stronger financial investigation. In the wake of a peace settlement in Northern Ireland, some found it odd that special provisions were being expanded rather than dismantled. However, these changes anticipated future trouble (Cornish 2005: 148–9; Moran 2006: 343).

Following the remarkable attacks on New York and Washington on 11 September 2001, the UK government moved to implement a new counter-terrorism strategy entitled 'Contest'. Confronted with terrorists that favoured mass casualty spectaculars and that seemed hard to deter, the official view was that merely increasing intelligence activity would not be enough. 'Contest' consisted of four main strands:

- Prevention: addressing the underlying causes of terrorism both here and overseas through, for example, support for moderate Islam;
- Pursuit: using intelligence effectively to disrupt and apprehend terrorists, with increased joint working and intelligence sharing internationally, tightened border security, and new measures to target identity theft and terrorist finance;
- Protection: using protective security precautions to minimize risks to the UK public at home and abroad; and
- Preparedness: improving resilience to cope with terrorist attacks or other serious disruption.

Arguably, we have seen a fifth 'P' in the form of 'pre-emption' that reflects government anxiety about large-scale attacks and the potential use of unconventional weapons. The security state is much less willing to allow potential terrorists to remain at large. Over the years, and reflecting its experiences in Northern Ireland, the UK had developed an intelligence strategy towards terrorism that might be described as 'watch and wait', hoping that terrorists who remained at liberty would continue to give off valuable intelligence. Since 9/11, the UK strategy has increasingly leant towards 'seize and strike'; however, once suspects are incarcerated, the flow of intelligence quickly becomes outdated (Omand 2005: 107–16; Innes 2006: 222–41).

The events of 9/11 also triggered significant changes in structure. During June 2002, the post of Intelligence Coordinator in the Cabinet Office was upgraded to become a Second Cabinet Secretary with wider responsibility for Intelligence, Security, and Resilience. The addition of 'resilience' greatly expanded the role and reflected Sir David Omand's desire to encourage joined-up government with many departments that had hitherto given little thought to resilience or security (Omand 2004: 26–33). The traditional view that security was the responsibility of specialist sections was at an end. This was reflected in a new mechanism for processing operational intelligence on terrorism, an all-source fusion centre called the Joint Terrorism Analysis Centre, located within the MI5 building at Thames House. This consists of participants from many different departments. Its inclusiveness has been widely praised and its has been emulated across Europe. MI5 itself has taken on an expanded coordinating role for a range of national security activities that go far beyond its traditional roles (Bamford 2005: 744–5).

New organizations were accompanied by new powers. Most controversial was the new Anti-Terrorism Crime and Security Act of 2001 which extended police powers against suspects (Fenwick 2002). The authorities were quick to use the new powers granted in 2000 and 2001 to arrest demonstrators who clearly had no relationship to terrorism, typically peace protestors outside a DSEi arms fair in London. In one case the police served a Section 44 Order (anti-terrorist order) on an eleven-year-old-girl. Similarly, the US Department of Justice has conceded that the Patriot Act has been little used against terrorism, but has proved useful against drug trafficking and organized crime. This reflects a deliberate corrosion of the boundary between intelligence and criminal investigation. The most obvious example of this in the UK has been use of intelligence presented to ad hoc tribunals regarding immigration, detention, or control orders. This material is of variable reliability and yet it is difficult to challenge (Moran 2006: 342, 345; Wada 2002: 51–9).

Notoriously, Part IV of the 2001 Anti-Terrorism Crime and Security Act allowed a significant number of people to be held indefinitely without charge by derogation from ECHR. For many, this recalled Ulster's dubious era internment under the Special Powers Act of 1972. By February 2004, some fourteen individuals were held under these provisions and kept at Belmarsh Prison. These were non-EU citizens detained on the basis of secret dossiers that often catalogued their associations rather than their activities. Returning to their country of origin was the only alternative to permanent detention. The following December, a nine-member bench of the House of Lords ruled this to be a contravention of their human rights. This system has been replaced by restraining orders that are akin to house arrest. Under further legislation passed in 2002 the Home Secretary gained the power to revoke citizenship (Bamford 2005: 748–9; Chirinos 2005: 265–76; Walker 2005: 400–1).

The Civil Contingencies Act of 2004 is the most remarkable piece of recent legislation and underlines the extent to which the whole UK state is now tinged with security. This Act replaces outdated cold war planning and allows the government to declare an 'emergency situation' and thence to restrict many civil liberties with the imposition of curfews, the prohibition of public protests, forced movement of people, and seizure of property. The original drafting of the bill set out a wide range of events that might trigger the declaration of an emergency, including threats to political, administrative, or economic stability. Although the phrasing was eventually tightened up, government remains at liberty to declare a 'state of emergency' as the result of threats that might disrupt transport or communications. Parliamentary criticism was fierce and the final version for the Act incorporated a sunset clause of thirty days and a requirement for approval by both houses within seven days (Bamford 2005: 750; Cornish 2005: 152–5; Sidel 2005: 153–4).

Detention without trial and civil contingencies, together with the period during which a suspect can be held for questioning, all created a political furore in the UK. ID cards have also formed a perennial subject for debate. However, equally important changes affecting UK citizens that have occurred outside the UK attracted almost no attention. After uneasy negotiations, the EU and the United States came to an agreement about the sharing of airline passenger data. A similar agreement gives US counter-terrorist investigators access to data on money transfers in Europe completed via the ubiquitous Swift system. There were also moves to require European telecom providers to retain data on their callers for a period of five years in order to assist investigators. These decisions resulted in the creation of vast warehouses of data relating to UK citizens, which can be aggregated and shared with private entities, but which are not within national control. Again, it is hard to resist the conclusion that the boundaries of the security state are expanding and increasingly blurred (Mathieson 2005: 1–2; Rees 2006: 231).

41.6 IRAQI WMD AND THE FOUR UK INTELLIGENCE ENQUIRIES

On 20 March 2003, the UK government joined the United States in a controversial invasion and occupation of Iraq that focused on non-compliance with UN resolutions on Weapons of Mass Destruction (WMD). Prior to this the UK government had decided to release two public dossiers on Iraq which it claimed to be based on intelligence material. The dossiers had been prepared for public consumption and were not actual declassified intelligence reports. Sceptical journalists could not believe that government press officers had been able to resist the temptation to enhance the dossiers. Subsequently, bitter arguments were played out in the full glare of publicity and rendered the security state more visible than ever before. In particular, the role of the JIC, a hitherto little-known organism, became the subject of national debate. Although the dossiers were in line with a long-term trend of allowing intelligence a more public profile, they also risked the charge that intelligence was being used to generate political support rather than to illuminate policy issues.

Following the invasion, no WMD were found, despite an intense search by the Iraq Survey Group. The controversy intensified and there followed an unprecedented 'season of inquiry' in Whitehall and Washington, with no less than four UK investigations between July 2003 and July 2004. Intelligence on Iraqi WMD was the subject of the first inquiry by the Parliamentary Select Committee on Foreign Affairs and the second inquiry by the ISC. The third, chaired by Lord Hutton, looked into the death of Dr David Kelly, a government scientist who had been closely cross-examined by the first inquiry. Finally, Lord Butler, a former Cabinet Secretary, was called in to conduct a more general investigation into the UK WMD intelligence. The Hutton inquiry, in particular, treated academics and journalists to a remarkably detailed view of the UK security state (Davies 2004: 495–520).

Was the Iraqi WMD fiasco a product of intelligence failure by the agencies, or deception by politicians and spin-doctors? Inevitably, the answer is 'both'. Having badly underestimated Iraqi WMD stocks in 1991, intelligence officers did not wish to be caught out a second time and so opted for 'worst case analysis'. Moreover, the allies cooperated so closely on WMD estimates that, far from challenging each other's findings, they succumbed to a form of 'Groupthink'. Only the Dutch and the Canadians expressed serious doubts. However, there was also government dishonesty. There was some plausible intelligence to suggest that the Iraqis might have hidden some old stocks from 1991. There was also some evidence that Iraq continued to seek WMD components on the world market and had future ambitions. However, there was no plausible evidence for the core claim that Iraq was engaged in 'continued' production of WMD. This latter assertion was made forcibly by the Prime Minister in his personal foreword to the Iraqi WMD dossier. ISC identified this mis-statement by Tony Blair, but curiously made little of it (Aldrich 2005: 73–5, 81). Equally, Butler noticed that there was no change in the intelligence reports on Iraqi WMD during the period between 2002 and 2003, when the UK shifted dramatically from a policy of containing Iraq to a policy of confrontation (Runciman 2004: 76–7).

These fourfold inquires into the security state deflected accountability downwards. Their remits did not allow an investigation of the relationship between intelligence and policy-making and so transparency translated into a hunt for minnows, while the big fish swam away. More importantly, by comparing these reports we can deduce much about the weak overall management of the burgeoning UK security state. The ISC pronounced UK intelligence on Iraqi WMD to be 'reliable' and credible, while Lord Butler's more thorough inquiry into the same issue pronounced the intelligence unreliable and its validation to be flawed. While Butler's conclusions were more accurate, his team was soon dissolved and oversight of the UK security state now remains with the ISC. Moreover, at Cabinet level there is supposedly a Ministerial Committee on the Intelligence and Security Services. Yet despite repeated exhortations, this body never met during the entire Blair administration. Arguably it is in the realm of experienced managerial oversight, as well as accountability, that the UK security state is impoverished.

41.7 Terrorism: After 7/7

The bombings in Madrid in March 2004 and then London in July 2005, together with the planned attack on airliners in August 2006, illuminate the scale of the current challenge faced by the UK security state. MI5 had taken an interest in radical Islamic groups in the UK during the 1990s but had not been greatly concerned about their presence. Each group was primarily interested in their own 'near enemy', namely their home governments in Saudi Arabia, Pakistan, and Algeria, and were regarded as inert from the point of view of London. However, Al-Qaeda was a new element in the security equation because it thought globally and sought to mobilize these parochial groups in a worldwide war against the 'far enemy'—the United States and its adherents (Gerges 2005; Bamford 2005: 739–40). Accelerated by the controversy over the Iraq War and the UK's closer association with the United States and Israel, radicalized Islamic groups that had hitherto been of only marginal interest to UK security agencies suddenly became a problem. The London bombings of 7 July 2005 also underlined the scale of a new indigenous threat (Gregory and Wilkinson 2005).

Shortly before the 7 July 2005 bombings, JTAC, the UK's intelligence fusion centre for terrorism, lowered the threat level. Subsequently, we have learned that two of the bombers, Mohamed Sidique Khan and Shazad Tanweer, had been the subject of attention by MI5 and may even have been filmed and recorded at meetings with other individuals of interest. While the events of 7 July 2005 probably contained some elements of intelligence failure, the more important lesson is that the efforts of Al-Qaeda, perhaps helped by current Western policies, have energized many constituencies that would not have thought to attack the UK a decade ago. As a result, the number of active individuals is beyond the capacity of even an expanded security state to keep under surveillance (Pythian 2005: 361–79).

Neither politicians nor the public recognize the limits of intelligence. During 2006, Elizabeth Manningham-Buller, Director of MI5, explained that there were 1,600 individuals of concern within the UK (Manningham-Buller 2007). Surveillance of one suspect requires the allocation of twenty operatives. Even with the expansion of MI5's A Branch, larger specialist police elements, and the occasional co-option of specialist military units it has not been possible to watch more than 200 people at any given time. The Metropolitan Police Commissioner, Sir Ian Blair, revealed in the Summer of 2005 that he was spending £500,000 a day over budget on terrorism-related security measures. The security state is at full stretch and this is also depleting the ability to counter organized crime and espionage (Harfield 2006: 743–61). More-over, counter-terrorist intelligence and the law do not make easy bedfellows. This has been underlined by a change in the attitude of the judiciary. During the cold war, commentators were inclined to observe that UK judges were cowardly when confronted with the spectre of national security rationales (Leigh and Lustgarten 1994: 321). However, following revelations about Guantanamo, Abu Graib, and 'spe-cial renditions', a new climate is evident. Equipped with the Human Rights Act of 1998 senior judges have become more robust in challenging the security state. The most obvious example is torture. On 8 December 2005, the House of Lords ruled that evidence obtained under torture from third countries was inadmissible in UK courts. The subject of torture has resonance. Some have alleged that the planned multiple attacks against airliners in the UK in August 2006 were thwarted by intelligence gained after the Pakistani security authorities had vigorously interrogated Rashid Rauf, a British subject (Danchev 2006: 587–95; Campbell and Ramesh 2006). More recently, the Venice Commission has underlined the importance of actively ensuring compliance with ECHR when cooperating with foreign services, a development that has profound significance.

Government has sought avenues by which it might discourage radicalization, but has moved uncertainly in this area. Efforts by the Foreign Office to engage directly with radicals have been dismissed as too timid by some and tantamount to appease-ment by others. Institutionally, the desire for a more sophisticated approach was signalled by the creation of a new Office of Counter-terrorism and Security within the Home Office in August 2007 under Charles Farr, a diplomat with extensive experience of counter-terrorism. Simultaneously, the post of Intelligence and Security Coordinator in the Cabinet Office has been downgraded. Farr's new office contains a Research Information and Communications Unit headed by Jonathan Allen, another diplomat who has a background in public relations. This represents an overt drive to win hearts and minds and parallels long-standing covert information activities. The creation of a Home Office unit run by diplomats also underlines deterritorialization and the end of a security state that has a largely domestic focus.

41.8 CONCLUSION

Globalization is now the fundamental security challenge for the UK. The porous nature of the market state has left government with little choice but to place its intelligence agencies on the front line in the struggle against terrorism, people trafficking, narcotics, and the other transnational pathologies of the early twenty-first century. This requires operations that are riskier, more kinetic, and often involve unsavoury partners. Activities against Al-Qaeda are an obvious example, but some of the operations led by MI6 in Colombia against the drug cartels from 1999 would serve equally well. The secret services are no longer the silent sentinels of the cold war; they have been recast as the 'toilet cleaners of globalization'. Yet at the same time Europeanization has presented a very different vista. Europe is still driving the new culture of regulation that overtook the security state in the 1990s. European institutions have worked with civil society in an effort to restrain the security agencies. As a result, the new security challenges that seem to call for more action, perhaps even a degree of beastliness, sit awkwardly with the rise of civil society and a complex legal culture. These contradictions do not augur well for the UK security state and its partners (Aldrich 2006: 158–61; Urban 2006: 24–5).

This, in turn, tells us something about the trajectory of the state in general. In the 1990s many had made confident assertions about the decline of the state, phrased in terms of marketization, the rise of consumerism, and the expansion of global governance (Marsh 1996; Paul and Ripsman 2004: 355–60). The catchphrase was the 'twilight of sovereignty'. Things look so different now. The long-awaited engines of global governance—much beloved of academics—are nowhere to be seen and, instead, muscular nation states are equipping themselves with arbitrary powers. The formidable growth of the UK security state might be unprecedented in national terms, but viewed through a comparative lens it is hardly unique. Enhanced military and intelligence capacity, together with extraordinary statutes that confer an intense cloak of secrecy, are now the spirit of the age. Political leaders who once embraced a neoliberal perspective on globalization have had to fall back on the Westphalian refuge of nation-state sovereignty. Accordingly, the security state that we thought had fallen out of fashion in 1989 is now very much 'back in' (Sidel 2005: 145–6).

REFERENCES

ALDRICH, R. J. 2005. 'Whitehall and the Iraq War: The UK's Four Intelligence Enquiries'. *Irish Studies in International Affairs*, 16: 73–88.

—— 2006. 'Setting Priorities in a World of Changing Threats'. Pp. 158–70 in Tsang 2006.

ANDREW, C. 2004. 'Intelligence, International Relations and "Under-theorisation"'. Pp. 29–41 in L. V. Scott and P. D. Jackson (eds.), *Understanding Intelligence in the Twenty-First Century: Journeys in Shadows*. London: Routledge.

—— and MITROKHIN, V. 1999. *The Sword and the Shield: The Mitrokhin Archive and the Secret History of the KGB*. New York: Basic Books.

ASH, T. G. 2008. 'Our State Collects More Data than the Stasi Ever Did'. *Guardian*, 31 Jan.

BAMFORD, B. W. C. 2005. 'The United Kingdom's "War against Terrorism"'. *Terrorism and Political Violence*, 16: 737–56.

BARNETT, H. 2002. *Britain Unwrapped: Government and Constitution Explained*. London: Penguin.

CAMPBELL, D., and RAMESH, R. 2006. 'Pakistan Says "Ringleader" Admits Link with al-Qaida'. *Guardian*, 14 Aug.

BETTS, R. K. 2007. *Enemies of Intelligence: Knowledge and Power in American National Security*. New York: Columbia University Press.

CHIRINOS, A. 2005. 'Finding the Balance between Liberty and Security: The Lords' Decision on Britain's Anti-Terrorism Act'. *Harvard Human Rights Journal*, 18: 265–76.

CORNISH, P. 2005. 'The United Kingdom'. Pp. 146–67 in K. von Hippel (ed.), *Europe Confronts Terrorism*. London: Palgrave.

DANCHEV, A. 2006. 'Accomplicity: Britain, Torture and Terror'. *British Journal of Politics and International Relations*, 8: 587–601.

DANDEKER, C. 1990. *Surveillance, Power, and Modernity*. New York: St Martin's Press.

DAVIES, P. H. J. 2004. 'Intelligence Culture and Intelligence Failure in Britain and the United States'. *Cambridge Review of International Affairs*, 17: 495–520.

DER DERIAN, J. 1993. 'Anti-diplomacy: Intelligence Theory and Surveillance Practice'. *Intelligence and National Security*, 8: 29–51.

FENWICK, H. 2002. 'The Anti-Terrorism, Crime and Security Act 2001: A Proportionate Response to 11 September?' *Modern Law Review*, 65: 724–62.

GEARTY, C. 1991. *Terror*. London: Faber and Faber.

GERGES, F. 2005. *The Far Enemy: Why Jihad Went Global*. Cambridge: Cambridge University Press.

GIDDENS, A. 1990. *Consequences of Modernity*. Cambridge: Polity.

GILL, P. 1996. 'Reasserting Control: Recent Changes in the Oversight of the UK Intelligence Community'. *Intelligence and National Security*, 11: 313–31.

GLEES, A., DAVIES, P. H., and MORRISON, J. 2006. *The Open Side of Secrecy: Britain's Intelligence and Security Committee*. London: Social Affairs Unit.

GREGORY, F., and WILKINSON, P. 2005. 'Riding Pillion for Tackling Terrorism is a High-Risk Policy'. ISP/NSC Briefing Paper 05/01, Chatham House. http://www.riia-org/pdf/research/niisBPsecurity.pdf.

HARFIELD, C. 2006. 'SOCA: A Paradigm Shift in British Policing'. *British Journal of Criminology*, 46: 743–61.

HC 314 2007. *Report of the Intelligence Services Commissioner for 2005–6*. London: House of Commons.

HENNESSY, P. 2000. *The Secret State: Whitehall and the Cold War, 1945–70*. London: Allen Lane.

INNES, M. 2006. 'Policing Uncertainty: Countering Terrorism thorugh Community Intelligence and Democratic Policing'. *Annals of the American Academy of Political and Social Science*, 605: 222–41.

LEIGH, I. 2005. 'Accountability of Security and Intelligence in the United Kingdom'. Pp. 79–98 in H. Born, L. K. Johnson, and I. Leigh (eds.), *Who's Watching the Spies: Establish Intelligence Service Accountability*. Washington, DC: Potomac.

——and LUSTGARTEN, L. 1991. 'Employment, Justice and Detente: The Reform of Vetting'. *Modern Law Review*, 54: 613–42.

————1994. *In from the Cold: National Security and Democracy*. Oxford: Oxford University Press.

LONDON ASSEMBLY 2005. 7 July Review Committee, Transcript of Item 3: 7 July—Lessons Learned, comments of Malcolm Baker, Superintendent, Anti-Terrorist Branch, Metropolitan Police Service. 1 Dec.

LYONS, D. 1994. *The Electronic Eye: The Rise of Surveillance Society: Computers and Social Control in Context*. Cambridge: Polity.

MANNINGHAM-BULLER, E. 2007. 'The International Terrorist Threat to the United Kingdom'. Pp. 66–73 in P. Hennessy (ed.), *The New Protective State*. London: Continuum.

MARSH, S. 1996. 'Technological Influences on Globalisation and Fragmentation: The Demise of the Nation-State?' *RUSI Journal*, June: 44–50.

MATHIESON, S. 2005. 'UK Seeks All-EU Traffic Data Retention'. *Computer Fraud and Security*, 7: 1–2.

MORAN, J. 2006. 'State Power in the War on Terror: A Comparative Analysis of the UK and USA'. *Crime, Law and Social Change*, 44: 335–59.

MORRISON, J. N. L. 2006. 'Political Supervision of Intelligence Services in the United Kingdom'. Pp. 41–54 in Tsang 2006.

NATIONAL CRIMINAL INTELLIGENCE SERVICE 2000. *The National Intelligence Model*. London: National Criminal Intelligence Service.

OMAND, D. 2004. 'Emergency Planning, Security and Business Continuity'. *RUSI Journal*, 149/4: 26–33.

——2005. 'Countering International Terrorism: The Use of Strategy'. *Survival*, 47: 107–16.

PAUL, T. V., and RIPSMAN, N. M. 2004. 'Under Pressure? Globalization and the National Security State'. *Millennium*, 33: 355–80.

PYTHIAN, M. 2005. 'Intelligence, Policy-Making and the 7 July London Bombings'. *Crime, Law and Social Change*, 44: 361–85.

REES, W. 2006. *Transatlantic Security Cooperation: Drugs, Crime and Terrorism in the Twenty-First Century*. London: Routledge.

——and ALDRICH, R. J. 2005. 'Contending Cultures of Counter-terrorism: Divergence or Convergence?' *International Affairs*, 81: 905–24.

RICE, G., and THOMAS, T. 1997. 'Men in Black: With MI5 now Moving in on the Drug Trade'. *Druglink*, 12: 14–15.

ROLSTON, B. 2006. 'Dealing with the Past: Pro-State Paramilitaries, Truth and Transition in Northern Ireland'. *Human Rights Quarterly*, 28: 652–75.

RUNCIMAN, W. G. (ed.) 2004. *Hutton and Butler: Lifting the Lid on the Workings of Power*. London: British Academy/Oxford University Press.

SCOTT-SMITH, G. 2002. *The Politics of Apolitical Culture: The Congress for Cultural Freedom and the Political Economy of Hegemony*. London: Routledge.

SIDEL, M. 2005. *More Secure, Less Free? Antiterrorism Policy and Civil Liberties after September 11*. Ann Arbor: University of Michigan Press.

SMITH, M. 2003. *The Spying Game: The Secret History of British Espionage*. London: Politico's.

TSANG. S. (ed.) 2006. *Intelligence and Human Rights in the Era of Global Terrorism*. New York: Praeger.

URBAN, M. 2006. 'The British Quest for Transparency'. Pp. 17–25 in Tsang 2006.

VINCENT, D. 1998. *The Culture of Secrecy: Britain 1832–1998*. Oxford: Oxford University Press.

WADA, K. 2002. 'Outline of Anti-Terrorism Legislation in Foreign Countries'. *Journal of Police Science*, 55: 51–96.

WALKER, C. 2005. 'Intelligence and Anti-Terrorism Legislation in the United Kingdom'. *Crime, Law and Social Change*, 44: 387–422.

PART V

PROCESSES

SECTION FOURTEEN:
SOCIAL CHANGE

CHAPTER 42

PARTICIPATION AND SOCIAL CAPITAL

PAUL WHITELEY

The political culture in Great Britain also approximates the civic culture. The participant role is highly developed. Exposure to politics, interest, involvement, and a sense of competence are relatively high. There are norms supporting political activity, as well as emotional involvement in elections, and system affect. And the attachment to the system is a balanced one: there is general system pride as well as satisfaction with specific government performance.

(Almond and Verba 1963: 315)

Popular engagement with the formal processes and institutions of democracy has been in long-term decline since the 1960s. Party memberships have been falling continuously since that time to the point where they stand at less that one-quarter of their 1964 levels. The number of people who say they identify with one of the main parties has followed a similar severe trajectory. Turnout for other elections—local and European parliamentary—have remained stubbornly low for decades.

(Power to the People 2006: 27)

42.1 INTRODUCTION

THESE two descriptions of the state of civil society in Britain are separated by nearly fifty years. The first comes from the classic study of participation by Almond and Verba undertaken in 1959. The second comes from the report of the Power Commission, an investigation of the state of democracy in Britain published in 2006. They characterize some of the important changes which have occurred in political participation in Britain over time. Political participation is essentially about ordinary citizens trying to influence the policies and the personnel of the state. So the relationship between the state and participation is central to the analysis. We know that key forms of participation such as voting and party membership have declined significantly over time (Clarke et al. 2004; Whiteley and Seyd 2002). At the same time other forms of participation, such as consumer involvement in buying or boycotting products for political reasons, are growing in importance (Pattie, Seyd, and Whiteley 2004). Unfortunately voting is much more important for democracy than boycotting, since it determines who governs the state, so these developments have not left the civic culture undamaged. Notwithstanding this point, why should we be concerned if some important types of participation have declined and the civic culture in Britain has deteriorated over time? What difference does it make?

Figure 42.1 illustrates why political participation is important. It shows the relationship between government effectiveness and political participation, using data from thirty-seven countries. The governmental effectiveness measure was developed by World Bank economists and combines indicators of the quality of public services and the effectiveness of policy formulation and implementation in each country into a single scale (Kaufmann, Kraay, and Mastruzzi 2006). The participation measure comes from the International Social Survey Programme Citizenship Survey of 2004, and combines eight different indicators of political participation into a single scale.[1] As the figure shows the relationship is quite strong, indicating that countries with high levels of civic engagement tend to have effective governments. It is noteworthy that the relationship gets stronger as participation increases, so that countries with very high levels of participation have very effective governments. By implication the public services are likely to be of poor quality and government is likely to be incompetent in states where participation is low.

Given the importance of participation, it is not surprising that the literature on this topic is vast and a number of different theoretical models have been used to explain why some citizens get involved in politics when others do not (Verba and Nie 1972; Verba, Nie, and Jae-On Kim 1978; Barnes and Kaase 1979; Muller 1979; Parrry, Moyser, and Day 1992; Verba, Schlozman, and Brady 1995; Pattie, Seyd, and

---

[1] Respondents were asked if they had participated in eight different activities: signing a petition, boycotting certain products, taking part in a demonstration, attending a political meeting, contacting a politician, donating money to a political cause, contacting the media, and joining in an Internet forum about politics. The scale used in Figure 42.1 is derived from a principal components analysis of these items.

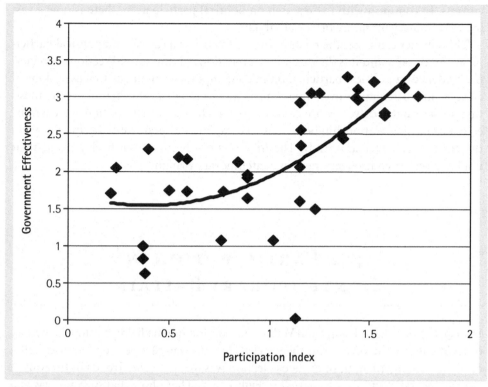

Fig. 42.1 The relationship between political participation and government effectiveness in thirty-seven countries, 2004

Whiteley 2004). A comprehensive review of this literature is beyond the scope of this chapter, and instead we will concentrate on examining a prominent theory of participation which has been influential in recent years. This is social capital theory.

The term social capital was introduced into modern social theory by the sociologist James Coleman who viewed it as a set of obligations and expectations on the part of individuals as well as a set of information channels linking them together (1988). In Coleman's interpretation social interaction generates 'credit slips' of obligations and fosters norms of reciprocation in society. In a trustworthy environment these credit slips can be acquired and used by third parties, and they facilitate social and political interactions of all kinds. In a similar approach Robert Putnam defines social capital as 'features of social organizations, such as trust, norms and networks that can improve the efficiency of society by facilitating co-ordinated actions' (1993: 167). Social capital is concerned with the extent to which individuals embedded within communities interact, support, and trust each other. Localities rich in social capital have many citizens who are active in both formal and informal community groups and, according to the theory, they are characterized by high levels of trust between citizens. In common with the research on political participation, there is now a vast interdisciplinary literature on social capital.[2]

This chapter examines the relationship between social capital and political participation in Britain, and it is divided into four sections. In the second section we review the evidence on political participation in contemporary Britain, as well as looking at changes in participation over time. This is followed by an examination of the thesis that social capital drives political participation. In the fourth section we examine evidence on the relationship between social capital and political participation from the 2005 British Election Study. The final section discusses the findings and their implications for civic engagement in contemporary Britain.

42.2 PARTICIPATION IN CONTEMPORARY BRITAIN

In 1959, the year that Almond and Verba were conducting the fieldwork for their study of civic culture, the turnout in the general election was 78.7 per cent; almost half a century later, the turnout in the 2005 election was 61.5 per cent. Trends in turnout in British general elections are charted in Figure 42.2. They show that turnout was at a maximum in the first fully post-war election of 1950, and thereafter it gently declined over time before dropping dramatically after the 1997 election.[3] Low turnouts have also been a feature of recent elections to the European Parliament, in local government elections, and elections to the Scottish, Welsh, and London assemblies, as well as the London mayoral election. The evidence shows that electoral participation among young people has declined faster than among the old, and there has been a corresponding decline in the norms which support voting among the young (Clarke et al. 2004).

Another development is the decline of party membership and party activism, which has been documented by more than fifteen years of surveys of grass-roots party members in Britain (Whiteley and Seyd 2002). Tony Blair's success in recruiting an additional 40 per cent of new members to the Labour Party between 1994 and 1997 has not been sustained. Figure 42.3 shows the trends in party membership over the period 1983 to 2005, and it is evident that all three parties have been shrinking in size during this period. Rates of activism among the surviving members have also declined.

---

[2] David Halpern provides an excellent and comprehensive introduction to this literature (see Halpern 2005).

[3] It has been suggested that turnout in general elections followed 'trendless fluctuations' prior to the 1997 general election, but this is not the case. The decline in turnout from 84 per cent in 1950 to 71 per cent in 1997 is highly statistically significant.

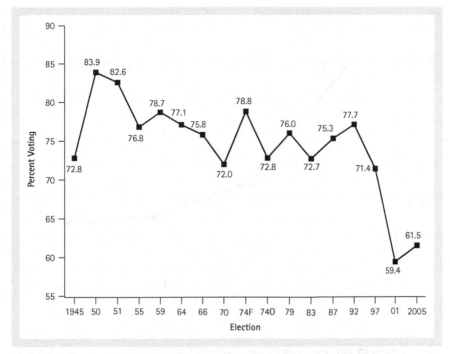

Fig. 42.2 Turnout in United Kingdom general elections, 1945–2005

Source: UK Election Statistics 1918–2004, House of Commons Research Paper 04/31, p. 17; General Election 2005, House of Commons Research Paper 05/33, p. 1.

The common characteristic of these trends is that they are related to voting and party activity. But the repertoire of participation in contemporary Britain is much wider than that. Before one can draw definite conclusions about the state of participation in Britain, it is necessary to examine a wide range of activities which constitute participation. To understand the state of contemporary British democracy it is necessary to cast the net fairly wide, in order to get a full picture of what is happening. A useful distinction in examining political participation is between macro- and micro-participation. The former refers to actions designed to influence directly government policies or personnel, while the latter refers to actions seeking to improve the services delivered to particular individuals. Traditionally research into political participation in Britain has focused on macro-participation (Parry, Moyser, and Day 1992) and rather neglected micro-participation. Macro-participation can be classified into individualistic, contact, and collective forms (Pattie, Seyd, and Whiteley 2004). These distinctions relate to the extent to which citizens have to work with others to make their participation effective. Thus individualistic forms of participation, such as boycotting goods, do not require any particular organization, and can be done easily by individuals acting on their own behalf. In contrast, collective action such as taking part in a demonstration, or attending a political meeting, involves organizationally based cooperation. Contact participation can be individualistic or collective, but it

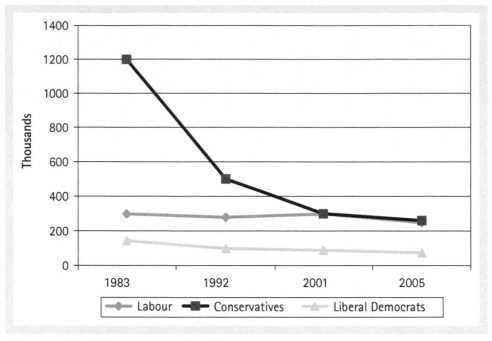

Fig. 42.3 Trends in party membership 1983–2005

Source: Beetham (2002) and party sources.

commonly takes an individualistic form, with citizens seeking help and advice from officials to navigate the complexities of the modern state.

Micro-participation is about individuals obtaining specific benefits for themselves rather than about changing the law or influencing local and national policies. In the past some of this has not been fully recognized as participation, but in a growing consumerist society and in the context of government advocating choice as a desirable goal for delivering public services, this form of participation is becoming more important.

We can get an overview of the different forms of participation in Britain using data from the Citizen's Audit conducted in 2000 (Pattie, Seyd, and Whiteley 2004). Table 42.1 shows that macro-political participation in Britain most commonly takes individualistic rather than collectivist forms. Thus, voting, donating money to a voluntary organization, signing a petition, displaying posters, and boycotting goods are the most common forms of political action. Acting collectively to organize a political group, to participate in a demonstration, or to organize a strike are much less common. These findings are unsurprising, since the modern era is characterized by individualistic consumerism which stresses the importance of market relationships. A number of sociologists have suggested that a decline in community solidarity and cohesion has occurred across the advanced industrial democracies and these developments are linked to growing affluence and to the pervasiveness of market-based relationships and the 'individualization' of modern society (Bellah et al. 1985; Beck 1992; Etzioni 1995). These developments sit alongside the decline of many large

Table 42.1 Acts of political participation in Britain (%)

	Actual participation	Potential participation
Individual actions		
Donated money to an organization	62	75
Voted in a local government election	50	71
Signed a petition	42	76
Boycotted certain products	31	59
Raised funds for an organization	30	55
Bought certain products for political, ethical, or environmental reasons	28	49
Worn or displayed a campaign badge or sticker	22	49
Collective actions		
Attended a political meeting or rally	5	26
Taken part in a public demonstration	5	34
Formed a group of like-minded people	5	23
Taken part in a strike	2	27
Participated in illegal protest activities	2	13
Contact actions		
Contacted a public official	25	59
Contacted a solicitor or judicial body	20	60
Contacted a politician	13	53
Contacted an organization	11	50
Contacted the media	9	43

Actual participation: 'During the last twelve months have you done any of the following to influence rules, laws, or policies?'
Potential participation: 'Would you do any of the following to influence rules, laws, or policies?'

collective organizations, such as trade unions, political parties, and pressure groups, which used to provide the framework for collective action. In this situation it is not surprising that traditional forms of collective politics are gradually being replaced by individualistic forms.

Notwithstanding this point, Figure 42.4 shows that many people are involved in diverse types of political action. More than three-quarters of the respondents in the Citizen's Audit had engaged in one or more political actions over the previous twelve months, and about a third had taken five or more actions. The mean number was 3.6. Thus it appears that most people in contemporary Britain participate in some form of political action, even if most of these are individualistic in nature. It might be that voting or party activity are in decline, but it would be wrong to assume that people in general are not interested in or involved in politics viewed from a broad perspective.

Who are the participants? What are the social background characteristics of those who get involved? In order to distinguish the non-participant from the active participant, we classify the respondents into those who engaged in no political actions, those involved in between one and four, and those participating in more than four actions. We can see in Table 42.2 that there are significant differences between various groups of people in their rates of participation; the young and the old are more likely

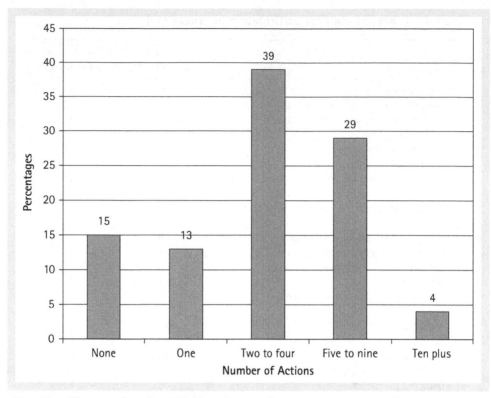

Fig. 42.4 The number of political actions undertaken in a year

to be disengaged than the middle-aged. The poorest members of society, manual workers, and those with little education are less likely to be active than the affluent professionals and the highly educated. Thus respondents with an annual household income of £50,000 or more are twice as likely to be very active as those with an income of less than £10,000. Professional and managerial workers are about twice as likely to be active than manual workers. Interestingly enough, people's gender and ethnic backgrounds appear to be unrelated to their rates of participation, since women participate at the same rate as men, and ethnic minorities are similar to the ethnic majority. However, there is a clear geography to political participation in Britain, with Londoners and people living in the south-east of England more likely to participate than people living in the north, Scotland, or Wales.

We have introduced the distinction between individualistic and collectivist forms of participation. Are there differences between people in relation to these different modes of participation? If we take typical examples of the three types of participation, individualistic participation defined in terms of buying goods for political and ethical reasons, contact participation measured by communications with officials and politicians, and collective action by involvement in demonstrations, we discover in Table 42.3 that the types of participant do differ. Those engaging in individualistic forms of action are found among the middle-aged professionals who tend to be rather

Table 42.2 Variations in political participation by social backgrounds (%)

Number of political actions undertaken in 2000	None	One to four	Five plus
All	15	52	33
Age			
24 and under	17	55	29
25–44	15	49	37
45–64	13	50	37
65 and over	16	60	24
Gender			
Male	15	53	33
Female	15	51	34
Class			
Professional and managerial	8	45	47
Intermediate	14	51	36
Manual	18	58	24
Religiosity			
Religious	12	52	36
Non-religious	17	52	31
Household income			
Under £10,000	19	56	25
£10,000 up to £19,999	15	54	31
£20,000 up to £29,999	10	51	39
£30,000 up to £39,999	10	47	44
£40,000 up to £49,999	9	41	50
£50,000 and above	3	43	54
Education			
15 years and under	19	57	24
16–18	15	52	33
19 years and over	7	43	50
Ethnicity			
White/European	15	52	34
Black/Asian/Caribbean/Other	18	56	26
Location			
Greater London	11	51	38
South West	16	50	34
East/West Midlands	21	54	25
North West/North/Yorkshire	14	54	31
South East/East Anglia	13	47	40
Scotland	17	54	29
Wales	6	73	21

affluent, highly educated, and live in London and the southern counties. The contrast is most marked in relation to educational backgrounds, where the highly educated are three times more likely to be engaged than those who left school at age fifteen. Similarly, professionals are about twice as likely to be individualistic participants as manual workers.

Table 42.3 Variations in individual, contact, and collective actions by social backgrounds

	Individual % yes[a]	Contact % yes[b]	Collective % yes[c]
All	28	13	5
Age			
24 and under	28	6	10
25–44	33	11	5
45–64	29	17	4
65 and over	16	13	3
Gender			
Male	27	14	6
Female	29	12	4
Class			
Professional and managerial	43	19	7
Intermediate	31	13	4
Manual	18	9	4
Religiosity			
Religious	28	14	4
Non-religious	28	11	6
Household income			
Under £10,000	18	11	4
£10,000 up to £19,999	24	14	5
£20,000 up to £29,999	34	12	7
£30,000 up to £39,999	41	15	4
£40,000 up to £49,999	57	13	8
£50,000 and above	56	18	7
Education			
15 years and under	17	11	2
16–18	27	12	5
19 years and over	52	19	10
Ethnicity			
White/European	28	13	5
Black/Asian/Caribbean/Other	27	13	5
Location			
Greater London	38	14	6
South West	28	13	6
East/West Midlands	22	10	4
North West/North/Yorkshire	25	14	5
South East/East Anglia	34	14	4
Scotland	20	13	6
Wales	14	7	4

[a] Percentage who had 'bought certain products for political, ethical, or environmental reasons'.
[b] Percentage who had 'contacted a politician (for example, a member of parliament or a local councillor)'.
[c] Percentage who had 'taken part in a public demonstration'.

The profile of contact participants is rather similar to that of individualistic partic-ipants. Again, they are more likely to be affluent professionals and managers, highly educated, and middle aged. However a person's gender, income, ethnicity, religiosity, and geographical location do not appear to influence their contact participation. This may be because it is about seeking help and advice rather than taking initiatives primarily of an individualistic nature. In focusing on the relatively small number of people involved in collectively organized political actions, differences in their social characteristics are rather less apparent. The only two significant differences in this group are age and education; the young and those with higher education are much more likely to be engaged in collectively organized actions. The educational effect is huge, with the highly educated being five times more likely to participate in a demonstration than the uneducated, and the young about three times more likely to do this than the old.

Table 42.1 understates the importance of collective action, however, since it says little about organizational involvement. A very important aspect of collective participation is organizational membership and this is examined in Figure 42.5 and Table 42.4. Respondents were asked if they had been members of a set of different

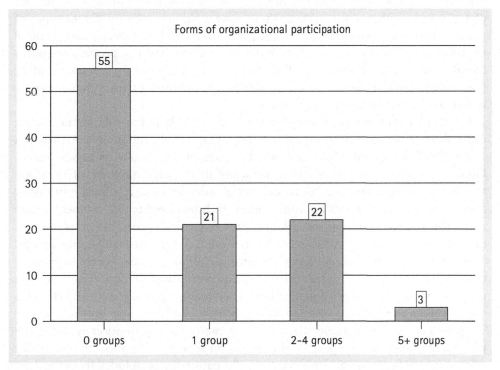

Fig. 42.5 Membership of organizations

Question: 'In the last twelve months, have you been a member of this type of organisation (in other words have you paid a membership fee if it is required), have you participated in an activity arranged by this type of organisation, have you donated money as an individual to this type of organisation, or have you done voluntary or unpaid work for this type of organisation?'

Table 42.4 Types of organizational membership

Percentage of people who are members of:			
Motoring	29	Youth	1
Trade union	9	Environmental	1
Sports/outdoor activities	8	Animal rights	1
Gymnasium	6	Business/employers	1
Residents/housing/neighbourhood	6	Women	1
Professional	5	Humanitarian aid/human rights	1
Social	5	Medical patients/illnesses	1
Conservation	4	Consumer	1
Religious/church	3	Parents and teachers	1
Hobby	3	Disabled	1
Cultural/music/dancing/theatre	2	Other	5
Ex-service	2		

voluntary organizations during the previous twelve months, where membership is defined as paying a fee to the organization. Figure 42.5 shows that the majority of the public are not members of any organization, but there are nonetheless four out of ten people affiliated. On average these joiners belong to two different types of organization, with only 3 per cent of the population being members of five or more organizations. These figures tend to underestimate the extent of people's organizational involvement, because they distinguish between *types* of organizations rather than specific interest groups. Clearly, people may be members of more than one *group* within any particular type of organization.

What types of organizations do people belong to? Table 42.4 reveals that people are most likely to join a motoring organization (for example, the Automobile Association or the Royal Automobile Club), followed by sports, fitness, and work organizations. Other types of organizations which attract relatively large numbers of members are the residential and neighbourhood, social, conservation, religious, and hobby groups. Some organizations are concerned with human rights (e.g. women's rights and animals rights), and others seek to represent particular constituencies (e.g. the disabled and consumer groups). Yet others represent cultural, arts, and hobby groups. The 2001 Census reports an adult population of 44 million in Great Britain, suggesting that almost 13 million people are affiliated to a motoring organization, about 3 million to sports or outdoor activity organizations, 2 million to a gymnasium, and between a quarter and a half million to human rights, women's, and consumer groups.

Many people would argue that joining a motoring organization is not really political participation at all, since the main aim is to provide an insurance policy against vehicle breakdown. If this category of membership is excluded from the data, we find that almost one in three people (31 per cent) are members of at least one voluntary organization. But what do they do in these organizations? Do they pay their membership dues and do nothing else, or are they actively involved in various ways? Respondents were asked to describe their activities in the one organization which was

Table 42.5 Participatory activities in the 'most important' organization (%)

	Often	Sometimes	Rarely	Never	Don't know
Attend meetings	32	14	10	41	3
Participate in decision-making at meetings	22	13	11	51	4
Speak at meetings	16	13	11	57	4
Plan/chair meetings	8	6	5	77	4
Write report about meetings	6	6	6	78	4
Talk about organization problems/goals	25	22	10	39	4
Call upon fellow members for practical help	18	21	12	45	4
Disagree about organization problems/goals	12	24	14	47	4
Meet socially	24	22	12	38	4

Questions: 'Thinking about the one organisation which is most important to you, how often do you...?' 'Again, thinking about the one organisation which is most important to you, how often do you do any of the following with other members of the organisation?'

most important to them. Not surprisingly, as Table 42.5 reveals, membership for a large number of people involves no real participation in the organization's activities nor any interaction with other members. This point is relevant to the later discussion of social capital. However, about one in three often attend meetings and one in five often participate in decision-making. Furthermore, outside of the meeting, about a quarter regularly talk with other members of the group, and a similar proportion often meet socially with their fellow members. In total, around four out of ten group members are involved in personal interchange with their fellow members at some point. One can see therefore that associational life provides a meeting point and a source of social interaction for millions of people in Britain. This is very relevant to the issue of social capital, a theme which we shall return to below.

The earlier discussion showed that election-related and party-related forms of political participation have been declining. However, it is important to stress that this is not true of all types of participation. Table 42.6 compares the responses to a set

Table 42.6 Changes in participation, 1984–2000 (%)

Type of activity	1984	2000
Voted in a general election	83	72
Signed a petition	63	42
Contacted a public official	25	25
Boycotted products for ethical reasons	4	31
Contacted the media	4	9
Attended a political meeting	9	6
Attended a demonstration	5	5
Attended an illegal protest	1	2

Source: Parry, Moyser, and Day (1992) and Pattie, Seyd, and Whiteley (2004).

of questions asked in a national survey of the population conducted in 1984 (Parry, Moyser, and Day 1992), with the same (or similar) questions asked in the Citizens Audit survey of 2000.

Table 42.6 shows that voting has definitely declined in importance, but boycotting or buying goods for ethical and political reasons has grown rather dramatically in importance. Young people, in particular, are attracted to this type of participation and many buy things like 'fair trade' coffee and boycott the fur trade. Similarly, contacting the media has become more common, something which is related to the proliferation of new media outlets that has occurred in recent years. There is also tantalizing evidence that illegal protest activity may have increased as well, but so few people are involved in this type of activity that it is difficult to be sure how much of an increase has actually taken place. Other indicators of political activity such as attending a political demonstration show no change from 1984. But if we look back further in time, the potential for protesting, if not actual protesting, appears to have grown in importance. In 1979 some 20 per cent of respondents in the British Election Study survey stated that they would be willing to go on a protest demonstration. By 2000 this had risen to 33 per cent. The campaign against the Iraq War saw upwards of 1.5 million people on the streets of London in 2003, and the previous two years had seen major nationwide protests occurring over fuel prices, and over rural issues by the Countryside Alliance. Campaigns against road schemes and airport expansion plans are now commonplace and have become a standard feature of the planning process in Britain. Such demonstrations and campaigns have all been made easier by the Internet which allows people to mobilize and organize protests much faster than was the case a generation ago. In one sense a willingness to join in a protest demonstration is an indicator of civic health, rather than civic decline, except that it might be argued that people demonstrate when they find orthodox channels of influence weak or ineffective. It is interesting to note that the evidence from Citizen Audit suggests that young people are more likely to get involved in demonstrations than their older counterparts, while at the same time being much less likely to vote.

Another development is that the norms supporting political activity have weakened over time. When asked 'what part do you think the ordinary person should play in the local affairs of his town or district?' some 70 per cent thought that citizens should be participants in their communities in the 1959 survey (Almond and Verba 1963). When asked to respond to the statement, 'Every citizen should be involved in politics if democracy is to work properly', only 44 per cent agreed or strongly agreed in the Citizen Audit survey of 2000 (Pattie, Seyd, and Whiteley 2004). This may explain why the numbers willing to serve on public bodies seems to be declining, and there are often difficulties in attracting people onto parish councils, school governing boards, or community health councils.

The focus up to this point has been on macro-participation. However, as the earlier discussion indicates, there is a whole dimension of participation which is very important. When citizens come into daily contact with the institutions or representatives of the state, this can generate its own type of participation. For example if a person spends time in hospital, regularly visits the dentist, has children in school, helps a relative who is drawing social benefits, or has occasion to report a crime to the police, they are interacting with representatives of the British state. Such interactions will often involve attempts on their part to influence the behaviour of state representatives. This does not involve changing the law or altering official policies, but it does involve trying to influence the implementation of these policies at the local level. The Citizen's Audit of 2000 sought to measure aspects of this micro-participation world. It focused on three areas: education, health, and the workplace. After finding out if respondents had children in school, if they had recently obtained medical treatment, or if they were in paid employment, follow-up questions were asked about these areas. They were asked if they had tried to influence their child's education, their medical treatment, and their working conditions during the previous year.

As Figure 42.6 shows, about one in four respondents with children had tried to influence the way their child's education was provided; one in ten who had sought medical treatment tried to influence that treatment; and almost half of employed

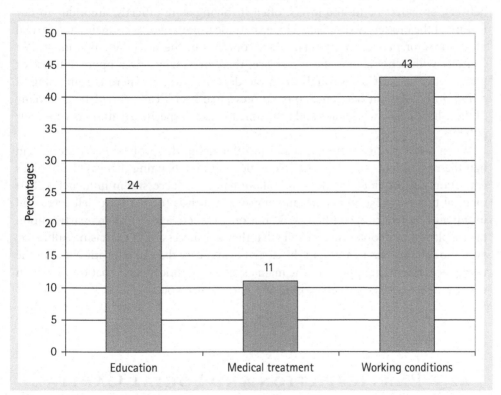

Fig. 42.6 Attempts to influence education, medical treatment, or working conditions

Note: The chart shows the percentages of parents with children in schools, the percentages of individuals seeking medical treatment, and the percentage of people in work who tried to influence their conditions and treatment over the previous year.

Source: Pattie, Seyd, and Whiteley (2004).

people had taken action to try to improve their working conditions. Much of this type of action is not 'political' in the traditional sense of the word, but it nonetheless has an important influence on people's day-to-day lives, and when they take this form of action they are often trying to influence state policies as they are applied in practice.

The differences in Figure 42.6 are striking and are explained by the quality of the service provided on the one hand and the opportunities available to take action on the other. Thus people will take action when they are dissatisfied with their treatment and also when the opportunities for involvement are available. The opportunity structures for involvement are particularly important (Tarrow 1998). Parents have many opportunities to be drawn into the daily life of their children's school via parent–teachers' associations and with school visits. In addition to organizing parent evenings, teachers will often encourage parents to become involved in informal ways in their children's education. Thus the opportunity structures for participation exist. In relation to the workplace, a complex legal framework exists to regulate workplace rights, working conditions, and health and safety issues. Negotiations between employees and employers, often involving state officials, are a day-to-day feature of the modern workplace. There are trade unions, works councils, and formal procedures for people to articulate their concerns in the working environment. In contrast with schools and the workplace, there are many fewer opportunities for patient involvement in hospitals or in the doctor's surgery. There is something of a tradition of patient deference to the professional health care providers, and many of these have heavy workloads and little time to discuss specific treatments with their patients.

When asked if they were successful in influencing the professionals, more than half the respondents said that they were successful in changing the way their child's education was provided (59 per cent), about half were successful in influencing their medical treatment (50 per cent), and almost two-thirds (62 per cent) felt successful in influencing working conditions. So not only is there a lot of micro-participation taking place, but people feel generally that they are successful in exercising influence, even though this was less true in the case of health care than in education and in the workplace. Having mapped out the main aspects of political participation in Britain we turn next to the task of explaining why participation occurs.

42.3 PARTICIPATION AND SOCIAL CAPITAL

There is no shortage of theoretical explanations for political action. In the analysis of the Citizen Audit six alternative models of participation were examined (Pattie, Seyd, and Whiteley 2004). Broadly speaking, these theoretical models divide into two categories: those linked to choice behaviour and theories of decision-making, and those linked to structural or sociological accounts. Choice theories emphasize the role of the individual as a decision-maker who makes choices about his or her level of involvement. Issues such as the costs and benefits of political action loom large in these accounts. Structural theories, in contrast, focus more on the social backgrounds of individuals and socialization processes which might account for their participation. In the present context we will focus on social capital theory, which provides a structural account that has been quite influential in recent years.

Putnam's explanation of the relationship between social capital and participation is best known. He explains social and economic differences between the Italian regions and between American states in terms of their different levels of social capital (1993; 2000). He finds that in areas like Minnesota or Emilia-Romagna, people are socially active, join groups, and take part in a wide variety of activities, both formal and informal, which put them in close contact with their fellow citizens. This builds a reservoir of social capital in these active communities. Feeling able to trust one's fellows most of the time on most issues helps reduce the costs of political interaction and helps to develop 'norms of reciprocity'. People come to expect broadly fair dealing, both from their fellows and from government. By contrast, in areas like Mississipi or Calabria civic life is not conducive to building social capital. In these places associational life is less active and norms of reciprocity and trust are relatively weak.

According to the theory interpersonal trust and voluntary activity are linked in a virtuous circle, so that as people mix with others in a voluntary setting, they come to know and trust each other, and this in turn promotes even more voluntary activity. As this happens those feelings of trust begin to extend to people beyond an individual's immediate circle of acquaintances. These interactions produce what the economists call 'externalities', which arise when cooperative behaviour spills over into the wider society. Because they know and trust their fellow citizens individuals are more likely to trust and to help strangers. As social capital develops, society works more efficiently by reducing the transaction and policing costs associated with widespread mistrust between citizens. Societies poor in social capital display only weak associational ties and exhibit limited mutual trust, and as a consequence they fare worse and work less efficiently than their more fortunate neighbours.

It is important to note that voluntary activity is much broader than political participation, and so the two concepts are not the same thing. In Putnam's interpretation, social capital can be built in all types of voluntary organizations such as sports clubs, cultural organizations, choral societies, and informal groups, all of which have little to do with political participation. The social capital model argues that these relatively non-political forms of voluntary activity can stimulate political participation by building trust between individuals, and political participation is encouraged by high levels of trust.

Social capital appears to have major consequences for society. Empirical research suggests societies where levels of trust in other people are high tend to perform better on a range of economic and political indicators than do societies where trust is lacking

(Knack and Keefer 1997; Knack 2002; Inglehart 1999; Whiteley 2000; Newton and Norris 2000). Putnam claims that social capital in America delivers many benefits to localities where it is high, including better economic performance, improved health and education, reduced crime, and higher levels of life satisfaction and happiness (Putnam 2000).

But social capital may not be an infinitely renewable resource. There is evidence of a decline in citizen activism and in social capital in the United States since the 1960s: in an influential argument, Putnam blames television for this development (Putnam 1995; 2000). Television now constitutes the main leisure pursuit for very large numbers of Westerners. The trend towards privatized television watching has grown rapidly over time, isolating people in their own homes, and reducing the time available for precisely the various kinds of social networking and associational activity which are claimed to be conducive to developing social capital. This claim about the importance of television is controversial, however, and has been challenged (Norris 1996).

The social capital argument has been subject to considerable critical scrutiny, both theoretical and empirical (Tarrow 1996; Newton 1999; Claibourn and Martin 2000; Milner 2002; Halpern 2005). One important finding is that while social capital may have been declining in the United States, it does not seem to have declined much in Britain (Hall 1999). One implication of this finding is that social capital cannot therefore account for the decline in turnout and in party activity (Franklin 2004). There is also evidence to suggest that social capital has declined in Sweden during a period in which electoral turnout actually increased in that country (Rothstein 2002). Thus social capital might be important for explaining some forms of political participation, but it may not be relevant for others.

Another finding relates to the link between local government and social capital in Britain. It appears that while service outputs at the local level are not influenced by social capital, service outcomes are. The former refer to the amount of money spent on services by local authorities, while the latter refer to the effectiveness of those services in delivering outcomes. In the case of education, for example, which is the biggest item in the budget for English and Welsh local authorities, the best pupil performances in GCSE are found in areas with high levels of political participation and associational activity (Pattie, Seyd, and Whiteley 2004: 189–223). While the geographical distribution of social capital does not appear to influence local government spending on services, it does influence the effectiveness of those services. Other case studies of real estate development and urban management schemes in the United States have shown that social capital significantly improves the quality of policy delivery in areas where it is high (Saegert and Winkel 1998; Glaeser and Sacerdote 2000).

These findings all suggest that social capital is an asset to government, but its relationship to political participation is more ambiguous. Putnam (2000: 31–64) produces a lot of evidence to support the idea that social capital and political participation have both declined at the same time in the United States. Moreover, individual-level analyses of civic participation repeatedly show a correlation between personal affluence and education on the one hand and indicators of social capital such as trust and voluntary activity on the other (Parry, Moyser, and Day 1992; Brady, Verba, and Schlozman 1995; Verba, Schlozman, and Brady 1995; Franklin 2004). Since affluence and education are determinants of political participation, this establishes an important indirect link between social capital and participation. Extending this to the community level, the implication is that the more affluent the community, the more social capital and the greater the level of civic involvement. However, as Oliver (2001) points out, social capital is not the same thing as affluence and other, subtler relationships are possible. He suggests that participation varies systematically across different types of American suburban communities. Even after controlling for individual-level factors such as personal affluence, political participation is greater, *ceteris paribus*, in economically mixed communities than in very poor or very rich communities. It is also greater in racially mixed than in near all-black or all-white communities. Both reflect the greater political stakes in 'mixed' rather than in homogeneous communities. Politics in diverse communities involve a battle between potential 'winners' and 'losers', whereas in homogeneous communities residents have similar interests, and hence the risks of non-participation and the potential gains from participation are not so great. This is a challenge to social capital theory, since it is often the most homogeneous communities which have the most social capital.

Another important factor in explaining participation is community size. People living in less populous communities are more likely, other things being equal, to participate in politics than are people living in larger urban centres (Oliver 2000; Frandsen 2002). This, it is claimed, reflects the relatively smaller prospects of free-riding in a small community than in a large one. Equally, the smaller the authority the more people living there trust their local government (Denters 2002). Again these findings are inconsistent with the social capital model, which suggests that there is no necessary relationship between the size of a community and its levels of social capital.

An important problem associated with research into social capital is to establish the causal processes at work. Does social capital explain participation, or is it the other way round? There may be virtuous or vicious circles at work in these relationships, but unless the starting point of the interaction can be identified, social capital runs the risk of being a theory without any solid foundations. To be fair, given that voluntary activity is a much broader concept than political participation, it is not tautological to argue that the former drives the latter.

All this suggests that while Putnam's (2000) evidence supports the idea that social capital drives participation there is evidence which clearly contradicts this hypothesis. With this point in mind, it is interesting to explore the relationship between social capital and political participation in Britain in order to establish just how strong the links are in practice. We do this using data from the 2005 British Election Study (Clarke et al. forthcoming). The analysis is cross-sectional and so is unable to identify the causal sequences at work. Rather than testing a fully specified causal model, the aim is a more modest one of establishing if social capital and participation are actually related.

42.4 MODELLING THE RELATIONSHIP BETWEEN SOCIAL CAPITAL AND PARTICIPATION

A series of indicators of political participation were included in the British Election Study post-election survey of 2005. In that study the focus was on voting and party-related political participation and, since these have been in long-run decline and they are particularly important for democracy, it is interesting to focus on their relationship to social capital. In the survey respondents were asked if they had voted in the 2005 general election and they were also asked about their likelihood of voting in future elections to the European Parliament and also in local government elections. The latter two scales varied from zero to ten, so that respondents were being asked essentially to assign a probability that they would vote in these secondary elections. In the case of the European parliamentary elections, for example, just under a third assigned a score of ten indicating that they were very likely to vote, and 37 per cent assigned a score of five or less, suggesting that they were not. The three measures can all be regarded as observable indicators of an underlying latent 'probability of voting' scale. In addition to the indicators of voting, there were three measures of party activism included in the survey. The first measure asked respondents if they were currently members of a political party. The second asked about the likelihood of their giving money to a party, and the third about working for a party in a future election. These were measured with zero to ten probability scales, and they can all be regarded as indicators of an underlying latent 'party involvement' scale.

Social capital was measured with indicators of interpersonal trust and also voluntary activity. One question asked, 'On balance, would you say that most people can't be trusted or that most people can be trusted?'; and another, 'Do you think that most people you come into contact with would try to take advantage of you if they got the chance or would they try to be fair?' Again, responses were measured using zero to ten scales, and can be regarded as indicators of an underlying latent interpersonal trust scale. The voluntary activity aspects of social capital were captured by three different questions in the election study. The first asked, 'Over the past few years, have you volunteered to get involved in politics or community affairs?' In addition two zero to ten scales were used to measure the respondent's views on voluntary activity in the future. One asked, 'how likely is it that you will be active in a voluntary organisation, like a community association, a charity group, or a sports club?'; and the other, 'how likely is it that you will work actively with a group of people to address a public issue or solve a problem?' Taken together the three items provide measures of an underlying 'propensity to volunteer' scale, a key indicator in the social capital model.

Figure 42.7 shows the results of a confirmatory factor analysis which shows the relationship between the participation and social capital measures.[4] The observed

---

[4] This was produced by LISREL 8.0. See Joreskog and Sorbom (2001).

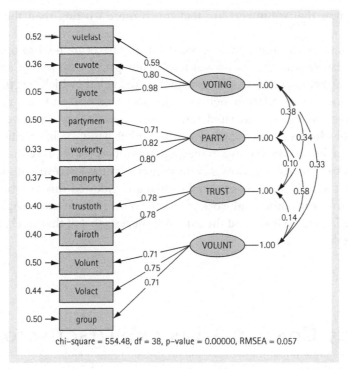

Fig. 42.7 The relationship between indicators of participation and social capital in the British Election Study, 2005

variables appear in the rectangles on the left and the latent measures in the ovals on the right. The magnitude of the coefficients linking observed and latent variables show how effective the former are in measuring the latter. While we do not see perfect relationships of 1.0, the links between the observed and latent variables are nonetheless very strong, indicating that the former are good indicators of the latter. The relationship between social capital and participation is captured by the correlations between the latent variables. The strongest correlation (+0.58) is between party activism (PARTY) and voluntary activity (VOLUNT). There is a strong tendency for individuals who are active in political parties to be active in other types of voluntary organization as well. Party activism can be viewed as a special type of voluntary activity, although it is by no means inevitable that involvement in sports clubs and cultural organizations should carry over to participation in parties.

The correlations between electoral participation (VOTING) and the social capital indicators (TRUST and VOLUNT) are much weaker. Individuals who trust others are a bit more likely to vote than their fellow citizens (+0.34), and the same point can be made about volunteers (+0.33). But neither effect is very strong. The weakest relationships are between party activism and trust (+0.10), and trust and volunteering (+0.14). Since social capital theory suggests that interpersonal trust should be closely linked to voluntary activity, this tends to undermine the credibility of the model. It does not appear that volunteers are that much more trusting than the rest of the population.

In fairness to social capital theory, the strongest effects are held to operate at the community rather than the individual level. Thus places with lots of social capital should have higher rates of political participation than places which lack this resource. If we examine the correlation between the social capital and the participation measures when they are aggregated into constituencies, they are generally higher than the individual-level coefficients.[5] On the other hand, social capital cannot be divorced from the people who live in these communities. Widespread distrust among these individuals inevitably means that the community has low levels of social capital. Communities with high levels of social capital are endowed this way because their inhabitants trust each other and work together. So the roots of social capital must be found at the individual level, and the evidence suggests that at that level key links are relatively weak.

42.5 CONCLUSIONS AND DISCUSSION

There are a wide variety of types of political participation taking place in Britain, from standing for public office at the high intensity end of the scale to voting at the low intensity end. A broad overview suggests that political participation in Britain is relatively healthy. But a narrower focus on elections and political parties reveals a different picture. A long-term decline in electoral participation in Britain has been taking place, something which has been happening in other advanced industrial democracies as well (Wattenberg 2000). Linked to this is a long-term decline in grass-roots party activity. Since political parties and electoral participation play such an important role in making democracy work, these developments can only be regarded as problematic for the future of civil society. One influential theory of participation, social capital, produces a rather mixed picture as an explanation. While voluntary activity and party activity are closely related to each other, relationships between trust and participation are much weaker. The forms of participation examined in this chapter are important but rather specialized, and it may be that social capital does a better job of explaining other forms of participation than voting and party involvement. However, the Achilles heel for the theory is the very weak relationship between voluntary activity and interpersonal trust. This is a key relationship which is thought to be at the core of the social capital model.

These findings tend to support the evidence of other research into the determinants of political participation in modern democracies. Increasingly citizens are

---

[5] The aggregate correlation between the first of the trust indicators and voting in the 2005 election was +0.48, and between volunteering and voting was +0.25.

instrumental in their approach to participation, and they will get involved if this furthers their interests, and avoid involvement when it does not. This is why choice models of participation tend to explain things better than structural models like the social capital model (Pattie, Seyd, and Whiteley 2004). A number of developments in society reinforce these trends. In addition to the rise of consumerism referred to earlier, there is the point that governments are increasingly constrained by global and regional forces in policy-making. If citizens conclude that governments cannot do very much to influence, for example, the state of the economy, they may very well decide that economic voting is a waste of their time. Equally, modern campaign strategies which emphasize the importance of capturing the middle ground of politics reduce the range of alternatives open to the voter, and this reduces the incentives to vote (Clarke et al. 2004: 267). On the other hand, if a local planning proposal threatens house prices in a community, a rapid mobilization of that community is likely to ensue. This will involve a lot of voluntary activity, as well as petitions, demonstrations, and contact participation. Social capital may play a role in explaining these kinds of developments, but it is probably a minor role in comparison with more instrumental considerations.

References

ALMOND, G., and VERBA, S. 1963. *The Civic Culture: Political Attitudes and Democracy in Five Nations*. Princeton, NJ: Princeton University Press.

BARNES, S., and KAASE, M. 1979. *Political Action*. London: Sage.

BECK, U. 1992. *The Risk Society*. London: Sage.

BEETHAM, D., et al. 2002. *International IDEA Handbook on Democracy Assessment*. The Hague: Kluwer.

BELLAH, R., MADSEN, R., SULLIVAN, W., SWINDLER, A., and TIPTON, S. 1985. *Habits of the Heart*. Berkeley: University of California Press.

BRADY, H., VERBA, S., and SCHLOZMAN, K. 1995. 'Beyond SES: A Resource Model of Political Participation'. *American Political Science Review*, 89: 271–94.

CLAIBOURN, M. P., and MARTIN, P. S. 2000. 'Trusting and Joining? An Empirical Test of the Reciprocal Nature of Social Capital'. *Political Behavior*, 22: 267–91.

CLARKE, H. D., SANDERS, D., STEWART, M., and WHITELEY, P. 2004. *Political Choice in Britain*. Oxford: Oxford University Press.

————— forthcoming. *Performance Politics*. Cambridge: Cambridge University Press.

COLEMAN, J. 1988. 'Social Capital in the Creation of Human Capital'. *American Journal of Sociology*, 94, supplement: S95–S119.

DENTERS, B. 2002, 'Size and Political Trust: Evidence from Denmark, the Netherlands, Norway, and the United Kingdom'. *Environment and Planning C: Government and Policy*, 20: 793–812.

ETZIONI, A. 1995. *The Spirit of Community: Rights, Responsibilities and the Communitarian Agenda*. London: Fontana.

FRANDSEN, A. G. 2002. 'Size and Electoral Participation in Local Elections'. *Environment and Planning C: Government and Policy*, 20: 853–69.

FRANKLIN, M. 2004. *Voter Turnout and the Dynamics of Electoral Competition*. Cambridge: Cambridge University Press.

GLAESER, E. L., and SACERDOTE, B. 2000. 'The Social Consequences of Housing'. *Journal of Housing Economics*, 9/1–2: 1–23.

HALL, P. 1999. 'Social Capital in Britain'. *British Journal of Political Science*, 29/3: 417–62.

HALPERN, D. 2005. *Social Capital*. London: Polity.

INGLEHART, R. 1999. 'Trust, Well-being and Democracy'. In M. E. Warren (ed.), *Democracy and Trust*. Cambridge: Cambridge University Press.

JORESKOG, K., and SORBOM, D. 2001. *Lisrel 8: User's Reference Guide*. Lincolnwood, Ill.: Scientific Software International.

KAUFMANN, D., KRAAY, A., and MASTRUZZI, M. 2006. *Governance Matters V: Aggregate and Individual Governance Indicators for 1996–2005*. Washington, DC: World Bank.

KNACK, S. 2002. 'Social Capital and the Quality of Government: Evidence from the States'. *American Journal of Political Science*, 46: 772–85.

—— and KEEFER, P. 1997. 'Does Social Capital Have an Economic Payoff? A Cross-Country Investigation'. *Quarterly Journal of Economics*, 112: 1251–88.

MILNER, H. 2002. *Civic Literacy: How Informed Citizens Make Democracy Work*. Hanover, NH: University of New England Press.

MULLER, E. 1979. *Aggressive Political Participation*. Princeton, NJ: Princeton University Press.

NEWTON, K. 1999. 'Social and Political Trust in Established Democracies'. In P. Norris (ed.), *Critical Citizens*. Oxford: Oxford University Press.

—— and NORRIS, P. 2000. 'Confidence in Public Institutions: Faith, Culture or Performance?' In S. Pharr and R. D. Putnam (eds.), *Disaffected Democracies: What's Troubling the Trilateral Democracies?* Princeton, NJ: Princeton University Press.

NORRIS, P. 1996. 'Does Television Erode Social Capital? A Reply to Putnam'. *PS: Political Science and Politics*, 29/3: 474–80.

OLIVER, J. E. 2000, 'City Size and Civic Involvement in Metropolitan America'. *American Political Science Review*, 94: 361–73.

—— 2001. *Democracy in Suburbia*. Princeton, NJ: Princeton University Press.

PARRY, G., MOYSER, G., and DAY, N. 1992. *Political Participation and Democracy in Britain*. Cambridge: Cambridge University Press.

PATTIE, C., SEYD, P., and WHITELEY, P. 2004. *Citizenship in Britain: Values, Participation and Democracy*. Cambridge: Cambridge University Press.

POWER TO THE PEOPLE 2006. *The Report of the Power Commission: An Independent Inquiry into Britain's Democracy*. London: Power Commission.

PUTNAM, R. 1993. *Making Democracy Work: Civic Traditions in Modern Italy*. Princeton, NJ: Princeton University Press.

—— 1995. 'Tuning In, Tuning Out: The Strange Disappearance of Social Capital in America'. *PS: Political Science and Politics*, 28: 664–83.

—— 2000. *Bowling Alone: The Collapse and Revival of American Community*. New York: Simon and Schuster.

ROTHSTEIN, B. 2002. 'Social Capital in the Social Democratic State'. In R. Putnam (ed.), *Democracies in Flux: The Evolution of Social Capital in Contemporary Society*. New York: Oxford University Press.

SAEGERT, S. G., and WINKEL, G. 1998. 'Social Capital and the Revitalization of New York City's Low-Income Housing'. *Housing Policy Debate*, 9/1: 17–60.

TARROW, S. 1996. 'Making Social Science Work across Space and Time: A Critical Reflection on Robert Putnam's *Making Democracy Work*'. *American Political Science Review*, 90: 389–97.

——1998. *Power in Movement*. Cambridge: Cambridge University Press.

VERBA, S., and NIE, N. 1972. *Participation in America*. Chicago: University of Chicago Press.

——— and JAE-ON KIM. 1978. *Participation and Political Equality: A Seven Nation Comparison*. Cambridge: Cambridge University Press.

—— SCHLOZMAN, K., and BRADY, H. 1995. *Voice and Equality: Civic Voluntarism in American Politics*. Cambridge, Mass.: Harvard University Press.

WATTENBERG, M. 2000. 'The Decline of Party Mobilization'. In R. J. Dalton and M. P. Wattenberg (eds.), *Parties without Partisans: Political Change in Advanced Industrial Democracies*. Oxford: Oxford University Press.

WHITELEY, P. 2000. 'Econonomic Growth and Social Capital'. *Political Studies*, 48/3: 443–66.

——and SEYD, P. 2002. *High Intensity Participation: The Dynamics of Party Activism in Britain*. Ann Arbor: University of Michigan Press.

CHAPTER 43

....

POLITICAL MARKETING

....

HEATHER SAVIGNY

POLITICIANS increasingly behave like celebrities (Street 1997; 2004; Higgins 2008), appearing on TV programmes such as *Richard and Judy*, *Have I Got News for You*, *Parkinson*, etc., and a plethora of spin doctors advise politicians on their interactions with the media. Political actors need to be 'telegenic' (Newman 1994: 17); how politicians look is as (if not more) important than what they say. This emphasis upon image and media management form, however, just one part of a broader set of strategies, referred to within the academic literature as political marketing.

Political marketing, while played out in and reliant upon a media environment, is not simply about media management strategies. Political marketing is something which has become much more than a 'trendy buzzword'; it has become an integral part of the practice of contemporary politics. Labour and the Conservatives routinely and extensively employ marketing in their electioneering and as Newman observes, in the current environment, the question becomes whether it is conceivable for a candidate *not* to adopt a marketing perspective (Newman 1994: 21). In this sense, it is important to establish not only what political marketing is, what it does, why and how it has become so prominent, but also what the implications of the application of marketing to politics might entail. As such, the aim of this chapter is to reflect critically upon these issues in relation to

I would like to thank: Lee Marsden, John Street, Mick Temple, Colin Hay, and the *Handbook* editors, Matthew Flinders, Andrew Gamble, and Mike Kenny, and the anonymous reviewers, for their constructive and insightful comments on earlier versions of this chapter.

political marketing as both as set of political practices and an academic discipline. It will also highlight the tensions and areas of contestation in this development, particularly with respect to the potential impact on the democratic process.

Broadly speaking political marketing is informed by a set of assumptions and models derived from management, which start from the premise that parties can be conceived of as businesses and voters as consumers. This fundamental premise has given rise to a divergent set of literature which details contemporary elite-level political behaviour, largely but not exclusively, in election campaign practice. The term 'political marketing' is used in this chapter to detail this use of business assumptions, models, and practices in politics as both (a) a set of practical strategies used by political actors, and (b) an academic literature which has charted these developments.

As a literature, political marketing draws from communications studies, political science, and management marketing literature (Scammell 1999), and has been able to capture and describe the changing nature of electioneering. This literature has proliferated, with a wealth of books, articles, and a specialist journal (*Journal of Political Marketing*) which detail, describe, and analyse contemporary elite-level political behaviour. This has also meant that alongside traditional election studies such as the Nuffield series, elections for more than a decade have been accompanied by books and special issues of journals (e.g. *European Journal of Marketing*; *Journal of Marketing Management*) devoted specifically to 'political marketing'.

As will be noted below, however, this literature has not only described campaign practice, but has also been used by some prescriptively, as justification for normative claims about the benefits to (a) political actors—that marketing is a necessary template for electoral success (e.g. Kotler and Levy 1969; Egan 1999); and (b) that it enhances the democratic process (e.g. Harrop 1990; O'Cass 1996; Lees-Marshment 2001a; 2001b). One of the main points of critique within this chapter is the extent to which the more prescriptive literature commits a logical fallacy, conflating evidence consistent with its models as evidence of its normative contribution to political practice[1] and the potential problems this raises for the democratic process.

The chapter proceeds by placing the growth and use of political marketing, in literature and practice, in its broader communications context. It then provides a historical overview of the trajectory of political marketing, as both political practice and a disciplinary subfield. Attention is then turned to the specific models and concepts, derived from business, which underpin and inform this development, and illustrates how these have been used to both describe and prescribe practice. The final section places political marketing in its broader context and explores its structural

---

[1] Paradoxically, given the empiricist/positivist nature of the more prescriptive literature, and yet the positivist emphasis on observer neutrality. For further discussion of this point see Savigny (2007).

basis. Throughout, the underlying assumptions are teased out (which have often been uncritically accepted within much of this literature), and key areas of contention and debate are also highlighted.

43.1 BACKGROUND

Political marketing has informed and influenced election campaigns in the USA, UK, Austria, Denmark, Germany, the Netherlands, New Zealand, Canada (Bowler and Farrell 1992; Lilleker and Lees-Marshment 2005), Australia (O'Cass 2001), Sweden (Nord 2006; Strömbäck 2007), and China (Sun 2007). For some, marketing strategy lies at the heart of electoral success (Kotler and Kotler 1999: 4). Commentators suggest we have reached an era of the 'permanent campaign' (Blumenthal 1980), and so in turn political marketing has been viewed by some as a method of governance (O'Shaughnessy 1990; Newman 1994; Lees-Marshment 2001a; for a more critical account see Needham 2005).

The term political marketing has been more widely used ambiguously as a 'catch-all' phrase to characterize a variety of changes that have been taking place in the practice and presentation of politics. For some political marketing is: 'smoke and mirrors' (Palmer 2002); synonymous with spin (Jones 1997); the packaging of politics (Franklin 1994); and the 'professionalisation of political communication' (Negrine and Lilleker 2002). This activity has also been described as representative of the behaviour of a 'public relations state' (Deacon and Golding 1994) or the workings of a 'public relations democracy' (Davis 2002). This for some has come to represent a 'crisis in public communication' (Blumler and Gurevitch 1995), and Franklin suggests that this attention to presentation has been at the expense of political substance, and has led to a 'dumbing down' which stifles democratic debate (1994). Although in contrast some suggest it enhances opportunities for political participation (Temple 2006; see also Brants 1998). While this emphasis on professional media strategies conforms to Panebianco's (1988) electoral–professional party, what is qualitatively different in the contemporary environment is that the presentation of politicians and policy has become at least as significant for political actors as the policy content. As Gaber notes, a spin doctor for New Labour was quoted after the 1997 election saying: 'communications is not an afterthought to our policy. It's central to the whole mission of New Labour' (1998: 13).

While media and communications do play an integral role in the marketing process, political marketing is, as the term suggests, extensively informed by marketing. What differentiates 'political marketing' (in the academic literature) from other analyses of the relationship between politicians and the media, or election campaigning per se, is the explicit emphasis upon 'marketing'; that is, the explicit acceptance and usage of assumptions, methods, and practices developed within and associated with both business practice and the academic management marketing literature. Thus the chapter proceeds by detailing the use of political marketing in practice, in order to provide the historical context from which the academic literature has developed.

43.2 HISTORICIZING POLITICAL MARKETING AS PRACTICE

If political marketing in practice is about the art of persuasion then it could be argued that this goes back to the days of Aristotle. Its historical antecedents are widely noted; for Harris (2001) these date back to Machiavelli. Wring charts the historical developments of marketing techniques in Britain back to the early twentieth century (1996: 102). In its contemporary form, however, the development and refinement of marketing in practice can be located in the USA, with Britain following closely behind. Maarek argues that while political marketing is 'entirely rooted in the history of political communication in the United States' (1995: 7) its modern manifestation coincided with the emergence of television, when Eisenhower became the first candidate to make use of this technology as a means of persuasion (1995: 7–21). Shama describes how, in the early 1960s, political campaigning was 'viewed and practiced as the *selling* of candidates' (1976: 767–8), but in the USA it was the Reagan campaigns of the 1980s that marked the wholesale adoption of marketing (as pursued by commercial companies) (Newman 1994: 25).

The development of marketing in Britain closely followed the American lead. It was the advent of Thatcher as leader of the Conservative Party, in particular the election campaign of 1987, which is generally regarded as changing the manner of British electioneering (Wring 1996: 107; O'Shaughnessy 1990: 218). While the Conservatives had previously employed advertising agents Saatchi and Saatchi (1979: 'Labour isn't working') (Lock and Harris 1996: 21), it was in the 1980s that marketing strategies were used to determine which *policies* would be electorally unviable. Scammell notes that, 'In 1987 . . . the manifesto and electoral strategy closely followed the analysis of marketing research' (1996: 124), and the Conservatives led the way on the use of marketing to inform their 'market positioning'. Labour followed and during the leadership of Neil Kinnock the term marketing also became part of Labour's organizational thinking (Wring 1996: 102; see also Gould 1998). This recognition and description of marketing as a set of practices employed by political elites is also paralleled by an academic literature, the origins and development of which are charted below.

43.3 HISTORICIZING POLITICAL MARKETING AS AN ACADEMIC LITERATURE

The phrase 'political marketing' was first used by Kelley in 1956, but it was the seminal article by Kotler and Levy (1969) which marked the origins of the embedding of this term as a feature of contemporary academic discourse and the foundation for the subfield. Kotler and Levy argued that marketing could be extended to other areas of endeavour whose primary aim was not the making of profit; that marketing could be extended to services/persons and ideas (1969: 10). Indeed, their words seem somewhat prophetic now that managerial thinking and marketing has become a feature of many areas of public life (for example health and higher education).

Kotler and Levy argued that marketing is not something that is confined to business practice, but 'political contests remind us that candidates are marketed as well as soap' (1969: 10). For some, the use of these strategies is a response to the context political actors find themselves in. Proponents suggest that there is a similarity in political and commercial contexts, as political actors find themselves in an electoral marketplace where they have to 'sell' their 'product' to a consumer. As such they assume that business managers and political campaigners face similar challenges, in a similar context (of a marketplace), and therefore similar responses/methods are appropriate (Reid 1988; Newman 1994: 34; Butler and Collins 1996). The acceptance of the assumption that politics is as amenable to commodification as any other kind of commercial 'product' has profound implications, not only for the reshaping of the way in which politics is conducted, but also raises broader issues about the role and function of democracy. Does it matter, for example, if all citizens do not participate in formal politics, as long as enough of the 'product' gets 'sold' in order for politicians to win elections? As will be evident from the discussion below, while some of the literature espouses the benefits to politicians of adopting marketing, these more fundamental normative questions are only just beginning to be addressed.

43.4 UNDERLYING DEFINITIONS WITHIN THE POLITICAL MARKETING LITERATURE

In some senses, one of the many difficulties for students of political marketing is in delineating what it actually is, as there is no agreed definition of the term (Scammell 1999; O'Cass 2001; Lock and Harris 1996). Operating with an implicit commitment to pluralism, the political marketing literature describes what politicians do to get elected, but crucially this is through the use of strategies and techniques derived from business. Consistent with the positivist thinking which underpins much of the management marketing literature, political marketing has been defined as the 'science of influencing mass behaviour in competitive situations' (Mauser 1983: 5).

The focus within the literature is largely upon election campaign practice rather than electoral outcomes. Election campaigns are viewed 'as, in all its essentials, a condensed consumer-product marketing campaign' (O'Shaughnessy and Henneberg 2002: p. xi) and so methods and strategies from marketing are deemed appropriate. Simply put, the existing research into political marketing highlights 'where, why and how a party positions itself in the electoral market' (Harrop 1990: 277). This draws heavily on management marketing literature, where scholars define '[m]arketing [as] the delivery of customer satisfaction at a profit' (Kotler et al. 2005: 5). While there are a variety of definitions of political marketing within the literature, all accept that marketing entails two actors (the organization and the consumer) and the desire for the organization to achieve their ends (for non-profit organizations this is to maximize utility rather than make a profit).

In this way, the political marketing literature differentiates itself from other forms of analysis of media and professionalized political behaviour, with its explicit emphasis on marketing. That is, it accepts the fundamental principle of marketing that 'the essence of marketing is reciprocity: "consumers" themselves bring something to bear on the selling' (O'Shaughnessy 1990: 2). The adoption of this central assumption suggests that consumers (voters) are elevated from being passive recipients of a political 'product' to playing an interactive role in its production. This is achieved through public opinion research (such as polls and focus groups) so that public opinion is identified and fed back into, thereby shaping, the political 'product'. In marketing this same process takes place, in order that the business can then sell the product to a receptive consumer and make a profit. In politics, the means are regarded as the same, but the aim for the political party is simply viewed as winning the election (Lock and Harris 1996: 18).

Henneberg argues that a formal analytical definition of political marketing is that it 'seeks to establish, maintain and enhance long term voter relationships at a profit for society and political parties. So that the objectives of the organisation are met' (Henneberg 2002: 102–3). In politics, this translates into a focus on the strategies and techniques employed by political actors in a competitive (and minimally specified) context to achieve their goal: electoral victory. Although, as will be discussed later in the chapter, it is worth noting that the key point here is that relationships with voters are viewed as instrumental and necessary insofar as they enable organizations to achieve their goal (Wring 1997: 652; see also Sackman 1992). As such this assumption introduces a tension between, on the one hand, the idea of a voter as a citizen, informed, engaged, and playing a participatory role in the political process, and on the other, functioning instrumentally simply enabling political actors to achieve their goal.

The basic premise within these definitions, and accepted by the more positive literature, is that candidates and/or parties can be positioned and marketed in a manner analogous to that of businesses in the commercial sector. Policy content is formulated and communicated within an assumed 'political market place' (e.g. Newman 1994;

Worcester and Baines 2006). This analogy is extended and the ontological and analytical supposition is that political parties can be conceived of as businesses and voters as consumers, who purchase (exchange their vote for) a political product (party or candidate) on the day of the election. This simplistic starting point clearly resembles that of Downs's (1957) spatial model of electoral competition. The economic roots of Downs's model are acknowledged within the literature (Mauser 1983; Newman 1994; Wring 1996; Butler and Collins 1999: 55; Scammell 1999: 726, 739; Lees-Marshment 2001b: 694) and while for some political marketing is viewed as a contemporary variant of rational choice theory (Savigny 2004) others claim that political marketing goes beyond Downs, through the detailing of *how* parties identify voter demands (Lees-Marshment 2001b: 694).

For those who advocate political marketing as practice, as well as an academic literature, there is the claim that it provides parties and candidates with a method that facilities the 'ability to address diverse voter concerns and needs through marketing analyses, planning, implementation and control of political and electoral campaigns' (O'Cass 1996: 48). There are two aspects to this process: the first is concerned with the techniques of marketing which include e.g. advertising, market research, and media management. The second is at the level of strategy, and as leading marketing scholars note, in order for an organization to be successful a marketing 'mindset' must be adopted (Kotler and Andreasen 1996: 37). That is, management marketing includes prescriptive tenets: marketing is not only about a set of tools and techniques, but a way of thinking. The ultimate philosophy for organizational success is claimed to be marketing (Webster 1992) and electoral success has also been linked to adherence to marketing ideals (e.g. O'Cass 2001; Lees-Marshment 2001a; 2001b). The difficulties with this are discussed later in the chapter.

43.5 MODELS AND CONCEPTS WITHIN THE POLITICAL MARKETING LITERATURE

In simple marketing terms, what distinguishes marketing from selling is the emphasis on the consumer. For example, while Labour's 1987 election campaign might have been regarded as highly professional, according to marketing scholars the distinction was that the emphasis was upon 'selling', whereas the Conservatives placed greater emphasis on the 'marketing'; that is, a response to public opinion and the successful communication of that response (O'Shaughnessy 1990; Scammell 1995). One framework that is widely used in the academic literature, to describe this organizational transition from 'selling' to 'marketing', is Keith's three-stage evolutionary model (1960). Keith's model claimed that firms went through three interlinked stages: product, sales, and market orientations. These stages overlapped and, Keith argued, once a firm reached market orientation, that is it adhered to the marketing concept (detailed below) and placed the consumer at the centre of the product, it would be successful. What this model highlights is the differing stages of fluidity in the process: in the selling stage, public opinion is thought to be malleable and subject to persuasion (through, for example, advertising); in the marketing stage, however, it is the product that is thought to be malleable, responsive to public opinion.

This three-stage model of evolution has been widely used and adapted to describe and analyse how political actors have moved towards and employed marketing in election campaigns. The literature uses these stages to reflect differing points of emphasis. In marketing accounts, the descriptor is the managerial 'product, sales and market orientation' of parties/candidates (Shama 1976; Smith and Saunders 1990; Newman 1994; Lees-Marshment 2001a; 2001b; see also Mauser 1983). In accounts which privilege communications and technology, the media provides the context to describe development from 'premodern' to 'television revolution' and then as a 'telecommunications revolution' (Farrell 1996); for Norris (2000) these stages are characterized as 'premodern, modern and postmodern'. Wring combines these different aspects with internal organizational learning, defining these stages as the 'propaganda, media and political marketing' phase (1996; 2005). Despite differing foci of analysis, what the application of this model highlights is the way in which political marketing is conceived as a process implying continuance over time, rather than a static, one-off phenomenon. This three-stage approach highlights historical, temporal, and contextual factors; electioneering being influenced by both endogenous factors (such as organizational learning from electoral successes and losses; party leaders and members) and exogenous factors (such as a densely populated media environment; behaviour of opposition parties; a changing societal base; advice from strategists from 'sister' parties such as in the USA and Australia).

43.5.1 The Marketing Concept

As management guru Peter Drucker argues, 'the aim of marketing is to make selling superfluous. The aim of marketing is to know and understand the customer so well that the product fits him and sells itself. Ideally, marketing should result in a customer who is ready to buy. All that should be needed then is to make the product or service available' (Drucker 1974: 64–5). At the heart of this lies the marketing concept, which is premised on the notion that 'the consumer, not the company, is in the middle' (Keith 1960: 35). While its utility has been debated (see e.g. Houston 1986), the 'marketing concept' is used within the political marketing literature to suggest that the consumer (voter) is at the centre of the process. As such, parties/candidates listen to (targeted) public opinion, and provide the electorate with a 'product' that they want, in order to achieve electoral victory (Mauser 1983; Reid 1988; Shama 1976; O'Cass 1996; Egan 1999; Lees-Marshment 2001a; 2001b).

These concepts, however, have been employed as more than heuristic devices. In practice, advocates argue that adherence to the marketing concept enables parties/candidates to 'find out who the voters are and what they want the candidates to stand for. Candidates can then feedback to the voters the ideas that they know will sell in the marketplace' (Newman 1994: 16). From here, once voter preferences have been identified, advertising and other promotional strategies then form part of the marketing process of both relaying the refined 'product' to 'consumers', and seeking to persuade them that their wants have been incorporated into the 'product'.

Labour's electoral victory in 1997 provides a clear example of this process in practice. Labour's use of opinion research to inform their repositioning meant that focus groups became a key element in the planning of electoral strategies and assessment of policy proposals (Gould 1998). Extensive opinion research was undertaken which enabled Labour to identify Tory 'switchers', particularly in marginal seats, who were necessary for a Labour victory (see Gould 1998: 204, 329, 350). The emphasis on the importance of both the perception of the electorate that their wants had been accommodated and the demands of a densely populated media environment are highlighted by Mandelson's statement that: 'If a government policy cannot be presented in a simple and attractive way, it is more likely than not to contain fundamental flaws and prove to be the wrong policy' (1997, cited in Franklin 2001: 131). The appearance of responsiveness to public opinion has been evidenced more broadly, with strategies such as Labour's 'Big Conversation'; the Conservatives' 'Listening to Britain'; the use of new media technologies such as blogs and petitions on the Downing Street website. Consistent with a 'permanent campaign' approach to government, this process has continued throughout Labour's period in office; Brown's maiden speech as Prime Minister reinforced this: 'As I have travelled around the country and as I have listened and I've learnt from the British people, and as Prime Minister I will continue to listen and learn from the British people, I have heard the need for change' (24 June 2007, cited in Lilleker and Scullion 2008: 1).

The desire to present the appearance of a visible engagement with the voters illustrates for some the centrality of the 'consumer' (voter) to the political process. In this way, advocates advance the normative claim that marketing ensures accountability and responsiveness and, as such, is a beneficial force for democracy (Shama 1976; Harrop 1990; Scammell 1995; O'Cass 1996; 2001; Kotler and Kotler 1999; Lees-Marshment 2001a; 2001b). Lees-Marshment observes that political parties in Britain 'no longer pursue grand ideologies, fervently arguing for what they believe in and trying to persuade the masses to follow them. They increasingly follow the people' (2001a: 1); and while this is presented as evidence of the responsive nature of political marketing, some warn of the potential for negative effects on the political process. This is in terms of both the dangers of populism (e.g. O'Shaughnessy 1990; Scammell 1995; Henneberg 2004), and the anti-democratic nature of this method of listening to voters who are necessary for electoral victory rather than the polity as a whole (Savigny 2007).

43.5.2 Implementing Marketing

Once public opinion has been identified, according to marketing, and fed back into the 'product', the next stage in the electioneering process is to 'sell' the 'product' to the public in an attempt to mobilize electoral support. One of the key ways in which this is done is through market segmentation. First introduced by Smith (1956), the notion of 'market segmentation' draws attention to the heterogeneity of the marketplace. Acknowledging that political 'markets' are not homogeneous (Butler and Collins 1996: 35), and consistent with management marketing, voters are 'segmented' into target groups (in practice this has been evident in categories such as 'Mondeo Man' or 'Worcester Woman'). Here, the assumption within the literature is that the electoral 'market' can be divided into subcategories building upon traditional variables such as class and gender. Segmentation means that parties can identify voter attitudes and beliefs, so in turn the message can be 'tweaked' to fit the profile of the voter whose support is being targeted. It is also assumed that this enables parties to gain a priori insights into voter behaviour (Smith and Saunders 1990; Smith and Hirst 2001). Technological developments, refinement of marketing strategies, advice from international strategists, and greater availability of information about voters' lifestyle choices and consumer trends have meant that, in practice, voters are now segmented into much smaller groups, leading to a much more specific individualized refining of the targeted campaign message.

Segmentation, while detailed in the literature, has also been widely used in political practice and, again, it is worth looking to the USA for some historical background. Clinton, aided and advised by strategist Dick Morris, relied on opinion research, but extensive voter profiling enabled him to focus in an unprecedented way on localized markets (Newman 1999: 6–7; see also Morris 1999). Clinton bypassed traditional media forms to communicate directly with the voters, for example through cable channel TV shows, and employed researchers to provide detailed opinion research based on 'lifestyle' analysis (Novotny 2000: 18). American strategists Penn and Schoen have also advised the Labour Party, and so again there has been a transfer of American strategies and technologies to the UK.

In 2005, both the Conservatives and Labour used comprehensive voter profiling software. The former, following consultation with the (now former) Republican strategist, Karl Rove, used US Republican software, 'Voter Vault'; Labour used the 'labour.contact' database. This technology and collaboration with international strategists enabled both parties to build up highly detailed personal profiles of aggregated groups (Wintour 2005). Target voters were no longer identified simply by traditional demographic social class, but by much more distinct and discrete categories. In 1997, campaign resources had focused on ninety key seats (Seyd 2001: 54). In 2001, further refinement had meant that there were 'no key seats only key voters' (Seyd 2001) and by 2005 over sixty-one different categories were identified. Those targeted by Labour included 'symbols of success', 'upscaling new owners', and 'affluent blue collar' (Wintour 2005). This in turn led to highly individualized campaigning, according to voter profiles and their likelihood of impact on the electoral outcome.

Here the conflation of analytical and ontological assumptions of voters as consumers seems to be most obviously accepted in political practice. Indeed, profiling of voters through reference to their purchasing habits and lifestyle choices suggests a perception by politicians that voters can be equated with consumers (for further discussion of voters/citizens as consumers see Scammell 2003; Schudson 2006; Lilleker and Scullion 2008; and more broadly see Lewis, Inthorn, and Wahl-Jorgensen

2005). Crucially however, and directly undermining the normative claims that marketing benefits democracy, this means that campaigning then becomes focused on a small segment of the electorate. In 2005 only 2 per cent of the electorate were considered strategically significant (Wintour 2005) as such; campaigning was directed at them rather than at the electorate as a whole. In this sense, if only 2 per cent of the populace were considered strategically significant for elites to achieve their goals, this potentially serves (a) to disenfranchise the broader electorate and (b) to undermine the claims of the marketing concept that the consumer is at the centre.

43.6 THE BROADER CONTEXT OF POLITICAL MARKETING: LITERATURE AND PRACTICE

While the political marketing literature draws attention to political actors and voters, clearly they do not operate in a minimally defined context. Moreover, given the prescriptive nature of some of the political marketing literature, this might suggest a one-way relationship where marketers are able to influence politicians and politicians simply able to influence the electorate. But politicians operate in a densely structured context which affects the course(s) of action available to them (cf. Giddens 1984). This is not to deny autonomy to political actors, nor deny their complicity in the marketing of politics, but rather to suggest that they interact not only with the electorate, but that this is done via the media (who have their own agendas and constraints), in the context of broader political structures and the rules of the electoral 'game'. As has been highlighted throughout, the international context is important, not only in terms of electioneering strategies, but in terms of defining the parameters of possibility of the promises that political actors may make, in terms of the constraints and opportunities afforded by the influence of institutions such as the European Union; international agreements; and (academically contested) processes such as globalization. The same is true for the influence of business (such as the relationship between politicians and, for example, the CBI). The relationship between politicians and their electorates is clearly not as straightforward as implied by the political marketing literature, and so while politicians may respond to public opinion, there are other constraints which mean that politicians cannot simply accommodate expressed voter preferences into their 'product' without consideration of potential loss of support from, or opportunities to engage with, for example, the media, international leaders, and/or business leaders.

43.6.1 The Media

The media are assumed to be so significant that Harrop suggests the media are the causal mechanisms for political marketing, making the use of marketing in contemporary political practice 'inevitable' (Harrop 1990: 284). Whether causality for this phenomenon lies with the media or not, here the political marketing literature departs from other academic literature which discusses the relationship between politicians and the mass media in a democracy, in terms of both what that relationship is and what it should be (e.g. McNair 1999; Street 2001; Lloyd 2004; Louw 2005). The media clearly are of key importance in the communication to the masses of election campaigns and political strategies. Labour's experience of a hostile media environment and their subsequent media-friendly behaviour suggests that they perceive the media to have an enormous influence on voting behaviour (irrespective of academic debates, see for example Newton and Brynin 2001). Clearly, too, so do the media. For example, consider Blair's studious courting of Murdoch, and subsequent favourable newspaper coverage, which led to Britain's biggest selling newspaper to proclaim in 1997: 'The *Sun* backs Blair'. This suggests that the media can become political actors while at the same time setting the context for the conduct of electoral competition.

However, as has been observed, the political marketing literature has yet to acknowledge the agency of the media in the marketing process, assuming media compliance when politicians present their message (Savigny and Temple 2008). While in liberal theory, the media in a democracy function to hold elites to account, this would suggest that some scepticism within the media towards political elites and their messages is almost to be expected. Notably, however, the media do not hold businesses to account in the same manner. In this way, politicians may also be responding to the behaviour of the media. If the press and media are more favourably disposed to business interests, is it a surprise if in the pursuit of positive and favourable media coverage (perceived by political elites as necessary for electoral support) parties attempt to position themselves as businesses?

43.6.2 Political Structures

Some suggest that marketing is ubiquitous in the UK, because, like the USA, there is a two-party system (although more broadly it is recognized that this is debatable). The first-past-the-post system means that electoral competition occurs between a number of key seats and marginal constituencies. In 1995, Kavanagh concluded that it was the strength of the British party system itself (in large part due to the nature of party/candidate funding) which meant that 'pollsters and experts on public relations and communications still have an insecure relationship with the politicians', preventing British politics from becoming completely Americanized by the marketing process (Kavanagh 1995: 7). However, as marketers and marketing become increasingly influential, if both Labour and the Conservatives are employing marketing strategies, then differences between them become, almost by definition, stylistic and presentational. Systematic studies have noted and debated the centrist tendencies of electoral competition in the UK (see for example Hay 1999), and if there is little to distinguish political parties then party competition, problematically, potentially becomes about who is the better at marketing strategies rather than about formal political substance.

43.6.3 Societal Structures

Whatever the debate—partisan dealignment (Sarlvik and Crewe 1983) or realignment (Heath, Jowell, and Curtice 1985)—clearly there has been a profound shift in public behaviour towards formal political activity, and parties are no longer able to rely on high levels of partisan support. Demographic changes in voting behaviour have been widely noted (e.g. Heath, Jowell, and Curtice 1985; Crewe 1986; Miller et al. 1990; Franklin 1992: 121; Parry, Moyser, and Day 1992; Dalton 2004). Party membership has fallen. Estimates suggest decreasing Conservative Party membership with figures around 290,000 in 2006 (Helm 2006). In July 2005 Labour's membership figures had fallen to 210,374 (*Guardian* 2006). This is consistent with the view of the perceived decline of political parties as relevant vehicles for the expression of public interest (see for example Lawson and Merkl 1988; Webb 1995). For some, marketing is presented as a method to reconnect with this increasingly diverse and volatile electorate. According to the literature, opportunities arise through the marketing process to build 'brand loyalties' (e.g. Smith and Saunders 1990), to replace partisan loyalties. This support is necessary within the marketing literature, because without it (returning to the definition of marketing) organizations (parties) are not able to achieve their aims.

43.6.4 Voters and Participation

Participation, according to the political marketing literature, is assumed to occur in two sites: where the public influence the construction of the political product; and in the act of voting. In formal political terms, this implies a participatory rather than a representative form of democracy. This participation by voters is what is assumed, within the political marketing literature, to keep political elites responsive and accountable. But for this analogy to work, participation by the electorate is crucial. However, the picture in the UK and other Western democracies is one of declining electoral turnout and increasing disaffection and lack of trust in both politicians and the process of politics (see for example Dalton 2004; Newton 2006; Hay 2007).

Advocates argue that marketing provides increased responsiveness to the public and hence enhances accountability (Shama 1976; Kotler and Kotler 1999; O'Cass 1996; Harrop 1990; Lees-Marshment 2001a; 2001b). But the empirical reality is that marketing has not proved a panacea to the difficulties of mobilizing electoral support and arguably has contributed to a 'marketing malaise'; a source of public disconnection from politics (Savigny 2008). Despite, or maybe because of, extensive marketing, the last two general elections show an alarming degree of non-participation. Following the post-war record low turnout of 59 per cent in 2001, turnout improved only marginally in 2005 to 61 per cent (compared also to 76 per cent in 1979).

In some senses this changing electoral base conforms to the fairly negative view of voters held within the political marketing literature. Voters are seen as fulfilling an instrumental function for parties, being the means through which politicians can achieve their goal. In terms of motivation to vote and choices for whom to vote, voters are not assumed to vote on the basis of party loyalty (Newman 1994: 29). Voters are assumed to regard policy content as secondary; for some, it is thought this is incidental (Harrop 1990: 280). Within the political marketing literature there is the assumption that 'voters are unable to unbundle the electoral product offering, the vast majority therefore choose on the basis of overall political package, concept or image' (Lock and Harris 1996: 17). Indeed, as implied throughout this chapter, it would seem, whether there is an awareness of academic literature on this topic or not, that political actors do indeed behave in a manner consistent with this assumption of voter behaviour.

O'Shaughnessy and Henneberg further argue that 'Political marketing works because of the apoliticality of most voters who are cognitive misers and who are thereby inadvertent consumers of political information' (2002: p. xviii). This claim would suggest that marketing is used because that is what the public want: that the public are uninterested in the minutiae of policy detail and political debate; they want their voices heard but at the same time want information relayed in a cost-saving 'soundbite' and an identifiable brand or image. Despite the claimed centrality of the consumer (voter), paradoxically, the voter has received little attention in the political marketing literature apart from the instrumental role afforded to them as a means through which organizations can achieve their goal. The assumption that the public want marketing thinking to influence their politics to the extent that politics needs to be delivered in soundbites, images, or are simply disinterested, while a fundamental supposition about how and why marketing should inform politics (both in literature and practice), has yet to be rigorously either theorized or empirically tested.

43.7 THE PRESCRIPTION OF POLITICAL MARKETING

There is nothing new in the adoption of management literature to the practice of politics. New public management informed many of the changes to public-sector services in the 1980s (see for example Christensen and Laegreid 2002) and other literature premised upon rationalist economic assumptions, notably public choice theory, has been heavily influential in policy practice. This attempt to influence the political process is also evident within some of the political marketing literature, where, for some scholars, marketing is not simply an analytic or descriptive framework, but provides practical advice for political actors. Here, again, management marketing provides the influence. In management marketing the marketing concept is not only a means to operationalize models, but also functions as a philosophy:

a template for thinking and guiding organizational behaviour (Kotler and Zaltman 1971; O'Leary and Iredale 1976). This prescriptive element has been accepted by some within the field of political marketing, and in turn analytic assumptions become rendered ontological. O'Cass argues the marketing concept is 'both a philosophical and practical guide for the management of marketing' (1996: 48). Marketing models and frameworks are regarded by some as 'pragmatic and realistic' (Mauser 1983: 1) which have practical utility (see also Reid 1988; Smith and Saunders 1990: 304; Butler and Collins 1996: 42).

Lock and Harris argue that political marketing 'has to develop its own prescriptive and predictive models if it is to inform and influence political action' (1996: 23). Lees-Marshment highlights how 'political marketing can enable us to observe how organisations may lose touch with their market; maybe even to advise them how not to do so' (2001b: 706–7). Political marketing claims to be able to show a political party what they 'ought' to be doing (O'Cass 1996: 56) to manage their campaigns more effectively (Maarek 1995). While Henneberg (2004; see also Henneberg and O'Shaughnessy 2007) highlights the need for greater theoretical and conceptual development within the field, Butler and Collins argue that 'research into the field of campaign/marketing management *must* be dominated by questions of practicality' (1994: 32; emphasis added). Indeed this is nowhere more clearly emphasized than in Egan's view that politicians need marketing, lamenting the difficulties in getting politicians to accept the utility of such models in practice: 'Political marketers do not, however, always have it their own way. Politicians have a habit of taking back the reigns of electoral management particularly when things do not seem to be going to plan. This is largely political arrogance' (1999: 496). This quotation highlights the desire for marketers both to influence that which they describe and to have a direct influence on the strategic behaviour of politicians. As Scammell notes, 'as the techniques of market research and market prediction become more "scientific" and precise, the more influential marketing and marketing experts are likely to become in politics' (1995: 19). However, to model and prescribe political behaviour from frameworks and assumptions developed in management is to work within the constraints of these management marketing assumptions, in effect to subordinate politics to marketing. For those concerned with the impact marketing has upon democracy, this is an alarming trend.

43.8 CONCLUSION

As the historical location of political marketing (as a literature and in practice) suggests, for some, marketing represents a continuation of existing techniques and practices which are simply enhanced and refined in accordance with developments in technologies. For others, while there is a historical component, the use of political marketing also represents a fundamental change in party thinking. That is, while parties may have adopted these strategies in the past, what is qualitatively different is the extent to which marketing, as a set of guidelines, now dominates organizational behaviour.

Some argue that, in practice, the UK is simply following trends in the USA, both in the use of marketing and also as marketing has become entwined with a permanent campaign approach to government (Sparrow and Turner 2001), which could be seen to reinforce the Americanization thesis (cf. Mancini and Swanson 1996). But the changing character of contemporary electioneering is not that straightforward. Politicians operate in opportunity structures which both constrain and facilitate action, and include: a densely structured media environment, which brings with it a demand for twenty-four-hour news; a changing demographic base from which to draw electoral support; and declining electoral turnout. Political marketing, as practice, has been a method through which political actors have responded to, and played a role in reconstituting, this changing environment.

As has been argued, the political marketing literature is far from homogeneous. Within this literature, differing starting points mean that some scholars focus on election campaign strategies (the external presentation of parties), while others draw attention to the internal behaviour of parties and party membership. Some focus attention on the role of the media as driving this process, some on the methods of marketing and marketers, and others on political parties themselves as agents of change. Some see marketing as a positive phenomenon for politics, while others adopt a more critical approach. What this fragmentation in the literature suggests is the existence of a healthy debate around a set of ideas, practices, and techniques that have extensively altered and reshaped the nature of elite-level political activity. This not only relates to presentational or stylistic concerns in electoral campaigning but also to the methods and ways of thinking about what politics is, and how it is and should be conducted. Within the political marketing literature, the driver of political change is viewed as the 'campaigners' strategic understanding of the political market' (Scammell 1999: 723). This overt emphasis on markets as shaping the activity of politics arguably, and problematically for some, however, reflects a much broader fundamental change in the conceptualization of politics, what its form and function is, and what politics should be.

REFERENCES

BLUMENTHAL, S. 1980. *The Permanent Campaign*. Boston: Beacon.

BLUMLER, J., and GUREVITCH, M. 1995. *The Crisis in Public Communications*. London: Routledge.

BOWLER, S., and FARRELL, D. 1992. 'The Study of Election Campaigning'. Pp. 1–23 in S. Bowler and D. Farrell (eds.), *Electoral Strategies and Political Marketing*. London: Macmillan.

BRANTS, K. 1998. 'Who's Afraid of Infotainment'. *European Journal of Communication*, 13/3: 315–35.

BUTLER, P., and COLLINS, N. 1994. 'Political Marketing: Structure and Process'. *European Journal of Marketing*, 28/1: 19–34.

————1996. 'Strategic Analysis in Political Markets'. *European Journal of Marketing*, 30/10–11: 32–44.

————1999. 'A Conceptual Framework for Political Marketing'. Pp. 55–72 in B. Newman (ed.), *Handbook of Political Marketing*. London: Sage.

CHRISTENSEN, T., and LAEGREID, P. 2002. *New Public Management: The Transformation of Ideas and Practice*. Aldershot: Ashgate.

CREWE, I. 1986. 'On the Death and Resurrection of Class Voting: Some Comments on *How Britain Votes*'. *Political Studies*, 35: 620–38.

DALTON, R. 2004. *Democratic Challenges, Democratic Choices: The Erosion of Political Support in Advanced Industrial Democracies*. Oxford: Oxford University Press.

DAVIS, A. 2002. *Public Relations Democracy: Public Relations, Politics and the Mass Media in Britain*. London: Sage.

DEACON, D., and GOLDING, P. 1994. *Taxation and Representation: The Media, Political Communication and the Poll Tax*. London: John Libbey.

DOWNS, A. 1957. *An Economic Theory of Democracy*. New York: Harper and Row.

DRUCKER, P. 1974. *Management: Tasks, Responsibilities and Practices*. London: Heinemann.

EGAN, J. 1999. 'Political Marketing: Lessons from the Mainstream'. *Journal of Marketing Management*, 15: 495–503.

FARRELL, D. 1996. 'Campaign Strategies and Tactics'. In L. LeDuc, R. Niemi, and P. Norris (eds.), *Comparing Democracies*. Thousand Oaks, Calif.: Sage.

FRANKLIN, B. 1994. *Packaging Politics*. London: Edward Arnold.

————2001. 'The Hand of History: New Labour, News Management and Governance'. Pp. 130–44 in S. Ludlam and M. J. Smith (eds.), *New Labour in Government*. Basingstoke: Palgrave.

FRANKLIN, M. 1992. 'Britain'. Pp. 101–22 in M. Franklin, T. T Mackie, and H. Valen (eds.), *Electoral Change: Responses to Evolving Social and Attitudinal Structures in Western Countries*. Cambridge: Cambridge University Press.

GABER, I. 1998. 'A World of Dogs and Lamp-Posts'. *New Statesman*, 19 June: 13.

GIDDENS, A. 1984. *The Constitution of Society*. Cambridge: Polity.

GOULD, P. 1998. *The Unfinished Revolution*. London: Little, Brown.

GUARDIAN 2006. 'Where's the Party?' 7 Apr.

HARRIS, P. 2001. 'Commentary: Machiavelli, Political Marketing and Reinventing Government'. *European Journal of Marketing*, 35/9–10: 136–54.

HARROP, M. 1990. 'Political Marketing'. *Parliamentary Affairs*, 43/3: 277–91.

HAY, C. 1999. *The Political Economy of New Labour*. Manchester: Manchester University Press.

————2007. *Why we Hate Politics*. Cambridge: Polity.

HEATH, A., JOWELL, R., and CURTICE, J. 1985. *How Britain Votes*. Oxford: Pergamon.

HELM, T. 2006. 'Cameron Boosts Party Members by 16,000'. *Daily Telegraph*, 7 Jan.

HENNEBERG, S. C. M. 2002. 'Understanding Political Marketing'. Pp. 93–170 in N. J. O'Shaughnessy and S. C. M. Henneburg (eds.), *The Idea of Political Marketing*. Westport, Conn.: Praeger.

————2004. 'The Views of an *Advocatus Dei*: Political Marketing and its Critics'. *Journal of Public Affairs*, 4/3: 225–43.

———— and O'SHAUGHNESSY, N. J. 2007. 'Prolegomena to Theory and Concept Development in Political Marketing'. *Journal of Political Marketing*, special issue 6 (2/3).

HIGGINS, M. 2008. *The Media and its Public*. Maidenhead: Open University Press.

HOUSTON, F. 1986. 'The Marketing Concept: What it is and What it is Not'. *Journal of Marketing*, 50/Apr.: 81–7.

JONES, N. 1997. *Campaign 1997*. London: Indigo.

KAVANAGH, D. 1995. *Election Campaigning: The New Marketing of Politics*. Oxford: Blackwell.

KEITH, R. 1960. 'The Marketing Revolution'. *Journal of Marketing*, 24: 35–8.

KELLEY, S. 1956. *Professional Public Relations and Political Power*. Baltimore: Johns Hopkins University Press.

KOTLER, P., and ANDREASEN, A. 1996. *Strategic Marketing for Non-Profit Organisations*, 5th edn. Englewood Cliffs, NJ: Prentice Hall.

—— and KOTLER, N. 1999. 'Political Marketing: Generating Effective Candidates, Campaigns and Causes'. Pp. 3–18 in B. Newman (ed.), *Handbook of Political Marketing*. London: Sage.

—— and LEVY, S. 1969. 'Broadening the Concept of Marketing'. *Journal of Marketing*, 33: 10–15.

—— WONG, V., SAUNDERS, J., and ARMSTRONG, G. 2005. *Principles of Marketing*. Harlow: Prentice Hall.

KOTLER, P., and ZALTMAN, C. 1971. 'Social Marketing: An Approach to Planned Social Change'. *Journal of Marketing*, 35: 8–12.

LAWSON, K., and MERKL, P. (eds.) 1988. *When Parties Fail: Emerging Alternative Organizations*. Princeton, NJ: Princeton University Press.

LEES-MARSHMENT, J. 2001a. *Political Marketing and British Political Parties: The Party's Just Begun*. Manchester: Manchester University Press.

—— 2001b. 'The Marriage of Politics and Marketing'. *Political Studies*, 49/4: 692–713.

LEWIS, J., INTHORN, S., and WAHL-JORGENSEN, K. 2005. *Citizens or Consumers? What the Media Tell us about Political Participation*. Maidenhead: Open University Press.

LILLEKER, D., and LEES-MARSHMENT, J. 2005. *Political Marketing: A Comparative Perspective*. Manchester: Manchester University Press.

—— and SCULLION, R. 2008. 'Introduction'. In D. Lilleker and R. Scullion (eds.), *Voters or Consumers: Imagining the Contemporary Electorate*. Cambridge: Cambridge Scholars.

LLOYD, J. 2004. *What the Media are Doing to our Politics*. London: Constable and Robinson.

LOCK, A., and HARRIS, P. 1996. 'Political Marketing: Vive la difference'. *European Journal of Marketing*, 30/10–11: 28–9.

LOUW, E. 2005. *The Media and Political Process*. London: Sage.

MAAREK, P. J. 1995. *Political Marketing and Communication*. London: John Libbey.

MANCINI, P., and SWANSON, D. L. 1996. 'Politics, Media and Modern Democracy: Introduction'. Pp. 1–28 in D. L. Swanson and P. Mancini (eds.), *Politics, Media and Modern Democracy: An International Study of Innovations in Electoral Campaigning and their Consequences*. Westport, Conn.: Praeger.

MANDELSON, P. 1997. 'Coordinating Government Policy'. Speech delivered to the conference on Modernizing the Policy Process, Regent's Park Hotel, 16 Sept. Cited in B. Franklin, 'The Hand of History: New Labour, News Management and Governance'. Pp. 130–44 in S. Ludlam and M. J. Smith (eds.), *New Labour in Government*. Basingstoke: Palgrave.

MAUSER, G. 1983. *Political Marketing*. New York: Praeger.

McNAIR, B. 1999. *An Introduction to Political Communication*, 2nd edn. London: Routledge.

MILLER, W. L., CLARKE, H. D., HARROP, M., LEDUC, L., and WHITELEY, P. F. 1990. *How Voters Change*. Oxford: Clarendon Press.

MORRIS, D. 1999. *Behind the Oval Office: Getting Re-elected against All Odds*. Los Angeles: Renaissance.

NEEDHAM, C. 2005. 'Brand Leaders: Clinton, Blair and the Limitations of the Permanent Campaign'. *Political Studies*, 53/2: 343–61.

NEGRINE, R., and LILLEKER, D. 2002. 'The Professionlization of Political Communication: Continuities and Changes in Media Practices'. *European Journal of Communication*, 17/3: 305–23.

NEWMAN, B. 1994. *The Marketing of the President: Political Marketing as Campaign Strategy.* London: Sage.

NEWTON, K. 2006. 'Political Support: Social Capital, Civil Society and Political and Economic Performance'. *Political Studies*, 54/4: 846–64.

—— and BRYNIN, M. 2001. 'The National Press and Party Voting in the UK'. *Political Studies*, 49: 265–85.

NORD, L. 2006. 'Still the Middle Way: A Study of Political Communications Practices on Swedish Election Campaigns'. *Press/Politics*, 11/1: 64–76.

NORRIS, P. 2000. *A Virtuous Circle: Political Communications in Postindustrial Societies.* Cambridge: Cambridge University Press.

NOVOTNY, P. 2000. 'From Polis to Agora: The Marketing of Political Consultants'. *Press/Politics*, 5/3: 12–26.

O'CASS, A. 1996. 'Political Marketing and the Marketing Concept'. *European Journal of Marketing*, 30/10–11: 45–61.

—— 2001. 'Political Marketing: An Investigation of the Political Marketing Concept and Political Market Orientation in Australian Politics'. *European Journal of Marketing*, 35/9–10: 1003–25.

O'LEARY, R., and IREDALE, I. 1976. 'The Marketing Concept: Quo Vadis?' *European Journal of Marketing*, 10/3: 146–57.

O'SHAUGHNESSY, N. 1990. *The Phenomenon of Political Marketing.* London: Macmillan.

—— and HENNEBERG, S. C. M. 2002. 'Introduction'. In N. J. O'Shaughnessy and S. C. M. Henneberg (eds.), *The Idea of Political Marketing.* Westport, Conn.: Praeger.

PALMER, J. 2002. 'Smoke and Mirrors: Is That the Way it is? Themes in Political Marketing'. *Media, Culture and Society*, 24: 345–63.

PANEBIANCO, A. 1988. *Political Parties: Organisation and Power.* Cambridge: Cambridge University Press.

PARRY, G., MOYSER, G., and DAY, N. 1992. *Political Participation and Democracy in Britain.* Cambridge: Cambridge University Press.

REID, D. M. 1988. 'Marketing the Political Product'. *European Journal of Marketing*, 22/9: 34–47.

SACKMAN, A. 1992. 'The Marketing Organisation Model: Making Sense of Modern Campaigning in Britain'. Presented at the UK PSA Annual Conference, Belfast, April. Cited in Wring 1997.

SARLVIK, B., and CREWE, I. 1983. *Decade of Dealignment.* Cambridge: Cambridge University Press.

SAVIGNY, H. 2004. 'Political Marketing: A Rational Choice?' *Journal of Political Marketing*, 3/1: 21–38.

—— 2007. 'Focus Groups and Political Marketing: Science and Democracy as Axiomatic'. *British Journal of Politics and International Relations*, 9/1: 122–37.

—— 2008. *The Problem of Political Marketing.* New York: Continuum.

—— and TEMPLE, M. 2008. 'The Great Political Marketing Debate: What Ever Happened to the Media?' Unpublished paper.

SCAMMELL, M. 1995. *Designer Politics: How Elections are Won.* London: Macmillan.

—— 1996. 'The Odd Couple: Marketing and Maggie'. *European Journal of Marketing*, 30/10–11: 122–34.

—— 1999. 'Political Marketing: Lessons for Political Science'. *Political Studies*, 47/4: 718–39.

—— 2003. 'Citizen Consumers: Towards a New Marketing of Politics?' In J. Corner and D. Pels (eds.), *Media and the Restyling of Politics*. London: Sage.

SCHUDSON, M. 2006. 'The Troubling Equivalence of Citizen and Consumer'. *Annals of the American Academy of Political and Social Science*, 608: 193–204.

SEYD, P. 2001. 'The Labour Campaign'. Pp. 43–59 in P. Norris (ed.), *Britain Votes 2001*. Oxford: Oxford University Press.

SHAMA, A. 1976. 'The Marketing of Political Candidates'. *Journal of the Academy of Marketing Sciences*, 4: 764–77.

SMITH, G., and HIRST, A. 2001. 'Strategic Political Segmentation: A New Approach for a New Era of Political Marketing'. *European Journal of Marketing*, 35/9–10: 1058–73.

—— and SAUNDERS, J. 1990. 'The Application of Marketing to British Politics'. *Journal of Marketing Management*, 5/3: 295–306.

SMITH, W. R. 1956. 'Product Differentiation and Market Segmentation as Alternative Marketing Strategies'. *Journal of Marketing*, 21: 3–8.

SPARROW, N., and TURNER, J. 2001. 'The Permanent Campaign: The Integration of Market Research Techniques in Developing Strategies in a More Uncertain Political Climate'. *European Journal of Marketing*, 35/9–10: 984–1024.

STREET J. 1997. *Politics and Popular Culture*. Cambridge: Polity.

—— 2001. *Mass Media, Politics and Democracy*. Basingstoke: Palgrave.

—— 2004. 'Celebrity Politicians: Popular Culture and Political Representation'. *British Journal of Politics and International Relations*, 6/4: 435–52.

STRÖMBÄCK, J. 2007. 'Antecedents of Political Market Orientation in Britain and Sweden: Analysis and Future Research Propositions'. *Journal of Public Affairs*, 7/1: 79–89.

SUN, H. 2007. 'International Political Marketing: A Case Study of its Application in China'. *Journal of Public Affairs*, 7/4: 331–40.

TEMPLE, M. 2006. 'Dumbing Down is Good for you'. *British Politics*, 1/2: 257–73.

WEBB, P. 1995. 'Are British Political Parties in Decline?' *Party Politics*, 95/3: 299–322.

WEBSTER, F. 1992. 'The Changing Role of Marketing in the Corporation'. *Journal of Marketing*, 56/Oct.: 1–17.

WINTOUR, P. 2005. 'Campaign Planners Buy into Supermarket Tactics'. www.spinwatch.org.

WRING, D. 1996. 'Political Marketing and Party Development in Britain: A "Secret" History'. *European Journal of Marketing*, 30/10–11: 100–11.

—— 1997. 'Reconciling Marketing with Political Science: Theories of Political Marketing'. *Journal of Marketing Management*, 13: 651–63.

—— 2005. *The Politics of Marketing the Labour Party*. Basingstoke: Palgrave Macmillan.

WORCESTER, R., and BAINES, P. 2006. 'Voter Research and Market Positioning: Triangulation and its Implications for Policy Development'. In P. J. Davies and B. Newman (eds.), *Winning Elections with Political Marketing*. Philadelphia: Haworth Press.

CHAPTER 44

TECHNOLOGY AND RISK

HENRY ROTHSTEIN

44.1 INTRODUCTION

BIOTECHNOLOGY, pesticide residues, and global warming are for many people an expression of our contemporary preoccupation with risk and our urge—for good or for bad—to seek to control threats to health, safety, and the environment. Popular concern with risk is not new; in nineteenth-century Britain public outrage at a series of food scandals, such as the adulteration of flour with white lead and sugar with ground glass, led to the 1875 Sale of Food and Drugs Act, which introduced basic controls on food safety. In recent decades, however, risk has achieved a heightened salience within the UK in a number of ways.

Animal health crises have hit the UK hardest. BSE contributed to the downfall of the Conservative administration in 1997 and rocked the EU, whilst, in 2001, foot and mouth disease brought parts of the country to a standstill and cost the public and private sectors £8bn. New technologies, such as bio- and nanotechnology, have created public anxieties and international trade disputes, fed by alarming images of Big Brother style genetic databases, 'Frankenstein foods', and globally creeping 'grey goo'. Scientific uncertainty has even caused public panics, such as that caused by a claimed, but later discredited, link between the MMR vaccine and autism, which resulted in outbreaks of measles as parents stopped vaccinating their children.

Such events have called into question the capacity and effectiveness of the institutions of UK risk governance and have prompted a wide range of sometimes controversial reforms. Dedicated risk regulation agencies have been created, the precautionary principle has been embedded into policy frameworks, and there have been attempts to open up policy processes and to bring the public into decision-making. Most recently, we have seen the emergence of risk-based governance as a central theme of regulatory reform. Opinion is divided, however, about the impacts of such reforms, or even whether they have amounted to little more than window dressing.

For some, the heightened salience of risk has had negative impacts on the UK economy and culture. In 2005, the then UK Prime Minister Tony Blair claimed the public and private sectors were too driven by society's 'wholly disproportionate attitude to the risks we should expect to run as a normal part of life' (Blair 2005). The PM was anxious that the UK was failing to exploit key technologies and was losing business to countries like India and China that were less risk averse. For others, however, risk politics mediate deeper anxieties about the shifting character of risks, conflicts between the public, the state, and business over technological progress, and deeper structural failures in governance (e.g. Irwin and Wynne 1996). From that perspective, the problems posed by technology and risk cannot be solved by simple changes of attitude.

These different dimensions of risk have attracted a range of disciplinary interests across the social sciences. The following chapter will attempt to bring together some of those insights in order to understand the character of risk politics in the UK and contemporary governmental responses. The chapter will then go on to consider why risk has become such a significant concept for governance across policy domains and organizational settings, and what this tells us about the character and future of UK risk governance more generally.

44.2 THE RISK SOCIETY

One popular explanation for the character of contemporary risk politics relates to the kinds of risks faced by advanced industrial democracies. Science and technology may have solved many problems associated with traditional societies, at least in the developed West, but for some the promise of modernity has revealed its Faustian nature. Beck (1992) and Giddens (1991), for example, argue that the risks of late modernity are different in type and scale to those of previous eras. Indeed, Beck argues that in what he calls the 'Risk Society', the distribution of 'bads' has assumed more significance than the distribution of wealth and has generated a new kind of risk politics and consciousness that has supplanted that of class.

Others argue that the problems risks pose today are not so different from those posed in previous centuries. Turner (2001: 13), for example, points out that in the fourteenth century, the Black Death travelled on the backs of international trade and warfare from Mongolia to Greenland, destroying a third of Europe's population, irrespective of social class, and brought with it a new 'baroque vision of death'. Yet in an era of high expectations that risks should be managed, it is fairly clear that, at the very least, the pace and character of scientific and technological innovation poses serious governance challenges. For example, risks that extend their reach beyond national borders and threaten global catastrophe, such as climate change, necessitate global political solutions. The irreversibility of some risks, such as nuclear contamination, have focused governance attention on future generations. And the creation of risks that affect both rich and poor, such as long range air pollution, has made risk politics cut across those of class.

The emergence of advanced technological and production systems has also increased the salience of risk in advanced Western societies. As technologies have become increasingly complex and interconnected, so they have become vulnerable to what Perrow (1984) termed 'normal accidents' in which trivial events rapidly snowball into major disasters. For example, incidents have alarmingly demonstrated how the security of national IT databases can be catastrophically vulnerable to the loss of just a few compact discs containing the records of millions of individuals. Equally, intensification of the UK's food supply chain has made it vulnerable to food contamination incidents that can rapidly propagate across the country.

Moreover, contemporary risks often pose difficult questions that touch the horizons of human knowledge, where potential harms and/or their probabilities of occurring are uncertain. Such uncertainties pose problems for governance as decision-makers have been forced to rely on what Weinberg (1985) has termed 'trans-scientific knowledge' in which the norms of proof occupy an often contested meeting ground between science and politics. One need look no further than debates around genetically modified crops to see the ample scope for conflict as governments are torn between precautionary and resilient stances. Such uncertainties have created a new politics of expertise in which it is no longer clear who the experts are, or who should be trusted to give advice.

44.3 RISK AND THE PUBLIC

A second factor that has shaped the politics of technology and risk in recent years is not so much the kind of harms that society has faced, but rather concerns public perceptions of those harms. Decision-scientists and social psychologists, for example, have long observed that public perceptions of risk are shaped by factors such as perceptions of control, familiarity, dread, voluntariness, and impact—rather than probability—of harm (Fischoff et al. 1978; Slovic 2000). For example, research suggests that public perceptions are shaped by an 'availability bias' that leads people to overestimate the likelihood of risks that are most easily remembered or imagined, perhaps because of a media story or personal experience.

Indeed, public perceptions of risk can be readily amplified or attenuated by the way in which risk is communicated to the public by government, social institutions, and, in particular, the mass media (Kasperson et al. 1988; Pidgeon, Kasperson, and Slovic 2003). The media, for example, will readily focus on risks where there are easy stories to be told about failure, blame, or personal tragedy, especially where they reinforce other current stories or play on public anxieties. Such 'social amplification of risk' can help explain the occasional public panics seen in the UK in recent years, especially when journalists are faced with 'slow news' days. In 1995, for example, intense but flawed media coverage of research suggesting that third-generation oral contraceptives could cause deep vein thrombosis created considerable anxiety and use of the pill dropped significantly (Breakwell et al. 2001).

Not all public anxieties about risk, however, can be related to media coverage. Cultural theorists, for example, argue that societal attitudes to risk are shaped by specific 'world-views' related to fundamentally distinct types of social organization (Douglas and Wildavsky 1982;Thompson, Ellis, and Wildavsky 1990). Risk politics, for cultural theorists, reflect broader cultural battles between hierarchical world-views of science and the state, individualist world-views of business, and egalitarian world-views of civil society groups. From that perspective, for example, the conflict between Shell, Greenpeace, and the UK government over the sinking of the Brent Spar oil platform in 1995 was not just about the possibility of environmental contamination, but reflected broader contested notions of the exploitability and resilience of nature, scientific authority, and decision-making legitimacy.

Other sociologists, however, caution against putting too much weight on a deficit model of public understanding of science or overly deterministic cultural heuristics. Instead, they argue that risk debates serve as a cipher for a broad range of legitimate and often well-founded public concerns, such as the handling of uncertainty, regulatory effectiveness, and trust in governments and professionals that go beyond any one issue (Irwin 1995). Certainly, the image of John Selwyn Gummer, the Minister of Agriculture, Fisheries and Food, feeding his daughter Cordelia a beef-burger during the BSE crisis became an indelible metaphor for a loss of trust in government that rippled across policy domains, from vaccination to mobile phone masts. Indeed, risk politics, as Langdon Winner (1980) observed, can give voice to wider anxieties about the way in which technologies embody particular institutionalized patterns of authority, power, and social organization, but which are often beyond the remit of risk governance mechanisms to address. For example, public anxieties about genetically modified food in the UK have not simply been about human and environmental harms, but have embodied wider anxieties about the distribution of benefits, the ethics of genetic modification, and the impacts on global food production systems.

These diverse explanations suggest that public perceptions of to risk are complex and cannot be reduced to a single measure. Snap opinion polls, for example, are likely to reveal different attitudes to more reflective reasoning. Yet, such subtleties have often been lost in practice in the UK, where politicians or regulators have been driven to respond to proxy indicators of public attitudes, such as front-page news stories, rather than considered public judgements in order to protect their short-term reputation. Well-known examples include the greater attention paid by government to widely reported multi-fatality accidents on the railways than lives lost in unreported smaller but more numerous incidents. Indeed, the UK Health and Safety Executive now builds in a 'societal concerns' factor into its decision-making to give greater weight to such high-profile problems (HSE 2001). Yet in-depth research suggests that when the public make reflective judgements they are indifferent to such differences in the manner of death (Slovic, Fischoff, and Lichtenstein 1984; Burton et al. 2001). Such research suggests that decision-making can be driven in perverse ways if the spotlight of media attention is confused with more considered public judgements.

44.4 RISK AND INTEREST GROUP POLITICS

Whilst general public attitudes towards risk can help explain something of the character of risk politics, account also needs to be taken of the distributions of risks, costs, and benefits of scientific and technological advance. The configuration and mobilization of affected societal groups (such as business interests and green and consumer lobbies) in trying to shape those distributions can go a long way to explain particular patterns of risk politics in the UK (Peltzman 1976; Wilson 1980; Breyer 1982; Hood, Rothstein, and Baldwin 2001; Vogel 2003). The creation of a panoply of national and supranational risk regulation frameworks in recent decades, for example, has provided a wide range of lobbying opportunities for organized interests. Equally, organized interests can seek to mould organizational and public behaviour in order to shape markets in their own interests.

In some cases, concentrated business lobbies have exploited their comparative advantage in organized lobbying to obtain gains at the expense of diffuse groups of consumers. Until the late 1990s, for example, UK food safety policy was a classic case of 'client politics' where food agri-business lobbies 'captured' the Ministry for Agriculture, Fisheries and Food (MAFF), capitalizing on its conflicting responsibilities for food safety and its promotion of food and agriculture business; a conflict that many observers linked to a series of food safety failures that culminated in BSE. Other examples include businesses that profit from small relaxations in regulatory standards that have vanishingly small impacts on the health of individual consumers, such as on drinking water contaminates; or, conversely, businesses that profit from tougher safety rules such as companies operating bedside phone services that benefit from controversial restrictions on mobile phone usage within hospitals.

In other cases, where technologies have offered diffuse societal benefits but imposed risks or costs on a small group, NIMBY-style risk politics have emerged. Common examples have included the formation of local groups to oppose the siting of incinerators, mobile phone masts, or nuclear waste facilities. Similar patterns of activity have emerged where scientific and technological advances have identified previously unidentified risks, such as genetic predisposition to disease or vulnerabilities to natural disasters. In such cases, the creation of new populations deemed 'at risk' has provoked often heated debates about their rights and responsibilities, for example in relation to health or flood insurance. The emergence of such groups and their success, however, has been dependent on their effectiveness at mobilizing support, and success has often been at the expense of others less able to organize. UK waste policy, for example, has been marked by exports to the developing world, siting incinerators in poorer areas, or leaving legacies for future generations to solve.

Risk controversies have also reflected tussles between organized interest groups. Sometimes, such 'interest group politics' have been between business lobbies seeking to protect their markets or increase their market share. Well-known cases include the spat between British and French farmers over BSE when the French banned British beef towards the end of the 1990s, despite the European Commission having given British beef a clean bill of health, or the controversial EU ban on American hormone treated beef (Ansell and Vogel 2006). Interest group politics has been particularly evident with the emergence of green and consumer lobbies, which have strong incentives to concentrate on those issues that gain public and media attention, such as high-impact, low-probability risks. Such tactics proved effective, for example, in the late 1990s when Greenpeace successfully campaigned against a proposal to relax the controversial EU standards on drinking water quality, against a backdrop of hard lobbying by the water utilities and the agrochemical industries. However, gains at the policy formulation stage can be accompanied by failures in implementation. For instance, in the 1990s, the transport lobby managed to delay by many years the implementation of European rules on vehicle exhaust emissions that had been subject to extensive bargaining between the vehicle and petrochemical industries and green groups.

Such interest group perspectives can help explain the underlying dynamics of many risk controversies. Whilst it is often assumed that risk controversies have their origin in inherent scientific uncertainties, competing interest groups can also 'manufacture' controversies by constructing and amplifying uncertainties through the selective use of scientific evidence and expertise (Nelkin 1975; Jasanoff 1990). Typical examples include businesses trying to gain market share over rivals, environmental and consumer groups keen to raise their public profile, or scientists seeking publicity for their research. In the early 1990s in the UK, for example, the 'cling film' controversy over the safety of chemicals leaching from plastic food wrap into food was driven, in part, by rival firms selectively highlighting safety concerns over each others' products. Or later, the absence of computer crashes at the turn of the millennium was evidence for some that the Millennium Bug risk had been exaggerated by an opportunistic IT industry eager for new business, but was evidence for the IT industry that mitigation strategies had been successful (Quigley 2004). Such dynamics help explain why risk controversies are not always readily resolved by 'more' or 'better' science and 'rational' discussion as regulators and politicians regularly wish for, since judgements of what stands for those concepts is often the subject of controversy itself.

44.5 RISK GOVERNANCE FAILURE

Another important explanation for contemporary preoccupations with risk lies not so much in the demands of the public and interest groups, but in the problems and failings of governance regimes in managing threats facing society. Risk politics in the UK is often mediated through complex and highly varied multi-level governance regimes, with their various functions such as standard setting, monitoring, and enforcement sometimes dispersed from across the supranational level of the World Trade Organization and the EU down to the level of local government (Hood, Rothstein, and Baldwin 2001). Risk politics can vary widely across such dispersed governance settings, sometimes having quite a different character at the policy formulation stage from that of the delivery stage, and that has often introduced irrationalities and incoherence into risk governance within the UK.

In recent years, for example, much of the hard politics of risk governance decision-making in many policy domains has shifted to the supranational level, where the dynamics of risk politics reflect different patterns of interests and public attitudes from those found within the UK. In some cases, the UK has proved reluctant to abide by EU decision-making; for example, the 1980 Drinking Water Directive was not implemented in the UK for ten years because of concern about the cost of meeting its strict standards. Since then the UK has taken a more active lead in risk decision-making at the EU level in a wide range of domains. British regulators subject to the discipline of 'full cost recovery' have been especially keen to lead in domains such as pharmaceuticals and pesticides, because mutual recognition rules have created a competitive market in product approval amongst member-state regulators. Indeed, supranational risk governance has even provided convenient blame-shifting opportunities for the UK government and regulatory agencies, which on occasions have proved happy to pass the buck to the EU when faced with politically difficult decisions.

The national level is still important in many domains of risk governance in the UK, but it has often been marked by sluggishness, incoherence, and failure. For example, the machinery of UK risk governance has sometimes proved ill-suited to the fast pace of technological advance, particularly in the biosciences, where policy often seems to be in a constant game of catch-up. Equally, its architecture has proved ineffective in handling trade-offs between risks within different policy domains, such as the closure of part of the UK rail network with little regard for the dangers of increased road traffic following the Hatfield train crash in 2000. Sometimes, the same risks have been handled in contradictory

ways in different domains; exposure to artificial sources of radiation is strictly controlled, for example, but exposure to the natural radioactive gas radon is subject
only to lax recommendations in the UK that could result in 1,500 lung cancer deaths
annually. And in some domains, such as chemical and pharmaceutical safety, the traditional style of UK risk governance in which select experts advised ministers behind
closed doors lent a whiff of secrecy to policy-making that all too easily spiralled
into conspiracy theories. A series of risk governance failures increasingly made that
paternalistic and opaque style untenable, most notably when MAFF reassured the
public that BSE was not transmissible to humans, despite accumulating evidence to
the contrary.

Sometimes risk controversies have emerged not so much from rule-setting failures,
but rather from implementation failures. Many risk governance regimes in the UK are
fragmented vertically between national policy-making and regional or local enforcement, making it difficult to ensure appropriate enforcement. Indeed in some cases,
that fragmentation has provided opportunities for central government ministries to
'throw policy problems over the fence', landing local authorities with often unfunded
or unworkable mandates. And sometimes rules have been under- or over-enforced
because of the way in which inspectors' understandings of problems, responsibilities,
and ways of working have been filtered through organizational pressures and cultures
(Lipsky 1971; Hutter 1988). Traditional occupational 'health and safety' culture, for
example, has held employers more culpable for tractable safety risks such as slips and
trips than less tractable long-term health risks, such as low-level exposure to chemical
fumes (Baldwin 1987).

Enforcement failure, for example, was a significant contributing factor to the BSE
crisis during the early 1990s, when infectious meat found its way into the human
food and animal feed chains because local authority inspectors failed to enforce rules
on the removal of specified bovine offal from cattle carcasses (Rothstein 2003). In
that case, MAFF designed rules that were difficult for inspectors to enforce. Abattoirs
were often working at the margins of economic viability and were resistant to further
regulation, and inspectors were sometimes subject to violence or intimidation. In
addition, the coping and fatalist implementation culture of local authority inspectors
was ill-disposed to the assiduous enforcement of the BSE-related rules on spinal
cord removal in abattoirs, particularly in the context of unwarranted government
reassurances about the threats BSE posed to the public.

44.6 REFORMING UK RISK GOVERNANCE

Perceived failures in the capacity and competence of politicians and the state to
manage risk adequately have prompted an often linked set of reforms to risk governance. For many, the answer has been to try to improve the scientific and economic rationality of decision-making (e.g. NRC 1983; Royal Society 1992; House of

Lords 2006). Since the BSE crisis, considerable effort has been put into separating out processes of risk assessment and risk management, and improving the quality of scientific advice and how it feeds into policy-making (e.g. May 1997; European Commission 2002). Interest has also increased in cost–benefit analysis, which has long been used in transport safety and has had considerable success in countering local political pressures and motoring lobbies over local road safety measures. Over the years, related approaches have found favour elsewhere. The UK Health and Safety Executive's 'Tolerability of Risk' framework, for example, broadly requires marginal increases in safety in the workplace to be proportionate to the costs, and the National Institute for Health and Clinical Excellence now assesses the cost—as well as the clinical—effectiveness of drugs, before recommending their use by the NHS.

Such attempts, however, face the kinds of constraints already discussed above. Better science advice is always welcome, but more scientific evidence can serve to open up debate, as much as close it down, and it cannot be expected to address more broadly grounded public anxieties. Similarly, political anxiety about retaining public support can conflict with the economic rationality of valuing human life. After the Ladbroke Grove train crash in 1999, for example, the Deputy Prime Minister John Prescott declared that 'cost will not be a consideration' in introducing Automatic Train Protection systems even though the costs implied a value of life of £14m. That figure was ten times the accepted figure for road safety (and 100 times the figure that is spent in practice). Other kinds of reform to risk governance, therefore, have proved necessary.

One approach to reform in the UK, as well as elsewhere in the EU and North America, has been institutional, most prominently the creation of risk regulation agencies for diverse policy domains such as food, environment, and pharmaceuticals. In the UK, agencies have proved attractive as ways of healing the scars of crises such as BSE that have left politicians badly burnt. Agencies have offered the opportunity of improving policy-making stability against the changing preferences of parliament and ministers, enhancing the expertise and the efficiency of policy processes, and perhaps most importantly of all providing a blame conduit for difficult policies or policy failure (Thatcher and Stone Sweet 2002). The pattern and success of institutional reform has been variable across sectors, however, with some agencies having greater powers, coherence, and independence than others.

One recent example was the creation of the UK Food Standards Agency (FSA) in 2000, by the relatively new Labour administration, which was keen to avoid the blame the previous Conservative administration had suffered for its failures in managing food safety. The FSA has successfully gained some support from the public, consumer groups, and the food industry, at least in part by consolidating food safety respon-sibilities and expertise from across central government and having no conflicting responsibilities for business promotion (NAO 2003). The agency's scope for action has been constrained, however, by the multi-level governance regime within which it sits. FSA proposals have been rejected by the EU, such as its BSE-related ban on sausage casings made from sheep intestines, which would have deprived Germans of their daily diet of eleven million such sausages (Rothstein 2004). At the national level, the FSA has been constrained by other major government departments, such as the media regulator Ofcom, which constrained the FSA's scope for action on food promotion to children, arguing that a ban on TV advertising to children would be 'ineffective and disproportionate' (Rothstein 2007). Moreover, the FSA has only had limited levers for changing food safety surveillance and enforcement behaviour, because those activities are still the responsibility of local government.

Another kind of reform, ostensibly designed to respond to public anxieties about the uncertainties of risk assessment, has been the embedding of the 'precautionary principle' within UK, EU, and international regulatory frameworks in the last twenty years (Lofstedt 2003). Those frameworks have broadly adopted the formulation of the principle found in the 1992 UN Rio Declaration, which states that, 'where there are threats of serious or irreversible damage, lack of full scientific certainty shall not be used as a reason for postponing cost-effective measures to prevent environmental degradation'. The principle is, however, infamously poorly defined; there are at least nineteen formulations of it that are often vague and incompatible and have given rise to considerable controversy (Sandin 1999).

For some, the precautionary principle is a way of ensuring that decision-makers award the benefit of the doubt in ways that best reflect the interests of the public and the environment. Shrader-Frechette (1991: ch. 9), for example, argues that policy-makers tend to have an in-built cultural preference for the conservative bias in science and law that presumes innocence until proven guilty. In contrast, others argue that the principle, at least in its strongest form, is incoherent and can have perverse consequences, for example if proven therapeutic benefits of drugs are outweighed by uncertain evidence of carcinogenicity (Majone 2002; Sunstein 2005: 26). Indeed, some observers are concerned that the principle is simply an instrument of trade protectionism, as American policy-makers claimed when the EU banned hormones in beef and milk and genetically modified food. In the absence of any agreed consistent definition of the precautionary principle or method of application, however, there is little hard evidence that the precautionary principle has changed policy outcomes. Instead, the regular references to the principle in UK and EU policy documents with little accompanying analysis very likely reflects its use as rhetorical justification for decisions that have been shaped by other more conventional factors already discussed in this chapter (cf. Heyvaert 2006).

A final significant trend within risk governance in the UK has been the move towards greater transparency and participation across governance domains. Greater access to information and engagement in governance processes is argued to have the potential to enhance the quality of decision-making, improve the representation of the public interest in governance decisions, and build trust and support for policy processes and outcomes (Dryzek 1990; NRC 1996; Funtowitz and Ravetz 1996). For example, public access to environmental information and decision-making has been enshrined in the Aarhus Convention (1998) and such ideas have been actively promoted by a range of bodies in the UK, such as the Royal Commission on Environmental Pollution (1998). Innovations in the UK have included public access to information on local environmental risks, monthly open meetings of the Food Standards Agency

Board, and 'GM Nation'—a government sponsored nationwide debate on genetically modified foods in 2003.

There is some limited evidence of success. The FSA, for example, prides itself on its open decision-making procedures, which appear to have helped it take difficult decisions and improve public trust. For example, in 2005 the agency reassessed the BSE-related rule that prevented cattle over thirty months entering the food chain, which carried high costs for the state in compensation payments to farmers, but delivered only an estimated small safety gain for the public (Royal Society 2005). After extensive public meetings and consultation, the FSA was able to relax the rule without attracting public controversy.

Such reforms, however, have only had limited impacts. Public information is of only limited use if it is ignored, misinterpreted, or creates further confusion, such as has been found with flood maps and exhaustively detailed food labels. Such innovations clearly require greater attention to the way in which risk is communicated. Moreover, greater openness and accountability have led to perverse 'blame-games' as organizations and individuals have attempted to deflect their enhanced liabilities. Such responses have included increased proceduralization; shifting decision-making to less scrutinized contexts, such as from the proverbial meeting-room into the corridor; or fudging accountability by diffusing responsibility, and hence blame, amongst multiple organizations (Hood 2002; Hood, Rothstein, and Baldwin 2001: ch. 9). For example, whilst much has been made of UK scientific advisory committees holding their meetings in public, often the important work and discussions are undertaken by subcommittees out of view of the public.

Moreover, greater public participation has only had limited success because of a number of institutional constraints (Irwin 2006; Rothstein 2007). For example, the impacts of participation on policy outcomes have been dependent on the fit between participative processes and the practical demands and needs of governance, the strength of other drivers shaping decision-making, and the degree of consensus on the goals of participation. Such constraints have meant that participation can improve some aspects of risk governance, such as building awareness or support, but simultaneously fail in others, such as improving equity of outcomes or the evidence base. The inevitable trade-offs between these goals have sometimes created disillusionment and conflicts, for example, when participation has been used to raise awareness but participants have expected to have policy impacts, or when public opinion-gathering exercises have been used to balance pressures from consumer group lobbies.

The Food Standards Agency, for example, experienced such problems when it established a Consumer Committee in 2002 to help the agency achieve one of its core objectives of 'putting consumers first'. In practice, the Committee's contributions only had a limited impact on decision-making and did little to improve support for policy processes because, amongst other things, the representativeness and value of the Committee's contributions were contested, it was poorly integrated into the policy process, and it had a poorly defined role and purpose (Rothstein 2007). As a consequence, it was abolished as a failure after just three years.

44.7 THE EMERGENCE OF RISK AS AN ORGANIZING PRINCIPLE OF GOVERNANCE

This chapter has so far focused on a range of traditional explanations to understand the contemporary political salience of risk in the UK and the problems it poses for governance. In recent years in the UK, however, the concept of risk has evolved from a simple concern with harms to individuals and the environment to become a key organizing principle for regulation and extended governance regimes across policy domains and organizational settings. 'Risk-based regulation' has become a central feature of the Labour administration's third term, and risk-based corporate governance has become standard practice in organizations across the public and private sector (ICAEW 1999; Cabinet Office 2002; Hampton 2005). Analysis of this conceptual shift in the use of the term 'risk' sheds light on the way in which risk has been intimately related to changing patterns of governance in the UK.

At first glance, risk-based governance offers a beguilingly simple rationale for decision-making by prioritizing activities according to the impact and probability of events. Indeed, it is often promoted as a means for cutting through entrenched organizational cultures to aid entrepreneurialism within both the public and private sectors. The emergence of risk-based governance, however, has not just been related to the management of what might be termed 'public risks'—such as threats to the environment, or health and safety. Instead, risk-based governance has additionally emerged in response to what might be called the 'institutional risks' of governance; that is, threats to organizations themselves in trying to manage public risks—such as liabilities and loss of reputation. In other words, there has been a growing emphasis on the risks of risk management (Rothstein, Huber, and Gaskell 2006; Power 2007).

The emergence of 'institutional risk' can be related to the increasing need to account for the limits and failures of governance. Governance regimes only have a limited capacity to achieve their intended goals because they operate within a range of common institutional constraints such as scarce resources, cognitive uncertainties, regime incoherence, ungovernable actors, and unintended consequences. Within weak governance structures, such problems can go undetected, unmanaged, or unaccounted for until too late. Recent years, however, have seen both the public and private sectors in the UK caught in a grip of audit and target cultures and exposed to greater external transparency and accountability (Power 1997; Hood et al. 1999). This change has amplified and routinized the management of institutional risks, as failures are recorded, potential failures are anticipated, and new categories of failure are defined. 'Good governance', paradoxically, has become a source of risk itself.

The use of the term 'risk' to describe both the objects of governance and threats to governance institutions is more than a linguistic coincidence. As Luhmann (1993) argued, modern societies frame decisions in terms of risk in order to manage the inherent uncertainties of rational decision-making. The concept of risk, according to Luhmann, anticipates and legitimates the possibility of failure by transforming decision-making into probabilistic assessments of success and failure. Framing governance objects as risks, therefore, is an attempt to manage threats to society, whilst reflexively managing the negative institutional externalities of governance itself.

This process has been well illustrated by the rise of the regulatory state in which the creation of numerous regulatory agencies in the UK has been accompanied by the introduction of tighter systems of scrutiny and accountability to compensate for the inherent democratic deficits of outsourcing the state's policy functions. In that context, risk has become a valuable concept for regulators in justifying their activities and performance, as the US Environmental Protection Agency found in the early 1980s when faced with a barrage of adversarial legal actions (NRC 1983). Such dynamics help explain the development of risk assessment and management tools by independent regulators such as the UK Health and Safety Executive (HSE) in the 1980s, and more recently a swathe of agencies from the UK Financial Services Authority to the Housing Corporation (e.g. HSE 1998; Black 2005). The cliché that 'there is no such thing as zero risk', beloved by regulators, neatly expresses not just an obvious practical reality, but also their need to find a way of rationalizing the practical limits of what governance can achieve, and to render given degrees of failure acceptable.

Attempts to manage the negative institutional externalities of governance has transformed problems not conventionally understood as risks into risk problems. Within the technological domain, for example, regulators are conceiving policy problems within ever more differentiated categories of risk, such as attempts to recast ethical dimensions of the biosciences in terms of ethical risks, or public anxieties in terms of reputational risks. In policy domains far removed from technological risk, offenders on probation, mental health patients, and child welfare have been turned from welfare problems into risk management problems as state agencies have been increasingly held accountable for ever more visible failures. Even more widely, as government has delegated decision-making to the public by empowering them to exercise 'choice', be it through food labelling, hospital infection league tables, or flood risk maps, it is perhaps unsurprising that the public has become more conscious of risk and its inseparable bedfellow, blame. Such examples of risk 'colonizing' governance suggests that the emergence of risk is driven less by Beck's new distribution of ills in society than by a new distribution of ills in governance.

Framing problems in terms of risk may reflexively manage the associated institutional threats, but equally, such framings encounter the same kinds of problems found in more conventional risk debates. Risk assessment, for example, is often an inexact science, especially in softer areas of social policy, and can strain institutional capacities to the point that it provides little more than a lingua franca for decision-making while making little impact on actual organizational practices. Second, risk-based decision-making can pose normative challenges for stakeholders and founder on a clash of cultural understandings about risk. Third, decision-makers may elide distinctions between public and institutional risk and choose to manage their own institutional risks at the expense of risks to society, such as responding to front-page news stories, irrespective of societal impacts. Such problems suggest that risk-based governance may have unanticipated consequences. But if risk holds out the promise of displacing the concept of failure within modern regulation and governance more generally, it is not hard to see why it is provoking such excitement.

44.8 CONCLUSIONS

This chapter has attempted to show how studies of risk politics can help understanding of changing patterns of politics and governance in the UK in three ways. First, the chapter has explored the factors shaping the politics and governance of risks associated with scientific and technological innovation in the UK. Popular commentary is prone to convenient generalizations when it comes to risk politics, but in practice the politics of risk may have more in common with Tolstoy's dictum that 'Every happy family is the same, but unhappy families are all different'. There is no one single factor that can be identified as the sole shaper of risk politics; rather, each case is shaped by a collection of often interacting factors that include the transactional characteristics of risk itself, complex patterns of public concern, and interest group lobbying and sometimes problematic, if not dysfunctional, governance arrangements.

Such factors are common to all advanced industrial democracies, but their salience and configuration varies across risks and across the complex policy, organizational, and societal settings within which those risks are handled. There are undoubtedly UK dimensions to some of those factors, such as the legacies of past crises that have shaped public attitudes; the particular configuration and mobilization of private and public organized interest groups; or the institutional specificities of UK risk governance. Equally, the profile of those shaping factors may vary across governance regimes, so that the politics of risk involved in shaping policy-making in Brussels or Whitehall, for example, may be very different to the kind of politics that shapes the implementation of that policy by local authority enforcement officers. The variable 'push and pull' of risk politics across risk governance regimes can have important effects on the overall management of risk.

Second, the chapter has examined a series of contemporary reforms to risk governance in the UK that have mirrored changes across many advanced industrial democracies. These changes have included reforms to governance architectures, such as the delegation of decision-making to dedicated regulatory agencies; changes in decision rules, such as the embedding of the precautionary principle within regulatory frameworks; and changes in governance style, such as greater openness and participation. In some respects, these changes represent a new mode of risk governance where the need to establish institutional legitimacy in the wake of past failures has become a central concern.

At the same time, these reforms have been constrained by a range of institutional factors that have limited their impacts on policy-making processes and outcomes. For example, risk regulation agencies have sometimes had only limited levers for shaping policy and implementation. The precautionary principle may be little more than a rhetorical justification for decisions that are shaped by more powerful drivers. Equally, greater openness and participation has triggered a range of blame-shifting responses and trade-offs between various conflicting goals in ways that have reduced the potential value of such reforms.

Finally, the chapter has tried to show how the contemporary salience of risk is as much to do with its emergence as a general organizing concept for governance, as its centrality to the politics of scientific and technological innovation. The chapter has argued that risk has emerged as a key feature of contemporary governance as tighter systems of scrutiny and accountability across the public and private sectors have forced decision-makers to find ways of rationalizing the practical limits of what governance can achieve. Risk has proved valuable as a way of framing policy problems that reflexively manages the negative institutional externalities of governance itself, and in so doing has transformed problems not conventionally understood as risks into risk problems. That dynamic process suggests that the seeming proliferation of risk may be less driven by societal conflicts over traditionally conceived harms arising from scientific and technological innovation, than as a by-product of the increasing need of politicians, regulators, and other decision-makers to account for the limits of their success.

Risk has the potential to shape and change politics as it colonizes wide domains of governance by offering a new rationale for decision-making. The value and success of risk instruments, however, is limited by a range of fundamental challenges that can reopen issues of knowledge, competence, acceptability, and blame. Studies of the politics and governance of risks associated with scientific and technological innovation, therefore, may be able to offer useful insights into the character of risk politics and governance strategies in policy domains that seem far removed at first glance. At the very least, the lessons from the technological domain can act as a sensitizing device for the dynamics that are underlying the colonization of politics by risk.

REFERENCES

ANSELL, C., and VOGEL, D. 2006. 'The Contested Governance of European Food Safety Regulation'. In D. Vogel and C. Ansell (eds.), *Why the Beef? The Contested Governance of European Food Safety*. Cambridge, Mass.: MIT Press.

BALDWIN, R. 1987. 'Health and Safety at Work: Consensus and Self-Regulation'. In R. Baldwin and C. McCrudden (eds.), *Regulation and Public Law*. London: Weidenfeld and Nicolson.

BECK, U. 1992. *Risk Society*. London: Sage.

BLACK, J. 2005. 'Risk-Based Regulation: Policy Innovation and Policy Transfer in Financial Services'. *Public Law*, Autumn: 512–22.

BLAIR, T. 2005. 'Future Challenges: Living with Risk'. Institute of Public Policy Research, London, 26 May. http://www.number-10.gov.uk/output/Page7562.asp.

BREAKWELL, G., BARNET, J., LOFSTEDT, R., KEMP, R., and GLASER, C. 2001. *The Impact of Social Amplification of Risk on Risk Communication*. London: HSE.

BREYER, S. 1982. *Regulation and its Reform*. Cambridge, Mass.: Harvard University Press.

BURTON, T., CHILTON, S., COVEY, J., GILBERT, H., JONES-LEE, M., LOOMES, G., PIDGEON, N., ROBINSON, A., SPENCER, A., and TWIST, J. 2001. *Valuation of the Benefits of Heath and Safety Control*. Sudb: HSE Books.

CABINET OFFICE 2002. *Risk: Improving Government's Capability to Handle Risk and Uncertainty*. London: UK Cabinet Office.

DOUGLAS, M., and WILDAVSKY, A. 1982. *Risk and Culture: An Essay on the Selection of Technical and Environmental Dangers*. Berkeley: University of California Press.

DRYZEK, J. 1990. *Discursive Democracy: Politics, Policy and Political Science*. Cambridge: Cambridge University Press.

EUROPEAN COMMISSION 2002. *Improving the Knowledge Base for Better Policies*. COM (2002) 713 Final. Brussels: European Commission.

FISCHOFF, B., SLOVIC, P., LICHTENSTEIN, S., READ, S., and COMBS, B. 1978. 'How Safe is Safe Enough? A Psychometric Study of Attitudes towards Technological Risk and Benefits'. *Policy Studies*, 9: 127–52.

FUNTOWITZ, S., and RAVETZ, J. 1996. 'Risk Management, Post Normal Science and Extended Peer Review'. Pp. 172–80 in C. Hood and D. Jones (eds.), *Accident and Design: Contemporary Debates in Risk Management*. London: UCL Press.

GIDDENS, A. 1991. *Modernity and Self-Identity: Self and Society in the Late Modern Age*. Cambridge: Polity.

HAMPTON, P. 2005. *Reducing Administrative Burdens: Effective Inspection and Enforcement*. London: HM Treasury.

HEALTH AND SAFETY EXECUTIVE (HSE) 1998. 'Changing Times'. *Nuclear Safety Newsletter*, 15.

—— 2001. *Reducing Risks, Protecting People: HSE's Decision-Making Process*. London: HSE.

HEYVAERT, V. 2006. 'Facing the Consequences of the Precautionary Principle in European Community Law'. *European Law Review*, 31/2: 186–7.

HOOD, C. 2002. 'The Risk Game and the Blame Game'. *Government and Opposition*, 37/1: 15–37.

—— ROTHSTEIN, H., and BALDWIN, R. 2001. *The Government of Risk: Understanding Risk Regulation Regimes*. Oxford: Oxford University Press.

—— SCOTT, C., JAMES, O., JONES G., and TRAVERS, T. 1999. *Regulation inside Government: Waste-Watchers, Quality Police, and Sleaze-Busters*. Oxford: Oxford University Press.

HOUSE OF LORDS 2006 *Government Policy on the Management of Risk*. London: House of Lords.

HUTTER, B. 1988. *The Reasonable Arm of the Law? The Law Enforcement Procedures of Environmental Health Officers*. Oxford: Clarendon Press.

Institute of Chartered Accountants in England and Wales (ICAEW) 1999. *Internal Control: Guidance for Directors on the Combined Code*. London: ICAEW.

IRWIN, A. 1995. *Citizen Science: A Study of People, Expertise and Sustainable Development*. London: Routledge.

—— 2006. 'The Politics of Talk: Coming to Terms with the "New" Scientific Governance'. *Social Studies of Science*, 36: 299–320.

—— and WYNNE, B. (eds.) 1996. *Misunderstanding Science? The Public Reconstruction of Science and Technology*. Cambridge: Cambridge University Press.

JASANOFF, S. 1990. *The Fifth Branch: Science Advisors as Policymakers*. London: Harvard University Press.

KASPERSON, R., RENN, O., SLOVIC, P., BROWN, H., EMEL, J., GOBLE, R., KASPERSON, J. X., and RATICK, S. 1988. 'The Social Amplification of Risk: A Conceptual Framework'. *Risk Analysis*, 8/2: 177–87.

LIPSKY, M. 1971. 'Street Level Bureaucracy and the Analysis of Urban Reform'. *Urban Affairs Quarterly*, 6: 391–409.

LOFSTEDT, R. 2003. 'The Precautionary Principle: Risk Regulation and Politics'. *Trans IChem E*, 81/B: 36–43.

LUHMANN, N. 1993. *Risk: A Sociological Theory*. Berlin: de Gruyter.

MAJONE, G. 2002. 'What Price Safety? The Precautionary Principle and its Policy Implications'. *Journal of Common Market Studies*, 40/1: 89–102.

MAY, R. 1997. *The Use of Scientific Advice in Policy-Making*. London: Parliamentary Office of Science and Technology.

NATIONAL AUDIT OFFICE (NAO) 2003. *Improving Service Delivery: The Food Standards Agency*. HC 524 Session 2002–3. 28 Mar.

NELKIN, D. 1975. 'The Political Impact of Technical Expertise'. *Social Studies of Science*, 5: 35–54.

NRC (National Research Council) 1983. *Risk Assessment in the Federal Government: Managing the Process*. Washington, DC: National Academy Press.

—— 1996. *Understanding Risk: Informing Decisions in a Democratic Society*. Washington, DC: National Academy Press.

PELTZMAN, S. 1976. 'Towards a More General Theory of Regulation'. *Journal of Law and Economics*, 19: 211.

PERROW, C. 1984. *Normal Accidents: Living with High-Risk Technologies*. New York: Basic Books.

PIDGEON, N., KASPERSON, R., and SLOVIC, P. 2003. *The Social Amplification of Risk*. Cambridge: Cambridge University Press.

POWER, M. 1997. *The Audit Society*. Oxford: Oxford University Press.

—— 2007. *Organized Uncertainty: Designing a World of Risk Management*. Oxford: Oxford University Press.

QUIGLEY, K. 2004. 'The Emperor's New Computers: Y2K (Re)Visited'. *Public Administration*, 82/4: 801–29.

ROTHSTEIN, H. 2003. 'Neglected Risk Regulation: The Institutional Attenuation Phenomenon'. *Health, Risk and Society*, 5/1: 85–103.

—— 2004. 'Precautionary Bans or Sacrificial Lambs? Participative Regulation and the Reform of the UK Food Safety Regime'. *Public Administration*, 82/4: 857–81.

—— 2007. 'Talking Shops or Talking Turkey? Institutional Constraints to Proceduralising Consumer Representation in Risk Regulation'. *Science, Technology and Human Values*, 32/5: 582–607.

—— HUBER, M., and GASKELL, G. 2006. 'A Theory of Risk Colonisation: The Spiralling Regulatory Logics of Societal and Institutional Risk'. *Economy and Society*, 35/1: 91–112.

ROYAL COMMISSION ON ENVIRONMENTAL POLLUTION 1998. *Setting Environmental Standards*, Twenty-First Report, Cm. 4053, London: HMSO.

ROYAL SOCIETY 1992. *Risk: Analysis, Perception and Management*. London: Royal Society.

—— 2005. *Social Science Insights for Risk Assessment*. London: Royal Society.

SANDIN, P. 1999. 'Dimensions of the Precautionary Principle'. *Human and Ecological Risk Assessment*, 5/5: 889–907.

SHRADER-FRECHETTE, K. 1991. *Risk and Rationality*. Berkeley: University of California Press.

SLOVIC, P. 2000. *Risk Perception*. London: Earthscan.

—— FISCHOFF, B., and LICHTENSTEIN, S. 1984. 'Modelling the Societal Impact of Fatal Accidents'. *Management Science*, 30: 464–74.

SUNSTEIN, C. 2005. *Laws of Fear: Beyond the Precautionary Principle*. Cambridge: Cambridge University Press.

THATCHER, M., and STONE SWEET, A. 2002. 'Theory and Practice of Delegation to Non-Majoritarian Institutions'. *West European Politics*, 25: 1–22.

THOMPSON, M., ELLIS, R., and WILDAVSKY, A. 1990. *Cultural Theory*. Boulder, Colo.: Westview.

TURNER, B. 2001. 'Risks, Rights and Regulation: An Overview'. *Health, Risk and Society*, 3/1: 9–18.

VOGEL, D. 2003. 'The Hare and the Tortoise Revisited: The New Politics of Consumer and Environmental Regulation in Europe'. *British Journal of Political Science*, 33: 557–80.

WEINBERG, A. 1985. 'Science and its Limits: The Regulator's Dilemma'. *Issues in Science and Technology*, Fall/II: 68.

WILSON, J. 1980. *The Politics of Regulation*. New York: Basic Books.

WINNER, L. 1980. 'Do Artefacts have Politics?' *Daedalus*, 109: 121–36.

SECTION FIFTEEN: DYNAMICS

CHAPTER 45

EUROPEANIZATION

KEVIN FEATHERSTONE

45.1 INTRODUCTION

CONTEMPORARY debate recognizes the relevance of globalization to policy and party programmes in Britain—even of 'Americanization', in the context of Bush and foreign policy or Clinton and social policy, for example—and thereby the penetration of the domestic political system. Set alongside these, in a manner that introduces much complexity, are the more structured and often more visible impacts of European Union (EU) membership. These involve distinctive features such as 'hard' and 'soft' law, the revision of existing competences, judicial interpretation, budgetary transfers, and diverse forms of representation. Whilst it is often accepted that membership has had a pervasive impact, charting its contours and depth is a daunting task. The study of the interrelationship between the domestic and the EU system commonly refers to processes of 'Europeanization'.

The task of the present chapter is to review recent scholarship on the effects of Europeanization on British politics to assess what has been learned to date. The discussion offers a brief survey of research straddling policy, political actors, and institutions, leaving the matter of party politics to the separate chapter by Buller. It is important to distinguish what has changed and what has not, as well as 'why, when and how?', for studies of Europeanization are sometimes criticized for being too ready to attribute causality to the EU, without adequate discrimination. To critics of Britain's EU policy, there might be incredulity in the face of claims as to her 'Europeanization'. Yet, this chapter will argue that, though Britain generally does indeed represent a distinctive case, the evidence of recent literature signals that Europeanization here has had a far more complex and varied character than popular images might suggest, and that there has been change over time.

45.2 THE STUDY OF 'EUROPEANIZATION'

'Europeanization' as a term, even as an object of study, can appear faddish. Past scholarship often used the term without definition, assuming the meaning to be self-evident. This has left some scepticism as to the rigour of its causal explanations. 'Europeanization' here should not be seen as a synonym for 'integration': the latter indicates the creation of new institutions, processes, and policies at the EU level; the former signifies how member states adapt to the EU. It is useful, then, to open with a résumé of the conceptual literature. A synthetical definition of 'Europeanization' has been provided by Dyson and Goetz:

> Europeanization denotes a complex interactive 'top-down' and 'bottom-up' process in which domestic polities, politics and public policies are shaped by European integration and in which domestic actors use European integration to shape the domestic arena. It may produce either continuity or change and potentially variable and contingent outcomes.   (Dyson and Goetz 2003: 20)

This stresses the contingent nature of the national–EU relationship and that the direction of activity, pressure, and resource opportunities are both to and from the national system. Yet, 'Europeanization' does not constitute an independent theory; rather, it is an 'attention-directing device' (Olsen 2002) to a distinct set of processes in need of explanation (Featherstone and Radaelli 2003: 333). The ontology is complex and may not easily fit with positivist notions. In any event, to explain what occurred, how, and why, 'Europeanization' needs to borrow from established theories of political science. Most writers on the subject have followed some variant of 'new institutionalism', with their distinct interpretations of ideas, interests, and institutions (Hall and Taylor 1996), though Boerzel and Risse (2003) have argued persuasively that rationalist and constructivist logics can occur simultaneously or sequentially in reality.

Crucial to such explanations are the links between the EU and domestic levels (Goetz 2000: 222). A number of typologies have been developed to identify them. Knill and Lehmkuhl (1999) refer to three: positive integration (where the EU prescribes policy models); negative integration (where EU commitments dismantle national regulations); and framing integration (where EU involvement alters beliefs, expectations). Dyson and Goetz specify dynamics of: coexistence (where both levels exhibit high mutual autonomy and there is little effective impact); co-evolution (where there is mutual interaction leading to accommodation between the two levels); and contestation (involving a clash of beliefs and preferences between the two levels). Clearly, the latter two offer the greatest interest: both involve a degree of change, rather than 'no effect' (though this might involve surprises of its own on a comparative basis). More recently, Bulmer and Radaelli (2005) identified three modes of governance in the EU, associated with distinct types of policy, to produce different mechanisms of Europeanization. These range from the hierarchical and coercive— where EU competence is strong and enforcement mechanisms limit the scope for 'cheating' or non-compliance, though their exact nature varies between 'positive' and 'negative' integration—to the competitive and horizontal—involving regulatory competition between states and actors where the EU plays a very limited role—and the non-hierarchical/voluntary nature of facilitated coordination, as in the Open Method of Coordination linked to the Lisbon Programme of 2000. The empirical application of such a framework is not unproblematic: as Bache and Jordan (2006a: 25) point out, not all EU policies can be singly and neatly categorized in this fashion. They themselves suggest a matrix distinguishing the intended 'direct Europeaniza-tion' from the inadvertent 'indirect Europeanization', and 'voluntary' and 'coercive' Europeanization according to the acceptance or resistance of domestic actors to EU stimuli (2006a: 24). The Bulmer and Radaelli typology seems more nuanced and, like Dyson and Goetz, conveys the main theme of relevance here: that the linkages between EU stimuli and domestic politics vary and that these are related to the type of governance existing at the EU level.

Moreover, culture and agency are relevant to how Europeanization is communi-cated and received. EU pressures are translated and interpreted within the domestic cultural setting, creating scope for much variation (Morth 2003). Falkner et al. (2005) have similarly argued that differences of domestic culture will determine the degree of domestic compliance to EU legislation. They posit 'three worlds of compliance': their *world of law compliance* (in which priority is attached to law compliance above domestic concerns) seems the closest fit to the UK.

45.3 REVIEWING THE EVIDENCE: THE UK EXPERIENCE OF EUROPEANIZATION

45.3.1 Policy

For the UK, as elsewhere, it is generally assumed that the impact of Europeanization has been most evident in terms of public policy, rather than politics or the polity. Yet, this differentiation is somewhat simplistic: each domain shows variation (Bache and Jordan 2006b: 278). Differentiation cannot be consistently made between type of policy or of policy process. A *first category of cases* is defined with reference to timing and tempo, an important defining element of Europeanization (Radaelli 2003: 47–8). Here, the UK adopted policy change in advance of the EU developing a similar agenda and/or requiring such reform. Deregulation, as well as privatization, under the Thatcher governments of the 1980s went further and faster than in the rest of the EU (Schmidt 2006). Financial market liberalization—the 'Big Bang' in the City of London in 1986—was well ahead of any EU decision. Similarly, the liberalization of the air transport sector in the mid-1980s, telecommunications in 1984, and electricity in 1990 each pre-dated EU action. British Airways was privatized in 1987, a year ahead of a sequence of three EU packages of reform spread over the following decade (Graham 1997). The EU did not introduce market liberalization in electricity supply until two directives in 1996 and 2003 (Jamasb and Pollitt 2005). Thatcher (2004: 293) found the EU stimulus to reform the regulation of telecommunications was 'very limited', differing sharply from the cases of France, Germany, and Italy. Indeed, BT and the government were strong supporters of 'exporting' the domestic model. Lehmkuhl (2006) examined the impact of the EU's Common Transport Policy and found that 'it is almost impossible to identify a European influence in the regulation of the British road haulage market', though there were on some minor aspects (e.g. the acceptance of bigger trucks) (2006: 9). Similarly, 'the British Railways Act of 1993 represents the most radical and far-reaching railway reform in Europe', with no impact of the EU noted on its scope or timing of implementation (2006: 10).

It is sometimes suggested that the UK was a policy leader on privatization, with other member states emulating its model and it being 'uploaded' to the EU level. Yet, in a comparative study examining the relevance of different stimuli to privatization across Europe, Clifton, Comin, and Díaz Fuentes (2006) find that the UK was more an anomaly in this area. Britain's partners did not embark seriously on privatization until 1993 (and often in response to EU directives) and rather than copying the UK, few others went as far. London had some influence on the EU directives, however.

The fact that Britain was in advance of EU liberalization could also create problems for harmonization later. Baldi (2006) examined the area of competition policy and found that Britain was actually the last of the large and medium-sized member states to harmonize its anti-trust laws with those of the EU. The 'pre-existence of an anti-trust system actually made harmonisation more difficult for Britain by allowing British industrial interests to develop preferences for the domestic system' (2006: 503). Pressure for UK harmonization stemmed, however, from an increasing recognition of the success of the EU policy and the inadequacies of the UK regime, and this influenced the Blair government in its introduction of the Competition Act 1998.

A *second category of cases* involves contestation and a deliberate British decision to reject participation in a common EU policy, securing some type of 'opt-out'. The most prominent case is that of Economic and Monetary Union (EMU), where Britain's opt-out was part of a protocol agreed in the context of the Maastricht Treaty negotiated in December 1991 (see Dyson and Featherstone 1999). It had, however, occurred after a limited Europeanization of Britain's monetary policy, when sterling was placed in the then Exchange Rate Mechanism (from October 1990). To a section of the Conservative Party, the media, and the relevant policy community, UK participation in the ERM met a policy need, a governing style, and offered greater international influence: thus, Europeanization was welcomed (Buller 2006). Yet, the extent of domestic adjustment was little and late, and soon the experience of the 'Black Wednesday' ERM exit (16 September 1992) provoked much bloodletting in the Tory party. The relatively better performance of the British economy over the last decade; the perception that a 'one-size-fits-all' monetary policy could seriously damage the British economy, given the lack of synchronization in the respective 'economic cycles' of the UK and its continental partners; and the debate surrounding the rules of the Stability and Growth Pact—each of these have been seen as strengthening the case for staying out (cf. Hay, Smith, and Watson 2006). As if to celebrate Britain's detachment, Gordon Brown as Chancellor rarely attended meetings of the Council of Ministers, preferring to send deputies instead, and frequently preached the UK reform model to his EU partners. As a result, Britain has been little affected by EU monetary regulations and directives—otherwise a key stimulus for domestic adaptation in other member states (Featherstone 2004).

In the other sector in which Britain obtained an 'opt-out' at Maastricht in 1991—social policy—the pattern has been more varied. The Thatcher government had refused to sign the Social Charter in Strasbourg in December 1989, much to the frustration of the TUC and the Labour Party. By contrast, one of the first moves of the Blair government was to agree in June 1997 that the Charter be incorporated into the EU's Amsterdam Treaty. The EU's Working Time Directive had also been rejected by the Conservative government when it was first proposed in 1993. Again, Labour and the unions protested. But, although it was introduced into the UK in 1998, the Blair government sought to retain the right of individual workers not to be bound by one of its core elements: that an employee could *not* be forced to work more than forty-eight hours a week (Arrowsmith et al. 2001). The agenda here highlighted the conflict of social models between Britain and her major partners. The Major and Blair governments saw the forty-eight-hour rule as increasing labour costs and stymieing employment growth. EU partners stressed the values of social solidarity. In other areas, EU action has been more directly consequential, as with the rulings of the European Court of Justice on gender rights in relation to pay and pensions. By contrast, the recent agenda of fighting social exclusion is one where British policies were largely formed in advance of the EU taking action. The impact of the latter on the formation of domestic policy appears to have been modest, competing with other sources of influence (Armstrong 2006). Moreover, in the 'National Action Plan on Inclusion' it was obliged to submit and share with its fellow EU governments, the Blair government chose to stress its success on growth and employment, rather than on poverty.

A *third category of cases* is of limited adaptation (shifting from coexistence to co-evolution), but one paralleled by strong reservations about the format or application of policy. Here, the ambiguous stance of Britain towards EU foreign policy cooperation is a prime example. The disputes between the Blair government and its EU partners over the invasion of Iraq, whilst at the same time being viewed as slavishly pro-USA, are well known. And, whilst there have been a number of clashes over the substance of policy, there has also been a consistent line to defend the intergovernmental character of EU foreign policy cooperation. Some years ago, Hill commented that the UK had sought to insert its leadership and to exploit the benefits of cooperation under the old system of 'European Political Cooperation' (1996: 77). More latterly, Oliver and Allen (2006: 197–9) noted that the UK had maintained its commitment to intergovernmentalism and that it had continued to refuse to have its hands tied. Yet, under the 'Common Foreign and Security Policy' (CFSP), there have been 'numerous foreign policy issues (that) show evidence of adaptation (by Britain) to a European norm' (2006: 197). A shared outlook was evident in the content of the EU's 'European Security Strategy' (ESS) of 2003, which reflected much British thinking, and the Blair government's own subsequent national strategy documents. Moreover, the ESS showed the differences of policy perspective between Britain and the EU, on the one hand, and the USA, on the other (Oliver and Allen 2006: 195).

A second, though distinct, case in this category may be agricultural and rural policy. Paradoxically, given its overall importance for the EU, few political science studies have been made of the Common Agricultural Policy (CAP) in general or in relation to the UK, in particular. A policy study by Ward and Lowe (2004) considered how the Rural Development Regulation (RDR)—the CAP's 'second pillar' agreed in Berlin in March 1999—has been implemented in England. They noted the disadvantageous funding settlement for the UK under this policy and the subsequent Whitehall decision to cross-subsidize the RDR for England from production subsidies to environmental subsidies, a mechanism known as 'modulation'. They accept that 'an increasingly Europeanised approach to rural development funding, programming and administration is being developed' in general, but that it risks 'distorting sub-national priorities [in England] to spread rural development support beyond the farm gate' (2004: 121), a feature to which Britain had objected.

A *fourth category of cases* are those where there have been clear domestic impacts on framing and prescribing the content. A prime example here is environmental policy. It is also a sector that has been relatively well researched across the EU in terms of 'Europeanization' (see Knill 1998; Boerzel 2000; Haverland 2000; 2003). Jordan (1998) in his study of coastal bathing water policy—focusing on actor participation—found that EU action had significantly restructured a relatively stable policy area. It had been dominated by engineers and scientists and governments had defended the practice of depositing raw sewage into the sea. In combination with the pressures arising from privatization, however, EU environmental ideas and policies shifted the British policy process by opening it up to environmental groups and helped to redefine policy goals and instruments. Again, Jordan (2000: 3) argues that UK policy here has been 'irrevocably transformed'. Yet Knill (1998), following a historical institutionalist/rationalist approach, had found greater institutional resistance to implementation in (other aspects of) environmental policy in the UK than in Germany (cf. Bugdahn 2005).

A *fifth category of cases* is of unilateral initiatives with a European frame. With respect to policy on internal EU migration, Britain for a period was seen as being more pro-Europe than most of its partners. Prior to the accession of eight countries from central and Eastern Europe to the EU in 2004, most EU member states applied long transition periods before allowing free movement of workers—a basic EU principle—from these states. By contrast, the UK—along with Ireland and Sweden—decided not to introduce any such restrictions. The effect was to open UK borders to thousands of migrant workers from Eastern Europe, epitomized in stereotypical images of Polish plumbers entering the market. Gajewska (2006) argued that the difference of response between EU governments was the result of different official reactions as to how to deal with the far right and anti-immigrant political campaigns. In any event, Britain was not the 'awkward partner' (George 1998). The optimistic assumption was the faster growing, liberalized British economy needed an influx of new skilled labour.

Britain's exceptionalism became a problem, however, with the larger than expected influx of migrant workers. The estimates of the likely *net* inflow from the new member states ranged between 5,000 and 13,000 per year (Dustmann et al. 2003). However, a total of 579,000 workers actually registered for employment between 1 May 2004 and 31 December 2006—and this figure excludes those coming as self-employed workers. Nevertheless, this huge total represents the number entering and does *not* take account of those leaving the UK (or their employment).[1] The increased political sensitivity about the greater numbers led John Reid, as Home Secretary, to announce (on 24 October 2006) that a more restrictive policy would be maintained for Bulgarian and Romanian workers when their states joined the EU in January 2007, with subsequent reviews.

The shift of policy was prompted by a domestic backlash which saw Britain as being a 'soft-touch'. The same theme had long been evident in the UK's politics of immigration. Britain had maintained a tough stance on border controls by refusing to accede to the Schengen Agreement signed in 1985 by five EU states and subsequently expanded. The Agreement lifts border controls on individual travellers within the EU to random checks. The Blair government had also resisted placing immigration and asylum policy within traditional EU policy-making (with no national veto) in the context of the Amsterdam Treaty of 1997. Moreover, in 2003 Blair proposed that asylum seekers wishing to enter the EU should have their claims processed in camps located outside the EU—Romania and Albania were suggested as possible locations (Geddes 2005).

This brief overview suggests a differentiation in the relevance of the EU—from UK action in advance of the EU, to UK opt-outs, limited adaptation, and resistance to some aspects of form, clear impacts on framing and content, and unilateral initiatives that were more in advance of her partners. Further differentiation is necessary according to timing and tempo, as well as the make-up of the government in office. Moreover, within each policy sector the significance of impact varies according to the type of EU policy instrument. There is little consistent pattern across the typology. A contrast may be made between areas of greater domestic political importance—such as EMU and foreign policy—where the policy impact is limited and areas of lesser political salience such as environmental policy, where the impact appears greater. Political sensitivities have changed over time, however. Few would have predicted, for example, the St Malo Declaration of December 1998 when the UK agreed with France to the establishment of the European Security and Defence Policy. Indeed, a number of authors note that the general reality of adaptation is much greater than

---

[1] I am grateful for the advice of my colleague Evgenia Markova on this matter.

that suggested by the image and discourse. This contrast is perhaps even more evident in the behaviour of actors and the operation of institutions.

45.3.2 Polity

EU policy processes have drawn in an increasing and varied number of domestic political actors from the UK. Though research in this area is rather limited, a number of studies have focused on those involved in subnational public authorities and NGOs. Here the impact of EU initiatives and funding can be significant, though generally short of the 'multi-level governance' depiction (Marks, Hooghe, and Blank 1996). Local actors can gain unprecedented access to information and resources, with parallel gains of legitimacy, features that were seen as in short supply under the Thatcher governments of the 1980s. Marshall (2005) examined the cases of Birmingham and Glasgow—both recipients of large amounts of EU structural funds—and the evidence of Europeanization on local government and local actors (in urban renewal, regeneration partnerships). He found significant impacts in terms of the engagement of councils in EU lobbying, building local working partnerships, and developing long-term strategic planning in order to benefit from EU funds (2005: 676). Moreover, the EU had affected the behaviour of NGOs concerned with regeneration initiatives (a greater EU awareness) and had restructured pluralistic politics at the local level (new forms of inclusion). In addition, the form and content of local regeneration partnerships had changed to accommodate EU Commission norms. The two city councils had sought to 'upload' their preferences and practices (to input into future EU policies) and to engage in sharing best practice in an EU context.

If local councils willingly circumvented Whitehall in the period of the Thatcher governments, the same has been even more apparent in the case of British NGOs. The expansion of EU competences into broader policy areas and the policy style of the EU Commission to seek coalitions of supporters across member states have provided a new dimension of political activity for NGOs. Indeed, British NGOs have been more responsive in this regard than many of their counterparts in other EU member states. They have joined EU-level campaigns, promoted European-level lobby organizations, and often provided the leadership personnel for such bodies. Pugh found that voluntary sector groups concerned with children's rights, infant health, disability, and the elderly were extending their advocacy strategies to take on an important European dimension (Pugh 1998). In the case of the pro-migrant sector, Gray and Statham found that British NGOs had built 'pathways' and 'linkages' to a new European political dimension (e.g. via the European Council on Refugees and Exiles), though national governments still maintained their grip on decision-making (2005). In his study of social exclusion policy, Armstrong (2006) found that participation in the EU-level process of the 'Open Method of Coordination' (OMC) significantly affected the domestic process of interaction between Whitehall, regional executives, and NGOs. Fairbrass (2006) focussed on British business and environmental groups in terms of their choice of targets and routes and drew a distinction on the basis that the latter saw the EU as a welcome alternative whereas the former was generally closer to the stance of the British government.

This willingness to act at the European level and the relatively high profile of British personnel in the relevant fora indicate a degree of engagement that contrasts sharply with Westminster-centred images of Euro-scepticism and detachment. The deeper reality is of a stratum of personnel whose schedules involve regular European inter-actions. For local authorities, much of this is seen as managerial and administrative, rather than being overtly political. For NGOs, it is a matter of creating and exploiting new lobbying opportunities and wider coalitions. The motivations are undoubtedly instrumental—seeking strategic advantage—but it is unlikely that a normative and socialization aspect is totally absent.

45.3.3 Institutions

The consequences of EU engagement are most often discernible in the modus operandi of governmental institutions. A common assumption in the UK is of their persistence and of incremental change. The long-term picture of Whitehall's manage-ment of EU policy, indeed, suggested that the administrative machine had absorbed the new demands without significant shifts of culture (Bulmer and Burch 1998). Fol-lowing a 'historical institutionalist' approach, Bulmer and Burch noted that 'The new challenges posed by EC/EU membership have simply been absorbed into the existing institutions and into the characteristic methods, procedures and culture of Whitehall' (1998: 613). Surprisingly, the 'critical juncture' in this respect had occurred in 1960–1 at the time of Britain's first application to join the then EEC. When Britain actually did join, the consequence was of adaptation of what had been established, rather than a reform of the administrative machinery. So, no 'big bang' but two 'quantum leaps' did occur much later. The single European market programme (1985–92) led to an 'intensification of adaptation in particular areas of Whitehall' (1998: 613), as did the Maastricht Treaty's extension of the EU's role into matters of 'Justice and Home affairs', which brought the Home Office more fully into the coordination process. In addition, the onset of the European Council meetings—regular 'summits' of heads of government from 1975—brought in the Prime Minister and the Cabinet Office much more. Yet the framework and principles established at the point of Britain's entry were not altered, just adapted. Thus, 'Europeanisation and the Whitehall model have proven to be quite compatible thus far' (1998: 613).[2]

At the centre of the EU's impact on Whitehall is the Foreign and Commonwealth Office (FCO). Earlier portrayals saw the FCO as an institutional loser: ceding respon-sibilities to departments concerned with domestic policy, as the agenda of the EU broadened. Yet, Allen and Oliver (2006) see the FCO as having been able to revise the format of its 'gate-keeping' function, via the role of the UK's Permanent Rep-resentation ('UKRep') in Brussels and coordination by embassies. The FCO retains significant influence over major policies: it is both a winner and a loser. Moreover, internally, the EU has had a range of impacts on the FCO: on the office of the Political

---

[2] A similar situation was found to apply to the Scottish Office, with the prevailing culture and approaches not exhibiting major changes (Smith 2001).

Director and Permanent Under-Secretary; the management of EU policy; the growth of UKRep as a 'mini-Whitehall'; the increased prominence of Europeanists in the FCO; and the greater role played by the PM and Downing Street (Allen and Oliver 2006: 63–4).

Whitehall processes have had the reputation of being very well coordinated, establishing coherent negotiating mandates. The system is geared up to establish 'an early, agreed, cross-departmental European policy position on major issues' and this is 'a feature which sets the British governmental machinery apart from most of its partners in the EU' (Bulmer and Birch 1998: 617; see also Rometsch and Wessels 1996; Wallace 1996; Wright 1996). Internal coordination in Whitehall may not be matched, however, by an alertness to wider agendas or the ability to forge coalitions with partners in EU negotiations (Dyson and Featherstone 1999: 758).

For one of the most important policy areas affecting Britain's relationship with the EU—EMU—Dyson stressed the strength with which the institutional culture of HM Treasury enveloped the policy agenda (Dyson 2000). Issues were embedded in the structures of belief and of meaning emanating from the Treasury and its surrounds, and these were powerful, independent factors. Moreover, the 'Treasury is much less Europeanised in outlook than either the Bank [of England] or the FCO and very cautious on EMU' (Dyson 2000: 913). Following a constructivist approach, Dyson highlights the differences of discourse on EMU in Whitehall—the impact of Europeanization varied between departments. The incentives to join EMU also differed for the UK in comparison to its partners: Britain had already had an economic policy revolution independent of EMU and the granting of (de facto) independence to the Bank of England in 1997 further decoupled domestic interests from the European constraint. The lack of Europeanization was thus not attributable to an innate conservatism: rather, the cycle of reform differed again and the ideational setting contrasted with those of major partners.

The EU stimulus has not remained static, of course. Bulmer and Burch (1998: 622–4) noted that changes under way in the early period of the first Blair government could lead to significant shifts. Labour's agenda of constitutional reform—notably devolution and human rights—looked set to reduce the disparities between the British state and its major partners. It was ironic, they noted, that whilst Whitehall had absorbed Europeanization pressures relatively easily, it was the EU that was challenging the very constitutional framework in which Whitehall patterns were embedded (1998: 624). More recently, the same authors concluded that in fact Whitehall, under Blair, was engaged in a 'step-change' with respect to Europeanization. The government, at both the ministerial and the official level, was able to take a more 'proactive, directive and strategic approach to Europe', partly because Labour was not so divided on Europe as were the Tories (Bulmer and Burch 2005: 886). This approach was qualified to some extent by the control wrought by Gordon Brown and the Treasury. Nevertheless, the government had seized the institutional opportunities and cultural change had been promoted to overcome the passive and defensive approach of the John Major years. The potential for projecting British interests onto the EU stage was greater than ever before, government personnel were more aware and engaged, and there was leadership and a strategic vision. It was not clear, however, whether these changes would endure, given the impact of Iraq and of Merkel and Sarkozy as more assertive rival leaders.

Somewhat paradoxically, given its reputation for Euro-scepticism, the UK has had quite a good record in transposing EU law into national law. There are few studies of parliamentary scrutiny of EU legislation in the UK. However, in a detailed study in the area of utilities and food safety regulation, Berglund, Gange, and van Waarden found that there was little delay in the UK's transposition and that this was due to advantages in terms of the existence of administrative routines for effective, efficient, and fast production of law (2006: 698, 712). Kaeding in a study of the transport legislation of the EU, though, reported that the average delay in transposing the legislation into domestic law was around thirty weeks in the UK, whereas—perhaps counter-intuitively—in Spain it was just ten weeks (2006: 235). The overall picture is very positive (e.g. Mbaye 2001 on compliance). As previously noted, Falkner et al. (2005) explained the UK performance in terms of the strong prevailing culture of law compliance.

Beyond Whitehall, researchers have examined the impact of EU membership in the context of devolution and on the English regions. Smith (2001) found the prevailing culture and approaches of the Scottish Office exhibiting much continuity. His later study (2006) examined the impact of the EU on the work of the new Scottish Executive after 1999, confirming again the relevance of the embedded culture and arguing that whilst there was no convergence to a European model of administration, there was some change—including an apolitical bureaucratic enthusiasm for European engagement. Burch et al. (2005: 474) examined each of the devolved administrations in the UK and concluded that change was evident not so much in policy outcomes as in the handling of EU policy. The devolved administrations were being drawn into the centre of Whitehall policy-making and they 'have more channels of access and are applying more resources in a more focussed way' on EU matters than in the past or in comparison to the English regions. Yet, the EU impact varied between policy sectors and access to UK policy-making appeared conditional on trust and agreement on fundamental aspects.

Burch and Gomez (2002; 2006) analysed the impact of the EU on institutional change on the English regional authorities. They distinguish impacts across two periods: 1990–7 and 1997–2006. The impact was 'often primary and predominant' in the first phase (a result in the main of the changes made by the EU in 1988 and 1993 in the regulations for its structural funds) and 'significant but secondary' in the second (2006: 95). In absolute terms, the EU had grown after 1997 but in the context of a far greater expansion of regional activities. The programming concept of the European Regional Development Fund had 'helped to both develop and consolidate the regional tier by creating a clear focus for activities and opportunities for engagement and activism'. The formal requirement for partnerships similarly exerted a 'powerful regionalising effect'. Post-1997, the EU effect was sustained but became secondary to that emanating from central government. However, wider EU effects became more apparent, as with rural development policy and environmental policy. They stress gradualism and variability in EU effects and also that over time small changes had the potential to emerge as transformative.

Long-term patterns have displayed small, incremental change. However, the onset of the Blair government in 1997 prompted a number of reforms with substantive implications: notably a step-change in Whitehall and a strong engagement from devolved administrations. Much of this change appeared conditional and contingent—not least on the political lead from on high—but, even so, it qualifies notions of deeply embedded institutional cultures.

45.4 EXPLAINING BRITAIN'S RELATIONSHIP

What explains this complexity—of contrasts and change? This is a huge agenda and one difficult to resolve. It is worth considering the arguments that have been deployed, however, in order to gauge the possible intervening variables standing between EU stimulus and domestic response.

The most all-encompassing starting point is to consider the nature of the political discourse in Britain on Europe. Meanings and images are attached to 'Europe' in speech and text and these structure political options and action. It is widely asserted that 'Brits' talk and write about the EU in markedly different terms from the 'continentals' (Wallace 1997). The British, it is argued, have never really adapted to EU membership in terms of their mindset. Schmidt (2006) compared Britain to France, Germany, and Italy. To explain the British problem, she argues, it is necessary to 'consider how the EU challenges traditional ideas about democracy and how national leaders have responded to such challenges in their discourse to the general public' (2006: 26). Britain and France share concerns about the EU threatening executive autonomy, but only in Britain is this linked to parliamentary sovereignty, via the traditional notion of 'Crown in Parliament'. Moreover, the EU depoliticizes policy issues—it involves 'policies without politics' (2006: 25)—and this poses a bigger shock to highly charged, majoritarian, and simply-structured polities like Britain. The arguments for joining the EU and, on occasion, deepening its integration have been primarily economic—in contrast to France, for example, which saw it as an opportunity for political leadership. The result of each of these factors, Schmidt argues, is that the British public has been made 'maximally aware of the drawbacks to Europeanization, but of few of the benefits' (2006: 29). Wallace has enlarged the point: the symbolic resonance of European integration—the ideas, concepts, and values associated with the project—has been much more positive than negative for France, Germany, and Italy, framing the judgement on individual issues. By contrast, for many in Britain this dimension has either been absent or negative (1997: 686). This largely leaves the response to new EU initiatives without a supporting normative discourse of a political kind. By default, issues are a cost–benefit analysis in terms of trade, investment, and the economy, with limits set anxiously on domestic political encroachment. Few British politicians have been described as 'Europeans of the heart', to use a phrase of Jacques Delors', and more have been closer to the pragmatic calculations of John Major or Gordon Brown.

The absence of a legitimating political discourse can be explained by reference to a host of other factors. Unlike most continental nations, the legacy of the Second World War was not one of seeking to exorcize history, as Jean Monnet himself commented (1978: 450). With this came the 'price of victory': successive governments assumed a weight for Britain in the world that became increasingly out of step with economic realities (Charlton 1983). Nevertheless, a continuing feature of the British discourse has been that 'Europe' is too small to meet her interests: variously, the emphasis has been on the importance of the Commonwealth, the 'special relationship' with the USA, the liberalizing economic logic of globalization. Strategic calculations left Britain uncertain about the value of a deepening European tie (Allen 2005). The focus can be further extended to cover differences of history, geography, and culture: some would identify a near endless list. Such explanations can appear too static and general, however, insensitive to change over time. If Britain lacks a narrative to explain its political engagement with Europe, the same can be said increasingly of the EU as a whole (Garton Ash 2001).

How the British political elite have managed the relationship with the rest of Europe has been the source of much dispute. The political bias of the media has been cited to explain the pro-European vote in the June 1975 referendum and, more recently, the Euro-scepticism of public opinion since the 1980s. The Euro-sceptic Lord Beloff argued that Britain's European policy was based on deceit: the public had been repeatedly misled about the real integration agenda by a Whitehall elite that lacked confidence in Britain's ability to go it alone (1996). By contrast, the ex-EU diplomat Roy Denman has written of a litany of strategic mistakes made by successive governments that have undermined Britain's influence in Europe (1996). More recently, former EU Commissioner Peter Sutherland (2008) argued that the politics of Westminster and its associated press coverage has cut Britain off from a wider European debate. Strong views on the desirability of integration can colour explanations of how it has occurred. Taylor (2008) sought to explain how and why the EU had a bad press in the UK. More generally, Allen (2005) has described the UK as having a Europeanized ruling elite, but a non-Europeanized polity given the absence of a public consensus and an aversion to debate about initiatives on the EU's long-term future.

Systemic features mediate responses to the EU at a general level: the political discourse, the perceived threat to established traditions and principles, the motivation for 'cost–benefit' analysis, the 'Euro-scepticism' of the media, etc. 'Europe' remains a divisive, emotive issue and engagement and adaptation are often kept low profile, sensitive to public images. Yet, differentiation and change was evident from the earlier brief survey. Whilst these may be more the result of strategic calculation, ideational shifts were also apparent. The UK setting—from various 'institutionalist' perspectives—is not as resistant or as impermeable to 'Europeanization' processes as generalized, systemic images suggest. Instead, the intervening variables at play appear far more varied and particular.

45.5 CONCLUSION

The foregoing has painted a picture of differentiation and change. Britain has experienced rather more adaptation than many might suspect and this has been evident across policy areas, political actors, and institutions. Yet, within each domain there are significant asymmetries: many policy areas display only limited direct EU impact; institutions exhibit much incrementalism and continuity; different types of actor have been drawn into EU processes. The extent of Britain's exceptionalism seems more difficult to gauge today than at any time previously. Some important dynamics of the British system are being reshaped, whilst settings appear more contingent and fungible. 'Every which way, but loose' may be an appropriate epithet here.

The agenda for Europeanization research in the UK is broad and, whilst scholarship to date has dwelt on particular cases, it has done so to varying degrees of empirical depth. There remain major gaps and limitations. There is limited empirical evidence of institutional adaptation across Whitehall; the impact of the EU on local policy-making; the effects of EU policies in key areas like the CAP and immigration; the strategies and perceptions of NGOs; the ideational influence of the EU on core national policies, etc. Moreover, there is much more research to date on the 'top-down' impacts of the EU, rather than the strategic effectiveness and substantive contribution of UK actors 'uploading' ideas and interests at the EU level. To some extent, scholarship remains 'ghetto-ized': analysts of EU effects are likely to be EU specialists drawn to the study by a European, rather than a domestic, interest. Domestic politics specialists instinctively have a different vantage point. 'Europeanization' studies are susceptible to the prior expectations of impact on the part of EU specialists, but the same is also true for experts on domestic politics. Further, the argument over the extent of EU impacts is closely tied to the choice of alternative methodological approaches—historical continuities, the policy relevance of increased interaction and socialization, for example—rather than contesting evidence within the same tradition. This means arguments over Europeanization impacts are more disputes over methodology.

The ontology of Europeanization explanations face much complexity, not least in the context of considering alternative causal factors or depth or permanence of change. Outcomes are not seen as consistently determinate across cases and settings; rather the interest stems from their differentiation and asymmetry. 'Europeanization' offers no theory of its own and it must rest on standard tests of rigorous research design. As such, 'imported' methodologies reflect the assumptions, the wider strengths and weaknesses of their approaches. Institutionalist explanations need to be adapted to two levels—the EU and the domestic—and to reveal the linking mechanisms of influence between them—to answer the 'how?' question. Much research to date has settled for the circumstantial and fails to penetrate a 'black box'. Conceptualizations of Europeanization processes are developing a more sophisticated 'tool kit', drawing important analytical distinctions.

Studies of Europeanization dynamics in Britain are concerned with an important and diverse phenomenon. With the increasing and broadening activity at the EU level, few would predict such studies would become less important in the future. The task is therefore to extend the research findings and to do so with a robust analytical design. At the same time, the expectations of such research should be consistent with those applied to other approaches: it lacks determinacy, so what's new?

REFERENCES

ALLEN, D. 2005. 'The United Kingdom: A Europeanized Government in a non-Europeanized Polity'. In S. Bulmer and C. Lequesne (eds.), *The Member States of the European Union*. Oxford: Oxford University Press.

——and OLIVER, T. 2006. 'The Foreign and Commonwealth Office'. In I. Bache and A. Jordan (eds.), *The Europeanization of British Politics*. Houndmills: Palgrave Macmillan.

ARMSTRONG, A. K. 2006. 'The "Europeanization" of Social Exclusion: British Adaptation to EU Co-ordination'. *British Journal of Politics and International Relations*, 8/1: 79–100.

ARROWSMITH, J., FRENCH, S., GILMAN, M., and RICHARDSON, R. 2001. 'Performance-Related Pay in Health Care'. *Journal of Health Services Research and Policy*, 6/2: 114–19.

BACHE, I., and JORDAN, A. 2006a. 'Europeanization and Domestic Change'. In I. Bache and A. Jordan (eds.), *The Europeanization of British Politics*. Houndmills: Palgrave Macmillan.

——— 2006b. 'The Europeanization of British Politics'. In I. Bache and A. Jordan (eds.), *The Europeanization of British Politics*. Houndmills: Palgrave Macmillan.

BALDI G. 2006. 'Europeanising Antitrust: British Competition Policy Reform and Member State Convergence'. *British Journal of Politics and International Relations*, 8/4: 503–18.

BELOFF, M. 1996. *Britain and European Union: Dialogue of the Deaf*. Basingstoke: Macmillan.

BERGLUND, S., GANGE, L., and van WAARDEN, F. 2006. 'Mass Production of Law: Routinization in the Transposition of European Directives. A Sociological Institutionalist Account'. *Journal of European Public Policy*, 13/5: 692–716.

BOERZEL, T. A. 2000. 'Why there is no "Southern Problem": On Environmental Leaders and Laggards in the EU'. *Journal of European Public Policy*, 7/1: 141–62.

——and RISSE, T. 2003. 'Conceptualizing the Domestic Impact of Europe'. In K. Featherstone and C. Radaelli (eds.), *The Politics of Europeanization*. Oxford: Oxford University Press.

BUGDAHN, S. 2005. 'Of Europeanization and Domestication: The Implementation of the Environmental Information Directive in Ireland, Great Britain and Germany'. *Journal of European Public Policy*, 12/1: 177–99.

BULLER, J. 2006. 'Contesting Europeanization: Agents, Institutions and Narratives in British Monetary Policy'. *West European Politics*, 29/3: 389–409.

BULMER, S., and BURCH, M. 1998. 'Organising for Europe: Whitehall, the British State and the European Union'. *Public Administration*, 76/4: 601–28.

—— —— 2005. 'The Europeanization of UK Government: From Quiet Revolution to Explicit Step-Change?' *Public Administration*, 83/4: 861–90.

—— and RADAELLI, M. C. 2005. 'The Europeanization of Public Policy'. In C. Lesquene and S. Bulmer (eds.), *The Member States of the European Union*. Oxford: Oxford University Press.

BURCH, M., and GOMEZ, R. 2002. 'The English Regions and the European Union'. *Regional Studies*, 36/7: 767–78.

—— —— 2006. 'The English Regions'. In I. Bache and A. Jordan (eds.), *The Europeanization of British Politics*. Houndmills: Palgrave Macmillan.

—— —— HOGWOOD, P., and SCOTT, A. 2005. 'Devolution, Change and European Union Policy-Making in the UK'. *Regional Studies*, 39/4: 465–75.

CHARLTON, M. 1983. *The Price of Victory*. London: BBC Publications.

CLIFTON, J., COMÍN, F., and DÍAZ FUENTES, D. 2006. 'Privatizing Public Enterprises in the European Union 1960–2002: Ideological, Pragmatic, Inevitable?' *Journal of European Public Policy*, 13/5: 736–56.

DENMAN, R. 1996. *Missed Chances: Britain and Europe in the Twentieth Century*. London: Cassel.

DUSTMANN, C., FABBRI, F., PRESTON, I., and WADSWORTH, J. 2003. 'Labour Market Performance of Immigrants in the UK Labour Market'. In *Home Office Online Report 05/03*. London: Home Office.

DYSON, K. 2000. 'Europeanization, Whitehall Culture and the Treasury as Institutional Veto Player: A Constructivist Approach to Economic and Monetary Union'. *Public Administration*, 78/4: 897–914.

—— and FEATHERSTONE, K. 1999. *The Road to Maastricht: Negotiating Economic and Monetary Union*. Oxford: Oxford University Press.

—— and GOETZ, K. H. 2003. 'Living with Europe: Power, Constraint and Contestation'. In K. Dyson and K. H. Goetz (eds.), *Living with Europe: Germany, Europe, and the Politics of Constraint*. Oxford: British Academy/Oxford University Press.

FAIRBRASS, J. 2006. 'Sustainable Development, Corporate Social Responsibility and Europeanization of the UK Business Actors: Preliminary Findings'. School of Management, University of Bradford, Working Paper (02).

FALKNER, G., TREIB, O., HARTLAPP, M., and LEIBER, S. 2005. *Complying with Europe: EU Harmonisation and Soft Law in the Member States*. Cambridge: Cambridge University Press.

FEATHERSTONE, K. 2004. 'The Political Dynamics of External Empowerment: The Emergence of EMU and the Challenge to the European Social Model'. In M. Andrew and R. George (eds.), *Euros and Europeans: Monetary Integration and the European Model of Society*. Cambridge: Cambridge University Press.

—— and RADAELLI, C. M. (eds.) 2003. *The Politics of Europeanization*. Oxford: Oxford University Press.

GAJEWSKAA, K. 2006. 'Restrictions in Labor Free Movement after the EU-Enlargement 2004: Explaining Variation among Countries in the Context of Elites' Strategies towards the Radical Right'. *Comparative European Politics*, 4/4: 379–98.

GARTON ASH, T. 2001. 'Is Britain European'. *International Affairs*, 77/1: 1–14.

GEDDES, A. 2005. 'Chronicle of a Crisis Foretold: The Politics of Irregular Migration, Human Trafficking and People Smuggling in the UK'. *British Journal of Politics and International Relations*, 7/3: 324–39.

GEORGE, S. 1998. *An Awkward Partner: Britain in the European Community*. Oxford: Oxford University Press.

GOETZ, K. H. 2000. 'European Integration and National Executives: A Cause in Search of an Effect?' *West European Politics*, 23/4: 211–31.

GRAHAM, A. 1997. 'The UK 1979–95: Myths and Realities of Conservative Capitalism'. In C. Crouch and W. Streeck (eds.), *Political Economy of Modern Capitalism*. London: Sage.

GRAY, E., and STATHAM, P. 2005. 'Becoming European? The Transformation of the British Pro-Migrant NGO Sector in Response to Europeanization'. *Journal of Common Market Studies*, 43/4: 877–98.

HALL, P., and TAYLOR, R. C. R. 1996. 'A Political Science and the Three New Institutionalisms'. *Political Studies*, 44: 936–57.

HAVERLAND, M. 2000. 'National Adaptation to European Integration: The Importance of Institutional Veto Points'. *Journal of Public Policy*, 20/1: 83–103.

—— 2003. 'The Impact of the European Union on Environmental Policies'. In K. Featherstone and C. Radaelli (eds.), *The Politics of Europeanization*. Oxford: Oxford University Press.

HAY, C., SMITH, N. J., and WATSON, M. 2006. 'Beyond Prospective Accountancy: Reassessing the Case for British Membership of the Single European Currency Comparatively'. *British Journal of Politics and International Relations*, 8/1: 101–21.

HILL, C. (ed.) 1996. *The Actors in Europe's Foreign Policy*. London: Routledge.

JAMASB, T., and POLLITT, M. 2005. 'Electricity Market Reform in the European Union: Review of Progress toward Liberalization and Integration'. *Energy Journal*, 26 (Special Issue on European Electricity Liberalization): 11–42.

JORDAN, A. 1998. 'European Community Water Policy Standards: Locked in or Watered Down?' Centre for Social and Economic Research on the Global Environment (CSERGE) Working Paper (1).

—— 2000. 'The Europeanization of UK Environmental Policy, 1970–2000: A Departmental Perspective'. Centre for Social and Economic Research on the Global Environment (CSERGE) Working Paper (16).

KEADING, M. 2006. 'Determinants of Transposition Delay in the European Union'. *Journal of Public Policy*, 26/3: 229–53.

KNILL, C. 1998. 'European Policies: The Impact of National Administrative Traditions'. *Journal of Public Policy*, 18/1: 1–28.

—— and LEHMKUHL, D. 1999. 'How Europe Matters: Different Mechanisms of Europeanization'. European Integration online Papers (EIoP). http://eiop.or.at/eiop/texte/1999–007a.htm 3 (7).

LEHMKUHL, D. 2006. 'Harmonisation and Convergence? National Responses to the Common European Transport Policy'. *German Policy Studies*, 3/1: 1–26.

MARKS, G., HOOGHE, L., and BLANK, K. 1996. 'European Integration from the 1980s: State-centric v. Multi-level Governance'. *Journal of Common Market Studies*, 34/3: 341–78.

MARSHALL, A. 2005. 'Europeanization at the Urban Level: Local Actors, Institutions and the Dynamics of Multi-level Interaction'. *Journal of European Public Policy*, 12/4: 668–86.

MBAYE, H. 2001. 'Why National States Comply with Supranational Law: Explaining Implementation Infringements in the European Law 1972–1993'. *European Union Politics*, 2/3: 259–81.

MONNET, J. 1978. *Memoirs*. London: Collins.

MORTH, U. 2003. 'Europeanization as Interpretation, Translation, and Editing of Public Policies'. In K. Featherstone and C. M. Radaelli (eds.), *The Politics of Europeanization*. Oxford: Oxford University Press.

OLIVER, T., and ALLEN, D. 2006. 'Foreign Policy'. In I. Bache and A. Jordan (eds.), *The Europeanization of British Politics*. Houndmills: Palgrave Macmillan.

OLSEN, J. P. 2002. 'The Many Faces of Europeanization'. *Journal of Common Market Studies*, 40/5: 921–52.

PUGH, A. 1998. 'Seeking a Voice: The Voluntary Sector, Social Policies and the European Union'. Ph.D thesis, University of Bradford.

RADAELLI, C. M. 2003. 'The Europeanization of Public Policy'. In K. Featherstone and C. M. Radaelli (eds.), *The Politics of Europeanization*. Oxford: Oxford University Press.

ROMETSCH, D., and WESSELS, W. (eds.) 1996. *The European Union and Member States: Towards Institutional Fusion?* Manchester: Manchester University Press.

SCHMIDT, V. A. 2006. *Democracy in Europe: The EU and National Polities*. Oxford: Oxford University Press.

SMITH, J. 2001. 'Cultural Aspects of Europeanization: The Case of the Scottish Office'. *Public Administration*, 79/1: 147–65.

—— 2006. 'Government in Scotland'. In I. Bache and A. Jordan (eds.), *The Europeanization of British Politics*. Houndmills: Palgrave Macmillan.

SUTHERLAND, P. 2008. 'Fog in Westminster, Europe Cut Off'. *Federal Trust for Education and Research*, European Essay (41).

TAYLOR, P. 2008. *The End of European Integration: Anti-Europeanism Examined*. London: Routledge.

THATCHER, M. 2004. 'Winners and Losers in Europeanization: Reforming the National Regulation of Telecommunications'. *West European Politics*, 27/2: 284–309.

WALLACE, H. 1996. 'Relations between the European Union and the British Administration'. In Y. Meny, P. Muller, and J.-L. Quermonne (eds.), *Adjusting to Europe*. London: Routledge.

—— 1997. 'At Odds with Europe'. *Political Studies*, 45/4: 677–88.

WARD, N., and LOWE, P. 2004. 'Europeanising Rural Development? Implementing the CAP's Second Pillar in England'. *International Planning Studies*, 9: 121–37.

WRIGHT, V. 1996. 'The National Coordination of European Policy-making: Negotiating the Quagmire'. In J. Richardson (ed.), *European Union: Power and Policy-making*. London: Routledge.

CHAPTER 46

GLOBALIZATION

COLIN HAY

THIS chapter provides a critical review of the substantial and growing literature in British politics on globalization. It assesses the extent of the exposure of the British state and economy to the pressures associated with globalization and the appropriateness of the adaptation to such pressures that has increasingly come to characterize domestic policy-making in Britain over the last two decades. Its argument unfolds as follows.

In a short introduction the ubiquity of the appeal to globalization, both in elite political discourse and in contemporary British political analysis, is established. Yet it is demonstrated that this is still a relatively recent phenomenon, associated in particular with the 'modernization' in opposition of the Labour Party and the tenure of the Blair and now Brown administrations in government. Before 1995, the concept of globalization appeared only rarely in British political discourse and, though often assumed as a contextual factor in British political analysis, it was rarely a focus of analytical attention. The diversity of the various senses of the term globalization appealed to in both academic and elite political discourse is demonstrated. This provides the context for a discussion of the semantic confusion that invariably surrounds the term. Whether globalization is an accurate description of the challenges faced by the British state and economy in an age of political and economic interdependence depends, unremarkably, on what globalization is taken to imply. A range of potential definitions are considered and the importance of differentiating clearly between regionalization on the one hand and globalization on the other is established. A relatively exacting definition of globalization is proposed and defended

* I am deeply indebted to David Held, Grahame Thompson, and the other editors of this volume for their characteristically perceptive, incisive, and encouraging comments on an earlier version of this chapter.

and the need to disaggregate the concept—particularly in terms of the scope, scale, 'intensity', and 'extensity' of the flows it entails (Held et al. 1999)—is established.

This provides the conceptual basis from which to move to a rather more empirical treatment of the question of globalization as it impacts on contemporary British politics and political economy. Here the chapter is concerned with three central issues: (i) the extent to which the British state and economy can indeed be said to be exposed, and increasingly exposed, to the (competitive and other) pressures associated with globalization—i.e. the extent of the globalization of the British economy since the 1960s; (ii) the extent to which the reform trajectory of the British state and economy since the 1980s provides a model of the adaptation of an advanced liberal democratic welfare state to the competitive pressures of an ever more integrated global economy; and (iii) the extent to which that reform trajectory rests on a particular understanding of globalization and the nature of the British state and economy's exposure to globalization.

The chapter shows that the characterization of the British economy in terms of globalization is both inaccurate and increasingly so. It argues, moreover, that the reform trajectory on which the British state and economy has embarked is based on assumptions about the extent and nature of the exposure to globalization that are difficult to reconcile with the empirical evidence. Finally, it suggests that, far from providing a model of adaptation to globalization which other advanced liberal democratic regimes might benefit from emulating, such a reform trajectory may well contribute towards the growing vulnerability of an increasingly debt-financed and predominantly service-oriented post-industrial economy on the edge of an expanding European Union.

46.1 THE PUBLIC DISCOURSE OF GLOBALIZATION IN BRITAIN

In no other developed economy has globalization been invoked so frequently and so consistently as a source of constraints and imperatives which domestic policy-makers must negotiate and internalize. Yet, however characteristically Anglo-liberal such a discourse now appears, it is still a relatively recent phenomenon—and one associated very clearly with, first, the modernization, in opposition, of the Labour Party and, subsequently, with its tenure in office as New Labour. Indeed, arguably nothing better defines New Labour than its interpretation and internalization of the constraints on domestic policy-making latitude arising from globalization (Driver and Martell 2003; Hay 1999).

New Labour's new political economy has invariably been presented as a logical correlate of internalizing the lessons of globalization. Appeal has consistently been made to processes beyond the control of political actors which must simply be accommodated—and hence to a logic of economic compulsion which is non-negotiable. In this way, a wholesale rethinking of its political economy was presented, first in opposition and then in government, in almost technical terms as a pragmatic response to the constraints imposed by globalization. Yet whilst this was certainly given a distinctly New Labour inflection in the appeal to the language of globalization, it arguably echoed themes already present in British public discourse—in particular, the DTI's turn to the discourse of competitiveness under the tutelage of Michael Heseltine in the early 1990s. At that time, of course, the concept of globalization was largely unheard of in public discourse. But both the DTI's understanding of competitiveness and New Labour's of globalization were predicated on a highly conserved set of open economy macroeconomic assumptions. From these were derived a common set of general policy commitments—to monetary discipline, to fiscal prudence, and to the elimination of labour-market rigidities and other microeconomic disincentives to innovation and entrepreneurialism. Such a conception of globalization, understood in terms of the challenge to competitiveness that it poses, continues to be extremely influential (see, for instance, HM Treasury 2004; 2005a; 2005b).

This much is already well documented. Yet, less widely acknowledged is that the appeal to globalization as a non-negotiable external economic constraint does not exhaust the public discourse of globalization in Britain today. Indeed, in government, New Labour's appeal to globalization has diversified considerably—as is shown in Table 46.1. This maps the range of potential discourses of globalization, differentiating between them in terms of whether they depict the process as positive or negative (judged by its effects) and in terms of the whether the process is seen to be inevitable or contingent upon political interventions. Those present in contemporary British political discourse are highlighted in bold.

Limits of space prevent a more detailed analysis, but a number of points might be noted:

- New Labour's public discourse of globalization is consistently positive— globalization is, or at least has the capacity to be made, beneficial for all.
- New Labour's appeal to the discourse of globalization is inconsistent.
- In domestic contexts, globalization is invoked as a non-negotiable process necessitating structural reform.
- Yet in international fora it is repeatedly presented as a more contingent and open-ended political project whose (potential) benefits to all need to be secured and more effectively communicated to a sometimes sceptical audience (see also Williams 2005).
- Consequently, the appeal to globalization is depoliticizing domestically yet politicizing in international fora.

It is certainly tempting to attribute this discursive inconsistency in the appeal to the language of globalization to confusion or, more simply, a lack of sustained reflection on the part of those deploying it. Yet that temptation should perhaps be resisted here. For, though inconsistent if taken as a whole, there is in fact a consistent internal

Table 46.1 The public discourse of globalization in Britain

	Globalization as unambiguously positive	Character of globalization contingent upon political choices	Globalization as unambiguously negative
Inevitable/inexorable process (non-negotiable)	1—globalization as a non-negotiable external economic constraint—globalization circumscribes the parameters of political and economic choice (New Labour's domestic political economy)	2—globalization as inevitable but a process whose content is amenable to political influence (no appeal to such a discourse)	3—globalization as threat of homogenization (no appeal to such a discourse)
Contingent process or tendency to which counter-tendencies might be mobilized	4—globalization as a political project which should be defended—globalization as liberalization is potentially beneficial for all (New Labour's foreign economic policy)	5—globalization as a political project which must be made defensible—a socialized globalization is, and must be made, beneficial for all (New Labour's development policy)	6—globalization as a political project which must be resisted (no appeal to such a discourse)

Source: Adapted from Smith and Hay (2008).

pattern in the appeal to globalization exhibited here—with different contexts and policy domains yielding predictably different appeals to the discourse of globalization. Moreover such differences endure changes in office holders (Smith and Hay 2008). This suggests perhaps a rather greater degree of strategic deliberation. This is reinforced by the way in which the appeal to globalization has served to depoliticize domestic reform agendas, thereby disarming opposition, whilst politicizing issues at a transnational level where arguably the responsibilities and capacity of domestic political actors to deliver is rather less. The appeal to globalization, it seems, has served to depoliticize contentious issues domestically whilst drawing attention and rendering more contentious issues beyond the immediate purview of domestic authorities. The success of such a strategy is certainly suggested by Eurobarometer (2003) public opinion survey data. This shows that the British public has one of the lowest levels of recognition of the term 'globalization' (second only to Luxembourg, with only 62 per cent of respondents claiming to have heard of the term). But it also shows that it is one of the most resigned to globalization and one of the most positive in attributing to it benign economic consequences (here second only to Ireland, with 64 per cent of respondents seeing globalization as having positive economic effects).

46.1.1 Elite Political Understandings and Attitudes Towards Globalization

There is, of course, only so much that can be said about elite political understandings of globalization by focusing solely upon *public* discourse—on what Vivien Schmidt terms the 'interactive' or 'communicative' dimension of discourse. Here it is particularly instructive to examine the (albeit limited) attitudinal survey data on elite understandings of globalization—to reveal, in Schmidt's terms, the genuinely 'ideational' dimension of discourse (Schmidt 2001: 249–50).

Summary findings from the only study conducted to date on elite political attitudes towards globalization are shown in Table 46.2. The study took the form of a postal attitudinal survey of parliamentarians and senior civil servants. This sought to solicit responses to a series of closed questions with identical answer formats ('strongly agree', 'agree', 'neither', 'disagree', or 'strongly disagree').[1] Table 46.2 shows net support for each of a series of statements about globalization. Again, limits of space prevent a detailed analysis, but a number of points might nonetheless be made:

- These responses seem, in general, to indicate the prevalence amongst senior civil servants and MPs of all major parties of what, in Table 46.1, was referred to as a type 1 understanding in which globalization is seen as principally economic, non-negotiable, a significant constraint on policy-making autonomy, and benign (see questions 1, 2, 3, 7, 8, 9, 11, 12).
- Such a seeming consensus, however, cannot hide a series of significant—and in some cases quite stark—differences in understandings of globalization between respondents (see questions 4, 6, 10).
- These seem to relate in particular to confidence in the capacity of political institutions to manage globalization effectively, sensitivity to the potential distributional asymmetries arising from globalization, and the consequences of globalization for social policy choices in particular.
- Moreover, these differences seem to divide respondents along pre-existing ideological lines, with Liberal Democrat and Labour MPs more likely to retain confidence in the capacity of political and regulatory processes to deliver solutions to problems of global governance, more likely to associate globalization with distributional asymmetries, and less likely to see welfare retrenchment as an imperative summoned by globalization.
- As this suggests, and perhaps rather ironically, it is the attitudes and understanding of Conservative MPs and, perhaps less remarkably, those of senior civil servants that chime most closely with the public discourse of globalization in Britain.

[1] For further details, see Hay and Smith (2007); Smith and Hay (2008).

Table 46.2 British policy-makers' understandings of, and attitudes towards, globalization

	Net agreement (number of respondents)			
	Civil servants	Conservative MPs	Labour MPs	Lib Dem MPs
1. 'Globalization [is] … the integration of world markets'	+98.2 (165)	+100 (62)	+100 (105)	+100 (24)
2. 'For Britain, the benefits of globalization outweigh the costs'	+75.9 (166)	+79.0 (62)	+57.6 (106)	+72.0 (25)
3. 'Globalization increases economic prosperity in Britain'	+86.7 (166)	+83.9 (62)	+69.8 (106)	+80.0 (25)
4. 'Globalization benefits the poor in Britain'	−1.2 (163)	+47.4 (59)	−17.5 (103)	−12.4 (24)
5. 'Developed countries have a responsibility to ensure that the benefits of globalization are more equally distributed'	+89.2 (166)	+63.2 (60)	+93.3 (105)	+100 (25)
6. 'Globalization can be regulated effectively'	−8.0 (164)	−21.0 (61)	+11.0 (105)	+44.0 (24)
7. 'The anti-globalization movement seeks to reverse the irreversible'	+65.5 (164)	+65 (61)	+56.3 (103)	+65.3 (24)
8. 'Globalization undermines the autonomy of British policy-makers'	+33.6 (164)	+16.1 (62)	+8.6 (105)	+50.1 (24)
9. 'Globalization makes economic competitiveness a precondition for all other policy goals'	+57.2 (164)	+74.2 (62)	+55.6 (106)	−8.0 (25)
10. 'Globalization increases the need for reduced social spending'	−49.3 (164)	+24.6 (61)	−69.0 (103)	−78.3 (23)
11. 'Globalization promotes convergence in labour-market policies'	+70.6 (164)	+75.0 (62)	+66.6 (105)	+75.0 (23)
12. 'Globalization increases the need for public investment in skills'	+27.0 (165)	+73.7 (61)	+91.2 (102)	+95.5 (22)

Notes: Net agreement = % agreeing or strongly agreeing minus those disagreeing or strongly disagreeing with the statement. Number of respondents in parentheses.

These findings are very interesting, and certainly suggest the value of further and more detailed attitudinal-based research on globalization amongst political elites. They also serve to indicate that, understood as it tends to be in the British context as a source of market-conforming imperatives, globalization has a more natural affinity with the traditional ideological and policy preferences of Conservative MPs than it does with those of Labour or Liberal Democrat MPs. The Conservatives may well be the 'natural party' of globalization thus understood.

46.2 GLOBALIZATION AND BRITISH POLITICAL ANALYSIS

As I have sought to show, the concept of globalization is a relatively recent addition to British political discourse. Yet we would be wrong to assume that the concept has had a long prior history in the analysis of British politics. It is a relatively recent addition to the lexicon of British political analysis too. Indeed, it is really only with the growing prevalence of the term in British political discourse that analysts of British politics have turned to the question of globalization in any sustained fashion. Yet if the concept scarcely appeared in the literature on British politics until the mid-1990s, it has since become the single most significant contextualizing factor in the analysis of domestic political dynamics. Policy-making and policy-makers must, it is widely assumed, answer not just to the concerns of domestic constituents and interests but to the imperatives of globalization. Indeed, as we shall see, in much of the literature the two are increasingly counterposed—internalizing the imperatives of globalization may come at some price in terms of the capacity to respond to the preferences of domestic constituencies. A significant aim of this chapter is to assess the claim and the tension between democratic and economic imperatives to which it points with particular reference to the British case.

But in order to do so, we need first to establish what globalization is. And herein lies an initial problem. For the increasing prevalence of the term has certainly not led to greater clarity as to what the concept of globalization entails. Indeed, if anything, it has led to a proliferation of the senses in which the term is used. This is problematic in itself. But such problems are merely compounded by the fact that authors often switch interchangeably between different senses of the term and, even where they invoke the term consistently, rarely consign their understanding of globalization to the page.

In general, understandings of the term can be arrayed along a continuum from the least demanding to the most exacting. Unremarkably, perhaps, those with the least exacting of definitional standards tend to find more evidence of globalization, whilst those with rather more demanding definitional standards tend to be more sceptical as to claims, say, for the globalization of the British economy. As this suggests, it is not just the evidence (and the various interpretations to which it gives rise), but crucially also questions of semantics that divide protagonists in debates over the more or less global character of Britain's economic, political, and cultural interdependence. Even where they agree on what is going on, they may describe that common understanding in terms which are, seemingly, diametrically opposed (compare, for instance, Hirst and Thompson 1999; 2000; and Perraton et al. 1997; or O'Rourke and Williamson 1999; 2002; and Frank and Gills 1993).

For many, then, globalization is merely a synonym for openness—the greater the volume of trade, foreign direct investment, and financial flows and the higher the level of migration between economies the more credible the claim that we have experienced a process of globalization. Yet, for sceptics, this is not enough. For them, openness is not, in and of itself, an indication of globalization; rather, it is a (potential) description of the geographical character that such openness may (or may not) exhibit. In order to be seen as globalized, economies must not only be open but the economic flows to which they give rise must genuinely (or, at least, increasingly) span the globe.[2]

The preceding paragraphs might be seen to imply that, in the end, how we define globalization is a purely semantic choice. And to some extent that is right. However, the point is that it is not an innocent choice and one with significant analytical consequences. Two observations might here be made. First, if we allow any and all evidence of cross-border flows, regardless of their source or destination, to count as evidence of globalization we may lose our analytical purchase on the geographical character and composition of such flows. In particular, we are rather less likely to identify trends in the always uneven patterns of economic interdependence which characterize an economy if we treat any regionalization or 'colonialization' of economic flows as evidence of globalization.[3] The more interested we are in the changing geographical character of Britain's economic interdependence and the specific configurations of opportunities and constraints for domestic policy-makers and businesses with which it may be associated, the less we can afford to treat globalization and openness as synonymous. Second, it is very important that we are consistent in our use of the term globalization—the more so, in fact, the more inexacting the definitional standard we deploy. The point is a simple one. If any evidence of cross-border economic activity is taken as evidence of globalization, then to point to the globalization of an economy is to say precious little in terms of domestic policy-making autonomy, for instance.

---

[2] This is, of course, to look at globalization simply in terms of flows. If we look at globalization, in contrast, in terms of processes of standard setting (as some now do), then globalization may well occur without a proliferation of cross- (or trans-)border flows. For, the extent to which global standards are set (and implemented) is the extent to which no flows are required to deliver common outputs. I am indebted to Grahame Thompson for pointing this out to me.

[3] By regionalization and colonialization in this context I refer simply to the tendency for membership of a regional bloc (whether formally constituted or not) or a colonial bloc (whether extant or historic) to become ever greater predictors of volumes of cross-border flows. The identification of any such tendency or tendencies implies an increasingly uneven geography of economic, political, or cultural interdependence.

Yet if, by globalization, we mean a process by which regional and colonial patterns of integration are (or are in the process of being) dissolved to be replaced by a single world market—with, perhaps, convergence in the prices for which commodities are traded and in interest rate differentials—then the consequences of globalization are of an altogether different order. What we cannot afford to do—as arguably many have done—is to conflate the two. In other words, we must be extremely careful not to take evidence of growing openness as an indication of globalization and then to infer from this identification of globalization the need to adapt domestic economic management to the imperatives we might associate with a perfectly integrated world economy. It is my argument in this chapter that much of the academic analysis of the British political economy and, indeed, much of the public discourse of globalization in Britain has been predicated on precisely such a conflation.

In order to show this, it is important to adopt an empirical approach to the question of Britain's economic interdependence. And it is equally important to be explicit about how that evidence is to be interpreted. That, in turn, entails a clear and consistent definition of globalization. In what follows, then, as in earlier work (Hay 2006; 2007), I define globalization in contrast to terms like regionalization and colonialization (see also Held et al. 1999: 16). If an economy becomes more open by trading an ever-growing share of its GDP, but with only one or two countries, whilst its trade volume with other countries falls then this is not globalization. To count as evidence of globalization, the process under consideration must be genuinely *global*-izing. As deployed here, then, the term globalization is taken to refer to processes which reinforce the tendency for economic and political relations to become more global in character over time. The advantages of such a conception of globalization are that it is precise and that it is easily operationalized empirically. It also serves to focus our analytical attentions on the changing geographical character of the process of economic interdependence. It is to the evidence for globalization, thus understood, and to the geographical character of Britain's economic interdependence that we now turn directly.

46.3 Britain's Economic Interdependence: Globalization or Regionalization?

It is conventional to date globalization from the 1950s or 1960s and to cite, as evidence of globalization, an exponential increase in trade volumes (imports plus exports expressed as shares of GDP) since that time. And if one plots such raw data most leading economies do show an impressive growth in openness. Yet the British case is something of an exception here, as Figure 46.1 suggests.

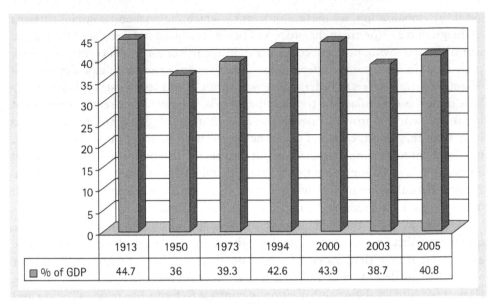

	1913	1950	1973	1994	2000	2003	2005
▩ % of GDP	44.7	36	39.3	42.6	43.9	38.7	40.8

Fig. 46.1 Ratio of merchandise trade to GDP at current prices 1913–2005

Sources: Calculated from Maddison (1987, table A-23); Hirst and Thompson (1999: 27, table 2.3); HM Treasury Pocket Book Data (June 2007 edition).

The openness of the British economy certainly increased between 1950 and 2000, but judged even by contemporary standards Britain was already a very open economy in 1950. Moreover, the ratio of merchandise trade to GDP was in fact lower in 2003 than at any point since 1950. It has since risen, but has yet to return to the level it reached in 2000, far less to its historic peak in 1913. This is a story of cyclical fluctuation around what, in comparative terms, is a high and relatively stable mean (of approximately 40 per cent of GDP); it is certainly not a story of an epochal shift or of *inexorable* pressures leading to *unparalleled* degrees of economic integration. That having been said, Britain is undoubtedly an open and international trading economy. Indeed, when compared to its G7 counterparts, Britain is, in Paul Hirst and Grahame Thompson's memorable terms, 'an over-internationalised economy in an under-globalised world' (2000).

Yet, whilst data like these might lead us to be suspicious of claims of an epochal shift to an era of globalization, they cannot tell us whether the British economy has experienced a process of globalization or not. For that, we need to consider the geographical composition of economic flows. Figure 46.2 is here particularly revealing. It shows the destination of British exports, plotting the ratio of exports bound to the EU to those destined for all other markets.

Since the early 1960s Britain has seen a very significant transformation in its trading relations, with a tripling in the share of its exports to the EU. In 1960, 23 per cent of British exports went to the EU; by 1980 that has risen to 50 per cent; today it stands in excess of 60 per cent. If Britain has indeed experienced an epochal shift since the 1960s in terms of its economic interdependence, it is surely this—a Europeanization

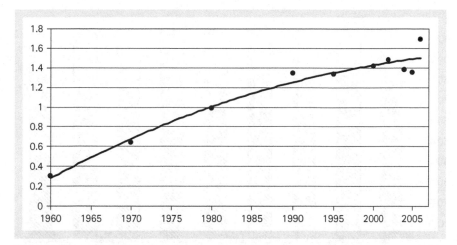

Fig. 46.2 Ratio of British exports to the EU to those to the rest of the world

Source: Calculated from European Commission (1996), *European Economy*; *UK Trade Information Dataset*
(www.ukintrastat.com).

(strictly speaking an EU-ization) of its trading relations, not a globalization (for a similar conclusion using rather different source data, see Overman and Winters 2004). This impression is only reinforced if we look in more detail, as in Figures 46.3a, 46.3b, 46.4a, and 46.4b, at the composition in recent years of British imports and exports in goods and services.

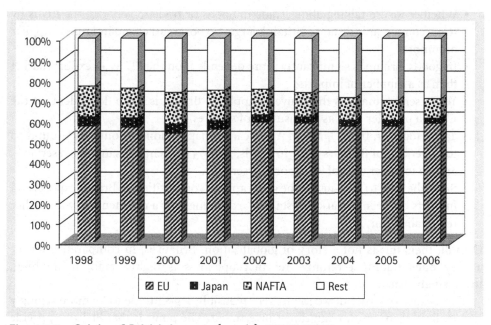

Fig. 46.3a Origin of British imports (goods), 1998–2006

Source: Office of National Statistics' Trade in Goods Data (various years).

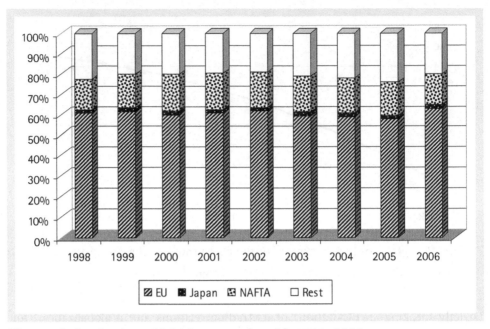

Fig. 46.3b Destination of British exports (goods), 1998–2006

Source: Office of National Statistics' Trade in Goods Data (various years).

A number of interesting points emerge from these data:

- Whether we are talking about trade in goods or trade in services, the EU is by some considerable distance Britain's largest export market and its largest supplier of imports.
- In goods, Britain is significantly more dependent on the EU as an export market than as a supplier of imports.
- Yet in service markets the converse applies—Britain is more dependent on the EU as a provider than as a consumer of services.
- Taken together, the EU, North America, and Japan alone account for around 70 to 75 per cent of Britain's trade in goods, 70 to 75 per cent of its imported services, and 60 to 65 per cent of its exports in services.
- Since the early to mid-1990s, the geographical composition of British exports and imports has been remarkably stable—exhibiting only a mild tendency to further regionalization;

Overall, then, this is not a story of globalization. Britain is, in comparative terms, a very open trading economy. Yet that openness is highly—and, if anything, increasingly—uneven.

This is all very well, but we might very plausibly expect trade to be more strongly regionalized than, say, foreign direct investment. The point is that FDI can provide a substitute for trade over long distances. Rather than import cars directly from South-East Asia why not build an assembly plant in the EU, exporting cars to Britain

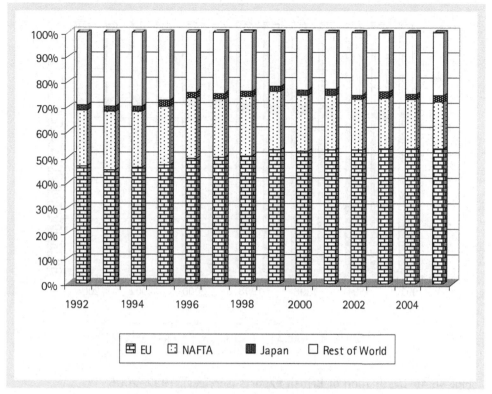

Fig. 46.4a Origin of British imports (services), 1992–2005

Source: Office of National Statistics (2001, 2006).

from that regionally located plant? Transportation costs are reduced, any tariff and non-tariff barriers to entry to the EU market are overcome—and, in the process, interregional foreign direct investment (and the intra-regional trade to which it is likely to give rise) replaces interregional trade. In other words, we are likely to paint a somewhat skewed picture of Britain's economic interdependence if we concentrate solely on trade. So what do the FDI data show? In fact, the geographical distribution of such flows is remarkably similar to that for trade in goods and services, as Figures 46.5a–d demonstrate.

As one might expect, since these figures show annual levels of new investment, they fluctuate far more from year to year than those for trade volumes—in terms of both their volumes and their geographical composition. Yet they show a strong Europeanization of inbound FDI since the mid-1990s and very high proportion of both inbound and outbound FDI coming from and going to the EU, North America, and East Asia.

In terms of trade and foreign direct investment, then, Britain is undoubtedly an open economy. Yet the geographical character of that openness is both highly uneven and, if anything, increasingly so. Since the 1960s a somewhat more global geographical distribution of imports, exports, and FDI, associated with Britain's colonial past,

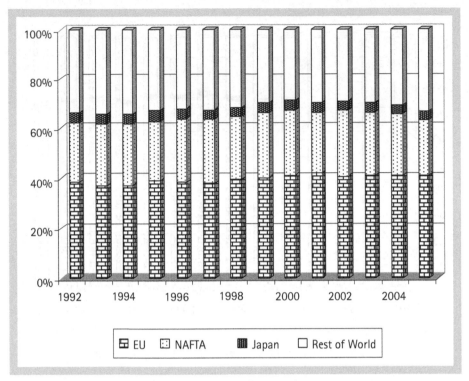

Fig. 46.4b Destination of British exports (services), 1992–2005

Source: Office of National Statistics (2001; 2006).

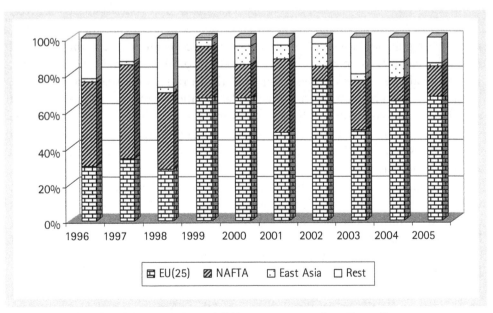

Fig. 46.5a Origin of British inbound FDI, 1996–2005 (% of total)

Source: Office of National Statistics, *Business Monitor*.

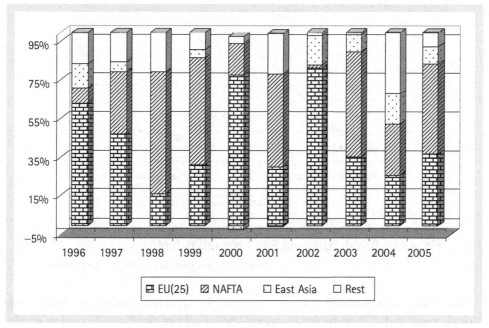

Fig. 46.5b Destination of British outbound FDI, 1996–2005 (% of total)

Source: Office of National Statistics, *Business Monitor.*

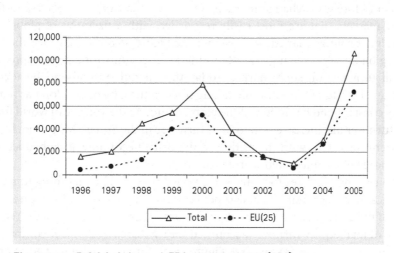

Fig. 46.5c British inbound FDI, 1996–2005 (£M)

Source: Office of National Statistics, *Business Monitor.*

has given way to a far more regionally concentrated economic interdependence. It is this dual process of decolonization and regionalization of trade and FDI, rather than any process of globalization, that represents the most significant transformation of the British economy in recent decades.

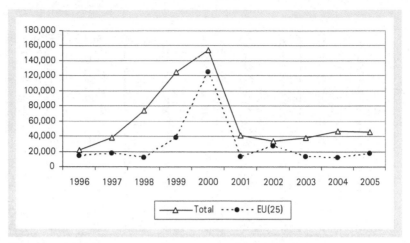

Fig. 46.5d British outbound FDI, 1996–2005 (£M)

Source: Office of National Statistics, *Business Monitor*.

But what about finance? Whatever one might say about the regionalization of British trade and FDI in recent years, the global role of the City of London surely cannot be denied? Up to a point that is certainly true. Yet even here there is need for some caution. It is important here to differentiate between three types of market, each very significant for the British economy—equity markets (the stock market), capital, markets, and foreign exchange markets. Of these, it is capital markets and foreign exchange markets that are most easily reconciled with a narrative of globalization. Take foreign exchange markets for instance. As Figure 46.6 shows, whilst the trading of sterling on foreign exchange (FOREX) markets accounts for a smaller proportion of overall turnover on such markets today than it did throughout the 1990s, the proportion of world FOREX trading taking place in the City of London has remained relatively constant and has followed the global trend. As the volume of world financial market turnover has increased, so too has turnover in the Square Mile. Data like these would seem consistent with the notion of the British economy as embedded within an ever more tightly integrated world economy.

Yet the evidence for the stock market is very different. The first thing to note here is that stock market capitalization (123 per cent of GDP in 2004 and as high as 198 per cent of GDP in 1999) is far greater than for any other leading economy. Yet, whilst the share of total equity turnover accounted for by shares in non-UK companies has risen significantly in recent years (see Figure 46.7), foreign holdings of equity remain low when compared to other leading exchanges (Hirst and Thompson 2000: 346).

Yet there is one respect in which UK market actors are rather more internationalized than their G7 counterparts. The equity and bond portfolios of Britain's institutional investors—pension funds, for instance—are typically far more diverse than those of their US or Euro-Area counterparts. This is shown very clearly in Table 46.3.

But this is a story of internationalization not globalization. As for the trade and FDI data already considered, even where there has been a clear internationalization

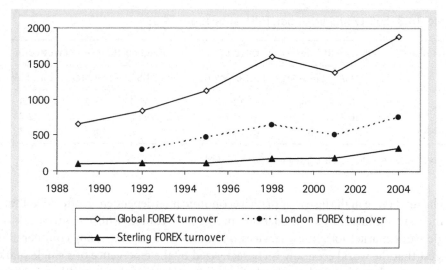

Fig. 46.6 Daily average foreign-exchange turnover, 1988–2004 (billions of $US)

Source: Calculated from BIS (2004); turnover expressed at April 2004 exchange rates.

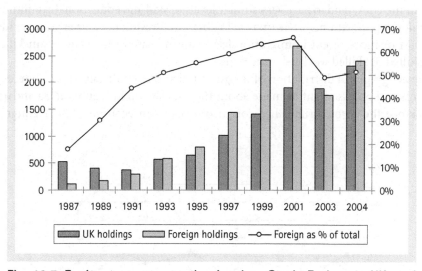

Fig. 46.7 Equity turnover on the London Stock Exchange—UK and foreign holdings, 1987–2004

Source: London Stock Exchange Market Information and Analysis (various years).

of activity (through, for instance, the growth of foreign equity holdings or the diversification of the bond and equity portfolios of institutional investors), this is largely a result of increased economic interdependence with the EU and North America—it is hardly evidence of the emergence of a genuinely global market.

Table 46.3 Equity and bond portfolio allocation, 2003

Portfolio	Equity portfolios—% invested in				Bond portfolios—% invested in			
	UK	USA	Euro-Area	Rest of World	UK	USA	Euro-Area	Rest of World
UK	69.7	8.9	8.1	13.3	59.7	11.0	18.8	10.5
US	2.8	86.2	3.3	7.7	1.2	94.8	1.3	2.7
Euro-Area	3.3	6.6	83.5	6.6	2.1	3.3	88.4	6.2

Source: IMF Coordinated Portfolio Investment Survey (2005).

The final piece in the jigsaw of British economic interdependence, often overlooked in the existing literature, is the labour market. Of course, whilst many speak of a single work market for goods, services, FDI, and finance, few if any commentators suggest that the world economy is characterized by the emergence of a single market for labour. Labour is a far less mobile factor of production than any other. Yet, since 1997 and, in particular, the passing of the Nationality, Immigration, and Asylum Act in 2002, Britain has one of the most open labour markets of the advanced liberal democracies (Hatton 2005). Moreover, despite much populist public rhetoric to the contrary, all the evidence suggests that immigrants into the UK, unlike their counter-parts in the USA, tend to have very similar levels of skill and educational attainment to the resident population. As Dustmann, Fabbri, and Preston note, 'there is no evidence that past or more recent immigration led to an increase of the ratio of unskilled to semiskilled or skilled workers' (2005: 331).

The geographical distribution of migration to and from Britain is very interesting. A number of points might be made about the data shown in Figures 46.8a and 46.8b. First, since the 1970s, Britain has gone from being an economy of net emigration

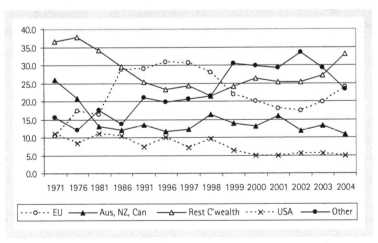

Fig. 46.8a British in-migration, 1971–2004 (% of total)

Source: Office of National Statistics, *Population Trends* (2007).

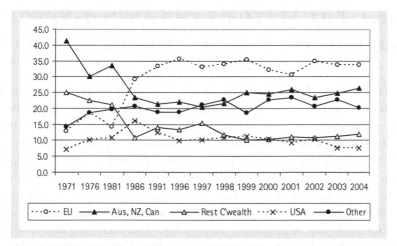

Fig. 46.8b British out-migration, 1971–2004 (% of total)

Source: Office of National Statistics, *Population Trends* (2007).

to one of net immigration (of around 100,000 per annum). During this time there has been a significant rise in the EU as a destination for British emigrants. The EU accounts for close to 35 per cent of all out-migrants from Britain today, three times the proportion in 1970. During this time, total levels of emigration to the Commonwealth have fallen, though those to Australia, New Zealand, and Canada have risen somewhat in recent years. Taken together, emigration to the EU, the Commonwealth, and the USA account for close to 80 per cent of all out-migration from Britain. This compares to some 88 per cent in 1971. Nonetheless, despite some diversification in migration destinations, the key change in the geographical distribution of migration from Britain is a strong Europeanization. Moreover, historic ties to the Commonwealth have proved more enduring in patterns of out-migration than they have in trade and FDI.

The in-migration data by no means directly mirror these trends. Levels of in-migration from the EU have certainly increased since the 1970s, but they have exhibited a more cyclical pattern, linked to successive waves of EU enlargement (Geddes 2003).[4] In Figure 46.8a the EU is the second-most significant source of in-migration, behind the developing Commonwealth economies. Interestingly, these still account for over 30 per cent of all immigration to Britain—a proportion that is rising steeply at present, as immigration from other developing economies is falling. Immigration from the developed Commonwealth economies and the USA has fallen consistently since the 1970s. Taken together immigration from the Commonwealth, the EU, and the USA represents close to three-quarters of all immigration to Britain. This compares to a figure of 84 per cent in 1971. Once again, though, there has been a mild diversification of patterns of in-migration, but no pronounced globalization.

---

[4] Here it is important to note that the data in Figure 46.8a run only to 2004. Since then it is clear that there has been quite a steep rise in both the level and proportion of UK in-migrants from EU member states, linked to the most recent phase of EU enlargement.

46.4 THE MYTH OF THE ANGLO-SAXON MODEL OF ADAPTATION TO GLOBALIZATION

The British economy has been widely touted, not least by the government itself, as a model of—and for—European competitiveness in an era of globalization. Its unquestionably impressive record (until 2008 at least) of steady and uninterrupted growth, stable and low unemployment, and, certainly in comparative historical terms, low inflation is typically attributed to its lean and flexible labour markets, its fiscal and monetary discipline, and, in European terms, its light-touch regulatory environment. It is, in short, widely seen as a model of adaptation to the imperatives of globalization—and one which other more reform-averse European economies can benefit from emulating. Arguably precisely such an understanding of Britain's growth trajectory since the early 1990s underpins much of the Lisbon strategy for EU labour-market and welfare reform.

Yet the evidence presented in this chapter suggests otherwise. There are two elements to this. The first, developed in some detail in the preceding section, challenges this now well-established orthodoxy on the grounds that the British economy cannot be seen as a model of competitive adaptation to the pressures and imperatives of globalization since the British economy has not experienced a process of globalization in recent decades. Britain is, undoubtedly, an open economy. But, as we have seen, there is nothing terribly novel or recent about that. Indeed, as Paul Hirst and Grahame Thompson have documented exhaustively, Britain has since the 1870s (if not before) been the most internationalized of the world's leading economies. And, as they have also shown, its experience since then is one of quantitative continuity, even if it is one of qualitative change (1999; 2000). Britain's early internationalization was a product of its imperial role and is still reflected today in patterns of trade, investment, and migration which are remarkably 'colonial'. Yet, since the 1960s in particular, there has been a pronounced decolonialization of Britain's economic interdependence, paralleled by a yet more pronounced regionalization. As I have sought to show, *it is Europeanization*—whether it be in trade in goods, trade in services, investment, finance, or the labour market—*that is the key driver of Britain's changing patterns of economic interdependence in recent decades, not globalization*. If the British economy can today be judged a competitive success, it is to competitiveness in European markets not in global markets that we should increasingly be looking for the sources of that success.

But this, too, would be to mischaracterize the British economy. This brings me to the second element of my critique of the familiar idea of Britain as a model of adaptation to globalization. This is concerned less with globalization per se than it is with the characterization of the British economy as a model of competitiveness. The point is a relatively simple one. That the British economy has performed well in recent years in terms of the headline indices of growth, unemployment, and inflation does not mean that it has done so *because* it has proved increasingly competitive in global

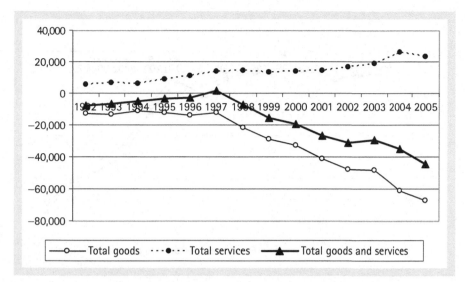

Fig. 46.9 Britain's balance of trade in goods and services, 1992–2005 (£M, constant prices)

Source: Calculated from Office of National Statistics (2001; 2006).

(or even European) terms, far less that the model of labour-market flexibilization that it has embraced is the source of that competitive advantage. Here, as elsewhere, the evidence is illuminating.

Consider, first, Britain's balance of trade statistics, as shown in Figure 46.9.

Though far less the focus of attention today than they were in the 1970s, these make exceptionally depressing reading and are very difficult to reconcile with the image of a modern, dynamic, lean and mean competitive economy which might serve as a model to be emulated (see also O'Mahoney and de Boer 2002). Arguably more alarming still are the data contained in Figure 46.10. These show Britain's balance of trade position in trade and services with the EU. Given the pronounced Europeanization of Britain's economic interdependence in recent years, it is particularly worrying that the British economy has a growing trade deficit with the EU in both goods and services. Indeed, this suggests that any competitive advantage that Britain may have enjoyed in service markets with the EU has now been significantly eroded.

A no less depressing picture is painted if we turn from trade to foreign direct investment. As is more widely noted, though Britain attracts a substantial amount of European inward-bound FDI, it has long been a net exporter of FDI. Thus, as Paul Hirst and Grahame Thompson again note, 'despite all the official rhetoric about the UK being the best home for FDI in Europe, because of its basic competitive advantages, in fact there has been a consistent hollowing out of UK domestic investment as better opportunities for competitive success seem to have presented themselves abroad' (2000: 342–3). Moreover, with approximately one-quarter of all British manufacturing employment (and a rather higher proportion of wages and

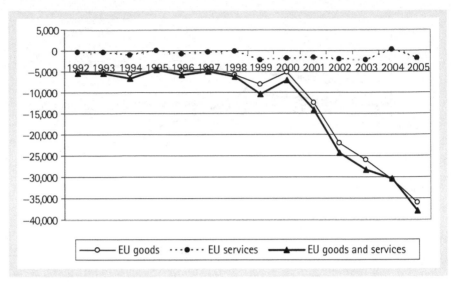

Fig. 46.10 Britain's balance of trade in goods and services with the EU, 1992–2005 (£M, constant prices)

Source: Calculated from Office of National Statistics (2001;2006).

output) arising from foreign investment, the British economy is extremely vulnerable to external shocks and the vagaries of international investors. Somewhat ironically, this is merely compounded by the highly flexible character of the British labour market when contrasted to that of other European economies. For, as and when excess capacity emerges in the European economy (regardless of levels of demand in Britain), it is far simpler to make cutbacks in Britain. Labour-market flexibilization is, as this suggests, a powerfully pro-cyclical policy instrument; whilst it may well be beneficial when demand is high, it predisposes an open economy like Britain's to labour shedding when demand falls (Hay 2004).

If Britain is rather less the model of export-led competitiveness in an era of globalization than is often depicted, then to what can we attribute its indisputably good aggregate economic performance since the mid-1990s? And, more to the point, how stable is this likely to prove? Again, the evidence is not particularly encouraging.

Since 1992 Britain's good headline economic performance has been driven to a significant extent by consumer demand (Watson 2003). This, in turn, has been funded out of unprecedented levels of personal debt and the release of equity arising from sustained house-price inflation. Indeed, house prices have been rising at, on average, 12 per cent per annum since 1997 (Council of Mortgage Lenders 2005). At present the average home increases in value by well over £20,000 per annum. This compares to average wages of around £30,000 per annum. Given these figures it is not difficult to see how dependent Britain's long-standing debt-financed consumer boom has become on sustained house price inflation—and the release of equity to fuel consumption that this has allowed. But there are limits to house price inflation and hence to the sustainability of this new, if unannounced and presumably inadvertent, growth model.

Indeed, at the time of writing, inflation is now once again a concern, interest rates are rising, and house prices are somewhat less predictable than they were. What is more, the anxiety engendered by this sense of fragility is, arguably, now beginning to interfere with the Bank of England's ability to control inflation and with consumer confidence. The Bank's Monetary Policy Committee seems today increasingly nervous to use interest rate hikes to bring down inflation for the fear of puncturing an unstable house-price bubble and, with it, the consumer boom it has sustained almost uninterrupted since 1992.

46.5 CONCLUSION

If we piece together the jigsaw that I have sought to assemble in the preceding sections, a very different picture of the British economy emerges to that with which we are familiar. Britain is, most definitely, a dynamic and open economy whose headline economic performance in recent years has been both impressive and sustained. But it is not a model of adaptation to globalization. For, as I have sought to show, its economy has simply not experienced a process of globalization by any but the least exacting of definitional standards. Moreover, and more worryingly perhaps, its good economic performance in recent years owes far less to competitive success in the markets (largely European and North American) in which it is most exposed than is invariably assumed. The determinants of Britain's growth trajectory are rather more peculiarly domestic and rather more fragile than this would imply—and they have tended to mask a continuing deterioration in its trade balance with the rest of the world. British growth is not the product of competitiveness but has been achieved largely despite a lack of competitiveness. That growth has been fuelled by an increasingly unsustainable consumer boom predicated on an ever more precarious asset-price bubble. Despite the rhetoric, Britain is, in short, no model of adaptation to globalization.

REFERENCES

BANK FOR INTERNATIONAL SETTLEMENTS 2004. *Triennial Central Bank Survey of Foreign Exchange and Derivatives Market Activity in April 2004.* Monetary and Economic Department, BIS.

COUNCIL OF MORTGAGE LENDERS 2005. *UK Housing Review 2004/2005.* London: Council of Mortgage Lenders.

DRIVER, S., and MARTELL, L. 2003. *The Labour Party: Continuity and Change in the Making of New Labour.* Basingstoke: Palgrave.

DUSTMANN, C., FABBRI, F., and PRESTON, I. 2005. 'The Impact of Immigration on the British Labour Market'. *Economic Journal*, 115: 324–41.

EUROBAROMETER 2003. *Flash Eurobarometer 151b: Globalisation*. Brussels: European Commission.

FRANK, A. G., and GILLS, B. (eds.) 1993. *The World System: Five Hundred Years or Five Thousand Years?* London: Routledge.

GEDDES, A. 2003. *The Politics of Migration and Immigration in Europe*. London: Sage.

HATTON, T. J. 2005. 'Explaining Trends in UK Immigration'. *Journal of Population Economics*, 18: 719–40.

HAY, C. 1999. *The Political Economy of New Labour*. Manchester: Manchester University Press.

—— 2004. 'Credibility, Competitiveness and the Business Cycle in New Labour's Political Economy'. *New Political Economy*, 9/1: 39–56.

—— 2006. 'What's Globalisation Got To Do With It? Economic Interdependence and the Future of European Welfare States'. *Government and Opposition*, 41/1: 1–23.

—— 2007. *Why We Hate Politics*. Cambridge: Polity.

—— and SMITH, N. J. 2007. 'Les Européens face à la mondialisation: recherché comportmentale sur les perceptions de l'élite politique et du grand public quant à la mondialisation au Royaume Uni'. In E. Fabry (ed.) *Les Européens face à la mondialisation: sondage international analyses qualitatives comparées*. Paris: Fondation pour l'Innovation Politique.

HELD, D., McGREW, A., GOLDBLATT, D., and PERRATON, J. 1999. *Global Transformations: Politics, Economics and Culture*. Cambridge: Polity.

HIRST, P., and THOMPSON, G. 1999. *Globalisation in Question*, 2nd edn. Cambridge: Polity.

—— —— 2000. 'Globalisation in One Country? The Peculiarities of the British'. *Economy and Society*, 29/3: 335–56.

HM TREASURY 2004. *Long-Term Global Economic Challenges and Opportunities for the UK*. London: HM Treasury.

—— 2005a. *Global Europe: Full Employment Europe*. London: HM Treasury.

—— 2005b. *Responding to Global Economic Challenges: The UK and China*. London: HM Treasury.

OFFICE OF NATIONAL STATISTICS 2001. *UK Balance of Payments: The Pink Book*. London: HM Stationery Office

—— 2006. *UK Balance of Payments: The Pink Book*. London: HM Stationery Office.

O'MAHONEY, M., and DE BOER, W. 2002. 'Britain's Relative Productivity Performance: Has Anything Changed?' *National Institute Economic Review*, 179: 38–43.

O'ROURKE, K. H., and WILLIAMSON, J. G. 1999. *Globalisation and History*. Cambridge, Mass.: MIT Press.

—— —— 2002. 'When Did Globalisation Begin?' *European Review of Economic History*, 6/1: 23–50.

OVERMAN, H. G., and WINTERS, L. A. 2004. 'The Geography of UK International Trade'. CEPR Discussion Paper No. 4529.

PERRATON, J., GOLDBLATT, D., HELD, D., and McGREW, A. 1997. 'The Globalisation of Economic Activity'. *New Political Economy*, 2/2: 257–78.

SCHMIDT, V. A. 2001. 'The Politics of Economic Adjustment in France and Britain: When Does Discourse Matter?' *Journal of European Public Policy*, 8/2: 247–64.

SMITH, N. J., and HAY, C. 2008. 'Mapping the Political Discourse of Globalisation and European Integration in the UK and Ireland Empirically'. *European Journal of Political Research*, 47/3: 359–82.

WATSON, M. 2003. 'The Politics of Inflation Management'. *Political Quarterly*, 74/3: 285–97.

WILLIAMS, P. 2005. *British Foreign Policy under New Labour, 1997–2005*. Basingstoke: Palgrave.

CHAPTER 47

··

MARKETIZATION

··

COLIN CROUCH

MARKETIZATION implies offering a good or service for sale, and therefore allocating a price to it that can in principle be compared with the prices of all other goods and services. The quantity and quality of it that is traded will depend on the intersection between the price at which the producer wants to offer it for sale and the price that consumers are willing to pay for it. In the context of contemporary British politics, marketization refers specifically to the process of taking goods and services that had previously been provided under bureaucratic, political, or professional means of resource allocation and transferring them to market arrangements.

The concept does not necessarily imply private ownership of the means of production; it is possible for services to remain in public ownership, and even to remain delivered by public agencies, but for consumers to obtain them through purchase. The quality and quantity of their provision can then be governed by consideration of the prices that consumers are prepared to pay. Alternatively, marketization can be a process carried on within an organization, whether in the public or the private sector; the markets that develop in such cases are known as 'internal' markets (Le Grand, Mays, and Mulligan 1998; OECD 1995; Osterman 1984; Rugman 1981). Organizations of all kinds have a choice as to how they allocate resources among their different departments. There may be a system of decisions by the organization's leadership, based on certain principles and desired outcomes, often preceded by a process of bargaining with the departments; or the leadership may permit market forces to determine how these resources flow. Often there is a combination of the two, with market forces operating only after the leadership has fixed certain parameters, such as prices. (For a more detailed discussion of these different approaches to intra-organizational resource allocation, see Williamson 1975). Frequently the marketization that has taken place in British public services refers to these internal markets.

Marketization must therefore be distinguished from privatization, which refers to selling or otherwise handing to private owners the assets of a formerly public service. This, in turn, might or might not imply marketization; a public service can be sold to a private monopoly, with ultimate consumers having little or no ability to affect the provision through their market behaviour. (This is the case with the privatization of the water industry in the UK.) Discussion of marketization needs to pay careful attention to these differences.

The idea that many public services would be improved by being marketized—and possibly also privatized—entered British politics through the wave of changes that accompanied the shift from a Keynesian to a neoliberal political economy in the mid-1970s. The general circumstances and character of that change are described elsewhere in this *Handbook*. Central to the neoliberal account was a strong criticism of the role of public services. The following can be seen as the main limbs of the critique, and of the associated new policies then advocated. Table 47.1 summarizes the perceived failures, the preferred marketization remedies, and problems occurring with those. This discussion has by no means been confined to the United Kingdom. However, since our focus here is on British politics, exclusively British examples will be used; also, the general wave of marketization around the world was in many ways pioneered in this country.

47.1 TACKLING PERCEIVED UNRESPONSIVENESS TO USERS

Because they respond primarily to a governmental and political agenda, public services are often considered to become unresponsive to users' actual preferences. They are said to be dominated by producer interests, as government policy-making is made by the officials and professionals who deliver the services; these provide what they like providing and are equipped to provide, not necessarily what consumers want. This is also a remote, centralized process—at least within the British political context where local government is weak and most power lies with the central ministries.

Arguments of these kinds flourished in the 1970s. Expansions of public services under the Labour government 1974–9 seemed to many to have been associated with increasing union militancy among public-sector workers, including some spectacular strikes. Public employees tend to be more strongly unionized than private ones, because public employers in a democracy cannot refuse the right of workers to organize themselves. Also, public provision is usually monopoly provision, imparting particular power to producers. This became particularly salient during that decade, when high inflation was leading different groups in society to reach for whatever means they could of protecting themselves.

Table 47.1 Marketization strategies in response to public service failures, and newly emerging problems

Public service failure	Marketization response	Limits to marketization
47.1. Unresponsive to consumers; dominated by producer interests; centralized and remote	47.1.1. Privatization, with regulation where competition remains imperfect	Scope for extensive marketization often limited by technical, etc. features, with little reduction in need for public action via regulation
	47.1.2. Market-making within public service, with direct consumer choice guided by performance data	Market failure problems of information inadequacy, resolved by top-down control of performance data
	47.1.3. Private providers compete with public ones, but within publicly funded system	Limited use of price mechanism
47.2. Unwanted services; inadequate cost effectiveness; high taxes	47.2.1. Internal markets	Limited use of price mechanism
	47.2.2. Private subcontracting	Central authorities control pricing
		Small numbers of contractors; loss of responsibility through contract chain; long contracts inhibit use of markets; development of 'insider' firms
47.3. Public service out of touch with business	47.3.1. Encouragement of intensive interaction with, and learning from, private sector	Development of insider firms, return to market failure of inadequate barriers between polity and economy
	47.3.2. Adoption of business criteria in government practice	Limits to and inappropriateness of pure markets in public service
	47.3.3. Public–private financing partnerships	Doubts over financial advantages to public sector

More generally, the neoliberal critique considered that virtually all economic activity would be more effectively conducted within profit-maximizing firms with clear incentives to satisfy their customers rather than provide quiet lives for producers, as neoliberals believed to be the case in public service organizations.

To these problems, the public service reform strategy offered a number of responses.

47.1.1 Privatization with or without Marketization

This involves selling the service to a number of competing private owners, who will then operate in the market, in principle bringing consumer sovereignty to the service in question. Privatization of the provision of manufactured goods and public utilities has today become an international orthodoxy, but it was originally highly controversial. Particularly after the 1930s, when the general protectionist wave provoked by the slump led to a major growth of monopolies which abused their position, parties from all parts of the political spectrum had come to believe that certain goods and services, particularly those that seemed to be 'natural' or inevitable monopolies or somehow 'essential' public services, should be in public rather than private hands. US economic theory had started to provide a new rationale for private monopoly under certain circumstances in the 1970s (Bork 1978; Posner 2001). But it was in the UK that the first major experiments in privatization were conducted. The reason for British primacy may be found partly in the arguments about British union militancy noted above. Also relevant was the fact that, during the 1980s, the British Labour Party, which was at that time the primary guardian of the public ownership project, had become virtually unelectable in national elections. It was torn by internal conflict and had actually split, as described elsewhere in this *Handbook*. The Conservatives were therefore left more free to pursue a strong radical agenda than had normally been the case for post-war governments, or governments in most other advanced democracies at that time.

A final important factor was that privatization was a means whereby governments could attract private finance into the funding of major capital projects, instead of relying on taxation or public debt. This was occurring at a time when it was believed that taxation rates, especially on higher incomes, needed to be reduced, and when counter-inflation strategy was considered to require a tight rein on public debt.

In practice, it was rarely possible to create pure markets for the privatized industries, problems of oligopoly and limited opportunities for competition usually having been important reasons why these activities ended up in the public domain in the first place. An exception was telecommunications, where technological change had expanded enormously the means of transmission of signals, making possible competition where there had before been very restricted provision possibilities. Other public utilities are major examples of where competition remained restricted even after privatization by the Conservative governments of the 1980s and 1990s. In many areas it became possible to have more than one supplier of gas or electricity, but usually only a small number. It did not prove possible to provide for alternative water suppliers drawing from the same reservoirs, and the privatization of water has (as already noted) not been a process of marketization, but of licensing private monopolies.

Privatization of railway track provision and maintenance by the Conservatives in 1994 was also an example of passing a service to a non-market monopoly. This proved unsatisfactory, partly for reasons of rail safety, and the track was then, in 2002, placed by the Labour government into an unusual form of ownership, designed to avoid giving the appearance of renationalization while also avoiding the market failures of a monopoly. An organization called Network Rail was created, which calls itself a private company acting on a commercial basis. But it was established by government, has no shareholders, and reinvests all its profit into the rail network. Its board comprises 'members' appointed from the rail industry and from users. It is subject to a regulatory agency, the Office of Rail Regulation (ORR), and it is underwritten by the government. Provision of rail *services* remains privatized. In some cases there is not enough trade on a particular service to allow for anything other than monopoly; on popular lines there may be limited competition, with two or possibly three providers.

In virtually all cases the weakness of marketization in these privatizations has been recognized by successive governments through the establishment of public regulation of the service concerned: such agencies as ORR for the railways, Ofcom for the telecommunications industry, or Ofwat for water. Regulation is a classic 'old' public service response to market failure, but modern regulatory procedures are based on sophisticated economic modelling, trying to reproduce what a true market would have produced had it existed rather than on the implementation of bureaucratic rules. Privatization is therefore typically not a case of 'back to the market', but an attempt at providing a new compromise between markets and regulation, with private ownership and a form of regulation based on market principles, but a continuing strong role for government agencies.

One result of this has been that controversies arising in these industries continue to be highly political. At the time of railway privatization the then Prime Minister, John Major, had offered as one of the benefits the fact that rail travel would cease to be a political issue. His prediction has been falsified by subsequent history. Where markets are highly imperfect, the service concerned important to daily life, and regulation continues to be required, the public continues to see government as involved somewhere in the service.

47.1.2 Market-making within Public Service, with Direct Consumer Choice Guided by Performance Data

Initially the privatization programme was seen as stopping at manufacturing industries, utilities, and some of the smaller welfare services that did not attract political attention—particularly homes for the elderly. Conservative governments were far more wary about touching the core of the health and education services, though they also took steps to encourage small extensions of the private sector (for example, the establishment of grant-maintained schools, and fiscal encouragement of private pensions). They mainly experimented with enabling customer choice via marketization within public services, but it was principally the Labour government elected in 1997 that took the customer choice agenda forward, and which also took bolder steps to include outright privatization within this strategy.

Historically this has been a shift of major proportions for the Labour Party, which, like all socialist and social democratic parties, has been rooted in suspicion of the private sector where basic public services are concerned. There have been three aspects to this suspicion. First, there was an early general hostility towards profit-making capitalist enterprise as such. In reality, by the 1960s this had become mainly limited to hostility to private monopolies, but basic public services were seen as completely inappropriate to the profit motive. Second, the party was historically concerned to ensure that, where important services were concerned, there should be near-equality in access. This meant exclusion of the price mechanism at the point of purchase, which seemed at that time to have excluded the role of the market. Finally, socialist and social democratic parties, historically representing sections of the population who are not major owners of private property, have had a concern to see resources publicly owned and available, and are particularly sensitive to ways in which markets cannot take account of externalities.

Labour's change of position can be explained by three factors, all of which are involved in the 1990s shift to 'New Labour'. First, the decline in the size of the Labour Party's old voting bloc of manual workers left it bereft of one of its main population bases. Its second and more recent bloc, public service workers, were deeply attached to the maintenance of existing public service approaches, but the party leadership had come to see them as a liability, tying the party to a 'tax and spend' image and associated with the problems of the 1970s mentioned above. Disenchanted with both of its sets of core voters, Labour was in search of new sections of the electorate, those in the past who had been 'natural' Conservative voters. Imposing reforms on public services, even—or indeed especially—if they were unpopular with those working in the sector, could help Labour's image with these other voters.

Second, far more than the Conservatives, Labour was strongly committed to improving the quality of public service delivery. Here the party had not at all changed from its earlier position as the principal political guardian of health, education, and social care services. This had in fact become the main political dividing line between the two parties. It was partly a question of Labour being more willing to spend money on the services, but there were limits to the extent that this could be done. The party therefore sought new ideas, which led it to emphasize consumer choice and the development of new (private) providers.

Third, Labour, like the Conservatives, interpreted inadequacies of public services as being the fault of the staff working in them, in particular professionals. The Conservatives had regarded schoolteachers as a 'guilty' profession, believing that left-wing teachers had dragged down educational standards. Labour extended the suspicion to medical practitioners, but for different reasons. It here leaned on an element in its own past traditions that mistrusted professional elites who were seen as having contempt for their clients. According to a leading social policy expert who became the Labour Prime Minister's health policy adviser, the old model of the professions required the public to believe that all practitioners were 'knights' who could be trusted to work to the best of their abilities because of their professional commitment (Le Grand 2003). But, argued Le Grand, few people were thoroughgoing knights. It was better to err on the side of caution and treat everyone as potential 'knaves', who would behave well only when given a financial market incentive to do so. Acceptance of this idea necessitated establishing market relationships between providers and their customers wherever possible, replacing reliance on professional ethics.

This all led to a customer choice agenda. Many (both Conservative and Labour) marketization initiatives do not actually give much choice to consumers; government typically place contracts for the monopoly provision of a service with private providers, consumers using them just as they had used traditional monopoly public services: the 'customer' in the market here is the government, not the ultimate users. Eventually however the Labour government began to use customer choice as a means of securing service improvement, particularly in health and education. If users could choose from among a range of providers, and if budget allocations followed their choices, weak providers would have a strong incentive to improve their services, or close down. Under the School Standards and Framework Act 1998, parents were given a range of schools from which they could choose to send their children; and under the National Health Service Act 2006 patients had to be offered a choice of hospitals for medical treatments. To guide their choices government required service providers to publish details of selected aspects of their performance (for example, examination success rates for schools; success rates for surgery for hospitals). The objective was to give providers an incentive to raise their achievement levels on these indicators, their budgets being dependent on their ability to attract customers.

The degree of marketization here remains limited. Services are still provided free or at nominal charges at the point of use, so there are no actual prices to adjust demand and supply. Government or local government, not the market, decides at what point demand for a particular school or health centre has dropped so low that the facility should be closed. The continuing importance of the typical market failures of poor information flow and difficulty of introducing true pricing for 'vital' services has continued to inhibit a stronger reliance on market forces. A public policy elite continues, through the indicators it chooses to publicize, to shape what users 'ought' to regard as important information on which to base choices; but it is now much more a political elite, not a professional one.

47.1.3 Private Providers Compete with Public, but within Publicly Funded System

The second model can be restricted to competition among public providers (as in choice of schools and hospitals among those provided by a public authority.) In a more radical version of this approach, private providers have been invited to compete with existing public ones. This introduction of an element of privatization may bring new capital to the disposal of the public service in question, and may also bring new ideas for delivery of the service.

Again, the Labour government has been associated with the most radical steps. By the early twenty-first century the party had abandoned all belief that some services required public provision. This belief had been based on the assumption that there was such a thing as a public service professional ethic that constituted a motive for the provision of such things as health care superior to the maximization of profits. Acceptance of the Le Grand doctrine that it was better to suspect people of being knaves rather than trust them to be knights led necessarily to preference for the profit motive over any so-called ethical conduct. In fact, the government logically began to favour private providers: markets could only be made in policy fields where they had not previously existed if firms could be encouraged to enter them. Local education authorities were permitted to bid to build new schools only if no private contractors wanted to do so. In 2008 the government embarked on a programme to encourage the merging of general practitioner and related health services into large 'polyclinics'. This is the form of health provision favoured by the US health-service firms who were wanting to enter the British market.

The Labour government did hold fast to its core belief that services should be free (or subject to nominal cost) at the point of receipt. In marketized public services (whether provided by public authorities or by private firms) users choose, and providers receive income as a result of their choice, but this is paid by government not by the user. This limits the extent to which users rather than government are the true 'customers'. There is also a problem that the universal service required by public health and education policy is not immediately attractive to private providers. An important element of firm strategy in the true market consists in finding niches: in the market it is not only customers who choose providers, but providers who choose customers too. Firms often need inducements in terms of generous and lengthy contract terms if they are to manage without this important component of entrepreneurship. On the other hand, lengthy contracts to provide services, demand for which is completely guaranteed by government, are highly attractive to firms. At a time when markets in general are becoming increasingly competitive on a global basis, public contracts have major advantages. This also explains the strong pressure being exerted by representatives of private business on governments and international organizations to encourage privatization of public services.

47.2 TACKLING PERCEIVED UNWANTED SERVICES

The marketization moves discussed above all assume that the public wants the services in question, but seeks more choice and better quality. Some other arguments for marketization are almost the reverse of this. It is argued that, because they are funded by taxation and decided by producer interests, public services are provided in 'excess'. If, rather than being compulsorily taxed in order to fund services, people had the ability to choose how much they personally spent on, say, fire services, they might spend less on these than taxation requires them to do. A more consumer-oriented system might therefore be associated, not so much with better public services, as with fewer of them. These arguments are difficult to make politically, but the growth of many new forms of spending by left-wing Labour councils in the 1970s and 1980s on services that could not easily be called 'essential' enabled Conservative governments of the 1980s and 1990s to venture some of these arguments. They eventually reduced the level of public service provision to an extent that became unpopular and was instrumental in their eventual fall in 1997. The ensuing Labour governments continued to enjoy political reward for increasing public spending and service provision, at least until around 2008, and in opposition the Conservatives began to accept that line.

However, even if criticism of unwanted services is not as popular as it once seemed, there are still concerns that there are inadequate pressures on public services to provide value for money, and people would still prefer to pay lower taxes. The most obvious way to square this circle is to improve efficiency. Government has recently tended to believe that the best ideas for doing this are likely to be found in the private sector, which is more immediately exposed to competitive pressure on costs. Marketization lies behind responses to this agenda in a number of ways.

47.2.1 Internal Markets

Most important is the use of internal markets, a resource allocation option open to organizations of all kinds, private and public, as mentioned above. It is easy to confuse this with the idea of offering market choices to consumers within a public service. The two can certainly be combined, but while the latter is targeted at the issue of consumer choice, the internal market per se is more focused on managerial concerns over efficiency, and may have no reference to the consumer. The internal market is a means of ensuring that departments within an organization relate to each other as though they were all separate firms in the real market, and not colleagues within the same organization. These markets may or may not be 'true' in that central authorities can 'rig' the notional prices used within them, which are not necessarily tested against external markets.

In practice, neither Conservative nor subsequent Labour governments relied on marketization alone to achieve the goal of efficient resource utilization, but on a more traditional approach to improving public service efficiency: calling in experts— though the role of the experts was now to introduce private-sector practices into government. The Conservative government used the services of the chief executive of Marks & Spencer, Derek (later Lord) Rayner, unleashing a round of changes in working practices. The Labour government appointed Sir Peter Gershon, who established savings targets for each department and agency. Nevertheless, the internal market has been used too.

The first objective of the internal market is to make managers think hard about whether they really need to use a service, by charging them for it. It can be, and is, also used as a preparation for privatization. Some of these supply units, especially if they might find work with more than one customer organization, might well be sold off to a private firm.

A major example has concerned changes imparted to the role of schools in general and headteachers in particular by the Education Act 1986. This removed from the teaching profession to central government agencies responsibility for the curriculum, but gave to headteachers and school governors greater responsibility for financial and managerial decisions. There was therefore a shift away from the role of professional autonomy and a move to managerial autonomy. At the same time, salary scales of teachers were elongated so that the salaries of headteachers and other senior teaching staff moved away from those of their non-managerial colleagues. These moves were not directly related to marketization as such, but they were part of a move from professional to managerial forms of leadership. By giving individual schools a deal of financial autonomy they were encouraged to think more seriously about the relationship between income and expenditure. In the National Health Service (NHS) there was a more explicit move to marketization with the development of internal markets (Le Grand, Mays, and Mulligan 1998). Again, this marked a shift from a professional to a managerial form of decision-making. Whereas in the past different units in the chain of patient treatment (e.g. from general practitioner to hospital specialist) had related to each other as professional colleagues, with links based on locality and personal acquaintance, they would now do so as purchasers and providers. Primary health care units would have notional budgets with which they would purchase services from service providers further up the supply chain. This is therefore another example of partial marketization, with central authority able to decide how far it will use the market, and how far it wants to continue to assert its own priorities.

In opposition in the 1990s the Labour Party had opposed the introduction of the internal market into the NHS, claiming that it would distort professional clinical judgement in favour of financial criteria in judgements about patient care. When in office however it renamed the exercise but maintained its essential features. The Labour government did however also establish a range of expert services, such as the National Institute for Clinical Excellence, to advise medical decision-makers on how to reconcile clinical and financial assessments.

47.2.2 Private Subcontracting

Just as private providers can be invited to compete with public ones in order to increase consumer choice, so too can private firms be used by public service managers to try to find cheaper provision than is available within public service itself. This is something that happens within the private sector, as managers contract out various activities to supplier firms able to operate more cheaply than the contracting firm itself. Normally an important determinant of whether to do this will be which services are so central to the core business of the firm and its reputation that it must handle them itself, and which are sufficiently marginal for cost to be the principal consideration. Indeed, one can sometimes assess what a firm regards as its core business by seeing what it does not contract out.

For private firms the biggest savings are to be found when activities can be contracted to suppliers in second- or third-world countries with low labour costs. UK government has not yet started to do this, though in principle such services as vehicle registration or the administration of the state pensions system could be carried out more cheaply by subcontracting them to firms in India. Until now, government has preferred to reserve such activities for providing employment in depressed areas of the UK, a matter which is important to political success and therefore itself 'core business'. But within the UK, government has been eager to encourage private firms to contract for public service delivery. By the nature of much public service work, the contracts involved often have to be for several years: it is not feasible to change the identity of a firm running a city's schools every year, though this is more possible for contracts to police local car-parking schemes. Contracts involving capital expenditure may need to last twenty or so years to be attractive to contractors.

This is therefore another limited, compromised form of marketization. The contracting authority itself loses its chance to exercise a customer's power for the duration of the contract, and there is not necessarily any element of market choice to be exercised by the ultimate consumer. The subcontractor's customer is the public authority placing the contract. The subcontractor has no relationship to the users, while, as Freedland (2001) has argued, the public also loses its 'citizenship' relationship to the public authority where provision of the service is concerned. In some cases, where a lengthy chain of sub- and sub-subcontractors develops, any responsiveness to the user becomes a matter for lawyers for the various corporate partners to the contracts. This became a major issue in the early 2000s, when government wanted to apportion responsibility for a series of railway accidents, the matter becoming confused by the terms of contracts between Railtrack and the firms to whom it had subcontracted repair and maintenance work. This was one of the reasons why government transferred the provision and maintenance of railway track from a private firm to the unusually structured Network Rail discussed above.

The length of some contracts also weakens the strength of the market mechanism, displacing the relationship to one of negotiation of the contract rather than providing the subsequent service. One consequence of this has been the emergence of a group of firms who have expanded their businesses to cover a wide range of public services. For example, firms that started as road-building contractors (where customers are almost entirely public authorities) have become providers of administrative support services to local government. The core business of these enterprises is winning government contracts, almost irrespective of the substantive activities involved. Such firms achieve this position not just by learning how to complete contract forms correctly, but by developing close relationships with government officials and politicians at national and local levels, which brings us to some issues raised in the next section.

47.3 Tackling Perceived Remoteness from Private Sector

In classic British (and many other) public service traditions, it was necessary to maintain an arm's-length relationship between public officials and private firms. This was designed partly to protect markets from political or administrative distortions through interventions designed to help 'friendly' firms, and at the extreme to prevent actual corruption. It is in fact a concept closely associated with a belief in free markets: if markets are to function properly, there must be an absence of mutual interference between personnel in governments and private firms. However, one of its consequences is considered to have been that public service became cut off from developments in the private sector, where competitive pressures lead to constant innovation in ways of working. Governments have responded to this in three ways.

47.3.1 Encouragement of Intensive Interaction with, and Learning from, the Private Sector

The idea of a protective layer between public servants and private business people has been almost completely discarded. Private-sector consultants have been taken deep into government, not only offering advice but designing policies, and not being placed under inhibition about using their consultancy role to recommend their own products for purchase. This has, for example, happened with government purchase of a number of computer systems. Similarly, staff seconded from US health firms have been appointed to advisory posts in the Department of Health in order to assist in the construction of a role for private firms in health provision.

The relationship between these developments and marketization is paradoxical. On the one hand, by seeking advice from individuals and organizations in the private sector, government is trying to get close to market-oriented forms of behaviour. On the other hand, by so doing it runs the risk of weakening the market: too close a relationship between public officials and individual enterprises, leading to the construction of entry barriers around a privileged group of insider firms to the exclusion of others. This issue, which has historically been a major concern of economic theorists, has not been raised as a serious issue in British political debate, which rarely distinguishes between 'the market' and 'the private sector'.

47.3.2 Adoption of Business Criteria in Government Practice

Public bodies have been increasingly urged to behave as though they were firms acting in the market. This is encouraged by many of the practices discussed above, such as internal markets, the introduction of competition among units, and most commonly by the adoption of performance targets for public service organizations and employees.

In general this approach is seen as constituting New Public Management (NPM). This began with attempts in the USA to improve public services by modelling their approaches to management on certain kinds of private-sector examples rather than on classic bureaucracy (Osborne and Gaebler 1992). It is never clear exactly what is meant by private-sector approaches, as the private sector of the economy contains an enormous diversity of managerial styles, ranging from highly sophisticated processes to so-called 'macho management', and from transnational corporations to small firms. However, the images of the private sector that have most influenced NPM have been a strong focus on matching action to managerially determined objectives, as opposed to either the rule following associated with traditional bureaucracy (public and private) or the acceptance of professionally determined goals and practices associated with the more skills-based public services (mainly medicine and education)— the knights and knaves problem again.

Behind this model of principal (political leadership) and agent (public service top management) stands the analogy of the neoliberal concept of the firm, in which the principal (the shareholders) requires the agent (top corporate management) to maximize share values. There is a problem of finding a public service analogy for the maximization of shareholder value. If politicians are the principals, then their maximization strategy is aimed at electoral success; put simplistically therefore 'votes' are the equivalent of shareholder value. But democracy does not operate like profit, providing a single measurable indicator. It constantly has to be interpreted by politicians, their advisers, and other public opinion makers. In the end, therefore, the ethics of professions and public service are displaced, not by the market, but by the ethics of politicians.

NPM, starting with US and British experience, has subsequently become a transnational orthodoxy. It is officially commended by the OECD, and countries seeking assistance from the International Monetary Fund or the World Bank are expected to follow its implications. It is also linked closely with privatization at these levels, with countries being required to show that certain percentages of public service delivery are in the hands of private firms. There is therefore no longer anything distinctive about the UK's pursuit of an NPM and marketization agenda. However, the country continues to be a major example of it.

Adoption of the approach started with the post-1979 Conservative government, and continued right through the subsequent Labour period. Several of the initiatives described above are associated with it, particularly the use of internal markets to drive up performance standards. A further feature is the removal of functions from control by a government department itself and placing them in the hands of an agency. For example, vehicle licensing, previously an activity of the Department of Transport, was hived off to the DVLA. More controversially, the management of prisons was removed from the Home Office to a Prisons Agency. Agencies are not necessarily a product of NPM: they were in fact pioneered in Scandinavia in the 1970s. However, they clearly fit the principal–agent model of the NPM approach. Ministers set the parameters of policy; the managerial heads of the agencies agree to maximize fulfilment of their requirements. An important aim is to clarify the distinction between political decision-making and managerial execution; another is to protect ministers from blame for operational failings. (The Prisons Agency was established when the government was exasperated at receiving political blame for a series of prison escapes.)

It is doubtful whether either of these goals is achieved. As we know from the private sector (Williamson 1975), there is no clear division between principal and agent but frequent interaction between them. And the nature of party competition is such that oppositions rarely let governments use the argument that a failure is purely operational and nothing to do with ministers. Nevertheless, agencies do permit a greater focusing of tasks within government.

Another central feature of NPM and of the principal–agent relationship has been government by objectives, which means the establishment of targets by the principal for performance by the agent. Targets have proliferated under the Labour government, in particular. They are an attempt at providing output rather than input measures of policy success. Instead of saying 'We have spent £x million reducing child poverty', government says 'we have met our target to remove y children from poverty by the end of this year'. However, targets and quantifiable performance management have a number of disadvantages (Radnor and Barnes 2007; Radnor and McGuire 2004). Some of these are in fact found in private firms, too, where senior managers may set targets in ignorance of the realities of the business on the ground, leading to both a distortion of activities and a perverse incentive to employees to 'game'— that is, to find ways of boosting the measured performance score without actually improving performance. This commonly happens because a target focuses on one aspect of a task at the expense of others; performance can therefore be improved by concentrating on measured tasks and ignoring those that are not measured.

Management can respond to this by increasing the range of activities for which it sets targets, but if this reaches a point where it is trying to measure and set targets for nearly everything that a service does, there are two negative consequences. First, the initial aim of priority setting becomes lost as everything is prioritized; second, the record keeping and reporting necessary to monitor performance targets consumes serious resources, especially of staff time, at the expense of the front-line activities of the service. In other words, performance management has transaction costs.

The problem of a lack of a true analogy for profit maximization is also relevant here. Public service goals are multiple; there is no obvious way to prioritize them. Targets establish priorities, but by political or managerial decision, not in response to markets. This increases the scope for gaming around targets and provokes irresolvable debates around relative priorities.

47.3.3 Public–Private Partnerships

In recent years government has encouraged joint ventures for funding public capital spending projects between public authorities and private firms. Most of these are covered by the Private Finance Initiative (PFI) (Akintoye, Beck, and Hardcastle 2003; Audit Commission 2001; Lonsdale 2005; Mumford 1998; National Audit Office

1999). This is an example of a more general phenomenon known as public–private partnerships (PPPs), a concept invented by UK government but now widely imitated around the world. An important motive of government in adopting PFI has been to be able to fund building projects that it regards as important, such as new schools and hospitals, without distorting its budget by raising taxes or increasing government borrowing. The private sector finances the project, and therefore owns the facilities. It leases these back to the public sector for a sum to be repaid over a period of years. During this period the project is managed jointly by the firm and the public service concerned.

However, this is not the only way in which governments can attract private finance for public projects: they can simply issue repayable bonds to private purchasers. The difference is that a bond holder is simply a passive holder of assets; firms involved in public–private partnerships remain active in the management of the asset. For this reason, these initiatives should be considered as the public sector seeking the involvement of private-sector expertise and not just funds. An important example was the funding of the modernization of London Transport. The Greater London Authority wanted to finance this through the issuing of bonds to the private sector, as had the New York and Paris underground railway systems when engaged on similar modernizations. The government overruled this and insisted on a PFI arrangement, in order to ensure the continued engagement of private firms in the management of the assets (National Audit Office 2004).

A problem that has occurred with PFI arrangements is a rigidity induced by the terms of the deal. If a school or hospital is being funded by a PFI, it is very difficult for the public authority concerned to change its use or the organizational arrangements surrounding it for twenty or (in the NHS) thirty years, because the original uses tend to be enshrined in the initial PFI contract. Also, the market operates at the single moment of establishing the contract; there is then a private monopoly for a lengthy period.

47.4 CONCLUSION

The above has shown how marketization is a multifaceted strategy. It is not the same as privatization, but overlaps with it. In several respects it is a purely technical device, an attempt at finding ways of achieving efficiency and focusing activities within large public service organizations in ways that cannot be reached by the bureaucratic rules that governed classic public service. At the same time, it has been an intensely political process. Initially it was part of the political offensive of first Conservative and then Labour governments against public-sector trade unions. Gradually the target shifted to being the alleged elitism of public service professions, whether taking trade union form or not. For the Labour government of 1997 greater use of markets was also considered to be a way in which a clear political demand for more and better public services could be reconciled with public aversion to high taxes. More recently that goal has had added to it the possibility of providing more individual choice to consumers, so that they might access public services similarly to the way in which they buy goods in shops.

As much of the above discussion has shown, the strategy has a number of weaknesses, several of them resulting from the fact that public provision had historically taken a non-market form because of certain market failures, some of which return to prominence when attempts are made to introduce or reintroduce markets. Controversy therefore continues to surround marketization. However, this is mainly organized by user and campaign groups, professional associations, political commentators, and some marginal groups within the Labour Party. The leaderships of both major political parties, and to an increasing extent the Liberal Democratic Party, are committed to the strategy, which is therefore largely beyond the reach of electoral conflict or debate.

References

AKINTOYE, A., BECK, M., and HARDCASTLE, C. 2003. *Public–Private Partnerships: Managing Risks and Opportunities*. Oxford: Blackwell.

AUDIT COMMISSION 2001. *Building for the Future: The Management of Procurement under the Private Finance Initiative*. London: HMSO.

BORK, R. H. 1978. *The Antitrust Paradox: A Policy at War with Itself*. New York: Free Press.

FREEDLAND, M. 2001. 'The Marketization of Public Services'. In C. Crouch, K. Eder, and D. Tambini (eds.), *Citizenship, Markets, and the State*. Oxford: Clarendon Press.

LE GRAND, J. 2003. *Motivation, Agency, and Public Policy: Of Knights and Knaves, Pawns and Queens*. Oxford: Oxford University Press.

——MAYS, N., and MULLIGAN, J.-O. (eds.) 1998. *Learning from the NHS Internal Market: A Review of the Evidence*. London: King's Fund.

LONSDALE, C. 2005. 'Risk Transfer, the UK's Private Finance Initiative and Asymmetric Post-Contractual Lock-in: The Cases of National Savings and Investments and the Lord Chancellor's Department'. *Public Administration*, 83/1: 67–88.

MUMFORD, M. 1998. *Public Projects, Private Finance: Understanding the Principles of the Private Finance Initiative*. Welwyn Garden City: NPV/Griffin Multimedia.

NATIONAL AUDIT OFFICE 1999. *Examining the Value for Money of Deals under the Private Finance Initiative*. London: HMSO.

——2004. *London Underground Public Private Partnerships: Were They Good Deals?* London: HMSO.

OECD 1995. *Internal Markets in the Making: Health Systems in Canada, Iceland and the United Kingdom*. Paris: OECD.

OSBORNE, D., and GAEBLER, T. 1992. *Reinventing Government: How the Entrepreneurial Spirit is Transforming the Public Sector*. Wokingham: Addison-Wesley.

OSTERMAN, P. (ed.) 1984. *Internal Labor Markets*. Cambridge, Mass.: MIT Press.

POSNER, R. A. 2001. *Anti-Trust Law*, 2nd edn. Chicago: University of Chicago Press.

RADNOR, Z., and BARNES, D. 2007. 'Historical Analysis of Performance Measurement and Management in Operations Management'. *International Journal of Productivity and Performance Management*, 56: 284–397.

—— and McGUIRE, M. 2004. 'Performance Management in the Public Sector: Fact or Fiction?' *International Journal of Productivity and Performance Management*, 53: 245–60.

RUGMAN, A. M. 1981. *Inside the Multinationals: The Economics of Internal Markets.* London: Croom Helm.

WILLIAMSON, O. E. 1975. *Markets and Hierarchies: Analysis and Antitrust Implications: A Study in the Economics of Internal Organization.* New York: Free Press.

—— and MASTEN, S. E. (eds.) 1999. *The Economics of Transaction Costs.* Cheltenham: Edward Elgar.

SECTION SIXTEEN: ECONOMY

CHAPTER 48

....

NATIONAL ECONOMIC POLICY

....

HELEN THOMPSON

DECLINE was the dominant motif in the academic analysis of British economic policy during the twentieth century (Gamble 2000: 1–2). Whatever their view about the viability of the post-war settlement, or its apparent demise during the 1970s and 1980s, most scholars perceived the politics of the half-century after the end of the Second World War as something that failed to find a means to solve the problem of relative economic decline (e.g. Gamble 1994a; Coates 1994; Sked 1987; Wiener 1985; Cain and Hopkins 1993). Although the causes of this were contested, few disputed that the story of economic policy from 1945 to the early 1990s was one of disappointment. That analytical narrative, however, is now spent (Gamble 2000: 17–20). Nonetheless, the legacy of past failures haunts much of the academic literature on British economic policy with many scholars unconvinced that anything has fundamentally changed in the economic and political dynamics of the economy from the period of relative failure.[1]

Much of the intellectual effort of the past forty years to explain Britain's relative economic decline until the mid-1990s has begun with some theoretical conception of the exceptional nature of Britain's economy, culture, politics, or society. For many years this debate was primarily an ideological one. For the right, Britain's culture since the second half of the nineteenth century had produced an anti-business bias that made the economy ill-equipped to adapt to economic change (Wiener 1985). Its governing elite, Correlli Barnett argued, whilst aspiring to imperial grandeur was in its habits unworldly. This left British politicians fatally exposed by the economic and political problems of the last third of the nineteenth century, the inter-war years, and

[1] See e.g. Coates (2002).

the Second World War. Their post-war successors, Barnett continued, proved unable to escape the great power delusion and added unsustainable social commitments to the burden of the British state (Barnett 1986). For the left, the cause of decline lay either in Britain's peculiar class development, which in missing out on a bourgeois revolution had left significant remnants of pre-modern politics and a weak industrial class (Anderson 1964; 1987; Nairn 1963), or a long-standing financial bias in British capitalism, which gave the City a distinctive commercial character that privileged short-term gain in secondary markets over long-term industrial investment (Ingham 1984).

After the end of Thatcher, the tone of the academic debate about Britain's political economy became less stridently ideological and more grounded in comparative economic and political analysis. Yet out of these new perspectives one of the left's old arguments persisted. By the mid-1990s, the thesis that the character of Britain's financial sector was the cause of many of Britain's economic problems had become an academic commonplace. Many argued that even if the City's position was not to be explained by some version of absolute exceptionalism, it was still what distinguished Britain's Anglo-Saxon style of capitalism from that which prevailed elsewhere in Europe. With a financial system based around capital markets rather than banks and in which government played a limited role, the British economy was condemned to suffer from low investment in the manufacturing sector and relatively poor growth (Pollin 1995; Zysman 1993; Coates 2000; Hutton 1996). For some the consequences of this financial bias in the structure of British capitalism were compounded by the willingness of British governments to accept the primacy of external financial interests around sterling's status as an international currency over the domestic economy in deciding macroeconomic policy (Pollard 1982). Starting from these premises, Britain's economic problems could only be solved, these scholars argued, by moving to a developmental state that would make possible greater investment in the productive economy, improved manufacturing competitiveness, and an exchange rate policy detached from the City's financial interests.[2] Those like David Marquand who lamented the absence of a developmental state focused their explanation on the unsuccessful efforts of governments in the 1960s and 1970s to modernize the British economy, and the Thatcher government's repudiation of that modernization project and acceptance of an economy divided between a booming financial and services sector and manufacturing decline (Marquand 1988; Gamble 1994b; Newton and Porter 1988). From this perspective, the Thatcher government's approach had reinforced the old problems of the economy and created new ones.[3]

For all their strengths in diagnosing the apparent weaknesses of the British economy, the problem with these arguments was that they did not always distinguish between politically explaining why economic policy had been as it was and normative condemnation and aspiration. The urge to dismiss the Thatcher years for moral reasons and because of what they did not attempt meant that less scholarly attention

---

[2] See Marquand (1988).   [3] See Hutton (1996); Pollard (1992); Overbeek (1990).

was focused on explaining the Conservatives' relative political success in economic matters as a political party in a contested democratic politics with a troubled economy. Yet what politically distinguished the Thatcher governments from their predecessors since 1961 was that for at least a five-year period they turned the economy into a positive asset for the governing party in British politics (Bulpitt 1986). This would have seemed highly unlikely in 1981, and the first Thatcher government only stumbled its way to electoral success after initially embarking on a set of disastrous policies from which it had to seek a rapid retreat. Yet from 1982 to 1988 the Thatcher government found a way of managing the economy that did not threaten the Conservative Party's grip on power.[4] Strikingly that political success did not rest on a clear reversal of relative economic decline. Measured against the performance of the other major EC states, the British economy ended the 1980s at best modestly, and in some areas— the proclivity for growth to produce rising inflation, a large current account deficit, and an unstable currency—with the same liabilities as it had accumulated during the previous decade.[5] This paradox left a problem for those scholars who argued that it was the absence of a developmental state that defined the problem confronting British politicians over the economy. If politicians could succeed in economic policy in the terms that mattered to them—governing competence and electoral victory—without a developmental state that might have given the economy a larger industrial base, why would they have reason to think that the existing structure of the British economy was a political problem?

This paradox was compounded by the relationship between the performance of the British economy and the political fate of the final Conservative government. Under John Major's premiership, there was an end to relative economic decline but the Conservative Party reaped no political reward for the achievement. The end of decline was not the result of restructuring the economy through a developmental state, but the construction after the exit from the European Exchange Rate Mechanism of anti-inflationary credibility through monetary and fiscal policy and the good fortune of serious problems befalling the German and Japanese economies.[6] Yet by the time the Major government had figured its political way to a macroeconomic policy that procured sustainable, non-inflationary growth that created jobs, sterling's short-lived membership of the ERM had destroyed the Conservatives' reputation for governing competence. Whilst the political failures of British governments had been directly tied to the relatively poor performance of the British economy, the developmental critique of Britain's economic and political problems had considerable resonance. Once, however, as became the case during the long period of Conservative rule, economic success appeared to be neither a necessary nor a sufficient condition for political success for British governments, the kinds of empirical explanations Britain's political economy required became more demanding.

---

[4] See Smith (1987).   [5] See Johnson (1991).   [6] See Burnham (1999).

48.1 THE BRITISH ECONOMY AND THE INTERNATIONAL ECONOMY

Wherever the burden of explanation was placed for understanding what had happened during the Thatcher and Major governments, from the mid-1990s the language of globalization provided a new theoretical framework for analysis. It opened up a new version of the exceptionalist argument: Britain, many argued, had an economy that was different from other large EU states because the Thatcher governments had embraced the internationalization of capital flows and, in contrast to the other large EU states, accepted the Anglo-Saxon model of capitalism on which a central thrust of globalization rests. As a consequence, the Thatcher governments' successors were less capable of pursuing non-orthodox economic policies than other European states (Gamble 2003: 104–7). Even some of those who were generally sceptical about globalization saw Britain as having a distinctively internationalized economy compared to the other G7 states with the financial sector standing at the centre of that internationalized economy (Hirst and Thompson 2000: 335–6).

Yet whilst the British economy was indeed more internationalized than other European states, the emphasis some scholars have placed on the Conservative governments' active encouragement of that openness has risked missing some important political nuances about the 1980s and the first half of the 1990s. The Thatcher governments do have to be understood in the context of the post-Bretton Woods international economy but it is erroneous to assume that they were strategically and tactically rational in dealing with the constraints and opportunities of globalization because they wished to procure a more open British economy. The Thatcher governments' primary political project was not to restore a particular kind of British capitalism that could thrive in an open international economy but, as Jim Bulpitt always insisted, to re-establish the primacy of the Conservatives as Britain's governing party (Bulpitt 1986). Rather than relying on international market forces to squeeze labour, their success was in good part dependent on using the coercive power of the British state to break the trade unions at the moment when the opportunity arose with the National Union of Mineworkers' strike. Moreover, the Thatcher governments never got to grips with the problems created for exchange rate management in a financially liberalized international economy. The ERM disaster that eventually politically destroyed the Conservatives was a sterling accident waiting to happen because Thatcher and her Chancellors never accepted that without capital controls, macroeconomic prudence required letting the exchange rate constrain both monetary and fiscal policy (Thompson 1996: 218–22). Whilst the Conservatives escaped the electoral consequences of the sterling-induced recession that decimated the manufacturing sector in the early 1980s, and reaped electoral reward in 1987 for the inflationary boom that began in 1986, their luck was never likely to last indefinitely. ERM membership might have taken the blame for the Conservatives' final fate, but continuing non-membership in the autumn of 1990 would have served them no better because high interest rates alone could not have sustained confidence in sterling as it waned under inflation and they had already pushed the economy into recession (Thompson 1996: 163–77). In macroeconomic terms, British economic policy had been at odds with the openness of the international economy for more than a decade. After Black Wednesday, the Major government found a means of macroeconomic adjustment, but one in which a substantial burden to restore credibility had to fall on tax increases, which was something that the openness of the British economy was supposed to deter. What in many ways made British macroeconomic policy in the 1980s and early 1990s exceptional was not how far it embraced globalization, but just how ill-suited it was to the exchange rate constraints generated by the financial openness of the post-Bretton Woods international economy.

48.2 New Labour and the International Economy

The political beneficiaries of the Major's government's post-Black Wednesday economic success were New Labour. Unlike any previous Labour government, New Labour assumed power without having to confront an immediate economic crisis. Against that backdrop, it presided over ten years of continuous growth, low inflation, modest interest rates, and what had become by early 2007 the second-lowest unemployment level in the European Union. Rhetorically, and in many of its actions, New Labour's economic success was premised on acceptance of the constraints of an open international economy. During Labour's first term of office, Gordon Brown insisted that there was no room for a discretionary macroeconomic policy by immediately giving the Bank of England operational independence and, in 1998, enshrining fiscal prudence in a Code for Fiscal Stability. For the first term anyway, Brown made macroeconomic decisions according to rules as if the government were a non-political agent of a new economic consensus (Burnham 2001). Those, like Ed Balls, who theorized Labour's approach justified it as 'open macro-economics in an open economy' (Balls 1998). On the supply side, the government accepted from the outset what were said to be the constraints of the existing structures of the British economy in relation to the international economy, and looked to exploit Britain's existing comparative advantages in openness and labour market flexibility rather than attempting to establish an indigenous investment ethic around the manufacturing sector. International openness, in New Labour economic thinking, has been an asset rather than a problem to escape. As Gordon Brown put it in his 2006 Mansion House speech, 'we can demonstrate that just as in the 19th century industrialization was made for Britain, in the twenty first century globalization is made for Britain too' (Brown 2006).

By Labour's third term in office, New Labour's policies had reinforced the internationalization of the British economy across a wide range of areas. In 2005, Britain absorbed more FDI than the United States, and FDI constituted 45 per cent of Gross Fixed Capital Formation, compared to an average of 16.1 per cent across the EU and an average for all developed economies of just 8 per cent (UN Conference on Trade and Development 2006). In contrast to furious political debates in other developed-economy states about foreign ownership, including the United States, at no time since 1997 has the New Labour government made a serious issue of this matter. Most symbolically, in 2005, it accepted without fuss the acquisition of the assets of the last British-owned car manufacturing company by the Chinese firm Nanjing Automobile Group. Meanwhile the government's immigration policies have been more open to highly skilled migrants than the United States since 2001, and to foreign labour generally than most other EU states, producing more than 600,000 new workers since 2004.[7] This has reinforced the flexibility of British labour markets and probably acted as an anti-inflationary wage discipline in certain sectors. Perhaps most revealingly, the financial and services sectors have become more, not less, important to the British economy since 1997. From 1997 to 2006 manufacturing growth totalled 4.5 per cent compared to 36.8 per cent for the financial and service sectors (HM Treasury n.d.).

New Labour's embrace of the financial sector and Britain's traditional comparative advantages in international openness have been crucial to the growth of the economy over the past decade given the continuing weakness of the manufacturing sector. It also remains central to Britain's balance of payments. In 2005 the financial sector contributed £19 billion of net exports compared to a deficit in traded goods of £68 billion (Brown 2006; HM Treasury n.d.). When New Labour came to power, London's position as the premier European financial centre appeared vulnerable. The prospect of the euro's arrival excited many in Frankfurt to believe that they could take business from London when London had already been damaged by the early 1990s recession that hit the financial sector hard and the collapse of Barings. By Labour's third term London had not only seen off the threat of Frankfurt but re-established itself at New York's expense as the pre-eminent financial centre in the world, enjoying the biggest share of international bond markets, over-the-counter derivatives, foreign exchange turnover, and cross-border bank lending (*Economist* 2007c). More foreign banks operate now in London than in any other city, and six of the ten largest international law firms are located in London (Brown 2006). The government's own approach to the financial sector was instrumental to London's success. Early in the first term, Brown moved to change the regulatory environment in which the City operates, creating a single regulator, the Financial Services Authority, which quickly established a reputation for 'light-touch' regulation. When in 2002, in the wake of Enron's downfall, the United States' Congress passed the Sarbanes-Oxley Act tightening accountancy regulation for American companies, London as a market for new listings pulled significantly ahead of New York. Since 2003 a growing number of American start-up

---

[7] See OECD (2006).

companies have chosen to list on the Alternative Investment Market (AIM), which has a market-driven governance regime, rather than the NASDAQ Stock Market where Sarbanes-Oxley rules apply. The New Labour government has, meanwhile, proved just as at ease with the growing foreign ownership of large City firms as of significant parts of the manufacturing sector.

Given the magnitude of New Labour's electoral success and the intellectual critique developed by the left, and the social and economic fallout, of the Thatcher governments' embrace of openness, it is not surprising that much of the academic debate about New Labour has focused on whether Brown's economic management was a missed opportunity for national economic renewal. This debate has been shaped by different theoretical understandings about just what globalization means for economic policy in any state and indeed how far the international economy is globalized at all. If New Labour has turned its back on creating the kind of developmental state that might boost indigenous investment and non-orthodox economic policies, was this a necessity produced by the prudence that the openness of the international economy requires of all states, or a contingent and erroneous political judgement for which New Labour can be reasonably censured? This question has become for the left part of a larger one about the possibilities of social democracy in today's international economy, with some arguing that this kind of politics is simply no longer viable in a world in which capital is so mobile (Gray 1998), and others insisting that the international economy is far less policy prescriptive than the globalization thesis supposes (Garret 1998; 2000; Pierson 2002; Hay 2000). For those who are pessimistic about the prospects for social democracy today, New Labour's economic policy has been either grounded in a clear understanding of the structural limits created by the openness of the international economy (Wickham-Jones 1997), or operated in the shadow of the historical failure to create a developmental state at a moment when the international economy was conducive to such a strategy (Coates 2002). For the more optimistic, New Labour has imprisoned itself. As a matter of its own political judgement, it has chosen to cultivate mythological global economic constraints that do not exist. For Colin Hay in particular, there has been a culpable failure to restore an indigenous investment ethic to British capitalism and to use fiscal policy as a counter-cyclical tool in an international economy in which there remains the discretion to act in these ways (Hay 1999; 2004; Watson 2002; Watson and Hay 2003).

This debate has some of the same limitations as that around the Thatcher governments, focused as much of it is somewhere between normative aspiration and political explanation. But regardless of whether prescriptive judgement can offer much to political explanation, both the optimists and the pessimists are right that the New Labour governments have left some of the old weaknesses of the British economy untouched. Unit labour costs in the manufacturing sector have risen by more than the G7 average in every year since 1997 (HM Treasury n.d.). Meanwhile productivity remains low. The annual increase in productivity from 1997 to 2005 has been lower than Germany's and the United States' in every year but one, and in absolute terms in GDP created per hour worked, Britain lags behind the USA, Germany, and France

(HM Treasury n.d.; OECD 2006). Whilst the Treasury's 2000 paper promised policies to increase investment in physical and human capital and promote innovation and research and development (HM Treasury 2000), a range of initiatives has reaped little reward. On investment, the British economy fares little better with Gross Fixed Capital Formation as a percentage of GDP behind Germany, France, and Italy for the whole period from 1997 (HM Treasury n.d.). And even the fall in unemployment disguises a substantial rise in the number of people claiming incapacity benefit since 1997. The crucial question is how consequential these indicators suggesting continuing relative failure are in practice. On investment they may be less significant than those who saw this weakness as central to Britain's previous relative economic decline believe. The service sector is less capital intensive than manufacturing, and consequently continuing growth is less dependent on investment. Elsewhere in today's world economy, the relationship between investment and growth does not suggest that low investment is necessarily a liability. For example, between 1997 and 2006 investment as a percentage of GDP has been between 11.9 and 7.1 per cent lower in the United States than in Japan but American growth has been higher in every single year (HM Treasury n.d.). Nonetheless, Britain's sizeable current account deficit which rose from £0.8 bn in 1997 to £29.5 bn in 2005, or 0.1 per cent of GDP to 2.2 per cent of GDP (HM Treasury n.d.), and is a symptom of Britain's low investment and low savings economy, is a serious long-term vulnerability. Whilst this deficit has been financed with some ease for the past decade, even the Americans have found that a burgeoning current account deficit eventually diminishes the external value of the currency and is likely to put upward pressure on interest rates at domestically awkward moments. If Britain's current account deficit eventually places sterling under strain, a whole set of external economic questions that have been laid to rest for more than a decade will resurface.

Yet if these potential weaknesses are in part the consequence of a supply-side approach that left the structure of the British economy much as New Labour found it, the government's macroeconomic policies have been more politically distinctive. During the first term, as Peter Burnham has described it, Brown succeeded through a strategy of depoliticization born out of an understanding of the consequences for incoming centre-left governments of open short-term capital flows and the political problems that macroeconomic policy caused to previous post-war governments. By giving operational independence to the Bank of England, and setting fiscal rules in 1997 that allowed the government to borrow only to invest to keep national debt at a prudent level, the government set out to establish its governing competence by lowering expectations about what it could deliver and differentiating itself from the approaches of not just previous Labour governments but reckless Conservative ones too (Burnham 2001; Butler and Flinders 2005).

However, the depoliticization strategy allowed for more political discretion than originally met the eye. In stark contrast to the terms on which the euro was created, the framework for monetary policy allowed politicians to determine the inflation target. Operational independence for the Bank of England did not deny the validity of political debate about short- to medium-term trade-offs between inflation and growth. In eschewing the euro and making clear that he regarded Britain's monetary model as superior to the subordination of all political judgement to the supremacy of price stability, Brown was explicitly rejecting any notion that the current international economy prescribes specific monetary policies.

On the fiscal side, even during the first term, the government's tax policies contained elements that would have been deemed risky if one started from the premise that anything that smacked of redistributive tendencies or of penalizing business would be punished in the financial markets, not least the windfall tax on the privatized utilities and the end of tax relief on the dividends of company pension funds.[8] After the 2001 election, Brown appeared to jettison his earlier strategy of depoliticizing important parts of fiscal policy in several respects. In 2003 he raised National Insurance contributions. He also allowed Britain to move from having the third-lowest rate of corporation tax among the EU's old members in 1996 to the sixth highest by 2006 (*Economist* 2006). Meanwhile public expenditure grew in real terms by 4.6 per cent a year from 2000–1 to 2006–7, which was more than 170 per cent the rate of average growth during the same period. This serious boost to public expenditure was paid for by borrowing as well as rising taxes. Having established a budget surplus during the first term, the Chancellor allowed borrowing to rise to 2.8 per cent of GDP by 2007 (*Economist* 2007b). There is a serious argument to be made, as Clift and Tomlinson have done, that the sum of New Labour's fiscal policy has been decidedly Keynesian in approach.[9]

As fiscal depoliticalization has unwound, it has become increasingly clear that the New Labour government has wanted to redistribute wealth. This has been disguised by the form redistribution has taken. Without any increase in the top rate of taxation, few of Brown's tax moves have hurt the rich. They have taken money away from middle-income earners in the South-East, who have found themselves above the 40 per cent threshold for income tax as earnings have risen, and given it to the working poor with children. In part this might seem a response to the supposed constraints of the international economy on the top rate of income tax, but it is also at least as much the product of the specific electoral geography that put New Labour in power.

48.3 NEW LABOUR'S POLITICAL SUCCESS IN ECONOMIC POLICY

Crucially, in its political consequences, New Labour's economic policy was for ten years extremely successful judged by any standards from the past century. It turned

---

[8] See Clift (2002).   [9] Clift and Tomlinson (2007). For a critique of this argument see Hay (2007).

the economy into Labour's primary electoral advantage for two consecutive general elections and was the basis of the party's claim to governing competence.[10] This was despite the fact that various of the government's moves, not least over pensions, created the kind of problems for a section of the population that earlier Labour governments would probably not have survived unscathed. In crucial ways, New Labour both found and made the economy less politically problematic than any governing party since the introduction of full-franchise representative democracy after the First World War.

Perhaps most surprisingly given the Conservatives' travails with ERM membership, the New Labour government turned Britain's non-participation in the euro into virtually a non-issue. From 1919 to the late 1990s, sterling stood at the centre of British politics. Much of the story of both internal political crisis and external decline can be told through the fate of sterling. From the gold standard crisis of 1931 that tore MacDonald's Labour government apart to the destruction of the Conservatives' six-decade-long electoral dominance in the wreckage of the ERM in 1992, sterling has had the capacity not only to undo governments but in its consequences to shape the political landscape for a generation. From the humiliation of Suez in 1956 after Eisenhower terminated American support for sterling to the fallout of Black Wednesday for ratification of the Maastricht treaty in 1993, it has also had the ability to derail a government's foreign policy. New Labour inherited impending non-membership of the euro, and did not have the time, if it had so wished, to reverse course by January 1999 when monetary union began. With London's position as the premier European financial centre threatened by Frankfurt, Tony Blair and Gordon Brown always likely to disagree on the issue, and any overt uncertainty risking speculation in the foreign exchange markets, how to handle sterling was a potential minefield for the Labour government.

From the onset, however, Brown found considerable room to manoeuvre. Despite Blair's efforts, especially after 2001, to turn the issue into one of general EU policy, Brown was able to retain Treasury control over the issue and block the Prime Minster's desire to make macroeconomic policy adjust to his ambition for greater British influence within the Union.[11] Brown's five tests for membership were politically driven, but the sheer weight of the economic facts gave Brown ammunition that ultimately Blair could not counter with non-economic considerations. The problems of the major euro-zone economies between 2000 and 2005, and the clear political difficulties of the one-size-fits-all interest rate policy demanded by the single currency when British interest rates were already on a different trajectory to the Continent, made the prospect of jettisoning the existing monetary framework a tremendous risk.[12] Having avoided even the hint of a financial crisis around sterling, Brown could insist that the context of macroeconomic policy would be decided by

---

[10] See Wickham-Jones (2002); Butler and Kavanagh (2005).   [11] See Peston (2005).
[12] See Sinclair (2007).

macroeconomic considerations, and in rejecting Blair's overtures to membership, Brown freed exchange rate policy from the eighty-year-old shackles of aspirations to international monetary status, imperial ambitions, and the illusory temptations of European influence without sufficient common interests with one of Germany or France.[13]

Whilst there remains for some a plausible economic case for membership,[14] there is a more plausible case against it. This goes back to some of the enduring difficulties of British national economic policy in an open international economy in which monetary power lies elsewhere, and where in a range of political contexts British governments have had to try to accommodate themselves to decisions made by others that impact on sterling as in 1926, 1947, 1956, and 1992. The euro will always be something that Britain can join only on monetary terms that were agreed by others. That was already true in 1997 but any British government that now wished to enter the euro-zone would have to abandon sterling after the New Labour government had spent a decade demonstrating that the way of the European Central Bank is not the only way, and indeed perhaps far from the best way, to conduct monetary policy for developed economies in a world of open short-term capital flows. The New Labour government has not just coped with the euro issue for itself but set effective political constraints on the context of macroeconomic management for future governments.

The paradox of New Labour's political success in economic policy over a decade was that it became so comprehensive that it was for a long time taken for granted. It carried the government through a second re-election in 2005 despite an unpopular war that drained the Prime Minister's credibility with a significant section of the electorate. Until Brown's tribulations as Prime Minister after he botched the election of the autumn of 2007 that wasn't, it left the Conservatives with no clear idea of how to exploit the economy as part of a strategy to reclaim power and govern in a different kind of way. Even after Brown gifted them a second chance, the Conservatives seem unlikely in the run-up to the next general election to offer significant tax cuts beyond inheritance tax, or promise to spend much less, or abandon the legal framework for monetary policy, any more than they would seek to reconstruct an indigenous manufacturing sector or regulate labour markets more tightly. Even if the performance of the economy in 2008 costs Labour the next election, Labour's success still exhausted most of the substantive party-political debate about economic policy after at least forty years when the two main parties have battled bitterly on this territory. That for over a decade the Labour Party had come to assume that the economy was unequivocally safe political territory for the party and that this was a natural state of political affairs was, in historical perspective, a rather extraordinary development.

[13] On the European dimension see Bulpitt (1996).
[14] Kettell (2004); Hay (2003). But cf. Hay, Smith, and Watson (2006).

48.4 NATIONAL DISCRETION, THE END OF DECLINE, AND THE INTERNATIONAL ECONOMY

British national economic policy had to be understood within the constraints and opportunities fashioned by the international economy long before the globalization fetish made this a fashionable insight. This does not mean, however, that there is no debate to be had about national economic alternatives, or that the actions of British governments over the past two decades should be understood as inevitable responses to an international economy in which Britain has found a circumscribed role. For different domestic political purposes, both the Conservative and New Labour governments exercised considerable macroeconomic discretion whilst doing little to try to change the structure of the British economy. Whilst the foreign exchange markets and the failure to find a credible underpinning for exchange rate policy finally curtailed the monetary and fiscal discretion of the Thatcher governments, the Major government after 1993 and New Labour were both more prudent and more fortunate. In May 1995, with sterling floundering, the Major government's post-ERM monetary policy was in some difficulty. But after the minutes of the Monthly Monetary Meeting revealed that the Chancellor, Kenneth Clarke, had ignored the advice of the Governor of the Bank of England to raise interest rates, sentiment in the foreign exchange markets suddenly hitched sterling to an upwardly floating dollar, and the pressure for higher interest rates to prop up sterling abated (Elgie and Thompson 1998: 87–9). Similarly, the New Labour government has escaped any consequences for sterling of the burgeoning current account deficit for reasons that would seem to have more to do with the dollar's weakness than any permanent indifference of investors in the present international economy to current account weakness. Although this fortune may well not last, and sterling may yet come once again to haunt British politicians as a constraint on economic policy, any government of either party has acute domestic political incentives to enjoy it whilst it does, regardless of what many regard as the damaging consequences of the present structure of the British economy that the current account weakness reflects.

Whilst relative economic decline is over, important aspects of the exceptionalism that was frequently held responsible for it remain. After a decade of centre-left government, Britain still has both a heavily internationalized economy and one that is in part removed from the core of the European Union. It is neither like the economy of other EU states nor, despite the rhetoric of Anglo-Saxon capitalism, like that of the United States, where trade and Foreign Direct Investment are a far less significant proportion of GDP (*Economist* 2007a) and technologically-advanced manufacturing production is much more important. It stands unabashedly outside the euro-zone, and conducts monetary policy in a unique legal framework. After the failed attempt to achieve at least macroeconomic convergence with the other EU economies through the ERM and the option of opting in to monetary union, successive governments of different parties appear to have laid to rest any notion of strategic restructuring via the EU. They have also presided over what is still an increasing internationalization of the British economy without producing a significant backlash in domestic politics against globalization of the kind that in different ways is firmly part of American, French, and Japanese domestic politics, and has some echo in German and Italian. The internationalized nature of the British economy may well have some serious deleterious long-term consequences, especially given the financial sector's consumption of so much scientific and engineering talent. However, it could only be undone by a government with a comprehensive agenda for domestic economic, cultural, and educational change that would severely test the limits of where the discretion for significant supply-side restructuring for developed-country states in the present international economy now lie. It would also be a serious domestic risk for either party in government when one finally found a way of making a political success of economic policy from a sustained period of relative economic achievement in a polity in which for more than eighty years this seemed extremely difficult and for much of the time impossible.

REFERENCES

ANDERSON, P. 1964. 'Origins of the Present Crisis'. New Left Review, 23: 26–54.
—— 1987. 'The Figures of Descent'. New Left Review, 161: 20–77.
BALLS, E. 1998. 'Open Macro-Economics in an Open Economy'. Scottish Journal of Political Economy, 45/2: 113–32.
BARNETT, C. 1986. The Audit of War: The Illusion and Reality of Britain as a Great Nation. London: Macmillan.
BROWN, G. 2006. Speech at the Mansion House, London, 21 June. www.hm-treasury.gov.uk/ newsroom_and_speeches/press/2006/press_44_06.cfm.
BULLER, J., and FLINDERS, M. 2005. 'The Domestic Origins of Depoliticisation in the Area of British Economic Policy'. British Journal of Politics and International Relations, 7/4: 526–43.
BULPITT, J. 1986. 'The Discipline of the New Democracy: Mrs Thatcher's Domestic Statecraft'. Political Studies, 34/1: 19–39.
—— 1996. 'The European Question: Rules, National Modernisation and the Ambiguities of Primat der Innepolitik'. Pp. 214–56 in D. Marquand and A. Seldon (eds.), The Ideas that Shaped Post-war Britain. London: Fontana.
BURNHAM, P. 1999. 'The Politics of Economic Management in the 1990s'. New Political Economy, 4/1: 37–54.
—— 2001. 'New Labour and the Politics of Depoliticisation'. British Journal of Politics and International Relations, 3/2: 127–49.
BUTLER, D., and KAVANAGH, D. 2005. The British General Election of 2005. Basingstoke: Palgrave Macmillan.
CAIN, P. J., and HOPKINS, A. G. British Imperialism, ii: Crisis and Deconstruction. London: Longman.
CLIFT, B. 2002. 'Social Democracy and Globalisation: France and the UK'. Government and Opposition, 37/4: 466–500.

CLIFT, B., and TOMLINSON, J. 2007. 'Credible Keynesianism: New Labour, Macroeconomic Policy and the Political Economy of Coarse Turning'. *British Journal of Political Science*, 37/1: 47–69.

COATES, D. 1994. *The Question of UK Decline: The Economy, State and Society*. Hemel Hempstead: Harvester Wheatsheaf.

—— 2000. *Models of Capitalism*. Cambridge: Polity.

—— 2002. 'The New Political Economy of Postwar Britain'. In C. Hay (ed.), *British Politics Today*. Cambridge: Polity.

Economist 2006. 'Bill, Ben and Gordon'. 9 Nov.

—— 2007a. 'Britannia Redux'. 1 Feb.

—— 2007b. 'Browned Off'. 1 Feb.

—— 2007c. 'Living by their Wits'. 1 Feb.

ELGIE, R., and THOMPSON, H. 1998. *The Politics of Central Banks in Britain and France*. London: Routledge.

GAMBLE, A. 1994a. *Britain in Decline: Economic Policy, Political Strategy and the British State*, 4th edn. New York: St Martin's Press.

—— 1994b. *The Free Economy and the Strong State: The Politics of Thatcherism*, 2nd edn. Basingstoke: Macmillan.

—— 2000. 'Theories and Explanations of British Decline'. In R. English and M. Kenny (eds.), *Rethinking British Decline*. Basingstoke: Macmillan.

—— 2003. *Between Europe and America: The Future of British Politics*. Basingstoke: Palgrave.

GARRET, G. 1998. *Partisan Politics in the Global Economy*. Cambridge: Cambridge University Press.

—— 2000. 'Capital Mobility, Exchange Rates, and Fiscal Policy in the Global Economy'. *Review of International Political Economy*, 7/1: 153–70.

GRAY, J. 1998. *False Dawn*. London: Granta.

HAY, C. 1999. *The Political Economy of New Labour: Labouring under False Pretences*. Manchester: Manchester University Press.

—— 2000. 'Globalization, Social Democracy and the Persistence of Partisan Politics: A Commentary on Garrett'. *Review of International Political Economy*, 7/1: 138–52.

—— 2003. 'Macro-economic Policy Co-ordination and Membership of the Single European Currency: Another Case of British Exceptionalism?' *Political Quarterly*, 9/1: 91–100.

—— 2004. 'Credibility, Competitiveness and the Business Cycle in Third Way Political Economy: A Critical Evaluation of Economic Policy in Britain since 1997'. *New Political Economy*, 9/1: 39–56.

—— 2007. 'What's in a New Name? New Labour's Putative Keynesianism'. *British Journal of Political Science*, 37/1: 187–92.

—— SMITH, N. J., and WATSON, M. 2006. 'Beyond Prospective Accountancy: Reassessing the Case for British Membership of the Single European Currency Comparatively'. *British Journal of Politics and International Relations*, 8: 101–21.

HIRST, P., and THOMPSON, G. 2000. 'Globalisation in One Country? The Peculiarities of the British'. *Economy and Society*, 29/3: 335–56.

HM TREASURY 2000. *Productivity in the UK: Evidence and the Government's Approach*. London: HM Treasury.

—— n.d. *HM Treasury Pocket Data Bank*. www.hm-treasury.gov.uk/economic_data_ and_tools/latest_economic_indicators/data_indic_index.cfm.

HUTTON, W. 1996. *The State We're In*. London: Verso.

INGHAM, G. 1984. *Capitalism Divided: The City and Industry in British Social Development*. Basingstoke: Macmillan.

JOHNSON, C. 1991. *The Economy under Mrs Thatcher*. Harmondsworth: Penguin.

KETTELL, S. 2004. 'Why New Labour Wants the Euro'. *Political Quarterly*, 75/1: 51–9.

MARQUAND, D. 1988. *The Unprincipled Society: New Demands and Old Politics*. London: Jonathan Cape.

NAIRN, T. 1963. 'The British Political Elite'. *New Left Review*, 23: 19–25.

NEWTON, S., and PORTER, D. 1988. *Modernisation Frustrated: The Politics of Industrial Decline in Britain since 1900*. London: Unwin Hyman.

OECD 2006a. *International Migration Outlook*. Paris: OECD.

——2006b. *Labour Productivity Growth—Data: GDP, Annual Hours Worked, Total Employment, Total Hours Worked, GDP per Hour Worked, September 2006*. www.oecd.org/topicstatsportal/0,2647,en_2825_30453906_1_1_1_1_1,00.html.

OVERBEEK, H. 1990. *Global Capitalism and National Decline: The Thatcher Decade in Perspective*. London: Unwin Hyman.

PESTON, R. 2005. *Brown's Britain: How Gordon Runs the Show*. London: Short Books.

PIERSON, C. 2002. *Hard Choices: Social Democracy in the 21st Century*. Cambridge: Polity.

POLLARD, S. 1982. *The Wasting of the British Economy: British Economic Policy 1945 to the Present*. London: Croom Helm.

——1992. *The Development of the British Economy: 1914–1990*. London: Arnold.

POLLIN, R. 1995. 'Financial Structures and Egalitarian Economic Policy'. *New Left Review*, 214: 26–61.

SINCLAIR, P. 2007. 'The Treasury and Economic Policy'. Ch. 10 in A. Seldon (ed.), *Blair's Britain 1997–2007*. Cambridge: Cambridge University Press.

SKED, A. 1987. *Britain's Decline: Problems and Perspectives*. Oxford: Basil Blackwell.

SMITH, D. 1987. *The Rise and Fall of Monetarism*. Harmondsworth: Penguin.

THOMPSON, H. 1996. *The British Conservative Government and the European Exchange Rate Mechanism*. London: Pinter.

United Nations Conference on Trade and Development 2006. *World Investment Report 2006*. http//www.unctad.org/sections/dite_dir/docs/wir06_fs_gb.en.pdf.

WATSON, M. ' "Sand in the Wheels", or Oiling the Wheels of International Finance? New Labour's Approach to a "New Bretton Woods" '. *British Journal of Politics and International Relations*, 4/2: 193–221.

——and HAY, C. 2003. 'The Discourse of Globalisation and the Logic of No Alternative: Rendering the Contingent Necessary in the Political Economy of New Labour'. *Policy and Politics*, 30/4: 289–305.

WICKHAM-JONES, M. 1997. 'Social Democracy and Structural Dependency: The British Case. A Note on Hay'. *Politics and Society*, 25/2: 257–65.

——2002. 'Exorcising Ghosts: How Labour Dominated the Economic Argument'. Pp. 103–12 in A. Geddes and J. Tonge (eds.), *Labour's Second Landslide: The British General Election 2001*. Manchester: Manchester University Press.

WIENER, M. 1985. *English Culture and the Decline of the Industrial Spirit 1850–1980*. London: Penguin.

ZYSMAN, J. 1993. *Governments, Markets, and Growth: Financial Systems and the Politics of Industrial Change*. Ithaca, NY: Cornell University Press.

....

CHAPTER 49

EUROPEAN ECONOMY

....

BEN CLIFT

49.1 EUROPEAN ECONOMY AND COMPARATIVE CAPITALISMS

....

THE broad distinction between more regulated Continental (European) capitalism and more free-market-oriented Anglo-American capitalism is a powerful undercurrent of nearly all discussion of economic policy-making in Europe. In the 1980s, Delors's 'European model of society' (1992: 157–8) championed a European variety of capitalism better able to reconcile economic liberalism and social justice than an Anglo-Saxon neoliberal Thatcherite British 'other' (Wincott 2003: 288). The British political economy, despite its geographical proximity to Europe, continues to be characterized by its typological proximity to US capitalism. Between them, these two form the archetypes of the 'liberal market economy' (LME) (Hall and Soskice 2001), with a limited role for the state, decentralized wage bargaining, and reliance on market mechanisms as the organizing principle within capitalism.

As such, the British political economy is closely aligned with the liberal political economic model which has in part driven the process of European economic integration since the 1980s. In the realms of financial market liberalization, privatization, deregulation, and opening up of markets, the UK was ahead of the European game. As a result, the British political economy has been able to adapt with relative ease to these aspects of the Single Market programme. Britain has also opted out of the euro, guaranteeing enduring macroeconomic policy autonomy.

However, EU economic governance has always been a complex, multifaceted amalgam. Liberal market-oriented elements akin to the UK model, many enshrined in the Single European Market, coexist with social solidarity and redistributive elements, more reminiscent of Continental European models of regulated capitalism. Both are institutionalized within European economic governance. It is discomfort with the more generous social minima of many Continental conceptions of the European social model, and regulatory aspects of European coordinated capitalism, which explains the highly charged European economic policy debate within British politics.

These debates are either explicitly or implicitly situated within the 'models of capitalism' frame of reference, pitting liberal British capitalism against a more regulated, coordinated Continental European capitalism. A second, related, conceptual framing of European economic policy debates is the nature of (and conceptions of necessary reform to) the 'European social model'. The chapter challenges the analysis and assumptions underpinning the prevailing analysis and prescription (diagnosis and cure) for European economic reform within British politics. These two discursive framings inform and shape the relationship between British politics and the European political economy. The British tendency is to assert the superiority of its capitalism (and social model) in terms of economic performance, and degree of 'fit' with the global economy. On the back of this, there is a proselytizing desire to redescribe (reinvent) the European political economic space in the UK image. This explains successive UK governments' civilizing mission to 'modernize' the European political economic space (in the UK image) to respond to globalization's challenges.

This account questions the view that the reason for weaker economic performance on the Continent is insufficiently flexible labour markets, and the assumed necessity of reform along 'British' lines. Secondly, it problematizes the notion of the British model's superiority, especially in relation to inequality. Analysis explores the clash of capitalisms and social models within the implementation, successes, and failings of the 'Lisbon agenda'. The relation between welfare state regime and economic performance is examined, before considering attempts to tackle unemployment through 'flexicurity' reforms to labour market institutions, and the framing and content of macroeconomic policy.

49.2 EUROPEAN ECONOMIC GOVERNANCE AND THE 'CLASH OF CAPITALISMS'

Attempts at European economic policy reform should be interpreted against a backdrop of the 'clash of capitalisms' (Callaghan and Hoepner 2005; Hoepner and Shafer 2007), crystallizing into 'contending conceptions of the internal market' and 'contending conceptions of capitalism in Europe'. The resultant ideological struggle pits 'the neoliberal project' against 'regulated capitalism' and Europe as an 'organized [economic] space' (Hooghe and Marks 1999: 74–9, 82–91; Wincott 2003: 292–4). The role, nature, and logic of state regulation is one battleground. For example, the EU takeover directive (inspired by the UK's 'City Code') ignited this 'clash of capitalisms'. The directive was perceived on the continent (notably in Germany) as enshrining an excessively 'Anglo-Saxon' view of takeover as a necessary discipline against inefficient management which ignored valued European corporate governance traditions. This, and some none too subtle 'divide and conquer' tactics by the European Commission (EC) seeking to isolate Germany, explain its failure in 2001 (Callaghan and Hoepner 2005. The subsequent 2004 directive avoided asserting that Anglo-Saxon capitalism was 'better', which appeased opposition at the expense of emasculating the directive (Clift 2009).

Important ammunition in this capitalism 'versus' capitalism skirmish is provided by stylized facts summarizing relative economic and employment performance. Higher growth and lower unemployment in the decade preceding the 2008 crisis in Britain (and the USA) compared to most of Continental Europe thus nourished the 'clash of capitalisms' axis. The reason, extrapolated from this observation, is that the more nimble, flexible, liberal model adapts better to international competition. The European economy is weaved into the UK political narrative as an undesirable other in terms of its organizing political-economic principles. This informs a proselytizing desire to reinvent the European political-economic space along UK lines. Yet New Labour's 'hubristic interpretation of the domestic record' (Hopkin and Wincott 2006) requires interrogation. Such interpretations, especially when told by policy elites advocating a particular course of action, need careful unpicking because they are painted with broad brush strokes and are selective in their inclusion of yardsticks by which success is judged.

Firstly, Blair plays fast and loose with his comparative statistical evidence, noting for example that European productivity is inferior to US levels, neglecting to mention French and German *superiority* to UK productivity levels (Blair 2005; contrast with UK Treasury 2001: 20; Taylor 2005: 200–1). Another neglected statistic in UK success storytelling is the UK 'trade gap' and its deteriorating balance of payments position. This is because the UK balance of payments position over the last two decades has been dire and is getting worse (Clift and Tomlinson 2008). The UK current balance in 2006 showed a deficit of $79.85 billion, whilst the German economy enjoyed a surplus of $146 billion (OECD 2007).

If, synchronically, at a given point in time, the construction of a comparative economic success story needs unpacking, then diachronically, across time, still further nuance is required. For example, in the mid-1990s, after comparatively strong economic performance by 'coordinated economies', notably Germany, Blair and others were enviously eyeing the economic institutions, welfare state, and labour market norms of Continental capitalism, convinced of their superiority. This was the crux of the 'stakeholder' debate which preceded (by only a year) the election of the first New Labour government in 1997 (Kelly, Kelly, and Gamble 1997).

The difficulty is that economic success comes and goes, but the institutions of capitalism are enduring, and change only incrementally. This illustrates the dangers of inferring direct causal performative significance from these capitalist institutions, which cannot be the only independent variable acting upon economic performance (see Coates 2000). Evidence amongst developed countries indicates that the institutional impact on performance is secondary, but that institutions do have a key impact on *distribution* of income (Clift and Perraton 2004), a point to which we shall return. Thus the characterization of Europe as stagnating and ridden with high unemployment because of excessive labour market rigidities does not do justice to the complexity of European economic experience, nor is it likely to stand the test of time.

For example, Germany in the mid-to-late 1990s has been portrayed as the 'sick man of Europe', encompassing all that is wrong with coordinated social market economies (sluggish growth and high unemployment). Recently, however, the German economy has shown strong growth, burgeoning exports, and improving employment performance, with unemployment dropping from 9.5 in 2005 to 8.4 per cent in 2006 (OECD 2007). Some argue Germany is re-emerging 'like a phoenix from the flames' as the 'economic motor' of Europe (Créel and Le Cacheux 2006: 10). Whilst we should be equally sceptical of over-exuberance about the German economy, the ebullient self-confidence of UK policy elites in advocating (Anglo-Saxon) 'solutions' to European economic problems should be tempered. As Blanchard's impressive survey of European unemployment policy notes, 'the history of the last 30 years is a series of love affairs with sometimes sad endings, first with German and German-like institutions—until unemployment started increasing in the 1990s—then with the United Kingdom and the Thatcher–Blair reforms, then with Ireland and the Netherlands and the role of national agreements, and now with the Scandinavian countries, especially Denmark, and its concept of "flexisecurity" ' (Blanchard 2006: 45). Should the worldwide economic downturn which began in 2008 undermine Danish economic and unemployment performance, this may dampen the ardour with which European economic policy elites have embraced 'flexicurity'. The depth of recession in the UK and US economies has certainly damaged faith in the liberal model.

49.3 EUROPEAN WELFARE CAPITALISMS

The urge to cluster political economies into types and models exerts a powerful gravitational pull on comparative political economists. Thus alongside different varieties of capitalist institutions, there are several 'worlds' of welfare state institutions (Esping Andersen 1990). The number of identifiable European clusters is disputed, but oft-identified welfare capitalism types include the 'Nordic', Continental/Bismarkian', 'liberal', and 'Mediterranean' poles (Pierson 2001; Hemerijck and Ferrera 2004; Ferrera, Hemerijck, and Rhodes 2000). It is a peculiarity of sub-disciplinarity within contemporary comparative political economy that, with a small number of honourable exceptions (e.g. Stevens and Huber 2001), the rich literatures on comparative capitalisms and comparative welfare states do not, as a matter of course, 'speak to' each other. This is problematic because both analyse 'welfare capitalism'.

There are too few attempts to explore the interrelationship between comparative capitalisms and welfare institutions and policy, or indeed comparative welfare state theorizing. Yet, on the ground, the European 'clash of capitalisms' is echoed within a clash of social models. The variety of welfare state 'families' feeds clashing conceptions of the correct shape and trajectory of a singular asserted notional European social model. Relationships between employment policy and social policy initiatives and economic and employment outcomes remain contested. The ability of each welfare capitalism type to combine economic competitiveness and social justice is variously decried and lauded. Always infused with a strong normative element, the European social model's beauty lies in the eye of the beholder. Each discussion has in mind a particular configuration, and a particular trajectory for its evolution. This explains the absence of *either* an agreed definition of the European social model, *or* an agreed blueprint for its evolution.

The identification of four welfare state 'families' (Hemerjick and Ferrera 2004: 252) begs the question whether there are specific trajectories in the changing global political economy for particular welfare families. Scholars have explored the 'goodness of fit' between different sets of welfare policies, programmes, and institutions and changing conditions of complex economic interdependence. An initial hypothesis was that globalization was bearing down on all welfare states with equal force, inducing retrenchment of programmes and convergence on minimalist neoliberal welfare norms (see Schwartz 2001 for a discussion and critique).

This crude conception of the relation between globalization and welfare provision (assuming more minimal provision is a necessary condition of international economic competitiveness) underpins the UK government's vision for the future shape and trajectory of the European social model. The accuracy of such assumptions has rightly been questioned. Closer empirical inspection showed that welfare state retrenchment pressures had been overstated (see Swank 2002; Hobson 2003; Hay 2006). Subsequent studies suggested that such retrenchment as is occurring within European welfare states is distributed differently across different welfare state clusters. This indicates *differential* vulnerability of extant EU welfare state 'clusters'. Significantly, the liberal model is not alone in (fairly) successfully navigating the choppier waters of increasing economic interdependence. The (more generous and more egalitarian) Nordic model is fairing well, too. 'Bismarckian' welfare states, on the other hand, face greater retrenchment pressures (Hay 2006: 9–13; Sapir 2006; Palier 2007).

Social rights are at the core of any welfare state regime. Looking at social rights to unemployment insurance, sick pay, and public pensions, analysed in terms of *replacement rates* and *coverage*, Scruggs assesses levels of benefits, duration of benefits, and conditions necessary to qualify for and gain access to benefits. In this way he unearths 'social programme dynamics' with more nuance than crude spending measures can, enabling a more fine-grained assessment of 'welfare state resiliency' (Scruggs 2006: 349–50). Evolutions in aggregate spending levels can conceal significant changes in the logic and character of welfare state provision. Analysis of evolving European social rights leads Scruggs to reject unambiguously the notion of a 'race to the bottom' (2006; see also Hobson 2003). Retrenchment (for example of replacement rates) is a reality in all welfare states, and this retrenchment is greater in the most generous social democratic welfare states (Scruggs 2006: 355). However, 'it is worth noting that all of these (social democratic) countries had higher expected benefits in 2002 than in 1972' (Scruggs 2006: 362). The story is a complex one; 'while welfare state programmes are more generous than they were a generation ago, there has been a shift away from expanding entitlements and towards retrenchment' (Scruggs 2006: 362).

Significantly, New Labour's other core assertion, that 'Anglo-Saxon' capitalism and welfare institutions display more compatibility with globalization, is also inaccurate. The relatively generous Nordic welfare states display *superior* compatibility with globalization than the UK; 'by some conventional analyses, all of Scandinavia should have long ago collapsed under the weight of its public spending. Yet in 2005, three of the four most competitive economies in the world, according to the *Global Competitiveness Index*, were in Scandinavia; the United States is the other one' (Scruggs 2006: 349).

Thus the British superiority complex is built upon decidedly shaky foundations as the impact of the 2008 credit crunch and recession have demonstrated. This is especially true in terms of the 'welfare properties' of British capitalism. The Joseph Rowntree foundation's 2007 report on changing wealth distribution in Britain over the last forty years found that Britain is regressing towards inequality levels last seen more than forty years ago. Indeed, the 'breadline poor' represented 23 per cent of the population in 1970; this dropped in the 1970s, but rose to 27 per cent by 2000 (Dorling et al. 2007: 16). Glyn notes, 'differences between the most and least egalitarian OECD countries have been and remain huge ... unexciting sounding differences in Gini coefficients measuring income inequality mask really enormous differences in distributive patterns' (2001: 6). In a West European context, the UK is a uniquely unequal society, and this inequality has been exacerbated, not reduced, under thirteen years of New Labour in government (Hopkin and Wincott 2006).

For all New Labour's hubris about its 'successes' as an economic and social policy model, there are dissenting voices. Perhaps unsurprisingly, for those analysts and policy elites contemplating reform within Bismarckian models, the more generous and egalitarian Nordic model is a more attractive beacon than the UK (even if movement towards either is unlikely given the complexity of welfare state restructuring—see Pierson 1994). A common continental riposte to British hectoring over labour market reform is that not all accept that realigning labour market institutions on the UK model is a necessary condition of solving unemployment problems and achieving growth. On closer inspection, it becomes clear that good employment performance *can be* compatible with a variety of types of labour market, including those more regulated, and securing higher minimum standards, than the UK economy (Blanchard 2006; Hopkin and Wincott 2006). Sweden and Denmark are often invoked in this context.

49.4 LABOUR MARKET INSTITUTIONS AND UNEMPLOYMENT

The political salience of welfare state reform has been augmented by persistent high unemployment (and its fiscal consequences) in Europe. In this context, welfare reform in the new European and global political economy becomes inseparable from discussions of 'appropriate' labour market institutions, and their (un-)employment effects. Dovetailing with New Labour's underlying premises about the kinds of welfare state compatible with globalization are assumptions about the necessary flexibilization of labour markets. Here they align with a pillar of the dominant European macroeconomic policy orthodoxy in the 1990s and early 2000s, whose essence was distilled in the 1994 OECD *Jobs Survey* (Dostal 2004; OECD 1994). This prevailing 'wisdom' identified 'labour market rigidities' as *the* cause of persistent high unemployment in Continental European countries, notably France, Germany, Italy, and Spain (Blanchard 2006: 26).

Layard, Nickell, and Jackman (1991) had previously placed considerable emphasis on the role of institutions in explaining high unemployment, yet it is the focus on labour market institutions (and rigidities) *to the exclusion of all else* which is striking. All unemployment, in this reading, is accounted for by excessive rigidities of labour market institutions. The European Central Bank (ECB) explicitly aligns with this compartmentalization of economic policy, seeing supply-side measures or 'structural reforms' as the only option (Martin 2004: 24–7). Any role for macroeconomic policy (or demand-side policy) in tackling unemployment is denied. New Labour anachronistically align with this European consensus (for a critique see Hopkin and Wincott 2006: 53–5; Taylor 2005), despite combining demand- and supply-side approaches in pursuing domestic full employment (see below).

As already noted, the empirical record does not support this simplistic reading. The variety of recent employment experience across Europe (good and bad) does not correlate with the variety of labour market regimes (less and more regulated). Many mainstream economists agree that macroeconomic policy *does* have an impact on unemployment. Blanchard, for example, explains how monetary policy (first accommodating, then contractionary) helps account for the initial rise and long-term duration of European unemployment in the 1970s and 1980s (2006: 21–3). Even *Financial Times* economists note the excessive complacency in interpreting all unemployment as resulting from labour market rigidities, and ignoring the possible role of macroeconomic policy errors (Munchau 2006).

The labour market rigidity-unemployment causal assumption is confounded by research offering little evidence of Continental labour market institutions increasing aggregate unemployment levels (Nickell and Layard 1998), with differences in unemployment protection 'largely unrelated to differences in unemployment rates across countries' (Blanchard 2006: 30–1). Martin's analysis finds that labour market institutions did not have the impact on the NAIRU (the non-accelerating inflation rate of unemployment) that some economics literature credits them with. He finds 'no consistent relationship...between economic outcomes and labour market institutions' (2004: 40), and little correlation between the extent of labour market reforms and changes in the NAIRU. Labour market reform *may*, he concludes, help reduce unemployment, alongside demand explanations. It is these interactions between institutions and macroeconomic factors, assessing the relative weight to attach to each, which is crucial.

Thus it is erroneous to assert (as New Labour does) that rigid labour market 'equals' poor economic performance and high unemployment. That is not to say that labour market institutions may not benefit from reform, and that they may well be one contributing factor (amongst many) to unemployment performance. Yet, as we shall see when we look at 'flexicurity' debates, views differ on to what extent labour market reform should erode job security, and the generosity and automaticity of benefits. In short, how much social justice can be retained whilst seeking to reinvigorate economic efficiency? The kind of labour and welfare institutions seen as 'necessary' in a global economy in Britain are regarded as threatening cherished norms and *acquis sociaux* in many European countries. Their defenders are comforted by countries like Sweden and Denmark who have achieved success in a global economy without the root and branch retrenchment of welfare and labour market flexibilization seen in the UK since the early 1980s (Taylor 2005: 198).

49.5 MACROECONOMIC POLICY, UNEMPLOYMENT, AND POLITICAL-ECONOMIC IDEAS

The 1994 OECD *Jobs Survey* approach takes a particular and very restrictive view of the limits of the possible for macroeconomic policy in tackling unemployment. Macroeconomic policy priorities have evolved in recent decades, with increasing priority afforded to 'stability' (low inflation), and a decreasing conviction on the part of policy-makers (in particular central bankers) that macroeconomic policy has an active role to play in securing full employment. More unites European governments than divides them in their pursuit of macroeconomic policy. In terms of public finances, within and outside the euro, all share the commitment to 'sound' public finances and low inflation, deemed by all a necessary condition of economic credibility with deregulated financial markets (see e.g. Green-Pedersen, van Kersbergen, and Hemerijck 2001: 309; SAP 2002).

The lessons drawn from earlier macroeconomic policy errors (such as the Lawson boom of the 1980s, or Swedish policy in the 1980s and early 1990s—see Ryner 2000: 341–5; 2002: 150–3) is that activist macroeconomic policy, whilst potentially beneficial, is also capable of doing considerable damage. Therefore ambitions are modest, seeking to deliver stability as priority number one. This is often interpreted as an 'abandonment' of Keynesianism and an 'embrace' of neoliberalism or monetarism. However, it makes sense to add more nuance, since elements taking inspiration from both approaches are present within European policy mixes, and the quantities put into the mix (and the policy infrastructure which delivers it) can vary cross-nationally.

The euro's institutional architecture has hindered the use of activist macroeconomic policy in tackling long-term unemployment on the Continent. The ECB's view of the 'appropriate' (non-inflationary) growth rate of the euro-zone at 2–2.5 per cent assumes that monetary policy cannot have a (positive) impact on unemployment without generating higher (and accelerating) inflation (Martin 2004: 24). The UK, some European policy-makers have noted, has less unemployment and a macro-policy infrastructure built on different assumptions which grants policy-makers greater autonomy. This correlation may explain why UK policy elites' desire to provide a model for European fiscal and monetary policy governance finds a more receptive audience than their welfare reform exhortations. Labour's macroeconomic policy approach is a pragmatic combination of monetarist ideas (particularly setting targets for inflation) and New Keynesian ideas, particularly that policy activism can improve economic performance (Annesley and Gamble 2003).

Gordon Brown established a rules-based macroeconomic policy framework consistent with this outlook, characterized by Bank of England independence and stability and credibility-centric fiscal 'golden rules' (Clift and Tomlinson 2004), a macroeconomic stance which nevertheless allows considerable scope for activism to support full employment, notably through expansionary fiscal policy (Clift and Tomlinson 2007). For all the apparent 'neoliberalism' of New Labour, the UK's 'golden rules' are more supple and less draconian than the stability and growth pact (SGP), and the UK stands on a more 'Keynesian' footing than do many of its euro-zone counterparts. Indeed, New Labour's fiscal activism in the early 2000s attracted both admiring glances from some European governments and the disapproving glare of the European Commission (who took exception to New Labour breaching their 3 per cent deficit target in 2001, 2002, and again in 2008). Gordon Brown attacked the 'over-narrow' and 'mechanistic' interpretation of the SGP for taking insufficient account of the economic cycle, public investment needs, and national debt levels.

At issue was the political economy model underpinning the economic architecture of the euro. Many felt it drew too heavily from 'monetarist' orthodoxy, insufficiently balanced by 'Keynesian' elements. As then Commission President Romano Prodi and EU Trade Commissioner Pascal Lamy attacked the SGP in 2002, the reform debate gathered pace. This became a central issue in European politics between 2003 and 2005, when France and Germany exceeded SGP targets, heralding a crisis of European economic governance. This was only resolved when the Commission and member states secured an uneasy peace over a (much less restrictive) revised SGP in March 2005 offering more fiscal policy latitude to euro-zone economies (see Clift 2006).

Yet the appetite for reform of the euro's economic policy architecture is not yet sated. Once again, those advocating reform cast an approving eye upon British monetary policy institutions. Many argue that the EU has to acquire institutions ensuring a monetary and fiscal policy mix without a deflationary bias (Pisani-Ferry 2006). Part of the reason for high euro-zone unemployment may well lie with the political-economic underpinnings of the euro, and the restrictive monetary policy stance holding back growth (Martin 2004: 32–41; Ball 1999). Blanchard also questions assumptions by the ECB that low European inflation 'proves' that European unemployment is at its 'natural' level, on which expansionary macroeconomic policy cannot have a beneficial effect, except at the expense of (substantial and accelerating) rises in inflation: 'it may be that, in fact, an expansion of demand might decrease unemployment without leading to steadily higher inflation' (2006: 47).

In this light, the British model of an independent Bank of England with a *symmetrical* inflation target (in theory, at least, the central bank has to *reflate* the economy if inflation falls too low) may be a step in the right direction. The rebalancing of priorities between inflation and growth could alleviate the deflationary pressure of the ECB (Pisani-Ferry 2006; Lamy and Pisani-Ferry 2002: 109–16; Martin 2004: 29). By contrast, arguments for a 'growth spurt' induced in part by macroeconomic policy to give an impulse to growth (and employment) (Ball 1999) fly in the face of the ECB's statutes which enshrine neoliberal orthodoxy on this point. Calls (from political parties, trade unions, and employers' organizations) for the ECB to change its statutes to incorporate a priority for jobs and growth alongside its constitutional obligation to keep inflation low continue to fall on deaf ears. In the meantime, more activist-oriented European macroeconomic policy reformers may continue to gaze wistfully over the Channel.

49.6 THE LISBON PROCESS AND EUROPEAN ECONOMIC REFORM: FROM FLEXIBILITY TO FLEXICURITY?

If ECB monetary policy is unlikely to solve Europe's unemployment problems, the thinking goes, then social policy and labour market reforms will have to. Centrally focused on labour market and social policy, the Lisbon summit ambitiously committed to make Europe 'the most competitive and dynamic knowledge-driven economy by 2010 capable of sustainable economic growth with more and better jobs and greater social cohesion'. This attempt to 'operationalize' the concept of the European social model was launched in 2000 and relaunched in 2005 (Annesley 2007: 195–6; Daly 2006). The method to achieve this 'Lisbon agenda' was not 'hard' law (directives and treaties) but the 'open method of coordination' (OMC), a 'soft' law approach involving moral suasion, reporting, disseminating best practice, and benchmarking. The OMC sees policy-making as involving 'problem-solving and policy development and learning through peer review, dialogue, soft incentives, normative reflection and experimentation' (Daly 2006: 466; Wincott 2003: 283).

The Lisbon process has been interpreted as an 'interrogation of the orthodox assertion that a "big trade-off" exists between equity and efficiency' (Hopkin and Wincott 2006: 51). There is a broad consensus on the need to scale back 'passive' welfare provision spending which makes no discernible contribution to economic growth (Annesley 2003; Bonoli, George, and Taylor-Gooby 2000). However, not all welfare spending is tarred with the same brush. Ideas of 'activation' within employment policy and social policy reform became widespread throughout Europe in the 1990s and early 2000s and are at the heart of the Lisbon agenda (Vandenbroucke 2002). This emphasis on 'active' welfare spending, and investment in human capital formation through education and training, suggests a very different set of priorities for social and labour market policy than the OECD's *Jobs Study*. The Lisbon process has political-economic foundations in ideas such as 'supply side egalitarianism', 'competitive solidarity' (Streeck 1999), and 'competitive corporatism' (Rhodes 2001). Slightly removed from the rigidity/flexibility dichotomy, the approach is more nuanced as to the kind and degree of labour market reform desired, as well as its interrelationship with other reforms.

The emergent employment-centred social policy consensus accepts 'the market and employment' as 'the primary *loci* of integration' to solve social exclusion (Daly 2006: 469). It is, in welfare state literature terms, concerned with recommodification (returning citizens to the labour market) not decommodification (Esping-Andersen 1990). Similar activation strategies have been pursued in many European countries, including Denmark (Campbell and Pedersen 2007), France (Clasen and Clegg 2003), Holland (Hemerjick and Visser 1997), and Portugal (Costa Lobo and Magalhaes 2004: 91–2) to name but a few, since the mid-to-late 1990s (see Bonoli and Powell 2004).

The European economic consensus should not be overstated, however. Conceptions of that 'market' differ widely in relation to its flexibility, and the degree of generosity and redistribution of the regulatory institutions which frame it. Although all champion employment-centred social policy, there are very different views on the relative importance of flexibility and job security as policy objectives, and the interaction between activation and the distributive consequences of welfare policies. Thus whilst all advocate activation, some remain more committed to redistribution than others. This difference of view explains why more familiar social policy objectives, such as redistribution, are 'at best implicit' in the objectives which underpin the

Lisbon process (Daly 2006: 470), and have been further marginalized in 'Lisbon II' since 2005.

The OMC provides opportunities in terms of 'uploading' social policy ideas. The Blair governments sought to be the source, rather than recipient, of lessons on social model reform. New Labour continued to drive home a particular framing of European economic problems and challenges, and a (British) solution, placing 'Britain at the leading edge of EU development, shaping its form, not "taking" policies shaped elsewhere' (Wincott 2003: 297). Most recently, this 'uploading' exercise has been facilitated because New Labour's ideas about the necessity of UK-style flexibility to social model reform have found favour within an EC seeking to frame a pan-European debate about 'flexicurity'. The EC's role within the OMC identifying and disseminating 'best practice' (Keune and Jepsen 2007: 10; Casey and Gold 2005) gives it significant discursive power. Through the EC's deliberately narrow (New Labour-esque) interpretation in seeking to develop an EU-wide set of flexicurity principles, particular reform trajectories are prioritized, others marginalized (Keune and Jepsen 2007: 8).

Drawing on Dutch and more recently Danish experience, the mooted combination of flexibility and security within 'flexicurity' has been the central focus of 'market-making' regulatory social policy reform in recent years. Danish 'flexicurity' combines three elements in a context of increasing flexibility of work contracts and work practices, as well as institutional decentralization of wage bargaining. Firstly, there is limited private-sector employment protection (e.g. hiring and firing), and thus high job mobility. Secondly, there are generous universal unemployment and health insurance and other welfare benefits. These were increasingly closely tied to employment seeking, levels were reduced, and eligibility restricted through reforms in the 1990s. Thirdly, there are extensive retraining opportunities to help workers acquire new skills, as well as assistance and support in locating new employment opportunities (Campbell and Pedersen 2007: 316–19). This model's combination of welfare generosity with an 'activating' role for the state attracts admiring interest from other European countries with high unemployment, such as France.

The fact that both poster children of flexicurity enjoyed employment rates 10 per cent above the EU25 average has bolstered the case for the merits of flexicurity. The support from academic studies, imparting causal significance to this correlation, served to add a scientific, technical quality to EC discourse on flexicurity. However, its appropriation and deployment by the EC was a deeply political process, emphasizing the flexibility elements and downplaying welfare generosity. The EC interpretation involves a very particular understanding of 'security'. This in turn rests on a distinctive conception of the European social model, and the relation between competitiveness, flexibility, and social cohesion within it. The EC's flexicurity agenda is framed, like New Labour's, by the perceived flexibility imperatives of labour market and welfare reform in the global economy.

For the EC, flexicurity provides bridges between labour market situations of employment, unemployment, and inactivity within 'the increasingly transitional nature of today's labour market' (CEC 2004: 159), whilst tackling problems of labour market segmentation and job precariousness. The key elements to deliver this are work contracts providing adequate flexibility (i.e. facilitating hiring and firing), active labour market policies, lifelong learning, and social security systems providing support during absence from the labour market and facilitating transition and mobility (CEC 2006: 31, 39; Keune and Jepsen 2007: 12–13).

Significantly, job security is *not* a priority from an EC perspective, and dismissal protection is deemed damaging to flexibility. It is people, not jobs, which are to be protected. What the EC takes as the core of flexicurity is to prioritize increased mobility, use of non-standard employment, and *reduced* job protection. In the process, 'old' security will reduce, supplanted by 'new' security. The EC has redefined security, no longer as 'protection against risk', but rather 'the capacity to adapt to change by means of a process of constant learning' (Keune and Jepsen 2007: 15). The EC understands flexibility primarily in terms of hiring and firing. The agenda which flows from this is 'a tightening of benefits schemes where they are "generous", and a reduction of employment protection' (Keune and Jepsen 2007: 15). This erodes security (certainly 'old' security) without a 'compensatory' bolstering of redistributive provision mitigating the effects of labour market transition.

Since the Lisbon relaunch, adapting and specializing education and training systems and raising employment and employability have been increasingly central to the agenda (Daly 2006: 466). As with 'Lisbon II' more broadly, social and redistribution commitments are decreasingly visible within the EC's flexicurity agenda. Given the redefinition of security, the 'balance' between flexibility and security is decisively skewed towards the flexibility side. The irony is that the OECD has, in the light of evidence and analysis since its 1994 *Job Study*, departed from its myopic flexibility-obsessed interpretation of labour markets and employment performance (OECD 2006: 96–100). The EC has moved onto precisely the terrain the OECD recently vacated.

49.7 THE EUROPEAN SOCIAL MODEL AND BRITISH POLITICS: 'UPLOADING' OR 'DOWNLOADING'?

Whilst New Labour's flexibility agenda has found favour with the EC, there is no guarantee it will reshape the European political economy. The lack of agreement and dissent from the relation between flexibility and economic and employment performance espoused by New Labour and the EC is significant given the nature of the OMC. In many member states, views depart from UK/EC norms over the degree and nature of the emphasis on flexibility (and the status of job security as a policy priority). Thus there has not been a seamless 'uploading' of the flexible LME

UK vision to the Lisbon agenda 'mainframe'. New Labour's attempt to shape the future form of the European social model, whilst well aligned with the EC vision, faces competition from other European visions and models which many deem more attractive. British economic and social policy initiatives have to hold their own in a battle of ideas. One's policy record is a key weapon in this battle for ideas. Here, given the poor inequality performance of the British social model, the UK policy advocacy loses ground vis-à-vis Nordic variants. The Danish model, more than New Labour, is evoked as the virtuous European path to 'activating' labour market reform.

Another Nordic source of inspiration is the Swedish activation approach and the 'adult worker model' (AWM) in which 'all adults—male and female, old and young, abled and less-abled—are required to take formal employment to secure economic independence' (Annesley 2007: 196). This heralds an evolution away from the old 'male breadwinner model' (of which the post-war UK was a prime example) to an 'emerging Europe-wide AWM' seeking to integrate all economic inactive citizens—be they women, older citizens, the disabled—into the labour market (Annesley 2007: 196–8). Within the European employment strategy, and the Lisbon process more broadly, Annesley identifies (halting) progress towards a Swedish-inspired 'supported' AWM with state provision of, for example, childcare and parental leave entitlements (2007: 199–202).

In practice, of course, no amount of enthusiasm for any of these models will induce a high degree of convergence in social policy and labour market institutions and programmes across Western Europe. The differentiated labour market and welfare institutions, programmes, and histories are sedimented into their national landscapes. The impact of EU economic governance on Europe's social models involves the complex interplay of endogenous and exogenous pressures, with 'domestic' ideational and institutional variables playing a key mediating role (Featherstone 2004). The prevailing depiction is of a differentiated 'hybridization' of Europe's welfare and labour market institutions, programmes, and policies (see Clift 2007).

The OMC highlights the limitations of the EU as a geological force eroding national particularities. This has implications, of course, for the extent of change to UK social and labour market policy *induced* by Europe. Many point to the lack of 'teeth' and change-inducing mechanisms within the OMC (Annesley 2007; Wincott 2003) and dissonance between the weakness of the Lisbon method and the very ambitious Lisbon agenda (Sapir 2006: 386; Daly 2006: 478). Indeed, the OMC is arguably little more than a 'discursive bandwagon' (Radaelli 2003: 32). Within the OMC, Europeanization takes on a 'voluntary form' (Wincott 2003: 297), and national policy elites choose to 'learn' those policy elements which align closest with their existing practice.

Analyses of UK social policy in the 1990s and 2000s indicate hybridization, drawing greater inspiration from *both* the USA (see e.g. King and Wickham-Jones 1999) *and* the 'growing influence of the European Union's social policy agenda on the UK' (Annesley 2003: 144), principally through signing up to EU social protocol (Annesley 2003: 158). EU influence is most evident on the industrial relations settlement, where there is evidence of UK *re*alignment with European union recognition and employment and unfair dismissal rights norms (Taylor 1998).

The establishment of a national minimum wage was also a major structural change for the UK labour market. Its original positive redistribution effect, Metcalf suggests, was underestimated in most studies (1999: 184). After modest increases between 2002 and 2004, it was more dramatically increased in 2004–5, and by 6 per cent again in October 2006 to £5.35; 'according to DTI figures, these increases will improve the pay of over 1.3 million low paid workers, the majority of whom are women' (EIRO 2006a). The partial empowerment of employees vis-à-vis employers and improvements in employee rights doubtless result from the ending of the opt-out to the EU Social Chapter (Undy 1999: 332) and the acceptance of the Employment Chapter at Amsterdam. Recalling Annesley's AWM, there are 'family friendly' policies extending rights to parental leave which are a direct result of the social chapter.

Yet the degree of change should not be overstated. A 'pattern of initial rejection of EU social legislation, followed by minimalist interpretation and implementation, has repeated itself since 1997' (Howell 2004: 8). Pierson and Liebfried (1995) point to how the EU (through Commission activism and ECJ jurisprudence) is potentially a powerful actor in welfare policy change, rendering member welfare states 'semi-sovereign' (see also Ferrera 2005; Annesley 2003: 151–2). There is some evidence of this in relation to working time. On rest periods, where the Commission felt UK application invited non-compliance, the ECJ ruled in September 2006 that the UK had 'failed to fulfil its obligations under the directive, with the implication that the government should amend the offending parts of the guidelines' (EIRO 2006b). Yet the degree of change induced by such rulings is limited, and the generalized opt-out remains. This leaves the UK as an outlier in Europe, not least because of New Labour's unswerving commitment to labour market flexibility.

49.8 CONCLUSION

Underlying UK government understandings of the appropriate EU priorities of economic and social policy reform have been conditioned by the hubristic, self-congratulatory interpretation of the British social model, the British model of capitalism, and New Labour's economic policy record between 1997 and 2007. Doubtless, there have been conspicuously successful aspects to the policy record, but there are clouds in the sky. The after-shocks of the sub-prime crisis (hitting the UK's more deeply financialized economy comparatively hard) have caused faltering growth and eroding consumer confidence. The falling pound relative to the euro, and the ongoing balance of payments deficit, beg further questions about the UK as Europe's economic success story. At present, international financial markets are sanguine about the balance of payments deficit. However, it is clear that policy-makers do not control (and possibly do not fully understand) the conditions under which that situation could change. Increased uncertainty and the post-sub-prime global downturn could herald a re-emphasis on 'economic fundamentals'. On those grounds, Germany looks a safer bet than the UK, and the inflows which offset the UK deficit may be harder to attract.

The UK's export record of political-economic ideas to the European continent is considerably better than its actual economic performance in terms of exports in the last decade. Regarding the macroeconomic policy architecture, in relation to both fiscal and monetary policy, the UK case is regarded with approval on the continent. Whilst it is difficult to assess what degree of positive employment performance can be traced to these macroeconomic policy institutions, there are some grounds for thinking UK institutions are 'right', perhaps 'better', than the current EMU framework. Yet since the economic architecture of EMU is not liable for reform, it is not here but on social policy and labour market reform that UK governments concentrate their reforming zeal. In these areas, their lessons fall on less receptive ears. International competition is stiff, with Denmark and Sweden cornering a sizeable market share of the economic and social reform agenda. This is partly because of the ambiguity about how much of the UK comparative economic success results from the labour market institutions it tries unsuccessfully to foist on the rest of Europe. Economic performance and political-economic institutions display a more complex interrelation than New Labour's superiority complex chooses to admit.

Moreover, New Labour hubris conceals a comparatively poor redistributive performance. New Labour has picked the 'low hanging fruit' by pulling those just below the poverty line just above it. More structural problems of poverty and inequality in British society remain unaddressed. Wincott and Hopkin's analysis indicates that the UK uniquely has an extremely poor inequality score, such that 'the UK remains an unusually unequal society by general European (never mind Nordic) standards' (Hopkin and Wincott 2006: 59–61, 65). For all the commonality between aspects of the UK social model and the EC's desired direction of travel for labour market reform, this gremlin seriously hinders the uploading of British social policy to the EU 'mainframe'.

The UK model was successful in terms of employment between 1997 and 2007, but this success has been bought at what many consider too high a price in terms of social inequality. Furthermore, the sub-prime crisis has highlighted the fragility of an economic growth model predicated so heavily on consumer debt. This hinders the effectiveness of first Blair then Brown as latter-day 'fishwife Britannias' (Clarke 1991: 317), when they emulate (in style if not content) Margaret Thatcher in haranguing European policy elites about their failings to pursue the Lisbon agenda with more vigour, and in a direction more closely aligned with New Labour's vision of economic and labour market institutions compatible with the new global economy.

Yet the Lisbon process lacks the mechanisms to induce the convergence it exhorts. The process is an exercise in what Campbell calls 'bricolage', or 'translation', 'the combination of locally available principles and practices with new ones originating elsewhere' (2004: 65). When one looks closer, it becomes clear that commonalities of direction of travel mask widely divergent starting points (Hay 2004), and differential degrees of commitment to activation. The result is differences in how much of the pre-existing (protected, less reformed) labour market remains, and different relative importance of 'new' activation-oriented contracts and programmes. Social minima, welfare programmes, and labour market institutions will continue to differ widely. The likely future trajectories of European economic and social policy involve cross-fertilization and hybridization of models. Within the protean comparative capitalisms (and European social model) debates, the relative merits of 'regulated' versus 'neoliberal' capitalism remain disputed, with little sign of the liberal convergence British politicians so enthusiastically advocate. With the recession deepening in 2008–9, and biting particularly hard in the UK, British export performance, at the level of both goods and services, but more importantly at the level of political-economic models, looks under threat.

References

Annesley, C. 2003. 'Americanised and Europeanised: UK Social Policy since 1997'. *British Journal of Politics and International Relations*, 5/2: 143–65.

——2007. 'Lisbon and Social Europe: Towards a European "Adult Worker Model" Welfare System'. *Journal of European Social Policy*, 17/3: 195–205.

——and Gamble, A. 2003. 'Economic and Welfare Policy'. Pp. 144–60 in M. J. Smith and S. Ludlam (eds.), *Governing as New Labour*. Basingstoke: Palgrave.

Ball, L. 1999. 'Aggregate Demand and Long-Run Unemployment'. *Brookings Papers on Economic Activity*, 2: 189–251.

Blair, T. 2005. Speech to the European Parliament. 23 June. Available at http://www.number-10.gov.uk/output/Page7714.asp.

Blanchard, O. 2006. 'European Unemployment: The Evolution of Facts and Ideas'. *Economic Policy*, Jan.: 5–59.

Bonoli, G., George, V. and Taylor-Gooby, P. 2000. *European Welfare Futures: Towards a Theory of Retrenchment*. Cambridge: Polity.

——and Powell, M. (eds.) 2004. *Social Democratic Party Policies in Europe*. London: Routledge.

Brown, G. 2005. *Global Europe: Full Employment Europe*. London: HM Treasury.

Callaghan, H., and Hoepner, M. 2005. 'European Integration and the Clash of Capitalisms: Political Cleavages of Takeover Liberalisation'. *Comparative European Politics*, 3: 307–32.

Campbell, J. 2004. *Institutional Change and Globalization*. Princeton, NJ: Princeton University Press.

——and Pedersen, O. 2007. 'The Varieties of Capitalism and Hybrid Success: Denmark in the Global Economy'. *Comparative Political Studies*, 40/3: 307–22.

Casey, B., and Gold, M. 2005. 'Peer Review of Labour Market Programmes in the European Union: What Can Countries Really Learn from One Another?' *Journal of European Public Policy*, 21/1: 23–43.

CEC 2004. *Employment in Europe 2004*. Luxembourg: CEC.

——2006. *Proposal for a Council Decision: Guidelines for Employment Policies of the Member States Presented by the Commission*. COM 2006.32. Brussels. 25 Jan.

Clarke, P. 1991. *A Question of Leadership: Gladstone to Thatcher*. London: Hamish Hamilton.

Clasen, J., and Clegg, D. 2003. 'Unemployment Protection and Labour Market Reform in France and Great Britain in the 1990s: Solidarity versus Activation?' *Journal of Social Policy*,

32/3: 361–81.

CLIFT, B. 2006. 'The New Political Economy of *Dirigisme*: French Macroeconomic Policy, Unrepentant Sinning, and the Stability and Growth Pact'. *British Journal of Politics and International Relations*, 8/3: 388–409.

——2007. 'Europeanizing Social Models?' *Journal of European Integration*, 29/2: 249–54.

——2009. 'Second Time as Farce? The EU Takeover Directive, the Clash of Capitalisms and the Hamstrung Harmonisation of European (and French) Corporate Governance'. *Journal of Common Market Studies*, 47/1: 55–79.

——and PERRATON, J. 2004. 'So Where Are National Capitalisms Now?' Pp. 195–261 in B. Clift and J. Perraton (eds.), *Where Are National Capitalisms Now?* Basingstoke: Palgrave.

——and TOMLINSON, J. 2004. 'Capital Mobility and Fiscal Policy: The Construction of Economic Policy Rectitude in Britain and France'. *New Political Economy*, 9/4: 515–37.

————2007. 'Credible Keynesianism? New Labour Macroeconomic Policy and the Political Economy of Coarse Tuning'. *British Journal of Political Science*, 37/1: 47–69.

————2008. 'Whatever Happened to the UK Balance of Payments 'Problem'? The Contingent (Re)Construction of British Economic Performance Assessment'. *British Journal of Politics and International Relations*, 10/4: 607–29.

COATES, D. 2000. *Models of Capitalism*. Cambridge: Polity.

COSTA LOBO, M., and MAGALHAES, P. 2004. 'The Portuguese Socialists and the Third Way'. Pp. 83–101 in Bonoli and Powell 2004.

CRÉEL, J., and LE CACHEUX, J. 2006. 'La Nouvelle Désinflation compétitive européenne?' *Revue de l'OFCE*: 9–36.

CROUCH, C. 2005. 'Models of Capitalism'. *New Political Economy*, 10/4: 439–56.

DALY, M. 2006. 'EU Social Policy after Lisbon'. *Journal of Common Market Studies*, 44/3: 461–81.

DELORS, J. 1992. *Our Europe?* London: Verso.

DORLING, D., RIGBY, J., WHEELER, B., BALLAS, D., THOMAS, B., FAHMY, E., GORDON, D., and LUPTON, L. 2007. *Poverty, Wealth and Place in Britain, 1968 to 2005*. London: Joseph Rowntree Foundation and Policy Press.

DOSTAL, M. 2004. 'Campaigning on Expertise: How the OECD Framed EU Welfare and Labour Market Policies: And Why Success Could Trigger Failure'. *Journal of European Public Policy*, 11/3: 440–60.

ESPING-ANDERSEN, G. 1990. *The Three Worlds of Welfare Capitalism*. Cambridge: Polity.

EIRO (European Industrial Relations Observatory) 2006a. 'Government to Increase National Minimum Wage'. 31 Aug. http://www.eurofound.europa.eu/eiro/2006/04/articles/uk0604029i.html.

——2006b. 'European Court Finds UK in Breach of Working Time Directive'. 20 Nov. http://www.eurofound.europa.eu/eiro/2006/10/articles/uk0610029i.html.

FEATHERSTONE, K. 2004. 'The Political Dynamics of External Empowerment: The Emergence of EMU and the Challenge to the European Social Model'. Pp. 226–47 in Ross and Martin 2004.

FERRERA, M. 2005. *The Boundaries of Welfare: European Integration and the New Spatial Politics of Social Protection*. Oxford: Oxford University Press.

——HEMERIJCK, A., and RHODES, M. 2000. *The Future of Social Europe*. Oeiras: Celta Editoria.

GLYN, A. 2001. 'Aspirations, Constraints, and Outcomes'. Pp. 1–20 in A. Glyn (ed.), *Social Democracy in Neoliberal Times*. Oxford: Oxford University Press.

GREEN-PEDERSEN, C., VAN KERSBERGEN, K., and HEMERIJCK, A. 2001. 'Neo-liberalism, the "Third Way" or What? Recent Social Democratic Welfare Policies in Denmark and the Netherlands'. *Journal of European Public Policy*, 8/2: 307–25.

HALL, P., and SOSKICE, D. 2001. 'An Introduction to Varieties of Capitalism'. Pp. 1–70 in P. Hall and D. Soskice (eds.), *Varieties of Capitalism*. Oxford: Oxford University Press.

HAY, C. 2004. 'Common Trajectories, Variable Paces, Divergent Outcomes? Models of European Capitalism under Conditions of Complex Economic Interdependence'. *Review of International Political Economy*, 11/2: 231–62.

—— 2006. 'What's Globalisation Got to Do with It? Economic Interdependence and the Future of European Welfare States'. *Government and Opposition*, 41/1: 1–22.

HEMERIJCK, A., and FERRERA, M. 2004. 'Welfare Reform in the Shadow of EMU'. Pp. 248–77 in Ross and Martin 2004.

—— and VISSER, J. 1997. *A Dutch Miracle: Job Growth, Welfare Reform and Corporatism in the Netherlands*. Amsterdam: Amsterdam University Press.

HOBSON, J. 2003. 'Disappearing Taxes or the "Race to the Middle"? Fiscal Policy in the OECD'. Pp. 37–56 in L. Weiss (ed.), *States in the Global Economy*. Cambridge: Cambridge University Press.

HOEPNER, M., and SHAFER, A. 2007. *A New Phase of European Integration: Organized Capitalisms in Post-Ricardian Europe*. MPIfG Discussion Paper 7/4. Cologne: Max Planck Institute.

HOOGHE, L., and MARKS, G. 1999. 'The Making of a Polity: The Struggle over European Integration'. Pp. 70–97 in H. Kitschelt et al. (eds.), *Continuity and Change in Contemporary Capitalism*. Cambridge: Cambridge University Press.

HOPKIN, J., and WINCOTT, D. 2006. 'New Labour, Economic Reform, and the European Social Model'. *British Journal of Politics and International Relations*, 8/1: 50–68.

HOWELL, C. 2004. 'Is There a Third Way in Industrial Relations?' *British Journal of Industrial Relations*, 42/1: 1–22.

KELLY, G., KELLY, D., and GAMBLE, A. 1997. *Stakeholder Capitalism*. Basingstoke: Macmillan.

KEUNE, M., and JEPSEN, M. 2007. *Not Balanced and Hardly New: The European Commission's Quest for Flexicurity*. European Trade Union Institute for Research, Education and Health and Safety ETUI-REHS, Working Paper 2007.01. http://etui-rehs.org/research/publications.

KING, D., and WICKHAM-JONES, M. 1999. 'Bridging the Atlantic: The Democratic Party Origins of Welfare to Work'. Pp. 257–80 in M. Powell (ed.), *New Labour, New Welfare State? The Third Way in British Social Policy*. Bristol: Policy Press.

LAMY, P., and PISANI-FERRY, J. 2002. 'The Europe We Want'. In L. Jospin (ed.), *My Vision of Europe and Globalization*. London: Policy Network/Polity.

LAYARD, R. NICKELL, S., and JACKMAN, R. 1991. *Unemployment: Macroeconomic Performance and the Labour Market*. Oxford: Oxford University Press.

MARTIN, A. 2004. 'The EMU Macroeconomic Policy Regime and the European Social Model'. Pp. 20–49 in Ross and Martin 2004.

—— and ROSS, G. 2004. 'Introduction: EMU and the European Social Model'. Pp. 1–19 in Ross and Martin 2004.

METCALF, D. 1999. 'The British Minimum Wage'. *British Journal of Industrial Relations*, 37/2: 171–201.

OECD 1994. *The OECD Jobs Study*. Paris: OECD.

—— 2006. *Employment Outlook: Boosting Jobs and Income*. Paris: OECD.

—— 2007. *Main Economic Indicators, March 2007*. Paris: OECD.

MUNCHAU, W. 2006. 'Commentary on European Unemployment: The Evolution of Facts and Ideas'. *Economic Policy*, Jan.: 5–59.

NICKELL, S., and LAYARD, R. 1998. 'Labour Market Institutions and Economic Performance'. In O. Ashenfelter and D. Card (eds.), *Handbook of Labour Economics*. Amsterdam: North-Holland.

PALIER, P. 2007. 'A Long Goodbye to Bismarck?' Seminar at the CEVIPOF, Sciences-Po. Paris, March.

PIERSON, P. 1994. *Dismantling the Welfare State?* Cambridge: Cambridge University Press.

—— (ed.) 2001. *The New Politics of the Welfare State.* Oxford: Oxford University Press.

—— and LIEBFRIED, S. 1995. 'Multi-tiered Institutions and the Making of Social Policy'. Pp. 1–40 in S. Leibfried and P. Pierson (eds.), *European Social Policy: Between Fragmentation and Integration.* Washington, DC: Brookings.

PISANI-FERRY, J. 2006. 'Only One Bed for Two Dreams: A Critical Retrospective on the Debate over the Economic Governance of the Euro Area'. *Journal of Common Market Studies,* 44/4: 823–44.

RADAELLI, C. 2003. *The Open Method of Co-Ordination: A New Governance Architecture for the European Union?* Stockholm: Swedish Institute for Policy Studies.

RHODES, M. 2001. 'The Political Economy of Social Pacts: "Competitive Corporatism" and European Welfare States'. Pp. 165–98 in Pierson 2001.

ROSS, G., and MARTIN, A. (eds.) 2004. *Euros and Europeans: European Integration and the European Model of Society.* Cambridge: Cambridge University Press.

RYNER, M. 2000. 'Swedish Employment Policy after EU-Membership'. *Österreichische Zeitschrift für Politikwissenschaft,* 29/3: 341–55.

—— 2002. *Capitalist Restructuring, Globalisation and the Third Way: Lessons from the Swedish Model.* London: Routledge.

SAP 2002. *Working Together for Security and Development: The Election Manifesto of the Swedish Social Democrats 2002–2006.* Stockholm: SAP.

SAPIR, A. 2006. 'Globalisation and the Reform of European Social Models'. *Journal of Common Market Studies,* 44/2: 369–90.

SCHWARTZ, H. 2001. 'Round up the Usual Suspects! Globalisation, Domestic Politics, and Welfare State Change'. Pp. 17–44 in P. Pierson (ed.), *The New Politics of Welfare.* Oxford: Oxford University Press.

SCRUGGS, L. 2006. 'The Generosity of Social Insurance, 1971–2002'. *Oxford Review of Economic Policy,* 22/3: 349–64.

STEVENS, J., and HUBER, J. 2001. *Development and Crisis of the Welfare State: Parties and Policies in Global Markets.* Chicago: Chicago University Press.

STREECK, W. 1999. 'Competitive Solidarity: Rethinking the "European Social Model"'. MPIfG Working Paper 99/8. September. Available at http://www.mpi-fg-koeln.mpg.de/pu/workpap/wp99-8/wp99-8.html.

SWANK, D. 2002. *Global Capital, Political Institutions, and Policy Change in Developed Welfare States.* Cambridge: Cambridge University Press.

TAYLOR, R. 1998. 'Annual Review Article 1997'. *British Journal of Industrial Relations,* 36/2: 293–311.

—— 2005. 'Mr Blair's Business Model: Capital and Labour in Flexible Markets'. Pp. 184–206 in A. Seldon and D. Kavanagh (eds.), *The Blair Effect.* Oxford: Oxford University Press.

UK TREASURY 2001. *European Economic Reform: Meeting the Challenge.* London: HMSO.

UNDY, R. 1999. 'Annual Review Article: New Labour's Industrial Relations Settlement: The Third Way?' *British Journal of Industrial Relations,* 37/2: 315–36.

—— 2002. 'Foreword'. In G. Esping-Andersen with D. Gallie, A. Hemerijck, and J. Myles, *Why We Need a New Welfare State.* Oxford: Oxford University Press.

WINCOTT, D. 2003. 'The Idea of the European Social Model: Limits and Paradoxes of Europeanization'. Pp. 279–302 in K. Featherstone and C. Radaelli (eds.), *The Politics of Europeanization.* Oxford: Oxford University Press.

CHAPTER 50

....

INTERNATIONAL
ECONOMY

....

PETER BURNHAM
STEVEN KETTELL

In an influential study published in 1968, Richard Cooper argued that the trend towards growing economic interdependence since the late 1940s had made the successful pursuit of national economic objectives much more difficult. Interdependence had increased the number and magnitude of the disturbances to which each country's balance of payments was subjected thereby directing policy attention to the importance of the restoration of external balance. Interdependence had also slowed the ability of national authorities to act independently to reach objectives, and finally the number of effective policy instruments available to national authorities had been reduced by the spread of international agreements (Cooper 1968: 148). Since the deregulation of financial markets in the late 1970s it could, with some plausibility, be argued that the international economy has become more constraining than was the case in the late 1960s, although the impact of this 'constraint' on individual nation states varies considerably. In the case of Britain this chapter will argue that whilst Cooper's economic observations are broadly valid they are nevertheless incomplete and need to be supplemented by a political analysis of how the notion of 'growing economic interdependence' has enabled state managers to use the idea of 'international economic constraint' to achieve domestic policy objectives. In so doing it will explore a number of key themes including the utility of the 'politicization–depoliticization' couplet; the changing character of state–economy relations; and the notion of the specificity of British capitalism.

The history of governing the political economy of Britain since 1900 is one of state managers attempting to survive the shocks delivered by the international economy whilst simultaneously trying to exploit the opportunities provided by such shocks for realizing policy objectives at home. In this view, national states exist as aspects of the international system and state managers are under constant pressure to make more efficient use of resources, particularly labour power and money. Failure to achieve stability of the currency and productivity growth will inevitably result in a loss of reserves precipitated by balance of payments problems and inflationary pressure provoking international exchange instability and financial crisis (Bonefeld, Brown, and Burnham 1995: 2). National state managers cannot of course resolve this crisis tendency which lies at the heart of capitalism but they can seek to manage its manifestations within their territory in such a way as to avoid an 'economic' crisis becoming a crisis of political authority itself. In Britain, one of the most popular methods used to achieve this end (and to restructure social relations more generally) has been the attempt to disengage the state politically from management of the economy so as to 'depoliticize' economic policy formation (Burnham 2001; Clarke 1990: 27). This strategy has met with varying degrees of success and has been most obvious in the areas of monetary and exchange rate policy (Buller and Flinders 2005; Flinders and Buller 2006; Hay 2007). 'Externalist' strategies have focused in particular on linking the British economy to international economic rules—so-called 'rules-based' approaches (Kydland and Prescott 1977). The well-known logic here is that if such rules are credible (governments cannot easily renege on them), visible (rooted in clear, simple regulations), and serve as the anchor for policy, then the public forms expectations assuming that the rules are followed (Giovannini 1993). International regimes, usually international monetary mechanisms based on a fixed exchange rate, set definite rules and thereby build 'automaticity' into the system. In this way state managers have the opportunity to secure a counter-inflationary strategy by altering expectations concerning wage claims and 'externalizing' responsibility for the general imposition of financial discipline. Depoliticized strategies achieved through the adoption of rules-based international arrangements (Gold Standard, ERM, EMU, WTO) generally have greater credibility than 'domesticist' approaches (such as granting operational independence to the central bank) since in the latter case the regulatory mechanisms are not widely perceived to be beyond the control of individual governments. The British state has a long history of linking the management of the domestic economy to international economic rules, in part in order to deal with some of the most difficult governing consequences of long-term economic decline. This chapter will explore aspects of the relationship between long-term decline and externalist strategies before returning in the conclusion to consider some of the broader theoretical concerns raised by an analysis of state–economy relations. Whilst there is of course a potentially limitless source of topics and issue areas that could be discussed under the rubric of 'Britain and the international economy', we have chosen to focus on some of the most high-profile policy decisions affecting sterling over the last century. The choice of the inter-war gold standard, Bretton Woods, post-war recovery, Lawson's externalist strategies, the exchange rate mechanism, and aspects of New Labour's economic policies is neither uncontentious nor is it meant to be totally comprehensive. It does however reflect a concern to engage with some of the most significant external economic policy events of the last century and indicate how an interpretation can be developed which challenges many orthodoxies (and which could, for instance, given more time and space, be extended to other areas such as the relationship between Britain and Europe).

50.1 THE RETURN TO GOLD

The decline of the staple industries and the implications of this for the international use of sterling are issues that have long preoccupied British state managers. In a wide-ranging review of Britain's commercial and industrial policy at the close of the First World War, the government produced a report concluding that unless economic decline could be halted and the fall in the export trade checked, British governments would suffer acute and recurring fiscal and balance of payments crises that would put paid to Pax Britannica (HMSO 1918). The decline of coal, cotton, textiles, shipbuilding, and iron and steel had been exacerbated by the rise of foreign competition (particularly German) in other branches of industry that profited from increased productivity, large-scale production, scientific advances, and investment in training. By contrast, Britain suffered from the handicap of traditional organization, liberal trade regimes, and small-scale production processes. The message was clear: in the short term foreign competition could only be kept at bay by a low-wage strategy. This however could give rise to industrial conflict on a grand scale—as had already been seen in the so-called Great Unrest of 1910–12 (Aris 1998). A mechanism would have to be found to impose discipline on both capital and the working class, and it would need to be consistent with Britain's continued international ambitions. The restoration of the gold standard was widely seen as a policy measure that could achieve both objectives.

The political economy of Britain during the inter-war period was dominated by the events surrounding its return to the gold standard in 1925, and by its subsequent departure from the system for a second time in 1931. In the conventional narrative of this era, two core assertions stand out. The first of these is that the decision to return to the gold standard (a fixed exchange rate system founded on the interconvertibility of national currencies and gold) was motivated by a desire to restore the British economy to its pre-war level of prosperity. The main considerations here, so it is claimed, were to provide the conditions on which Britain's international trading and financial activities depended: namely, exchange rate stability and anti-inflationary discipline. With sterling relinked to gold, any balance of payments weaknesses would lead to an outflow of bullion, providing the trigger for a corrective rise in interest rates by the Bank of England (for example see Pollard 1976; Winch 1969; Moggridge 1972; Sayers 1976). The second key element of the prevailing narrative concerns the effect of the return. For the most part, the decision to restore the link to gold at the pre-war exchange rate of $4.86 is considered to have been a mistake. This, it is argued, overvalued the pound by around 10 per cent, undermined the competitiveness of British exporters, put employers under pressure to reduce wages, and required high interest rates to avoid losses of gold, leading to economic stagnation (although the City of London prospered), chronically high unemployment, and outbreaks of industrial unrest, the apogee of which was the General Strike of 1926 (see Keynes 1925; Winch 1969; Moggridge 1972). Those offering a more sympathetic view of events, namely that the return to gold was not a mistake, pin the blame for Britain's subsequent economic malaise on external factors, most notably the poor state of the world economy during the inter-war period (for example, Youngson 1960; Howson 1975).

A central premise of the conventional view of Britain's return to the gold standard is that the decision to return, and its effects, were both largely shaped by Britain's external relations; principally by its high level of exposure (industrial, commercial, and financial) to world economic conditions. Largely absent from this picture, however, are considerations of the domestic politics involved in this policy (for a limited exception see Williamson 1984). The key factor in this was the desire of state managers to address a series of problems resulting from an expansion of the state's regulatory apparatus during the war. This had undermined the mechanisms of the market, turned economic conditions and policy-making into overtly political issues, and had made state officials directly responsible for economic affairs. On this level the return to gold was chiefly designed to enhance competitiveness by returning control of economic conditions to the market, and to ease the political difficulties of so doing by displacing responsibility for economic conditions away from state managers. The 'automatic' anti-inflationary mechanism of the regime would effectively preclude any activist policy measures on the part of the government and the Bank of England, each of whom could legitimately maintain that such activities were incompatible with the rules and procedures of the gold standard (Kettell 2004).

While the economic effects of the return to gold were less than impressive, in political terms the policy was more successful than is usually appreciated. The issue of unemployment remained politically contentious (leading to the defeat of the Conservatives in the 1929 general election), but economic policy matters were for the most part effectively displaced from the political agenda and the pressure on state managers over economic policy-making remained lower than at any time since the war. Responsibility for the poor state of the British economy was also seen by the majority of domestic opinion to lie with producers themselves (with employers blaming trade unions and vice versa), as well as conditions in the world market more generally. Concerns over high interest rates were also successfully deflected onto the gold standard regime, with Chancellors Winston Churchill and Philip Snowden both declaring that the sole responsibility belonged to the Bank, with the Bank highlighting the constraints imposed on its own actions by the necessity of maintaining the value of the pound, and with the gold standard policy itself attracting no significant criticism from any section of British society until the onset of the 1931 crisis. The level of industrial unrest, too, was dramatically reduced compared to pre-return levels, and while the General Strike remains the single largest outbreak of unrest in British history, the role of the gold standard in provoking this was, contrary to popular wisdom, limited at best (Kettell 2004: 57–78).

Britain's exit from the gold standard, following a calamitous run on the pound in September 1931, required the construction of a new framework for economic management. This new regime, effectively in place by mid-1932, consisted of several core components: a tariff on imports from non-empire countries, a 'cheap money' policy of low interest rates, a balanced budget commitment, and a floating exchange rate, kept (as much as possible) at around $3.50 by the Exchange Equalization Account and the establishment of the Sterling Area. As with the return to the gold standard, this new framework is typically seen to have emerged as a response to external conditions; an attempt to secure the greatest possible degree of national economic prosperity in the face of a global depression and the collapse of the world's trade and financial systems. For some, this response also signifies the slow, but steadily rising influence of Keynesian ideas of policy activism in Britain and an acceptance of greater state responsibility for economic affairs (Winch 1969; Howson 1975; Middleton 1985; Booth 1987).

While this new framework for economic management bore no resemblance to the gold standard regime, a strong thread of continuity in terms of the underlying policy objectives linked the two together. For state managers the central aims in this respect were to revive Britain's sluggish economy through a mild inflationary stimulus while avoiding measures that risked undermining the competitive pressure on domestic producers, and, in the face of greater calls for state action to ameliorate economic conditions, to avoid any overt measures that might lead to a repoliticization of economic policy-making. Aligned to this, for most of the 1930s, the ultimate policy aim of state managers remained that of securing another return to the gold standard at an exchange rate of $4.86. Unlike the 1920s, however, neither external nor internal factors were now conducive to such a move. Sustained global economic and financial instability, combined with domestic opposition to the prospect and political fears of the social discontent that may follow a renewed bout of deflation induced by a high pound, ruled out the possibility (Kettell 2004).

The slow recovery of the British economy from mid-1933, aided by the new policy framework, also eroded the possibility of a return to gold, though the upturn was never decisive and unemployment remained high and economic growth uneven. Similarly, while impressions of an era of growing state activism are misplaced (the Bank of England, for example, retained its operational independence vis-à-vis the Treasury throughout the 1930s), the prospects for promoting a restructuring of the British economy through the reimposition of competitive discipline remained elusive. This was a dilemma that would subsequently re-emerge, though would not be resolved, in the years after the Second World War.

50.2 FROM BRETTON WOODS TO THE 1976 IMF LOAN

International trade and financial relationships between 1944 and 1976 were dominated by discussions surrounding the Bretton Woods Agreement, the move to currency convertibility and non-discrimination in trade, the implication of the fluctuating fortunes of the dollar, and the creation of the European Common Market. In terms of domestic policy, British state managers operated in a context of increasing politicization in an effort to stabilize sterling, regulate public expenditure, and control inflationary wage settlements. In conditions of relatively full employment successive governments sought to regulate labour through moral exhortation (always couched as 'in the national interest'), centralized authority over wage determination, and the creation of new surveillance and guidance machinery. Indicative planning and official incomes policies were combined with the discretionary management of money in an attempt to maintain the value of the pound, contain prices, and stave off recurrent balance of payments crises.

Bretton Woods sought to enshrine the following multilateral objectives: currencies freely convertible at fixed exchange rates, with controlled capital movements; no discrimination in trade (except by the formation of full Customs Unions); and the abolition of quotas (except to meet temporary balance of payments difficulties), the reduction of tariffs, and the progressive elimination of preferences (although there was no obligation to reduce preferences except in return for tariff concessions of equivalent value). The aim of the Articles of Agreement of the International Monetary Fund, the International Bank for Reconstruction and Development, and the Havana Charter for an International Trade Organization was to translate these objectives into international rules of behaviour in the economic field and establish institutions to administer the rules and promote further action towards the objectives (Burnham 2003). The ITO was of course stillborn, but the commercial policy provisions of the draft Charter for the ITO were incorporated into the General Agreement on Tariffs and Trade (Irwin 1995: 130–2; Curzon 1965: 6–8). It was envisaged that after a relatively short 'transitional period' (which allowed members to maintain restrictions for a five-year period in order to adapt to changing circumstances), a smoothly working international system would be established (HMSO 1944: 33). It was anticipated that balance of payments difficulties would arise but it was thought that such problems would, over time, be the exception rather than the rule. The Articles of Agreement indicated that in such cases, there should be no pressure on countries to deflate (for this would jeopardize full employment). Rather, difficulties could be rectified by import restrictions and short-term borrowing from the IMF. Universal discrimination against a persistent creditor was permissible, in theory, under the provisions of the Scarce Currency clause, if the IMF's resources of that country's currency were approaching exhaustion. In short, the architects of Bretton Woods assumed that, provided import and exchange restrictions were removed—and their reimposition in time of emergency strictly controlled—and provided that there were no discriminatory blocs, a smoothly working multilateral system would come about automatically.

At the close of the Bretton Woods conference on 22 July 1944, as a band played the 'Star-Spangled Banner', Keynes and Morgenthau spoke of the creation of a new 'brotherhood of man' and of the Bretton Woods signpost 'pointing down a highway broad enough for all men to walk in step and side by side' (Van Dormael 1978: 2, 222). However, this objective was never met, clear international rules were not established, and British policy instead was dominated by the same concerns that had been outlined by the government in 1918. In a review of the post-war situation produced in the early 1950s, British Treasury and Bank officials concluded that the architects of the 'new system' had failed to appreciate six key factors (PRO: T236/3071). Firstly, the scale of the disruption in Europe and Asia and the double advantage which North America had gained by both escaping physical damage during the war and having developed its production of essentials under the forced drought of wartime necessity. Secondly, the revolution in the international economy resulting from the impoverishment of the UK and the transformation of Britain from the world's biggest creditor to the world's biggest debtor—including the weakening of sterling and competitive power. Thirdly, the move towards industrialization and development in the 'underdeveloped' countries of the world, and the effect which this would have on world trade. Fourthly, the abnormality of the great surpluses of primary products in the 1930s and the major change in the terms of trade between primary products and manufactures. Fifthly, the great demand for investment in the disrupted world, and the resulting rapid world inflation. Finally, the inadequacy of the gold reserves outside the United States in view of the rise in prices and the size of the balance of payments deficits. The worldwide demand for food, consumer goods, fuel, and capital goods—which could be supplied in sufficient quantities only from North America—created the 'world dollar shortage' with the United States amassing balance of payments surpluses of $7 billion and $10 billion in 1946 and 1947 respectively. As US aid was rapidly exhausted, the world's gold reserves flowed back to Fort Knox; European economies were plunged into crisis; trade began to seize up around the world; and bilateral trade and payments systems were reactivated.

Although the British problem was of course an aspect of the world dollar problem, the Treasury recognized that a solution to the world problem would not necessarily carry with it a solution to the special problem of the United Kingdom—in fact, under certain circumstances it might have the reverse effect. Britain's freedom of choice in external economic policy in the post-war period was limited by three factors which emerge from a consideration of the crises of 1947, 1949, and 1951 (PRO: T236/3071; Burnham 2003). Firstly, any policy would have to attend to the problem of the reserves. Even achieving a level of nearly £1,400 million in June 1951 could not, Treasury officials noted, stop a loss of confidence in sterling three months later. The first problem therefore was to adjust to this situation, either by acquiring substantial resources to strengthen the gold reserves or by altering the external financial situation in a way which reduced the strain on the gold reserves (or, of course, both). Secondly, the balance of payments problem could only be solved in the long term by expanding exports and invisible earnings, and by obtaining an increased share of world trade. The third, and what the Treasury perceived to be the hard-core, problem of Britain's external economic policy was to provide an effective basis for eliminating the UK's large and increasing deficit with the dollar area, either by direct action or by multilateral earning of gold or dollars.

A similar diagnosis was produced by the US State Department, who conducted a number of surveys into 'the British problem' in the early 1950s (US National Archives: RG 56/450). Inflation and over-full employment had 'deranged' the balance of payments by creating excess demand for imports and diverting resources from exports to domestic markets. Business had become inefficient because of the atmosphere of a seller's market and the tight labour market had encouraged restrictive practices and impeded the transfer of labour to essential industries. According to State Department economists, studies of British productivity showed that in the fourteen-year period 1935–1948, for twenty-two key industries, productivity in eight had declined (including coal, coke, cotton spinning, and paper), productivity in seven had increased less than 10 per cent, and in only seven had it increased by more than 10 per cent. In general it was found that real product per man hour was rising very slowly and by the end of 1951 was only 5 per cent higher than in 1938. The State Department concluded, 'Restrictive practices of industry and labour are primarily to blame for the inflexibility of the British economy. These practices impede production and cause prices to be kept at artificial levels, either through price agreements or inflated costs. Psychology of labour is dominated by fear of new techniques which might jeopardise jobs or wages'. Britain's competitive power in export markets was in decline principally because newer industrial rivals had a higher rate of growth of labour productivity and lower wage levels. According to the US State Department, action needed to be taken in the sphere of 'domestic British politics' to reduce the scale of the welfare programme (which had adversely affected incentives), reduce the level of direct controls, and introduce greater flexibility.

In short, a solution to the problems of Britain's long-term external economic policy would have to be consistent with increasing industrial potential and competitive power, and relieving pressure on the reserves to enable confidence in sterling to rise. Alternatives to a one-world multilateral trade and payments system, such as bilateralism, permanent discriminatory groups, and extended preference arrangements, would, in the long term, be inconsistent with these objectives. Hence the Bank and Treasury's commitment by the first quarter of 1952 to Operation Robot: to the creation of a multilateral system in which sterling was freely convertible (except for residents of the Sterling Area), discriminatory or quantitative restriction of imports were kept to a minimum, and market forces, through a floating exchange rate, were allowed to effect a structural adjustment of the domestic economy and a restructuring of the global economy, to enhance overall competitiveness (Bulpitt and Burnham 1999). The debate over Robot was not a dry discussion of the merits of exchange rate regimes or the technicalities of convertibility, although, of course, it encompassed both. At heart, Robot was about the future direction of British, and by implication global, capitalism. In one fell swoop Robot would demolish what remained of Bretton Woods and re-establish Britain as a leading power alongside the United States. At home, market forces would destroy the 'rigidities' set up under Attlee and help cure the economy of the 'creeping paralysis' induced by over-full employment and the lure of 'soft' markets for uncompetitive goods.

The decision to reject Robot left state managers grappling with successive balance of payments crises and the spectre of heightened industrial action throughout the post-war period. In terms of broad macroeconomic policy, the gradual relaxation of direct controls in the late 1940s initially placed a greater burden on fiscal policy. Although during the 1950s monetary policy played an enhanced role in the form of credit restrictions and movements in short-term interest rates, the Radcliffe Report of 1959 confirmed the view that interest rates were an uncertain tool for demand management (Hatton and Chrystal 1991: 68; Dimsdale 1991: 89; HMSO 1959). However, balance of payments difficulties, experienced particularly under Wilson in the 1960s, led to increased reliance on monetary restriction to stabilize the external balance. Even a 14 per cent devaluation of the pound on 18 November 1967 (from $2.80 to $2.40) offered little more than a temporary respite to state managers whose efforts to find a politicized solution to the major governing problems were looking increasingly futile (Cairncross 1996). By 1975 the Treasury was forced to admit that post-war management, and in particular incomes policies, 'must be judged a failure' (PRO: T267/28). Inflation, in February 1975, reached 20 per cent and wage rates were rising at 29 per cent (Browning 1986: 65). The Treasury now pushed Healey to re-examine public expenditure, lay down a norm for pay increases, and drastically deflate domestic demand (Wass 2008: 323). In July 1975, a system of 'cash limits' was introduced as a means of controlling public expenditure and, before the agreement with the IMF in 1976 (which granted Britain $3.9 billion from the Fund and endorsed another $3 billion from the BIS), Healey decided to publish the undisclosed monetary targets that had been in use since 1973 in an attempt to placate the markets (Grant 2002: 97). Although the IMF package temporarily restored confidence in sterling, unemployment and inflation continued to rise with predictable consequences for the Labour government in the early months of 1979. By the early 1980s the new Conservative government gave a clear signal that it would no longer adjust demand to accommodate inflation. The credibility of this strategy, as Hatton and Chrystal (1991: 74) emphasize, was established by the imposition of cash limits, by the commitment to medium-term budgetary objectives, and by the refusal to reflate the economy using fiscal policy in the early 1980s. Whereas in general in the 1950s and 1960s changes in monetary and fiscal policy were not closely related, the adoption of targets for monetary aggregates led to explicit coordination in the 1908s and the increased importance of exchange rate considerations dominating monetary policy (Dimsdale 1991: 137–40). In summary, the international economy had delivered significant 'external' shocks to the British economy in the post-war period manifest in recurrent balance of payments, fiscal, and monetary crises alleviated in part through extensive international borrowing, and in the later phases close control of public expenditure. Politicized management techniques allowed little room for state managers to deflect the political consequences of economic crisis, hence the charges of 'overload', 'ungovernability', and 'legitimation crisis' (Hay 1996: 98–101). The mid-1970s are therefore accurately seen by Grant (2002: 96) as a transitional period in which policy-makers were increasingly led towards depoliticized solutions designed in part to reassert the operational autonomy of the political executive by placing at one remove the political character of decision-making (Burnham 2001). This is the context in which to understand economic policy under Thatcher and in particular the move towards more explicit externalist approaches under Major.

50.3 FROM THATCHER TO MAJOR

Conservative statecraft from 1979 to 1997 is, for many observers, chiefly characterized by its concern with domestic factors (Bulpitt 1985). Although the strategies employed by the Thatcher and Major governments are located within the overarching context of reversing Britain's post-war economic sclerosis relative to its main global competitors (see for example the notion of a shift to 'post-Fordism' in Overbeek 1990; Jessop et al. 1988), the central theme is that of an attempt to achieve this by removing domestic blockages to economic growth. This is set within a broad-ranging narrative of decline in which the principal cause of the political-economic crises of the 1960s and 1970s was seen to have stemmed from the inherent weaknesses of Keynesian social democracy itself: namely, an over-extended and overly interventionist state combined with overbearing trade unionism and a parasitic public sector. Present too, although sitting somewhat uneasily with this theme, is a critique of the City for its pervasive and anti-dynamic culture of 'gentlemanly capitalism'. In this setting, Thatcherism is seen to constitute a process of 'rolling back the state', freeing up hitherto constrained market forces, a process of deregulation and liberalization designed to improve the flexibility, dynamism, and competitiveness of the national economy (Gamble 1988; English and Kenny 2002). In reality, however, the situation was a much more nuanced affair. Domestic-based reforms designed to ensure a greater degree of 'fit' between the British economy and the imperatives of the world market were mixed with 'externally-based' measures designed to stimulate a restructuring of domestic political and economic relations by directly exposing producers to global pressures.

The initial cornerstone of Conservative statecraft combined an attempt to reduce inflation, raise productivity, and reduce the direct economic involvement of the state through the imposition of explicit domestic policy rules in the form of monetary targets (Smith 1991). In a similar fashion, the numerous trade union reforms implemented throughout the period of Conservative rule, along with the processes of privatization, deregulation, and public-sector reform, were all essentially 'domestic' in nature. However by the mid-1980s it was clear that although the Medium-Term Financial Strategy had achieved a degree of success in combating inflation, it had been discredited in theoretical terms and it increasingly seemed that state managers lacked a coherent approach to economic policy (Smith 1993; Johnson 1991). Lawson now switched his attention to 'externalist' strategies—in particular linking the pound to the German Mark. From 1987 onwards Lawson 'shadowed the deutschmark' within a range between DM2.75 and DM3.00, apparently without Thatcher's agreement (Grant 2002: 99). Other 'outward facing' measures adopted during this period included the process of financial deregulation that culminated in the 1986 'Big Bang', designed to improve the competitiveness of the City by opening it up to external competition; and the signing of the Single European Act, one of the core aims of which was to expose British producers to the competitive disciplines of a Single European Market. The impact of the external environment was also felt in other ways. Indeed, the initial monetarist turn was itself largely undermined by global forces, the ability to control or even measure the domestic money supply being compounded by the instability of sterling, and by the liberalization of world credit markets (Tomlinson 2007). The decline of the world economy during the early part of the 1980s also played a key contributory role in the onset of a fierce domestic recession, one effect of which was to undermine the government's attempt at scaling back the state by prompting a large rise in unemployment and increased levels of welfare spending (Gamble 1988).

Without question however the most notable attempt to secure domestic restructuring via external means under the Conservatives centred on the use of the exchange rate following John Major's appointment as Chancellor in October 1989. The issue of Britain's relationship with the European Exchange Rate Mechanism (ERM) had already led to deep divisions within the government following Lawson's suggestion that Britain should enter the German dominated semi-fixed rate system. For those in favour (most ministers as well as Treasury and Bank officials), fixing the value of the pound within an externally constituted system of rules offered a useful means of tackling inflation, enhancing competitiveness, and reducing the direct involvement of the state in economic affairs. Entry to the ERM would make the exchange rate floor more credible, providing a new anchor for economic policy, thereby underwriting the anti-inflationary resolve of the government. Thatcher, however, viewed this and other externalist strategies as a sign of weakness and instead favoured the by now largely discredited 'domestic' approach to tackling inflation (Bonefeld, Brown, and Burnham 1995: 76–81). While membership of the ERM (achieved on 8 October 1990) arrived too late to provide salvation for Thatcher, its benefits were not lost on her successor, John Major.

According to received wisdom, membership of the ERM is considered to have been a policy disaster. As with Britain's return to the gold standard in 1925, joining the regime at an overvalued exchange rate (DM2.95) is seen to have forced interest rates to be held at onerously high levels, to have exacerbated the severity of the downturn, and to have dealt a fatal blow to the governing credibility of the Conservative Party—epitomized in sterling's ignominious withdrawal from the system on 'Black Wednesday' 16 September 1992—from which it has still to fully recover (Thompson 1996; Budd 2005). This view however ignores several indicators of relative policy success. Although the economy stagnated, unemployment reached chronically high levels, and there was no real breakthrough in productivity in relation to Britain's main international rivals, the goal of lowering inflation was secured to notable effect (dropping from 10 per cent in October 1990 to 3.7 per cent by September 1992), clearing the way for a sustained period of low-inflationary growth in subsequent years. Moreover, in political terms, notwithstanding the long-term damage to the Conservatives' reputation for economic management, ERM membership initially proved to be still more beneficial, providing state managers with an effective means of deflecting pressures over the condition of the economy and helping the Conservatives to a fourth consecutive general election victory in April 1992 (Kettell 2008).

Britain's exit from the ERM presaged a return to 'domestic' policy rules, with a regime of inflation targets setting the core framework alongside attempts to give the Bank of England greater autonomy. While much of the Conservatives' remaining years in office turned on domestic affairs, most notably the continuation of the privatization and deregulation agenda, the international context continued to exert a defining influence. Growing pressures for ever-closer levels of economic and political integration within the European Union, for instance, provided an ever-present site of contestation in British politics, while the increasing pressures of 'globalization' and the shifting nature of the world economy, replete with notions of a 'hollowing out' or a decline of the state (Holliday 2000), formed the backdrop to the ongoing process of domestic economic change. Defined most notably by the rise of the service-sector economy, by the processes of 'offshoring' and contracting-out, and by the continued decline of Britain's industrial base, the theme of necessary adaptation to uncontrollable global forces would become one of the more enduring legacies of the Conservative era.

50.4 NEW LABOUR

Despite its professed adherence to strike a 'Third Way' between Thatcherite free market capitalism and 'Old Labour' social democracy, in terms of external relations the form of statecraft pursued by New Labour since 1997 bears a striking resemblance to previous modes of governance. As with the strategic approach pursued by the Thatcher governments, for example, many of the measures taken by New Labour have focused on distinctly domestic matters. The mainstay of these has been an effort to combine socially progressive policies such as the introduction of a minimum wage and a large rise in public-sector spending (relabelled 'investment' in Third Way discourse) from the second term in office, with a neoliberal commitment to ensuring the effective operation of the free market (Grant 2002: 229–30). The maintenance of the trade union reforms, economic deregulation, and privatization processes implemented by the Conservatives have been accompanied by efforts to secure a closer involvement of the private sector in public service reform, and by an openly professed eagerness to be as business friendly as possible—a desire expressed in initial efforts to establish governing credibility by adhering to the restrictive spending plans of the outgoing Conservative regime (Ludlam and Smith 2004).

The two themes of the free market and progressivism, however, were not considered to be incompatible. Indeed, at the core of the New Labour project has been the assertion that it is possible to transcend these apparently irreconcilable opposites (Fairclough 2000). Here, Old Labour conceptions of the state as an instrument for shielding society from the adverse effects of the market, primarily through the provision of welfare and public services, were supplanted by a notion of the state as a facilitative and enabling agency, the task of which was to equip members of society with the means to make their own way within the free market, chiefly via the provision of opportunity, macroeconomic stability, and the requisite access to skills, education, and training (Ludlam and Smith 2004). All this was embedded within a system of domestically constructed policy rules; both fiscal, in the form of the Treasury's golden and sustainable investment rules, and monetary, in the form of Bank of England operational independence and a symmetrical inflation target. The avowed aim here was to establish a credible framework for economic management that would provide the necessary stability for long-term growth (and thus the required fiscal revenues for public investment); the less obvious being the displacing of responsibility for any potentially difficult and unpopular decisions away from state officials (Burnham 2001).

The attempt to achieve these goals also linked together the domestic and the international. Central to this, at least initially, was closer engagement with the European Union (though not to the extent of joining the Single European Currency), and, more enduringly, a strong discursive emphasis on notions of external change deriving from the process of 'globalization'. Presented as an uncontested reality of political and economic life in the modern age, the much vaunted spread of globalization has served as an ever-present banner under which is carried the need for unceasing national economic adaptation in the form of improved competitiveness, productivity, and dynamism (Hay and Watson 1999). As a key means of justifying the government's commitment to extending and deepening the marketization of British life, this discursive construct has thereby served clear political ends even though as Panitch (2001: 374–5) emphasizes, 'nation states are not the victims of globalisation, they are the authors of globalisation'.

To a large degree the successes and the failures of the New Labour project have been inextricably linked to conditions in the global economy. Initial economic success was founded on a large degree of fortune deriving from the updraft of a sustained period of rising world economic growth, buoyed by an enormous expansion of credit, which helped the government to avoid serious economic difficulties and to expand investment in public services. Indeed, this latter point, along with rising levels of consumer and national debt, provided the main reason why Britain was able to avoid the worst effects of a global downturn that accompanied the arrival of the millennium. The counterpart to all this however, a global 'credit crunch' presaging a sharper and far more serious downturn in the world economy, and one from which Britain is not able to insulate itself, threatens to bring an end to the New Labour era. Yet even here it is the external context to which governmental hopes are pinned. New Labour's strategy for mitigating the fallout from the downturn has been unabashed in its displacement of blame and responsibility onto the exigencies of the world market; an insistence that the core drivers of discontent, namely higher prices for food, fuel, energy, and credit, are inherently international in nature and beyond the purview of any single government to solve.

50.5 CONCLUSION

This chapter has highlighted the complexity of the relationship between domestic policy-making and the international economy. In so doing it has confirmed the sense of Block's call for a unidisciplinary intellectual approach that brings together the study of politics, economics, sociology, and history (Block 1977: p. x). British policy, for example, cannot be understood in abstraction from the international economy since capitalism is a single global relationship of class antagonism in which state power is allocated between territorial entities. The accumulation of capital within the domestic economy depends on the accumulation of capital on a world scale. National states founded on the rule of law and money are at the same time confined within limits imposed by the accumulation of capital on a world scale— the most obvious and important manifestation of which is their subordination to world money (Marazzi 1995; Bonefeld, Brown, and Burnham 1995: 28). The international monetary system, as Block (1977: 1) notes, is simply the sum of all the devices by which state managers organize their international economic relations. The construction and maintenance of global circuits of accumulation is an ongoing task, built upon national states providing the 'domestic' political underpinning for the stability and the movement of capital, and is one that requires constant effort at the international level to guard against the restriction of trade and payments systems.

In many respects the recent history of Britain's articulation with the international economy is one of a movement from relative 'openness' in the nineteenth century to relative 'closedness' in the period 1930–60 (whilst always maintaining the ideology of multilateralism) and thereafter regaining 'openness' as market forces were given a key role by state managers in determining international transactions. As we have seen, the principal methods of 'adjustment' open to state managers have tended to focus either on changing the level of domestic economic activity and/or on altering the exchange rate. Both methods, as Block (1977: 2–3) further indicates, result in applying downward pressure on real wages and affect levels of employment with the likely result being 'a breakdown of social order and an intensification of class conflict'. In such circumstances governments are well served by strategies that will 'depoliticize' the process of economic policy-making, thereby helping to reduce the likelihood of a political crisis of the state. The more state managers embrace 'openness' with respect to the organization of their international transactions, the greater becomes the need for depoliticized strategies since increased reliance on market mechanisms carries an enhanced threat of heightened social conflict (Goldthorpe 1978). As already noted, however, the international economy is not an 'external given' but is a carefully constructed achievement representing distinct power relations and as such is both fragile and subject to change and crisis (Block 1977: 221). This emphasis on the crisis-ridden character of the intenational economy has definite implications for commentators such as Douglas Wass (2008: 356–8) who argue that economic policy in Britain has now changed fundamentally and that neither the balance of payments, nor unemployment, nor pressure from the trade union movement is of any great importance in terms of policy-making. It is certainly true that the freeing of restrictions on capital movements has made it easier for debtor countries to finance deficits and that in recent years Britain has had greater foreign exchange reserves to manage its market interventions. However, the delicate character of the international economy has been revealed once again with the contraction of international finance, the return (even temporarily) of inflation, and a widening UK trade deficit which many economists regard as unsustainable. Periodically in the last fifty years arguments have been advanced that changes either in the international economy or the British political economy have rendered redundant 'old style' economic crisis and its management (Crosland 1956; Hirst and Thompson 1996). On every occasion such arguments have been shown to be overly optimistic (and in many ways have been a reflection of both the politics of the time and time-bound academic fashion). The form of Britain's integration into the international economy may change slowly but the means available to state managers to deal with the manifestation of crisis at international and domestic levels remain broadly constant. It is here that the political analyst can contribute directly to the development of a unidisciplinary intellectual approach by charting the political strategies employed by state managers in response to economic crisis and indicating in particular how notions of 'external constraint' are consistently employed in an effort to secure 'domestic' policy objectives.

REFERENCES

Aris, R. 1998. *Trade Unions and the Management of Industrial Conflict.* London: Macmillan.

Block, F. 1977. *The Origins of International Economic Disorder: A Study of United States International Monetary Policy from World War II to the Present.* London: University of California Press.

Bonefeld, W., Brown, A., and Burnham, P. 1995. *A Major Crisis.* Aldershot: Dartmouth.

Booth, A. 1987. 'Britain in the 1930s: A Managed Economy?' *Economic History Review*, 40/4: 499–522.

Bordo, M., and Eichengreen, B. 1993. *A Retrospective on the Bretton Woods System.* London: University of Chicago Press.

BROWNING, P. 1986. *The Treasury and Economic Policy 1964–1985*. London: Longman.

BUDD, A. 2005. *Black Wednesday: A Re-examination of Britain's Experience in the Exchange Rate Mechanism*. London: Institute of Economic Affairs.

BULLER, J., and FLINDERS, M. 2005. 'The Domestic Origins of Depoliticisation in the Area of British Economic Policy'. *British Journal of Politics and International Relations*, 7/4: 526–44.

BULPITT, J. 1985. 'The Discipline of the New Democracy: Mrs Thatcher's Domestic Statecraft'. *Political Studies*, 34/1: 19–39.

—— and BURNHAM, P. 1999. 'Operation Robot and the British Political Economy in the Early-1950s: The Politics of Market Strategies'. *Contemporary British History*, 13/1: 1–31.

BURNHAM, P. 2001. 'New Labour and the Politics of Depoliticisation'. *British Journal of Politics and International Relations*, 3/2: 127–49.

—— 2003. *Remaking the Postwar World Economy*. London: Palgrave.

CAIRNCROSS, A. 1996. *Managing the British Economy in the 1960s*. London: Macmillan.

CLARKE, S. 1990. 'Crisis of Socialism or Crisis of the State?' *Capital and Class*, 42: 19–29.

COOPER, R. 1968. *The Economics of Inter-Dependence: Economic Policy in the Atlantic Community*. London: McGraw-Hill.

CROSLAND, A. 1956. *The Future of Socialism*. London: Cape.

CURZON, G. 1965. *Multilateral Commercial Diplomacy: The General Agreement on Tariffs and Trade and its Impact on National Commercial Policies and Techniques*. London: Michael Joseph.

DIMSDALE, N. H. 1991. 'British Monetary Policy since 1945'. Pp. 89–140 in N. Crafts and N. Woodward (eds.), *The British Economy since 1945*. Oxford: Clarendon.

ENGLISH, R., and KENNY, M. 2002. 'British Decline or the Politics of Declinism?' *British Journal of Politics and International Relations*, 1/2: 252–66.

FAIRCLOUGH, N. 2000. *New Labour, New Language?* London: Routledge.

FLINDERS, M., and BULLER, J. 2006. 'Depoliticisation: Principles, Tactics and Tools'. *British Politics*, 1/3: 293–318.

GAMBLE, A. 1988. *The Free Economy and the Strong State*. London: Macmillan.

GIOVANNINI, A. 1993. 'Bretton Woods and its Precursors'. Pp. 109–54 in Bordo and Eichengreen 1993.

GOLDTHORPE, J. 1978. 'The Current Inflation: Towards a Sociological Account'. In F. Hirsch and J. Goldthorpe (eds.), *The Political Economy of Inflation*. London: Martin Robertson.

GRANT, W. 2002. *Economic Policy in Britain*. London: Palgrave.

HATTON, T., and CHRYSTAL, K. 1991. 'The Budget and Fiscal Policy'. Pp. 52–88 in N. Crafts and N. Woodward (eds.), *The British Economy Since 1945*. Oxford: Oxford University Press.

HAY, C. 1996. *Re-stating Social and Political Change*. Buckingham: Open University Press.

—— 2007. *Why We Hate Politics*. Cambridge: Polity.

—— and WATSON, M. 1999. 'The Discourse of Globalisation and the Logic of No Alternative: Rendering the Contingent Necessary in the Political Economy of New Labour'. *Policy and Politics*, 31/3: 289–305.

HIRST, P., and THOMPSON, G. 1996. *Globalisation in Question*. Cambridge: Polity.

HMSO 1918. *Commercial and Industrial Policy: Final Report*. Cd. 9035. London: HMSO.

—— 1944. *United Nations Monetary and Financial Conference: Bretton Woods, New Hampshire, USA, July 1 to July 22, 1944*. Cmd. 6546. London: HMSO.

—— 1959. *Committee on the Working of the Monetary System (Radcliffe Report)*. Cmnd. 827. London: HMSO.

HOLLIDAY, I. 2000. 'Is the British State Hollowing Out?' *Political Quarterly*, 71/2: 167–177.

Howson, S. 1975. *Domestic Monetary Management in Britain 1919–1938*. Cambridge: Cambridge University Press.

Irwin, D. 1995. 'The GATT's Contribution to Economic Recovery in Post-war Western Europe'. Pp. 127–50 in B. Eichengreen (ed.), *Europe's Post-War Recovery*. Cambridge: Cambridge University Press.

Jessop, B., Bonnet, K., Bromley, S., and Ling, T. 1988. *Thatcherism*. Cambridge: Polity.

Johnson, C. 1991. *The Economy under Mrs Thatcher 1979–1990*. London: Penguin.

Kettell, S. 2004. *The Political Economy of Exchange-Rate Policy-Making: From the Gold Standard to the Euro*. London: Palgrave.

—— 2008. 'Does Depoliticisation Work? Evidence from Britain's Membership of the Exchange Rate Mechanism, 1990–1992'. *British Journal of Politics and International Relations*, 10/4: 630–48.

Keynes, J. M. 1925. *The Economic Consequences of Mr. Churchill*. London: Hogarth.

Kydland, F., and Prescott, E. 1977. 'Rules Rather than Discretion'. *Journal of Political Economy*, 85: 473–92.

Ludlam, S., and Smith, M. 2004. *Governing as New Labour*. London: Routledge.

Marazzi, C. 1995. 'Money in the World Crisis'. Pp. 69–91 in W. Bonefeld and J. Holloway (eds.), *Global Capital, National State and the Politics of Money*. London: Macmillan.

Middleton, R. 1985. *Towards the Managed Economy: Keynes, the Treasury and the Fiscal Policy Debate of the 1930s*. London: Methuen.

Moggridge, D. E. 1972. *British Monetary Policy, 1924–1931: The Norman Conquest of $4.86*. Cambridge: Cambridge University Press.

Overbeek, H. 1990. *Global Capitalism and National Decline*. London: Unwin Hyman.

Panitch, L. 2001. 'Reflections on Strategy for Labour'. *Socialist Register 2001*: 367–92.

Pollard, S. 1976. *The Development of the British Economy 1914–1967*, 2nd edn. London: Edward Arnold.

Sayers, R. S. 1976. *The Bank of England 1891–1914*, vol. i. Cambridge: Cambridge University Press.

Smith, D. 1991. *The Rise and Fall of Monetarism*. London: Penguin.

—— 1993. *From Boom to Bust*. London: Penguin.

Thompson, H. 1996. *The British Conservative Government and the European Exchange Rate Mechanism*. London: Pinter.

Tomlinson, J. 2007. 'Mrs Thatcher's Macroeconomic Adventurism, 1979–1981, and its Political Consequences'. *British Politics*, 2/1: 3–19.

Van Dormael, A. 1978. *Bretton Woods: Birth of a Monetary System*. London: Macmillan.

Wass, D. 2008. *Decline to Fall*. Oxford: Oxford University Press.

Williamson, P. 1984. 'Financiers, the Gold Standard and British Politics, 1925–1931'. In J. Turner (ed.), *Businessmen and Politics: Studies of Business Activity in British Politics, 1900–1945*. London: Heinemann.

Winch, D. 1969. *Economic and Policy: A Historical Study*. London: Hodder and Stoughton.

Youngson, A. J. 1960. *The British Economy 1920–1957*. London: George Allen and Unwin.

Author Index

Subject Index

Note: page numbers in *italic* refer to figures, those in **bold** to tables.

CPSIA information can be obtained
at www.ICGtesting.com
Printed in the USA
LVOW03s1222141216

517215LV00003B/3/P